THE OXFORD
━ HISTORY OF ━
NEW ZEALAND
LITERATURE
in English

THE OXFORD
—HISTORY OF—
NEW ZEALAND
LITERATURE
in English

Edited by Terry Sturm

Auckland
OXFORD UNIVERSITY PRESS
Oxford   New York   Toronto   Melbourne

Oxford University Press

Oxford University Press, Walton Street, Oxford OX2 6DP

OXFORD   NEW YORK   TORONTO
DELHI   BOMBAY   CALCUTTA   MADRAS   KARACHI
PETALING JAYA   SINGAPORE   HONG KONG   TOKYO
NAIROBI   DAR ES SALAAM   CAPE TOWN
MELBOURNE   AUCKLAND
and associated companies in
BERLIN   IBADAN

Oxford is a trade mark of Oxford University Press

First published 1991
© Oxford University Press 1991

Published with the assistance of the Literature Programme
of the Queen Elizabeth II Arts Council
of New Zealand

ISBN 0 19 558211 X

Jacket illustration, 'The Untidy Verandah' by Olivia Spencer Bower,
in the collection of the Aigantighe Gallery, Timaru, used with permission
Jacket designed by Neysa Moss
Photoset in Bembo by Rennies Illustrations Ltd
and printed by Sovereign Print, Christchurch
Published by Oxford University Press
1A Matai Road, Greenlane, Auckland 5, New Zealand

Contents

List of Contributors   vii

Introduction   ix

Acknowledgements   xvii

1 Māori Literature: A Survey   1
Jane McRae

2 Non-fiction   25
Peter Gibbons

3 The Novel   105
Lawrence Jones

4 The Short Story   203
Lydia Wevers

5 Drama   271
Howard McNaughton

6 Poetry   335
MacD. P. Jackson and Elizabeth Caffin

7 Children's Literature   449
Betty Gilderdale

8 Popular Fiction   493
Terry Sturm

9 Publishing, Patronage, Literary Magazines   545
Dennis McEldowney

10 Bibliography   603
John Thomson

Notes   710

Index   735

Contributors

Jane McRae is Librarian in the Department of Māori Studies University of Auckland

Peter Gibbons is Senior Lecturer in History at the University of Waikato

Lawrence Jones is Associate Professor of English at the University of Otago

Lydia Wevers is Lecturer in English at Victoria University of Wellington

Howard McNaughton is Reader in English at the University of Canterbury

MacD. P. Jackson is Professor of English at the University of Auckland

Elizabeth Caffin is Managing Editor of Auckland University Press

Betty Gilderdale, formerly Lecturer at Auckland College of Education, is a historian and critic of children's literature

Terry Sturm is Professor of English at the University of Auckland

Dennis McEldowney, formerly Managing Editor of Auckland University Press, is a writer and critic

John Thomson is Reader in English at Victoria University of Wellington

Introduction

The idea for the *Oxford History of New Zealand Literature in English* took initial
shape during discussions between the General Editor and Anne French, of
Oxford University Press, in 1982-3. From the outset it was clear that the
comprehensiveness of what was envisaged, a 750-page volume offering for the
first time a history of all the main genres of writing in English, as well as a
history of publishing, patronage, and literary magazines and an introductory
survey of writing about literature written in the Māori language, would
require a team of specialist contributors. In most genres a substantial amount of
primary research needed to be done, in order to recover what had been lost or
marginalized in earlier accounts of the country's past, which have always been
highly selective, and strongly biased towards the promotion of canonical
authors and texts; hence, the collaborative nature of the undertaking, and the
six-year time scale during which it was written, beginning in 1984 with the first
of a series of annual meetings of the ten contributors. The terminal date for the
period covered by the history was set at 1986, some two years in advance of the
start of the project, but adjustments were later to include, on a more selective
basis, new writing which appeared in the later 1980s, especially, work by
established authors, and by new authors of the early 1980s whose work after
1986 had given them a much stronger presence on the literary scene.

From the beginning the contributors had little doubt of the need for a large-
scale general literary history, scholarly in approach, addressed not simply to
specialist readers but to the rapidly expanding body of educated general readers
of New Zealand books in New Zealand and overseas. A market survey of the
reading habits of New Zealanders in the early 1980s showed that one in three
books purchased in New Zealand was a New Zealand book, a dramatic increase over a period of little more than a generation. The survey included all
kinds of books, however, not literature in its more restricted sense, and in 1985
J.E. Traue, then Chief Librarian at the Alexander Turnbull Library, drew
attention (in his booklet, *New Zealand Studies: A Guide to Bibliographic
Resources*) to the paucity of scholarly books in the country's annual output,
approximately one per cent of the total titles published per annum compared
with ten per cent in the United States. Literary history (and criticism) has been
no exception. Wystan Curnow was perhaps only slightly exaggerating when,
in introducing the first anthology of New Zealand critical writings in 1973
(*Essays on New Zealand Literature*) he commented, 'Until recently book
reviewing has been almost the only kind of literary criticism practised in New
Zealand'.

Australia and Canada, older Commonwealth countries whose colonial
origins and history are closely related to New Zealand's, both have at least a

dozen substantial general literary histories. Before 1990 New Zealand had only one, the pioneering 160-page survey by E.H. McCormick (*New Zealand Literature, A Survey*), which appeared three decades earlier in 1959, and was, in the main, simply an expansion of his earlier 1940 Centennial volume, *Letters and Art in New Zealand*. Although New Zealand literature in English has much in common with Australian and Canadian literature, there are also significant differences. Since the population is much smaller, and European settlement began later, the total body of literature is considerably smaller, and forms like the novel and poetry, which were vigorous in Australia and Canada in the nineteenth century, remained relatively weak in New Zealand until the twentieth century. The literatures have also developed differently in relation to the indigenous cultures of each country. There is a much stronger consciousness of Māori culture in New Zealand writing than of Aboriginal culture in Australian writing; and Canadian literature in English has been shaped in special ways by the parallel presence of the country's French-speaking culture, and by the powerful cultural pressure of its near neighbour, the United States. Furthermore, over the past two decades in New Zealand a considerable amount of writing has appeared, especially by Māori writers, whose affinities are less with the older white Commonwealth than with the new post-colonial literatures in English. For overseas readers, this volume aims to provide the most comprehensive account yet of one of the significant 'new literatures in English'.

Since McCormick's survey, a considerable amount of more specialized literary criticism has appeared, in local and overseas literary magazines and in series like the Twayne World Authors Series and the Oxford University Press's New Zealand Writers and their Work Series. The main model for this critical literature, which deals primarily with individual authors, and occasionally assembles a variety of articles into an anthology, was formalist academic criticism overseas, and its main achievement has been to consolidate a smallish canon of perhaps a dozen of New Zealand's 'best' writers, grouped around the central figures of Katherine Mansfield, Allen Curnow, Frank Sargeson, James K. Baxter, and Janet Frame. A brief glance at the entries for individual authors in the Bibliography at the end of this history gives some indication of how selective the critical focus has been: of the 144 authors listed, the five mentioned above attract more than twenty per cent of the total entries, and Katherine Mansfield alone accounts for ten per cent of them. Since McCormick, there have also been a small number of histories confined to particular genres (Joan Stevens on the novel, Howard McNaughton and John Thomson on drama, and Betty Gilderdale on children's literature), and the 1980s also saw a significant expansion in literary biography and the beginnings of revisionist theoretical approaches to earlier accounts of New Zealand poetry and fiction.

However, the absence of any strong tradition of general literary historiography in New Zealand, compared with Canada and Australia, has meant that what might be called the empirical aspect of the project (the mapping, simply, of *what* has been written in English, and largely lost to view, over nearly two centuries) has loomed much more importantly in this history than might otherwise have been the case. The enormous expansion of bibliographical resources of all kinds, which were primitive at the time McCormick wrote his first book half a century ago, has been an indispensable aid. One of the history's main aims is thus to be a comprehensive work of literary reference, working on inclusive rather than selective principles, the first such history to appear in New Zealand.

Although the proportions vary in each section, about forty per cent of the book as a whole is devoted to the last three decades, to the period after McCormick's 1959 survey appeared, during which there has been a major expansion of writing of all kinds. A related aim has been to revisit writing before the 1920s and 1930s (that time from which so many received accounts date the 'real' beginnings of a national literature), not in order to unearth forgotten nineteenth century masterpieces, but to ask different questions about it. What were its most vital forms? (Certainly not poetry and fiction.) In what ways was writing involved (as Peter Gibbons puts it in his discussion of non-fiction) 'in the processes of colonization, in the implementation of European power, in the description and justification of the European presence as normative'? What continuities and disjunctions can be discerned both within it and in relation to literature that came later, prompting a need to re-read and re-think *later* writing? About one third of the book deals with literature prior to 1920.

Furthermore, more than half the book is devoted to writing other than poetry and 'serious' adult fiction — to drama, children's literature, popular fiction, literature in Māori, and the various genres of non-fiction (including exploration and travel narratives, history, natural history and ethnography, and biography and autobiography). With rare exceptions such writing has been largely ignored or marginalized in the past. For this reason, much of the research that has gone into them, as into the history of publishing, literary magazines, and patronage, is of an exploratory nature, designed to open up territories which need further investigation, to provide the beginnings of a more broadly based and diverse critical discourse.

Literary history is never simply, of course, the 'innocent', value-free provision of information. Indeed, what it defines *as* its object of enquiry implies judgements and attitudes, and is itself an intervention in contemporary literary debate, which needs to be made with as strong an awareness of that particular fact as can be mustered. Nor can literary history pretend to be a dispassionate, magisterial activity, handing down definitive judgements from on high. It is, invariably, as much a provisional statement about the present, as about the past. In fact, in the 1980s *all* the terms in the notion of a 'history of New Zealand literature' are problematic in ways that would not have been recognized as recently as two decades ago. Not only has the very possibility of literary history come under challenge, but there are new uncertainties surrounding the term 'New Zealand literature'. In a recent lecture on 'Pacific Maps and Fiction(s)' published by the Stout Research Centre, Albert Wendt drew attention to the ways in which maps of New Zealand literature which ignored the fact that the country is part of Polynesia and the Pacific 'have determined even such things as the canons and content of so-called New Zealand Literature and Art, and their language and vocabulary'. Even the notion of 'literature' itself has come under scrutiny. Does it privilege the written over the oral? If so, was not the introduction of writing itself into 'New Zealand' one of the main acts of colonization? And what is the relationship between literature and such major twentieth century cultural forms as film, radio, and television?

The new international discourses of post-colonialism and post-modernism, of linguistic theory, and of feminism, which have begun to find their way into debate about New Zealand literature, are also part of this contemporary context. 'Serious' writing by women has expanded dramatically in the past two decades, not only in poetry and fiction, where it tends to be most visible, but in drama, and especially in the field of non-fiction (history, sociology, biography, and autobiography). It is a diverse, exploratory literature, written from a wide variety of perspectives, but its main tendency has been oppositional, challenging male accounts of New Zealand society and culture. Most urgent of all, however, have been the cultural questions posed, with increasing intensity throughout the 1980s, by debate about relations between Māori and Pākehā in New Zealand, fuelled by the resurgence of Māori claims to cultural self-determination under the terms of the Treaty of Waitangi. The 1980s began with a Springbok Rugby Tour which polarized New Zealand society, then plunged at its mid point into an economic recession which accentuated racial inequalities, and ended in a sesquicentennial year full of reminders, for most Māori and many Pākehā, of longstanding injustices still to be redressed. A comment by Mark Williams, in his recent study of New Zealand fiction in the 1980s (*Leaving the Highway*), could be applied with equal truth to every genre of New Zealand writing during this latest, troubled decade: '[A]t no time since the 1930s has fiction in this country been so directly involved with crucial and unresolved questions of national self-definition and evaluation as was the case in the late 1980s.'

Individual contributors address this contemporary context in a variety of ways, and from different angles, as they explore questions of shape and direction, periodization, coherence and conflict, change and disjunction, political, social and cultural context, and (most problematic of all) meaning and value, in their particular genres. They also consider earlier seminal accounts of New Zealand literature — such as Allen Curnow's influential arguments about the development of New Zealand poetry (1945 and 1960), R.M. Chapman's long essay, 'Fiction and the Social Pattern' (1953), with its central focus on the nature of the institution of the family in New Zealand, or Bill Pearson's essay on attitudes to the Māori in Pākehā fiction (1958) — all of them, now, a part of the literary history they once challenged and re-interpreted. As well, there is continuing reference to the more dispersed and ephemeral discourse of reviews and articles, and to the practices and policies of editors and anthologists, through which — less spectacularly — New Zealand's literary culture continually defined and re-defined its values and beliefs. A homogeneous account of the country's literature, from ten contributors exploring different kinds of writing in the light of such issues, was hardly to be expected. There has been no attempt to force all genres into a single pattern of periods, a single pattern of leading ideas or themes or movements, a single model of evolutionary progress, or a single model of aesthetic value. Variations among genres — time-lags and disjunctions of theme and preoccupation, and the varying strength and weakness of particular genres (and of particular kinds of writing within genres) at different times — are seen as at least as important as continuities and similarities.

Although a diversity of approach amongst individual contributors was encouraged, overall coherence was promoted through the method of organization and the way the structure of the book defines the field of New Zealand literature. The first, and most important, of these general aims is implicit in the limited definition of field conveyed by the last two words of the book's title. It is a history of New Zealand literature *in English*, and thus of only one (and that the more recent) of the country's two main literatures. A comprehensive history of literature in Māori, and of pre- and post-European Māori oral culture, would be a huge project, requiring its own team of Māori scholars, and, most likely, a quite different methodology. What this volume offers, in the section by Jane McRae entitled 'Māori Literature: A Survey', is not a history of the kind attempted in the other sections, but a primarily descriptive survey of the main archival sources and published collections of writing in the Māori language, the major forms it has made use of since the introduction of the technology of writing and print (especially, in the nineteenth century, the newspaper, the journal, the letter, and the handwritten record), and the large body of published work, mostly written in English by both Māori and Pākehā, about the Māori language and its traditional and contemporary forms of artistic expression. 'Published work', in the broad sense used above, includes dictionaries, bibliographies, educational texts, translations (of myths, legends, prose narratives, and the many oral forms of poetry and prose), as well as commentaries, surveys and interpretative studies of oral and written texts. The section thus provides a comprehensive guide to published and archival resources for readers who wish to explore the literature further.

Within the field of New Zealand literature in English, the decision to organize the history into genres (rather than adopting other kinds of organization — thematic, chronological, or author-based, for example) also aimed to emphasize a number of general perspectives. The first of these is an expanded definition of the term 'literature', taking it in the direction of the much more inclusive term, 'writing'. Over the past half century a powerful hierarchy of genres has dominated critical discourse about New Zealand literature, with poetry and 'serious' adult fiction (the novel and the short story) enjoying largely undisputed possession of the field, the genres of non-fiction and drama on the margins, and children's literature and forms of popular writing largely invisible. (The recent *Penguin History of New Zealand Literature*,

1990, is a representative instance: almost wholly uncontaminated by any reference to drama, non-fiction, or popular literature, it relegates one of New Zealand's major writers, the children's author Margaret Mahy, to a footnote.) At least until recently this narrow hierarchy of genres has carried with it a strong gender division (since children's literature and popular literature have always been written mainly by women); it has also carried with it a high-cultural distaste for popular culture as 'escapist' and 'inauthentic', and a tendency to marginalize non-fiction as a kind of lesser discourse concerned only with 'facts', rather than (like any writing) a discourse whose narratives (historical, biographical, ethnographic, and so on) have contributed powerfully to the invention of the myths by which the country lives.

Organization of the history into genres enables these fields to be brought more directly into focus than would otherwise be the case (though the large field of journalism, except where it bears on the other genres, has had to be omitted for reasons of space). It also means that the sections on non-fiction, popular fiction, and children's literature are of a more exploratory nature than the rest, since (as a glance at the bibliography reveals) there is hardly any secondary literature devoted to these fields. Betty Gilderdale, the author of the section on children's literature, has written the only book in the field. In the field of popular fiction, another exception is Heather Roberts's *Where Did She Come From? New Zealand Women Novelists, 1862-1987* (1989), which works across the divide between high culture and popular culture and contributes to the growing body of feminist criticism of New Zealand literature. The section on non-fiction posed special problems, since so many different genres of writing are subsumed under the somewhat unsatisfactory term 'non-fiction' (unsatisfactory, because it concedes so much to the 'positive' pole, 'fiction', against which it is defined). The *Oxford History of Australian Literature* (1980) excluded it altogether, although a considerable effort was made to find a contributor able and willing to take it on. The three-volume *Literary History of Canada*, published by the University of Toronto Press in 1965, employed a large number of specialist contributors (eighteen altogether), each of whom wrote relatively brief, unrelated sections on the various genres of non-fiction. This had some advantages, but it also meant that the larger questions Peter Gibbons raises in his section — about the relations between different genres of non-fiction, the importance of particular genres at particular times, the meanings carried by the emergence of writing as a *subject* of writing in the relatively recent genres of literary biography and autobiography — remained largely unasked.

Organization of the history according to genres was also designed to encourage contributors to explore the genealogies of texts: not simply the ways in which writers vaguely 'influence' their successors, but the ways in which, as MacD.P. Jackson puts it in his section on poetry up to 1945, traditions are defined 'when texts begin to respond to their predecessors'. Naïve thematic or interpretative studies of the 'content' of texts, and author-focused studies of a writer's work as the expression of an 'individual' intention or 'vision', obscure the extent to which all writing is re-writing. A writer's choice of genre, and selection from the variety of given conventions within a genre (narrative, stylistic, linguistic), immediately engages the writing dynamically with the powerful cultural meanings and values such conventions carry. The connection of so much women's writing with the conventions of writing about children, for children, is an obvious instance, but it is in the genre of poetry that the connection between form and wider cultural meaning has been most powerfully explored. As Elizabeth Caffin comments in her section on poetry since 1945, Allen Curnow's anthology introductions 'initiated a discourse about the practice of poetry in New Zealand which still continues and which has no parallel in other literary genres'. Indeed poetics has provided the main discourse, the primary instance, through which general theories about the relationship between New Zealand literature and the society and culture (the theory of literature as an articulation of national identity, for example) have been pursued and debated.

The vigour of this discourse, and the intensity of the debates it has continued to generate, provide a distinctive context for the sections on poetry contributed by MacD. P. Jackson and Elizabeth Caffin. However, it has been much thinner in the case of the novel, the short story, and drama. In each of these sections, written respectively by Lawrence Jones, Lydia Wevers, and Howard McNaughton, the opportunity to explore the internal history of a particular genre has thus been used as a springboard to generate ideas about the relationship of changing narrative or dramatic models, and changing fictional or theatrical conventions, to the broader context of social and cultural change in New Zealand: to investigate how, as Lydia Wevers puts it, 'an ascendancy of type, such as the romance, or the sketch, may indicate the preoccupations of its time', or how, as Lawrence Jones puts it, 'themes and modes and conventions' are interrelated. In Howard McNaughton's account of New Zealand drama, an additional context for New Zealand's playwrights has been provided by the growth of the media of radio and television.

In all of the sections on particular genres there is thus a focus on the broader social, political, and cultural contexts in which New Zealand literature has been written. Although emphases vary amongst contributors, the tendency in the volume has been to read New Zealand literature as a body of related texts interacting with contexts, rather than as the product of individual authors carrying suitcases bursting with themes. In one section, however, by Dennis McEldowney on the history of publishing, patronage, and literary magazines in New Zealand, context is the explicit subject. Very little has been written about the history of these important institutional networks, which in the most fundamental ways shape what is written (and what is *not* written) at any particular time, not only through their impact on the economic circumstances of writers, but through the exercise of editorial policies about what to publish (and what *not* to publish), and, in the case of government patronage of writers, through the philosophies and policies that lie behind the provision (and division) of resources amongst particular individuals and groups and institutions. In the past the absence of any strong sense that such institutional networks have *histories* has meant that a relatively small number of literary journals and publishers has tended to dominate the field of vision: journals like *Phoenix* and *Landfall* and publishers like the Caxton Press, whose function as touchstones of cultural value largely reflects the dominance of poetry and poetics in the hierarchy of genres in New Zealand. Dennis McEldowney's section, like the others, places such significant institutional moments within a much broader, much more diverse context, opening up the field for the more detailed investigations that are needed.

Lastly, the special character of the Bibliography prepared for this history by John Thomson should be mentioned. It is not an alphabetical listing of resources, but a detailed bibliographical essay, a discursive guide to the various kinds of material available, and to the literature about individual authors. It has the essential function, in an exploratory history of the kind this volume aims to be, of providing a guide to other perspectives, other kinds of discourse about New Zealand literature. The structuring of any history places some questions at the centre, and marginalizes others. This history places genres and texts at the centre, and disperses individual authors amongst them, so that authors who write in more than one genre (and there are a considerable number of them) are discussed, in different ways, in different sections: collisions and variations of perspective, if they occur, have been seen as wholly desirable. The bibliography thus plays a role complementary to the other sections in providing readers with an informed guide to the many perspectives of other scholars and critics who, to adapt a phrase of Allen Curnow, have taken the literature of this country as a 'point of departure for the imagination'.

Terry Sturm
Matapouri
February 1991

Acknowledgements

A book as large as this incurs many debts of gratitude to individuals and institutions during the course of its writing.

Dr Peter Simpson contributed much to the planning of the non-fiction section before he entered Parliament and had to withdraw as a contributor. Peter Gibbons agreed to replace him mid-way through the project. Special thanks are also due to Elizabeth Caffin, who came into the project at an advanced stage to write the poetry section for the period after 1945.

Many libraries were used by contributors during the course of their research, but thanks are specifically due to the staff of the following libraries: the Alexander Turnbull Library, Wellington (especially J.E. Traue, Philip Rainer, and Janet Horncy); the Auckland Institute and Museum Library (especially Peter Hughes); the Auckland Public Library, especially the staff of the Rare Books Room and the New Zealand Room, and Cathy Williamson of the Children's Room; Auckland University Library, especially Cathie Hutchinson, and the staff of the New Zealand and Pacific Room; the General Assembly Library; the Hocken Library, Dunedin (especially David McDonald); the National Archives, Wellington (especially Ray Grover); the University of Canterbury Library; the University of Waikato Library; and the Victoria University of Wellington Library.

Thanks are also due to the University of Auckland and to Otago University for providing contributors with periods of study leave for the purposes of research, and with research grants; to the Alexander Turnbull Library for a Research Fellowship for Lawrence Jones; and to the Stout Research Centre and the English Department of the Victoria University of Wellington for residencies for Lawrence Jones. Grateful acknowledgement is also made to the Department of Internal Affairs, Wellington, for funding assistance which enabled contributors to attend several meetings in Auckland.

Many individual people assisted contributors in scholarly, practical, or personal ways during the writing of the book. Some are acknowledged in individual sections; others are acknowledged with warm appreciation here: Dr Susan Ash, Vivienne Ballantyne, Dr Cleve Barlow, Dr T. H. Beaglehole, Jean Bertram, Professor Bruce Biggs, Alistair Bisley, Sebastian Black, Dr Trevor Burnard, Jim Caffin, Mary Caffin, Maud Cahill, Dr R.A. Copland, Marietta Coulter, Murray Edmond, William Elderton, James and Margaret Garrett, Professor Ian A. Gordon, Dr Janine Graham, Kathryn Hastings, Helen Heazlewood, Rachel Jewell, Professor Timoti Kāretu, Professor Hugh Kawharu, Dr Michele Leggott, Dr E.H. McCormick, Professor Hirini Mead, Bill Manhire, Dr W.H. Oliver, Dr Bill Pearson, Hugh Price, Ray Richards,

Bruce Ringer, Bert Roth, Dr Kendrick Smithyman, Sir Keith Sinclair, Helen Sturm, Cathrine Waite, and Ian Wedde.

Finally, appreciation is recorded here to Oxford University Press for its sponsorship of the book, especially to Anne French, for her continuing enthusiasm for the project, expert editorial guidance, and care and patience in the book's production, and to Gillian Kootstra, whose copy-editing skills were invaluable in the final preparation of the manuscript.

Māori Literature: A Survey

JANE McRAE

Historical and Contemporary Setting

Before there was a literature of New Zealand, there was a Māori oral tradition of Aotearoa with an ancient history which began in the Polynesian homeland of Hawaiki. A Māori literary tradition has a recent history which tells of the effect on the people of the occupation of New Zealand by the European immigrants who brought the technologies of writing and print. The two traditions have become inextricably linked, although the oral tradition remains a vital part of Māori society. There has been a written form of Māori since 1815, but the benefits of writing were attenuated by the reduction in the use of spoken Māori which occurred in the wake of a predominance of English speaking colonists. A long tradition of orality, a recent history of literacy, and a decline in the spoken language might suggest a paucity of literature in Māori. There is, however, a considerable literature which is of great significance to Māori people and which is increasingly appreciated by Pākehā New Zealanders.

Archeological, linguistic, and historical evidence suggests that about AD 800 the ancestors of the Māori people came by canoe from East Polynesia to the land which they called Aotearoa. The voyagers spoke a Polynesian language and in the isolation of the new land it developed, with some regional dialects, into the form known as Māori.[1] In occupying Aotearoa these people established tribal kin groups in defined territories. Each group, following the pattern of the Polynesian heritage, produced a rich and complex oral tradition concerning all aspects of its life — common and esoteric lore about customary skills and practices, tribal history, relationships between people, sacred and secular etiquette, and the concerns and feelings of individuals. Amongst many kinds of composition there were the main genres of whakapapa (genealogy), karakia (incantations), whakataukī (sayings), waiata (sung poetry), and kōrero (narratives). The language of these texts was poetic and striking so that they could be easily memorized and recited. Respect for the words of the ancestral composers created conservative and ritual-bound transmission and use of texts (for example, word perfect recitation of karakia), but compositions changed with the passage of time or were re-worked to suit special occasions and audiences.

Most texts of an oral tradition were exclusive to the tribe which composed them, but some came to be known and used universally. Although the fame of certain composers lingered, compositions were not always attributed to individual authors because they were first and foremost vested in the public forum. There were specialists in different fields of knowledge and forms of

1

texts — priests who knew karakia appropriate for particular occasions, women skilled in the composition of waiata, and orators versed in tribal history, genealogy, and time-honoured quotations and sayings. Prompts to the oral tradition existed in carvings and decorations on meeting houses, in named and treasured possessions, in the patterns of weaving and other crafts, and in the mountains, rivers, and other named features of the tribal landscape. The primary record of the tradition, however, lay in the memories of the people and was preserved by regular use.

The oral tradition remains in many ways unchanged, although it is a less powerful force in Māori society. It is an essential introduction to literature in Māori because it complements that literature. To speak of the oral tradition is not only to speak of a legacy of customary lore but also of knowledge acquired in post-European times and from written material. Similarly, to speak of literature in Māori is to speak of the stylistic forms and subject matter of oral and literary traditions. Written texts of the traditional knowledge are regarded as a revered inheritance from the ancestors, but the oral form is arguably more important to Māori people.

The growth of a literature has been limited by a decline in spoken Māori. The language was spoken universally in the nineteenth century and by most Māori in the early decades of the twentieth, but a dramatic reduction in speakers had occurred by the 1970s, when a survey revealed that most native speakers were over thirty years of age and only about two per cent of the children were growing up speaking Māori as their first language. Such rapid language loss has prompted predictions that Māori will cease to exist as a living language.[2] Māori people took the survey results as a challenge to revive the language and sought recognition of its official status and the institution of bilingual education. An Act of Parliament in 1987 declared Māori an official language of New Zealand and conferred the right to speak it in certain legal proceedings; it also established a Māori Language Commission to give effect to the Act and to promote use of the language. Most hope for Māori as a living language is vested in educational initiatives targeted at the young: the Kōhanga Reo (pre-school 'language nests'), the Kura Kaupapa Māori (independent Māori schools), and other bilingual schools and programmes.

Although the number of fluent speakers of Māori is small, and English is used for written and spoken communication in most situations, the language is vitally important to Māori people principally because of its use on the marae. It is on that ground and in the whare hui (meeting-house) which stands upon it that Māori cultural values and practices are affirmed and expressed through the oral tradition. In the rituals which take place when tribes or groups meet, on the marae and away from it, the oral arts of speeches, chants, and songs are paramount, although the texts recited are composed, memorized, and preserved by the use of written documents and sound recordings. Fluency in Māori and knowledge of historical and contemporary lore are essential for any orator on a marae or for any composer of the genres of the oral tradition which are recited there. There is much about Māori society that can only be learnt by listening to the speeches given at hui, or at tribal whare wānanga (schools) where it is sometimes required that students memorize texts without the use of pen and paper. The tribal territory, with its heart in the marae, is also a source from which Māori composers and writers gain inspiration for their work. It could be said that for Māori people the value of most literature in Māori lies in its contribution to maintaining the ceremonies of the marae which express the essence of Māori culture.

The oral tradition, therefore, is not simply a precursor to the literature but exists in and alongside it. The Māori literary tradition incorporates the oral and grows beyond it, as will be evident in this survey of the published and unpublished texts that have been produced since Māori was first written.

Writing and Describing the Language

An orthography for Māori was created by the early 1800s, soon after the arrival in Aotearoa of the first European voyagers, missionaries, and settlers. The orthographical conventions established then have remained remarkably stable, though in recent years a debate has arisen (still unsolved) over the use of double vowels or macrons to represent long vowels.[3] Missionaries were especially active in promoting a written form of the language, and Māori literacy, as part of the programme to convert the 'New Zealanders' to Christianity. Once an orthography was available the mission schools taught classes in Māori, a practice which was brought to a close by government policies requiring that the medium of instruction in schools be both English and Māori (from 1847) and from 1867 onwards, English only. The longer-term effect of these policies was deeply detrimental to the survival of spoken and written Māori.[4]

It is apparent from extant literature that Māori people found immediate and profitable employment of writing and print. Reports from the 1830s tell of a rapid acquisition of literacy, prompting a suggestion that 'by the middle of the century a higher proportion of Maori than of settlers were literate in their own language'.[5] How accurate the reports were remains a matter of debate. In *Oral Culture, Literacy and Print in Early New Zealand: the Treaty of Waitangi* (1985), D.F McKenzie examined the reports in the context of the signing of the Treaty and concluded that the historical record had exaggerated the extent of Māori literacy at that time. McKenzie supported his case by referring to the hesitant use of literacy in the twentieth century,[6] but historians — while acknowledging the continued importance of orality in Māori society — replied that he underestimated abundant evidence of functional and sophisticated Māori writing from the 1840s onward: incomplete literacy in the twentieth century was primarily the result of language loss caused by an English-language dominated educational policy and the power of English as the general medium of communication.[7]

Whatever the outcome of such debates, there can be no doubt that Māori people experienced writing and print in the context of profound social change.

In a study of the early effect of literacy, for example, Michael Jackson[8] documented a shift from the desire for literacy as a key to European religious and technical knowledge, to a recognition of its practical value for effective political negotiation with the colonizers. He also marked a number of social and cultural changes resulting from literacy: challenges to traditional chiefs from the literate who acquired a prestige that had no precedent in custom; questioning of traditional knowledge under the impact of new information and beliefs encountered in printed literature; testing of the authority of the oral tradition, since literacy altered the content and communal setting in which texts were composed and published. It might be expected that such social changes would have a profound effect on the character of literature in Māori.

The book in which an orthography for Māori first went to print was *A Korao no New Zealand* (Sydney, 1815). This attempt to write the language was made by Thomas Kendall, a schoolteacher and lay-reader of the Church Missionary Society who had arrived in the country in 1813. Kendall followed up that work five years later in England, together with Professor Samuel Lee of Cambridge University and the Ngapuhi Māori chiefs Hongi Hika and Waikato. The result was an improved orthography for Māori and the beginnings of a grammar, published in Lee's *A Grammar and Vocabulary of the Language of New Zealand* (London, 1820). After some changes over the next twenty-five years, the Māori alphabet was standardized, and there began the descriptions of the grammar of the language which contribute to the progress of a literature.

The influential grammars of Māori published in the nineteenth century came from other incumbents of the Church Missionary Society, in the Rev. William Maunsell's *A Grammar of the New Zealand Language* (Auckland, 1842) and the exceptional contributions from the Williams family. These began with William Williams's grammatical sketch in *A Dictionary of the New Zealand Language, and A Concise Grammar; to which are Added a Selection of Colloquial Sentences* (Paihia, 1844), and continued with the influential *First Lessons in the Maori Language with a Short Vocabulary* (London, 1862) compiled by W.L. Williams, of which there were several editions, with revision also undertaken by his son Herbert W. Williams.

In the twentieth century the first grammar of the language to be written by a native speaker was produced by H.M. Stowell, with the engaging title *Maori-English Tutor and Vade Mecum* (Wellington, 1913). Other books published by Māori on the structure of the language have taken the form of teaching guides and workbooks: for example, K.T. Harawira's *Teach Yourself Maori* (1950) and the teacher's manual by S.M. Mead, *We Speak Maori* (1959), both published by Reed; and, from the Government Printer, Hoani Waititi's *Te Rangatahi* (1962), with its emphasis on prose pieces and dialogue, and *Te Reo Rangatira* (1974), a course written in the Tuhoe dialect by Timoti Karetu. In the 1980s, too, material for teachers was a priority, as exemplified in Merimeri Penfold and Linda Holdaway's *Ngaa Hiikoi Tuatahi* (University of Auckland, 1981) with its sample conversations and simplified texts from the oral tradition, and in the language

4

courses compiled by J.B. Foster, *He Whakamarama* (Auckland, 1987), and John Moorfield, *Te Kakāno* and *Te Pihinga* (University of Waikato, 1987).

Additional descriptions of the language followed from university study in the 1960s promoted by the scholar and linguist Bruce Biggs, whose *The Structure of New Zealand Maori* (University of Indiana, 1961) and *Let's Learn Maori* (Wellington, 1969), along with Pat Hohepa's description of the syntax of the language, *A Profile Generative Grammar of Maori* (University of Indiana, 1967), gave impetus to national and international studies of Māori. There have since been a number of unpublished postgraduate dissertations concerning syntax and grammar.[9] A new departure for the language came when the first description of grammar was published in Māori. *Me Ako Taatou i Te Reo Maaori* (Auckland, 1990) is a translation, by native speaker and linguist Cleve Barlow, of Biggs's *Let's Learn Maori*.

Dictionaries of Māori are few. Assorted vocabulary lists appeared from time to time in early nineteenth century publications on Māori society, but the first extensive list appeared in 1844 in William Williams's *A Dictionary of the New Zealand Language and a Concise Grammar*. In its fifth edition it became Herbert W. Williams's *A Dictionary of the Maori Language* (Wellington, 1917), and after a thorough revision for the seventh edition (1971) this work remains the standard Māori-English dictionary. Another substantial listing was compiled by Edward Tregear as *The Maori-Polynesian Comparative Dictionary* (Wellington, 1891), in which each Māori word was given with translation and Polynesian comparatives, and an English key to the Māori words added. The first English-Māori dictionary of the twentieth century was Bruce Biggs's *English-Maori Dictionary* (Wellington, 1966). His second compilation, *Complete English-Maori Dictionary* (Auckland, 1981), contains the English meanings taken from the Māori headwords in Williams's dictionary, supplemented with entries from Tregear and others' listings. A small work by P.M. Ryan, *The Revised Dictionary of Modern Māori* (Auckland, 1989), with Māori-English and English-Māori sections, has remained popular over many editions for its transliterated words and contemporary usage. Two special listings are Richard Benton's *Ko Ngā Kupu Pū Noa o Te Reo Māori. The First Basic Maori Word List* (Wellington, 1982), comprising words most frequently encountered in Māori speech and writing, and the only dialect listing, Ray Harlow's *A Word List for South Island Maori* (Linguistic Society of New Zealand, Auckland, 1985), compiled from a vocabulary kept by a South Island missionary in 1844. The limited extent of writing of all kinds in Māori is suggested by the fact that there is no dictionary of words explained in Māori.

Nineteenth Century Publishing

The earliest printed works in Māori, indeed most of what was published up to 1900, were produced by Church and State. The scope of these publications (and a brief history of the presses on which many of them were produced) has been documented by Herbert W. Williams's *A Bibliography of Printed Maori to 1900* (Wellington, 1924) and its *Supplement* (1928). Arranged chronologically these catalogues of nineteenth century Māori literature provide bibliographic description and a brief summary of contents for all works printed wholly or substantially in Māori. Additional works (and a listing of titles from 1901 to 1946) are contained in A.D. Sommerville's unpublished supplement available in main libraries (N.Z. Library School, 1947).[10]

A wide range of religious matter was printed in Māori — books of the Bible, orders of service, catechisms, prayer-books, hymnals, and almanacs. There were tracts on church doctrine, on topics as varied as the Antichrist, the errors of the Church of Rome, and the happy deaths of converts to Christianity. The translation of the Bible into Māori has its own history, touched on in the Introduction to Williams's *Bibliography* and by citations throughout it. Parts of the Bible were printed from 1827 with the first complete edition in Māori being issued by the British and Foreign Bible Society in 1868. Revisions to this translation led to new editions prepared by Rev. Maunsell and W.L. Williams in 1887, by Herbert W. Williams in 1924, and by a committee of Māori scholars who worked from 1946 to produce an extensively revised version in the 1960s.[11] Newspapers in Māori were also issued by the churches. The Wesleyan Mission's *Te Haeata* went out monthly from 1859 to 1862 and featured articles on the scriptures, instructions on bringing up children, moral tales, reports of meetings between chiefs and government, and international news. The churches' production of Māori newspapers was maintained through to the twentieth century with, for example, *Te Korimako* (1882-1890), *Te Pipiwharauroa* (1898-1913) and *Te Waka Karaitiana* (1934-1966).[12]

Material translated under government sponsorship was selected to inform Māori readers about the civilizations of Britain and Europe and about government policy. As can be read from the chronological arrangement of Williams's *Bibliography*, official publications grew from the short texts of circulars, letters, proclamations, and the Treaty of Waitangi, to the large texts of newspapers. Māori newspapers issued under direction of the government ran from 1842 to the 1870s, beginning with the all-Māori *Te Karere o Nui Tireni*, which went through various changes of format and title, including the addition of English translation. The last of the government newspapers was *Te Waka Maori o Niu Tirani* (1871-1877). Such newspapers reported on local, national, and international events. They minuted meetings between chiefs and government officials (often recording the speeches given) and gave notice of policy relating to native affairs; the correspondence pages were an important avenue of communication between the Māori people and government. The papers also printed some texts from the oral tradition, songs, myths and legends, excerpts from tribal histories, and biographical details about renowned chiefs. Other printed matter in Māori prepared by the government included translations of Acts of Parliament[13] and, from 1865 to 1930, *Te Kahiti o Niu Tireni*, an equivalent to the *New Zealand Gazette* for official notices to Māori people. Some speeches of Māori members of the Legislative Council were printed in a form similar to *Hansard* from 1881 to 1906. In addition to explanations of specific English laws and customs, the government directed the translation of a large and curious selection of texts to foster understanding of the Europeans' culture. Amongst these were didactic moral stories by Samuel Wilberforce, an account of Peter the Great, a treatise on the care of bees and the working of honey and wax, a short history of Britain to the end of the Roman occupation, and the novels *Robinson Crusoe* and *The Pilgrim's Progress*.

The published record of a writing system for Māori, the grammars and dictionaries of the language, and the production of a large corpus of printed material by Church and State, combined to present a nineteenth century literature in Māori which largely represented the religious, political, and intellectual life of the British colonizers. A literature which represented Māori culture emerged from the written and printed forms of the oral tradition and from the political documents which Māori people produced in response to colonization.

The Written Oral Tradition

Although writing has become a means of preserving the oral tradition, no widespread practice of publishing the traditional knowledge has been established by Māori people. In the nineteenth century books about the oral tradition were published by Pākehā. From the 1860s newspapers under the control of Māori printed some of the traditional material, and around the turn of the century there was some Māori participation in the publishing of texts of the oral tradition, principally through journal articles.

This limited publication by Māori people is explained to some extent by factors such as their recent history of literacy, a decline in the use of the language, and publishers' reluctance to pursue a literature with a small readership. But it is also explained by cultural conventions about access to the traditional knowledge. Books (at least potentially) allow common access to knowledge. There has never been free and open access to the texts of the oral tradition. The acquisition of these texts has been bound by rituals and restrictions, such as the limiting of historical and genealogical texts to tribal members, the keeping of sacred (tapu) manuscript books away from common (noa) items and activities, and the use of incantations during the transmission of knowledge from elders to chosen individuals. Time and the influence of new ideas have modified the power and universality of these rituals. Opinion about the use and dissemination of knowledge, whether transmitted orally or in writing, varies. The most conservative view is that because traditional knowledge is tapu it must be dealt with seriously and with due regard for the ritual requirements, and even those who do not hold rigidly to the traditional beliefs are likely to make a careful selection of texts for the purposes of teaching or publishing.[14] It is not uncommon for written records of traditions to be kept close to the tribal home and to be made available only to selected readers.

Published literature in Māori recording the oral tradition is, therefore, relatively rare and not always easily accessible. What books there are tend to be old and out of print; newer publications have often been produced by small presses or by institutions and in small quantities. Journal articles have to be searched out, and other material (for example, typescripts prepared for specific occasions) has a limited circulation. A rich source of the oral tradition, however, lies in manuscripts. Substantial collections of Māori manuscripts, a great number of which have never been published, are held in the Auckland Public Library, the Alexander Turnbull Library in Wellington, and the Hocken Library in Dunedin. Such collections in the public domain have come from two main sources; first, from collectors of traditional lore, and secondly, from the family papers of Māori people.

The majority of Māori manuscripts in public institutions are the result of the interest of nineteenth century Pākehā settlers, missionaries, and government officials in Māori society. Motives for their recording of the oral tradition were varied and of the times: the need, for instance, to understand the language and oral history in order to promote Christianity or effect government policy, or the desire to document the customs of a dying race. They acquired material either by writing out texts as they heard them, or by inviting Māori acquaintances to write for them, sometimes offering inducement by payment and provision of paper, pens, and ink.

A typical collection in terms of the type and content of this manuscript legacy, but outstanding in terms of its size and the quality of much of the writing, is that accumulated by Sir George Grey, twice Governor of New Zealand during 1845-1853 and 1861-1868, and Premier from 1877-1879.[15] During his terms of office Grey took a keen and scholarly interest in the Māori language, not least because he believed that it would help him to govern, but also because he admired the poetry of the oral tradition, sufficiently in fact to publish extensively from the texts he collected. Grey kept his own records of what he heard as he went about the country, and he also sought out others to write for him. His manuscripts contain notes on the language and its vocabulary, lists of sayings, tribal histories, popular and legendary stories, songs, chants and incantations, genealogies, accounts of customary practices, and reports of meetings between government and chiefs. The texts came from many tribal areas, but especially from Te Arawa, Ngati Kahungunu, Waikato, Ngati Toa, Ngati Raukawa, and Te Atiawa.

Some of the manuscripts in Grey's collection show that the authors were new to the conventions of writing. This is evident in erratic or non-existent punctuation and paragraph breaks, a failure to indicate direct speech, and the joining together of words. Some writing, too, presents difficulties for the reader because the authors employed the oral style of composition which assumed the understanding of an immediate audience conversant with the tradition. But there are also the fluent and sophisticated writings of the most practised scribes whom Grey contracted to write for him — Matene Te

Whiwhi, Tamihana Te Rauparaha, Piri Kawau, and especially Wiremu Maihi Te Rangikaheke.

The work of Te Rangikaheke, of the Ngati Rangiwewehi tribe of Te Arawa, can be singled out for both its quantity and quality. He wrote some 800 pages on many topics — language usage, the origin of man and the universe, religious rituals and ceremonies, customary practices, and historical events in the life of his tribe. He compiled lists of sayings, wrote out the texts of waiata, and produced 234 pages of commentary on the meanings of words and customs referred to in the songs published in Grey's *Ko Nga Moteatea me Nga Hakirara o Nga Maori* (Wellington, 1853). Te Rangikaheke worked for Grey between 1849 and 1853, and formed a close friendship with him, and his writings were a primary source for other publications by Grey. A bibliographic listing of all of Te Rangikaheke's writings, a brief biography, an evaluation of his accounts of history, and transcription and translation of manuscripts concerning the evolution of the universe, the origin of gods and mankind, the ancestors in Hawaiki, and the voyage of the Te Arawa canoe to Aotearoa, are provided in Jenifer Curnow's unpublished thesis 'Te Rangikaaheke: His Life and Work' (University of Auckland, 1983).

Te Rangikaheke's writing[16] is some of the finest Māori literature, and it came about from the kind of close relationship which often occurred between those Pākehā with a keen interest in Māori society and their colleague-informants. Extracts from the oral tradition written down by knowledgeable nineteenth century Māori are also to be found in the papers of writers such as Edward Shortland, John White, Elsdon Best, S. Percy Smith, and George Graham, all of whom edited the material for publication in books about the Māori race.[17]

Personal manuscript books of family and tribal traditions expressed in narrative, song, and genealogy, have been kept by Māori people since the 1850s when it was recognized that writing was a necessary means of preserving the traditions. These books are a valuable repository of the oral tradition, but because they are in private possession many of them are known only to those who can claim descent from the genealogical history they describe. Although it is not possible to provide an accurate assessment, these manuscripts probably comprise the largest single body of writing in Māori. Some have been deposited in public libraries and archives and some are known to have been buried with their authors. However, most are likely to remain in private ownership, and in some cases are kept in sacred storehouses in the tribal territory. Heightened interest in traditional history, and the desire for tribal control over the dissemination and publication of the literary heritage, suggest that this material will eventually become more accessible. Two examples of such manuscripts from the northern tribes of Ngapuhi and Te Rarawa, which are open to be read in public libraries, are discussed here as representative of writings that exist amongst all tribes.

A fine personal record of tribal history is to be found in a manuscript book which belonged to Ngakuru Pene Hare of Ngapuhi and Te Rarawa.[18] This book, dated in the 1920s, contains some 200 pages of the author's handwritten accounts of over sixty incidents of tribal fighting in the early 1800s amongst the northern Māori tribes. It is likely that the information for these came from both oral and written sources. The accounts are written fluently and with a clever use of language and pertinent quotations. Each account includes some or all of the following features: an explanation of the reasons for the fight, the naming and genealogical description of notable people who took part, texts of the incantations, songs, and chants recited at the time, a description of the action that took place (giving special attention to dramatic or memorable incidents), and an explanation of the reason for a name or saying which originated on the occasion. In addition, conversations and remarks are reported verbatim, and references and quotations allude to other historic events concerning the tribes involved. Hare's writing is forceful, picturesque, and persuasive in arguing the case for his version of the historical record; it is also typical of the oral narrative style.

The second set of private papers, which belonged to Himiona Kamira of Te Rarawa, reveals the tribal influence on the content of the literature.[19] Texts of genealogies, histories, songs, and incantations make up the collection. Amongst the papers there are minutes of meetings of elders who, from 1930 to 1950, convened to settle on the correct versions of the tribe's history and genealogies as written in the texts of the collection. A short piece by Kamira, concerning Kupe, one of the first northern ancestors to arrive from Hawaiki, has been published with a translation by Bruce Biggs.[20] Again, features of the oral style are evident in this writing, which is a compact narrative of episodes that move backward and forward in time, linked by the relationships of the people taking part. The antiquity of the story is accentuated by the insertion of ritual chants and the long and allusive names of people and places, while immediacy and vivacity are achieved through frequent quotations of direct speech.

It is in these private records, often the work of those well-versed in traditional knowledge, that some of the best literature in Māori is to be found. Because of their concentration in a tribe, such texts take readers to the heart of the traditional knowledge by acquainting them with the characters in the genealogies and with the recurring themes and historical references which give the tradition its special meaning. Moreover, narratives written for personal use are less likely to have the conscious changes to them that were made, for example, by those writing for Pākehā in the nineteenth century who omitted material distasteful to the Christian reader, or who interrupted the flow of an intricately constructed narrative to explain a custom. At their best these are complex texts, demonstrating an astute and economical use of language, and skill in the use of such poetic devices as rhythmical repetitions, figurative and metaphoric expression, and symbolic imagery.

The oral tradition also absorbed new information which had been learned from the printed literature of the Pākehā. The influence of the Bible on Māori prophet leaders was such that they created new, and eventually written, doctrines of faith. Te Ua Haumene, the prophet leader of the Pai Marire movement of 1862, left a record of his teachings (with prophecies and prayers drawing on Biblical references) in a notebook entitled 'Te Ua Rongopai' (The Gospel of Ua).[21] The Ringatu faith was established during the 1860s and 1870s by the visionary leader Te Kooti Arikirangi Te Turuki. Te Kooti composed prayers and songs which, along with his prophecies, sayings, compilations of Biblical texts for recitation during services, and some Church records, were written down by secretaries to ensure their preservation. Some of those texts are still known only to a few, and his predictions continue to be passed on orally. Much literature concerning the faith and its founder remains in manuscript form and in private hands.[22] It was not until 1960 that the Ringatu Church decided that the memorizing of texts for its long services could not be maintained without the aid of written texts, and published a service book, *Te Pukapuka o Nga Kawenata e Waru a te Atua me Nga Karakia Katoa a Te Haahi Ringatu*.[23] The prophecies of Tahupotiki Wiremu Ratana, founder of the Ratana Church, and of other Māori prophets, have also been printed in the Church's newspaper, *Te Whetu Marama o Te Kotahitanga*.[24] The new religions followed the pattern of the old, in requiring faithful recitation of texts and in using writing and print to record the sacred knowledge only when it was in danger of being lost. The manuscripts of the oral tradition, the writings of the prophet leaders, and the publications from their churches represented one literature of adjustment to Pākehā settlement; another literature was created in the adjustment to Pākehā government.

Political Literature in Māori

A separation between literature of the oral tradition and of politics is a convenient way to describe the origin of new forms of Māori text, but it is not an indication of Māori labelling or use of the texts. Categorization into, for example, political, scientific, or literary writing has no exact parallel either in the terminology of the language or in tradition. The nineteenth century political literature in Māori — letters, newspapers, minute books — followed Pākehā models for a Māori purpose and often in a way which was in keeping with tradition.

Letter writing had a special attraction because for the first time it made possible communication with those at a distance; it was also appreciated as a means of circulating notices and arranging meetings. But the greatest value of letters, to judge from those extant, was in enabling communication with government about matters of law. Scores of letters in Māori which were sent to government administrators to express opinions on personal and public matters remain to be read. They can be found in the files and letter books of government departments, printed (along with petitions) in the *Appendices to the Journals of the House of Representatives*, and in great quantity amongst the papers of government officials.

The Auckland Public Library holds 750 letters written to Sir George and Lady Eliza Grey between the 1850s and 1890s. They contain diverse topics and writing styles, and demonstrate that the Māori letter had its own distinctiveness. Many were marked by the formalities customary in performance of the oral arts, for example, in being prefaced with mihi or ritual greetings and concluded with waiata in the way of whaikōrero (formal speeches). Writers, too, would often advert to tribal history, quote from ancient chants, or express their feelings through a waiata. Signed by either individuals or groups the letters sent to the Greys expressed critical and appreciative assessment of action planned or taken by the government, described domestic difficulties, conveyed expressions of goodwill and affection, and outlined problems over the sale or use of land.

The land question more than any other was the subject of nineteenth century letters to government officials. This is obvious from those that remain in the papers of, for example, W.B.D. Mantell, who was appointed in 1845 as Commissioner for purchases of native land in the South Island, and of Donald McLean, a land purchase officer and native secretary during the 1850s. A number of letters to McLean have been published in transcription.[25] The letters combine to form a literature of historical record and they also demonstrate the application of the rituals of oral communication to the conventions of the written.

The ongoing process of resolving problems over land generated another important literature in Māori with the institution of the Native Land Court. The Court was established in 1865 with the principal function of investigating customary ownership of tribal land and assigning it title in English law. Verification of rights to land was in large part based on family and tribal relationships. Genealogies were therefore recited during Court hearings to justify claims to ownership. Otherwise in English, the Court minutes are a major source of tribal genealogies.[26] Genealogical texts are a valuable, in many ways essential, part of Māori literature. Despite their terse and even cryptic form, they are rich with meaning. They serve functions of specifying chronological order for generations and events, establishing the identity of speakers and their right to recount tribal history, and defining social and political relationships. They are also a succinct form of descriptive analysis: for example, in the cosmogonic accounts which list in sequence the names given to the phenomena of nature to picture the evolution of life. Recitals of genealogies may also be elaborated on by brief explanations such as the meaning of a name or a saying about a particular individual. The Land Court continues to preside over all transactions involving Māori land, some of which depend on proof of family connections. Genealogies are therefore written down as evidence for the Court as well as for personal records of family history. It was also a nineteenth century practice for those attending the Court to keep minutes in Māori of claimants' speeches, and these books have come to be regarded as valuable documents of tribal history.

Tribal committees also deliberated on rights to land and kept minutes in Māori. The Papatupu Block Committees, for example, were empowered by legislation in 1900 to investigate claims to papatupu land (held in Māori ownership without title in English law) before confirmation by the Native Land Court. Proceedings were conducted and minuted in Māori. Some thirty minute books from committees formed amongst northern Māori tribes survive as a remarkable record of local histories.[27] In putting a case for ownership to a particular block of land, a claimant before the committee would recite the genealogy of the ancestor who commenced settlement on the block, describe the boundaries, and detail the history of occupation. Songs, chants, and sayings were also recited to substantiate a claim. Knowledge of the land was attested by explaining the meanings of place names and the reasons for sacred and named landmarks, and by recollection of the memorable events which occurred there. Claimants' speeches and the cross-examination following them were minuted verbatim. The Land Court has documented and endorsed the shift of land from Māori ownership. The literature produced from the Land Court and its related institutions preserves knowledge about life on the land that was lost. Another similar literature is accruing from the documentation of claims to the Waitangi Tribunal, which was established in 1975 to hear Māori claims against the Crown for breaches of the Treaty of Waitangi.

Another medium for expression of Māori opinion about land and the Land Court were the newspapers produced on Māori-owned presses and under Māori editors. In the 1860s a press was acquired from Austria by the Māori King movement. When two Waikato chiefs, Wiremu Toetoe Tumohe and Te Hemara Rerehau Paraone, through an acquaintance with the geologist Ferdinand von Hochstetter, visited Austria in 1859, their interest in the Imperial Printing House prompted a gift of a press from the Austrian Emperor. The two chiefs kept diaries of their trip which were published with a translation almost a hundred years later.[28] The press was set up at Ngaruawahia where it produced the newsletter of the King movement, *Te Hokioi O Niu Tireni e Rere Atu Nei* (1861-1863). Issued monthly, its primary purpose was to communicate the King movement policy of refusal to sell land. In December 1862 the Government, in opposition to this Māori voice, set up a press nearby, and issued the newspaper *Te Pihoihoi Mokemoke i Runga i Te Tuanui*. It was edited by John Gorst, the Resident Magistrate for the Waikato, and censured the King movement's stand over land. In response to this criticism of their kinsmen, a Ngati Maniapoto war party removed the press in March 1863.[29]

Newspapers under Māori control were issued from time to time, some ceasing due to a lack of funds. With the encouragement of a Pākehā, C.O.B. Davis, money was collected from tribes for the papers under his editorship, *Te Waka o Te Iwi* (1857), *Te Whetu o Te Tau* (1858), and *Ko Aotearoa* or *The Maori Recorder* (1861). They followed the format of English papers of the time, with foreign and local news, correspondence columns, and advertisements. *Te Waka Maori o Niu Tireni* (1878) and *Te Waka o Aotearoa* (1884) were established in opposition to the government papers, as was *Te Wananga* (1874-1878) which was owned, printed, and published by Māori, and was openly critical of government policy for native affairs. The Kotahitanga (Unity) movement which led to the formation of a separate Māori Parliament, put out a newspaper, *Huia Tangata Kotahi* (1893-1895), reporting on both Māori and New Zealand Parliaments, land issues, local and world news. The Māori Parliament, which sat from 1891 to 1897, printed the proceedings of at least four of its sessions, held between 1893 and 1895, listing names of the participants and recording the speeches given and the bills proposed.[30] From 1891 to the 1920s the King movement produced a second newspaper and a series of notices under the title, *Te Paki o Matariki*. These papers carried the pronouncements of King Tawhiao, notices and policies of the King movement, comment on government policy, and general news. Newspapers under control of Māori continued up to the 1930s, with, for example, *Te Tiupiri* (1898-1900) and *Te Toa Takitini* (1921-1937). Māori newspapers had a central concern to ensure that Māori viewpoints were heard throughout the colony, but they also followed the custom of English newspapers and reported on matters of general interest. The papers published some excerpts from tribal traditions, and many waiata which were a forceful and expressive form for communicating feelings and opinions.

The Oral Tradition in Print

It has already been mentioned that a good deal of published literature in Māori originated from Pākehā, or from the joint work of Māori and Pākehā. Sir George Grey led the publication of texts of the oral tradition with selections from the manuscripts he had collected. The first of his books was *Ko Nga Moteatea me Nga Hakirara o Nga Maori* (1853), a listing of 533 waiata texts and some narrative pieces subsequently printed in *Ko Nga Mahinga a Nga Tupuna* (London, 1854). Grey was aware that much could be learnt from the waiata about history, relationships between people, customary etiquette, and current events. He put out a second collection, *Ko Nga Waiata Maori*, published in London in 1857. *Nga Mahinga* was Grey's edited version of the writings of some of his informants. It comprised a series of short narratives concerning the creation of man, legendary heroes and heroines, and episodes of the arrival and settlement of the ancestors in Aotearoa. In its fourth edition (1971), after revisions by Herbert W. Williams and a change of title in the third edition (*Nga Mahi a Nga Tupuna*, 1928), it remains well used as a text for teaching the language. His English version, *Polynesian Mythology* (London, 1855), has had a wide readership, being reprinted in 1885, 1906, and with editing and illustrations in 1961. It was reproduced in 1988 under a new title, *Legends of Aotearoa* (Silver Fern, Hamilton), with an introduction by S.M. Mead in which he noted that the translation is neither exact nor complete. The English version fails to convey the complexity of the Māori texts, their dramatic and poetic qualities and expression of Māori values and custom, and in the opinion of some has had a somewhat unfortunate influence on New Zealand writers and on general knowledge and understanding of Māori oral tradition.[31]

Grey was also a collector and quoter of the sayings which he published in *Ko Nga Whakapepeha me Nga Whakaahuareka a Nga Tipuna* (Cape Town, 1857).

He organized these in an alphabetic listing, each entry accompanied by some explanation: a translation, an interpretation, or an account of the situation a saying applied to or derived from. An appendix contained narratives to explain the circumstances in which some sayings had arisen. As a collection it has not been equalled. It includes examples of the different forms of whakataukī, and conveys the breadth of their subject-matter as well as touching on particular customs relating to their use.

Grey's contribution to the writing and publication of the oral tradition is greatly valued. There has been criticism of his work — for making additions and deletions to the manuscripts, for the joining together of several accounts to form one narrative, for omitting passages considered impolite, and for failing to acknowledge his writers.[32] But these criticisms have been made in the light of improved methods of collecting oral history and of a more equitable exchange of knowledge between Māori and Pākehā. It should also be appreciated that Grey not only collected this literature but helped to generate it. As Governor he became the subject of many compositions in Māori, exemplified in C.O.B. Davis's collection *Maori Mementos. Being a Series of Addresses, presented by the Native People, to His Excellency Sir George Grey, K.C.B. F.R.S.* (Auckland, 1855) which, as well as sayings, stories, and reports of meetings he had attended, prints songs and speeches composed on his departure in 1853 to take up the governorship of South Africa.

Prominent among nineteenth century publishers of the oral tradition was John White. White began collecting in the 1840s, gathering material from informants by specifying topics to be written about, providing them with exercise books, and writing himself as they talked. In 1848, for example, he asked a Ngapuhi chief, Aperahama Taonui, to write down the history of his tribe. The following year Taonui wrote 43 pages in a notebook which gave a description, interspersed with genealogies and chants, of events surrounding the arrival and settlement of Ngapuhi ancestors in Aotearoa.[33] As holder of several government offices relating to Native Affairs, White acted as a translator — in 1867 Grey requested that he translate into Māori a booklet giving instructions on the best method of growing tobacco.[34] His first major piece of Māori writing appeared as 'The Legendary History of the Maori'. This consisted of a series of articles on the canoe voyages, which drew heavily on accounts provided by informants, whose authorship was acknowledged: Hoani Nahe and Wi Te Wheoro contributed on the Tainui canoe, for example, Nepia Pohuhu on the Horouta, and Aperahama Taonui on the Mamari.[35] Later, he was sponsored by the Government to compile a history of the Māori, which appeared as the six-volume *The Ancient History of the Maori, His Mythology and Traditions* (Wellington, 1887-1890). The time span of the history reached from the life of the gods and creation of human life, through stories of famous ancestral figures, to tales of migration and inter-tribal battles in Aotearoa and some early incidents involving Europeans. Each volume had a Māori and English section, and waiata and genealogies were given throughout. Volumes 7 to 13 remain unpublished.[36]

White's work, like Grey's, has failings if judged against the criteria of modern scholarship, and has received some harsh criticism — for his rewriting of informants' material, his unacknowledged borrowings from Grey and others' work, and his inadequacies as a translator. After an examination of his methods of collection, the authenticity of his material, and his detractors' views of him, M.P.J. Reilly concluded that he is to be credited for a remarkable achievement in recording material from reliable sources.[37]

Another publication which derived from manuscript sources and appeared in an edited form was the two-volume work, compiled by S. Percy Smith, entitled *The Lore of the Whare-wānanga* (New Plymouth, 1913, 1915). The text was taken from manuscripts believed to have been transcripts of the teachings of eminent priests at an East Coast school of learning held in 1865 for the purpose of preserving traditional knowledge. Smith edited the material, which he claimed to have transcribed from the manuscript books of H.R. Whatahoro (one of the scribes at the school), adding a free translation and commentary on the content. The first volume, subtitled 'Te Kauae Runga or Things Celestial' deals with esoteric lore concerning the evolution of the world and the gods, and the second, 'Te Kauae Raro or Things Terrestrial' covers the migrations by canoe from Hawaiki and the arrival and settlement in Aotearoa. The provenance of the manuscripts used by Smith, some of which are extant in the Alexander Turnbull Library and Auckland University Library, is complicated, and has been partly explored by Bruce Biggs and David Simmons.[38] The book is still consulted by teachers for its substantial body of text in Māori, and for its content which has influenced both Māori and Pākehā understanding of Māori tradition.

Books wholly in Māori are few, but many Māori texts have had prominence as quotations. Waiata, karakia, whakataukī, whakapapa, and excerpts from tribal histories have always been published in books written in English about Māori society. Early publications such as Edward Shortland's *Traditions and Superstitions of the New Zealanders* (London, 1854) and Richard Taylor's *Te Ika a Maui* (London, 1855) featured such quotations, and this practice was followed through to the turn of the century and beyond. S. Percy Smith in *The Peopling of the North* (Wellington, 1897) and *Maori Wars of the Nineteenth Century* (Christchurch, 1910), and Elsdon Best in his series of monographs published by the Dominion Museum and in his tribal history *Tuhoe* (New Plymouth, 1925), used generous quotations of sayings, direct speech, genealogies, and songs. Twentieth century writers, too, have had the habit of illustrating their works in this way — Te Rangi Hiroa (Sir Peter Buck) in *The Coming of the Maori* (Wellington, 1949), David Simmons in *The Great New Zealand Myth* (Wellington, 1976), and Anne Salmond in *Hui* (Auckland, 1975). The traditional texts are quoted extensively and the meanings of them explored in Margaret Orbell's *Hawaiki* (University of Canterbury, 1985) and *The Natural World of the Maori* (Auckland, 1985). Tribal histories in English, such as Leslie G. Kelly's *Tainui* (Wellington, 1949), John Te H. Grace's *Tuwharetoa* (Wellington, 1959) and J.M. McEwen's *Rangitāne* (Auckland, 1986) have texts of songs, chants, genealogies, sayings, and reported speech. This selective quoting from the oral tradition has brought attention to the value and variety of texts, but it reveals only part of the tradition and as it is not often possible to go to literature to explore the quotations in their larger context, it can leave an impression of a fragmented and unfinished literature.

Twentieth Century Literature

From the 1890s to the first decades of the twentieth century texts of the oral tradition appeared in journals, often contributed by Māori working in collaboration with Pākehā writers who provided translation and commentary for them. From 1879 to the 1890s the *Transactions and Proceedings of the New Zealand Institute* counted a small number of articles in Māori amongst its issues, including a collection of sayings and two accounts of tribal history, one submitted by S. Percy Smith from a manuscript written by Hami Tawaewae, and another which had been written down by W.L. Buller as told to him by an elder.[39] From 1892 until the 1950s there was a steady output of articles in Māori from the *Journal of the Polynesian Society*, several coming from Māori members of the Society. There was an emphasis on tribal history, as in Timi Waata Rimini's description of the fall of a Ngati Kahungunu pā, Takaanui Tarakawa's series about the canoe voyages from Hawaiki, and Paora Tuhaere's historical narrative concerning Ngati Whatua.[40] Since the 1950s the number of articles in Māori has declined, there being the occasional contribution of transcription and translation of manuscripts.[41]

A journal with the particular object of publishing Māori language texts, *Te Wananga*, was begun in 1928 but ran to only two volumes with an article on the building of the Waikato meeting house 'Mahinarangi' by Pei Te Hurinui Jones, some writings by Nepia Pohuhu (one of the priests said to have been involved in the whare wānanga or 'school of learning' from which Smith's *Lore* was compiled), waiata with explanatory notes, and a listing of sayings. From 1952 the quarterly journal *Te Ao Hou*, published by the Maori Affairs Department, offered its readers a variety of material in Māori: local stories, tribal histories, sayings, songs and incantations, legendary tales, biographies of famous ancestors, and reports on contemporary events. Since it ceased in 1975 there have been other serials, some short-lived, which have carried writing in Māori, either on topical or traditional matters. These include the Maori Affairs Department journal *Tu Tangata*, the all-Māori school journals *Tautoko* and *Te Wharekura* produced by the Department of Education, and occasional pieces in a newspaper initiated in 1987, *Te Iwi o Aotearoa*. Since 1985 the journal of the Canterbury Maori Studies Association, *Te Karanga*, has regularly printed transcription and translation of manuscript texts — letters, song texts, historical narratives, and folk-tales. Special publications such as souvenir booklets prepared for the opening of meeting-houses or centenaries of schools, sometimes print introductory greetings in Māori, genealogies, and song texts.

Through the work of the Māori Language Commission there has been an increase in the number of printed Māori texts in circulation: pamphlets, newspaper advertisements, and government documents; and the Commission also issues a newsletter in Māori. In 1990 papers in Māori were planned for *Matawhaanui*, the journal of the Maori University Teachers' Association.

That there were many Māori readers of the journals up to the 1950s is suggested by the fact that between 1924 and 1951 *Te Toa Takitini* and the *Journal of the Polynesian Society* were chosen as a means of circulating the large number of waiata which Sir Apirana Ngata (of the Ngati Porou tribe) had collected from books, journals, manuscripts, and individuals. He published them through the journals in the hope of eliciting information on archaic words and historical references which would help with his translation and explanation of them. Ngata died in 1950 before completing the work, and Pei Te Hurinui Jones, a Ngati Maniapoto scholar, took up the task of revising, translating, and annotating the texts which came to be published as the three-volume *Nga Moteatea* (A.H. & A.W. Reed, Wellington, 1959; Polynesian Society, Wellington, 1961, 1970). The collection comprised 300 song texts, covering a range of song types from many tribes, with full notes to explain the meaning of names, sayings, and historical references; information for the annotations was drawn from books, manuscripts in public and private ownership, and from colleagues and correspondents. Prefaces in each volume discuss the conventions of composition and the song classes and characteristics. An introduction by Mervyn McLean in the third volume describes the music of the songs. A fourth volume, containing another 100 texts, remained in manuscript until it was published in 1990. *Nga Moteatea* represents an exceptional record of the sung poetry, and a significant body of writing on tribal history, genealogy, and custom. There are English translations throughout.

Sir Apirana Ngata and Pei Te Hurinui Jones were accomplished writers in Māori. Ngata wrote numerous articles and letters, notices and reports of meetings for the serialized papers *Te Pipiwharauroa* and *Te Toa Takitini*; he published a paper on the Treaty of Waitangi (1922) and a short article about printing (1940).[42] Pei Te Hurinui Jones wrote a history of the Tainui tribes (the manuscript of which was prepared for publication, with translation and annotations, by Bruce Biggs in 1990), quoted traditional texts in his tribal histories *Mahinarangi* (Hawera, 1946) and *King Potatau* (Wellington, 1960), and chose some formidable works to translate into Māori, including *The Merchant of Venice* (*Te Tangata Whai-rawa o Weniti*, H.L. Young, Palmerston North, 1946) and the *Rubaiyat of Omar Khayyam* (*Nga Rupai'aha a Oma Kai'ama*, P. Jones, Taumarunui, 1975).

From the 1960s a new lease of life was given to the publishing of Māori language texts through the work of scholars in the Maori Studies departments of New Zealand universities. Ethnographic monographs by Bruce Biggs, *Maori Marriage* (Wellington, 1960), and Roger Oppenheim, *Māori Death Customs* (Wellington, 1973), cited, with translation, passages from Te Rangikaheke's writing. Material for *Selected Readings in Maori* (Wellington, 1967) by Biggs, Pat

Hohepa, and S.M. Mead, and Margaret Orbell's *Maori Folktales* (Auckland, 1968), was taken from manuscripts and publications that were out of print. Work on manuscripts of tribal traditions brought the publication of *The Puriri Trees are Laughing* (Auckland, 1987), a study of the political history of Ngapuhi sub-tribes by Jeffrey Sissons and Pat Hohepa, based on a 70-page historical narrative written by Wiremu Wi Hongi in 1935; and of Manu van Ballekom and Ray Harlow's edition of *Te Waiatatanga Mai o Te Atua* (University of Canterbury, 1987), a South Island version of the creation of the world and human life written by Matiaha Tiramorehu in 1849. In 1983 a series of monographs initiated by the Canterbury University Maori Department offered an avenue for publication of manuscript texts.[43]

Māori scholars have generally chosen to publish material which is from their own tribal areas. There are, for instance, the transcriptions of letters written by Te Kaahui Kararehe of Te Atiawa to S. Percy Smith compiled by Ruka Broughton (1984), the writings by Hamiora Pio of Ngati Awa transcribed by Hirini Mead (1981) and, in the field of the oral arts, the study by Te Kapunga Dewes of haka (a posture dance with chant) composed by Henare Waitoa (1974).[44]

Language teaching at the universities has supported the writing of theses in Māori, resulting in the unusual occurrence of original writing in prose. Again, studies have focused on the writers' own tribal areas, as in Wharetoroa Kerr's community study 'Te Tahaaroa a Ruapuutanga' (University of Auckland, 1983), Ruka Broughton's investigation of the origin of his tribe 'Ko Ngaa Paiaka o Ngaa Rauru Kiitahi' (Victoria University, 1979), and Waerete Norman's tribal history 'Muriwhenua' (University of Auckland, 1987).

Some discourse about the literature, although seldom in Māori, has come from Māori university teachers. Commentaries in English by Māori scholars on style, conventions, and form in the oral tradition are to be found in Robert Te Kotahi Mahuta's analysis of the structure of whaikōrero (1974), in Mead's article on imagery and symbolism in Māori chants (1969), and in articles by Karetu on language use on the marae and by Dewes on the oral arts.[45] There is no Māori equivalent of the literary criticism of European tradition, but there is assessment of compositions when performed and discussion about the meaning and correctness of references in them. It is an assessment which is made to ensure that the texts reinforce the image of the tribe and the values of Maoridom.[46] Some comment in Māori about types of texts and the cultural value of them was made by past Māori scholars — Te Raumoa Balneavis writing in *Te Wananga* about whakataukī, and Ngata and Pei Te Hurinui Jones's introductions to *Nga Moteatea*, but there has been little expansion of this, apart from remarks by Arapeta Awatere and Koro Dewes on the use of sayings in formal speeches, and by Dewes and Karetu in their collections of waiata and haka.[47] An important development in discourse about the literature has come from the recent work by Agathe Thornton. In her articles, and particularly in *Maori Oral Literature* (Dunedin, 1987), she has brought experience as Emeritus Professor of Greek and Latin to bear on her analysis of Māori texts.

Sayings have long been well documented by lists and by frequent quotation in books and journals. There have been studies in English on the contextual use of sayings and on their role in the oral tradition.[48] A twentieth century collection published by Reweti Kohere, *He Konae Aronui* (Wellington, 1951), was intended for schoolteachers, listing sayings by subject with translation and explanation of meanings, and giving appropriate emphasis to the sayings of his own East Coast tribes. A.E. Brougham and A.W. Reed's popular *Maori Proverbs* (Wellington, 1963), with texts arranged by subject and followed by translations and occasional explanation of origin or application, has seen several editions. A collection published by the Department of Maori Affairs, *He Pepeha, He Whakatauki no Taitokerau* (Whangarei, 1987), listed sayings which applied to a group of closely related northern tribes. The wealth of the proverb literature is confirmed by the publication of 3000 examples culled from published and unpublished literature and listed, as the Māori text only, in Neil Grove's *Ngā Pepeha a Ngā Tupuna* (Victoria University, 1981). With their witty and metaphoric language and the historical and cultural references which they encapsulate, the sayings make up an important component of the oral tradition, invaluable to Māori orators and to their audiences who must know them to appreciate their proper use.

Of all the texts of the oral tradition the many forms of sung and chanted poetry have most often seen publication in print. The collections by Grey and by Ngata and Pei Te Hurinui Jones remain invaluable, as does *Maori Songs* (Auckland, 1893) and its supplements (1898, 1903, 1905, 1908), prepared by John McGregor, who had befriended Māori prisoners under his guard during the Land Wars of the 1860s and who agreed to publish the songs they wrote down for him. An interesting and broad range of texts (including samples of their use in letters of last century), with translation, notes on their content, the composers and music, and the change from a traditional to modern style of song, appeared in Barry Mitcalfe's *Maori Poetry: The Singing Word* (Wellington, 1974). Intensive analysis of the sung poetry has been carried out by Margaret Orbell. The style, content, and function of 100 texts were closely examined in her Ph.D. thesis 'Themes and Images in Maori Love Poetry' (University of Auckland, 1977). She has published texts with translation and commentary in numerous articles, and given further illustration of the song types, their literary qualities and cultural meanings in the selections published in *Maori Poetry* (Auckland, 1978) and, with musical transcription and annotation by Mervyn McLean, in *Traditional Songs of the Maori* (Wellington, 1975).

Literature in Māori published since the 1960s indicates that there is a great reliance on the manuscript bank from last century as a source of Māori writing. New compositions in prose are rarely seen, but original compositions of the sung and chanted poetry flourish. Even if they are first composed in writing (and serious collectors of Māori literature never throw away the handwritten or typed text of a waiata given to them), they are intended for oral performance, but some contemporary texts also reach publication in print. The study of Henare Waitoa's haka edited by Te Kapunga Dewes (1974) offers one example, as does Timoti Kāretu's collection of the waiata and haka performed by the Māori culture group at Waikato University.[49]

The tradition of composing waiata is a long one and famous composers from last century, like Topeora of Ngati Toa, and Puhiwahine of Ngati Tuwharetoa, are still honoured.[50] Perhaps the most prolific twentieth century composer whose work reached book form was Tuini Ngawai of Ngati Porou. An account of her life and the texts of many of her waiata are to be found in Ngoi Pewhairangi's *Tuini. Her Life and Her Songs* (Te Rau Press, Gisborne, 1985), a book compiled and published by members of her tribe who wished to preserve her work for future generations. The scope of the subject-matter of her songs is broad — from love songs and laments for the dead, to political and religious songs, and songs about sheep shearing (at which she was skilled) and everyday activities. There are many other composers of waiata who have been seldom, sometimes never, published but who are known and admired through the performance of their songs.

The range and nature of poetic compositions have become more widely known in the 1980s, and in conjunction with the publication of English literature. *Into the World of Light*, edited by Witi Ihimaera and D.S. Long (Auckland, 1982) aimed to present works in English by Māori writers, but it also printed song texts by composers well known to their tribes but not necessarily to Pākehā readers: for example, Wiremu Kerekere, Arapeta Awatere, and Dovey Katene-Horvath. Three years later Harvey McQueen and Ian Wedde, editors of a new edition of *The Penguin Book of New Zealand Verse*, deliberately chose to include poetry in Māori with translations. The inclusion of Māori poetry was not new; in the 1960 edition Allen Curnow had presented a sample of representative texts in English translation (for example, a genealogical text of creation, a ritual chant, a flute song, and a lament). These he placed before the English verse, together with a short introduction and notes which he wrote with Roger Oppenheim on the history and sources of the poetry.[51] Not surprisingly, given the emphasis on the revival of the language, the editors of the 1985 edition chose to have Māori texts alongside the translations. Margaret Orbell's introduction pictured the use of the songs in pre-European life, outlined the discovery and collection of texts by Pākehā, and gave a summary of song types and their uses.[52] Texts date from the 1820s to 1980s. There are a range of song types, including oriori (lullaby), waiata tangi (lament), pao (song of derision), and haka, and also of themes — love, religion, history, and modern politics. The composers are from many tribes and the order in which they are listed provides a genealogy of twentieth century poets, from the elders, Te Puea Herangi of Waikato, Apirana Ngata of Ngati Porou, Kohine Ponika of Tuhoe, and Kingi Ihaka of Te Aupouri, through the 'composer-teachers' Ngoi Pewhairangi, Merimeri Penfold, Katerina Mataira, and Arapera Blank, to the new generation, Pita Sharples and Hirini Melbourne. The chronological arrangement of the collection clusters some Māori texts first before the insertion of the first English text; thereafter Māori and Pākehā poets are listed together.

Four years later the same editors, this time with a Māori colleague, Miriama Evans, published Māori texts and translations in *The Penguin Book of Contemporary New Zealand Poetry* or, in its Māori title, *Nga Kupu Titohu o Aotearoa* (Auckland, 1989). In her introduction Evans explained that she made her selection by enquiring about poets' work at hui and by listening to performances of waiata, reporting that a number of composers declined to publish while others altered texts to omit parts relating to their tribes. Her choice centred on poets of the decade and aimed at an equitable distribution among tribes, sexes, and forms of texts.[53] There are the composers of the previous volumes and others: Ruka Broughton, Te Okanga Huata, Kuini Reedy. The book acknowledges Māori as a living language, and the texts indicate a strong and confident command of the ancient tradition of composition subtly adapted for the contemporary world. Both anthologies are innovative in their presentation of the distinct literatures of Māori and English verse side-by-side, for in the past the two literatures have developed largely apart.

In comparison with poetry, new writing in prose has been much slower to find its way into print. It can be expected that the writing of tribal history and genealogies goes on, but very little of it reaches publication. Two histories in Māori produced by tribal groups in the 1980s are edited compilations of manuscript material. *Te Tumu Korero* (Turongo House, Ngaruawahia, 1982) was published by the Māori King movement on the occasion of the dedication of a carving on one of the tribal marae. The book describes the images depicted in the carving, giving biographical and genealogical details of the people represented; summary translations in English are included. Manuscripts in the private collections of the King movement were the source of information for the book, which was produced in limited quantity.

A publication of a more substantial nature was *Karanga Hokianga* (Motuti Community Trust, Hokianga, 1986), an edited transcript (by Father Tate) of the minutes of the Papatupu Block Committee which sat at the turn of the century to debate rights to land in the Hokianga district. The testimony of claimants recorded in the minutes describes the history of the locality. The minutes were edited by members of the local tribal community while a new meeting-house was being built. Events described in the written texts were depicted in the carvings for the meeting-house (the carvings themselves becoming a public text), and incorporated in songs for the ceremonial opening of the house. The process by which this book came to be published — the reading of the written words of the ancestors and the giving of public expression to their teachings through artwork, song and, finally, a book — exemplifies both the use of writing to generate oral material and the slow, perhaps hesitant, move to publication in print.

A number of prose works are in progress at the time of writing. In the 1990 publication of the second volume of *The Dictionary of New Zealand Biography* there are 161 Māori biographies written in Māori. This work, which has addressed many issues of style in the writing and printing of Māori, is likely to establish a precedent for future writing. There are also plays by Pat Hohepa, a three-volume autobiography by Hemi Potatau, and a collection of articles, in Māori and English, on cultural topics being edited by Pakariki Harrison, a Master Carver of Ngati Porou. These and other writers were encouraged by the establishment of the Maori Publication Fund in 1989, which gave priority to funding original material generated in the Māori language rather than to translations of existing work. Writers like Witi Ihimaera, Patrica Grace, Keri Hulme, and Apirana Taylor will continue to write in English while incorporating Māori language and the influence of the oral tradition in their work. There may, too, be more translations of their works — like Jean Wikiriwhi's Māori version of Ihimaera's *Pounamu, Pounamu* (Auckland, 1986).

Lastly, but not insignificantly, in this survey of literature in Māori there is a 'new generation' of Māori language readers which have been prepared in the 1980s for those growing up speaking or learning to speak the language. Such books are being produced regularly and in quantity, some originating from small, independent co-operatives committed to the publication of Māori language texts.[54] Many are written by well-known Māori writers and composers — Hirini Melbourne, Patricia Grace, Katerina Mataira. They cover ordinary, everyday topics as well as subjects of relevance to Maoridom. Since the future of Māori as a spoken and written language lies with the children who grow up able to read these books, this indeed is crucial literature.

Literature in Māori is a large, vital, and compact literature including texts of an ancient oral tradition, translated works, and a well-defined body of historical and contemporary documents. Yet, in its physical form, it appears to be a small, antiquated, and fragmented literature, a scattered mass of published and unpublished texts, some of which are inaccessible to readers. Because of conventions about dissemination of the oral tradition and the unsympathetic climate into which a published form of the tradition might have emerged, a public literature in Māori (except for the material translated and collated by Pākehā) has grown slowly and tentatively while a private literature has prospered. This is why the path to this literature leads as often, if not more often, to manuscripts as to books and journals, why it traverses other texts such as newspapers and official documents, and why it also leads to individuals versed in the oral tradition.

Taking a summary view of the scope of the literature, it might be seen to fall into two categories, neither entirely exclusive of the other. One category comprises the outward-looking and public literature created by innovation (the interaction with Pākehā) rather than by tradition. This includes publications describing the language, translation of English works, and the political literature of letters and official records. The second category comprises the inward-looking and personal literature of the oral tradition which is spread widely, sometimes thinly, over a variety of texts — manuscripts, books, journals, and official documents. In this category, too, there is the new writing in Māori which, like the oral tradition, is self-conscious and primarily concerned with securing Māori values, but which is also open to changes which are acceptable to Māori conventions.

The future of literature in Māori can be pictured through these two categories. The literature of the first category will survive in reference works, and as public documents of the historical record. Some of it will grow: publications about the language will be added to by scholars and teachers, official documents will be generated in continued attempts to create a mutually effective political relationship between Māori and Pākehā. In the second category of literature the texts of the oral (and written) tradition will be preserved, by public institutions and by individuals and tribes, as a treasured heritage embodying the cultural wisdom and knowledge of Maoridom. There will be an effort to sustain the current level of new compositions and encourage further writing. The future of that writing is, however, precarious because it depends on a new generation of Māori speakers. The appearance of original prose and poetry in the 1980s is a promising sign. It is supported by evidence of a greater appreciation of the language and literature by sections of the Pākehā community. But if the future of new literature is precarious, the future of the existing literature can be said to be assured.

Māori people speak of the language as 'te reo rangatira' (the language of chiefs) and a fine use of words, especially by an orator but also by a writer, is highly valued. If the spoken language and the rituals associated with its use should diminish further, there will still be a substantial body of literature composed in that chiefly language, a rich classical literature which exhibits the pre-eminent skill of its authors and which will satisfy and inform readers for a long time.

Non-fiction

PETER GIBBONS

'Books about New Zealand are numerous enough', wrote William Pember Reeves in 1898. 'A critic need not be fastidious', he continued, 'to regret that most of them are not better written, useful and interesting as they are in the mass. Every sort of information about the country is to be got from them, but not always with pleasure or ease. To get it you must do a good deal of the curst hard reading which comes from easy writing.'[1] Reeves's judgement about easy writing making hard reading remains apposite a century later, and the books are much more numerous. The great bulk of New Zealand writing published in the form of books and pamphlets is non-fiction — 'books about New Zealand' to use Reeves's phrase; and even excluding works with a prominent statistical or graphic component there is still a very large archive to be considered.

The customary method of reducing an archive to manageable proportions is to select for discussion those writings estimated to be 'great books'. The yardstick is usually either aesthetic quality or significant innovation, and what measures up is literature in the more exclusive sense of that word. As long as the canon is not too rigidly maintained it is a useful as well as conventional device for literary historians; but because non-fiction includes a multiplicity of genres the delineation of a canon is less easy and less justifiable than for, say, novels or verse. New Zealand non-fiction writings, moreover, have been subjected to very little scholarly investigation. What follows must therefore be regarded as a very provisional account.

Non-fiction is an awkward term. Taken in its most literal sense it defines prose writing that is not fiction, and thus to some extent is a negative category in any literary universe which privileges fiction, or works of the creative imagination more generally, in contrast to work which is 'factual'. Alternatively, non-fiction is a label of approbation in the world of positivist scholarship where the fictive aspects of writings are either held to be of small importance or are not recognized — indeed, it is usual for local reviewers of New Zealand non-fiction works to be more concerned with veracity in the restricted sense of factual accuracy than with literary aspects of writing. Though the will to convey 'the truth', or at least a verisimilitude, is one important motivation in most non-fiction composition, the veridical dimensions of the writings are not of primary importance in this essay. Books appear in the exposition below because they are 'cultural events', or are of major influence in form or content for the development, maintenance or revival of a genre, or are typical of an important or simply bulky form of writing, or are recurrent representations of persistent subjects — or for combinations of these reasons. The essay does not attempt any Leavisite

27

prescription of a canon. On the other hand, some attention is paid to certain works which because they have a kind of canonical status exercise a notable influence upon later writers. There is a marked but not exclusive concentration upon various biographic writings (journals, reminiscences, memoirs, biographies, and autobiographies), and upon works of history and ethnology. These kinds of productions seem to have a broad currency beyond the specialized conformations in which they first appear, while other materials are, in general, ephemeral or are influential primarily within more or less discrete epistemologies — some of the important exceptions find a place in this essay.

The literary history of colonial or settler societies such as New Zealand is commonly explicated as the evolution of a 'national literature'. This is often the stated programme of writers and critics in colonial societies, but to regard the programme as the performance is to fail to recognize the ideological scaffolding. While there is discourse regarded as normative at different times, there can be no 'authentic' New Zealand literature in any absolute sense, and no omega point towards which writing proceeds. In this essay there is a chronological exposition in the sense that the sections into which the discussion is divided deal in turn with non-fiction writings from the earliest to the most recent 'periods'; but this sequence should not be read as indicating a broad progress from writing of a lesser quality or significance to writing of a greater quality or significance. Each section deals with the inauguration and elaboration of a different discursive strategy which may be said to have dominated or strongly influenced the majority or the most significant of the writings of one 'period'. The dates of these 'periods' it should be said, are indicative rather than prescriptive.

Part of the task of literary history is to explore textual genealogies. Where one might begin is difficult to decide; all texts reformulate pre-existing texts, all writing is rewriting, and the horizon of beginnings recedes beyond New Zealand. There is something to be said in favour of starting at the point where the consciousness of a local tradition (or the need to assemble one) can be shown to exist. But long before then the basic conditions which generated non-fiction writing had been established. These conditions were the extension of European power into non-European territories and the way in which writing was intimately engaged in expressing that power; writing, like Marx's capital, arrives in New Zealand 'dripping from head to foot, from every pore, with blood and dirt'.[2] Writing in and about New Zealand was henceforth involved in the processes of colonization, in the implementation of European power, in the description and justification of the European presence as normative, and in the simultaneous implicit or explicit production of the indigenous peoples as alien or marginal. At the same time writing was instrumental in classifying, mythologizing, and gendering experience within New Zealand.[3] There have been and are many important contestatory elements within this discourse. A major one is writing which 'corrects' the discourse of colonization by asserting the legitimacy, vitality, and persistence of the indigenous peoples; another is writing by women which seeks to revalue those experiences eliminated, denigrated, or misrepresented by male writers.

The discourse of colonization, the textual production of 'New Zealand', is here regarded as the predominant discourse; and most of the discussion is taken up with describing the formation of this discourse and tracing some of its various manifestations. The essay is divided into five major sections, four of which deal with the discourse of colonization. The first, the 'Archive of Exploration' extends through the period 1642 to 1840 and gives a brief description of the ways in which New Zealand was textualized by maritime explorers and by visiting or resident missionaries, traders, and adventurers in the period before British sovereignty was imposed. The 'Literature of Invasion' covers the period 1840 to 1890 and provides examples of writing by European colonists who were 'settling' the country, often finding themselves profoundly unsettled by the experience. The third section is called the 'Literature of Occupation', and concentrates on the period from 1890 to the 1930s. This section indicates how writers incorporated local phenomena in their texts, in an attempt to make themselves indigenous writers by concentrating upon indigenous subjects. The 'Literature of National Identity' discusses the textual definition of 'New Zealand' from the 1930s, and examines the ways in which women have sought to establish a cultural space of their own in non-fiction writings. It also notes briefly resistance by Māori to cultural colonization through print.

There is, however, at least the outline of a discursive formation which is more than a critical reformulation of the predominant discourse of colonization. The fifth section deals with 'Literary Biography and Literary Autobiography', concentrating largely though not exclusively on works published in the 1970s and 1980s. Writers themselves, their writings, and their struggles to wring meaning and livelihood from writing are the subjects of these texts. This other discourse, or potentially distinctive discourse, in some small measure also derives from the scholarship of empiricism: from the need to establish the transparency of textual sources, to create 'reliable' critical editions, to make manuscript materials available as printed texts; and from revisionist readings of materials which have previously been seen (and utilized) as unproblematic 'sources'. In this process texts are revealed as *writing* rather than merely 'evidence'. Thus New Zealand non-fiction works can be seen to inhabit the same terrain as works of the 'creative imagination' wherein writing does not simply represent, as if transparently, an apparently fixed and given 'real world' but is itself an act of making, continually inventing — and re-inventing — provisional notions of 'New Zealand'; of its past and present, its 'place' in the world.

The Archive of Exploration, 1642-1840

Up to 150 years before, read the instructions of the Dutch East India Company to Abel Tasman and his councillors who were preparing to sail in 1642, only a third of the globe was known. The sea-heroes Columbus and Amerigo Vespucci had discovered the new world, and the Portuguese captains had sailed to the east, and what inestimable riches and great might and powers had since accrued; now it was time to seek similar fruitful and rich lands in the southern part of the globe. The mariners were enjoined to observe the lands, the inhabitants, the resources, and to keep 'a full, and suitably extensive journal' in which all their encounters were to be 'completely noted'.[4] A scribe duly kept the journal. He wrote of the discovery of a land, and of the deaths of four mariners in Murderers Bay after an exchange of trumpet-calls. In time the information was summarized for inclusion in various printed texts listing voyages of 'discovery', and thus Nieuw Zeeland/Zeelandia Nova (as the land was called) was entered as another curiosity in the archive of exploration.[5] It was more than 125 years after the clash at Murderers Bay before any other European navigators arrived, two expeditions almost simultaneously; and though the presence of each was unknown to the other, they knew where Nouvelle-Zélande/New Zealand was to be found because the information collected by Tasman's scribe had been disseminated through print.

These then are the circumstances under which the 'literary history' of New Zealand may be said to have begun. There was writing in New Zealand before Tasman's scribe made his log-book entries: the local people had their incised glyphs and carvings which were written and read, and, if they had chosen to, the inhabitants could have monumentalized their victory over the strangers in 1642. But they did not have an alphabetical script which could readily be transformed into other grapholects (as Dutch accounts of the voyage could be and were made into accounts in French and English), and they did not have the technology of print. The information and communications systems of incumbents and invaders were not equivalent: the invaders had a technology which allowed the Other to be recorded and classified, to be *managed* in particular ways through the material accumulation of knowledge. And even before the Dutch set eyes on New Zealand the actions of the local people had been prefigured in the written instructions: the sailors should always be on their guard because trust of barbarous people had 'caused many treacherous murders' in the discovery of America.[6] All European experiences from the first were mediated by aggregations of existing knowledge drawn from the archive of exploration.

The journals of the English navigator James Cook and his companion, the gentleman-naturalist Joseph Banks, were the earliest extensive accounts of the land and its people. For the most part Cook and Banks recorded their observations in straightforward language (Banks was tempted into occasional philosophizings about women and anthropophagy) but their accounts include passages which foreshadow European penetration. 'Should it ever become an object of settleing this Country', writes Cook, 'the best place for the first fixing of a Colony would be either in the River Thames or the Bay of Islands'; and he then lists the various advantages, concluding that the people 'seem to be too much divided among themselves to unite in opposing, by which means and kind and gentle usuage the Colonists would be able to form strong parties among them'. Banks makes similar remarks in his journal. He also writes that they saw 'an immense quantity of Woodland, which was yet uncleard, but promisd great returns to the people who would take the trouble of Clearing it'. Cook and Banks made these comments in sections of their journals which stand apart from the day-by-day recital of experiences and events and which summarize the information of several weeks into a handy compendium. Such a process of abstraction, the 'liberty', as Banks said, 'of conjecturing and drawing conclusions', was possible only with writing in the European sense.[7]

Nevertheless, the journals of Cook and Banks were not presented to the public in the forms in which they were composed. They were delivered by the First Lord of the Admiralty to John Hawkesworth, recommended as 'a proper person to *write the Voyage*'.[8] Hawkesworth, a friend of Samuel Johnson and a person of some literary repute, rendered the various accounts of the voyage into a single narrative, smoothing out the angularities of the rough journals and adding some philosophical fancies of his own. Just as the separate observations were drawn into one narrative, so were the individual observers reduced by the editor into a single omniscient persona. Cook for one was not very happy with the result; and Hawkesworth was roughly treated by the literary critics. But the work was widely read and went into several editions. Hawkesworth's version became the standard printed account of Cook's voyage and thus of 'New Zealand'.

During the next seventy or so years (there were occasional examples beyond the 1840s) several major European expeditions visited New Zealand as part of a more general maritime exploration: Cook on his next two voyages, Vancouver, the Spaniard Malaspina, the Russian Bellingshausen, several French expeditions, FitzRoy (on the *Beagle* with Darwin), the American Wilkes, and, virtually at the end of the sequence, James Clark Ross on his way to the Antarctic. In most cases governments or learned societies published a handsome series of volumes to record the general enterprise and (more particularly in later years) the collection of scientific materials. The space given to New Zealand and its phenomena depended on the length of the visit and upon the industriousness of the observers and scientists, but in aggregate the reports are considerable and mark the start of a scientific discourse about New Zealand. In fact, New Zealand (or a few parts of it) was primarily an occasion for accumulating information to be added to the scientific inventories. In addition, peripatetic missionaries and sundry adventurers made New Zealand a port of call, and their experiences are recorded in such books as Daniel Tyerman's *Journal* (1831) and Peter Dillon's *Narrative* (1829). In these accounts New Zealand was simply one more place visited in the course of exploring what others called the 'South Sea Islands'.

During the early decades of the nineteenth century there were published the first books of which New Zealand was the exclusive subject and was thereby established as a discrete textual presence. John Savage's *Some Account of New Zealand* (1807) is of interest primarily as 'the first work devoted entirely to New

Zealand'. Savage had been a surgeon in the colony of New South Wales and spent six weeks at the Bay of Islands during his return voyage to Britain. He found that New Zealand, unlike other islands of the Pacific, 'had not been spoken of by a voyager since the time of Captain Cook' — which suggests (despite the inapposite reference to speaking) that he was conscious of a textual space to be filled.[9] Most of Savage's slight essay is made up of speculation about the local inhabitants, and the little reliable information he offers was largely derived from conversation with 'Moyhanger', a local man whom he persuaded to accompany him to England. In many later works Europeans would arrogate to themselves the title of author for knowledge freely provided by the indigenous people.

A decade later, in 1817, J.L. Nicholas produced his *Narrative,* two volumes based on a journal he had kept while spending several weeks in New Zealand with the missionary Samuel Marsden. Nicholas, like Savage and the scientific explorers before him, writes optimistically of the New Zealanders in the fashion of the Age of Enlightenment; but he is also fascinated by local customs of sexuality, warfare, 'superstition', and cannibalism. These European obsessions are evident in many accounts, even in R.A. Cruise's *Journal* (1823) which is otherwise a matter-of-fact record of a trading visit; and Cruise adds infanticide to the list. When these textual deposits were drawn upon as authoritative texts, a highly distorted account could result. Sixty years after Cook's first visit the printed materials were sufficiently plentiful for the textualization of the indigenous inhabitants without actual experience of them. G.L. Craik's *The New Zealanders* (1830), a volume in the 'Library of Entertaining Knowledge', is written around the reminiscences of a shadowy European figure who had lived for a time among the local people, with amplifications by way of Cook (in Hawkesworth's version), Nicholas, Cruise, and other published accounts.

The way in which New Zealand and the New Zealanders were rendered in print changed as did literary and philosophical tastes. The evangelical missionaries saw the South Seas world in a very different way from the recorders in the Age of Enlightenment; and the Romantic movement in art and letters, a movement which in some measure drew inspiration from the reported experiences of the navigators, gave the peoples and landscapes of the Pacific new literary and graphic roles.[10] The contrasting works of William Yate and Augustus Earle reflect in part these distinctive influences. Yate's *An Account of New Zealand* (1835) claimed the authority of seven years' missionary activity by the author; he also drew information from the published and unpublished journals and reports made by other members of the Church Missionary Society. First he writes an extensive and highly favourable report on the landscape and the flora and fauna. The central section of the book is a description of the 'manners, customs, prejudices, and superstitions' of a 'savage and barbarous people'; though Yate is not too censorious in his observations of their material culture, he makes a frightful catalogue of their unregenerate practices.[11] In the final chapters the mission is established and the conversions begin, with the gloss of appropriate testimonies written by New Zealanders. What purports to be a realistic account is, in fact, carefully plotted to denigrate the New Zealanders in their natural state, to glorify the mission, and to amplify the success of evangelism.

Earle's *Narrative of a Residence* (1832) is by comparison less contrived and far closer to experience, perhaps because the text is (as far as can be guessed) not too much elaborated from the journal on which it is based. An artist, Earle took up 'temporary residence' amongst the natives in the hope of finding new subjects in their 'peculiar and picturesque style of life'. At times his prose renders the New Zealanders as actors on a classical stage, and his description of Hongi Hika and his entourage has been quoted frequently. To Earle the scene 'almost seemed to realize some of the passages of Homer, where he describes the wanderer Ulysses and his gallant band of warriors'. This conceit, if not singular, was not altogether typical of Earle either; more than any of the other early writers he expresses his immediate emotions. When he and a friend hear that a young woman has been killed, and that her remains are right then being cooked: 'we felt sick almost to fainting', he records, and he organized a raid on the oven and an interment for the victim closer to European practice. Earle evinces an honest revulsion for certain local customs but admiration for the people, and the complex judgement is given piquancy by his malign criticism of the missionaries.[12]

J.S. Polack was more prolix. His *New Zealand, Being a Narrative* was published in 1838 in two volumes; he then reworked his materials into a kind of ethnological survey for another two volumes, *Manners and Customs,* in 1840. Polack was a trader and did some travelling around the northern half of the North Island in the course of business; he makes minor comic epics out of these humdrum expeditions, with himself always the centre of attention. His overstated descriptions which sometimes pass as broadly humorous in fact mock his hosts and travelling companions: 'The abomination of the tangi commenced, in which the early sobs rose to shrieks and outcries that were truly dismal to hear . . . . This howling lasted an hour; and as we had passed through many adventures (in the ideas of a native), it took some time to chant over.'[13] Polack expresses disdain for rather than dislike of the New Zealanders; for the trees and the birds there is warm appreciation. The central thesis (fitfully expounded) of both his works is that colonization is the right and proper circumstance for New Zealand and the New Zealanders.

New Zealand was a British colony by the time J.C. Bidwill, a visiting Sydney merchant with a speculative eye for real estate, brought out his short *Rambles in New Zealand* (1841), but his exploration of the central North Island took place in 1839 and he may be included alongside Polack. Bidwill's prose is compact and plain, even when describing the flora. He was an amateur botanist, and his observations are precise. His writing reveals his impatience with the laws of tapu, which he more than once infringed, most spectacularly in his ascent of Mount Tongariro; and he finds the reluctance of New Zealanders to do precisely what he wants irksome. Like Polack, he writes of the

New Zealanders with deprecatory amusement and a degree of contempt. William Wade's *Journey in the Northern Island of New Zealand,* published in 1842 but based on the missionary's diary of travels during 1838, with interpolations of other contemporary material, is also marked by suspicion of and contempt for the New Zealanders. These are attitudes absent from the writing of Savage, Nicholas, and other early writers, even the censorious Yate. It seems reasonable to suggest that such attitudes arise from an expectation or (in the case of Bidwill and Wade) knowledge of the establishment of British sovereignty.

It is not altogether satisfactory to draw a line through 1840 and say that the change in the political circumstances in New Zealand can also be seen in the literary history. One might suggest, for example, that J.H. Kerry-Nicholls's *The King Country* (1884) is in content, scope, and form simply an expanded version of Bidwill's *Rambles* (Kerry-Nicholls also recounts breaking the Tuwharetoa prohibition on climbing mountains). But the establishment of British sovereignty and the beginnings of organized colonization alter the circumstances of writing. What had been written hitherto belongs to the archive of exploration, an archive which was a consequence of European power but which while operating upon New Zealand and the New Zealanders was largely external to them. After 1840 European power is symbolically, legally, and materially installed in New Zealand, and writing is directly or indirectly constitutive of that power: the textual space and the geopolitical space thenceforth coincide, at least for Europeans. Indeed the Treaty of Waitangi, a written document, signifies this coincidence. Thus, the archive of exploration is succeeded by what may be called the literature of invasion.

The Literature of Invasion, 1840–1890

The literature of invasion concentrated on three interrelated subjects: the indigenous inhabitants, the natural phenomena and resources of New Zealand, and accounts of European settlement experiences. The major genres were those common to the first decades of colonization: personal accounts in the form of letters, diaries, journals, narratives, and reminiscences; history; natural history; political essays, pamphlets, and polemics; ethnological writings; and the various publications which make up the propaganda of migration. Nevertheless, many works do not fit neatly into these categories. Much scientific writing, for instance, contains accounts of exploration as well as descriptive and taxonomic matter.

With certain exceptions the more sophisticated works were written by people educated in the 'old world', the books were published in Britain, and they were addressed primarily to an audience beyond New Zealand. In this period, literature written by and for New Zealanders (without defining any of those words too carefully) is a variety of official papers, almanacs, institutional reports, printed addresses, essays, booklets, and the assorted contributions published in periodical journals and newspapers, sometimes also issued in pamphlet form. This typographical undergrowth requires literary study, but until it receives detailed consideration it must be left to one side in general discussions. Therefore, this section concentrates on a small number of works which are either typical of the most substantial forms of the literature of invasion or which exercise a continuing influence.

Essentially the literature of invasion has an instrumental purpose: it is bound up with the imposition and extension of European power in New Zealand, and supplements the formulaic writings which (in the shape of Acts, ordinances, gazette notices, proclamations, and so on) are the fundamental prescriptions of European colonization. The literature of invasion thus forms a prose commentary or gloss upon the basic tabulations of power. It is the discursive explanation and legitimation of the central act of violence, the insertion of an alien people and polity into an already inhabited land.

The New Zealand Company, a speculative group which hoped to reap rich profits from the sale of land to colonists, sent its first ship, the *Tory*, to New Zealand in 1839. Among those on board were three men who published books on New Zealand in the early 1840s: Charles Heaphy, Edward Jerningham Wakefield, and Ernest Dieffenbach. Their works were directly related to the colonizing activities of the Company, and may serve to introduce some of the major features of the literature of invasion.

Charles Heaphy's *Narrative of a Residence in Various Parts of New Zealand. Together with a Description of the Present State of the Company's Settlements* (1842) is not in itself an especially significant work; it finds a place here as an early example of the literature of emigration. Heaphy's subtitle indicates the purpose as well as the content of the book. 'From the circumstance of my having been in the service of the Company', admits Heaphy, 'it may be imagined that I am interested in upholding its principles, and am now writing by dictation.' This, he protested, was not the case; but his disclaimer is disingenuous: Heaphy's descriptions of the settlements and adjacent lands and resources were designed to persuade potential migrants that the Company's settlements deserved their favourable attention. At the same time, Heaphy used textual sleight of hand to reduce the importance of the indigenous people and to inflate the power and significance of the colonists. Just one chapter out of twelve is devoted to the New Zealanders, and their future declension is sketched — many will in time be 'labouring for the settlers', in half a century 'the interests of the two races will be one', and 'the extermination of the aborigines will only take place in their amalgamation with the Europeans'.[14] Later works would contain more recondite information than Heaphy provided, such as what goods migrants ought to take on the voyage, what the wage rates were for different kinds of employment in the different settlements, what return a man might expect on this or that investment in land. Often there were testimonials from satisfied migrants, some doubtless solicited if not written to dictation: these letters form an *ad hoc* commentary on the progress of settlement. Eventually there was a divergence between the tracts written in Britain from a limited knowledge of New Zealand (Arthur Clayden's numerous works of the 1870s and 1880s are a

35

good example) and those works written by long-term residents of New Zealand, which show a more precise knowledge of colonial conditions, and which, while addressed to emigrants/immigrants, not only map prospects for settlers but move towards defining what is different and even special about New Zealand. *The Official Handbook of New Zealand* (first published in 1875) prefigures *The Official Year-book* (annually from 1893) which combines prose and statistical materials, and later includes pictorial matter. The other progeny of emigration literature are the innumerable guides for tourists dominated by photographs of scenic attractions but often accompanied by prose which tries to characterize the distinctiveness of New Zealand.

Whatever its precise format, a general feature of emigration propaganda is its optimistic perspective. It seems likely that the consistently positive view of colonization which was maintained came to be read as an account of what actually happened; thus the failures and tragedies were regarded as the exception rather than the rule. There were, of course, contrary views. Alexander Marjoribanks, a New Zealand Company settler who quickly returned to Britain, wrote in *Travels in New Zealand* (1846) that the country appeared to be 'a singular paradise . . . unlike what mankind in general look forward to, — being composed chiefly of mountains, hills, ranges of mountains, ridges of mountains, tops of mountains, snowy mountains, creeks, bays, lagoons, and mangrove swamps'.[15] In later years the tartest comments were made by short-term visitors, and their criticisms, often perspicacious, were not applauded in New Zealand. Notable examples were Anthony Trollope (less sharp than his mother had been about Americans) and J.A. Froude. The pseudonymous 'Hopeful' (evidently a woman, as the letters which make up the book are signed 'Maggie') in *'Taken In'* (1886) is as condemnatory of the social and cultural landscape as Marjoribanks had been of the physical: 'Maggie' noted there were problems with drink and that wife desertion was 'very common'. People not suited to colonial life included, in her opinion, 'all those who delight in music, poetry, art, nature, all those who worship the beautiful'; she needed only to raise her eyes 'and look out on the common squalid looking little wooden shanties' to remind herself that she was not at Bruges, Ghent, Brussels, Geneva — 'seats of beauty and civilisation'.[16] Most non-fiction writers even when they were not deliberately writing promotional literature felt constrained to be more equivocal about the disadvantages of colonial life.

*   *   *

The second of the *Tory* trio is Edward Jerningham Wakefield. His *Adventure in New Zealand* (1845) is aptly titled. The son of Edward Gibbon Wakefield (sometimes called the theorist of colonization), he kept a detailed diary of his experiences, partly (it has been suggested) to be able to provide his father in Britain with full details of how the theory translated into practice, and partly to use as a basis for regular instalments of Company propaganda which were published in a London journal. On his voyage back to England he turned the diary into both a defence of the Company and a vigorous account of his official and unofficial experiences. Wakefield was young (nineteen when he disembarked from the *Tory* in 1839), and there were no parental and few self-imposed restraints on his behaviour. He travels and trades with gusto; he feels few inhibitions in his dealings with the New Zealanders, and at times lives a bohemian kind of existence. Wakefield's prose is bright and vivacious, both when he is describing his own experiences, and also when he is defending the point of view of the Company and attacking missionaries, officials, and governors who hold different views. His book is, as he admits at its end, partisan; it is also a close-grained account of the impact of New Zealand and the New Zealanders upon the youthful Englishman: 'Close to my home was a warm spring, so shallow that you could lie down on the sandy bottom, holding your head out of water. In this bath all the natives assembled, morning and evening . . . . I soon learned to join them; and used to remain there for hours, smoking and playing at draughts, at which game all the natives have learned to be extremely expert.' Yet his mission was, in effect, to see that this congenial world passed away. Wakefield left 'with the conviction that the brave colony of Englishmen planted on its sunny shores had taken a firm root in the fertile soil' while at the same time deriding Governor FitzRoy for being 'so foolish as to encourage the savage in his infantile ambition to maintain himself in a rivalry with the White man'.[17]

Ernest Dieffenbach, ship-board companion of Heaphy and Wakefield, was employed by the Company to make an inventory of New Zealand which was published as *Travels in New Zealand* (1843). Dieffenbach, a German scientist for whom English was a second language, is precise, careful, and measured in his expression; but by contrast with Wakefield his writing is clumsy. However, Dieffenbach's brief was to collect and classify information, and such a compendium had the potential to be a great deal duller than it is. What Wakefield felt and experienced physically, Dieffenbach observed and tabulated intellectually. The scientist, too, is entranced by what he finds, the people and phenomena, and his prose does not altogether conceal the delight: 'Sometimes a parrot would perch on one of the trees embowering our huts, as if curious to ascertain who had ventured to disturb his repose. During the night a solitary cry from one of these birds might be heard from time to time, after which everything again became quiet.'[18]

The first volume of *Travels in New Zealand* is the register of what the scientist sees as he moves through the North Island; the second volume is an ethnography of the New Zealanders with a substantial section on their language. Dieffenbach believed that the people could be fully understood only through a knowledge of their language, and he therefore sets down not just a grammar but also versions of their songs. (Wakefield's view was different; it was while camped with Dieffenbach at Moturoa that Wakefield was 'first struck with the absurdity of maintaining the native language' because of the common practice of transliterating European personal names and other English words.) Diligent though the scientist is, he expresses, not too obliquely, dismay at the juggernaut of colonization and the treatment, actual or potential, of the New Zealanders; in the end he hopes the worst effects will be mitigated by 'amalgamation', that is, assimilation.[19]

In prose style, organization of the texts, and ideology Dieffenbach's and Wakefield's works are distinctively different; but in subject-matter there are similarities. Both authors deal with the present and possible future relationships of New Zealanders and colonists, European exploration of the landscape, flora, fauna, and other local phenomena. In addition, Wakefield's *Adventure in New Zealand* is a kind of narrative of pioneering. These are major themes of the literature of invasion. Each is discussed below with reference to important or representative texts.

*   *   *

In the 1840s and 1850s several major works were published which sought to textualize the New Zealanders, though none were as comprehensive as Dieffenbach's survey. The general purpose of most of these works was put very plainly by George Grey in his Preface to *Polynesian Mythology* (1855). Grey explained that when he arrived as Governor of New Zealand he had found some of 'Her Majesty's native subjects engaged in hostilities with the Queen's troops'. He could, he believed, 'neither successfully govern, nor hope to conciliate, a numerous and turbulent people, with whose language, manners, customs, religion, and modes of thought' he was 'quite unacquainted'. He discovered that in their speeches and letters they 'frequently quoted, in explanation of their views and intentions, fragments of ancient poems or proverbs, or made allusions which rested on an ancient system of mythology', and that 'the most important parts of their communications were embodied in these figurative forms'. It was in order to govern his subjects more effectively, therefore, that Grey collected legends, proverbs, and songs. The songs he did not publish in translation; but Grey believed that some of the legends (though he called them 'puerile') would be of interest to European readers, and he made translations of more than twenty. His versions employ the diction he thought appropriate for tales of other creatures and other worlds. *Polynesian Mythology* became, and has remained, the *locus classicus* of local myths and legends; nearly all subsequent published collections derive, in whole or part, directly or indirectly, from Grey. 'Hine-moa' in particular has been popular among Pākehā, either in Grey's own words or retold with modified language but repeating the structure of Grey's story. In 1987 Antony Alpers pronounced this 'New Zealand's earliest piece of tourist trash . . .. Grey's sentimentalised version of 1855 is regrettable for what it started — the cheapening of the Maori in a popular tourist location.'[20]

Richard Taylor, who worked as a missionary, was also a university graduate, and he indulged his interests in natural history and various other intellectual matters as a kind of hobby in New Zealand. His *Te Ika a Maui* (1855) is a collection of his papers and essays. Taylor does not display the rigour of enquiry of Dieffenbach, but he ranges widely through geology, botany, and other scientific subjects as well as the mythology and the material culture of the indigenous people. He was by no means the first to speculate on ultimate origins but his suggestion, made with due seriousness and appropriate exegesis, that the culture and beliefs of the New Zealanders indicated they were akin to and very likely descended from the 'long lost tribes of Israel' is an example of how in print the New Zealanders could be subjected to all sorts of theoretical fancies. Taylor argued that they had 'degenerated', but were 'Naturally a noble race'. He was concerned that they not suffer the fate of the Tasmanians, 'hunted with dogs and exterminated'. To correct the common settler view of New Zealanders as savages 'we must have a more perfect acquaintance with them'. Though Taylor goes on to applaud the process of colonization, he wants some official regard paid to Māori custom, and he argues that at least in the short term there should be a bi-racial legislature; thus his perspective, like Grey's, is guardedly bicultural.[21]

Edward Shortland is a contrast to both Grey and Taylor in that his sympathies are less calculated. He had been sent by the government in the 1840s to spy out the southern part of the South Island, and he duly made his reports. Later he turned those experiences into *The Southern Districts of New Zealand* (1851): the text includes a description of the land but the writer's interest is engaged more by the people and their utilization of the land's resources. Shortland's subsequent experiences in the North Island are embedded in a more analytical work, *Traditions and Superstitions of the New Zealanders* (1854, revised 1856). Shortland is careful to maintain separate tribal traditions, and to show that the local culture is complex and complete in itself, not 'primitive' or 'simple'. In one passage he recounts his experience of an atua speaking: 'the whistling voice of the *Atua* was easily enough traceable to the old woman's mouth. But how the rustling noise, which seemed to creep along the thatch of the roof and the side of the hut was caused, I could not comprehend.' Ultimately the writer places the episode in a sceptical European perspective; the 'supernatural agency' is as 'easily credible' as the miracle of Saint Januarius regularly repeated at Naples, and thus he belittles the presence of the atua.[22] Nevertheless, that Shortland so sampled the supernatural suggests his openness to experience. On the other hand (and in this he is similar to Grey and Taylor), in recording these fundamentals of the practice and beliefs of the New Zealanders, Shortland makes them accessible to all readers, thus desacralizing knowledge customarily transmitted, with the appropriate protocols, by the elders.

The first two substantial histories of New Zealand were published in 1859. William Swainson's *New Zealand and its Colonization,* in part a republication of his earlier books and printed lectures, concentrated on the European invasion and its impact upon the New Zealanders. He had no doubt that the Māori were becoming 'civilized' (all praise to the missionaries) but he worried about their future, especially at the hands of the settlers. Was it possible, Swainson asked nervously, 'that two distinct portions of the human race, in the opposite conditions of civilization and barbarism, can be brought into immediate contact without the destruction of the uncivilized race?'[23]

A.S. Thomson's weightier and more sophisticated *The Story of New Zealand: Past and Present — Savage and Civilized* (1859) contains a bibliography, which lists more than 500 publications (including official papers and newspaper and journal articles), striking evidence of the existence of a considerable literature 'relative to New Zealand'. Nevertheless, Thomson 'could find no book containing a general history of the colony; and, at present, several professing to be accounts of New Zealand limit their information to one settlement and one race, while others are evidently written for political, colonising, or religious purposes, and not a few are flattering mercantile advertisements.' He had hopes, rather like Savage fifty years earlier, of 'filling up' a 'literary gap'.[24]

Thomson's history is presented as a comprehensive and nonpartisan narrative, a view of New Zealand as a whole, based on the critical use of a wide range of published material and informed by the author's own knowledge and experience gathered during a decade as an army surgeon with a regiment then serving in New Zealand. The tone is one of detachment: Thomson begins with 'Geography and Natural History', then 'Climate', both matters which can be dealt with in a scientific manner. The indigenous people he also discusses scientifically. He authoritatively judges their ancestors to have been Malays; and by some clever arithmetic offers 'about A.D. 1419' as the date for the arrival of Polynesians in New Zealand, 'a date corresponding with that of the arrival of the gipsies in Europe'.[25] Thomson goes on to measure the people in the clinical fashion that befits a surgeon. By the end of four chapters he has established the 'scientific' nature of the discourse which he maintains throughout his dissection of the Māori and their customs, and his narrative of colonization.

Part III of Thomson's *Story* is entitled 'On the decrease of the New Zealanders. Their progress in civilisation, with hints to emigrants.' Perhaps the 'hints to emigrants' was an afterthought to increase the potential readership (or to fatten the second volume). Nevertheless, the title of Part III epitomizes the programme within the 'scientific' *Story*. The land, which Thomson admires, is inhabited by an estimable but savage people who do not, until the arrival of Europeans, appear 'on the stage of the civilised world'. Thereafter they make progress, and their 'progressive Civilisation' between 1770 and 1859 is demonstrated in a table. But the civilized New Zealanders will not maintain their autonomy, it seems: 'In all conquests, whether by the mind or the sword, which have terminated in good to the weaker party, the conquerors have invariably amalgamated with the conquered.' Once again, only in 'amalgamation' will the New Zealanders survive.[26]

From 1860, shortly after Thomson's *Story* was published, there was more than a decade of conflict between, on the one hand, some tribes of New Zealanders and, on the other, troops of the imperial forces, volunteer and militia units drawn from the settler communities, and other tribes of New Zealanders. Though there were substantial casualties among all contending parties, probably almost as much ink was spilt as Pākehā blood. The debate over the justice and legality of the Waitara land purchase produced some fine prose written in the heat of indignation, expressed particularly in despatches and in pamphlets. William Martin's documented analyses of government chicanery, for example, are clever expositions. The plainest, most direct brief statement was made by Octavius Hadfield in *One of England's Little Wars* (1860), the title itself a sardonic commentary upon the imperial mentality. Hadfield was not an uncritical defender of all Māori people (he calls the King movement a 'conspiracy'), but over the Waitara business he was in no doubt. He begins, 'When a flagrant act of injustice has been commmitted by the Governor of a British colony in the name of Her Majesty the Queen, it is not easy to determine on what course to pursue' — a powerfully composed accusation which directly juxtaposes the injustice with the royal power. And if the dispute should be resolved by the use of force: 'No doubt Great Britain has men and money wherewith to carry on against the native race a war of extermination. But is this to be the issue of the endeavours to establish Christianity and civilization among one of the most intelligent and tractable of races? Are we in the middle of the nineteenth century to confess to the whole civilized world that our Christianity and our civilization have given us no advantage over these people but that of a more scientific use of material force?' Twenty years, he thinks, 'would not end a war of races'. Hadfield, a missionary, also indicates the European obsession about the truthfulness of written materials: 'The commissioner's admission, as contained in this letter,' he notes, while reviewing the evidence, 'has filled intelligent natives with amazement, and destroyed all confidence in the veracity of official documents.'[27]

John Gorst's *The Maori King* (1864) is more detailed and analytical, the most considered contemporary account of antipathies. 'To view men whose skin differs in colour from our own as "damned niggers", is a weakness of our Anglo-Saxon character', writes Gorst in his catalogue of racist attitudes and actions. The 'affronts' which appear in the newspapers are not unknown to the Māori either. The Auckland *Southern Cross*, for example, was regularly read aloud in Ngaruawahia 'by a native girl who understood English perfectly'. Gorst's conclusion is that the colonists should be kept out of Māori districts, and the Imperial Government should place those districts under the direct administration of imperial officers. 'The native province or provinces thus created would have to be governed on some such principles as the countries of the semi-independent Rajahs in India.' In all of these texts it is, as the paternalistic Gorst puts it, 'the old question — How are the Maories to be managed?'[28]

Those who were not settlers but 'outsiders', whether of long residence (such as the missionary Hadfield) or *ad hoc* officials like Gorst (who spent a short time in New Zealand), were more sympathetic, or at least less antagonistic, towards the New Zealanders. This applies even to soldiers in the British regiments like James E. Alexander, who pronounces himself an 'Aborigines-protectionist'. Alexander, a regular participant in England's little wars, wrote extensively about his soldiering and travels, and he made two books out of the campaigns in New Zealand. 'I take no credit for being able to deal agreeably with Maories,' writes this magnanimous Alexander, 'for it had been my fortune to be placed on terms of intimacy with brown and black races from early life in the east and west and in Africa, and the same rules prevail every where; if one is kind to the natives they will be kind to you.'[29] This is not quite the advice implicit in the most celebrated of the books which have their origin in the wars of the 1860s. F.E. Maning had been in every sense intimate with the Māori from the early 1830s through the 1840s; his *nom de guerre* for the first issues of the *History of the War in the North* (1862) and *Old New Zealand* (1863) was 'A Pakeha Maori', the term indicating a European who had crossed to the other culture.

Old New Zealand is perhaps the best known and most widely read of all works on early New Zealand. For a century at least it was quoted freely in other books so that those who had never read the full work knew it through characteristic quotations, especially phrases taken from the start of Chapter One: 'Ah! those good old times, when first I came to New Zealand, we shall never see their like again . . . . Pigs and potatoes have degenerated; and everything seems "flat, stale, and unprofitable". But those were the times — the "good old times" — before Governors were invented, and law, and justice, and all that.'[30]

Old New Zealand is customarily read as an incomparably entertaining account of the state of New Zealand and the New Zealanders 'before Governors were invented'. Maning's unravelling of the complexities of such concepts as muru, utu, tapu, and mana became standard definitions, popularly preferred to more technical and tentative versions. For a good many Pākehā New Zealanders *Old New Zealand* was and is a kind of ethnography, its reliability founded upon the author's own experiences. Maning lived for many years in close contact with the Ngapuhi people, his spouse was a Ngapuhi woman, and he had an extensive knowledge of the language. What makes the book more convincing for readers is Maning's apparent acceptance of the New Zealanders as human equals, talking of them with affection but without sentiment. He seems to identify with their aspirations too. Almost at the beginning of the book he talks of when he 'first cast eyes on Maori land' and adds, in contemporary reference to the King movement, 'It *was* Maori land then; but alas! what is it now? Success to you, O King of Waikato.'[31]

Maning's exposition is highly digressive, and reminiscent of Sterne's *Tristram Shandy*. To tell his tale Maning must go ashore to begin living it, and two chapters are required to convey him from boat to beach, with many half-relevant discussions on the way; and then his grand arrival ends with an anticlimactic spill in the surf. Throughout his exposition Maning interrupts the action in his 'real' life long ago, addressing the reader directly to point up a moral or make a humorous comparison. Such evidently careless retelling is in fact contrived. The contrivance is signalled, for instance, in that celebrated opening passage: the literary reference ('flat, stale, and unprofitable'); the 'good old times' of the first sentence enclosed in quotation marks by the end of the paragraph, so that it becomes a cynical repetition. A few pages thereafter he mentions Falstaff, Achilles, and Hector; later we meet Mr Pickwick, Shakespeare, Jason, Adam Smith, and certain other literary and political characters and allusions.

Much of *Old New Zealand* is concerned with violence or the threat of violence, and this does not accord with the narrator's statement of intent: 'Now if there is one thing I hate more than another it is the raw-head-and-bloody-bones style of writing, and in these random reminiscences I shall avoid all particular mention of battles, massacres, and onslaughts, except there be something particularly characteristic of my friend the Maori in them.' It is the last phrase which is the most important: Maning does indeed mean to convey the sense of violence, the turbulence and warlikeness of Māori society, which he sees as 'particularly characteristic' of the Māori people. There is a succession of robbings, fights, and despoliations, all, it is suggested, according to Māori custom. That was in the good old times, but, he says, pointedly, 'Since the introduction of firearms the natives have entirely altered their tactics, and adopted a system better adapted to the new weapon and the nature of the country.' And the grandson of his old rangatira has recently told him certain things in confidence which he can't disclose, he can 'only hint there was something said about the law, and driving the pakeha into the sea'.[32]

Maning's book, it would seem, was written to arouse settler society, especially politicians and leaders of opinion, to a realization of the violence of Māori society, both in the good old days (when there was no law but custom) and currently (when there is British law which is ineffective), and to prepare for war: 'I am sure we shall have fighting', he insists. Reconsidered as a call to arms, a tract for the times rather than a memoir, Maning's humour becomes mordant, mocking, his contempt for the Māori horribly clear. It is possible that the continuing appeal of this 'classic' was not based simply on Maning's attractive prose style but in large measure rested on his carefully crafted production of the stereotypical Māori that the settler society wanted to believe in — cunning, shrewd, lacking in compassion, careless of life, unregenerate.[33]

There were many accounts of the fighting of the 1860s — some contemporary, others retrospective — but all, as James Belich has indicated, were affected in some measure by the 'expectation of victory'.[34] The success of imperial and colonial troops in battle was in several cases ambiguous and they certainly did not manage to destroy the autonomy of all the groups which made armed resistance. The victory was partial; and in terms of anticipations amounted to a defeat, or at least a stalemate. The texts, nevertheless, deliver what the soldiers could not: those Māori provoked into resistance are 'rebels' (as the *printed* proclamations designated them) who, after a fair fight, are driven from their lands, the remnants pursued until they are beyond causing further trouble; after which they are left in the interior wilderness to brood sullenly upon their defeat. In this literature a variety of episodes are gradually conflated into a broad narrative of conquest, eventually to be called 'the Maori wars'. Just as in Virginia in the seventeenth century the 'massacre' of 1622 allowed the narrativization of colonial history as the justifiable subjugation of a 'treacherous' people in place of the missionary narrative of civilization, conversion and redemption, so the 'Maori wars' of the 1860s allowed the colonists to narrativize their aggressive history as the just defence of their persons and property against 'rebels' and 'fanatics'.[35]

An early example of the narrative of conquest was William Fox's *The War in New Zealand* (1866), a full-length book with the directness and polemical force of a pamphlet. Fox was anxious to spell out a difference between the war of 1860 in Taranaki, which he (like Hadfield and many others) deplored, and the war of 1863 and 1864, in the Waikato, Bay of Plenty, and East Coast districts, which he applauded, supported, and, as a government minister, helped to carry through. The book is full of special pleading and specious argument, and puts the point of view of the settlers very cogently: '[H]ad the colonists from the first been allowed to arrange their own relations with the native race . . . no serious difficulty would have arisen between the two races.' Fox believes all 'the troubles' are attributable to 'the representatives of the Imperial Government'. On the title page he gives a quotation from John Smith's *The General History of Virginia, New-England, and the Summer Isles* (1624), which raises a few questions about the literary influences upon Fox's policies if not his prose.[36]

In the 1880s G. W. Rusden, resident in Australia, tried to rework the narrative of conquest in a consistently critical way. His three-volume *History of New Zealand* (1883) provides ample documentation of a story marked by deceit, broken promises, bad faith, and unprovoked aggression on the part of the settlers, particularly in the 1860s. This was followed by his *Aureretanga: Groans of the Maoris* (1888) in which he further itemizes the savagery of the colonists, including the inglorious victory in 1881 at Parihaka. Rusden's version of the past, based largely upon documents with some assistance from 'Philo-Maoris' such as Hadfield, proved to be as intolerable to some colonists as the passive resistance at Parihaka of Te Whiti and his followers. John Bryce, the Native Minister who had insisted on a vigorous policy at Parihaka, took Rusden to court, ostensibly over a brief passage indicating Bryce's complicity in killing women and children during an engagement in 1867. It appeared that Bryce, though present or thereabouts, had not hacked down the victims himself, and in any case Rusden had exaggerated — young males only and not women had been murdered. Bryce was awarded a very large amount in damages; Rusden's *History,* consequently amended before being reissued, was thereafter slighted or ignored. With its great slabs of quotation it was never likely to be a popular work; but its greatest offence was in not conforming to the accepted ideology.

Writings on the past, present, and future of the Māori people did not cease altogether after the bitter conflicts of the 1860s. Nevertheless, the more or less sympathetic textual exploration of their manners and customs, and the sometimes optimistic rehearsals of a bicultural society (even if 'amalgamation' and 'civilization' were harbingers of a slow obliteration of the indigenous people and their mores) were now, after the wars, irrelevant for European writers and readers. The Māori were for Europeans no longer the Other in any sense of an alternative people and polity, whether rendered attractive or repulsive; but were reconstituted as enemies or friends, cowardly or brave, barbaric or chivalrous, actors within the theatres of British and colonial power. Moreover, the indigenous people were rapidly losing their designation as 'New Zealanders' and becoming, more frequently, 'Maoris' (or 'Maories') in the printed materials. This change of nomenclature had begun before the 1860s and was not completed until many years thereafter. The shift is evident, for example, in the title of Shortland's book of 1854 (*Traditions and Superstitions of the New Zealanders*) and that of his last major work, published in 1882 and called *Maori Religion and Mythology*.

*   *   *

John Rochfort wrote his *Adventures of a Surveyor* (1853) in the hope that his 'little gleanings' would 'give the reader some insight into colonial life'; and this seems to have been the broad purpose behind most pioneer narratives. Some of these accounts are picaresque, like Rochfort's own, which includes a visit to the Victorian goldfields; and Charles L. Money's *Knocking About in New Zealand* (1871), published in Melbourne with an approving preface by Marcus Clarke, which introduces a variety of rogues as Money turns his hand to storekeeping, gold prospecting, exploring, and eventually fighting 'niggers' in the Wanganui conflicts.[37]

Samuel Butler's *A First Year in Canterbury Settlement* (1863) was put together out of letters sent from New Zealand to England by Butler and out of revised portions of periodical articles (themselves edited from Butler's originals), not by Butler himself but by his father. The pieces were fitted together with some care and a little skill, but the book had not the blessing of Butler, nor his active participation, and there were times when he greatly regretted its existence. These several provenances, and the different audiences Butler addresses in separate portions, are fully visible even in an unannotated text. Some of the matter is epistolary; some takes the form of (or is clearly derived from) a journal; and there are portions which are more like inventories of the life within the landscape. The text is by turns a shipboard diary, the journal of a new settler, a handbook for migrants, a guide to the economics of pastoralism, a register of natural history, a pioneer narrative, a dramatic depiction of the landscape, an autobiography, and the memoirs of an explorer: *A First Year* is almost an anthology of a wide range of typical migrant-settler texts of invasion. Nevertheless, it has a certain unity, and although this may come in part from a reader's familiarity with the work (and few New Zealanders reading the work for the first time will not have seen quotations from it in other books and articles), it perhaps arises primarily from the sense of freedom which Butler experiences, and expresses, as he moves from the confines of the boat, beyond the 'scattered wooden boxes of houses' of the towns, across the plains and over the rivers into the ranges beyond. His route can be plotted topographically but essentially it is a spiritual journey from the confines of civilization to high places occupied by a handful of men — though there is high culture there too; he finds Tennyson's *Idylls* under the bed of his companion. (It is this same laconic fellow who replies 'The lake' when Butler asks where he might wash.)[38]

In much of the book Butler, like other writers in this period, measures local phenomena by British (and Continental) norms. His first view of the mountains disappoints, for 'they were not broken up into fine forms like the Carnarvonshire mountains'; the sandpiper is 'very like the lark in plumage'; the grand scenery in the Alps 'wanted, however, a chalet or two, or some sign of human handiwork in the foreground; as it was, the scene was too savage'. In another place Butler writes: 'Snow-grass, tussock grass, spaniard, rushes, swamps, lagoons, terraces, meaningless rises . . . . It is so hard for an Englishman to divest himself, not only of hedges and ditches, and cuttings and bridges, but of all signs of human existence whatsoever, that unless you were to travel in similar country yourself you would never understand it.' Nevertheless, in several passages Butler does depict the country without exterior references and succeeds in creating a world with its own integrity. His enthusiastic passage on the sight of Mount Cook has been much quoted; it ends with the ironic comment: 'I am forgetting myself into admiring a mountain which is of no use for sheep.' It is hardly too much to say that Butler forges a literary relationship between men and the Canterbury terrain; he makes the country less 'savage' (to use his word), and renders it in prose in a way others would find exemplary when they followed the same trail.[39]

J.L. Campbell's *Poenamo* (1881), long considered a classic, is derived from the first part of a lengthy manuscript written to inform his children of the circumstances of the early years of his life. Campbell had hoped to make his fortune in New Zealand and then return to Europe for good. *Poenamo* suggests otherwise. Through material added to the earlier manuscript and placed at the start and finish of the published text, Campbell makes his early days in New Zealand the 'first chapter' in the life of a young colonial city, Auckland. He numbers himself as one of the pioneers, indeed, by the 1880s 'almost the only remaining link that binds the long-ago past with the present time'. He has lived 'to see the great fern wilderness reclaimed' and 'the infant settlement' of Auckland 'grown into a city and proudly marching along the great broadway of civilisation'. But *Poenamo* does not deal with the reclamation of the 'fern wilderness'; it begins with Campbell's early life in Scotland, and then details his early months in New Zealand in 1840 at Coromandel and on the Waitemata harbour. Much of the appeal of the book is in Campbell's evocations of the unspoiled isthmus: 'Ah! never can I forget that morning when first I gazed upon the Waitemata's waters. The lovely expanse of water, with its gorgeous colouring, stretched away to the base of Rangitoto, whose twin peaks, cutting clearly into the deep blue sky, sloped in graceful outline to the shore a thousand feet below.' But it is by no means all respectful salutes to a past landscape. There is a great deal of humorous incident, and the Māori people are the butt of most of it; they are shrewd, simple, devious, naïve, and Campbell enjoys their company. The largest joke is 'Our first Maori scare': the rumours become palpable information, the settlers organize, the sentries are posted and detail by detail Campbell builds the tension for a frightening denouement.

> And then there came a terrible and fierce cry from the enemy from out the darkness of the waters.
> 'Hullo on shore there! What the devil are you up to, bang, banging away with bullets in your guns? Do you want to kill some of us?'

A sawyer with Māori companions has brought a great raft of timber from the nearby ranges down the harbour. There is a touch of Maning in this sort of broad farce.[40]

Both Campbell's *Poenamo* and Butler's *A First Year* deal with the world of men outside the pale of civilization. In that sense *Poenamo* and *A First Year* represent one kind of pioneer narrative, though few other examples provide the same kind of interest. Women wrote rather different narratives of pioneering.

Lady Barker, the name under which Mary Anne Stewart presented *Station Life in New Zealand* (1870) and *Station Amusements in New Zealand* (1873), composed her books in England. Even if the letters of *Station Life* rest upon original correspondence they have been worked over later, and the epistolary form is largely, perhaps entirely, a device. The narrator gives point to her experiences by constantly indicating that behaviour in the town and in the sheep country of Canterbury is *déclassé*, or at least that the conventions of social intercourse are either absent or so uncertain that all contact is charged with misunderstanding. Nothing in colonial life in fact works out as anticipated and Barker's own attempts to civilize those around her are fraught with the nearness of catastrophe. Likewise with her expeditions: the scenery may be grand, but her anxious concern is fixed more upon the steep track, and as a dampener there is rain during the return. Even on a more or less satisfactory Christmas Day picnic one of her companions falls through a temporary bridge and is drenched, and Barker herself, relaxing after lunch, suffers the sharp attentions of a weka. Her zest remains undiminished, except perhaps in her experiences with domestic servants.

Barker's artful prose is most fully demonstrated when her books are read as comedies of manners rather than as transparent documentary episodes. Other writers depict in more detail the difficulties of the landscape, the ravages of weather, the contrariness of 'nature' — L.J. Kennaway's *Crusts* (1874) is the most realistic and humorous of these chronicles of recurrent disaster — but Barker's eye is generally for the people within the landscape, not the terrain itself except where it participates in and exaggerates the absurdities of colonial life. If there is any point in considering Butler and Barker side by side, it must be to observe this: that they appear to be early examples of, and even perhaps formative influences in, two broad traditions of New Zealand nonfiction writing. Butler invents a world of vast spaces, sparsely occupied by men who pit their wits and strength against the rivers and mountains and find freedom in the absence of society; Barker's territory is a social one, full of people relating to each other with awkwardness, with expressions of excessive sentimentality, or even with sullen but palpable silence, yet communicating or trying to.

The subject-matter of Sarah Amelia Courage's *'Lights and Shadows' of Colonial Life* (1896) is similar to Barker's works, but the account is less cheerful. Courage chronicles the trials of life on a sheep station. The scenery 'was beautiful', she found at the start, 'but oh, so dreary — not a house nor a tree to be seen anywhere — and a thick pall of depression descended upon me. I felt so terribly alone, as it were — the sort of feeling one would imagine of those who were transported for life.' In her final pages she addresses intending immigrants: 'It only remains for people coming out here not to expect too much, for then they will not be disappointed.' Colonial life fills her with a kind of horror, and so do the colonists: she is enmeshed in the web of domestic and social responsibilities, unable to strike out for mountains or goldfields, forbidden the solace of withdrawal. It was not just for herself she was sorry. Todd beat his wife, at least 'occasionally'. Mrs Todd 'sighed dejectedly' as she told Courage that 'she had buried all her children, three babies'. Mrs Todd's words 'came between spasms of pain'. For Courage, writing was therapy as well as record. She had promised friends in England she would keep a journal to show them when she returned, as she intended, inside the decade — in fact, she did not return for twenty-six years. 'However long a day may be, it comes to an end at last, and I retired at half-past nine, but not before I had written a couple of pages in a book I called my diary.' The diary was 'a source of great comfort' to her — she 'looked upon it as a confidential friend'. These manuscript diaries she eventually used as 'books of reference' for *Lights and Shadows*.[41]

Courage's view of colonial life was kept well hidden. Fewer than twenty copies of *Lights and Shadows* were published originally, and apparently several of those copies were destroyed by acquaintances who did not like what they read about themselves. Not until 1976 was a new edition made available.

A broad mythology of the pioneering past was well established by the later years of the nineteenth century, and whatever the individual reactions to Courage's local characterizations may have been, her critical view of colonial life was at odds with accepted pieties set out in local and regional histories. James McIndoe, in *A Sketch of Otago* (1878) wrote of the worthy settlers of Otago:

> Asked to leave their homes for an unknown country, relying altogether on the testimony of men who had obtained their evidence from others, knowing there were no civilized inhabitants to receive them or provision made for their necessities; on the contrary, that they were asked to go to a country of savages, where they would require to plant and grow the food necessary for the subsistence of themselves and families, it needed faith of more than ordinary strength, a courage peculiar and above the common, and a self-reliance rarely met with, to induce prudent, honest, conscientious men — for such only were selected — to hazard such a step, to take such a leap in the dark.

The phrases are similar to those in William Bradford's *Plymouth Plantation* (1856), the account of the *Mayflower* Pilgrims arriving in North America in the seventeenth century. 'The pioneers of the settlement', McIndoe piped, 'were neither daunted nor discouraged by their difficulties . . .. The hardships endured are now looked back on with pleasant reflection.'[42] The lives of both men and women were to be buried under such banal incantations recited by generations of local historians.

*   *   *

The most celebrated European explorer is Thomas Brunner, and his diary of a journey in 1846-8 from Nelson down the West Coast of the South Island, reckoned his greatest achievement, was published not only in Nelson newspapers and as a local pamphlet, but also in British parliamentary papers and in the Royal Geographical Society's *Journal*. If the suggestion that Brunner was a modest man is correct, he certainly had much to be modest about. As chief surveyor of the Nelson province in later years he was incompetent. His famous journey to the West Coast took 550 days, but for various reasons he travelled only half that time. Without geological expertise, he reported that there was nothing on the West Coast to warrant expenditure on further exploring: within twenty years the Coast was the scene of a major gold rush. Brunner lost his sketches before he got back. He went by land in places of extreme difficulty when he might have travelled, like the local people, by canoe.

Brunner's account is very straightforward, without any airs or graces: its merits lie in avoiding the pitfalls of cliché and hyperbole. He rarely breaks into applause: 'Some of the bends of this river I passed to-day are as beautiful, in my opinion, as nature can possibly make them. The river is clear and deep, and runs over a bright shingle bed; the undergrowth on the banks is a beautiful mixture of shrubs, and the adjoining bush fine lofty rimu, rata, and black birch, with scattered patches of fern land. I was so pleased with the Grey river, that I should not object to visit it again.' That is unusually sublime for Brunner. Some journal entries are as brief as: '13th. Alternate rain and sunshine'; or simply, '15th. Rainy.' Perhaps it is the relentlessness of both journey and journal that excites admiration: '17th. Another dirty day, at least too wet for leaving our shed to brave the rain, but we managed to procure for supper a fine eel and two woodhens. A sharp frost at night, and very cold.'[43]

The contemporary appeal of Brunner's journal and of accounts by other explorers is in their function as colonizing texts. The land was not felt to be fully a European possession until it had been travelled through and catalogued, and the published accounts allowed readers to traverse the same territory and thus to 'know' it. (There was also a transfer of knowledge in a more fundamental sense: Brunner and other explorers usually had Māori guides through all or part of their journey, and Brunner acknowledged the assistance of his guide, Kehu. At the very least information was acquired directly or indirectly from the local

49

inhabitants before proceeding, and in nearly every case the explorers were travelling through plains and beside rivers and over mountain passes which were well known to Māori people. The achievement during this 550-day journey was not so much Brunner's as that of Kehu, who in various ways helped Brunner to find his way and supplied him with food and shelter.) In addition, the account probably suggested to the reader that Brunner learnt to live 'off the country': the European had become a true indigene, just as the frontiersmen in North America were reputedly as adept as the Native Americans in forest lore and woodcraft.

Julius von Haast provides a contrast to Brunner's plain prose. Von Haast held various official posts, including that of Canterbury Provincial Geologist, he provided reports on several journeys of exploration, and later combined much of this material in his *Geology of the Provinces of Canterbury and Westland* (1879). Von Haast was given to superlatives when the vista appealed to him: 'But the beauty of the magnificent scenery did not fade away even after the glorious orb of day had disappeared, because, as the night advanced, the full moon threw her soft silver light over the whole picture, and lake and sea, forest and snowy giants, still were visible . . . .. It was late at night before I could leave this glorious view, and my heart swelled with such a pure delight as only the contemplation of nature can offer to her admirers.'[44]

Later in the century, Arthur Harper, in his *Pioneer Work in the Alps of New Zealand* (1896), followed largely the plain style of Brunner rather than the striving for effect of von Haast. He writes, 'How feeble this pen feels when attempting to describe such wondrous scenery'; he says (possibly echoing Butler, though Harper, too, had climbed in Europe) that the Southern Alps in some cases exceed in grandeur the scenery of Switzerland, and the only thing lacking is 'the presence of human interest, for there are no picturesque peasants and *châlets* to give an added charm to the wild and glorious scenes'; but there is no awkwardness in his depiction of the less dramatic moments.

> In the evening we generally had a game or two of cribbage, discussed various items of news three or four months old, which we had just gleaned from the papers, and at soon after 8 o'clock boiled the billy again, and made a small drink of cocoa. At 9 P.M., having made up a large fire, we rolled into our respective blankets, and dreamed of city banquets and good living until daylight.

Such careful understatement was to be the customary prose of men in the mountains in the future; and when climbers celebrated their achievements in prose without proper modesty, as Samuel Turner did in *The Conquest of the New Zealand Alps* (1922), they were regarded as 'egotistical' and 'vainglorious'.[45]

Though some explorers were, like Brunner and Arthur Harper, essentially topographers, others made major contributions to natural history — Julius von Haast, for example, or William Colenso, who included extensive botanical records in his *Excursion* (1844) and *In Memoriam* (1884) which detailed lengthy journeys into the rougher country of the North Island in the 1840s, or J.C. Crawford, whose *Recollections of Travel* (1880) has a chapter on his field of expertise, geology. Many of those who wrote scientific accounts, however, were not explorers in any grand sense. They were for the most part amateurs who gathered information either day by day or on short trips, observing phenomena around them. They wrote articles for newspapers, or read learned papers at meetings of local philosophical societies in the major towns, the papers being subsequently published in the *Transactions and Proceedings of the New Zealand Institute* (1868-). Their work was fundamentally descriptive. The colonial scientists saw their function as adding to the general scientific knowledge of the world by collecting species or specimens, and detailing their properties — science was organized at the centre, which was Europe, and in the outposts of the empire the workers in the field supplied materials for the taxonomic and theoretical engines. On the other hand, the locally-published accounts describing soils, rocks, birds, insects, trees, shrubs, and so on particularized New Zealand phenomena, and thus further defined 'New Zealand'.

Two larger works of natural history were especially influential. T.H. Potts's *Out in the Open* (1882) is a compilation of articles printed in the *New Zealand Country Journal*, in *Transactions*, and in other publications. Potts writes on introduced and indigenous birds, ferns, the Māori (including a meeting with King Tawhiao in the company of Grey), and briefly on the Moriori. His prose is at times as leaden as some of the birds he describes: 'Less fleet on the wing than the blue rock pigeon, the heavy fruit-consuming kuku (*carpophagus*) urges its sounding pinions vainly in its efforts to escape, nor does the darting erratic flight of the parroquet — swift, dodging, evasive as it is — avail to save it from the claws of its destroyer.'[46] Nevertheless, his capacity for careful observation of birds in their natural habitats was appreciated by some contemporary and many later local readers, and his arguments for 'national domains' where indigenous flora and fauna could be preserved was a harbinger of the celebration of New Zealand phenomena.

Potts provided information for Walter Buller, whose bird-snatching he abhorred. Buller's *A History of the Birds of New Zealand* (1873, revised and amplified in 1888, with a *Supplement* in 1905) has been, from the first day of publication, the most famous of all New Zealand works of natural history. It is notable for several reasons, some of which are somewhat aside from, though not altogether unrelated to, matters of concern to literary history. The book, like many of its subjects, is a *rara avis;* and it is famous for the pictorial images of indigenous birds it contains, images which became standard for people who had not seen the birds alive and never would. The images, in fact, become icons of identity. But the images were not produced by Buller; they were the expert work of J.G. Keulemans and his assistants, with advice from Buller.

While Keulemans' striking pictures have been reproduced in many publications over the years, Buller's text is now largely forgotten, superseded by other ornithological writings. None the less, for two generations his information was quoted or drawn upon frequently, not only for books but also in newspaper articles by enthusiastic naturalists such as James Drummond. Thus, portions of Buller's writing were known even to people who had no ready access to the sumptuous originals. Unlike most of the writers mentioned so far, Buller was born and brought up in New Zealand. Perhaps as a result of this, one of his many ambitions was to succeed in Britain, and the *History* was a means of self-promotion (he was eventually elected a Fellow of the Royal Society and awarded a knighthood). Buller's prose is vigorous and anecdotal; but the prose style is less significant than the attitudes Buller incorporated into his text. Some of his remarks on the piopio (New Zealand thrush) illustrate these attitudes concisely. First he recounts his own destructive activities: 'In the wild state this species subsists chiefly on insects, worms and berries. I have shot it on the ground in the act of grubbing with its bill among the dry leaves and other forest débris.' Within a few sentences Buller can be eloquent about the singing of another piopio: 'Commencing sometimes with the loud strains of the Thrush, he would suddenly change his song to a low flute-note of exquisite sweetness.' But the sound of the piopio, Buller regrets, is now rare, for the bird is hardly ever seen.

> The last accessible place in which I met with it was Horokiwi, about twenty-five miles from Wellington. This was some twenty years ago — when riding through this lovely valley — at a time when the road passed through the primitive forest, all untouched by the hand of man, disclosing to the eye new beauties at every turn as it followed the course of a tortuous mountain stream. From the time of my first visit up to the present . . . I have never tired of this beautiful sylvan scenery . . . . Even now it is a delightfully refreshing resort. The tawa rears its feathery branches of soft pale green, and beside it rises, like a sentinel, the cone-shaped top of the darker *Knightia excelsa*; the bright green of the rimu with its graceful, drooping boughs is everywhere present . . . — the whole presenting a beautiful picture, in ever varying tints, and almost sub-tropical in the luxuriance of its growth . . . . but the hand of civilization is upon the wilderness, the virgin forest is receding more and more, the axe of the woodman is incessant, and the bushman's fire is doing every season its further work of devastation. A few years hence, and the sylvan beauty of Horokiwi with all its sweet memories will have passed away for ever![47]

Buller sees the triumph of 'civilization' as inevitable. Nevertheless, he still feels some sadness that the New Zealand in which he has grown up is vanishing; though not entirely, for his writings will provide a record of what once was. Paradoxically, the result was a book that specified New Zealand, and greatly assisted European New Zealanders in the development of the idea that New Zealand was a separate, indeed special, part of the world. Buller's *History* is in this way a cultural event which impinges upon New Zealand literary history.

The Literature of Occupation, 1890-1930

By the 1890s there had been a shift in cultural perceptions for a considerable number of European New Zealanders. Britain was still 'Home' even for those born in New Zealand, but New Zealand was 'home' too. The census of 1886 recorded a majority of locally-born residents for the first time, and during the 1890s Natives' Associations flourished briefly in several major centres. In the same period inspectors of schools reported a demand by primary teachers for the inclusion of New Zealand subjects in parts of the curriculum, and for 'readers' and other textbooks to contain some local materials. These kinds of developments were in part a result of the passage of time, as the experiences or memories of Britain became less immediate, or, for later generations, were vicarious. There were influences from Australia as well, where a much-debated call for the federation of the separate colonies led, eventually, to the formation of a single political entity. If Australia were to be a nation, it ought to have a national literature — New Zealand readers of the Sydney *Bulletin* were aware of these arguments, and no doubt wondered whether New Zealand was in a similar case.[48]

In addition, New Zealanders experienced major political and economic changes in the 1890s. The economic upturn which began in 1895 gradually spread prosperity and a general feeling of well-being around the community. There was more ambivalence about legislative changes but when overseas commentators suggested that New Zealanders were worthy of notice for the radical enactments they supported, local people felt some pride. New Zealand was perhaps not simply a 'Brighter Britain' but a distinctively special place and society. Inevitably there was talk of national identity, and even of a 'national literature' for New Zealand.

Hitherto, writers of non-fiction had emphasized contrasts between metropolitan norms and the alien New Zealand world. For many of the next generation of writers New Zealand would be a place of habitation rather than islands of exile. A considerable amount of non-fiction writing from the 1890s is concerned with fabricating New Zealand by creating an inventory of its phenomena. The 'native-born' colonists were trying to depict themselves as the indigenous people. To 'belong' in New Zealand they must regard the place and its phenomena not as alien but as normal. The earlier colonial attitude, on the other hand, had been to normalize New Zealand by destroying what was 'alien' (i.e., indigenous) and substituting in the space left by this destruction the social and material forms of the metropolitan world. It is a view concisely expressed by E.M. Bourke in her *Little History of New Zealand* (1881). In the Preface to the second edition (1882) the writer regrets 'the ignorance prevailing amongst many New Zealand children concerning the history and early settlement of their own country.' She hopes the book will be of 'practical benefit to the young people of New Zealand' who will 'learn some particulars of the settlement of their own country, with the names of those instrumental in colonizing it'. One hundred years ago, the conclusion states, 'New Zealand was a wilderness, fertile and beautiful indeed, but utterly unknown to civilization, inhabited only by wild and untaught savages, incessantly at war, and in the constant practice of cannibalism and many other barbarous customs. To-day we see fair cities and fertile, cultivated plains.' Now, too, there were railways, and steamboats. The vast forests had disappeared, having been replaced by farms and homesteads. 'English fish, such as salmon and trout, introduced by the colonists, exist in many rivers; and English birds may be seen on every side. The skylark, thoroughly acclimatized, makes his voice heard as loudly as in an English meadow.'[49]

The attitude of a number of writers at the turn of the century was that 'New Zealand' might be best expressed as the aggregate of its distinctive phenomena. Not only the native born held this view. Some of those who celebrated the indigenous were recent migrants. Long-term colonists and their descendants might feel that colonization was proceeding apace, and that the rough outlines of civilization had been sketched out; but later migrants could be appalled by the roughness of the outline, the squalor and ugliness of towns and farms. The world the colonists had created was almost a parody of the metropolis. More inspiring by far was what was yet unchanged — mountains and bush, and the local fauna which still survived in those fastnesses. B.E. Baughan's earlier non-fiction writings, eventually collected together as *Studies in New Zealand Scenery* (1916), are examples of a migrant's efforts to celebrate local scenic attractions through word-pictures; the contributions of Leonard Cockayne and Herbert Guthrie-Smith are discussed later in this section.

A national literature could in some measure be devised from materials to hand — the writings of the past one hundred years or so which dealt largely with New Zealand. Both bibliographers and collectors were at work from the 1880s. Thomas Hocken first began collecting out of an antiquarian interest in researching Otago history; Alexander Turnbull's initial motivations are less clear; but after the turn of the century both men eventually saw their collections as having national significance and by gift and bequest delivered them to the people of New Zealand. The Hocken and Turnbull libraries demonstrated the existence of a 'New Zealand literature' in the most monumental way. For those at a distance from these great accumulations there was Hocken's *A Bibliography of the Literature Relating to New Zealand* (1909), a chronological listing of more than 600 pages.

Some works had already acquired classic status as 'New Zealand' books. This is shown, for example, in the *New Zealand Reader* (1895), published by the Government Printer for use in the higher standards in schools. A number of pieces were written especially for the *Reader*, and there was a new translation of Tasman's log-book. The samples of verse were almost all from Alfred Domett. The remainder, with one exception, consisted of non-fiction, including extracts from Augustus Earle, F.E. Maning, J.L. Nicholas, Vincent Pyke, Samuel Butler, G.L. Craik, T.H. Potts, William Wade, and John Savage. The selection was made with the sympathetic encouragement, perhaps even active assistance, of the Minister of Education, W.P. Reeves. Reeves hoped the *Reader* would 'tend to make our children more patriotic and foster love and pride for their country'.[50]

Reeves himself was shortly thereafter to write a work of singular importance. *The Long White Cloud: Ao Tea Roa* (1898) became a popular history of New Zealand. It gave contour and coherence to the New Zealand past; it gave currency to what was understood to be the Māori name for New Zealand; and it fostered New Zealanders' 'love and pride for their country'. Yet the book was originally written for a British audience — that 'minority' in the 'Mother Country' which took 'a quickening interest in the Colonies'.[51]

From 1896 Reeves was Agent-General for New Zealand in London, and he was approached by an English publisher to write a short account of New Zealand for a Story of Empire series. Having thus cleared his throat, he set out to write for the same publisher a longer work to be called 'The Fortunate Isles', the title of the first chapter in the earlier essay. It happened that the phrase had already been attached to another book on a slighter archipelago, hence *The Long White Cloud*. It was not, like previous histories, a catalogue of the successes and failures of the colonists in their efforts to shape a brighter Britain; there was no constant measurement of New Zealand by metropolitan standards; New Zealand was not an offshoot or outgrowth, a regeneration or degeneration, but had its own integrity: 'It is my country', said Reeves.[52]

The geographical distance from his subject no doubt sharpened Reeves's perceptions, and perhaps heightened his sense of loss. The opening chapter, which depicts land and landscape, resonates with feeling for what has been left behind: 'How could a photograph even hint at the dark, glossy green of the glistening karaka leaves, the feathery, waving foliage of the lace bark, or the white and purple bloom of the koromiko?' And those things which had been introduced were for Reeves as much a part of the landscape as the indigenous: 'The dark eucalypt of Tasmania, with its heavy-hanging, languid leaves, is the commonest of exotic trees.'[53] In London (and in France where some of the writing was done) New Zealand could be conjured up entire.

Reeves tells an entertaining story, and a colourful one, in a narrative stripped of extraneous incident, detail, and inessential chronological codes. His chapter headings indicate the successive tableaux: the Navigators; No Man's Land; Mission Schooner and Whale Boat; the Muskets of Hongi; and so on. Some of the myths were not his invention; but he made them such an essential part of the story that they became entrenched as verities: Edward Gibbon Wakefield ('The founder of the Colony now comes on the scene') and the New Zealand Company receive more than their due;[54] the Company by its initiatives forces the hand of the British Government in the matter of annexation; Hobson sends the *Britomart* in haste to Akaroa ahead of *L'Aube* to forestall a French colony.

Much of *The Long White Cloud* is expressed in irony and paradox. Reeves piles up the paradoxes at the very start:

> Though one of the parts of the earth best fitted for man, New Zealand was probably about the last of such lands occupied by the human race. The first European to find it was a Dutch sea-captain who was looking for something else, and who thought it a part of South America, from which it is sundered by five thousand miles of ocean. It takes its name from a province of Holland to which it does not bear the remotest likeness, and is usually regarded as the antipodes of England, but is not. Taken possession of by an English navigator, whose action, at first adopted, was afterwards reversed by his

country's rulers, it was only annexed at length by the English Government which did not want it, to keep it from the French who did.

Reeves accords virtually every person of importance similar ironic treatment. 'Captain Fitzroy was one of those fretful and excitable beings whose manner sets plain men against them, and who, when they are not in error, seem so. Often wrong, occasionally right, he possessed in perfection the unhappy art of doing the right thing in the wrong way.' Grey ('Good Governor Grey' is the wry chapter title) receives more extensive treatment, some four pages. Grey 'had the knightly virtues — courage, courtesy, and self-command'. 'Naturally fond of devious ways and unexpected moves, he learned to keep his own counsel and to mask his intentions; he never even seemed frank. Though wilful and quarrelsome, he kept guard over his tongue, but, pen in hand, became an evasive, obstinate controversialist with a coldly-used power of exasperation.'[55]

The succession of ironies that gives parts of the work a mesmeric quality is less evident in the final chapters which deal with recent politics. Here Reeves reports more matter-of-factly. The men and measures were alive, and so was he, and perhaps in 1898 there was still a political inheritance to come. However, he contrasts the 'Progressives' (the Liberals) with the 'Conservatives' and thus sharpens the political distinctions, though he is careful to indicate that both groupings shared certain general principles. In the revised edition (1924) he added new chapters: in 'The End of the Oligarchy' he insists on the 1890 election as a watershed, and 'King Dick' deals with the Prime Minister who had been, in Reeves's view of things, his political rival as well as mentor and cabinet colleague. The ironies are still there, but muted, touched with affection (compared with the treatment of, say, Grey). Seddon 'scarcely ever asked for advice, but was prepared to listen to it, and sometimes took it in important matters'.[56] Of course Reeves was now in part following a myth rather than wholly formulating one. Nevertheless, the chapter on Seddon, which provided a more detailed account of his personality and practices than any of the longer eulogies, provided a suitable coda for the book, and for Reeves's era. Most later politicians would claim to be progressive, like the Liberals, and the particular Liberal they often had in mind was not Reeves but Seddon, and perhaps even Reeves's Seddon.

Reeves's other major prose work, *State Experiments in Australia and New Zealand* (1902), is quite different in scope and in style to *The Long White Cloud*, and it had neither the immediate popularity nor the long-term influence of the earlier book. It is nevertheless a considerable accomplishment. Reeves compares and contrasts 'the more interesting experiments in law and administration' in the Australasian colonies between the early 1880s and 1902.[57] The ironies are rare; and the clarity of the prose means that it can still be read without much sense of anachronism — excepting the rabid denunciations of 'Asiatics', then a standard part of the intellectual rhetoric of 'progressives'. Reeves marshalls a wealth of detail in a logical and interesting manner, enlivening the whole with both judicious criticism and sympathetic characterizations of colonial life. The work can perhaps be called 'sociological', one of several such studies produced in or about Australasia around that time — other New Zealand examples included H. Broadhead's *State Regulation of Labour* (1908), and J.E. Le Rossignol and W.D. Stewart's *State Socialism in New Zealand* (1910), though these had neither the distinction of expression nor the trans-Tasman breadth of *State Experiments*. Reeves's achievements in non-fiction were without parallel in his generation; others lacked his intellectual breadth and depth, and they were more concerned with an insular celebration of 'God's own country' and its indigenous phenomena.

*   *   *

In *The Long White Cloud* Reeves could not decide whether the Māori people were dying out, but most colonists believed that they were. Some regretted the passing of the Māori people and wanted as much as possible about them to be placed on record: in print, if not in life, they might be preserved. The former missionary, William Colenso, wrote a good deal in weighty pamphlets and scientific papers, dry, scholarly stuff. George Grey retained an interest also; and when he was premier in the 1870s he persuaded the Cabinet to fund John White's collection of tribal traditions. White paid various people to fill up exercise books, collected extant manuscripts, rewrote the material in his own style ('White Maori' it has been called),[58] and made an English translation. Six bilingual volumes of *The Ancient History of the Maori* were issued between 1887 and 1890, and this matter became a basic source for European New Zealanders to utilize. When White died in 1891 almost as much remained in manuscript, but the series was not continued.

The cessation of the *Ancient History* (and perhaps even its appearance in what many thought was an unsatisfactory form) may have made the need to record Māori traditions seem even more urgent. At any rate, the Polynesian Society was founded shortly afterwards. Its major concern was to preserve information about the indigenous peoples of the Pacific, including the Māori, primarily through publication in the quarterly *Journal of the Polynesian Society*. A small number of Māori people were members, but the Society was essentially a cloak of scholarly respectability under which the functionaries of imperialism, old soldiers, surveyors, and clergy, could indulge their fascination about 'primitive' people. The Society both sanctioned and encouraged the textual objectivization of the Other; even when the Society was not directly involved in the processes of compilation and publication, it indirectly authorized a large body of literature. Most of this literature was undistinguished as writing but important for the particular topoi and genres which it established.

Edward Tregear, one of the founders of the Society, had produced *The Aryan Maori* in 1885. 'Comparative Philology and Comparative Mythology', he wrote, were 'the two youngest and fairest daughters of Knowledge' and he 'hasted' to make his discovery known. The apparent linguistic affinities of certain Māori words with those of Sanskrit and Sanskrit-derived languages indicated a Central Asian pedigree for both Māori and Anglo-Saxon. In particular, the bull was 'embalmed' in the Māori language though Māori people had no traditional knowledge of large quadrupeds. In the colonization of the Pacific, writes Tregear, 'the two vast horns of the Great Migration have touched again; and men whose fathers were brothers on the other side of those gulfs of distance and time meet each other, when the Aryan of the West greets the Aryan of the Eastern Seas'. The philological excursions drew a devastating response from A.S. Atkinson who, in a clever parody, reversed the migrations of words and people by deriving the phrase cock-and-bull story from kākāpō, the Māori word for a native parrot. *The Aryan Maori* is perhaps the most spectacular example of how writers could indulge their theoretical fancies about the Māori. Tregear took his intellectual inspiration in this case from F. Max Muller; like the other major local ethnologists, he read widely, if eclectically, in a variety of ethnographic and related literature from Britain and other countries. Tregear was also at one with his Polynesian Society colleagues in his preference for studying the unacculturated Māori. 'The degraded Natives who hang about our towns', he decided, 'have little of the appearance or the character of the true Maori.' *The Maori Race* (1904), in which Tregear eschewed the comparative method, was for twenty years the standard handbook on 'the true Maori', forerunner of many such compendiums, some scholarly, some less so.[59]

S. Percy Smith, the leading light of the Polynesian Society until his death in 1922, published much of his work initially in the *Journal of the Polynesian Society*, of which he was editor; and the accumulated instalments of his most substantial efforts, revised and enlarged, subsequently appeared as books. It was Smith's opinion that 'the European Ethnologist' (as distinct from the New Zealand ethnologist) was 'too apt to discredit tradition' and he pronounced it to be 'an axiom that all tradition is based on fact'.[60] Such an approach allowed him to construct a past for the undocumented period before the European incursion: Pākehā New Zealanders were being provided with a history located in the Pacific, stretching back hundreds of years. His speculations on the 'original home' of the Polynesians, the subject of *Hawaiki* (1898, final version 1921), were a matter of great interest to amateur ethnologists; several other books in the same period addressed the subject at length, and there were many slighter pieces in the learned journals. But it was Smith's production of a past for the Pacific which was to grip the popular imagination. Smith assembled a Polynesian story which is (no doubt unconsciously) contrapuntal to the history of the colonists — a series of notable Polynesian navigators (at least a couple sailing into the high latitudes of the Antarctic seas), a homeland, conflict in the homeland (or perhaps competition for its resources) which leads to migrations to other islands, a precursor of Cook in Kupe's discovery and circumnavigation of New Zealand and his reports of the new land Aotearoa to his people; later the Great Migration, a Fleet of canoes with people to colonize Aotearoa. Even the subjugation of the Māori by the 'superior race' of Europeans is rehearsed in the subjugation of an aboriginal people, the Moriori (perhaps, the experts suggested, Melanesian or part-Melanesian and therefore 'inferior'), by the invading Polynesian-Māori.[61] This was not all Smith's doing: Elsdon Best also played an important part in the creative process, and proved to be a more effective disseminator of the ideas than Smith, whose writings were aggregations of evidence rather than the straightforward telling of a dramatic story. Nevertheless, Smith constructed the crucial chronology which authenticated the broad narrative. Smith made another kind of contribution which was more valuable. His *Peopling of the North* (1897) and *History and Traditions of the Maoris of the West Coast, North Island* (1910) were the first examples of 'tribal history' which focused primarily on the Māori people rather than on the colonists, and was essentially a compilation, in English, of Māori materials. This genre, peculiar to New Zealand, was developed later by both Māori and Pākehā writers.

The works produced through the Polynesian Society (predominantly but not exclusively those of Smith) in the generation after its founding had a considerable formative influence upon New Zealand non-fiction writings. Even though the indigenous people are imprisoned within the texts, and their traditions are distorted by being reduced from oral performance to print, nevertheless they are accorded a participatory role within the text, and thus in the historical sequences. Moreover, the textualization of traditions is in effect a demonstration that indigenous traditions have a place within the discourse. Once the indigenous people were located in the textual world as participants, and their traditions were accorded status within the discourse, they could not be erased. On the other hand, the texts could be manipulated by Pākehā. Smith translated and edited the *The Lore of the Whare-wānanga* (1913 and 1915) which became a major printed source of traditional beliefs. Later scholars discovered the provenance of a major section was of doubtful authenticity.

Besides his collaboration with Smith in inventing a grand design for Polynesian history, Elsdon Best made the most substantial contribution to creating 'the Maori as he was' in written form. He gathered information in the field, especially from Tuhoe people but also from other areas, and drew upon manuscripts and published works left by earlier observers. For some subjects, particularly religious beliefs, he read widely in the contemporary anthropological literature from overseas. Though he wrote up his notes for articles in newspapers and learned journals from the 1890s, much of his composition was carried out in the last twenty years of his life while he worked as an ethnologist at the Dominion Museum. The programme he set himself he completed before his death (and two more books were published posthumously); it amounted to more than a dozen weighty volumes (*Tuhoe*, the largest, runs to over 1000 pages) and half a dozen 'monographs' of lesser size as well as scores of popular and learned articles.

Apart from speculations about monotheism and the Moriori (he called them 'Maruiwi'), Best was careful to stay close to his evidence, usually if not invariably noting his sources (personal or published), and often incorporating or appending Māori language materials verbatim in his more detailed works. He was, nevertheless, not simply the objective observer he professed himself to be. His earlier writings, including *Waikare-moana* (1897) and *Tuhoe* (published in 1925 but at least in part written around 1907), attempt to evoke an atmosphere of romance and mystery, and *Tuhoe,* in particular, begins as if it were to be a prose epic. Later his style became terser, even vehement. However, by his use of the past tense (occasionally the historic present for dramatic effect), phrases such as 'old-time Maori' and 'barbaric folk', archaisms like 'era', 'yore', 'anent', and adjectives such as 'curious', 'peculiar', and 'puerile', Best so successfully contrives to distance his subjects from the present that even when he reports contemporary practices (by way of illustrating the customs of earlier times) those practices are made to appear anachronistic.

There was another way in which Best 'produced' the Māori rather than simply recording their culture 'as it was'. He was very aware of the distinctions in lore and custom of different tribes and in his more detailed studies the different traditions and lexicons were carefully recorded. However, in some parts of his summary work, *The Maori* (1924), he tends to suggest a single homogeneous Māori culture, as the title of the work indicates; and in the popular survey *The Maori As He Was* (1924), the process is taken further and the Māori way of life is stereotyped.

*   *   *

Smith and Best saw themselves primarily as recorders. It so happened that in the course of their recording they felt the need to tidy up, classify, tabulate, and resolve the contradictions they perceived in the materials they collected, and, perhaps largely inadvertently, they created new intellectual mythologies. But they also saw their ethnographic work as having a specific purpose in the creation of a Pākehā cultural identity. We might call this process primitive accumulation of cultural capital. Best himself gives a hint of the greediness with which Pākehā appropriated information: in *Waikare-moana* he reports a 'strange sensation of vivid interest and pleasing anticipation which is felt by the ethnologist, botanist, and lover of primitive folk-lore when entering on a new field for research. For the glamour of the wilderness is upon him, and the *kura huna* — the "concealed treasure" (of knowledge) — loometh large in the Land of Tuhoe.' *Waikare-moana* also includes a preface by Smith, in which he explains that the work had been printed 'with a view of furnishing information to tourists as to the various scenes of beauty on the lake' and, he goes on, 'at the same time an attempt has been made to invest the different places with a human interest by preserving the old Maori history relating thereto. Young countries like New Zealand', declared Smith, 'are often wanting in the historic interest associated with so many of the sights of Europe. This is not because New Zealand has no history, but because the guide-books fail to touch upon it.' Thus the land might be invested with a history through the stories 'gathered together in the following pages'.[62] In effect, Smith is saying that Māori lore, disseminated through print, could be utilized to make the Pākehā feel 'at home'.

This is close to the thesis James Cowan puts forward in the *New Zealand Illustrated Magazine* in 1901. In New Zealand, writes Cowan, 'we have infinite advantages over Australia in the way of material for literature, a national literature. Our country has a history; Australia has none — at any rate none that can equal our own in all those stirring elements which invest the past with a halo of romance, and make food for the poet, the painter, and the novelist.' This comment was made in an article about Domett's *Ranolf and Amohia* — Domett, Cowan suggests, showed the way to others in using Māori material and the New Zealand landscape as subject matter for literature. Cowan also mentioned James Fenimore Cooper and Longfellow: he had in mind a New Zealand literature which would draw upon indigenous subject-matter, and have the same cumulative cultural effect as the works of certain United States writers of the early national period.[63]

The pictorial artistry Cowan had to leave to other people, though he took the opportunity to add an accompanying text to a publication of Gottfried Lindauer's paintings on Māori subjects; but he carried through a massive writing programme over the next forty years, despite the demands of journalism, and later in life, much ill health. To the aims he outlined in 1901 he remained faithful, restating his ideas sometimes in later works, most fully perhaps in *Hero Stories* (1935). Cowan had been irritated by O.N. Gillespie's preface to a collection of *New Zealand Short Stories* (1930). Gillespie had written that 'The pioneers had an easy task' and that New Zealand 'lacks much romantic material usually found in a new land'. It had had 'no frontiersmen, no epic struggle with mighty forces' and the 'settlement victory was prosaic and swiftly won'. Not so, says Cowan: 'This country has a history, in its first century as a British land, adventurous and romantic in the widest senses of those words', but the 'ignorance of that story' is 'widespread'. 'Patriotism', he declares, 'flourishes best upon the soil of history'. Further: 'The New Zealander perhaps is not sufficiently conscious of the fortune that is his in being able to call this country Home. He is too apt to look over the seas to the lands of his forefathers for leadership instead of cultivating the spirit of nationhood for himself.'[64]

Cowan grew up on a farm which included the site of the battle of Orakau, on the 'frontier' which the Armed Constabulary still patrolled when he was a boy. The yarns of Māori and Pākehā, and later of Pacific mariners he met in Auckland, were his early sources of knowledge, and he always relished oral testimony; 'written documents', he believed, did not give 'the real meat of history'.[65] His 'New Zealand' is so plotted that the conflict between Māori and settler becomes formative rather than destructive. Pākehā who crossed cultural barriers are prominent as Cowan's biographical subjects: *A Trader in Cannibal Land* (1935) is the story of Hans Tapsell who made the first marriage to a Māori woman according to missionary rituals and who later traded at Maketu; *Sir Donald Maclean* (1940) is the story of a government agent and cabinet minister ('statesman' Cowan calls him) who was in constant contact with Māori people. *The Adventures of Kimble Bent* (1911) celebrates more than censures a soldier who deserted the British forces to serve with their foes and stayed in a Māori community thereafter. In his tourist guides Cowan constantly searches out the Māori presence, often through the place-names and their associated myths and legends. Cowan's largest work was a commissioned history, *The New Zealand Wars* (1922 and 1923). From both Māori and Pākehā he collected stories (he was able to find and talk with two nonagenarians who had fought against each other at Ohaeawai in 1845), and he stalked the old battle sites himself. Once again he found literary models in North America: 'It is to the pages of Francis Parkman, Theodore Roosevelt, and Henry Cabot Lodge that the New Zealander must turn for historic parallels in the story of the nations, rather than to those of Macaulay, Green, or Freeman.' The 'white conquest in America' offers a 'remarkable similarity' to the New Zealand experience. The *Wars* includes passages which appear to imitate Parkman. For example, Cowan's evocation of a concealed assault party and the unsuspecting defenders at Kororareka during the night before the early morning attack in March 1845 is probably inspired by Parkman's account of the attack on Deerfield. However, Cowan could not maintain the kind of controlled dramatic narrative that gives Parkman his lasting literary interest; on the other hand, though his language can be lurid, Cowan is not as racist as Parkman.

The scholarly interests of ethnologists like Smith and Best, and the more popular celebration of Māori subjects as a basis for a distinctive New Zealand literature which Cowan advocated, converged in the extensive *œuvre* of Johannes Andersen. His first bulky work, *Maori Life in Ao-tea* (1907), a characterization of the traditional Māori way of life, was dedicated to 'the older Maori people of Ao-tea-roa and to the younger poets and artists of New Zealand, with hopes for the immortality of the one at the hands of the others'.[67] Subsequently he produced books on myths and legends and on Māori place-names. With the encouragement of Elsdon Best, he compiled ethnological studies, including *Maori String Figures* (1927) and *Maori Music* (1934).

Andersen's espousal of indigenous themes extended beyond Māori topics to include local fauna and flora, and as well as *Bird-song and New Zealand Song Birds* (1926), which besides descriptive matter contained the 'songs' of New Zealand birds in orthodox musical annotation, he published numerous articles, popular and more serious, on the birds and the bush. If one of the more notable and prolific writers on such topics, Andersen was by no means unusual in his attempts to make the birds and the bush subjects for significant nonfiction. Quite apart from scientific manuals, there were several works which, while basically handbooks, contained a good deal of prose designed to be evocative as well as informative: influential examples were F.W. Hutton and James Drummond's *Animals of New Zealand* (1904), in which most of the animals were birds; and R.M. Laing and E.M. Blackwell's *Plants of New Zealand* (1906). Some works, such as G. M. Thomson's *A New Zealand Naturalist's Calendar* (1909) and Marguerite Crookes's *Plant Life in Maoriland* (1926), combined reliable scientific data with enthusiasm for local flora and fauna. Others, like Mona Gordon's *Children of Tane* (1938) and *The Garden of Tane* (1944), dealing with birds and plants respectively, were little concerned with science and sought to evoke a positive emotional response from readers. But two works of natural history had a more general impact, in rather different ways.

The first edition of Leonard Cockayne's *New Zealand Plants and their Story* (1910) was an accumulation and enlargement of newspaper articles; the second edition (1919), Cockayne calls 'virtually a new book'. He begins with a review of earlier botanists and their literature, sets out some general principles and explanations, and then examines in turn the plant communities of different habitats, with an emphasis always on the ecological relationships. He dispels drily the prejudices he is aware people have acquired: 'A mangrove swamp is supposed to represent all that is most hideous on earth — alligators in crowds, a fearsome odour, crabs waiting to pick such of the victim's bones as are left by the alligators, malaria, and deadly "microbes" in vast abundance.' Throughout there are punctuations of delight: of the snow-groundsel Cockayne writes that he 'will never forget the wet herb-field near the source of the River Poulter, gleaming like a snowfield with the multitudes of its pure blossoms.'[68]

Cockayne impresses upon his readers both the special nature of New Zealand vegetation and its relationship to the flora of other lands. The forest 'is a unique production of nature, found in no other land' — he thinks this 'not a matter of common knowledge' even though there were few New Zealanders who were not able to raise 'some enthusiasm regarding the "bush"'.[69] In the final chapter he cautiously speculates on a geophysical history which might explain wider botanical relationships. *New Zealand Plants* is scientific but accessible to the knowledgeable layperson. The scientists drew material from Cockayne through his more detailed scientific books and papers; but amateur naturalists and popularizers of natural history in this and in the next generation gathered inspiration as well as information from *New Zealand Plants*.

Herbert Guthrie-Smith's *Tutira* (1921) also took what could be called an ecological perspective. Guthrie-Smith was a Scotsman educated in England whose literary ambitions first took shape in *Crispus*, a blank verse drama set in classical Rome. As the proprietor of a sheep station in Hawke's Bay he found an understanding of the land and vegetation important for successful management of the property, and this blended with his interests as a naturalist. Though he wrote four highly-regarded books of ornithological observation, it is *Tutira*, a very detailed account of his own property, which is considered his finest accomplishment. *Tutira* deals with geology, Māori occupation, original vegetation, Pākehā intrusion, the impact of introduced flora and fauna — 'Nothing pertaining to the station seems to have been omitted, save perhaps the earthworms', was Elsdon Best's opinion. Guthrie-Smith's detail is personalized: 'In the spring of 1902 I noticed near Petane a cock chaffinch (*Fringilla coelabs*). A week later on Tutira I saw a hen chaffinch on the road between the wool-shed and homestead. Four days afterwards I marked a third chaffinch, and almost at the same instant a redpole (*Acanthus linaria*), the first of its breed seen by me in New Zealand.' He then notes the dates these species were introduced into New Zealand and plots their migration over the years to his own property. Or, to take another example, he is able to deduce from the initial distribution of the weed 'viscid Bartsia' that a pack-load of grass seed had been ripped open at a particular point on its journey. 'After the boundary gate the plant altogether ceased. There, where the horses had been stopped, the packman had doubtless noticed the rent, and stuffed or plugged it. No more specimens at any rate appeared, until three miles further on', where it grew, undesirably but not unexpectedly, amongst the sown grass seed.[70]

Elsdon Best thought *Tutira* was 'an entirely new departure in the recording of reminiscences by an old settler', the first time the 'breaking-in of new country in New Zealand' had been well described. 'It is a story of a long fight against nature and poverty, of a great and enduring faith, of patience and determination.' He concluded a review: 'Old-time veterans of the fern lands and modern land-breakers alike will be well-advised to peruse it.' This is to make *Tutira* a kind of pioneer narrative. Others read the book more as a critique of settler destructiveness, and as an account of a migrant turning into a New Zealander through his identification with the land, a prose re-enactment, on an epic scale, of multiple acclimatizations, or a natural history of New Zealand in microcosm.[71]

Guthrie-Smith was in fact a thoroughgoing conservationist by the time he wrote *Tutira*, and in the third edition, prepared in the late 1930s but not published until 1953, he added two new chapters which dramatically contrasted sequences of regeneration after a fire in the 'hanging wood'. In the first the bracken cover is succeeded by mānuka, and then larger native trees (māhoe, five-finger, cabbage-trees) begin to penetrate and pierce the 'manuka jungle'. The 'hanger' had been burnt in the 1880s: Guthrie-Smith could report that by 1939 the process of regeneration was well advanced. In the second, wholly imaginary sequence, introduced honeysuckle, blackberry, climbing roses and convolvulus would smother the native plants since the 'balance of ancient nature' had been 'upset by the importation of aliens'. Only by the agency of such a tree as the macrocarpa could this 'abomination of desolation' be corrected, over many years, 'to pristine conditions existent ere Tasman, Cook, Banks, and Solander were born or thought of'.[72]

*   *   *

The literature of occupation entailed the construction of an appropriately detailed New Zealand past. Reeves's contribution has already been noted. Two men who happened to be his parliamentary colleagues in the 1890s also became prominent historians. Robert McNab, a lawyer and farmer, and like Hocken and Turnbull a collector of books and manuscripts, was as an author essentially a compiler of materials. *Murihiku* (standard editions 1907, 1909) is a history of early European activities, especially sealing and whaling, in the Southland region and around the southern coasts and islands. The book was expanded and republished several times as fresh information came to hand, incorporating, often verbatim, newspaper items, journals, and log-books which McNab located not only in New Zealand but also in Australia, North America, and Europe. Two other works, *Old Whaling Days* (1913) and *From Tasman to Marsden* (1914) are similar aggregates of evidence.

Lindsay Buick also made considerable use of documentary records, but unlike McNab, who eschewed speculation, Buick deliberately added imaginative colour to the documentary framework. His first two books were regional histories of Marlborough and the Manawatu. Subsequently he wrote three works on the moa, a study of the conflicts in the north during the 1840s, another on Te Rauparaha, and (his most influential work) *The Treaty of Waitangi*, first published in 1914, then, substantially rewritten, in the 1930s. Though Buick was prepared to revise popular misconceptions — his study of *The French at Akaroa* (1928) which argued there had been no 'race' between the British and French for possession of the South Island was repeating what had already been established by other historians — his own interest was in myth-making, and his histories were attempts to depict a glamorous and dramatic past.

There was a quickening interest in New Zealand history during the 1930s: people with an eye for significant milestones looked forward to the centennial of British sovereignty in 1940, and the more knowledgeable could mark interesting anniversaries in the 1930s — 100 years since this or that event, such as the arrival of the British Resident in 1833. Writers both responded to this interest and helped to promote it. A particularly significant publication was *The Letters and Journals of Samuel Marsden* in 1932, edited by J.R. Elder. Some of Marsden's writings had been available in contemporary missionary journals, but these were not readily accessible and the materials were scattered; some letters and portions of reports had not thus far been printed at all. Elder added useful notes and supplementary material from other sources. The result, which took up a mammoth 580 pages, was a revelation: Marsden had written of New Zealand and the New Zealanders in clear, vigorous prose which provided latter-day readers and researchers with an intimate view of the first period of mission activity. The appeal of Marsden's account was probably heightened by his insistent adumbration of a christianized and regenerate New Zealand nation; this non-European future had since been hidden or at any rate overshadowed by the subsequent narrative of conquest. This perspective was opened up by a number of writers in the 1930s, including Eric Ramsden, who, beginning with *Marsden and the Missions* (1936), informed several historical works with his bicultural sympathies.

The most numerous historical accounts were local histories. Local history may be taken as a generic term for large and small texts which set out the past of an area defined geographically — province, region, district, parish, or locality. The production of many of the slighter efforts and some of the larger was linked to jubilees and anniversaries, so the purpose was often explicitly commemorative, and usually exhortatory as well. 'Our fathers', write Henry

Brett and Henry Hook in the *Albertlanders: Brave Pioneers of the 'Sixties* (1927), 'laid foundations. What they endured, suffered, and bravely accomplished takes up the story of example and achievement handed down to us to-day, and which is worth more than all our material gains. We remember the Past with admiration and gratitude.'[73] The brave pioneers had transformed a wilderness and thus had earned their title to the land: explicit or implicit is the notion that the dispossession of the indigenous inhabitants is just. In some local histories — for example, J.G. Wilson's *Early Rangitikei* (1914) — the acquisition of the land by war or purchase is recounted in great detail; the text re-enacts the passage of the land from one people to another. Local histories are thus colonizing texts in a very direct sense, since they justify the European appropriation of the land.

The local histories left out the defeats and the personal tragedies: 'We have not retailed the faults and frictions of Albertland life, which are common to human nature and every community,' admit Brett and Hook. 'We have rather aimed to draw attention to the noble traits which are calculated to edify and inspire.' When the less savoury aspects of life are recounted, they are presented as colourful incidents. Robert Gilkison's *Early Days in Central Otago* (1930) and *Early Days in Dunedin* (1938) with their racily-told anecdotes are examples of this approach. Of course the gold-seekers of Otago were, Gilkison reminds the reader, basically 'noble fellows', and 'the diggers as a body were extremely well behaved'.[74]

The reluctance to write of 'faults and frictions' was probably one reason why so few biographies were published, and why those which were published were almost entirely without merit. Books which featured missionaries and statesmen as their subjects (for example, Marsden, E.G. Wakefield, Seddon, Sir Francis Dillon Bell) were either solemn or adulatory. The most significant biographical work was carried out by G.H. Scholefield. Over a period of some thirty years he collected a vast amount of material on national and provincial luminaries and, in imitation of the British model, produced *A Dictionary of New Zealand Biography* (1940). The subjects of the 2500 entries were almost all male and European, and the majority of them had been politicians: textually the entries constituted New Zealand's pantheon.

Autobiography was rare. Men engaged in medicine and law could write reminiscences which included sin and sickness because these were related to their professional duties. The best of these was O.T.J. Alpers's *Cheerful Yesterdays* (1928). There were also some dreary pioneer narratives, most of them dry, colourless, and self-effacing. An odd exception was E.E. Vaile's *Pioneering the Pumice* (1939). Vaile's account emphasizes his own hard work, his foresight, and his rectitude; he inflates, without any trace of wit, his slight erudition; his views on local Māori people are extremely racist. It is the quintessential pioneer legend.

Celebration of the indigenous — birds, bush, the Māori; evocation of the 'colourful' early history of New Zealand; praise for the pioneers — all these major themes of New Zealand nonfiction writing from the 1890s to the 1930s were designed in various (and sometimes contradictory) ways to make New

Zealand writers (and readers) feel 'at home' in New Zealand. Nevertheless, writers continued to identify themselves as British and occasionally wrote of the Empire with a proud warmth that dismayed a later generation. It was Alan Mulgan who made the most explicit effort to sort out the personal, cultural, and literary incongruities.

Mulgan tried a variety of literary forms — drama, verse, fiction; his non-fiction includes local history, travel, autobiography, essays on New Zealand literature, and (with A.W. Shrimpton) a general history of New Zealand. He wrote carefully, if digressively, rather like an essayist, even in his larger works. He had more influence perhaps as a 'man of letters' in general than through the particular ideas disseminated by his writings; but two of his works, *Home* (1927), and a much later book, *The Making of a New Zealander* (1957), gave voice to the multiple identifications of his generation. Mulgan grew up in Katikati, an Ulster settlement: 'The tendency of life in Katikati was to bind us to Britain and her established order: her politics, her Navy and Army, her Empire, her literature, her ways of thought.' Despite his Ulster antecedents, it was England which intrigued him and when he eventually visited Britain in the 1920s he found in England all of the idealized images stored up over half a lifetime. A village in the Cotswolds lay 'between a brook at the bottom of the steep valley, and a manor house at the top of the hill, a fragrant and authentic bit of old England, nodding through the years in the shade of its trees and the twilight of its memories.'[75] From New Zealand settler society Mulgan was unable to derive equivalent stereotypes, though *A Pilgrim's Way in New Zealand* (1935), in which Cowan's influence is explicitly acknowledged, was an attempt to combine people, places, indigenous and exotic flora and the Māori presence into a prosy guidebook which left out the asperities.

Mulgan's books, if unexciting, were at least written clearly. But much of the non-fiction written between the 1890s and 1930s, however much it specified 'New Zealand', either in celebrating indigenous phenomena or praising the pioneers, was poorly crafted. The major exceptions were Reeves's works, and perhaps Guthrie-Smith's, and a handful of writings by expatriate New Zealanders.

Raymond Firth's *Primitive Economics of the New Zealand Maori* (1929) was originally written as a doctoral thesis in London. R.H. Tawney contributed a considerable preface. Making extensive use of the printed materials on the Māori, including Best's work, Firth reinterprets Māori society as a coherent traditional system, and indicates in a coda the adaptations which occurred when Europeans intervened. In one way it is as much an artificial rendering as Best's: Firth draws upon modern scholars in anthropology and economics to provide a framework for exposition and analysis. Otherwise it is a striking departure from the usual treatment of the Māori way of life as being curious, quaint, and deficient. Firth stayed overseas; his research and his writings on other Pacific peoples and their social and economic systems became an important contribution to the development of British anthropology.

Peter Buck (who often placed his Māori name, Te Rangi Hiroa, above P.H.

Buck on title pages) had gone overseas about the same time as Firth, not to London but to the Bernice P. Bishop Museum in Hawaii; he was later Director of the Museum, and a visiting professor at Yale. His major writings delineated the material culture of several areas of the Pacific; and he produced a popular book (originally for a United States audience) in 1937, *Vikings of the Sunrise,* a celebration of the Polynesian peoples and of his own Polynesian ancestry. He had long intended to revise his paper 'The Coming of the Maori' (1925, 1929) and eventually decided to rewrite it entirely. The result, *The Coming of the Maori* (1949), deals with much more than the title indicates: it is in fact a full-scale ethnology which in some aspects superseded Best's *The Maori.* Years of practice had perfected Buck's ability to write simply and clearly about sophisticated techniques of design and manufacture. While precise and scholarly, *The Coming of the Maori* is a work of great charm, full of humour, personal asides, and quiet correction of earlier absurdities.

J.B. Condliffe's *New Zealand in the Making* (1930), a 'survey of economic and social development' as the subtitle indicated, was also written, or at least completed, while the author was an expatriate. It can be called the first comprehensive history of New Zealand, and it complements, while not supplanting, Reeves's *Long White Cloud.* It is vastly superior to any other contemporary history — A.W. Shrimpton and Alan Mulgan's *Maori and Pakeha* (1922), for example. The examples of Firth, Buck, and Condliffe might suggest that expatriate circumstances made the difference between accomplishment and aspiration. No doubt, as with Reeves, exile sharpened their perception; but other works of non-fiction by expatriates such as Hector Bolitho and A.J. Harrop do not display any outstanding qualities. Some allowance must no doubt be made for individual talent. What Firth, Buck, and Condliffe did have in common was experience of research institutions, and therefore intellectual debate, outside New Zealand. Condliffe, indeed, was very critical of educational and intellectual standards in New Zealand. By contrast, a great number of prominent New Zealand non-fiction writers from the 1890s to the 1930s were autodidacts or journalists.

The literature of occupation did not fade away as a new discursive strategy was inaugurated in the 1930s and 1940s. Many of the established writers continued to publish into the 1950s and 1960s, and younger writers followed the paths which had been shaped from the 1890s. Books on the Māori, flora and fauna, local histories, celebrations of the 'colourful' early days of New Zealand — these kinds of works were increasingly numerous in the succeeding decades. In fact, the literature of occupation is still being written and published in 1990.

The Literature of National Identity, 1930s-1980s

At the end of his essay, *New Zealand: A Short History* (1936), J.C. Beaglehole wrote that New Zealand was not, 'with any deep feeling, a nation'.

The tenderness of place, the *genius loci,* in no large sense, it appears, is part of the life of the European born in our country — for the Maori, the ancient conqueror, it is different — the sense of intimacy, quietude, profound and rich comfort is not yet indestructibly mingled with the thought of a native soil, an habitual and inseparable surrounding. There is glad recognition, there is love even; but there is not identity.

It was a process that could not be forced, but would come 'quietly and unconsciously'. Nevertheless there was, Beaglehole indicated, an important role for art and letters in crystallizing and ennobling New Zealand life. These concerns, however improved in Beaglehole's phraseology, are similar to those of writers in the 1890s and 1900s: earlier writers had hoped to develop a sense of 'belonging' to New Zealand by incorporating into their works indigenous subjects, especially the birds, the bush, and the Māori. Beaglehole and his contemporaries wanted to construct identity out of other materials, but the purpose of the exercise, whatever the materials, was essentially the same: to take colonization a stage further and inhabit the land more completely than hitherto.[76]

The changed emphasis in prose style and subject-matter of the younger generation is evident in several of the centennial surveys. The subject-matter is European New Zealand — exploration, politics, education, history, agriculture, 'external affairs'. The sources are documentary materials, the residues of the articulate past, not oral evidence. The prose is shorn of the hyperbole and bombast that marked and marred earlier writings, and is concise and plain, yet still elegant. The younger writers did not simply compose their works in reaction to the faults of their predecessors, but they were aware of their aesthetic failures and no doubt were ashamed that such work had for many years stood *faute de mieux* as New Zealand writing.

Among the materials for constructing identification with the land, for writers at any rate, were earlier writings. This strategy allowed the latest fashioners of national identity to pay less attention to Māori subjects than their immediate literary predecessors. What Beaglehole himself had in mind is evident not only in his exemplary works on exploration, *The Exploration of the Pacific* (1937), and *The Discovery of New Zealand* (1940), and in his editions of the journals of James Cook and Joseph Banks, but also in a Foreword he contributed to Nancy Taylor's collection, *Early Travellers in New Zealand* (1959). England had been written about so much, thought Beaglehole, 'that the ordinary literate Englishman, even if no traveller, has generally something in the back of his mind compounded of the observations of travellers like Defoe and Arthur Young and Pennant and Cobbett.' From the *Early Travellers* 'New Zealanders . . . may learn something essential about our own country . . .. We can clutch onto the yarns; and as they become known, we shall enlarge and deepen our tradition, the tradition of a particular people in a particular land, whose mutual workings have given us ourselves.'[77] This strategy may be contrasted with that of writers of the previous generation who had collected the Māori place-names and their meanings to give historical and human depth to the landscape.

Beaglehole asserted the vigour and particularity of the New Zealand experience *within* the wider perspective of the British (and European or 'western') framework. New Zealand was for Beaglehole a provincial product of the metropolitan world and its story carried the impress of that world. His views had a substantial impact upon a wide range of people connected with the centennial publications and also among his students. For example, John Miller's *Early Victorian New Zealand* (1958) combines the literary residues of the Cook Strait settlements of the 1840s with Miller's own graceful writing in a way that exemplifies as well as expresses the literary relationship between metropolis and periphery. Ruth Allan's *Nelson: A History of Early Settlement* (1965), which also deals with the 1840s, is a demonstration of Beaglehole's demand 'for technical accomplishment, for professional standards, even to the point of pedantry', but it contains as well the fine writing he valued.[78] John Dunmore's *French Explorers in the Pacific* (1965, 1969) is another major work within the Beaglehole tradition; and his *The Fateful Voyage* (1969) is a reconstruction of the tribulations of the adventurer Jean de Surville, an excellent example of how the imaginative techniques of fiction may be imported into an historical account without distorting the documentary evidence.

F.L.W. Wood, a colleague of Beaglehole's, explored the relationship of New Zealand with the metropolis in a way that provided a context for reconsidering the emotional ties of empire. As its title suggests, *New Zealand in the World* (1940) ranges much more widely than imperial relations. The vantage point is New Zealand rather than Westminster, and Wood identifies the intricate web of interests within which politicians moved. His conclusion is judicious: since history has 'shaped New Zealanders into a people British in sentiment, tradition and economic interest', the 'permanent basis of New Zealand's relations with the outside world' is 'close co-operation with the mother country'. However, New Zealanders have had 'honourable contacts in peace and war with other countries and other cultures.' New Zealand's history, therefore, has 'equipped her to live a life of her own as a small but not subservient member of the British Commonwealth'.[79] Wood further detailed the development of New Zealand as an independent nation with its own foreign policy in *The New Zealand People at War: Political and External Affairs* (1958), the first major account of the 'high policy' of a New Zealand government.

Several general or short histories likewise clarified the sense of nationhood. Reeves's *Long White Cloud* was republished in 1950; it was then still the best short history of New Zealand but Reeves's text remained as it had been for the 1924 edition, and the section which took the story from Seddon's death in 1906 was an uninspired résumé by another hand. Harold Miller's *New Zealand* (1950) was part of a series published by Hutchinson University Library. Miller depicted the past as, first, the tragic destruction of Māori society by settlers just as the Māori had begun to develop a christianized and agricultural basis for life, and, secondly, the 'remarkable political experiment' which European society had tried thereafter. J.B. Condliffe and W.T.G. Airey's *A Short History of New Zealand*, extensively rewritten by Airey in 1953 and essentially his book thenceforth, contained a left-liberal interpretation of political and social changes, and raised perspicacious questions about the future influence of world markets and international political systems upon New Zealand's economy and society. W.H. Oliver's *The Story of New Zealand* (1960), in the Faber series of national histories, was more philosophical, abstract, and analytical in expression. Oliver saw 'a history of adaptation and improvisation'. 'Nothing has remained quite as it was when it crossed the seas', he wrote, 'neither political institution nor social custom nor literary and artistic form. Nor does anything exist in to-day's New Zealand which does not preserve something of the character of its overseas origin.' The last part of the *Story* raised a series of unresolved questions about 'society at mid-century' — 'Like and Unlike' was the ambiguous British heritage expressed in the title of the last chapter. At the end of his book Oliver discussed New Zealand writing; he judged that it had 'achieved a modest maturity'. 'The spiritual pioneer', he concluded, 'is beginning to populate the land.'[81] It is a phrase which hints at the entire discursive programme.

None of these works was as influential in the long term as Keith Sinclair's *A History of New Zealand* (1959), a volume in the Pelican history of the world series. The book was an immediate success and by the end of the 1980s had been constantly in demand and almost continuously in print since its first publication. It superseded (though it did not immediately supplant) all other short histories of New Zealand then in print, including Reeves's *Long White Cloud*. Quite apart from its impact on academics and on students of history, Sinclair's *History* has been widely read by writers and artists, and indeed by what may be called the general public, and has been a major influence on New Zealanders' perceptions of their pasts. In short, the *History* was not just a text but a cultural event as well.[82]

It was still possible in the 1950s for a diligent individual to read all the significant works of research, including unpublished theses, which dealt with New Zealand's past; and Sinclair's knowledge of these materials, as well as his own considerable researches in the primary sources, is evident in the text. The *History* was therefore authoritative in the sense that it rested on the whole body of historical scholarship then available: this accuracy and comprehensiveness was part of its appeal. It was not, however, primarily a compendium of research: Sinclair formulated a complex mythology of national identity expressed in vivid prose. Sinclair interprets New Zealand history as the growth of a nation and emphasizes the evolution of national consciousness as indicated in such varied activities as politics, war, patterns of speech, and writing. The British or European background is not eliminated but the focus of the story is what takes place *in* New Zealand. The Prologue, 'The Fish of Maui', begins with myth and legend and includes recent ethnological and archaeological investigations; the first chapter sets New Zealand in a Pacific context as an 'Australian colony', and when later the British emigrants arrive there is less emphasis upon what they bring with them than on the ways they adapt themselves to new circumstances. On occasion there is something close to scorn for those who might have made New Zealand other than it has (in Sinclair's depiction) become. He writes of the 1940 centennial, for example, 'To celebrate the event the Labour [government] ministers turned back, not to the "common colonist", but to Wakefield, Godley, Featherston, FitzGerald, to the cultural ambitions of the systematic colonizers and the colonial gentry.'[83]

The conflicts between Pākehā and Māori are given considerable space, but rather more than hitherto the blunders of officials and the antagonisms of settlers are made the causes of hostilities: Governor Browne's 'ignorance of the rights of the tribe and the chiefs was inexcusable'; 'The investigation of the title to the Waitara by McLean and Parris was a farce'. At least in the period before 1870, Māori people play as great and as positive a role in New Zealand history as the invaders. This was not a new perspective by any means, but the execution struck a new note, or perhaps there were fewer of those customary false notes of contempt and paternalism.[84]

Thereafter Sinclair concentrates on cultural identifications, on governments and people and the relationships between them, especially the communal renewal of hope and progress with the advent of the Liberals in 1891 and Labour in 1935. By the 1950s there seemed to be solid accomplishment in both material and cultural terms: New Zealand was not a classless society but Sinclair thought it 'must be more nearly classless . . . than any other society in the world'. He wrote that 'New Zealanders belong to a branch of New World civilization the main centres of which are Sydney, San Francisco, and Auckland — the Pacific Triangle'.[85]

Sinclair's *History* tells a story in the form of a narrative, sometimes in a series of closely related scenes or episodes, at other times in more general characterizations of people and places — verbal snapshots. (In a later essay, Sinclair suggested the author of a short history must think of it 'as a piece of literature' and see the shape 'clearly, steadily and whole, as a composer might hear in his mind an unwritten symphony'.) He makes good use of epigrammatic statements: 'Ideas were as destructive as bullets'; 'Many a "Kiwi" drinker must look into his nine-ounce glass, only to discover there the disapproving face of his Primitive Methodist ancestor'; in 1930 Sir Joseph Ward 'was succeeded by New Zealand's most improbable Premier, G.W. Forbes, a Canterbury farmer, and a good, honest man whose political merits will doubtless, one day, be uncovered by some dogged researcher'. Sinclair's George Grey is as complex as Reeves's, but less obscured by prose pyrotechnics.[86]

Sinclair had Reeves's work in mind as he wrote his *History*: he lists his predecessors in the dedication — Reeves, Condliffe, Beaglehole, Airey, 'pioneers in whose tracks I have laboriously followed'. There is also an Australian influence. Sinclair has maintained an active interest in the Australasian dimension of New Zealand's past, and he is aware of Australian literary nationalism and poetry as well as writings on history. Before he went 'into production', Sinclair has recorded, W.K. Hancock gave him 'the best advice'.[87] Hancock's short history, *Australia* (1930), had been a major cultural event in that country, and Sinclair's *History* has been, as he doubtless intended, a cultural event of similar magnitude in New Zealand.

The *History* concludes with an Epilogue called 'The search for identity'. To many it must have seemed that Sinclair had completed that search, had given a satisfying and complete historical definition of New Zealand's identity. The Epilogue has been changed only slightly through several editions, though Sinclair has expanded his main ideas on the formation of identity in *A Destiny Apart* (1986), subtitled 'New Zealand's search for national identity'.

*   *   *

Although most local histories continued to be compiled by antiquarians who combined the rhetoric of the pioneer legend with about as many names as the district's telephone directory, there were some important works which displayed both scholarship and careful writing. The books provided a provincial or regional counterpoint to the general histories. In the late 1940s the organizers of the Otago centennial encompassed both the local piety and the scholarly overview in a massive project. Each district (the city of Dunedin excepted) arranged its own author and volume, with advice from a general supervisory committee: there are more than a dozen of these local histories emphasizing as was felt appropriate gold or sheep or kirk or exploration. In the centre was A.H. McLintock's *The History of Otago* (1949), immense in size and scholarship, correcting both smaller and larger pieties with some astringency and copious annotation; it concentrates almost entirely on the nineteenth century.

In Canterbury the plan was more sophisticated: a comprehensive history of the province written by different hands but drawn into a coherent whole, to be published in a single volume. The first instalment appeared in 1957, seven years after the centenary of organized settlement; it took the story to 1854 and deftly demolished the last of the Wakefield mythology while entrenching the enormity that the Ngaitahu people had not been cheated of their lands. Deaths and consequential reorganizations delayed the last volume until 1971, yet the authors and editors maintained throughout a perspective that was provincial without being parochial. Perhaps no other region is suitable for such treatment; at any rate no other region has followed the Canterbury model. One of the later editors of the Canterbury history, W.J. Gardner, produced a very satisfying record of the Amuri district in the nineteenth century. Gardner draws the reader into the vast spaces of *The Amuri* (1956) by way of a meticulous rehearsal of early European exploration. Philip May, a student of Gardner's, wrote what was possibly the most popular local history of all. May's *The West Coast Gold Rushes* (1962) eschews conventional hyperbole; the text is invested with the excitement of a few short years through the finely-organized accumulation of detail and incident.

In most local histories Māori people, the tangata whenua, are made to retreat (or disappear) from the text by salutary infusions of what is usually called civilization. This writing-out of one people and the writing-in of another is a textual re-enactment as well as recapitulation of colonization. A bicultural local history may be a contradiction in terms. Nevertheless, Evelyn Stokes's *A History of Tauranga County* (1980) maintains the presence of the Māori communities throughout her exposition in an exemplary manner. So, in a rather different way, does W.H. Oliver in his history of the Gisborne East Coast region, *Challenge and Response* (1971). Oliver treats his subject as 'a set of variations upon a New Zealand theme', thus seeking to link local and national history. 'The distinctiveness is there,' he admits, referring to the region, 'but it would be rash to push it too far.' No doubt aware of the tendency for sponsors of these works to consider the settler story as central, there is an element of strain in Oliver's insistence upon both the differences and (for the modern period) the similarities between the two communities, Māori and Pākehā: 'The general conclusion is inescapable: that the management problems of bringing deteriorated land into better production are generally regional, and not specifically Maori, in their nature.' He distances himself from his subject: 'To visit the East Coast will normally be an agreeable experience; to live there would be to have prolonged personal contact with the limitations of a region with considerable problems.' Such a statement of detachment, almost disengagement, is rare in local histories. By contrast Stokes writes, 'I am also tangata whenua of Tauranga and this book is coloured by my experiences.'[88]

In *Seven Lives on Salt River* (1987), Dick Scott makes no political, geographical or cultural definitions, but illustrates life in the Kaipara district through a multitude of incidents and people connected with the seven subjects. There is William Gittos, a relentless missionary and patriarchal father: when Edwin Fairburn arrives to court his daughter Esther, the unfortunate Fairburn is held down by a male servant and horsewhipped by three women. Ted Pook is a fisherman: he uses the whip, too, to get his way with his children, and there are a good many of them, twenty-six altogether, nineteen by Kohinga Mika Haira. Ellen Blackwell is the forgotten co-author of Laing and Blackwell's *Plants of New Zealand*. Gordon Coates is the local politician who becomes Cabinet Minister and for a time Prime Minister of New Zealand: he has children, acknowledged and unacknowledged, in both the Pākehā and Māori communities. All of these people and their friends and enemies Scott brings to vigorous life with the use of documentary and oral evidence and a style of reportage that celebrates the diversity of human experience.

*   *   *

While the historians shaped the past into a national story, or a regional variation, other writers attended to what they considered characteristic of the New Zealand way of life. It is possible to begin the discussion with reference to one of the centennial surveys. Whereas most of those volumes were firmly based on documentary materials, Oliver Duff's *New Zealand Now* (1941) was more a work of intuition and experience. Duff suggested as sources for students just a handful of books (the *Yearbook,* the Bible — which Duff noted, rather curiously, as 'still the best explanation of the New Zealand way of thinking' — Guthrie-Smith's *Tutira,* H.C.D. Somerset's *Littledene*), as well as the newspapers; but if students wanted to 'see and hear "New Zealand" more specifically', he prescribed 'any church, any school, any parliamentary debate, any racecourse, any football ground, any picture theatre, any camp, any conference, any wrestling match, any street corner, saleyard, railway station, woolshed, sewing meeting, tea-room, or backblocks hut'.[89] His five 'people' selected for pen portraits are a public servant, a teacher, a farmer, a policeman, and a soldier, all males. There is hardly a woman in the book, and only two oblique references to Māori people. Long before John Mulgan's *Man Alone* was very widely known and before Frank Anthony's Taranaki peasant-farmers had been rewrapped as 'Me and Gus' for a post-war generation, Duff had depicted with warmth what he regarded as the ordinary male New Zealander.

It proved possible in 1956 to reprint *New Zealand Now* unchanged (except for a very brief postscript) without any sense of anachronism. The social and political landscape was dominated by men in the post-war years — or that at least was the cultural illusion, reflected and promoted in the texts. Those male amphitheatres catalogued by Duff were elaborated in non-fiction works on war, on sport, on rural and outdoor life generally. Such subjects were drawn together into a generalized mythology, and John Mulgan, writing at the end of the war in a memoir published posthumously as *Report on Experience* (1949), stated the ethos concisely. The fellow New Zealanders he met as soldiers in Egypt were 'quiet and aloof and self-contained'.

> They had confidence in themselves . . . knowing themselves as good as the best the world could bring against them, like a football team in a more deadly game, coherent, practical, successful . . . .. Everything that was good from that small country had gone into them — sunshine and strength, good sense, patience, the versatility of practical men.[90]

There is in many texts this convergence of masculinity, personal identity, and national identity.

The Second World War was the subject of a great deal of writing. The most popular memoir was Jim Henderson's *Gunner Inglorious* (1946), his own story of battle, the loss of a limb, and life as prisoner of war, told with much understated dialogue. Howard Kippenberger, a senior officer who was crippled by a mine, produced the most considered autobiography, *Infantry Brigadier* (1949). The gunner and the brigadier in their very different ways talked of the comradeship of New Zealanders in uniform. Kippenberger was appointed editor-in-chief of the official war histories. Both the campaign and unit histories of this drawn-out series were an improvement on the order-of-battle compilations after the Great War, and Kippenberger kept his more wayward writers honest and on their topics, but there were pieces of the less glorious past which were left out. Some of the best prose is to be found in *Crete* (1953), written by the novelist Dan

Davin. His brief characterization of the morning of 20 May 1941, when the German parachutists hung in the sky ('each man dangling carried a death, his own if not another's'), indicates what might have been done if the histories had been less official and not so marmoreal.[91] Works of fiction (including Davin's) reveal more about the war.

The personal experience of war remained largely unwritten. It may be glimpsed in Denis Glover's essay on D-Day and in his sketches published in *Penguin New Writing*. It can be seen clearly in the straightforward account of a conscientious objector dragged to the front line in the First World War, Archibald Baxter's *We Will Not Cease* (1939). In *Gallipoli* (1984) Christopher Pugsley reaches back to that earlier conflict; and though the question of national identity remains part of his agenda, he renders the campaign as a human experience. Maurice Shadbolt's *Voices of Gallipoli* (1988) continued this recent process of reclamation.

Sport was war carried on by other means. Books on 'football' (the predominant code of rugby union) described a series of battles and celebrated both collective and personal heroism. Track and field athletes were necessarily given more extended individual treatment than had been usual for rugby footballers, and gradually it became acceptable and not immodest for sports heroes to appear as living legends in biographies and even in what were called autobiographies. The number of books written about sport probably approached the number which, officially and unofficially, sought to describe the war, but they were even more undistinguished as writing, and significant mainly as a bulky reiteration of the archetypal New Zealand man. Though concerned with war rather than sport, the relevant values are epitomized in Kenneth Sandford's biography of Charles Upham, *Mark of the Lion* (1962).

Men also proved themselves in the uninhabited fastnesses. John Pascoe was the most influential writer among those who made the mountains and the climbers their subjects. He built his books out of his own experiences not only in the mountains but also in the libraries and in the archives. 'My narrative is to be concerned with country of which I have active knowledge', he wrote in *Unclimbed New Zealand* (1939). Into this warp he weaves the story of earlier climbers and their accounts of successes and failures. In later, more designedly historical works his personal knowledge is used to colour the exposition; like many significant non-fiction writers of this period he is diligent in the use of documentary materials, bringing to life unpromising quotations and spare reports by incorporating something of himself. His re-creation of human activity over several decades gives an impression of almost constant occupation. He stocks the territory beyond the sheep stations of the 'high country' with Europeans, but is also able to write, 'All too rare are the Maori names which survive', and add, 'Fortunate are the peaks which are blessed' with Māori names. He can quote from Heaphy and note, 'This account honours the characteristic debt to Maori guides.' Nevertheless the emphasis is on European achievements.[92]

Pascoe makes his writing programme very clear: 'I take my position . . . as a New Zealander whose purpose is to interpret his own country to his readers.' He sees himself as part of a literary tradition. In his second work, *Land Uplifted High* (1952), there is a chapter on 'The writers: mountain literature' which is evaluative as well as bibliographical. He gives high rank to Samuel Butler but his admiration is greatest for Arthur Harper. Pascoe also produced a new edition of Brunner's journal, and he located and edited the manuscripts of Arthur Harper's companion and mentor, Charles Douglas, as *Mr Explorer Douglas* (1957). He envisages a textual grid which friends and acquaintances might help to complete: 'If these men wrote they could in turn inspire professional deer killers, high-country musterers and guides to take their share of literary burdens and the broader stream of New Zealand literature could flow closer to its mountain regions and rugged frontiers.'[93] There was indeed a torrent of writings by and about musterers (the first of Peter Newton's many works, *Wayleggo* (1946), proved especially popular), and deer cullers; and a good deal, more carefully wrought, about the mountains (Phillip Temple's works, for example). Jim Henderson's collection of *Open Country* (1965; later collections also), a selection of materials originally written by a wide range of contributors for radio performance, preserved the vitality and variety of rural and back country folklore more generally.

There were elements of autobiography in the *Open Country* sketches, and in the books by musterers and mountaineers, but in nearly all of these works, as well as in more deliberately autobiographical volumes, the intricate detail of personal experience was apparently sacrificed to archetypal imperatives. There were exceptions: Toss Woollaston's *Sage Tea* (1980) and Douglas Stewart's *Springtime in Taranaki* (1983) depict their early lives with engaging honesty. Many of the better autobiographical works were by women, and these are discussed further below.

For biography the picture is different. Two works which appeared in 1948 form an instructive contrast. H.F von Haast's *Life and Times of Sir Julius von Haast* is a vast compilation, a work of filial piety more than a thousand pages in length, Victorian in size, style, and subject. A.G. Bagnall and G.C. Petersen's *William Colenso*, on the other hand, although also a wordy volume, is in places more like a modern biography: Colenso had been dismissed as a missionary for 'misconduct' — he fathered a child by a Māori woman in his household — and neither the detail nor the drama of this was excluded, even if it was almost obscured in the relentless retracing of Colenso's peregrinations about the ranges. R.M. Burdon was the first writer to explore biographical possibilities in a consistent way. His essays on *New Zealand Notables* (three series, 1941, 1945, 1948) deal with a variety of eccentric, flawed, and tragic characters, and include a little psychological probing. He also indicated what could be done in political biography: *The Life and Times of Sir Julius Vogel* (1948) is scarcely more than an outline, but his biography of Richard Seddon, *King Dick* (1956), is perceptive and substantial, even if far from comprehensive.

James Rutherford's *Sir George Grey* (1961) and P.J. O'Farrell's *Harry Holland* (1964), the latter researched and published in Australia, marked advances in scholarly and well-organized political biography; but, as with short history, Keith Sinclair's contribution was of major significance. Sinclair's *William Pember Reeves: New Zealand Fabian* (1965) is at once scholarly and entertaining, and rather more than a political biography without being an exhaustive life-and-times study. It is not always a warm portrait, but Reeves was not always a warm man; and Sinclair's clipped, sometimes terse prose is quite suited to the subject. The work set a high standard for other biographers; at the same time it removed almost all local doubts about the utility of biography as a significant form of historical study and literary expression in New Zealand, and demonstrated that questions of power and morality and matters of domestic detail could be treated with candour. Since then there have been several successful studies. They include Judith Binney's *The Legacy of Guilt* (1968), a life of Thomas Kendall which grew out of contemplation of an essay by Burdon and a poem by Sinclair and reveals the contorted intellectual apostasy of an evangelical; Jeanine Graham's *Frederick Weld* (1983), which places its subject within the setting of marriage and family and makes these relationships neither sentimental nor peripheral but a basis for understanding Weld's excursions into public and imperial affairs; Barry Gustafson's evocative study of M.J. Savage, *From the Cradle to the Grave* (1986), which reconstitutes through a single subject the personal and ideological migration from Australia to New Zealand in the early years of the twentieth century; R.C.J. Stone's biography of J.L. Campbell, *Young Logan Campbell* (1982) and *The Father and his Gift* (1987), a sensitive portrait of a merchant building a business empire and a personal mythology, with much of the history of Auckland city in the nineteenth century as a detailed backdrop; Ross Galbreath's *Walter Buller* (1989), which reveals that the energy of this interpreter, magistrate, naturalist, lawyer, and businessman was not altogether matched by his probity; and Frances Porter's *Born to New Zealand* (1989), which through a biography of Jane Maria Atkinson depicts in beguiling detail the domestic, cultural, and intellectual life of the Richmond-Atkinson clan. Sinclair himself made a second large offering with *Walter Nash* (1976). The substantial development in biographical writing can be measured by contrasting Burdon's *Vogel* with Raewyn Dalziel's *Julius Vogel* (1986), a carefully researched account of nineteenth century politics, finance, and ambition.

E.H. McCormick's *Alexander Turnbull: His Life, His Circle, His Collections* (1974) deserves more extensive comment. McCormick links Turnbull with William Pember Reeves, Katherine Mansfield, and Frances Hodgkins 'as another in the group of native-born New Zealanders that emerged in the colony's first half century'. Like the others, Turnbull spent time as 'a colonial domiciled not unhappily at "Home"'; unlike the others Turnbull returned to live and die in New Zealand, building up his collection of books, and contributing unobtrusively 'to the country's dawning intellectual life'. 'Above all' says McCormick, 'he laboured to perfect his library, extending it outside narrow national limits to take in the Pacific, Australia, and aspects of the larger world beyond.'[94] The biography of Turnbull, in terms of McCormick's *œuvre,* can be seen as a counterpoint to his earlier works on Hodgkins, especially *The Expatriate* (1954). Turnbull withdraws from 'Home' to live in New Zealand, and in time withdraws from life in New Zealand to a kind of self-incarceration in his library. But he draws the world of books with him, expatriates them it could be said, and ultimately enriches the cultural life of New Zealand by bequesting this archive which encompasses Shakespeare and Milton, de Bry and Thévenot, as well as Emily Harris and Margaret Bullock.

McCormick's biographical technique in *Turnbull* may be derived from the nature of the evidence — correspondence relating to business interests, book collecting, and personal life but with major gaps and little detail on several periods of Turnbull's life — rather than from any theories about the inapplicability of what James Clifford has called the 'myth of personal coherence'.[95] Nevertheless, his depiction of the subject is close to some notions of what modern biographic practice should be. Turnbull is presented not as a transcendent individual but decentred, a series of occasions and relationships within the social and intellectual structures which operated upon him. The subject is constituted through a presentation of the traces of his activities: McCormick keeps close to the documentary materials and forbears to speculate about what is unspoken, or at least unwritten. The result is very satisfying: 'Life' and 'times' are drawn together, instead of 'times' receding into the background; Turnbull is placed within the circumstances of family and library rather than separated out from them; and the text is left open to the reader beyond the point where documentation ceases.

*   *   *

The literature of national identity was not accepted without challenge. Social scientists, staffing the universities and parts of the public service in increasing numbers from the 1960s onwards, brought their social theory, including quantitative techniques, from overseas academies, and in great detail supplemented or questioned the generalizations which had been put in place from the 1930s onwards. The concept and the reality of class especially seemed to some critics to have been eliminated or at least devalued by the fabricators of national identity.

A 'left' interpretation restated the idea of class struggle much more strongly, or emphasized the failures of 'progressive' governments (the Liberals, the Labour Party) to deliver social equity to the extent that their rhetoric seemed to have promised. Such a view was set out in W.B. Sutch's books, which, originally published in the early 1940s, reappeared, much amplified, in the 1960s: *The Quest for Security in New Zealand* (1966) and *Poverty and Progress in New Zealand* (1969). Tony Simpson's *The Sugarbag Years* (1974), the first major work of oral history in New Zealand, provided documentation of this perspective through the memories of people who had endured the Depression of the 1930s. Simpson's *Te Riri Pakeha* (1979) and Dick Scott's *Ask that Mountain* (1975, a revision of his *The Parihaka Story* of 1954) extended what might be called the 'Rusden tradition' of relations between Pākehā and Māori. This leftish critique, which is not too far from the major left-liberal tradition of New Zealand historiography (pepper to their salt), is essentially a moral history. It has continued to exist between (and to inform) the writings of both the documentary historians and those social commentators who give a theoretical basis to their works. One comprehensive and short account which provided a coherent critique of both the predominant 'national identity' writers and those of the 'left', and placed New Zealand's development within orthodox Marxist discourse, was David Bedggood's *Rich and Poor in New Zealand* (1980).

The most concentrated, if often implicit critique of the literature of national identity has been made by women, especially in the 1970s and 1980s, a period when the women's movement generally became more prominent. This challenge could be seen as a reaction by women to a literature which almost completely excluded them. General histories, local histories, books on war, sport, the 'back country' — these works dealt primarily with the world of men. If women were also involved, their participation was overlooked. To take one spectacular example: though women had been trampers and mountaineers in considerable numbers, there was scant reference to them in the literature. From another angle, the domestic labour which has made possible much climbing activity by men is almost entirely overlooked. John Pascoe was unusual in allowing these considerations to enter his writing. In *Land Uplifted High* he explains that though his family had increased, 'the sympathy of a mountaineer-wife' enabled him 'to get back to the snows when less fortunate men had their wings clipped by the demands of paternity'. On one peak the mists cleared long enough for him to see the social landscape in the distance: 'I glanced at my watch, thought it was time for Dorothy to be bathing our third infant, and settled down to the tasks of descent that demanded caution.'[96]

While non-fiction writing by women in the 1970s and 1980s has been of greater volume than previously, and therefore more visible, there appears to have been a distinctive women's non-fiction tradition since extensive Pākehā settlement began in the nineteenth century. There may be a good deal of this writing to be retrieved from newspapers, or transformed from manuscript letters and journals into published form. The *Letters* of Charlotte Godley (1936) were a revelation when first published; and another striking example are the letters of Mary Taylor to Charlotte Brontë and others in England, edited by Joan Stevens in 1972. Jessie Mackay, Edith Searle Grossman, and B.E. Baughan, known primarily for their verse and prose fiction, all published non-fiction essays, articles or pamphlets. Among the notable non-fiction writers in the second quarter of the twentieth century were Ettie Rout and Mona Gordon; and Robin Hyde's *Journalese* (1934) provides a witty, socially-informed picture of New Zealand in the Depression which is not equalled in any non-fiction literature of that time. In slighter works the perspective of women is evident, too. N.E. Coad's *New Zealand from Tasman to Massey* (1934), the first general history of New Zealand by a woman since E.M. Bourke's small primer of 1881, makes quite clear the importance of women's activities in gaining the vote for women. 'New Zealand women', wrote Coad, 'achieved the franchise as a result of forty years' struggle. It was not, as some people assert, achieved easily.'[97] The textual and cultural genealogies which link the nonfiction of Godley, Taylor, Mackay, Rout, Gordon, Coad and others need investigation.

Three works by and about women published for New Zealand's 1940 centennial provide a useful starting point in the present discussion. Helen M. Simpson's *The Women of New Zealand* (1940), one of the centennial surveys, was the first historical work to specify a separate and significant past for Pākehā women. Simpson concentrates on the early generations of settlement and gives relatively small space to experiences in the twentieth century. Nevertheless, she examines contemporary occupations and emphasizes the range of work performed by women, adding that the 'statistics do not of course reveal against what opposition women may have had to struggle to gain an entrance into these various trades and professions, nor in the face of how great discouragement they have kept a footing, however precarious.' 'The Early Home-makers' makes apparent the exhausting nature of domestic labour. The final chapter, 'Women in Association', indicates the complex networks operated by women in various organizations. Simpson records as a difficulty for her work 'the comparative lack of records other than those written by men and from the man's point of view'. However, she is able to extract material by and about women from some of those materials, and to list several works by women: these include A.E. Woodhouse's *George Rhodes* (1937), Lady Barker's books, and Charlotte Godley's *Letters*.[98]

The other two important works produced at the time of the centennial were published by the major organizations of rural women, one by the Women's Division of the Farmers' Union, the other by the Women's Institutes. Both included material drawn from women throughout New Zealand and they are thus similar in form as well as in origin. The Women's Division volume, *Brave Days* (1939), was edited by Helen Wilson, Nina A. R. Barrer, and Flora Spurdle; the Institutes' volume, *Tales of Pioneer Women* (1940), by A.E. Woodhouse. The titles suggest something of the substance and tone of these recollections and reminiscences, which broadly conform to the 'pioneer legend' established by male writers, but many of the contributors specify women's particular experiences. Woodhouse indicates in her 'Editor's Note' that there is a transmission of information between different generations of women: 'This is not a history book, nor is it a collection of short biographies of the most outstanding women of our country; rather is it a book of simple tales, chiefly memories that have been handed down to us by our mothers and grandmothers.'[99]

There are some general points which may be made about *Tales* and *Brave Days*. First, although there is a measure of selection from the materials offered, and there has been some editing and rewriting of what is printed, the personal accounts are not submerged into or reduced to a single narrative: the integrity of the individual contributions and of the individual subjects is maintained. Secondly, the detail of women's experiences is preserved: no recollection of food or technology or human incident is considered too trivial to be included. Thirdly, the works are collaborative. Finally, the production of the two books suggests that women were aware of the need to establish their own separate textual space to ensure the recording of the distinctive experiences of women — an implicit recognition that this was something men would not do and could not do. These features of *Tales* and *Brave Days* — the biographical basis, the detailed accounts of women's lives, the collaborative effort, and the deliberate creation of textual space — are characteristics of much of women's non-fiction writing, whatever the precise subject-matter.

While men in the 1950s and 1960s laboured over the war histories, the books on sport, and celebrations of the 'back country', women produced reminiscences which dealt with a wider range of human experiences and conditions: it is, to some extent, that contrast between Samuel Butler and Mary Ann Barker or Sarah Amelia Courage once again. Women's writing is more concerned with people and their relationships than with national identity; the literary world of women writers is far more densely and variously populated than that of men; and New Zealand as a huge cultural artifact recedes or almost vanishes altogether in the verbal particularization of life. All these qualities may be found in a selection of autobiographical works from the 1950s and 1960s. Helen Wilson's *My First Eighty Years* (1950) tells a story of pioneering through detailed incidents rather than in rhetorical terms: she is very aware of the tragedies of life, and the social conceits of townspeople. Timaru in the 1880s was famous for its 'fraudulent bankruptcies which resulted in disappearances, imprisonments, and suicides'. There was so much 'wire-pulling' in getting elected to the gentlemen's club that men in financial difficulties would not resign: 'Timaru was noted for smart turn-outs and continued to be so long after the money to keep them up had vanished.' Te Kuiti in 1910 'resembled a gold-rush town', but there was nevertheless 'Te Kuiti Society, with a very big S . . . frilly, dressy, fashionable'. In the nearby Pio Pio district her own house 'stood in a sea of mud. Every animal seemed to have to walk past the back door several times a day . . .. The mud was often knee-deep. Stepping-stones alone made it possible for me to step outside.' Of all the changes which had taken place during her life she considered the altered place of women to be the 'most fundamental'.[100]

Nancy Ellison's *The Whirinaki Valley* (1956) is more sombre. She, too, writes of farming experiences (the financial as well as physical difficulties), of sickness, of death, of the births of her own children, and, near the end, of the conception of her memoir: 'The voice inside me spoke again saying, "Write a book." Oh, God, not a book. I can't. I'm here alone with six little children. The winter is coming on. We have no money. I have all the children's winter clothes to make. The pump is broken. The last few days I have had to carry all the water up from the creek in a bucket and will have to until Terry comes home to fix the pump. I can't write a book. But I knew I could do even that if I had to do so.' This is farming life in the prosperous 1950s.[101]

Jean Boswell regarded *Dim Horizons* (1955) as a biography of her mother 'rather than an autobiography', but both stories are woven together. Here again are 'pioneers', at the end of the nineteenth century, in Northland. The tone is bright and breezy, optimistic; yet the deeper hurts are in the text too. As a child all her sympathies were for the men who grumbled over the lack of 'farm conveniences', but when she is twelve she hears a neighbour talking: ' "Yes," said the woman wearily, "we can slave our soulcases into carcasses, with scarcely a convenience of any sort to help us. It's all 'the farm, the farm, the farm'." ' It is from confidences between her mother and women neighbours that she learns 'what fear and even terror the advent of each child meant to these poverty-stricken, overworked, backblock mothers'. The children of the farms resent so 'mightily' the children of the storekeepers who are able to go to high school and colleges that 'there grew in us a bitterness that time has never completely eradicated'.[102]

Amelia Howe's *Stamper Battery* (1964) is set in Thames in the 1880s and 1890s when the six hundred stampers smashing quartz for gold produced an 'all-pervading noise' which 'dinned in the eardrums, day in and day out'. Of this industrial town her memories are 'poignant yet happy, loving yet bitter'. One of Howe's brothers is crushed by a dray and dies, another loses an eye, Charity Anne's 'sweetheart' is whipped by her father, Howe's own father is trapped with others by a fall in the mine and the family must wait through the night until the men are brought to the surface on stretchers — and still alive. By then the only dream her mother has is of 'getting away from Thames before it killed both Dad and her'. 'The women of Thames worked all the time', writes Howe. 'No day was ever set aside for them to rest. I often think now that the real heroes of the goldfields were not the pioneers . . . or the miners . . . but the women who worked even longer hours.'[103]

In the reminiscences of Wilson, Ellison, Boswell, and Howe, and in other autobiographical writings by women before the 1970s, the accounts supplement the discourse of men, and perhaps correct, rather too gently, some of the grosser misstatements. During the 1970s and 1980s, on the other hand, as a result of the reinvigorated women's movement which drew upon overseas models of dissent, much writing by women became deliberately contestatory, used to create a textual-ideological space as an alternative to and as a displacement of patriarchal discourse. A good deal of this writing for tactical reasons has appeared in relatively ephemeral forms such as letters, articles, and pamphlets. The range of material, writing strategies, and subjects is displayed in the periodical *Broadsheet* (1972-), and in the publications of the Women's Studies Association, including the *Women's Studies Journal* (1983-). However, there have also been in the 1980s volumes of essays by several different writers, this arrangement in part reflecting the co-operative principles which the women's movement has tried to practice. An example which indicates the breadth of these works is *Public and Private Worlds* (1987), edited by Shelagh Cox, a book 'seeking to extend the known world of social analysis to encompass private life'.[104] It contains chapters by Rosemary Novitz (work and wages), Rangimarie Mihomiho Rose Pere (her whakapapa and waiora), Aorewa McLeod (fiction),

Anne Kirker (art), Bev James (wives of industrial workers), Marilyn Waring (unpaid labour), Alison J. Laurie (suppression of knowledge about lesbianism), Catherine Benland (religion), Jan Robinson (prostitution), and Katherine Sackville-Smith (women and the State). Many of the writers incorporate in their analysis theory and research from Europe and North America — Firestone, Rowbotham, Oakley, Cixous, Radway, Rich, de Beauvoir.

Likewise proceeding from the principles of the women's movement, much work is biographical and autobiographical. This writing seeks to remove the invisibility of women by insisting on the concreteness of individual lives. Some books are collections of life histories, such as *Celebrating Women* (1984), edited by Christine Cole Catley, which blends interview and biography. *Head and Shoulders* (1986) comprises eight autobiographical essays introduced and edited by Virginia Myers. By juxtaposition of subjects and unobstrusive editing, Myers draws from some powerful individual statements a work which makes a compelling collective story. The emphasis in these works is on the effort to achieve not material success but personal liberty, social esteem, and visibility. Sonja Davies's *Bread and Roses* (1984) is a very detailed account of one woman's struggles in various causes over a period of nearly sixty years. Davies gives an impression of constant travail, with little of the calm retrospection characteristic of reminiscences by women in an earlier period. Her concerns, like her travels, eventually become international in scope; her public and private lives are drawn together throughout.

Women have also been prominent in the recent enthusiasm for collecting and utilizing oral testimonies, either because their personal skills facilitate the creation and presentation of such materials, or because they significantly supplement the limited documentary archive of women's experiences, or perhaps for a mixture of ideological and methodological reasons. Eve Ebbett has used oral evidence and more conventional materials in her histories of women in the Depression, *Victoria's Daughters* (1981), and in the Second World War, *When the Boys were Away* (1984); while Lauris Edmond's *Women at War* (1986) contains both spoken and written memoirs. The biographical basis, nevertheless, remains significant in the reclamation of the past beyond the possibilities of oral evidence: Julia Millen's *Colonial Tears and Sweat* (1984) examines the experiences of the working class in New Zealand during the nineteenth century, illustrating general conditions as far as possible through individual examples, and in their own words where these are recorded in extant records.

A considerable amount of women's writing of the 1970s and 1980s has been concerned to empower women by revealing to them their subordination and by indicating how the subordinating structures might be transformed or destroyed. Such writing has an instrumental purpose. The article 'An Unfortunate Experiment', co-authored by Sandra Coney and Phillida Bunkle and published in the magazine *Metro* in 1987, is an important as well as spectacular example. This article, critical of clinical experiments upon patients at National Women's Hospital, led to a Commission of Inquiry and consequential reforms. The case is discussed, together with other investigations into 'the politics of women's health in New Zealand' in Phillida Bunkle's *Second Opinion* (1988). 'This book', writes Bunkle, 'is about women finding ways to bring power over their bodies and lives back to themselves.' Sandra Coney's *The Unfortunate Experiment* (1988) gives a detailed account of efforts to bring evidence before the Commission. Coney wants 'to place on record that this was a feminist effort', since from her own experiences she knows 'how women's endeavours can sink without trace if they are not recorded'.[105]

*   *   *

In the generation after Elsdon Best's death, scholarly Pākehā study of and writing on the Māori developed in several directions. One was concerned with what was eventually to be called prehistory. It initially derived very largely from H.D. Skinner's studies, in museum collections and, to a smaller extent, in the field, of artefacts of the Moriori people of the Chatham Islands and of the South Island Māori. In his monograph *The Moriois of Chatham Islands* (1923) and in articles, Skinner questioned the reliability of certain traditions as presented by S. Percy Smith in *The Lore of the Whare-wānanga*. Skinner persuaded others to carry out archaeological work, but his hypotheses were known to, or at least accepted by, a relatively small group of his students. One of them, Roger Duff, built upon Skinner's work as well as confirming its broad outlines in *The Moa-Hunter Period of Maori Culture* (1950). It is not a well-fashioned book: its dogged rehearsal of the details of material culture and the recapitulation and critique of 'tradition' are expressed in a manner more thorough than captivating. The excitement is in the narrative of excavating the remains of humans and moa at Wairau Bar, and in the title which established in the popular imagination an historical sequence for the Polynesian occupation of New Zealand: before the 'classic' Māori there had been the moa-hunters, and they had, quite clearly, hunted moa. In the three decades following Duff's work, archaeology, like the sciences earlier and the social sciences later, became more professional and more academic, and this was reflected in the detached, clinical prose of the writings which reported work on sites and in laboratories. The excavations and the literature were summarized in Janet Davidson's *The Prehistory of New Zealand* (1984).

The greatest public attention focused on Andrew Sharp's *Ancient Voyagers in the Pacific* (1956). Sharp elaborated an hypothesis which had been put forward many years earlier without winning widespread favour — that the islands of the Pacific, including New Zealand, had been populated through 'accidental' or involuntary voyages of the Polynesians, rather than by deliberate navigation. Sharp's crisp argument, buttressed with documentary annotations, set scholars throughout the Pacific upon a detailed review of all kinds of evidence, and even re-enactments of voyages. Of equal interest to the substantive debate is the alacrity with which many Pākehā New Zealanders accepted Sharp's reading of the documentary evidence in preference to Māori traditions, however much some of these had apparently been recast by S. Percy Smith. David Simmons, whose ethnological and archaeological knowledge and familiarity with the Māori language was much greater than Sharp's, authoritatively reinterpreted S. Percy Smith's migration myths in *The Great New Zealand Myth* (1976).

Much of the writing of Pākehā scholars has turned away from 'the Māori as he was' towards a consideration of contemporary Māori society. The writers are usually academics (sometimes students carrying out supervised research), many of them social scientists trained in or invigorated by overseas teachings and writings in social anthropology, from North America and Britain initially, later from Continental Europe as well. The first generation of these writers admired the constructive programmes inaugurated by Apirana Ngata, and their work was either encouraged or inspired by him. F.M. Keesing's *The Changing Maori* (1928) is notable primarily as the first of a long sequence of such studies. I.L.G. Sutherland's *The Maori Situation* (1935) is a reasoned, quietly passionate defence of Ngata and his schemes after that leader had been placed in a situation which required his resignation from the government; Ngata himself was a major contributor to a volume of essays edited by Sutherland in 1940, *The Maori People Today*. Ernest Beaglehole and Pearl Beaglehole's community study *Some Modern Maoris* (1946) was followed by a series of reports on 'Rakau' and other pseudonymous localities, culminating in James Ritchie's *The Making of a Maori* (1963). These works, and many others, are reports by participant-observers, people who eschew detachment for sympathetic promotion of their subjects, and much of the writing is collaborative in the sense that the subjects authorize the study and often actively contribute to it. Alternatively, the writing is mediatory, designed to inform Pākehā and elicit a positive response from them: Anne Salmond's *Hui* (1975), which takes the reader onto the marae, seems to be almost the last possible development in this direction, for the marae is the centre of the other world.

It is hereabouts that a discursive threshold is recognized, and a consciousness of certain ethical and political questions is more explicitly displayed in some texts. This is not something which occurs as a logical consequence of the unfolding of the discourse, but is a result of the subjects themselves expressing their resistance to discourse which textualizes them and which appears to turn them into objects. A measure of the impact of this resistance is the careful consideration given by some Pākehā writers to the appropriateness of their textual strategies. A concern for textual and cultural integrity is evident in Joan Metge's *In and Out of Touch* (1986), where the issue of the italicization or romanization of Māori words is carefully weighed. Metge's 'cross-cultural' disquisition on whakamā is drawn from the statements of Māori people, and the book invites an activist Pākehā response and the reorganization of Pākehā perceptions and cultural actions. Whakamā is shown to be not just a word, or a concept which can be defined, but a complex signifying system embedded in Māori culture. In another example, Judith Binney and Gillian Chaplin's *Ngā*

Mōrehu (1986) maintains the interviews with subjects as separate life histories rather than incorporating the materials in a narrative fashioned by the editors.

The problematic nature of the literature of identity and several fundamental questions about the discourse of colonization were revealed in a rather public way in and through the writings of Michael King, especially his *Being Pakeha* (1985). This work, which King calls an 'ethnic autobiography', focuses on 'elements of personal and national identity'. It is at once a retracing of the way King himself sought out his identification with New Zealand, an account of his career as a writer of works which plot and extend European New Zealanders' sense of identity, and a defence of his methods as a biographer and cross-cultural communicator. 'A sense of history' claims King, 'comes from three ingredients: early habitation, evidence of that habitation, and stories about it based on the evidence.' Paremata, where he lived for a time as a child, 'had all three'. It is in James Cowan's *New Zealand Wars* that King finds 'a detailed account of what had happened militarily in the neighbourhood in 1846'. One is reminded of the influence of Cowan upon Alan Mulgan: *Being Pakeha* is a latter-day equivalent of Mulgan's *The Making of a New Zealander*, but it is more eloquent and much less equivocal.[106]

King's exploration of Māori culture and history has been expressed in journalism, in television productions, and in several books. His most highly-regarded work is the biography *Te Puea* (1977). It was by no means the first biography of a Māori by a Pākehā writer but it was so superior to what had been offered hitherto that the book seemed (as in some senses it was) a work without antecedent. King successfully depicts the Tainui leader not just as an individual but also as a spokesperson whose activities are all directed towards the survival and vivification of the group of which she is member. The biography was authorized by Tainui leaders and King was given access to the collective information of the people — both written and oral sources. Moreover, in his knowledge of the language and of protocol King had cultural skills which few other Pākehā writers could claim or exercise. Altogether it might seem that King's book was a more ethical excavation of the past than the unauthorized appropriations of the Māori as subject-matter by so many earlier writers.

Nevertheless, there were objections from Māori people, mostly expressed obliquely and indirectly; and when King subsequently published *Whina* (1983), a biography of Whina Cooper, and *Maori* (1983), a series of essays to accompany pictorial matter, the criticism from some Māori was sharper, and more openly expressed, if not widespread. King's partial acceptance of the broad thrust of the critique, set out in *Being Pakeha*, has been regarded by a few critics as simply compounding the crime. Using the phrase 'being Pakeha' is of course in one sense King's way of saying that he is not Māori and is not trying to be Māori. 'Being Pakeha' from this perspective is a contraction of cross-cultural claims. Yet it is also a phrase which insists on a double heritage, which still claims that portion of experience and cultural identity constructed out of the colonizing discourse. Even so, it was ironic that King's sensitivity towards and sympathy for Māori should provide an occasion for the discourse of colonization to be seen in clearer focus than ever before *as* a discourse. Writing was not just writing, something apart from the 'real world'. Colonization had meant, and still meant, the dispossession of the tangata whenua, and writing had been utilized, and was still being utilized, as an instrument in that process; it was not innocent of the power it described and analysed but implicated in that power.

The discourse of colonization had been much disputed by Māori people in earlier times. For instance, Apirana Ngata took a not altogether genial swipe at the Polynesian Society in the late 1940s, and earlier there was a letter from Paora Temuera in the Society's *Journal* protesting against an article on funeral customs written by Ernest and Pearl Beaglehole. Over the years there have been many cases in the Land Courts, petitions to Parliament, and commissions of inquiry, in which Māori people have counterposed their own understanding of verbal and written agreements to Pākehā interpretations of documentary materials. When in 1863 John Gorst's newspaper *Te Pihoihoi Mokemoke*, established in opposition to the Kingitanga newspaper *Te Hokioi*, printed certain insulting remarks, a party of Ngati Maniapoto captured the printing press and ordered Gorst to leave the Waikato area. The incident has been made to carry even greater symbolic weight by the further story that the type was melted down to mould into bullets, though it appears that this detail is fanciful ornamentation. Nevertheless, the point is that much of the resistance to colonizing discourse has taken non-chirographic forms.

In the 1970s and 1980s, however, as well as the customary dissent expressed by gesture and spoken word, and by silence, some Māori have contested the discourse of colonization on its own terrain, that is to say, in printed materials, the subjects themselves disrupting the discourse by raising questions about its instrumental purposes. Donna Awatere's *Maori Sovereignty* (1984) may be mentioned as an important example. In New Zealand, she writes, 'white people have no real identity of their own apart from that which exists through opposition to the Maori'. The historical and political significance of writing is emphasized by Awatere: 'The written word allowed communication and information carrying that did not depend on oral tradition. However the tasks and skills of writing remained in the hands of the rulers.' Her view is that in the hands of Pākehā chroniclers 'The history of Aotearoa becomes the history of white occupation'. She proposes Māori sovereignty as a teleology in place of national identity.[107]

Among the responses to Awatere's *Maori Sovereignty* has been the accusation that it is 'racist'. It may be observed that Awatere constructs her countertext out of the discourse of colonization as well as out of the knowledge she has derived from her own people. Awatere's utilization of the rhetoric of the discourse of colonization in her countertext makes visible the linguistic figures of the conquerors. In the textual artefacts of the past which have been constructed by Pākehā they seem more conventional and therefore are less visible; out of context, or in a different context, such basic signs as 'race' appear to some Pākehā no longer conventional but offensive.

Literary Biography and Literary Autobiography, 1930–1990

Sometime in the middle of the 1930s D'Arcy Cresswell decided to make use of a letter of introduction to the Governor-General, Viscount Bledisloe. Eventually he arrived in the presence of His Excellency, who asked what Cresswell had written.

> So I told him; and in return he told me of his great interest in New Zealand, on which account his wife and himself had lately purchased the treaty-ground of Waitangi and presented it to the people. There was a great field for literature here; why couldn't I tackle a poem on this subject? . . . I said that something might be made of New Zealand history, although to attempt it didn't accord with my outlook on literature; nor did I think that the history of New Zealand offered any ground for a native poetry; and especially the Maori did not. He said he was sorry to hear me say so, and hoped I was mistaken. My background in letters was mainly classical, I said. Well then, what about Virgil? he asked promptly. But Virgil had seven hundred years of the Republic behind him, I said; he didn't write about the colonization of Britain. I think you're mistaken, Cresswell, he said, I hope so.[108]

A second interview was chillier: Bledisloe thought Cresswell was after money.

> 'You say here you won't commercialize your pen. Why, Cresswell, that's just nonsense!' And he went on to tell me for some time of the opportunities before me in journalism, and of the high level of newspaper-writing in New Zealand, while I listened and said nothing. Every Saturday he read excellent articles on New Zealand history and scenery, he said; and surely there was a field here for my pen. Not for *my* pen, I said; although now I had no wish to talk to him, nor to be in his presence, and wanted to go.[109]

Although Cresswell probably did not know it, Bledisloe himself had written about the Roman colonization of Britain; but that little irony is of no great matter. Bledisloe was in close contact with the local men of letters: Lindsay Buick helped the Governor-General with the historical matter for his speeches; Johannes Andersen entertained their Excellencies in the rare-book room of the Alexander Turnbull Library; James Cowan applauded in print the gift of Waitangi. Bledisloe had read much of the recent work on New Zealand history and natural history, as well as the articles on 'New Zealand history and scenery' in the Saturday papers: the proper subject of New Zealand writing was New Zealand — it was 'a great field for literature' and what more appropriate than Waitangi?

Throughout his life Cresswell had a great many encounters marred by misunderstanding, even with people less august and more sympathetic than Bledisloe, but this is an appropriate tableau, if a slightly ridiculous one, to indicate the prospective divergence between the discourse of colonization and a discourse which takes writing as its subject. For Cresswell writing was not a report on life, nor a distillation of life, but life itself; and he struggled to make it his livelihood. His chief concern was to be a poet and a philosopher. What stands as his greatest accomplishment, and even in his day was recognized as a notable (or sometimes notorious) achievement, is his literary autobiography, *The Poet's Progress* (1930) and *Present Without Leave* (1939). Both volumes consist of numbered paragraphs which make up a loose narrative. In prose variously described as 'poetic' and 'archaic' Cresswell invests mundane events with heightened personal import. When he reached the English town of Oxford he was 'so overawed' that he was unable to peddle his poems, 'and having no money to obtain a bed I sat out in the rain all that night, on a hill overlooking the town, where I was moved to consider how none that she had crowned with fame had she chosen to do so during their lives, but from Death alone would she deign to receive their names; wherefore I was a trifle consoled to be in such neglect and discomfort now.'[110] Cresswell avoids naturalistic prose and breaks the conventional distinctions between fiction and non-fiction.

'In New Zealand', Cresswell begins his second work, 'a great many natural fires and volcanoes exist, whereby much of the country is hot; and many rivers and lakes are heated and give off a great steam. Beside these there are others which issue from snow and ice, being mortally cold, and proceeding through forests of exceeding darkness and depth from the mountains whence they descend.' As for the New Zealanders: 'They have everywhere great natural qualities, such as honesty, courage, endurance, and an exquisite simplicity; for in business they cheat and defraud one another quite openly, and as it were honestly; wherefore their men are distinguished, but not their women, who lack art and complexity the more they assume them.'[111] This mannered *tour de force*, which echoes passages in Hakluyt's *Voyages*, continues for some forty pages before Cresswell recounts how he leaves again for Britain and there resumes his vagrant life as a poet; when he returns to New Zealand in the second half of the book his occasional company is that of other writers and lovers of literature; the end of the book is the beginning of another boat journey to England. It is possible to read *Present Without Leave* as a denunciation of New Zealand. Whether this is an appropriate reading is arguable: Cresswell's concern is with words, with rhetoric, with the poetry he can create, and the geography does not matter.

After Cresswell's work in the 1930s there was no major published literary autobiography until the 1970s — nothing at all, in fact, apart from Sargeson's memoir of the early 1950s (discussed below), and a graceful essay, *The Inland Eye* (1959), by E.H. McCormick. It is true that there were a few reminiscences by people who also happened to be writers; the most entertaining are Denis Glover's *Hot Water Sailor* (1962) and Nelle Scanlan's *Road to Pencarrow* (1963), but these works dealt with writing only incidentally. Even Alan Mulgan's *The Making of a New Zealander*, which shows the author to be very self-conscious about the production of 'Words for New Zealand' (one of the chapter titles), is not a work of literary autobiography in a consistent way.

An important initiative was taken by Charles Brasch who in the 1960s commissioned several writers (and one artist) to contribute essays on their 'Beginnings' to *Landfall*. Then in the 1970s and 1980s Frank Sargeson, Janet Frame, Sylvia Ashton-Warner, and Monte Holcroft produced a volume (or two or three) of autobiography in which their choice of writing as a vocation, their literary efforts, and their lives as writers are predominant or major themes.[112]

Brasch himself had written an autobiography; it was edited by his friend James Bertram, and published posthumously. *Indirections* (1980) is a chronological and factual account, but it is also reflective and contemplative, and the tone at times is elegaic. Brasch takes his story to the point where his decision to found *Landfall* is made, or at least crystallizes, so that the autobiography forms a kind of retrospective preface to the main text, the literary periodical he edited for twenty years. Brasch traces his relationship with the physical and cultural landscape of New Zealand, and it is out of his feelings of alienation, or at least unease, that he ultimately derives his prose and poetry. It is only towards the end of his memoir, after many years and much travel in other parts of the world, that Brasch, rather self-consciously, accepts New Zealand: 'New Zealand lived in me', he writes, 'as no other country could live, part of myself as I was part of it, the world I breathed and wore from birth, my seeing and my language.' He could help to formulate 'a distinct New Zealand literature' which would 'define New Zealand'.[113]

Whereas Brasch is quiet, Sylvia Ashton-Warner, in *I Passed This Way* (1979), is vigorous, colloquial, and polemical. Ashton-Warner begins with a prefatory statement of alienation: she writes from 'this country abroad' as 'one who's been both rejected by and who has rejected' her country; and she terms this 'a broken love-affair never again to be mended'. Her New Zealand is at once physical and emotional. When the family moves from the town of Hastings back to a rural area, she, with her brother and sisters, 'took to exploring New Zealand all over again: hills, paddocks, cliffs, creeks, a sulky temperamental river and a white pine forest, kahikatea, rearing from shallow water', and they were 'joyful as aliens returned to the homeland'. Ashton-Warner genders New Zealand as 'the girl spirit'; and describes a breed of men who have stopped living fully themselves or who try to stop life, and women who live their lives passionately and to the full, whose origins are in the descriptions of her own disabled father and strong mother.[114]

Ashton-Warner's book is literary autobiography in the sense that it is the account of a major writer's life, and includes her decision to become a writer, but writing itself does not loom large as a subject. (Louis Johnson and Monte Holcroft appear in the preface, and later, very briefly, Rousseau, Coleridge, and Herbert Read, but except for one concentrated listing there is little about books elsewhere.) For Ashton-Warner herself, writing is initially a 'skylight inching open' when the alternative 'escape hatches' from the teaching (which she refers to as the 'bloody profesh') shut about her. (The other escape hatches she lists are 'art, music, swimming and marriage'.) When she quits teaching (temporarily, as it happens) because the educational authorities are consistently antagonistic towards her methods, she decides she will 'take the writing road': this would be 'a channel through which to surface, clearing out on its way the delirium of both music and paint to enrich the main stream'. New Zealand publishers show no interest in the manuscript of what was eventually to be published as *Teacher* (1963), so she recasts it as fiction, 'employing drama, suspense, love, disaster, unrequited passion and dialogue', and creates the character of a spinster in place of herself, 'so that it might sell'.[115] The fictional version is also rejected locally, but *Spinster* (1957) eventually finds a London publisher, and is acclaimed in the United States. Ashton-Warner expresses pride in her own literary achievements, and she is both saddened and resentful that recognition of her artistry has, in her view, been so belated in New Zealand. In an echo of Robin Hyde, Ashton-Warner refers to the flight of the godwits at both the start and the finish of the autobiography.

I Passed This Way does not fully or explicitly present Ashton-Warner's views on language, words, and writing. For that understanding an acquaintance with *Spinster* or *Teacher* (or both) is necessary. Ashton-Warner worked primarily with Māori children, and she developed a successful pedagogy which utilized a 'key vocabulary': the children were encouraged to speak the words which signified their basic hopes and fears, and these spoken words were written by the teacher, and then read by the children. Writing was not therapeutic, nor civilizing (as it was for Brasch), but empowering — as indeed it clearly is for Ashton-Warner in writing her account of her own life.

The title of Monte Holcroft's *The Way of a Writer* (1984) is taken from a letter Jane Mander had written to him in the early 1930s. No one knew better than she did, Mander told him, 'that the way of the writer is long and hard'; and, in chronological order, Holcroft reports his difficulties very fully. The second volume, *A Sea of Words* (1986), details his busy life as literary editor (for many years, of the *New Zealand Listener*), occasional traveller, and constant writer. Both volumes contain a considerable amount of recondite detail; an index would list references to meetings or correspondence with a very large number of local journalistic and literary figures established before mid-century and some thereafter; and there is much by-the-way information on rejections and acceptances of his manuscripts and more than in most memoirs about remuneration.

Holcroft's first three published works were novels; he then wrote others he considered 'better novels' but they remained unpublished. After these 'setbacks' he 'moved to new and higher levels' as 'an essayist, a literary critic, a social historian'.[116] His nominations for the 'three great books' of New Zealand literature are *The Letters and Journals of Samuel Marsden*, Guthrie-Smith's *Tutira*, and Beaglehole's *The Life of Captain James Cook* (1974), all nonfiction writings. He makes a plea for the recognition of works of non-fiction and for less critical concentration upon prose fiction and poetry, wanting the historians to be remembered for their histories, and not because some of them were also significant poets.[117] The detailed recapitulations of his disputes with (and about) Frank Sargeson and Louis Johnson, first set down in *Reluctant Editor* (1969), might be read as evidence of Holcroft's wish to displace writers of prose fiction and verse from the centre of the literary world. Holcroft (quite reasonably) wishes to revalue the work of writers more broadly defined, including editors and journalists, particularly those who have literary aspirations or interests.

Though in his memoirs he reconstitutes a wider world of writers and writing — one which encompasses J.H.E. Schroder, a notable editor and essayist, Ian Donnelly, 'a book-loving journalist', and Pat Lynch, sub-editor of a newspaper — and though the material, social, and domestic circumstances of writing are set out fairly fully, Holcroft says little about the processes of writing. There are hints about the composition of leading articles for the *Southland Times* and editorials for the *Listener*, and about the scribbling that 'grew into paragraphs' and gradually became *The Deepening Stream* (1940); and he reports how he 'came to understand' that newspaper offices abounded in 'clichés and vogue words', allowing little time for revision, 'the true heart of writing'. There is also a suggestion that Holcroft sees fiction and non-fiction as quite distinct. In *The Way of a Writer* he refers to an earlier autobiographical account of his late teens, the *Dance of the Seasons* (1952), in which he depicts a migrant as out of place in a New Zealand community. The son of this migrant had written to Holcroft after reading *Dance of the Seasons* to say his father had lived out a long and happy life in New Zealand — and Holcroft, 'shaken' after receiving the letter, wonders if he has 'drawn on imagination as well as memory', warning that this is 'a practice against which writers must always be on their guard when they are not producing fiction'.[118]

In another and longer passage, nevertheless, Holcroft clearly indicates the creative or imaginative element in his non-fiction writing. He had been asked to undertake a history of Manawatu county at such short notice that he had no time for a lengthy research before writing. He 'feared a loss of nerve' unless he began to write immediately.

> Always, at the beginning of a new book, I have felt the need to make a start, to get the opening sentences, the first pages and chapter, safely on to paper. Everything grows from those beginnings, for words are alive and fertile, and whatever is needed in additional research will come as the theme determines — or afterwards, in revision. At such a time, as one is writing every day, unconsciously searching for sub-themes and new directions, the mind arouses itself until it is at full stretch, and the whole self is engaged, all thinking narrowed upon a single task which becomes a re-creation of experience, the past living again as people and events are summoned back to be looked at and known, and drawn finally into their places in a co-ordinated and advancing mesh of words.[119]

This is not, it may be added, the way most local histories are composed.

*   *   *

In the early 1950s Frank Sargeson's 'Up onto the roof and down again' was published in *Landfall*. The 'roof' in the title is the plateau of the central North Island. Sargeson travels by bus to the King Country in the hope of glimpsing a corner of the property his beloved bachelor uncle once farmed. At Rotorua he has not the money to proceed south, and returns to Hamilton, dozing in the back seat of the bus on the climb over the Mamaku hills. When the cold causes him to reach for a jacket, he sees in the twilight the 'ravaged landscape' of 'wrecked trees' and clear against the sky 'the tall and feathery shape' of a honeysuckle tree.[120]

Sargeson had first been told of this kind of tree by the King Country uncle on his initial visit to his uncle's farm, a visit which he did not at first enjoy — the bush 'was so positively dark and forbidding'. Sargeson had previously associated honeysuckle with a family friend who allowed it 'to grow all over her veranda because it brought back memories of Home'. It astonished him that there was another sort, 'a great tree that grew along the ridges of my own country'. Eventually it is his uncle rather than the native honeysuckle that becomes 'the permanent and unchanging symbol' of his 'new world', the uncle who carried out 'work that was rarely hurried and never scamped or ill-done, that was related to the seasons and the weather, but not to the day of the week or the time of the day'. At the end of the story Sargeson says: 'I can see now that his pattern of death was a worthy one also: refusing to lie down he died as he would have wished standing up — and unless my eyes deceived me there is somewhere on the Mamaku plateau at least one honeysuckle tree that still stands up, for me standing not for New Zealand as it is, but New Zealand as it might worthily have been.'[121]

'New Zealand as it is' is symbolized near the start of the reminiscence when Sargeson refers to another farming uncle, an uncle by marriage. As a boy he had been embarrassed by the way that uncle had been bossed around by the aunt: 'My aunt always made you feel that men were rough inferior creatures, useful for farm work but a nuisance inside the house.' During a boom in land prices the uncle had sold his farm and retired to live in town. 'After years of suburban boredom, relieved by bowls, newspapers, films, radio and library novels, my uncle died in a house surrounded by a desert of concrete, and crammed to the doors and windows with vast quantities of expensive rubbish. All decided upon and bought by my aunt of course. It was so fantastic you felt the place could only be inhabited by savages who had fallen for the Birmingham bead necklace in a big and alarming way.' Two uncles, two deaths; and between these memories a bus journey which Sargeson transforms into a 'pilgrimage' of vast interest by his intricate narration of personality and circumstance both present and recollected.[122]

In 1973 'Up onto the roof' became the first part of an autobiographical volume, *Once is Enough*, which was followed by *More Than Enough* (1975) and *Never Enough!* (1977). Throughout Sargeson uses the device of the ironical and omniscient narrator, a technique he had developed over some thirty years in his later stories and novels; and it proved to be perfectly suited to his autobiographical purposes, the distinctions between person and persona virtually eliminated. Sargeson seems to address the reader directly and intimately in long, episodic monologues, allusive and digressive, revelatory and discreet, punctuated by some very broad humour. The circumstantial detail adds to the impression of verbal authenticity, and so do the reported speech patterns, in subtly different registers, of the other people who enter into Sargeson's story. Nevertheless, Sargeson's trilogy is not oral performance reduced to print, but writing which is coloured by the cadences of speech. The elaborate phraseology and the slightly unorthodox punctuation draw attention to the text *qua* text; and so at times does the outrageous incongruity of dignified style and vulgar subject-matter: 'In the crowded bar the picture postcard of the nude girl could be handed round — well of course. But I remember an astonishing barman who, shown a photograph of a naked youth contemplating himself in a state of erection, was all for putting the disgusting material in the hands of the police. Argument was useless. Also he was insulted by the suggestion that he would never himself have got into the world unless his own father had put himself into a similar state of preparation.'[123]

The subject-matter is, very substantially, writers, books, Sargeson's own problems with composition, and his solutions, which the memoirs exemplify as well as describe: writing is simultaneously the subject and the practice. 'Life and work are one', writes Sargeson. 'To live has been to write. And I have lived besides in the work of other writers, and more especially the poets.' His account therefore includes reference not only to his own works but to a range of literary influences and literary experiences: Keats, Milton, Shakespeare, D.H. Lawrence and James Joyce appear in one passage, Maritain, Marx, and Engels in another close by, and Henry George immediately thereafter; and there is a clergyman who talks of Sophocles and Macaulay and Toqueville and who presents Sargeson with 'three thick late-Victorian volumes' of Hume's *History*, the short introductory autobiographical section of which, and one passage in particular, remains 'an especial vade-mecum over a lifetime'. (Hume's diction in this passage, which Sargeson uncharacteristically quotes, is remarkably similar to some of Sargeson's own.) The writers are present in Sargeson's life in person as well as in print — Greville Texidor, Maurice Duggan, Fairburn, Frame, Cresswell, and many others, most of them in Auckland, and usually at his small bach in Takapuna. On one of Sargeson's rare sorties further afield there is a journey in Alec Gaskell's car towards the Canterbury high country, and 'as we approached the mountains all was there at last before my eyes — I mean what had become one great composite *cliché* derived over many years from writings I much admired (Lady Barker, Samuel Butler, D'Arcy Cresswell . . .).'[124]

Though Sargeson 'cultivated his intellectual ties with Europe' and though he was pleased to provide hospitality to writers, certain convergences, he indicates, were less than entirely comfortable. He devotes much space to Cresswell, he praises his prose (the autobiographical works), and sees merit in the Lyttelton sonnets if not so much in Cresswell's other verse; but Cresswell was not altogether admirable in his inability to manage even the simpler aspects of living, like cultivating and cooking potatoes. And if Sargeson expresses a debt to him, it is the rather negative one that Cresswell was as a poet 'indissolubly wedded to hidebound notions about what he conceived the proper language for Poetry to be', and so Sargeson begins his quest for a new prose. Later, there is the German poet in exile: 'There were times with Karl Wolfskehl when I would feel myself overpowered, weighed down by so much civilisation'; this was a feeling Sargeson had felt in England many years before. In Europe he had discovered himself 'to be truly a New Zealander . . . and now here I was once again being overpowered by Europe, and this time *in my own country*'.[125]

Sargeson's search for 'an appropriate language' had led him beyond Europe: 'What was the European doing in this faraway Pacific ocean country anyway? Had he the right to be here? . . . Was a community being built which could continue to flourish, or was the European occupation a kind of tenancy which would eventually be terminated?' He looked to where 'The European had also established himself' — America, South Africa, Australia.

> I had never supposed myself capable of coming anywhere near the degree of excellence which I recognised in the great European novels, but now I thought myself obliged to include the New England novels of Nathaniel Hawthorne among the greatest of literary achievements. The America of Mark Twain and Sherwood Anderson was not perhaps, I thought, so very far beyond my range; and Australia had a very mixed bag to show indeed — but what was I to say for myself when I read Olive Schreiner's *Story of an African Farm;* or rather I should say re-read? For as a younger man I had read the novel when egotism and frustrated ambition had blinded me to its wonderful genius. And it was especially disconcerting that besides the genius I was confronted by a formal literary language which tended to upset all the theories I had so painstakingly been working out.[126]

There is more interest in this than the explicit acknowledgement of extra-European literary influences. The reference to 'when the European had established himself' seems to be related to literature; writing is seen as an index to the permanence of 'European occupation'. (This is close to W.H. Oliver's comment about the 'spiritual pioneers'.) And there is in another place his comment, referring to about 1945 or 1946, that 'it was fast approaching twenty years since I had made my discovery about being a New Zealander, and ever since I had been driven along by my ancillary purpose — to learn how to write so that I might memorably fix on paper in appropriate form as much as I could of what was implied by the awakening of that discovery.' It was then that he worried about Wolfskehl. Was this purpose 'to be disrupted, perhaps even destroyed, by too close a devotion to the interests of a great living representative of the European humanities?'[127]

It is not too remarkable that such traces of the discourse of colonization should appear within Sargeson's prose; and against this it is necessary to set his much weightier subversions which overturn or call into question or ridicule the conventional appurtenances of national identity. There is, for example, an account of a journey to the Bay of Islands in 1924 which faintly echoes Cresswell's conversation with Bledisloe. Sargeson and his friend are bound for Russell 'with some sketchy notions about historical associations'. Most of the other notable historical places in the district they omit to visit because they were not then aware of them — 'Perhaps the time for an adequate awakening to our country's past was still to arrive'. They 'failed to hear about Pompallier house'. They took the cream-launch trip about the Bay — 'which may well have taken us to the site of the famous sermon at Rangihoua (and yet I can't recall)'. Fifty years later he discovers that in 1924 he 'had been within a few hundred yards of what was to become a national marae'; in 1974, the Waitangi site is 'the scene of national multiracial junketings', the area littered with 'cars, tourist buses, cartons, Coca Cola bottles, beer tins, and plastics not biodegradable'.[128]

'New Zealand as it might worthily have been': while this phrase at the end of 'Up onto the roof' can be read as an antagonistic commentary upon New Zealand and New Zealanders, it is not what the autobiography as a whole is about. There is sourness at times, not least for the editor of the *Listener* who does not get mentioned by name but is placed in a paragraph which recalls the 1950s as 'years of the worst poverty' Sargeson has known;[129] but even the more puritanical family members are drawn with some compassion. What Sargeson carries through in his memoirs is the placing of 'New Zealand as it is' in the margins of his narrative. He produces 'New Zealand as it might worthily have been' by filling most of the textual space with his own, preferred New Zealand — the writers, the tramps and strays, the men and women who have suffered the disapproving attentions of the puritans; the fertile, less-than-tidy landscapes rather than the scenic attractions on a grand scale (and even Mount Cook is seen literarily rather than literally); the Takapuna bach, its fruitful if unruly garden. The suburbia beyond is rarely visited and otherwise only briefly glimpsed.

*   *   *

'It is for Janet Frame to tell the story of her days in my hut if she chooses' Sargeson writes towards the end of *More Than Enough*;[130] and Janet Frame did choose to tell the story, as part of her own three volumes of autobiography. The trilogies thus intersect, and they are parallel in that each tells the story of a writer seeking space and circumstance favourable for writing. But there are great contrasts also: whereas Sargeson seems to address the reader directly, Frame sounds more distant, her voice lower, a little secretive, almost unaware of the listener; yet the verbal clarity is spellbinding.

Frame's story is about words, their appearances, their sounds and the relationships between people and words. Her mother, she remembers, in *To the Is-land* (1983), spoke of the doctor who delivered Frame as '*Dr Emily Seideberg McKinnon*', and there was, too, her mother's 'lifelong repetition of names important to her — Henry Wadsworth Longfellow, Harriet Beecher Stowe,

John Greenleaf Whittier, William Pember Reeves . . . Michael Joseph Savage'. In the silent reading class at school she reads an adventure story, '"*To the Is-Land*"', she tells her sister. I-land, says Myrtle: '"It's a silent letter . . .. Like knee."' Frame reads more '"adventure" books' and discovers she can 'experience an adventure by reading a book'. The pleasures of life are in words, precious icons collected from experiences otherwise bitter. When Myrtle drowns, Frame finds that lines from Walt Whitman's 'Out of the cradle endlessly rocking' (from *Sea Drift*), describing the search for a lost bird by its mate, 'told everything I was feeling'.[131]

Whereas Sargeson draws attention to the artifice of writing through his use of an elaborate and mannered rhetoric, Frame does so by inscribing words upon the surface of her text, deliberately registering their significance with italics or by enclosing them in inverted commas. She is pleased when Dad asks her to help with the crossword, and remembers one evening 'searching and searching' for 'one word to be found'. Next morning her father gives 'a shout of triumph'. '"*Rattan*. It's *rattan*." And it was *rattan*, a word that was new to me but that remains memorable in my life with *decide, destination, adventure, permanent wave, O.K., skirting board, wainscot*, and others.' Especially in the first volume, *To the Is-land,* she explores the distinctions between what critics might call *langue* and *parole*.

> We had learned about the Maoris at school, but there were few in Oamaru. Mother had told us how she had been 'brought up among the Maoris' because her mother had step-sisters and brothers who were Maori. And Myrtle's friend was a Maori and yet not a Maori, for her father, Dad's work mate and fishing mate, was described as 'full-blooded' as if this were something better than his daughter, who was talked of as being 'only a half-caste' as if it were something to be ashamed of. I gave none of this much thought, only sensing the feeling behind people's words; I thought the word *half-caste* was related to Dad's fishing casts and cast sheep and the worm casts on the front lawn after the rain . . . .[132]

In *An Angel at My Table* (1984), the second volume, Frame recalls on learning of the death of her mother that her own life has been spent watching her parents, and listening to them, 'trying to decipher their code, always searching for clues'.[133]

Words also implicate people, and they have an instrumental power which can be destructive. In an essay submitted for a university course, Frame has mentioned her recent attempt at suicide; and as a result three worried mentors persuade her into Dunedin Hospital, 'just for a few days' rest'. It turns out that she is in a '*psychiatric ward*'. When her mother arrives at the hospital to take her home, Frame screams, and (she finds out years later) 'Refused to leave hospital' is the 'official note' of the incident. On the medical certificate is written, 'Nature of Illness; *Schizophrenia*.'[134]

The third volume, *The Envoy from Mirror City* (1985), is the definitive account of the expatriate New Zealander in Britain and Europe. Frame has with her the haversack Sargeson had used in Europe thirty years before; and she has the words and images of England just as Alan Mulgan had them; but England is not 'Home' as it was for Mulgan. In London she goes out with an Irishman, and with a Nigerian, and with a physicist who though an Englishman has (she primly observes) 'lapses of grammar' in speaking. When she sends poems to a magazine, she pretends to be a West Indian: 'In a sense my literary lie was an escape from a national lie that left a colonial New Zealander overseas without any real identity.' It is easier to be a foreigner out of England, in Ibiza, 'in good human company', and later in Andorra. Back in England again, she rents in Suffolk the kind of cottage that made Mulgan eloquent, but is burdened with the care of a dog, a ninety-foot lilac hedge, and for a time the presence at the weekends of the spinster owners.[135]

Though she inhabits the cottage, Frame finds herself living within 'cathedrals of the imagination', ' "real" experiences' hold diminishing interest for her, and what she calls Mirror City becomes 'the true desirable dwelling place'. Back in her birthplace, 'the Envoy' tells her that the 'city shining across the valley' is not Dunedin but Mirror City. 'I stare more closely at the city in my mind. And why, it *is* Mirror City, it's not Dunedin or London or Ibiza or Auckland or any other cities I have known.' The autobiography thus not only recounts the journey to Mirror City but also exemplifies 'the processes of fiction' in which 'the self' ('the Envoy as it were') is 'the worker, the bearer of the burden, the chooser, placer and polisher' who arranges and lists the treasures 'for shaping into words'.[136]

In such a manner Frame opens the prospect of dissolving 'New Zealand' as a subject, even if a little self-consciously, as though to indicate the process is not yet complete. In England she asks herself whether she should return to New Zealand. She considers Europe 'so much on the map of the imagination' that 'the prospect of exploring a new country with not so many layers of map-makers, particularly the country where one first saw daylight and the sun and the dark, was too tantalizing to resist.' 'Exploring a new country' is a metaphor of colonization; but Frame is not too insistent: 'The fact is that when I was about to go home to New Zealand I did not need reasons for returning; but others needed to know why, to have explanations.' Moreover, she felt she had found her place 'at deeper level than any landscape of any country would provide'. The truth, she says, is always painful to extract and express, 'whether it be the truth of fact or fiction'.[137]

*   *   *

The first substantial work of literary biography was Antony Alpers's *Katherine Mansfield* (1953). Alpers begins by placing Mansfield in the context of his own life. He was, Alpers said of himself, of a generation that 'acknowledged our land but repudiated our country' for its 'blatant materialism and its lack of style'. About to leave for Europe, he finds that Mansfield in her stories had given 'faultless expression' to his own feelings about New Zealand, and that the 'conflict' between 'life in a raw young country' and her spiritual and actual needs 'was the central situation in her life'. He discovered, too, that he had once lived in a house formerly owned by Mansfield's family, and that the room in which Mansfield had shut herself away from Wellington was the same upstairs room he had known as a child. He delayed his departure for Europe to begin his investigations.[138]

The biography may be seen in part as an analysis of the imperatives of expatriatism. Alpers corrects the earlier view of Ruth Mantz that in Mansfield's youth Wellington was a cultural desert, but suggests that 'a culture transported to a larger and little-known country, thinly held, is in danger of vanishing, and in its own defence becomes a fetish of memory, rigid and fixed.' In the gulf between 'freedom and convention, between life and its expression' Mansfield sensed a threat to her genius. London, then, was 'life'. In Europe she could deal 'unselfconsciously with the problem of relating character to environment and action to atmosphere in a raw, traditionless country' and create 'an authentic New Zealand literature'.[139]

'New Zealand' is therefore a subject within the biography. Alpers answers the critic who thought a weakness of Mansfield's stories was the lack of 'silent character in the background' by suggesting that 'the silent character was the stillness of the bush, the disdain of the lofty islands for their huddled little pockets of colonial intruders, the silence of the vast sea-deserts that encircled them'.[140] For the most part the themes of exile and identification are embodied in the relationships of Mansfield with her family, and particularly with her father: the Beauchamps in effect stand in for New Zealand. They are not reduced to metaphor, however; though there is some reticence in speaking of those still living, Alpers renders his New Zealand characters with as much particularity as available information would allow. The exposition is arranged in short episodes and this technique, a device of fiction, gives Alpers the opportunity to dramatize personalities and scenes in detail. The biography has the authenticity of fiction, and some of its revelatory characteristics. The facts of Mansfield's first marriage and her subsequent pregnancy, though the outlines of these situations were not unknown to Mansfield's acquaintances and to her later devotees, had not been committed to print in such detail hitherto. The discussion was discreet, but sexuality was a new subject in New Zealand non-fiction.

For the most part Alpers eschewed psychological analysis and literary criticism, and concentrated upon the life of the writer, the circumstances which were conducive to writing and those which were a hindrance. Throughout the book Mansfield's own writing appears, so that she gives, in some measure, her own account: the reader is in the presence of the writer. This effect is also generated by deploying the sources of information and considering their provenance and reliability within the exposition.

That the significant initial work of New Zealand literary biography should take Katherine Mansfield as its subject seems in retrospect to have a certain inevitability: Mansfield alone among New Zealand writers then had an international as well as a New Zealand reputation; there was a local mythology which required amplification or correction; and J.M. Murry, Mansfield's spouse, had edited extensive extracts from her journals and letters so that there was a corpus of literary and autobiographical writings available to supplement her published fiction. These are neither necessary nor sufficient conditions for literary biography, but they were not unhelpful circumstances. For other potential subjects the documentary materials in particular were not readily available and only very gradually was there the kind of growth of interest in New Zealand literature which required biographical studies to further inform critical judgements. Phillip Wilson, on his way through a self-imposed programme of reading New Zealand fiction, developed a curiosity about William Satchell: *The Maorilander* (1961) is predominantly an essay in appreciation and criticism but Wilson includes a preliminary memoir to set the scene. He repeated the exercise at greater length for a volume on Satchell in Twayne's world authors series; other writers contributed to the same series, and to the Oxford 'New Zealand writers and their work' series, published from 1975 to 1986. In some the biographical content is slight; in others more space is expended on the life of the writer, and personal reminiscences of acquaintanceship as sources are supplemented with material drawn not only from letters in private ownership but also from materials by then being deposited in some quantity (and sometimes under various access restrictions) in public collections. However dispersed and limited of access, an archive is coming into existence which will increase the possibilities of substantial literary biographies being published in the future. Only a fraction of the archive can be consulted in print: Helen Shaw has edited the letters of D'Arcy Cresswell, Lauris Edmond the letters of A.R.D. Fairburn. Mansfield continues to receive the most concentrated attention, and the first two volumes of a critical edition of her *Letters*, edited by Vincent O'Sullivan and Margaret Scott, appeared in 1984 and 1987.

Alpers made use of the wealth of further material collected and of the critical and biographical work of a generation of scholars in New Zealand and elsewhere in writing an entirely new version of *The Life of Katherine Mansfield* (1980). To a much greater extent than in the earlier biography, Mansfield inhabits a literary world, and several of the writers who were little more than names in the previous work become full-blooded contemporaries; Mansfield in the *Life* is no longer woman/writer/New Zealander alone. This shift in emphasis is in part a result of making the expatriate theme less significant, and indeed 'New Zealand' is a less intrusive subject in the *Life*. A.R.D. Fairburn has also received extensive treatment, in a carefully documented study by Denys Trussell, published in 1984. Like Alpers in the 1950s, Trussell leaves some personal matters to one side; so perhaps does Dennis McEldowney in his essay, *Frank Sargeson in his Time* (1976), and W.H. Oliver in another essay, *James K. Baxter, a Portrait* (1983). The two latter works, in which graphic materials are closely associated with the text, successfully and economically depict lives of writers without making larger authoritative critical judgements, but the authors remain aware that the creative efforts of their subjects are the substantive matter.

In *Sylvia!* (1988), a biography of Sylvia Ashton–Warner, Lynley Hood is less reticent about the personal life of her subject. She adds to the written evidence information drawn from correspondence or interviews with more than two hundred of Ashton–Warner's contemporaries and relatives, and contributes her own expertise in psychological and physiological matters. Ashton–Warner, it seems, mixed truth and fantasy both in her life and in her autobiography, and *Sylvia!* does indeed read 'like a novel', as the author intended.[141] As well as documentary materials and the testimonies of friends and relatives of the poet, Frank McKay draws upon his own memories for *The Life of James K. Baxter* (1990), a work which reveals in detail the complex intersections between Baxter's personal life and his literary artefacts. Baxter was also a public figure, constantly pronouncing upon as well as agonizing about the society in which he lived; and it is one of the great merits of McKay's biography that he characterizes in satisfying depth the cultural, political and spiritual landscapes through which the poet made his pilgrimages.

*   *   *

For most writers of non-fiction there is not the consciousness of the intricate relationship between words and 'reality' that informs the autobiographical works of Cresswell, Sargeson, and Frame and becomes a major theme in Hood's *Sylvia!* Writing, in the positivist view, represents 'the real world'; and in the discourse of colonization which constitutes 'New Zealand' the effect is to collapse the distinctions between sign and referent. It would, however, be misleading to suggest that there has been a total lack of interest in the literary or fictive aspects of non-fiction. Much of it has come, as might be expected, from literary critics and scholars: from Joan Stevens, for example, in her brief introductions to Campbell's *Poenamo* (1952, abridgement made some years earlier by James Cowan) and in her abridged version of Wakefield's *Adventure* (1955); and from E.H. McCormick, in his introduction and annotations to a new edition of Earle's *Narrative* (1966), and in his introduction for the first publication of Edward Markham's *New Zealand or Recollections of It* (1963), written about 1836. Markham's manuscript, as McCormick clearly indicates, had been marked in preparation for a printed version, with alternative renderings and contemplated excisions. Other notable works to situate a number of related non-fiction writings in a critical framework include M.P.K. Sorrenson's *Maori Origins* (1979), which traces the European mythologies incorporated in ethnographic works, and Margaret Orbell's *Hawaiki* (1985), which carries the same enquiry a stage further, though her work is largely concerned with revaluing as religious narratives those Māori traditions considered earlier to be history. With the partial exception of Hood's study of Ashton–Warner, there is no substantial biography of any non-fiction writer that makes the life of the *writer* the major subject, though there are useful sections in Gerda Bell's *Dieffenbach* (1976); and discussions of the relationships between Campbell's *Poenamo,* its antecedent manuscripts, and Campbell's own life recur throughout R.C.J. Stone's biography and its attendant footnotes.

Nevertheless, the writings of women have thrown into sharper relief the evasions, suppressions, and silences in works by men; and the disruption of the colonizing discourse by Māori people has also invited a critical reconsideration of the making of non-fiction texts. It is difficult to imagine how recent works by James Belich and Jock Phillips could have been produced without those discursive interventions. Belich, in *The New Zealand Wars* (1986), suggests that both contemporary and retrospective writings on the conflicts of the 1840s and 1860s reflect a 'dominant interpretation' derived from ideological preconceptions, and are at a variance with what actually happened. Whether his reinterpretation stands or not, the veridical status of the various works, and of the literature of the 'New Zealand wars' as a whole, has been questioned. In *A Man's Country?* (1987), Phillips echoes the biographical emphasis in recent writings by women with an autobiographical epigraph for each section of the book, though italicization separates these passages from the general exposition. He discusses in turn the pioneer, boozer, rugby player, soldier, and husband/ father ('the family man'), and draws out the contradictions between the stereotypes of literature and the suppressed realities. The ways in which the stereotypes are created and maintained is a major concern: he ranges across fiction and non-fiction, and includes a handful of cartoons and 'jokes' to indicate the topoi common to various media as well as different genres. Above all, the materials are identified not merely as writings but as gendered writings which privilege the experiences of males and project these experiences as 'New Zealand'. In addition, the approach of the 150th anniversary of the Treaty of Waitangi in 1990 occasioned a considerable number of publications, varying in size, scholarship, and sympathy, which sought to record, or establish, the 'meaning' of the Treaty. One of the most substantial of these works, Claudia Orange's *The Treaty of Waitangi* (1987), the first comprehensive history of the Treaty since the revised editions of Buick's *Treaty* had been published in the 1930s, proved to be the non-fiction bestseller of the 1980s. Some of those who purchased Orange's book no doubt anticipated a definitive 'reading'; but what Orange's *Treaty* and several other recent works seem to suggest is that 'readings' of this hallowed document, and by extension readings of other texts, are always provisional, the ultimate 'meaning' forever deferred.

It would not be entirely inappropriate to end with James Cook and J.C. Beaglehole, two writers whose linked texts form a kind of printed parenthesis around the discourse of colonization. 'Nearly forty years ago,' wrote his son in 1974, 'J.C. Beaglehole said he was going to write the life of Cook: the preliminary step — and how lightly that was once viewed — would be a new and scholarly edition of the Journals.' The preliminary step took twenty years. In the textual introduction to the journal of the first voyage J.C. Beaglehole himself wrote, in a characteristic phrase, 'The study of Cook's journals is not — to borrow a natural metaphor — all plain sailing.'[142] Cook had left, so his editor found, various drafts with interpolations and interleavings and deletions and rewritings. In 1967, Beaglehole had finally done with the journals and began to compose the *Life;* but in 1969, when he was invited to give an important lecture in Australia, he put the *Life* aside for a time and took the opportunity to make *Cook the Writer* his subject. The address is an illuminating supplement to the journals and, together with the editorial materials attached to the journals, it enables the reader to understand how problematic writing was for Cook.

As Cook worked up his drafts of the second journal, self-consciously making himself into a writer, he noted (no doubt with the travesties of Hawkesworth in mind) that his account was to be 'a work for information and not for amusement'. He felt, he reported of himself, 'obliged to give the best account he is able of his proceedings'. But the correspondence between journal and incident, between writing and 'his proceedings', was a difficult matter, and Cook was sometimes troubled to convey what he wished, or even to know what it was he wished to convey.[143]

The first two days he spent on the New Zealand coast were disfigured by bloodshed. In the third of these sanguinary incidents, Cook, with peaceful intentions, he insists, had caused a shot to be fired over the heads of 'Indians' in a canoe, in a clumsy attempt to persuade the people to make contact; and when the frightened people retaliated by attacking Cook's own small boat, he ordered further shots to be fired, and 'either two or three were kill'd'. The incident is briefly noted in the log-book, but there are three rather more extended versions drafted out for the journal as Cook tries to explain what had happened, and exculpate or justify or criticize himself. In the end he settles for a measure of self-criticism with a coda of justification.[144] It is to some extent a matter of chance that the drafts have been preserved; but it is now possible to read the separate formulations and 'open up' the text, and to see very clearly the complex relationships between writing and power.

Those who would write the literary history of New Zealand non-fiction in detail must read the texts as multiple drafts. When the texts are opened up, and the multiple drafts are revealed within the figures of language, it will be possible to log more precisely the tortuous voyages to 'Mirror City', and to understand how the words which purport to describe 'New Zealand as it is' have been so often rewritings of New Zealand 'as it might worthily have been'.

The Novel

LAWRENCE JONES

Introduction

The following sketch towards a history of the New Zealand novel is an 'internal' history, treating the novel as a particular form within the institution of literature. Although it exists in a complex relationship of reciprocal influences with other New Zealand forms and institutions and with the British and American novel (among others), it has its own history of themes and modes and related conventions. As with the history of many New Zealand institutions, this is a history which includes importation and adaptation. As Allen Curnow so famously reminded us, there are many examples of a 'failure to adapt on islands', and in its earlier history the novel appeared as if it might be one. It took longer to adapt than poetry or the short story; it was not until the late 1950s that successful adaptation seemed assured, and it is only in the last twenty-five years that there has been anything like an abundant production. Ironically, the novel came to act out the Pākehā cultural myths of 'adaptation' and 'progress' only when it became a vehicle for questioning those myths.

The history of the form falls naturally into four periods: the rough and uncertain beginnings of the 'Pioneer' or 'Early Colonial' period (1861-1889), the earnest and self-conscious but still rather discontinuous attempts of the 'Late Colonial' period (1890-1934), the painfully accomplished formation of native traditions of critical realism and impressionism in the 'Provincial' period (1935-64), and the productive developments of and reactions to these traditions in the 'Post-provincial' period (from 1965). The periods are defined by three interrelated factors: the major social and economic changes in New Zealand society; the novelists' relationship to and attitude towards those changes; and the novelistic modes and conventions that they evolved for depicting their society and expressing their attitudes towards it. The terms are provisional (although there is already if not a consensus at least an argument concerning them), and are intended to be descriptive only.[1] The dates, of course, are approximate and relate to the novel only. They indicate that the novelists' response to social change has usually lagged behind the change itself. Thus if 1929 was a crucial date in relation to changes in New Zealand society, it was not until the mid-1930s that novels began to appear depicting those changes and expressing changed attitudes that followed from them. Similarly, the profound social changes towards a more affluent and suburban society in the 1950s did not begin appearing in the novels until the mid-1960s.

The account that follows focuses not on individual novels or novelists, but on the establishment of the form, and on the development of its themes and modes through those periods. Only for the second period, when there was a small and readily identifiable group of significant novelists, is there a full critical account of individual novelists. For the first period, when there were too few novelists for such a discussion, and for the third and the fourth, when there were too many, there are no sections on individual novelists. Rather, for each period there are three sections: a brief chronological account of the careers of the primary novelists; an account of the primary fictional modes of the period, charting not only the relatively predictable rise of the dominant realistic mode but also the less predictable development of the didactic, impressionistic, and other modes; and an account of the primary themes of the period, with emphasis on the permutations of the recurring themes of the Pastoral Paradise (the taming of the land and remaking it as England's sheep station and dairy farm) and the Just City (the building of a new and better social order). For the first period, all longer fictions are discussed, including those in the melodramatic and other more conventional popular modes, but for the following ones a distinction has been made between 'serious' and 'popular' fictions, the latter being discussed in a separate section of this history. We should note, however, that this distinction is only a relative one in New Zealand fiction. While various clearly formulaic popular genres have been developed fully, especially since 1920, not many novels have appeared at the extreme 'serious' end of the scale. There have been only a few high modernist art novels in the impressionist mode, such as Janet Frame's, and rather more attempts at a sober, unadulterated realism, as in Bill Pearson's *Coal Flat* or David Ballantyne's *The Cunninghams*. However the dominant mode of the New Zealand novel has been a kind of middlebrow moral realism, dealing with serious themes in a basically realistic mode, incorporating some of the type characters and melodramatic plot devices of popular fiction, and aimed at a relatively wide audience. From William Satchell and Jane Mander through Dan Davin and James Courage, to Marilyn Duckworth and Fiona Kidman, such novels have been important in New Zealand literary history.

The Pioneer Period, 1861–1889

The indigenous novel did not appear in New Zealand until over twenty years after the first European settlement, with the publication of Henry Butler Stoney's *Taranaki: A Tale of the War* in 1861, and its first, 'Pioneer' phase of development — the product largely of emigrant authors born in England prior to 1850 — was pretty well completed by 1890. However, 'period' boundaries are never absolute, and some of the Pioneer novelists such as Dugald Ferguson or Alexander Bathgate continued publishing as late as 1912 or 1913, while some novels by others were written earlier but were posthumously published or (in the case of Sygurd Wiśniowski) translated.

This group of Pioneer fictions is very much a mixed bag, with no continuity of development, no conscious sense of a local literary tradition. Certain common character types, motifs, and themes do emerge, but these are the result of common factors of the pioneering experience and of imported Victorian conventions, not of direct influence of one New Zealand novelist upon another. Among these early fictions there are a few flawed works of interest, but not one entirely successful work, and in most cases only a few flashes of quality. Most were published in England and aimed at different segments of the English reading public, from the middlebrow readers of the Smith, Elder list to the readers of Religious Tract Society publications or 'the poorer populations of our town, the inhabitants of our coasts, and our soldiers and sailors in barracks and on board ship' (as well as those learning reading in night school) for whom 'Taking Tales' were intended.[2] However, others (including *Taranaki*) were published within New Zealand, often by newspapers, and seemed designed for home consumption.

* * *

Some of these Pioneer novels were by professional writers who, as a result of visits to New Zealand or reading about it, included a 'New Zealand' novel among their works. Examples would be Lady Campbell, Jules Verne, Hume Nisbet, Rolf Boldrewood, or Sygurd Wiśniowski. Benjamin Farjeon (1838–1903) actually began his career as a professional novelist in New Zealand with three novels between 1863 and 1866: *Life and Adventures of Christopher Congleton* (serialized in the *Otago Witness* in 1862-3, but left unfinished); *Shadows on the Snow: A Christmas Story* (1865); and *Grif: A Story of Colonial Life* (1865). However, he returned to London in 1868 and there established himself as a prolific popular novelist. Most of the Pioneer novels were written by amateurs, with fiction at best an occasional avocation in the midst of lives dedicated primarily to the more material concerns of a pioneer society. Only two of these writers had what might be considered 'careers' as novelists — Vincent Pyke and Dugald Ferguson. Pyke (1827-1894), in the intervals of a busy administrative and political career, published at least five novels: *Wild Will Enderby: A Story of the New Zealand Goldfields* (1873); *The Adventures of George Washington Pratt*, a sequel to that popular book (1874); *White Hood: A Tale of the Terraces* (1878); *Craigielinn* (by 'F.E. Renwick' 1884); and a 'lost' novel of the Land Wars, *Eustace Egremont*.[3] Ferguson (1833-1920) turned to the novel relatively late, publishing four novels between 1891 and 1912: *Vicissitudes of Bush Life in Australia and New Zealand* (1891; popular enough to have reached a fourth edition by 1908), *Sketches of Gossipton* (1893, by 'Daniel Frobisher'), *The King's Friend: A Tale of the Scottish Wars of Independence* (1905, reaching a third edition by 1908), and *Mates* (1912). Even the most significant Pioneer novelist, George Chamier (1842-1915), published his two novels, set in Canterbury in the 1860s, *Philosopher Dick: Adventures and Contemplations of a New Zealand Shepherd* (1891) and its sequel, *A South Sea Siren: A Novel*

Descriptive of New Zealand Life in the Early Days (1895), only as later diversions in a career as an engineer in Australia.

* * *

The primary modes of the Pioneer novel might be designated as naïve realism, exploitive conventionalism, and didacticism. The first is a fictional extension of the non-fictional 'literature of occupation' — slightly fictionalized accounts of the pioneer experience and of the land and its indigenous people as first encountered, not consciously didactic, but taking for granted the pioneer biases and values. The second is an attempt to exploit New Zealand materials by slotting them into existing conventional formulae, usually melodramatic ones — a literary version of the pioneer pattern of appropriation. The third involves the use of New Zealand materials in fictions designed primarily to communicate a moral, religious, or political message. All three modes are present in the first novel, Stoney's *Taranaki*. The naïve realism is implied by the descriptive subtitle: *A Tale of the War. With A Description of the Province Previous To and During the War; also an Account (Chiefly taken from the Despatches) of the Principal Contests with the Natives During That Eventful Period.* The didactic element is evident in the avowed aim to move the readers 'to form not only a correct impression of the war, but see the real cause in its proper light, of its origin and continuance'. However, the novel is held together by a melodramatic romance plot, which is probably what H.H. Lusk (who thought it the worst novel he had ever read) was referring to when he described it ironically as 'Thucydides-cum-Scott'.[4]

Some of the naïve realism is 'fiction' only in a minimal sense, as in C.M. Harkness's *Yorick's Walk from Wellington to Wanganui, Twenty Years Ago* (1874), adapted from a personal diary; M.H.A. Buchanan's *A Pilgrim of the Nineteenth Century: A Sketch in the Early Days of Canterbury, New Zealand* (1893), closely based on the writer's father's diary; or William Mortimer Baines's *The Narrative of Edward Crewe; or, Life in New Zealand* (1874), which reads like artlessly fictionalized autobiography. Other works involve more fictionalization, usually in the form of a romance plot to hold together the bits of observation and experience. Thus Robert H. Scott's *Ngamihi: or The Maori Chief's Daughter; A Tale of the War in New Zealand* (1895), although purportedly based 'directly' upon the author's diary 'written at the second Maori War'[5] has a conventional tragic romance of Māori and Pākehā lovers at its centre.

A recurring type of fiction is the clearly autobiographical novel in which the hero's career has been fictionalized and made more dramatically coherent by an admixture of melodramatic romance. Ferguson's two long Australia-New Zealand novels, *Vicissitudes of Bush Life in Australia and New Zealand* and *Mates*, are notable primarily for their realistic 'delineation of station life in Colonial backblocks', but are shaped by the conventions of melodrama, in contrast to his *Sketches of Gossipton*, which is simply loosely strung local-colour anecdotes. William Langton's *Mark Anderson: A Tale of Station Life in New*

Zealand (1889) and Bathgate's *Waitaruna: A Story of New Zealand Life* (1881) are similar in their sober depiction of Otago life, with Bathgate defining the formula when he says his book is a series of 'true pictures of life in the southern portion of the colony of New Zealand . . . strung together, as it were, by a story'. Thomas Cottle's *Frank Melton's Luck; or, Off to New Zealand* (1891) is a rather livelier North Island version, with 'a realistic and truthful description of station life in New Zealand' given shape by a melodramatic romance plot.[6] A more urban version of the type is Justin Charles MacCartie's *Making his Pile: A Colonial Story* (1891), where possibly autobiographical memories of Dunedin in the 1870s (including some score-settling with Dunedin's rapacious speculators) are mixed with romance. A variation on this mode is *Frank Leward Memorials* (1884), which purports to be a memorial volume of letters 'edited' by 'Charles Bampton' (Charles Hamilton Brophy), but which appears really to be a picaresque epistolary novel, with one section set in New Zealand in the early 1840s (possibly based on writings rather than on experience). J. Hall's *Potona; or, Unknown New Zealand* (1892) similarly purports to be the deathbed reminiscences of an old identity concerning his youthful experiences of being shipwrecked in Fiordland, but has a strong admixture of the conventionally melodramatic.

A related mode of naïve realism, but with a stronger didactic element, is found in the many fictional chronicles of pioneer families, most of them aimed at children or beginning readers, such as Joseph Spillmann's *Love Your Enemies: A Tale of the Maori-Insurrections in New Zealand* (translated from the German, 1895). A less condescending naïve realism is found in some of the slightly fictionalized accounts of Māori life and history. The impulse to write such fiction was present as early as in the French explorer Dumont D'Urville, who wrote an unpublished ethnographic novel, *Les Zelandais Histoire Australienne*, immediately following his first visit in 1824. The best of these novels are John White's *Te Rou; or, The Maori at Home* (1874) and *Revenge: A Love Tale of the Mount Eden Tribe* (1891; published 1940). In the preface to the first novel White insists that it is not really fiction, but rather a series of pictures which exhibit 'truthfully the everyday life, habits, and character of the pre-civilisation Maori . . . woven together in the form of a tale, as that most convenient for lifelike representation'. In the second novel the 'love tale' is more important, although the description of Māori peacetime life is central. More documentary and even less literary is Capt. J.C. Johnstone's *Maoria: A Sketch of the Manners and Customs of the Aboriginal Inhabitants of New Zealand* (1874), described by its author as making 'no pretence to the character of a work of fiction', but rather as being 'an attempt . . . to put on record the rare military qualities that for so long a period enabled a few handfuls of half-armed barbarians to resist the dominion of the white man'.[7]

Many of these works of naïve realism are held together by bits of conventional plot: the conventions are at the service of the material. The emphasis is reversed in the largest group of Pioneer fictions, where New Zealand materials provide topical subject matter for the conventional patterns.

The difference can be seen by comparing *Te Rou* with George Wilson's *Ena; or, The Ancient Maori*, published the same year. There is an element of naïve realism in *Ena*, but it soon becomes clear that the book is less documentary than literary, an attempt to exploit Māori materials for the purposes of an Ossianic tragic epic, replete with epic similes and picturesque description, a prose *Ranolf and Amohia*. Less poetic but similarly built on the model of epic tragic melodrama is Nisbet's *The Rebel Chief: A Romance of New Zealand* (1896), which purports to be based on personal experience in the 1880s as well as on the writings of White and Sir George Grey, but which uses the materials for conventional tragic melodrama (with racist comedy for light relief).

It is the pattern of melodramatic romance that is found most frequently in these conventional fictions, with the New Zealand scene providing an exotic locale, some useful plot gimmicks (capture by Māori, volcanic eruptions, hidden caves, shipwrecks, the discovery of gold, and so on), and often a Māori villain (as well as a Māori tragic second love, who can play the Rebecca role in the *Ivanhoe*-type romances, and a 'good Māori' friend, on the model of James Fenimore Cooper's 'good Indians'). These elements, mixed with the usual lost heiresses, secrets, and kidnappings form the basis of Alexander Fraser's two New Zealand melodramas written for the Religious Tract Society, *Daddy Crips' Waifs: A Tale of Australasian Life and Adventure* (1885) and *Raromi or The Maori Chief's Heir* (1888). Rather more artful commercial exploitations of Māori material can be found in the two Australian-written Māori romances, Robert Whitworth's *Hine Ra; or, The Maori Scout: A Romance of the New Zealand War* (1887) and Rolf Boldrewood's *'War to the Knife'; or, Tangata Maori* (1899), and in Henry Brereton Marriott Watson's more mystery-oriented *The Web of the Spider: A Tale of Adventure* (1891). The Māori romance had become such a popular form that R. Ward could parody it in his *Supplejack: A Romance of Maoridom* (1894).

The South Island authors had nothing as handy for melodramatic romance as the literary Māori, but they did have the goldfields, and as Bret Harte was showing with California and Charles Reade with Australia, these provide a good setting for melodrama. Farjeon initiated New Zealand goldfields fiction with his *Shadows on the Snow*, later imitated in his *The Mystery of Roaring Meg: A Christmas Story* (1878), both involving Dickensian melodrama on the Otago goldfields, while his more substantial *Grif* put Dickensian melodrama on the Australian goldfields. Bathgate's *Sodger Sandy's Bairn: Life in Otago Fifty Years Ago* (1913) is a late entry in the same mode. The best of these goldfields novels are Pyke's *Wild Will Enderby* and *George Washington Pratt*. Both involve some vivid naïve realism, with anecdotes and observations from Pyke's time as secretary of the Otago goldfields (1862-67), but set within conventional melodramatic romance plots. His Christmas story, *White Hood*, draws on the same background, but there is less naïve realism, with a stronger emphasis on the melodramatic plot, with its traditional elements of the secret and the false accusation. Thorpe Talbot's *Blue Cap*, published in the same volume, also has a South Island setting, in Dunedin and the South Otago sheep country rather than the goldfields, and a more gothic plot (based on an absurd idea of pre-natal influence) that ends in tragic melodrama.

Pyke's *Craigielinn* follows a melodramatic romance pattern similar to that of his goldfields tales, but takes place in Scotland just before the migration to Otago. Two other novels use North Island materials for the construction of standard three-decker Victorian domestic melodrama: Clara Cheeseman's *A Rolling Stone* (1886) and W.B. Churchward's *Jem Peterkin's Daughter: An Antipodean Novel* (1892). Both incorporate interesting material in the interstices of the elaborate plots; the first about bush farms near Auckland in the 1880s, the second about race relations in Auckland in the 1870s, but both, as is typical of the genre, become totally taken over by plot machinery by the third volume.

The melodramatic romances looked at so far are mostly quite traditional in their conventions, the only new element being the use of New Zealand materials to demonstrate those conventions. However, in England in the 1860s through the 1880s a new form of melodramatic romance had arisen — the sensation novel, with its own set of conventions. The basic formula was that of the romantic melodrama, but the crimes and secret past that helped separate hero and heroine involved violations of Victorian sexual mores (adultery, bigamy, and illegitimacy). There was more emphasis on the unravelling of a mystery (often turning on substitution and false identity) involving detective work, with a 'documentary' method of telling the story through the partial perspectives of letters, journals, court evidence, newspaper reports, and so on (leaving a crucial 'pocket of time' to be revealed), and with the effects of shock and surprise heightened through the use of evocative settings and a psychological-physiological rhetoric of sensation. Novels in this new mode exploiting New Zealand elements appeared quite early and continued for thirty years, even after the mode had lost favour in England. The first, Lady Campbell's *Martin Tobin*, published in 1864 by Maxwell (one of the prime purveyors of the genre), is an action-packed farrago, more on the model of Charles Reade than of Wilkie Collins, and filled with sensation. Joshua Henry Kirby's *Henry Ancrum: A Tale of the Last War in New Zealand*, published in 1872 by Tinsley Brothers, (another prime purveyor of sensation), is not quite as sensational but still has its quota of murders, attempted murders, and violations of Victorian mores. Both authors use Māori elements in the sensation plots, whereas Charlotte Evans, in her two South Island sensation novels of 1874, *A Strange Friendship* and *Over the Hills and Far Away* (both subtitled *A New Zealand Story*), uses materials of domestic settler life in rather more tightly-plotted novels modelled on those of Wilkie Collins, as does W.M. Southan in his South Canterbury novel, *The Two Lawyers* (1881). William Ross's *The Riven Cloud: Being a Sketch Taken in New Zealand* (1889) is tamer and less elaborate, while *Alone in the World* (1886), 'by the author of "The Half-Caste Wife"', etc. etc. etc.' (which works seem to have been lost to the world forever), dilutes sensation material with Dickensian pathetic melodrama.

When the sensation novel first appeared in England in the 1860s there was some concern about the moral effects of the genre, and this was echoed in New

Zealand even before the home-grown sensation novel appeared. In 1862 Henry Lusk published a parody of a Wilkie Collins novel in *Chapman's New Zealand Magazine*, and five years later Edwin Fairburn included in his strange *The Ships of Tarshish: A Sequel to Sue's 'Wandering Jew'* (by 'Mohoao', 1867) an inset essay on the dangers of the 'feminino-sensationo-romancist' novel, with its 'copious cullings from the fruitful fields of Murders, Madnesses, Fraudulencies, Forgeries, Brutalities, and Bigamies'. A feeble satirical pamphlet of 1871, *The Very Latest News, Communicated through the Medium of Mr J. Smith*, by 'Algernon Reginald Hillend Mortimer', has the Otago inhabitants of 2871 still reading such sensational novels as 'The Benighted Bigamist, A Novel of Incident' in thirty-one and a half volumes. The strongest criticism did not appear until twenty years later in Gilbert Rock's *By Passion Driven: A Story of a Wasted Life* (1888), a modified sensation novel written in criticism of sensation novels, in which the heroine's sister through her addiction to 'novels of the most sensational kind' is led to commit murder.[8] The novel that gave Rock's character the fatal idea was entitled *Lucrezia's Revenge; or, A Story of Love and Hate*. In 1894 appeared the wildest of New Zealand sensation novels, with a very similar title: *Utu: A Story of Love, Hate and Revenge*, by 'Tua-o-Rangi' (Margaret Carson Bullock). The book exploits the story of the du Fresne expedition for the utmost of sensation and surprise. Frank Atha Westbury's incredible *The Shadow of Hilton Fernbrook: A Romance of Maoriland* (1896) puts more emphasis on the romance and less on the horror, but ends most sensationally with the villains killed in the Tarawera eruption. Another novel of the 1890s, Oliver Growden's *Matthew Redmayne: A New Zealand Romance* (1892; first serialized in *Zealandia* in 1889-90 as *The Mark of Cain* by 'Owen Graham'), puts the emphasis more on suspense and mystery, with a detailed application of Collins's narrative devices to New Zealand materials.

The exploitation of New Zealand materials for the purposes of conventional fiction was most apparent in the sensation novel and in the Māori romance. Other conventional modes appeared more sporadically: the pastoral romance in Frank Bartle's *An Idyll of the South; or, a Sketch in Dreamland* (1886), an Australian version in Pyke's 'Under the Wattles: A Pastoral Idyll', and a Sterne-ish play with the pastoral romance in Sir John Logan Campbell's anonymously published *My Visit to Waiwera-Baden: Things that I have Seen and Read, and Thought and Heard, in Passing Through the World* (1878).[9] Ferguson also produced an imitation of Scott in *The King's Friend*, and there was even an early space romance in *The Great Romance* (1881), by 'The Inhabitant' (identified by Thomas Hocken as one 'Honnor of Ashburton').

In addition to these fictions of naïve realism and of exploitive conventionalism, there is a small group of predominantly didactic fictions. Ellen R. Ellis's *Everything is Possible to Will* (1882) has an autobiographical origin, but the emphasis is on the moral, 'proved by the present narrative', that 'the will is absolute, for good and for evil', and the novel has appended to it an essay about will and colonization. The full title of Reve Wardon's short novel of 1892 indicates its didactic purpose: *Macpherson's Gully: A Tale of New*

Zealand Life, Containing Some Views of the Social Outlook from the Proletarian Standpoint. Wardon's grim tale of poverty, death, and madness is meant to encourage the reader to 'sympathise with, and wherever possible alleviate, the miseries of poor humanity'.[10]

Other didactic fictions use more conventional plots, but the emphasis is on the message placed within this frame. Robert Carrick's *A Romance of Lake Wakatipu* (1892) has a conventional plot which is almost lost amidst the didactic material on Otago's commercial future, while Fairburn's *The Ships of Tarshish* buries the conventional plot in essays about the value of iron warships and their relation to the British Israelite reading of biblical prophecy. Julius Vogel's *Anno Domini 2000; or, Woman's Destiny* (1889) is a bit more novelistic and a bit less mad, but it also uses a conventional plot only to further its ideas, and it ends with an essay making explicit Vogel's views on sexual equality, the British Empire, and a welfare state based on economic expansion and increased consumption.

Vogel's novel (and to a lesser extent Fairburn's) involves a projection into the future. A large group of only nominally 'New Zealand' fictions use as their starting place Macaulay's prediction about the New Zealander looking at the ruins of London Bridge, usually purporting to be written from a New Zealand of the future (any time from 1942 to 2990), and showing the decline of England and Europe and the rise of Australasia (Vogel had Melbourne as the capital of his future British Empire). However, these works were all published in London and lack any New Zealand content,[11] unlike two other didactic future fictions: Alexander Joyce's *Land Ho!! A Conversation of 1933, on the results of 'Nationalizing the Land of New Zealand', adopted in 1883* (1881), and John Featon's *The Last of the Waikatos: A Sensational Tale of the Province of Auckland* (1873, by 'Comus'), a piece of fictional 'history' purportedly written in the 1920s to show the positive results of the last round of the Land Wars, supposedly fought in 1874.

A somewhat different didactic strategy involves a move in space rather than time, to a hypothetical society in unexplored territory. This strategy was used by 'Hildebrand Bowman' in the first 'New Zealand' fiction inspired by Cook's voyages, *The Travels of Hildebrand Bowman, Esquire, Into Carnovirria, Taupiniera, Olfactaria, and Auditante in New Zealand; in the Island of Bonhommia, and in the Powerful Kingdom of Luxo-volupto, on the Great Southern Continent* (1778). Bowman's little-known satirical book anticipates the strategy of Samuel Butler's *Erewhon* (1872), as Butler moves from a realistic picture of the Canterbury high country in the first five chapters to 'Erewhon' found 'over the range' on the West Coast. Joseph Jones has shown how much Butler drew on the New Zealand that he knew for those first chapters.[12] However, the real focus of the Erewhon chapters is not New Zealand, but the England Butler is satirizing (including his own early beliefs and experience) through his picture of Erewhonian society. The same is true of *Erewhon Revisited Twenty Years Later, both by the Original Discoverer and by his Son* (to give the full title to the less successful sequel of 1901). Like the 'London Bridge' fictions, these works are only marginally New Zealand. However *Erewhon* may have had one possible outgrowth in John A. Barr's *Mihawhenua: the Adventures of a Party of Tourists Amongst a Tribe of Maoris Discovered in Western Otago* (1888, 'edited' by 'R.H. Chapman'). It is just possible that this strange book was conceived as a parody of Butler, but if it began as parody it seems to have ended as straight (and absurd) adventure narrative.

Of critical realism, the mode that was to become dominant in the New Zealand novel, there are few signs in the Pioneer novel. New Zealand settler society did not produce a minor Trollope, Thackeray, George Eliot or William Dean Howells, nor, (perhaps closer to the possibilities of the environment), a Mark Twain. Hints of a realism that could deal critically with New Zealand society can be found in the first volumes of *A Rolling Stone* and *Jem Peterkin's Daughter*, but the conventions of melodrama outweigh any nascent realism. An indication of what might have been done is Wiśniowski's *Tikera or Children of the Queen of Oceania*, which appeared in Polish in 1877 but was not translated into English until 1972. It is not a well-made novel, but is rather loosely picaresque (no more so, however, than *Man Alone*), and as such depends less on the conventions of melodrama to give it shape. There is no inheritance, no sensational action (except perhaps the death of Charles and William), none of the unitary characters of melodrama but rather the mixed human beings of realism that George Eliot had called for in English fiction; and there is no happy ending. Tikera, the half-caste heroine, does not die heroically nor does she marry the narrator. Rather, the narrator comes to see his mistake in rejecting her, she has an illegitimate child by the charming but amoral Charles, and she marries a decent man who accepts the child and takes her away. As in *Man Alone*, the real focus is on the society, viewed critically, even sardonically.

The writer who comes closest to critical realism of any of the writers in English is Chamier, but his two novels relate less to nineteenth century realism than to the eighteenth century picaresque novel. Like *Tikera*, they escape the imposed patterns of the melodramatic romance. Instead, they focus on the education of Richard Raleigh, his development from naïve expectations and lack of self-knowledge (he is one of the 'unconscious blind' who 'cannot see that they cannot see', at least 'where their own intentions and sentiments are concerned')[13] to a tempered realism and awareness. As their descriptive subtitles imply, and as is the case in many eighteenth century novels of education, the books (especially the longer and looser first one) are crammed with diverse materials loosely relevant to the hero's development — letters, a diary, philosophical discussions, detachable episodes and pictures of New Zealand life and society, and inset stories. The books are not so much reactions against the well-made Victorian melodramatic romance as throwbacks to an earlier, looser, more capacious form that has space for the expression of a critical, philosophical mind such as Chamier's.

*   *   *

While only a handful of novels interpreted New Zealand pioneer experience in any critical and coherent way, and while there was nothing to indicate the beginning of a conscious literary tradition, most of the fiction did at least reveal something about New Zealand, even unwittingly, and these revelations did gather around a few basic settler concerns. First, there was the land itself. Often it formed a sublime or picturesque backdrop, but what really interested most of these writers and their characters was not the beauty of the land but what could be made of it, or better, from it. Butler's narrator was merely blunter than most when he saw the land primarily in economic terms, describing the mountains as 'perfectly worthless' from a sheepfarmer's point of view, and the alpine country as of little interest because 'there was no money in it whatever, unless there should be minerals'.[14] To Baines's Edward Crewe (and evidently to his creator) the environment was simply something to plunder for money and adventure, a place in which to hunt pigs, catch fish, cut timber, dig gum, and mine gold.

More frequently, the land was seen as the raw material for the creation of a Pastoral Paradise that would be a paying proposition. Right from the first, in *Taranaki*, the landscape was something that 'nature had adorned . . . with lavish hand', but which 'art, taste, skill, and capital' could make into something much better. There was no doubt that the land was made for this purpose, with its 'fertility, salubrity, and general adaption to the needs of an Anglo-Saxon race', as Boldrewood put it in *'War to the Knife'*. Ellen Ellis spoke for many of these writers in seeing the land as 'calling loudly for the sower and the seed', just 'waiting to be reclaimed'. Some of the novels at least acknowledge the difficulties of the task. Clara Cheeseman, for example, comments that although the idea of carving a farm from the bush may be 'very charming to an imaginative mind', and 'these pioneer settlers, with their bush cottages and farms' may be 'picturesque figures in story or sketchbook', the reality is 'the labours, the privations, the poverty of their lives' that 'heaven only knows'. It is in this context of the difficulties faced by pioneers that Man Alone first begins to appear in New Zealand fiction. Even the happy-go-lucky Baines comments that 'a man requires to have his heart in the right place to live alone among the great trees' of the North Island bush, while MacCartie's Arthur Barton complains of Central Otago that '. . . insanity is extremely likely to overtake any man of intelligence who lives by himself in such vast solitudes as these'.[15] The only antidote is mateship, and although there is no mystique of the mate in this New Zealand fiction comparable to that found in some Australian fiction, the hero's friend and travelling companion is a character so common as to be taken for granted.

The goal of all this difficult and lonely endeavour with the land is, of course, material success, a goal that is uncritically accepted by most. Lady Campbell writes confidently that 'wealth is within the power of all who work for it; and the motto not only of Auckland but of all New Zealand must ever be "Onward!" '. Towards the end of this period, in 1889, Rachael MacPherson in *The Mystery of the Forecastle; or, A Restless Heart: A Colonial Tale of Fact and*

Fiction looks back with admiration on those early settlers 'who . . . by sheer indomitable courage, energy, and shrewdness climbed, one by one, the toilsome rungs of the ladder Success'. Along with this dream of individual success, there were also some hints of the dream of building a Just City. Vogel's ideal future society, and also H.C.M. Watson's, would at least spread the material success to all, while, more radically, Wardon's Neil Macpherson looks forward to a Christian Socialist society in which 'the selfish individualism now rampant in society will give place to a loyal regard for the common weal'. More frequent was the note sounded by Langton's Dr MacKinnon, who praises New Zealand for its 'absence of class distinctions and aristocratic exclusiveness', and its 'unrestricted opportunity given to every man of rising by his merits' (as Langton's hero and so many others do).[16]

Assumed in all of these fictions is a faith in progress, usually seen in the context of the Empire. W.L. Rees, in his *Sir Gilbert Leigh; or, Pages from the History of an Eventful Life* (1878), states this assumption most explicitly in his appendix, an essay passionately defending the policies of Sir George Grey in relation to New Zealand, South Africa, and India (the setting for most of the novel): 'Anglo-Saxondom, bearing the standard of the cross, lifts the whole earth and its nations towards knowledge, and peace, and happiness, and good.'[17]

Almost all of these writers, with their faith in progress, were confident of New Zealand's future and saw their present society primarily as a stepping stone to that future, without viewing it at all critically. The only sustained criticism is found in Wiśniowski and Chamier. The Polish novelist, writing from America in the mid-1870s and looking back on his time in New Zealand in 1864-5 (and probably drawing also on at least the memory of written accounts of New Zealand), presented a sardonic view of the use of the land and the scramble for material success. His narrator is clearly critical of the crude exploitation of the natural environment. To an Irish sawyer, for example, the giant kauris 'brooding paternally over the forest's growing youth' were only trees 'from which a certain number of boards could be sawn' to provide earnings for his 'Sabbatical drinking bouts'. As Dr Arabat tells the narrator, the Anglo-Saxon mode of colonizing is successful, perhaps 'the only practical way of conquering a new land', but it is arrogant and destructive: 'At first they have to plunder, exterminate, uproot, to make a desert out of a living country, and then they implant a new life there.' The economic means to this end are viewed critically, as the narrator observes the land speculation and shady business deals in a country where, as he is told by the soldier 'Tempski', 'what is legal is moral'.[18]

Chamier, writing from Australia in the 1890s and looking back on his New Zealand experience of 1862-8, viewed New Zealand society with a more humorous irony as he showed his naïve hero stumbling through it and discovering the truth about it. Richard begins with naïve hopes, but is soon disillusioned. He quickly discovers that the pastoral life involves not just communion with Nature, but also killing and skinning animals: 'too cold-blooded a performance for my nerves', he notes, for the 'post and rail fences

. . . hung with reeking sheepskins, and the slaughter-yard, with its blood-stained scaffold' are part of everyday life on the sheep station. He also discovers that the dream of gaining wealth and happiness through hard work as a pastoralist is delusive. He sees it embodied in a terrible Scot 'staggering under the load of an enormous swag', like an allegorical figure from Bunyan, who shows him that 'all it required was singleness of purpose, unfailing perseverance, and a lifetime of self-denial' and one could be as wealthy, unattractive, and crabbed as he was. He writes to his friend Dr Valentine that he is sick of the stories so beloved by the pioneer novelists of how 'our hardy pioneers went through unheard of trials and privations in converting a barren desert into smiling fields'; such a single-minded drive for success produces a town like Christchurch, 'absolutely wanting in all the attractions of a refined civilization, the beauties of art, or the charms of old associations'. In his view, 'The thorough colonial only believes in reproductive works', and he notes the 'wily schemers' who catch would-be pioneer farmers in their financial nets, as well as the 'sickening spectacle' of the hard drinking, 'the besetting curse of the whole community'. He had emigrated full of 'liberal tendencies' and optimistic hopes that such political and social reforms as universal suffrage, the ballot, payment of members, state education, would 'be productive of unmixed good', and instead finds that colonial politics is a 'pitiable exhibition' evoking disgust, and that the country progresses 'not in consequence of its laws, but rather in spite of them'. He had hoped to discover truth and self-knowledge in solitude, but discovers only doubt and disillusion: 'The only result of thinking is to unsettle our faith.'[19] By the end of *Philosopher Dick* his illusions are all destroyed, and the only value he has found is his friendship with Dr Valentine.

A South Sea Siren continues Richard's education, as he settles in a North Canterbury community and gets to know it. Again, there is the crude exploitation of the land:

> To fence in as much land as possible, to run a plough over it and obtain a few wheat crops from it without manuring and systematic cultivation, then to sow with English grasses and to paddock sheep, was the only rule recognised by the pioneer settler, and the only practice which was admitted *to pay*.

He observes the easy credit and doubtful business morality (as in the way in which the slippery Prowler, Tom Mutter, and the Wyldes take in a new chum), as well as the manners of a crude provincial society: the hard drinking by the men (the sad case of Tom Mutter's poor wife revealing the terrible domestic effects), the gossip and social hypocrisy of the women. His hopes for a 'fair and fresh field . . . free from all the corruption and hereditary taints of the Old World' are defeated, for 'the Englishman, away from his native land, carries with him all the customs, tastes, and prejudices, and most of the vices of his nationality'; instead of 'a purer, simpler and more primitive mode of existence', there is 'whenever circumstances would permit . . . a rather servile imitation of life in the Mother Country'.[20] Thus an important part of Richard's education is his coming to see clearly the actual nature and possibilities of New Zealand society.

No other novelists were as critical of New Zealand society as Wiśniowski and Chamier. However, some of the novels dealing with the expansive 1870s and the depressed 1880s show signs of a critical perspective. The hero of *Making His Pile* learns the hard way that, as his friend Barton tells him, 'it is not a good country for an honest man of any culture to live in'. However, MacCartie's contrast of 'grasping' Dunedin and 'honest' Melbourne (where his novel was published) is too simplistic to be taken seriously. Southan in *The Two Lawyers* shows sharp practice and land speculation more convincingly, if melodramatically, while Cheeseman in *A Rolling Stone* gives an effective portrait of the farmer-speculator Langridge, a sharp but not vicious operator, who finds that 'the way to gather in the "unearned increment"' is to 'put a thousand acres or so into grass, and sell them, just when the young fern was shooting through, with millions of stalks, tender, fresh, and green'.[21]

Also in the 1880s the first signs appeared of what was to become a dominant feminist theme in the next generation, with Ellen Ellis and, in a different way, Vogel. Ellis set the terms for the women's movement of the 1890s with her complaint that women 'are crippled by their enforced ignorance and degraded social position' from properly carrying out 'their God-given work to bless mankind' by teaching and exemplifying a simple, unselfish moral code of duty, will-power, and hard work. Vogel, on the other hand, looked forward to a time when progress would be greater, because it had been found that 'women bring to the aid of more subtle intellectual capabilities faculties of imagination that are the necessary adjuncts of improvement' and are thus 'the guiding . . . force of the world', while man serves best as 'the executive force'.[22] However, in most of these fictions the women are standard Victorian heroines, passive, submissive, and decorative.

The treatment of that other disadvantaged group, the Māori, was also viewed critically in some novels, especially in relation to the land and the Land Wars. Here a range of opinions were expressed. At one extreme were those who were critical only of the Government for being too soft on the Māori. Stoney makes clear in the Introduction to *Taranaki* that the Māori are 'little more than savages, but lately changed from open and direct cannibalism', and the story presents them as dangerous obstacles to the carrying out of the dream of converting New Zealand into a Pastoral Paradise. It is their fault that 'the smiling village and the blooming country' of the early settlement have been 'converted into an embattled town and wild waste around'. The only answer is 'the breaking down of the savage customs so prejudicial and opposed to those of the Colonists', and this must be done by harsh policies backed by vigorous military force. Similarly, to Kirby in *Henry Ancrum* the Māori 'has been weighed in the balance and found wanting — he must go', for it is only when 'the savage Maori has disappeared' that the country will become 'thickly inhabited and prosperous'. Kirby looked especially to the Waikato as an area for Pākehā settlement, and it is that process which Featon's *The Last of the Waikatos* urges and predicts. Featon's ending, showing the Waikato after his hoped-for final Māori War, is revealing:

> There was now a thorough understanding with the natives; the new territory was rapidly peopled with Europeans, roads cut in all directions, and everyone looked forward with confidence to the future. The hills that had formerly been solitary wastes were converted into smiling pastures, and fields of wheat bowed their golden heads to the summer breeze in place of the useless fern and ti-tree. A large stone monument now stands on the site of the High Hill pah; it was erected at the expense of the volunteers to mark the spot where fell THE LAST OF THE WAIKATOS.[23]

The implications are clear: the Māori are as 'useless' as the fern and ti-tree, and must be dispossessed to make way for the Pastoral Paradise.

In distinct opposition to this 'exterminate the brutes' philosophy were a few writers, mostly not English, who were extremely critical of Pākehā appropriation of the land and who saw it as the cause of the Land Wars. Verne's garrulous French geographer, Paganel, in *A Voyage Round the World: New Zealand* (1877), makes it clear that he views the Treaty of Waitangi as a fraud and the English as clever land-thieves. The Polish Wiśniowski was scathing about the use of promises of confiscated land to get volunteers to fight the Māori (his hero calls the volunteers a 'gang of freebooters'), and says of the New Zealand Settlements Bill that 'It took away the land belonging to the tribes and handed it over to a few grasping speculators'. The ambush of the Forest Rangers he refers to as 'the fitting end to this war of conquest'. The German Spillmann's Irish frontier farmer admits to a militant Māori that the latter has been 'very badly treated' by the Pākehā over the land, and although he fights for his family, refuses to join the militia, for he considers the war 'unjust' for 'The Maoris have been, for the most part, shamefully deceived, and they fight in defence of their home.'[24]

Hints of a similar attitude appear in some novels written in English. In Churchward's *Jem Peterkin's Daughter*, the hero, English soldier Jack Brett, fights in the war but is 'almost ready to condemn his own countrymen as unprincipled land pirates'. In *Frank Leward Memorials* the missionaries are seen as greedy for land and are blamed for rigging a fraudulent Treaty of Waitangi, while in Nisbet's *The Rebel Chief* it is stated that 'wars and massacres' were the inevitable outcome of 'nefarious trafficking' by some of the missionaries and early settlers who engaged in the 'cheating of the natives . . . out of their hereditary property'. The rebel chief Kawite is compared to Tell and Wallace, and his warriors are called 'patriots . . . who were not prepared to be friends with the invaders of their lands'. Boldrewood in *'War to the Knife'* speaks of the Māori determination to 'resist a foreign occupation to the death', and has a wise Pākehā Māori attack the 'folly and greed' of those who pushed through the Waitara purchase.[25]

Both Nisbet and Boldrewood, however, writing in the 1890s, viewed the Māori as none the less doomed. Boldrewood's Māori guide, Albert Warwick, states that 'It is idle to expect that New Zealand, able to support millions of civilized people, should be abandoned to less than a hundred thousand savages', and accepts that the Pākehā, 'stronger in war', can and ultimately should win. This is an extreme version of the ambivalence found in most of these novelists. On the one hand, there was admiration of Māori courage and a sense that they were fighting for their own land; on the other hand, there was the realization that the dream of the Pastoral Paradise could be achieved only by the defeat of the Māori, a defeat that was both excused and seen as inevitable by a kind of cultural Darwinism. Thus Archibald Hood's *Dickey Barrett* (1890), Nisbet's *The Rebel Chief*, Watson's *The Web of the Spider*, and Johnstone's *Maoria* all have laments from Noble Savage Māori chiefs for the future destruction of their people. Similarly, the Australian Daniel Pulseley's *Number One; or, The Way of the World* (by 'Frank Foster', 1862), Emilia Marryat's *Amongst the Maoris* (1874), Whitworth's *Hine-Ra*, Wilson's *Ena*, and Wiśniowski's *Tikera* all contain statements by the narrator or by an informed Pākehā character that the Māori, despite being 'the finest race of darkies in the world', as Pulseley crudely puts it, are doomed, for, as Wilson puts it, 'the colonizing and civilizing energies' of the Anglo-Saxon must inevitably supplant 'the retrogressive customs' of the Māori. Only Boldrewood and Scott see some hope of Māori survival, as part of a future British Empire whose justice might prove the fears of cultural Darwinists unfounded.[26]

The differing attitudes towards the Māori-Pākehā conflict over the land are paralleled in the differing attitudes towards Māori-Pākeha sexual relations. The beautiful Māori or part-Māori girl who loves the hero is a recurring character, but her role is not entirely constant. In *Martin Tobin* and *Henry Ancrum* the passionate part-Māori girl is a temptation, luring the hero away from his true Pākehā love. In *'War to the Knife'* the noble half-caste Erena Mannering is shown to be superior to the Pākehā heroine, but dies for the hero, leaving him free to return to his first love. In *Ngamihi* the daughter of the Māori chief dies heroically for her Pākehā love, leaving him heartbroken. In *Hine-Ra*, the chief's daughter marries the hero, but then spends five years with him in England to become thoroughly Anglicized before returning to New Zealand with him. Cottle's *Frank Melton*, on the other hand, marries the part-Māori Fanny with no question about race. The most explicit discussion of interracial marriage is in *Jem Peterkin's Daughter*, where the hero overcomes his fellow-soldiers' taunts about 'a touch of the tarbrush' and a 'tinted Venus' to come to 'appreciate natural dignity and true worth regardless of origin, country, or colour' and to marry the half-caste Jemima.[27]

Clara Cheeseman in 1903 complained that the 'field' of possibilities for the novel in New Zealand was 'as rich and varied as the scenery', but that it was as yet 'practically untouched'; while Maurice Shadbolt eighty-six years later said that one of his reasons for writing historical novels about nineteenth century New Zealand was to supply the novels that the period itself had neglected to write, the nineteenth century New Zealand novels that he would have liked to read.[28] Certainly the Pioneer novelists did not succeed in adapting the genre to New Zealand, and managed to illuminate only a few corners of the 'field'. Only Wiśniowski and Chamier, both short-term visitors to New Zealand, created coherent pictures to which one can return with any pleasure, and their unique and isolated works could scarcely be said to form the basis of any native tradition.

The Late Colonial Period, 1890-1934

The novels of this second period of New Zealand fiction are by authors born between 1850 and 1900, many of them native New Zealanders, and are mostly about New Zealand between the Jubilee and the beginning of the Great Depression. The chronological boundaries of the period are not clear, as there is some overlap with both the earlier and the succeeding periods. Although many retrospectively focused novels about frontier society such as Chamier's two or Ferguson's first one appeared between 1890 and 1895, those years also produced the first novels dealing with a more settled, 'late colonial' society, such as Jessie Weston's *Ko Meri; or, A Cycle of Cathay: A Story of New Zealand Life* (1890) or Lady Anne Glenny Wilson's *Alice Lauder: A Sketch* (1893). At the other chronological boundary, the period persists beyond the onset of the Depression into the early 1930s, effectively ending in 1934 with Alan Mulgan's retrospective *Spur of Morning*, a novel that summarizes most of the period's major themes. Mulgan's novel contrasts with John A. Lee's *Children of the Poor* of the same year, the first significant Provincial novel and one which, while it is likewise retrospective in its focus, anticipates later Provincial fiction in its critical stance towards the society which it depicts.

While there is an improvement in both the quantity and the quality of the novels in the Late Colonial period, the form can still scarcely be said to have established itself, since despite the hopes and efforts of at least some novelists there was still no significant local readership for New Zealand novels, no publishing and institutional infrastructure (only about a third of the novels were published in New Zealand, and they were mainly the lesser ones), and no coherent indigenous tradition of the novel. Rather, the period is marked by a series of separate struggles by talented individuals to become New Zealand novelists, with each finally withdrawing into silence or expatriation.

*　　*　　*

As with the Pioneer novels, many of the books of this period were 'oncers', isolated attempts at the genre — even some of the better ones such as Weston's or Mulgan's, or John Bell's *In the Shadow of the Bush: A New Zealand Romance* (1899). The only relatively continuous and prolific careers were those of writers of popular fiction such as Louisa Baker, Isabel Maude Peacocke, G.B. Lancaster, and, at the end of the period, Nelle Scanlan and Rosemary Rees. However, some middlebrow, if not entirely 'serious' novelists were able to advance beyond a single book: Alfred A. Grace (1867-1942), for example, published novels in 1908 and 1914, as well as volumes of short stories, and C.R. Allen (1885-1962) published six novels between 1925 and 1939, significantly moving from a depiction of the author's or the character's imagined England in his three novels of the 1920s to a depiction of New Zealand (although pre-World War I) in his three novels of the 1930s.[29] Other writers began a career with New Zealand novels, but then established themselves in another literature: Arthur H. Adams (1872-1936) published only one New Zealand novel in 1904 before establishing himself as an Australian writer; Harry Vogel (1868-1947, son of Julius) published two New Zealand novels (1898, 1909) but set most of his novels in Australia; Hector Bolitho (1898-1974) published two New Zealand novels (1927, 1929) but then established himself as a journalist, biographer, and royalty-watcher in England.

The period's four significant novelists — Edith Searle Grossmann (1863-1931), William Satchell (1860-1942), Jane Mander (1877-1949), and Jean Devanny (1894-1962) — all had New Zealand careers which were cut off in one way or another, but all produced bodies of work more substantial than those of any of the Pioneer novelists. Grossman published four novels in twenty years (1890-1910), although there was a fourteen-year gap between the second and the third, and the last was followed by twenty-one years of silence. Satchell likewise published four novels, between 1902 and 1914, followed by twenty-eight years of silence probably caused by the lack of commercial success of any of the novels.[30]

Mander published six novels in the relatively brief period between 1920 and 1928. New Zealand gave her the subject for her first four, the North Auckland in which she grew up, but it did not give her the audience or the intellectual sustenance that she needed to continue as a novelist. In her twenties she had found the 'brain-benumbing, stimulus-stifling, sense-stultifying, soul-searing silence' of provincial puritan New Zealand inimical to her growth, and had escaped the 'forces that hampered [her] individuality' and 'the barren wastes of Victorian Philistinism' to go first intermittently to Sydney, then more permanently to New York, and finally to London, so that she spent parts of 1907-11 and all of 1912-32 outside New Zealand. She had to escape New Zealand to write of it, and New Zealand's response, through the newspaper reviews of her work, was to attack her as 'sex-obsessed' and overly local and personal in her criticisms, charges she denied in a letter to the *Auckland Star*: 'I am simply trying to be honest and to be loyal to my own experience'. During her last seventeen years back in New Zealand she published no more fiction, although she completed at least one more novel about England before she returned, and often expressed the hope of writing another New Zealand novel. Her inability to continue writing must have been related to her disappointment in the direction New Zealand was taking. In 1934 she wrote in the Christchurch *Press* that when she went to America in 1912 New Zealand seemed to be 'a positively exciting country' in its social and political developments, but that by the 1930s New Zealanders had 'mentally and spiritually . . . become one of the backward peoples of the earth'.[31] Her earlier optimism had been destroyed, and it was left to the next generation of writers, whom she encouraged, to dissect the national *malaise*.

Devanny was the most prolific of these Late Colonial writers, with seven New Zealand novels (and one volume of short stories) appearing between 1926 and 1932. She alone achieved popular success, at least with her banned first novel, *The Butcher Shop* (15,000 copies were sold overseas), but she never won acceptance in New Zealand, and her last nine published novels were written and set in Australia. The achievement of these four writers stands out enough to warrant separate discussion, but it is best seen against a background of the predominant modes and themes of the period.

*   *   *

The naïve realism that marked so much Pioneer fiction is found less often in this period, although even as late as the 1930s there are a few autobiographical travelogues. Occasionally these works remain of at least historical interest: C.R. Browne's *Maori Witchery: Native Life in New Zealand* (1929), with its glimpses (amidst the melodrama) of the experience of surveying for the railroad in Māori country; Guy Thornton's *The Wowser* (1916), for its glimpses of frontier life in the King Country, 1905-12; poet Hubert Church's surprisingly urbane *Tonks* (1916), which uses the travelogue of visiting Englishmen as a vehicle for social satire and commentary; and Sir James Elliott's lightly fictionalized centennial chronicle, *The Hundred Years* (1939).

The didactic mode continues as an important one, especially between 1890 and 1910, when there was an outpouring of fiction focusing on temperance and feminism, and of utopias and dystopias. Some of this fiction is a crude mixture of biography and autobiography with explicit preaching, such as Bertha Cameron's *In Fair New Zealand* (1899) on prohibition, Davy Heber's *Netta; or A Plea for an Old Age Pension* (1894), Edward Hunter's *The Road the Men Came Home* (1920) on the Red Feds, Wilhelmina Sherriff Elliot's *Service: A New Zealand Story* (1924) on Christian marriage; or *Our Home in the Roaring Forties: A Story of New Zealand Life in the Early Days* by Walter Kerr (Jane Mander's uncle), which is, as the subtitle proclaims, 'a plea for home interests and a rational foundation in the knowledge of things' (1926). Other works of fiction of this period are built on the Horatio Alger pattern: John Christie's *A Prophet of the People* (1898), on Christian Socialism; Susan Mactier's *The Far Countrie: A True Story of Domestic Life at Home and in the Bush* (1901), on the Christian pioneer; or Herman Foston's earnest epics of Christian prohibitionist capitalists in the King Country, *In the Bell-Bird's Lair; or, 'In Touch with Nature'* (1911) and *At the Front: A Story of Pluck and Heroism in the Railway Construction Camps in the Dominion of New Zealand* (1921). Much more complex and readable is 'Kathleen Inglewood's' *Patmos* (1905), on John Saxon's campaign against alcohol, written from within the Temperance Movement by Kate Evelyn Isitt and obviously based on family experience.

Other works mix didacticism with strong doses of melodrama to further a variety of causes, from Spiritualism (Hélène Greenwood's *The Splendid Horizon* of 1931) to the marriage of true minds (*Two Women and Three Men, circa* 1899, the author identified by Hocken as being James O. Bryen Hoare), or the problems of small shopkeepers (Frederick Taylor Redman's *The Martyrdom of Jacob Rush: A Romance of South Wellington*, 1899). By far the most frequent cause is that of temperance, and the favoured pattern is that of tragic melodrama, with the innocent wife or daughter martyred to male alcoholism, as in G.M. Reed's *The Angel Isafrel: A Story of Prohibition in New Zealand* (1896), Susie Mactier's *The Hills of Hauraki or The Unequal Yoke: A Story of New Zealand Life* (1908), or Alie Kacem's *For Father's Sake* (1897), where the heroine is more apotheosized than martyred. The heroine of Bannerman Kaye's *Haromi: A New Zealand Story* (1900) is martyred to a racial and sexual double standard, and in Elsie Story's *The Tired Angel* (1924) she is a martyr to the marriage laws which tie her to a syphilitic philandering husband.

With the model of *Erewhon* before them, many writers attempted utopian or dystopian didactic fictions, although none were very successful. In George Bell's *Mr Oseba's Last Discovery* (1904) a traveller from Symmes Hole finds the best society on the surface of the earth to be Seddon's version of 'God's Own Country', while Edward Tregear in *Hedged with Divinities* (1895) presents a future New Zealand as a dystopia of feminine rule. Archibald Forsyth's *Rapara; or, The Rights of the Individual in the State* (1897) is a tedious utopia of 'equalistic individualism', while John Macmillan Brown's *Limanora: The Island of Progress* (1903, by 'Godfrey Sweven') is an equally tedious Platonic utopia, and his *Rialloro: The Archipelago of Exiles* (1897, also by 'Godfrey Sweven') was a dull attempt at Swiftian satire. J.M. Torrens in his *A Trip to Mars: An 'Awful Venture', a Curious Message* (1901) goes to outer space for a utopia, while G. Warren Russell in *A New Heaven* (published 1919, written 1902-3) presents a cabinet minister's version of heaven as a more highly evolved New Zealand.

The conventional mode of the Māori romance also continues in this period in various forms, from W.R. Hodder's H. Rider Haggard-influenced *The Daughter of the Dawn* (1903), through Grace's tragic melodrama *Atareta: The Belle of the Kainga* (1908), to Frank O.V. Acheson's epic of the pre-European Māori, *Plume of the Arawas* (1930), and A.W. Reed's novelization of Rudall Hayward's epic film of the Land Wars, *Rewi's Last Stand* (1939). Another group of historical romances deal with the exploration and pioneer periods, beginning with Robert Noble Adams's pious *The Counterfeit Seal: A Tale of Otago's First Settlers* (1897), and including the more melodramatic glorifications of the missionaries and early settlers in Sophie Osmond's *Ponga Bay: A Story of Old New Zealand* (1922) and Harvey Cook's *The Cave of Endor* (1927). A different kind of historical novel is Grace's *The Tale of a Timber Town* (1914), which incorporates the Maungatapu murders into its melodramatic romance structure.

Another group of melodramatic romances present some glimpses of contemporary New Zealand society: the Hawke's Bay 'squattocracy' in Ebba Stelin's *A New Zealand Pearl* (1896), Marlborough in William Sylvester

Walker's *Zealandia's Guerdon* (1902), the Manawatu bush frontier in Ellen Taylor's *A Thousand Pities* (1901), a Poverty Bay sheep station in W.H. Koebel's *The Anchorage* (1908), the Wanganui bush frontier in Charles Owen's *Philip Loveluck* (1909), the King Country in Harvey Cook's *Far Flung* (1925), the Canterbury high country and central North Island in Sir George Makgill's *Blacklaw* (1914), the Wellington province bush frontier in Bell's *In the Shadow of the Bush*, the best of this group. Vogel's *The Tragedy of a Flirtation* (1908) fits into the frame of melodramatic romance an interesting conflict of manners between an upper middle-class Englishwoman and a self-made New Zealand man on a North Island bush farm, while Wilson's two novels, *Alice Lauder* and *Two Summers* (1900) are romantic comedies of manners without any melodramatic complications. Three domestic novels stand out in the attempt to move away from melodrama towards tragedy: Weston's *Ko Meri*, set in Auckland's polite society of the 1880s, H. Musgrove's *Myola* (1917), set on a North Auckland bush farm, and Alice Kenny's *Alan McBretney* (serialized in the *The Triad*, 1915-16), set in a Coromandel town.

A move away from dependence on melodrama towards a quiet kind of realism can be seen in the period's many *Bildungsromane*. A popular novel such as Louisa Baker's *Wheat in the Ear* (by 'Alien', 1908) shows how melodramatic the form could be, but the use of autobiographical materials in many of these novels seems to check the tendency to melodrama. Even the melodramatic and didactic Susie Mactier, in her *Miranda Stanhope* (1911) includes some quiet but telling domestic realism of life among the poor in Auckland. Constance Clyde McAdam's more substantial *A Pagan's Love* (1905) uses melodramatic deaths to move the plot along at crucial points and has elements of didacticism but is built primarily on a realistic interplay of character and environment. Vogel in *A Maori Maid* (1898) and Eric Baume in *Half-Caste* (1933) both fall back on melodrama, but include realistic accounts of the growing up of part-Māori girls. Arthur Adams, in his substantial *Tussock Land: A Romance of New Zealand and the Commonwealth*, minimizes the element of melodrama while showing the maturation of his hero in Otago and Southland, Australia, and the King Country; in his last novel, the autobiographical and non-chronological *A Man's Life* (1929), which contains some finely realized scenes in Dunedin in the 1880s and 1890s, he foregoes melodrama entirely. Bolitho's autobiographical *Solemn Boy* (1927) provides a convincing picture of growing up in provincial and puritan Opotiki, but falls into melodrama in the end, as does his other New Zealand novel, *Judith Silver* (1929), in which only the scenes of growing up in New Zealand seem authentic.

The best of these autobiographical *Bildungsromane* is Mulgan's *Spur of Morning*, which requires a romance pattern to round it off, but which succeeds in integrating plot, character, and setting in a way that few other novels of the period achieve. Allen is equally unmelodramatic in his three Dunedin novels of the 1930s, *A Poor Scholar* (1936), *Hedge Sparrow* (1937), and *The Young Pretender* (1939), but there is less substance than in Mulgan's novel; this is true also of Pat

Lawlor's *The House of Templemore* (1938), a loving re-creation of a Wellington childhood.

*   *   *

None of these quietly realistic novels of growing up express a critical view of New Zealand society, although Mulgan at least raises most of the issues. In general the novels of this period continue to take a relatively positive stance towards the society they present, the dominant theme, following on from the Pioneer novelists, being what Mulgan referred to as 'nation building' — the carrying out of the dreams of the Pastoral Paradise and the Just City. Novels of all modes celebrate these tasks. The historical romances of the exploration period, such as Cook's *The Cave of Endor*, Owen's *Captain Sheen* (1905) or Stanley Wright's *Oak Uprooted* (1928), anticipate the transformation of the 'wilderness of "toi toi" and flax' (a 'profitless tangle') into 'wide belts of luxuriant grass'. The historical romances of the first Pākehā settlement, such as *The Counterfeit Seal*, and those of the contemporary bush frontier, such as *In the Shadow of the Bush* or *Tussock Land*, celebrate the struggle, 'undisguised and bitterly strenuous', to transform the wilderness into 'a garden of fertility and a centre of commerce'. One of the last of the novelists of the period, Helen Wilson (1894-1957), looks back in *Land of My Children* (1955) at the whole seventy-year process in relation to one piece of land and celebrates the long and varied effort it took 'to change a block of standing bush into the smiling farm it now was'.[32]

While celebrating the carrying out of the Pastoral Dream, these Late Colonial writers were aware of some of the costs. Even though a writer such as R.N. Adams could refer to the bush as made up of 'useless and noxious plants', to be replaced by something offering 'the full satisfaction of human wants', there was a perceived loss in the replacement of it with farms. Bell, A.H. Adams, and Mulgan all describe the 'dismal wreck of a once superb beauty' in the process of burning off, leaving the 'grim unconquered corpses' of the dead trees, but all see the ugliness as a temporary phase on the way to the building of a Pastoral Paradise. Many novelists treat the decline of the Māori in similar terms. The chorus of doomsayers mourning the necessary extinction of the Māori swells in the first twenty years of the period, as the 'resistless stream' of history is seen as sweeping over Maoridom. From *Ko Meri* in 1890 through *Zealandia's Guerdon*, *Captain Sheen*, and Annabella Forbes's *Helena* early in the century to *Maori Witchery* in 1929, Māori characters are made to articulate and mourn the coming doom of their race. Looking back to the turn of the century in 1934, Mulgan has his hero wonder 'What would be the fate of these quick-witted children of the captivity? Destruction or absorption?' A.H. Adams more romantically celebrates absorption, describing his part-Māori heroine Aroha as a representative of 'a newer people, a nation that had no past'; 'two long lines of conquerors fused and blended in her', the Māori blood in her bestowing 'upon the New Zealand race of the future a physique and a vitality that belong to primitive things, a gift that would carry the new race far'. If for Adams the Māori race's 'destiny was intermarriage with the pakeha', other Late Colonial writers were worried about the degenerative possibilities of miscegenation. Weston, Kaye, and Baume, whose writings span the period (1890, 1900, 1933), all deal dramatically with a perceived danger of Māori 'reversion' to savagery as an obstacle to interracial marriage.[33]

The bush and the Māori are not the only perceived victims of the struggle to carry out the Pastoral Dream. In 1903 Cheeseman complained that no New Zealand novelist had dealt with 'the "forty acre settlers" who had been worsted in the struggle', but it was not until the work of Frank Anthony in the 1920s that there was a reflection of failure, in this case that of the post-World War I soldier settlement farms, those last sad expressions of the Dream. Anthony's primary importance is for his contributions to popular literature in the 'Me and Gus' sketches; his novels have been published posthumously and thus had no contemporary impact, but they do provide a rueful literary record of failure, the 'weary, lonely, monotonous drag' of life, the difficulties with the soil and the mortgage. And even for those who succeeded, as Forbes commented, the Pastoral Dream 'was a dream that had cost to fulfil', for 'the very quality of the settler made the ordeal harrowing — the fight with petty necessity, the loneliness to be endured, the resource demanded till the desert was reclaimed'. Makgill in *Blacklaw* shows the mentally blighting effects of growing up on a bush farm, the 'half-finished feeling' of the landscape of 'charred stumps and half-cleared waste-land' becoming symbolic of a depressed inner state. Mulgan and Bell commented on 'the heavy burden on the women folk' of frontier life, while the temperance novelists such as Cameron, Mactier, Inglewood, and G.M. Reed show the sufferings brought upon women by the drinking culture of the frontier male, 'the root of all women's wrongs' according to Reed.[34]

The deficiencies of frontier society are revealed as not all compensated for by the more settled society that followed. From the rough life in the central North Island small towns shown humorously in Arthur Rees's *The Merry Marauders* (1913) to the ugliness of Dunedin business culture encountered in Prudence Cadey's *Broken Pattern* (1933), many of the novels of the period show the narrow, unfinished quality of life in Late Colonial New Zealand. Bolitho in *Solemn Boy* shows how the second generation after the pioneers made themselves more comfortable but did not restore the high culture that had been left behind in England, establishing instead a secularized puritan culture of respectable mediocrity. Timothy Shrove's mother thinks that '*originality, individuality* and *personality* were things to be avoided', sounding like Bolitho's own mother as he describes her in his autobiography, *My Restless Years*: 'My Mother's ideas of behaviour were as fixed as the pattern on a plate: her motto beneath the design was "What will the neighbours say?"'. The dark side of this culture was its repression of sexuality. Timothy Shrove 'had been brought up to believe that every part of the body that was covered by clothes was indecent and associated with some strange wickedness he did not comprehend';[35] Simon

Grantham's father in *Judith Silver* is a melodramatic model of the destructively repressed puritan, while the hero's father in Adams's *A Man's Life* is less dramatically shown as isolated and lonely in his puritanical rectitude.

In *Solemn Boy* Bolitho describes the coming of a third generation not satisfied with the 'content that came out of the early pioneer struggle', and developing 'the desire to paint, the desire to write and the urge to self-expression stirring in its bosom'.[36] However, he implies that the only immediate way to meet these needs is to import a bit of English high culture into New Zealand, or (like Timothy and Simon) to become an expatriate. Similar views underlie the desperate desire for things English in Mulgan's Philip Armitage, or in C.R. Allen's heroes. The implication of many of these Late Colonial novelists is that a lagging development of a high culture is part of the necessary price to pay for material progress in a new country, but in the future New Zealand will build its own version of English culture. In this, as in other areas, present imperfection is but a stage in a development towards a better future.

Underlying all of these ideas concerning New Zealand society, its future accomplishment and its present imperfections, is a faith in evolutionary progress, often tinged with a cultural Darwinism. From the sober belief of one of Adams's characters that it is humanity's 'stupendous task to tame and educate that hideously callous, strenuous, grim thing called Nature' to the ethic of evolutionary progress of Macmillan Brown's ideal state in *Limanora* or to the mystic religion of Humanity of Carlyle Ferguson's heroine in *Marie Levant* (1913), in most of these novelists there is a faith, implicit or explicit, in human evolutionary progress. This evolutionary ethic provides a goal for the process of colonization, and justifies the costs, including the regrettable but necessary destruction of the bush and the Māori, as well as the human costs for the settlers themselves. As G.B. Lancaster puts it in *The Law Bringers* (1913), the Anglo-Saxon colonists, driven by 'that great merciless inscrutable Power' which has made them rulers and 'the builders up of new dynasties', must go on 'fulfilling their destiny, destroying the lesser within or without the law, taking that which they can never replace'.[37]

The evolutionary imperative also justifies attempts to reform New Zealand society from within. The temperance novelists saw prohibition as a way to help the race go 'ever forward towards God's highest ideal for it'; feminist novelists justified female equality in terms of evolutionary advance. Baker, for example, looked forward to the 'Immaculate Conception' to be brought about by women aided by 'science, reason and religion,' the 'predestined birth of a larger broader purer love, that will triumph over minds illuminated with truth'; and Hunter's Red Fed hero proclaims 'I shall go on-on-on, until we behold a perfect race', justifying trade union radical action. Most interesting among these reform novels is Clyde's *A Pagan's Love*, with its attacks on puritanism (that 'coarse, church-belled heathenism'), economic exploitation and sexism, and its call for a new morality and religion of love rather than law, of fulfilment rather than denial ('we need our minds enlarged rather than our souls purified'), of sexual equality rather than 'enslavement': goals towards which the liberated, ex-puritan hero and heroine will move ('there was work to be done together'). Political and economic theories from Brown's conservative social order (the Limanorans know 'how necessary to all progress was the struggle for existence')[38] through Foston's Christian capitalism and Forsyth's 'equalistic individualism' to Christie's Christian Socialism and Devanny's Marxism are all justified by evolutionary arguments. The note of an ultimate faith in progress, in humanity controlling social evolution, and in the ultimate achievement of the dreams of a Pastoral Paradise and a Just City in New Zealand, provides the background bass for all the novels of the period.

*   *   *

The themes and modes of the lesser novels appear in a more developed form — though still unevenly and with varying degrees of success — in the four most important novelists of the age: Grossmann, Satchell, Mander, and Devanny.

Despite the discontinuous nature of her career as a novelist, Grossmann in her four novels — *Angela: A Messenger* (1890), *In Revolt* (1893), *The Knight of the Holy Ghost* (1907), and *The Heart of the Bush* (1910) — displays a process of development in her vision and mode of expression. Her vision develops from a relatively naïve and narrow feminism in *Angela* towards a grounding of it in an evolutionary Religion of Humanity in *The Knight of the Holy Ghost*, where the struggle for female equality is seen as part of 'our efforts to emancipate the race from the past and to make way for its evolution in the future'. This process of evolution is seen as the true meaning of the Resurrection, the human ideal 'made flesh after generation upon generation of higher life', as Hermione, the martyred heroine, states. However, from first to last there remains an ambivalence about material and technological progress, a tendency to want to retain a kind of pastoral innocence while espousing evolutionary progress. Thus the nostalgia in *Angela* for 'those golden days of the old colonial times' before the railroad brought corruption reappears in more complex form in *The Heart of the Bush*, when Dennis McDiarmid, the hero, is persuaded by Adelaide, the heroine, to forego working for economic growth and the new agricultural technology and instead live a quiet and retired life with her on a small farm. Almost alone among Late Colonial writers, Grossmann implies that their 'limitless hopes for our social future',[39] which she shares, need to be qualified by fears concerning the results of material development.

In her mode of expression Grossmann seems to aim at something less like realism than like the heightened symbolic moral melodrama of *Jane Eyre*, as appropriate to her vision and didactic purpose. Her first three novels espouse the kind of 'Tragic Art' she described in an article of 1906 ('The Decadence of Tragedy') as 'a truthful and sympathetic picture of life' which 'shows us the significance of other lives, and . . . nerves us to bear our own pain'. In *Angela* the result is an oversimplified tragic melodrama, the too good and innocent heroine set against the stock villain, and finally martyred by an alcoholic male. *In Revolt* deepens and complicates the melodrama, for Hermione has her own pride and will to set against those of her husband. However, the conflict finally becomes a simple opposition of the suffering Hermione and the brutal Bradley, in an unjust world where 'he had *the right* to torture her at his brutal will, the right, confirmed by law, sanctified by scripture, and applauded by society' (the novel is set before 1884, when married women had no property rights).[40] *The Knight of the Holy Ghost* continues Hermione's story, taking it to its final tragedy with her death. The oppositions are somewhat less simplistic, for Hermione is shown as disappointed by some of her allies as well as persecuted by her enemies, (and there are hints that her idealism is tinged with pride and blindness), but by the end her martyrdom is that of absolute good trampled under by absolute evil.

In *The Heart of the Bush* there is a mellowing, and a change from tragic melodrama to a kind of symbolic *Bildungsroman*, although the emphasis remains didactic. The absolute oppositions modulate into a kind of dialectic, as Adelaide tries to bring about 'the marriage of the leisured and the labouring class, of art and nature, of civilisation and barbarism' in her relationship with Dennis. However it requires quite a bit of manipulation of the plot (as well as some high-flown nature symbolism in the long honeymoon sequence in 'The Hidden Vale') to bring Adelaide and Dennis to an idyllic existence on a small farm where they can be 'children and lovers together for life'[41] — a state which would seem neither possible nor desirable in the real world of South Canterbury in which they ostensibly live, whatever its status in the world of melodramatic romance. Perhaps Grossmann's search for a mode of expressing her vision had finally brought her up against contradictions implicit in the vision itself.

Satchell's career as a novelist may have been a truncated and disappointed one, but his four novels — *The Land of the Lost* (1902), *The Toll of the Bush* (1905), *The Elixir of Life* (1907), and *The Greenstone Door* (1914) — when read together do give a sense of completeness, a vision achieved and adequately if not superlatively expressed. The vision, even more than Grossmann's, is an evolutionary one, rooted in the late Victorian understanding of the implications of Darwinism. Geoffrey Hernshaw and Mrs Gird in *The Toll of the Bush* probably speak for Satchell in their agnostic rejection of the traditional explanation of the course of things, and in their assumption of the indifference of nature to human values. However, Geoffrey probably also speaks for Satchell when he states his hope that the 'formed road' of scientific knowledge, which has crossed and superseded the 'old worn track' of religion will finally lead to 'the fountain of Truth, the Absolute'. Philip Westland in *The Elixir of Life* raises one possibility as to that Truth when he cites Alfred Wallace's evolutionary faith (in *Man's Place in the Universe*) that 'man is the *raison d'être* not merely of this earth but the whole universe . . . .. Here . . . is the nursery of spiritual beings, for whose production the whole universe was designed.' Alan Vincent in that novel speculates that we are evolving toward 'a perfect type', and the elixir that he discovers can be read as a symbol of science's role in aiding that evolution.[42] 'Progress', then, can take on a cosmic meaning.

But progress for Satchell also has a more limited, historical meaning, for in the novels he develops a myth of New Zealand history. First there was Māori society, vital but primitive and technologically undeveloped. The Pākehā brought the technology that the Māori needed, and the immediate result was the Māori 1850s in the Waikato, 'the halcyon time of the race', when European agricultural technology was absorbed into Māori life, as described in *The Greenstone Door*. However, Pākehā greed for land, the disparity between the societies, the pace of change, and the ecological effect of the introduction of Pākehā plants, animals and diseases meant that 'the Maori was doomed; that his best hope was extinction in the blood of the conqueror', for in the Darwinian workings of 'the Inevitable', the less developed culture would be overcome. Thus the Land Wars were inevitable: 'The road to peace ran through the iron gateway of war.' The new society to be built on the ruins of the Māori culture would absorb within it what remained of the Māori, and evolve its own pattern. In the process it was necessarily destroying the bush, for, as Geoffrey states, 'civilisation is a ruthless thing. One is sometimes tempted to ask if it is worth the cost, but we are bound to think so. That is a thing we dare not disbelieve'. The process of social evolution is rough and painful, but the result could be the Pastoral Paradise that Jess Olive foresees in *The Land of the Lost*, 'the apple orchards and vineyards of the future' over which 'rests the peace of God'. At the end of *The Toll of the Bush*, Major Milward proposes a toast to 'the country of our children — the Fairest Land in the World',[43] and each of the novels ends in a marriage looking forward to that better future.

In his search for a mode of expression for that final optimistic vision, Satchell tried various ways of combining realism with romance, including elements of the melodramatic romance of the sensation novel, the philosophic romance of Hawthorne, and the historical romance of Scott. In all cases the temptation was to use the romance elements to push his materials to a more positive resolution than might have been implicit in them if treated realistically. The disjunction between realism and romance is greatest in *The Land of the Lost*. The realistic elements of the natural and social setting of the gumfields do not sit too oddly with such elements from the philosophic romance as the visionary character of Jess Olive, but they do not work well with the sensation novel plot by which the book is organized, with its villains and detectives, sensational plot devices, and melodramatic techniques; and it is the sensation novel that finally dominates. *The Toll of the Bush* involves a similar mix, but with the elements better integrated. Again there is a convincingly realistic social and natural setting (the Hokianga bush frontier), and the minor characters and even the secondary pair of lovers, Robert and Lena, are plausibly related to it. The romantic lovers Geoffrey and Eve are more problematic, and seem more at home in a philosophic romance than in a realistic novel, as do the villains Fletcher and Wickener, who seem to owe something to Hawthorne's Arthur Dimmesdale and Roger Chillingworth. The sub-plot involving Robert and Lena grows naturally out of the setting, but the primary plot once again depends on the tired devices of the sensation novel, both in its melodramatic motifs and in its stagy techniques. The novel is a stronger one than *The Land of the Lost*, and the flaws are less important, but they are the same kind of flaws.

The Elixir of Life changes the balance more in favour of the philosophical romance, and with its central symbolic device of the elixir is directly derived from Hawthorne. The mode allows Satchell to express some of his ideas about evolution more clearly than in the earlier novels, but it does not allow adequate scope for his capabilities as a realist, and the result is the least memorable of his novels. *The Greenstone Door* takes Satchell in a different direction again, this time towards the Scott of the Border romances set in a time of social conflict and transition. As in Scott, the opposing forces are convincingly drawn: the Māori in a time of intense change through culture contact, the settlers divided between the hardy and courageous pioneers and the petty and grasping business people of Auckland, with Purcell as the one caught between Māori and settler societies, and with Governor Grey as a finally ineffectual mediator. As in Scott, the background and the sub-plot are most effective, while the organizing plot of the Cedric and Helenora romance is as feeble as Scott's romance plots. As in the three earlier novels, romance is used to force a positive resolution that does not arise from setting and character. The inadequacy of this device is indicated in the way in which the greenstone door image associated with Rangiora and Cedric is shifted inappropriately at the end of the novel to the Helenora and Cedric relationship, implying a broader positive resolution than the romance can carry. As with the earlier novels, the failure to find a convincing mode of expression may be an implicit commentary on the vision, casting doubt on Satchell's attempt to find a positive meaning in evolution.

Jane Mander's six novels present an optimistic Late Colonial period vision. Even more than with Satchell and Grossmann, there is an excitement with 'the new way of thinking about God as force, or sin as defective education', a sense of liberation from a puritan past, and a faith in evolutionary progress, 'the flow of the great human current that carries all men, great and small, towards some goal of understanding and goodwill which they see as in a glass darkly'. While Mander could ruefully write in 1938 that her first novel revealed that she had had 'too much of reading Bernard Shaw and Nietzsche' and was 'too enthusiastic about social movements — the bogus and fuzzy ones — without waiting to see how they'd affect the future', that was hindsight, not evident in the novels of the 1920s. In *The Story of a New Zealand River* (1920) she celebrates the 'Zeitgeist' which at last was giving 'the impulses and instincts . . . their innings', and which was felt especially in a New Zealand which 'seethed with the atmosphere of social and moral experiments'. Of course she was also aware of 'the organised prudery and artificial and anaemic chastity' of New Zealand puritanism, from which she herself had fled, but trusted that this was a vestigial remnant from Victorian England that the country would outgrow. Beneath the novels is a nascent sense of New Zealand's historical development, a three-stage process. The first, the pioneering stage, was still evident in the Northland of her youth, and is represented by men such as Tom Roland of *The Story of a New Zealand River* and Jack Ridgefield of *The Passionate Puritan* (1921), men with a crude vitality, vigorously involved in clearing the land and sacrificing the bush to the 'great adventure' of building a new country, fired by 'plans for future greatness'. It is to one of the last pockets of this stage of development that Allen Adair eagerly turns, feeling the joy of taking part in 'an exciting procession of events in the transmutation of bushland into prosperous farms, of isolation into settlement, of lonely tracks into railway lines'. As Redman Feltz comments in *The Besieging City* (1926), such a 'pioneer and fighting age' demands a strongly developed 'masculine element', but for the further growth of civilisation 'the artists and the feminine elements in the race' must be cultivated.[44]

As Mander saw it, the second stage in New Zealand's development involved a misapplication of the 'feminine element', the imposition on the crude society of a false secularized puritan code of respectability imported from Victorian England, represented by such characters as Alice Roland and Marion Adair. This is the development that Sidney Carey discovers in the bush village of Puhipuhi. Hoping to find 'treasures of native wit and philosophy', she finds instead 'bourgeois respectability', for the women 'had evolved from the crude state that produces native philosophers into the state of "getting on in the world" wherein philosophers rapidly perish and die'. What she finds in Puhipuhi is the beginning of something that she has already encountered in a more developed state in Auckland. Similarly, Valerie Carr finds that in Dargaville people strive to be 'poor copies of other imitations, all straining their imaginations in the process of worshipping "the correct thing"'. Mander's young heroines — Sidney, Valerie, Asia Roland — represent the third stage, a stage of revolt against the 'awful disease' that is puritanism, a freeing of the emotions and intellect and behaviour, and an insistence on feminine equality and fulfilment. Sidney 'expected great things of herself and of the world', Valerie 'carried an internal dynamo', and Asia, having helped to educate her mother out of puritanism, is ready to go off with her lover to Sydney to work 'for the intellectual dynamiting of the unthinking masses'.[45]

Less didactic than Grossmann, less philosophic than Satchell, Mander was not looking for a mode of expression beyond realism but rather was trying to free her realism of the vestiges of melodramatic romance. For her the temptation was to use melodrama to force a more definite and positive resolution, and perhaps to use romance to make her fictions more commercially viable (she admitted that both *The Passionate Puritan* and *The Strange Attraction* (1922) were the result of a 'misguided' attempt to 'write books that would film'). All of her novels except her last one are basically realistic *Bildungsromane*. As Satchell did in his Hokianga novels, Mander in her first effort, *The Story of a New Zealand River*, builds a strong realistic sense of place and society, a Northland timber community. This is an appropriate 'New World' environment for the focus of the novel, the education of Alice Roland, since as Mrs Brayton observes, she 'must be cured' from the 'awful disease' of puritanism. The symptoms of the 'disease' are well captured in the everyday interplay of character and environment, but the process of education is forced by a series of melodramatic actions, culminating in the heroic death of Tom Roland, so that the *Bildungsroman* is diluted with popular romance. The elements of romance are stronger in the next two novels, perhaps because of the desire to make them readily adapted to film. In *The Passionate Puritan* the Northland setting is again convincingly evoked, but Sidney's learning to abandon the last remnants of puritan morality in her relationship with Arthur Devereux requires some melodramatic plot-manipulation on the part of the author, including even that staple of New Zealand romance, the bush fire. As with the departure of both Alice and Asia in *The Story of a New Zealand River*, the departure of Sidney for England sacrifices something of the point of the *Bildungsroman* to the desired romantic ending. Again in *The Strange Attraction*, Mander renders that 'solid realism' of setting that Frank Sargeson found to be her 'greatest strength as a writer'.[46] Dargaville is convincingly sketched: rough but striving for respectability, hard-drinking but puritanical and gossipy. However, again there is melodramatic manipulation to bring about the marriage of Valerie to Dane Barrington (the obstacle this time is not vestigial puritanism but rather her 'liberated' stand against bourgeois marriage, which does not take into account the need to adapt to her small-town environment). Mander goes beyond the romance by subsequently showing the difficulties of a relationship between two such individualists, but gains her pathetic ending (Dane's noble acceptance of his own death in order to free Valerie) only by lapsing once again into melodrama.

It is with her last New Zealand novel, *Allen Adair* (1925), that Mander finds a more successful mode, although even here the realism is to some extent marred by melodrama. Perhaps because there is less overt description than in the earlier novels (in the first one, especially, there was the tendency that Katherine Mansfield noted to separable descriptive set-pieces),[47] the Northland setting is most successfully evoked: the small farms on the Wairoa, the gumfield, the small timber settlement. Frontier values and manners are consciously chosen by Allen over those of Auckland, and play an important part in dividing him from Marion. The novel traces Allen's development, his initial liberation from his Auckland family in Northland, and then his anti-romance with Marion. In this novel for the first time, Mander is able to make characters interact with each other and the environment to bring an unforced development. Although the author's sympathies are obviously with Allen, the part played in the decline of his marriage by his own blindness and neglect is also clearly portrayed. The one flaw in the novel is Dick Rossiter, a character right out of melodramatic romance, who brings with him a string of unnecessary plot devices (and who provides an unearned let-out at the end for Allen). This melodramatic evasion of the implications of Mander's own realism is serious, but it does not prevent *Allen Adair* from being the finest novel of its period and the most successful New Zealand novel before *The Godwits Fly* and *Man Alone*.

After the achievement of *Allen Adair*, the last two novels are an anticlimax. *The Besieging City* is an accomplished novel; the milieu of New York around

World War I is sketched well, the story of Chris Mayne is handled with little melodrama, and the Darwinian view of sexuality as the process of 'sexual selection' carried out by 'a ruthless Nature entirely occupied with the perpetuation of its manifold forms' is frankly stated. However, the book lacks the social significance of *Allen Adair* and remains primarily a novel of one character's idiosyncratic choices. The London novel *Pins and Pinnacles* (1928) is equally accomplished, but is obviously aimed at a commercial market. Sardonically regarded by Mander as her 'most saleable book',[48] it is really an intelligently modified melodramatic romance, an attempt to accommodate the mode to feminism. As a last novel it is significant only in showing that Mander had given up on New Zealand and a New Zealand audience. That 'awful disease' was stronger than she had thought.

In her seven novels relevant to New Zealand literature — *The Butcher Shop* (1926), *Lenore Divine* (1926), *Dawn Beloved* (1928), *Riven* (1929), *Bushman Burke* (1930), *Devil Made Saint* (1930), and *Poor Swine* (1932) — Jean Devanny, like her writer-character Lenore Divine, was attempting to write books 'instinct with the germs of progress, vital to achieve, a real fighting force for the good of the race'. As is indicated in that somewhat breathless phrasing, she shares the Late Colonial novelist's faith in evolutionary progress, which in her case is focused on feminism and socialism, with special emphasis on the question of bourgeois property-marriage. Drawing on Engels, she formed her own vision of the three evolutionary stages of history into which she fitted her characters. The first was the primitive stage of Nature in which there was no private property, no artificial checks to passion and desire, and men and women were equal in their struggle for survival. Pre-European Māori society she thought approximated this stage. The second stage was the current age of bourgeois capitalism, an age in which private property dominated all, including marriage, where the wife was viewed as the property of the husband and the children the property of the family, thus putting artificial checks on desire and passion; it was also an age of technology, but one in which Art was in conflict with Nature. This stage she saw as a process of breakdown everywhere, including in New Zealand, as a result of a revolt against inequality and repression. The third stage was that of the socialist future, with no private property, and with no monogamous marriage or nuclear family, so that there would be male and female equality, 'a race of emancipated women, free in body and mind, economically independent, choosing their own mates, marching onward to that goal which the finite mind of man cannot even now perceive' (as Ian Longstairs rather grandly puts it in *The Butcher Shop*).[49]

In such a society, with technology put at the service of the race instead of being chained to private property, Art and Nature would be harmonized. This new age would come 'when order has again evolved out of the present social chaos'. As Lilian sees in *Poor Swine*, conduct in the present is to be judged by how well it adapts to 'the necessities of an ineluctable material development'. Highest on the scale are the Nietzschean individuals 'who refuse to draw their actions and ideas from a common mould', and who are 'bright enough to see short cuts to ultimate advancement and are brave enough to take them and blaze the trail for the slow-thinking masses to follow' (as Dawn Haliday's brother explains to her in *Dawn Beloved*). Those who most hinder the coming of a new age are those 'more likely to relish retrogression to the ways of [their] primitive progenitors than to sigh for the perfection of a society as yet unborn'. A recurring problem for Devanny was where to fit the contemporary Māori on this evolutionary scale. At times, as with the handling of Jimmy Tutaki in *The Butcher Shop*, she seems to accept the views of contemporary cultural Darwinism in seeing the Māori as tending to 'reversion' and thus doomed, but at other times, as with Kowhatu Ngatoro in *Lenore Divine*, she sees the Māori as capable of overcoming 'the call of the pah' and aligning themselves with progress.[50]

Devanny attempted to find ways of expressing this strongly held if rather muddled vision through revealing not only the conscious values but also the deepest currents of feeling in her characters, currents that aligned them with the forces of progress or retrogression, and that might be dammed or temporarily diverted by the artificial checks of a bourgeois society. The aim was ambitious, and bears some resemblance to that of D.H. Lawrence. Unlike Lawrence, however, she never found the means of effecting the aim. She was capable of rhetorical excesses even more blatant than Lawrence's, but she was not capable of his successes, and her career shows no pattern of growth towards achieving her goal but rather a series of false starts and unsuccessful experiments. The discrepancy between aim and accomplishment is spectacularly evident in *The Butcher Shop*, an attempt at tragedy that does not rise above melodrama. The aim was to show Margaret Errol as a potentially superior person driven finally to murder because of the interplay of her husband's inadequacies, her lover's bourgeois view of property-marriage, and the interference of the 'regressive' Miette Longstairs. To achieve this aim Devanny needed to evoke the deepest forces moving the characters so that the tragedy would seem to be inevitable. Instead, passions are asserted through imprecise, generalizing, and inflated language and the crude iterative imagery of butchery, underlined by abstract and preachy set speeches by Margaret and by Ian Longstairs.[51]

Lenore Divine is very different, an attempt at a serious romance. The romantic quest of Lenore for her true mate is counterpointed, somewhat in the manner of *Women in Love*, with the search of Lafe Osgood for a successful relationship with Alle Wishart. The characterization is thin and assertive, the ending forced (Kowhatu never comes alive as a character), but the novel is an interesting attempt to turn the romance pattern to more radical uses, somewhat on the model of *The Passionate Puritan*. *Dawn Beloved* is another new departure, an attempt at a female *Bildungsroman*. In many ways it is the best of Devanny's New Zealand novels, with a realistic setting and an unforced plot. Tasman Bay and Golden Bay of 1900-1920 are evoked in detail: the poor farming community with its narrow puritan morality, 'base materialism', and 'somnolent minds', and the mining town, rough, vigorous, with an element of radicalism, but 'an environment offering no outlet for human reactions'.[52] Dawn Haliday comes alive as a character (although her fineness of soul is too explicitly insisted upon), and her childhood, adolescence, and early marriage experiences emerge naturally from the interplay of character and environment, so that even her conversion to socialism by Duke seems probable and not simply asserted. However, having shown Dawn trapped in an unsatisfactory marriage that she has learned to see through, Devanny forces a melodramatic ending with a convenient murder.

In *Riven* the emphasis changes again, this time to the presentation of the time of crisis in which a middle-aged woman learns to get beyond her primitive maternal feelings and move towards her own fulfilment. The focus is more domestic than in the previous novels, the socialism not evident at all, and the feminism rather more subdued. The most interesting change, however, is the attempt to capture the interplay of emotions through free indirect thought, interior monologue, and Lawrentian metaphors of feeling. The methods are rough and imperfect, but there is some sense of the ebb and flow of emotion within a character and in the interplay between characters. However, in *Bushman Burke* these potential gains in method are not consolidated (the order of composition is not clear, for Devanny reports in her autobiography, *Point of Departure*, that she entered both novels in a publisher's competition in 1928). There is some use of a shift in omniscient point of view to reveal the mutual incomprehension of the two main characters, but the approach to character is in general more external. The structure is that of an educative romance, as Flo Wallace, in this most conventional of Devanny's novels, learns to give up her Jazz Age selfishness and come to share Burke's 'stirring of the deep-rooted yet hidden impulses of the pioneer stock to "break in the land": to fell and to burn, and to sow and to reap and to build, to love and to wed'.[53]

Devil Made Saint is another swerving, an attempt to show how the passions which, when they are suppressed and perverted lead Mrs Safron to kill her husband, when freed can work positively to encourage the genius of her daughter's husband. There is an attempt to capture the flow of the deepest passions, but the result is often lurid rhetoric, and the climax is absurdly melodramatic. The setting of the novel is vague, whereas in *Poor Swine* the towns of Granity and Denniston on the West Coast are clearly drawn. The latter town especially is caught with its ugliness, gossip, and odd mixture of puritanism and political radicalism. The focus of the book is the development of Lilian, whose repressed creativity, initially finding an outlet only in promiscuity, is finally transmuted into art. There are flashes of a Lawrentian kind of rhetoric which does not fully succeed: 'and suddenly, from her whole personality, it seemed, a stream of something vivid, personal and profound, flashed out from her and enveloped him'.[54] There is no real advance on the previous novels, the dominant impression still being that of something serious and intense which fails to find adequate expression.

As a novelist Devanny seems never to have found her voice and mode, and her achievement always falls short of her intention. But her importance lies in the fact that she was the only New Zealand novelist of the 1920s to attempt to deal with contemporary social reality (from the historically unusual perspectives of Marxism and feminism). Devanny and Mander together provide a link between the evolutionary faith of the Late Colonial writers and the anti-puritanism of the 'provincial' writers who emerged in the mid-1930s.

The Provincial Period, 1935-1964

In a review of Nelle Scanlan's *Pencarrow* in *Phoenix* in 1932, Rilda Gorrie noted the inadequacy of the novel but saw it as an attempt to meet a genuine need, for 'we have need of the novelist in our midst, but it must be the good novelist'. Four years later, in an essay on the New Zealand novel written for New Zealand Authors' Week in 1936, Alan Mulgan found that few good novelists had yet arrived: Satchell and Mander were worth noting, but if the novel was to flourish in New Zealand the writer would have to 'seek his subjects in the life about him', and find 'something more than facile sentiment against a background of tree-fern and tussock'. Only two years later, O.N. Gillespie proclaimed that 'we are on the eve of a Golden Age in New Zealand literature', and in the novel pointed not only to the reprints of *The Story of a New Zealand River* and *The Toll of the Bush*, but also to the 'boldly original work' of John A. Lee, the 'opulent imagination and riot of fantasy' of Robin Hyde's work, and the varied accomplishments of Allen and Lancaster among the older writers and Gloria Rawlinson and Ngaio Marsh among the more recent ones. Another two years later, in his Centennial survey, *Letters and Art in New Zealand*, E.H. McCormick saw the fiction of 1934-40 as one of the 'signs, few but positive, of adult nationhood', singling out Hyde's Starkie novels (1936, 1938), John Mulgan's *Man Alone* (1939), and Frank Sargeson's *A Man and His Wife* (1940). However, although there were 106 entries for the novel section in the Centennial Literary Competitions (1939-40), only Beryl McCarthy's *Castles in the Soil* (third equal) achieved publication. J.C. Reid writing six years later in his *Creative Writing in New Zealand: A Brief Critical History* was less enthusiastic than McCormick but found that the only fiction of 'any real interest' began to appear in the 1930s, and that the work of Sargeson and Mulgan the reader could at least 'recognise as being a faithful reproduction of certain aspects of the New Zealand character'. By 1953 in his 'Fiction and the Social Pattern' Robert Chapman spoke of the 'quantity of considerable fiction' that had appeared since 1940 and devoted a considerable essay to it.[55]

When McCormick returned for a second look in 1959 in his *New Zealand Literature: A Survey*, he thought that the fiction writers of the 1940s and early 1950s, with the exception of Dan Davin, James Courage, and David Ballantyne, had not followed up the achievements of the later 1930s as well as might have been hoped, but he ended on a note of 'mild optimism' in looking at 'four novels of marked distinction' that had appeared in 1957-58: Janet Frame's *Owls Do Cry*, Sylvia Ashton-Warner's *Spinster*, M.K. Joseph's *I'll Soldier No More* and Ian Cross's *The God Boy*. Charles Brasch, observing those same novels in late

1958 (and implicitly adding Ruth France's *The Race* to the list), thought that they might mark the beginning of 'a steady if small flow of good fiction of our own', finding favourable signs in the acceptance by British publishers of unapologetically New Zealand novels (for joint British-New Zealand publication), and in the evidence that 'there is now an audience here ready for and responsive to the work of New Zealand novelists'. Joan Stevens was similarly optimistic in 1960 in her book on the New Zealand novel, entitling her chapter on the novels of the 1950s 'The Harvest Begins', seeing the 1930s as 'the years in which the New Zealand novel began to take root', and the 1950s as the time when a 'crop of . . . high quality' began to appear in some abundance. By 1964 Brasch could state that New Zealand fiction was 'visibly coalescing at last into a body of work', and could point to the career of Courage and the accomplishment of Bill Pearson's *Coal Flat* as evidence: Courage had 'made himself a thoroughly professional writer' with the publication of seven novels between 1948 and 1961, and Pearson had succeeded in 'doing consciously for his time what Jane Mander, William Satchell and others attempted for theirs, but more easily and fully, with greater complexity'.[56]

In unconscious corroboration, in the same issue of *Landfall* M.K. Joseph, in a review of Philip Wilson's *Beneath the Thunder*, acknowledged that 'the publication of a New Zealand novel is no longer a singular event' so that the reviewer must 'learn to live with the problem of How to Review the Average Novel'. He could see Wilson's novel as 'a fair specimen of our average, serious novel, and in every way representative', implying that a set of conventions had been established. Thomas Bettica, reviewing Neva Clarke's *Behind Closed Doors* in the *New Zealand Listener* the next year, commented that if the novel 'had been published a decade ago it would probably have received critical attention at some length', but that 'so much has happened in New Zealand writing since then that it now appears to be just another attempt to write seriously about ourselves'. As if to illustrate the point, in the same issue there was a review of Frank Sargeson's *Memoirs of a Peon*, and the following week one of Noel Hilliard's *Power of Joy*. A.J. Gurr, reviewing Hilliard's novel and one by Gordon Dryland that same year, commented that 'The archetype of the New Zealand Novel is slowly fixing itself' and did not like what he saw — a humourless, portentously critical, self-consciously New Zealand mode of 'inexorable realism' that took too little account of 'private realities and the problems of communication that follow from the lack of common ground' (only Janet Frame was seen as free from the mode and its conventions). By 1968 in a review of Ray Grover's *Another Man's Role* in *Landfall* Denis Taylor could refer to some of those conventions as worn out, as part of 'the whole New Zealand documentary tradition . . . the literature of egalitarian dismay' with its 'familiar pieties', its 'conscientious, dogmatic reproduction of experience in its confined New Zealand dimensions of apprehension', and Brasch could agree that the view of New Zealand society and behaviour in the novel was 'wholly conventional' and gave 'renewed currency to a damaging, deadening stereotype'.[57] The review and the response to it are significant not so much for what they say about Grover's novel as for what they reveal about the state of the New Zealand novel, which had become so 'established' that conventions and even stereotypes could be discerned.

Something significant had happened to the New Zealand novel in this thirty-year period. For the first time, some more or less established novelists had emerged, and they had formulated a local tradition, developing characteristic themes and modes. Those themes, involving a sharply critical stance in relation to their society, and those modes, a predominant one of critical realism and a more slowly developing one of impressionism, set them off sharply from their predecessors. Although only five years separate the publication of Alan Mulgan's *Spur of Morning* from his son John's *Man Alone* (1939), there is a great gap in attitude and mode: the one is the production of a Late Colonial sensibility; the other of a sensibility that has come to be termed 'Provincial' (although the term has been used pejoratively, it is intended here to be purely descriptive). Those 'Provincial' themes and modes persisted through two generations of 'serious' novelists (the first born between 1900 and World War I, the second born mostly in the 1920s), reaching their culmination with Pearson's *Coal Flat* in 1963, which stands in relation to other Provincial novels as *Spur of Morning* does in relation to Late Colonial ones. While there is no sharp dividing line, and some 'Provincial' novels continued to be written even into the 1970s, it is in the mid-1960s that a 'Post-provincial' sensibility begins to emerge in the novel as the conventions of the earlier period are recognized as conventions and increasingly seen as outworn, no longer appropriate for dealing with an increasingly affluent, suburbanized, and pluralistic society.[58] In the face of that change in the structure of feeling, some of the surviving Provincial novelists such as Cross and Pearson retired into silence, while others (most spectacularly Frank Sargeson), moved their art in new directions.

*   *   *

Simon Gregg, the narrator and central character of Guthrie Wilson's *Sweet White Wine* (1956), boasts that he is 'author of thirteen novels, four volumes of essays and many short stories, better known by name in my own country than the Minister of Education, not without reputation in the English-speaking world and the world of outlandish languages'. At the time of publication, the possibility of such a New Zealand novelist appeared an absurd fiction, but within thirty years it would not seem so absurd. Already by 1960 Stevens noted a 'feature of the literary landscape' was 'the number of serious *established* writers' (among whom she numbered Guthrie Wilson). However, the foreshortened and broken careers of most of the novelists testify to the difficulties in becoming 'established'. Cross, who was to have one of the foreshortened careers, pointed out some of the difficulties in 1959 — the claustrophobia and the lack of material in a 'homogeneous' society where the 'community's vitality is low', the lack of a large and informed audience, the 'rather sneering hostility' of reviewers; these factors meant that 'novelists worthy of the name haven't yet been able to survive in New Zealand' (the one exception being Sargeson).[59]

None of the novelists who began writing in the 1930s had a long, uninterrupted career as a novelist. John A. Lee, who was the oldest (born 1891) and the first to appear on the scene with *Children of the Poor* in 1934, was in a sense also the longest on the scene, as his *The Politician* appeared posthumously in 1987. However, all of his serious fiction originated between 1932 and 1937, as not only *The Hunted* (1936) and *Civilian into Soldier* (1937) but also *Soldier* (published 1976) and *The Politician* were first written then. His later fiction was all popular literature, mostly written for serialization in one of his periodicals. Robin Hyde's five novels come from about the same time as Lee's, but all were published in a single three-year period: *Passport to Hell* (1936), *Check to Your King* (1936), *Wednesday's Children* (1937), *Nor the Years Condemn* (1938), and *The Godwits Fly* (1938). Her short life (1906–39), cut off by suicide, left a question behind as to what she might have gone on to do. A similar question mark stands by the name of John Mulgan, his short life (1911–45) also terminated by suicide, author of only one novel, *Man Alone*, before the war claimed his energies and finally his life. Sargeson, on the other hand, through a long life (1903–82) managed to publish six short novels and four novels, in addition to his short stories, autobiography, plays, and essays. However, his was anything but a straightforward career, and it divides into two distinct parts in relation to his longer fiction. His 'Provincial' longer fiction was published between 1943 and 1952, made up of the short novels 'That Summer' (1943–44), 'When the Wind Blows' (1945), and 'I for One . . .' (1952), and the novel *I Saw in My Dream* (1949), which incorporated 'When the Wind Blows' as its first section. His other very different 'Post-provincial' fiction appeared between 1965 and 1979 and will be discussed in the next section. Sargeson's near contemporary, Roderick Finlayson (born 1904), similarly began with short fiction and published his novels at odd intervals, *Tidal Flat* (a novel made up of short stories) appearing in 1948, *The Schooner Came to Atia* in 1953, and *Other Lovers* (made up of three short novels) in 1976.

Brasch pointed to Courage (1903–63) as a novelist with a 'professional' career, but that career also shows a long hiatus. His first novel, *One House*, was set in England and appeared in 1933; there was a long break until the next (his first New Zealand novel, *The Fifth Child*) appeared in 1948. It was followed relatively quickly by four more set in New Zealand — *Desire without Content* (1950), *Fires in the Distance* (1952), *The Young Have Secrets* (1954), *The Call Home* (1956) — and then a final pair set in England — *A Way of Love* (1959), and *The Visit to Penmorten* (1961). Like Mander, he wrote all of his New Zealand novels overseas, looking back on an earlier time. The same is true of Davin (1913–90). Those of his novels that are primarily set in New Zealand look back mostly to the 1920s and 1930s: *Cliffs of Fall* (1945), *Roads from Home* (1949), *No Remittance* (1959), *Not Here, Not Now* (1968). Those set in a contemporary time deal either with New Zealanders overseas — soldiers in *For the Rest of Our Lives* (1947) and expatriates in *The Sullen Bell* (1956) — or with overseas visitors to New Zealand (*Brides of Price*, 1972). Although each writer achieved a considerable *œuvre*, Davin's and Courage's careers may show also the inherent limitation of the expatriate drawing on a diminishing capital of youthful experience.

The other significant novelist to appear in the 1940s, Ballantyne, was considerably younger (1924–87), the first of the second generation of Provincial novelists, and although he had a long stay in London, spent most of his writing life in New Zealand. Like Sargeson's, his was a broken novelistic career. *The Cunninghams* appeared in 1947, and seemed as if it would be the beginning of an immediately prolific career. He had finished the first two novels of a planned trilogy by 1947 (*The Cunninghams* is made up of the first and part of the second) and was at work on the third section as well as on another independent novel. However, his second published novel, *The Last Pioneer*, did not appear until 1963, although 'Blood and Sand' (an 'extract from a novel' which never eventuated) appeared in *Landfall* in 1951.[60] It was followed by *A Friend of the Family* (1966) and *Sydney Bridge Upside Down* (1968), but then there was a second long hiatus before he came out with his last two novels which, like Sargeson's later fiction, will be dealt with in the next section.

Guthrie Wilson (born 1911) was the only substantial novelist to emerge during the early 1950s, a barren period in which only Davin and Courage among earlier writers published much. Wilson appeared with *Brave Company* (1950), which was followed by *Julien Ware* (1952), *The Feared and the Fearless* (1954), *Sweet White Wine* (1956), and *Strip Jack Naked* (1957). However, at this point Wilson moved to Australia, and although two more novels, set in Australia, appeared quickly, there was nothing published after 1960.

The late 1950s saw a number of significant debuts by 'second generation' novelists (born after 1920), the five from 1957–8, and Marilyn Duckworth's *A Gap in the Spectrum*, Errol Brathwaite's *Fear in the Night* and Gordon Slatter's *A Gun in My Hand* in 1959. Not all of these debuts led to significant careers: France published only one more novel (*Ice Cold River*, 1961) before her death at fifty-five in 1968, although she left behind two unpublished novels; Slatter has published only one other novel (*The Pagan Game*, 1968); Ian Cross (born 1925), after *The Backward Sex* (1960) and *After Anzac Day* (1961) published no more novels, announcing in 1959 that his third, on which he was then working, would probably be his last because he liked 'eating, drinking, a reasonable degree of comfort', had to 'provide for these and other satisfactions for five people', and was finding that even successful novels did not earn enough for him to do this.[61]

Of the other debut novelists of the 1950s, Joseph (1914–81) had the most broken career, following *I'll Soldier No More* with *A Pound of Saffron* in 1962, then with his quite different 'Post-provincial' novels between 1967 and 1977, and a final posthumously published novel in 1988. Marilyn Duckworth (born 1935) published three more novels in the 1960s — *The Matchbox House* (1960), *A Barbarous Tongue* (1962), *Over the Fence is Out* (1969) — and then there was a long hiatus until the 1980s, with five published so far between 1984 and 1989. Brathwaite (born 1924), on the other hand, seemed to work out his seams of material relatively rapidly, adding two more crisis novels (*An Affair of Men* in 1961 and *Long Way Home* in 1964), and then a trilogy of historical novels on the Land Wars: *The Flying Fish* (1964), *The Needle's Eye* (1965), and *The Evil Day* (1967). Sylvia Ashton-Warner, the oldest of this group of novelists (1908-83), produced four more novels — *Incense to Idols* (1960), *Bell Call* (1964), *Greenstone* (1966), *Three* (1970) — without giving a sense either of building on previous efforts or of exhausting a vein of material. Finally, Janet Frame (born 1924), went on to complete her 'Provincial' period with *Faces in the Water* (1961), *The Edge of the Alphabet* (1962), and *Scented Gardens for the Blind* (1963), before launching into a new phase with five novels between 1965 and 1972. By 1988 she had added two more novels and three volumes of autobiography, which, together with her four collections of short stories, lift her at least near to the productivity of Wilson's fictional Simon Gregg.

At least four other significant novelists who are best viewed in the context of the Provincial period began in the early 1960s. Noel Hilliard (born 1929) began a tetralogy with *Maori Girl* in 1960, added *Power of Joy* in 1965, but did not complete the tetralogy until *Maori Woman* in 1974 and *The Glory and the Dream* in 1978, with his one separate novel, *A Night at Green River*, coming between the two halves of the tetralogy in 1969. Philip Wilson (born 1922) made a relatively late debut as a novelist in 1963 with *Beneath the Thunder*, and continued to write in what had become by then a conventional mode of realism, in *Pacific Flight* (1964), *The Outcasts* (1965), *New Zealand Jack* (1973), and *Pacific Star* (1976). Ronald Hugh Morrieson (1922-72) had in many ways the saddest career of these Provincial novelists, achieving immediate success in Australia with his first two novels, *The Scarecrow* (1963) and *Came a Hot Friday* (1964), but remaining relatively unknown in New Zealand, despite the efforts of C.K. Stead and Sargeson to publicize his work. Unable to get his later novels published in his lifetime (*Predicament* was published in 1974, *Pallet on the Floor* in 1976), he became, as he had confided to Maurice Shadbolt that he feared, 'one of these poor buggers who get discovered when they're dead'. By 1982 all of the novels had been reprinted and he had joined Mulgan, Sargeson, and Frame as one of the few novelists represented in the 'New Zealand Writers and Their Work' series of critical studies.[62]

The 'big' novel of the period, the one that Sargeson had implicitly called for in his radio talks of 1950 on 'Writing a Novel', the novel that would 'seek out the threads of our lives, and show us where they all lead to', did not appear until Pearson's *Coal Flat* in 1963. However, it had had a long incubation period. Pearson (born 1922) published a chapter of it in *Landfall* in 1951 under the pseudonym 'Chris Bell'; he published his classic account of the New Zealand Provincial mind, 'Fretful Sleepers: A Sketch of New Zealand Behaviour and its Implications for the Artist', in *Landfall* the next year, thus laying out the major themes the novel would take up; by 1953, he had completed only three chapters; a first draft with the original conception by then much modified, was finished 1953-4; further revisions and a new ending were added in 1957 and 1958; finally there were local revisions made in the early 1960s.[63] Pearson's one novel, then, took something like thirteen years from conception to publication, worked on in the time allowed during graduate study and school and university teaching.

Pearson's long struggle to write *Coal Flat* epitomizes the effort and the accomplishment of the Provincial novelists. The New Zealand novel was finally established and there were some established novelists. But those who could not or would not live on the fringe of society in relative poverty, as Sargeson (and others such as Finlayson and Frame) did, had to put in at times the 'eighty-hour week' that Cross describes, if they were to earn a living,[64] and not many could sustain such an effort for very many years. Hence the pattern of broken and aborted careers. Whatever the personal cost, however, the result was a significant and coherent body of work, with distinctive themes and modes.

*   *   *

The novelists of the Provincial period indeed sought their subjects in the life about them, as Alan Mulgan had urged, but they mostly did not like what they saw — not 'God's Own Country' nor even an imperfect society developing into that, but rather a sick society, 'homogeneous, dull, conformist, philistine, puritanical, bourgeois, materialist, Anglo-Saxon, and hostile', in Peter Simpson's terms. Previous novelists, from Chamier through Mander and Devanny, had been critical of New Zealand society, but never so unremittingly and almost unanimously as were these writers. The rapidity and extent of the change can be seen if one places Gillespie's introduction to his selection of New Zealand short stories, from 1928, next to Chapman's account of the Writers' Conference in Christchurch in 1951. Gillespie had written of the single purpose of all Pākehā New Zealanders 'to refashion in these islands the homeland they had left', and boasted that the purpose had been fulfilled in part at least in creating a society with 'a standard of material comfort . . . possibly unequalled anywhere'. He assumed that the writers shared this common purpose and that their fiction reflected it. Chapman, only twenty-three years later, referred to Gillespie and Alan Mulgan and their generation as 'literary pre-Adamites' whose work 'continued to conform to the major pattern and opinions of New Zealand life', and contrasted them with the majority of the prose writers under fifty at the Conference, who 'were agreed on an assumption and thus on a theme — the formative, constricting and distorting effect of the mores and values of New Zealand puritanism on our human scene'.[65]

The year before, Sargeson, in 'Writing a Novel' had made the same point: 'one of the very first things the New Zealand novelist must be aware of, is the large number of distortions he has to deal with', brought about by the 'particular variety of puritanism' that is 'pervadingly characteristic of New Zealand'. Chapman in his 'Fiction and the Social Pattern' (which seems to have come out of the experience of the Conference) defined the writer's function in such a society as to expose 'what lies beneath the crust of everyday', offering a 'clinical report . . . on the state of the patient'. The generational divide that

Chapman had earlier noted is clearly evident in Alan Mulgan's response to Chapman's essay: 'deliberate sociological probing and exposure' was not the 'main business of the novelist', for the novelist should entertain and uplift by showing 'what is *right*' with society. But Mulgan's own son John, in his one novel, *Man Alone*, which became one of the key works of the period, did probe and expose what was wrong with New Zealand society. One of his characters, Robertson, uses a revealing image of the Queen Street riots: they 'brought too much out into the open that people didn't like to think about . . . like if you had a body in the cellar you didn't want known about and suddenly you found it laid out on the table when your friends went in to dinner'.[66] The image would hold for the Depression in general, which brought the body out in the open where Mulgan and his fellow novelists insisted on calling attention to it and dissecting it.

The dissection of society, unlike that which emerged from the Depression in Australia or the United States, did not come from a Marxist critique of socio-economic causes, but rather from a sympathetic study of the human effects. As Sargeson put it in 1937, 'There are places in the human spirit where the Marxian word doesn't run', and most of this fiction issues from those places. Even Lee, the author of *Socialism in New Zealand* and the most political of these writers, has recounted how *Children of the Poor*, arguably the first of the Provincial novels, began from a primarily humanitarian impulse: it was immediately after seeing 'one of those relief processions' of 'lean hungry starving men' that, 'heart wrenched with the awful suffering unnecessary poverty imposes on innocents', he 'started right in on *Children of the Poor*'. The humanist note is there in his references to 'awful suffering' and the 'innocents', although for most of the writers the suffering would be seen as caused less by poverty than by (in Chapman's terms) 'an irrelevant puritanism of misplaced demands and guilts'.[67]

Chapman commented that for the writers up to 1950 their 'way of examining the society that they depict' was primarily through 'the isolated individual, isolated in every sense, who may or may not explode into violent gestures under the distorting weight of a society he does not understand'.[68] Although John Mulgan's novel gave this Man Alone pattern its name, it had appeared earlier in the novels of Lee and Hyde, and even its later appearances may not have been influenced by Mulgan, for his novel was not widely available in New Zealand until reprinted in 1949. The prevalence of the pattern is probably less a matter of direct influence than of different writers independently discovering a pattern written into the life around them. Hyde found it in Douglas Stark, whom she encountered through her work as a journalist for the *New Zealand Observer*. *Passport to Hell* and *Nor the Years Condemn* trace his life from his childhood and adolescence in poverty and crime, through his experiences as hero and rebel in World War I, to his life as an itinerant labourer in the boom of the 1920s and as one of the unemployed in the early 1930s. In showing his varied experiences and in counterpointing his post-war life with that of Sister Bede Collins and others, Hyde gives a very full and implicitly critical picture of New Zealand society. Lee found his Man Alone in himself, for although the name of the hero of his novels changes, he is always a Lee persona. His own experience of poverty and of the war in many ways parallels Starkie's, but he emerges from it with a developed political sense, and the element of social criticism in his novels is more explicit than in Hyde's.

While Lee and Hyde were publishing their Man Alone novels, John Mulgan in England was working on his. Although his Johnson is a veteran of World War I, we do not see that part of his life. Rather, it is the 'bit in between' that war and the beginnings of the next one that the novel focuses on. Johnson undergoes experiences in the New Zealand of the 1920s and 1930s not unlike Starkie's (both are in the 1932 Queen Street riots, both work as itinerant labourers, both get into trouble with the law), and the picture of the country that emerges is of a narrow, materialistic, puritanical society with a great deal of latent animosity and violence.

Hyde and Mulgan set the basic Man Alone pattern, but later writers modified it to suit changing emphases. Sargeson's first Man Alone novel, *That Summer*, was begun in 1938, about the same time as *Nor the Years Condemn* and *Man Alone*, but was not completed until 1941 and was published in 1943-4. Bill, the central character, has something in common with Johnson as a drifting labourer who finds that things get tough in the Depression, and he also has his run-in with the law, but he is a more passive character and a gentler one, and there is no explosion of violence. Nevertheless, his story is also an implicit criticism of his society. Like Johnson, he asks only for the most basic goods, with mateship more central than it was for Johnson, and like Mulgan's character he is disappointed. He is less conscious, less articulate, but all the more moving for that: a good man surrounded by quarrelling, grasping, unloving people, who deserves much better than he is ever going to get from his environment. There is no overt social criticism, but as much as Johnson, Bill provides a test for New Zealand society that it fails. More spectacularly, Finlayson's Frankie (in the novella 'Frankie & Lena' from *Other Lovers*) is gunned down by a society of sexually frustrated puritans projecting their sexual shadow on him.

The manhunt motif central to *Man Alone* and 'Frankie & Lena' is taken from the historical example of Stanley Graham (1941) in at least three of the Man Alone novels: R.M. Burdon's *Outlaw's Progress* (1943), Erik de Mauny's *The Huntsman in his Career* (1949), and Jack McClenaghan's *Moving Target* (1963). Although de Mauny's existentialist interpretation differentiates his novel somewhat from the other two, all three essentially treat the Man Alone figure as a victim of society driven to violence.[69] A similar pattern appears in Grover's *Another Man's Role* and a variation occurs in Finlayson's *A Schooner Came to Atia*, where the Man Alone who explodes into violence is himself a puritan whose religion denies his own sexual needs. Peter, the sensitive hero of O.E. Middleton's 'Confessions of an Ocelot' (1979), is another kind of Man Alone, a homosexual who becomes aware of his sexual orientation only after being cruelly raped. And yet another kind is the physically or intellectually handicapped character, such as Frame's Toby Withers in *Owls Do Cry* and *The Edge of the Alphabet*, or Dell Adsett's Bennie in *Leave Me in the Park* (1974).

Bennie achieves a kind of victory over a society that abuses him, but Toby remains the unhappy outsider, desperately trying to conform to the mores of the society that rejects him.

Men Alone are not the only recipients of what Chapman calls 'the writers' attitude of unjudging pity for their driven and socially damned characters'. There are other 'bent pennies' which show the cost of the 'social milling machine'.[70] There are, for one thing, solitary and suffering women. Bede Collins, whose lonely existence is counterpointed with Starkie's later life in *Nor the Years Condemn*, is the central focus of the fragment 'A Night in Hell' (1937), a vivid account of the pains of drug addiction. This fragment does not put the experience in a social context, but the glimpses of Bede in *Nor the Years Condemn* and the account of Hyde's own life in *A Home in This World* (1937) show the kind of social pressures driving Bede (and Hyde) to drugs. Hyde also dealt with social pressures on the sensitive individual in a quite different way in *Wednesday's Children* (1937), where the sometimes whimsical and often fantastic surface only partially covers a kind of desperation. Wednesday Gilfillan is oppressed by her super-respectable sister-in-law Brenda and Brenda's priggish brother Crispin, and is able to find space to be herself only in her role as fortune-teller in the slums and in the world of her imaginary children on her island. But even this precarious existence is destroyed by her well-meaning but too unimaginative 'rescuer', Mr Bellister, so that she is driven to suicide. Aroha, the alienated heroine of Gloria Rawlinson's slighter *Music in the Listening Place* (1938), is 'cured' by some authorial fantasizing, but only when she agrees to leave her 'magic isle' for the mainland.

Hyde's and Rawlinson's heroines might have been labelled as schizophrenic by society; Frame's Daphne Withers in *Owls Do Cry* was so labelled, with the result that her imagination was cut out of her by a leucotomy. Istina Mavet of Frame's *Faces in the Water* is threatened with a similar fate in the institutions New Zealand society provides to 'remove the foreign ideas, the glass beads of fantasy, the bent hair-pins of unreason embedded in the minds' of those it considers mad.[71] Both Daphne and Istina take refuge in interior worlds not only from a conformist and judgemental society, but also from a natural order of Time and Death which they find terrifying. Vera Glace in *Scented Gardens for the Blind* invents her own fantasy world, which is itself shadowed by Time and Death, but is at least her own creation. Zoe Bryce of *The Edge of the Alphabet* is not institutionalized but is driven to suicide by a life that is too much for her, as is her metafictional 'creator' Thora Pattern, the Woman Alone as artist who creates Zoe's and Toby's world. Even Sargeson created a sympathetic Woman Alone figure in *I For One . . .* in Katherine Sheppard, imprisoned in her socially respectable role and not aware of her own repressed lesbian desires. A more traditional Woman Alone, a throwback to Grossmann's Hermione, is Joanna Denniston of Florence Preston's *The Gallows Tree* (1956), driven to suicide not by an alcoholic brute but by a super-respectable physician husband.

'If you attempt to deal with the natural inclinations of human beings in the wrong way, then certain results are inevitable — something that is clearly understood by those whose job it is to deal with children . . . and in New Zealand, you have the results staring you in the face.' So said Sargeson in 'Writing a Novel'. Sargeson undoubtedly had in mind his own novel *I Saw in My Dream*, published the previous year, but he was pointing to a subject area at least as important to all of the Provincial novelists as that of Man or Woman Alone. As Patrick Evans has stated, among the most important character types in the New Zealand Provincial novel are 'parents who are puritans, and children who are alienated'.[72] The child or adolescent as social victim is central to Lee's *Children of the Poor* and *The Hunted*, to Ruth Park's melodramatic picture of a King Country town in the 1920s, *The Witch's Thorn* (1951) and to Margaret Jeffery's somewhat less melodramatic *Mairangi* (1964). More typical of the period is Sargeson's Henry Griffiths in *I Saw in My Dream*, victimized not by beating but by the nay-saying ethic of his parents. He is finally able to liberate himself from it by his own sympathetic imagination, saying 'YES' to life and creativity and becoming a new man, Dave Spencer (as Norris Davey became Frank Sargeson). Hyde's *The Godwits Fly* similarly shows Eliza Hannay as a potential artist in a puritan environment, who must fight free of it, but she does not arrive at Henry/Dave's 'YES' to life, only at the role of the defeated outsider who is sensitized by the experience so as to make poetry of the defeats she sees around her.

While the danger of growing up puritan for such characters as Eliza Hannay or Henry Griffiths is that the growing branch will be warped, for some more active adolescents the danger is that repression will lead to an explosion, as with the Men Alone. Jimmy Sullivan in Cross's *The God Boy* is driven to the edge of violence by the tensions of his puritan family, but the final explosion is his mother's not his, releasing him from the situation but leaving him scarred. Robbie Thompson in Cross's *The Backward Sex* explodes into a kind of sexual violence as a response to the pressures of puberty in a puritan society, but emerges relatively whole (Mrs Ranier, the catalyst for his explosion, is the one who is hurt). Harry Baird, the younger protagonist of Ballantyne's *Sydney Bridge Upside Down* is not so fortunate (nor are his victims): the onset of puberty, complicated by the actions of his sex-mad cousin and his irresponsible rebellious mother, leads to multiple murder and a schizophrenic removal from reality. Caroline Culzean in Preston's *The Gay Pretensions* (1959) is driven to attempted murder not by puritan repression but by a hypocritical and self-indulgent stepmother.

Robbie Thompson's view of sex as a 'race' and a 'struggle', Harry Baird's sicker equation of it with the killing of animals ('the squeals and groans are the same. Like the cries of dying animals. Hit by hammers, stabbed')[73] — these are provided as the characters' views, not the authors', and thus as evidence of the distorting effect of their environment upon them. The implied authors of the novels, standing behind their first-person narrators, may themselves show the marks of the same upbringing in their intense interest in adolescent sexuality, but they are standing outside puritanism, placing it in a critical perspective. The case is rather different with the novels of Morrieson, which tend to enact, to contain within themselves, the tensions of puritanism, rather than to reveal them critically. Neddy Poindexter in *The Scarecrow* and Cedric Williamson in *Predicament* experience the pressures of puritan repression on nascent sexuality, but both, by acts of authorial manipulation and scapegoating, are allowed to emerge unscathed, ready to adapt to the community. The two books are quite different in impact. *The Scarecrow*, despite its finally 'comic' shape, gains great power through the acting out of the narrator's, the community's, and perhaps even the author's repressed sexual violence in its textual unconscious, while *Predicament* remains a 'boys' own' narrative romp with gothic overtones.

Some of these novels of growing up in a provincial puritan society widen their focus beyond the single adolescent protagonist to take in an entire family. Although *The Godwits Fly* is primarily Eliza's novel, Hyde included more about the sad relationship of her parents than would have been strictly necessary to determine their effect upon her. They become significant characters in their own right, as does Eliza's sister Carly, the 'good girl' whose life has its own pathos. In *Owls Do Cry* Frame took a further step to widen her focus so that a novel that might have been Daphne Withers' comes to be the whole family's, all victims in different ways of society's schools, woollen mills and mental hospitals. Even Chicks, the 'successful' daughter, comes off little better than Hyde's Carly, having lost the childhood world of imagination that is the book's only positive value.

The fullest picture is created in David Ballantyne's *The Cunninghams*, where father, mother, son, and daughter among them provide a depressing portrait of secularized puritanism in the working class in the mid-1930s in a community marked by a hypocritical religion, furtive sexuality, small-minded social judgement, rigid sexual roles, a superficial borrowed popular culture, political apathy, and the lack of any vision of alternatives. Of an early draft of the book, Sargeson said he had been 'overpowered by the dullness of [the] characters' lives', which seems to have been the effect for which Ballantyne was aiming. Anne Holden's *The Empty Hills* (1967) presents a family very much like the Cunninghams twenty-five years later. Her terrible Lockwoods carry on with their dull work, their bad marriages, their futile search for trivial pleasures because they cannot imagine anything else. Ballantyne had to a great extent been his own sociologist in describing the Cunninghams, but Holden and her generation of writers had read Chapman, and could refer to a 'frontier cult of masculinity together with a lack of outlets for it'.[74]

Chapman had commented on how difficult it was in a monocultural society to undertake 'the whole task of drawing the social diagram', and saw this as the reason for the more restricted focus on the Man Alone or, at most, the family. *Man Alone* and *Nor the Years Condemn* take this method to its social limits. However, as the novelists gained in confidence there were attempts to move beyond these limits: to encompass a larger section of their society within their critical vision. One strategy was simple enough — to focus on two different, contrasting families. This is essentially Cross's method in *After Anzac Day*, a novel with a broader social scope than seemed possible before the early 1960s.

As Evans has shown, there is an attempt to get beyond the limitations of the novel of growing up in small-town New Zealand, an attempt to deal critically with a range of adult experiences in a provincial society and to put it in historical perspective.[75] Cross's title implies an attempt to catch a 'national' consciousness, and the year of the action, 1951 during the Waterfront confrontation, is a crucial national moment when the Labour dream of the Just City seemed to have died as the country embraced the Cold War consensus and the values of consumer-driven affluence that were to be the pattern for the next thirty or more years. Through four representative characters from three different generations, three different social classes and two different races, caught in their present state and in their memories of the past, Cross attempted to show where his society was in 1951 and how it had got there. The novel is not entirely successful, its characters often becoming stereotypes, its ending forced into a vague optimism, but it is significant in its ambitions, the kind of novel that could have been attempted only towards the end of the Provincial period.

Jenny Page, the part-Māori girl, is one of Cross's ways of widening his scope, introducing Māori urban experience (while old Henry Creighton, in his memories of his and his father's past, explores its historical roots in the loss of land to the Pākehā settlers). The fictional novelist in Robin Muir's *Word for Word* (1960) prophetically pointed to Māori deracination as a theme in her *Wahine* (but Muir's own melodrama of the part-Māori woman novelist reflects earlier stereotypes of Māori 'reversion'). In the next few years there were a number of sympathetic attempts to deal with contemporary Māori experience, both rural and urban: Charles Frances's self-destructive protagonist in *Johnny Rapana* (1964), caught between cultures; Jim Hotene in Philip Wilson's *The Outcasts* (1965, but from the 1958 story 'One World'), destroyed by an interracial love affair in a racist community; O.E. Middleton's Sonny King in 'Not for a Seagull' (1964), more like a Māori version of Bill in Sargeson's 'Last Summer' as he drifts through a number of failed relationships during an Auckland summer in an implicitly racist society, whose betrayal of him he can sense but not fully articulate; the young part-Māori protagonist of Anne Holden's *Rata* (1963), learning to accept and affirm her mixed heritage; the three generations of Māori women in Doris Addison's *Mara* (1964), with their painful experiences of interracial love; and the half-caste hero of her *A Greenstone of Two Colours* (1965), who succeeds in interracial love, pointing towards a biculturalism which is perhaps only marginally differentiated from assimilation. Preceding all of these in 1960 was Hilliard's *Maori Girl*, the first novel to focus on a contemporary Māori character, a sympathetic account both of growing up Māori in a rural community and of the dangers and temptations of Māori urban migration. When it was followed in 1965 by the story of Paul Bennett's experience of growing up Pākehā puritan, in *Power of Joy*, it seemed that Hilliard had written two quite separate novels, unrelated except in their general pattern of a rural upbringing and a painful attempt at adaptation to an urban environment. It was not until *Maori Woman* in 1974 and *The Glory and the*

Dream in 1978 that the full ambitiousness of Hilliard's scheme became evident: the Māori Netta Samuel of the first novel and the Pākehā Paul Bennett of the second come together, moving through difficulties to an interracial marriage, and then working their way through their differences within that relation to arrive at mutual acceptance and understanding. The tetralogy as a whole draws a significant section of the 'social diagram' (especially in *Maori Woman*, where the scope is widened to include Jason Pine, Netta's lover, a Man Alone at home in neither culture, and Henry Rushbury, her employer, a frustrated business man as Man Alone), covering a period of thirty years. In the tetralogy, and on a smaller scale in Hilliard's one other novel, *A Night at Green River*, there is a kind of dialectic, a synthesis of Māori and Pākehā, but it is a relatively one-sided one, for almost all of the learning and renunciation is on the Pākehā part. Māori values are more an antidote than a corrective to Pākehā culture.

While Cross and Hilliard widened their social focus primarily by dealing with two contrasting representative families, other novelists attempted to focus on a whole small community. There had been earlier attempts, but usually in a satiric mode. John Guthrie's *The Little Country* (1935) is the best of these in its breadth and liveliness. His *Paradise Bay* (1952) is thin and contrived in comparison to that brave first effort to write 'a book in which we, as a country, should know ourselves and be known as we really were'.[76] Julian Mountain's *In Love is Vanity* (1948) is more forced and feeble in its satire on Christchurch than Guthrie was on New Plymouth, while John Gillies's *Voyagers in Aspic* (1957), on a cross-section of New Zealanders visiting England, is livelier but still quite thin. Gordon Johnston's The *Fish Factory* (1978), a humorous satire on a small fishing town, is a late example of the mode, while William Owen's *Tryphena's Summer* (1974) is a more serious attempt to treat the society of Great Barrier Island as a kind of microcosm of narrow, provincial, self-defeating New Zealand. Florence Keinzly's *Tangahano* (1960) attempts to show a cross-section of a hydro community of the 1950s, with some superficial success, as a kind of updating of *The Story of a New Zealand River*, but like Mander's novel it lapses into a melodramatic positive conclusion, as do C. Merton Wentworth's more violent *Mill Town* (1963), with a stereotyped Man Alone as victim, and Addison's *Valley In The Clouds* (1963) and *Bird of Time* (1965), portraits of tiny Northland communities. Jeffery's *Too Many Roses* (1956) begins with domestic realism in the vein of *Cranford*, but declines into melodrama, as does Clarke's *Behind Closed Doors* (1964), in the process finally supporting the suburban pieties it first criticized. Adsett's *A Magpie Sings* (1963) eschews melodrama in its quiet realism, succeeding in capturing, albeit diffusely and superficially, a King Country community of about 1915, while F O. Bennett in his *The March of the Little Men* (1971) loosely builds a historical portrait of a small Canterbury town from 1910 to 1960 around the contrasting lives of two men.

There is much more narrative tightness in Morrieson's *Came A Hot Friday*, another novel treating a cross-section of Provincial society, with Wes Pennington's mad schemes bringing together a whole range of characters in South Taranaki in the late 1940s in closely plotted interrelation. As in his novels of growing up, Morrieson does not so much analyse the contradictions of his world as enact them, but it is doubtful whether the anti-puritan underside of New Zealand small-town life, turning on gambling, alcohol, and sex, has ever been so vigorously caught. It is significant that Morrieson's one attempt to deal with the post-provincial society of the late 1960s, *Pallet on the Floor*, is a relative failure in its mix of uncontrolled violence, crude social analysis, and sentimental escapism. Morrieson's creative imagination seemed to spark only when he had the puritan and anti-puritan poles of small-town society for the current to flow between. Ballantyne's contemporaneous *The Last Pioneer* deals with another North Island small town immediately after the war in a much more consciously critical way. The attempt of Charlie Wyatt, the 'last pioneer', to make a new life in Mahuta for himself and his son is Ballantyne's occasion for revealing the pattern of life in the town: the male culture of drinking and wild driving, the female one of gossip and petty pleasures, the poverty of imported popular culture, the narrowness of vision and anti-intellectualism.

Reviewing *The Last Pioneer* in *Landfall*, R.A. Copland conceded that Ballantyne had caught 'the social facts' and tone but contended that they had not been 'refashioned within a critical and philosophical imagination', and that the conflict was 'feeble' because a hero of 'decidedly reduced stature' offered no real challenge to the dull environment. *Coal Flat* the same year met a very different reception. Although Stuart Johnston was only lukewarm in *Landfall*, Allen Curnow in *Comment* found that 'It embodies more human lives, and more of the life in the lives, than any New Zealand novel before it.' Here at last was the 'project in fiction on the major scale' that the Provincial novelists had been reaching towards. As we have seen, Brasch concurred editorially in *Landfall*, and Winston Rhodes took the novel as evidence that 'New Zealand fiction is reaching a mature level of provinciality', while Sargeson a few years later was to describe the novel as 'a detailed demonstration of what has happened to European civilization transported to this country'. This response indicates that Pearson succeeded in establishing an adequate conflict between protagonist and environment, and in putting that conflict in the perspective of a 'critical and philosophical imagination'. The balance in the conflict between protagonist and community was consciously worked at by Pearson. During the course of various drafts he decided to keep Paul Rogers and his personal problems 'at a greater distance', instead 'brought the town forward', and dropped plans for a positive resolution in favour of the present 'purged and purgatorised' ending.[77] The result was a novel which, in Paul Rogers, was a more adequate protagonist than Charlie Wyatt, a character of energy and idealism but also of naïvety and confusion, and which shows in convincing detail the real weight of the inertia of a community of 'fretful sleepers' in opposing change.

In its reconciliation of breadth and depth the novel is the culmination of the critical realism of the novelists of this generation, the closest that they could get to their greatest English progenitor, *Middlemarch*. Sargeson had commented in 1953 on the similarities between George Eliot's situation as provincial novelist and that of the novelists of his time in New Zealand, and implied that the best that New Zealand fiction could hope for in its present situation was something not unlike *Middlemarch*, however distantly it might follow behind. At just that time Pearson was writing *Coal Flat* to bear out Sargeson's prediction. Ironically, Pearson had not then read *Middlemarch*, but direct influence was not necessary. As Sargeson said, 'Given a certain kind of society, you may reasonably expect a certain kind of novelist',[78] and the kind of society New Zealand had become in the first half of the twentieth century had finally been embodied in a novel not unlike that which had best embodied the provincial, puritan society of the nineteenth century Midlands.

A common 'structure of feeling' underlies all of the novels discussed so far in this section, a dualism of the sensitive individual against the repressive community. This dualism has a social-historical aspect, 'New Zealand as it might worthily have been' (or might yet be) versus 'New Zealand as it is', in Sargeson's terms. It also has an implicitly metaphysical aspect which Sargeson defines as 'Creation (which is positive)' versus 'Rules (which so often and so distressingly turn out to be negations)'. There is a kind of residual romanticism in most of these writers, an assumption that puritan society and its values are finally 'unnatural' while sexuality, mateship, art, the sensitive individual are 'natural'. This residual romanticism takes many forms: the Rousseauian primitivism of Finlayson (explicit in *Our Life in This Land*, implicit in *Tidal Creek*); the Shelleyan idealism of Hyde ('the things that aren't right only exist for the moment, but the things that could be and ought to be right exist for eternity'); or the Wordsworthian idealism of Hilliard, by which at the end of his tetralogy Netta is associated with the natural cycle and with Paul's redemption ('her body harmonised with the convolutions of the earth and made its symmetry complete'). It is also implicit in *Coal Flat* in an episode singled out for praise by Curnow and Sargeson, the 'whitebaiting pastoral', where a 'natural' life brings some healing to the tormented young victim of puritanism, Peter Herlihy. Usually this 'natural' versus 'unnatural' dualism implies hope: Chapman, for example, calls for the walls of Jericho, the puritan fortress, to fall in order to free human potentialities, and Pearson in 'Fretful Sleepers' looks forward to 'a social system that makes possible the meaningful liberation of the talents and energies of the common people'.[79] The darkness of vision found in so much modernist writing appears among these writers only in the work of Frame, where the dualism is of a more radical sort, between human wishes and values on the one hand and both the social and natural world on the other. In Frame's world nature is not on the side of the rebels against society, but rather *is* the terrifying reality which society tries to avoid facing and which the sensitive characters see in all its terror. There is an absolute division between the realm of 'treasure' (the world of childhood and the imagination) and the realm of Time and Death, and it is the latter that inevitably must prevail: there is finally no protective cowslip's bell in the world where owls do cry.

The dualistic structure of feeling, setting the worthy individual against the unworthy society, does not appear in the novels dealing with World War II.

These tended to be written, as Chapman commented, by those 'who remain inside the pattern [of New Zealand society] and share its values'. Those written during the war tended to be realistic documentaries, the most interesting being J.H. Fullarton's *Troop Target* (1943), a wide-focus novel showing an entire fictional Company in the Middle Eastern campaigns. The Company includes a critical intellectual within its ranks, but he is integrated into the Company as one of a harmonious group sharing common goals within the war situation. Later war novels such as Ian Cameron's *The Midnight Sea* (1958) and Brathwaite's *Fear in the Night* likewise celebrate collective male accomplishment. The best of these is Guthrie Wilson's *Brave Company*, which does for the Italian campaigns what Fullarton's novel did for those of the Middle East. Brathwaite's *An Affair of Men* and Olaf Ruhen's *Scan the Dark Coast* (1969) focus on Men Alone operating in Japanese-held territory in the Solomon Islands. In each case, the hero faces and passes a difficult test, with Brathwaite's Islander facing down a Japanese commander and Ruhen's New Zealander handling a difficult situation brought about by an impulsive Australian airman. Philip Wilson's *Pacific Flight* is the only one of these novels to be written from a Provincial perspective, showing the war experience as but another aspect of the hero's unhappy relationship with his social environment. Guthrie Wilson's *The Feared and the Fearless* also attempts to show some of the psychologically destructive aspects of the war, but lapses into sensational melodrama. The two best of the war novels, Davin's *For the Rest of Our Lives* and Joseph's *I'll Soldier No More*, put the war experience into a philosophical or religious perspective. To Davin the war, with its sudden deaths, its sharp contrasts of action and inaction, its sexual temptations, simply brings out more clearly the basic human condition, that we are 'children moving to extinction through the ambush of life'.[80] The meditations and experiences of his three main characters in the desert campaign bring out Davin's tragic, agnostic view of life. In contrast, the experiences of Joseph's three characters in the European theatre bring out his Christian view of life, as only the Christian Peter Bonham fully passes the tests posed by the war experience.

These two novels point ahead to a group of post-war novels in which the criticism of New Zealand society, while not necessarily denied, is not central; in which the focus is much more on individual moral choice than on the power of the environment. The influence of existentialism is strong in such novels, whose characters, as Ian Reid states, are not Men Alone but rather 'still essentially isolated individuals whose dilemmas are personal ones of belief and behaviour'.[81] The structure of feeling has shifted in these writers. There is often the assumption of an indifferent universe with no 'natural' values. Human beings have a margin of freedom in which to attempt to define their own values (even if not necessarily to make them prevail), and the emphasis is on how individuals adapt or fail to adapt to their situation.

This shift in attitudes can be seen in some of the later Man Alone novels. Jack Stevens in Guthrie Wilson's *Strip Jack Naked* gains some sympathy as a social victim, but is shown more as the perverse architect of his own destruction.

Similarly, Ron Sefton in Slatter's *A Gun in My Hand* is used by Slatter as mouthpiece for cathartic diatribes against his puritan society, but is finally shown to be self-pitying and self-deceived, crippled by his failure in the testing crucible of war. In a different way Paddy Hogan, the Man Alone of McClenaghan's *Travelling Man* (1976), has some of the same experiences as Mulgan's Johnson, but is shown not as a victim but as a kind of crudely existentialist free agent. More consciously existential is Davin's Mark Burke in *Cliffs of Fall*, who rejects not only his Irish Catholic puritan upbringing but any restraints on his ambition, and destroys himself in the Raskolnikov-like gesture of murdering his pregnant lover. The awful Gregory of Duckworth's *Over the Fence is Out* similarly rejects the constraints of conventional conscience and finally destroys himself.

Less melodramatic and more convincing are the young provincial males struggling to rise within or above a limiting environment. Among the overreachers are Joseph's Machiavellian academic James Rankin in *A Pound of Saffron* and Guthrie Wilson's Paul Mundy in *Sweet White Wine*. Among those who keep their cool and succeed are Martin Cody of Davin's *Not Here, Not Now* who (like his creator) wins a Rhodes Scholarship and flies by the nets of his provincial society; Michael Anderssen, the cool young hedonist of Laurence Baigent and Charles Spear's *Rearguard Actions* (1936), an early example of the type; and Peter Henessey of Redmond Wallis's *Point of Origin* (1962). Henessey points the existential moral for all of them as he steers his way between unquestioning conventionality and unbounded anarchy: 'man is on his own and must draw his own chart, but it does not exclude him at the same time from devising rules for charting'.[82] Pat Booth's Steve Barlow, in *Sprint From the Bell* (1966), like Davin's earlier Ned Hogan in *Roads From Home*, frees himself from his mother's dream that he will become a priest, but then goes on to both adapt to, and ultimately free himself from, the demands of commercialized athletics.

Ashton-Warner's strong heroines who come into conflict with their provincial environment are more problematic, neither social victims nor existential free agents. The novels simply enact the ebb and flow of emotion, the great force of natural human desires, and the conflicts that come when they interact with environmental constraints and the desires of others. Desire, conflict, and emotion are what matter, not any judgement that we may pass on the characters or the environment. Anna Vorontosov in *Spinster*, Germaine de Beauvais in *Incense to Idols*, and Tarl Prackett in *Bell Call* are very different characters, but all are artists of a sort, all are 'under the strain of . . . those who determine to walk counter to the common', and all come up against New Zealand society, with its 'suicidal cult of the Average Man', its worship of 'the grim god Utility', and its 'insular, wool-brained, mutton-fed, butter-spread, rugby-bred, beer-blind' people.[83] In each case the final outcome is not clear and there is no definite judgement, only an intensely-realized process of conflict. The same is true of *Three*, a novel set in England which deals with the interaction between a strong-minded mother, her son, and her daughter-in-law.

Ashton-Warner's focus on strong female characters distinguishes her from most of the novelists of the time. More typical of the 1950s and early 1960s is the hapless anti-hero in the Lucky Jim mould. The most engaging of these is Horse, in James K. Baxter's novel of that title (probably written in the 1950s but published posthumously in 1985). Horse oscillates between his puritan home, the anti-puritan underworld, and the vocation of art. John Hill, the anti-hero of R. Casey's *As Short a Spring* (1953), carries pathos and melodrama as well as comedy, but follows the same trajectory, away from respectability and towards existential freedom. Stan Patchett, the narrator of Philip Andrews's *Terese* (1967), is less funny and more pathetic in his drifting, while Jacob Small of John Hooker's *Jacob's Season* (1971) more energetically brings his own downfall. The middle-aged anti-hero of Diarmid Cathie's *She's Right* (1953) is a sadder case, sinking into suicidal alcoholism in his inability to handle his existential freedom in a hostile social environment. In contrast, Graham Tarden, the repressed immigrant anti-hero of Nicholas Armfelt's strangely uneven *Catching Up* (1971), finds himself through his misadventures in South Otago.

The female equivalents of these anti-heroes tend to be more passive, and at the same time more earnestly engaged in a search for their own identities. Duckworth's Jean Dobie in *The Matchbox House* shirks that task for a fantasy world and is left bereft when it collides with reality, while Diana Clouston in *A Gap in the Spectrum* refuses such escapism and asserts her own definition of herself in a world where she has lost her memory. Frieda of *A Barbarous Tongue* is weaker, but finally faces up to her terrifying existential freedom and her responsibility for herself in a world where the old puritan imperatives and anxieties no longer hold even as something against which to revolt. Sarah in Jean Watson's *Stand in the Rain* (1965) drifts through a similar world, finding no meaning except in living her feelings of the moment. These drifting anti-heroines had been strangely anticipated in Margaret Escott's one New Zealand novel, *Showdown* (1936), with its sad account of a free sexual relationship, 1920s version.

Marcus Klein has described how the American novel of the 1950s tended to concentrate on 'accommodation', the attempts of the characters to adapt to a given social environment rather than to be victimized by it or to transcend it.[84] Many post-war New Zealand novels have a similar emphasis. Some are analogous to the war novels in putting the characters in extreme situations that test them. Brathwaite's *The Long Way Home*, set in the Canterbury foothills, and McClenaghan's *The Ice Admiral* (1964), set mostly in Antarctica, are both peacetime 'war' novels of the kind, focusing on rescue operations that test the characters. France's *The Race* is similar, except that the test is both of the men on the boat and of the women ashore. France's *Ice Cold River* tests the members of a family in a flood, focusing on the middle-aged daughter, Julie, who faces and overcomes her fears of birth, death, and contingency. The protagonists of Philip Wilson's *Beneath the Thunder* and *Pacific Star* similarly confront and overcome fear and guilt, while the astronaut hero of Booth's *Long Night*

Among the Stars (1961) proves himself as an updated Man Alone, seeing through the self-serving military and political establishments and meeting the challenge of space flight on his own terms.

Another kind of accommodation is evident in novels showing their protagonists learning to adapt to and live within a society that they have found limiting. Davin's *No Remittance*, a kind of historical chronicle, shows Richard Kane making such an adjustment to rural Southland's Irish Catholic society. Booth's *Footsteps to the Sea* (1964) reads at first like another exposure of small-town provinciality, with its set-piece scenes on rugby, pub, and RSA, but instead goes on to show its protagonist giving up his rather empty rebellion and adapting. Philip Wilson's *New Zealand Jack* less dramatically shows its protagonist, the angry young man of *The Outcasts*, at least making a separate peace with his society.

The expatriates Courage and Davin are the two most significant novelists of accommodation. In Courage's novels social, psychological, and natural forces are all givens, to be faced and accepted in their complex interaction: his characters learn (or fail) to adjust to their own natures, the natures of others, the facts of heredity and blind sexual desire, and their social situations. Adjustment always means compromise, and maturity is a rueful recognition of its necessity. The young Walter Blakiston, in Courage's best novel, *The Young Have Secrets*, the young adult Catherine Wanklin in the early *One House*, the middle-aged Florence Warner in *The Fifth Child*, the entire Donovan family in *Fires in the Distance*, the older homosexual protagonist of *A Way of Love* — all must make their less than fully satisfactory accommodations to reality. The characters in *Desire without Content* who do not face their own limitations bring disaster on themselves, while Norman Grant, in *The Call Home*, by facing his responsibility for past tragedy is able to move to make something of what is left.

In Davin's novels the process of accommodation is given a more existential flavour. *The Sullen Bell* is perhaps the archetypal novel of accommodation, as a group of expatriates and others in post-war London learn to accept responsibility for the past, face their own limitations, give up impossible political or romantic ideals, and live without illusions in an imperfect present. Hugh, the central character, defines the task for all of them as to 'admit the deficiencies in themselves instead of attributing them to accidents of time and place and circumstance'. In the later and more mellow *Brides of Price*, Davin plays the process again as comedy. The aptly named Adam Mahon achieves a happy accommodation because he believes in nothing 'except how complex everything was',[85] recognizes limits, and does not expect too much.

*   *   *

As the novelists of the period developed their attitudes towards their characters and their society, they developed the fictional modes for presenting character in relation to society. Some of the earlier modes continued, but only peripherally. Naïve realism or reporting became briefly relevant again during World War II, in journalistic fiction such as Fullarton's and later in fictionalized autobiography focusing on special occupations such as Michael Davis's *Watersiders* (1964), Nola Thompson's *The Share Milkers: A Novel of the Waikato* (1966), or Bennett's *The Tenth Home* (on life in a home for the aged, 1966). An engaging late example of the mode is Norman P. H. Jones's autobiographical *Jonesy* (1981), reminiscent of Lee in its critical treatment of Southland in the Depression and in its vivid (if overwritten) accounts of battle in World War II. The didactic mode is much reduced in importance, with G.R. Gilbert's allegorical future fiction, *Glass-sharp and Poisonous* (1952) standing almost alone. The melodramatic romance persists in historical novels such as Joyce West's *Sheep Kings* (1936) or Beryl McCarthy's *Castles in the Soil* (1939); and the melodramatic Māori adventure story in J. F. Cody's *The Red Kaka* (1959) or, in the tradition of *The Greenstone Door*, Leo Fowler's *Brown Conflict* (1959). However, Georgina McDonald and Florence Preston show in their historical novels how it is possible to eschew melodrama for a more sober realism.[86]

More important is the well-made realistic novel on English lines, which could be seen as developing from or at least paralleling the efforts of Mander to reconcile realism with a conventional narrative structure. Such novels feature realistically conceived, individualized central characters in a concrete New Zealand environment, interacting in a well-made plot that rises to a recognizable climax (often with the aid of a bit of melodramatic contrivance), usually told from an omniscient point of view or as a straight retrospective first-person narrative, often in a relatively formal literary English. It is the favoured mode of John Guthrie, Davin, Guthrie Wilson, Courage and, increasingly from the mid-1950s, of the many writers such as Addison, Jeffery, Clarke, Booth, Brathwaite or, more interestingly, Duckworth, who work in the large area of middlebrow moral realism. Guthrie's *The Little Country* is an early virtuoso performance in the mode, using an omniscient point of view to control the interweaving of multiple plot strands which involve conventional elements of romance and melodrama, and incorporating descriptive and satirical set-pieces. Davin is more interesting in his attempts in the mode. His style is more consciously literary, often elaborately metaphorical and allusive in passages reporting the meditations of characters, usually with an omniscient point of view allowing him access to the minds of all of the characters. Throughout his career he had trouble organizing the characters and their thoughts into a plot that would be shapely without being too artifical. In *Cliffs of Fall, Roads from Home, The Sullen Bell*, and (more playfully) *Brides of Price* he opted for a well-made plot moving towards melodramatic climax, and with all of the loose ends tied up. Perhaps in reaction to their neat artificiality, he attempted looser chronicles in *For the Rest of Our Lives, No Remittance*, and *Not Here, Not Now*, all of which tend to sacrifice unity of pattern to meditation and detail. Guthrie Wilson's novels present similar problems, except that the melodramatic contrivance and the flat chronicle appear in different parts of the same novels, as he manipulates his plots to move things on when the chronicle gets bogged down. Only *Strip Jack Naked* achieves economy and unity, although *Brave Company* is given adequate shape by the military campaign.

Courage was not as ambitious in his aims as Davin, but was somewhat more successful in carrying them out, using a version of the well-made novel adapted from E.M. Forster and L.P. Hartley, as well as from the well-made play (he was an unsuccessful dramatist). From Forster he took the sudden (and often offstage) death or accident to move the plot and shake the characters; from Forster and Hartley he took the foreground iterative symbol; from the well-made play the rising sequence of two- or three-character confrontation scenes. The result is usually a competent novel, but with the artifice a little too evident, although in *The Young Have Secrets* he integrated all the devices well. In the later middlebrow writers, there is less use of consciously literary symbolism and more use of realistically grounded melodramatic contrivance to resolve the plot. In Jeffery's *The Forsaken Orchard* (1955), for example, the husband's accidental death allows the heroine out of an unhappy marriage, much as Tom Roland's accidental death frees Alice in *The Story of a New Zealand River*.

It is significant that the mode most dependent on English models was developed by expatriate novelists and by those such as Guthrie Wilson, and most of the later middlebrow novelists, who tended to be less critical of the New Zealand social environment. Among the more socially critical writers there was a move away from the well-made novel and English models, arguably because such forms assumed an agreement with stable social norms and values. Thus the New Zealand critical realists turned towards a mode without the clear resolutions and plot manipulations of the well-made novel, with a more restricted point of view (often involving character revelation through free indirect thought, and avoiding the formal literary language favoured by Davin and Courage), and with the dialogue in the New Zealand idiom and the narrative prose in keeping with it. Sargeson spoke for such formal possibilities in his 'Writing a Novel' when he talked of the search for 'an appropriate New Zealand language to deal with the material of New Zealand life', language which would be not only 'the tool that the novelist worked *with*', but also 'the raw material of life which he worked *upon*', a language unlike that of his predecessors, 'which did not differ a very great deal from that used by English novelists'. In 1934 A.R.D. Fairburn had suggested that New Zealand writers might find in American literature models giving 'form and consciousness' to 'the anarchy of life in a new place', and he pointed especially to the Mark Twain of *Huckleberry Finn* ('from the point of view of the New Zealand writer . . . the most important novel ever written') and to Ernest Hemingway and William Faulkner. Mander disagreed ('good writing means the fine use of one's own language, and our language is English and not American'),[87] but Fairburn turned out to be the better prophet, and it was to American models that Mulgan, Sargeson, Ballantyne, and later Cross turned in developing a local mode of critical realism.

Mulgan in *Man Alone* drew on Hemingway for his narrative prose, with its simplicity and understatement, its emphasis on sense impressions and avoidance of abstractions, and for his point of view, basically a restricted third-person one, with access limited to the mind of Johnson (although there is a first-person frame narrative). The plot structure is of the type favoured by Hemingway and the American realists, a relatively loose one, with the climaxes (the Queen Street riot and the death of Stenning) emerging 'naturally' from the interplay of character and environment, and with little sense of overt shaping. The result was something different from any previous New Zealand novel, leading James Bertram to say at the time: 'I close the book with the unspoken comment: "Here, at any rate, is one novel that tells the truth about New Zealand". There haven't been many.' Sargeson had turned not to Hemingway but to Sherwood Anderson for his model in attempting to tell 'the truth about New Zealand' in his early short stories, and when he first attempted a 'novel' (really a novella) in *That Summer* he kept to that model. He has said that the work arose from his 'desire to write something longer, to write a novel', and that it came from combining the notes he had for possible short stories into a single work built on the theme of mateship.[88] It is thus an attempt to push the short story mode to its limits in a novella, using a first-person point of view with a relatively uneducated narrator, and adapting the style accordingly to the New Zealand idiom. The novella differs from the stories in its more sustained plot structure, but it is still relatively simple, a loose chronicle of the curve of Bill's attempts to form a relationship with Terry.

Ballantyne in *The Cunninghams* turned to yet another American realist for a model, James T. Farrell. He began the first draft of the novel three weeks after reading *That Summer* in typescript. Although he admired Sargeson's work it revealed to him 'how little [Sargeson] knew about conventional relationships, family life, ordinary toilers, and all that', and he was bothered that Sargeson sometimes seemed condescending. He had also been concerned to see how the Sargeson mode, that of 'splendid miniaturist', had 'travelled the longer distance'. His own aim was to capture the ordinary life he thought Sargeson missed, to integrate the revelatory 'minutiae' into a larger narrative framework, and to retain a kind of *impassibilité* that could not be seen as moralizing or as condescension:

> . . . as an investigator of human existence, [the novelist] must try to understand the way in which average people live out their time; it is only incidental that he may not approve of all that he sees, may feel that it is shameful that people live the way they do; for this, for better or for worse, is reality; and he is the observer.

Farrell seemed to provide an answer. Ballantyne read *Father and Son* from Farrell's Danny O'Neill sequence just before beginning *The Cunninghams*, read *Studs Lonigan* while writing it, and discovered that he had 'switched' to 'the Farrell wavelength' (although he was also reading Hemingway, Anderson, Thomas Wolfe, and others at the time).[89] What he worked out was a method in which the narrator was totally effaced (not only no comment but not even any narrative summary), with the point of view moving from character to character to give a greater range and to capture the relationships that Sargeson had missed, using free indirect thought with the third-person often modulating into the second and occasionally into direct first-person interior monologue. The plot, made up of a series of discrete scenes each of which worked as a revelatory 'slice of life' story, moved through the natural interaction of character with character and with environment. There was no contrived climax, no conventional plot pattern, and perhaps the most moving scene was one in which nothing at all happened, not even speech — 'Husband and Wife', in which the failing Gil Cunningham and his wife Helen carry on their separate interior monologues, each thinking about and remembering the relationship with the other, but neither able to communicate.

Many of the novels of the 1950s and early 1960s use aspects of the Mulgan, Sargeson, and Ballantyne models in various ways. Cross in *The God Boy* might have seemed to have drawn from the Sargeson of the stories of childhood and adolescence such as 'A Good Boy', but in actuality went directly back to Anderson. He felt 'a strong sense of kinship' with a group of American writers because he shared 'the same problems and the same experience as a colonial people', and named Anderson ('like hearing another brother talk'), Wolfe, Hemingway, Ring Lardner, Salinger, and, of course, the Twain of *Huckleberry Finn*, as among his literary relatives (and *The God Boy*, like *The Cunninghams*, was first published in the United States). The idea for the narrative method of *The God Boy* came from watching a television version of Anderson's 'I Want to Know Why' and then going back to the story. What he discovered in Anderson's technique was the kind of structural irony that Sargeson had also found there, a 'double focus' which enabled him to 'have the boy tell his own story, but in such a way that the reader could take an adult view'. In practice he gave the story a triple focus, having the thirteen-year-old Jimmy tell the story of his eleven-year-old self, with the implied author behind him understanding more than either Jimmy could. The appeal of the American writers was that they were dealing with a 'colonial' experience in a 'colonial' language. As he saw it, New Zealand writers were in a similar position, for New Zealand English was not just 'a kind of provincial variation . . . significant only as a colloquial phenomenon' (which was the way Davin tended to use it — a kind of local-colour 'slumming' in the dialogue quite different from his narrative language); rather, 'it goes much deeper than that', for 'it is concerned with our responses to what we have seen and heard since the day we were born'. Thus the New Zealand writer must 'start with the way people use it here'.[90] Cross was in a sense rediscovering for himself Sargeson's discoveries about point of view and language. He may also have rediscovered something about plot structure, for the way in which the violence arises naturally from tensions that are seen obliquely, and the way it takes place offstage, remind one of a Sargeson story such as 'I've Lost My Pal' writ large. *The God Boy* in fact started as a short story. But by dealing with a family, as Ballantyne did, and in relation to the ordinary institutions and relations of New Zealand society

163

(school, church, neighbours), Cross was able to develop his situation into the depth and breadth of a novel.

Cross used this method again in *The Backward Sex* and in so doing may have discovered its limits. Norman Harvey exploited it for more superficial effects in *Any Old Dollars, Mister?* (1963), while Morrieson used it for his own purposes in *The Scarecrow*, with the triple layering of Neddy-as-character, Neddy-as-narrator, and implied author used more for ironic humour than for social criticism. Slatter also used it in *A Gun in My Hand*, with the structural irony of the fallible narrator more a device for Slatter to contain his own contradictions (to criticize his society but dissociate himself from the critic) than to expose those of his culture. Grover in *Another Man's Role* is closer to the Mulgan model, but uses a first-person narrator. The method of *The Cunninghams* as a means of portraying a whole small community is there in Ballantyne's own *The Last Pioneer* (perhaps *his* discovery of the limits of his mode) and in Adsett's *A Magpie Sings*. It may also lie behind Booth's somewhat more conventionally plotted *Footsteps in the Sea*.

The careers of Sargeson, Ballantyne, and Cross would seem to indicate that all of them reached the limits of the modes they helped to form. The method of the early Sargeson seemed eventually to confront him with two technical barriers: how to extend the social range and the variety of relationships beyond his lonely narrators on the social fringe, and thus make a more complex, extended fiction possible; and how to get into the fiction something of the author's intelligence and language — in R.A. Copland's terms, 'how to reconcile the authorial range and the character range' so that the author need not always 'stoop'. Ballantyne got beyond the first barrier, but not the second. When *The Cunninghams* first appeared, Chapman noted that it left Ballantyne nowhere to go: his method, applied to such limited and typical characters meant that the author's critical intelligence was there only in the selection and arrangement ('the Cunninghams are the self-defeated who cannot rise above an inadequate and impossible aim or realise that this is what is bedevilling them'). And, as with Sargeson, the author's language could not appear at all: 'Shorn of all comment, the pace and the depth of the story are correspondingly delimited by this convention of telling it in the anonymous cramped patter of a class.'[91] Cross attempted to transcend these limits in *After Anzac Day*. The method adopted — the use of a limited third-person point of view which moves among four characters, with much free indirect thought — is basically that of Ballantyne, but the characters are more diverse in their experience, more intelligent, less verbally limited, and they have rich stores of memory. Cross does not have to 'stoop' so much, and can include more of the authorial intelligence. However, he also manipulates his plot rather more (reverting to the well-made novel at the end) and at times uses the characters as a means for presenting his own views too directly.

At the same time as Cross, Pearson was also struggling with the means of dealing with an expanded social range. Although he was drawn to the modernist mode (especially Dos Passos's in *USA*), what he finally settled for was something pretty close to George Eliot's traditional realist method, with an omniscient point of view that not only shifts rapidly from character to character but also allows the narrator to tell the reader things about the characters that they do not know about themselves, to inject general and evaluative commentary, and to provide large blocks of narrative summary, especially to fill in the characters' past. This method avoids the temptation of planting authorial thoughts in the characters, but at the cost of a loss of interiority and intensity. Still, Pearson did succeed in his stated aim of devising 'a traditional structure that would be large enough to comprehend a community and sensitive enough to reflect the crises of feeling and conscience that might come to a man who was out of sympathy with the materialist values of the community'. He was even more successful in his aim of creating a plot that 'would grow easily from the initial situation and by its own logic would reach a satisfying outcome without any of the tricks and evasions or improbabilities by which some of the 19th century English novelists reached their answers', and that would at the same time achieve 'the noble symmetrical curve' of *Troilus and Criseyde* or *Wuthering Heights*.[92] Better than Cross and most of his contemporaries he avoided melodramatic plot manipulation and achieved the crises naturally, while the 'curve' was achieved partly by the simple device, borrowed from Arthur Koestler's *Arrival and Departure*, of having similar opening and closing paragraphs call attention to continuing natural and human rhythms.

In the twenty-five years between *Man Alone* and *Coal Flat*, a couple of generations of novelists had worked out a range of methods and conventions by which to present their generally critical views of New Zealand society. By the end of the period they had found ways to widen their range to present something approaching that 'social diagram' that Chapman had thought impossible for the novelists of the 1930s and 1940s. However, the kind of criticism that Virginia Woolf made of Arnold Bennett and John Galsworthy might have been made of these writers: that they tended to sacrifice the uniqueness of individual vision and the intensity of moments of individual experience to social realism; or, as Gurr put it, they were not aware enough that 'a writer's individuality matters more than his locality'. If, as Brasch stated, a novelist such as Pearson succeeded more fully in doing what Satchell and Mander had been moving towards, it was at the (probably necessary) cost of not attempting the kind of thing that Mansfield had done in 'Prelude' or 'At the Bay'. Sargeson was aware of this, and spoke of the difference between a 'masculine' tradition with its 'sense of social tradition' and a 'feminine' tradition which depends on personal sensibility and the individual perception of 'isolated details and moments of life'.[93]

However, the opposition between modes is not so great as Sargeson implied, a difference in emphasis rather than a difference in kind (and certainly not a difference that would permit the 'masculine' to be labelled 'major' and the feminine 'minor', as Sargeson did). The emphasis in this impressionist tradition shifts from what David Lodge calls the 'common phenomenal world' of realism, 'located where the private worlds that each individual creates and inhabits partially overlap', to the uniqueness, interiority, and intensity of those private worlds.[94] Such an emphasis does not preclude a critical treatment of society, but rather it changes the focus of criticism from the external effects of society on the individual to the internal experience of those effects. Hence setting becomes not so much externally observed 'environment' as something that impinges on individual consciousness, caught in the process of impingement; character is not so much public persona as private consciousness and feeling; action is not so much a chronological, causal chain of public events as achronological moments of consciousness, often epiphanies of realization; structure tends to be as much 'spatial' as temporal, with recurring images and motifs. Thus the impressionist narrative method differs, with point of view coming more from within the character, less filtered through an omniscient narrator, with more use of interior monologue and stream of consciousness to catch the intensity and privateness of inner states, and with a more poetic, allusive, metaphorical style to catch the evanescent moment.

In the person of Katherine Mansfield, New Zealand literature has one of the creators of this international mode of modernist psychological fiction, but for the novel the key local figure is Hyde. She described the aim of her own fiction as 'to write from the inner centre of what people think, hope and feel', to catch what Bede Collins thinks of as her own experience in *Nor the Years Condemn*: 'what I have seen . . . what I have touched and tasted', what no one could tell from the outside 'by looking at us'. Her novels are a series of attempts to find means of writing from that 'inner centre'. In *Passport to Hell*, her 'object in writing . . . was not to portray the outside world looking at Starkie, but to portray Starkie looking at the outside world'.[95] The point of view is mostly third-person but restricted to Starkie, with occasional direct first-person 'testimonies', and with the narrator's own personal explanations and impressions interspersed. There is a sense of the narrator as a personality, not a disembodied authority, one who sympathetically or empathetically moves in and out of the mind and feelings of Starkie, with a second-person 'you could see' sort of construction often running together Starkie's impressions with the narrator's imagined ones. The method is especially successful in capturing the confusing horror of battle experience.

In *Nor the Years Condemn* Hyde broadened her focus, the aim being to convey 'the "boom and bust" period in New Zealand' to 'tell as exactly as possible what happened, and the types of people who were caught up in a mounting wave, sank down into its pit, and are now struggling up again'.[96] The period covered is that of *Man Alone*, but whereas Mulgan used Johnson as a kind of lens through which to see the period in hard, clear outline, Hyde uses Starkie, Bede Collins, and others to catch the inner feel of moments of the experience, what it felt like for this person at this or that moment in the 'wave' or the 'pit', the total pattern forming a kind of mosaic. The result is a novel that is in many ways as 'social' as *Man Alone*, with as strong an implicit criticism of society, but with a very different feel to it. The difference is evident if one puts Mulgan's description of the Queen Street riot next to Hyde's 'Riot Reported', the narrative *tour de force* of her novel. Even more fully than Mulgan she presents the pressures leading up to the riot, but she does so through a fugue of voices, from public occasions including Communist, Social Credit, Legion and Pentecostal meetings, from private meetings of lovers and families, and from individual monologues. The riot itself is re-created from a montage of speeches, reports, conversations, and thoughts, with an emphasis on Bede Collins's personal experience, her impressions being captured especially by metaphors of a fish on a line, and of electricity.

Check to Your King, like the Starkie novels, is based on documentary sources, but here de Thierry's written account (instead of personal interviews), and the narrator's struggle with the materials and her attempts to enter into de Thierry's mind and feelings by an effort of historical imagination become part of the narrative itself, as in more recent 'metafiction'. *Wednesday's Children* is the least inward and impressionistic of these novels, the playful, ironic narrator playing a kind of game with the reader, who does not realize until the end that many of the scenes are taking place only in Wednesday's imagination (a narrative trick that Janet Frame will pick up in her later fiction). *The Godwits Fly* is the most important for its influence on later fiction and the closest to the psychological novel as it had developed in Great Britain and America, but the model is not so much Virginia Woolf or Faulkner or Joyce as Mansfield — it is a kind of novel that she could conceivably have written had she lived. The narrator is more effaced than in the other novels; the point of view is usually that of Eliza Hannay, but sometimes belongs to John, or Augusta, or Carly, or Timothy Cardew, or even one of the minor characters; and occasionally it shifts to the first person with Eliza. There are no transitions, no narrative summaries, but a kind of continuously unrolling present-in-the-past, with metaphor and simile used to capture impressions and feelings of the characters.

Rawlinson used some similar devices in her *Music in the Listening Place*: a quickly shifting point of view, interior monologue, and a metaphorical, impressionist style. However, the next significant text in the impressionist tradition is, surprisingly, by Sargeson: *I Saw in My Dream*. The model is not Mansfield but rather the Joyce of *A Portrait of the Artist as a Young Man*, especially in the first section, 'When the Wind Blows', where the vocabulary and syntax of the free indirect thought and interior monologue of the central character develop as he develops from childhood to adolescence and young adulthood. This first section especially is much more interior in its emphasis than *That Summer*, the aim being to find words for inner experiences rather than implying them through laconic narration and dialogue. Italicized sections, moving from third-person to second-person free indirect thought and then into first-person interior monologue, present feelings at the deepest level, the search for a personal identity, and a movement from the fears and anxieties of a negative puritanism to a positive acceptance of the possibilities of life.

The impressionist mode was only a way station for Sargeson, who developed in a different direction in his later novels. It was also taken up by Keinzly in

Tangahano, which resembles *Nor the Years Condemn* in its use of free indirect thought and interior monologue combined with a shifting point of view, to capture a social cross-section impressionistically. A more restricted focus, with a first-person version of the method, was used by Jess Whitworth in her novelized memoir, *Otago Interval* (1950). However, the real heir to Hyde was Frame, who in *Owls Do Cry* wrote the best impressionist novel of the period and developed fully the mode of *The Godwits Fly*. Frame adopted a flexible method which allowed her to capture individual experience in its intensity, each scene being sharply focused, and at the same time to fit the experiences into an implicit pattern. The effect of the point of view is kaleidoscopic, a constant shifting of perspective to juxtapose the different feelings and attitudes of the members of the family and some of the community: there are the narrator's own views, shifting in mood from the lyrical to the ironic; the shared perspective of the Withers children, contrasted to the public perspective of the town ('they say'); the individual pespectives of each of the children, and sometimes of the parents; and the occasional individual perspectives of outsiders such as Fay Chalklin or Flora Norris. This shifting third-person point of view, involving both free indirect speech and free indirect thought, sometimes modulating into interior monologue, is supplemented by Daphne's italicized inner lyrics from the 'dead room', and by her occasional first-person narration, as well as by the italicized stream of consciousness of Toby or Chicks, and by the first-person diary of Chicks, with its ironic self-revelation. The action moves from scene to scene, with no transitions and no narrative summaries, with brief time gaps between most scenes, and with twenty years between Parts I and II. The order is roughly chronological, but the songs of the adult Daphne and scenes from her adult experience in the mental hospital are inserted in Part I, bringing a sharp juxtaposition of perspectives, the world of childhood and the world of adult loss, and there is some movement back in time in Part II through memory and some parallel chronology as the lives of Toby, Chicks, and Daphne are taken up. The effect is to pick out moments along the curve of loss that characterizes the lives of the Withers family (and, as the Epilogue implies, of all of us), without tracing the entire curve as would have been done in a family chronicle belonging to the realistic tradition. The pattern of loss is further captured in the spatial structure of images, offering a contrast between those associated with true treasure (spring, summer, warmth, flowers, bright colours, birds, the Songs of Innocence, fairy tales) and those associated with Time and Death (winter, cold, darkness, erosion, knitting, the sea, the eel, the dead hedgehog). And it is ultimately the second group that prevails. This rich and coherent spatial pattern is Frame's greatest contribution to the impressionist novel.

Frame continued to experiment in her next novels, replacing the narrator's comments and Daphne's lyrics in *The Edge of the Alphabet* with the metafictional presence of Thora Pattern, who comments on the world she has created, adds her own lyrics concerning it, and calls attention to the process and conditions of creation. *Scented Gardens for the Blind* uses a rather different method, with the 'Vera' sections in a limited third person employing some interior monologue, and the 'Edward' sections in a traditional omniscience. However, the most striking development is the sudden change in focus in the last chapter, when we see that all three 'characters' are projections of aspects of the mute Vera Glace, and that all has taken place in her head.

At the same time as Frame was developing her method, Sylvia Ashton-Warner was working out her rather different, less complex kind of impressionism, involving a first-person present tense point of view: not a retrospective story-telling, but more like a diary or a running interior monologue, with a metaphorical style and a loose, immediate syntax. Her plot structures follow the ebb and flow of feeling and relationship (with the temptation to use the occasional bit of melodrama to shake them up), and she also employs a kind of spatial structure of images less dense and elaborate than in Frame. The result is intense immediacy, especially in capturing the flow of emotion between characters (*Bell Call* and *Three* are best at this), but a less structured world than Frame's, and certainly with a looser texture.

Although at their extremes the critical realist and the impressionist traditions are quite different, they are not mutually exclusive. In the 1960s especially there was a coming together in some texts, as the realists seemed to take up some of the devices of the impressionists to move their fictions towards interiority. The most striking example is Ballantyne's *Sydney Bridge Upside Down*, where the method of Cross and Sargeson is modified by the method of Frame, as Ballantyne moves the story of 'all the terrible happenings up the coast that summer'[97] more within Harry Baird's mind and feelings. The point of view is the retrospective first person of *The God Boy*, with Harry as a relatively naïve narrator. Jimmy Sullivan was to some extent a reflexive narrator, aware that he was telling a story, but Harry is much more so, consciously manipulating his story ('I start with . . ., I go back now . . .'), partly in imitation of his cousin Caroline's way of writing her 'autobiography', but also as a way of avoiding the things that worry him most. Like Caroline, who invents things to meet her own needs, Harry also invents, so much so that by the last two chapters (in his narrative present) he raises doubts about the reliability of the previous narrative and forces the reader to enter his thought processes and do some decoding. The reader is further pushed directly into Harry's mind by two dream chapters, told in the present tense, with inset inner addresses to Caroline (anticipating Frame's method in *Intensive Care*), and those serve to bring out his repressed fears, guilt, and desire. With its use of dreams, recurring images, projected wishes, and repressed knowledge, the novel incorporates some of the devices and preoccupations of the impressionist novel into the realist novel, gaining greatly in the process, and showing how strong had been the technical advances of the New Zealand novel since the early 1930s.

The Post-provincial Period, from 1965

The name 'Post-provincial' perhaps implies more of a reaction against the previous 'Provincial' period than has actually been the case, for the novelists who have emerged since the mid-1960s have not been involved in any wholesale repudiation of their predecessors, but in a variety of responses, some carrying on a modified critical realism in relation to a changed society, others moving into other modes. The distinguishing characteristic of the period has been the recognition that the puritan monoculture no longer prevails (it is treated as past history or as an anachronism by most of these novelists). All of these novelists deal directly or indirectly with the tremendous social and cultural changes the society has been undergoing in this period — what Maurice Shadbolt has called 'that Pacific sea-change which began to overtake the country in the 1960s' and that 'stunning and perplexing change of climate' of the 1970s.[98] Increasing affluence, (and latterly the threats to it), the move to a consumer society, increasing urbanization and suburbanization, the sexual revolution, the feminist revolution, the growth of racial and cultural consciousness, the emergence of a more distinctive youth subculture, and changes in family patterns — these and related phenomena have given the novelists material very different from the more narrow, monocultural society of the previous period. Such change has also presented them with problems, for the conventions and explanatory patterns developed by the previous generations of novelists would not necessarily work for these new materials.

The recognition of the breakup of the puritan monoculture has brought with it a changed stance in relation to society. The relatively simple oppositional stance of anti-puritan humanism that united especially the first generation of Provincial writers was no longer appropriate. The novelists assume a less alienated position in relation to society, remaining critical, but from within rather than on the edge. The critical perspective is still that of humanism, but usually modified by the kind of existentialism that began to appear in the 1950s, and often given sharper focus by such later attitudes as feminism and Māori nationalism. The result is a greater diversity, with neither the single target of criticism nor the relatively simple positives of the earlier Provincial writers. That diversity of theme and attitude is expressed through an even greater diversity of modes. Critical realism remains, but is not so dominant, while the impressionist mode has been developed and expanded, and a new post-modernist metafictional mode has appeared.

As this diversity and the sheer quantity of published fiction indicates, the New Zealand novel has in these years established itself thoroughly as part of the national culture, receiving more public attention than ever before within this country (symbolized by the Wattie Book of the Year Award, initiated in 1968, and the New Zealand Book Awards, initiated in 1976), and also receiving more overseas recognition (the James Tait Black Memorial Prize for Maurice Gee's *Plumb*, the Booker McConnel Prize for Keri Hulme's *The Bone People*). Although full-time professional writers are still relatively thin on the ground, an increasing number of novelists have persisted, joined by younger writers who give promise of continuing the range and level of accomplishment.

*   *   *

Some of the important novelists of the previous period went on to complete their careers with new accomplishments in this period. The most significant and surprising was Sargeson, who moved into a strikingly different second career, publishing no less than three novels and four novellas between 1965 and 1978, as well as a three-volume autobiography. *Memoirs of a Peon* (1965) was actually written in 1957-9, and at the time Sargeson thought of it as his 'literary last will and testament'. However, its publication proved to be the opening of a period of rich creativity. When he finished it he became increasingly aware of 'a new environment, one that was now appearing momentously different from what had served [him] well for literary material so far', and after a few years of near-total involvement in drama, he returned to fiction feeling 'a sudden interior pressure of a whole new mass and range of material for writing which [he] had never foreseen except perhaps very sketchily'.[9] Some of this new material was from that changed social environment, as in *The Hangover* (1967) and 'A Game of Hide and Seek' (in *Man of England Now*, 1972). Another part of his 'new range' was dealing with the survivors of the earlier society, beached high and dry in a new affluent age, as in 'Man of England Now' (1972), *Sunset Village* (1976), and *En Route* (1978). His third stratagem was to deal with the puritan past as a distant historical past, viewed with comic detachment, as he had done in *Memoirs of a Peon*; *Joy of the Worm* (1969) continues in this vein.

Ballantyne was another novelist who found a new subject in the changed society. After a decade's hiatus following *Sydney Bridge Upside Down* (1968), he dealt with a society utterly changed from the one of that novel in *The Talkback Man* (1978) and *The Penfriend* (1980). M.K. Joseph found new subjects in a different way, turning to a kind of philosophical future-fiction in *The Hole in the Zero* (1967) and *The Time of Achamoth* (1978), returning to a distanced World War II in *A Soldier's Tale* (1976), and moving into historical fiction with the posthumously published *Kaspar's Journey* (1988).

Several of the novelists who began writing in the 1950s have continued or resumed their career in this period. Frame, after *Scented Gardens for the Blind* in 1963, turned to a variety of new modes and subjects in an intensely prolific period from 1965 to 1972, producing five novels: *The Adaptable Man* (1965), *A State of Siege* (1966), *The Rainbirds* (1968), *Intensive Care* (1970) and *Daughter Buffalo* (1972). There was a long hiatus until *Living in the Maniototo* (1979), followed by her three volumes of autobiography, which ended with a promise that she would return to fiction: afterwards met by *The Carpathians* (1989). Duckworth, on the other hand, produced no novels for fifteen years after *Over the Fence is Out* (1969), her belated final Provincial novel, but began again in the 1980s with what is already a substantial second career: *Disorderly Conduct* (1984), *Married Alive* (1985), *Rest for the Wicked* (1986), *Pulling Faces* (1988) and

A Message From Harpo (1989). Watson similarly had a gap of ten years before she followed up *Stand in the Rain* with *The Balloon Watchers* in 1975, and has since added *The World is an Orange and the Sun* (1978) and *Address to a King* (1986).

Another group of novelists began to emerge in the early- to mid-1960s. Born (as Duckworth was) in the 1930s, but appearing in print rather later, these novelists became the first to be closely identified with Post-provincial themes. Maurice Shadbolt (born 1932) from the first defined himself as being 'in antagonistic reaction' to the Provincial themes, believing that 'New Zealand fiction was stuck in rather a rut; a rut running directly out of the 1930s', and wanting to leave off dealing with 'the country's puritan underside' in order to show something of contemporary society. His first novel (after several volumes of short fiction), *Among the Cinders* (1965), began as 'a pastiche of New Zealand writing', intended 'to turn some literary preconceptions about this country inside out or upside down', but 'this attempt to subvert our native orthodoxies and mythologies' became itself a novel. It was followed by several novels arising out of immediate personal experience, *This Summer's Dolphin* (1969) and *An Ear of the Dragon* (1971), and the novellas of *The Presence of Music* (1967). In 1972 Shadbolt published his synthesis to that point, *Strangers and Journeys*, a large novel incorporating some of his short fiction going back to 1956, his 'attempt to pull into the pages of one book an account of the New Zealanders [he] knew best, and the New Zealand [he] knew, in this 20th century'.[100] It was followed by two less ambitious novels, *A Touch of Clay* (1974) and *Danger Zone* (1975), then another synthesis, in a different key, the historical *The Lovelock Version* (1980), followed by two 'straight' historical novels, *Season of the Jew* (1986) and *Monday's Warriors* (1990). Supplementing the fiction with journalistic writing and with drama, Shadbolt has built an exemplary career as a professional writer.

Shadbolt's near-contemporary Maurice Gee (born 1931) began as a novelist a little earlier with a late-Provincial novel, *The Big Season* (1962), but did not establish himself as a full-time professional writer until later. His next three novels were all written within the intervals allowed by his career as librarian: *A Special Flower* (1965), *In My Father's Den* (1972), and *Games of Choice* (1976). With the trilogy of *Plumb* (1978), *Meg* (1981), and *Sole Survivor* (1983), he established himself as a major novelist and full-time writer, and continued with *Prowlers* (1987) and *The Burning Boy* (1990). Joy Cowley, another full-time writer (born 1936), came on the scene as novelist a bit later with *Nest in A Falling Tree* (1967), and followed it with *Man of Straw* (1970), *Of Men and Angels* (1972), *The Mandrake Root* (1975), and *The Growing Season* (1978). The other significant novelist to emerge in the 1960s was Graham Billing (born 1936). He began with *Forbush and the Penguins* (1965), followed by *The Alpha Trip* (1969), *Statues* (1971), *The Slipway* (1973), and *The Primal Therapy of Tom Purslane* (published 1980, but completed in 1973), but he has not to date established himself in the way that Shadbolt and Gee have. The 1960s and 1970s also saw the appearance of further novelists in the middlebrow area, many using elements of romance and melodrama to deal with significant themes. Some, such as Alice Glenday, Shona Michael, Brent Penberthy, or Jane Wordsworth, published only one or two novels, but others continued to publish without ever quite receiving recognition. Gordon Dryland published four novels between 1965 and 1977 while receiving only peripheral critical attention. Peter Bates published four between 1966 and 1973 (moving from late-Provincial to Post-provincial concerns) and William Taylor six between 1970 and 1974 without ever being noticed in any of the literary periodicals.

A rather larger group of novelists have emerged since 1970, indicating an increasing diversification. James McNeish (born 1931) and Philip Temple (born 1939) both began with nonfictional works and went on to write a range of very diverse novels as well as works in other genres. McNeish began with the historical myth *Mackenzie* (1970), following it up with the more literally historical *The Mackenzie Affair* (1972), several 'straight' novels, including *The Glass Zoo* (1976) and *Joy* (1982), and then the novelized 'autobiography' *Lovelock* (1986) and the novel of contemporary New Caledonian politics, *Penelope's Island* (1990). Temple began with two historical novels, *The Explorer* (1975) and *Stations* (1979), followed by the wildlife novel *Beak of the Moon* (1981) and the autobiographical *Sam* (1984). C.K. Stead (born 1932), Ian Wedde (born 1946) and Peter Hooper (born 1919) established themselves first as poets before turning to fiction. Stead's first novel, *Smith's Dream* (1971), was an important one, but he really came into his own as a novelist with two very different works in the 1980s, the metafictional *All Visitors Ashore* (1984) and *The Death of the Body* (1986), followed by *Sister Hollywood* (1989). Wedde's first extended fiction was the novella *Dick Seddon's Great Dive* (1976), followed ten years later by *Symmes Hole*, and then by *Survival Arts* (1988). Hooper began as a novelist rather later in his career, but made a substantial contribution with his future-fiction trilogy, *A Song in the Forest* (1979), *People of the Long Water* (1985), and *Time and the Forest* (1986). In the 1980s several other poets appeared to be moving into the novel: Elizabeth Smither (born 1941) published *First Blood* (1983) and *Brother-love Sister-love* (1986), Rachel McAlpine (born 1940) published *The Limits of Green* (1986), *Running Away from Home* (1987) and *Farewell Speech* (1990) and Mike Johnson (born 1947) made a striking debut as a novelist with *Lear* (1986), followed by *Antibody Positive* (1988).

An important aspect of the 1970s was the emergence of the first Māori novelists, Witi Ihimaera and Patricia Grace, both of whom had begun with short stories. Ihimaera (born 1944) was silent for a period after *Tangi* (1973) and *Whanau* (1974) to allow other Māori writers to emerge to present a more politicized vision, but he resumed writing in 1982, and in 1986 *The Matriarch* appeared, followed by a short novel *The Whale Rider* (1988). Patricia Grace (born 1939) published her first novel, *Mutuwhenua: The Moon Sleeps* in 1978, followed by *Potiki* (1986). In 1984 Keri Hulme joined them with *The Bone People*.

Hulme, Grace, McAlpine, and Smither are, of course, women novelists, and the predominance of women writers has been another feature of the novel in the 1970s and 1980s. Joining them (and Frame, Watson, Cowley, and Duckworth) as significant women novelists have been Margaret Sutherland, Fiona Kidman, Sue McCauley, Yvonne du Fresne, and Colleen Reilly. Sutherland (born 1941) appeared first, with *The Fledgling* in 1974, followed by *The Love Contract* (1976) and *The Fringe of Heaven* (1984), while Kidman (born 1940) has published *A Breed of Women* (1979), *Mandarin Summer* (1981), *Paddy's Puzzle* (1983), *The Book of Secrets* (1987) and *True Stars* (1990). McCauley (born 1939) has published *Other Halves* (1982) *Then Again* (1986) and *Bad Music* (1990); du Fresne (born 1929) *The Book of Ester* (1982) and *Frédérique* (1987), and Reilly *The Deputy Head* (1986) and *Christine* (1988).

*   *   *

The most obvious challenge faced by the Post-provincial novelists was to develop new themes and explanatory patterns to deal with the great social changes of the period. The problems can be seen most clearly in the first novels of Gee and Shadbolt, the novelists who have done most to define this cultural transition. Gee's *The Big Season* is a traditional Man Alone novel, confronting the rebellious young Rob Andrews with a small-town conformist culture of rugby, drinking, and small business for the males, marriage and motherhood for the females. As Copland pointed out, Gee is clear about what he opposes but not about an alternative, since 'The menace of the Welfare State is to leave our rebels without a cause'. Shadbolt, on the other hand, began *Among the Cinders* as a satire on 'the childhood-adolescence nonsense', the 'unnatural naturalism' of the novel of growing up puritan (he seems to have had *The God Boy* and *The Backward Sex* especially in mind). He also aimed satirical barbs at the attitudes towards the land and history identified with Curnow and exemplified by such a poem as 'The Unhistoric Story'. However, Shadbolt knew the Provincial mode so well that he ended up writing a kind of modified Provincial novel, Nick becoming a serious character as well as an instrument of satire, so that Shadbolt finally admitted that he 'tried to have [his] cake and eat it too'.[101]

An important feature of Shadbolt's novel was grandfather Hubert Flinders, a figure from the colonial period living on in a society which no longer had a place for him. Sargeson's aged survivors in *Sunset Village* and *En Route*, like Hubert, vigorously resist being marginalized, demonstrating that sexual activity is not the monopoly of the liberated young. However, some of the survivors of the puritan past place a dead hand on the present. Alan's mother in *The Hangover*, like her cottage 'an anomaly — something left over from last century',[102] imposes her sexual repression, joyless hard work, and narrowly utilitarian values on her son. Unable to integrate her values (internalized as the puritan conscience) with the joys of poetry and the Aladdin's Lamp of sexuality (both homosexual and heterosexual) that he encounters in the bohemian subculture around the university, he explodes spectacularly into multiple murder. Puritan Mum encloses Joy Cowley's middle-aged Maura Prince (in *Nest in A Falling Tree*) in a more genteel prison, and Maura's revolt comes in the quieter form of a doomed love affair with the coarse adolescent Red, followed by a decline into neurotic seclusion. As Red was an attempt at a way out for Maura, so is the crude Coralie for Donald Pinnock in Gee's *A Special Flower*, a prisoner of his mother's and his sister's lifeless gentility. When he cannot hold her, he chooses to die. Lydia, in Alice Glenday's *Follow, Follow* (1973), somewhat unconvincingly escapes from the dead hand of Mother, but it is Mother's ability to control everything from the most trivial to the most important aspects of her family's life that is the strongest force in the book.

Follow, Follow is built around the juxtaposition of Lydia's traumatic experience of ten years before with her present attempts to free herself. Another body of fictions juxtapose a somewhat more distant puritan past with a present to show the influence of one upon the other. John Summers's novella *Earthenware* (1977), a recycling of Sargeson's 'Old Man's Story', shows the protagonist's final stage of liberation from 'that sunday-school type' that he had been, as he moves beyond society's negative judgement of the old homosexual who had first encouraged him to step outside puritan patterns. Ellen Shaw, in Yolanda Drummond's *Meeting the Americans* (1983), likewise in the present finally comes to terms with her past, but the emphasis is on what has been lost through the agency of her puritan stepmother and respectable brother. Gee dealt with a similar theme in *In My Father's Den*, juxtaposing Paul Prior's puritan past, dominated by his self-righteous mother, to his seemingly liberated present. But Gee in this, his third novel, rises above the anti-puritan dualism of his earlier fiction in making Paul, the rebel Man Alone, recognize that his 'libertarian habits . . . were Presbyterian after all, by simple inversion. Everything took its tone from Mother'.[103] Paul arrives at escape, not liberation, and in the process young Celia Inverarity is destroyed by the interplay of Paul's 'libertarianism', his brother's bitter puritanism, and her father's narrow business values.

Both Drummond and Gee juxtapose a twenty-year-old past with the narrative present, with little attention to the area between. Another way to show the transition from the Provincial to the Post-provincial is to trace the curve of a life. Sargeson's 'Man of England Now' shows how Johnny, 'a thoroughly good person without any qualifications whatsoever',[104] lives varied New Zealand experiences, from scrub-cutter in the 1920s to 'Zone Caretaker' in a shopping centre in the 1960s, with an attitude of acceptance and responsibility, never receiving the rewards he deserves, his role always that of the exploited 'Men of England' of Shelley's poem. Kidman, in *A Breed of Women*, traces Harriet's life through a somewhat shorter time span: an unconscious victim of repressive puritanism and male domination in Northland in the 1950s, she becomes a naïve rebel against respectable racism in small-town Weyville, then a convert to late-1960s liberation in Wellington in 1968, and finally a somewhat compromised 'survivor' of the temptations of affluent society in the narrative present. Dryland's *Balloons* (1973), with rather less emphasis on social change, traces the waste of Max Jenner's life from his conformist puritan adolescence in 1940 to his loss of his family and finally of his life in the 1960s. William Taylor's *The Persimmon Tree* follows the unhappy life of Gerald Parrott, poisoned by a miserable childhood dominated by his parents' terrible puritan marriage, made worse by his own bad marriage, and contrasted to the success of his cynical and selfish younger brother, an accountant who is successful in the world of affluence from which Gerald is shut out.

Two first novels, Michael Henderson's *The Log of a Superfluous Son* (1975) and Lloyd Jones's *Gilmore's Dairy* (1986), take their protagonists through shorter time-spans (about ten years) in which the move from adolescence to independent young manhood is acted out against a background in which the same social and cultural transitions occur. Henderson shows Osgar Senney in 1965-6 freeing himself from the nets of a puritan father, a possible bourgeois marriage, and a government job that would require him to accept New Zealand's role in the war in Vietnam. Henderson sees contemporary New Zealand as inheriting an earlier conformism, but the conformity is now to a consumer rather than a puritan ethic, and the dependence is on America instead of England. Jones symbolizes change in Gilmore's Dairy, transformed from neighbourhood shop to video games parlour. His hero, Moss Tolley, rejects the change and finds his alternative values in the working-class provinciality represented by his mother and an old school friend. There is almost a nostalgia for the more innocent days of puritanism.

Although the time-spans of their fictions are very different, Sargeson, Kidman, Dryland, Taylor, Henderson, and Jones all focus on the development of a single character. Shadbolt and Gee, in two of the period's major works, widen the focus to trace social change through three generations. Shadbolt's *Strangers and Journeys* takes two families, the Freemans and the Livingstones, from 1919 to 1970. Despite his complaint about the 'rut' of Provincial writing, Shadbolt is strongest in dealing with the earlier period in terms established by Sargeson and Mulgan. In Part 1, Ned Livingstone's failure to achieve the Pastoral Dream on his King Country farm is effectively counterpointed by Bill Freeman's failure to carry out his Marxist dream of building in New Zealand 'the turrets and spires, the fountains and parks, of the just city',[105] with the two coming together briefly on opposite sides in the Queen Street riots in 1932. Part 2 traces the parallel but different revolts of the sons, Tim Livingstone and Ian Freeman, against their father's dreams, with the two coming together on the same side in the 1951 Waterfront confrontation. There is some falling off after the 'luminous' first section, but the book holds together to that point. However, when Shadbolt attempts to show the transition to contemporary New Zealand in the last two sections, the book comes to pieces. The focus is on Tim, whose friends try to force him into playing the cultural role of rebel visionary that they need from him (a theme Shadbolt first explored in the novellas 'The Voyagers' and 'The Presence of Music'), but the design will not contain all the material, so that in the end a successful Provincial novel is yoked to a mediocre Post-provincial one.

Gee's Plumb trilogy is a more successful attempt to trace several generations up to the narrative present (1982 in this case), but it also exhibits similar problems. The first two volumes, *Plumb* and *Meg*, are extremely successful, the first tracing George Plumb's development from the 1890s to 1949, the second his daughter Meg's from World War I to the 1950s. Plumb as radical public-spirited clergyman takes part in the great political and economic events and intellectual and social currents of his age, while Meg presents a domestic perspective. Each in a quite different way is a fully-realized character, more so than any in *Strangers and Journeys*, with their development structuring each novel while bringing into its orbit a rich and convincing range of secondary characters. It is with the third volume, *Sole Survivor*, that problems set in. Raymond Sole, Meg's son, is adequately realized as protagonist, although not fully-drawn, as is the case with Plumb and Meg, and his interplay as observer with his cousin Duggie Plumb, amoral manipulator and politician, structures the book adequately. However, the plot is forced, the social background skimpy and uncertain (Gee omits both the Vietnam War and the Springbok tour of 1981 in dealing with more recent political events), so that the synthesis of character, social setting, and plot which Gee achieves so well in the first two volumes breaks down. Like Shadbolt, Gee seems unable to deal with the contemporary setting as well as he does with earlier periods.

Other novels attempt to deal directly with aspects of contemporary society without going back to the transition from the Provincial. The drug culture that appears as part of the contemporary background in *Sole Survivor* is in the middle background in Stead's *The Death of the Body*, but from the supply rather than the consumption side, and is brought into the foreground as a political issue in Bates's *Old Men are Fools* (1970), and, more strikingly, at the end of Ballantyne's *The Pen Friend*, when the young reporter-protagonist discovers that what he thought were clues to UFOs were actually evidence of drug-smuggling. The culture of pop music, another feature of the time, is dealt with in Taylor's *The Mask of the Clown* (1970), where the lives of youthful Kiwi pop stars 'Kristal' and 'King William V' are contrasted with that of the ageing traditional showman 'The Great Marco'. The politics which provided a background in *Sole Survivor* and the last part of *Strangers and Journeys* are foregrounded in the period's few overtly political novels. In McNeish's *Joy*, the political point about the potential dangers of government exploitation of the conformity and political ignorance of the populace is at times almost buried in a complex narrative, in which historical figures and events (Dr G.M. Smith of the Hokianga, the prosecution of Dr W.B. Sutch) are oddly mixed with fantasy. More directly, Keith Ovenden's *Ratatui* (1984) deals with discreet corruption in domestic politics, while Billing's political thriller, *The Alpha Trip*, deals with the American alliance, as does Bates's *A Kind of Treason* (1973), more peripherally. Ovenden's second novel, *O.E.* (1986), Don Binney's *Long Lives the King* (1985), and Shadbolt's *Danger Zone* all deal with French nuclear testing in the Pacific.

In Shadbolt's novel the real 'danger zone' is human relations, not the nuclear testing area: in a society lacking a religious or political faith, or without the challenge of pioneering, personal relations are the primary source of meaning and the area of greatest potential pain. Most of the novels dealing with the Post-provincial Pākehā present focus on personal relations, with political and social issues in the background, as occurs with the Springbok tour in Duckworth's *Disorderly Conduct*. Patrick Evans, in a symposium in *Landfall* in 1977, constructed a hypothetical (and by implication nonexistent) 'major New Zealand novelist': 'someone whose novels accept that most of us live in suburbs and that our destiny, for better or worse, lies somewhere there; and that the people found in the suburbs are fit material for fiction, not as the blind monsters of some of the fiction we already have, but as human beings who may just have real limitations and aspirations'. A fair number of recent novelists seem to have been aiming to show something like that in focusing on the usually suburban middle-class Pākehā family. Several avoid stereotyping characters as 'blind monsters' while presenting rather sharply the break-up of a suburban family. John Thomson remarked of Gee's *Games of Choice* when it first appeared that 'It is a delight . . . to recognize suburban life of the sixties and seventies so sharply observed, so deftly and economically delineated.'[106] At the centre of the novel is Kingsley Pratt, caught between his working-class father who remembers the 1932 Queen Street riots, and his daughter, Miranda, born in the post-war age of affluence and at home in the brave new world of recreational drugs and sex and radical chic. At home nowhere, Kingsley arrives at painful self-knowledge, facing the implications of his choice, through the process of family break-up. Frame's *The Rainbirds*, very different in many ways, shows an even more painful break-up, more the result of social pressures than of personal choices, with Godfrey Rainbird victimized by an affluent, escapist society for possessing the forbidden knowledge of death.

Another group of novels deal with the near break-up of suburban marriages. Frank Neate's *The Hour-Glass Girl* (1966) plays with the theme of marital discontent but ends affirming suburban virtues. More ironically, Catherine McLeod's *Fortunately There was a Haystack* (1970) shows the upset brought to a North Shore world of adultery and the marriage market by a graceless daughter writing a successful book (until the daughter is brought back into the fold of hypocrisy and materialism by psychoanalysis, which cures her of any dangerous artistic tendencies). Billing's *The Primal Therapy of Tom Purslane* deals more intensely with extramarital sex as the result of a kind of demonic possession, and Stead's *The Death of the Body* makes adultery into anti-feminist comedy.

Most of these novels of marital difficulties are by men, and in all of them women are portrayed primarily as objects of desire and/or updated versions of the traditional mother-wife, guardians not of puritan virtues but of consumption and status. But there are other novels of the period, written by women, which show the strains in marital relationships from a woman's point of view. The earliest of these is Anne Mulcock's *Landscape with Figures* (1971), a novel dealing not with suburbia but with Courage's North Canterbury squirearchy, updated. The social constraints of a genteel late puritanism defeat Hester Carrington, the protagonist, although an uncertain narrative distance between implied author and character leaves unclear how much Hester is a victim, and how much she traps herself with her quixotic, self-destructive behaviour. In *The Love Contract*, Sutherland gives a detailed picture of a marriage in one of the new suburbs of West Auckland from the point of view of a trapped and frustrated wife. The approach is that of sympathetic realism, not satire, with Kate's search taken seriously, and with no melodramatic plot devices to force a climax. As Rachel Nunns states, the book is 'a valiant and generally successful attempt to show the pressures that suburban life imposes on that very institution upon which it depends for its existence'. However, although the dust jacket of the first edition indicated that the novel was to be the first in a sequence (and some characters are introduced who seem to require another volume before their relevance would be made clear), no sequel has followed, perhaps because too many readers may have agreed with Kirsty Cochrane's crticism that 'Kate's inadequacies and problems, which should involve us — there is nothing else to do it — are too boringly related to arouse a reader's sympathetic attention, despite the general accuracy of the picture'.[107]

Perhaps because of that problem of 'narrative interest', no other novelist has attempted as sober and unspectacular an analysis of a suburban marriage. Closest in its case-study approach is Alison Gray's *The Marriage Maze* (1979) (singled out, incorrectly, by Sue McCauley as 'the first New Zealand novel that looks at the *ennui* and isolation of suburban motherhood from a woman's point of view'), which sympathetically traces the movement of its protagonist from a puritan childhood and adolescence through an early and unsatisfactory marriage, into the difficult but freer life of a solo parent. More on the edge of society is Irene, in Watson's *The World is an Orange and the Sun*, who finds that life with two small children, even in the counter-culture, 'is sordid, sticky, there is no shine, no polish on it', as she rather enviously watches her older neighbour throw over her marriage and run off with a younger man.[108] Duckworth's *Rest for the Wicked* takes place in England rather than New Zealand, but the heroine has the same symptoms of entrapment: her recurring dreams are of suffocation or of being drowned with her children upon her back. However, her attempted escape with a lover turns to a nightmare, and she finds no way to reconcile her need to love and be loved with her need to have some freedom away from family pressures. Olive, the trapped housewife in Lisa Greenwood's *The Roundness of Eggs* (1986), sticks with her marriage but is driven over the edge by it into withdrawal and fantasy.

A related group of novels deals with refugees from marriage attempting to make new lives. Watson's Deirdre Pining, in *The Balloon Watchers*, has been so hurt by her failed relationship that she treats it as something that happened to someone else, but through her fellowship with the symbolic balloon watchers comes to accept herself and her past. Naomi Carter, in *Address to a King*, on the other hand, is learning how to recapture moments from her past marriage by a kind of Proustian recall, aestheticizing her own life. Rose, in Phyllis Gant's *The Fifth Season* (1976), another divorcee as Woman Alone, finds her life invaded by the unspeakable Ferdie, and is forced to assert herself and refuse the 'caring' role in order to get rid of him. Sophie, in Duckworth's *Disorderly Conduct*, is at the other extreme, a gregarious widow, survivor from the radical 1960s and 1970s, coping with the joys and frustrations of children, lovers, and ex-lovers. Olga, in Sutherland's *The Fringe of Heaven*, is another survivor of that era, an ageing solo mother who must learn to give up trying to take lame ducks under her wing. The focus of Sutherland's comedy of manners extends beyond Olga to show her children, her boarder, and her neighbours making their adaptations to a reality that falls short of their needs and their wishes. McCauley's focus is wider yet in *Then Again*, but not for the purposes of comedy. She deals with a whole group of fringe people, refugees from the 'rancorous and fearful' society of Auckland in 1984,[109] on 'Motuwairua' (Waiheke) Island. In the background are racism, economic exploitation and inequality, and the 1984 election with its nuclear and other issues; in the foreground is simmering sexual warfare, men against women and lesbians against heterosexuals. Her escapees from broken marriages conduct a desperate dance of relationships in which some reach an equilibrium, one is driven to suicide, and another ends trapped in an exploitive lesbian affair that will damage her and her children. The book emphasizes the theme of many of these novels — the difficulty of making and sustaining satisfying relationships in a confused, exploitive, rapidly changing society, with special emphasis on the harm done by bad parenting and the chain-reaction effect this has on other relationships.

Cowley in several of her novels deals with hurtful parent-child relationships, and also with sibling relations. *Man of Straw* shows the unintentional destruction of thirteen-year-old Ros Jonsson by her family, through the interplay of various acts of selfishness, irresponsibility, and indifference, so that the narrator can say that 'what happened, just happened, no blame, no fault unless one can talk of geological fault, a sort of subsidence that was an act of . . . an act of circumstance'.[110] There is more obvious blame in *The Mandrake Root*, for Elizabeth Stilwell is a victim of dominating parents and an exploitive drug-dealing brother who pushes her into incest, but she is able to fight through to a kind of liberation, aided by her counter-culture friends. *Of Men and Angels* deals with a different kind of 'family', when two female refugees from unsatisfactory relationships decide to raise a child. Although there is a rather anachronistic assumption that women can be fulfilled only with children, the novel does show how great has been the social change in this period, when the expectation of an illegitimate child can be read as a happy ending.

Sutherland's first novel, *The Fledgling*, also deals with the desire of an unmarried woman for a child, as the protagonist moves beyond trying to fill her life with another and learns to accept responsibility for her own freedom. In a sense both Sutherland's and Cowley's novels are about taking control of one's own life, but the means for doing this are quite different. Frame's *A State of Siege* is likewise about a single woman taking responsibility for her own life, a process which is given geographical and historical dimension, as it involves moving from the 'provincial, prejudiced, puritanical background' of her South

Island town to a new existence on an island in the Hauraki Gulf. Like Sutherland's Clodagh Pilgrim, Malfred Signal has finally been freed by the death of a parent and is attempting to make a new life for herself, to move from the state of being 'bound in someone else's dream, as she had read that some Eastern children had their limbs bound to set them in the shape desired by their parents and by tradition', to find a 'new View' that included her 'own essence, the pebble-core and simplicity of it'.[111] What she discovers, however, in her brave but doomed attempt, is that existence precedes essence, that we become what we do: there is no hidden essence or true self, but only the self we have made by our choices, even if the choices have been to act on someone else's choices. Her inward journey ends not in the discovery of a true essence but in the mystery of death. At the other extreme from Frame's tragic parable is Heather Marshall's light *A Nest of Cuckoos* (1985), in which a widow with grown children struggles through a series of problems like those of a television situation comedy, attempting to make an independent new life and to refuse the roles that her children and her well-meaning friends and neighbours would thrust upon her.

From Marshall's pleasant but superficial sketches to Frame's dark exploration of the unconscious, these domestic novels by women tend to focus on women. There is one notable exception: Colleen Reilly's *The Deputy Head*, which focuses on Henry George Williams, a humourless, repressed middle-aged schoolteacher who is a disaster to every woman in his life — his ex-wife, his grown-up daughters, and his female colleague who falls in love with him. However, most of the novels focusing on Men Alone are by men. Some, like Henry, come from broken marriages, Raymond Sole in *Sole Survivor* being a good example. Perhaps the most effectively drawn of these divorced males is Paul Pike in Shadbolt's *A Touch of Clay*, who runs away from the destruction of his own marriage, only to contribute to the destruction of a young woman through his fear of committing himself to any other relationship. Shadbolt's focus is considerably wider in the earlier *This Summer's Dolphin*, in which a diverse group of outsiders are briefly brought together by a 'visiting' dolphin before being returned to themselves to make the best of the burden of their existential freedom. Shadbolt's and Gee's lone males point to a real change in the Post-provincial writers in the handling of Man Alone figures: they are seen less as social victims than as agents responsible for the use they make of their existential freedom, and they are viewed with authorial criticism as well as sympathy. Often, like the protagonist of Edith Campion's novella 'The Chain' (1979), they are prisoners of their own self-made shackles and usually, like Harris, the ex-preacher seeking liberation in Brian Taylor's *The Other Shore* (1975), they are held responsible for their use of their existential freedom in an absurd and indifferent world, a theme most darkly explored in John Sligo's violent novel *The Cave* (1978). Ben Brown, the convict protagonist of Ken Berry's autobiographical *First Offender* (1980), is a less conscious existentialist, having more in common with the earlier Men Alone of McClenaghan. A more conscious Christian existentialist view underlies Bates's novels. The embittered late-Provincial Men Alone of *The Red Mountain* (1966, a belated World War II novel) and *Man Out of Mind* (1968) both learn to get beyond their bitter alienation and to choose solidarity, as does the adolescent protagonist of *Old Men Are Fools* (1970), although Harry Lash and John Coleridge in *A Kind of Treason* (1973) opt out of Cold War society in a 'Smith's Dream' gesture. Even the old-fashioned Man Alone hero of Ross Doughty's *End of the Circle* (1980), reminiscent of an Ayn Rand hero in his uncompromising stand against a corrupt town, has to accept responsibility for the unexpectedly violent results of his stand.

Billing especially has dealt with Men Alone viewed from an existentialist perspective that is both critical and sympathetic. The hero of *Forbush and the Penguins* is the least ambivalent of these Men Alone, arriving through his lonely experience in Antarctica at a kind of existential affirmation that all living things are victims of an indifferent natural process, but that 'human beings were free only if they knew', and asserted their knowledge with love and creativity in the face of indifference and absurdity. Duncan Bracken in *Statues* is more complex, repenting of the egotism that caused him to hurt others in the past, and making an obscure gesture of refusal to be tempted again. Geoffrey Targett in *The Slipway* is a more damaged individual, self-destructive in his alcoholism, but he makes a symbolic descent into his self-imposed Hell to retrieve 'his own lost soul', and finds the courage to give up the last vestige of his lost family grandeur, to make his gesture and take responsibility for his own life.[112] Ballantyne's Phil Rhodes in *The Talkback Man* is another alcoholic, haunted by past failures and, unlike Geoffrey, unable to save himself, although he at least goes down to defeat with dignity. Dryland's protagonist in *An Absence of Angels* (1965) is Man Alone as semi-Bohemian cynic; self-alienated, he fails the great test of his life when he cannot face up to the passionate (if absurd) spiritual search of his lover, but he is able finally to face himself, his own failures and limitations and their roots in his response to a puritan past (somewhat like Gee's Paul Prior, though not so clearly drawn).

Dryland, especially in the character of David Stanhope in *Multiple Texture* (1973), but also as a minor theme of *An Absence of Angels* and *Balloons* (1973), has dealt sensitively with the homosexual as Man Alone or as a person on the edge of society, as has Taylor in *The Persimmon Tree*. Barry Nonweiler in *That Other Realm of Freedom* (1983) focuses on homosexual relationships and shows his protagonist achieving a kind of existential salvation as he learns to recognize and accept his homosexuality, to give up his romantic dream of a perfect relationship and to accept the difficulties of responsible relationships to fallible fellow human beings in a complex and imperfect world. In contrast, the charming but weak pederast of Jeffery's *Cabin at Your Gate* (1973) is unable to come to terms with his compulsive behaviour; however, the true existential protagonist of the novel (a novel very different from Jeffery's earlier fiction) is the widowed narrator, who does achieve a kind of sad knowledge of herself through her relationship with him. Ivan, the homosexual narrator of Sargeson's 'A Game of Hide and Seek', is a different kind of Man Alone, fallible, a bit ridiculous, neither social victim nor self-destructive, viewed from a distant but humane and accepting comic perspective. Also viewed with a kind of sympathetic humour is the hapless protagonist of Stevan Eldred-Grigg's much slighter *Of Ivory Accents* (1977), an adolescent Man Alone who is not seen as a victim, while the Man Alone of J. Edward Brown's *The Glass Arm* (1982) is literally left adrift in a mad world, like the protagonist of Patrick Evans's even darker *Being Eaten Alive* (1980), who is left consuming himself in a mad consumer society.

Ivan, Phil Rhodes, and Malfred Signal are all failed or frustrated artists. Several other novels deal with the somewhat equivocal place of the artist in contemporary society, no longer the total outsider as in the past, maybe even too much at ease in Zion. The sculptor Hollinius in Dryland's *Balloons* is an old-fashioned Provincial artist, in whom 'the God-force . . . must constantly increase its efforts to make its statement and be acquitted', leading him to assert his creativity against an uncaring society and his own mortality. However, Dryland's Martin Baylis in *Curious Conscience* (1977) is much more the Post-provincial version (leading Belinda Robinson in the *Listener* to see him as 'proof positive that the New Zealand novel has come of age'),[113] a compromised Man Alone who escapes the pain of his own life and the challenge of his creativity in writing detective novels. Shadbolt's Frank Firth in *An Ear of the Dragon* also takes the easy way out, becoming a facile culture commentator instead of creative artist. Smither's Angus in *Brother-love Sister-love* keeps his independence by thumbing his nose at the wealthy who would patronize him. Smither's intention is comic and satiric, whereas Graeme Lay is serious in his somewhat implausible literary thriller, *The Mentor* (1978), with the protagonist's betrayal of the Sargesonian writer James Patterson perhaps dramatizing a guilty sense that the contemporary writer has had it too easy compared to his alienated elders.

Nigel Cox returns to the image of the artist as Man Alone in his *Waiting for Einstein* (1984), but as one who chooses such a role in an affluent society in order to cultivate a vision of new personal and environmental relationships. His Lawrentian search for a mode of sexual relationship beyond 'that old, totally bonded together way'[114] places him as a survivor of the 1970s counter-culture. Sue Freeman's *Fat Chance* (1982) deals superficially from the woman's point of view with a rather casual attempt to form such a counter-culture relationship, as does B.V. Bell's *Hôtel des Voyageurs* (1983) from the man's perspective, while Wedde's *Dick Seddon's Great Dive* deals at greater depth with the tragic failure of such a relationship, resulting in suicide. Wedde's novel raises questions about how to live life to the full spontaneously, intensely, taking risks — without exploiting or destroying others and burning out the self — but it leaves them as questions. It is really an elegy to the counter-culture of the late 1960s and early 1970s, a look backwards rather than a hopeful anticipation of the future like *Waiting for Einstein*.

From the suburbs to the counter-culture fringe, all of the novels discussed so far have dealt almost exclusively with Pākehā society. However, Māori society, both in its relation to Pākehā society and in its own inner development, has been an important concern of both Pākehā and Māori writers. Some novels have focused on Pākehā–Māori sexual relations, such as Jane Wordsworth's *Four Women* (1972) and *Reunion* (1975), which deal rather superficially with interracial marriage from a liberal Pākehā point of view, or Brent Penberthy's *The Shallow End* (1972), less hopeful, showing how the very process of making a film about an interracial marriage brings its ruin. William Taylor has returned to the theme of interracial sexual relations several times. It is a minor theme in *Pieces in a Jigsaw* (1972), where the gang-rape murder of the Māori girl, Alana Kingi, is but one consequence of the unhappy adolescence of the bitter, unloved, but ultimately redeemable protagonist. It is the central theme in *Episode* (1970) and *Chrysalis* (1974). The first deals with the rescue of its hurt Pākehā protagonist by a relationship with an understanding Māori woman, the second with the failure of a Pākehā teacher in his attempts to save an abused, street-wise Māori girl. Finlayson's novella, 'Jim and Miri', from *Other Lovers* (1976), connects an interracial marriage with the land issue. Joan Rosier-Jones in *Cast Two Shadows* (1985) also makes such a connection. Emma (of Dalmatian/Māori birth), is moved by the Bastion Point confrontation of 1978 to accept and act on her Māori identity — the crucial part of accepting responsibility for herself as a woman — and in the process she breaks out of a suburban marriage which offers her only a false and reductive role. The Pākehā protagonist of McCauley's *Other Halves* moves from a failed suburban marriage to begin to discover herself and her society in a sexual relationship with a Māori street kid. Grace's *Mutuwhenua: The Moon Sleeps* (the only one of these novels of interracial relations to be written by a Māori) addresses the harder questions of bi-culturalism: the Pākehā husband must learn to accept not only his Māori wife's sense of tapu but also her sense of whanau, which leads her to give their first child to her widowed mother to raise.

The other novels by Māori authors deal less with personal relationships and more with the survival of the Māori community and Māori culture within a Pākehā-dominated world. Ihimaera's earlier 'pastoral' novels, *Tangi* and *Whanau*, were written, he has said, 'with three purposes: the 'first priority' being to help communicate the nature of their Māori heritage to young urban Māori, 'the ones who have suffered most from the erosion of the Maori map'; the 'second priority' being to communicate to Pākehā that 'cultural difference is not a bad thing and that, in spite of the difference, [they] can incorporate the Maori vision' into their own personalities; and the third, to make all New Zealanders 'aware of the tremendous value in Maori culture and of the tragedy for them should they continue to disregard this part of their dual heritage'. Central to all three purposes is a focus on 'the landscapes of the heart, the emotional landscapes which make Maori people what they are', seen especially in the love for father and for whānau in *Tangi* and in the aroha felt in the community's search for its kaumātua in *Whanau*. However, the struggles of Tama's family in *Tangi*, as well as his own move to the city, show some of the difficulties of retaining a Māori culture, while in *Whanau* there is much more evidence of cultural decline than there is of renewal, despite the obvious intention to emphasize the latter. Ihimaera later analysed the underlying faith of these 'pastoral' novels as the belief that 'even if all the land were taken away, our maraes razed, our children turned into brown pakehas . . . nothing could take away the heart, the way we feel'. However, he went on to say that an emergent 'political reality assumed a higher profile', a political reality of 'hardening of attitudes on both sides. Of inflexibility. Of infighting'. It is this political reality that Ihimaera turned to after his ten-year hiatus, in the present-day sections of *The Matriarch*. The focus there is more on the infighting, part of the Matriarch's ambiguous legacy to Tamatea, but it is clear that her goal for him is to 'become a Pakeha, think like him, act like him and, when you know you are in his image then turn your knowledge to his destruction'.[115] How Tamatea will deal with this charge is still unclear at the end of *The Matriarch*, and a promised second volume has yet to appear.

While Tamatea has not yet been shown undertaking the political battle with the Pākehā world, Grace in her second novel, *Potiki*, shows a skirmish in that battle (a skirmish in that although there is a Māori victory, the book ends with a shadowy prediction of more desperate battles to come). Pākehā society is seen only from within the Māori community, in the person of 'Mr Dollarman' and his enterprises: 'Dollarman' is unable to appreciate any values but the economic and the individualistic, blind to the Māori sense of land, community, history, myth, and ritual, and willing to use any methods to gain economic goals. If it is a melodramatic vision of Pākehā society, it is one that is supported both by current actions and by past history:

Money and power, at different times and in many different ways, had broken our tribes and our back, and made us slaves, filled our mouths with stones, hollowed the insides of us, set us at the edge and beyond the edge, and watched our children die.[116]

What is seen from within in the novel (more fully than in any of Ihimaera's fiction) is the Māori community, its roots in myth and ritual, its relation to the natural cycle of the seasons and of birth and death, its inclusiveness and its determination to fight to hold on to the bit of land and heritage that it still retains.

Myth is important to *Potiki* (with Toko incorporating elements of both Maui and Christ), and it is central to those novels that attempt to point beyond cultural battles to a bicultural future. Robert de Roo's *The Eye of the Thorn* (1984), the first part of a planned trilogy, uses the night journey of its Māori and Pākehā protagonists and their encounter with Moana, the goddess figure, to point towards a new 'New Zealand mind or identity . . . created from both the Maori and European heritages', but it succeeds primarily in creating the present hell of racial tensions and self-indulgence and competing ideologies, the road to the future not clear but existing only as myth and dream. Hulme's *The Bone People* succeeds much more on a personal level, presenting intensely and convincingly the painful personal struggles of its three protagonists. However, it loses credibility when it takes off into myth (Simon, like Grace's Toko, is a foundling incorporating something of Christ and Maui), first to resolve the personal struggles and then to gesture vaguely towards a future beyond sexual and racial categories, its central trio becoming 'the bone people', 'the people who make another people', 'the heart and muscles and mind of something perilous and new, something strange and growing and great', 'the waves of future chance'.[117] The positive values remain primarily symbol and adjectival assertion, whereas the intense joy and suffering of personal interaction are vividly realized, as they are in Hulme's two short stories dealing with triangular adult-child-adult relationships, 'Hooks and Feelers' and 'Nightsong of the Shining Cuckoo'.

While the Post-provincial novel has had much to say about the situation of the tangata whenua, it has also dealt with newcomers, recent immigrant groups from areas other than the British Isles. The protagonist of Albert Wendt's *Sons for the Return Home* (1973), son of a Samoan immigrant family, becomes a new kind of Man Alone as, alienated both from the New Zealand society which will not accept him and the Samoan society he can no longer accept, he returns to New Zealand at the end of the novel, asserting, like Camus' Sisyphus, his painful existential freedom. The protagonist of T. F Dorman's *The Islander* (1974), on the other hand, returns to Samoa to try to rebuild his life after his stay in New Zealand ends in disastrous violence (as had occurred in *Sons for the Return Home*), in contrast to the Rarotongan family of J. Edward Brown's condescending comedy *The Luck of the Islands* (1963), who return home triumphantly after succeeding all too well in New Zealand. Much more inward is the struggle of du Fresne's Ester in *The Book of Ester* as she searches back to her Danish and Huguenot roots in order to 'steady' her grip on New Zealand after the death of her husband in a car accident. More externally and superficially, with an emphasis more on the past, Jye Kang's *Guests of the New Gold Hill* (1984) deals with the Chinese immigrant experience, while Amelia Batistich's *Another Mountain, Another Song* (1981) deals with a Dalmatian girl's assimilation into New Zealand in the 1930s.

Craig Harrison's *Ground Zero* (1981) reverses the emigrant experience, counterpointing the English experience of Bradford-born Joe Chapman with that of his New Zealand mate Koro Ngati, as both discover in England that they belong in New Zealand. That issue is never in doubt in Smither's *Brother-love Sister-love*, which treats Isobel's visit to England as just that — a visit to an interesting place, not an experience of 'Home'. Sue Freeman's *Wales on a Wet Friday, I Cried in my Do-nut* (1982) takes its Kiwi alternative-lifestyle heroine through a series of casual relationships in England and Wales, while Barbara Ewing's *Strangers* (1978) records the more unsettling experience of its Australian heroine in London when she falls in love with a Black South African political activist and has an abortion rather than present him (and herself) with the political and social difficulties of a child. McNeish's *The Glass Zoo* and Ian Middleton's *Faces of Hachiko* (1984) focus on New Zealanders' discovery of the human deficiencies of other cultures through their work within those cultures

— the first showing the waste of the 'hidden intelligent' student in the English school system, the second the tyrannical power of family and business over private lives in Japan. Stephanie Dowrick's *Running Backwards Over Sand* (1985) is a kind of contemporary feminist updating of a Provincial novel of expatriation such as *The Sullen Bell*, showing its heroine, a refugee from a Catholic version of a New Zealand puritan upbringing, learning to deal with her own needs and her past in the sophisticated societies of London and Berlin in the 1960s. Ovenden's *O.E.* is the only one of these overseas New Zealand novels to deal explicitly with the cultural meaning of the experience indicated by its title, seeing such experience as a necessary means of discovering what is missing from New Zealand, not a 'matter of national identity or of growing up' so much as 'the act of becoming complete'.[118]

If this period is rich in depictions of contemporary New Zealand society and people, it is also rich in historical novels, for an important part of the contemporary consciousness is an awareness of the New Zealand past as history, with its own myths, dreams, and disappointments (the previous period itself increasingly seen as part of that history). Some of the historical novels about the nineteenth century and earlier continue earlier traditions of historical fiction, although with different emphases, especially in dealing with the Māori past. Brian Mackrell's *Only the Land Endures* and Barry Mitcalfe's *Moana* (both 1975) continue the tradition of Maori romance, the first dealing with the pre-European period, the second with the period of culture-contact. Heretaunga Pat Baker's *Behind the Tattooed Face* (also 1975) gives a more realistic, less melodramatic picture of a Māori society just before Cook's arrival, and K.W. Ritchie's *From the South* (1972) deals with the contact of the Murihiku Māori with the first European sealers. Laurence Jackson's *Mana* (1969) is more traditional and melodramatic in dealing with the early period of European settlement, but treats Māori pain from loss of land more sympathetically than do earlier romances. More interesting are two quite different novels dealing with Māori-Pākehā interaction in the Otaki area in the age of Te Rauparaha and Te Rangihaeata. The first, June Mitchell's *Amokura* (1978), stresses the individual impressions and experience of its narrator, a Māori woman married to a Pākehā trader. The second, Ray Grover's *Cork of War* (1982) is narrated by such a trader, but emphasizes public history rather than private experience. Each shows in a different way the destructive impact of Pākehā land-greed on Māori society.

Traditional historical novels of pioneering continue to be written in the period, as in Ivy Hutchinson's *Forbidden Marriage* (1971), on the Thames and Coromandel area, or Iris Nolan's *Bells for Caroline* (1986), on the Norse settlement in Hawke's Bay. Philip Temple's two novels of South Island pioneering, *The Explorer* and *Stations*, are more toughly realistic in showing the struggle with powerful and indifferent nature. Smither's *First Blood* focuses more on human relations in early New Plymouth, showing the interaction of a variety of human causes behind the new colony's first murder. Smither's and Temple's historical novels, purging the genre of romance and melodrama

187

without falling into documentary chronicle, are noteworthy accomplishments, but are not as significant as those which radically reinterpret dominant historical myths and attitudes. One such is McNeish's *Mackenzie*, which questions the myth of the Pastoral Dream and offers a counter-myth. The questioning of the Pastoral Dream comes through the more conventional panoramic historical novel of the first section, 'The Station', in which Amos Polson's idealistic dream of a homeland for the dispossessed Māori is played off against the greed of the squatters and the town businessmen. The counter-myth is established in the symbolic quest narrative of the second section, 'The Journey', in which the historical Mackenzie is daringly reinterpreted not as a folk-hero who democratizes the Pastoral Dream but rather as the archetypal quest-hero who brings back a religious vision of the land and the Life Force which his society (and the corrupted Māori) reject. Thus McNeish uses Mackenzie as the central figure in a kind of myth-history of South Island Pākehā settlement. Its re-enactment of the Fall (the curse put on Pākehā settlement from the beginning) is analogous to the historical myth constructed for North Island settlement in Cross's *After Anzac Day*. McNeish's other treatment of Mackenzie, *The Mackenzie Affair*, is a kind of footnote, a semi-documentary but basically novelistic account of the historical Mackenzie, showing how his society projected its own needs and values onto the interpretation of his story.

Shadbolt, who had dealt with the historical myths of the recent past so well in *Strangers and Journeys*, and had vividly evoked the nineteenth century in the grandfather's diary in *A Touch of Clay*, took a quite different approach in *The Lovelock Version*, playing narrative games in a kind of New Zealand version of Gabriel Garcia Marquez's *One Hundred Years of Solitude*, with his tongue-in-cheek account of one hundred years of the Lovelock family in New Zealand (1860-1960). In the process he presents comic versions of the failures of the dreams of the three Lovelock brothers for 'peace' (the Pastoral Dream), 'perfection' (the dream of the Just City), and 'profit' (the dream of El Dorado), and incorporates references to historical figures and events from Mackenzie to George Wilder, from the death of Von Tempsky to Chunuk Bair. In *Season of the Jew*, New Zealand's most powerful historical novel to date, Shadbolt takes history straight again, using the story of itinerant soldier-artist George Fairweather to present a revisionist version of the Te Kooti rebellion and its aftermath in which no one comes off well, neither the greedy Pākehā settlers, nor the ambitious and ruthless Te Kooti, nor the State which indulges in the cynical judicial killing of Hamiora Pere. The comparison with Brathwaite's historical trilogy is illuminating, for while Brathwaite allows no simple judgement, he none the less ends at a position not far from Satchell's or James Cowan's, while Shadbolt's vision is altogether darker and more ironic.

Ihimaera, in the central historical section of *The Matriarch*, 'The Song of Te Kooti', offers a more radically revisionist reinterpretation than Shadbolt. Te Kooti's life is set in the framework of a larger pattern of myth-history, from the Creation, through the pre-European Māori millenium and the Pākehā invasion, to the present decline of Māori culture. Te Kooti's career is set in this framework so that his actions at Matawhero are interpreted as a 'retaliation', not a 'massacre'. The parliamentary career of Wi Pere is seen as a continuation of Te Kooti's battle by political means, and the Matriarch continues his battle and prepares Tamatea to take part in it, with Rongopai the painted meeting-house as the symbol of the retention of Māori identity, the source of 'the strength to recreate the Maori nation'.[119]

Much of the effect of *The Matriarch* comes from the layering of time, the playing off of different pasts with different narrative presents. Two other historical novels of the time depend similarly on the counterpointing of past and present: Binney's *Long Lives the King* and Wedde's *Symmes Hole*. In the first, the defeat of the absurd but generous and expansive George de la Roche (a fictionalized de Thierry) by narrowminded British puritan colonialism is counterpointed with the experiences of his descendants in the present. *Symmes Hole* is a much more complex book, counterpointing the narrator-Researcher's mock-epic journeys in the present with stories of those he is studying in the past: primarily James Heberley's search for a home in the New Zealand of the 1830s, but also Herman Melville's formative experiences in the South Pacific at the same time. Beneath the sometimes comic surface of Wedde's novel is a binary view of history involving a radical historical revisionism. On one side are ranged the 'successes', the people who get the attention of the historians and the accountants — the Wakefields, the United States navy, or Ray Kroc of McDonald's, the people of power and consumption and imperialism; on the other side are the 'failures', those who, like Heberley or Melville or, in a comic way, the Researcher, see the futility and ultimate destructiveness of 'success' and opt out, resisting in their own ways, perpetuating an anarchistic kind of life.

The nineteenth century is the focus of these historical fictions by Wedde, Ihimaera, Shadbolt, and McNeish. There is also a group of novels that focus on the earlier parts of the twentieth century as history. Eric Beardsley's *Blackball 08* (1984) is an ambitious attempt to evoke the mining community of Blackball on the West Coast at the time of the famous strike, the events framed by the sad comments of an ageing Bob Semple, looking back on the strike from the disillusioning perspective of the society of fretful sleepers of the 1950s: 'We killed poverty and the revolution never came.'[120] More joyful and less concerned with public history are Sargeson's two novels of the early twentieth century, *Memoirs of a Peon* and *Joy of the Worm*. The former presents the mock-heroic adventures of Michael Newhouse, an absurdly out-of-place Casanova in puritan New Zealand of 1900-22. The latter follows the comic adventures of James and Jeremy Bohun in rural North Island during the same period, both utterly out of place in their society because of their excessive sexuality and intellectuality.

The period of the Depression and World War II has increasingly become the object of historical, or at least consciously retrospective, 'period' fiction for later writers. As might be expected, there are some autobiographical novels by writers born in the 1920s or earlier, looking back on childhood or adolescence in the 1930s. James Sutherland's *The Elver* (1978), Marshall's *Second-hand Children* (1984), Batistich's *Another Mountain, Another Song*, and, more intensely, Gant's *Islands* (1973) all deal with the experience of growing up in the Depression (the last being set in Melbourne). Ian Middleton's *Pet Shop* (1979) and Temple's *Sam* deal with adolescence in Auckland and childhood in England during World War II, the latter being notable for its sensitive evocation of the child's confusions and needs, while McLeod's *Dorinda* (1967) deals with the protagonist's painful adolescence in relation to her charming yet ultimately destructive mother in post-war Auckland. The best of these novels of the homefront is Kidman's *Paddy's Puzzle*, in which the protagonist's passionate assertion of self against death and repression is contrasted to her older sister's sacrifice of self to 'respectability'. The war itself is dealt with in Shadbolt's *An Ear of the Dragon*, in which Pietro Fratta's experiences with the Fascists and Partisans in Italy (based on Renato Amato's) are vividly re-created, and in Joseph's *A Soldier's Tale*, in which a contemporary narrator imaginatively re-creates a haunting and appalling story of love and war that had been told to him by a fellow soldier in 1944. Elspeth Sandys in *Love and War* (1982) deals more conventionally both with the home front (with its conscientious objectors and its patriots) and with the war with the New Zealand division in Egypt, Greece and Crete.

When Dryland's *A Multiple Texture* (1973) first appeared it raised from reviewer Len Wilson the 'uneasy question' whether the choice of a 1950s setting was to indulge 'the author's tendency to patronise'. However, in retrospect it can be seen as the first New Zealand novel to treat the 1950s as (like the war) something finished, a different age. Dryland's historical point was that the easygoing, unambitious, unpuritanical Wallace (17 in 1957) is the wave of the New Zealand future; as Elsa (the alienated expatriate Provincial intellectual) observes, he is 'entirely adapted', one of a new generation, unlike hers, who 'have achieved their environment'; Barton Hollinbroke, the Provincial poet, agrees. Poet Lauris Edmond, in her first novel, *High Country Weather* (1984), has her protagonist looking back on her experience of thirty years before, judging a younger self engaged in an abortive extramarital affair, although even the later judgement has a 1950s feel to it, emphasizing commitment and responsibility rather than romantic ideals of 'happiness'. Stead, in *All Visitors Ashore*, on the other hand, exploits to the full the thirty-year gap between Curl Skidmore, the young hero, and Curl's older self, looking back on his younger self with what Stead has called 'a kind of avuncular detachment and irony'.[121] Hunger for O.E., an enthusiastic rebellion against puritanism, the satirical art of 'Melior Farbro' (Sargeson transposed into a painter), the intense inward art of 'Cecelia Skyways' (the young Frame fictionalized), Skidmore's own vague ambitions, a backstreet abortion, Prime Minister Holland, and the 1951 Waterfront confrontation — all are viewed from a distance, vividly re-created, but placed as 'period' experiences.

From the straight critical realism of the historical sections of *Strangers and Journeys* to the ironic metafiction of *All Visitors Ashore*, many of the finest novels of the period have been at least in part historical. The range of accomplishment — including such works as the Plumb trilogy, *The Lovelock Version*, *Season of the Jew*, *The Matriarch*, *Memoirs of a Peon* and *Joy of the Worm*, *A Soldier's Tale* and *Symmes Hole* — is remarkable.

In future fiction (at the other extreme from historical fiction) there has also been some fine work. A genre which previously flourished only for a brief time at the turn of the century has undergone a renaissance. One group of future fictions, mostly satirical and/or political in emphasis, has extrapolated trends into the near future. The best known is Stead's *Smith's Dream*, a straightforward 'it could happen here' account of the 'Vietnamization' of New Zealand after economic collapse, a resultant dictatorship, guerilla opposition, and American involvement in counter-insurgency warfare. Rather less convincing, *Broken October* (1975) draws on the same elements from 1932, 1951, and Vietnam for a similar political situation, but adds a racial element, making the guerilla movement Māori. On the other side politically is Norman Harvey's *One Magpie for Sorrow* (1967), which posits a Chinese invasion, and soon develops into a predictable Cold War political thriller. McAlpine's *The Limits of Green* involves foreign intervention again, from 'RUSA', and projects the Think Big programme of the early 1980s into a future in which the society of fretful sleepers (the 'Sleeping Islands') allows the economic and military imperialists to build not only a nuclear power station and pesticide plants, but also a secret base for missile guidance and for chemical weapons, before they are defeated by the liberated heroine and her ecologist lover, who have Nature on their side. Colin Gibson's *The Pepper Leaf* (1971) involves a rather darker view of human nature, as an off-key *Lord of the Flies* is re-enacted in a post-1984 New Zealand that is hit by a major earthquake rather than nuclear war, with the stresses on an isolated group bringing out 'the turbulent slimy mire within themselves where they had never thought to reach' (the novel must be the last in a long line to include a reversion to savagery on the part of a Māori character).[122] Harrison's *The Quiet Earth* (1981) posits a post-catastrophe New Zealand in which the only two survivors are a Māori carrying with him the guilt of participation in a Vietnam massacre, and a paranoid Pākehā scientist whose mad revenge scheme has caused the catastrophe. Less apocalyptic is Vincent O'Sullivan's *Miracle: A Romance* (1976), a playful satire in which the primary targets are rugby as the national religion, the sexual contradictions of a residually puritan culture, and political subservience to the United States. Deadly serious is Adrian Hayter's *A Man Called Peters* (1977), which moves from fictionalized autobiography into a future in which the Man Alone hero overcomes his corrupt New Zealand affluent society and leads the way to a brave new future of Jungian integration and individual fulfilment.

Three other fictions of the near future are less fanciful. Duckworth in *Married Alive* imagines a New Zealand of the late 1980s in which a faulty vaccine has caused an epidemic of instant insanity, accelerating the breakup of close personal relationships. Bob Jones's *The Permit* (1984) is more a straight didactic fiction, imagining a New Zealand in which state power has become more concentrated, so that the libertarian, individualist hero is ground under. Russell Haley's *The Settlement* (1986) is a much more substantial novel, but shares the postulate of a centralized, totalitarian state against which the free individual makes his gesture of protest.

The most impressive of these future fictions, and one of the major novels of the period, is Frame's *Intensive Care*. The novel looks back as far as 1918 and ahead to the twenty-first century after a nuclear war has destroyed the North Island. It moves from the individual tragedies of Tom Livingstone and his grandson Colin Torrance, who impose their dreams on others and then strike out when the dreams are not realized, to the social tragedy represented by Milly Galbraith, declared a 'non-human' and sacrificed to the dream of recovering affluence after nuclear war. In Frame's world, not only do 'all dreams lead back to the nightmare garden' of personal need and pain,[123] but forward also to a social nightmare when the attempt to impose the dream on reality results in war and destruction. *Intensive Care* is the darkest as well as the most powerful of these future fictions.

Johnson's *Lear* is another dark and powerful post-catastrophe fiction. Against the background of a world fallen into barbarism and suffering from a terrible AIDS-like plague, a travelling theatrical company that carries within it both the hopes and the sickness of its society acts out a version of *King Lear* that becomes nightmarishly real. Sandi Hall and Lora Mountjoy's radical feminist future fictions are less dark, more hopeful. Hall's *The Godmothers* (1982) interweaves action from a Toronto feminist group in the near future with that from a feminist communications group of 2095; the common thread is the movement of the world away from a hierarchical, competitive, war-and-business society run by men ('conceited, arrogant, prick-driven' in the words of one of the characters) towards a new society informed by radical feminist values in tune with the Life Force, the Great Mother (women are 'the vessel and its water, the source of life, the bearer of the flame, the guardian of the flesh through which the spirit wells').[124] Mountjoy's *Deep Breathing* (1984), another didactic moral melodrama but with less narrative drive and moral energy, is set in a post-catastrophe New Zealand and deals with the education of its central character into bisexual radical feminist values. Its concept of a tribal, post-catastrophe New Zealand is also central to Hooper's much more substantial Tama trilogy, which traces the development of its hero from young nonconformist to priest to dying visionary outcast, in relation to his own male-dominated hunting society and the neighbouring gentler pastoral society. Although the trilogy contains tragic elements of culture clash and human error and waste, Hooper's vision is not as dark as Frame's or Johnson's, for the wisdom that Tama finally attains persists although it does not prevail.

Joseph's two future fictions are closer to the science fiction tradition than any of those discussed so far, but like Hooper's involve a strong philosophical element. *The Hole in the Zero* is a space fiction, but involves a philosophical fantasy of alternative worlds based on alternative premises. *The Time of Achamoth* is time-machine fiction, with scenes set in the past, the near future, and many forward futures, most of which are used to point towards Joseph's relatively conservative religious and political views. Philip Mann's future fictions, *The Eye of the Queen* (1983) and the duo that make up 'The Story of the Gardener' (*The Master of Paxwax*, 1986, and *The Fall of the Families*, 1987), are likewise strongly philosophical, but without the Christian colouring. They present a strong attack on humanist hubris.

Joseph's Christianity, although it surfaces only occasionally, is a strong implicit element in both his 'straight' novels and his future fiction, and sets him off from most of the other novelists of the time. However, although there is little overtly religious fiction (Michael Brown's *The Weaver's Apprentice* of 1986, with its focus on the doctrine of transmigration of souls, is an exception), an implicit non-Christian religious structure of feeling underlies the work of a significant minority of contemporary novelists. The statement of Hooper's Tama that 'all is open to us only if we would open ourselves to the All' of which we are a part is like that of McNeish's Mackenzie when he states 'I am in God'; similar insights come to de Roo's Simon when he feels 'the pulse of life, the exuberant energy of it, the dance of it', or to Ihimaera's Tamatea when he feels that 'he was in the universe and the universe was in him', or to Grace's Toko when he speaks from his 'now knowing as if everything is now'.[125] Especially in the writers influenced by Jung, such as McNeish, de Roo, and Hooper, in radical feminist writers such as McAlpine, Hall, and Mountjoy, and in the Maori writers there are assumptions about the Life Force, the cycle of birth and death, and the human relation to it, often presented through myth and symbol.

A dark version of this religious vision underlies Frame's fiction. There is a strong sense of the Life Force and of the cycle of birth and death, but it is death that is emphasized, and the human place within the system is felt as frightening because of the Life Force's indifference to human consciousness and human values, as in Godfrey Rainbird's terrifying vision of the grass: once he had been aware of being at one with it in the sexual act, 'the grass-heads knocking, shaking, leaning so intimately upon him and Beatrice as they leaned upon each other, grass and bodies intent on crushing and being crushed'; but after his 'death education', he is most aware of 'the writing of the grasses that could not distinguish between life and death, that would wave against your cheek, eavesdrop on your thoughts with the same sparkle and grace as they waved across your dead body or found a path through your flesh to the sky and sun; in all innocence'.[126] This dark vision is frightening but necessary; technological society tries to avoid recognizing it, but wisdom and humility, if not salvation, lie in accepting it, as Turnlung learns in *Daughter Buffalo*.

Despite this strong religious undercurrent, New Zealand novels remain primarily expressions of what James K. Baxter called 'our determinedly secular culture'. The dominant structure of feeling beneath the novels is a continuation of that existentialism that first began to appear clearly in the 1950s, the assumption that human beings live in an absurd universe with no religious significance, and that meaning is something one makes for oneself by exercizing one's existential freedom and choosing commitment and responsibility.

Sometimes it is implicit, as in Gee's fiction; sometimes it surfaces explicitly, as occasionally in Billing's or Shadbolt's. A feminine (if not always feminist) version of this liberal, agnostic existentialism runs through the work of writers as diverse as Edmond, Sutherland, or Kidman, appearing most succinctly in the flippancy of Sophie in Duckworth's *Disorderly Conduct*: 'What she suffers from is the human condition, no less . . . . Life is a sexually transmitted terminal disease.' As Gee's Raymond Sole concludes, 'Get on with it.'[127]

*   *   *

Most of the writers expressing an agnostic, existential structure of feeling operate within the mode of critical realism, as set by Sargeson, Mulgan, Ballantyne, and Cross, although they extend its boundaries. Some of the extensions are simply stylistic, as Sargeson himself showed in the opening up of his style in *Memoirs of a Peon* and *Joy of the Worm*. Another extension is in the handling of time. Many of the novelists move back and forth between different chronological layers, perhaps most effectively in Gee's *In My Father's Den* and Shadbolt's *A Touch of Clay*. There is a complementary cutting back and forth in space to capture a group or community, as in Sargeson's *Sunset Village*, Shadbolt's *This Summer's Dolphin*, and Sutherland's *The Fringe of Heaven*. At the same time in most of these writers there is an internalization of realism, in order to catch the inner life while keeping the focus social. Free indirect thought, idiomatic but not so self-consciously 'New Zealand' as in the Provincial writers, is in everyone's technical repertoire, often modulating into moments of direct interior monologue. Memory, dream, and recurring metaphor and symbol are again found everywhere. The innovations of Ballantyne and Cross have become common property.

Two of the major extended realist fictions, *Strangers and Journeys* and the Plumb trilogy, show clearly the attempts to expand realist methods for greater stylistic range, historical coverage, social breadth, and psychological depth. In *Strangers and Journeys*, Shadbolt cannot quite get it all to work. In the first sections, an omniscient point of view shifting back and forth between two parallel and contrasted narrative lines, with a basically chronological approach (after the achronological 'Preludes') works well, and there is a nice balance between rigorously selected external detail and brief internal glimpses, with some free indirect thought. However, when the focus shifts to Tim Livingstone, treated indirectly, Shadbolt fumbles for new methods and fails to make them work to organize his increasingly disparate material. He has Ian Freeman voice the thought that after World War II 'the conventional and omniscient novel began to perish',[128] and himself tries to accommodate the post-war uncertainty with partial points of view, 'documents', and shifting layers of time that build up a tentative picture out of detail; but still the novel falls to pieces.

Gee in the Plumb trilogy is more successful in modifying the conventions of critical realism to meet his needs, perhaps partly because he found a viable model in the Joyce Cary trilogies. The interaction of three different first-person points of view, written from different sexual, generational, and social perspectives, provides a means to express the relativism and 'uncertainty' that Shadbolt felt increasingly characterized the age. Because of narrative overlap, events and characters are often seen from two or three perspectives, and there is no sense of a too certain view of 'truth'. Each narrator has a distinctive personal style, and operates within three interwoven layers of time — the historical past, the immediate past, and the narrative present — with the narrator in the advancing narrative present learning more as he or she talks about the past. Individual volumes and the trilogy as a whole are stitched together into a spatial as well as a temporal pattern, with recurrent motifs and images giving a rich musicality. The trilogy shows clearly how far the resources of critical realism have been developed.

Although critical realism has remained the dominant mode, there has also been much development in the impressionist mode, with exploitation of free indirect thought, interior monologue, and occasionally stream of consciousness, psychological time-shifts, dream, myth, and recurring images to capture the inner life of the characters. The mode has been used not only by women writers, as in the earlier period, but also by many male writers, and has been the preferred mode of Māori writers. It appears in its simplest form in novels with a first-person, present-tense narrator, such as Mitchell's *Amokura* or Cowley's *Nest in a Falling Tree* or any of Watson's novels (all of which focus on the importance of individual subjective perception), although it can be complicated by time-shifts, as in Grace's *Mutuwhenua* (through the narrator's memory and association) or Ihimaera's *Tangi* (through systematic alternation of time-levels). A related form is the use of third-person narration limited to a single consciousness, with the emphasis on inner life and impressions, as in du Fresne's *The Book of Ester* or Greenwood's *The Roundness of Eggs* or Gant's *Islands* (in the latter the diction is often restricted to the child's vocabulary and Australian idiom). A more elaborate literary use of this method, modelled on Malcolm Lowry's *Under the Volcano*, with extensive use of allusion and myth, can be seen in Billing's *The Slipway* and in Henderson's more Joycean *The Log of a Superfluous Son*. De Roo's *Through the Eye of the Thorn*, also Joycean in its texture, complicates the method by moving the point of view from character to character but always keeping it within, as Hulme also does in *The Bone People*, with a rich texture of dream, myth, and symbol. The two methods, first and limited third-person, are combined somewhat clumsily in Johnson's *Lear* (again with a rich texture of metaphor, symbol, and allusion), and more gracefully in Wedde's *Dick Seddon's Great Dive*, with shifts in both person and tense. Perhaps the densest in texture of these impressionist fictions is Wedde's *Symmes Hole*, with its freewheeling syntax (sometimes loosely periodic, sometimes with multiple parallel structures) and with its wealth of metaphor and allusion from a Pynchonesque range of reference.

The two most complex works in narrative method in this mode are Ihimaera's *The Matriarch* and Grace's *Potiki*. In Ihimaera's book the variety of method is so great that the narrative threatens to fragment. The point of view shifts between first and third-person with various 'reflectors', and there is a highly complex multiple layering of time (some key events, such as the 1949 hui, being broken up into many parts and inserted amidst other layers), as well as a complex web of allusion to Verdi's operas and Māori mythology. Perhaps when the sequel is completed all will come together, but the impression from *The Matriarch* in isolation is one of fragmentation, of a narrative complexity that hinders as often as it aids comprehension. The case of *Potiki* is quite different, for the final impression is one of oral simplicity and unity, although the method reveals itself upon analysis to be quite complex. Grace varies her method to make it appropriate to the 'reflector' in any given chapter, from the external third-person dialogue for 'Dollarman', through reported action and monologue for Mary, to third-person limited for Hemi, to a retrospective first-person for Toko and Roimata. The chronology moves back and forth through memory and association quite naturally, and the underlying mythic substructure of Christ and Maui (which Grace has said was her only preliminary 'plan')[129] is unobtrusively unifying.

The writer who has done the most substantial work in the impressionist mode in this period is, of course, Frame, building upon her previous work. In the first three of her five novels between 1965 and 1973 there is a kind of indecisiveness, with *Adaptable Man* almost in a realist mode (if it is taken straight), *A State of Siege* moving progressively back inside a single character, and *The Rainbirds* coming part way out again, with a multiple focus. However, in the fourth, *Intensive Care*, her most complex and substantial fiction to date, Frame puts it all together. The first two sections are in a shifting third-person omniscience, supplemented by individual characters' lyrics and arias and unwritten 'letters'. In the last section there is a change to the first person, with Colin Monk's account framing Milly Galbraith's journal (which may be Monk's invention). Frame exhibits her full variety of styles in the narrative, and her densest pattern of images and motifs — suggestive names, submerged puns, crossword puzzle clues, literal and figurative images, dreams, fantasies. After that *tour de force*, *Daughter Buffalo*, although complex by most writers' standards, seems relatively simple, almost a reprise of *Scented Gardens for the Blind*.

In many of these works there is also a strong mythic element: the dream imagery of *The Primal Therapy of Tom Purslane*, the references to Rangi and Papa in *Tangi*, and to Maui and Christ in *The Bone People* and *Potiki*, and the symbolic night journeys in *The Slipway*, *People of the Long Water*, *State of Siege*, and *Through the Eye of the Thorn*. In such novels motif moves towards substructure, and in the second section of *Mackenzie* substructure becomes primary structure, as the quest-journey moves into the foreground.

Although critical realism and the impressionistic and mythic modes have been the primary modes of Post-provincial fiction, there have also been other developments. Black humour for the purpose of satire has been used in O'Sullivan's *Miracle*, in Wayne Innes's *The Department* (1983), a broad attack on various psychological schools and dogma in William Maughan's *Good and Faithful Servant* (1974), a broader and feebler satire on the civil service (and other targets), and in Evans's *Being Eaten Alive*, with its darker satire on contemporary education, the mass media, and consumption society. Fantasy has been used for less satiric and more didactic purposes in McAlpine's, Hall's and Mountjoy's feminist novels and Joseph's and Mann's science fiction. However, the most important new development in mode has been the rise of the metafictional in narratives explicitly concerned with their own narrativity and fictionality. Although emphasis on metafictionality has been a relatively recent development, often associated with post-modernism, writers operating primarily within the realist and the modernist mode of impressionism had previously incorporated elements of it in their work. Shadbolt was aware as early as his first novel, *Among the Cinders*, that realism is a set of conventions, and he played games with this, having Nick Flinders as narrator tell the reader that he is telling the story in order to pre-empt his brother's making a novel of it. In the first edition he even cons a character named 'Maurice Shadbolt' into ghost-writing it for him. Later, in *The Lovelock Version*, Shadbolt plays games with fictionality: from the epigraph 'quoting' spurious entries from his own Shell *Guide to New Zealand* concerning his fictional Porangi River and Lovelock Junction, right through to the conclusion of his narrative romp through a playfully fictionalized New Zealand history, with a self-conscious narrator who wonders who is creating him.

Frame, from the impressionist side, experiments with metafictionality. Narrative tricks at the end of *Scented Gardens for the Blind, Daughter Buffalo*, and *Intensive Care*, when we learn that the narratives are 'really' the inventions of the characters, raise epistemological questions about the very nature and status of fictionality. *The Adaptable Man* seems to have been an attempt to show her publisher that she simply could not work within the confines of the well-made English novel, which was as foreign a country to her as England itself: so that the book that he hoped would become her first bestseller became instead a subversion of the conventions of the middlebrow English novel. As Stead has said, Frame 'planted landmines everywhere in those bogus English fields'.[130] Thus there is a self-conscious narrator exposing the artifice, the elaborate plot-preparations that are then short-circuited, and a character who wants to write the kind of novel her publisher desires but who instead (after undetected murder and incest) becomes a journalist writing fake letters from places he has never been to. In *Living in the Maniototo* metafiction becomes the dominant mode, as the main character, a novelist, discovers that the people among whom she has been living are her own fictional creations, and that she herself is perhaps someone else's creation. Frame, however, unlike Shadbolt, is not so much playing a game with her metafiction as exploring the difficult question of the relation between the artist's 'real' life and her life in the 'Mirror City' of the imagination, the question of whether it is necessary for the artist to insulate herself from the pressures of the outside world in order to sustain the creative life.

While Shadbolt and Frame have moved in and out of the metafictional mode, Joseph was a visitor only once, in *A Soldier's Tale*, perhaps less by intention than as a necessary result of his complex narrative method: the unnamed narrator, a New Zealand ex-bombardier, retells in 1973 a story that Saul Scourby told him in late 1944 about Saul's experience with Belle in mid-1944, an experience which further involved Belle telling Saul what had happened to her earlier in the war, including a story told to her by a German officer. In reconstructing these narrative layers the narrator is forced to fill in and interpret and thus face the implications of his own narratorial role. Further, in raising questions about his own interpretation of Saul and Saul's interpretation of Belle, he implicitly raises the question of the implied author's interpretation of him. He views himself as an educated and sensitive man of thought filling out the implications of what is told him by an inarticulate and violent man of action, and in doing so he seems to condescend to Saul. Is he speaking for the implied author in this, or is the implied author's distance from him as great as his from Saul? Is the implied author through his narrator revealing his own class bias in his treatment of Saul (as Allen Curnow assumes in his poem about the novel, 'Dichtung and Wahrheit') or, as K.K. Ruthven assumes, is he standing back and implying a criticism of his narrator?[131]

Ian Wedde raises similar questions with his handling of the narrative in *Dick Seddon's Great Dive*. On the surface Kate seems to be trying to understand what happened between her and Chink by telling the story of it; but the third-person narrative sections hint that maybe what we are getting is someone else's attempt to tell the story of her telling the story — perhaps 'Curtis', a character with whom she stays as she reconstructs the story, who quotes as his own some of Wedde's poetry, and who incidentally carries the author's own second name. In *Symmes Hole* Wedde plays even more elaborate metafictional games, inventing an anthropologist to write the 'introduction' to his novel (even copyrighting it in the character's name), and creating a hapless persona of himself in his 'Researcher'. This Researcher then creates the historical sections of Heberley and Melville in his own head, drawing on actual historical documents, while spaced out from a 'history drug' he retrieves from the harbour.

In several other recent novels, the metafictional mode is so strongly present as to be inescapable. Haley's *The Settlement* has a self-conscious omniscient narrator who at one point gives up on the story he has been telling and starts over again (leaving 'evidences' of the first version in the fictional world of the second version, to puzzle the characters), while the story he tells may itself be a 'perithanatic fantasy', the 'oneiric spasm of a dying brain' in his central character,[132] who may be dreaming it all as he lies dying (and he confides to his psychiatrist in the story — who may not after all be a psychiatrist — that that is his fear). Various disquieting details in the story's narrative present relate to the character's past life in England and imply that this future fiction may be constructed from elements of his fictional past (which resembles Haley's own past).

Stead, in a different way, has emphasized the metafictional in *All Visitors Ashore* and *The Death of the Body*. The first can be read as a modernist-impressionist historical novel of the 1950s, but Stead moves 'behind' this fictionalized world to show that all is 'really' taking place in the head of the fifty-year-old Curl Skidmore as he thinks about his experience of thirty years before and makes a novel out of it, exaggerating and embroidering the supposed prior reality, calling attention to alternative ways of presenting it and to his own artfulness, and carrying on imaginary dialogues with past images of himself and his lover. For the English reader to whom *All Visitors Ashore* was first presented, such references to its own narrativity would be enough for it to be seen as a metafiction. But for New Zealand readers there was another dimension, indicated by the dedication, 'To whom it may concern', for the 'faction' obviously 'concerns' Frame, Sargeson, and Stead, among others. It is a conflation of Stead's own experiences in relation to Frame and Sargeson in 1954, and in the Waterfront dispute of 1951, applying varying degrees of fictionalization. Fact and fiction weave in and out in a wondrous manner which becomes its own justification. The metafiction finally becomes a kind of romantic irony by which Stead can have his novel, with its tendency to nostalgia, and at the same time undercut the nostalgia by drawing attention to its arbitrariness and literariness.

Stead pushes metafictionality even more to the forefront in *The Death of the Body*, as the story of the telling of the story becomes at least as important as the story that is told, with its own setting, characters, plot, and theme. The narrator explicitly acknowledges the difficulties of story-telling — transposing simultaneous experience into a linear mode, the problems of selectivity, the different way things might be handled in the medium of film, the falsifying effect of conventions, the necessary collaboration of the reader — while the implicit problem of the 'reality' of the characters and actions is related to the philosophical problems with which the main character occupies himself throughout. Thus the book becomes a different kind of novel from merely an account of the drug and university worlds of Auckland in the 1980s.

Stead's novel is an appropriate place to end this account of the New Zealand novel, not because it is a high point to which all has been building, but because it shows how the novel, after its long struggle to establish itself in New Zealand, has become so firmly established that it can play with its own conventions, make serious fun of what Henry James called the novelist's 'sacred duty' to preserve the illusion of the fiction. That *The Death of the Body*, *The Settlement*, and *Symmes Hole* could appear in the same year (1986) as *Potiki*, *The Matriarch*, *Season of the Jew*, *Time and the Forest*, and *Lear* is an indication of the range of accomplishment that has become possible as the novel has become naturalized in New Zealand in the 125 years since *Taranaki*.

The Short Story

LYDIA WEVERS

The proliferation of short story anthologies in New Zealand over the last ten years lends substance to a recent claim that New Zealanders have a 'longstanding preference for the short story'. Mark Williams claims the eminence of the short story is due both to the 'continued force of the Sargeson tradition' and to the 'smallness and homogeneity' of the reading public.[1] The quantity of published short stories and of writers who have specialized in the short story suggests that as a form the short story has enjoyed a privileged status in New Zealand and, more than the novel, been the genre in which the preoccupations of a colonial and post-colonial literature have worked themselves out. To write short stories for a local periodical press, often a discontinuous and fragile publishing forum with many journals and magazines surviving only for a short time, is to address an explicitly local readership. This was especially so prior to the 1950s when most New Zealand novelists still published in Great Britain. A longstanding preference for the short story can then be seen as something of a cultural choice, a resistance to the more usual practice of writing 'Home' for a British readership.

For a number of writers, particularly Sargeson, Duggan, and most of the writers publishing in periodicals, the short story is where New Zealanders have placed themselves; away from Europe but within European hegemonic cultural discourse. Clare Hanson, commenting on Frank O'Connor's remark that the short story flourishes best in an incompletely developed culture, has suggested that it 'seems to be the mode preferred by those writers who are not writing from within a fixed and stable cultural framework'.[2] This comment would seem to suggest that short fiction is peculiarly marked and characterized by cultural preference, that its very brevity speaks for the absence of other, larger certainties, encoding the problematic context of colonial and post-colonial literatures. If breaking away from Great Britain is articulated in a hunger (as the literary magazine *Phoenix* put it in 1932) for words that give us a 'home in thought', the characteristic fictional form of these words in New Zealand for a long time was the short story, perhaps because the problematic questions of separation, race, culture, and identity which constrain and shape an emerging national literature can be more comfortably articulated in a genre which does not imply resolution. In discussing the history of the short story in New Zealand I hope to raise some of these questions and to suggest the ways in which particular types of short fiction become prominent at different times.

The history of the short story has tended to be the history of writers who specialize in the genre and are therefore seen as reactive upon each other. What is often ignored is the great bulk of short fictions published in magazines, newspapers, and journals, which provide a local context for individual writers, particularly as they begin their careers. Unless short fictions are collected or anthologized, they remain relatively unread. The history of the genre then becomes the history of writers who distinguished themselves from the wider context, and this can obscure the relationships, for example, between the work of Katherine Mansfield and colonial short fiction in local magazines. The following discussion refers outwards from well-known writers to the wider context of publication in which particular kinds of stories are pre-eminent for a time, suggesting the narrative models which a writer like Mansfield or Sargeson may use, or the ways in which an ascendancy of type, such as the romance or the sketch, may indicate the preoccupations of its time. Its focus is the short story as a form of cultural history, the sign by which 'New Zealand' is produced, as well as the preoccupying narratives of some of our significant writers. The discussion is divided into three sections: Colonial Short Fiction up to and including Mansfield; Nationalism and Social Realism, 1920s-1950s; and Writing as Other; Other Writing (1960s and after).

Colonial Short Fiction to Katherine Mansfield

Colonial short fiction begins in New Zealand as the occasional publication of small groups and literary societies whose effort is directed mainly at documenting and recording the local environment. *Literary Foundlings* (1864), a collection of verse and prose edited by Canon George Cotterill in aid of the Christchurch Orphan Asylum, may suggest in its title a metaphor of separation from the 'Mother' country, but is mostly addressed to an audience of known tastes and interests. Its accounts of travel and humorous anecdotes of colonial life represent the adventurous colonist as someone who is doing credit to his British origins, but there is one story that begins to suggest a larger preoccupation of nineteenth century colonial fiction. 'A Tale I Heard in the Bush' is framed, like many colonial stories, as an oral narrative, authentic word of mouth. It is a tale of romance and money told by two men travelling through the Australian bush, who have the following conversation about one of the characters:

> 'Is he a gentleman?'
> 'Yes and no. He is as good as many a gentleman in a drawing-room; but he is not gentleman enough for the bush.'
> 'You're right there; it's only when the polish is off you can see the real fibre.'[3]

The distinction made between gentlemanly qualities necessary to a drawing room and those for the bush becomes in later fiction part of a larger distinction between colonial culture and the culture of origin. Appearances can be cultivated. It is only when the 'polish is off' that people identify themselves as showing 'real fibre'. Importantly, the mark of distinction that separates the colonial from the civilized world he has left is his lack of 'polish'; he remains a gentleman and thus affirms his British origins, but 'real' gentlemanly qualities are more clearly recognized out of the drawing room. Ultimately this distinction is between values and manners, and it becomes clear that the discourse of colonialism represents itself repeatedly in short fiction in distinctions which question European social identity while reaffirming its underlying moral value. In order to register as colonial, some form of separation must take place (usually a difference in social form, or in manners), while at the same time European moral and cultural hegemony is asserted. Short fiction typically reveals the ambiguities and anxieties inherent in the colonial condition.

Colonial stories begin as tales and yarns which represent experience as orally authenticated and basically documentary even if realism is heightened or exaggerated for comic or dramatic effect. A typical example is the work of Lady Barker. A *Christmas Cake in Four Quarters* (1872) contains a description of Christmas Day in New Zealand on her station in North Canterbury, which frames a story told by 'old Bob', a shepherd, about a working Christmas Day in the high country in the 'old days' of the colony. Although the point of Bob's narrative is comic, in the context of Lady Barker's recording presence it takes on the character of archive, life as it is lived rather than literary experience. This suggests a distinction characteristic of colonial short fiction between 'real' tale-telling and fiction, which explicitly signalled itself as story, and perhaps most commonly as romance. Tale-telling typically adopts an oral frame, as in Henry Lapham's *We Four and the Stories We Told* (1880). Lapham, who with his sister Mrs Nugent Wood had published an earlier collection, *Waiting for the Mail* in 1875, published in the *Australian Journal* and in local newspapers, and wrote stories firmly located in a male environment and in male experience. In the later collection, the yarns are told by four men holed up in a pub. Lapham's storytelling environment is an early version of mateship; his fictions are less about places than about the behaviour of men in those places and the incomprehensible nature of women:

> It's strange the way women have; they cry when they are sorry, and they cry worse when they are glad. I can't make it out, but then there's a deal to understand about a woman.[4]

In a prefatory note to *We Four* Lapham explains that these four stories are 'on the subject of frights in general', a general classification which suggests the use of conventions associated with ghost stories and stories of the unknown. Conventional ghost stories are common in colonial short fiction and act as a frame for colonial discourse. The consequences of cultural separation and instability can be suggested very easily in a narrative specifically engaged with experience that is out of the ordinary, exotic, inexplicable, and takes place in the overtly unfamiliar landscapes of the Empire. Lapham's stories employ familiar colonial motifs such as the lost child, trouble on the goldfields, conflict between a good man and a bad man over a woman; and the collection ends explicitly on the question of 'frights' with a ghost story. This story is said to derive from 'the Pater', for whom storytelling is a 'special accomplishment' and whose art is said to encompass an exotic world of experience, 'his reminiscences sounding like pages from "The Arabian Nights" '.[5] The story is about sleeping with a corpse, which so effectively 'frights' the drinkers that they go home, closing the narrative. Such stories of mystery and adventure told by men to each other form a central complex in colonial fiction right through to *Heart of Darkness*. Ghost stories, often framed as oral narrative, represent experience of otherness in its most unequivocally 'written' form: the Pater's reminiscences sound like 'pages from "The Arabian Nights" '. By presenting the alien as both a fictional reading of the unknown and as tales that are orally transmitted (and thus accounts of experience), ghost stories suggest the containment of the unfamiliar within a deeply familiar cultural context; in Lapham's case the pub. The presence of the narrator, who is often in his club or, like Sherlock Holmes, his professional rooms, contextualizes the story he is about to tell, so it is read as fiction, distant, legendary, and unlike the cultural context in which it occurs. Both the teller and his audience are fascinated by the tale, but not a part of it.

Ghost and mystery stories are a regular part of the fiction published in annuals and magazines during the 1880s and after. The usefulness of the ghost story is clear in a literature using conventional forms of tale-telling to describe unfamiliar but fascinating experience. Ghost stories are about types of knowledge. The colonizing narrator, speaking from an environment suggestive of conventional social structures (the club, the pub) and often smoking a pipe, is a thinker associated with empirical knowledge and rationality. The story he tells, very often about Māori in the 1890s and 1900s, defines itself in opposition to this context: social conventions and structures are violated, events are irrational and inexplicable, and governing impulses are emotional not ratiocinative. Very often it is a story of desire, the desire of colonial characters to assimilate or be assimilated by the other, the colonized race, which possesses primitive powers, supernatural knowledge, and powerful emotion. A typical example is 'The Disappearance of Letham Crouch'[6] which was published in the *New Zealand Illustrated Magazine* in 1901. In this story an overzealous missionary who is 'mad about his priesthood' is received by Māori as a 'new tohunga'. In order to tread their pagan beliefs underfoot, Crouch lives in a tapu house, and after a period in which his eyes become 'sunken and wild' and he develops a fanatical appearance, he vanishes, leaving the house in a state of destruction, to reappear as a Māori 'stripped for dancing'. The narrator's comment shows the extent to which the missionary has crossed a boundary: 'As a Maori he was as sane as possible.' Actions that would suggest madness in a European become 'sane as possible' when their perpetrator is reconstituted as Māori. Letham Crouch crosses a cultural divide by becoming fanatical. He engages in a battle with superstition, to tread it underfoot, when his own rationality is under threat; he is already in the territory of otherness which is signalled by the Māori's readiness to see him as a new tohunga. Without the protection of his culture, he is assimilated — 'Letham Crouch, preacher of

Christ, turned heathen'. The story is typical of nineteenth century colonial ghost stories in its attribution of mystical powers to the heathen and in its representation of colonial anxiety about identity.

Attitudes to the Māori were closely associated with the whole problem of how to represent the distinctiveness of colonials within the conventions of the appropriating culture. In short fiction, distinctiveness is often expressed in a discourse of exteriority; when the polish is off, the fibre shows. Appearance, for example, provides the basis for comic distinctions between the colonial and the New Chum, emphasizing the multiple associations of dress, place and work. In a story by G.B. Lancaster, 'God Keep Ye, Merrie Gentlemen' (1901),[7] the association of dress, place and ownership is explicit. 'Teddy had worn pinafores in Australia, wide collars in England, and dungarees from one end of New Zealand to the other.' Teddy is also 'strong in the knowledge gained as indubitable owner of a nine-by-fourteen sod *whare*, and a two thousand acre run many miles down the river'. Dress and work legitimize property in colonial fiction. By emphasizing visible connections between work and land, competence and identity, colonial fictions represent appropriation as assimilation, and economic and cultural domination as the legitimate consequence of hard work. Clothing, work skills, and the physical environment in which the colonial works, indicate forms of knowledge that separate him both from his place of origin, which is signalled by the New Chum, and also from simpler acquisitive motives. Most yarns which document and describe colonial life are firmly based on the work of settling or on the characters of settlers shaped by their work, such as some of the stories in the collection by B.E. Baughan, *Brown Bread from a Colonial Oven* (1912) whose title suggests a pastoral and even nostalgic dimension of colonial work. Identification by work and the appearance which that work causes allows a degree of flexibility about social convention in colonial yarns. Polish, or manners, don't matter as much as 'fibre'. Characters quickly became stereotypes: 'the rough diamond', the 'New Chum' who needs to be tested, the girl whose 'worth' is shown by her preference for horse-riding over ball-going. Even in recent short fiction, the country person characterized by work is less likely to reveal ambiguities of behaviour than the urban dweller.

In the Preface to his *Stories of New Zealand Life* (1889), William Davidson explained that 'A love for his adopted country has induced the author to make this humble attempt to draw attention to a land which Nature has endowed so lavishly with fair gifts.' Davidson's urge to draw attention to the land is one shared by most colonial writers, though the problem of how best to go about creating a distinctive literature (or whether such a thing was desirable) was frequently addressed. William Freeman established *Zealandia* in 1889 as a 'distinctively national literary magazine' and a letter from John C. Thomson to *Zealandia* described colonial literature as 'the formative power of true colonialism'. However, there were others who believed that colonial writing illustrated too wide a gap between colonial life and the established conventions of British culture and writing: by definition, colonial writing was fettered to the narrow circle of the colonies and should be rejected in favour of English literature. Too much local colour, too great a distinctiveness, as Clara Cheeseman pointed out in an article in the *New Zealand Illustrated Magazine*, represented the colonial in damaging ways, more particularly so if the writer was a woman:

> The saddest and most unflattering accounts of colonial life are to be found in the books written by those who ought to know it best . . . . Many women invent situations which they ought to be ashamed of, and write down language which surely they would not have the hardihood to read aloud. Sometimes this is done through ignorance, or under the mistaken impression that they are making their writings forcible. And so they are in one sense — too forcible. Everyone admires strength; but we do not want to be struck with a sledgehammer.[8]

Anxiety about what, if anything, constitutes colonial literature indicates a real problem. To guarantee cultural distinctiveness, the term colonial must signify some separation from the originating culture. Colonial fiction signifies this separation in external and stereotypic difference; people look different and are valued differently. But narrative structures, the kinds of stories that are told about people, increasingly suggest the difficulty of maintaining change and separation as purely exterior. The ways in which predominant types of short fiction work at defining colonial identity suggest how problematic it is, and this is particularly evident in stories which deal with Māori, especially when such stories are not simply describing and documenting Māori customs, as are some early stories, but *include* the Māori in a conventional narrative structure, in which the only possible narrative definitions are as stereotype, caricature, or supernatural Other. As Bill Pearson has pointed out:

> At worst, the Pakeha attitude was that he had every right to occupy the land of uncivilised heathens and the sooner they died out the better. At best, it was one of indulgence, as in two of Blanche Baughan's stories: being kind to them, showing yourself as cunning as they are, and then giving them some tobacco. Naughty, lovable children, but you could manage them if you understood them.[9]

Alfred Grace's *Maoriland Stories* (1895) and *Tales of a Dying Race* (1901) were widely published in periodicals (*Bulletin*, *The Triad*, and *New Zealand Illustrated Magazine*) before being published as collections, and indicate a sympathetic writing of the Māori in fiction, though (like all forms of 'writing the Māori') appropriative in their transference of a distinctive culture into the forms and conventions of another. Grace was the son of a Taupo missionary and knew the local tribes well. One of the stories in *Tales of a Dying Race*, 'A White Wahine', purports to relate his mother's experience during the Land Wars, how she and her children were saved from a hostile war-party by the heroic action of a chief friendly to Pākehā. Grace's stories are written from a perspective that generally values Māori freedom from Pākehā convention and puritanism. Nevertheless as narratives the stories assert cultural superiority unequivocally, and racial stereotypes are unquestioned. As Pearson remarked:

> His attitude is a little like that of a Pakeha-Maori, who, as he calls it, 'speaks the lingo'. He takes it for granted that they are rogues, but he prefers to write of their way of living rather than of conventional and self-righteous Pakeha life for which he had little sympathy.[10]

In Grace's stories Māori are war-loving and vengeful, and many of the narratives take place in, or as a result of, 'deadly tribal wars'. According to the Preface to *Tales of a Dying Race* Grace saw this as the natural condition of the Māori and the main cause of their dispossession:

> When the white man arrived, he found the islands rent from end to end by internecine wars; but instead of seeing in him their common enemy, the Maoris welcomed the *pakeha*, because he could supply them with powder and shot with which to exterminate each other.[11]

Furthermore, in Grace's fictions it is frequently the white man who rescues the Māori woman from the ill-treatment or prejudice of her tribe; the Māori practise diabolical arts and are represented as animalistic and brutal. In one story a Māori woman, rejected by her Pākehā lover, exacts a long-distance revenge by giving her Māori suitor a task to prove his worthiness: 'In after time, Hira, when the thought of the faithless Giles came upon her, would lift from a box, sunk in the floor of her hut, a woman's head with long yellow hair, embalmed with all the horrors of the Maori art.' Māori are governed by their tohunga, and the narrative context in which they are shown emphasizes qualities which are at odds with European culture and often stresses the liberating function of the Pākehā male. Although Grace refers to the dispossession of the Māori, his argument places less emphasis on the inequitable act performed on one race by another, and more on man's essential commonality 'before the white man had dispossessed his brown brother'. At other times he romanticizes it: 'Villiers was on good terms with the dispossessed lords of the soil. He had a sort of romantic regard for them.'[12] In 'Te Wiria's Potatoes' Villiers refers to the local Māori, whom he has dispossessed, as his 'pet tribe', and when they offer to dig up his crop of potatoes and then steal it from him, his protestations are met with ironic and imperturbable humour by the chief Tohitapu. In this story the Māori are allowed to steal on a small scale from those who have stolen on a large scale, and both Villiers and Tohitapu regard the other as their own, their protégé or possession. This narrative emphasis thus stabilizes and normalizes the existing economic, social, and cultural hierarchy; it is by 'permitting' a humorous theft, that Villiers establishes his moral and cultural ascendancy.

Grace frequently refers to young Māori men as 'braves' or writes about Māori ownership systems in language which suggests Arthurian romance. Stories published in the *New Zealand Illustrated Magazine* and other journals

(*The Huia, Lone Hand, Zealandia, Bulletin,* and *Current Thought*) use language and literary conventions which represent the Māori as exotic and primitive, but familiar enough to be assimilated into received Anglo-European and American literary traditions. There is already a vocabulary within which the Māori are seen to fit, whether the form is Victorian comedy, Arthurian romance, or some version of supernatural Other. Sometimes language represents the Māori as shrewd and lovable, but speaking a childlike corruption of English. In Blanche Baughan's 'Pipi on the Prowl', an old woman looking for tobacco is to be nurtured and cared for, her tricks and practical jokes allowed and enjoyed by a benevolent Pākehā who can speak her language. The *New Zealand Illustrated Magazine* published a considerable number of stories about Māori which combine a childish spoken English with a comically formalized descriptive vocabulary, emphasizing the gap between the erudition of the narrative and the simple-mindedness of its subjects, who act entirely on instinct and appetite. Alice A. Kenny's 'The Justice of the Kaianga [*sic*]', about the consequences that overtake an impulsive Māori youth who steals a tomahawk from a Pākehā store, is framed as a mock-heroic comedy. The Māori chief who brings the boy to justice has 'myrmidons'; 'Nemesis' waits on him; he is apprehended from 'Honeymoon Cottage or whatever he called his little whare on the banks of that excellent though peat-stained creek where he sojourned'. But though Kenny's narrative signals a comic reading to the subscriber of the *Illustrated Magazine*, it ends with a trader, Alf Taylor, rescuing the young offender from the utu of his tribe, who offer his life as he is a slave. Alf Taylor repudiates this offer in a narrative climax characteristic of colonial short stories about Māori. By rejecting the Māori solution he emerges as the generous benefactor, saving the thief's life and demonstrating civilized humanity to savages who make inhuman distinctions between people. And Alf Taylor's reward is also typical of short fiction which, even when critical of Pākehā behaviour as are Grace's stories, morally endorses the European colonist as light-giver, mercy-bringer and rescuer:

> Iria, the culprit, grey-faced and dazed, flinched away from Alf Taylor's knife as his bonds fell from him, and followed him out of the kaianga in silence with his small wahine at his heels. But later on, when the fear of death had passed further from him, he went to the pakeha and said to him in a touching and child-like manner, 'I am ashamed.'[13]

Other stories represent the Māori only as bloodthirsty and savage, and often purport to be 'historical' accounts of the Land Wars, amounting to little more than propaganda. Less simplistically, like William Baucke's *Where the White Man Treads* (1905), they may claim to be constructing a Māori history from oral narrative. Baucke claims that his intention is to 'enter into the inner life of the Maori', but after listening to 'stories of fairies and gnomes, ghosts and creatures fearful to look upon; of customs and witchcraft', he is confirmed in his *distance* from his subjects; he is the 'undeveloped savage':

what wonder then that the undeveloped savage in me — which regardeth neither race nor colour — found here excuse to loiter on my errands.[14]

The Māori as child in need of a father, as savage ready for enlightenment, as romantic hero within his own legends — these are the tropes of colonial short fiction. Incorporating Māori within the conventional literary genres of ghost/ mystery story and romance allowed the kinds of racial problems encountered in colonial life to receive a formulaic narrative expression which encoded cultural distinctions and moral hierarchies.

The huge popularity of romantic short fiction in the periodicals of the 1890s and 1900s also indicates its peculiar suitability as a framing device for colonial discourse. Romance is perhaps the most conservative of narrative structures in that it represents desire and the fulfilment of desire as natural and normal. In the process, racial, cultural, and gender differences tend to be written out, in favour of preserving essential unities and existing systems. This is particularly so in the most common kind of colonial love story, whose nexus is the interaction of love and money. Very frequently, the motivation of those who marry for money, as in Clara Cheeseman's 'Married for his Money', is contrasted unfavourably with those who marry for love; the general objective of such stories is educative and addressed specifically to the problems associated with wealth that are seen to flourish in a new, land-based, and imperialist economy. Cheeseman's story, set in fashionable provincial Auckland, comes straight out of the heartland of Victorian fiction; Mr Repton, whose income is 'quite inadequate to supply the wants of a fashionable family' intends to resolve his difficulties by marrying his daughter to a young man who has recently inherited a fortune, even though this involves the humiliation of seeing his daughter marry beneath her. The story satirizes the way in which wealth cuts across social classes and their associated 'values'. The Reptons educate the young man in middle-class manners; even the appearance of his disreputable brother can be accommodated for £40,000 — revealing, as a visiting baronet puts it, the 'hollowness and corruption of colonial society'.[15]

The acquisition and distribution of wealth is always central to the structure of nineteenth century romance melodrama, and in colonial literatures the power of wealth and/or the desire for it is explicitly fictionalized, though in love stories involving Māori it is implicit rather than explicit. Some writers use the conventional structures of romance and melodrama to express metaphorically the materialist dimensions of cross-cultural and interracial romance. Edith Lyttleton, who before she left New Zealand wrote for a number of periodicals both in New Zealand and Australia under the names Keron Hale and G.B. Lancaster, and who also published a considerable number of novels, wrote short romantic fiction in which women were clearly associated with the land. Desiring them was to desire, by metaphorical and economic extension, territory and wealth.

In one of Lancaster's stories, published in *The Huia*, romance as signifier of a discourse of possession is asserted in the association of the land with a Māori woman. In 'His Daily Work', narrative oppositions are established between man and woman, desire and duty, Māori and Pākehā, and work/reason and love/soul. Strickland, a railway engineer, is helping drive a new railway line through the country. He meets and falls in love with a Māori woman, Amira, who disturbs his certainty about his occupation, about the value of work and the meaning of duty. The story expresses an opposition between the Pākehā male and the Māori female that stands for the opposition between colonizer and colonized (both people and landscape) and is also a moral opposition, between work and love and between owning territory and *being* it. As a commentary on the legitimizing of colonial identity through work, 'His Daily Work' is explicit. In her final insistence on the power of love, Lancaster affirms essential romance conventions, but also suggests the underlying tensions by focusing on inevitable separation.

> 'You are my dear love,' she said, with all the dignity of her race. 'It is quite true. You were not for me. I knew. The hills knew. The pakeha drives through the hills and the river, and he goes away. I am the hill and the river. But we have loved — much.'[16]

The great majority of romance writers were women. It seems that for women, writing love stories (or poetry) was an acceptable literary activity, and to some extent the genre gendered its authors and its audience. Although G.B. Lancaster wrote romances, the majority of her short fiction was, as her pseudonym is clearly intended to suggest, written as if by a man. Almost always from a male point of view, Lancaster's early New Zealand narratives are about men engaged in masculine activity (the majority are engineers, surveyors, or stockmen) and troubled by women only to the extent that a female presence introduces complication and ambiguity into male environments and male values. In a sense Lancaster's fiction is the natural successor of William Davidson's stories of young Dunedin men, or Henry Lapham's yarns. The authors she most admired at this time were Kipling and Stevenson. In 1904 she published *Sons o' Men*, a collection of stories about stockmen and mateship on a back-country run in the Southern Highlands. Perhaps more emphatically than anything written by a colonial man, *Sons o' Men* documents and praises the colonial stereotype. Tough, hardworking, truthful and upright, Lancaster's men are framed in biblical language which affirms the heroic nature of their work:

> For, after all, a man must serve his work faithfully, uncounting the cost. This is the lesson of the hill-country, and the Mindoorie boys had learnt it.[17]

Work, in the connected narratives of *Sons o' Men*, constitutes the bond and moral strength of male society. Toughness is a moral quality, and mateship is the emotional expression of it; most of the men have their mates. Lancaster's fictions explicitly connect the terms 'work' and 'mate' to colonial identity, but also outline the conditions by which it is defined. Her stories take place in the country and usually in rugged bush; the characters are men who live alone or in the company of other men, never in a family situation (though this is usually the result of some past emotional unhappiness) and the preoccupying rationale of existence is work, which alone is proof of moral identity, and which is always hard, lonely, and the context in which moral dilemmas are defined, tested, and resolved. In a broader context, colonial means away from 'Home', which accounts for the nature of the colonial's existence and also for some of his attitudes, and the oppositions which cause them: 'A colonial is not a product of civilisation; he is a product of the soil.'[18]

Being a product of the soil means that only what is connected with the soil is valued. Lancaster's stockmen are anticlerical, immoral in that they do not conform to the conventional social expectations of 'Home' but to their own hierarchies and to the standards of the stockyard, the hill country, and mateship. A recurring character in *Sons O' Men*, Harry Morel illustrates the difference between the conventions of established social institutions and the social code of the stockman, who represents the frontier, the colonial who has left 'Home' behind, even as it exists in the local township. Harry has 'gone to the bad' over a woman, and his whistle is 'the one pure and perfect thing left him':

> The curate down at the township called Harry a man of sin. But neither the curate nor anyone else could better Harry Morel's seat on a horse, or the turn of his whip wrist as he swung the mob, unbroken, into the yard.[19]

In the colonial man, traditional loyalties and conservative values have been displaced and relocated. Lancaster's fictions, while glamorizing and stereotyping the colonial male, also participate in a mythologizing process of identification that is the foundation for colonial literature in New Zealand as it is elsewhere: man heroically subdues the environment, and is anti-domestic, moral and tough, while woman, (as she is represented by female colonial writers) remains in her proper landscape of romantic love (also anti-domestic; there are very few mothers or working wives amongst the women of nineteenth century short fiction) embodying the emotional rewards of civilized leisure which promise hope and joy to those without them.

Sons O' Men can be read as establishing a prototype of the tough colonial man, but in B.E. Baughan's *Brown Bread from a Colonial Oven* and Alice Webb's *Miss Peter's Special* (1926) the ascendancy of stereotype is marked, especially since it exists within a context of nostalgia. In the Preface to her collection, Baughan remarks:

> The reason why I want to put into book form efforts so fugitive and meagre is, that, with all their faults, they do yet seem to me honestly to delineate in some degree a phase of New Zealand life that is already passing, and that, so far at least as I have been able to gather, lacks not only an abler chronicler, but any chronicler at all.

'Pipi on the Prowl' belongs to the kind of fiction established by Grace, serving (as W.H. New has pointed out) the 'reigning public image' of the Māori as 'wily

— but comic, figures of pathos and entertainment'.[20] It was published in the first number of *Current Thought* (a Christchurch monthly begun in 1908) under the title 'Pipi, a Maori character sketch', complete with photographs allegedly of Pipi and her home. The story illustrates the increasing use of the 'character' sketch for documentary purposes, rather than the plotted story, in response to the pressure to record what was felt to be passing. Baughan's stories have their origins in the idea of character as history: they work to record places as they were, and the people who inhabited them. Her interest in the Māori is marginal; 'Pipi' comes perilously close to satire and is written from a paternalistic European cultural perspective, made even more pointed in this story by the fact that Pipi, an elderly Māori woman, receives her benefactions from a young Pākehā woman. But in a story like 'Grandmother Speaks' Baughan's subject is close to that announced in the Preface. Grandmother represents a 'phase of New Zealand life that is already passing', the early settlement at Akaroa, and she speaks in a language which suggests a kind of demotic memory of the past:

> I reckon there's a good word to be said for these days, as well as them days . . . . but for my part, I must own as I'm glad it was in them I mostly lived.[21]

'An Active Family' reaffirms the colonial past as a place of 'danger and excitement', of 'sore straits' endured during the process of transforming a piece of bush into an idyllic mimicry of English country life, a result of the unceasingly cheerful effort of 'Mum', 'Dad', and their children.

By the early 1900s colonial life was represented in literature as 'real' life characterized by work and a disregard for unnecessary social convention, in which the colonial could be recognized by his appearance, his speech and 'unpolished' moral qualities. The literary conventions of oral narrative and 'real' descriptive context occupied a privileged position in fiction. The 'colonial' was also now seen to have a history, defined through a series of distinctions between past and present, town and country, Māori and Pākehā, the uncivilized and the civilized. Such oppositions constituted a stereotyping of the forces of change. Very often the larger questions they implied were subsumed into character study; and the recognition of 'type' became a major preoccupation of short fiction. Alice Webb's collection, *Miss Peter's Special* is characteristic of this kind of short fiction, which was to be so subtly transformed by Sargeson in the following decade. The titles of Webb's stories ('The Patriot', 'The Mother's Help', 'The Prophet's Wife', 'The Food Hoarder') reveal her concern to identify the typical, and as the dustjacket pointed out, their authenticity had been verified by the mere fact of local publication:

> These fourteen stories of New Zealand life have all first seen the light in Dominion newspapers, which in itself assures them to be true to life in their local colour.

Webb's sketches are dominated by New Zealanders' experience of the First World War. At the same time they illustrate the colonial preoccupation with 'local colour', which, in the context of the Great War, is colour seen from Great Britain. Webb's stories claim a distinctive regionality, but define their distinctiveness by reference to events occurring elsewhere.

The conventions of colonial short fiction work at containing the problematic questions of race, culture, selfhood, and nationhood within acceptable distinctions, distinctions which represent both the presence and the experience of the colonial as normal, recognizable, and knowable. It is the experience of romance and adventure represented in anecdote, narrative, and character sketch: literary forms whose conventional structure limit or control unfamiliarity by creating stereotypical recognitions of event, character, sequence and ultimately, meaning. A story by Mona Tracy, published in 1928, provides a description of Te Rauparaha which suggests that the Māori chief is a kind of text, read and understood by the writer. He is 'an old man whose nature was stamped on his tattooed face. Craft was marked; treachery, rapacity and cruelty; and gluttony'.[22] Such recognitions of type, in settings emphasizing 'local colour', and framed in familiar romance and adventure narratives, all served to write the colonial story in acceptable terms.

*   *   *

In his study of the New Zealand short story, W.H. New states that 'The problem, in writing a history of New Zealand short fiction, is Katherine Mansfield':

> She not only produced a substantial body of high quality work, she also produced much of it while writing abroad in England and France, was claimed by English criticism and so given honorary English citizenship, died young and became a cultural icon, and managed all of this so early in New Zealand's social history that her very existence cancels all easy generalisations about cultural and historical 'progress'.[23]

The argument about where Mansfield belongs in literary history is certain to remain inconclusive. Part of her attraction, as a writer and as a phenomenon, is her displacement. In self-imposed exile from the country of her birth, she is never really at home as a writer, and her stories disturb the conventional certainties represented in short fiction. The phenomenon of Katherine Mansfield's work could never be contained by the term 'New Zealand colonial' as is the fiction of Blanche Baughan, her near contemporary, nor can it sit comfortably under the term 'English modernist'. Distance seems to have been the necessary condition of her work.

None the less, there are distinctive ways in which her role relates to the colonial literature she left behind (though these are not separate from her achievement as a modernist writing in a European context). It is perhaps helpful, in a history of the New Zealand short story, to look at her firstly from the ground of New Zealand colonial writing. The stories Mansfield wrote for *Rhythm* in 1912 and 1913 in response to a request from her husband, John Middleton Murry, are the most obviously 'colonial' of her *œuvre*, specially categorized as such by Ian Gordon in his collection, *Undiscovered Country* (1974). 'The Woman at the Store', 'Millie', 'How Pearl Button was Kidnapped', 'Ole Underwood', and 'Old Tar', collected with other early work and published by Murry as *Something Childish and Other Stories* (1924), are all stories which show a familiarity with the subjects and conventions of colonial literature. Mansfield had published short sketches and fictions in local publications (*The Triad, The Native Companion*, and the *Dominion* newspaper) before she left New Zealand permanently in 1908; her first published pieces were either stories about children written as anecdotal or fairytale narrative, or what Clare Hanson and Andrew Gurr have called 'imitative pieces in the Symbolist manner'[24] — prose poems and vignettes. Her early writing was published under a variety of names, mostly variations on her given name, Kathleen Beauchamp and her eventual writing name, Katherine Mansfield, but one of them, 'Julian Mark', reflects the same objective as Edith Lyttleton's use of the pseudonym G.B. Lancaster: to be taken seriously as if she were male, where to write as a woman would have restricted her to certain subjects.

It was not until the group of stories written at Murry's request that Mansfield engaged with colonial narrative models. Commentators generally connect these stories with the biographical underpinning of her travels in the Ureweras in 1907. Antony Alpers remarked that 'one New Zealand notebook proved of use in 1912 when she wrote "The Woman at the Store"', although Ian Gordon considered that in stepping outside the 'pastoral world' of her later stories to the kind of real life that may or may not have derived from her observations while travelling in rough bush country, Mansfield 'loses touch':

> She can only reproduce what she overheard or read in the more sensational pages of the local newspaper. What could a girl of her background know of Millie or Ole Underwood or the Woman in the Store, she with her fastidious distaste for the smell of cooking mutton chops, 'commercial travellers and second-class, NZ'?[26]

Whether or not a girl of Kathleen Beauchamp's background could have known of Millie or the woman at the store is beside the point; what is striking about these stories and their subjects is how closely they fit the colonial desire for description of 'real life' and 'local colour' and how Mansfield uses in them the typical literary conventions of colonial writing (oral narrative framing, melodramatic romance plot, character sketch) as well as picking up fictional motifs typical of colonial literatures: the lost or stolen child, landscape as subject, the New Chum breaking down (in 'Millie'). These stories demonstrate a highly conscious use of convention and stereotype, complicated by a deliberately ambiguous narrative context.

'The Woman at the Store' is full of details which describe an explicit setting. The heat, the wind, the tussock grass, the pumice dust, the horses, the mānuka bushes, the discomfort: these are the customary external details of colonial regional dressing. The characters, too, announce their identity in dress; Jo wears a 'blue galatea shirt, corduroy trousers and riding boots', and has a spotted scarf and a wideawake. Hin is dressed in a 'Jaeger vest — a pair of blue duck trousers fastened round the waist with a plaited leather belt'. All dressing is self-representation, as Mansfield's Bertha in 'Bliss' is well aware, but in the kind of clothing, associated with work, and in the specification of material and type of garment, Mansfield places herself alongside the colonial model.

The frame of the story suggests the conventions of romance melodrama: three travellers in a lonely landscape have as their destination a yellow-haired, blue-eyed woman with a reputation for amorousness. But Mansfield begins to subvert readers' expectations almost as soon as the convention has been suggested. Far from being an object of desire the woman is a 'figure of fun':

> Looking at her, you felt there was nothing but sticks and wires under that pinafore — her front teeth were knocked out, she had red pulpy hands, and she wore on her feet a pair of dirty 'Bluchers'.

Not even in Baughan's 'An Active Family' (published in the same year as 'The Woman at the Store'), where the women of the family work as hard as the men, does their work disfigure and mutilate them. If anything it makes Baughan's women more desirable; their faces glow with exertion. As an object of desire the nameless woman at the store exists only in fantasy, and the 'whare' in which she and her child live is a place of cultural dislocation. Out-of-date English periodicals are plastered to the walls, there is a 'coloured print' of Richard John Seddon, and it is a place of work, the work of the colonial woman which stands in the foreground of the more 'civilized' but distant environment implied by the wall coverings. In such a room the narrator becomes afraid, conscious of it as a foreign and hostile place. At this point in the story the fragility of the woman's existence as a cultural transplant, a colonizer in a savage and frightening landscape, is evident to the narrator: 'Imagine bothering about ironing — *mad*, of course she's mad!'[27] As the narrative proceeds, the visible cultural identity of the woman at the store reveals as much substance as the flesh behind her pinafore: it is a kind of dressing concealing what she has become — a murderer, 'mad' as the country she inhabits (and which in another sense inhabits her). The barmaid, pretty as a wax doll, has been doubly displaced, from wax doll to sticks and wires to savage, removed from the conventional narrative expectations she initially invokes, and rewritten as a line drawing by a child. She is no longer woman as heroine of romance, though she has been (knowing as she did one hundred and fifty different ways of kissing), nor is she woman in command of her territory; rather she is unwoman, characterized by the environment she inhabits.

'The Woman at the Store' invokes colonial melodrama and then subverts its narrative model. Romance is about the attainment and possession of an object of desire, but Mansfield's story represents that object as a form of dressing concealing something undesirable; the puppet-like sticks and wires of a woman shooting at a man with a rook rifle. The story is further complicated by Mansfield's destabilizing of the narrative model. The reader's initial assumption that it is three men who are riding alone through rough bush country, places the story within the oral narrative/adventure frame so characteristic of colonial short fiction. When it suddenly becomes clear that the narrator is a woman, a great many questions are raised about her position in the narrative which are left unresolved. How to understand the woman at the store as an object of desire when it is a woman who describes her? The text becomes a site of uncertainty as the narrator is effectively placed outside the categories of cultural and gender stereotype by which such stories are read. The disordering of convention, both social and narrative, occurs within a specific cultural and regional context: the story is distinctively 'New Zealand' and 'colonial' and so what happens to the woman at the store, and by extension to the men associated with her, serves as a further definition of those terms.

'Millie' is framed as an oral narrative and eponymous sketch, based on the colonial motif perhaps best known in the Australian writer Henry Lawson's 'The Drover's Wife': a woman alone in the landscape, threatened by an unknown male. In 'Millie' the narrative structure is inverted so that the young English johnny — on the run after murdering his employer — is threatened by Millie, the large powerful colonial woman. But the story is less about Millie or Harrison than about belonging. Harrison's speech identifies him as of a higher social class than Millie: what he has done in murdering his employer confirms his position as an outsider for whom class is irrelevant, just as Millie's reaction to him confirms her as a colonial, for whom 'home' is represented by a photograph of Mt Cook. 'How Pearl Button was Kidnapped', a story about a child taken on an expedition to a marae and to the beach by two big (Māori) women, inverts a typical colonial narrative about a child who is lost, or stolen by indigenous people, a story which expresses colonial fear of appropriation by the Other. 'Pearl Button' is written from Pearl's point of view, which allows a simple cultural contrast to develop; Pearl enjoys herself with the Māori women as she never has in the 'House of Boxes'. In 'Ole Underwood' the emotional pressures which might drive a man to violence and mad obsession are presented within the frame of the colonial character sketch.

In all these stories Mansfield signals the conventions of colonial short fiction, positioning her narratives within the stereotypes that identify colonial culture in order to challenge them. It is perhaps significant that each of her 'colonial' stories is of a distinctive type and not repeated, and their small number suggests the limited repertoire of colonial fiction as well as its limited usefulness as a source of models for Mansfield's talents. When she returned to New Zealand as a subject in her stories several years later, it had become the emotional centre for the complex indirect multi-voiced narrative form she developed. In her famous journal entry of 22 January 1916, written after her brother's death in France the previous year, Mansfield saw New Zealand as a landscape she must recollect, rediscover, and renew in writing, a landscape in which she could relive the country of her early life.

Mansfield's letters, journals, notebooks, and stories have been the subject of a vast quantity of psycho-biographical speculation and critical commentary which began after her death and still continues. A history of New Zealand short fiction is not the place to deal in detail with all this material, and in any case, the complexity of Mansfield's work is such that it is constantly being re-invented according to critical preoccupation, and this will no doubt continue to be a fruitful exercise. My concern here is firstly to see Mansfield from the standpoint of colonial literature, and secondly to indicate some possible readings of her work, particularly of the later New Zealand stories, which suggest a subtler metaphorical bearing on the meaning of the term 'colonial' than is found in other local writing. When Mansfield declared her ambition (in the Journal entry mentioned above) to 'make our undiscovered country leap into the eyes of the Old World', she defined an intention common to colonial writers. Hanson and Gurr identify that remark as decisive in her development:

> From this point on, when she began to see her New Zealand background as an artistic
> positive . . . she gained enormously in confidence as a writer.[28]

Although Mansfield meant something different from the simpler impulse to document that occurs in much nineteenth century short fiction, the desire to discover her country in writing, to force it into the vision of the Old World, argues a sense of New Zealand as an unwritten, 'undiscovered' territory, which links her with her countrymen and women. Mansfield, in renewing 'all the remembered places' in her writing, also re-knew them, brought New Zealand into the context of modernist European fiction and reviewed it, culturally and textually.

It is clear that Mansfield felt herself to be a displaced person. Both in New Zealand and in England she suffered a sense of exile common to all colonial literatures.[29] Her well-documented difficulties with social relationships, the fact that a substantial part of her adult life was spent out of England, and remarks in the notebooks all bear witness to dislocation. In her fiction the sense of displacement functions in two ways: physically, in the locations of her stories; and figuratively, in the recurrent motif of transit. A surprising number (close to half) of Mansfield's stories are located in New Zealand.[30] Next to New Zealand, Continental Europe is the setting for the largest number of stories, and only a comparatively small number are set in England. As a whole, Mansfield's fiction suggests that cultural identity is a kind of baggage carried around in hotels and on trains, constantly on the move. This shifting location markedly distinguishes Mansfield's fictions from those of Virginia Woolf, with whom she is often compared. However, Mansfield's location of her fictions repeatedly outside England is even more specifically directed to a context of transit. A large number of both the European and the New Zealand stories take place on trains or boats, in foreign hotels or at stations, or on the brink of voyages, at wharves; 'Prelude', a story about shifting house, and 'At the Bay', about a holiday house, are both stories set in a condition of impermanence. Mansfield's fictions characteristically occur within the context of travel, they are the text of travelling, of change and dislocation. If colonial literature has a preoccupying context, it is that it is always addressed elsewhere; somewhere else is the 'real' against which colonial literature must prove its 'realness'; it is always a discourse of transit, and of the anxiety of transitoriness.

As a writer influenced by the symbolists and one who began her writing career with symbolist pieces, Mansfield was concerned in her stories with transmitting the moment which might signify the whole, or, as Raoul Duquette, perhaps the slyest of her narrator-frames, puts it:

> There does seem to be a moment when you realise that, quite by accident, you happen to have come on to the stage at exactly the moment you were expected . . . . There I had been for all eternity, as it were, and now at last I was coming to life . . . .

For Mansfield, the context of the moment of significance is often one which structurally defines its transitoriness: a boat, a train, the eve of a voyage, a hotel abroad, a café, a taxi. There is clearly a metaphorical dimension to the transitoriness of Mansfield's settings, and it may also be associated with her practice as a writer. Like Joyce, she is concerned with 'life purified in and reprojected from the human imagination'; according to Murry she ' "saw", and wrote, in flashes', and it is the epiphanic, concentrated focus on the particular as suggestive of something beyond itself that is the most complex and typical aspect of Mansfield's short fiction. It also suggests an association between the terms colonial and modernist. Mansfield hated 'plotty' stories, like colonial ones, and did not write them, but in her fictions concentrated on a point of significance which gives meaning to the changing and unstable context in which it occurs. This might also be said to be the seldom-realized objective of colonial fiction.[31]

In her most famous New Zealand stories, the fiction which displays her talent at its most commanding and indescribable ('Prelude', 'At the Bay', 'The Doll's House', 'The Garden Party'), Mansfield's use of her own childhood past has been well documented. They are stories which Mansfield saw as part of a 'novel' to be called 'Karori', and which in fact form two story cycles, one about the Sheridan family, and one about the Burnells. Apart from *In a German Pension* and her earliest pieces, only the New Zealand stories feature children other than adult children, so that with one or two exceptions ('Sun and Moon' and 'The Young Girl') children, in Mansfield's later fictions, live in New Zealand. Obviously there is a biographical reading for this, but it does indicate a major difference between the New Zealand stories and the English stories, and suggests different concerns. Single-layered families or couples (as in 'The Escape' or 'The Man Without a Temperament'), and double-layered families of adult children and parents (as in 'The Daughters of the Late Colonel') give way to the multi-layered extended family of the Burnells who, correspondingly, occupy a great deal more space (house, garden, beach house, beach) than do Mansfield's Anglo-Europeans. In their colonial location, Mansfield's stories are both more expansive and structurally more extended, so if the 'Burnell stories are about discovery and the growth of . . . awareness'[32], it is the discovery of a more extensive and complex awareness metaphorically associated with a larger space.

The country discovered in 'At the Bay' is not the country of colonial fiction. Nothing dramatic happens, there is no plot, descriptions of native bush are kept to a minimum; yet as a story it is both culturally distinctive and distinctively modernist. Written in thirteen sections, 'At the Bay' progresses through a day spent by the Burnells at the beach; the narrative opens and closes with an unpeopled landscape, the frame through which the family and beach society are seen, and the frame of a day acts to contain the fluid projections of past and future and present that take place in the minds of the characters. Like many New Zealand colonial families, the Burnell family has an Australian past. Linda, lying under the mānuka tree, feels with intense emotion the pleasure of solitude, but no sooner has the word 'alone' been articulated, than she has a recognition of time and life, passing, sweeping her away:

> Along came Life like a wind and she was seized and shaken; she had to go. Oh dear, would it always be so? Was there no escape?

The image of escape that comes to Linda is her Australian childhood, and the dream of travel, 'cutting off' with her father, as if they were 'two boys together', enjoying the mateship of colonial itineracy, anti-domestic and rootless. For what imprisons Linda, in time and in circumstance, is her gender: 'She was broken, made weak, her courage was gone, through child-bearing. And what made it doubly hard to bear was, she did not love her children.'[33]

But though Linda is swept away by Life, constrained by her family, though the whole Burnell clan exists only momentarily as it is, in the narrative present, the story's structural focus on transitoriness is paradoxically as close to an affirmation of stability and permanence as is possible in Mansfield's fiction. Linda's angry thoughts about motherhood are succeeded, at the next moment, by an unexpected 'new' feeling about her baby; as time sweeps past it brings discoveries in the mind quite as much as in the actual physical world, the 'vast dangerous garden . . ., undiscovered, unexplored'[34] that waits outside Jonathon Trout's office. The country of discovery of 'At the Bay' is both the country of 'Life' and the unexplored country of possibility that is metaphorically associated with an expansive colonial environment, even though the characters' ability to discover it is constrained by their circumstances and relegated to their fantasies.

In the narrative detail of 'At the Bay', precise colonial location occurs: Linda and Stanley grew up in Tasmania, Kezia's Uncle William died of sunstroke at 'the mines', Alice goes to tea with Mrs Stubbs who is like a thrilling older version of the woman at the store, and there are numerous positioning descriptive details in the references to paddocks, mānuka, and so on. Figuratively, 'At the Bay' represents its peaceful domestic structures as metonymic for journey, voyage, change; the road on which Alice walks to Mrs Stubbs's shop or the road bringing Harry Kember to Beryl, is insistently present, and the traveller can, like the narrator at the end of 'The Woman at the Store', 'turn a bend and the whole place disappears'.[35] In 'At the Bay' the signifying journeys are inward, as they are for the colonist, journeys that occur as moments of concentrated focus within the discontinuities, divisions, and ambiguities of individual life.

Nationalism and Social Realism, 1920s-1950s

More than that of any other writer, the work of Frank Sargeson signifies New Zealandness in our literature. Even though his stories can hardly be said still to reflect a familiar society, his fiction, like Henry Lawson's of Australia, offers a reading of New Zealand. Mansfield's transformation of the short story took place in Europe and in the context of modernism; though she was considered to have interpreted accurately and beautifully a segment of New Zealand life and a part of the New Zealand landscape, the short story as it was written and read in New Zealand was the fiction of a different country from hers. Mansfield's complex disguisings of self were not representative of a literature still engaged with problems of context, of readership, and of self-representation. In 1930, the 'first collection ever made of short stories by New Zealanders' opened with an apology for the lack of 'any national outlook or distinctive atmosphere', which the editor, O.N. Gillespie, took to be a consequence of New Zealand's homogeneous society, ('Except for the delightful Maori race . . . our stock is Anglo-Saxon')[36] and of its environmental and cultural closeness to 'Home'. More than half the stories included by Gillespie are by women (including Mansfield's 'The Voyage') and the majority are romances, while the stories by male writers mostly conform to oral tale-telling patterns: the yarn, the adventure story, the racing story, or the comic · sketch as in Arthur H. Adams's 'The Last of the Moas' (from *The New Chum*, 1906), which enjoyed some satirical play with colonial stereotypes and legends.

However, by the late 1920s romance had outlived its usefulness as a simple narrative ground of short fiction, though it remained strong in popular fiction. Although 'local colour' (with an eye on an English readership) still seemed the best means of participating in the production of the 'real' to many writers, more sophisticated attempts to locate short fiction in a regional context, both in terms of its readership and its content, began to appear. The stories published in the *New Zealand Illustrated Magazine* implied a reader originally from 'Home', if not actually living there, but by 1936 local reviewers such as 'Quivis' in the *Evening Post* regarded local readership as the imperative condition of a national literature.

Some day we shall have stories of New Zealand people by New Zealand people for New Zealand people and, given the requisite art, the beginnings of a truly national literature; but so long as our best writers, however pardonable the motive of making a living, tell this tale with a telescope to one eye, bearing on the distant market in London, and the other eye half-shut to their readers here, that day will be deferred.[37]

In 1927 Jean Devanny's *Old Savage and Other Stories* was published in London. Devanny's stories were not included in Gillespie's anthology, even though they might seem to provide a 'distinctive (local) atmosphere', and though they are based on the romance model, being mostly stories about love. But Devanny re-wrote romance as a vehicle for her political convictions. She was a communist and a feminist, and the stories in *Old Savage* vary between more romantic and more political treatments of the relationship between men and women. Even in stories such as 'The Soul of Black Bill Hogan' and 'Tui With Added Years', whose narratives are structured on conventional romance objectives, Devanny introduces class distinction or insists on the sexuality of the woman as a motive force in her behaviour.

A cluster of Devanny's stories are written about coal-mining settlements on the West Coast, which evoke a New Zealand unfamiliar to the educated middle-class readers of colonial romance: an environment of pubs and mines and townships without sewage systems, in which the 'refuse piled up and rotted in the sun till the stinks of it lay like a loathsome blanket upon the townships',[38] and in which miners drink all their hard-earned pay, leaving their wives to support the children by prostitution. Devanny's fictions are based on a Marxist view of social conditions, and challenge the conventions of romance by insisting that the relationship between the sexes is political: woman as the property of man, woman constrained by powerlessness to exploit her body as a commodity (which, however, she does for selfless reasons, for love of her children). Devanny's use of narrative as overtly political distinguished her from the writers of the late nineteenth and early twentieth century, more especially as she emphasized the gender of her subject — one of the reasons no doubt for the hostile reception her writing received. She signals a crucial change in direction for short fiction, away from the squattocratic *beaux champs* of Mansfield's fictional locations to the plain-speaking, truth-telling, hard-drinking, and hard-up rural New Zealander.

Frank Anthony's sketches, later published as *Me and Gus* in 1938, appeared in periodicals in the 1920s. These comic sketches of Taranaki dairy farmers not only formed a popular audience but were also highly praised by critical commentators for their 'direct and masculine' qualities. E.H. McCormick attributed to Anthony a 'minor' revolution in New Zealand fiction:

The broad masculine humour of the sketches, their unfailing gusto, and their wholesome bucolic flavour had been absent from New Zealand writing since pioneer days.[39]

Where Devanny used romance and melodrama as her structure for the representation of the social problems of 'real' working class people, and to undermine conventional romance stereotypes, Anthony's sketches of Taranaki dairy farmers are written as oral narrative, vernacular accounts of two young men in a dominantly masculine environment, anti-domestic, afraid of women and either suspicious or conventionally romantic in their attitudes towards them, preoccupied with ambitious but uncompleted projects, practical jokes, and horseplay. As a view of rural New Zealand, Anthony's sketches represent 'real' work on the farm, but work that is humorously difficult, comically mismanaged by men as little boys. Anthony explodes expectations associated with the colonial Pastoral Dream and romance conventions by focusing on the unglamorous work and financial difficulty of inexperienced farmers. At the same time the sketches of *Me and Gus* frame the New Zealand male as inarticulate and emotionally constrained, 'authentic' in his inadequacies. Anthony's implied reader is as gendered as Devanny's, but Anthony's emphasis is on the satirical possibilities of a rural society. Undemanding as their stories are, Devanny and Anthony share an interest in creating a fictional environment that makes some claim on the reader to acknowledge the relationship between characters and institutions, experience and convention. Whether it is Devanny exposing the perfect mother of colonial society or Anthony's Mark in combat with the agent, they function as predecessors to Sargeson in this fictional shift away from local colour to the 'real' idiom and conditions of the social context, though with the advent of Sargeson in the 1930s, feminist political romance gave way to masculinist oral narrative as the dominant short fiction of New Zealand literature.

In its first number in July 1932, the Auckland University College literary magazine *Phoenix* declared: 'We are hungry for the words that shall show us these islands and ourselves; that shall give us a home in thought.' Finding a 'home in thought' explicitly preoccupied New Zealand writers throughout the 1930s and 1940s, and has dominated both fictional and critical writing throughout our literary history. What is 'New Zealandness'? How New Zealand is written and thought must also be how it is read, and that story, like text and meaning itself, can only exist within changing and impermanent boundaries, no sooner marked out than redefined. But literary history can demonstrate that some writers have been considered more significant than others, constructing fictions in which 'we recognise (however obliquely) something of ourselves'.[40]

In a celebratory issue of *Islands* for Sargeson's seventy-fifth birthday a large number of writers and friends paid tribute, and it was apparent that he had provided a major context for the work of many of his successors, particularly as a writer who 'invented New Zealand'. C.K. Stead remarked in his 'Letter to Frank Sargeson':

On my desk at this moment I have an essay by a research student troubled by the fact that your fiction doesn't represent New Zealand as it really is. Isn't this the inevitable next step when for so many years you have been plagued by the good will and praise of critics who have found New Zealand perfectly represented in your work?[41]

That Sargeson should have been seen for so long as a writer who 'perfectly represented' New Zealand raised some questions about the kind of fictions he wrote and about who might have recognized nationhood in them (even in 1978 the contributors to *Islands* are overwhelmingly male); but it also points to the historical and political context in which his fiction was produced.

Sargeson's sketches were first published in *Tomorrow*, an independent weekly edited in Christchurch, in 1935. By far the largest part of *Tomorrow* was given over to political commentary, on both internal and international politics. As time passed, political commentary became more pressing and more critical; in 1940 the journal was effectively forced to close by the Labour Government. It was in this anti-provincial, political, and internationalist context that Sargeson's realist, nationalist, and provincial sketches were first published. All the fiction published in *Tomorrow* was sketch-length, clearly due in part to *Tomorrow*'s constraints of space. But the sketch also has some structural advantages as a piece of short fiction published in a political context. It can function as an illustration of stereotype in the vernacular or as a parable or anecdote which gives sharp focus to a particular question. In comparison to the psychological sketch of the 1890s, used as the basis of free indirect discourse by Mansfield in order to create emotional depth, Sargeson's sketches and the sketches or parables of other writers published in *Tomorrow* concentrated on educative anecdotes:

Sargeson chose not to make his art subservient to the popular stereotypes of society; but to use those stereotypes in his art — in the process subverting the stereotypes and teasing nuance from the vernacular.[42]

To the readers of *Tomorrow*, or perhaps more precisely, the contributors and producers of *Tomorrow*, it was the accuracy of Sargeson's political eye which was so compelling, as its literary editor, Winston Rhodes, later recalled:

If I stood by the long drawing board at the window with my back to the baby grand piano and looked down into Hereford Street, more than a few of the passers-by seemed to my uncharitable eyes exact replicas of the narrator's uncle who 'couldn't suppose'.

But after *A Man and His Wife* came out as a collection in 1941, a reviewer in the *Dominion*, commenting on McCormick's praise of Sargeson, remarked that 'the dialogue is certainly convincing, but do not their weak structure, their appalling sentimentality, spoil them?' While Sargeson's stories did not receive wide acclaim when they first appeared, his representation of local idiom eventually functioned as a coercive frame for the 'real' to a very wide readership, though, as Roger Horrocks has observed of *The Penguin Book of*

New Zealand Verse edited by Allen Curnow, what strikes one readership historically as 'reality' may well strike later readers quite differently.[43]

Not all of Sargeson's contemporary readers were comfortable with his realities. When a popular monthly like the *New Zealand Railways Magazine*, which began in 1933 'with a truly national outlook' could claim to its readers that its adventure and romance stories 'present to New Zealanders the story of the life and colour of their own land', Sargeson's sketches of Depression life on the margins hit a nerve. Oliver Duff, editor of the *New Zealand Listener*, made a distinction, no doubt not an uncommon one, between what 'most of us' see and what Sargeson 'can't help' suggesting about New Zealand:

> That New Zealand during the last twenty years has been a kind of rural slum . . . most of us don't see it like that. We don't see our neighbours as morons, our young people as sensual louts, our teachers and preachers as liars and hypocrites, our patriots as profiteers. We know, however, that such people exist, and their place in the picture need not worry us if Sargeson sees them, can't take his eyes off them, and can't help presenting them as they are. It is his affair and not ours if he chooses to be laureate of hoboes.[44]

The great majority of stories published in the periodical press in the 1930s followed conventional narrative patterns, and were directed at a conservative and implicitly untroubled readership. Sargeson's target is precisely that audience, the New Zealand he referred to as 'Little Bethel', a 'raw, aesthetically hostile' environment, puritanical and 'proper', exhibiting a 'combination of frightful crudity and even more frightful refinement'. What is remarkable about Sargeson's fiction is not that he chose to attack a society he perceived as morally deficient and artistically negligible, but that he chose to attack it in an idiom that made such demands on his readers, by forcing them into political recognitions of stereotype and attitude as they represent themselves in vernacular speech. It is for his 'convincing' dialogue that Sargeson received tribute; it is in the construction and shaping of that dialogue that Sargeson is at his most political. However, as he was always at pains to point out, he was writing fiction, not social commentary, and though his fictions work to return the reader to a kind of social and moral imaginativeness both about fiction and what it might be taken to represent, as a writer Sargeson stressed that 'all I can do is be aware of this terribly complicated and difficult situation, and I can only make marginal comments in the form that seems to suit me best — that is, by creating fictions'.

In 1935 Sargeson wrote an article for *Tomorrow* about Sherwood Anderson, which might also be read as a description of his own narratives. He stressed the 'value of repetition', the 'short suggestive sentence', and Anderson's use of words to 'liberate the imagination':

> Histories are told in the commonplace words and phrases that you find in the Old Testament, but they have nothing of the flatness of life. In life the third dimension often appears to be missing. Anderson makes it his job to put it in.[46]

Sargeson's fictions also have the effect of having 'put in' the 'third dimension'. The texture and surface of his fictions are incomplete, not fully self-referential; instead they initiate a process in which the reader must participate in order to 'make sense' of the fiction, in order, indeed, to 'make' the narrative.

In the sketch 'A Piece of Yellow Soap', the 'facts' presented by the narrative are minimal and sketchy; only the outline of a story is told, without explanation, so that what is not said between the facts is left to the reading process itself. The milkman knows what it is like to have bloodless and shrunken fingers, and the sight of a piece of yellow soap arouses in him an identification with the woman holding it that blocks his speech, an identification participated in by the reader, who like the narrator is blocked from 'knowing' any more about the woman than her piece of soap suggests, and who can only 'understand' the narrative by feeling, like the narrator, what it signifies.

'A Piece of Yellow Soap' restricts the information, points of view, and narrative explanation given to the reader to an image and an anecdotal voice. But the effect of that image on the narrator and his attempt to understand it is to represent both the milkman and the woman as participants in a social relationship suggestive of larger moral and economic questions than those explicitly raised. It is the power of the particular (the cheap yellow washing soap) to signify an economic discourse, a discourse of the 'real' concrete world, and the power of the individual (the narrator) to signify a moral one, that define the characteristic structures of Sargeson's sketches. In the play between the image and the narration, which typically sets up incomplete contexts for the image, the reading process is the connecting and educative force. The will to understand Sargeson's stories lies in the will to 'read' his idiom. Though Sargeson's fictions represent themselves as speaking of the lives of working-class white males, often poor, ill-at-ease with the language, recounting anecdotes with incomplete or uncertain understanding, they speak *to* the reader who is none of those things (except perhaps male), but who is, like God, a Person of Sensibility. When he looks at that piece of yellow washing soap, he feels, or is made to feel, ashamed; the fiction infects the 'real' context of the reader. Sargeson's fictions are overtly political and educative in their narrative intention; in his hands short stories became, in his own phrase, 'marginal comments' on the complicated social fictions of history.

'That Summer' is Sargeson's major narrative of the 1930s. Located in a shifting male environment of boarding houses and pubs, it begins with an image of rural New Zealand as the place of origin that has been left behind. Even though 'things couldn't be worse in town', that is where Bill's itchy feet take him. The move into town places Bill in an environment where the things that identify him are gradually removed; from having been a good farm worker he becomes one of the many unemployed (cooks, sailors, barmen, farm workers) awash in the pubs and in the registry offices of Auckland; from having plenty of chips in his pocket, he is without the price of a tram fare after Ted has robbed him; from being a man on holiday enjoying looking at the sheilas in the park, he is arrested on a charge of sexual assault and imprisoned; from being a man trying to pick up a girl at the pictures he becomes someone whose emotional motivation is love of another man and whose possible relationships with women have contracted to his landlady, her small daughter, and a transvestite. As the story unfolds, all the reader's assumptions about Bill are undermined — not so much by Bill's proving to be other than he appears, as by the gradual and inevitable constriction of his circumstances; his power to choose steadily retreats. It is this constriction and confinement that the text enacts.

Some of Sargeson's titles, like 'The Making of a New Zealander' or 'White Man's Burden', explicitly signal cultural discourse, and almost all of his stories and sketches represent the relationships between men and women as destructive, often violently so, as in 'Sale Day'. But it is the commonplace words and phrases used by an anecdotal voice apparently only half-engaged with the narrative that produce the cultural significance of Sargeson's texts. When Bill in 'That Summer' hears he has won the double on Boxing Day, after knocking off work at the Dally's, it is a 'bit of All Right'. Not even at a moment of triumphant celebration can his language expand. Bill expresses himself only in recounting the sequence of events as he experiences it; his speech contains almost no modifiers, few intensifiers, scarcely any adjectives or adverbs, no similes or metaphors; in other words Bill has no language with which to speak anything other than 'factual' reporting, and what he narrates demonstrates his limited ability to articulate his understanding of what he reports. The absence of a metaphorical, emotional, and cognitive dimension to Bill's narrative prompts, in the reader, an insistent reading-in of that dimension; the reader's presence in the narrative is a product of the absence in Bill's narrative, but also conditioned by Bill's constriction. The reader can read Bill, and 'know' his story, but that knowledge confirms its 'realness'; by supplying the absent discourse, the reader authenticates and re-imprisons Bill: there is no other world in which to understand him.

These recurrent locations of Sargeson's stories indicate a preoccupation with identity in his fiction; gender identity, national identity, economic identity, social identity, and cultural identity, all locations in which the 'real' can be constructed and deconstructed, and textual identity destabilized. Simon During has demonstrated, in what he calls an 'overreading' of 'The Hole That Jack Dug', that that story is a number of different texts, deconstructing in the process not just its own narratives, but also its implied reader(s).[47] In 'The Making of a New Zealander' the inconclusiveness of narrative events is reflected back to the definition promised by the title; the text as a text of cultural identity is thus called into question. The story functions to create uncertainty about what the term 'New Zealander' might signify, at the same time as it presents a narrator whose speech assumes a common identity with the 'real' reader.

As a story about cultural identity and as a story which illustrates some qualities of Sargeson's narratives, 'The Making of a New Zealander' shows how uncertain the boundaries of meaning become once conventional contexts are subverted or questioned. Having to construct the meaning of a narrative from a narrator who doesn't know whether or not there is any meaning in it, in the context of a title which suggests another agency to whom meaning is apparent, puts responsibility for the 'real' meaning of the story onto the reader without foreclosing on other possibilities. Neither Sargeson, Nick the Dalmatian, nor the narrator are going to make any big claims about cultural or national or gender identity, even as the narrator seems to revert to stereotype and forgets his problems in booze, leaving the question to the reader.

It is this kind of politically educative destabilizing of narrative and narrator while 'writing' his fictions in a provincial realist idiom deeply familiar to his audience that characterizes Sargeson's best work. It is ironic that his work should have been acclaimed for its convincing realism when his narratives consistently work to undermine notions of the real; but in the process, the identification of the reader with the narrator by completing the narrative and supplying the lack in the narrator's speech, forces an affirmation of the 'realness' of uncertainty (about voice, objects, images, and events) that is as expressive of a cultural context as it is of the fragmented and incomplete meanings of texts, in which nothing, not even the reader, is taken for granted: 'Well, that's it. If these pages ever have a reader I would expect them either to ring a bell, or not to.'[48]

Sargeson's later stories, such as 'City and Suburban' or 'Just Trespassing, Thanks', focused more on the 'writerly' aspects of fiction, with educated, linguistically self-conscious narrators and much more play with language. His stories moved away from the sketch model and also from the characteristic narrative subject of his early fictions — the isolated, socially marginal, apparently stereotypical Kiwi jokers of 'A Good Boy', 'I've Lost My Pal', and 'A Pair of Socks' — but stories like these remained the location of New Zealand realist fiction for a long time, and still carry iconic freight in our cultural history. The male writers who followed Sargeson positioned themselves, as Lawrence Jones has put it, 'under my uncle's hat'.[49]

In an extended interview in 1970, Sargeson claimed that he was never conscious of writing in the shadow of Katherine Mansfield or of reacting against her, but that Mansfield 'imposed a pattern on our writing . . . .. Hosts of young women wrote Mansfield stories.' There has long been a tendency in New Zealand literary history to see Sargeson and Mansfield as progenitors of divergent though coexisting traditions. Sargeson himself in the same interview registered unease about its consequences:

> When I came along a lot of people felt, I think . . . that because of a certain amount of power in these early sketches they seemed to relate so much to New Zealand. And that's right, *relate* — it wasn't New Zealand itself; it related. But people felt, 'Ah, this is the way you write.' So therefore, instead of opening up something for New Zealand, both Mansfield and myself have tended to be constricting influences. I mean who wants all of New Zealand life to be seen in terms of Mansfield or in terms of Sargeson?[50]

But for twenty or more years after the first publication of 'Conversation With My Uncle' the short story in New Zealand's literary magazines, anthologies, and published collections was dominated by Sargeson's presence and by male writers. Although women kept writing short stories, as shown by C.R. Allen's London-published collection, *Tales by New Zealanders* (1938), which includes stories by Robin Hyde and Eileen Duggan, as well as by a number of lesser-known women writers, they tended to write romances directed to a homogeneous readership neither sharply local nor political, but loosely middle-class, educated, and white, who were as comfortable with the idea of Great Britain as a fictional environment as with a pastoral and affluent New Zealand. The New Zealand short story feature which appeared weekly in the *New Zealand Herald* was entirely dominated in 1936 by romance and adventure stories, mostly by women (Mary Gurney, Joyce West, and Lucy Winn are recurrent names), and while it is probable that most of these writers were aware of Mansfield (and possibly of Sargeson), the short story in the popular press and in popular journalism remained, as it does today, confined to particular narrative models (the romance, the yarn, the adventure story) in which fundamental types of human experience were reaffirmed as essential and universal.

Women writers clearly could not (or would not) use Sargeson's stories as literary models, even though he was extremely helpful personally to a number of women writers, including Greville Texidor, Helen Shaw, and Janet Frame; and although Mansfield's work provided the heartland for a sentimentalized view of early New Zealand common in magazine romance, none of her formal innovations (her symbolist prose techniques, or her use of complex layered narratives) was taken up in the work of her successors in New Zealand. With Sargeson, the focus of the short story shifted to the idiom of men. His characterization of New Zealand as a puritanical, narrow-minded, and provincial society, torn by conflict between the sexes, framed by the point of view of a young man or a boy, and expressed in an orally impoverished, repetitive, and largely non-figurative idiom, became the realist ground on which the short story flourished. But whereas an explanatory context in Sargeson's fiction was the Depression and the social structure of a depressed provincial economy, many of the writers of the 1940s and 1950s narrowed down the broad critique of social institutions and systems that is the subtext of Sargeson's narratives, to the war, and to the game-playing preoccupations of the New Zealand male. A.P. Gaskell, G.R. Gilbert, John Reece Cole, Dan Davin, James Courage, O.E. Middleton, and Roderick Finlayson have all been termed 'Sons' of Frank Sargeson.[51] What is common to their work is a general reliance on a 'real' New Zealand invented by Sargeson and a willingness to push the terms of that invention into more formal and definite shape. Where Sargeson's narrative method worked to destabilize assumptions, the work of Gaskell or Davin affirms them. In the stories of A.P. Gaskell, the typical New Zealand male likes football and beer, finds relationships with women difficult, and has rural connections even if he doesn't actually farm.

Gaskell's stories are typically presented through a first person narrator 'like someone talking', but without the kind of deconstruction of the narrator by his narrative that occurs in Sargeson's fiction. In 'The Big Game', Bernie's consciousness of his preparations for the big game represent him as typical of a society for whom such games are deeply serious. His straightforward and humble appreciation of his part in the team acts as both record and affirmation of the relationship between men seen as a group, in pursuit of a common objective, and as an icon for a social structure much larger than themselves: they represent their university, their names are in the paper, a tram conductor recognizes them, crowds queue to see them play. In fact nationhood itself is the metaphorical context of 'The Big Game'. The narrative closes as the players move out into the roar of the crowd, about to be tested and proved; their identity and success as people are unquestioned, and the outcome of the particular game is irrelevant. The real point is that Bernie and his team-mates are culturally tested and proven.

Gaskell's later story, 'All Part of the Game' is a more complex treatment of game-playing as social metaphor, and employs a narrative that established a paradigm for many subsequent short stories. Although Bernie in 'The Big Game' proves his maturity by his willingness to match up to the rest of the team, he is in fact adult, has a girlfriend, and is at university. Gordon, in 'All Part of the Game', is still at primary school (though perhaps pubescent) when he is propelled into an environment of difficult adult emotions and masculine occupations. The game in this story is more explicitly associated with living, though it is articulated as horse-racing; winners and losers in the actual race are also winners and losers in the larger context of adult sexual relationships; and the story functions as a piece of observation about adult society as it is understood partly by a male child. When Norman, the unsuccessful jockey and lover, is found hanged in the loft, Gordon is forced into a sad, adult recognition that 'someone always had to be the loser'. His transition into an adult environment, in which those who don't succeed or conform are ignored or rejected, functions as a critique of that environment in a way that is typical of the male realist tradition. Gordon's shock on seeing Norman, and his sympathetic and simple affection for him, are an indication of his sensibility, like Bill's caring for Terry in 'That Summer', or the cheerful comradely affection of the rugby team in 'The Big Game', or the sore hearts of the boys and their father in Dan Davin's 'Death of a Dog'. Emotional sensibility and a kind of solidarity and truth are located in young boys and in male environments. Very often the knowledge that marks the child's transition to emotional awareness is caused by or associated with the behaviour of women. In Sargeson's stories, in Davin's stories of childhood, and in many of Gaskell's, women are often figures of power, especially emotional power (though Sargeson's women tend to be also physically large and strong), who care too much for social distinctions, like Gordon's aunt in 'All Part of the Game', or are not emotionally honest, like Mrs Connelly in Davin's 'Death of a Dog'.

The middle-class family as a place of constriction and gender battle is a commonplace in the realist short story, whose narrative model of escape is found in the sensitive young boy or in the kind of male environment offered by sport or war; an environment of generic names (Ted, Joe, Mac, Bill), intense physical activity, and incompletely expressed emotion. This stereotypical masculine environment is at the same time challenged and affirmed by its narrators, who record it (thereby asserting the authenticity of the stereotype) but also challenge it through the very nature of their activity, since the man who writes and in particular the man interested in exploring emotions and ideas is, according to the stereotype, unmale. As a result narrators are often younger, or sexually ambiguous, or 'outside' in some distinctive but non-disabling way.

The fictions of John Reece Cole are, as Cherry Hankin has remarked, only indirectly about war, unlike Davin's stories which are about actual combat as experienced by New Zealand soldiers on active duty in Crete or Italy, who remain assertively and expressively grim with their 'narrow hearts' and their regional idiom. The further Davin's soldiers are displaced from home, the more at home this travelling environment becomes: when off-duty, the men read *Free Lances* round the billy. Cole's stories take place on the edge of war, back home with the survivors and the damaged. Unlike Davin's, his fictions are not picaresque or documentary, but associate war-related damage with the kinds of damage experienced by outsiders in civilian societies. In the eponymous story of the collection *It Was So Late* (1949), a town welcomes back its returning soldiers with a reception in the local grand house where one of the returnees, Flight Lieutenant Brent, had grown up as the child of the maid. The conjunction of past and present acts as a commentary both on the kind of childhood he experienced and the loss it represents, and on the different kinds of war fought in civilian and military contexts. In Cole's stories there is a liberation for men in going to war, since real emotional bonds are established as distinct from conventional social ones. In 'The Sixty Nine Club' a returned soldier visits his friend's mother to tell her about his death:

> Jimmy's mother was sitting with her head resting against the back of the chair, her eyes closed. He wondered whether tears were coming and felt emotion knot up in his stomach. She opened her eyes suddenly. 'I did everything possible for him, didn't I?'
> It came out more like a challenge than a question. He thought, where is the sorrow? Where is the grief?[52]

However in Cole's most sharply focused fictions, 'Up at the Mammoth' and 'A Babble Between', the return of soldiers into civilian society reveals it as alien, combative, anxious, its citizens living at cross purposes, unable to pay service to the myths of honour and duty and love. The return of the stories is not away from the desert but back to it, to use a simile that occurs at the end of 'A Babble Between':

> He pressed back into the dark seat, silent as the car settled into the long fast drive into the city, his own inadequacy stretching before him like a desert.[53]

The inadequacy of oral language to express anything other than conventional attitudes, or its identification with an 'approved' code of speech that permits only a certain kind of expression, provides the functional frame of short narrative after Sargeson. Sargeson's minimalist dialogue which acts as an ironic dialect for the reader, forcing recognition of the unexpressed, took on the status of a 'real' language in the work of Gaskell, Davin, Middleton, and others. As part of the official language of war, it becomes in Davin's war stories a kind of truth-telling, as if undecorated and unexpressive prose bears witness to the kinds of moral qualities valuable in soldiers, a sign of national and personal character. With the return of the short story to the timber yards and community picnics of small-town New Zealand life, the constriction of spoken language takes on, textually, a more complex meaning. In Greville Texidor's story 'Epilogue', it is used ironically, as Rex tells Jim's pacifist parents about his heroic death as a combatant. In John Reece Cole's 'Up At the Mammoth', the speech of a displaced and (un)returned fighter pilot suggests an inability to locate meaning in language.

In Davin's anthology, *New Zealand Short Stories* (1953), Gaskell's sketch of racial opposition, 'School Picnic' was juxtaposed with Greville Texidor's 'An Annual Affair'. In Gaskell's story, Miss Brown's pejorative, stereotyped, officially 'correct' language to her Māori pupils and their families is set against their colloquial speech, the frame in which her 'civilized' behaviour is ironically defined by their generosity and affection. In Texidor's story, the clichéd and truncated dialogue is framed by Joy's unofficial, youthful comprehensions of what is not intended or expressed, the fullness on the other side of speech, the significance of non-vocal expression, signalled to her by her emotions or her observation. In 'An Annual Affair', all speech becomes a coding of what cannot be said either because it is too complex, or because no one wants to hear it, or because there is a refusal, on the character's part, to engage in anything more than the expression of conventional attitudes which do not require thought, or which disguise emotional realities. Simple speech is not evidence of plain truthfulness, but rather a masking of a truer or more difficult response. At the same time, people who speak in simplistic truisms wish to be heard to conform, even when (like Mum) they are in a situation of unexpressed conflict, or when (like the Reverend Allum) their speech is not dialogue but egotistic monologue.

Texidor places her stories at a kind of intersection between the rural, puritanical New Zealand of 'An Annual Affair', where the community is attempting to hold off change, and the 'outside' world of her later stories: 'outside' either because their fictional scene is away from New Zealand altogether as in 'These Dark Glasses', or because the appearance of foreigners in wartime Auckland generates uncertainty about who or what New Zealand might be. In Texidor's stories the homogeneous society is a myth like any other, and New Zealand is a foreign country writing its necessary fictions, all the way from farce to tragedy:

Fred had once bought a little rocky island up North. He meant to farm it. I think he pictured himself as a sort of Gauguin, only beneficent, bringing health and enlightenment to the Maoris. He'd even been meaning to marry a Maori girl and had had her to housekeep as a tryout, but after three weeks she'd run away.[54]

Texidor's fictions force a recognition that cultural identity is *invented* in language and image, through her introduction of outsiders, who bring with them, like Lilli in 'Goodbye Forever', the photographs and stories and language of another world. By contrast, the New Zealand stories of James Courage, discontinuous narratives of squattocratic Canterbury, affirm cultural identity by focusing on a small boy's view of the tensions of a closed family environment. Courage moved to England as a young man, but published stories in *Landfall* during the 1940s. Just as Texidor's fiction enacts a shift from the outskirts of the Spanish Civil War to provincial New Zealand, and Cole's a movement from English air raids to bleak Auckland suburbs, Courage's stories also document personal and family transitions. However both Texidor and Cole focus on the intersection of individuals with wider social structures and systems. Courage, as Charles Brasch indicated in the title he chose for a collection of Courage's stories, emphasizes the subjectivity of individuals: 'We are all of us — each of us — such separate creatures.'[55]

Although Courage's settings and subjects are quite different from the doss-houses, farm labourers, and Kiwi soldiers of his contemporaries, his narrative structure shares their typical focus on the perception of a young boy, and his stories require the reader to interpret his protagonist's observations. There is little attempt at regional distinctiveness: their idiom is a class idiom, and the narrative environment is self-contained and hierarchical, solidly white, upper-class and pastoral. The kinds of conflict Walter witnesses and participates in are those that exist between genders and in families; he is confined by his father's expectations of him. What connects Courage's fiction to that of his contemporaries is not the social environment he writes about but the unresolved antagonisms that exist between the sexes in families (between husband and wife, and mother and son), amongst which the child Walter is asked to identify himself as masculine. Sometimes these antagonisms are displaced on to animals and children. In 'Uncle Adam Shot a Stag', Courage's first published story, Uncle Adam's hostility to women is displaced on to the stag he had shot, which 'ran like a ruddy stag-woman'; Walter is overcome by the spectacle of Uncle Adam, angry and laughing, waltzing with the carcase. In 'After the Earthquake', Walter's knowledge that he had seen a horse tied to Miss Duncaster's verandah is denied by the adults around him in order to conceal evidence of adult sexuality: Miss Duncaster is supposed to be in mourning for her mother, not receiving visits from her lover on his bay horse.

The group of stories Courage wrote about Walter Blakiston and his parents focus so intensely and exclusively on the relationships between father, mother, and son, and on the structures of subjective identity, that broader questions like class, nation, and race appear to be simply accepted as part of the unquestioned cultural and social identity within which the characters live. Neither the

Depression, nor the war, nor motorized transport have disrupted affluent pastoral life; battle is gender-based and contained within the family group; but by locating the colonial past in Walter's perception, the perception of a child for whom gender is still fluid and adults complex, fearful, and incomprehensible, Courage re-invents the Canterbury settler as a dominating, angry, and fearsome father. His 1940s child is sensitive, curious, questioning, unwilling to conform to the stereotype expected of him, uncertain about what is right or wrong — the child of a new country.

Sargeson's stories wrote of New Zealand as a place where romance and adventure had been supplanted by the hole that Jack dug. In doing so he presented his successors with a narrative model that proved irresistible. Few writers were able to resist the realist, socially committed narrative of a young boy's version of cultural truth, and few possessed Sargeson's narrative subtlety. In the process, invention became stereotype, and complex ambiguity turned into iconic platitude, as in the stories of Barry Crump. For better or for worse, realism in the New Zealand short story stayed within the terms in which Sargeson was seen to have invented it, for at least twenty years. But there were some writers who engaged with questions other than those of gender and cultural stereotype.

It is perhaps a reflection of the dominant realist model that Finlayson's stories of Māori life between the wars had difficulty getting published. In his introduction to a collection of Finlayson's stories published in 1973, Bill Pearson remarked:

> Editors of most of the New Zealand journals of the time were not interested in his stories. *Brown Man's Burden* and *Sweet Beulah Land* were published at the author's expense .... There were no more than a few hundred of each book printed, distribution was poor, and the two collections between them attracted no more than six short reviews.[56]

Unlike Sargeson's stories, Finlayson's short stories are 'plotty'. Written in third-person vernacular, the drive of the fiction is not on the play between the narrator's account of events and the reader's interpretation of them, but on the outcome of the story. Formally, Finlayson's stories are a hybrid derived from the tale-telling mode (very often cast into an ironically-treated romance frame, as in 'Hemi's Daughter') and the idiomatic sketch, and the narratives mix spoken Māori/English idiom with a third-person idiom suggestive of heroic tale, and of a legendary cultural past. Like Alfred Grace, Finlayson also writes of the Māori as a dying race. There is a continuous background of death through consumption, drink, poor health, violence, or accidents; and most of it, directly or indirectly, is associated with dispossession by the Pākehā. But unlike Grace, Finlayson does not sympathize with the Māori while simultaneously characterizing them as bloodthirsty, diabolical, and alien. In a story like 'The Totara Tree', the effects of dispossession are subtly shown to have developed over generations, and the kind of racial and cultural conflict that all the stories describe does not, as it does in Grace, assume the ultimate superiority of one culture over another. In 'The Totara Tree', the variety of Māori attitudes to the Pākehā who want to cut down a tapu tree to make way for an electricity pylon, suggest that tribal systems are in decay, with a younger generation weary of Uncle Tuna's exploits, and men and women boasting around a barrel of home-brew about what they'll do to the Pākehā. However, there is no sense of the Pākehā inspector and his men as anything but other. If Māori resistance degenerates into a rubbish fire and drunken shouting until only the dead old lady is a figure of dignity, the Pākehā, with their red faces and their blustering and their wasted money have no more dignity and are considerably more alien, associated not with trees and drunken camaraderie but with Power Boards and concrete foundations.

Finlayson's stories do not sentimentalize the Māori, nor do they represent the Māori as less complex or ambiguous than the Pākehā. In 'New Year', 'Māori matters' are opposed to institutional procedures. But the local Māori youth represent themselves as characters in a western, with 'dark heavy coats and wide-brimmed hats pulled down over their eyes'; and the pretty girls think of one of them as a 'sort of Arizona Kid hero'. In 'Hemi's Daughter', Ripi and Huia's romance begins in the colouring language of legend ('For Ripi the strong had looked upon her, and Ripi the handsome had set his spell upon her'),[57] but soon collapses into the comic ironies of realist narrative.

Whereas in Alfred Grace's stories the clash of cultures and races is signified by the conflict of individuals or groups of individuals, in Finlayson's stories the narrative frames the Māori as individual but the Pākehā as institution or representative of an institution, as in 'Johnny Wairua's Wonderland'. Johnny has his eyes opened in Rotorua by the fine big cars the Māori are driving, and opens his valley to the tourist trade. Eventually his valley is taken over by a host of Government Departments and Johnny is rigged out as Official Caretaker in a peaked cap, deprived of his valley and of '*all* the half-a-crown from *all* these big tourists', but able to buzz off to Rotorua for a bit of a spree. Māori speech in Finlayson's fictions signifies cultural dislocation and is fundamentally at odds with Pākehā systems and institutions. In 'A Man of Good Religion' Henare Tinirau demonstrates his 'good religion' by getting married to several different women; in 'Wi Gets the Gospel' Wi's conversion deprives Meri of her husband. The appropriations of language are deeply ironic in Finlayson's stories, where the tourists 'smiled sweetly and said "kia ora"', but 'the youngsters cried, "Atta boy!" as they raced to the store to buy bright-red fizzy drinks'.[58] But though the Māori are comic, tragic, cheerful, drunken, dying, polluted, and corrupted, characterized by the muddled ambiguities of a colonized existence, the stories affirm a culture whose loss brings deprivation and caricature and absence to those Māori who reject or forget it. Finlayson's fictional environment is rural Māori, with city Pākehā looming on the margin and infecting the speech, beliefs, and systems of Māori life. In Noel Hilliard's stories, most of which were written a decade or more later, the rural Māori is displaced even further into the Pākehā system by leaving the country for the town.[59]

*   *   *

C.K. Stead's edition of Maurice Duggan's *Collected Stories* (1981) shows the movement of Duggan's fiction over thirty years of publication. His stories travel from Sargeson to Wedde, from the modernism of James Joyce to the post-modernism of his last published story 'The Magsman Miscellany': thirty stories in thirty years, from 1945-75. Duggan's early fictions signal their intertextuality explicitly. 'Conversation Piece', published in 1947, is a parodic sketch of Hemingway; 'Faith of our Fathers', Duggan's first published story (1945), rewrites early Joyce; and 'Machinery', first published in *Anvil* in 1945 and again in *Irish Writing*, is written in a Sargesonian idiom. Interestingly, Sargeson himself chose, for his suggestively titled anthology *Speaking for Ourselves* (1945), a story of Duggan's which is far removed from the prevailing realistic 'free' story Sargeson established as New Zealand idiom. 'Notes on an Abstract Arachnid', a story in which the texture of language attempts to drive 'beyond words', is not a story Duggan later liked, or thought successful,[60] but Sargeson's aim was to promote a range of 'voices' which might speak for 'us'. In his own work, Duggan's recognition of a variety of textual models shifted the ground of the short story. The rich textual surface of his stories, feeding off other texts, insisted on itself not as mediator of locally recognizable idiom and regional or social 'reality' but as a medium of narratives. As Duggan himself commented, referring to these qualities in his writing: 'in what else could a culture be embalmed, enfolded or expressed?'[61]

Duggan's complex 'enfolding' of culture in language provided the focus both of his own, more extended later fiction and of critical commentary on his work.[62] His fictions travel away from the familiar, relatively simple Joycean precedents in the early Lenihan stories (or in the sketches of Roman Catholic childhood such as 'Guardian' or 'In Youth is Pleasure') to stories in which there is a much richer play of textual surface, away from the representational clarity of a story like 'Race Day' to the concentration of the puzzle in 'The Magsman Miscellany'. Like the stories of Janet Frame, Duggan's later stories challenge the narrative expectations of realism. The chronological sequence of Duggan's work suggests a writing environment in which the historical proximity of Sargeson affected the kinds of narratives he wrote. His first collection, *Immanuel's Land* (1956) is prefaced by a quotation from *The Pilgrim's Progress* containing the title of the collection. The stories that follow, while acknowledging a 'most pleasant mountainous country', also take as their object Sargeson's puritanical society, most obviously in 'Chapter' and 'Towards the Mountains', where the constrictions of public attitudes as they are expressed by parents and schoolteachers, and in the courtroom, force the young or the dispossessed into antisocial, sometimes violent behaviour. In most of the stories of *Immanuel's Land* language mediates the 'real', representing its sequence of events as a narrative in which characters' experiences of the unreal can be distinguished *within* the real, confirming the significance of its context. A cluster of stories are written around the Lenihan family, from the point of view of the children and particularly of Harry, who grows from a small child in 'A Small Story' to a young man in 'Chapter'. Like Davin's 'stories about the Connollys, or Mansfield's about the Burnells, Duggan's Lenihan stories constitute a discontinuous narrative in which individual stories function epiphanically; within a general process of transition, some moments signify.

When Harry sees from a train a weeping Māori woman, a child, and a dog, 'He felt that should he return this way in years to come he would find this scene unaltered, still beyond any ravage of time or season'; the moment in which he sees the child, woman, and dog, is more 'real' than Harry's existence in the train. As a spectator of a scene in which he will never participate, Harry is also a signifier for the artist, predecessor of Duggan's Magsman, witness to the textual frame fixed at its point of clearest signification, but excluded from it. For Harry Lenihan, seeing the woman and the objects and beings which surround her 'fixed within that frame beyond which was only chaos', it 'was as if he had walked into a cinema to confront a scene without movement, the players grouped and their last words still echoing, and must construct from that all he was ever to know'.[63] All Duggan's fictions engage, explicitly or metaphorically, with such 'construction' of knowledge in language; where Sargeson's language offered an apparently transparent screen through which the real was transmitted, Duggan's fictions increasingly concentrate on the problems and uncertainties of language.

'Along Rideout Road That Summer' is Duggan's best known story. As a fiction it engages immediately and directly with textual experience. The context of Buster O'Leary's narrative is the knowingly literary medium in which it is transmitted: a bookish lad shouting Coleridge's 'Kubla Khan', observed by milk-white unicorns. Buster O'Leary's account of experience recognizes the problem of 'how to cope with the shock of the recognition of a certain discrepancy between the real and the written', but the narrative is complicated by further uncertainties about the narrator and the status of his narrative, which serve in the end to destabilize everything but the subjectivity of the narrative and the textual experience it represents. Buster O'Leary's ornamented prose account of his encounter with Puti Hohepa's beautiful daughter Fanny is deeply conscious of problems of connection. How to connect Coleridge's dulcimer with Fanny's ukelele suggests cultural discrepancies as well as the 'discrepancy between the real and the written', and implies a further difficulty of connection between Buster and his audience, addressed in the plural as 'gentlemen'. How to 'read' Buster O'Leary is the real problem posed by the text. The 'gentlemen' to whom the text is addressed provide a knowingly ironic perspective on Buster's romantic and sexy story, but even though Buster's youthful emotions are placed within an adult frame of knowledge, memory, and repetitious experience ('so few variations to an old, old story'),[64] their significance, both to the adult narrator and the reader, is preserved, buried as it were, in Buster's compulsive and prolific retelling of his story. Hearing Buster put tongue to the narrative shows what he is: the volume, energy, and multiple self-representations of his language, within which the 'story' is consumed, rewritten, retold, and finally escaped from, suggest the difficult connections between age and youth, memory and desire, language and experience, story and story teller, narrator and audience.

In a general sense, it is the problem of connection, with all the gestures of 'Rideout Road' towards narratives of passion, adventure, and cultural conflict, that the body of Duggan's fiction is concerned with. All his stories centre on loss and what follows after. Loss is the condition of living and also the context of remembered happiness, whether it is the loss of a mother and the uncertain change in families as in the Lenihan stories, or the loss of youth that Buster O'Leary's adult commentary voices. The process of transition typically provides the narrative structure of Duggan's fictions, voyages, uncompleted journeys, real or fictive departures, or what has been described as Duggan's 'repeated plot': 'some ritual of beginning, another act of breaking out and departing'. This context of transition is reiterated both in the human relationships his stories represent and in their stylistic variety, which Duggan once described as 'the problem of hanging whatever it is on the conventional peg, finding the machinery'.

Duggan's story, 'The Magsman Miscellany', which appeared posthumously, is about texts and fictions and partial views; the problems of knowledge and its transmission in language. The story of Ben McGoldrick and Rosie Finan is written around by marginalia, written across their two lives, written within their differences, their different writings; all the time the miscellany draws attention to its own incomplete, possibly random, variable existence, the separations in the printed text acting metaphorically as a marginal comment on fiction, on human existence, and on language:

> Language is so much a part of what defines and imprisons and paroles us . . . in a world where riddles and metaphors may serve a certain purpose.

While Rosie irons, Ben writes. The gap between their activities can be measured as 'fourteen feet and some inches', or as a work of fiction, a fantasy, or a gap that is 'not bridged'. 'The Magsman Miscellany' draws attention to process, to gaps and silences and alternative selections, shifts of view, territories of promise signposted but unexplored. In the course of his thirty-year writing span, Duggan moved away from the pastiches of his early writing to a looser, more textual prose medium, in which narrative and plot are less the objective of writing than 'a way of putting people into our mouths, of giving substance to our many voices'.[66] In Duggan's hands, the short story, ample, literary, self-reflecting, moved firmly away from the realist sketch, instead drawing deliberate attention to itself as a product of epistemological and literary conventions as much as of the workings of social forces.

If the construction of a canon can be tracked through anthologies such as the series published since 1953 by Oxford University Press, then the short fiction of Janet Frame is a continuous presence in New Zealand literary history, with each of the four collections published over forty years including a Frame story. Although the bulk of Frame's work consists of novels and autobiography, she began publishing in 1952 with a collection of short stories, *The Lagoon*, the first of the four collections of short fiction she has published over her career. In *An Angel at My Table* she described how the publication of *The Lagoon* redeemed her from a projected leucotomy, while she was a patient in a mental hospital.[67] Such interactions of text and world, the power of language to express difference and earn survival, recur in Frame's fictions and in her accounts of the events of her life. Constantly in her writings Frame explores problems of meaning; all her fictions are journeys in words, experiments with identity, inscriptions of being, repeated attempts to write the real. But whereas Sargeson's construction of the real takes place in a locally recognizable context, Frame continually redefines her contexts so that apparently normal narrative situations are suddenly menaced, and illustrate the fragility of existence; or, in her later sketches, questions of truth and knowledge can be approached only in fantasy and fable.

The Lagoon (1951), is a collection of twenty-four short stories, some sketch length, almost all written from the point of view of a child. The few that are not are mostly either about people in mental hospitals (such as 'The Pack') or, as in 'A Beautiful Nature', about someone who is 'simple'. The world the stories construct is one in which understanding is limited, either because the protagonists are children, or because they are segregated from properly adult society and live in the foreign world of a mental hospital, or because things are simply too puzzling. In 'Swans' Mum does not understand the railway system and ends up at the wrong sea, confused about what she has done. In Frame's fictions the surfaces of existence are always confusing and unstable, liable to turn out, at any moment, to be something else. It is clear that there are rules and customs, but for those who do not understand them, appearances only temporarily disguise waiting menace, the breakdown of stability, corruption, and mortality. Language itself provides perhaps the least stable surface of all. The eponymous story of Frame's first collection signals preoccupations which have remained central in Frame's work. The lagoon of the title is a shifting presence, for 'at low tide the water is sucked back into the harbour and there is no lagoon'. It is a place where you can find unexpected treasure, or 'see your image tangled up'. It is also a place where the grandmother lives. Family history in Frame's narratives is often female, and her visionaries and storytellers are also often female, like Daphne, singing from the dead room in *Owls Do Cry*. Although the grandmother talks about the lagoon, its seaweed, drifting wood, and smells, she does not tell a 'proper' story about it to the child, who finds out the 'real' story only when she is grown-up and the grandmother is dead. It proves to be a story of murder and passion, 'the sort of story they put in *Truth*'.[68]

This distinction between 'real' stories, which in *The Lagoon* correspond to the official encodings of the adult world (films, books, newspapers), and 'unreal' comforting stories that children like (such as, 'This is my castle we said you be father I'll be mother and we'll live here and catch crabs and tiddlers for ever . . .')[69] repeats itself in various forms throughout Frame's work. It generates later distinctions between environments and codes of behaviour, between autobiography and fiction, but it never loses its textual focus. 'Real' stories are the fictions and events in which people recognize their violent behaviour, their hypocrisies, the nature of their illusions. Other stories rewrite the world as a place of safety and comfort, where children can be brave, confront fear, and 'know' the real, as in the later story 'The Reservoir'. The gaps between speech and meaning, between narrative and event, between individual understanding and publicly sanctioned codes of explanation, are the unstable, difficult territory Frame explores throughout her fiction.

Frame's two collections of stories published in the 1960s, *The Reservoir* and *Snowman, Snowman*, reveal a movement away from the realistically framed narrative based on childhood to sketches, fables, and fantasies explicitly concerned with the unreal, the visionary. W.H. New expressed reservations about these later stories:

> While these experiments produced some of Frame's finest work — 'The Reservoir', for instance — the fables proved largely end-closed and mechanical, serving a preconceived and rigid scheme of judgements rather than serving as the medium of narrative discovery that the earlier stories had promised.[70]

But it is clear in Frame's work as a whole that realism did not suit her purposes, and the kinds of knowledge she works to undermine are represented as much by the comfortable stabilities of 'proper' stories and straightforward narrative language as by the rules of, for example, hospital life. There is an intermittent but fairly constant stream of stories about writing from 'Jan Godfrey' in *The Lagoon* to 'The Triumph of Poetry' in *The Reservoir*, which suggest that the context of the stories, their means of production, is also their subject. Correspondingly, they give the impression of being more and more consciously written. They seem less a transparent medium for the transmission of lived experience and more a place where identity is actively constructed, mysteries acknowledged, truths questioned. Frame's later fictions rewrite the urban domestic and personal environments of her earlier stories as places where nothing certain can be known, and in which the only reliable shape or form is the end-closed fable, with a narrative persona delivering a fabulous verdict.

Many of the later sketches have as their focus an 'I' persona observing some small event. In 'The Linesman', a woman alone at her window in a suburb crowded with people, watches a linesman up a power pole. Far from being afraid for the linesman's safety, the narrator hopes he will fall; and she is herself prey to 'marauding despair'. Frame's hard, shaped little stories are a parodic rewriting of fable, legend, and fairytale, instructing rather than engaging the reader. But the main point is not so much their overt didactic purpose as the destabilizing effect of their parodic form. A tension exists between the seemingly closed narrative with its didactic authorial voice and the apparently disordered world of emotions and events it describes. The overall effect is to emphasize the incomprehensible relationship between acts and responses, between the authorial voice's isolation and the busy world she observes, between the world that language claims to represent and the slippery fluid difficulty of language in use, between those who belong and understand what is around them and those who do not. There are many examples of the failure to make comprehensible connections, from the realism of Olive in 'The Bull Calf' (who worries why no one 'formed twos' with her when her teacher called out 'Form Twos': 'Is it because I stink? she thought') to the narrator in 'Royal Icing' who asks:

> Is it better to want and get an icing-forcer, a mincer, than to walk for the remainder of our lives about the house with a little dagger in our pocket trying to catch Death bending over the coal in the coal house . . . [?][71]

Both Duggan and Frame in their early stories use the narrative perspective on New Zealand (established by Mansfield) of the experience and point of view of a child. Where Mansfield's children are middle-class and Protestant, well-off, and living within an extended family, Duggan's are middle-class, Catholic, and their father has married again, and Frame's are working-class, poor, and visited by illness and death. It is possible to read processes of social change into these shifting family circumstances, but the real point seems to be the persistence of the child's point of view in New Zealand writing. In the colonial story, writing about children explored questions about dependence and cultural identification which functioned as a metaphor for larger issues of colonial relationship to the 'parent' culture. In the later short story, the focus on children may suggest a reinforcement of the earlier narrative emphasis on dependence. In Duggan's and Frame's stories, however, children are placed outside, or at the edge of, a largely incomprehensible 'adult' world, an environment of rules and codes and beliefs that remain quite 'foreign' to the child. A typical instance is the behaviour of their father and stepmother to the Lenihan children, whose distance from the world of adult events in 'Race Day' is suggested in the miniaturized scene they observe through the wrong end of a telescope. In Frame's stories, the focus on children is often a recognition of difference which may be sexual, economic, behavioural, or based on age, and it may also include the family, as in *Owls Do Cry*, where almost all the members of the Withers family are on the outside of 'normal' life.

In the stories of Frame's contemporary, Helen Shaw, whose first collection, *The Orange Tree and Other Stories*, was published in 1957, the focus is largely on family remnants (especially the elderly and the unmarried), who represent a vanished society. Many of Shaw's stories explicitly refer back to a colonial generation whose disappearance has marooned their descendants in large houses on subdivided estates. In 'The Blind' the family has contracted from large beginnings in another country, to two elderly daughters, one unmarried and one abandoned, caring for their senile mother in a large, old, once grand house. The only children are phantom children, or the dead children of the past. The journey towards a new life has thus reached a dead end in the lives of these women, and though one has a grown-up son, he has disowned her, like his father before him. 'Praise the Lord, Wilson' is a more direct representation of colonial conflict between generations. When young Wilson at last persuades old Miss Barclay to sell him a half-acre of her wilderness, he declares ownership by cutting down all the trees. In Miss Barclay's terms he is a vandal, and she loudly and powerfully resists his progress; Wilson, after felling the poplars, vanishes to the pub. Most of Shaw's stories are built around family and generational structures and the possession or dispersal of property, and they imply colonial discourse as it has been transmitted to the daughters and granddaughters of pioneers. Significantly, Shaw's narrative focus stays with the women. 'The Orange Tree' is one of the few stories which ends with the defeat of the hopeful acquisitor, perhaps because the owner of the section Jack and Mercy wish to buy is an old Māori woman who refuses their bribe of an orange tree. But in most of Shaw's fictions, the elderly women left in possession of estates see their inheritance going, and are left childless and marooned. As the large family networks break up, such characters are increasingly enclosed by their large houses, which bear the decayed signs of their inhabitants' once powerful cultural heritage, wealth, and skills. In 'The Gypsies', a later story, the 'pillared house with its stone portico and verandas and balconies' built by Paolo Rosa is now run down and inhabited by itinerant young people.[72] The house of culture has become nothing more than a memorial to its past, an oddity, irrelevant in a society which wants a motorway more than a house and garden.

Mansfield's concentration on family structures and children's points of view in her New Zealand stories suggested the possibility of growth beyond the kinds of entrapment and conflict experienced by the adult (especially female) characters. Shaw's fictions are constructed around families in which the children are themselves elderly, and in which growth is a youthful but external and destructive force, demolishing the artefacts of past generations and the cultural power they once expressed.

Writing as Other; Other Writing (1960s and after)

Short fiction in English by migrant writers and by Māori writers began in the 1950s with the publication of stories by J.C. Sturm in *Te Ao Hou, Numbers*, and the second volume of the Oxford *New Zealand Short Stories* series, and with Amelia Batistich's *An Olive Tree in Dalmatia*. These writers and those who followed them, particularly Yvonne du Fresne, Patricia Grace, and Witi Ihimaera, used the short story to explore New Zealand as if from the outside, constructing narratives about people distinguished by their cultural and racial difference, which function both as a commentary on the official homogeneity of New Zealand literary history and culture, and as an expression of heterogeneity.

An Olive Tree in Dalmatia, which appeared in 1963, is about origins. Many of the stories are set in New Zealand, but it is a landscape and society as seen from a Dalmatian perspective — a place in which to make money and 'get on', but which never seems, as with the earlier British settlers, quite right. Batistich's stories re-create the villages, family networks, social customs, and complicated historical memories of the Balkan States as the background of displacement; her characters know New Zealand as a place where the local people are kind, where they themselves are hardworking and not poor, where the hills are burnt and hard, and from which, to borrow one of her titles, 'It's a Long Way to Dalmatia'. The narrative tide of the stories is all back — back to the villages where the men send for wives, back to see the olive tree Stipan planted as a boy, back to the place all the stories are about, where words take on their final meaning.

'Having all that and being poor?' I wonder.
'It's a different kind of "poor" from here,' Mama says. 'In Dalmatia you have everything but money.'[73]

Batistich's local fictional environment is still that of pioneer and settler: gumfields, clearing the bush, carving farms out of swamps so that a young, strong bride can be sent for. Yvonne du Fresne's stories are more characteristically placed in the schools, farm settlements, and historical events of New Zealand, and in this sense her writing constitutes a new generation. *Farvel and Other Stories* (1980) and *The Growing of Astrid Westergaard and Other Stories* (1985) are mostly linked stories representing the life of a girl from a Danish family living in rural New Zealand. A great many of the stories take place at school, which provides a paradigm of society itself: a place of institutional rules and codes, group identities, and individual differences; a place, also, in which the infant class learns that words make 'experience' real: 'Our Experience Sheet', said Miss Bates, 'must be filled up with good words.'[74] Much of Astrid Westergaard's experience is also written experience. The fictions which contextualize and represent her are both literary and oral narratives. The words in which she writes of herself are, like those in 'Astrid of the Limberlost', from '*Girls'* Books . . . of the Colonies, the Antipodes and so on', their potency testified to by Tante Helga who becomes 'vague' and 'drugged' as she reads them. But there are also the stories her family tells, stories of heroic ancestors, of Danish myths, of a landscape populated not by the Carson Gang, but by Danes who were legendary workers, draining and clearing the swamps, surviving hardship.

Like Batistich's, du Fresne's stories are densely imbued with cultural texts. Stories told by her Grandtante, the history of Jutland, and the myths and ghosts of Denmark are superimposed on the Manawatu; Cherry and Astrid with their raffia purses become English princesses, and Astrid as Peter the Great gives orders to her playmates. Du Fresne's fictions work towards the acceptance and reconciliation of difference, which is made in typically colonialist terms. In 'Houses', Astrid's fear of Cherry's grandmother gives way to astonishment that she knows their names and generations; her Moder explains that they 'were pioneers . . . here long before we came from Jutland.'[75] The work of the pioneers thus legitimizes them, and the Danish/English difference in du Fresne's stories is historically familiar, and comfortably accommodated. It stops short of any larger questions about the ways in which colonizing and pioneering peoples impose their narratives on the colonized, but draws attention to the heterogeneity of 'their' New Zealand, written in foreign tongues.

In the 1950s, the first stories in English by a Māori writer were published in a number of periodicals. Although it was not until 1983 that the stories of J.C. Sturm were collected and published as a volume, they are set firmly in the social realist country of Sargesonian narrative, writing of New Zealand as it looks and feels to a Māori woman in the 1950s. Sturm's stories, along with those of her successors, Patricia Grace, Witi Ihimaera, Keri Hulme and others, engage directly with cultural oppositions as do those of immigrant writers. Like Batistich and du Fresne, Māori writers speak in a different language, but by giving voice to the silent other, the other who most explicitly and uncomfortably challenges cultural hegemony and given social structures, Māori writers rewrite New Zealand in English, their fictions breaking out of and therefore signifying their silence. Although Ihimaera's collection of short stories *Pounamu, Pounamu* was the first to be published by a Māori writer in 1972, earlier writers like Sturm, many of whose stories do not explicitly identify themselves as expressions of a Māori voice, from the vantage point of hindsight indicate the breaking of silence. Sturm's *The House of the Talking Cat* (1983) is divided into two parts, which trace a kind of progression towards writing as a Māori. The stories collected in Part 1 have an implicit chronological connection, moving from a young woman in her first sexual encounter, to a woman alone with her small children, a mother taking an afternoon off, a woman contemplating an affair, a woman running a family and talking to the cat. They are narratives of women alone, caring for children, working, and tied to husbands who come home late, drunk, unable to offer comfort or protection from the threatening world outside the home.

Although Sturm's women narrators are not explicitly identified as Māori until the stories collected as Part 2, their isolation and their imprisoning domestic circumstances put them on the edge of the society they inhabit. In 'Where to, Lady?' a woman takes the afternoon off from her family, but finds, as is ironically pointed out in the title, that she has no destination: 'You can't just move out of one world and into another simply by boarding a tram.' Eventually, caught in the rain, she enters a cheap restaurant, full of men shovelling food, but at a side table is a half-caste Māori woman by herself who beckons to the young woman to join her. This kind of metaphorical positioning, at the table with the Māori woman in a room full of men, is typical of Sturm's stories. There is only one story in the collection which openly and explicitly deals with racial conflict (at a children's birthday party), but the whole collection is concerned with characters on the edges of conventional society; women, cleaners and hospital workers, and the illiterate. Though Sturm's women tend to be well-educated, literary, and relatively well-off, in important ways they are seen as outsiders. Their husbands are only footsteps coming up the path, their only real conversation is with the cat, and there is no answer to the question 'Where to, Lady?'.

The title of Witi Ihimaera's *Pounamu, Pounamu* (1972) suggests that writing is a kind of cultural wealth, a taonga. Ihimaera's earlier stories represent young Māori men as individually and successfully bridging cultures. The stories in *Pounamu, Pounamu* are mostly stories about rural Māori life. They stress community, family and tribal networks, and children. Cultural and racial difference, as in 'The Other Side of the Fence' or 'Beginning of the Tournament', is expressed in difference of behaviour, attitude, or convention, and the social problems these cause can be resolved by essential human emotions: love in 'The Makutu on Mrs Jones' and basic decency in 'The Other Side of the Fence'. Although in the story 'In Search of the Emerald City' there is a narrative frame for the drift of young Māori to the city, and the stories as a whole refer to Pākehā and in particular American culture,[76] the Māori is presented as being still connected to, and secure within, rural and tribal life. Like Patricia Grace, Ihimaera is concerned to stress the importance of the whanau, and to construct a language that represents some of the spoken idioms of Māori English and incorporates Māori words as customary and unexplained. In *Pounamu, Pounamu* there is also frequently a division in Ihimaera's language between an 'official' Pākehā narrative voice (as in 'The Other Side of the Fence', which is told in the third person using complex sentences and a formal vocabulary), and a spoken first-person idiom, repetitive, often spoken by a child, dense with Māori phrases and vocabulary. Such an idiom 'speaks' Māori to a Māori readership, telling of the social context of the tribe and family, and of the physical context of the land by which, far more successfully than by cultural and racial opposition, the Māori is identified. Whereas in Sturm's stories (Māori) women are isolated and silenced in a confusing, threatening society, in Ihimaera's rural narratives there is an assertion of happiness in numbers, in the feeling of common origins. Racial conflict is a problem that can perhaps be distanced by the affirmation of a counter-culture: the good-humoured rural Māori community.

Ihimaera's second collection of stories, *The New Net Goes Fishing* (1977) shifted from rural to urban settings, framed by two stories ('Yellow Brick Road' and 'Return to Oz') which allude to the 'perfectible fantasy world of the American writer L. Frank Baum',[77] and which had been prefigured by the story 'In Search of Emerald City' in *Pounamu, Pounamu*. Allusions to the fantasy land of Oz frame stories of dislocation, poverty, family disintegration, violence, and racial discrimination of all kinds. The move into the city is a move away from home, and the dream of the Emerald City that prompted it is an illusion. Yet once the possibility of journeying to Oz has arisen, it has to be taken, as Jimmy Jackson Heremaia acknowledges in 'Catching Up':

> He had been pushed this far, led this far. And now? He could not stop now. He had to keep on going. He *wanted* to. He'd seen beyond the horizon. He hadn't known what was there, but he had to find out. He had to.

When Ihimaera's characters achieve Pākehā success, as in the story 'Cousins', the Māori self is submerged but does not vanish. In fact it is the re-invention of the Māori in a Pākehā context that Ihimaera focuses on, the recovery of the displaced, not as it was, but as it pushes through and infects the experience and language of change:

> You seem to be living two lives at once — sometimes fragments of one life and then of the other and, more and more often, both at the same time until you are not sure which is the reality.[78]

The power of language to silence or to rewrite cultural identity is never more evident than in the work of Māori writers, who identify their writing as 'foreign' by burying in it the spoken idiom of another language, suggesting in that other language another version of the 'real', of 'home', and another cultural identity. Patricia Grace's story 'A Way of Talking', which opens her first collection, *Waiariki* (1975), focuses explicitly on the self constructed in language. When Rose and her sister visit a Pākehā neighbour who refers to 'the Maoris' who are scrubcutting as if they are an indistinguishable group without individuality, Rose attacks her in what her sister thinks of as 'Pakehafied' talking. Just as the neighbour's language reveals her cultural assumptions, so Rose's adoption of Pakehafied talking acknowledges the weapon of domination with which she must fight her battles. Grace's stories, like Ihimaera's, imply that writing Māori in Pākehā language re-invents the Māori subject, allowing cultural and racial stereotypes to be parodically challenged.

> 'It's fashionable for a Pakeha to have a Maori for a friend.' Suddenly Rose grinned. Then I heard Jane's voice coming out of that Rohe's mouth and felt a grin of my own coming. 'I have friends who are Maoris. They're lovely people. The eldest girl was married recently and I did the frocks. The other girl is at varsity. They're all so *friendly* and so *natural* and their house is absolutely *spotless*.'[79]

Grace's stories also concentrate, like Ihimaera's, on extended family relationships among cousins, grandparents, aunts, uncles, children, and elders. She has written of the need to represent the Māori, and particularly Māori women, in relationships other than sexual. In *Waiariki*, the fictions which represent the Māori range from stories which affirm traditional Māori social structures and values, and are framed as realist (often oral) narratives, to stories like 'At the River' or 'And So I Go', which emphasize relationships with history and landscape, articulating the mythological and elemental context in which Māori cultural identity is affirmed:

> And I lie on soil in all my heaviness and trembling. Stretch out my arms on wide Earth Mother and lay my face on hers. Then call out my love and speak my vow.[80]

'Parade', published in the influential anthology of Māori writing, *Into the World of Light* (1982), was referred to by the editors (D.S. Long and W.H. Ihimaera) as the story which best described the volume's purpose. A Māori girl performing action songs in a parade looks back at the crowd: 'I kept thinking and trying not to think, "Is that what we are to them?" Museum pieces, curios, antiques, shells under glass.' In the story Grandpa Hohepa says to her, 'It is your job, this. To show others who we are.'[81] Grace's fiction originates from the same impulse; her stories show 'others' who 'we' are with a significant inversion of conventional terms. Both *Waiariki* and Grace's second collection, *The Dream Sleepers* (1980), use social realism to show the Māori as an underprivileged race. The title story of *The Dream Sleepers* describes the lives of children whose mothers and grandmothers go out to clean office blocks at 3 a.m. Grace's narrative world, however, includes not only the menial or meaningless work her characters are obliged to do, but also the monumental pregnant woman celebrating her condition in 'Between Earth and Sky' and the energy and intelligence of the children in 'Kepa' and 'Drifting', who inhabit land and sea without any restrictions on their freedom and vitality.

When *Pounamu, Pounamu* appeared in 1972, followed by *Waiariki* in 1975, the writers were characterized respectively as the first Māori writer in English and the first Māori woman writer in English. But both Ihimaera and Grace's writing had been appearing for some time in *Te Ao Hou*, 'the Maori magazine'. This quarterly began in 1952, published by the Department of Maori Affairs and edited by E.G. Schwimmer, and announced itself as 'a magazine for Maori people . . .. *Te Ao Hou* should become like a "marae" on paper'.[82] From the beginning *Te Ao Hou* explicitly encouraged Māori creative writers and artists to produce texts which would help to affirm a collective identity amongst its readers. Initially the texts it published were tribal legends, translated into English for *Te Ao Hou*'s readership. Legendary fiction continued to occupy space in the quarterly throughout its publishing history, but as early as the fifth number (Winter 1953) a short story competition was announced, aimed at fostering Māori writers. Instructions for the competition suggest a prevailing view of the kind of story thought desirable — that it should be mimetic, documentary, educational, and concerned to demonstrate group identity: 'It is hoped that the stories will help to increase awareness of what Maori life today really is.'

Subsequently, stories were submitted in Māori and English; most numbers published at least one story and often several, and the magazine advertised ceaselessly for writers and artists, holding literary competitions every year. At the end of 1955 a series of stories by Māori writers was opened by J.C. Sturm's

'For All the Saints'. By the time Grace and Ihimaera published in *Te Ao Hou*, the magazine had already established itself as a publishing forum for Māori writers, and in doing so, explicitly recognized that cultural identity is textual as well as racial, ceremonial, historical, and linguistic. Heretaunga Pat Baker, Riki Erihi, Rowley Habib, Arapera Blank, J.C. Sturm, S.M. Mead, Rora Paki: a great many names appear whose writing constructed a context for the writers whose work progressed from periodical to book publication. The story models that emerge in *Te Ao Hou* also act as a comment on New Zealand's then-authorized version of unproblematic race relations, based on an assertion of equal opportunity and mutual goodwill.

For some time, stories sponsored by *Te Ao Hou* remained obedient to the official version of race relations while focusing on a point of great tension — the departure of the young to another cultural environment. The Judge's Report on a Literary Competition held in 1961 commented:

> Every story was concerned in some measure with the basic problem of Maoridom today — adaptation to a new and sometimes bewilderingly complex way of life . . . . Somewhere, either directly or by implication, every writer insists that the Maori must learn to take his rightful place in the Pakeha world, and more significant — that such a place is waiting for him.[83]

Increasingly the stories in *Te Ao Hou* are narratives of Māori failure in both cultures: alienated from one and excluded, by lack of education, money, and opportunity, from the other. The stories are mainly written in the first person. Like colonial writing by Europeans, Māori writing in English is predominantly oral narrative, representing itself as authentic experience. This may be read as a response to the frequent calls in *Te Ao Hou* for Māori writers to 'increase awareness of what Maori life today really is'; the text positions itself within the speaking voice of such 'real' life. *Te Ao Hou* stories are always located in the extended family, with considerable emphasis on grandparents. Sometimes the frame of the story consciously extends into whakapapa, and the post-European Māori family is shadowed by its larger, older, pre-European structures with their attendant values and responsibilities. But as in the early work of Ihimaera and Grace, the great majority of such stories focus on grandparents as a way of signalling cultural difference from the Pākehā family. Again and again in the stories of *Te Ao Hou*, a connection to a different past is reinforced by the active presence of grandparents, whose roots are tribal and suggest a larger context for the immediate family. Representation of the Māori family in this way inevitably emphasizes internal conflict, since the generations signify oppositions destructively inherited during the progress of Pākehā society: rural/urban, pastoral/technological, rural labour-based economy/income-wage earning economy, tribal knowledge expressed in legends, beliefs and behaviour, as opposed to acquired knowledge of Pākehā education and behaviour, especially behaviour induced by the ability to earn money: drinking, smoking, or being fashionable.

As if to give emphatic point to the experience of transition and conflict that Māori stories describe, from the 1950s to the 1970s, many actually take place at a bus-stop, as the son or daughter of the family leave for the city, or the university, or some equally powerful location of difference. Although they are very often stories of failure, regret, and nostalgia, it is significant that once the move away from grandparents and the rural and tribal environment has occurred, return is almost always impossible. The focus on grandparents suggests inevitable loss, through death, of the older culture.

In 1959 *Te Ao Hou* published a special Māori Writer's Issue. Addressing 'some dozens of Maori' who had started to write, the editorial posed some special problems: should writing be in Māori or in English, and if in English, to a specifically Māori or more general readership? The editorial also asked if Māori were to see themselves primarily as 'Maori or New Zealand authors'. Such questions became increasingly pointed in *Te Ao Hou* and the publications that succeeded it, *Te Kaea*, *Te Maori*, and *Tu Tangata*. *Te Ao Hou* provided a separatist context, announcing itself as specifically for a Māori audience. As Māori writing moved increasingly into Pākehā forums over three decades it became redefined as English-language writing, with the Māori language remaining in the text only as macaronics, dispersed fragments of a superseded cultural identity. At the same time, as if to counter this absorption, Māori writing in English became more politically militant and confrontational in the late 1970s and 1980s. In 1959 a story called 'Goodbye', by Tirohia, won the literary competition in *Te Ao Hou*. It is about a boy leaving the family farm and local community to go to the city and train as a doctor. His departure is opposed by his Granny. ' "The Maori belongs on his land," she would argue, forgetting that there was no longer enough land for them all.'[84] That there is not enough land is, in this story, something that Granny has 'forgotten', and the boy's departure argues his superior understanding of necessity. But in the stories of Apirana Taylor and Bruce Stewart in the 1980s, the loss of land is an insistent political subtext, underwriting the violence and the racial and gender conflicts in the narratives.[85]

It is possible to make a number of interesting comparisons with stories by Pākehā writers of the same period. Māori writers seldom write about gender conflict. Patricia Grace's stories often celebrate gender roles, such as in 'Between Earth and Sky', an often-anthologized story, as do Witi Ihimaera's and the majority of the stories in *Te Ao Hou*, but race relations are always present, providing a point of conflict in the text. Many Pākehā writers do not write about non-Europeans at all, whereas in fiction by Māori, race is invariably the foreground of identity. In the more recent stories of Bruce Stewart, gender is closely associated with race. Stewart's typical narrator is a person of mixed race, whose own identity is at a point of transition from one race to another, rather than fixed in an external movement from one culture into another. In 'Mangu', for example, the narrator's Pākehā father is identified as Pākehā by the maleness of his behaviour (his deer hunting, trophy collecting, and general acquisitiveness), in opposition to the Māori mother (herself regarded as a trophy by other deershooters), whose family are tribal landowners and practise conservation and resource management in their living habits. In Stewart's fictions such identification of cultures by gender is quite explicit, but throughout Māori writing in English since 1952 the oppositions explored by the stories imply the masculinity of Pākehā culture.

As used by Pākehā writers, especially in popular short fiction, cultural identification by gender can also prompt racist stereotypes. The stereotype of the fat, lazy Māori who fails to meet male standards of success is a familiar figure, but in Māori writing the opposition is more generally articulated as one between nurture and its associated forms of knowledge (conservation, tribal economy, the land as text for identity), and use, characterizing Pākehā culture as greedy, obsessed with material success, violent, and destructive. Māori texts tend to be both pastoral and past/oral: the past is where identity lies, and its text is the land, and oral language is the medium in which identity is expressed.[86] Māori written texts constantly reach back to oral language and voiced narrative, but do not employ dialect as Pākehā writers about Māori often do. Rather, Māori writers tend to stress the orality of the written, the function of language as a medium for voice rather than for the kind of abstract or linguistic play that characterizes language in, for example, post-modern stories. Read in bulk, Māori stories in English illustrate a remarkably consistent narrative of dispossession, conflict, and eventually anger. The writers who preceded and accompanied Ihimaera and Grace represented Māori identity as past/oral, spoken as it was disappearing. It is in a sense a linear narrative, from 'One by one the elders passed on, and we who were once richly endowed with Kaumatua, are now without a background',[87] to the stories in Apirana Taylor's *He Rau Aroha*, which mix violence and comedy, generating humour from and affection about their characters as well as expressing anger about the situations in which they are placed. Taylor's characters may be 'without a background', but they are also claiming a place in the world.

*   *   *

The predominant form of the short story in New Zealand in the last thirty years, which flourished as a successor to Sargeson's social realist sketches and novellas amongst the major short fiction writers of the 1960s and 1970s, as well as providing the vast bulk of periodical fiction publication, might be described as the 'free' story. Clare Hanson derived the term from the English writer Elizabeth Bowen, drawing a distinction between the 'free' story and symbolist or modernist short fiction:

> Character and locale . . . are usually closely delineated by free story writers who are attracted to the particular rather than the general. They rarely use description for symbolic purposes: the emphasis is on the particular, concrete subject . . . .. The free story also shows far more response to social pressures than does modernist short fiction.

Maurice Shadbolt, describing his own attitude to the short story, drew approvingly on a definition provided by Frank O'Connor which uses very similar terms. 'The short story,' O'Connor had said, 'is the art form that deals with the indiviual when there is no coherent society to absorb him: when he has to exist, as it were, by his own inner light.' Shadbolt added, 'Or when (my antipodean codicil) a coherent society has hardly begun to exist.'[88]

Shadbolt's *The New Zealanders* (1959) explores, illuminates, and transmits a 'vision of the national sensibility'[89] by means of fictions which are in effect explorations of types: the Englishwoman pining for 'Home' and passing her cultural identification on to her daughter, the Depression family man unable to get work because of his politics, teenagers in a small town set alight by sexuality, men whose manliness is a cover for their latent homosexuality. Most of the stories are end-closed, and because their focus is not on plot, nothing very much happens. Shadbolt uses events to reveal character, and by extension, society. At the end of 'Love Story', for example, when Gloria's rape has resulted in her pregnancy and Ralph's rejection by his mother, their only course of action is to ride their bicycles out of town, away from a puritanical and violent society.

In both *The New Zealanders* and *Figures in Light* (1978) — the latter including stories from *Summer Fires and Winter Country* (1963) and *The Presence of Music* (1967) — characters are placed in narratives by arrivals and departures. The society they represent and the national sensibility they illumine is one in which voyaging is endemic, homecomings ironic and ambiguous, and social conflicts and divisions frequently a consequence of departure or change. In 'Homecoming', a successful London journalist returns home to her parents on a remote North Auckland farm, and eventually moves in with a Māori man, the lover of an old friend. He is associated in a dream with 'the country' and becomes, in his rather sinister sexual presence, an object of desire for whom she betrays her friend. Coming 'home' has multiple associations in Shadbolt's stories. Despite the fact that they often represent 'home' as rural and Māori, and thus also a reflection of Pākehā and European culture, they are framed as explorations of character and sensibility, 'about people', to use Shadbolt's own phrase. A story like 'The People Before' explicitly engages with cross-cultural and racial questions, so that when at the end of the story the narrator feels 'robbed' of something which was rightfully 'mine', his sense of loss suggests less about him as an individual than about the historical and racial questions raised by his brother's possession of ancient greenstone adzes. In practice, then, despite Shadbolt's insistence that in his stories 'the essence is human',[90] his characters represent cultural identities as much as personal ones, a textual dimension which other writers of the 'free' story develop even more overtly. Philip Mincher's picaresque linked stories in *The Ride Home* (1974) of a young man and his girl on their bikes, travelling, fishing, and hunting, celebrate the self-sufficient possibilities of an alternative lifestyle, but also function as a commentary on the puritanical social environment which in a larger sense they inhabit.

In Maurice Gee's stories, as in Shadbolt's version of the 'free' story, the behaviour of individuals is similarly suggestive of larger social pressures (as in his story 'The Losers'), but it is the characters' psychological and motivational distinctiveness that governs the narratives. Published over twenty years, his stories have culturally significant locations: the racecourse, the town council, the beach resort, the bowling club. It is an environment of small-town families and businessmen, and the narratives are constructed on antagonistic relations between the sexes, within families, and between generations. Usually written from a male point of view, and with an increasingly elderly central character, Gee's fictions are always focused on an event which isolates its protagonists from their social context but also reinstates the power structures which sustain it. In 'Eleventh Holiday', anxiety and aggression amongst males expresses itself competitively in a game of tennis between a bodgie and a middle-aged man. The tennis match is the overt representation of a number of conflicts (generational, sexual, economic, racial, and political) and when the bodgie, who is the person without power in the social context, wins the game, he becomes a target of violence. Such violence is never far away in Gee's New Zealand, where sexual relationships are constrained by personal limitations or public disapproval, where men are territorial and underdeveloped emotionally, and women are managing and possessive. In the stories Gee's male characters age; the last four stories of his collection, *A Glorious Morning, Comrade* (1974), focus on elderly men, retired and finally senile, who represent powerlessness and are victims of constraining social forces. In every case they are opposed by or to women. In the title story, Mr Pitt-Rimmer's escape from his daughter's bridge party, incontinent and wearing his dressing gown, suggests both the need felt by individuals to escape social structures and the futility of their efforts.

In a general sense, Gee is one of a group of male writers whose stories share the cultural locations that produce (male) New Zealand — racing, rugby, and beer — with their attendant gender divisions, small towns, and orthodoxies. Vincent O'Sullivan and Owen Marshall also focus on this familiar New Zealand fictional environment, though their stories are framed by irony, satire, and parodic re-invention. Throughout the 1970s *Landfall*, the *New Zealand Listener*, and anthologies based on the short fiction published in such periodicals, were dominated by the 'free' story, with its emphasis on socially realistic settings and character-based narratives. Perhaps partly as a successor to the 'voice' Sargeson established as 'New Zealand', the 'free' story as written by Gee, O'Sullivan, and Marshall functions not so much as a spoken idiom signifying a culture, but as the idiom of a culture identifying itself. The extent to which short stories had become recognizable types is suggested by A.K. Grant's parody, published in the *Listener* in 1973. 'An Inquiry into the Construction and Classification of the New Zealand Short Story' includes such parodies as: 'The ordinary Kiwi working bloke short story' and 'The sub-Katherine Mansfield 'At the Bay' short story'.[91] O'Sullivan and Marshall share with Gee, and with many uncollected short story writers, a concern with the way individuals mark themselves out from, or capitulate to, group identities, which may be based on gender, race, religion, politics, economics, or class. The typical focus of the 'free' story is the signifying individual, whose behaviour opens up a number of discourses that characterize the larger environment. O'Sullivan's stories are less concerned with overt masculine locations than those of Gee or Marshall, but all three writers represent New Zealand as a territory of division and conformity, and local short story writing as the province of a brand of realism in which individual character is made the vehicle of social criticism.

O'Sullivan's first collection of stories, *The Boy, The Bridge, The River* (1978) provides a number of variations on people who locate themselves, or are located, outside norms. Sometimes they are Catholics, outsiders in a Protestant society, and sometimes they are foreigners, like Latty in the title story. Others are marked out in some other, perhaps more mysterious way: Grove with his head dented in, or Mr Foster (in 'Letter from Orpheus') rewriting the lives of his workmates in a shoeshop. In the later collections, *Dandy Edison for Lunch* (1981) and *Survivals* (1985), the reader is invited to recognize the narrative process by which fiction is created, (the 'story' which is like a lie told by a professional as described in 'The Professional': 'It's the arc where you control the appearance of things'),⁹² as well as its relation to the world, 'the appearance of things'.

O'Sullivan's stories typically take place at a point of transition, which often also entails (as in 'Dandy Edison for Lunch') a recognition of loss. The smart talk between Kevin and Karen, their successful careers and their wealth, are thrown into a different focus by lunch with Dandy Edison, an old man and a childhood neighbour, whose honesty functions as a kind of visionary subtext to the coded languages adopted by the narrator. O'Sullivan's stories often use a conflict or a confrontation in individual histories to suggest such larger subtexts. The story of Dandy Edison's prostituted daughter and her early death is received by the narrator's famous and successful wife Karen as if 'what [she] looked at was a kind of veil and what [she] sought was on the other side'.⁹³ The story of prostitution becomes a counterpoint to the marriage of Karen and Kevin, both of whom are good at 'being vile' to each other, their relationship providing the text for Kevin's successful commercials.

Although the bulk of fictions in *Dandy Edison* were set in New Zealand, a number moved offshore to New York, the effect being to emphasize cultural rather than regional boundaries. Other writers of the 'free' story in the 1970s and 1980s (including Joy Cowley, Shonagh Koea, and Fiona Kidman) also located some of their short stories outside New Zealand, with similar effect. In O'Sullivan's *Survivals* (1986) the settings shift geographically between Australia and New Zealand, but their unchanging focus is middle-class pretension, aspiration, and self-representation; the cultural boundaries they draw are unaffected by geographical transition. The title of *Survivals* indicates both the ironies of the collection and its narrative preoccupations. In 'The Last of Freddy', the life of a famous painter is reconstructed by three lovers who 'survive' him. In many of O'Sullivan's fictions death signifies the absence of life around the dead: in the title story, 'Survivals', the dying man Richard and his lover Monica represent intense emotion, hope, grief, in a milieu where belief and passion are absent. O'Sullivan's stories present estrangement, division, and emotional hypocrisy as a narrative that has supplanted the 'real' story. The subtext of his narratives is often a story which is not being told, and which, when it emerges as a shadowy reflection of the 'real' story, creates a re-reading, a refocusing on moral questions. *The Snow in Spain* (1990) engages in such moral questioning through satire of social pretensions (several of the stories were first published in fashionable Auckland magazines) or black comedy. The title story is about dwarf-tossing and is narrated by a dwarf whose story reflects on a grotesque audience:

> the lovely bit, never mind it's only a second or so, the bit when arms out and all i'm really flying. then the racket starts up again and i thud on the foam mattresses and they're shouting out fucken beauty.⁹⁴

In Marshall's 'Body and Soul' a man tries to talk to his brother, a painter, about painting, but the conversation is abortive: 'They talked no more of it: not because it was too theoretical, but because it was too personal. The inner landscape of belief is hazardous ground.' Marshall's fictions signal only indirectly the 'inner landscape of belief'. His first three collections of short stories, *Supper Waltz Wilson* (1979), *The Master of Big Jingles* (1982) and *The Day Hemingway Died* (1984) are on culturally familiar ground: Anzac ceremonies, rugby matches, schoolboy battles, farms, farming families. Like Sargeson, Marshall also writes sketches, ironically framed moral parables (like 'The Homily of Mr Poose') which function as a commentary on narrative method when published alongside the longer, realist stories. Characters recur from book to book, and there is a loose clustering of stories set in a small rural South Island town, Te Tarehi, which gives the fiction a regional frame and suggests historical 'reality'. His stories hint at discontinuous narrative, (perhaps just at the level of metaphor), so that though the 'inner landscape of belief' can only be approached indirectly, in repetitions and silences, it exists as a subtextual profile, occasionally glanced at in the fictional surface. 'New Zealand' is produced, in Marshall's fictions, by small towns like Te Tarehi, by characters like Raf or Simon who are distinguished by their passion and their nonconformity, and by the stories and histories in people's lives that reach out and populate the past and the present. As one of his characters thinks:

> All of us had lived together in the place, yet each had a separate experience of it: in the same way we share life, I suppose.⁹⁵

Whereas O'Sullivan's fictional world is characterized by ambiguities and antagonisms, Marshall offers 'a lesson about human nature presented with an almost magisterial authority'. His fictions emphasize the social patterns and codes by which individuals live, and the landscapes into which histories and memories settle. As David in 'Bravo Echo Victor' puts it: 'Some places are stained with the sweat of our minds'.[96] Time, language, memory, experience; the constructions of personal and cultural identity in New Zealand; journeying back to Te Tarehi to the bedrock of the national [male] self: these are the physical and verbal landscapes of Marshall's fictions.

Marshall's later collection, *The Lynx Hunter and Other Stories* (1987), pushes more explicitly at the shapes of realism. In the title story there is no mediation between the narrator and the narrative, no orderly sequence of possible events which might allow a reader to construct the narrator by or against the narrative. 'The Lynx Hunter' is the free indirect discourse of a narrator through whom a walk to work functions as deliberate self-representation: 'See me stand respectably dressed . . . .. See me smile back to my wife.' Such injunctions identify the reader as the paranoid 'seeing' self addressed by the subject: 'Mirrors catch mirrors catch mirrors'. As the divided self is its own audience and performance, so the view through its eyes mirrors back what is inside the head: a daughter rides past to school while a dromedary waits beyond the breakwater, and the snout of the lava-flow smokes by the Farmers' Co-Op. If the world is constructed in language, then a man walking to work can have many dimensions of possible experience in the storage of his skull. In 'Joining the Ishmaelites' Marshall parodically relocates the small-town man walking to work with his head full of history, paranoias, and galaxies, as the middle-class writer who inhabits fictions, matching 'life' and 'experience' to the typewriter's need for authenticity: an 'inexorable bounty hunter of reeking copy — and fame'.[97] This story comments satirically on the notion that fiction is something that occurs outside 'real' life, as 'The Lynx Hunter' emphasizes the fictionality of appearance and the de-forming constructions of language. Marshall's stories trace a movement from the recognizable codes and practices of masculine small-town South Island New Zealand to an idiosyncratic, unfamiliar, and menacing environment, in which his narrators are deprived of such comfortable identifications.

The 'free' story in New Zealand fiction, especially as it is written by Pākehā men, is deeply preoccupied with gender relationships, and in particular, with sexual relationships. Exploring character as a signifier of a larger cultural context, the stories of male writers focus on male locations which can only achieve definition by reference to gender-based difference. As a result, cultural identity is represented as sexual identity, difference as gender difference, and signs of anxiety and unease express themselves in bad marriages, unforgiving partners, failed or inadequate sexual performance, and conflicting emotional claims. Marshall's 'Mumsie and Zip', a black comedy about an elderly couple locked in paranoia and sadism, with Mumsie placating and managing Zip's violence, provides an extreme, sinister vision of suburban New Zealand marriage, premised on the gender-based violence and antagonism expressed by husbands. The antagonisms are not always directed *at* women, but are often presented as a function of sexual identity in a puritanical and hypocritical society which at its most extreme punishes difference of any kind.

C.K. Stead's 'A New Zealand Elegy', whose title clearly suggests a culturally central experience, opens with a family discussion of 'Freedom' somewhere in suburban Mt Eden, during which the narrator's father remarks: 'It's all very well for poets . . ... Some of us have to live in the real world. And that means you, my boy.' The 'real world' the story engages with consists of teenage boys, bikes, beach resorts, suburban Mt Eden, the freezing works, *Hamlet*, dances, a Norton motorbike — the story speaks for Auckland in the 1940s when the prize for being the first to have sexual intercourse is six milkshakes. The narrator, Ian's friend, is identified formally only as 'I', which perhaps allows him to be read as a signifying type (and perhaps as fictional autobiography) representing youth and male sexual desire. 'A New Zealand Elegy' narrates a 'real' world in which the actions of the youthful male narrator are governed by sexual longing so intense that it functions as identity, in an environment where other people's sexual behaviour is the occasion of hypocrisy, prurience, and puritanical judgement, and where the narrator's neighbour Marion, engaged in an extramarital affair with a truckdriver, symbolizes the freedom and pleasures of adult life. The object of both the narrator's and Ian's desire is not an individual woman, but a sexual encounter; women are undifferentiated and simply represent potential objects. But the story does differentiate between the narrator and his friend in two ways. Ian is the first to achieve sexual intercourse, and he is killed in a motorbike accident which is a macabre parody of sexual experience. Accelerating round a corner, he runs 'up the tailpipe' of a parked truck where Marion is meeting her lover. Ian's death is both a vicarious consummation for the narrator, an experience which makes him adult and signals the end of desire, and a commentary on the society which they inhabit. Death is less significant than extramarital sex in the world that Marion perceives:

Nobody cares about the kid anyway. All they care about is that it was us in the truck, and that's given them a lot to chat about hasn't it?[98]

In Stead's 'New Zealand Elegy' the elemental taboo is sex, which is also the governing condition of desire in which all men and a very few, socially outcast, exceptional women, live. In Stead's earlier story, 'A Fitting Tribute', New Zealand is also represented as a puritanical and conventional society, but his focus is less on sexual taboos than on a comic or satiric view of social norms and values. In the story, Julian Harp, who changes from an eccentric to a National Hero by inventing engineless flight, exposes a society which is unimaginative, intolerant of difference, and opportunistic.

By the early 1980s, what has come to be called the post-modern story was well established in New Zealand, published regularly in periodicals (*Islands, Mate, Landfall, Climate, Untold, Sport*, and *Parallax*), and challenging the domination of short fiction by the realist-humanist or 'free' story. It also began to be visible in anthologies and collections. Like modernism, post-modernism began as an international phenomenon. Initially characterized by John Barth as a 'literature of exhaustion', it subsequently came to be used as an umbrella term for a more general cultural and economic shift, described by Frederic Jameson as the 'Cultural Logic of Late Capitalism'.[99] In short fiction there is a breakdown of unitary narrative, and of the structures of meaning which sustain conventional story-telling realities: character, time, plot, social and historical experience, and language.

In New Zealand the case for the post-modern story was presented in an anthology (*The New Fiction*), edited by Michael Morrissey and published in 1985. Morrissey's lengthy introduction was less a preface to the writers whose stories appeared there than a history of post-modernism and an attack on the writing which had preceded it in New Zealand. While conceding that a writer like Frame had always produced 'new fiction', Morrissey attacked the 'New Zealand short story' for having had a largely non-innovative, almost oral, history:

Story after story has had the same beige moral tone . . . the same dreary humanism . . . the same truncated, banal dialogue occupying itself with similar issues, confrontations and characters.

In Morrissey's view the result was a procession of look-alikes: 'Writer has imitated writer like the boy on the Bycroft biscuit tin.' Post-modern consciousness, on the other hand, heralded a 'new aesthetic fearlessness', placing its practitioners in 'the international context — to which the writers of *The New Fiction* belong'.[100]

The writer who introduced New Zealand readers to the post-modern story was Russell Haley, whose *The Sauna Bath Mysteries and Other Stories* appeared in 1978. Haley's fictions broke with both modernism and realism, avoiding the 'difficult scholarly density' of a writer such as Joyce, refusing to confirm the 'special, usually alienated, role of the artist',[101] concentrating instead on an essentially playful breakdown of narrative certainties. Like the succeeding work of Ian Wedde, Chris Else, Morrissey, and others, Haley's continually draws attention to the fictional nature of subjectivity, to language, and to writing itself as subject-matter. Since no distinction between the 'real' and the 'unreal' is allowed in such fiction, it is often preoccupied with shifts in time and place that complicate and undermine the boundaries between memory, dream, experience, and knowledge. Haley's 'Barbados — A Love Story', which opens Morrissey's anthology, suggests in its title and opening sentences a typical pattern of displacement and fictional complication:

I have chosen to call this room Barbados. Ah — I can feel you shrink back already. Oh God am I going to be nagged by another of these madmen who is so confused about reality that he imagines his fireplace is a white sandy beach and that the brown bottle of beer on his table is a character named Nick Tromso?[102]

The narrator's stress on his environment as fictional, a product of imaginative will ('I have chosen') directly addresses the reader, who remains dependent throughout on the version(s) of reality constructed by the choices of the narrator. 'Barbados — A Love Story' is an anti-linear narrative. Owing to failures or uncertainties of memory, understanding, and knowledge, it is not possible to untangle fully the events of the story; in any case, all of its events occur only in the context of the multiple possibilities presented by the narrator's mind, and the story is thus 'about' the narrator's consciousness of himself as the story's subject. His narrative is punctuated by the phrase 'let me tell you': another story, one of my favourite stories, a real joke. He keeps notebooks, begins to interpret himself, and feels he is the subject of 'some fully coherent plot' understood, presumably, elsewhere. His referent for reality, in a bar, is Literature (Michael Anthony and V.S. Naipaul), and he eventually provides an 'account' of the story's events with a conclusion.

While the narrator's narrative insists on the fragmented and uncertainly known or perceived nature of 'reality' transmitted through language, Haley's story, like many other post-modern stories, insists equally on the presence of the body in experience and knowledge. Tortillas eaten in Acapulco pursue the hapless narrator with increasing urgency on the bus and into a washerwoman's privy. Physical existence is never in doubt. The body eats, defecates, has erections, swims, drinks, and experiences sensations, but all in the context of a multi-directional narrative in which the narrator resists definition other than by the most primary terms: male, not elderly, travelling in the Caribbean, lived or living in Auckland. Think of a person and 'they' exist. Haley's narrator recalls a friend thousands of miles away, and he appears in the next paragraph: language makes no distinction between thought or fantasy and event. A post-modern fiction like 'Barbados — A Love Story' thus leaves the reader with minimalized certainties. Stories have been told, but all the other questions which might be asked of a fiction — what happened? to whom? where? when? what does it mean? — can be answered only partially, if at all.

The experience of post-modern fiction is a special experience of language, and post-modernism sets out to demonstrate the primacy of the text. Consequently there is often a great deal of play with highly formalized textual strategies, with codes, abstract vocabulary, scientific language, and the language of facts. Post-modern fictions also play with historical events or people, juxtaposing incompatible historical realities, as in Michael Morrissey's 'Jack Kerouac Sat Down By the Wanganui River and Wept' or 'A Very Timid Little Boy Called Franz Kafka'. Such stories directly challenge notions of probability, and exploit the possibilities offered by discontinuities of space, time, and place, collapsing the conventions of meaning normally shared between reader and text. The post-modern text is continually interrupted and invaded, deflected from the narrative it appears to offer at any one point as its principal concern. The only constant factor is the process of transformation itself, which never concludes, and remains obstinately self-referential, emphasizing its own artifice.

In doing away with the possibility of fiction's providing an answer to the mysteries of existence, post-modernism has thrown much greater emphasis on the mysteries. The stories of Chris Else, Ted Jenner, Ian Wedde, and Michael Gifkins focus on puzzles, either as explicit forms of brainteasing (some of the shorter pieces in *The New Fiction* play with language in the form of visual puzzles) or by presenting codes of information which, when detached from structures of meaning, assume a puzzling, comic, or bizarre character. In Else's stories, quixotic characters search for truths amongst mathematical equations, popular songs, religious rhetorics, or the paraphernalia of spy novels. Post-modern fiction often plays with the formal strategies of texts, using footnotes, scholarly references, research data, even parallel texts, in order to break down the boundaries between fictional and other texts. Bill Manhire, Wystan Curnow, Ted Jenner, and Malcolm Fraser have all explored such possibilities, replicating the formal writing procedures of non-fictional modes in order to fictionalize them. Malcolm Fraser's 'The Original Community of James Fox' was reprinted in the *New Zealand Whole Earth Catalogue* as a genuine account of a polygamous community on the Hauraki Plains. Many post-modern stories create 'factions' in which real events or people occur in fictional contexts. At the same time, they exploit a highly topical and culturally specific environment. The references to popular songs, contemporary drugs, and topical events and personalities that occur in the work of Wedde or Gifkins tie it closely to the time at which it was written, even as the stories collapse the boundaries of time and space and create a kind of fictional world in which any number of conditions and possibilities can coexist within the text. In the Preface to his collection, *The Shirt Factory* (1981), Wedde observed, 'You think of fiction as a kind of rhythm beneath the endless obsolescence of fact; a swell beneath the surface chop.'[103] His stories reproduce in detail the surface chop, and the many specific dialects and registers that identify people. The postman in 'Paradise' notices seasonal changes on the surface of the ground on which he urinates. Otto's loathing of the bourgeoisie in the title story, and the drugs and booze and food and songs and desire which course through Herman Flag in 'Snake', spread 'character' so thickly with 'culture' that they become indistinguishable aspects of each other. In the end, it is the textual density of the surface chop, its stops and starts and accumulations, that suggests a kind of deep flow, an underlying process.

Post-modern fiction in New Zealand has mainly been the province of Pākehā male writers. However, during the 1980s its influence was gradually diffused through the story writing and reading environment, shifting and altering the main short story forms, so that by the end of the decade it was rare to find social-humanist-realist stories in major periodicals. But though it challenged a number of orthodox literary concerns and expectations, post-modern fiction did not disengage itself from the masculine. From Haley to Wedde and after, the narrators of post-modern fiction are identified with their masculinity. Their desire is predominantly heterosexual and their identification of the languages and codes of power, as well as their social relations and fictional contexts, are defined by their sexuality. Post-modernism, in its origins, was a masculine act, and gender is a continuing preoccupation, as it had been with writers of the 'free' story. If race is not a form of difference which it explores, gender is.

By transferring the scene of the post-modern story out of the partially specified regional context of *The New Fiction* and into an environment of multiple socio-economic signifiers, Michael Gifkins locates his fictions and his reader in the atmosphere of high fictionality that characterizes late capitalism. All three of Gifkins' collections suggest wealth as the ultimate signifier of Western culture. *After the Revolution* (1982) remained onshore, mostly in Auckland (although in the title story, Antony's introduction to the social scene is a journey into foreignness), but subsequent collections, *Summer is the Côte d'Azur* (1987) and *The Amphibians* (1989), moved into ironic and geographical distance. His characters inhabit the densely inscribed landscape of Southern Europe; cosmopolitan, international, wealthy, often artistic or engaged with the arts. The sexual configurations into which couples and communities fall act as analogues for their imaginative and artistic lives, and sexuality and spirituality are closely connected. In 'Mediatrix', Lucy's inability to paint is associated with difficulties in her relationship with her husband, and when she decides not to accompany him to London but instead enters the sea with the dolphin she has been trying to paint, the boundary between human art and animal life vanishes: 'the code was starting to change, become infinitely subtle'.[104] Lucy's painting is swimming before her eyes.

The stories play with ideas of mediation and with the points at which difference vanishes to re-emerge as something else, something 'fictional'. They pursue a narrative deceptively familiar in its linearity but at the same time located in a highly 'novelized' environment where counts, young heiresses, and the eccentric rich meet in apartments and villas and cafés along the Côte d'Azur, subject to the textuality and epistemological insecurities of their surroundings. The titles of Gifkins' collections suggest both the fictional code by which we recognize their play, and their mimetic reference to a recognizable real world of novels and tabloid magazines (*After the Revolution, Summer is the Côte d'Azur*), as well as the fluid transmission of fiction from one dimension to another (*The Amphibians*). Gifkins has marginalized New Zealand as a location for his fiction in a way that makes nationality, as a point of origin, as fictional as any other notion of place; a number of stories contain a spoken reference to New Zealand as a place suggesting the exotic, the foreign, the mystical, far off: a place where dolphins *do* play with children without accident or ill-feeling.

In Gifkins' work the post-modern story creates an undifferentiated continuum on which 'Art' and 'Life', 'fiction' and the 'real', 'home' and 'away' coexist. The displacements of his characters which result in a kind of circumstantial self-reflexivity always return the linear narrative to circularity; the reader is returned to fictionality however much the story may suggest that a transition from narrative to commentary can be effected. In the end the text reasserts itself as text in which the reader, too, must be constructed. The stories close, not with conclusiveness or with endings, a sense of resolution, but with the camera clicking its shutter on the perfect shot, a moment of immobility chosen by the imaginative will, in which the reader is compelled to acquiesce; the text imaged as memento, souvenir, holiday snap, the moment of reflection:

> You pause before the mirror but the mirror lets you pass. You are wearing your small black dress. You smile. You toss back glistening curls. The Mediterranean proceeds to Africa. Mimosa is close outside the window and light reflects its calm back to the world.[105]

Although the stories in John Cranna's *Visitors* (1989) pursue a more linear narrative than those of Haley or Gifkins, their realist surface is also based upon unknown or unknowable conditions. In 'Archeology', a lack of information about the wider environment forces the reader to construct a possible reading for 'that summer of the war', the events of the story, and eventually for the title. In 'Accidents', the story transgresses the boundaries of acceptable 'real' behaviour, but without any of the glosses which might provide a causal or psychologically interpretive context; instead the story sharpens its focus with claustrophobic hyper-realism. Cranna's narratives combine geographical with cultural and temporal mobility, and mix an apparently recognizable world with inexplicable irruptions of 'outside' events which come from nowhere, and are never interpreted by the narrator. Like the grandfather's stories in 'Visitors', information, contexts, and sequences remain incomplete:

> A story that began in Djakarta might end in Santiago without his being aware that the location had changed, and fragments and characters from one tale would find their way into others, so that his monologues were jigsaws of confusion that held me entranced for hours, but which I could never fully understand.[106]

Cranna's fictions affirm the incomplete understanding of the reader while representing an apparently familiar, richly detailed world. 'Soft Targets', for example, contains some parodic reworking of familiar New Zealand literary landscapes (including 'Along Rideout Road that Summer'), and 'History for Berliners' refers to the political and historical map of the late twentieth century. Cranna's stories enact the post-modern fictional environment by constructing the reader as a visitor to the narrative, unable to fully possess and comprehend it, while playing with a mimetic referentiality to the 'real' world of history, geography, literature, politics, and behaviour.

Bill Manhire's stories (*The New Land: A Picture Book*, 1990) resist textual classification (entries in the mock-index reference the text to a plurality of comically disparate categories of writing), but they are conceptually connected by their frequent allusions to different versions of cultural identity. New Zealand is thus presented as invented, transmitted, and known through and across 'texts', from Janet Frame's autobiography which invades the 'real' world of New Zealand House ('South Pacific') to adventure stories of the South

Pacific ('Cannibals'). Manhire's stories reveal a shift from a post-modern to a post-colonial consciousness. Texts are seen as leaving their traces in other texts, and as inventing new lands, authors, fictions, and literatures. Since their focus, throughout, is the South Pacific, the reader is continually engaged in a post-colonial process of recognition and discovery:

> That is how it is, adventure and regret, there is no getting away from it. We live in the broad Pacific, meeting and parting shake us . . . .[107]

The growth of anthologies of women's writing in the 1980s reflected an interest in gender-based categories of writing as distinct from traditional generic groupings. The short story is a form practised by many women writers perhaps because, though it is less durable than the novel, and more easily lost in the great bulk of periodical publication, it is marketable and does not necessarily require an extended commitment. For decades the *New Zealand Listener* carried stories by women whose names seldom appeared in major anthologies such as the Oxford series. *Landfall* and *Islands*, which set literary standards for substantial periods of their publishing history, at times published few women writers, and it was not until collections began to appear in the late 1970s and early 1980s which reconstructed literary history outside the major publishing forums that the extent of writing by women became more visible. It is easy to infer from the bulk of largely unnoticed published writing by women that some forms of discrimination have been practised by editors and publishers of anthologies in New Zealand as elsewhere. Having said that, it seems pointless to pursue the vexed question of separate traditions as if it were a process consciously undertaken by women writers. Nevertheless, the work of women does reveal some common preoccupations and literary choices, which are as suggestive of the constraints women writers may have felt themselves to be under in a restricted market as they are of anything that might stand for a collective identity. Women writers, perhaps even more markedly than men, fall into two distinct groups: those who have published a collection and those who have not. In the 1970s, the short story writers who achieved the status of a collection were generally also novelists: Joy Cowley, Margaret Sutherland, Fiona Kidman, Patricia Grace, Yvonne du Fresne. In the later 1980s, a number of women emerged initially as short story writers (Shonagh Koea, Barbara Anderson, Anne Kennedy, Stephanie Johnson, Sue Reidy), and anthologies like *Women's Work*, *In Deadly Earnest*, the *New Women's Fiction* series, *Shirley Temple is a Wife and Mother*, and *Goodbye to Romance* indicate the extensive territory occupied by short fiction written by women.

The predominant kind of fiction written by women in New Zealand until very recently has been social realism with a close domestic focus. Since the 1930s, women's fiction has been concerned with the family as the *Realpolitik* of female experience, most often in Pākehā writers as a place of restraint, repression, and conflict. While the social roles of women have been largely determined by family — wife, daughter, mother — short fiction by women is particularly concerned with the meticulous investigation of the female condition and its emotional landscape rather than with connections between the individual and society. Cowley's description of her practice as a writer suggests a view of language as a medium for emotion, and of storytelling as an articulation of the territory of the self:

> [S]ince stories must begin with the heart, the intellect can know little about them until the work is finished. Then the mind reads them, as it were, for the first time.[108]

Very often the narrative concerns of fiction of the 1970s and early 1980s identify selfhood as a product of emotional self-knowledge, and stories delicately investigate where the boundaries in social relations lie, giving metaphorical density to the identification with particular social roles that women see themselves as making. In Cowley's 'The Silk' a little man waving from the bridge in the piece of Chinese silk affirms the point of Mrs Blackie's wifeliness, and all her competencies, qualities, and strengths are directed towards celebrating the woven silk landscape which signifies her successful marriage. At the same time Cowley's fiction, like that of Sutherland and Kidman, is effectively anti-romantic. Post-marital rather than pre-marital, its choices and possibilities occur in the competing self-interests of marriages and families, where selfhood is so closely identified with role that the playful constructions of a Herman Flag or a Julian Harp have no space in which to exist.

A great many stories by women are preoccupied with territorial space. Settings are often quite literally interior, walled, defined, the narrative taking place in domestic environments which function metonymically to signify women, and seldom moving into a larger or less controllable terrain. There is no equivalent of Man Alone in the fiction written by women. Cowley's 'The Colonel and South America' explores its differences (age, gender, nationality) almost entirely within the metal walls of a bus as the clear air and colourful environment of the Andes unrolls outside. In 'Distances', marital warfare occupies a no man's land inside the house; it is not until the female character stops ironing and goes out onto the lawn that she can express herself in feelings. In 'Heart Attack' the spatial analogy is similar: 'There was no room in the house for his grief. It was a pain too big to be contained within walls and yet there was nowhere else to go.'[109]

'Home' in short fiction by women is represented as the place in which female selfhood is most clearly recognized and where it is most at risk, perhaps because, in its accommodation of the shifting identities that include daughter, wife, and mother, it is a continuous re-invention of place and condition. In Fiona Kidman's story 'Mrs Dixon and Friend' Bethany and her house are indistinguishable, from the point of view of Bethany's ex-husband; the house represents for him both what he has lost, and the characteristics of his ex-wife which threaten to disorder or rearrange his own existence:

> For wasn't it Bethany who had resisted the flat lawns and bevel-edge hedges and the

new wallpaper in the hallway each spring where she had let the children put their dirty hands, and the kitchen repainted annually because the fat splashed over and her cigarettes burned holes while she read books?[110]

Kidman's stories are representative of the work of many women writers in that they make domestic space into a metaphor and identify female subjectivity with its area of occupation. More specifically, female sexuality is often identified with the possession of enclosed space. What alarms the ex-husband about Bethany in Kidman's story is that her house reveals the extent of her self-possession; her fat-splashed kitchen, her body spilling out of its dress in the sun, and her open books, suggest the extent to which she is not confined to the role or identification her suburban house and her wife/motherhood might seem to predicate.

In Sutherland's 'Dark Places, Deep Regions' a young journalist recently arrived in Papua New Guinea finds himself able to record in language the facts of his new life, the 'known ground' of his profession, but not his 'feeling of openness, compared with which his past life seemed a static, half-lived state'.[111] The inability of men to manage or articulate feeling, or to accommodate ambiguity, is commonplace in fiction by women, particularly during the 1970s. Sutherland's journalist experiences Papua New Guinea as a journey into sensation and loneliness, eventually alleviated when he rents a room from the wife of an army sergeant who is absent on a jungle training course. Moving into her house he moves irresistibly into the absence contained within her domestic structures, which is both represented and affirmed by her feeding baby. As the journalist succumbs to the dark places and deep regions of his own selfhood that Joy opens for him, he is 'annointed' by drops of milk spilled from her breast. The significance of entering a new land is emphatically repeated in his entering a new house, a new woman, and a new self-knowledge. House, woman, and country of the senses are thus metaphorically connected in Sutherland's story. In Sutherland's story of adolescent sexuality, 'Codling-Moth', the enclosed space of teenage knowledge and possibility is suggested in the intense focus that two girls have on each other, in their insistent consciousness of their bodies, and in their rituals, a friendship unable in the end to withstand the reconditioning of female sexuality that Mother carries out. The focus of both Kidman and Sutherland on the metaphors of female sexuality and on the structures by which it is regulated and contained can be seen as the groundwork from which short fiction in the 1980s reformulated and reshaped the connection between female identities and roles.

The first anthology of lesbian writing (*The Power and the Glory*) appeared in 1987, edited by Miriam Saphira. By the mid-1980s the process of investigation of gender roles, which was often a process of affirmation, had started to shift into more fluid representations, a shift represented at its most politically radical in lesbian writing, which surfaced in feminist periodicals: *Broadsheet*, *Hecate*, and *Spiral*. Lesbian short fiction typically challenges the heterosexual family by rewriting romance as lesbian. In this respect it adopts in order to subvert what has been the dominant model for both male and female writers (though romance is mostly written by women) for representing heterosexual gender roles. Lesbian romance preserves the essentialist attributes of heterosexual romance (recognition of selfhood and value in the discovery of oneself as a lover or as beloved) but transfers them to a liaison which threatens the social fabric. Conventionally literary as it may often seem, lesbian romance inscribes difference on the dominant structures of social experience and gender conditioning: by redefining the environment of short fiction it radically extends the territory of 'women's writing'.

Lesbian fiction is also colonizing. The stories in Saphira's collection are very often about the discovery of collective female identity. Like the writing of all minority groups (much the same thing occurs in Māori writing), lesbian texts are concerned to represent the extent of homogeneity, rather than difference, amongst women. Other women writers of the later 1980s are concerned to dismantle the idea of gender itself in order to pursue difference. The stories in Saphira's anthology contain many moments of recognition, perhaps not so much moments of colonization, as recognitions of an extension of selfhood, a repeated 'I am' that sets up a different social structure:

> And I remembered a time on the patch all those months ago when a women's voice, two rows away, was heard saying, Maudie's gay you know. And I stood up and shouted, so am I, I'm gay. And Nikki next to me instantly straightened and said, I am too, I'm a lesbian. And shouts from the other three came to us as they stood — me too, I'm a lesbian. I am. I am. I am. And the whole patch stopped work and unfolded like a pack of cards righting itself.[112]

Janet Frame's anti-individualistic, anti-essentialist fiction, which questions all given structures of knowledge, is the most radical of all New Zealand writing, and in the specific ways in which she deconstructs gender roles and the importance of the individual self her texts are reference points for recent writing. In a story entitled 'Jan Godfrey', the narrator observes:

> Alison Hendry. Margaret Burt. Nancy Smith. We cling to our names because we think they emphasize our separateness and completeness and importance, but deep down we know that we are neither separate nor complete nor very important, nor are we terribly happy . . . .[113]

Such an observation might have prefaced Barbara Anderson's 'Up the River with Mrs Gallant', a story written without a narrator and composed entirely of reported speech of the flattest kind, the speech of provincial newspapers. Almost every sentence opens with a proper name (Mr Lewis invited them, Mrs Gallant said, Mrs Kent said, Mrs Kent remarked, Arnold said), a device which draws attention to the absence of a narrative frame, inviting readers to 'read' the story for themselves. It also subordinates the name of the speaker to what is said, for it is not the use of proper names which differentiates the characters but how they define themselves in language. Anderson's first collection, *I Think*

We Should Go Into the Jungle (1989), uses a highly ironic and flattened language to suggest the detachable surface of the text. Cut loose from the traditional anchoring of a narrative point of view, located mostly in the social occasions and defining situations of middle-class white New Zealand, the stories re-view the familiar as strange, composing their narratives from foreshortened perspectives, with an emphasis on picture, texture, colour, collage, and leaving structures of meaning and knowledge to the effort and will of the reader:

> The sunporch was made as a sergeant's billet. A Royal Stuart rug given them as a wedding present covered the low bed. An alarm clock, a small Swiss army knife, a yellow Gollancz, a blue plastic glass of water shared the kitchen chair alongside. Una lay awake each night listening for his snores.[114]

As well as removing emphasis from the narrator and (under the influence of post-modernism) moving away from unitary narrative, recent writing has also burst out of the domestic post-romance frame characteristic of earlier writing by women. Shonagh Koea, Sue Reidy, Stephanie Johnson, Anne Kennedy, and Fiona Farrell Poole have all published collections of stories which take place outside the family and outside New Zealand. In the title story of Koea's *The Woman Who Never Went Home and Other Stories* (1987), a woman in pursuit of a man she fancies in a New Caledonian hotel recuperates from her past in an environment where she is anonymous. Travel, afloat in another culture, as if on a metaphorical journey away from home, is perhaps the most commonly represented condition of recent fiction by women. Johnson's fictions are set in Sydney, Reidy's in Indonesia, and Poole's travel between Europe and New Zealand, across historical time and geographical space.[115] As the expansion of the physical environment of fiction by women breaks down the metonymic association between 'home' and 'woman', gender roles, particularly in the work of Johnson and Reidy, become conscious game-playing. In Johnson's 'The Invisible Hand' the narrator earns her living receiving obscene phone calls from men. It is her deliberate adoption of the role of sex-object, her commercial investment in the marketability of her gendered voice and the telephone's receptivity to male fantasies, that earns her an income, and gives the story its point: gender exploited as a commercial asset threatens the acceptability of sex roles by making them explicit. Robyn's friend Sue leaves in disgust when she discovers Robyn's occupation, telling her she is unfit to be a mother. On the wall of Robyn's bedroom are signs: 'I am a Strong, Free-Spirited Woman. I Control My Own Destiny.'[116]

Being female is to exist in a conjunction of impossibilities, as Johnson's title story, 'The Glass Whittler', with its image of concentrated effort and pain, might suggest. Far from giving gender roles or the domestic location of women some kind of metaphorical affirmation, the stories of Johnson, Rosie Scott,[117] and Sue Reidy attempt to unsettle preconceptions about gender. The musicians, solo parents, and travelling adventurers are located outside the home, and represent anti-domesticity. The scientists, artists, and entymologists who appear in the stories of Wendy Pond, whose environment is constructed wholly in terms of their work, redefine subjectivity in occupational terms.[118] Frame and Anderson explicitly, and all female writers implicitly, redefine it as textual. In Reidy's magic realist stories, strange events invade and interrupt apparently realistic surfaces so that possibilities are extended. In 'Alexandra and the Lion' Alexandra's nocturnal voyages on the lion's back break down the apparently stable structures of marriage (where gender occupations are reversed), job, and apartment living; in 'Modettes', Rose 'does not question why a Hindu goddess should be eating a Chinese meal in the middle of the night in her apartment'. Anything can and does happen in magic realism. Rose travels through Indonesia in a number of the stories in *Modettes*, and there is no such thing as improbability. Her clothes are appropriated by a beautiful Japanese man, to whom she becomes '*Rangda* the Queen returned from the dead'.[119] Any construction of the self is possible in an environment where cultural and social definitions are abandoned. In recent writing by women, gender, role, nationality, and culture, like the text itself, have burst out of containment, calling into question all the terms which might precondition identity: wife, mother, daughter, lover, woman, New Zealander, narrative, story.

Drama

HOWARD McNAUGHTON

More overtly than other literary forms, the dramatic text is the product of its surrounding society; while the process of scripting assumes the existence of an immediate audience, the realization of the text in the theatre is also an expression of audience values, attitudes, and norms. In New Zealand, as elsewhere in white settler societies, dramatic production has been itself an act of colonization, with no clear chronological boundaries between the drama of colonial imposition and the drama of post-colonial hybridity.[1] The first section of this chapter, on the nineteenth century, refers loosely to colonial drama, in which the power of colonization does not acknowledge the voice of the colonized; although Māori themes and characters recur, they are never problematized, and are generally reduced to the stature of postcard curiosities.

The first four and a half decades of this century (the subject of the second section) were a period of protracted amateurism, marked fitfully by the efforts of individuals in a theatrical environment which lacked the resources and professionalism, and hence the audiences, necessary for their survival as playwrights. It was only towards the end of this period, in the sponsorship of one-act plays by the New Zealand branch of the British Drama League and in the activities of left-wing theatre groups, that a more receptive climate began to emerge, and in a handful of plays some of the older colonial certainties began to be challenged. The remaining four sections, on drama after 1945, trace the shifting patterns of this emergent post-colonial dramatic consciousness: the cultural dictates of the parent culture begin to be questioned, new (or suppressed) social perspectives are opened up, and a more complex probing of cultural identity occurs. In this process the voices of minorities and marginalized groups come to be acknowledged, and drama becomes increasingly diverse; earlier preoccupations and attitudes are displaced or become decentred, with Māori, women, and gays choosing their own target audiences.

Two other factors require that a description of New Zealand drama should give the bulk of its attention to the period since the Second World War. The nineteenth century, the major era of British colonization, was also a period in which the dramatic text was not particularly valued as literature. All dramatic writing was affected, and the relative dearth of verifiable records means that an expansive coverage would necessarily be speculative. Also, New Zealand has always had a low-density population, with the result that the theatre's primary objective has tended to be to find *any* audience; a narrowing of focus — on locally-based New Zealand drama, for example — would often have been seen as an unrealistic, if not suicidal, luxury. Since 1945, however, a few cities have grown large enough to make such specialization possible, helped considerably by the introduction of government funding and support.

In a timespan as relatively short as the four and a half decades since 1945, during which the great majority of New Zealand plays have been written and performed, any division into periods has to be seen as indicative rather than prescriptive. The most prominent playwrights continued writing over two or more decades, and at any one time newer impulses existed alongside (and often in conflict with) older continuities. In what follows four periods are provisionally defined, on the basis of new 'generations' of playwrights whose emergence was often closely linked to new institutional developments. From 1945 to the early 1960s, despite the continuing shortage of resources and professionalism, there are the first distinct signs of change in the theatrical environment: writers who in earlier circumstances might have confined themselves to other forms of imaginative expression began to explore the possibilities of the stage. In the mid-1960s a new generation of playwrights appeared in the wake of the establishment of state-subsidized professional community theatres; a further expansion occurred in the early 1970s, this time after the founding of the professional writers' agency, Playmarket. The final section explores new impulses of the 1980s. Throughout the whole period relationships between the stage, radio drama, and then television drama have been significant, and these provide a recurrent background in each section.

The Drama of Colonization

In New Zealand, as in other British colonies, the theatrical activity which quickly followed first settlement was essentially a showcase for Old World fashion. No regard was shown for new environmental factors or for the artistic interest of the extensive performance tradition within Māori culture (though this did not include impersonation or dramatic characterization in the European sense). In the townships of the 1840s and 1850s entertainment focused on the farces, melodramas, and variety programmes which were generally offered at night in makeshift hotel annexes by performers who had limited experience of the English or Australian stage. In order to draw the same audience several nights a week, extravagant claims were often made for the novelty of the plays mounted, and it was this impulse which led to the presentation of the first 'original' New Zealand play: *Marcilina, Or The Maid of Urnindorpt* was a two-act play written by James Marriott (manager of Wellington's Britannia Saloon), which premièred on 11 July 1848. The production was followed by a 'Shakespearian festival' and a return to English melodrama, with acting assistance from members of a locally-stationed regiment.

In the 1860s the military continued to be a stimulus to theatre in the North Island, while the South Island gold rushes attracted numerous itinerant groups of performers to the cities and to the goldfields. Several Dunedin literary gentlemen, including Benjamin Farjeon (manager of the *Otago Daily Times*) and Julius Vogel (then editor of the same newspaper, later New Zealand premier), wrote plays on mainly European subjects which had considerable stage success. Vogel's version of *Lady Audley's Secret* was staged in 1863, only a year after the London publication of Braddon's novel and two months after its first (unpublished) West End dramatization. Reviewers, while praising performances, were largely non-committal about the achievement of the anonymous author, but considerable attention was paid to dramatic theory and to comparisons with Braddon, Eliot, Collins, and Charlotte Brontë. The cultural climate of Dunedin, with an increasingly unstable goldfields population being viewed in dismay by the puritanical settlers, is also reflected in one condemnation of Braddon's story:

> The principal incident is not merely vulgar, but so repulsive that the dramatist rejects it as unmanageable. The murder at the ruined well might form the *point d'appui* of a Porte St. Martin melodrame, but is out of place in a piece addressed to refined audiences.[2]

Possibly in acknowledgement of Dunedin's colonial refinement, Vogel's play accentuated the theme of repentance as well as the title character's madness. When *Lady Audley's Secret* was revived later in 1863, it was double-billed with *Aurora Floyd*, another Braddon adaptation by a Dunedin journalist, possibly Farjeon. In the 1860s Farjeon gained a local reputation as the author of the drama *A Life's Revenge* and three burlesques including *Faust* (1865) and *Guy Fawkes* (1867) written for the stock company which had premièred the melodramas. His own dramatization of his goldfields novel *Grif* was produced in Dunedin in 1866 to coincide with the book's publication, and it was revived in 1881; set in Victoria, the action follows an already traditional Australian pattern in which weak-willed young men on the fringes of bushranger society are sustained by the devotion of a pure woman.[3]

Auckland was the port of entry for most performers coming to New Zealand, and colonial theatrical activity there dates back to 1841. By the early 1870s Auckland audiences were receptive to original plays on local themes, seven of which were premièred in 1870-71.[4] The most successful of these, Laurence Booth's *Crime in the Clouds* (1871), is remembered mainly from a description of a Christchurch revival in 1875.[5] Three of the four acts were set in England, and consisted of a clandestine marriage and romantic intrigue. These precipitated the chief sensation (in the Boucicault tradition): a knife attack by a jealous rival, ending with the victim being hurled from a balloon hovering twelve feet above the stage. Before the retribution of the final act, the characters visit New Zealand where they become involved in the Land Wars, and experience another sensation: torture and burning at the stake. The New Zealand act included specific historical allusions, with Booth himself playing the part of Von Tempsky, whose actual death and Hauhau cremation in 1868 may have formed the basis of the tribal torture scene. Since the action recalled such a recent past, the use of Māori actors (remarkable in itself at the time) must have contributed to an atmosphere of topicality. A few months after the première of *Crime in the Clouds*, Booth wrote *Guided by the Auckland Public, or The Fortunes of a New Chum*, a farce with a satirical edge sufficient to antagonize part of the Auckland public.

Topical farce, in which the absurdities of colonial Auckland were exposed, was the mode of another substantial success, F.L. Davey's *Potagold's Peep* (1871), ostensibly about the courtship of a sailor's supposed widow, but also accommodating observations on 'the City Board, the railway, the scrip mania, Queen Street sewer, and other subjects that possess special interest to an Aucklander'.[6] Similarly, the anonymous *The Tomahawk, or Auckland and its Insolvent Laws in 1870* (1870), satirized local politicians and, presumably, the public works with which they were associated.

One play which moved well beyond parochial concerns to make a larger statement about New Zealand society was A. Western's *Philo Maori, or New Zealand as it Is* (1870), which anticipated Booth's device of using Māori performers for war scenes. Contemporary attitudes to the use of Māori material are reflected in a brief newspaper preview stating that 'Real Maoris are to be introduced, and go through the war dance, and such other little arrangements as aboriginals are liable to.'[7] In production, however, this emerged as the only popular element:

> [H]ad it not been for the novelty of several 'real Maoris', who played the parts of the savages, the piece would have been a complete failure, but these gentlemen kept the audience in a pretty good humour by their dance — the first of which by-the-way, was anything but a pleasing exhibition — and general movements.[8]

The play's themes raised complex issues to do with the consciousness of New Zealand audiences, particularly through the title reference to a character type with an idealistic belief in racial harmony. Balancing (or perhaps parodying) this was the portrayal of the Pākehā Māori and a situation of intermarriage which complicated the central action of lust, massacre, and betrayal. The only substantial review attacked the work for its simplistic portrayal of drunken Māori, cowardly constabulary, and lustful Europeans, arguing that these were neither typical nor the cause of the wars, that the reality of such massacres was too recent a memory for them to be burlesqued, and that the work as a whole amounted to a 'libel upon the Maoris'. It seems unlikely that the play's tone was satirical. Western seems to have drawn uncritically on the ethnic and social types of northern hemisphere melodrama, with their related stock company values of confirming assumed audience prejudice. This is supported by the final tableau, 'representing a young and very pretty Britannia very triumphant, amidst flags and crimson fire, with Maoris sticking their heads into the dust in token of subjection'.[9] The production thus offers an important index to contemporary audience feeling: its failure was due not solely to bad writing but also to its insensitive depiction of race relations, a tone which would not recur as blatantly in the more successful New Zealand melodrama of the 1890s.

The exceptionally large number of local scripts mounted in Auckland in 1870-1 (though they comprised only a fraction of the total output of Auckland theatres) reflects a theatre in a state of evolution, and indicates that audiences were becoming increasingly receptive to the novelty of local plays. The difficulties of sea transport around New Zealand meant that resident stock companies frequently accommodated a single touring celebrity, and New Zealand's isolation made for easy evasion of copyright. By the 1880s, improved steamer services across the Tasman would make commonplace the touring of whole companies, with up to a hundred members and dozens of sets. The management of such enterprises was perfected by J.C. Williamson, who first toured New Zealand in 1881 (if only to look after his investment; it was necessary for Williamson to protect his copyright). In 1880, Williamson was reported to have paid £1000 for the Australasian rights to *The Pirates of Penzance*,[10] the same amount as he would pay to transport a company across the Tasman.

The first local play to be published in New Zealand appeared under the pseudonym 'Grif', but had nothing to do with Benjamin Farjeon; it was the work of a Mr Griffen of Wanganui.[11] His 'New Grand Semi-Maori Christmas Pantomime' was an extravaganza fully entitled *Kainga of the Ladye Birds, or Harlequin Prince Tumanako, the Fair Ataahua, and The Demon of Colonial Finance* (1879). The style of the lyrics is heavily derivative of Gilbert's *H.M.S. Pinafore*, often to the point of parody, but the directness of the satirical aggression against the Colonial debt (and its named political perpetrators) is remarkable, especially as the work was produced at the Wellington Academy of Music. All of the dramatic characters are Māori (played by Europeans) and the locations are tribal, with a secondary romantic theme. However the main characters, concerned with colonial finance, are clearly pursuing European careers, and Koura (the Demon) introduces himself with an autobiographical song modelled on Gilbert's 'Now I am the ruler of the Queen's navee'. Te Whiti's prophecy of decolonization is an oddity of the past, the Parihaka railway is seen as a cultural bridge, and Matatu (the good spirit) looks forward to New Zealand becoming 'the Britain of the South' (a slogan of Vogel's). At such an early stage of colonial development it may seem surprising that a Māori perspective was used at all, but the ethnic content is extremely superficial, little more than a romantic personification of the world of the ladybirds, an appropriately elastic structure to accommodate the political satire. Apart from a possible reference to the Wanganui chief Te Mamaku in the character of Tumanako (Prince of Zealandia) the topical focus is entirely on politicians, and the satirical style a lively mixture of colloquial prose and musical lyrics. The unsuccessful manoeuvrings of Premier Hall in 1879 are described thus:

And served him right, too. May all such political traitors be similarly treated. In return for his vote, he reckoned on getting the Agent-Generalship, at the very least; but in this he has been bitterly disappointed, as Julius Vogel doesn't intend to give that up for some time to come. When Wood complains to Johnny Hall, about the way he has been treated, the Premier politely replies (chorus)

> Hurst, Swanson, and Colbeck, perhaps,
> Are still more unfortunate 'flats'.
> Didn't Hall set a nice little trap
> To catch these political rats?
> They laid themselves out to be bought,
> And become the most pliant of tools;
> But I don't know how ever they thought
> To 'squat' on the Government stools![12]

The play also shows satirical audacity with a reference to Graham Berry premier of Victoria, who would shortly become involved in Australia's most celebrated case of political stage censorship. Griffen produced another extravaganza, with no apparent political content, the following year: *Hinemoa* (1880) was favourably received but not published, although one journalist predicted that it would

form the groundwork of a permanent entertainment, which might be worked successfully throughout the Colonies, one of the principal features being the introduction of a series of panoramic views, illustrating the Middle Island Sounds and the Hot Lakes of the North Island.[13]

The plays of Gilbert formed a popular model for satire throughout British colonies. Marcus Clarke's localized version of *The Wicked World* was banned by Berry in Melbourne in January 1880 (and produced only in modified form),[14] and the same play formed the basis of *The Happy Land*, written anonymously by a Christchurch journalist in February 1880, revised with a Wellington location a month later, and with a Dunedin location in September. In the opening scene of the Christchurch version the fairy queen describes New Zealand as 'a land (the fairest surely 'neath the refulgent sun) that rises sparkling from the radiant southern seas in many islets', inhabited by a people 'sober, industrious, and frugal, and well deserving of the blessings plenteous they enjoy'. A listing of the blessings, culminating in 'scientific Hospital Boards', provides the first opportunity for satire, but more opportunities occur when the queen sends for 'three bright specimens of humanity' to educate her fairies in these blessings, and is sent three prominent New Zealand parliamentarians; the premier John Hall, the treasurer Major Atkinson, and the minister for Lands William Rolleston. Though assessments of the originality of the satirical allusiveness varied, it was immediately recognized that the play drew extensively from the 1879 election debates and that it was supportive of Sir George Grey. However, even in 1880 it was felt that the point of many of the allusions had been 'lost by the time which has elapsed'.[15]

Kainga of the Ladye Birds was published in Wellington to coincide with the première, in the common Victorian format of programme and annotated lyrics.

The first play to be published in book form followed soon after, and was also a work of political satire. Josiah Clifton Firth's *Weighed in the Balance: A Play for the Times* (1882) appeared under the pseudonym of Arthur Fonthill, possibly because the author already had a reputation under his own name as a religious moralist.[16] Again, the play's satirical thrust is contained within a curious amalgam of local allusion and English manners; the action, resembling a Socratic debate, begins and ends in a cavern on Kawau Island, with intermediate scenes in the baronial hall at Kawau and in the Wellington House of Representatives. The main character is the Knight of Kawau (a reference to Sir George Grey) whose pretence to egalitarian principles is questioned by the King of the Witches, with the support of a chorus of witches. Their reactionary arguments on social and political theory, in verse and rhetorical prose, allude to specific local politicians such as Grey, Vogel, Browne, and Stout, but there are also stereotypes like Spluttermuch and Lowdown. There is no record that the play was ever staged.

New Zealand's other published drama of the late Victorian period is stilted and formal in style, eurocentric in location and social perspective, and directed primarily at a reading audience. Eleanor Montgomery's one-act *Madame Béranger* (1887) is a short romance with a French setting, rich in passionate bombast; however, with only three characters and some awareness of stagecraft it may well have reached a cultured audience in Wanganui where it was published. W.H. Guthrie-Smith's *Crispus* (1891) is a full-length blank-verse play derived from Gibbon, in which the title character, a son of Constantine, is the innocent victim of machinations by his stepmother and a eunuch; the play's pretensions to tragedy are emphasized by extensive use of soliloquy. James Izett's tragedy, *King George the Third* (1899), was developed from Thackeray and is rich in intrigue, sensation, and imperialist patriotism (he also published a collection of 'patriotic songs' in 1901, 'The Blood that Makes for Empire'). In the play's final scene the king briefly regains his sanity to eulogize a statue of Victoria at her coronation before he resumes his raving, and dies to the accompaniment of the Hallelujah chorus. The play does show some concern for historical accuracy, and the notes on the characters suggest that the author was hopeful of production. R.T. Hammond's *Under the Shadow of Dread* (1908) is a five-act drama about King Alfred, with a literary competence in its prose, lyrics, and predominant blank verse that does not obscure its Shakespearian model. Though these plays had no theatrical significance, their publication at least reflects the persistence of the minority consciousness noted earlier in connection with Vogel's refined version of *Lady Audley's Secret*: colonial taste could encompass the 'higher' traditional British forms of heroic and classical drama, as well as the more popular contemporary forms.

Amateur theatres such as the Auckland Garrick Club had existed in most townships since the 1860s and, unlike the professional commercial stage, had often mounted literary productions of some ambition, particularly Restoration plays. The amateur approach to play selection was not, however, governed by a quest for novelty, and so there was little interest in finding original scripts.

That the social function of the amateurs could occasionally go beyond the pretensions of literati is illustrated by the work of E.W. Seager with the Christchurch Workingmen's Club and the Sunnyside Dramatic Class. In 1885 he wrote and staged *Vivants Variants*, a collection of tableaux vivants illustrating 'the life and vicissitudes of a drunkard, from the cradle to death'. The concept was not new to New Zealand; fifteen years earlier *Philo Maori* had been double-billed with a three-act teetotal drama illustrated by living tableaux. However Seager's work, performed by asylum inmates, had a function as much therapeutic as didactic, and was drawn from Seager's long service working in the Police, Gaol, and Lunacy departments of the colony.[17]

Published literary drama appears in a colonial context almost in defiance of available production and publishing resources, and the early published playwrights seldom if ever shared the objectives of the writers who were popular in the nineteenth century theatres, none of whom showed any interest in publication for posterity. The central model for ephemeral sensation playwrights was the Irish writer Dion Boucicault.

Boucicault did not visit New Zealand until 1885, when his major work was behind him; but his methods were already thoroughly familiar to Australasian audiences, both through productions of his plays and through the work of local imitators (an early example of these was Laurence Booth). Pre-eminent among Boucicault's disciples was George Darrell, who was born in England in 1841, travelled to New Zealand in 1865, and worked as a journalist and bookseller before committing the rest of his career to the Australasian theatre, as actor, manager, and playwright.[18] It was in Christchurch that Darrell spoke his first line professionally, and wrote his first successful play, *Transported for Life* (1876), which established the dominant characteristics of his most popular work to follow. The script of the play has not survived, but reviews show that it exploited the transportation theme already popularized through fiction, notably in Marcus Clarke's *For the Term of His Natural Life* (1874), which it closely resembled in several other respects. The potential for melodrama is obvious: a plentiful supply of villains, a gold rush economy in which fortunes could change suddenly, an overtaxed administrative system in which justice was almost accidental, and an untamed environment where disasters were commonplace. In Melbourne in 1883 Darrell premièred his greatest success, *The Sunny South*, the only one of his scripts to have survived; Anglo-Australian in theme and location, it includes only one reference to New Zealand.

Darrell only once gave a whole play a New Zealand setting, with *The Pakeha* (1890), the material of which derived from his experiences as a reporter on the West Coast of New Zealand. The play's qualities were advertised as

of the sensational order, replete with exciting scenes and incidents, the most notable being the sticking up of the gold escort on the route between Christchurch and Hokitika. In this scene a coach and horses will be driven on the stage, with mounted troopers.[19]

Darrell was reported as stating that 'the main incidents of the play are founded on fact':

> The escape from the gaol he avers that he witnessed himself, whilst the escort robbery and the 'roll up' are taken from events well within the author's recollection.[20]

It has been suggested that the beginning of *The Pakeha* duplicated the beginning of *Transported for Life*, and this would be consistent with Darrell's respect for the Boucicault method of localization. But it is also clear that Darrell was making a gesture towards autobiographical play-writing in *The Pakeha*, since he developed the part of a cavalier stage journalist for his own performance.

The responses of Darrell's Australasian audience were often confused because, as a colonial playwright, he experienced a sense of cultural ambiguity. Ultimate success, he hoped, would come on the London stage, and he did in fact tour his companies through both America and England. His Australasian seasons were frequently billed as farewell tours prior to northern hemisphere commitments, although this generally amounted to nothing more than wishful thinking; his moderate London success in 1884 was greatly inflated in subsequent New Zealand advertising.

Much more directly attuned to New Zealand audiences was George Leitch's *The Land of the Moa* (1895), another sensational melodrama in the Boucicault tradition — the only such New Zealand work to have survived in script.[21] The action takes place in New Zealand in the period of the Land Wars, and involves a complex structure of intrigue, revenge, and romance. Corrections to the manuscript show that the original version used historical Māori characters who were fictionalized, presumably to allow more narrative freedom, but the resultant characterization is close to the stereotypes of stock company melodrama. Leitch's concern for immediacy is reflected in the way that the first scene of the play was always set in the town in which the company was playing, with completely repainted scenery. The final two acts involve the dispensation of natural justice as the characters converge on the boiling mud-pools of Rotorua and then happen to be present at the Tarawera eruption.

The Land of the Moa toured much more extensively in New Zealand than any other locally-set melodrama. Its main impact was as a scenic spectacular, with an impressive reconstruction of the famous Pink and White Terraces (destroyed in the 1886 eruption), the lowest of which were strong enough to support actors and horses. There were three 'practical' thermal pools, but the geyser produced only a cascade of 'rice and spangles'. The eruption scene was not the only one to use pyrotechnical sensation: earlier in the play a bridge was blown up as the villain rode over it on his horse, in a scene which also used a real waterfall, a 'fount of fire', and an airborne flock of alarmed waterfowl.

There was some criticism of the show's dependence on pictorial effect, and within a decade such a style of theatre would be completely obsolete with the advent of film and other photographic entertainment. However, the postcard technique of *The Land of the Moa* was frankly acknowledged by the use of two 'accessibility' characters (through whom the audience could move into the dramatic world) — young holidaying Englishmen who get caught up in the colonial adventure and return to Old World security in the final scene. So, although none of the action is set in Britain (as was the case in antipodean adventure melodramas like *The Sunny South* and *Crime in the Clouds*), the perspective is completely British. New Zealand is seen as a country to be visited rather than lived in, and stereotypes of pioneers allow no acknowledgement of any sense of an emergent local identity. However, the young Englishmen have another function which is unusual for melodrama. They are in New Zealand because they have heard it is an 'absolute wonderland where exceptional material and character can be found for their unrivalled pens and brushes', and one of them pretends to be engaged in writing a popular romance which 'caricatures' his friend's 'passions and lovey-dovey hopes'. The play's action emerges as a projection of this romance, so that there is a strong tone of self-parodying satire in the introductory situational comedy about a good-for-nothing old ship's pilot who has taken his orphaned niece out of her English finishing school so that she can share his assumed life of colonial grandeur in New Zealand. The triteness of this situation is blurred by the eagerness of the young writer, who is actually in love with the niece; and the presentation of the uncle as a low comic, unscrupulous but scarcely menacing, eases the introduction of the major villain, 'the Black Angel', who is pursuing a career of indiscriminate harrassment of a whole Māori tribe (which has sworn revenge on him) and various Europeans (including the niece).

Audience values assumed in *The Land of the Moa* do not, however, pivot on the crude racist and patriotic prejudice that informed much northern hemisphere melodrama. The villainous characters are variously English, American and Māori, while the two heroines are English and Māori; apparently by 1895 there was no longer the market for simple dramas of racial antagonism that there had been twenty years earlier. Similar values characterize the locally-set melodramas of Barrie Marschel, which were being premièred in the South Island at about the same time. *The Murder at the Octagon* (1895) was praised for its murder scene in the snow of Dunedin's Octagon, complete with Town Hall and Burns Statue, and for a spectacular scene at the Otago Heads, where the hero, wrongfully convicted through the machinations of an evil French woman, works in a prison gang. French villainesses were relatively uncommon in Dunedin society of 1895, but for his next work Marschel resorted to an even more recherché melodramatic stock: *Humarire Taniwha* involves the murder of a Dunedin Corsican industrialist, an event which causes his Corsican-Māori daughter (the title character and heroine) to go blind with grief. The play's most famous concession to realism comes when blindness causes the heroine to lose interest in horse-racing and she sells the horse named after herself which wins the Dunedin Cup, ostensibly run before the audience. Even here, however, the drama pivots on a scheme (perpetrated by an Irishman and a Jew) to drug both horse and jockey. In terms of their social dimensions, the plays of Marschel and Leitch were seen as naïve beside the work of Robertson, Pinero, and Jones which was at the same time being toured by Australasian companies.

The scenic spectacular survived the turn of the century in Arthur H. Adams and Alfred Hill's opera *Tapu* (1904), and reviewers reflected that 'the marvellous lost Pink Terrace almost exists again for those who thank their blessed stars that they once saw it in all its glory'.[22] A more interesting development in the direction of New Zealand social drama came with *The Growing of a Rata* (1904) by Charles Owen and Alfred Dampier. Critics, accustomed to the values of melodrama, complained that its morality implied a 'strange perverseness'. The exposition established a debtor-creditor tension in an early settlers' context, between a squatter and his neighbour (played by Dampier), to be resolved by an arranged marriage (to Miss Lily Dampier). One reviewer complained that this was 'not heroic; nor is it indicative of a liberal mind that the settler should shoot his brother-in-law's bullocks for trespassing'.[23] The main confusion of moral assumptions, however, came when the much-wronged squatter was shot by his reprobate part-Māori son (played by A. Dampier, jun.) from a previous marriage:

> The father is held up to the scorn and hatred of the audience for no just cause, while his brother-in-law and his wife's lover, who have both vowed, in a hesitating sort of way, to kill him, are glorified. It is only because Wiremu, the half-caste, presumed to be typical of the rata, gets ahead of them, that one or the other does not become a murderer. The morality of all this is not very apparent. The tragedy is too ignoble, and the passion is not the real stuff, but spite masquerading as such.[24]

Again, however, pictorial impact was important, particularly a fern bower and a scene 'of the Devil's Gorge, near Otomoa'.

Dampier's involvement in drafting *The Growing of a Rata* came towards the end of a long career on the Australian stage, and epitomized this late Victorian colonial actor-manager's strenuous promotion of local scripts. Dampier was well known throughout Australasia for his adaptations of novels, but in this case he appears to have been offered a dramatic script which related very precisely to the North Island, and he worked to widen the focus of the script so that Australian touring would also be feasible. The underlying presumption that trans-Tasman colonial experience was broadly homogeneous was in fact inconsistent with some of his Australian plays which articulated local problems, and would certainly be dispelled by the first phase of post-colonial thinking, in which nationalism would generate a more subtle awareness of social identity.

The Amateur Movement, 1900–45

The period 1900–20 saw a rapid increase in amateur theatre in Australia, and several New Zealand writers continued their careers there. Most notable of these was Arthur H. Adams, who had published *The Minstrel*, a one-act medieval play clearly intended for the stage, in 1899. Similar developments also occurred in New Zealand, with the emergence of theatres such as the Christchurch Comedy Club (1909) and Auckland's Grafton (1912). Most cities and some towns had a Shakespeare Club, and the universities and technical colleges occasionally produced plays. Some original scripts also appeared from amateur groups working in school and parish halls; Ngaio Marsh's first play, *The Moon Princess*, premièred on the Victorian-style raked stage of St Michael's School hall, Christchurch, in 1913.

It was in the following two decades that New Zealand amateur drama really gathered momentum, with the foundation of 'Repertory' theatres in most cities and towns, and the establishment of the New Zealand branch of the British Drama League. University drama societies were also more systematically organized, and it was out of this milieu that Alan Mulgan's *Three Plays of New Zealand* appeared in 1920, with a preface by James Shelley drawing parallels between Mulgan and the Australian realist Louis Esson, as well as with intellectually fashionable European playwrights. Even greater similarities might have been found with the later plays of Arthur Adams, published in 1914 as *Three Plays for the Australian Stage*, but probably deriving from his New Zealand experience. Mulgan's work reflected a trend towards realism (away from the Boucicault sensation melodrama) which would become the dominant mode of New Zealand drama for two decades. However, compared with Esson's whole-hearted commitment to an Australian drama, Mulgan's gesture towards national identity is at best tentative. *For Love of Appin* depicts a Cockney migrant in backblocks New Zealand cushioning a feud between her homesick Scottish husband and a Stranger who turns out to be his boyhood enemy. New Zealand is a land of egalitarian opportunity where the Old World social hierarchy is neutralized or inverted: the Stranger comes from Highland gentry, but is now reduced to a drunken beggar. Interestingly, it is uncertain whether it is in the name of Scottish or New Zealand hospitality that the men retreat to the whisky bottle; there is no strong affirmation of a new society welding itself together. In *The Daughter*, the educated wife of a dairy farmer is visited by an old university friend whom she almost married; the drama pivots on the disillusionment of impoverished rural life for a woman. References to farming and to the universities indicate that the play is located in New Zealand, but its main impact is in its brutal undercutting of glamorized images of colonial country life. In *The Voice of the People* a reactionary New Zealand member of parliament proposes marriage to a woman who is about to blackmail him before standing as a Labour member herself. The satirical thrust is mainly against the man, whose discourse locates him firmly in the world of English politics, but again there is little suggestion of a more relevant local alternative emerging.

The writing and production of one-act realistic plays were promoted on a very substantial scale by the Repertory theatres and by the British Drama League, but Mulgan's achievements in this area, slight as they were, had not been bettered by 1939, and his plays continued to find production throughout the Depression. B.D.L. and *Art in New Zealand* competitions in the 1930s drew large numbers of similar plays, echoing Mulgan's themes, with an efficient network for production throughout the country. Groups of these plays were published annually, but within a few years it became apparent that the bulk of such scripts scarcely merited such publicity, and only a couple were revived after the war. One of the judges commented of the plays submitted in the first B.D.L. competition that

> the majority dealt with the deadly boredom of life on a New Zealand farm, the itch to forsake the farm for the city and the snobbishness of the townsfolk to those who live in the backblocks. Last year, close on a hundred plays were submitted, and it appears that having worked the irksomeness of farm life out of their systems, the authors have broadened their scope.[25]

Themes of cultural displacement, homesickness for Britain, economic uncertainty, and rural poverty were also common in the poetry of the period, but much of the drama had a particular emphasis on women's issues — a reflection of the growing numbers of women in drama societies and universities. Most of the one-act plays were in fact written by women.

The most successful writer in the early years of the B.D.L. was Violet Targuse. Two of her plays were placed first equal in the first competition (1933), which was judged on criteria of 'dramatic construction, characterization, quality of dialogue, idea, pace, climax and actability'.[26] *The Touchstone* is set in a farmhouse kitchen where the main characters make strawberry jam while discussing local issues such as the Gabriel's Gully gold rush, the influenza epidemic of 1918, and a topical sheep-stealing mystery. The mystery is solved with the arrival of an old, pipe-smoking Māori woman who in a slow, suspenseful narrative in Māori and pidgin English reveals the culprit. *Fear* is set in the residence of a freezing-works manager. He discovers that his wife is being persecuted and blackmailed by her sadistic first husband, who has miraculously survived being buried alive by an earthquake. Escape to Auckland or to the iris-clad marshes of her native Cornwall is mooted, but this decision is circumvented by the curtain-line news that the villain's powers of survival have deserted him and he has apparently been crushed in a machine at the works. Targuse was praised because 'her plays have a sound psychological base; they grip because the characterization is true, evidencing her instinctive knowledge of elemental facts and her keen observation of her fellow-men'.[27]

It is an illuminating reflection of the values of the decade that such plays were rated above another of Targuse's, *Rabbits*, in which a middle-aged woman loses her mind under the pressure of nothing more dramatic than life in a South Canterbury railway siding. Her dreams are focused not on a cliff-top cottage in Cornwall but on a transfer to the Addington railway suburb of Christchurch. Her ultimate disappointment in this is profound, and the play achieves a final resonance precisely because there is no facile assumption that all the problems of psychology can be remedied by a single machine at a freezing works. It seems clear that the factor which relegated *Rabbits* to a secondary achievement was the requirement for tightness of 'dramatic construction', which implied a fully-resolved action and characterization so stereotypically defined as to evade wider questions of the consequences of behaviour. There was, however, some resistance to B.D.L. assumptions: Professor James Shelley, who as a leading proponent of university drama had championed Mulgan's plays, is reported to have regarded *Rabbits* as 'the high water mark of New Zealand drama at that time'.[28]

Targuse's plays received extensive production within the B.D.L. and Repertory network until her death in 1937. An indication of how quickly her style became formulaic, and also of the 'broadening' of playwrights' 'scope', may be seen in Ilma Maude Levy's *God Made Two Trees* (1934), which provides another instance of an assumed-dead first husband walking into a New Zealand household. Here the treatment is comic, and the situation can be resolved by his departure, without his wife but with his good-for-nothing son who has been leading a life of Wildean inertia at Silverstream. The growing pretensions of B.D.L. audiences are reflected in the fact that house-parties of the East Riding Pendlethorpe no longer have the magnetic appeal of the marshes of Cornwall, but the young people of this play have assimilated urbane Old World decadence to the extent that they quote Lawrence and Freud, censuring them as unadventurous. In fact the relevance of issues of local or regional identity is explicitly rejected. Asked if his mother likes living in New Zealand, the eldest son replies that she 'likes gardening and going to Church. You can do that almost anywhere, can't you?'[29] The daughter observes that 'no one ever seems to belong here, and no one seems to have any intention of remaining. Those who aren't English are Scotch or Irish, or Australian. You only meet New Zealanders at the other end of the world.'[30] Though such opinions are not presented as authorial, there is a clear assumption that audiences are likely to identify with them.

Full-length play-writing competitions were less popular, partly because the B.D.L. system was not fully geared up to promote them, and partly because longer plays attracted a different group of authors, many of whom had literary rather than theatrical priorities. In 1937 a play by Robin Hyde failed to win an *Art in New Zealand* one-act play-writing competition because it was too long.[31] The first full-length prize-winning script was *Rose Lane* (1935) by Edith Howes, already well known as a children's author. A farm on the outskirts of Dunedin in 1858 is ruled by a patriarchal tyrant who subjects his wife, four sons, and daughter to a brutally pleasureless labouring existence. His daughter Rose is the first to rebel, eloping to Invercargill with Dancy Lane, a bank clerk, who leaves her there with two babies while he joins the Central Otago gold rush. In the second act, set at the Dunstan rush, her father's assessment of Lane is confirmed when he resumes a relationship with a prostitute. By the last act Rose's youngest brother has turned twenty-one: the sons rebel against their father, heading for the goldfields only a few minutes before the entrance of Rose, who has walked from Invercargill with the news that Dancy has a broken leg. The melodramatic poignancy of the last scene finds Rose, reluctant to think anything but the best of her husband, thanking the prostitute for nursing him and then, after a grim realization, telling Fred, the devoted neighbour she rejected, that her life will be fulfilling as long as she has 'the children for comfort, and a man to rescue and console, and a home to make again'.[32] The same thesis could scarcely apply to Rose's mother, whose children are banished and whose husband defies rescue or consolation. For Howes, multiplying out a crude plot to three-act duration meant emphasizing the pre-war playwrights' general disregard for the causes and consequences of behaviour, and although the setting clearly aimed at historical realism, the distancing of the action in time also allowed an evasion of socially relevant issues. Implicit in the play's ethical perspective is the notion of salvation through a stoical adherence to the values of 'Home'. The first description of the 'still-faced' mother itemizes the features of her clothing, stating that they 'all denote that quality in her which not even the unremitting labour and rough life of a pioneering farmer's wife has been able to destroy nor to coarsen'.[33]

Two writers did successfully defy the constraints of realism, with experimental one-act expressionistic plays. After a series of pieces which tentatively incorporated stylized features, Eric Bradwell wrote *Clay* (1936), an ambitious nine-scene play which splices together a simple love narrative and a frenetic portrayal of a shattered mind, dramaturgically achieved through choric use of fragmented sentences. As a vehicle for dramatizing the insight into psychological issues which had been attributed to Targuse, Bradwell's hybrid style could accommodate a vastly greater range of modulations of tension and suggestion in his subject. Targuse had announced her psychoanalytical propensities in the title of *Fear*, but had portrayed it through the extensive use of smelling-salts and the husband's assertion 'through clenched teeth' that his wife must 'shake off this soul-destroying depression'[34] which he subsequently identifies as an 'obsession', a 'grotesque fear', and a 'hallucination'.[35] Bradwell similarly has his stage dominated by a woman whose 'whole attitude is one of utter despair',[36] but he makes no overt attempt to analyse that despair; instead, he relies on expressionistic stage effects, using phatic utterances from a chorus to imply the woman's inability to account for herself. The chief technical influence here was the radio drama of the 1930s, of which little has been recorded because of the lack of archives. Bradwell did not attempt radio writing until later; his radio play, *The Last Station* (1937), presented telepathy as a deterministic force governing character convergence in a remote location, but achieved little of the psycho-expressionistic impact of *Clay*.

A much more extensive career in experimental drama was that of J.A.S. Coppard, who also achieved a measure of international recognition for plays depicting the social ramifications of mental anguish rather than framing it within a single personality. *Sordid Story*, which premièred at the Scottish Drama Festival in 1932, has a colossal cranium on stage, suggesting a wholly internalized action, but the play also attempts to demonstrate the force of social conditioning in generating delinquency. *Machine Song* has the popular German theme of mechanization and dehumanization, while *Candy Pink* uses expressionism for the dramatic analysis of delinquency. *The Axe and the Oak Tree* is a poetic, choric work similar to the Canadian Herman Voaden's 'symphonic theatre'.

The 1930s was a period in which many New Zealand writers showed an awareness of the international stage. Coppard was reticent about his aims and models, but the range of his experimentation strongly suggests that like Bradwell he was familiar with German and American expressionism as well as with the theoretical writings of Voaden. Other people working in the theatre also brought the momentum of European innovation. Ngaio Marsh returned from Fine Arts studies abroad with a set of theatrical axioms which would govern her work, and that of the actors she directed throughout her career. Arnold Goodwin, who established a remarkable marionette theatre in Auckland during the war, referred frequently to his contact with Picasso's circle as an art student in Paris in the first decade of the century, and journals such as *Tomorrow* gave substantial review coverage to the theatrical avant-garde. However, whereas Bradwell used his models critically, to develop writing idiosyncracies of his own, none of Coppard's work moves far beyond that of the playwrights he clearly admired.

The amateur theatre flourished in the 1930s, and the growing receptiveness of audiences to technically adventurous scripts is reflected in the substantial public interest in *Clay*. However, the touring commercial companies which were dominant at the turn of the century became all but extinct with the Depression and the rise of the cinema. From George Darrell to Bruce Mason and Roger Hall, there have always been New Zealand playwrights who looked towards West End success, and these impulses have in general been at least partially satisfied by local professionalism. However, for the playwright of the 1930s and 1940s there was no local supply of the glamour of touring professionalism. It was inevitable that the young Merton Hodge, who as a student in the 1920s had developed a taste for the style of Noel Coward and John Van Druten, should set his sights on the London stage, and his remarkable three-year run there with *The Wind and the Rain* (1933) meant that on his return after the war he was completely incapable of adapting to a style which could be accommodated on the New Zealand stage. *The Wind and the Rain* is a well-made, full-length realistic play, under-written in that its slight romantic narrative could not survive the fragility of its pre-war West End context. Hodge's other London plays were equally ephemeral. *Grief Goes Over* (1935) has the sensationalism of the young Coward — prurience compounded with a well-made morality — while *The Island* (1937) establishes a powerful human atmosphere only to puncture it by a reassertion of mannered normality. Hodge's later work was grandiose in scale, an archaism by London standards and irrelevant to the conditions of New Zealand theatre.

Hodge wrote like a showman, offering vehicles for famous actors (such as Marie Tempest), and meticulously preserving his records through the use of clipping agencies. He provides a spectacular contrast with the methods of New

Zealand's pioneer socialist playwrights of the 1930s, who circulated their (often anonymous) scripts in duplicated form for reading and production through the Left Book Club, Wellington's Unity Theatre, the Workers' Educational Association, and The People's Theatre (Auckland). Productions were rarely advertised or reviewed in daily newspapers, but there is evidence that the phenomenon of the workers' theatre was comparable in scale with the British Drama League. Left Book Clubs, modelled on the London organization of Victor Gollancz, opened in most New Zealand cities in 1938, and a national conference in 1939 was attended by about twenty branches, including small townships such as Blackball and Ruawai, most of which had an active drama group. The objectives of the left-wing theatre groups directly opposed the work of the British Drama League, and the divergence of values was clearly stated in Ian Hamilton's review of the 1938 League national finals in *Tomorrow*.[37] Attacking the use of imported English judges and their patterns of assessment, Hamilton asserted that New Zealand was 'in the position of being capable of evolving a culture of its own', and that the League's affiliation with England in drama should be considered 'in name only': the type of drama promoted by the League would inevitably lose its audience to the cinema, and the public would only return 'when they realize that the theatre has become "a cathedral of the spirit" putting forth fables of its own time and hour'. Looking at the League's national showcase, Hamilton could anticipate a time when 'the public, sick of seeing itself portrayed in its meanest and silliest aspect, has merely walked out of the theatre and stayed out. When that day appears the foundation stone of another cathedral is laid.'

The workers' theatre, committed to staging plays of immediate social relevance, subsisted mainly on sketches, satirical revues, and agitprop scripts. Only one prominent literary figure contributed to the movement: the poet R.A.K. Mason wrote a number of sketches most of which have survived in manuscript. *To Save Democracy* (1938) is set in a cell near the front line in France during the First World War, and involves four male characters. Two privates have been torturing a pacifist in civilian clothes, and their dialogue turns on their misgivings and self-justification until a sadistic officer enters, brutalizes the victim further, and asserts the need for conscription. The pacifist speaks at some length, protesting and accusing, but the play ends with the officer hysterically threatening to bayonet the Labour Party after the war. For such a short play, character differentiation is remarkably efficient, especially between the two privates, an Irish immigrant whose garrulousness outstrips his intelligence and 'a rangy, uncommunicative New Zealander' who 'takes everything very literally and tests it judicially before he decides whether it is a fair thing or not'.[38] The narrative development is slight, and the two privates serve as an on-stage audience for the violence and the longer speeches; and though the ending, with its very abrupt truncation, is unresolved in terms of dialogue, a structural cohesion occurs as the theatre audience finds itself gradually given the moral responsibility for the position of the privates. The play's ending, an emotional speech from the officer which the audience cannot possibly condone, is in the most strident tradition of agitprop. Most of Mason's numerous other plays have an international reference, but the dance drama *Refugee* is a theatrically ambitious treatment of the evolution of New Zealand society through various kinds of migration, presented through the device of bringing a group of refugees from overseas oppression to a meeting of returned servicemen.

Among the most substantial scripts of the workers' theatre movement is *The Reichstag Fire Trial* by Alun Faulkner, written and produced under the pseudonym Alun Morgan.[39] Copies of the play were held in gestetnered form in the libraries of the Communist Party of New Zealand. The form of the play is governed by an insistence on historical accuracy, with real names used even for peripheral figures. Though it lacks the broad stylistic features of English and American agitprop theatre, the play capitalizes heavily on assumed audience attitudes by the use of amplified propaganda from Nazi radio before each of its three scenes. The atmosphere is established for a display of brutally heavy-handed Nazi justice, including an appearance from Goering, and the audience's sympathies are channelled entirely towards the eloquent Dimitrov, one of the accused Bulgarian communists. *The Reichstag Fire Trial* has no theatrical sophistication: there is very little scripted movement, and the cast includes supernumeraries in the form of police, counsel, reporters, and judges whose only function is an occasional display of 'consternation'.

Much more adventurous technically is *Falls the Shadow* (1939) by Ian Hamilton, who was already known as the author of a radio play on the theme of national identity, and of three one-act plays, one of which was a dramatization of aspects of the mind, following a mixture of Freudian and Jungian principles. *Falls the Shadow* is a full-length fictional play with a variety of strategies for presenting its socialist pacifist perspective. In the first two acts the style is realistic, with a British family facing the impending war; in the last act the family is shown as being destroyed by a year of Fascist government. The chronological transition is assisted by a blackout, during which there are set speeches from representative social types such as a recruiting officer, a politician, a strike leader, and a strike breaker (with audience boos and cheers), and these are followed by the sound of an air raid, anticipating the play's end (where a fly-over symbolizes an ambiguous year of peace). The play also starts boldly, including an introductory monologue in which the playwright coaxes an awkward actor in Marxist first principles. In view of Hamilton's conviction that B.D.L. plays could not survive competition from the cinema, it is interesting that Frank Sargeson, in a review of the 1939 People's Theatre première of *Falls the Shadow* in *Tomorrow*, considered that the technique of using symbolic figures with set speeches during the blackout derived from the cinema, and should be staged with a cinematic rapidity. In the play's ending Sargeson detected a thesis that 'Violence breeding violence is losing caste in favour of non-resistance breeding tolerance', a resolution in which the playwright 'avoided defeatism, but not altogether convincingly'.[40] Whether such optimism is latent in the play's ending is questionable; within a web of romantic and domestic relationships very like the dramatic world of Merton Hodge, Hamilton demonstrates R.A.K. Mason's point in *To Save Democracy*: that fascist and pacifist tendencies coexist in any society and must be recognized at home.

At the outbreak of the Second World War the one-act play industry had dwindled, and most theatre societies were soon to be hampered by a serious decline in male membership. Left-wing and university drama were able to show some growth during the war, and several women playwrights were active (including Isobel Andrews). Although continuity in the fragile local tradition of play-writing was lost, the place of theatre as a means of cultural expression was securely established. This is reflected in F.G. Soper's and Lilian McCarthy's *Pageant Dealing with the History of the Women's Franchise in New Zealand from 1870 to 1893*, which was staged as part of the Women's Franchise Jubilee Celebrations in Dunedin in 1943. A Herald's succinct prose narration of the annals of the cause is punctuated by lightly satirical songs and verse dialogue from a group of only slightly individualized women. All the tunes are taken from the Savoy operas, and the extensive use of mime and tableaux (with the figure of Zealandia prominent) echoes the traditions of Victorian theatre. However other features of the style, particularly the unpretentious historical satire, also anticipate techniques which would regain popularity in the 1970s.

The *Pageant* was staged in the year of the foundation of New Zealand's most famous left-wing theatre, Wellington's Unity Theatre, which in its early years presented several one-act plays by women showing an uncompromising approach to social conditions. The most severe piece of realism to come from Unity at this period was Kathleen Ross's *The Trap* (1950), a study of four women from three generations faced with a near-hopeless problem of survival in a world of male exploitation and hostility. Sympathy is initially with the mother, who has just got her five youngest children off to school and who now turns her attention to her two eldest daughters and her mentally-handicapped aunt. In the early action the eldest daughter (who wishes to escape her working-class upbringing) reveals that she is pregnant, and the other daughter is again sacked from her job. From this situation Ross develops a complex interlocking depiction of each character's dilemma. For the mother there is still a residue of pride which will be frustrated by whatever her children do, and strained further by the revelation that she was herself pregnant when she married the husband who later deserted her. The eldest daughter reveals that she could not bring her boyfriend to the house she was ashamed of, and consequently reduced her relationship to street-corner level, thus making the man's desertion easier. The other, worldly-wise daughter welds them together with a sly perception of the instinctive attitudes behind the stubbornness and bluster, and even the aunt's role is much more than a vehicle for pathos; it is she who states that they are better off without men, and it is she who at the end comforts the eldest daughter, replacing argument with feelings. Of the many types of trap implied in the women's various conditions, the most deliberately articulated is that of the pregnant daughter who rejects her mother's grudging offer to look after the baby, insisting that adoption would bring better chances in life; but she too is finally subordinated by the mother's well-rehearsed hypochondria.

The Early Post-colonial Period

Ross's play — and the left-wing theatrical movement of which it was a distinguished example — represented one kind of challenge to residual colonial habits and assumptions. Other impulses — more ambiguously élitist in their theatrical assumptions and style — took root during and after the war. The élitism may be explained partly by the overseas experience of returned servicemen, many of whom had seen London and the Mediterranean, and partly by the growing importance of the universities. At Canterbury University College, Ngaio Marsh established a tradition of Shakespeare production based on English models, firmly avoiding New Zealand speech, and it was in this context that the poet Allen Curnow wrote *The Axe* (1948), a verse play based on a Polynesian anthropological subject. The story was taken from a study of Mangaia in the Cook Islands by Sir Peter Buck (Te Rangi Hiroa), and concerns tribal conflicts in 1824 associated with the introduction of Christianity and western technology, symbolized in the axe itself. Within this social context Curnow introduced a sub-plot about two young natives whose love is destroyed by the axe, and a chorus of two masked ancestral figures from the island who, with more allusive poetry, explore themes such as time, the island, the sea, and mutability. The complexity of thought contained in the choric passages contrasts with the simplicity and occasional banality of the human action, where rudimentary motivation and general incomprehension of wider issues generates a great deal of poignancy but little that approaches tragedy. It may also seem remarkable that Curnow, whose poetry had been much concerned with New Zealand's nationhood and social identity, should choose a dramatic subject that was geographically and historically distant from his Christchurch audience of 1948; the dramatic world seemed to some theatre-goers as remote as that of Greek tragedy. However he himself was not conscious of the subject's remoteness in this sense, and paid scrupulous attention to the cultural appropriateness of the imagery, so that it is arguable that his vision shows a precocious awareness of post-colonial Pacific identity.

Writing twenty years later Curnow argued that Mangaia is 'a metaphor for New Zealand' and for the 'state of world war':

> By shifting the scene to another island, I might mirror New Zealand: if the glass reflected us darkly, among the shadows of greater events, at least it would not be one of those magnifying gadgets which, like so much of our historical writing, shows pores and pimples with remarkable distinctness, but neither the features nor the expression of a human face.[41]

Curnow's argument, however, does not account for the fact that his poetry had not pivoted on such distancing metaphors, and it may be deduced that in the 1940s audiences were felt to be less receptive to self-images on the stage than in a book of poetry. A simple explanation for the Mangaia location has been offered by Alan Roddick: it enabled Curnow 'to move out of New Zealand in thought, which he had not yet done in person, to explore the theme of "discovery" '.[42] *The Axe* is important in Curnow's poetic development, and served as a vital index to the aspirations of serious student actors at the time, but it has been revived little. D'Arcy Cresswell's *The Forest* (1952) deals with the love of nature and the threat of commercial exploitation in a similarly erudite verse form, with appearances from Lucifer and the archangel Gabriel. The same literary values are apparent in *Life Sentence* (1949) by Howard Wadman, editor of *The Year Book of the Arts in New Zealand*. This is a mountaineering drama with a romantic sub-plot, contained in a taut, poetic mode. Even Charles Brasch, founding editor of *Landfall* and a highly influential arbiter of literary taste, attempted drama in *The Quest* (1946), the verse script of a mime play.

The élitism of such writers was paralleled in the post-war tendency of young actors and directors to go to Britain for training. This was partly because professional training was not available in New Zealand, but there was also a cultural cringe perpetuated through the poetic drama movement. A few unpretentious full-length plays were appearing, such as the nine generally well-made plays which Claude Evans wrote for the Canterbury Repertory Theatre Society between 1946 and 1961, but these were not performed in other cities. Perhaps the most illuminating articulation of contemporary values is the correspondence between Bruce Mason and John Pocock, published under the title *Theatre in Danger* (1957). Here, amateur Repertory theatre and some touring professional drama are vigorously deplored.[43] Mason's yardstick is the Old Vic's 1944 London season, and Pocock's his admiration for Ngaio Marsh's London-modelled Shakespeare productions. That their stance was élitist was frankly acknowledged. Mason's attitude of cultural superiority on his return to New Zealand after the war in fact echoed that of the first wave of colonizers, exhibiting a contempt for much local drama that was of a completely different intensity from that of most other writers who were conscious of overseas models. However, since both writers were committed to the evolution of a healthier New Zealand drama, their position was a transitory one, and the exchange ends propitiously with Mason describing a full-length play on a Māori theme which he had just completed.[44]

Mason's artistic instincts had received stimulus in Europe during the war, and he had acted in Wellington's socialist-orientated Unity Theatre on his return. Unity's emphasis on plays of social significance meant that realism was subjected to a closer scrutiny than in most amateur theatres, although other left-wing theatre groups also survived the war, and some intensified in commitment as Unity began to forget its ideology. The Association of People's Artists was particularly active in Auckland in the mid-1950s, and performed a considerable number of locally-written sketches with aggressively direct satire. But it was in the Unity Theatre environment, which had premièred Ross's *The*

Trap, that Mason wrote his first short realistic plays, including *The Bonds of Love* (1953), a forcefully blunt study of a Wellington immigrant prostitute, and *The Evening Paper* (1953), a depressing portrait of New Zealand domestic life. In *The Verdict* (1955), the focus on a recent murder trial provides a sensational core for the action, and at the end the characters move assertively into the future. This play marks a tendency towards a more fully resolved action which would typify Mason's mature work.

The *Pohutukawa Tree* (1956), whose completion Mason triumphantly announced to Pocock, was the first of five plays on Māori themes, and it quickly became popular through amateur production and study in schools. Aroha Mataira, the old widow of a fire-and-brimstone preacher, is in the ambivalent position of honouring both Māori tradition and European puritanism. This conflict of moral imperatives is activated by what she sees as the delinquency of her children, and her pregnant daughter finally finds accommodation not in her home but on the marae. The humanism of tribal values is described (by an Anglican clergyman) rather than dramatized — which led some early critics to object that Aroha is an atypical Māori. The assumption behind such an objection is that dramatic behaviour should be broadly representative of social norms, and that a play should give a recognizable sampling of local life and scenery, as was imagined to be the case with *The Land of the Moa*. The same premise lay behind adverse reviews of Mason's later Māori plays as well as of domestic works like the television adaptation of *The Evening Paper* (1965). Mason, however, was constantly aware of the biracial nature of New Zealand society, of the fragmentation of both Māori and European traditional values, and of the conflicting conditioning forces that operate on all characters aware of the complexity of their heritage. Though his next Māori play *Awatea* (1965) revolved around a tribal hui, the imminent European presence created an obvious irony, and the wedding scene of English festivity in *The Pohutukawa Tree* is clearly parodic. Social behaviour provides the context rather than the focus of the Māori plays, each of which is dominated by the figure of the Māori elder at its centre, a figure of such dignity and authority that his dilemmas and mistakes are widely felt; his stubbornness may constrict his whole family or community, and any opposition to his stance must be persistent. Moreover, the elder's social stature is reinforced by the power of his rhetoric, which allows Mason to indulge his propensity for baroque, sometimes florid utterances. In *Awatea* the blindness of the old protagonist heightens the resonance of his speeches and reinforces his stubborn intractability to the police and other characters who are trying to bring him to an awareness that his son is a liar and a criminal.

All of Mason's plays on Māori themes after *The Pohutukawa Tree* were written for the voice of Inia Te Wiata, the internationally-famous operatic bass who had, however, relatively little experience as a stage actor. This certainly influenced the larger-than-life stature as well as the vocal presence of the elders, but the tendency was with Mason even in the 1950s, evidenced by Aroha's son's perception of her: 'Ma. You're too big. The world can't hold you.

It's too small out there. You tried to make me as big as you. I tried, Ma. But me: I'm not big. I'm just a Maori boy who wants to live in his own way, easy, quiet.'[45] The sometimes suffocating conservatism of these elders is more than just a character trait; dramaturgically, it emphasizes Mason's interest in social evolution, often with historical parallels which are rich in irony. In the last act the dying Aroha is seen as a battlefield occupied by Christ and her ancestor Whetumarama:[46] she becomes, explicitly, a personification of the defeat of the Europeans on her land last century, a battle frequently referred to in the first act. A similar conflict is historicized in *Hongi*, where the tentatively-converted Māori chief is taken by the missionary Kendall to visit George IV at Windsor Castle. The hypocrisy of European values, particularly regarding warfare, drives Hongi back into tribal values, into something resembling the context of Aroha's ancestors' victory over the Pākehā at Te Parenga. The implication of both plays is that European civilization means duplicity, naïvety, and shallowness; Aroha's son finds the Robin Hood legend the most appealing facet of Pākehā culture, and in places it seems not far removed from Aroha's own perception of Christianity.

Mason's two other radio plays on Māori themes are more contemporary in focus, although the elders' ethos again draws heavily on the past. *The Hand on the Rail* has some sociological emphasis, and might be read as a case study in delinquency which explores at greater depth a predicament similar to that of Aroha's son. The emotional resonance of the play, however, is almost entirely located in the elder, whose conflict with his European wife is presented, through memory episodes, as a vital conditioning influence on the son. *Swan Song* allows more extravagant stylistic flourishes: the Māori protagonist is a terminally-ill opera lover who has defiantly immersed himself in Māoritanga By his Pākehā wife, now dead, he has an austerely puritanical daughter who is now marshalling him around various New Zealand tourist resorts she feels he should see before leukaemia kills him. The absurdity of the situation generates more comedy than any of the other Māori plays, but there is also a strong sense of contemporary relevance: the old man's instinctive affinity with Māori culture is not bound up in a heroic past, but is prospective, identifying with his people as he sees them today.

All of Mason's Māori plays were written between 1956 and 1968, a period in which the New Zealand stage offered few production opportunities. Such professional theatre as existed was tentative or weak, and Mason's faith in amateur companies had declined after Unity Theatre began to lose impetus. It was thus largely for practical reasons that in 1959 he mounted the first of his solo works, *The End of the Golden Weather*, which (like its successors) was scripted by him for his own unaccompanied performance in theatre buildings with minimal resources. The solo works were thus ideal touring material, and in the following twenty years Mason appeared throughout the country in many townships which did not have even an amateur organization. Mason was also influenced in his use of this form by the overseas example of solo performers like Emlyn Williams, and by his own experiences on radio, where he had given semi-dramatized readings of some of his prose writings. *The End of the Golden Weather* itself grew out of short stories and anecdotal material initially presented (and well received) on radio, which Mason then shaped into a collage of poignant reminiscences on the theme of adolescent self-awareness. Because of the nature of such performance, using very few props or costume details to represent about forty characters, the writing style is heavily charged, especially in its emphatic assertion of dominant imagery, and much of it appears florid on the page. In the theatre, however, literary style was subsumed by a vigorous performance rhetoric which manipulated the audience response through many emotional modulations, so that material which had initially been not far removed from intimate autobiography developed into a collective experience.

It is notable that although Mason's performance models were British, the inspiration for his literary style was American: the title of *The End of the Golden Weather* was taken from Thomas Wolfe's novel *The Web and the Rock*, a work which clearly had an influence on the play's theme, imagery, and atmosphere. During the 1960s Mason became increasingly interested in facets of American culture and politics (particularly the Cold War, the peace movement, and the ramifications of student counter-culture), and corresponded with numerous American writers and theatre directors. These inclinations are reflected in his second solo work, *The Counsels of the Wood* (1965), a title taken from a Ronald Duncan poem. The first half of this work, which was often performed separately under its own subtitle ('To Russia, with Love'), is based on Mason's visit to the Soviet Union in 1958 and consists of three sustained, related monologues, all set in Moscow, delivered from the perspectives of a Texan tourist, a Californian student, and a young Russian member of the 'loyal opposition'. The three segments constitute a single story, and the considerable technical interest of the work lies largely in its audacious approach to stage narration. The second half of the programme, entitled 'The Last Supper', deals with nuclear contamination and is set in America; its source was factual (an article in *Look* magazine) and it is not related to the first half in terms of the plot. Another solo work from the same year, *The Waters of Silence*, is also a study in political pessimism, this time based on Vercors' famous work on the French Resistance, but in Mason's version narrated from the perspective of the German officer billeted with a hostile French family.

The solo works after *The End of the Golden Weather* were critically successful, but had lost touch with the New Zealand scene. Mason's popularity in the theatre waned somewhat in the late 1960s, and his only substantial stage work of this period was *Zero Inn* (1970), which attempted to repeat the success of his earlier full-length social comedy *Birds in the Wilderness* (1958). In 1973 he returned to more limited touring of the solo works, and in 1976 premièred two more, *Not Christmas, but Guy Fawkes* and *Courting Blackbird*. The first of these was similar in conception to *The End of the Golden Weather*, reworking for the stage a number of prose works (autobiographical in varying degrees) which were already known from radio and periodical publication; one of them, 'The Conch Shell', was originally written as a play for television. *Courting Blackbird* was a wholly new work, with the most immediate dramatic unity of all the solo works: a linear sequence of episodes tracing the eccentric career of a friend of the narrator. Even this play, with a lightly picaresque tone in some of its early episodes, finds a political resolution as its protagonist dies a victim of a Soviet work camp.

Operations for cancer terminated Mason's solo tours in 1978, although *The End of the Golden Weather* reached the stage again in a revision for a full cast. Before his death in 1982 he completed *Blood of the Lamb* (1980), a full-length stage play about a lesbian couple with a child, and three television plays which were presented posthumously. *Blood of the Lamb* was a highly successful synthesis of the distinctive qualities Mason had developed as a writer throughout his career, and much of its theatrical impact came from operatic monologues which indulged his propensity towards a baroque allusiveness. This tendency was also evident in one of the television plays, *Daphne and Chloë* (1983), but the most resonant of the series on the screen was *The Garlick Thrust*, which counterpointed an action set during the Springbok tour of 1981 with poignant scenes of boyhood frustration.

More graphically than any other New Zealand playwright's, Mason's work shows a development from a crude colonial perspective towards a post-colonial awareness. Although he began writing late enough to eschew the simplistic nationalism of the 1930s, he initially took the role of an Old World missionary in the wake of his wartime European experience. His plays on Māori themes, however, began to explore many post-colonial issues, re-opening questions of cultural identity and introducing a multiplicity of social perspectives which were then unfamiliar on the stage. His commitment was towards the definition of New Zealand identity, an identity which he was never naïve enough to expect to articulate, but which would be premised on notions of cultural fragmentation and diversity, and on the possibilities of new, unique kinds of synthesis. His first Māori play attempted an audacious syncretization of tribal and Christian values with the Robin Hood legend, but the motivating image was that of the colonial gaze:

> both plays are dramatic exercises in a well-known nineteenth-century *genre*, the panoramic painting . . . . The artist has set up his easel on the beach and looks up into the bush-dense hills. He paints it all in a heavy green, with tattooed faces peering out at the strangely-clad Europeans with their mounds of chattels . . . . I am surprised that more plays have not been written on a theme intrinsically dramatic: the clash of the continuous and contained eye culture of the European with the resonant ear culture of the Maori.[47]

In his solo works there is a constant search for new forms, and fragmentation becomes a structuring principle, with a collocation of dramatic worlds that shows his leaning towards a post-modernist position. Ironically, though Mason acquired a reputation for self-promotion (partly because of his isolation and lack of organizational support), he came to minimize the achievement of his Māori plays:

All I would claim to have done is turn over the ground. Total theatre is upon us, with its larger resonances, dramatic and musical together, and Jenny McLeod's splendid *Earth and Sky* accomplishes more in its first half hour than my whole five plays. My task, as I see it, has been to chart a century of displacement and fragmentation; hers to redeem it in barbaric splendour.[48]

Later post-colonial criticism would sharply question the terms in which Mason defines McLeod's objective, while accepting the appropriateness of his description of his own. The rhetoric of a 'redemption' of the past in 'barbaric splendour' has scarcely survived later, more sophisticated cultural analysis, but his more sober assessment of himself — as charting a century of displacement — does provide an appropriate measure of his place in the development of New Zealand drama.

Although the diversity of his artistic activities was remarkable, Mason's primary commitment was to the theatre. He wrote relatively little for television and came to radio drama late, suspicious of its editing procedures, offering material such as *Hongi*, *The Hand on the Rail*, and *Swan Song* which could not find production as stage scripts. By the time these were produced, in 1967, New Zealand radio drama had been flourishing for nearly a decade and had sponsored a number of new dramatists, several of whom would later make substantial contributions to the stage. The most notable of these in the evolution of the New Zealand theatre of the 1970s was Joseph Musaphia, but the new playwright who most immediately attracted public attention was the poet James K. Baxter.

Baxter's *Jack Winter's Dream* in 1958 was in effect the beginning of internationally respectable production of radio drama in New Zealand, and was seen as a sample of the potential of new studios, equipment, and staff education. The script itself is an expressionistic presentation of the drunken reverie of an old dead-beat whose death is observed at the end, and it incorporates many of the themes, and some stylistic traits, of Baxter's early poetry. The subject is based on a New Zealand goldfields yarn, located in the Naseby area, and the action is melodramatic, with superficial characterization. The radio medium, however, allowed Baxter to use an elasticity of time and range of allusion similar to Mason's *The End of the Golden Weather*, and to mask the limitations of his portraiture (even more evident in his subsequent stage plays) by a fluid poetic texture.

In the following decade Baxter wrote more than twenty plays for stage and radio, drawing themes from Greek myth, Catholicism, and his own experience of alcoholism. All of them, even those ostensibly distanced into Aeschylean or New Testament archetypes, are governed by a poet's subjectivity, so that some areas of the script generate a lyrical intensity while others appear crudely under-written, requiring sympathetic bulking-out by the director's skills of visual realization. Remarkably, Baxter had been aware of this as a problem for the poet-turned-playwright from the start of his career: Curnow's *The Axe*, he wrote, illustrated 'the tendency of poets to conceive of a given speech as a total poem, not, as it were, as a single unit in the total dramatic poem which is the play'.[49] Baxter suspected that his first stage play, *The Wide Open Cage* (1959), was weakened by the same defect as Curnow's because one character articulated an authorial viewpoint: 'Thus the play was stalled nearly every time the priest spoke. At best I had tried to give him poems to speak.'[50] In fact the problem was more complex than this (how to sustain the dramatic momentum during the characters' vatic phases, when they dwell at length on religion or drunkenness), but Baxter's awareness of the perils of self-consciously 'poetic' drama meant that his only attempt at verse drama was the brief and unproduced *Requiem for Sebastian*.

In a late interview Baxter said that some of his poems reflect 'the rather multiple world of experience':

Of course there are contradictions — that is the drama. Men just live in contradictions — that's the nature of man.'[51]

In various covert ways, many of his plays explore this principle as the basis for dramatic interaction. The clearest examples are the stage plays on alcoholic subjects: *The Day that Flanagan Died* (1967) attempts to objectify his ballad 'Lament for Barney Flanagan' by giving each element of the 'multiple world of experience' a separate voice, so that a whole dramatic cast is generated from the various perspectives used in the poem. Of *The Band Rotunda* (1967) Baxter insisted, 'I am not Concrete Grady, though Concrete Grady is one of my secret selves.'[52] This character had already been developed in 'The Ballad of Grady's Dream' and other poems, and even *Jack Winter's Dream* had expanded a ballad structure in a similar way.

Baxter's need to see his characters as simplified elements of his own identity explains why his female characters are rarely developed much beyond crude stereotypes, and his notion of drama as the interplay of 'secret selves' recalls the Strindbergian technique of hallucinatory dramaturgy. *The First Wife* (1966) shows a simple form of this: the authorial main character is deprived of the comforts of domesticity and thrust into a dream world in which fragments of his own identity are in conflict (both the domestic and dream actions are set at Brighton, south of Dunedin, where Baxter was brought up). This hallucinatory method is further complicated in *Jack Winter's Dream*, where an ancestral figure is fragmented to generate a period melodrama, and the alcoholic dreamer is taken to the point of death by the intensity of his vision.

By 1966-7, when his most intensive period of play-writing was beginning, Baxter saw radio as a suitable vehicle for a didacticism which would be wholly unacceptable in the theatre:

Human stupidity, not divine illumination, is the communal foundation of dramatic art. If man's intellect were not partially blinded, he would reject the spectacle of the theatre . . . . It is precisely the element of doubt and possibility, both moral and intellectual, which enables the dramatist to 'corrupt' his audience with illusions.[53]

Baxter's stage characters are all illustrations of 'human stupidity', — most obvious, in many of the plays, in the drunken stupor of a victim of society to whom all action seems pointless. However, even in his last plays, such as *The Temptations of Oedipus* and *The Starlight in Your Eyes*, the central characters are blind or crippled, so that sensory awareness is accentuated by a process of privation. Baxter's articulate and urbane Greek characters also are revealed as groping towards an elusive truth, dependent on the same process of rationalization as Jack Skully in *The Wide Open Cage*. Baxter's use of the 'stupidity' principle was valuable for the dramaturgic exploitation of suspense and ambiguity, and it provided a dramatically powerful means to explore his various philosophies about human nature. But it also heightened the intellectual bias of his drama: the later plays in particular flattered the audience's powers of recognizing carefully structured mythical and biblical allusions through an elaborate strategy of distortion, inversion, and recapitulation. Heroic stupidity on the stage too easily became an index of intellectual nimbleness in the auditorium, so that in production poignant observations on the human condition could easily be lost in a sophisticated game of interpretation, especially in the élitist atmosphere of Dunedin's Globe Theatre, where most of the Greek plays were premièred. *The Bureaucrat* (1967) is about life in the government department of School Publications; Baxter himself had worked there, and the play might have accommodated anecdotal material such as he often used in talks and prose writings, generating the sympathetic satirical laughter at a commonplace New Zealand experience that Roger Hall would later exploit in *Glide Time*. Instead, he imposed a veneer of intellectual distance on the material by making extensive parallels with the Prometheus legend.

In plays drawing New Testament parallels, however, the theatrical dynamic was not always diminished in this way. In *The Band Rotunda*, set on Good Friday, several of the alcoholic characters try to move into crucifixion roles; there is considerable psychological effectiveness in that at least one of them is experiencing delirium tremens, and there is also a cogent pathos in their helplessness, since their role-playing represents a frustrated need to believe. A similar tension occurs in both *The Wide Open Cage* and *The Day that Flanagan Died*. Only once did Baxter dramatize the anxieties surrounding the need to believe without resorting to archetype, in a play immediately recognized as one of his most effective: *The Devil and Mr Mulcahy* (1967) is a powerful study of the way contemporary religious taboos may precipitate domestic tragedy.

The remarkable critical interest in Baxter's early plays reflected a growing attitude that drama, as literature, was a severely under-developed genre of New Zealand writing. E.H. McCormick's *New Zealand Literature: A Survey* appeared in 1959, the year of *The Wide Open Cage* and *The End of the Golden Weather*, yet drama occupies less than one page. In his 1920 preface to Mulgan's plays, Professor Shelley had been unaware of any previously published New Zealand play, and forty years later there was still a widespread assumption that such plays as had appeared did not merit attention as literature. This notion of an underpopulated genre, coupled with what some felt to be an over-generous reception for Baxter and Mason as dramatists, led several other writers who were already well known in other fields to move sideways into drama; the most successful of these, in the years around 1959, were Frank Sargeson and Allen Curnow. After *The Axe* Curnow did not attempt drama again until *Moon Section* (1959), an unpublished play which was given a professional tour of the North Island by the Community Arts Service Theatre; it achieved notoriety for what was seen as sordid naturalistic detail, and was not revived. During its turmoils on tour Curnow wrote a more urbane verse comedy, *The Overseas Expert*, which in spite of a contemporary local setting and a good deal of relatively gentle satire did not find stage production and was eventually broadcast on radio in 1961. The theme is again colonial exploitation, except that the context is contemporary Auckland, where a gullible, pretentious bourgeois family is duped by a supposedly titled Englishman. Rejecting the stage as unaccommodating, Curnow wrote both of his later plays specifically for radio. *The Duke's Miracle* (1966) is a dramatic expansion of Browning's monologue 'My Last Duchess', using eleven characters, while *Resident of Nowhere* (1969) is an historical verse play about James Busby, presented from the perspective of his old age, as — bedridden in London — he reflects on his experiences as the official British Resident in New Zealand in the 1830s. The conception of the play is audacious, but in the central action there are few indications that the release of historical information is being governed by Busby's faltering memory. The manner is more that of an objective pageant, reflecting the play's origin as a special commission for the Cook bicentenary.

Both Sargeson and Curnow had followed the theatre closely as young men, writing occasional drama reviews for *Tomorrow* and the *Press* respectively. The dramatic values which they formed then have been modified little in their later careers as playwrights. This is particularly noticeable in the case of Sargeson, who wrote dramatic sketches in the 1930s but did not complete a stageable full-length play until 1960. *A Time for Sowing* is a biographical play about Thomas Kendall, the early Bay of Islands missionary. Rejecting much of the available sensational detail about Kendall's life, Sargeson produced a taut character study with a considerable subtextual dimension which was less effective in its stage première than in a radio production of 1967. Although the dialogue is meticulously weighted the play is technically unadventurous, its conservative realism allowing only a limited portrayal of Kendall's mind. As if to correct this, Sargeson quickly wrote *The Cradle and the Egg* (1962), a fictional work with slighter characterization but heavier in symbolism and philosophy. The three acts show a family in different stages of evolution, in the 1880s, in the 1950s, and in a vague future after an aeroplane explosion has propelled them on to a rock in space. As élitist intellectual theatre at the Auckland Art Gallery the play had an appeal similar to Baxter's Greek plays in the South, and it too had a much publicized radio production in 1968.

Domestic realism of an unspectacular (though often well crafted) kind had been common in the one-act plays of the 1930s and had reached some degree of refinement in the short plays of Isobel Andrews and Marie Bullock after the war. At the same time as Sargeson and Curnow were finding new dramatic energies, two other writers were unpretentiously achieving some stature in this older mode with full-length plays. Stella Jones was the better known of these, reaching a wide audience with her first play but failing to repeat the success, while Campbell Caldwell developed a more regional popularity with four plays, all of them developed under the aegis of his Wellington director, Nola Millar.

Critical evaluation of Stella Jones's *The Tree* has been coloured by its production history. Rejected by several New Zealand companies, it was eventually premièred in 1957 by a professional theatre in Bristol, after which it was seen as an illustration of philistinism in the New Zealand arts and received a compensatory tour of forty North Island towns in 1959 by the New Zealand Players (who had previously rejected it), as well as publication with a subsidy from the New Zealand Literary Fund in 1960. The New Zealand Players, however, have been unfairly censured for their unadventurous approach to local plays. As a professional company conceived on a grand, somewhat archaic style, they achieved a remarkable record of touring lavishly mounted productions throughout the country, supported by sporadic grants from lottery funds, from the Department of Internal Affairs, and (towards the end) from a system of debentures.[54] Suspension of grants by the Department effectively precipitated their collapse soon after touring *The Tree*, for debts which seem negligible beside the funding that would be given to other companies by the Queen Elizabeth II Arts Council within a few years.

The Tree is a domestic homecoming drama of a kind that is particularly familiar in America: O'Neill and Miller are the clearest predecessors for an action in which a small-town family uneasily awaits the return of a child and struggles to reassert continuity. Jones was already known as a short story writer when the play appeared, and her dramatic style was based on a spareness that was more fashionable in fiction than in drama. It also demanded greater subtlety of acting than was generally available on the amateur stage. Drawing the inevitable comparison with Mason's *The Pohutukawa Tree*, James Bertram found that *The Tree* read much more 'smoothly and easily', observing also:

> So much is this a women's play, so firmly is it planted in the Katherine Mansfield, or for that matter in the Lady Barker tradition, that the literary critic no less than the social analyst should be delighted at the merely vestigial roles here allowed to the men.[55]

Bertram's description of the central male character as 'a shabby domestic totem' ('His role, in such Amazon country, . . . [is] strictly biological') nicely countered the lack of balance in plays such as Baxter's, but audience sensitivity to gender issues in the late 1950s was insufficient to make this the focus it might have been had the play emerged in the 1970s. Like Curnow and Sargeson, Jones expressed her dissatisfaction with the treatment she received from the local stage by writing her subsequent plays for radio; the most substantial of these, *Between Season* (1966), also shows studied female characterization and a bold approach to controlling atmosphere through subtext and apparent under-writing.

The New Zealand theatre's general expectation of the playwright in the years around 1960 was of someone who would produce a stageable literary product from a typewriter and then retire to begin drafting another play. The only prominent director who engaged in sustained collaborative dialogue with dramatists was Richard Campion, founder of the New Zealand Players, and his creative contribution to plays such as *The Pohutukawa Tree* and *The Wide Open Cage* was acknowledged at their premières; yet his workload was such that he was unable to continue working with single playwrights for successive plays. Later, in 1967-8, Patric and Rosalie Carey exercised a similar influence over Baxter's Greek plays at Dunedin's Globe Theatre — an influence which came so late in Baxter's career that he was not particularly receptive to finer issues of stagecraft. But in 1960 the concept of the dramaturg was virtually unknown in the English-speaking theatre, and this makes more remarkable Nola Millar's sustained creative support for Campbell Caldwell; she directed his first play *Flowers Bloom in Summer* in 1962, and her commitment to his work was such that she directed his fourth play when she was conscious of her imminent death in 1973. In some respects Caldwell's plays show an affinity with the realistic tradition from between the wars: three of them have a rural setting, and their actions tend to reduce behaviour to the dictates of a crude economic determinism, with the result that the plays' resolutions veer towards the implausible. However, Caldwell also showed a determination to address uncomfortable issues, with a post-colonial focus on the margins of society, and his characters sometimes find themselves in moral dilemmas reminiscent of the world of Ibsen.

In *Flowers Bloom in Summer* a free-thinking schoolteacher tries to survive in the face of the entrenched conservatism and flagrant racism of a North Island township; he is caught between a sense of public and private responsibility, conscience, and institutionalized morality, uncertain whether to take cases of child abuse to the Department of Social Welfare. The hero's social conscience makes parts of the play appear melodramatically sentimental, but in *After the Wedding* (1964) the focus is on the obverse side of Kiwi morality, on the wartime origins and post-war domestic consequences of the more boorish variety of mateship. There is nothing heroic and much that is disturbing in this study of physical and emotional violence; there is effective use of vernacular dialogue, and careful depiction of rural society, including the ethos of the Returned Servicemen's Association. In *The Prisoners* (1967) New Zealanders in a German prisoner-of-war camp reveal facets of their rural conditioning under the pressures of incarceration, while *A Southerly Wind* (1973) is a less successful attempt at domestic comedy, a period piece without the aggressive dialogue of *After the Wedding*.

Although Caldwell (like Jones, Curnow, and Sargeson) represented an older generation of playwrights, Nola Millar followed Ngaio Marsh's example as a director in working extensively with younger actors; she was the founding director of the New Zealand Drama School, a development of the School of Drama attached to the semi-professional New Theatre which she launched in Wellington in 1968. Arts Council funding enabled selected students to enrol for a full-time one year course (later expanded to two years) in which they learnt most aspects of theatre skills and participated in major productions, and so most of the scripts Millar handled were subjected to the scrutiny of a younger generation.

As in Australia, the 1960s in New Zealand saw the rise of a new wave of enthusiasm for university drama, with a particular taste for material which could be loosely located within the perimeters of 'the absurd'. Numerous younger writers wrote such plays, almost all one-acters, as a direct assault on the traditions of suburban amateur theatre, and on occasion entered them provocatively in British Drama League competitions. The most prominent of these playwrights in the early 1960s was Alexander Guyan, who also became known as a short story writer.

Conversations with a Golliwog was premièred in Dunedin in 1962, the year of *Flowers Bloom in Summer*. It would be difficult to imagine two plays more dissimilar. Guyan's play has no sense of a social setting, no moral implication in the action, and no specific register in the dialogue other than a parodic Cockney. The main characters are a sophisticated and precocious girl and her golliwog, which serves (when talking) as a catalyst for expressionistic regression and (when silent) as a buffer to distort contact with the rest of her family. The script is witty and iconoclastic, and remained in the repertoire of student drama for more than twenty years. Surprisingly, in view of the success of the play and Guyan's own abilities as a satirical actor, all of his subsequent plays have been premièred on radio or television. Several of these were produced in 1965, mostly dark comedies, often with a fantasy element. *The Arrangement for Thursday* (1966) was an especially sinister work, exploiting the spatial uncertainties of radio to create a complex study of a personality disorder, reflected in a violent, menacing world. Guyan's later plays (including two for television) have been lightweight, mostly on amorous themes in a playful atmosphere.

As a performer and revue writer in Dunedin, Guyan was associated with Michael Anthony Noonan, whose *The Rattle* (1963) was also an exercise in absurdist comedy. In the 1970s Noonan became a highly influential figure in New Zealand television as a scriptwriter and drama editor. Christchurch student drama in the early 1960s was still heavily influenced by Ngaio Marsh's continuing work as a Shakespeare director, but in 1966 Max B. Richards began writing brief, plotless, abstract plays dealing with an aspect of collective behaviour such as boredom, old age, or routine. The succinct, existential tone of Richards' work immediately attracted a student following, but his attempts to reach a more popular audience were not immediately successful. Working in North Island professional theatres in 1969 and 1970 he followed Guyan's pattern of development in producing a grim comedy of menace (*The Messengers*, 1969) and then a series of whimsical radio plays on simple romantic themes. He subsequently lived in Melbourne for a long period, writing prolifically, but very little of that work reached the New Zealand stage.

The Foundation of the Community Theatres

In Wellington, much of the energy that might otherwise have been available to student drama was diverted into the first of New Zealand's professional 'community' theatres, Downstage Theatre, founded in 1964 as an intimate venue offering a buffet dinner and play. The milieu was particularly suitable for experimental short plays, revues, and satirical work, so that the theatre quickly became a focus for university audiences. Several of Bruce Mason's plays were premièred there, but the first new playwright to emerge was one of its founders, the poet Peter Bland. Apart from revue scripts, Bland's first play was *Father's Day* (1966), a three-act naturalistic study of tensions among three women (a mother and her two pregnant daughters) living together in a state house. There are no concessions to light entertainment, and the play's social urgency reflects the uncompromisingly high objectives of Downstage's early years. A year later, however, box-office considerations led Bland to reduce the social comment in his second play, *George the Mad Ad-Man*, accentuating the comic absurdity of a photographer who brings a female model home for an evening's work while his wife nonchalantly continues domestic chores. The compactness of this play, along with Bland's inability to ignore social issues even when trying to write farcical comedy, meant that it was widely produced, reaching both educational and popular audiences. Bland spent the 1970s in his native England, where his considerable success as an actor led to a discontinuation of play-writing, but before leaving New Zealand he wrote two radio plays, both of which show a careful exploitation of the medium in their expressionistic use of memory and fantasy. *'Shsh! He's Becoming a Republic'* (1968) is an absurdist farce about another fanatic who buys a state house from the government, declares it a republic, and defends even his air space. *I'm Off Now* (1968), a study of the mischievous inner life of an English teenage boy who is pondering leaving home, was Bland's farewell to New Zealand drama: an imaginative return to the world of his boyhood.

For writers who were not concerned to reach a university audience, and who did not perceive themselves as contributing to New Zealand literature, the most important production opportunity (and source of income) in the 1960s was provided by the increasingly active Radio Drama department of the New Zealand Broadcasting Corporation (later Radio New Zealand). Unless a radio writer had the established literary stature of a Sargeson or a Curnow there was little likelihood of a play being published, and a common pattern was for a play to be forgotten after perhaps a single repeat broadcast. Under such circumstances playwrights inevitably tended to view their work as ephemeral, sometimes taking unpretentiousness to the extreme of concealing their identity behind pseudonyms. The dominant figure to emerge through radio drama in the 1960s, who went on to establish a significant reputation in stage drama in the 1970s, was Joseph Musaphia.

After a variety of mechanical occupations Musaphia decided to become a professional writer in the early 1960s, and submitted his first play (*Free*, 1961) to *Landfall* — a sign of the seriousness of his literary ambitions. *Free* was staged as part of a double bill with a minor Baxter work, but although it received critical recognition it was to be Musaphia's last stage play (and virtually his last serious play) for a decade. *Free* is typical of Musaphia's dramatic world in that it is a male-centred proletarian drama (almost the inverse of Bland's *Father's Day*): a study of the bachelor habits and aspirations of three young men — a driver, a mechanic, and a painter — who sit in their flat discussing a forthcoming wedding. The masculinist emphasis in this and subsequent plays seems commonplace beside New Zealand poetry and fiction of the 1930s, but in its intensity it was a remarkable innovation in drama: it is at least arguable that the vigorous involvement of women in acting and directing had over several decades effectively achieved a tradition of gender balance. For the professional theatres of the 1980s, writers such as Greg McGee and Vincent O'Sullivan would be able to write for large male casts, but in the 1960s radio was found to have a special tolerance for unbalanced casts. Baxter was quick to exploit this, and Musaphia's shift to radio obviously allowed him to indulge the character range he preferred. *Free* received radio presentation in 1962. By this time Musaphia had completed six similar radio plays, of which *A Seat in the Sun* is a representative example: in this play three male factory workers ogle women during their lunch-hour and amuse themselves with frivolous role-playing. The plays of the next few years consist mainly of amusingly ironic studies of the predicaments and expectations of the beer-swilling male world. In the late 1960s his radio work became more commercialized, with even less subtlety, and he became involved in television acting and scripting (mainly for children) before his major stage achievements in the community theatres of the 1970s.

Although he gradually learned the essentials of radio technique, Musaphia showed little interest in exploring the extremes, always giving the impression of a stage writer who was reluctantly dependent on radio. Warren Dibble and Alistair Campbell, on the other hand, wrote radio plays from the start, which would be impossible to stage without major rethinking, and only turned to the stage after a special invitation at the end of the decade. Dibble's *Loser on Drums* (1962) is a complex presentation of a subnormal boy's obsession with drumming; his psychological disorder is reflected in the structural elasticity of the play, in which reality is often lost in a blur of distorted memories and hallucinations. Several less ambitious radio plays followed, but in *A Recital* (1965) the absence on radio of a concrete visual world is exploited even more boldly to depict a woman who is completely out of touch with reality: she talks to a man, but seems uncertain whether they have been lovers previously; she talks of her plans for the afternoon, but cannot find where they are to be carried out. Because of the dislocation of her memories and fantasies, the causes of her confusion are impossible to unravel. *Carnovan* (1966) deals with a suicidal headmaster from South Africa on holiday in New Zealand, interrogated in his mind by an Examiner. In the same year Dibble's first stage play (*'Lord, Dismiss Us . . .'*) was produced, an undistinguished school drama which was almost immediately produced on radio in a double bill with his best-known work, *Lines to M*.

Lines to M, which was eventually staged in 1969 at Downstage and subsequently at numerous other professional and university theatres, combines the complex questions of causation from *A Recital* with the motif of mental collapse under inner interrogation from *Carnovan*. At the start Victor Spilman speaks directly to the audience, and quickly establishes himself as a morose middle-aged man with a neurotic obsession manifested most clearly in a need for absolute precision as he outlines his life and circumstances. Suddenly, he reveals what seems to be the traumatic origin of his condition — the fact that he recently murdered his daughter — and he uses a blackboard diagram to trace events leading up to 'M' (Murder). Other characters emerge for brief scenes as functions of his memory or guilt (in what is referred to as the 'prosecution of the imagination'), and a pivotal episode seems to be one in which he allegedly sexually abused a girl to whom he was teaching the cello. The courtroom of his mind is objectified, containing a schizoid Barrister very like the Examiner of *Carnovan*, until mental disorder leads him to speculate that the 'M' might stand for 'Mistake'. The play's structure thus follows the Strindbergian model for hallucinatory dramaturgy, presenting a gradual intensification of chaotic, associative thinking whose final outcome is a state of psychological collapse. With a minimal setting and many devices to puncture any illusion of stable location in time or place, the play strategically exploits the referential vagueness that Dibble had found in radio, and this made it a particularly effective work for New Zealand's new intimate community theatres.

Alistair Campbell's period of dramatic productiveness almost exactly parallels Dibble's, and although the two writers do not seem to have been particularly aware of each other, Campbell also used radio to explore the theme of mental collapse before producing his one stage play (for Downstage) in 1969. Campbell's reputation as a young New Zealand poet had been high through the 1950s, and he made a tentative venture towards radio drama in *Sanctuary of Spirits*, produced as 'a tone poem for voices' in 1963. Though its published versions suggest some doubt that the work is properly a play, the use of a variety of voices on radio suggested otherwise, offering a vigorous internalized action in which the implied author struggles unsuccessfully to accommodate historical elements of his Polynesian identity; at the end his psyche is invaded by Te Rauparaha. In *The Homecoming* (1964) Campbell used radio for a more orthodox memory drama with a contemporary autobiographical tone, exploring the thoughts of a young Māori travelling home by train in the hope of reconciliation with his European wife who has recently been in an asylum; at the end they meet happily on a beach, but this is ambiguous, and possibly just hypothetical wish-fulfilment. In the next two years Campbell wrote three surrealistic radio plays dealing with asylum situations, plays completely divorced from realism and autobiography: he admitted the influence of an Ionesco play at Downstage, and his own poetry of the same period was also surrealistic. *The Proprietor* explores the delirium of a mental patient lost in the world of Greek mythology, *The Suicide* is a study of a split personality (in which an educated New Zealander tries to dislodge an over-familiar ordinary Kiwi), and in *The Death of the Colonel* a surreal collage is projected from an insane colonel.

Like Dibble, Campbell had written for British Drama League production in the middle of the decade, but his first substantial opportunity for stage writing came when he extensively revised *The Homecoming* as *When the Bough Breaks* for Downstage in 1969. This time, he presented the action from the perspective of the wife, in an asylum bed from the start of the play. The episodes are detached from any chronological structure and secondary characters appear as functions of her delirium. However the husband, recognizable as an authorial figure, gains a degree of autonomy because of his caring, reasonable approach to her (at least on occasion), and when he recites Alistair Campbell poems as his own his stature becomes even more independent of her delirium. For this reason, it has been questioned whether Campbell achieved the depth of sympathetic female characterization that he was aiming for in both plays, although the work certainly does succeed in exploring the inner tensions often created in interracial marriages. Campbell's plays are essentially subjective, and his awareness of his own mixed-race ancestry is articulated with particular clarity in his plays, whose main purpose was to come to terms with 'the dark side' of himself.[56] Only the most superficial reading of Campbell's work could find its function to be the 'redemption' of the 'barbaric splendour' which Mason attributed to McLeod. The post-colonial search for identity is central to Campbell, but origins are an elusive concept in his plays.

Two other playwrights of the 1960s with a slighter but nevertheless significant output used radio for complex psychological dissection of characters: Graham Billing and Owen Leeming. Billing's first play was a radio adaptation in 1966 of his novel *Forbush and the Penguins*, and traces the experiences of a man fighting to preserve his sanity while left in Antarctica for the duration of the penguin breeding season. The radio version is in the tradition of symphonic theatre: voices expressive of Forbush's inner conflict are given not only to human figures like Scott but also to elemental forces (like the sun and the mountain) in the physical environment. In *Mervyn Gridfern Versus the Baboons* (1966), written expressly for radio, Billing achieved an unusual dark comedy about the growth of a man's fantasy to the point where it overwhelms his perception of reality; much of the wry comedy comes from the nature of his fantasy self (the subversive zookeeper of the title), and there is an engrossing ambiguity in the function of the man's girlfriend, who starts as an audience for the Gridfern yarn but whose presence dissolves as the zoo animals become more prominent in the fantasy.

Owen Leeming became known as a radio producer and showed an experimental approach to the medium from the start. *Order* (1969) is about a retired army man who controls his domestic life with military meticulousness; the play uses a Describer to splice into the action various climactic episodes of army life in Africa. *Yellow* (1969) is written in a more orthodox mode of expressionism, using fifty minutes to explore the moment of death of a young soldier in Vietnam. Like Dibble's radio drama, the play is built on interior conflict — the man is interrogated throughout by his own brain — and the constant intrusion of extraneous detail and military data in a highly formal style greatly intensifies his anxiety. Like Richards, Campbell, and Dibble, Leeming also had a play (*The Quarry Game*) mounted at Downstage in 1969 in a series of New Zealand plays sponsored by the Gulbenkian Foundation. Its impact, however, was weakened by the stage cliché it adopted: an attempt to combine audience involvement with a science fiction time-slip situation.

Television had reached most New Zealand towns by the mid-1960s, but it was regarded with some suspicion by educated audiences, who still expected depth and subtlety in recorded drama — as in current affairs coverage — to come only through the radio. The few attempts at television drama production were hampered by inappropriate training of actors, writers, and directors, and this reinforced audience resistance. In recognition of the fact that radio drama was reaching a special audience, the Concert Programme supplemented classical music with plays of a more intellectually demanding nature than were generally presented on the then-popular National Programme. Leeming, Campbell, and Baxter were typical Concert Programme playwrights, and there were several other prolific writers such as Dora Somerville who exploited cleverness and allusiveness for their own sake within contrived story-lines. The Radio Drama Department's greatest success in developing an unpretentiously popular playwright was Julian Dickon, who was gradually encouraged to abandon verse drama and atmospheric ambiguity in favour of a full-bodied naturalism and an adroit manipulation of suspense. The main achievement of Dickon's early period was *Brindle* (1967), a forestry drama which provided the basis of New Zealand's first successful television drama series, *Pukemanu* (1972). Disagreement over television editing reaffirmed Dickon's commitment to radio, and he remained very productive for several years, but a diminishing audience and more attractive rates of payment led him increasingly back to television in the late 1970s, with particular successes in writing children's series.

If television drama was still embryonic in 1970, the professional and semi-professional stage was beginning to assert itself in seven cities. Some of these theatres, especially those in Auckland, showed a nervousness about using local scripts, even though the Downstage model had demonstrated that there was now a significant audience for them. In 1969 Downstage mounted a series of eight New Zealand plays by authors most of whom were better known in other genres; it was sponsored by the Gulbenkian Foundation, and imitated the Royal Court system of productions without décor for emergent dramatists. Dibble, Somerville, Richards, Leeming, and Campbell were included, but the most controversial new writer was Edward Bowman, who had recently won a television play-writing competition run by the *London Observer* with his first play, *Salve Regina*. One of the judges, Kenneth Tynan, had condemned it as a television script, while admitting that it would work on stage,[57] and this was tested — again drawing an ambiguous critical response — in the Gulbenkian version, which was also influenced by Bowman's recently-produced radio script. Bowman's general inclination towards science fiction is reflected in the futuristic situation of *Salve Regina*, where the basement of a department store, wrecked by a nuclear war, provides a refuge for three survivors from the violent world outside, ravaged by starving dogs. The woman (who calls herself the Queen) has sterilized herself, and humanity seems to be nearing extinction when an obviously fertile young woman appears, having escaped the war in a space vehicle. The characters and situation are very similar to William Saroyan's *The Cave Dwellers*, but without any of the American's optimism; here, sexual aggression — from the men and between the women — is the basis of the action, and by the end most recognizable elements of humanity seem to have been abandoned as the characters approach the dogs' terms of survival.

Tynan's belief in the play's theatrical potential may have been prompted by the pervasive use of a clownish style both in the men's behaviour and in their dialogue, but this has never been more than a qualified success on stage, and some productions have chosen to accentuate the sinister aspects of the situation. It was probably the very long radio version, with its fluidity of location and tone, which best integrated all of Bowman's stylistic intentions. He moved more deliberately towards science fiction in his next radio play, *Solus* (1973), a space fantasy in which only one character seems to have any residual humanity. The expansive nature of these works contrasts severely with the economy of two monologues, which were both produced on radio and stage: their compactness and carefully-controlled suspense interested audiences, despite their bizarre content. It is only at the end that *John*, with its contemporary action of a woman painting her husband's portrait, reveals itself as a re-enactment of the decapitation of John the Baptist. *Iscariot*, on the other hand, reveals its terms of reference at the start: a latter-day Judas, trapped in a Nazi brothel, defends himself with a frenetic awareness of the proximity of Auschwitz. Bowman's interest in situations, themes, and sensation rather than motivation means that he has had little chance of gaining popularity with actors, although his monologues have been used for displays of stage virtuosity by young actors.

Much more acceptable to audiences has been the combination of Bowman's graveside savagery and theatrical aggressiveness with a degree of developed characterization such as Brian McNeill achieved in *The Two Tigers* (1973), a biographical play about John Middleton Murry and Katherine Mansfield which fades out with her death. McNeill's play has a brutality, announced in the title, which seems subtle in the script but becomes intense in production because of the story's basis in biographical fact, and there is a strong ingredient of the sensational as the ironies of Katherine's imminent death of tuberculosis accumulate. Though the play ends with dialogue derived from 'At The Bay', the focus of the action is on the 'other' Mansfield: the mature, assertive woman in whose existence many sentimental New Zealand readers refused to believe, even in the 1970s; a further aspect of the play's appeal was that it allowed a voyeuristic insight into the intimacies of death.

With two fully-drawn characters, and two actors playing a variety of secondary parts on a stage that used light and variations in level rather than an elaborate fixed set, *The Two Tigers* was an ideal piece for the intimate milieu of most of the new Community theatres. Although Downstage did not serve as a direct model for any other New Zealand theatre, its success left no doubt that the viability of professional theatre lay not in nationally touring companies doing brief seasons behind huge proscenium arches, but in locally based groups serving an immediate community in a small auditorium which would allow considerable flexibility in staging and seating. The Arts Council gave considerable funding support to the scheme, and by the early 1970s almost every larger city (and some smaller ones) had at least one such theatre. The main auditorium of Auckland's Mercury Theatre was the only one of these with a seating capacity substantially above two hundred, and it is indicative of the relation between production conditions and the dramatic text that *The Two Tigers* was premièred not there but at Auckland's other, very much smaller, professional venue, Central Theatre. This coincided almost exactly with the first Mercury main-bill production of a local play, James McNeish's *The Rocking Cave*, an expansive historical saga requiring lavish presentation.

The young playwright who most adventurously explored the economies of intimate theatre was Robert Lord, who for several years was recognized as the most promising and innovative New Zealand dramatist. At Downstage in the early 1970s Lord was encouraged and influenced by two directors, Sunny Amey and Anthony Taylor. Amey had recently returned from London, where she had been assistant to Olivier and director for BBCTV,[58] and was the first woman to become artistic director of a New Zealand professional theatre, Downstage at the Hannah Playhouse, a new theatre constructed specifically to continue the presentational flexibility of Downstage in its earlier makeshift locations. Though Amey did not use a New Zealand play for the opening of the new theatre, her stance as artistic director contrasted strongly with Ngaio Marsh's earlier deference to London models: her support for local writers was extensive, and she became a stimulating contributor to playwrights' workshops. Anthony Taylor was a highly respected radio producer who occasionally worked on stage; his own earlier plays were all written for radio, and developed simple interview situations to explore behaviour enigmas within very stark dramaturgic structures. Such tendencies are very noticeable in Lord's early work, the period when he was most committed to dramatic experimentation.

It Isn't Cricket (1971) established dramatic idiosyncrasies that would occur in almost all of Lord's plays: character is pared down to the essential, and the audience is denied a precise positioning of the action in time or place, so that there is no possibility of building up case histories. Although the eighteen scenes are consecutive, there is deliberate vagueness about how much time passes between them; and although the characters all belong to a single generation, their ages are regarded as unimportant. Each scene focuses on a different piece of behaviour, generally a confrontational game; the ethics generated by such games are then shown as gradually permeating the rest of their lives, so that the worst kind of antisocial behaviour is cheating or lying. A mannerism apparent even in this play (and which irritated some critics) is Lord's method of fading scenes out with a catch-phrase, often a variation on a cliché. *Friendship Centre* (1971) uses all of these techniques even more deliberately, but the most substantial achievement of Lord's early period is the full-length *Meeting Place* (1972). Here, even the chronological sequence of scenes defies unravelling, and the characters talk as much in monologue as in dialogue. Instead of the simplistic game-playing and relationship-building of the earlier plays, a more poetic ambiance is built up through vivid allusiveness and imagery, and the vagueness of the action's location brings into sharp relief Lord's use of suddenly violent or assertive behaviour. Memory and imagination provide the dynamics of the play, so that there is often an uncertainty about the level of reality represented; this applies even to the ending, when the four characters have coupled homosexually.

Meeting Place was a critical success but a box-office failure at Downstage, and this led Lord to cross the fine line between character reduced to an essence and a frank indulgence of stereotype. *Balance of Payments* (1972) is a black comedy which illustrates this transition, especially in the way that a balanced sympathy with all the characters is replaced by a more clinical, satirical overview. The ultimate target of the satire is in fact the audience, since the characters function as a parodic extension of popular social values in the manner of Albee's *American Dream*. In the same year Lord's first radio play, *Moody Tuesday*, used stereotypes with less satirical edge by deriving its characters and their aspirations from the genre of popular fiction. This anticipated a vogue in New Zealand drama that would become widespread in the mid-1980s, and Lord developed it in four police dramas, two for stage and two for radio, written in 1973. The banality of the crime situations is matched by the portrayal of the police, who range from exploitative picaroons to absurdly heroic supermen. In the other characters there is always at least a suggestion of human fragility, and sometimes this invades the police. *Well Hung*, the best known of these plays because of its allusions to the Crewe murder investigation, presents police life as an amalgam of corruption, laziness, and brutality, but jolts into a surprise ending when a young constable hangs himself in disgust. The play's structure, blending farce with sudden blackness, drew widespread criticism on its première at Downstage, even though the work was certainly Lord's most direct effort to address social issues on the stage. The more abstract style of *Heroes and Butterflies* (1974) returns to the vagueness of the earlier plays in its nightmarish creation of a civil war situation in which social morality seems to have dissipated. A feeling of urgency runs through much of the disconcertingly non-specific action, but the very large cast and problematic fluctuations in tempo meant that its two professional productions, though quite dissimilar, were unpopular.

After 1974 Lord lived for a long period in New York and remained productive, although only a few of his plays, domestic comedies, reached the New Zealand stage. *High as a Kite* (1979) has an American setting, but is loosely based on a play written five years earlier, and as David Carnegie has noted, it reflects Lord's earliest style:

> [It] is more like the strong and distinctive early plays *It Isn't Cricket* and *Meeting Place*. It shares the shifting quadrille structure of *Meeting Place*, and the sense of isolation of each individual on the shifting and treacherous sands of personal relations. Like Arthur Mamet, Lord . . . depicts the alienation of individuals in a fragmented society.[59]

The obsessive construction of the large box kite (a birthday present for one of the characters) itself functions symbolically during the play, as the characters form new, heterosexual relationships; and there are other physical correlatives of the characters' personalities, all of which imply 'play' and insulation from reality. *Unfamiliar Steps* (1983), retitled *Bert and Maisy* for its Australian première, is a gentle satire of the aspirations of very ordinary family people for whom commonplace problems become magnified into controlling obsessions and anxieties, reflected in the absurd edge which the action assumes in the second act. Lord's affinities with American drama had been obvious to critics from the first, but living in New York gave him greater stylistic confidence, and the distance clearly enabled him to find greater satirical clarity in his perception of life in New Zealand.

Max Richards and Robert Lord were both initially recognized (perhaps sometimes over-lavishly) as writers whose talent deserved encouragement, and both were appointed writers-in-residence for major professional theatres. Lord in particular received relatively large budget main-auditorium productions in the early 1970s. However the departure of both writers overseas indicated a continuing dissatisfaction with the artistic support structure available to young writers within the theatres. Even in the early 1970s there was still no more provision for the systematic workshopping of new scripts than there had been in the time of Sargeson and Curnow, and there was still no organized structure for the professional reading, marketing, publication, and distribution of plays. Lord and Richards had to follow Bruce Mason's practice of typing and photocopying their scripts before beginning the demoralizing ordeal of mailing plays to every theatre that might be sympathetic, where an overworked artistic director might take months to read and then summarily reject them. The formation of Playmarket in 1973, which was designed to address these fundamental problems in the professional relationship between New Zealand playwrights and the theatre, was thus an organizational advance of quite exceptional significance in the history of New Zealand drama.

Playmarket and its Playwrights

The foundation of the Queen Elizabeth II Arts Council of New Zealand in 1964 provided funding from government and lottery sources to foster the arts generally; the community theatres as well as Playmarket would become heavily dependent on the Council for finance, but although it has always included staff with a specialist interest in drama, the Council's function has primarily been restricted to providing and assessing funding. The New Zealand branch of the British Drama League merged with the New Zealand Drama Council in 1970 to form the New Zealand Theatre Federation, which continued to operate a script lending library used mainly by schools and amateur theatres. Although the library always included some New Zealand material, the organization had never attempted to act as a professional authors' agency able to collect the substantial royalties accrued by a successful full-time writer. The Drama Council had also since 1947 published a monthly magazine, *New Zealand Theatre*, which was an important news source and contained brief critical items. In 1973 this merged with *Act*, a magazine established at Downstage by Bruce Mason in 1967, which (under Nonnita Rees's editorship in particular) had begun systematically to foster a larger-scale awareness of New Zealand drama.

Playmarket realized many of the largely unfulfilled aims of these other organizations. It began as a free script advisory service and authors' agency, taking over the management of *Act*, which became *Act Bulletin* (until it ceased publication in 1986). It organized workshops and encouraged major productions, liaised with similar organizations in Australia and Canada, published and encouraged the publication of many New Zealand plays, and mounted New Zealand playwrights' conferences and weeklong residential workshops which in the 1980s became a biennial event. Most important, it created a sense of solidarity among New Zealand playwrights, and with it a tentative professional morale. Within a year Playmarket could claim that it acted 'for the majority of established and new playwrights in the country', although its future as an organization would not be assured until the advent of its first major commercial success in Roger Hall.

The playwrights whom Playmarket regarded as its leading assets in its early years were Campbell, Lord, McNeill, Musaphia, and Mason, as well as Craig Harrison, Eve Hughes, Gary Langford, Gordon Dryland and Dean Parker. Of the latter group, Langford had recently gone to Australia where he would achieve a reputation as a stage and television writer, and Eve Hughes had written a short Brechtian satire *Mr. Bones and Mr. Jones* (1971) which was widely produced. However her next play, an unsuccessful outdoor stage version of Verne's *Around the World in Eighty Days* (1974), signalled the virtual end of her play-writing. Harrison, Dryland and Parker would also all have in effect severed their connection with New Zealand drama through Playmarket within a decade, but the reasons for their disaffection were more complex.

Gordon Dryland was a contemporary of Baxter, and had written one successful novel when his first stage plays were produced in 1967-8. His first professional stage production, *If I Bought Her the Wool* (1971, later retitled *Wool*), was typical of most of his work with its themes of bisexuality and physical abnormality (here a hydrocephalic child), and its tone of acid comedy distilled from the dialogue of highly articulate but defensive characters. *Dark Going Down*, an earlier full-length stage play with most of these qualities, was produced on radio in 1971, and in the mid-1970s Dryland wrote several lighter radio plays. The moral cynicism that pervades his work has always given him a special popularity with younger actors, and it was for such a cast that he wrote *Fat Little Indians* in 1976, another domestic comedy which was staged by several student groups but grudgingly accepted by older critics who found some of the wit distasteful or self-indulgent. In the same year *Think of Africa* was also premiered at Auckland's amateur New Independent Theatre, arousing controversy because of the moral iconoclasm implicit in its comic approach to taboo subjects, in this case a hideous birthmark. In this play the adult characters seem propelled by varying combinations of hatred, resentment, and avarice accentuated by an awareness of the commercial potential of some family wasteland.

Dryland's critical reception parallels that of the British playwrights Peter Nichols and Dennis Potter or of the New Zealander John Banas, but the sour wit of his dialogue was more acceptable in *Think of Africa*, since the cynicism of the older characters was itself explored as the effect of a conditioning process. For Dryland's most supportive critics, such as Paul Day, the formula works well: 'Beginning as a light family comedy, it develops in Act II into an Ibsen-like debate on the ethics of civic development; its final apotheosis is something between Gothic horror and Greek tragedy.'[60] Dryland wrote a considerable number of similar plays for stage and radio before his departure to live in Australia in 1984. The most substantial of his later works is *Unlikely Places* (1979), in which a middle-aged nymphomaniac and her male homosexual friend are tourists on a tiny Pacific island, where they compete sexually for the same local Casanova. The comedy of these relationships is gradually overshadowed by the play's emergent focus on the island's horrifying history of economic — as well as sexual — exploitation. Although the ambitious attempt to create a metaphoric alignment of personal relationships with the larger exploitation theme is imperfectly achieved (its structural weaknesses are partly caused by the difficulties of sustaining a long play with only two characters), *Unlikely Places* is notable as virtually the only play to address cultural friction between New Zealand and the Pacific, with the New Zealanders cast as corrupt Old World predators, unscrupulous in their use of economic power. The oil slick which surrounds the island and threatens its mainly half-caste population suggests both the specific New Zealand presence and the vulnerability of all Pacific nations to industrial exploitation by superpowers.

A more polemical assault on audience morality as well as on theatre-going assumptions came with the work of Dean Parker, who suddenly attracted public notice in 1974 with a group of outspoken radio plays, mostly social comedies. His first stage play, *Smack*, belongs to the same year, and was immediately praised by critics. Bruce Mason commented on its 'ear for New Zealand dialogue' and also saw in its more stylized passages of obscenity and poetry a strong similarity to Baxter's dramatic language.[61] The action of *Smack* pivots on the counter-cultural motif of a youth trying to blackmail a bank manager into supporting a drug deal, and killing him when he refuses; the play fades out without hint of consequence or retribution, as the man, his girlfriend, and a hitchhiker drive south. As in Dryland's play, there is an implicit parallel between interpersonal behaviour (drugs and blackmail) and economic circumstance (capitalism) — an unappealing thesis to conservative audiences, which may account for the relatively limited stage history of a play so eulogized on its première. The theatricality of Parker's talent was apparent to all critics, but his provocative use of language and argument was even less acceptable on radio, for which an expurgated version of *Smack* was produced in 1975. Since then, however, Parker has written only sporadically, and in a minor vein, for the stage; and in 1984, dissatisfied with his reception in the established theatres, he withdrew his work from the Playmarket agency.

On radio, Parker has continued to produce remarkable work, winning the Radio New Zealand Mobil 'best drama' award for 1981 with *Engels F: A History of the Ould Sod*, a highly entertaining treatment of a serious subject (Ireland through the eyes of Engels), complete with songs, vaudeville routines, and a flippantly anarchic ending, all of which succeeded on radio in spite of the fact that the techniques almost all derived from the stage. A completely different tone, without any overt entertainment devices, permeated *Strike* (1982), a radio trilogy dealing with three strikes of particular importance to the evolution of the socialist movement in New Zealand. The first play, 'Waihi 1912' showed a fictional worker and his family caught in the historical mesh. The second, 'Auckland Relief Workers 1932', showed the same worker, now older and a vociferous communist, laid off from the coalmines at Huntly. A woman's perspective is strongly articulated by his wife, and Parker achieves an effective dramatic balancing of political issues by allowing her father a deathbed speech against communism, from a more conservative Labour Party perspective. The final play focuses on a strike at Hellaby's Auckland meatworks in 1942. The family saga has advanced by a generation, and there are two sons, one in North Africa and the other at Hellaby's. The family's attitudes to the war effort are complex even before the strike, and the tensions and paradoxes it generates provide the thematic core of the play. The conflicting values of the characters recall those in Hamilton's *Falls the Shadow*, and Parker's political position as a writer also parallels Hamilton's. Politically committed playwrights of the left almost inevitably find themselves at odds with the institutions of established theatre, and in the absence of a sympathetic local climate for political theatre (such as existed in the late 1930s) Parker has suffered more than most from the lack of recognition of his talent and promise as a writer for the stage.

Beside Parker, Craig Harrison appeared as a strident but rather less polemical dramatic satirist who would often disagree with interpretations of his work, but after his first play, he abandoned the objective of unnerving his audience. It is this play, *Tomorrow Will Be a Lovely Day* (1974), which is nevertheless his main achievement. Conjecturing a situation in which two Māori extremists precipitate civil war by stealing the Treaty of Waitangi, the play episodically sketches their backgrounds in terms of Vietnam, penitentiaries, and racism, and projects the action forward to the point of American intervention. The satire is supported by Brechtian techniques which are not well coordinated; these include direct audience address by various characters, a dummy prime minister who literally falls to pieces, and considerable use of recorded media material. For the professional première of the play at Auckland's Mercury Theatre in 1978 the director Mervyn Thompson also used videotaped material, and ended with a confrontational indictment of the audience's attitude to racism. However, in the four years since the play had been written social circumstances had changed considerably. Harrison had initially conceived the events of the play as a 'fantasy'. Auckland audiences — acutely aware of recent government-prompted police action against Māori land protesters at Bastion Point — 'read' the play against these immediate events. The result was that its structure, 'a series of revue skits compered by a Narrator',[62] seemed to imply a superficiality of treatment which did no justice to the urgency of the theme.

Another futuristic political play of 1974, *The Whites of their Eyes*, also dealt with civil and racial unrest, but with a selection of stereotypes that did not generate the same controversial immediacy. Harrison's subsequent full-length plays have all been dependent on situational comedy, generally arising from cultural confusion. The prototype for these is *Ground Level* (1974), about a Yorkshireman and a Māori who is travelling overseas after winning a lottery. *Home Truths* (1975), *Perfect Strangers* (1976) and *Western Powers* (1977) all explore similar themes, resulting in comedy with an edge of social observation, but in the television series *Joe and Koro* the motif was reduced to innocuous entertainment. The virtual discontinuation of Harrison's dramatic writing reflects his dissatisfaction with the treatment and reception of several of his plays, but it is also an apparent reflection of his unwillingness to engage in a continuing social dialogue through his plays, in the light of dynamically changing race relations in the 1980s. Of his later work, the most provocative play is *Hearts of Gold* (1983) which, though historically distanced, explores some of the parallels between sexual and colonial exploitation developed in Dryland's *Unlikely Places*.

A playwright much more sensitive to the changing social climate is Mervyn Thompson, who evolved his own form of 'song-play' for the ironic analysis of contemporary New Zealand identity, and of the pressures which shaped it. His first play, *First Return* (1974), traces the process of self-discovery of a New Zealander in London, whose meeting with a young expatriate woman triggers an expressionistic journey through distorted memories of his boyhood experiences. The memories are represented by a 'menagerie' of sometimes grotesque stereotypes, including general types such as Authority as well as specific figures such as his parents. The protean nature of the menagerie reflects the haunting dimensions of the nightmare, but there are also powerful static images like the chains that hold the parents (the 'wild animals of the circus') together, and there is a gradual intensification of the sense of persecution as the memory probes closer to specific traumas such as his mother's death. However, although some episodes are horrifying, others are comic or sardonic, and there are excursions into New Zealand religion and horse-racing where the tone becomes lightly ironical, anticipating the mood of *O! Temperance!* (1973). Here documentary replaces fantasy, but although most of the characters are devoutly dedicated to the temperance movement as it existed in New Zealand around the turn of the century, their didacticism is clearly not authorial, so that a mischievous perspective qualifies all of their endeavours. If the play does not expound an authorial commitment, its tone is nevertheless gently sympathetic to the misguided vigour of the temperance workers, who are presented as an engaging eccentricity in the evolution of New Zealand society.

First Return and *O! Temperance!* both used songs extensively but incidentally, the former to express loneliness or choric antagonism towards the main character, and the latter for self-parodying expression of the temperance ideal. The short play *Songs to Uncle Scrim* (1976), however, is almost entirely sung, and the music offers a collage of Depression sentiments, sung to the radio uncle by the collective cast, in which individuals crystallize briefly before being absorbed back into anonymity. *A Night at the Races* (1977) is a full-length song-play, a celebration of the race-going instinct with a pervasive sympathy for the escapism of gambling. In this play there is also a fictional story involving characters who are more than stereotypes, and there is a good deal of dialogue as well as singing. Audience involvement is also more adventurous, with theatre-goers invited on stage to place bets.

None of Thompson's work is strictly Brechtian, although it does make a general assertion of the ambiguity of the world through the occasional use of alienation devices. The Brechtian ingredient becomes greater (but is still not dominant) in his major achievement in the 'song-play' genre, *Songs to the Judges* (1980), with its ironic motif of the theatre as a courtroom resounding with the melodies of the conventional theatre of escapism. In *Songs to Uncle Scrim* the central paradox was that the main theme — the Depression — seemed in itself completely resistant to musical celebration, and a similar paradox informs *Songs to the Judges*. Like his production of Harrison's *Tomorrow Will Be a Lovely Day*, this play was partly inspired by the events of Bastion Point. The play selects examples of racism from throughout New Zealand history, emphasizing the law as a primary arena of institutionalized injustice. The Judge is a farcical figure in the style of *Trial by Jury*, pronouncing mindless verdicts on the Māori characters in the dock, and offering absurd solutions such as genocide. The play's illustrations of injustice range from the Land Claims Ordinance of 1841 to the Maori Affairs Amendment Act of 1967, the presentation implicitly condemning self-justifying Pākehā attitudes. The European perspective is without a cogent apologist, and the Māori characters command sympathy because they are consistently brutalized. The play fades out with a musical version of the idealistic prophecy of Te Whiti, implying a better Māori future; some critics have considered this to be intended seriously and have judged it fatuous, but it is more consistent with Thompson's method to see it as parodic, assaulting the audience's wish for a happy ending, and this is supported by a stage direction emphasizing that the final grouping constitutes a 'warning' about the future.[63]

The New Zealand 'Truth' Show, written by Thompson and the 1982 Auckland University Drama Diploma students, also demythologizes New Zealand social history, scrutinizing 1931, 1941, 1951, 1961, 1971, and 1981 over the editorial desk of the weekly popular newspaper *Truth*. The audience thinks it is viewing New Zealand through the eyes of *Truth*, but gradually realizes that it is viewing *Truth* from the perspective of the perceived New Zealand. In the final segment, concerned primarily with the 1981 Springbok tour, the 'myopia' of *Truth* becomes insufferable; previously, it has fluctuated mainly between the amusing and the irritating, with tension being broken by slapstick techniques and token characterization, but as the absurdities of *Truth*'s reporting of the tour accumulate, roles are broken by the actor-journalists. When release comes from the nightmare a new ironic commitment emerges in the sung finale to *Truth*/Truth. Throughout his play-writing career Thompson has also had a strong creative influence over New Zealand drama as a director, teacher, and actor. Many of his leading roles (including the judge in *Songs to the Judges*) were created by him in the theatre, but only in 1984 did he take the logical step of writing a full-length solo work for his own performance. *Coaltown Blues* is a semi-autobiographical profile of working-class New Zealand from the election of the first Labour government to the repression of the unions in the 1950s. Songs, mostly ironical, maintain a tautly ambivalent attitude towards the miners' existence and values, an ambiguity announced even in the opening song, 'Labour Pains'.

The ambiguities in which Thompson's plays tangle his audience, and the complexity of their vision, has ensured their continuing social relevance, whether their focus is historical or contemporary. The Māori land issues of *Songs to the Judges* also prompted much more direct lines of attack, and the best known of these was the group-scripted *Maranga Mai* (1980) which, mainly in Māori, used agitprop techniques to confront its audience. Group theatre had been an important part of New Zealand drama since about 1970, when Francis Batten's touring 'Theatre Action' used Lecoq mime techniques to complement antipodean epics such as *The Best of All Possible Worlds* (1973). After several years of distinguished group work in New Zealand Batten moved to Australia to establish a training school. Paul Maunder, on the other hand, showed more persistence, founding the Amamus Theatre in Wellington in 1971, and immediately attracting wide attention with his group's poignantly low-key studies of working-class New Zealanders. The performance style was deliberately unpolished, using local accents exclusively, and the practice of collective scripting and adaptation (even when works were in performance) meant that there was never a sense of a subjective authorial perspective.

In 1973 a brief visit was made to New Zealand by Jerzy Grotowski, whose work Maunder respected, and Amamus did a special performance of *Pictures* for him, a play which explored New Zealand's involvement in the Vietnam War in a style of brutal confrontation of the national psyche. *Gallipoli* (1974) presents the situation of a young New Zealander in the campaign, whose boyhood memories are counterbalanced by the perspectives of the enemy, a group of five Turks. To them the Kiwi is an irrational and naïve barbarian, and the play explores in a stylistically adventurous manner a cultural impasse similar to that of Vincent O'Sullivan's *Shuriken*. For the Kiwi, however, the campaign is a process of self-discovery, and his self-esteem finally flourishes to the point where he sees his death as an affirmation of a new sense of identity. The Old World cynicism and decadence of the Turks is the catalyst for this process, but equally important is the play's decolonizing rejection of the adolescent Kiwi's models in the form of his parents, mate, and wife (all of whom appear as memory figures). The unusual cross-cultural gaze of this play, coupled with the post-colonial rigour of its reviewing of New Zealand history, made it an interesting choice to take to Poland, where further contact with Grotowski led the theatre into more extensive use of mythic material. When the group returned to New Zealand *Gallipoli* was used as the first part of *Song of a Kiwi* (1975-8), the major achievement of this period of Amamus's development. The other two parts develop images of violence and cultural disjunction in a more abstract manner, drawing their material from both ancient and contemporary myth. In the early 1980s Amamus was dissolved, to be replaced by the Theatre of the Eighth Day, also directed by Maunder but committed more specifically to Māori issues.

Although he was a pivotal figure in the alternative theatre movement, and occasionally received Arts Council funding for specific tours, Maunder has never prepared scripts for use outside his own company and has thus not really found Playmarket's objectives relevant to his own purposes. *I Rode my Horse down the Road* (1981), his only published script, was prefaced with the statement that 'it would be disastrous for someone else to learn these lines and the play to be performed in a normal fashion'.[64]

Thompson, on the other hand, has often written plays with the resources of a particular theatre in mind, but then modified them with the intention of reaching a wider audience through Playmarket. Other writers, less involved with the specific conditions of a local theatre, found an immediate use for the agency, and in the first three years of Playmarket the authors whose work sold most productions were Lord, McNeill, Harrison, Dryland, and Musaphia. All of them received some professional productions, but the author who seemed to have the greatest commercial potential was Musaphia, whose return to stage writing in 1971 was stimulated by the new wave in Australian theatre — a notable instance of the general incentive provided for the Playmarket movement in New Zealand by the Australian renaissance.

For *The Guerrilla* (1971) Musaphia adapted a recent factual story about a Sydney hostage drama in which the central figure was a frustrated and disillusioned worker. The worker (Adam) and his girlfriend are both intellectually limited, only partially aware of the seriousness of their situation, and Musaphia's skill in developing their characterization, with a tone of affectionate irony, almost compensates for the anticlimactic ending in which Adam surrenders his morale and his dignity. *Victims* (1973) was both Musaphia's most specific work of social commentary and his biggest box-office success, a fact which had a clear influence on other technically more adventurous writers including Robert Lord. The play is indirectly about the work of the Society for the Preservation of Community Standards — a name alluding transparently to a real organization which was generally unpopular with the liberal world of arts and entertainment in the early 1970s. Musaphia, however, historically distanced this element and set the whole action at the turn of the century, using a rich man's death to precipitate a complex intrigue of blackmail and licentiousness. Most characters (the prudes in particular) are compromised by events, and the farce is structurally more tidily resolved than any of the earlier plays, though at the expense of depth of characterization. Its large cast precluded the wide professional stage history that *Victims* otherwise deserved, and Musaphia's subsequent stage plays would alternate between the light comedy or farce which came easily to him, and the tonally ambivalent studies of society's underdogs to which he had developed a particular commitment.

It was to this vein that he returned in 1974 with *Obstacles*. In this play a heavy-drinking ex-boxer blunders into a domestic situation and becomes an unwitting agent of sexual harrassment as well as a victim of manipulation that verges on blackmail. As in *The Guerrilla*, the three characters have only the most rudimentary capacity for self-awareness, and the situational comedy is heavily tempered by the seriousness of the underlying themes: the abuse of power in personal relationships, and domestic and social entrapment. A powerful correlative to the interpersonal conflict is provided by the off-stage demolition machines which are steadily closing in on the building. In 1975 Musaphia moved back towards pure farce with *Mothers and Fathers*, a play about surrogate childbearing. At the time the subject seemed absurdly remote from reality. A social dimension is present, but is hardly pursued at any depth: a bourgeois couple wants to buy the breeding abilities of a woman whose economic circumstances do not allow her the luxury of debating the finer moral issues. The main exploitation of the subject is in terms of farcical inversions of the sexual situation, and the female characters in particular are only slightly developed. *The Hangman* (1978) ostensibly deals with the death penalty within the context of a South Island township a century earlier, and there is a great deal of satire against the small-mindedness of the citizens, who are more concerned with sexual scandal than with the moral issues involved in the hanging.

A year later Musaphia produced his most successful fusion of locally-coloured comedy and social awareness. *Hunting* (1979) presents two middle-aged divorced people who are living together and trying to preserve a sense of professional fulfilment and independence, he in art, she in journalism. A child of each visits their flat: the man's son is an insensitive male stereotype, while the woman's daughter is embittered after an abortion. The ensuing conflict is not, as in most of the earlier plays, concerned to explore and comment on stereotypes. Rejection of traditional gender roles is a premise from which the action starts, and the dramatized tensions focus on other issues: divided loyalties between children and partner; vulnerability, guilt, and isolation in fragmented families; the difficulties of pursuing new goals in middle age. If the predatory concept of relationships announced in the title implies a fundamentally serious study of sexual politics, there is also a great deal of thought-provoking comedy in the way that postures are challenged and undermined. Musaphia's subsequent stage plays have been much less complex. *Shotgun Wedding* (1980) is a light domestic farce with a typically down-to-earth pragmatism in some characters, but it also contains a quantity of incongruous one-line witticisms that suggests an attempt to widen the style. *Mates* (1986), a comic study of mid-life crises, attempts the socially-aware perspective of *Hunting*, focusing this time on the problems faced by working women accused by their husbands of being overachievers. However the earlier play's depth of character perception is absent, and Musaphia seems to return to a male view of the world which is now outdated.

Without question, the playwright whose commercial success gave Playmarket (as well as Wellington's new Circa Theatre) the security it needed was Roger Hall, whose *Glide Time* (1976) suddenly monopolized Playmarket's attention, achieving no less than fourteen productions in its first year of availability. Hall's previous experience was mainly in television and stage revues, and techniques derived from these sources recur in his full-length plays, where he manipulates his audience's laughter with a consistently professional strategy. In *Glide Time* a group of menial public servants try to assert their dignity through trivial gestures of anarchy and independence, such as exploiting the system of flexible working hours referred to in the title. The world of the office, where the whole play is set, is drawn with considerable detail; almost all audiences have close knowledge of this world, and so the satirical target is a popular one. Hall's character portrayal, however, achieves a texture that is much more complex than his early satire, and the anxieties of several characters generate a degree of poignancy. *Middle-Age Spread* (1977) is set around a dinner party hosted by a schoolteacher who has recently ended the only infidelity of his life; both wife and mistress are present, and the history of the affair is shown through flashbacks. The trigger for the immediate action is an antisocial, cynical teachers' college lecturer who finally reveals the facts of the affair. Again, there is considerable emotional poignancy in some aspects of the play, but the attempt to develop a generational theme (the lecturer's son is responsible for the pregnancy of the host's daughter) seems contrived (especially as the children do not appear on stage), and the depth of characterization varies: the hostess, for example, is close to a stereotypical matriarch whose menopausal rejection of her husband, it is implied, has pushed him into the affair.

Hall's first two full-length plays had numerous professional productions and revivals: *Glide Time* formed the basis of a number of radio and television series (which continued until 1985), and *Middle-Age Spread* had a long West End run as well as being filmed. His next few plays had much less success. *State of the Play* (1978) attempted a more serious tone, presenting a once-successful dramatist as he conducts a play-writing seminar and touches off various kinds of self-awareness among the participants, but the situation seems hackneyed and none of the characters has the vitality of the earlier plays. *Prisoners of Mother England* (1979) develops the migration motif of *Glide Time* into a satirical comedy in which eight English migrants are shown trying to adjust to New Zealand life. Many of the fifty-nine scenes (covering ten years) employ revue methods, and this relates well to the theme of dislocation. *Fifty-Fifty* is set in London. The main character is a meek, middle-aged nonentity in the process of abandoning his flat as the realities of divorce register upon him. The play lacks any satirical power because its social location is vague, presumably aiming to capitalize on the London stage success of *Middle-Age Spread*. On the other hand the short play *The Rose* (1981), focused on the 1981 Springbok rugby tour, directly and effectively targeted New Zealand attitudes. The play made considerable use of caricature and was scripted for its immediate (perhaps ephemeral) impact, but it indicated the commitment to serious themes that has always existed alongside Hall's remarkable skill as an entertainer.

With the exception of *Footrot Flats* (1983), a highly successful musical developed from the cartoon strip, Hall's work had limited production for a number of years after 1981. *Hot Water* (1982) is a crude and untidily resolved situational farce, built around a businessman's ambition to catch a trout, a deer, a swordfish, and a woman in the same day. The living-room of the Taupo holiday home is crowded with cosmopolitan visitors, most of whom are blatantly stereotypical, including a matriarch who seems very similar to the puritanical hostess of *Middle-Age Spread*. *Multiple Choice* (1984) returns to a more serious mode, dealing with the educational system. However the structure, with few props and numerous scenes, echoes revue techniques, and there are elements of comedy and farce which undermine the seriousness of its assertions about individuality. *Dream of Sussex Downs* (1986), based on Chekhov's *Three Sisters*, is a serious study of English expatriates in Wellington in the 1950s, the time of Hall's own arrival: echoes of *Prisoners of Mother England* are inevitable, but the defensive atmosphere is more urgent. The collaboration with Philip Norman and A.K. Grant which had been successful in *Footrot Flats* was repeated in *Love off the Shelf* (1986), ostensibly a play about a literary researcher writing popular romances to cover costs, but basically a musical parody of the True Love genre. A more substantial musical is *The Hansard Show* (1986), which draws on parliamentary archives to reflect the evolution of national self-consciousness. Much of the tone is ironical, but (as in

Mervyn Thompson's plays with a documentary basis) a great deal of feeling is invested even in the more grotesque absurdities. Hall's work of the late 1980s returned to the mode of light farce and achieved extensive production, especially *The Share Club* and *After the Crash* — complementary plays using the same characters from the world of private investors.

New Impulses in the 1980s

By the late 1970s the importance of Roger Hall in creating stability and continuity in the community theatre movement was obvious, but there was also a widely felt need for a more aggressive realism that would relate to the changing attitudes and tolerances which had become apparent in cinema audiences. Even before its workshop première in 1980, Greg McGee's *Foreskin's Lament* was seen to fulfil such a demand, with a severity that was new to New Zealand drama. On the literal level the play is about rugby, with one act in the changing room after practice and the second at an after-match party. At the start the audience hears the noise of the players, but no one is on stage. This establishes the fundamental element of the play's dynamics, the feeling that the stage should be populated by fifteen characters, and this vacuum principle draws the other characters on stage, each couple of players talking about others who have not yet entered. The team is a unit, with an arrogant spirit and an ethos of its own which lead to the rejection and victimization of non-members such as the homosexual masseur.

The solidarity of the team thus creates a metaphor for New Zealand society at large, and this becomes more explicit as the character nicknamed Foreskin argues that the rugby player is 'the heart and bowels' of society. The essential action consists of Foreskin isolating himself, articulating his individuality, and then being taken back into the collective context. Foreskin does not want to destroy the team or its game; he simply wants to teach it to transcend its violence and insensitivity and play altruistic rugby. His continuing participation, albeit with a missionary purpose, makes him and his sympathetic audience accomplices in the rugby phenomenon, sharing responsibility for its consequences. The coach, whose slogan is to 'kick shit out of everything above grass height', says that he 'does not understand the meaning of the word "altruism" ',[65] and at the end Foreskin, defeated, retreats from his university-derived articulacy into the coach's language which, turned on the audience, becomes an indictment of a whole society. As he realizes his failure, he begins his 'lament' as a serious parody of an after-match speech, although the subject now is the death of a team-mate; gradually, it becomes an elegy for the lost heroes of New Zealand rugby, and the style, with invented verbs implying loss and fragmentation, becomes highly allusive.

The play's dramatic action (which pivots on envy of the captain, resulting in his injury on the field and subsequent death) is pure sporting melodrama, but McGee's depiction of the team's organic nature, ethics, and language behaviour made it the finest piece of social realism in New Zealand drama to that point. Foreskin may be seen as a Promethean rebel, a martyr to his social precociousness, or a scapegoat who breaks one of New Zealand's most cherished taboos and by his defeat reinforces that taboo; in whichever capacity, however, his primary dramaturgic function is that of commentator. The central violence of the play would have occurred regardless of Foreskin's presence; he is irrelevant to the particular events leading to the death, and his importance is purely as a focus of interpretation. The game of rugby, and the patterns of social brutality reflected in it, will continue regardless of Foreskin's gesture, and there is no apparent way in which his crime of complicity is a civilizing crime. The lament is not for the death of a friend, but for the impossibility of individuality.

McGee's next two stage plays also set up large-scale metaphorical projections of New Zealand life. At the start of *Tooth and Claw* (1983) a screen provides a monochromatic image of street rioting, watched in disbelief by the only character on stage, a young lawyer. This suggests an interior nightmare; however, it soon emerges that street anarchy is an objective reality, and that the lawyer has recently been assaulted by a Māori activist (who appears as a grotesquely-masked mime). The screen at the back of the law office thus serves a dual symbolic purpose, used both as a window (suggesting that city life is being monitored by authority figures) and as a mirror of the young lawyer's mind, reflecting and compounding his anxieties. The on-stage action consists of covert blackmail from a former flatmate who is now engaged in shady business speculation, and a similarly manipulative relationship between the two senior partners. Various compromising secrets are discussed in detail, providing a strong dramatic contrast to the vagueness of the impinging public world of events. The play eventually takes its audience into an urban Armageddon, with civil disorder, racial unrest, and a holocaust which in the second act invades the set. However, McGee's strategy of transmuting the thoroughly personal nightmare of the start into a generalized collective nightmare in the second act is awkward, and the play as a whole fails to engage as a social vision.

In the same year as *Tooth and Claw*, *Out in the Cold* was premièred as a stage play, although its outline was already familiar from McGee's short story of the same title.[66] In broadest terms, it is a situation comedy: Judy, a former student and now a solo mother needing to support her children, tries to pass as a man in order to obtain a heavy labouring job in the chamber at the local freezing works. Her attempts at tolerance and compatibility with the two regular freezer hands lead to a general rethinking of attitudes when, inevitably, her true identity is discovered. However, like rugby in the first play, the freezing works here represents a stereotypical male world, and the ease with which it can be invaded means that the situational comedy contains an implicit indictment of that world and its values. A television version (1985) began with Judy sunbathing naked, getting up, cutting her hair and dressing as a man before competing for the job at the works; this eliminated the initial ambiguities in the stage version, and created strong sympathy with Judy from the start. The screen also paid close attention to the butchery process and the factory itself, which became even more clearly a concrete correlative to the social system. On stage, the freezing chamber where the action is located is a mechanical proletarian hell dominated by a single distorting light source, and the presentation of each of the three characters in turn moves through phases of exaggerated garrulousness and reflectiveness, with the formulaic banter generated by repetitive work creating a language world of its own. A similar bonding function is achieved by the adroit use of the languages of sport and law in the earlier plays, but unfortunately it is absent from McGee's fourth stage play, *Whitemen* (1986), which attempted to explore rugby politics through farce.

McGee's early plays attack traditional male values without positing in detail a more sensitive alternative; even Judy, McGee's most complex female character to date, is applauded as a demolisher of male boorishness more than she is felt for as a socially disadvantaged woman. Over the previous four decades numerous women had written plays with a strongly female perspective which often contained an implicit polemic against a male-dominated society; these playwrights were given considerable encouragement by the traditional British Drama League category of plays for all-female casts at festivals. Isobel Andrews was a most prolific playwright, best known for her one-act *The Willing Horse* (1941) in which the central stratagem is husband-hunting at a dance: the implication is that every woman will eventually get the marriage trophy she deserves. However, if the perspective means that men are viewed as commodities, marriage is regarded as the proper female fulfilment and a career is dismissed as an abnormal objective. Kathleen Ross's *The Trap* (1950) challenged this view, as did some of the plays of Marie Bullock and Stella Jones.

The playwright who led the move towards an uncompromisingly feminist theatre in New Zealand was Renée, a member of the *Broadsheet* collective, and author of satirical songs and sketches for their Roadshow. She had in fact more than twenty years of experience as a director with the Community Arts Service theatre before *Setting the Table* was premièred on radio. It then received a Playmarket workshop at Mercury Theatre in 1981 and became her first work to reach the professional stage. The action is set in a women's refuge centre for victims of rape and domestic violence. Though nearly half the characters are male, their aggressiveness (or, at best, insensitivity) makes them merely targets of the dramatic polemic, and the real dilemma involves the principles and consequences of the use of retaliatory violence by the women. The style is a simple realism, relieved occasionally by musical items that the women are preparing for a feminist satirical revue.

Secrets (1982) is a pair of short, complementary one-woman plays, initially performed by the same actor. The first monologue is in narrative terms similar to Dibble's *Lines to M*: a middle-aged woman wanders around her kitchen in the evening talking intermittently to a photograph of her daughter about a 'secret' which is eventually revealed to be a family history of sexual abuse. Although the woman is not given the psychological complexity of Dibble's

Spilman, she does have an obsession about hygiene which dominates her on-stage behaviour, as she compulsively sterilizes and polishes glasses and crockery. A television adaptation by Diana Rowan introduced secondary characters to dramatize the memory episodes, including the actual incidents of abuse. The second play is also a study of a middle-aged victim of male oppression, here a woman cleaning men's lavatories in a theatre, who is continuously reminded of the standards the boss demands. As she works, this time mechanically rather than obsessively, she interprets her life as a cleaning saga which has never taken her far away from lavatories. However, liberation has come in the form of a lottery win and, after ruminating on how she will tell the boss that she now has independent means, she ends the play with a triumphant gesture of defiance, throwing rubbish everywhere. *Groundwork* was another play prompted by the 1981 Springbok tour, and written soon after it, although it was not until the formation of Auckland's professional Working Title Theatre in 1985 that a group was found that was prepared to mount it. The setting, in Auckland police cells on the last day of the tour, is an obvious arena for the expression of social tension, but the play has a breadth of reference, and a complexity of characterization (based on the extensive use of memory flashbacks), which take it well beyond the polemics of agitprop.

Wednesday to Come (1984) was Renée's first work to be widely produced in both professional and university theatres, and its success prompted her to develop it into a trilogy, viewing the same character group at three points of historical crisis, as Dean Parker had done in his *Strike* plays. The first play is set in 1934, and with a simple and effective historical realism shows working-class women of four generations receiving the body of their 'breadwinner' who has committed suicide in a Depression relief camp. Although there are two male characters, the play's focus is on how the women respond to the stress related to the death, and by the Depression in general. A group on a hunger march wants to generate publicity from his martyrdom, harnessed like a horse to pull a plough. For the women of the family, however, the heroics of male sacrifice are an irrelevance, and the appearance of the dead man's mistress is a powerful device to undermine any sentimental reaffirmation of emotional and material dependence. *Wednesday to Come* is the middle play of the trilogy. The first play, *Jeannie Once* (1990) is set in the 1870s, and presents the title character (Granna in *Wednesday to Come*) as a young working-class woman in late Victorian Dunedin; more than any other part of the trilogy, this play reflects Renée's work in revues through a music-hall element, problematizing a theme of institutionalized oppression through the use of asylums as a facile solution to societal discord. The concluding play, *Pass it On* (1986) is concerned with the Waterfront strike of 1951. The adolescent children of the previous play are now married; the daughter is a Communist activist with an insipid husband, while the son's wife's gradual awareness of the principles at stake serves as an accessibility device for the audience. In this play the dramaturgic style changes from a studied naturalism to a more episodic sequence of thirty scenes, allowing for much greater variations of tempo but with less emphasis on the meticulous portrayal of character. Like Roger Hall, Renée has incorporated into several of her plays techniques derived from her early experience scripting revues, and these help to relieve their generally monochromatic realism; she has in fact continued writing feminist revues, with *What Did You Do in the War, Mummy?* (1982) and *Asking for It* (1983). None of her plays may be reduced to a simple thesis, even though there is seldom any difficulty in identifying oppressors and victims.

Of several women playwrights who emerged at about the same time as Renée, initially the best received was the poet Rachel McAlpine, whose *The Stationary Sixth Form Poetry Trip* (1981) derived from the same Playwrights' Workshop as *Foreskin's Lament*. Entirely in verse dialogue, the play presents eleven sixth-form pupils studying Coleridge's 'The Ancient Mariner', the teacher reading a few verses and the students responding by interpreting the culturally remote poem in the light of their own experience. Coleridge thus becomes a catalyst for an exploration of New Zealand adolescence, but the script is primarily auditory, showing very little awareness of the potential of stage production. One critic argued that in this play, for the first time in New Zealand drama:

> the female child's or adolescent's imagination has affected the choice of subject for drama, . . . her phobias, myths and fantasies (like anorexia nervosa) have been [seen as] worth exposing on stage. The revelations of the girls' dreams and expectations also throw some light on the other-than-technical restrictions upon the portrayal of women in the child-occupied years.[67]

Such a description might more aptly be applied to *The Life Fantastic* (1982), McAlpine's second play and her first for radio, which presents the playful fantasies of a thirteen-year-old girl, augmented when her family shifts to another town. Deliberately, she lets loneliness fire her imagination into exercises in wish-fulfilment, wryly entertaining to herself, richly amusing to the radio audience. The pattern of self-dramatization means that she propels herself into unlikely amatory contexts, to the anguish of on-looking sixth-formers and teachers. When one teacher thwarts her, the fantasy generates its own energy and finally gets out of control in a scene of desperate savagery against the teacher; the nightmare is relentless, and interruptions from parents only momentarily delay its progress. By this stage, there is no irony: audience and character are completely united in their attitude to the life fantastic. But if the climax is gruelling, there is an equipoise of tone in the way the girl's gratuitous self-delusion and her hysteria and mental anarchy are balanced, and it is a tribute to the quality of character creation in *The Life Fantastic* that even at the peak of the nightmare we remain confident that such a balance will be found.

Renée has said that her writing is politically motivated, and that one of its purposes is 'to present women's views of the world'.[68] By that yardstick *The Life Fantastic* seems a much more compelling achievement than *Setting the*

Table. Both plays reach a crisis about three-quarters of the way through, when central characters discover that violence has become addictive. McAlpine, with a fine instinctive sense of dramatic strategy, uses the crisis as an emotional watershed, refining and clarifying attitudes before a strong ending. Renée, on the other hand, following Ibsen's tradition of the discussion play, leaves most issues suspended at the point of crisis, so that the articulation of the title metaphor at the end seems a dramaturgic convenience. Of McAlpine's subsequent stage plays, *Driftwood* (1985) is about the aspirations of surfers and break-dancers, a large-cast play written for young actors, while *Paper Towers* (1986) is a dark domestic play dealing with the menace and stress of adult urban life.

One of the most complex historical plays with a female protagonist is *In Confidence: Dialogues with Amy Bock* (1982) by Fiona Farrell Poole, who in 1983 became the first winner of the Bruce Mason Playwrights' Award. Amy Bock, a celebrated transvestite confidence trickster, in her public context (a grotesque, who devastates Dunedin at the turn of the century) commands an audience's awe rather than sympathy. Elsewhere, Poole's imaginative structuring of the private character generates early scenes of frustration with parents, moving in and out of Cinderella roles, and a poignant penumbral scene at the end, where Amy measures herself against Melba, the true Antipodean Cinderella. Although the stagecraft of *In Confidence* is severely economical, it could accommodate two radically different production emphases, either as a social drama with a thesis to articulate, or as a primarily psychological play, probing the extraordinary recesses of the Amy Bock cranium. In *Passengers* (1985), written for high-school performance, Poole assembled twenty female working-class migrants on a ship to New Zealand last century; the choice of such a large cast and the extensive use of music preclude much character investigation, but the collocations allow a great deal of irony and a very broad view of a dislocated society. *Bonds* (1986), by contrast, is a fictional domestic play which requires three simultaneous interior sets to present discrete actions spliced together episodically. In each case, a couple has a visitor whose presence leads to a revaluation of their relationship and an examination of the bonds and goals carrying them into the future. The three narrative filaments involve an elderly couple, some middle-aged graduates, and a married woman with a lesbian sister, and there is an audacious strategy of truncation of the story to bring suspense to often mundane material.

The extent to which plays by women contribute to a feminist theatre varies considerably. Some plays, such as Sarah Delahunty's *Stretchmarks* (1985) and Kathleen Gallagher and Kate Winstanley's *Mothertongue* (1986), announce their gender focus in their titles and develop it through stylization, while Rosie Scott's *Say Thank You to the Lady* (1985) and Delahunty's *Loose Connections* (1986) introduce feminist issues into social drama similar to Renée's. A play developed at the 1982 Playmarket Playwrights' Workshop and later subjected to controversial productions was Carolyn Burns's *Objection Overruled*, a courtroom drama which dissects and indicts a stereotypical New Zealand life.

One review (entitled 'Hysterical cliché as art') began by describing it as 'the strident lament of a disappointed feminist',[69] and a unique series of generally negative reviews of various productions followed. The play's tonal diffuseness perhaps accounts for the confusion of response, and the ambiguity of the farcical elements also blurs feminist elements; the accused person is a man, but the dramatic portrayal of his conditioning, with a great deal of role-transfer, creates considerable sympathy for him, and the most serious focus on women is intermittent, as in the episode when his mother aborts herself with a knitting needle.

A much more provocative approach to a New Zealand feminist theatre, at least in dramaturgic terms, is Hilary Beaton's *Outside In*, which was regarded as the most stimulating script to come from the 1983 Playwrights' Workshop. As a prison play with an all-female cast, it is arguably the most intense work of naturalism in the history of New Zealand drama: there is a constant attrition of the characters' self-images (and thus of their self-esteem) to a level of animalistic survival, until even rudimentary stimuli like food trigger off violence, and this is closely paralleled by a reduction of their language to simple expletives. Prison conditioning, with the constraints of power, exploitation, and sexual abuse from warders as well as from other prisoners, gradually generates a prison mentality, so that even a new inmate is seen to be quickly assimilated into a type. On this immediate naturalistic level the play may be taken as a didactic illustration of the 'schools for crime' theory of the effects of incarceration, especially as it begins with a parody of law-enforcement: a mentally retarded character is punished by another prisoner for stealing the sugar. But there are other implications which carry the play beyond naturalism. In prison, behaviour is seen to start with 'criminals' evolving their own morality, and this is reinforced by the way they create their own microcosmic social hierarchy, quickly finding themselves in parent/child or boss/worker roles. Since their own culpability as 'criminals' is, for the first act at least, assumed rather than demonstrated, the foundations of the new society they are creating are at best fragile. As a result, the on-stage behaviour takes on a metonymic dimension, representing or parodying the world outside.

Critics and directors, however, have found different possibilities to focus on for this other world. If the play is simple naturalism, the other world is just the ordinary life of the audience's world, the latent bestiality of which may be accentuated by the severities of prison conditioning. However, since the characters are all women, it is difficult to evade the play's implications about gender roles. Michael Neill, while conceding the play's 'superficial naturalism', found that the characters

> . . . know, better than anyone, that the artificial female society of which they are both victims and creators is only a slightly distorted mirror of the male-dominated world outside. Here too relationships are organised by the supposedly 'male' values of competition, and love itself becomes a function of power.[70]

In places, Neill found that the play seems 'to embody a disillusioned Hobbesean view of the ungovernable human appetite for power'. More constructive qualities such as strength and assertiveness seem to have been lost, although Neill found that parts of the play celebrate 'the capacity of human love to survive the most degrading circumstances and the most intolerable betrayals'. Helen White, however, argued that the play contained more than 'male' values, and for her a comparison with *Foreskin's Lament* showed up 'a degree of compassion, a female element, that was conspicuously absent from the preferred world of the New Zealand male'.[71] Such consoling dimensions in the play, however, are at best vestigial, and the climactic celebration of Christmas followed by the most brutal piece of violence and a recapitulation of the parodic punishment gesture of the start, all suggest that Christian or even elementary human compassion has been withdrawn from the 'hell' of the prisoners.

The ambiguities of Beaton's prison world are explored and compounded by poetic allusiveness in the stage plays of Vincent O'Sullivan, who in 1981 had extended his reputation as a poet, short story writer, and critic with a group of short radio and television plays. *Ordinary Nights in Ward Ten* (1984) is a stage work similar to *Outside In* in its conception of characters subject to conditioning in an institutional setting (an asylum). New role relationships and new power structures are discovered, but the play becomes confused by religious dimensions and by farcical tendencies which have a trivializing effect. The play ends with the approach of death and a clinical statement of animalism as a non-speaking Mary/Madonna figure, bound and shaven for ECG treatment, is examined in the dehumanizing language of pathology. However, a final stage direction leaves a puppet dancing, a possible affirmation of survival and imagination. O'Sullivan's first stage play, *Shuriken* (1983), is more consistent in tone, though scarcely less complex in the parallelism of its structuring. As another prison play (this time with a large all-male cast) it raises questions about metaphor and sex roles similar to those raised by *Outside In* and *Foreskin's Lament*. The setting is non-fictional (the Featherston prisoner-of-war camp outside Wellington), and the concluding action represents an historical event: the massacre of Japanese prisoners by New Zealand guards in 1943. The characters, however, are fictional. The guards represent a cross-section of attitudes to the war (a Māori, an Englishman, an educated Pākehā, a pacifist, and so on), designed to complicate the central assertion that there is a basic ethical impasse between the New Zealand soldiers and the Japanese. The Japanese are initially presented as being lost, disowned by a field code which does not recognize surrender as legitimate; the New Zealanders feel a comparable insecurity because their authority figures are presented as ludicrous stereotypes. The audience, grappling with a pervasive problem of xenophobia, finds itself intermittently alienated by characters who had seemed sympathetic; the religious character, for example, is established as attractive in that he attacks racism, yet it is he who finds himself behind the machine gun at the end.

As in *Outside In*, group dynamics mean that a character who asserts his individualism seems doomed to be absorbed again into herd thinking (termed by the Japanese 'sheep mentality'); a pattern very similar to *Foreskin's Lament*. At a simple historical level (which has been called naturalistic by some critics) the play seems to be about a clash of authorities and a clash of cultures, with the common men stranded as uncomprehending victims. The Japanese position is further articulated by the use of Noh techniques, including a Spirit who presents a vision quite outside the perception of the New Zealanders. This masked Noh figure speaks for the body of a prisoner who has committed suicide, and confronts the New Zealanders with their incomprehension; the accusation is reinforced by the action of a New Zealand guard who stands over the corpse and tells a particularly tasteless yarn about a cadaver.

It has been argued that the play's tautness depends on more than a simple opposition. Sebastian Black pointed out that when the Māori soldier Tai sings his waiata tangi 'he taps sources of emotion that are as humanly recognisable as those in the haiku, but they are not any more comprehensible to the Pakeha community',[72] and extends his analysis to show that there are in fact three cultures which fail to relate. However, Black's implication that O'Sullivan 'the Pakeha playwright does not violate the unknown and unknowable Tai's privacy' by showing him 're-entering the Pakeha world' is questionable since (as in *Outside In*) the final authorial attitude is dissolved in a gesture of irrational violence. Tai's capitulation in the last act is also impossible to demonstrate from the script because he largely stops verbalizing his anger and grief after Act I, and falls back on physical violence which is easily absorbed into the massacre. Less contentious is Black's evaluation of O'Sullivan's achievement: 'Dramatists like Bruce Mason and Craig Harrison have previously incorporated these [Māori] elements into their plays, but only O'Sullivan uses them so openly as a comment on a largely monocultural audience.'[73]

The variety and complexity of responses to plays such as *Outside In* and *Shuriken* show that New Zealand drama has begun to play a significant role in articulating society's growing self-awareness, particularly about issues of gender, race relations, and human rights. This development is particularly clear when one compares McNeill's *The Two Tigers* (1973) and Cathy Downes's *The Case of Katherine Mansfield* (1980) with one of O'Sullivan's more recent stage works, *Jones & Jones* (1988) which also reworks the Mansfield story: though the substantial stage history of both earlier plays exploited a sometimes severe frankness and realism, *Jones & Jones* moved into the sphere of demythologization, using music hall devices to bridge the bizarre relationship between Mansfield and Ida Baker. The development in terms of audience receptivity is the more remarkable because *Jones & Jones* was accepted as a major contribution to the Mansfield centenary, just as Mervyn Thompson's *Children of the Poor* (1989) was staged in the 1991 Dunedin New Zealand Writers' Week to mark the centenary of John A. Lee's birth. Neither work is in any sense a simple celebration of the subject: the resources of the stage for immediacy are in both cases exploited to engage the audience in confrontational dialogue with a literary saint who for the moment defies monumentalization. Of Thompson's other recent works, *Lovebirds* (1990) is a structurally innovative view of the brutalities within relationships which is also an index to the change in climate since *The Two Tigers*, while his second one-man work, *Passing Through* (1991), is largely affectionate iconoclasm directed at the New Zealand theatre.

However, the production viability of such confrontational scripts has only been able to emerge within a context that has also supported — and drawn vitality from — the more popular theatre of social comedy generated by playwrights like Roger Hall and Joseph Musaphia. Just as the characters of *Glide Time* were extended into radio and television series, those of *The Share Club* have been revived not only in *After the Crash*, but also in the television series *Neighbourhood Watch* (1990). If new dimensions seem to have emerged in the theatre audience, there is also a constancy evident in the immediate popularity of Hall's stage play *Conjugal Rites* (1990), which seems in no way to deviate from the domestic comedy of *Middle-Age Spread*. It was for lack of this latter theatre, addressing the entertainment needs of the general public, that many earlier attempts at providing a culturally innovative theatre failed.

Hall, Musaphia, and other playwrights have at times addressed serious issues through a medium of farce or light comedy, but the most sustained attempt to revalidate the New Zealand comic tradition has occurred in Stuart Hoar's *Squatter* (1986). Hoar was known as the author of a number of radio plays when he offered *Squatter* as his first stage play at the 1986 Playwrights' Workshop under the direction of Mervyn Thompson. *Squatter* is an historical comedy, set on a Canterbury run in 1894, and uses incongruity, role confusion, social iconoclasm, and situational comedy to observe the collapse of power and authority structures in society. However, the recurrent use of anachronism and other devices of alienation leaves the audience wondering whether the drama is culturally and historically specific, making a statement about Cheviot in the 1890s which would not be as pertinent in any other context. As if to highlight the play's historicizing dynamic and its status as a parable for the theatre, Hoar actually introduces Nathan's Old Testament parable of the man with one sheep and the man with a hundred,[74] followed by an on-stage interpretation which is so transparently wrong that the audience is forced to decipher its meaning. The play's cumulative implications about class, power, and property come to a head in the last scene, where the dead characters appear, trying to find some meaning in the territory which was once the homestead. Their attempts at interpretation are either absurd or banal, and are epitomized by a character who reads the late-medieval *In Praise of Folly* in a futile effort to track down the meaning of life. The absurdity of such an aim is reflected not only in the play's dialogue but in many of its events and visual effects. The Victorian photographer Bracken, with his panoply of cumbersome equipment, symbolizes the absurdity of pretending that things can stay the same: everything changes, and social change and revolution are inevitable. The play's title is itself a statement of impermanence, as well as a denial of colonizing presence.

The historical and cross-cultural sweeps which are set up in the plays of Hoar and O'Sullivan are remarkable, and have been developed further in works like O'Sullivan's *Billy* (1989), a complex work which tests the parameters of class, race, and nation. Such plays do not resolve themselves in simple statements of monoculturalism or decolonization; rather, they are an acknowledgement of cultural and social confusion or absence such as Paul Maunder addressed in his Theatre of the Eighth Day, committed to 'the penetration of the confused and contradictory cultural experience of the people of Aotearoa since colonization'.[75]

Electra (Thoughts during the Tour) (1982) was the first major work of this new company, and Maunder used Orestes as an instrument for a polemic against apartheid and its supporting economic structure. The bilingual *Encounter at Te Puna* (*Te Tūtakitanga I Te Puna*, 1984) presented the advent of the first Christian missionaries from the perspective of a modern Māori woman groping through history to try to find her cultural identity. As in *Gallipoli*, the dream structure collates specific historical images which holistically develop a vision of a bewildering contemporary dilemma. Another bilingual play, *Ngati Pakeha* (1985), used a present-day narrative perspective to present memories and traditions from around the Hauhau period. Maunder has also on occasion exploited location to achieve a peculiarly intense New Zealand dimension in his drama. The early Amamus work had been scripted for performance in non-theatrical informal touring situations. The Gallipoli campaign, though presented indoors, placed the audience inside a huge canvas structure that represented the vulnerable, claustrophobic atmosphere of life at the front. *Encounter at Te Puna* was located in a Māori meeting house with the audience along the walls, and Keri Kaa described the setting of *Ngati Pakeha* at Wellington's Depot Theatre:

> The actual setting of the play was unusual but appropriate for the style of the production. The Whanau were grouped around the fire near the audience so that we identified with them. The pakeha colonists, settlers, immigrants, soldiers and surveyors were isolated at the far end 'for purposes of clarity'. Depicted as historical archetypes they emerged as victims of their own ideals, people of their time shaped by the forces of their own culture, determined to do what they thought was 'right for the natives' and ultimately satisfying their own ambitions.[76]

Electra took place in a clearing in the bush at nightfall, with just a few oil lights, making it perhaps the most direct rebellion to date against the theatre-going conventions of the parent colonial culture. This parentage Maunder has all but destroyed, but he has also demonstrated the paradox — fascinating but unviable — of attempting to re-enter a pre-colonial existence in dramatic works which Keri Kaa and Philip Tremewan have praised for their power of 'cultural dislocation'.[77]

Poetry

MacD. P. JACKSON

ELIZABETH CAFFIN

Poetry: Beginnings to 1945

MacD. P. Jackson

Introduction: Words and the Inner and Outer Worlds

When Pope John Paul II visited New Zealand in 1986, Māori Catholics were hoping that he would announce the appointment of a Māori bishop. The organizers of the Māori welcome for the Pope searched for a lost eyeless tiki with which to express this hope. On the right-hand gatepost at the entrance to a temporary marae set up in the Auckland Domain had been painted six small crosses, representing the six New Zealand Catholic bishops, and in the middle of the crosses was to be placed the eyeless tiki — the tiki symbolizing the Māori people and its eyelessness indicating the deprived state of Māori Catholics, their need for a spiritual leader who would see the way forward, guide his people, provide direction.

The poet James K. Baxter told a similar anecdote — of how Tahupotiki Wiremu Ratana, visiting Michael Joseph Savage in 1935, set before the Prime Minister a kūmara, a gold watch, a greenstone tiki, and a huia feather through which to make a political point — to illustrate the essence of poetic thought and associate it with a 'broad symbolic' language natural to the indigenous people of this land.[1] And while Pākehā poets, unable in any case to proffer material objects directly, have seldom deployed their verbal symbols in quite such single-minded ways, they have usually subscribed to a view of poetry that sees it as presenting images in order to convey feelings and ideas. Descriptions of things, scenes, and happenings in the external world have traditionally served as vehicles for — or, at the very least, been intimately bound up with — thoughts, emotions, attitudes, intuitions, and moods.

But the relationships between outer and inner, between 'poetic image' and 'meaning', to use a crude but convenient shorthand, have changed, and the history of New Zealand verse is, among other things, the history of these changes. A simple comparison will illustrate the point. 'The first [New Zealand] poets who almost consistently wrote well were R.A.K. Mason . . . and . . . Ursula Bethell', according to Vincent O'Sullivan, in the introduction to his influential anthology.[2] Mason's 'Sonnet of Brotherhood' has been frequently anthologized and much discussed:

Garrisons pent up in a little fort
  with foes who do but wait on every side
  knowing the time soon comes when they shall ride
  triumphant over those trapped and make sport
  of them: when those within know very short
  is now their hour and no aid can betide:
  such men as these not quarrel and divide
  but friend and foe are friends in their hard sort

And if these things be so oh men then what
  of these beleaguered victims this our race
  betrayed alike by Fate's gigantic plot
  here in this far-pitched perilous hostile place
  this solitary hard-assaulted spot
  fixed at the friendless outer edge of space.

The relationship between image and idea is perfectly explicit. Mason's poem straightforwardly compares the human inhabitants of earth with a garrison living in a fort under siege. Men in the desperate situation of being besieged, knowing that they cannot hold out against the enemy much longer, that no relief is at hand and that therefore they have only a short time to live, are united by their common plight. They do not quarrel among themselves, even if some of them are not normally friends. There is a rough feeling of solidarity in the face of their hopeless situation, their certain impending doom. Human beings in general, the poem goes on to say, are in precisely this condition, all victims of Fate in a hostile universe. The earth is on the very fringes of space, threatened by nameless disasters. And, it is implied, we are all mortal, doomed to death: *vita nostra brevis est*. Then surely, urges Mason, men should, like the garrison in the little fort, feel a sense of brotherhood in their common predicament. The image of the besieged garrison is the essential vehicle for the poet's attitude to life and his Marxist call to comradeship.

The poem is typical of its period in drawing on feelings of isolation that affected many Pākehā New Zealand poets in the 1920s and 1930s, when the country itself still seemed remote and solitary and far from the European centres of civilization. And a certain colonial disillusion, a conviction of having been lured to a false paradise, may lie behind Mason's obsession with betrayal, as it emerges here in the line about Fate's conspiracy against us. The poem is typical, too, in its use of a regular metre and rhyme scheme, and, most significantly, in its movement from the particular to the general. It is, of course, a sonnet of the strict Italian form: it divides neatly into octave and sestet. The octave establishes the image of the besieged garrison; the sestet goes on to apply the emotions evoked by the image to 'mankind' in general. The movement is from the particular image to the wider meaning, and the connections are made deliberately and explicitly, the participial adjectives 'beleaguered', 'far-pitched', and 'hard-assaulted' in the sestet linking back to the octave's image of the garrison under siege.

'Sonnet of Brotherhood' is, then, very much a poem of the 1920s in the straightforward and logical way it develops its single image, in its use of a conventional form — and also in its consciously literary diction, in such phrases as 'no aid can betide', and its earnest tone. It is also of its time in being thoroughly male-oriented. It expresses Mason's sense of 'brotherhood', his sympathy for his fellow *men*, and so on. Although Mason is addressing the human race and intends 'oh men' generically, those of his own gender are pretty clearly foremost in his mind: the basic military image suggests a spirit of mateship that runs from Roman legionnaires to Anzacs on Gallipoli.

'The May Bride', by young poet and playwright Anthony McCarten, provides a sharp contrast. It was published in the *New Zealand Listener* in 1987:

Who has ever lost something in a May
  as cold
  as an egg is smooth as the head of a bald man
  contemplating lifting his 65 kilo bride over the threshold?

Or have you smelt your lover approaching
  and it's stronger
  than a muscle man is cold saying "I do" in church,
  and he is very cold, and bald?

I tell you, I have smelt mine going and it's very heavy
  and cold
  as May is to all heads that resemble eggs
  but it is pointless to pursue this.

However, I might as well,
  sensing a clarity smoother than you know what
  or a lost lover's indentation on a white pillow
  which is cold as a church in any month
  and, "You shouldn't carry all those indentations
  in the same basket," advises the wife of the man
  with the muscles over the garden fence.

Simply,
  the lifting of the 65 kilos
  went smoothly as an egg,
  and since those newly-weds moved in next door,
  and you've gone like May on a cross-town bus
  to an unheated church, I get about as much sleep
  as an indentation is bald.[3]

McCarten's poem, unrhymed and with no regular metre, has nothing of the clear logical argument of Mason's, nor the simple relationship between an image and what it stands for. Rather, it tosses up an assortment of images and adjectives and juggles them, catching them with a dazzling display of skill at the end. We have the repeated adjectives 'cold', 'smooth', and 'bald', and the idea of heaviness, and the egg which is smooth like a bald head, and the indentation of a head on a pillow, and the month of May, and the muscle man and his new bride, and the church, and the poem's 'I' and 'you', and all these are worked into various syntactical patterns in constantly surprising, unexpected, odd ways. Those key adjectives have slightly different meanings each time they recur. Instead of walking a straight line, this poem seems to keep side-stepping. It teases and delights. Though it is 'about' the loss of a lover, it is witty and amusing and playful. It is colloquial and idiomatic. There is a casual air to the way the sentences are formed. The poem is very self-conscious. It has half an eye on its own performance, as in the lines 'but it is pointless to pursue this. / However, I might as well, / sensing a clarity smoother than you know what' — and, yes, we do know what: an egg that is like a head that leaves its indentation on a pillow; and so the new wife next door can advise the speaker not to carry all her 'indentations' in the same basket. Reading the poem is like receiving a series of mild electric shocks to the imagination, just strong enough to tickle.

Yet it is a serious poem, from which a narrative can be inferred. The speaker has lost his (or her) lover at the same time that a pair of newly-weds has moved in next door, and the poem builds on a contrast between the two relationships (the new one more obviously conforming to the social proprieties and marked by counsels of prudence and compromise). 'May' is the right month for this combination of losing and winning, ending and beginning, arriving and departing: loaded, from its use in English verse, with associations of spring and romance and new growth, it denotes autumn here. Imported literary connotations are set against a local denotation.

McCarten's poem differs from Mason's in its relation to its readers. 'Sonnet of Brotherhood' is a cry to the world at large; urgent self-expression is turned into a plea to humankind. McCarten, with his interest-arousing question, begins as if wooing an audience at a poetry reading, and quickly assumes a certain intimacy with the 'you' to whom his words are addressed. McCarten encourages us to juggle with his words and images ourselves, to engage in a lively kind of mental activity. His poem retains a shifting, tantalizing, elusive quality. It seems fair to say that, like Mason's sonnet, it still uses images, scenarios, dramatized events to convey inner feelings, but the relationship between verbal images and whatever they may be supposed to evoke is much more problematical. Indeed, whereas Mason seems impelled by a 'message' that is largely apprehensible through other means to find a suitable image in which to embody, realize, or encode it, McCarten's play with words and images and associations seems partly, if not wholly, to create the poem's reality, to which something may or may not have in some way corresponded before the existence of the poem itself.

Contemporary New Zealand verse by women is mostly more apt to give the impression of having originated in a specific 'reality prior to the poem'. Christina Beer's 'Waiheke 1972 — Rocky Bay', for instance, which is reprinted in the 1985 *Penguin Book of New Zealand Verse*, traces a single narrative line, telling us about something that happened to her.[4] Like 'The May Bride' it reflects a general movement in New Zealand verse away from rhyme and metre. The lines, varying from one to eleven words in length, appear to have been dropped onto the page — to the point where we feel an urge to push them around so that they are symmetrical on a vertical axis:

> i came
> heavy with child in the fierce sun
>   the house was a dull yellow
>   lying
>   below the road

The speaker when pregnant went to live alone in a house in Rocky Bay, Waiheke Island (in Auckland's Hauraki Gulf); her child was born but later died. The poem is full of the pain of this tragedy, but mentions it only in the spare line 'when he died'. The central experience that the poem is about is indicated just in that understated phrase. But it colours everything the poet describes as leading up to and following it. The details she records and the words she uses to record them are governed partly by her physical and emotional state while pregnant and the sense of foreboding that she had before her child's birth, and partly by hindsight. Here too, there is a repetition of key adjectives: the speaker was 'heavy with child' and came to a 'heavy house' where the bodies of cicadas were glued to the walls as if 'heavy' and the 'heavy' pods of the nikaus crash to the ground in the heat. Rats with shining eyes skim up trees. The atmosphere is oppressive, stifling, menacing. The baby is enclosed within her and she too feels trapped. And the images suggest fullness (the nikau pods) and emptiness (the clothes on the line). The details of the house, with its wire gate, chimney rising into the sky, and swaying wooden cross (which is presumably part of the clothes line, or the power pole or aerial) are in retrospect ominous, with suggestions of graveyards and crematoria and concentration camps. After the baby escapes, first from the womb and then from life, the speaker walks:

> down a long dusty road
>   at the end
>   was a shop
>   a telephone box
> and a little crushed beach
>   where the sea ran
>   in and out

That is a fair description of the real Rocky Bay, but at the same time the 'little crushed beach' is an apt correlative for the speaker's sense of herself: she feels crushed, inanimate, a mere thing to which a natural process has happened. The sea runs in and out as analogue to the poem's human comings and goings, and to the flow and ebb of the poet's own emotions. In form, Beer's poem is very different from Mason's, and the relation between images and feelings is less overt and direct, but it still conforms to a concept of poetry indicated in, for example, American poet Richard Wilbur's declaration: 'I like it when the ideas [or emotions] of a poem seem to be necessary aspects of the things or actions which it presents — stretching away and yet always adhering, like shadows'. The notion is an old one: poetry, wrote Wei T'ai, a critic of the Sung Dynasty, 'presents the thing in order to convey the feeling'; if it is 'precise about the thing and reticent about the feeling . . . the mind responds' and the poetry 'enters deeply into us'.[5]

Comparison between Mason's poem and the two more recent ones reveals chiefly a kind of development that might be found in poetry in English anywhere. But shifts in the relations between words evoking 'the external world' and words evoking 'the internal world' of states of mind — or between 'image' and 'feeling' or 'idea' — are inevitably bound up with phases in the assimilation of specifically New Zealand phenomena into our verse. In considering its history we will often be concerned with changing models of what constitutes a poem, where these models have originated, and how they have been developed locally by individuals and by groups. But a history of New Zealand verse will bear witness also to changes in the wider social and political context; a national poetic tradition evolves as the country itself evolves. Nothing in McCarten's poem brands it as 'made in New Zealand'. Mason's is perhaps shaped by an antipodean alienation. Beer's describes a place one can photograph, and it refers to the native nikau palm as familiar to her readers. More significantly, no New Zealand poet in the 1920s would have thought of writing a poem about being pregnant and losing the child. McCarten's poem is at a greater distance from Mason's in its manner (though Mason anticipated McCarten's 'hanging indent'), Beer's in its matter.

Social, intellectual, and political pressures within a particular time and place affect the language itself, and there is a sense in which 'The real history of poetry is . . . the history of the changes in the kind of language in which successive poems have been written.' Adapting this idea to the special problems of a literature with colonial origins, Ian Wedde has, in his introduction to *The Penguin Book of New Zealand Verse* (1985), made an ingenious attempt to subsume a variety of changes under a single rubric, arguing that 'the development of poetry in English in New Zealand is coeval with the developing growth of the language into its location, to the point where English as an international language can be felt to be original *where it is*': that the drift has been from the 'hieratic' towards the 'demotic', so that local culture has become 'internally familiar rather than willed'.[6]

'To introduce the language to the landscape' — not merely to a new geographical environment but to new lineaments of experience within it — was part of the New Zealand poet's task as Allen Curnow formulated it. But in focusing his own lively discussion of New Zealand poetry on changes in the 'language', Wedde tends to muddle at least three separate senses of the word: (a) English as distinct from French, Swahili, or Chinese; (b) New Zealand English; and (c) the way poets, as groups or individuals, use these. There have been changes at each level. Most of the time, Wedde implies the primacy of changes in (b), but these have been largely dependent on changes in (a), and the really important ones are those in (c). When Wordsworth, in pursuit of rustic plainness, proposed to replace a gaudily 'hieratic' Augustan poetic diction with a 'demotic' 'selection of the language of men', Coleridge demonstrated at some length how crucial was that word 'selection'. As he said, 'Every man's language has, first, its individualities; secondly, the common properties of the class to which he belongs; and thirdly, words and phrases of *universal* use'[7] — these three categories needing only slight adjustment to correspond, in inverse order, to mine. It is the way poets select from the global or national linguistic resources that most matters. The hailstorm of upper case ampersands that spattered the pages of *The Young New Zealand Poets* in 1973 — there had been none in Allen Curnow's *Penguin Book of New Zealand Verse* of 1960 — had next to nothing to do with any such impersonal process as could be described as 'the growth of language into its location', and almost everything to do with the productive influence of certain Americans. Of course one reason why New Zealand poets were attracted to these models was that the American modes of expression suited their own sensibilities and situations, just as Frank Sargeson had decided in the 1930s that a prose style indebted to Mark Twain, Sherwood Anderson, and Henry Lawson best conveyed his own sense of New Zealand life. Also, New Zealand English as a variety of the global language has acquired a significant American component, since it too is a product of selection, a distinctive blend from the international stock, with a few peculiarities thrown in; and we all use it in our own ways.

Wedde's all-inclusive generalization may, however, be broken down into limited and specific truths. It is true that poetry here, as elsewhere, has become less grandiloquent and more colloquial and easy-going, increasingly wary of anything that Ezra Pound might have mocked as 'sonorous — like the farting of a goose'. This change occurs in poets as different as James K. Baxter and Allen Curnow: from Curnow's 'paying / Out into our time's wave / The stain of blood that writes an island story' to 'That / will be all, I suppose'; or from Baxter's 'preaching the truth of winter / To the fallen heart that does not cease to fall' to ' "You bugger off", he tells me, / "Your Christianity won't put an end to death".' It is true that the cabbage tree that for Alfred Domett in 1872 was a 'strange asphodel' with bloom like 'sea-washed madrepore' could be calmly contrasted with rimu and kauri by Denis Glover in full confidence that his readers in the 1940s would respond to the connotations:

These songs will not stand —
The wind and the sand will smother.

Not I but another
Will make songs worth the bother:
   The rimu or kauri he,
   I'm but the cabbage tree,
     Sings Harry to an old guitar.[8]

From being an item of South Seas exotica to decorate Domett's 500-page epic, 'a pressed leaf in a visitor's collection', the cabbage tree has become a vital image, essential to Glover's poem's effect. It recurs often enough in later verse, notably on the last page of Leigh Davis's *Willy's Gazette*, where 'the cabbage tree claps / its swords over the setting sun'. The fact that here it is in the company of an 'armature', a 'daisywheel', and a 'liner' that is both part of an electric typewriter and an ocean-going ship is some measure of the distance New Zealand verse has travelled from Glover's simple lyricism. In Bob Orr's 'Cabbage Tree . . . Three Lamps', the native plant, growing 'between the pub & the police station / in Ponsonby', has been thoroughly urbanized: 'Above an asphalt yard / by the drive in bottle store / it sways above the beer crate stacks', to the sound of 'race results', and 'the blues / of Sonny Day'.[9]

Several other small truths huddle under the 'language into location . . . hieratic becomes demotic' umbrella. It is true that once New Zealand experience has worked its way into the vernacular (so to speak), the meeting of language and experience in a poem may be a less strenuously conscious business; that Vincent O'Sullivan's ear for crude male kiwi dialogue, evident in his play *Shuriken*, also serves him well in his 'Butcher' poems; that, like Ben Jonson before them, Baxter (in his 'Pyrrha' sequence) and C.K. Stead (in 'The Clodian Songbook') filter Catullus through sensibilities and modes of saying that are recognizably of their own time and place; that the poets whose first volumes appeared around 1970 were interested in a 'demotic' pop culture: rock music, movies, comics, TV; and that no New Zealand poet of the 1930s, for example, would have ended a poem (as Wedde does) with the maxim that 'living in the / universe doesn't / leave you / any place to chuck / stuff off / of'. It is true, too, that our state of mind in relation to our country can be reflected in linguistic choices, as Maurice Gee illustrates in Plumb's comment on his wife: 'I walked along by the creek or stream — Edie in the Englishness imposed on her by her mother would have it stream, would have the paddock field, would even have the ti-tree picnic hut Robert built on the lawn a summer-house. She never adjusted to colonial ways.'[10]

In amplifying his theme of the adaptation of poetic language to a new environment, Wedde concentrates on Hubert Church, Charles Brasch, and David Eggleton, as representatives of the early, transitional, and contemporary phases of twentieth century New Zealand verse. Church's late-Romantic 'hieratic' language utterly fails to engage with its local subject matter. Brasch in *The Estate* uses 'a more demotic Wordsworthian thought-language' to express his Eurocentric alienation in a poetry vitiated by a 'willed relationship of his art to its situation'. In David Eggleton's 'Painting Mount Taranaki', coming at 'a more integrated stage' in our literature, we reach at last 'a sense of consummation in location': the language is 'a confident . . . blend of vernacular, lyric, and "high demotic" ', and 'the poem immerses us in its process . . . . It is inside its history.' Other poets are implicitly valued for their 'demotic' elements and downgraded for their 'hieratic': the good bits are ironic, laconic, satiric, austere, blunt, curt, humorous, self-parodying, and are associated with confidence, freedom from anxiety, and a sense of natural relation and integration; the bad bits are literary, exhibit will-to-language and will-to-location, and are associated with insecurity. Although Wedde repudiates any glib notions of progress, his theory about the development of New Zealand poetry, and his critical vocabulary, are loaded against some of the country's finest poetic achievements.

But the advance from Hubert Church to Charles Brasch and his contemporaries does involve an improvement in poetic quality. Church was a poetaster, tippling on Tennyson. It is not just that his language is unsuited to a colonial subject-matter: it is not suited to anything, except mellifluous jabberwocky. Most nineteenth century New Zealand poets had not only brought with them moribund Victorian poetic modes and disabling conceptions of the poet's role as comforter, moralist, or dreamer, but also lacked talent, like their long-forgotten fellow versifiers back in England. But from the 1920s and 1930s onwards, the development of New Zealand poetry was not a matter of improvement, but of diversification — partly in response to modernism, and later to the various post-modernist movements which originated mainly in the United States. We need to register these shifts in poetics, but we also need to recognize the real achievements within them. Brasch was no less a New Zealander for having a patrician voice and a head full of the high arts — not only European but Chinese, Australian, Indian, Russian, Japanese, Egyptian, American, and African. And the countryside about Dunedin was among his 'internal familiarities': as he wrote in his autobiography, *Indirections*, it became 'an interior landscape of my mind or imagination . . . . The shapes, textures, scents, sounds . . . grew into me and grew with me';[11] and the poetry bears the evidence. Possibly there is about 'Painting Mount Taranaki' something more 'secure' and 'natural', less 'anxious' and 'willed' than about Brasch's 'Thurlby Domain' poems, for example. But unease is not a bad thing in a writer, and Brasch's language expresses — or, if you like, creates — his sense of life in relation to a place, no less adequately than Eggleton's.

Whether New Zealand poetry — poetry written by poets who have spent significant periods of their working lives within this country — is in some way 'distinctive' is not a question that need much trouble us. 'Like any other craftsman, a poet likes to work with materials that lie to hand',[12] and for a New Zealander these will inevitably include local flora, fauna, scenes, institutions, people, events, myths, practices, and habits of mind, along with much that is available to poets everywhere. And the peculiarities of New Zealand English and of New Zealand speech — with its 'accent' akin to but distinguishable from the Australian — doubtless influence the verse in scarcely definable ways.

In any case a poetic tradition can perhaps be said to have reached a degree of maturity when texts begin to respond to their predecessors. Among the best first volumes published by any New Zealand poet in recent years is Anne French's *All Cretans are Liars* (1987), which includes a poem called 'Eucalypts Greenlane'. As a sonnet it takes its place within a long English and European verse tradition. But for a New Zealander it is not just a sonnet, but a 'Baxterian' sonnet, since it consists of fourteen unrhymed, irregular, paired lines such as James K. Baxter used for his superb *Jerusalem Sonnets*, and which C.K. Stead (in

Twenty-One Sonnets) and other New Zealand poets have since imitated. French's poem, which sets up a resonant metaphorical association between the felling of some gum trees and the miscarriage of a human foetus, self-consciously quotes, as part of its overall strategy and to striking effect, snippets from well-known New Zealand anthology pieces by Allen Curnow and Ian Wedde, and ends with an allusion to a more recent Curnow poem in which death is linked to a descent 'into the surge-black fissure' of a rock formation at Auckland's west coast beach, Karekare (where Curnow is known to have a bach), and with a tribute to Curnow, foremost living New Zealand poet, as 'il migliore fabbro', echoing T.S. Eliot's dedication to Ezra Pound of the key poetic text of twentieth century modernism, 'The Waste Land'. Eucalyptus trees had in fact been felled in Auckland's Greenlane when French wrote her poem. The sonnet is specific and detailed in its referents on each side of the metaphorical equation. It is a powerful and moving poem, and its 'literariness' within both a national and an international tradition is a significant source of its power.

Victorianism Down Under: Nineteenth Century New Zealand Verse

'Eucalypts Greenlane' achieves satisfactory interrelationships between poet, readers, their common language, and a shared literary tradition, and between words signifying material realities and words conveying emotions. In nineteenth century New Zealand poetry such co-operation is hardly ever attained. 'There are few literary occupations more depressing, and less rewarding, than the study of New Zealand verse before 1890', as an earlier investigator lamented.[13] Nor is there much in the way of 'development' to be charted. But a great deal of solemn endeavour yielded a few poems of interest, and at the very turn of the century two poets appeared who can still, in parts, be read with pleasure and admiration today: Arthur H. Adams and Blanche Baughan.

It is often easy enough to guess what nineteenth century British poets their New Zealand imitators have been reading. Charles C. Bowen, impressed by *The Rime of the Ancient Mariner*, writes 'The Spectre Ship':

> I could not speak. I could not think.
>   No power was in me then.
> I seemed to slide adown the cliff
>   To join those strange seamen.
>
> .   .   .   .
>
> He raised his hand; the tall masts bent;
>   The white sails bellied free;
> I felt no wind, I heard no sound,
>   As we glided o'er the sea.

Frederick Napier Broome betrays his intoxication with Swinburne in 'Cleopatra: A Fragment':

> Seen of the sun in the south, languid for love of the shade,
> Queen! from the mint of thy mouth coin of kisses for kings there was made;
> Sharp-struck, clean cut from the press; and stamped with a tone
> Harp-like, and keen to excess, didst thou give of thine own.

The early spiritual life of the young hero of Alfred Domett's *Ranolf and Amohia* is described in distinctly Wordsworthian strains:

> Such sights and sounds inspired the growing Boy
> With wondering exultation; and the joy
> Of deeper thought and loftier feeling lent
> To the mere gladness of temperament.

Dunedin poets looked back to the last decades of the eighteenth century, and the revered Robbie Burns. Here is John Barr of Craigilee in 'My Ain Dearie':

> It's ower yonder hill, and it's through yonder glen,
>   Whaur the burn rins doun sae clearly,
> When the moon shines sae bricht, and the stars gie their licht,
>   I'll gang then and see my ain dearie.

Otago's womenfolk turned to the same model, as Marie R. Randle makes plain in 'Herdin' the Kye':

> The wild snaw-clouds were driftin'
>   Athwart the wintry sky,
> As thro' the gusty gloamin'
>   I went to herd the kye.
> I row'd my plaidie roun' me,
>   An' shiver'd in the blast;
> When o'er the knowe cam' Jamie,
>   An' clasp'd me close an' fast!

Jessie Mackay attempts Kiplingesque verses on the death of Gordon:

> Come quickly or we perish! Death is on every side;
> Ever the strong men fall, and floweth the crimson tide.
> The Mahdi strikes without with his dusky myriads strong;
> And the cry goes up from the city, 'How long, O Lord, how long?'

D.H. Rogers seems to have the refrain of Kipling's 'Tommy' ('Then it's Tommy this, an' Tommy that, an' "Tommy, 'ow's yer soul?"') ringing in his ears as he composes words for sailor Johnnie in 'Homeward Bound':

> Then it's Johnnie heave an' start her, then it's Johnnie roll and go;
> When the mates have picked the watches, there is little rest for Jack.
> But we'll raise the good old chanty that the Homeward bounders know,
> For the girls have got the tow-rope, an' they're hauling in the slack.

The one American poet to whom nineteenth century New Zealand versifiers frequently turned was Longfellow — especially when bent on immortalizing their local Hiawathas and Minnehahas, as was Joseph Earle Ollivant in one of innumerable accounts of *Hine Moa, the Maori Maiden*; the legend is 'sung by an ancient Maori' enamoured of the white man's trochaic tetrameters:

> Trees that shed the sere and faded
> Leaf in winter plants the stranger,
> But the ruthless strokes of hatchet
> Ring along the tracks entangled
> Of the forest hoar, primeval.

In all these cases indebtedness is obvious enough.[14] More common is verse that, while manifestly 'Victorian', is written in a kind of poetic *lingua franca* of the period. And Cowper's *The Task*, Gray's *Elegy*, and Thomson's *The Seasons* are among eighteenth century English poems that echoed in the heads of local practitioners.

'The Victorian age is the great age of fiction in English poetry': dramatic monologue and verse narrative served Browning, Tennyson, and their followers as vehicles for the expression of complex and often contradictory responses to the religious, political, psychological, and social tensions of the century. The richest poetic exploration of religious doubt is arguably not *In Memoriam*, in which Tennyson agonizes directly over his spiritual dilemmas, but Matthew Arnold's *Balder Dead*, 'where the distancing power of the Nordic myth . . . enables Arnold both to release and to control his deepest feelings about the Death of God'.[15] Anger, pessimism, aggression, bitterness, jealousy, despair — all those darker emotions that the ego repressed — found their poetic outlet through story-telling and the construction of imaginary characters and their monologues.

Until the end of the nineteenth century, New Zealand poets did not work these rich veins of the Victorian tradition, except by way of the many inept versifications of Māori mythology that drew on a superficial fascination with the picturesque and exotic without tapping any deeper creative sources. Nor were New Zealanders much given to the nonsense verse that is among the most original and imaginative of Victorian contributions to English poetry. Most of the 'hieratical' New Zealand poems of the period are lyrical or meditative, while the 'demotic' folk poetry consisted mainly of simple, rollicking, jocular commentary on topical issues and pioneer pursuits.

John Liddell Kelly's *Heather and Fern: Songs of Scotland and Maoriland* (1902) is representative of dozens of volumes published up until that time. Kelly includes a contents list that classifies his poems according to a system that any taxonomist of nineteenth century New Zealand verse as a whole could readily apply. There are Historical and Descriptive Poems, such as 'Tarawera; or, The Curse of Tuhotu' and an 'Apostrophe to Auckland' (from 'Zealandia's Jubilee') that begins:

> Auckland! Queen City of the Austral Seas,
>   Seated majestic on thy hundred hills,
>   Soothed by the murmurings of hidden rills,
> And songs of birds embow'red amid the trees

(Most poets had an incurable itch to confer instant dignity on their raw new towns.) There are Poems of Purpose, Philosophy, and Religion, with titles like 'A Dream of Perfect Beauty', 'Birth and Death', 'Nirvana', 'The Making of God', 'The Poet's Creed', and 'The Voice of Nature'; Poems for Special Occasions, such as 'Queen Victoria's Jubilee', 'St. Patrick's Day in Auckland', or 'Ode for the Centenary of the Death of Burns'; Songs on 'A Modest Little Maiden', 'Lost Love', or 'The Phantom Canoe'; Quatrains on 'Labour', 'Life', 'The Christian's Answer', or 'The New Woman'; Humorous and Satirical Poems called 'A Spiritualistic Seance', 'Marry or Burn', 'The Platypus', 'To Father Christmas', and the like; Poems of the Fancy and Imagination, such as 'Blackbirds at Caldervale', 'Dreams', and 'The Taniwha'; a single entry under Ballad, namely 'The Ballad of Ellinor'; Songs and Poems of Love, such as 'Hymn to Eros' and 'Love, the Conqueror'; Poems in Dialect, such as 'Barney Flynn at the Burns Club' and 'The Bonnie Braes o' Blantyre'; Odes on such topics as 'The Coronation of Edward VII'; and Sonnets, including 'In Maoriland', 'Renunciation', and — the obligatory excursion into the self-referential — 'Sonnets to a Sonneteer'. Several poems are categorized under more than one head. The whole volume is the epitome of local Victorianism in verse.

Kelly was represented by four pieces in the first national anthology, *New Zealand Verse*, intelligently edited and introduced by the youthful W.F. Alexander and A.E. Currie in 1906, when the colony's total population had barely reached 900,000. Although, like subsequent New Zealand anthologies, it is biased towards more recent work, this volume gives a fair picture of the country's poetic achievement over the previous seventy years. But New Zealand verse that 'comes well up to the level of modern minor poetry' written elsewhere, can make few claims on our attention now. As Alexander and Currie remark, 'the poetical element that a new land contains must always at first be small and of little power'. Migration and the setting up of a home at the other end of the world exhausted the creative impulse. 'In the generation of the pioneers that is passing away . . . men's energies were set too sternly to battle with the material facts of life to leave them time for cultivating its graces', while the second generation had 'still before it the task of establishing the nation whose foundations were set by our fathers' and was therefore also preoccupied with practical things: 'the columns must be set up before we turn to moulding the entablature'.[16]

The point is not so much that settlers were too busy wielding axe, grubhoe, saw, hammer, and spade to be bothered writing verse — Alexander and Currie draw on the work of fifty-five poets, while ignoring at least as many more — as that what Northrop Frye, in an outline of the history of Canadian poetry, calls a 'garrison mentality', which develops when people think of themselves as pitted against a raw and hostile environment, fosters a 'sub-literary rhetoric' bolstering shared moral and social values, discouraging any attempt to create 'a disinterested structure of words'. As Frye puts it, 'A rhetorician practising poetry is apt to express himself in spectral arguments, generalizations that escape the feeling of possible refutation only by being vast enough to contain it, or vaporous enough to elude it.'[17]

And Victorian poetry was in any case prone to such vices, too often being a result of 'thinking aloud, instead of making something', in Matthew Arnold's phrase. The New Zealand poetaster's 'thinking' was invariably commonplace. Reflex homage to the Beauty and Grandeur of Nature and pious musing about God, the Great Creator ('Wisdom's Great Dictator'), sentimentality, didacticism, pomposity, melodrama, vagueness — these are the hallmarks of the bulk of nineteenth century New Zealand verse. The spirits of Felicia Hemans and Martin Tupper haunted the antipodean air. To sit down to write a poem was, if one's pretensions went beyond those of the popular semi-humorous entertainer, to adopt a devotional frame of mind and produce familiar abstractions. Jessie Mackay praised Longfellow because 'his soul was ever straining up / Towards the noble, infinite, sublime', and she and too many of her fellows were apt, shunning observation and description of the particulars of their colonial environment, to indulge in what T.E. Hulme once called 'the sentimental escape to the infinite'. For critic David Will. M. Burn, writing in *The Monthly Review* in 1890, the function of the true bard was 'to sing . . . of what he sees when gazing awestruck into the deep chasmic secret of the Universe — gazing with those keen, stilly-glowing eyes of his that must see more than ours'. Less ambitious seers were enjoined to express the 'dumb emotion' of common humanity 'thrilled intensely in the presence of life's mystery' and 'entranced by the external beauty of the Universe'.[18] It was seldom effective poetry that emerged from pursuit of such lofty goals.

Poetry is made not with ideas but with words, as Algerian poet Ibn Khaldun asserted five hundred years before Mallarmé. But the words must be made to work hard. F.W. Bateson has argued that Victorian English was characterized by a diffuseness 'ultimately derived from a loosening of the connection between the connotations and the denotations of words'. In such a linguistic milieu, the natural hazard for a poet is prolixity. By way of illustration, Bateson notes that whereas William Cory's 'Heraclitus' expands a literal translation of the original Greek to twice the length, a modern poet's treatment of another epigram from the *Greek Anthology* contains about the same number of words as a straightforward English prose version. Much nineteenth century New

Zealand verse is marked by just this diffuseness and verbosity. Alfred Domett, said Tennyson, 'want[ed] but limitation to be a very considerable poet'. And the much more talented Blanche Baughan justly resolved in a private letter: 'I really must try to boil myself down.'[19]

Domett's prolixity might be illustrated in the same way as Bateson illustrates Cory's. Several sections of his 'South-Sea Day-Dream' are based on Sir George Grey's *Polynesian Mythology*. For example, four simple and effective sentences (amounting to just over one hundred words altogether) in Grey's English account of the legend of Tawhaki are expanded by Domett into seventeen rhymed trochaic octameters totalling nearly 200 words — and Domett's words are of a greater average length than Grey's — like this:

> Through the darksome Mansion — through and through those Sons of Darkness
> streaming
> Flash the spear-flights of the Day-God — deadly-silent — golden-gleaming!
> Down they go, the Pona-turi! vain their struggles, yells and fury![20]

Is it Edgar Allan Poe's 'The Raven' that echoes in these lines? Elsewhere in *Ranolf and Amohia*, Grey's 'So she sat down upon the ground to rest; and then soft measures reached her from the horn of Tutanekai, and the young and beautiful chieftainess felt as if an earthquake shook her to make her go to the beloved of her heart' is Domett's pretext for an epic simile that begins:

> As through the land when some dread Earthquake thrills,
> Shaking the hidden bases of the hills;
> Their grating adamantine depths, beneath
> The ponderous, unimaginable strain and stress,
> Groan shuddering as in pangs of world-wide death

and carries on with a further two dozen lines of seismological magniloquence before arriving at 'Even such a trouble smote in that wild hour / Our Maiden'.[21]

Whatever their weaknesses, New Zealand Victorians anthologized by Alexander and Currie could at least handle rhyme and metre. Iambics, trochaics, and trisyllabic feet; short lines, tetrameters, pentameters, alexandrines, the largely dactylic hexameters of Clough or of Longfellow's *Evangeline*, the fourteeners of Morris's *Sigurd the Volsung*, and the trochaic fifteeners of Tennyson's *Locksley Hall*; blank verse or rhymed stanzas of almost every kind; the sonnet, the roundel — local poets knew their nineteenth century prosody. To tell 'The Legend of Papa and Rangi', Domett even resorted to rhymed couplets with twenty-five syllables to the line! Alexander and Currie noted that in adopting 'the common narrative metres' for their recountings of Māori myths, poets had 'been unable to dissipate a certain incongruous English atmosphere that clings to the very movement of the lines'.[22]

The poems in *New Zealand Verse* are loosely arranged, not chronologically or by author, but according to theme and type. The volume begins with William Pember Reeves's 'New Zealand' — one of dozens of nineteenth century poems with this title — and follows with several pieces on emigration, exile, the colonial experience. There are descriptions of 'Maoriland' tourist spots, including Domett's attempt at a verbal equivalent of painter John Clark Hoyte's many pictures of the Pink and White Terraces, with Lake Rotomahana and Mount Tarawera; poets were as fond as the painters of this scenic wonder. Reeves's 'The Passing of the Forest', a lament for 'beauty swept away', is accompanied by Dora Wilcox's 'The Last of the Forest', a requiem for 'old worlds passing by'. There are poems on seasons and times of day ('A Winter Daybreak', 'In the Moonlight'), on life in the backblocks, on the sea, on New Zealand towns and places ('Picton Harbour by Night'), on birds (including three on the bellbird or makomako, the local stand-in for the Keatsian nightingale), on Māori themes, and on pre-Raphaelite ladies such as 'Maisrie' and 'Rosalind'; there are love songs and lullabies and dirges and sonnets, celebrations of Art and Beauty, some Hellenistic verses ('Pan', 'Ariadne Forsaken'), and several religious and philosophical musings. Some of the poems on specifically New Zealand themes have been reprinted by later anthologists, but others, to which we shall return, also deserve salvaging.

Much that is most distinctive in nineteenth century New Zealand verse coheres around ideas of 'absence' and 'difference'. The editor of a recent *Everyman's Book of Victorian Verse* notes that 'Victorian poets are often concerned with loss, the loss of loved ones, of loved places, of youth, of a belief in God', and especially singles out 'exploration of sadness at leaving a much-loved place' as 'a common feature of Victorian verse'. How much stronger must be this sense of loss when 'England, life and art' are exchanged for 'lonely islands' in an antipodean sea as 'shipless' as they are 'empty'! From the anonymous ballad in which 'David Lowston' laments the fate of a whaling crew marooned on a desolate island off the West Coast in 1810, to poems written well into the twentieth century, New Zealand is defined in terms of absence, of what it lacks. At its most maudlin, this theme becomes pure nostalgia for an English home fabricated out of cosy childhood memories of robins, village greens, rose gardens, and white Christmases, or a 'guid auld' Scottish 'hame' where 'the blue heather-bells bloom'd bonnilie'. The obverse to this poetic coinage was strained praise of a rugged new land, purified by 'winds of the masterless deep', and emphasis on the 'bright golden promise' of future greatness; or the satisfactions of honest toil within 'garrison' communities were simple-mindedly celebrated.[23]

As late as 1903, Mary Sinclair's *"Tena Koe"* was still harping on these themes, though the poems, dedicated to the Countess of Ranfurly, who had encouraged her, were 'written at intervals during more than half a century of a very trying life'. 'The Jubilee of New Zealand' (1890) calls on her 'fellow-countrymen' to 'sing the charms of this fair land, / So richly dowered by Nature's hand'. She proclaims 'The Dignity of Labour' and in 'The Daughters of the Empire' numbers herself among 'True scions of the grand old stock that made our Empire great'. But in 'The Homeland' she fondly recalls 'the land of the rocks and the heather, / The Northern Lights and the snow'.

Consciousness of 'difference' expressed itself largely as tourist's-eye description of an exotic scenic wonderland, in which kiwi ('strange brown-speckled would-be beast'), rātā, supplejack, Mount Cook, the Bowen Falls at Milford Sounds, geysers, glaciers, and the Māori are indiscriminately picturesque. Such attitudes are captured in the very titles that poets gave their books: Thomas Bracken's *Lays of the Land of the Maori and Moa* (1884), or *The Huia's Homeland and Other Verses* (1897) by 'Roslyn' (Margaret A. Sinclair). Often enough the effect is like that of the letters home of a teenage overseas traveller. But nineteenth century New Zealand poets were seldom sure where to locate their audience, even in the mid-1880s, by which time more than half the population was New Zealand-born. And if Victorian poetry generally suffered from 'a loosening of the connection between the connotations and the denotations of words', transportation of the language to the other side of the world exacerbated the malady: simple words such as 'spring', 'farm', and 'bush' had changed their denotations, while their connotations 'remained stubbornly rooted in centuries of English rural life'.[24]

Most of these points may be illustrated by Bracken's 'April Here and April There', which begins:

Through the realms of coral fairies,
  Down the ocean's sloping sides,
O'er the sea-god's swelling prairies
  There are lands where Spring abides,
    Linnets singing,
    Blue-bells springing,
Fragrance melting on the air;
    Friendly meetings,
    Kindly greetings —
April here, and April there.

April here is robed in shadows,
  Heralds of impending gloom;
April there sheds o'er the meadows
  Yellow, white, and purple bloom.
    Here, clouds flying,
    Nature sighing,
On her brow a shade of care;
    Wintry traces,
    Dreary places —
April here and April there.[25]

The contrast is elaborated over three more stanzas. Although Bracken is 'here', his muse is of the other hemisphere. It furnishes him with a wealth of poetic counters for spring in England, but has no such stock for autumn in New Zealand. Consequently, Bracken can particularize 'April there' in terms of linnets, bluebells, fragrance, blooms, larks, doves, daisies, cowslips, holly, ivy, warm showers, budding roses, lilacs, and lilies, while 'April here' is evoked only by shadows, clouds, gales over 'yon flax-clad mountain', rain flooding the rivers, reeds that 'rave', and breakers — none of which are peculiar to the month or the season. And it is to the English spring that Bracken's floating poetical sentiments attach themselves: 'friendly meetings', 'kindly greetings', 'old age talking', 'lovers walking', roses giving 'Thanks to Him who gave them birth'; 'Nature sighing' careworn and dreary is his one conventional poeticism for 'April here'. Of course Bracken's fellow settlers, young and old, were perfectly able to walk, talk, meet, and greet one another in their new country. But his poem registers a vague sense of emptiness — the loss of a mellow community, established social niceties, a serviceable language. He cheers himself up in the end with the prophecy that a familiar spring will eventually brighten New Zealand, and that in any case Heaven can be relied on somehow to make good the privations of a colonial existence:

> But we'll have a season here, too,
>   Borne on Earth's prolific breast —
> Effusive, beautiful, and clear, too,
>   As reigns now where our fathers rest.
>   Darkest sorrow
>   Hope should borrow —
> Winter should not bring despair;
>   Spring will follow,
>   Grief is hollow —
> Look up! the brightest April's there.

From William Golder to Blanche Baughan

William Golder (1810–1876) acknowledged outright that he hoped to extract 'some of the sweets which lie hid among the asperities of colonial life' and 'to endear our adopted country the more to the bosom of the *bona fide* settler'. He thought that a literature would make New Zealanders 'more connected as a people in the eyes of others'.[26] He had immigrated from Scotland in 1839. His *New Zealand Minstrelsy* (1852), 'the first book of verse published in New Zealand', was followed by *The Pigeon's Parliament* (1854), a crude but vigorous bit of topical and satirical balladry, *The New Zealand Survey* (1868), conceived when the author was 'assisting in the survey of the Mungaroa Swamp', and *The Philosophy of Love* (1871).

Golder writes conventional appreciations of the country's 'lofty ridges covered with evergreen forests, and its deep ravines from which issue many purling brooks', but the 'awe' chiefly inspired in him by all this pristine grandeur is that which comes from contemplating 'the amount of labour required before such can be subdued'.[27] A pragmatist, for whom the Māori is another obstacle to be cleared if 'British power' is to act as 'Heaven's messenger, diffusing peace, / And op'ning up new fields of outlet, where / Britannia's enterprising sons might come', he looks forward to the time when 'hills / And plains . . . shall be parcelled out / To active owners', and 'flocks and herds / Shall wake the dull air with their living sound'. Towns and hamlets marked by church spires populate his vision. Meanwhile, since 'where a clearing's formed, / A good beginning's seen', he encourages 'the *bona fide* settler':

> Come to the bush, my boys,
> Where Fortune's way's before ye;
> Leave the city's idle joys,
> And follow fame and glory

and in 'The Plough' (to be sung to the tune of 'Buy a Broom') he celebrates the rewards of physical work:

> How hard, in the outset, to clear off a forest,
>   With back often aching, and sweat bedewed brow;
> Such labours got over, I now can discover
>   How pleasing indeed 'tis to follow the plough.

So may the 'great monotony of scene' be enlivened and the 'desert . . . gladden'd'.

While resident in New Zealand, Golder never travelled more than sixty miles from Wellington. Another Scot, John Barr (1808–1889), who arrived in Otago in 1852, was even more firmly based within his provincial community. Written mainly in 'hamely Scottish jingle', his *Poems and Songs, Descriptive and Satirical* (1861), though published in Edinburgh, was sponsored by Dunedin settlers; a second edition was launched at a public benefit organized by the Caledonian Society of Otago and various local dignitaries. His favourite subjects are courtship and marriage, but he covers a fair range in versifying a comedy of manners. He is at his liveliest in such pieces as 'Rise Oot Your Bed', which dramatizes some humorous *badinage* between a 'worthless wretch' with a hangover and his nagging wife, or the ironic monologue 'Noo, Jock, My Man, Sit Doun by Me', in which a woman advising her son on the kind of girl he should marry exposes her own philistinism, or 'Crack Between Mrs Scandal and Mrs Envy', in which the two women trade gossip, or 'The Beagles They Came Round About' with its proletarian scorn of the tax-gathering and governing classes:

> O shame upon the lazy drone,
>   When days are warm and sunny O;
> When others strive to stock the hive,
>   They only lick the honey O.

For Barr, as for Burns, 'a man's a man for a' that'. In Otago 'The sluggard or the exquisite / Is but a noxious weed', but 'honest men soon stand upright / That bowed down have been'. Barr registers his environment as social setting and workplace, not as landscape; indigenous plants are little more than impediments to his spade:

> For either I'm mawin', or thrashin', or sawin',
>   Or grubbin' the hills wi' the ferns covered fairly.
> Grub away, tug away, toil till you're weary,
>   Haul oot the toot roots and everything near ye.

The rough struggles of pioneering life are caught in such rhythms and diction.

In the same year that Barr's *Poems and Songs* appeared, Gabriel Read discovered gold in Otago, and the province's population rapidly rose from 12,600 to 60,000. With the prospectors came, from England by way of Victoria, Charles Robert Thatcher, 'pre-eminent singer of the goldfields'. He toured the country's theatres and halls with his satirical 'locals' about 'lawyers and policemen, shipping agents and shipwrecks, unregistered dogs and hungry horses, fighting bailiffs and squalling boys'.[28] His irreverent verses crackle with imported slang. They are peopled by 'coves' who eat 'grub' and may be 'dressed very nobby' or 'togg'd up like a dandy'; New Zealand towns have 'various dodges' for making 'you spend your tin' till 'you're totally fleeced'; phrases such as 'sang out whoa!', the 'gaff was blown', 'give five bob', 'fight shy of', 'a deal too slow', 'can't stomach working', 'get cheeky', and 'making their piles' are standard.

The 'demotic' verses of Barr and Thatcher remain more readable than the 'hieratic' offerings of Charles C. Bowen (1830-1917) and Frederick Napier Broome (1842-1896). Nobody in Bowen's or Broome's poems would 'get cheeky' or 'grub away, tug away' at fern roots. For Bowen, the poet is not 'the man / Who can but picture what is seen' but 'he who builds / To reach as near as he may hope to do / Some fair ideal of his inward mind', and Broome has a similarly exalted notion of his office as cultivator of interior 'visions . . . lapped in liquid ecstacy'.[29] In practice this means that both men were far too apt to produce pompous or elegant late-romantic poeticisms about nothing at all. Bowen had the Victorian propensity for preaching as well as dreaming. In 'The Battle of the Free', composed during the Crimean War, he calls the outposts of empire 'To Arms! To Arms!', justly confident that 'When the battle rages fierce / . . . Young New Zealand shall be there'. 'The Old Year and the New' has lasted better, its romantic clichés and plaintive cadences conveying something of the Janus state of those who were 'the children of a far land, / And the fathers of a new'. And it is Bowen's musical sense that gives grace and poignancy to his elegiac 'Moonlight in New Zealand', which again balances 'Hope and Memory'.

In the work of Irish immigrant Thomas Bracken (1843-1898), who achieved laureate status in his new country, links between the connotations and the denotations of words are sometimes not merely loosened but altogether broken. This is how he describes 'Waiaronui':

When all the scene is tinted with the blood
  Of dying day, then is the silver sheet
O'erlaid with nameless glories, — then the bloom
  Of koromiko groves seems richer, and aglow
The rata flushes, and the sweet perfume,
   That floats from where the rich tawhirris grow,
Embalms the sunset treasures as they fall
  And melt upon the lake's clear bosom deep.[30]

Obviously we are not supposed to imagine real 'blood' on a 'sheet' or real 'treasures' being 'embalmed' before 'melting' on a 'bosom'. Bracken's ideal reader will be conscious only of a vague aura of suggestiveness. But this poet's imagery is a psychoanalyst's delight. There are bosoms everywhere in his verse. He is fixated on the maternal breast, and he likes to think of everything else as 'little'. It is perhaps a case of ordinary Victorian escapism being sustained by sentimental attachment to 'the mother country'.

His chief poetic strategies are Augustan, rather than Romantic. He personifies abstractions by conferring capitals upon Peace, Freedom, Nature, War, Wisdom, Plenty, Art, Commerce, and the like, and he revels in periphrasis, so that the sun, for example, is 'glorious king of light', 'day's bright pendant', 'the golden shield of God', and so on. For sheer mawkishness he is hard to match, and *Musings in Maoriland* (1890), with its fey illustrations, is the essence of kitsch. But he could extemporize topical doggerel, and rhyme a commonplace sentiment to the satisfaction of the crowd. 'Not Understood' received international acclaim when recited, to zither accompaniment, by American entertainer Mel B. Spurr; and 'God Defend New Zealand' has become the national song. The complete opportunist, he had Irish blarney enough to twice win the Caledonian Society of Otago Prize Poem competition with 'The Exile's Lament', 'in which he revealed more nostalgia for heather and glen than he had ever shown for a shamrock', and 'Guallin a Chiel'; and he exploited Māori material in such poems as 'The March of Te Rauparaha', while admitting to Grey that he knew 'little or nothing of the Maori race, never having mixed amongst them, nor travelled in their country'.[31]

Andrew Kippis, noting in 1788 that the voyages of Captain James Cook had 'opened new scenes for the poetical fancy to range in', advised that the 'Morais', in particular, afforded 'a fine subject for the exercise of a plaintive Muse'.[32] The most ambitious response to this challenge was that of Alfred Domett (1811-1887). His *Ranolf and Amohia* (1872), in twenty-five cantos of great metrical variety, is longer than *Paradise Lost*. The story it tells is simple enough. Erudite young British maritime adventurer, Ranolf, shipwrecked on the New Zealand coast, saves beautiful Māori princess Amohia from a pair of male tormentors, and having learned her language from her tribe, eventually elopes with her and marries her. They enjoy an idyllic honeymoon in a natural Eden stocked with fish and fowl and inspiring scenery, and exchange information about their cultures. Once back at the pā, Ranolf helps repulse an enemy attack. However, neither physical exercise nor domestic bliss can entirely assuage his hunger for the 'intellectual food' of Europe. Amohia, sensing her husband's discontent, initiates a period of self-sacrificial separation, during which she is reported drowned. But the lovers are reunited at the end, and set sail towards the sunrise.

Puccini might have made an opera out of such a tale. But it is too frail a structure to carry the weight of Domett's metaphysical ruminations, his elaborate word-paintings of bush, mountain, river, and lake, his zoological and botanical details, and his recountings of Māori myths and customs. The poem, which begins *in medias res*, is a series of digressions.[33] The opening lines of the second canto ask, 'But this "Ranoro" — Ranolf — who was he? / Let us a brief while turn aside and see'. This is the signal for sixty pages of intellectual biography. Domett's main handicap is his misconception about what constitutes 'significance' in poetry. He thinks of it as something to be added in. So the record of Ranolf's self-education is the pretext for a history of world philosophy and a comprehensive lesson in comparative religion: the ideas of Locke, Berkeley, Hume, Brahma, Kapila, Spinoza, Sakya Muni, Kásyapa, Kant, Fichte, Reid, Brown, Schelling, and Hegel are among those paraded before us. There are whole pages as laborious and arid as this, for example:

> As Abstract Space, for instance, cannot be
> Conceived as boundless, or as bounded either;
> Yet must be one, to be at all, you see,
> Then cannot be at all, because 'tis neither;
> A negative that meets denial clear,
> For space is something after all, and here.
> That last negation, then, the Idea revives,
> And real essential Being to it gives
> In the "Conditioned" where alone it lives.[34]

The Māori legends are more entertaining, but remain embellishments, and the descriptive passages are at best verbal brushwork by which sights are recorded — with painstaking accuracy at times, but without being turned to poetic account. In Domett's poetry the realm of ideas and feelings and the realm of things and events never really mesh. Nor does he have a story-teller's gifts. Action is clumsily recounted, and it is only as the reader begins to anticipate the Homeric (or Mills and Boon) recognition scene, that 'what happens next' becomes a matter of interest. The Māori figures are two-dimensional — portraits by Lindauer or Goldie — so that the cultural clash is reduced to a simplistic version of Art versus Nature.

But Domett's greatest weakness is his reliance on a hackneyed language of the sublime, inherited from Milton, Shelley, and others. His verse is overloaded with adjectives such as 'ponderous', 'grim', 'beauteous', 'rapturous', 'stately', 'haughty', 'darksome', 'gorgeous' 'downy', 'tumultuous', 'dusky', 'gigantic', 'mighty', 'ghastly', 'boundless', and with adverbs such as 'dimly', 'softly', 'majestically', 'tremulously', 'grandly', 'nobly', 'airily'. Participles dwell on 'spreading', 'glistening', 'arching', 'throbbing', 'palpitating', 'glimmering', and 'burning'. Sometimes the epithets pile up before and after the noun, as in 'horrible white gloom profound'. They are devastatingly predictable; this is a poetry of 'heavenly smiles', 'cavernous depths', 'murderous rage', 'fitful gusts', 'blinding tears', 'sombre clouds', 'funereal darkness', 'furious fight', and 'dewy vales'. Domett's sporadic attempts at novelty are bizarre:

> Just then the ill-omened Moon withdrew behind
> A sable cloud-stripe, sudden, as if dropped—
> Dead Nun! into a coffin snowy-lined.[35]

Allen Curnow thought that a few sections describing landscape were salvageable, but Domett is at his most winsome in his accurate observation of small things, especially birds:

> And near some river-mouth — shoal — marshy-wide —
> Would mark the swarming sea-birds o'er the waste
> Tremble across the air in glimmering flocks;
> Or how, long-legged, with little steps they plied
> Their yellow webs, in such high-shouldered haste
> Pattering along the cockle-filled sandbanks,
> Some refuse dainty of the Sea to taste;
> Or standing stupefied in huddled ranks
> Still rounded up by the advancing tide—
> White glittering squadrons on the level mud
> Dressing their lines before the enclosing flood.

There are several such vivid passages. In one lake scene:

> The wild-ducks' black and tiny fleet
> Shot in-and-out their shy retreat;
> The cormorant left his crowded tree
> And stretched his tinselled neck for sea.

Elsewhere the 'crimson-billed' pūkeko, with its 'velvet plumage' of 'jetty black and violet blue' is aptly characterized as a bird 'That jerking struts among the cool / Thick rushes by their rust-red pool'; and there are evocative lines about the hawk that 'soars in pride of place, / Stiff-wheeling with bent head in circles slow'. Domett's real forte was as poetry's equivalent of Walter Buller.[36]

Domett's poem was praised by his friend Browning and by Tennyson, and Alexander and Currie rated him 'incomparably the greatest' of the poets represented in their anthology. As late as 1929 Jessie Mackay yoked Domett and Bracken as 'the Castor and the Pollux of a new Pacific school'. In a booklet called *Thomas Bracken: An Appreciation* (1916), Louis H. Victory, a Fellow of the Royal Society, enumerated six 'qualities' that he looked for in evaluating a poet's work: Moral Philosphy, Sincerity, Sympathy, Imagination, Depth of Vision, and Fundamental Brain Work; on 'the technical side' he sought Verbal Power and Metrical Craftsmanship. His essay is offered as a demonstration that

Bracken scores highly on all counts. At about the same time, Ezra Pound in England was urging the aspiring poet to 'Use no superfluous word, no adjective which does not reveal something', and declaring, 'I believe in technique as the test of a man's sincerity'.[37] For Pound, there could be no distinction between a poem's 'qualities' and its 'technical side': the moral vision inhered in the language used, and the 'brainwork' manifested itself in the choice and ordering of words. But Victory's 'appreciation' is a useful reminder of the notions of poetry with which poets such as Bracken and Domett worked.

One poet who could have benefited from Pound's advice to avoid 'rhetorical din', 'luxurious riot', and 'emotional slither' was Jessie Mackay (1864–1938), the first poet of any importance to be born in New Zealand. 'Dreamer and Doer', which appeared in her second collection, *The Sitter on the Rail* (1891), is a dialogue between man of action, Eric Gray, who treks through jungles and enlists as freedom fighter in foreign climes, and poet Guy Brand, whose ear is cocked to 'catch the psalm of great infinity'; and throughout Mackay's career 'dreaming' and 'doing' were in conflict. An ardent prohibitionist, defender of the underprivileged, and 'advocate of Irish and Scottish Home Rule, of Liberalism, feminism, and internationalism', she at times felt an impulse to make her poetry serve a social function, but even 'Vigil: The Eve of April 10, 1919' (the date of New Zealand's first Prohibition Poll), is so dense with bardic jargon such as 'gloam-rift', 'silverfoot', 'ringed rune', 'bower maiden', 'Shekinah-light', and 'Rose of Eternity' as to be virtually incomprehensible. Her main poetic impulse is towards Swinburnian incantation, in which words lose their denotative value altogether and become a 'mystic miraculous moonshine' of pure association and sound; but her own Gaelic romanticism can complicate the mix. It is often genuinely intoxicating; as Pound conceded in connection with Swinburne, 'a certain kind of verbal confusion has an emotive value in writing'.[38] Mackay's poems are peopled by Lorelei, Naiad, Nereid, and Nixie, by 'the Maid of the Mist' and 'the Spirit of Past Days'. Her fancy plays around legend and history. On a visit to Great Britain she was thrilled by a trip to the ruins of Tintagel. She has greater metrical and verbal facility than any of her predecessors, and when she comes closest to using the page as a Ouija board for a kind of automatic writing — as in 'Moth and Candle' or 'The Night Song of the Sea' — she taps unconscious yearnings that a Freudian analysis might explore. In the dialect piece 'For Love of Appin', she indirectly gives expression to a New Zealand sense of exile through the voices of the Scots of Appin, deported to America in the eighteenth century, and her lines about the 'running rings of fire on the Canterbury hills' stuck in the minds of some readers. Before she died she was being hailed as a Grand Old Lady of New Zealand literature.

To turn from Jessie Mackay to David McKee Wright (1869–1928) is to exchange 'the psalm of great infinity' for the crackle of a speargrass fire under a boiling billy and the click of shears in the woolshed. Wright paid homage to Henry Lawson as 'the first articulate voice of the real Australia . . . sincere and strong and true', claiming that his verse had 'a rugged music that goes straight to the heart', and his own *Station Ballads and Other Verses* (1897) and subsequent volumes are in the vein of Lawson and 'Banjo' Paterson — bush ballads written in six- and seven-beat lines and aimed at an audience of nomadic diggers, rabbiters, shearers, and swaggers in the Depression years when the gold-fields were exhausted and the big sheep stations were 'mostly busted up'. Domett's flowering ratas, pohutukawas, and kowhais give place in Wright's verse to plain flax, fern, and tussock. Wright, who, though 'born under . . . brown Irish thatch',[39] had attended Otago University and became a Congregationalist minister, anticipated Frank Sargeson in employing naïve narrators who deliver their verse anecdotes, reminiscences, or homespun philosophies in a simple, colloquial style. The technique allows Wright to express the social values of this male subculture, with its respect for comradeship, resourcefulness, pluck, fair play, and physical prowess in the great outdoors. Even the odd sentimental touches are in character. When not using an imaginary narrator, he still adopts an unsophisticated persona. The self-imposed limitation frees him from dependence on Parnassian clichés; when, as in a few of his 'Other Verses', he drops the persona, he is just another dreamer.

In 'Our Cities Face the Sea', Wright evokes the familiar 'village' with 'steeple grey', 'cottages white', gardens of lavender and roses, thrushes and sparrows, and fields of hay and corn, only to dismiss them. 'We take our homeland with us, however we change our sky', as the 'he' of the poem remarks, but:

> He had learned the charm of the mountains, the breath of the tussocks he knew;
> He had lived in the land of sunshine, under skies of cloudless blue;
> And the charm of the old had faded, as the charm of the new had grown,
> Till he hailed the windy islands with their flax and fern as his own.[40]

The New Zealand landscape is far from adequately realized in those lines, but for the first time in New Zealand poetry, it is both a recognizable, unglamorized presence and the correlative for a positive emotion.

The argument of William Pember Reeves's best known poem, 'A Colonist in his Garden', is not so much that the charm of the old home can be replaced by that of the new, as that it can be imported into the new.[41] For Reeves we can 'take our homeland with us' *literally*. The poem is in two parts. In the first, the Colonist reads a letter from an Old Friend in England, urging him to return from 'A land without a past; a race / Set in the rut of commonplace' to the joys of a rich culture where 'beauty weds grey Time'. England has 'grace and colour'; New Zealand is 'lonely' and 'empty'. Then the Colonist speaks. His replies are not entirely consistent. He prefers, he claims, to let England remain an unspoilt image in his memory, associating it with 'dim romance'. The new land has been an arena for heroic endeavour, and who, having 'made the wilderness to flower, / Can turn, forsaking all?' New Zealand is a blank canvas on which the colonists 'paint the hues of life', which (in the poem) is largely a matter of bringing in English trees, birds, and flowers, though the Colonist and

359

his fellows are also 'rough architects of State'. The Colonist's garden is his England. He need not go back Home: Home has come to him. Reeves's poem is essentially a declaration of faith in the transplantability of English culture. It is not surprising to learn that he wrote the poem after he had already abandoned his antipodean garden for 'the old, green land'.

In a letter written a few years before he died, Reeves referred to poetry as 'a solace and delight' — for the practitioner, in particular, as he trudges 'the beaten and dusty thoroughfares of life'.[42] The brilliant ironies of Reeves's prose history of New Zealand, *The Long White Cloud* (1898), find no place in his verse, which, though competent, is the typical late nineteenth century medley of dreaminess and rant. He did combine with George Phipps Williams to produce two volumes of predominantly humorous 'occasional' pieces. Reeves was a key radical in Ballance's Liberal cabinet from 1891 to 1896. Domett rose to be Premier. Bowen became Minister of Justice, Bracken a Member of Parliament. Many of the poets represented in Alexander and Currie's *New Zealand Verse* were leading figures in the country's public life. But the full force of their personalities failed to enter their poems.

Arthur H. Adams (1872-1936), in contrast, lived as a writer — journalist, novelist, playwright, and poet. Born in Otago, he spent time in Australia, China, and England. In Sydney he was literary editor of the *Bulletin* and for a time edited the *Sun*. In Adams's verse, one senses a new degree of commitment: he writes because he must, and although the poetic mind on display has often, one feels, been thwarted by operating within hackneyed conventions, it is of a kind that engages with areas of experience ignored by more complacent spirits.

Maoriland and Other Verses (1899) includes many poems that had been published in the *Bulletin*, and seems to be aimed at an Australasian readership. Adams is unorthodox enough to characterize Maoriland as 'Land where all winds whisper one word, / "Death!" — though skies are fair above her'; to take a Māori perspective on the coming of the Pākehā; to see Britain (in the future) as 'grey old crone'; to look forward to the equality of 'The New Woman' with man; to empathize with 'The Anarchist' as he awaits the guillotine; and to imagine wife and paramour quarrelling over a corpse. There are affinities with British poets of the 1890s such as John Davidson and Arthur Symons. Poems of sensual passion, such as 'Antagonists' and 'Satana', with their *odi et amo* themes and women conscious of their sexual power over men, are very like Symons's, and point forward also to Rupert Brooke. Adams can surprise by writing an epitaph on a woman with 'peerless face' and 'paltry soul', and he can produce the unexpected phrase: 'palisades of self', a 'voice, with its tincture of tears', 'in my face the dead Past flaps its wings', 'the sullen blaze of rata-fire' — no earlier poet would have conceded the 'sullenness'. In 'The Brave Days to Be', Adams even describes the thermal region ('haggard country of the North / Between the uncouth hills of manuka') in refreshingly anti-touristic terms:

                                    The earth
Writhed with a scrofula of quivering sores;
Her thick warm blood, exuding sluggishly,
In pools of ugly reluctant bubbles oozed.

He goes on to describe the 'fret-work fantasies of silica' and other beauties that nevertheless issue out of the earth's 'agonies', and sketches an analogy with a poet who, 'wedded to his pain', creates 'spheral song'. The imagery is a bit muddled, but the suggestion of a relation between poetry and personal distress is apt for Adams.

'The Coming of Te Rauparaha', in trochaic pentameters, is a satisfying narrative that imagines its way into a particular situation. 'Written in Australia' is the first poem about exile *from*, instead of *in*, New Zealand. 'The Australian' begins 'Once more this Autumn-earth is ripe, / Parturient of another type', and proceeds to define the new colonial breed in a series of couplets, which end with lines of Yeatsian originality: 'So, toward undreamt-of destinies / He slouches down the centuries'. The one poem in the volume that modern anthologists have picked up is 'The Dwellings of our Dead', which reworks the theme of Wright's 'Nameless Graves' and carries, by way of its mournful music, a strong emotional charge. Despite the persistence of nineteenth century poetic counters, *Maoriland and Other Verses* is a promising collection.

In *The Nazarene: A Study of a Man* (1902) the promise is realized. In spare, blank verse it tells the story of a solely human Christ from the successive points of view of his mother Mary, John the Baptist, Judas Iscariot, the young man who followed Jesus in Gethsemane and fled naked from the soldiers, Pontius Pilate, and Mary of Magdalene. Christ's 'chiefest glory' is 'that he rose / No higher than the cross we built for him!' The poem's strength lies not only in its heterodoxy, but in its psychological insight. A motif is Jesus' craving to be loved as well as to love; in fact love that is as much torment as delight is the poem's true theme. Judas's motives for betraying his master are an especially complex blend of jealousy of John and Mary Magdalene, and desire to prove his own superior understanding of Christ's 'divinity'. *The Nazarene* remains one of the most vital religious poems written by a New Zealander.

Adams's *Collected Verses* (1913), which marked his abandonment of poetry for prose, contains many new poems. Allen Curnow judged that the first section exhibited 'exemplary . . . failures to assimilate Maori matter into pakeha verse',[43] but the longish blank verse pieces on 'Marama: The Moon God' and 'Puhihuia' use the legends naturally enough as vehicles for the expression of sexual desire and of intuitions about its kinship to violence. Adams smuggles a bold adolescent sensuality into his treatment of these figures of myth. In this volume, too, Adams cocks a snook at respectable attitudes. 'The Coming of Pan' sees Australia, rightly as it turned out, as site of a renascent paganism. The poems are sympathetic towards society's outcasts. They affect, as in 'Requiescat', a grim stoicism in the face of 'blind Fate'. Some of the sonnets are enlivened by strong last lines: in 'The Pacific' the ocean witnesses political struggles, 'but within his lair / the dreaming saurian lifts a listless claw'; in 'Night in England', 'from dark towers / Village to village calling, chime to chime, / The empty churches tell the empty hours'. Perhaps the most individual poems in the book are 'The Ballad of Judgement Day', in which a hanged criminal indicts his Maker, and 'The Tavern', which is analogue for the world and from which, when the 'grey Companion' claims us, we exit 'into the night / With a head upright, / And on ashen lips a song'.

Adams is interesting not only in himself, but in his foreshadowing of R.A.K. Mason, who had evidently read his verse and been influenced by it. There is a temperamental affinity between the two poets. Both wrote poems on Judas and celebrate a Christ of the Arian heresy, and Adams's Mary remembers the saying by her son that forms the basis of Mason's 'Footnote to John II 4', whose theme is also anticipated in the dedicatory poem to his mother that prefaces *Maoriland and Other Verses*. Mason's 'After Death' echoes Adams's 'After', and his 'Stoic Marching Song' has points of contact with Adams's 'Truce'. Mason, like Adams, empathizes with the condemned felon and the army of the unemployed, and feels the torment of carnal desire. 'Myself — My Song' looks forward to 'Song of Allegiance', and 'A Song of Failure' to 'The Lesser Stars'. The two poets share a sense of the insignificance of earth and human life within the universe, and a fascination with the immortality not of the soul but of matter. The relation between the two poets is the first instance in New Zealand of profitable influence: wherever similarities may be detected, Mason improved and refined on his predecessor.

But 'the best New Zealand poem before Mason' is Blanche Baughan's (1870–1958) 'A Bush Section', which, while vividly evoking physical realities of the New Zealand scene in the first decade of the twentieth century, charts with marvellous precision the 'inner landscape' that 'colonists so rarely and reluctantly . . . admitted to consciousness'.[44] The poem's distinction as image of a place, a moment in history, and a state of mind is in part a result of Baughan's technical adventurousness. Here at last is a substantial and serious poem in which manner and matter are as one. Language and its formal deployment on the page are instruments by which a vision of life is brought into being.

Blanche Baughan had already published *Verses* (1898) two years before she arrived in New Zealand, with her BA in Classics from the University of London, to settle on Banks Peninsula as housekeeper on a farm. *Verses* shows signs of her later ability to tell a story and dramatize a situation. 'Gaffer's Last Journey' and 'A Northern Maenad' are both brief dramatic monologues, and the latter, in particular, makes vigorous use of an exclamatory and interrogative rhetoric that was to form the basis for 'A Bush Section'. *Reuben and Other Poems* (1903) is a shorter and stronger collection. The long title piece derives from 'Michael' by way of 'Enoch Arden'. 'Outside o' the Mail into Mennen' is in the liveliest of Victorian verse traditions, deftly characterizing its good-humouredly stoical working-class speaker as she recounts, in her own vernacular and in galloping rhythms, the shared discomforts of a journey in a storm. 'The Ship at Sea' — in which the ship is something between Wallace

Stevens's jar in Tennessee and the Venerable Bede's sparrow flying through a hall — is one of the poems that stand out in the Alexander and Currie anthology as displaying a true poetic imagination at work. The two New Zealand pieces in the volume both use imaginary speakers and fashion a plausible literary version of a colonial idiom; and they reveal Baughan's quick understanding of the people she had joined. The hero of 'Young Hotspur' is a farm lad 'off to the war' for adventure. In 'The Old Place' a pioneer reflects on the 'place that's broken my heart — the place where I've lived my life'.

In *Shingle-Short and Other Verses* [1908], which Baughan introduced as a 'volume of New Zealand verse', narrative and dramatic techniques predominate. The longest poem, 'The Paddock', even has speaking and singing parts for White Clover, Sunbeams and Strawberries, Creek, Wind, Seeds, and Ti-tree; evidently conceived as a kind of pastoral oratorio, it unfolds the human drama of backblocks farmer Andrew, his wife Elizabeth, her young sister Janet, and an old Māori woman called Hine. It is too bizarre and ramshackle for modern tastes. In the title poem, a garrulous simpleton mutters to himself, from dusk till dawn, in a quaint colloquial lingo as he botches the making of a toy boat and meditates about Creation and the Creator who seems to have botched him. This poem, which may owe something to Browning's 'Caliban upon Setebos', does succeed in getting inside the addled mind of its protagonist. In 'Early Days', Granny, who has all her wits, re-creates pioneering life for her audience of grandchildren, right down to the reek of the slush-lamp; the stanza in which letters from 'Home' are read ('Uncle listen'd interested, Father with a frown; / Mother used to listen with her head bow'd down') is a more telling expression of the familiar nostalgia than the whole of Bracken's 'April Here and April There'. 'The Hill' presents a back-country killer, after twenty years still plagued by guilt and fear of discovery, and craving absolution.

In a letter to Johannes C. Andersen, Baughan commented on the mismatch between 'rhymed smooth metres' and the 'free genius of the Maori', and speculated on the possibilities of a long-lined and irregular version of the *Hiawatha* metre.[45] But her eventual solution, for retelling the legend of 'Maui's Fish', was to use trisyllabic and disyllabic pentameters and hexameters roughed up and redeployed under the influence of Whitman. Baughan tacks onto the story of Te Ika a Maui a moralizing section exhorting the country to 'Live! Dare!' The poem catches an authentically Polynesian note of the humorous grotesque, but remains a curiosity. But a similar style of verse admirably serves 'A Bush Section'. The poem is a five act mini-drama beginning with a scene of devastation:

Logs, at the door, by the fence; logs, broadcast over the paddock;
Sprawling in motionless thousands away down the green of the gully,
Logs, grey-black. And the opposite rampart of ridges
Bristles against the sky, all the tawny, tumultuous landscape
Is stuck, and prickled, and spiked with the standing black and grey splinters,
Strewn, all over its hollows and hills, with the long, prone, grey-black logs.

We are in another poetic world — more concrete, stark, and actual — from the 'ruined beauty' of Reeves's 'The Passing of the Forest', with its 'plundered and insulted kings' of the native bush. Baughan's images are of stasis, apt correlatives for a colonial, and indeed Victorian, predicament of being caught 'between two worlds, one dead, / The other powerless to be born'.[46] But in 'the little raw farm on the edge of the desolate hillside' lives, 'dependent on strangers', ten-year-old orphan Thorold von Reden; and though not dramatic monologue, the text intermittently associates itself with the boy's own consciousness. The ensuing sections insinuate potential for progress, life, and growth into this scene through imagery of motion, as the focus moves to river, mail-train, stars, and Thor himself. The poem's vision comprehends past, present, and future, with the repeated refrain 'Where does it come from? / Where does it go?', modulating to questions apostrophizing 'little Thor' himself:

> Ah, little Thor!
> Here in the night, face to face
> With the Burnt Bush within and without thee,
> Standing, small and alone:
> Bright Promise on Poverty's threshold!
>> What art thou? Where hast thou come from?
>> How far, how far! wilt thou go?

As a structure of sound and imagery the poem is beautifully organized; and as Curnow remarked, 'there is true feeling, not merely the facile optimism of her generation, in the interrogations with which the poem concludes'.[47]

Decades of Achievement

After an illness in 1909-10, Baughan was deserted by her muse and dedicated her life to penal reform. Close on two decades were to pass before her achievement was matched.

Looking back on the seventy years of English poetry in New Zealand before 'A Bush Section', one notes that the South Island cities, Christchurch and Otago, were the main centres of poetic activity. Among the most significant anthologies before *New Zealand Verse* had been *The Book of Canterbury Rhymes* (1866, second edition 1883), edited by Reeves and J. Ward, and *The Jubilee Book of Canterbury Rhymes* (1900), edited by O.T.J. Alpers. Most of the New Zealand daily and weekly papers had their poetry columns. The Sydney *Bulletin* provided an outlet from the time of its foundation in 1880, and the *New Zealand Illustrated Magazine* from 1899 till 1905.

Poets such as James Edward Fitzgerald, with 'The Night-watch Song of the *Charlotte Jane*', and Henry Jacobs, with 'The River Avon', hit off the odd poem that, reprinted in *Canterbury Rhymes* and *New Zealand Verse*, had enough local or national content to catch the attention of later anthologists or commentators.

And Tasmanian-born Hubert Church (1857-1932) shuffled Tennysonian clichés into verses melodious enough to seduce Oxford editors Robert Chapman and Jonathan Bennett as late as 1956.[48] But in terms of poetic achievement, the more interesting stray pieces rounded up by Alexander and Currie are two Kiplingesque ballads and two dramatic monologues. In 'What Used to Be', Edith Lyttleton, who under the pseudonym 'G.B. Lancaster' also wrote novels that were praised as 'virile', gives early expression to an ideal of male mateship through a stockman's lament for a pal trampled to death by stampeding cattle, and M.C. Keane finds the germ of a poem of some feeling and originality in a memorial for the 400,000 horses killed during the Boer War 'in a cause of which they knew nothing'. (Another ballad by Keane, 'Two Voices', reprinted in the 1926 edition of *New Zealand Verse*, shows his ability to evoke a bush scene in a few unpretentious words: 'Dark ratas stalking down the gorge (a-waiting for the day) / To the sheen of rippling waters in the shingle sweep below!'). Inspector of Schools and devoted classicist William Hodgson displays some psychological delicacy in creating for Homer's Nausicaa a piece of self-revelatory blank verse in which, on the day before her wedding, she recalls the charismatic stranger Ulysses, long since departed. And in 'Jael', Mary Colborne-Veel has her heroine, wife of Heber the Kenite and brutal slayer of Sisera, according to the biblical Book of Judges, meditate on her deed in long, largely dactylic lines of considerable power. Even the most fragile poetic talents flourished from time to time within narrative and dramatic conventions.

The enlarged second edition of Alexander and Currie's collection, published in 1926 as *A Treasury of New Zealand Verse* and including forty-three new poems and eighteen new poets, reveals little advance on the first. From the period separating Adams and Baughan from Mason and Bethell, Edward Tregear's 'Te Whetu Plains', with its evocation of 'the ghastly peace' of 'a songless land', has survived as an anthology piece, and Allen Curnow gave space in his Caxton and Penguin anthologies to Arnold Wall's 'vignettes of Christchurch' and amiable Edwardian musings about this and that. But it was the publication of R.A.K. Mason's *The Beggar* in 1924 that, in Curnow's judgement, announced the emergence of New Zealand's 'first wholly original, unmistakably gifted poet',[49] and one who (in 'Wayfarers') could people Lichfield, the Waitemata Harbour, Otahuhu and Papatoetoe with the wraiths of Mary Queen of Scots, Flora Macdonald, Chatterton, Gaius Marius, Herostratus, and Aeneas.

Over eighty per cent of Mason's *Collected Poems* (1962) were written before he turned twenty-five. The creative energy that at first found its natural outlet in the composition of verse was later channelled into political and trade union activities. C.K. Stead's impression that Mason's best poems were 'spontaneous expressions of feelings not always perfectly understood by the mind as it brought them forth' has been corroborated by the poet's own journals, where he notes that he does not so much invent the words as utter them 'at the bidding of some invisible prompter far back in the dark stage of my soul' and avers that his lack of conscious control over his gift was such that he 'just gave up and sort of trusted to luck'.[50]

The poet's youthfulness excuses a certain Byronic posturing, often ironically placed, and the genesis of his poetry accounts for its curious mixture of the stilted, the archaic, the overblown, the prosaic, the downright banal, the colloquial, the spare, the muscular, and the sharply observed. For all the heterogeneity of his diction, Mason, like Hardy, achieves a ruggedly individual voice that, as it puzzles over what it has to say, transforms even gaucheness into a kind of authenticity. Mason's is verse of peculiar intensity. To object to the floridities of epithet, the nineteenth century poeticisms, the manœuvrings towards a rhyme, the rhetorical inversions, the torturings of syntax would be to fail 'to meet truly the experience of reading the poems', which 'leave one . . . critically disarmed'. For all their limitations, they affect one as 'formidable living organisms, seldom graceful in movement, but always strong and swift'. 'The living part of a poem', declared Robert Frost, 'is the intonation entangled somehow in the syntax, idiom and meaning of a sentence' uttered within chosen metrical constraints.[51] Mason's verse has a distinctive dramatic life of this kind. 'O Fons Bandusiae', the translation from Horace that he wrote for his Latin master at Auckland Grammar School, already shows unmistakable evidence of this rhythmical zest and power.

Mason resembles Hardy in his frequent use of the very short line or the exceptionally long one or, most characteristically, both within a fairly complex stanza, the rhymes standing as solid markers in an utterance otherwise shifting and unpredictable. The rhymes often seem to act like a clinical psychologist's stimulus-words to engage the image-making faculty. For example, the sensuous content of 'After Death', which recalls Hardy's 'Afterwards' as well as Adams's poem, is almost entirely a response to the rhyme-words 'cull', 'dull', 'pull', 'beautiful', 'vine', 'sign', 'fine', 'line', 'brass', 'mass', 'pass', and 'grass'. And a simile such as 'The ointments I bring up to you my lord / gleam jewels like a steel-flashing beetle shard' in 'Oils and Ointments' has clearly been prompted by the need to find a rhyme with 'spikenard'.

Mason's poetic vision has been well enough characterized by his critics. Who could miss the urgent classical pessimism and dour stoicism, the Hamlet-like fascination with death and corporeal decay, the sense of human brotherhood that extends backwards through history, the compassion for the reviled and condemned, typically taking the form of obeisance before a Christ of the Arian heresy and defiant indignation at a persecuting or indifferent God, the outraged tenderness, the belligerent anti-clericism, the gloomy fixation on those pseudo-philosophical discoveries about time, self, and space that attend adolescence, the tortured sexuality lightened by infrequent moments of joy, the dwelling upon sufferings of the distant past and historic acts of desperation, the preoccupations with betrayal, sacrifice, and fame, the bitter and macabre humour, the Dowsonian drift towards negation?

The image that Mason projected of the poet as suffering consciousness and conscience of the race helped bring professionalism and a sense of mission to a verse tradition that had been dominated by earnest dilettantism. In 'Song of Allegiance' he places himself in line of descent from Shakespeare, Milton,

Donne, Coleridge, Wordsworth, Keats, Shelley, Byron, Tennyson, Beddoes, and Housman, and might have added the Latin poets, especially Catullus and Horace, and the Frenchman Baudelaire:

Little clinging grains enfold
　　all the mighty minds of old . . .

They are gone and I am here
　　stoutly bringing up the rear

Where they went with limber ease
　　toil I on with bloody knees

Though my voice is cracked and harsh
　　stoutly in the rear I march

Though my song have none to hear
　　boldly bring I up the rear.

The way that 'stoutly bringing up the rear' is repeated with variations in the last two couplets is characteristic: is this effective rhetorical patterning or sheer carelessness? In any case, as the imagery suggests, for Mason, to be a poet is not to indulge some harmless hobby but to join the troops for honourable battle. His Roman sword has, as he declares in 'Prelude', 'no fine cluster / on the hilt, this drab / blade lacks lustre— / but it can stab'.

Alienation and dispossession are in Mason's verse less evidently connected with his geographical and historical situation as a Pākehā New Zealander, than they are in poems of the 1930s and 1940s by Fairburn, Curnow, Brasch, and others. But his sympathy with the downtrodden was intensified by the Depression of the 1930s and isolated him from middle-class society, and his verse everywhere shows signs of that 'struggle with the austere anti-aesthetic angel of Puritanism' which James K. Baxter was later to see as the 'endemic problem' of the New Zealand writer.[52] Mason seems ever plagued by obscure guilt that requires expiation. Just as his talent as poet surrendered to a busy Marxist altruism, so within his poetic imagery the sexual and the social merge. Poems delve below the surface of the earth or plunge to the ocean's floor to discover the equivocal energies of the Freudian unconscious, or unsavoury social truths. The rebellion of the flesh against a Calvinist repression can shade into the uprising of repressed masses or the storming of a Christian citadel by pagan hordes. Even in the two poems surviving from *In the Manner of Men*, circulated in manuscript in 1923, archetypes of 'the Romantic agony' already appear: the disinterred corpse, the ocean base where ghastliness and opulence mingle in images of history, religion, poetry, and death. *Alter egos* and the ghosts of slain selves haunt Mason's pages. The dichotomy in the psyche may be expressed in terms of 'spark' and 'clay'. The beautiful love poem 'Be Swift O Sun', in which the beloved (muse, white goddess, Jungian anima figure) reconciles all opposites, has its counterpart in 'Ad Mariam', with its

367

momentary, half-comic vision of woman as witch, servant of chaos, and anti-Christ.

In its verbal texture, Mason's verse is relatively free of ambiguity, paradox, and irony, but the poems are often paradoxical in structure, incorporating the counter-statement to what they affirm or deny. In 'Arius Prays' the heretic addresses with religious devotion the Christ whose godhead he rejects. The middle stanza of 'The Lesser Stars' dramatizes the testimony to poetic promise and achievement that the poet's speaker claims 'can never be ours'. 'In Perpetuum Vale' avers that life beyond the grave is a myth, but it is the dead man who makes this assertion and who recalls the priest's benison upon his 'poor rotting soul'. In another miniature dramatic monologue, 'Footnote to John II 4', based on the biblical situation, the young male speaker reveals a rich nostalgia for a mother's loving care even as he melodramatically protests his desire for independence; the conflict is Oedipal and universal, but might also serve as symbol for a youthful colony's impulse to free itself from the mother country's apron strings. 'After Death' presents with such sensual pleasure those experiences of which we will be deprived, as to be essentially a celebration of life. The persona of 'Vengeance of Venus' imagines himself in the dock, making his 'plea of mitigation' to the goddess of erotic love who sits in judgement on him. His crime is to have failed to make love to a young woman. He comically excuses this sin of omission in the kind of language he might have used for a penitent acknowledgement, to puritanical accusers, of premarital misbehaviour. But this young tearaway's offence has been against pagan, not Calvinist, laws. A wide range of ambivalence is enacted in poems such as these.

'Judas Iscariot' stands at the centre of Mason's achievement. It makes its point with the strength and directness of one of Blake's *Songs of Experience*, 'A Poison Tree' for example. The intuition captured in Mason's poem is as broad as Hamlet's — that a man 'may smile and smile and be a villain'. But the poem arose out of a specific and local occasion. Mason and his friend and fellow poet A.R.D. Fairburn had been discussing the subject of political treachery, with a particular New Zealand context in mind.[53] By presenting arch-traitor Judas as a popular joke-cracking 'good fellow', Mason melds betrayal and social ease in a mordant little parable. Judas is the antitype of a Jesus identified with the despised and rejected. Smug, hedonistic, bourgeois, hearty, he is the cheerful conformist, perfectly at home in the world — and he betrays his master without a qualm.

> Judas Iscariot
>   sat in the upper
>   room with the others
>   at the last supper
>
> And sitting there smiled
>   up at his master
>   whom he knew the morrow
>   would roll in disaster.

At Christ's look he guffawed —
   for then as thereafter
   Judas was greatly
   given to laughter,

Indeed they always said
   that he was the veriest
   prince of good fellows
   and the whitest and merriest.

All the days of his life
   he lived gay as a cricket
   and would sing like the thrush
   that sings in the thicket

He would sing like the thrush
   that sings on the thorn
   oh he was the most sporting bird
   that ever was born.

There is something of the English public school old boy about this Judas. For the metric of his poem, Mason reaches back to the Old and Middle English four-beat alliterative line, here divided into its component halves, and he might have found a jolly jesting Judas among the Vice figures of medieval balladry and drama.[54]

If Mason's poetry is, as Fairburn noted, 'very masculine', Ursula Bethell's (1874-1945) has the virtues of much of the best New Zealand verse by women. In surveying the annual crop of local collections as late as 1984, John Needham found that the women poets were more apt than the men 'to speak to someone, rather than address the world at large, or the empty air'.[55] Bethell's earliest poems, not originally intended for publication, were enclosed in letters to a friend in England, and among the most valuable things she brought to New Zealand poetry was a lack of the pretensions of a Bowen or a Domett. Instead of a moribund epic, she began writing *little* poems — simple, direct, restrained, in her own voice and dealing with her own thoughts and feelings as she reacted to her immediate environment. The result is that she strikes a tone and manner that seem surprisingly modern and are perhaps more appealing to present-day readers than Mason's.

Bethell was born in England, spent her childhood in Rangiora in Canterbury, received a good classical schooling in Oxford and Geneva, several times revisited Britain and Europe, and eventually settled in Christchurch and began writing poems in her fifties, publishing *From a Garden in the Antipodes* in 1929. The garden of the title was at 'Rise Cottage', where she lived with her friend Effie Pollen, a cat called Michael, and a special orange tree christened Omi-Kin-Kan. The cottage, perched on the Cashmere Hills, commanded views of the Pacific Ocean in one direction and of the Canterbury Plains as far as the Southern Alps in another. It is a small domestic world that Bethell shares with us, but her garden, as she busies herself over digging, planting, weeding, and

369

pruning, comes to stand for all fields of fond human endeavour, and for all that we make and tend, and watch develop and mature; and the rugged and vast landscape and seascape that she surveys from her small cultivated space is a constant reminder of human impermanence. 'The Mother of all will take charge again' and obliterate what has been so diligently achieved. Bethell is intensely aware of the slow geological processes that have moulded mountains and plains. In her garden she works to keep chaos at bay, never forgetting that eventually 'our impulsive limbs and our superior skulls' will restore to the soil 'several ounces of fertilizer'. She knows that at her very fingertips are 'emblems, allegories, parables'. Even the nurseryman's catalogue describes daboecia, the Irish heather, as suitable for 'small gardens, for rock gardens, and for graveyards'. Bethell's garden poems benefit from a very specific subject matter that effortlessly raises large poetic themes: 'Just as a camera set with the smallest aperture will register the greatest depth of field, so Ursula Bethell, in her concentration on minute particulars always seems to get Time and Infinity in focus too, in a way never achieved by those like Jessie Mackay, who made a frontal attack on such imponderables.'[56]

Besides having something concrete and close at hand to write about, and a congenial audience of one to address, Bethell has other advantages over most of her predecessors. One is a connoisseur's fascination with words: 'I listen to them, try them — ring them on the counter, so to speak', she declared.[57] She collects rare ones, such as 'matutinal', 'aquarellist', 'fugacity', 'sessile', 'agisted', 'mattamore', relishes the effects within a single poem of a Latinism such as 'transmarine' ('swept by transmarine winds') and an unexpectedly prosaic noun such as 'heaps' ('rain-worn rocks strewn in magnificent heaps'), extracts the older senses from 'fond' or 'candour', self-consciously and amusedly considers the word 'established' or 'horticulturalist' or contrasts a 'pleasaunce' with 'a heterogeneous botanical display', experiments with the onomatopoeia of 'a soft susurration of small leaves in dessication, a rustling', and takes an almost sensuous delight in cataloguing the 'lovely-sounding names' of shrubs ('an ugly word') or bulbs. 'Solitary, after all, were the gardener, / But for the accompaniment of words', and in Bethell's poems, language and experience seem continually to enrich one another. Bethell displays a nice sense of humour, of a much gentler kind than Mason's. And she also benefits from having a painter's eye. She had enjoyed some training in art in her youth, and her talent shows in the vivid pictorial detail of her poetic world. In 'Nor'-West Evening, Winter' she sketches a scene with the delicacy of a Japanese print-maker; the poem needs little more than a hawthorn, a heifer, and the poet-observer to convey a whole way of looking at the world.

Bethell's own version of 'April Here and April There' is a distinct improvement on Bracken's; she entitled it 'Response':

When you wrote your letter it was April,
And you were glad that it was spring weather,
And that the sun shone out in turn with showers of rain.

I write in waning May and it is autumn,
And I am glad that my chrysanthemums
Are tied up fast to strong posts,
So that the south winds cannot beat them down.
And I am glad that they are tawny coloured,
And fiery in the low west evening light.
And I am glad that one bush warbler
Still sings in the honey-scented wattle . . .

But oh, we have remembering hearts,
And we say 'How green it was in such and such an April',
And 'Such and such an autumn was very golden',
And 'Everything is for a very short time'.

The understatements of the last stanza are perhaps a shade calculated for some contemporary tastes, but the rest of the poem moves with the unaffected ease of educated talk. It is doubtful whether Bethell's success here has much to do with 'the growth of the language into its location' — she is more concerned with the growth of her chrysanthemums. It seems rather a matter of fidelity to experience, of having something particular to focus on, of being so much more intelligent, sensitive, observant, and linguistically aware than Bracken. The poet is content to make her points by implication: the time that a letter from England takes to reach her is indication enough of her distance from her friend and the site of past experiences, and the fact that the winds threatening her plants are southerly establishes the antipodean location. The lines, as is typical of the garden poems, are in a free verse grounded in iambic pentameters, of a kind she might have found among Arthur Waley's translations from the Chinese. And while Bethell's 'remembering heart' may lure her momentarily back to England, she is nevertheless securely 'here': in her poem, in contrast to Bracken's, the local details predominate, and they are more specific than those evoking 'there'.

'Detail' seems so matter-of-fact as hardly to be a poem at all — until one ponders the repetition, with variations, of the last line:

My garage is a structure of excessive plainness,
It springs from a dry bank in the back garden,
It is made of corrugated iron,
And painted all over with brick-red.

But beside it I have planted a green Bay-tree,
— A sweet Bay, an Olive, and a Turkey Fig,
— A Fig, an Olive, and a Bay.

The trees, with their time-honoured associations, are living insignia for a whole Christian, humanist, and classical tradition. The poet's garage is totally utilitarian. The planting of the saplings of trees that flourished in ancient Greece and Palestine is emblematic of the other side of the colonial enterprise. How deftly and economically Bethell treats the theme belaboured by Reeves!

In 'Trance', the language becomes more literary and carries a higher emotional charge, as it re-creates an almost mystical experience, a profound sense of strangeness and timelessness, as the speaker's moonlit garden assumes in the stillness the unreal clarity of art, Platonic ideal form, mirage, or dream. She herself feels 'abstracted' from the temporal, as though transported to a vantage point in the distant future, from which she were looking back upon her present self through the haze of countless centuries, yet in the knowledge that the scene and the person whose aspirations and concerns seem so pressing have long since passed away. The poem thus holds in perfect equilibrium an intuition of the eternal and the consciousness of time.

'Trance' may serve as a bridge to the later volumes, *Time and Place* (1936), *Day and Night, Poems 1924-1935* (1939), and the posthumously published *Collected Poems* (1950), where the uninsistent rhythms, conversational tone, and straightforward syntax of the garden pieces give way to a more complex, oratorical poetic style in which Bethell grapples with the fundamentals of religious faith. She was an Anglican who had, as night waitress at the New Zealand Soldiers' Club and social worker with boys' clubs, witnessed the horrors of East London in the war. 'I never could slur over things, or take anodynes, I want to know it all — and this death and *destruction* that I *saw*, must be lived through and known', she told M.H. Holcroft. But 'the *consciousness* of God came to me . . . chiefly in the solitudes of Nature'. The death of the much loved Effie Pollen in 1934 gave increased urgency to her quest for the permanent and the meaningful behind life's vicissitudes. In *Time and Place*, her meditations are conducted through fine description of the Canterbury landscape as it changes with the cycle of the seasons; the poetry appropriates a region for the purposes of moral or mystic contemplation. 'Levavi Oculos', for example, imbues 'the hills of this country' with Christian symbolism. Into 'The Long Harbour' is compressed also a sense of the history of Akaroa; indeed, the poem — in which words such as 'cobbled', 'curvature', 'sea-bevelled', 'palm-feathery', 'sequestered', and 'ossuary' assume an almost palpable presence — serves as 'a summing-up of and benediction on the whole colonial adventure'.[58] The later poems are often more deeply inward, as 'the heart's anguish' yields to 'the sure purpose of eternity'.

In her later phase, Bethell inverts natural word order, compresses imagery into numerous hyphenated compounds, increases the proportion of polysyllables, and shapes her stanzas by means of a repetition and parallelism that owe much to bible and prayerbook. Often she uses rhyme and near-rhyme. The richly evocative 'Evening Walk in Winter' traces both an actual walk and a journey of the spirit. In 'Winter 1941. Kaikoura' Bethell sets 'this intimate Eden, this close anchorage' against 'the thunder of the waves' blind battering' and feels the lure of 'the dark crypt of the breakers'. A primal darkness beckons in many of these poems. 'Midnight' illustrates the Hopkinsian energy that Bethell can generate by using words as a composer of music might use notes and chords, or a painter the pigments on a palette:

All day long, prismatic dazzle,
Clashing of musics, challenge, encounter, succession;
Gear-change on the up-and-down-hill of hypothesis;
Choice, choice, decision, events rivetting shackles;
Hazardous tests, new wine of escape . . . oh, strange noviciate!
Bright stimulus, venture, tension, poised preparedness.

But at midnight, infinite darkness,
Opulent silence, liberty, liberty, solitude;
The acrid, mountainy wind's austere caresses;
Rest, rest, compensation, very suspension of death;
Deep stillness of death, dark negation . . . ah, thy heart-beat,
Origin, Signification, dread Daysman, Consummator.

That poem needs to be read aloud or with the inner ear alert to intonation, weight, and timing. There is nothing about it to suggest its country of origin, but it represents a remarkable enrichment of New Zealand poetry and a considerable extension of its range of effects.

Mason's *The Beggar* and Bethell's *From a Garden in the Antipodes* were the most significant first volumes of the 1920s, but many new voices were raised during this decade. Quentin Pope's *Kowhai Gold: An Anthology of Contemporary New Zealand Verse* (1930) included work by fifty-six poets, thirty-two of whom had not been anthologized by Alexander and Currie. The bulk of the verse in Pope's collection — which owes much to Edward Marsh's *Georgian Poetry* anthologies of 1912-22 — is fanciful, cosy, decorative, and precious.[59] These qualities evidently appealed to the editor, but strained attempts at the picturesque were in vogue at the time:

The hilltop street lamp, suddenly in jest
  Flicks out the pale flame of the climbing moon,
  And twilight, dropping from a cloud balloon,
Sets off as postman with a bag of rest.

So runs the first stanza of 'Six-Thirty' from O.N. Gillespie's *Night and Morning and Other Verses* (1927). Pope reprints seven of Gillespie's poems. One, typically beginning by comparing a hill to a troglodyte, dramatizes an incident in the life of a sheep-stealer. Another, 'The Court of Arches', is a cynical little fable about some frogs in a blood-polluted lagoon in the Somme, but even here the final effect is to trivialize the subject. The women poets in *Kowhai Gold* have (when 'the vision is upon' them, as Ishbel Veitch puts it) decorous thoughts about the beauty — or rather prettiness — of nature, are sentimental about children, mothers, and old folk, let their fancies play around pixies, elves, and sprites, and utter pathetically inadequate pieties when confronted with death. Mona Tracy's prettified 'Akaroa' provides an instructive contrast to Bethell's 'The Long Harbour'. The men's imaginations work in the same way. For Boyce Bowden, the city lights of Wellington are 'A glowing heap of jewels on a negro's palm'. Occasionally a more interesting note is struck, as in Marjory

Nicholls's 'Depression' (about the psychological state, not the economic one), J.C. Beaglehole's 'British Museum' and 'In the Cotswolds', D.M. Ross's 'The Flight', Alan Mulgan's 'Soldier Settlement', or Alison Grant's 'Shub-Ad, the Queen' (reminiscent of Victor Plarr's 'Ad Cinerarium', though lacking its formal elegance).[60] Grant's poems carry most conspicuously the typographical hallmark of the anthology: if poets of the 1970s were partial to the ampersand, the *Kowhai Gold* versifiers delighted in the dash and, above all, the ellipsis — three dots, like a moment's silence in church, to be filled in by appropriate reverie.

Pope included two poems by Mason, along with pieces by Mackay, Church, Baughan, and Adams. Also represented were Eileen Duggan, Katherine Mansfield, A.R.D. Fairburn, and Robin Hyde (pen-name of Iris Wilkinson). In fact, Eileen Duggan (1894-1972) was given more space than any other poet. Her *Poems* had been published as early as 1922, and *New Zealand Bird Songs* appeared in 1929. She continued to write over the next few decades, *Poems* (1937) being followed by *New Zealand Poems* (1940) and *More Poems* (1951). Hers is the epitome of *Kowhai Gold* verse, once religiosity has been recognized as part of the mix. She had been born in Marlborough of Irish Catholic parents. 'The individual response of Eileen Duggan's best poems subverts their Georgian decorum', says Ian Wedde, but to most competent readers Duggan will appear 'as subversive as a vicar's tea-party'. Too much of her work is marred by sentimentality, on the one hand, and a partiality for similes that are merely ornamental and for far-fetched conceits, on the other — as when (in 'Invasion') she likens New Zealand to a stag, or (in 'Cloudy Bay') a great aurora to a paddock-full of foals. And there is usually a triteness about the very movement of her verse within its tidy stanzas. Consequently, 'the whole effect is that of . . . emotional cliché', as Allen Curnow observed. This is true even of the 'lovely lyric' 'And at the End', which Alan Mulgan quoted to illustrate 'the miracle we call poetry' and which Fairburn judged to be 'of its kind . . . quite perfect'. James K. Baxter, reviewing Duggan's *More Poems*, found 'three levels in her poetry which rarely combine to make a completely satisfactory unit — the first whimsical, the second sensuous, the third religious and metaphysical'.[61] The praise that British and American reviewers showered upon *Poems* (1937), published in London with an enthusiastic introduction by Walter de la Mare, seems inexplicable today.

It is true that Duggan's verse is littered with 'local signs' — Māori words and legends, the names of New Zealand places and explorers, the flora and fauna of Aotearoa, back-country types — and that it shows a patriotic concern for New Zealand history and identity that is complicated by her sympathy with Irish nationalism. But Curnow's harsh judgement remains apt: Duggan's poems too often reveal 'the futility of "local colour" writing and the danger of a too energetic will-to-poetry'.[62] Duggan is yet another poet for whom dramatic monologue may be a key to unlock something a little different, as in 'A Maori to Mary', and the handful of her poems that remain memorable would certainly include 'Twilight', a recollection of childhood terror, 'Contrast', in which the approaches of the three Magi and the shepherds to the infant Jesus represent reason's and instinct's contrasting paths to truth, and 'Shades of Maro of Toulouse', which is wittily rude about modernism.

Katherine Mansfield's *Poems* (1923) add little to her literary reputation. Her three best pieces are those that have most often been reprinted, 'To Stanislaw Wyspianski', in which praise of the Polish patriot and dramatic poet allows her to define her relationship to her own native country, 'To L.H.B.', which records a dream about her beloved dead brother, and 'Sanary', with its elegantly woven suggestions of neurosis, oppression, sickness, and doom.

Robin Hyde's early poems, like many of Mansfield's, sit comfortably enough in the pages of *Kowhai Gold* — testimony to a sensitive soul, a lively fancy, and a head full of books, but scarcely worth a second glance. *The Desolate Star* (1929) was followed by *The Conquerors* (1935), and *Persephone in Winter* (1937). The last and best of these three volumes contains a fine free-verse monologue, 'They Consider the Crucifixion', about the perennial human craving for salvation from poverty, disease, and oppression; the poem obliquely reflects the economic Depression of the 1930s. But more often 'One has the sense that a true theme has not been found, that some actual knowledge is being suffocated', as Baxter remarked. He blamed 'a bad tradition': 'The Georgian dilemma had its roots in the structure of New Zealand society: in the great pressure towards conformity which prevented poets, and novelists also, from exercising a free and critical insight. They were quite literally afraid of what they might find themselves writing; and the demand by every newspaper reviewer for an optimistic, sentimental tone prevented them from following up their own best work.' Hyde, best known as a novelist, had supported herself through journalism. Throughout her brief life she suffered several physical and mental breakdowns, the last culminating in suicide. Her early poems were 'smiling painted masks covering a tormented face'.[63]

In 1937 she toured New Zealand, then sailed for England in 1938, but spent half the year in China. It was during this last period that she wrote her best poems, collected posthumously as *Houses by the Sea* (1952). Their forms are less regular, with much use of long-lined free verse. Out of Hyde's 'pilgrimage of self-discovery' came such poems as 'What is it Makes the Stranger?', where relocation in China challenges her sense of identity, 'The Deserted Village', where the Chinese village is a casualty of Japanese invasion, and the long title poem 'Houses by the Sea', in which Hyde seeks to recover the lost world of her Wellington girlhood — 'The Beaches', 'The Houses', 'The People' — with a care for detail and atmosphere that have reminded commentators of Mansfield's stories: against 'the background of sea and hill and sky' are re-created 'the physical sensations, the emotional discoveries, the moments of terror and precocious intuition' with 'sharply etched glimpses of the middle-class home', and sympathetic portraits of her parents and explorations of her ambivalent feelings towards them. Perhaps most striking of all Hyde's later and longer poems is 'Young Knowledge', which, in blank verse, accumulates around the nominal subject a kaleidoscope of images both of slow processes of maturation and of sudden, violent revelation; birth and death, creation and destruction, pleasure and pain, innocence and experience, beauty and ugliness are in the blend, and there are suggestions of the Garden of Eden, the Tree of Knowledge, and the corrupting serpent; a pun on 'carnal knowledge' lurks just below the surface. As in several of Hyde's later pieces, the connections between the vividly rendered phenomena and the abstractions that they are supposed to illustrate are tantalizingly elusive. But the richness of the imagery encourages re-readings. The poem ends with a coda, reminiscent of the coda to Matthew Arnold's 'The Scholar Gipsy', in which Heaphy, discovering 'the Greenstone People', 'half steeled his heart / To tell the cities there was no such world'. The poem thus catches the 'colonial dilemma' embodied in New Zealand's past. It is a remarkable synthesis of autobiography, national history, and sheer observation of the physical world. The title is, in fact, apt. The still youthful poet has succeeded in conveying what she knows; the poem taps that dark source of knowledge with which her earlier pre-Raphaelite fancies had failed to engage. *Houses by the Sea* also contains Hyde's strongest short lyrics, such as 'The Last Ones' and 'Image'.[64]

A.R.D. Fairburn's first collection, *He Shall Not Rise* (1930), even has a lyric called 'Kowhai', in which the flowers are 'golden'. Most critics have shared the mature Fairburn's disdain for the products of his youth, but the verse is extraordinarily good of its kind — a kind that may recall de la Mare or the James Joyce of *Chamber Music* or, beyond them, the early Yeats and his Rhymer's Club contemporaries. Perhaps the closest affinities are with Ernest Dowson, whose haunting melancholy cadences carry intimations of mortality, loss, and decay. The twenty-six-year-old Fairburn had Dowson's marvellous gift for a verbal music that can confound linguistic distinctions and blur images to create vague yet intense moods. In several poems he recalls Mason, and in 'Seasons' he manages to echo Keats, Shelley, and Swinburne within the space of a sonnet's fourteen lines. All Fairburn's later themes and techniques are foreshadowed in this volume, which ranges from diffuse lyricism to epigrammatic wit, and from rhymed quatrains to fluid free verse. The diction is mostly a matter of 'silver-throated birds', 'mournful vespers', 'grass-scented air', 'crying violins', and 'the cherry in bloom', but the poeticisms are woven into beautiful patterns of sound, and the tone may be complicated by references to 'the vulgar dead', 'the flat calm of death', or 'the slut / Mortality', or by the thought that 'Wisdom, with a winding-sheet / is coming here to tea'. The poem 'Release' begins 'It seemed that Time had died', and imagines 'all things' gathered into 'one immortal moment', but the depiction of this state is, paradoxically and inevitably, heavy with the language of mutability. Alun Lewis's famous summary of the one true lyric theme — 'love, death, and what survives of all the beloved' — points to Fairburn's persistent concerns. But the last poem in the volume announces the ritual murder of that 'lily-white lad' who 'lay a-dreaming . . . of pretty love-tales' and composing languid verses. Publication of *He Shall Not Rise* was meant to be an act of exorcism.[65]

In that volume's 'Odysseus', Homer's hero is imagined as, in a second voyage, arriving by chance on New Zealand shores, and 'Hellas' also shows Fairburn haunted, as his grandfather had been, by a vision of 'the isles of Hauraki' as 'the isles of Greece'; earlier writers had toyed with the notion. And Fairburn, a fourth-generation New Zealander of many talents and interests and with a personality compounded of exuberance and *Angst*, lived out a local twentieth century version of the ancient Greek ideal of the well-rounded man, restless in his quest for a view of life and a mode of being that would sustain him with a sense of meaning and purpose, but that grew naturally out of secular New Zealand experience. His poetry, the record of this lifelong 'search for meaning' by a man at odds with his society, was the product of a wide-ranging modern mind, a romantic temperament, an aesthetic sensibility, and a vigorous physique.[66]

Dominion, first published in 1938, had been written during the winter of 1935. As Fairburn explains, 'The world was recovering from the worst economic depression it could remember, and the poem bears the imprint of that period'. The Depression made it difficult for all but the most blinkered of poets to continue writing optimistic pieties and trivialities. A suffering and disrupted nation was no subject for conventional platitudes. Moreover, New Zealand poets were beginning to respond to the poetic revolution initiated by Pound and Eliot. *Dominion* shows the influence of *The Waste Land*, though Fairburn's closest kinship in manner and tone is with those British poets of the 1930s — Auden, MacNeice, Day Lewis, Spender, Warner, Allott, Roberts — who, though themselves indebted to Eliot's modernism and eager to confront realities of modern urban life, composed according to more conventional principles.[67] *Dominion*, written in irregular verse with some haphazard rhyming, consists of five sub-divided sections that amount to over 600 lines. The title points both to the nation and to true 'dominion over the earth', as opposed to various forms of exploitation. The poem offers snapshots of New Zealand in a state of economic and spiritual crisis, potted history, lyrical faith in the recuperative power of the land itself, tortuous philosophical debate, and a forecast of apocalypse involving 'the sacrament of death and renewal' whereby 'the seed shall spring in blackened earth / and the Word be made flesh'. There are memorable lines, striking passages, interesting ideas, but the effect is not of a coherent whole. The poem engages us when its findings are presented in fully developed images; the torrent of invective belongs to the generalizing surface effects of the caricaturist and satirical pamphleteer; and the metaphysics and economics fail to take firm hold on the imagination. However, *Dominion* is significant as the first New Zealand attempt to structure a long poem, on modernist lines, through the accumulation of disparate components.

Fairburn's *Three Poems* (1952) included, besides 'Dominion', 'The Voyage', 'a poem about faith, and works' that had been written for radio in 1948, and 'To a Friend in the Wilderness', written in 1949. In 'To a Friend' the latter-day romantic is given free rein. The poem dramatizes a recurrent conflict, between engagement and withdrawal, present even in the opening poem of *He Shall Not Rise* and in such later pieces as the surreal 'Full Fathom Five'. Here the ancient debate between town and country, the active and the contemplative life, assumes a personal urgency, as the poet wavers between a private Arcady on the Mahurangi peninsula, north of Auckland, and a metropolis where social concern sours into disgust and despair. Retreat is envisaged not as mere evasion, but as joyous submission to nature's imperatives. The poem has the bare minimum of intellectual structuring: it lives in its rhythms, in the rich particularity of its loving evocation of a northern littoral, in the ebb and flow of feeling as it moves through its resolution to the coda's dying fall. Few later New Zealand poets have risked such fullness of sentiment.

The shorter poems that Fairburn published over the years were brought together in *Strange Rendezvous* (1952), which incorporated *Poems 1929-1941* (1943). In the lyric style of the best of these, Fairburn 'reconciled in a singular way . . . the English and the traditional with the modern, the regional, and the personal'. The many love poems hold in balance an intense awareness of change and death, and a conviction of lasting value, affirming 'the visionary moment' in the very face of apparent oblivion. 'I believe that the meaning of life is to be realised in the tension between Time and Eternity', Fairburn once wrote.[68] 'Winter Night' (which was composed in England in 1931) delicately maintains this tension. The poet-persona and the woman he loves are indoors in front of a fire on a windy winter's night. There is the characteristic assertion that 'this moment holds / within its span the sum of life', that the lovers inhabit a self-sufficient microcosm, a 'small infinity'. The argument is similar to that of such seventeenth century poems as John Donne's 'The Sun Rising'. In Fairburn's poem the contraction of actual time and space becomes a mysterious expansion of the soul. Yet acknowledgement of the age-old passage of time is subtly conveyed in images relating to the fire, whose coals preserve the warmth of the sun shining on primeval forests buried and resurrected in this new form; the imagery shows time countered by its own processes. As the flames in the fireplace die down, the sense of space contracts even more, as the furthest wall of the room becomes invisible. The poem ends as the poet drifts towards sleep:

> Now lovelier than firelight is the gleam
>   of dying embers, and your face
> shines through the pathways of my dream
>   like young leaves in a forest place.

Time, death, and beauty are inextricably mingled in those lines. The young leaves of the forest that produced the coal in the fireplace have long since died. The embers themselves are dying; yet they are lovelier than the brighter firelight. And the woman's face 'shines through the pathways of [his] dream', young and fresh and beautiful like the long-dead leaves, as they used to be in an ancient springtime, glinting in the sun. There is the implicit recognition that the loved person too will age and wither; but her beauty and their love are nevertheless real and part of an eternally recurring process. Time is both triumphant and defeated. Although the poem contains words like 'snug' and 'lovelier', it is neither 'cosy' nor 'sentimental'. In its poise it is reminiscent of 'Trance': there are the same multiple perspectives on an intensely focused moment. As Curnow remarked, Fairburn's poems are 'written in such excellent, well-mannered English — are so readable, in fact — that their distinction may not immediately strike some readers'.[69] The strength of 'Winter Night', and of other such poems, lies in the faultless organization by which each detail in a situation or scene receives attention at the appropriate point. 'Song at Summer's End', another conventional lyric, shows the same care in the selection and ordering of particulars, besides great metrical skill as Fairburn quickens or retards the four-beat line.

The best known of Fairburn's love lyrics, 'The Cave', has a New Zealand setting. It seemed very bold when first published in 1943, being about an act of love-making in a cave by the sea — a 'brief eternity of the flesh' that 'transfigures' and 'redeems' the lovers' lives, links them with 'principles, essences, things that pervade the Universe . . . eternal and unchanging', relates them to the natural world and the whole history of the human race:[70]

> We left, and returned to our lives:
>
> the act entombed, its essence caught
> for ever in the wind, and in the noise of waves,
> for ever mixed
> with lovers' breaths who by salt-water coasts
> in the sea's beauty dwell.

'The Estuary' is also vividly localized, and the range of fine love poems includes 'Love Song', 'Poem', 'A Farewell', 'Tapu', 'To Daphnis and Chloe in the Park', 'Now', 'Sea-Wind and Setting Sun', and 'Wild Love' (in which energy is generated by the straining of the unruly romantic content against the bounds of the poem's heroic couplets). Related to these is the longer 'Disquisition on Death', which Fairburn called 'unfinished' and dated 1929. It is one of the few poems in which Fairburn the lyricist and Fairburn the wit peacefully coexist. He wrote much topical and comic verse, including mere squibs, the boisterous ballad 'The Rakehelly Man', and more serious pieces of satire and social commentary, such as 'Yes Please Gentlemen' (which benefits from posing as dramatized pub-talk), 'I'm Older Than You, Please Listen' (which expresses 'the tragi-comic plight of the New Zealander vacillating between his homeland and "overseas" '), and 'La Belle Dame Sans Merci'.[71] In 'Walking on my Feet' and 'Down on my Luck' Fairburn speaks as the gunny-toting vagabond that in spirit he remained, and in that mysterious poem 'The Sea' his thoughts revolve around the element in which his body delighted, and which served as complex symbol for both dissolution and transcendence of the self:

> The sun went down behind the hill,
> the sea grew pale, bewitched me with a semblance
> of something I had seen once in a dream
> or in the sweet sloth of my mother's womb.
> I plunged, and drowned.

The 1930s saw the emergence of groups of talented New Zealand poets concerned with the implications of their nationality, and with the social function of their craft. Among the coterie that gathered around Ursula Bethell in Christchurch was D'Arcy Cresswell (1896-1960), whose first collection of poems was published in London in 1928. Cresswell, who spent much of his life hawking his verses and his ideas in England, impressed many intelligent New Zealanders by the single-mindedness of his dedication to playing the role of poet, and the vehemence with which he rejected his native country and the twentieth century. His autobiographical prose works, *A Poet's Progress* (1930) and *Present Without Leave* (1939), are of more interest than his verse. A Luddite eccentric, he concocted a personal philosophy out of paranoia, nostalgia, and megalomania, and a poetic style out of miscellaneous archaisms. Fairburn, who admired the prose, thought that as poet, Cresswell deserved to be taken no more seriously than 'a piece of very good imitation period furniture' and joked about his 'pseudo-wordsworthian pipes-of-pansy water lilies'. Curnow rated *Lyttelton Harbour: A Poem* (1936) highly enough to include substantial excerpts in his anthologies, finding it 'rich in general insights' and in 'bristling local particulars', but the surface freakishness is all that any reader is likely to see in it today.[72] Cresswell managed plausible pastiches of Shakespearian or Miltonic sonnets, as in 'Time Lags Abed'.

One of the most significant associations of poets in the 1930s had as its initial focus the Auckland University student quarterly *The Phoenix*, which lasted for only four issues (1932-3). Edited first by James Bertram (with the help of J.A.W. Bennett) and later by R.A.K. Mason, and printed by typographer Robert Lowry, it included work by Mason, Cresswell, Hyde, Curnow, Fairburn, and Charles Brasch. At a time when the country struggled under 'a load of debt . . . the heritage of Empire', it was natural that writers should critically re-examine the very foundations of New Zealand society. Primarily literary and aesthetic in Bertram's two issues, *Phoenix* became more political and sociological in Mason's. The Canterbury University College counterpart was *Oriflamme*, edited by Denis Glover, who went on to establish the Caxton Press in Christchurch. Glover and Lowry between them printed much of the best verse of the next two decades, and Glover established lasting friendships with both Curnow and Fairburn. *Another Argo*, published by the Caxton Club Press in 1935, consisted of a poem by each of the three men, and the Caxton *Recent Poems* (1941) included verse by Curnow, Glover, Fairburn, and Mason. As early as 1930, flamboyant poetaster Geoffrey de Montalk, friend of both Mason and Fairburn, had been fostering overseas talk of an innovatory 'New Zealand movement' in poetry, of whom the central figures were alleged to be Cresswell, Mason, Fairburn, and himself. De Montalk's egotism now seems laughable, but the *Phoenix* generation of poets certainly wrote within a challenging new context of national assertiveness and self-scrutiny, intellectual ferment, and scorn for amateurish parlour versifying. A target for Glover's mockery (in *The Arraignment of Paris*, 1937) was *New Zealand Best Poems*, edited annually (1932-43) by C.A. Marris, who promoted the verse of gifted poets such as Duggan, Hyde, and the excellent J.R. Hervey, along with the kowhai-golden effusions of what Fairburn notoriously called the 'Menstrual School of Poetry'.[73]

By the end of the Second World War, Curnow, Glover, and Brasch were each the authors of a substantial body of verse. Glover's poetic response to the Depression was more succinct than Fairburn's: in 'The Magpies', a cross between ballad and grim nursery rhyme, the farm on which Tom and Elizabeth have laboured goes to 'the mortgage-man', as the birds chortle their ironic refrain. Glover's best early verse was collected in *The Wind and the Sand: Poems 1934-44* (1945). In poems like 'Holiday Piece' he showed an ability to evoke, with the utmost economy, South Island landscapes that included 'peaks perspective-piled beyond Ben Lomond' and 'at evening an Otago sky / where detonated clouds in calm confusion lie'. 'Always the simple, flat epithet where it ought to be, and the dynamic ("inventive") one where it ought to be. Hard-wrought and vigorous', as Fairburn remarked of his friend's technique. Glover apprehended the poetry in manual work and its 'gear and tackle and trim',[74] celebrating 'The Road Builders' who had 'pitted their strength and their cunning' against 'the obdurate strength of the land'. 'Leaving for Overseas' catches the experience of New Zealanders voyaging to the war. And 'Landing Field' is a much more substantial poem than Stephen Spender's 'The Landscape near an Aerodrome'. Already in evidence at this early stage is Glover's peculiar metric, which can, through the subtle mixing of rising and falling feet, and with the assistance of rhymes and assonances, produce a robust music unlike anybody else's.

Charles Brasch's manner was more reserved, the voice disquieted. *The Land and the People and Other Poems* (1939) was followed by *Disputed Ground: Poems 1939-45* (1948). Brasch's elegiac cadences expressed an uneasy feeling of rootlessness, exile, spiritual impoverishment. In 'The Islands', 'Waianakarua', 'Forerunners', 'A View of Rangitoto', 'The Silent Land', and other poems, he spoke for an immature island nation in which 'Lives like a vanishing night-dew drop away', without due sense of human continuity or of intimacy with the land. The Pākehā's, as distinct from the Māori's (in 'Forerunners'), was a 'shallow occupation' of the country. The longing was for what the Welsh call *cydymdreiddiad*, which has been glossed as 'that subtle knot of interpenetration, which . . . grows in time . . . between a territory and its people and their language, creating a sense of belonging to a particular stretch of the earth's surface'. Conducted mainly in terms of the South Island landscape, Brasch's poignant meditations reach beyond their local origins to touch 'the homelessness of the modern mind'.[75]

Always, in these islands, meeting and parting
Shake us, making tremulous the salt-rimmed air;
Divided, many-tongued, the sea is waiting,
Bird and fish visit us and come no more.
Remindingly beside the quays the white

Ships lie smoking; and from their haunted bay
The godwits vanish towards another summer.
Everywhere in light and calm the murmuring
Shadow of departure; distance looks our way;
And none knows where he will lie down at night.[76]

In his Auckland poem on the Waitemata Harbour's volcanic island, Rangitoto, Brasch offers a 'view' in both senses of the word: a verbal equivalent of a postcard seascape with the mountain at its centre and a vision that sets a city, a people, and an age within geological time.

Harshness of gorse darkens the yellow cliff-edge,
And scarlet flowered trees lean out to drop
Their shadows on the bay below, searching

The water for an image always broken
Between the inward and returning swells.
Farther, beyond the rocks, cuffed by pert waves

Launches tug at their moorings; and in the channel
Yachts that sprint elegantly down the breeze
And earnest liners driving for the north.

Brasch's scene-painting is very different from Bracken's or Domett's. The visual details with which he fills up his canvas are not only convincing pictorially, but also resonate in a realm of feelings and ideas: the pohutukawas, 'searching', like Narcissus, for the image of themselves, which comes and goes, hint at the poet's own quest for identity; the launches tugging at their moorings and the earnest northbound liners echo an island people's restlessness. Rhythm and the pattern of vowels and consonants enhance meaning, as in the subtle placement of the verb 'searching', so that the activity is enacted by the run of the verse. Yet these three opening stanzas are but preliminaries to the treatment of the central symbol, the extinct volcano, which still belongs to a primeval 'world of fire', living out its 'fiercer life / Beneath its husk of darkness, blind to the age / Scuttling by it over shiftless waters'.

The centenary, in 1940, of the signing of the Treaty of Waitangi, and the tricentenary, in 1942, of the first European sighting of New Zealand by the Dutch navigator Abel Tasman, were the occasions for a good deal of jingoistic bluster. Allen Curnow made more honest, more fully conscious attempts to relate the nation's present to its past. In such poems as 'The Unhistoric Story' and 'A Victim' in *Island and Time* (1941), and 'Landfall in Unknown Seas' in *Sailing or Drowning* (1943), he countered the self-congratulatory political speechifiers of the time with a dubious history of accident, miscalculation, failure, and tragic waste — the 'stain of blood that writes an island story'. 'The Unhistoric Story' sketched the country's Pākehā development, from Tasman to 'the chemical farmers', and found that at each stage 'It was something different, something nobody counted on'. In these remarkable poems, which represent an

intense imaginative response to the historic record, Curnow provided the New
Zealand counterparts of Yeats's 'Easter 1916'. With other well-known pieces,
such as 'House and Land' — a mini-drama in which octogenarian colonial exile
Miss Wilson, footloose cowman and rabbiter, ineffectual historian, and restless
dog on a chain play out their roles in 'a land of settlers / With never a soul at
home' — and the sonnet, from 'Attitudes for a New Zealand Poet', about 'The
Skeleton of the Great Moa in the Canterbury Museum, Christchurch' ('Not I,
some child, born in a marvellous year, / Will learn the trick of standing upright
here'), they are the fruition of 'geographical anxieties' already voiced in *Not in
Narrow Seas* (1939), and of poetic talents of which *Valley of Decision* (1933) had
afforded the first faint inklings.[77]

Curnow's language in his poems on national themes is clear, strong, and
concentrated, and he is served well by the sense of cadence and line that confers
distinction on short, minor pieces like 'Sentence' and 'Wild Iron'. Periods of
New Zealand history are evoked in a few pithy alliterative phrases and vivid
images, as in the fourth stanza of 'The Unhistoric Story':

> Green slashed with flags, pipeclay and boots in the bush,
> Christ in canoes and the musketed Maori boast;
> All a rubble-rattle at Time's glacial push:
> Vogel and Seddon howling empire from an empty coast
> A vast ocean laughter
> Echoed unheard, and after
> All it was different, something
> Nobody counted on.

'Landfall in Unknown Seas' — which had been commissioned by the
Department of Internal Affairs and was set to music by Douglas Lilburn — is
itself structured like a sonata in three movements: the first, in relaxed blank
verse, recounting Tasman's motives, preparations, and departure into the
unknown; the second, in staccato rhythms, conveying the mingled excitement
and disappointment of arrival in New Zealand waters and the fierce Māori
response; and the third, in elaborately rhymed stanzas, 'harmonising the vision
and action of the first two parts, and offering a possible meaning for the whole
to our own age and nation'.[78] In Curnow's description of the clash at Golden
Bay, which Tasman named Murderers' Bay, the particular and the general are
made to interact in a superb blend of eloquence and ironic understatement that
preserves the full complexity of the poet's attitude to the episode:

> Always to islanders danger
> Is what comes over the sea;
> Over the yellow sands and the clear
> Shallows, the dull filament
> Flickers, the blood of strangers:
> Death discovered the Sailor
> O in a flash, in a flat calm,
> A clash of boats in the bay

> And the day marred with murder.
> The dead required no further
> Warning to keep their distance;
> The rest, noting the failure,
> Pushed on with a reconnaissance
> To the north; and sailed away.

The paradox of Death's discovering the discoverer, the meiosis of the phrase 'noting the failure', and the thought that the dead 'required no further / Warning to keep their distance' create a tone utterly foreign to New Zealand's Victorian bards, none of whom would have had the restraint to narrate the killing, which is the climax of events, so elliptically and obliquely and hence so powerfully. No previous poet had exhibited such mastery over words.

In some observations on 'Poetry and Language', published in 1935, Curnow had explained that branches of a 'living language' may be 'quasi-dead', and hence unfit for poetry, as distinct from the making of 'meaningless noises' — which was why 'it is impossible for anything of importance to be communicated by the jargon of politicians'. Curnow's successes were achieved partly because, recognizing that it is through their medium that creative artists 'intuit their object' or discover what they have to say, he thought more acutely and strenuously than any previous New Zealand poet about the very nature of language as the medium of his comprehension and his art. He was to be a leader in shaping a New Zealand poetic tradition over the next few decades. The Caxton Press had added Basil Dowling and J.R. Hervey to its list of poets: Hervey, in 'Threnos', 'Two Old Men Look at the Sea', 'I Have Made Friends with Time', 'The Return', 'Children among the Tombstones', and 'Man of Crete' revealed a Georgian romanticism toughened by familiarity with Herbert, Donne, and the Metaphysicals.[79] By 1945 the time was ripe for the publication of Curnow's Caxton *Book of New Zealand Verse*.

Poetry 1945–90

Elizabeth Caffin

The Caxton Anthology, 1945

Allen Curnow's 'At Dead Low Water' was written in November 1944 and appeared in the *First Year Book of the Arts in New Zealand* the next year; it was collected in *Jack Without Magic*, published by Caxton in 1946, and finally gave its name to a 1949 collection to which new poems were added. Curnow must have seen it as a major work and it was so recognized by contemporaries as different as Fairburn and Baxter. With *A Book of New Zealand Verse* complete and the war near an end, it shows at once the powerful continuity of Curnow's poetry and his persistent determination to develop new directions. It repeats the images of sea and shore, the obsession with guilt and man's fallen nature, and the exploration of time and its meaning seen in the public themes of the early 1940s. But its source is a personal memory, not a national one, and its concerns are religious and philosophic rather than patriotic. And the father and son who walk by the water's edge are the same who appear in poems of the 1980s, the beach here an augury of the shore at Karekare where later a man collects mussels or a dead lamb lies.

It is a poem which, complete and satisfying in itself, is yet part of a dynamic process, moderating what went before and opening up possibilities ahead. *A Book of New Zealand Verse*, Curnow's anthology of recent New Zealand poetry prepared for the Caxton Press, occupies a similar place. It established almost without dissent the way in which the poetry of the previous twenty years was to be read. But in doing so, its introduction cast a long light (or for some, a shadow) forward on poetry yet to be written. Statements like 'verse has begun to be recognized as purposive, a real expression of what the New Zealander is and a part of what he may become' [81] led younger poets like James K. Baxter, Louis Johnson, Keith Sinclair, and Kendrick Smithyman to chide Curnow for prescribing a narrow nationalism as an essential test of value in New Zealand poetry.

Curnow makes here and elsewhere a clear distinction, indeed a celebrated one, between the poem and the world outside it, so-called 'reality'. The distinguishing character of the poetry of the 1930s was its responsiveness to the real world in which it was written. For Curnow this meant the physical, social, and historical realities of contemporary New Zealand, and it included the psychological realities of alienation and isolation felt by a migrant people: '[A]nyone capable of poetry, feeling his own land and people, his footing on the earth, to be in any way inadequate, unstable, unreal, is bound to attempt a resolution of the problems set by his birth.' [82]

By defining reality thus, Curnow was understood to be saying that good poetry had to be attentive to national preoccupations: description appeared to slip too easily into prescription. Searching for what linked the sixteen poets he had chosen, he instanced pervasive symbols, like the sea, repeated themes, like that of land and people, and an approach to history that was typically iconic in character. Although he later resisted the use of the word 'myth', it was something very like myth that he was after. A poet's task was not simply to reflect 'reality' but also to determine it, to 'invent' New Zealand, to create the idea of New Zealand: 'The good poem is something we may in time come to recognize New Zealand by'.[83] He several times uses of poets the word 'prophet', attributing to them the power to 'see' and articulate a national truth. The authority and confidence with which Curnow wrote and the way he presented the book as a pioneering work gave these ideas great potency.

But Curnow's approach was never as simplistic as his detractors often painted it. He firmly denied that he was recommending mere local colour, and he used a variety of criteria to judge the quality of poems. He also showed himself, particularly in the additions to the 1951 edition, willing to include good poems with no overt signs of their New Zealand origins. He fully recognized at several points the fact that individual poets must conduct their own dealings with the tradition and the contemporary practice of poetry in English as well as with their physical location. Further, he clearly believed that poetry is always changing, even improving, and that the stage revealed in the anthology was not a static ideal but a necessary step from which a more personal and universal poetry would follow.[84]

Curnow had laboured long in producing this essay, and several preparatory pieces had appeared in other places in the latter years of the war.[85] Controversial and challenging as it was, it initiated a discourse about the practice of poetry in New Zealand which still continues and which has no parallel in the other literary genres. In the years that followed, this discourse was marked by further introductions to further anthologies, usually by further poets; but many of the matters they discussed had already been raised by Curnow in 1945.

'Childhood and age in one green cradle joined': The Post-war Romantics, 1945–60

By looking for common characteristics, Curnow had forced a homogeneity on the poets of the 1920s and 1930s. It was not entirely an illusion, for they had grown into poetry together, developing their ideas and practice to some extent in concert. The 1930s did not end for New Zealand poetry when war broke out: fourteen of Curnow's sixteen selected poets were still alive in 1945 and several of them remained the grand panjandrums of the years that followed. (The two dead poets were women, Ursula Bethell and Robin Hyde, and though important volumes of work by both subsequently appeared and were greeted warmly, it would be some time before any woman poet learned again the trick of standing upright in a crowd of men.)

Mason's and Cresswell's best work was done, but Curnow, Glover, Fairburn, and Brasch exerted extraordinary power in poetic circles after the war. The founding of *Landfall* by Brasch in 1947 provided an outlet which was sympathetic, discriminating, and stable; Glover, back at the Caxton Press, immediately embarked on a series of Caxton Poets which by 1951 numbered eight; Fairburn became poetry editor of the new *Year Book of the Arts in New Zealand* (1945-51); M.H. Holcroft, friendly to poetry, became editor of the *Listener* in 1949; and Curnow was soon gathering material for the revised edition of his anthology.

In retrospect the importance of Curnow's 1945 anthology and its introduction was not so much as a national manifesto but rather as a statement of a modernist attitude to poetry. He reacted against a romanticism that had become sentimental and derivative, emphasizing tradition and the craft of the poem and preferring impersonal, indirect, and ironic ways of signifying. This was not, however, well understood by Curnow's contemporaries; few may have recognized that the real achievement of the 1930s poets was the development of a fresh approach to the relationship between poet and poem, to language and to diction, and to form as well as 'reality'. While the specific national imperatives of that generation were not long-lived, these modernist ideas would prosper. But not immediately.

Romanticism, in its Victorian and Edwardian hybrids, was a hardy and adaptable plant still flourishing in antipodean soil. Although Eliot and Auden were often visible, Yeats was surely the most pervasive influence on the post-war poets. Fairburn identified a swing back to romanticism during the war, and praised Curnow's 'At Dead Low Water' as if it were a romantic poem; and James Bertram, writing in 1952 on Robin Hyde, referred to 'the new romanticism'. Poets as different as the elderly clergyman, J.R. Hervey,[86] the highly successful Catholic writer, Eileen Duggan, the young part-Polynesian lyricist, Alistair Campbell, and the refined editor of *Landfall* himself, all saw one of the functions of poetry as the direct expression of personal emotion, moving through an apparently spontaneous lyric or a more measured personal meditation to harmonizing general statement.

Both Smithyman and Oliver wrote of the obvious attraction of Wordsworth to poets in an empty and beautiful land, Oliver claiming landscape to be an almost obligatory subject for the New Zealand poet.[87] And so it was for Ruth Dallas, a Southland poet who was an early protégée of Brasch (she was one of six young poets featured in *Landfall* in December 1948). The last verse of the title poem of her first collection, *Country Road* (1953), instantly declares her tradition:

> Over the grass and over, moves the wind;
> This moment will not come again, white dust
> Upon green leaves as innocent as snow,
> A wind that sings of nothing in the grass.

Already using clear and simple language and syntax, and with a strong rhythmic sense, she focuses directly on natural scenes and objects — a striped shell, a hedge, a beech forest, a tui. They are often associated with the passage of time, the movement of the seasons, the inevitability of death, the loss of childhood. The characteristic Wordsworthian urge to move from private epiphany to moral generalization is not too insistent here, but Dallas several times implies a contrast, also a matter for regret, between landscape and 'men and their sharp towns'. Figures in the landscape though are usually only that — distant shapes in 'The Land' or 'Farmyard', named as 'the woman', 'the man', 'the child', or as unspecified pronouns in lyrics that owe more to a literary tradition than to a particular situation. Dallas's sense of past poetic practice is in fact a strength because of her disciplined attention to making the words fit the object. Her poetry now seems like a skilful and still attractive attempt to tame the landscape within a well-mannered, unpretentious framework.

Brasch's encouragement of Dallas was not surprising, since though he was associated with the *Phoenix* poets and several of his poems were classic texts of the Curnow anthology, he continued, like Glover, to write in a largely romantic mode. Landscape certainly featured in his work, but his romanticism was a more complex and cerebral matter than Dallas's. His collection, *The Estate* (1957), gathered together poems written since 1945 and is a full expression of the romantic idiom. Its context is important. Brasch had returned to New Zealand after some years spent in Europe, to discover again scenes of family and childhood in a raw and empty land. He had just embarked on an exciting public endeavour to develop and nurture a New Zealand culture. His poetry is an honest and sometimes even naked expression of these somewhat ambiguous concerns. Isolation and alienation possessed him, as they had Curnow, but in a peculiarly intense and personal way. 'If you would sing,' he concluded, 'you must become news.' His characteristic approach then was to start from where he was, a natural scene or a friendship, and to extend out in ever-increasing circles of personal meditation towards national and ultimately universal themes. His natural tendency was to move away from immediacy towards abstraction, from the disturbing chaos of experience to 'an order sought by the imagination' ('In Memory of Willi Fels'). This movement is not away from the personal but offers a method of mastering it.

Three of the best poems in *The Estate*, 'The Ruins', 'Letter from Thurlby Domain', and 'Autumn, Thurlby Domain', begin with an image of ruined buildings — in the first poem, imaginary structures yet unbuilt; in the other two, the ruins of his great-grandfather's house near Queenstown. 'The Ruins' is close kin to the poems of the 1940s, and envisages not a flourishing civilization of the future, but a land possessed of an inhabited past (of a distinctly European kind — stone with ivy), a time of ghosts and memories, in contrast with 'the careless now' to which the speaking poet must return from his reverie.

In the Thurlby Domain poems Brasch evokes the decayed house of his forebears, describing it at first, but gradually moving the focus away from the external scene towards a moral interpretation whereby the picture of decay might yield up for poet and reader ('us') some consoling significance. By different routes the poems answer the questions posed by death and human imperfection in similar phrases:

> To make our peace on earth and become native
> In place and time . . .

('Letter')

and

> In celebration of death we consummate
> Our vows to place and time . . .

('Autumn')

The poet's austere acceptance of the world and the experience it brings echoes, without being limited to, the exploration of land and belonging of earlier poems.

Brasch's major poem of the post-war years, though, was a response to a person, not a place. 'The Estate', a lengthy and ambitious work written between 1948 and 1952, was addressed to T.H. Scott, scholar and mountaineer, and is the celebration of a friendship. As the title and the epigraph show, the poem returns also to the theme of the human condition, 'man's estate', expressed frequently in terms of natural imagery of mountains, trees, rocks, and flowers and framed throughout the poem by the rhythms of day and night and of the seasons. Although in its thirty-four sections swift changes of verse form and line length introduce pace and variety, the tone remains unremittingly serious and earnest — the plangent cadences of a cultivated mind — and in most respects, in spite of the beauty of some parts, this is a profoundly conservative poem.

Yet another South Island poet whose verse was frequently a response to the natural world, was Basil Dowling. His third volume, *Canterbury and Other Poems* (1949), revealed a modest and unassuming talent, at its best in simple landscape lyrics carefully made in traditional forms. Land is a benign Eden, a place of childhood innocence — 'I visited heaven here in holidays' — and only man is vile, memorably so in a poem like 'The Trapped Hare'. Vestiges of a prettified 'poetic' language hang about some of these poems and they sometimes fall prey to a complacent religious sentimentality quite foreign to Brasch.

These three southern poets, Dallas, Brasch, and Dowling, were closely associated, but the romantic temperament thrived further north too as the 1950s began. Hubert Witheford was a Wellington poet already admired for his wartime poem, 'Elegy in the Orongorongo Valley', precursor of elegies by other poets.[88] Two collections appeared in 1950 and 1951, but like Dowling, Witheford moved to Britain in the 1950s. His landscapes were chiefly of the mind, their features vague but endowed with high seriousness. A poem like 'Pine Trees in Mist' records with care how physical images of the external world enter the symbolic world of the subconscious:

> Now the eye receives them
> Loosed from earth and sun
> Pale emblems on the void
> And shadows of the mind.

The title poem of *The Falcon Mask* (1951) gives an interesting picture of the poet as priest and performer, master of the higher mysteries; and a self-conscious rhetoric appropriate to this stance is common. Devoted to the art of poetry, he is of all these late romantics the most heedless of the daily immediacy Curnow had sought, one reviewer describing the book as a 'flight from contemporaneity'.[89]

The post-war romantic temperament took luxuriant and extravagant root in the work of James K. Baxter and to a lesser degree of Alistair Campbell. It is hard to imagine the young Campbell could have written anything other than highly romantic poetry. Born in the Cook Islands to a Scottish father and Polynesian mother, orphaned as a child and brought to New Zealand, he had published little when his first book, *Mine Eyes Dazzle* (1950), became an instant success, reprinted twice, and welcomed enthusiastically by Baxter in particular.

This is poetry which evokes mood and atmosphere rather than encourages thought, by stressing associations of images and sounds rather than their syntactic structure. Baxter describes it as having 'glamour' or 'incandescence'.[90] Its power is more like that of chant, prayer, spell, lament, working at an intuitive level difficult to analyse. Though the most celebrated poem of this collection, 'Elegy', is set in a variety of South Island landscapes, they are never particular or identifiable; nor is the experience of loss on which the poem purports to be based at all personal, direct, or intimate. The sources of the poem are almost entirely literary, the beautifully handled motif of nature weeping for the lost youth thoroughly traditional, the whole poem stylized and artificial. The same can be said of the landscape and love poems making up the rest of the collection. The love poems are more exactly poems about women, or about romantic images of women, fleeting, imprecise, poignant, idealized. The landscapes are barren, isolated, and forlorn.

The finest poem in the book is 'The Return'. With all the clarity and strangeness of dream, it evokes seafarers on a beach, men or gods, but certainly Polynesian inhabitants of the land, and ends with a mysterious image of 'The drowned Dionysus, sand in his eyes and mouth, / In the dim tide lolling'. The poem is unusual for its time in remaining open to the varying apprehensions of its readers, and its ability to give verbal expression to a mythic impulse, deeply sensed but barely understood, links it with Campbell's more explicitly Polynesian poems of the 1980s.

In the late 1940s and early 1950s, at a time of many new and eloquent voices, the most celebrated was that of James K. Baxter. From the day at the end of August 1944 when his mother marched the eighteen-year-old into the Caxton Press with a sheaf of poems, until his death in October 1972 among strangers in an Auckland suburb, his work and his life, so intensely entwined, compelled public attention.

Beyond the Palisade appeared in early 1945 and was followed by *Blow, Wind of Fruitfulness* in 1948 and *The Fallen House* in 1953, both lavishly praised. *In Fires of No Return* (1958) firmly established him as a major poet. He wrote prolifically throughout these years, and no literary journal, no anthology, no publication of verse, was without Baxter poems. The intensity of his vocation, his creative energy, and his capacity to absorb the work of other poets and turn it to his own use prevailed against critical adulation, alcoholism, and temperamental gloom and restlessness, and the early collections contain some of his finest and best-known work.

Baxter was first a fluent and fertile maker of phrases and teller of stories. But he believed that such a talent carried social and moral responsibilities, and the young Baxter had a grandiose conception of the poet's role. Like Curnow he used the word 'prophet' and spoke of the poet as a 'cell of good living in a corrupt society'.[91] It is at this point that the interconnection between biography and art becomes so apparent. His inclination towards extreme behaviour was not mere dandyism, but the expression of a profound distaste for the hypocrisy of society and an attempt, naïve and confused perhaps but certainly courageous, to live out a personal integrity wherever that might lead.

Baxter drew on traditional romantic attitudes which placed value on 'the holiness of the heart's affections and the truth of the imagination', considered superior to the truths of reason. He saw the poem as confronting the primitive, irrational depths of human experience, 'the chaos inside people'.[92] Many of the early poems record personal experiences or impressions of places, scenes, the weather, or the seasons. In these poems, as well as in his love poems and poems directly addressed to others, the poet's sensibility is placed at the centre. This is a man speaking to men.

Or rather that is how it appears. For Baxter was also a highly skilled practitioner, familiar with a wide range of poets, not only the Romantics learned from his father but also Greek and Latin poets, Hopkins, Yeats, Hardy, and more recent English poets. He is also a writer with a fine sense of the theatrical. An authoritative voice, rhetorical, extravagantly gestured, pervades the poems of Baxter's first four volumes; and though its tone and manner change, it never quite leaves his poetry. For all their brilliance, many of the early poems seem designed to strike a pose, moving effortlessly and eloquently towards a resounding declamatory close.

The path from personal to universal is the same as Brasch's, the journey far more spectacular. In this writing about himself Baxter was, as has often been said, making myths, interpreting the daily and particular as a pattern of the human condition. The event is endowed with a significance beyond itself: a rocket show an image of life and death. To see the outward and physical world as signalling, through metaphor, symbol, parable, and allegory, an inner and spiritual truth, appears to have been a natural way of thought. Baxter's view of the world was religious in the broadest sense.

During the post-war years, he wrote landscape poems as frequently as any post-war romantic poet. 'Haast Pass', 'The Bay', 'Virginia Water', all start from the traditional romantic position of the poet alone with nature. But the focus is not the intensity of a personal experience, nor the characteristically New Zealand qualities of the scene (though both are elements), but a 'reading' of its symbolic significance.[93] The abiding pattern in these collections is that of the Fall, the loss of Paradise, its force for the poet clearly seen in the last lines of 'Wild Bees':

> But loss is a precious stone to me, a nectar
> Distilled in time, preaching the truth of winter
> To the fallen heart that does not cease to fall.

These and many other lines convey a pervasive sense of human imperfection, of the unremitting cycle of original sin. Mutability is a central part of such a vision, and the poems are often presented as acts of memory as well as of interpretation, conducting a journey back to childhood (another familiar romantic locale), a far-off image of the innocent, unfallen state, 'the city of instinctive wisdom'. Several of the poems explore strategies for escape from 'the grinding cycle of death and renewal', but nature is seen as hostile and alien ('Haast Pass'), love as subject to death ('To my Wife'), and in the beautiful lyric, 'Let Time Be Still', the momentary stay is recognized as a rhetorical device contrived by the voice of the poet and under constant threat.

The very accomplishments of Baxter's early work, however, seemed like an end rather than a beginning. It was as if European romanticism had taken root and flourished for the last time. Although his technical virtuosity is everywhere apparent, the art of poetry itself is not subject to creative critical scrutiny. He readily acknowledged his debts to other poets in his efforts to find a distinctive formal structure,[94] and recognized the essential conservatism of his way of making poems. He also took the way language performs in a poem for granted, seeing it as drawing on both ordinary speech and a poetic tradition, but controlled by the poet to create a clear rhythmic harmonious effect. However, though he often used a grand hieratic voice, there are interesting variations in tone. The second 'Letter to Noel Ginn' is written in a very tight form and mostly comes from the mouth of a poetic persona, yet the relaxed conversational tone allows the possibility of irony not much visible elsewhere. It was a straw in the wind, however, and the ballad-like 'Lament for Barney Flanagan' (1954), showed more clearly a way forward.

The major post-war poems of A.R.D. Fairburn, 'The Voyage' and 'To a Friend in the Wilderness', continue the romantic mode of his earlier verse. A persistent romanticism also informs the poetry of Denis Glover, who would become as much a legend, though of a robust, ribald, rollicking kind, as Baxter. The poems of *Sings Harry and Other Poems* and *Arawata Bill: A Sequence of Poems*, for which he is best known, seem also to belong to an earlier period among the verse of the Caxton anthology, but in fact they were published in 1951 and 1953 respectively. In their simple, unaffected way they attempt to sing the songs of a new land, the images of river, mountain, land, and sea starkly fulfilling Curnow's descriptions of earlier verse. But the nostalgia which pervades 'Sings Harry' surely has its source in the war, which affected Glover profoundly. 'Returning from Overseas', a deliberate riposte to the earlier 'Leaving for Overseas', is not one of the 'Sings Harry' poems but it sets the scene for those songs of innocence and experience by its rueful contrast between then, 'the land of our remembered past . . . nourishing its golden trees' and now, 'a sullen and perplexing coast' with its mundane urban present. The 'Sings Harry' poems regret the loss of an idyllic rural past, a simple, unpretentious physical existence when man was alone in harmony with nature. 'All of a beautiful world has gone'; 'I remember paddocks opening green'; 'Once the days were clear' run a succession of opening lines with their haunting memories of 'once', before war, before quarrels, before city and civilization existed. While there is clearly strong personal emotion here, it is controlled and broadened by the use of the persona Harry, the poet stepping into the poem as a simple balladeer (not a Baxterian rhetorician), as well as by the regular verse forms and the restraint of the language. Arawata Bill and Mick Stimson, heroes of two later sequences, are based on historical figures, a goldminer and a Banks Peninsula fisherman, and also express mythic themes of loss and yearning, but neither group of poems has, except intermittently, the surety of tone of 'Sings Harry'.

Romanticism, as Smithyman points out,[95] can generate its own ironic reaction, and Glover often enjoyed comic deflation of his own romantic leanings. However, sometimes the necessary tension between passion and mockery, between sentiment and bathos, collapses and the poems fall flat. At its best though, Glover's resistance to the intellectual or the pompous in poetry, and the emphasis on deliberate and modest craftsmanship that this implies, produces verse that is lucid, evocative, and close to actual speech: 'hard words / made crystal in clarity'.

*   *   *

Curnow's anthology and its revision were not hospitable to women poets, presumably because he did not find in the work of those currently writing much he admired (though he did endeavour, without success, to include Eileen Duggan in both his 1945 and 1960 anthologies). Chapman and Bennett in their 1956 anthology, and Louis Johnson in the *New Zealand Poetry Yearbook*, found more women poets interesting and worth encouraging. Baxter, who noted most things about the practice of poetry in New Zealand, observed that women struck difficulty in getting poems published (which seems likely) and wondered if this was because not only their subjects but also the tools they used to deal with them were rather different from those familiar to men.[96] It is certainly the case that publication outlets were entirely in the hands of men and that if the New Zealand male poet of the 1940s and 1950s brooded on his isolation and alienation, how much more acute was that of the woman poet seeking to enter the rarefied realm of the higher culture. The sparsity of publication, the almost casual, occasional air of many of the poems produced, the absence of intellectuality about poetry by women, go back beyond the narrowness of editors and publishers to speak of the timidity, loneliness, and guilt experienced by a woman who might be a serious poet in the post-war golden age of the suburban wife and mother.

Eileen Duggan succeeded by locating herself within the Georgian tradition and the Catholic community, and by a determined sense of a vocation. Not the least of the qualities of her last book, *More Poems* (1950), is a steely confidence. Indeed there is little lush 'feminine' romanticism here, and the book impresses most for its zeal in the pursuit of analogies and its boldness in their capture. Her tone was not always sure, and her work showed crashing lapses of taste even in this her most accomplished collection; her inclination to didacticism sometimes spoiled what might have been more complex moral exploration.

Of the women publishing frequently in the 1940s and 1950s Mary Stanley is clearly the one whose neglect is least justified. She did not appear in *Landfall*, Curnow ignored her in both his anthologies and so did Vincent O'Sullivan in his 1970 anthology. But poems were published occasionally in the *Arts Year Book* and in the *New Zealand Poetry Yearbook*, and her one collection, *Starveling Year* (1953), was well received at the time. Her subjects are those supposedly favoured by women poets, though they are simply human — the close relationships within families and the mortal condition before God. The poems are personal and particular in origin and retain that intimate quality throughout; they are about powerful and sometimes conflicting emotions and that too is recognized by the reader. But Stanley exercises a crafty intelligence in the making of the poem; she is interested in the deliberate formal organization of language indebted to a tradition but releasing its potential to startle or please:

> Night puts
> an ear on silence where
> a child might cry

or

> To crook
> Your finger knocks my heart

or

Our traitor breath makes sinners of us all.

This wit and polish, a sensitive and inventive use of language, contrasts with the often bland literalness of a poet like Ruth Gilbert, who, dealing in similar territory, too often falls from simplicity and directness into banality. Stanley's original and alert mind conducts a quiet subversion within the conventional stereotype of wife and mother, assumed sentimentalist. This kind of subversion is sometimes apparent in Gloria Rawlinson's work, but not reliably — there are some sharp, strong poems in her 1963 collection, *Of Clouds and Pebbles*, but equally some trivial, coy, and sentimental ones.[97] Her abilities were more naturally lyric: in the fragments of *The Islands Where I Was Born* (1955) she takes a typically romantic subject, memories of a Tongan childhood — 'in the apple of a heavenly eye' — to reach at moments something more challenging.

A heavily weighted opposition between reason and emotion or between nature and humanity appears facile and predictable in Rawlinson, and also in Ruth France, writing under the name 'Paul Henderson', in *Unwilling Pilgrim* (1955).[98] The reluctance to disclose her sex, however understandable, gives an odd quality to this poet's work, depriving it of passion and intensity, even when arguing for just those qualities. Her plain, serviceable language and syntax, deliberately unostentatious, work best in two narrative poems, 'After Flood' and 'New Year's Bonfire', which execute a natural and unpretentious switch from vivid event to potent symbol.

It is not possible to make any fruitful generalizations about these women poets. To say they write about families, gardens, landscapes is about as true as it is for male poets, and they write about other matters too: to suggest a narrower range of attention simply belies much of Duggan's last volume, for example. This is the difficulty with Baxter's remarks. To emphasize the central importance of personal feeling might be as close as one could get, if only to add immediately that the uses made of this slippery substance are extraordinarily varied in kind and in competence. Duggan and Stanley are both poets with strong romantic strains, but both at their best are capable of an intellectual detachment in fashioning the poem which puts them in another camp altogether. It is the failure to recognize this quality which has been responsible for their neglect until much later, and for the shallow stereotyping of rather complex verse as sentimental, domestic, or feminine.[99]

'Poetry as a present adventure': Modernist Poets, 1945-60

In contrast to the neo-romantic poets writing in New Zealand between 1945 and 1960 were others who might be called modernist. The distinctions between the two groups are not absolute. Brasch, for example, shares some modernist traits; all the modernists show some debt to the English Romantic movement and its later exponents, particularly Yeats; both owed something to Auden, Spender, and MacNeice. Some poets, like Witheford, moved during their careers from one group to the other. Furthermore, there are characteristics common to the poetry of both groups which were challenged only at a later period, most notably the authoritative, ordering role of the poet and the allegiance to a high-cultural tradition.

This division of post-war poets is not new: it was recognized with varying degrees of subtlety and emotion at the time.[100] As an analytic tool focusing on the poets' work, a variant was developed by Kendrick Smithyman in his 1965 study of recent New Zealand poetry, *A Way of Saying*. He makes a distinction between 'romantic' and 'academic' poetry; but while 'romantic' is a term broad enough and familiar enough to serve, 'academic' is too narrow in its implications and fails to acknowledge the links between these poets and movements in other places.

The difference, as proposed here, is to do with language. The romantic poets assume, and aim at, a kind of transparency of language — it works, powerfully or delicately, to convey a meaning apprehended without difficulty according to the usual rules of logic and syntax. The poem is a skilful means by which the poet shares thoughts, feelings, experiences with the reader or listener.

The modernist poet, on the other hand, regards the poem, the creation in words, as an object of interest in itself. The elements of language, sounds, words, phrases, sentences, and all their multifarious possibilities are seen afresh, made new: its history in the poems of the past, its present in other linguistic contexts, are noticed and exploited. This active attention to language makes the work of these poets more demanding; they require the intellectual complicity of their readers.

The difference is also a matter of the relation between poet and poem. In the romantic poem, the poet inside the poem and the poet outside it are never too far apart, even when the focus broadens out, as it usually does, towards a generalizing statement. The modernist poem begins in personal experience, but the poet in the linguistic act of making the poem depersonalizes its contents, removes himself/herself from it. The poem becomes something like a play in which invented voices speak. The poet's ideas and feelings, so vivid in romantic poems, are expressed in the modernist poem indirectly through irony, contrast, and allusion.

Both romantics and modernists recognize a separation between the poem and the world, or 'reality', outside it. But whereas the romantic poem is about reality, a kind of window on the world, the modernist poem is an analogue of reality, an image of what the world might be like.

Modernist attitudes to poetry were derived of course from Pound and Eliot, who were certainly read in New Zealand in the 1930s and 1940s; but they were taken up and developed much more vigorously in America by poets like William Carlos Williams, Wallace Stevens, Allen Tate, and John Crowe Ransom. Because New Zealand poets still looked to England, modernist ideas were slow to appear, as the strong romantic character of post-war poetry shows. However, some poets, notably Curnow and Smithyman, but also M.K. Joseph, Charles Spear, and at times Keith Sinclair, were now writing what could be called modernist poetry.

*   *   *

It seems increasingly clear that Allen Curnow will come to be regarded as one of the great modernist poets in the English language. His dominance over fifty years of New Zealand poetry, however, has sometimes been resisted by other poets, particularly in recent years, and he has never been a 'popular' poet. The complexity, austerity, and intelligence of his writing has also somewhat deterred critics, and his continuing achievement still awaits the critical attention it merits.

Jack Without Magic (1946), brief and bleak, was followed in 1949 by a larger collection, *At Dead Low Water and Sonnets*, which reprinted poems from his two previous volumes alongside twelve new ones. Joy is not easily wrung from this collection either, though its technical and verbal preoccupations make it important; and the shift towards the personal in the title poem shows the way Curnow's interests were moving. It was not until 1957 that he published a new volume, *Poems, 1949-57*, revealing the vivid effects of his first trip outside New Zealand, eighteen months in 1949 and 1950 spent in England and the United States. This collection is vigorous, confident, and varied in tone, subject, and especially form; and the characteristic Curnow voice, so familiar from later work, is clearly audible. The poems fall loosely into two groups: those written overseas or in association with his overseas journey, notably the elegy for his father; and those, including 'To Forget Self and All' and 'Spectacular Blossom', from the ensuing years in Auckland, where he moved in 1951.

Fundamental to Curnow's poetry, as to his criticism, is the relation he observes between the poet, the poem, and the 'real' world, always connected but always emphatically distinct. The effort of the poet is to capture the 'real', 'the obstinate *outwardness* of things and men', to attempt what memory fails to do: 'if memory were ever good enough — even of a moment ago! — would we want poetry?'[101] There is no question for Curnow that reality is 'prior to the poem', being in all its particularity what occupies us daily. This here and now (which is not of course merely the physical) is complex, confused, subject to time and decay, fascinating but elusive. The problem of how to grasp it is the focus of a number of poems in the 1957 collection, poems about poems, or poems about art-and-reality, a favourite modernist subject. They include

'A Leaf', 'To Forget Self and All', 'He Cracked a Word', and the two elegies on the deaths of fellow poets Dylan Thomas and Wallace Stevens.

Curnow regarded the poem itself as an artefact made in language. In a note written much earlier he had defined poetry as 'the skilful making of things with language, things which will please and stimulate the mind', and his attention to the craft of poetry was always rigorous and painstaking, each 'seedy word' being deliberately placed, nothing left to chance or habit.[102] The many sonnets of the 1940s gathered in *At Dead Low Water* are dense, concentrated, nimble, and witty in their use of language. In poems like 'With How Mad Steps', 'In Memoriam, R.L.M.G.', and 'Old Hand of the Sea', elaborate metaphysical conceits, multiple meanings, literary allusions, and unlikely conjunctions of adjective and noun, noun and verb, defamiliarize linguistic usage.

Curnow is technically accomplished, but his approach to form is inventive and flexible in contrast to Baxter's conservatism. His work of the 1940s shows an almost obsessive interest in the sonnet form — more than thirty from *Sailing or Drowning* through to the deft 'To Introduce the Landscape to the Language' in *Poems, 1949-57*, and including the last section of 'At Dead Low Water'. The concentration and precision of the form attracted him, particularly in its Shakespearean variant of three rhymed quatrains and a final strong couplet. Yet within that formal structure Curnow is bold and creative, varying length of line and rhythmical pattern, alternating rhymes with half-rhymes, allowing syntax to override quatrain breaks. As he plays with linguistic expectations in these poems, so he also plays with the reader's knowledge of the sonnet, not only its formal characteristics, but its usual subjects and contexts. A good example is 'Eden Gate', where the powerful strains in the form reflect the tension between order and chaos in the poem's image of the Fall.

T.S. Eliot's comment that the function of poetry was 'to transmute . . . personal and private agonies into something rich and strange, something universal and impersonal'[103] is highly relevant to Curnow's poetry in these years. The poet's own experience and emotion is where the poems start, as he suggests in 'He Cracked a Word', but they end as autonomous 'things which will please and stimulate the mind'. In the early 1940s he had expressed personal anxieties about identity and place in public poems attempting to form a national myth or tradition. In the two major post-war collections, there is an evident shift of attention away from public occasions to personal events. As well as the moving childhood memory in 'At Dead Low Water', there are two sonnets on his grandmother and great-aunt, one to the composer Douglas Lilburn, a group of love sonnets, and (in the later collection) the elegy for his father; and there are also the many poems about belief and knowledge which dominate the 1957 book.

The shift, as the poet himself notes, is in subject, not in style: these are still public poems — 'all poems, if any good at all, are public acts'; and it was not immediate nor complete.[104] Many poems up to 1962 can be read as explorations both of the individual and the national condition. In 'In Memoriam, R.L.M.G.' a personal tribute is also an image for the alienation of settlers — 'her clay chose that way home'; 'When the Hulk of the World' is a poem about separation, colonial or personal; in 'Elegy For My Father' the poet prays for atonement from the guilt of the imperial conqueror, or of the son absent at his father's death, or of sinful humanity:

> sweet relic atone
> To our earth's Lord for the pride of all our voyages,
> That the salt winds which scattered us blow softer.

The relatively brief period in which Curnow's poetry deliberately addressed national concerns obscures to some extent the continuing religious focus of his work, with biblical imagery as natural to him as breathing. The twin Christian myths of the Fall and the Atonement, of expulsion and sacrifice, pervade all his writing, providing not only a means of reading New Zealand's history but also an entry to those more private concerns, of which death is the most persistent. The Fall is a central subject in 'At Dead Low Water' (as it is in Baxter's poems of the same period), now something to be faced and accepted on an individual plane. One can observe in the late 1940s a process whereby the poet, no longer constrained by the doctrinal force of this myth, is endeavouring to recover affirmative values from the sombre facts of sin and dying. In 'A Sonata of Schubert', with its echoes of Nashe and Stevens, 'pain' is associated with 'joy':

> It is the falling brightness
>
> From keen unusual skies, omen of birds,
> Day breaking at the beach of sacrifice.

These powerful associations of death, beauty, sexuality, and sacrifice are most richly celebrated in 'Spectacular Blossom', a poem written in the mid-1950s which is at one level a response to the changed circumstances of his personal life; here flowering pohutukawas at the sea's edge function as dramatic and complex symbols.

For all Curnow's focus on the 'real', however, he is never a 'realist' poet, his landscapes never mere geography: 'Life is the wrong shop / For pictures, you say, having all points and no view'. He is profoundly interested in the interpretation of the real, in what we see and how we know. Particularly in the 1957 collection, there is an unwillingness to allow a single point of view, a holistic belief, to control the world of the senses. His delight in pun and multiple meaning is in part a recognition of the possibility of different ways of seeing, of contrary angles, opposing viewpoints. Images of vision, seeing, mirrors, and pictures are common, for example, in 'A Small Room with Large Windows' ('What it would look like . . .'), 'Old Hand of the Sea', 'Jack-in-the-Boat' ('Children, children, come and look'). In a number of poems (for example in 'Keep in a Cool Place' and 'When the Hulk of the World') the position from which the poem looks outward suddenly shifts, producing a clash of perspectives. 'The Eye Is More Or Less Satisfied with Seeing', with its opening image of a Janus-face and its jaunty couplets, reflects a similar ambiguity of vision. The use of alternating voices, as in the different sections of the longer poems, and of refrains as ironic comment on the main text, are all ways of representing this insecurity — or diversity — of view. They give the 1957 collection a sceptical cast, but lift it out of the gravity and density, the darker mood, of the previous book.

'A Small Room with Large Windows' addresses the problem of 'uncertainties, mysteries, doubts' directly, ironically positing a simple holistic answer to 'the questions that are always private and unanswerable'; to this is contrasted the muddied, muddled world, 'what you call a view', changing, dying; a third section mocks simplistic theories about how to live in such a world; but finally a series of epiphanies, momentary images of beauty and harmony, provide a solution which is a move from the discursive (and rational) to the iconic (and inexplicable). The see-sawing parts of the poem, its coastal setting, its epistemological concerns, loop back to 'At Dead Low Water' and suggest where the poet has come in these ten productive years. The 1944 poem is a more formal, more sombre work. Its language gains a theological gravity from the predominance of religious symbols and themes, and its mood is one of painful and poignant regret at the passage of time and the loss of innocence. The later poem is lighter in tone, more casual and detached in manner, the imagery less weighty with the past but retaining a brilliant clarity all the same, 'like a burst of accurate fire'. A phrase from 'To Introduce the Landscape to the Language', 'And where, from here, do you go?' was indeed the question for a poet who had already developed and perfected a distinctive style. Only one new poem, 'An Oppressive Climate, a Populous Neighbourhood', a bleak and bitter poem written in New York, was added to the 1962 *Selected Poems*.

Of the young poets who emerged after the war Kendrick Smithyman was certainly the most revolutionary. That was, however, little recognized at the time.[105] Always a prolific poet, he published widely in journals, both in New Zealand and abroad, from the early 1940s. Book publishers were less generous: *The Blind Mountain* (1950) was eventually followed by *Inheritance* (1962) and *Flying to Palmerston* (1968). The poems in *The Blind Mountain* were written between 1945 and 1948 and are abstract, intricate, and polished. Both the other books contain some poems of much earlier dates, often considerably revised; *Inheritance*, in particular, is an impressive and mature collection, with the poems of the late 1950s (like 'Waikato Railstop', 'Climbing in the Himalaya', and 'Muriwai 1957') the finest he had written. In an odd parallel to Curnow, Smithyman was less productive in the 1960s and re-emerged in the 1970s and 1980s writing a rather different kind of poetry.

We know something of the way Smithyman saw his work from *A Way of Saying*, which is, among other things, a modest apologia for his own poetic: the move he claimed to identify from romantic to academic poetry was as much desired as described.

Academic poems favour more complex, even baroque, structures and more ramified operations than is usual with romantic writing . . . . The academic writers are . . . more readily given to 'tragedy, irony and multitudinous distinction'. They like to capitalize on the pleasure of intellect in verbal play and wit. Their poems are based, if not on learning, then often on an active body of information.[106]

No better description could be given of Smithyman's poetry up till the 1960s. In these poems, the reader is an active participant in the process of the poem, not a passive receptacle into which simple sensuous waves flow. However, readers not used to bringing intellect and knowledge to bear on the understanding of poetry found Smithyman difficult, and wider appreciation of his importance came late in the day. A recent study of his poetry arguing for syntax as the key to his poetic method, shows the truly radical nature of this earlier work — each poem was an experiment to see what language could do ('to see how the machine worked'). But syntax was only one of the complex structures Smithyman bent to distinctive use; he was also master of a learned literary tradition of rhetoric, emblem, and verse form which he used to provoke syntax into meaning. His poetry is often the pursuit of elaborate analogies, a poetry, as he said of Donne's, 'of multiple reference and function', the mind darting 'variously' (a favourite word) in several directions at once, as something like an argument or more like 'an extensive grid of intersecting remarks' is erected.[107]

A further challenge to his audience was Smithyman's encyclopaedic mind. Curnow, describing him as 'that clever hedge-hopping pilot of his art', stressed Smithyman's loving and lifelong devotion to facts: 'I like to . . . have my feet on a fact before I start to write about the place'.[108] Facts about places are favourite beginnings, developed into plays of ideas using perhaps Jungian archetype or religious trope. His home territory, Northland and Auckland, has provided material for many poems. The most international of the post-war poets, Smithyman was also the most local: he saw himself as a regionalist poet and, like other contemporaries, had little interest in a poetry of national identity.

He is also a poet of the modern city (a Smithyman bar-room ballad is *sui generis*), and of the modern family, exploring the personae of parent and husband in a manner, to quote Pound, 'austere, direct, free from emotional slither'. There are many love poems, including some beautiful early lyrics, in the first two books; and Baxter justly describes Smithyman as a 'robust metaphysical love poet'. A poem like 'How to Dispose of Ajax' shows much of the confidence, elegance, and wit of its seventeenth century precursors.

However, for all their aplomb, many poems in these three books strike a self-mocking note. Ghosts and shadows haunt, there are many deaths by drowning, and doubts about truth and meaning persist. Above all, anxieties about language, 'the screen of our words', and about the adequacy of the fictions we make to live by, disturb Smithyman: 'none of my words will get it right'. His stern vow of impersonality ('I tried to be concerned with the poems rather than with me')[109] had perhaps led him as far as it could.

M.K. Joseph was a poet admired by Smithyman and considered typical of the 'academic' poets. Better known as a novelist, he first appeared as a poet soon after the war. He was also a poet for whom literature was a 'game of knowledge'. Ingenious, playful, highly structured, Joseph's verse has an ease and lightness of touch which might suggest the hand of a skilled amateur. Its direct and polished surface has nothing like the density of Smithyman or Curnow. But appearances can deceive. The series of poems on painters, for example, is a brilliant and urbane *tour de force*. 'A Riddle: of the Soul', on the other hand, is the kind of poem which might divide readers: a highly patterned poem, depending on precision and paradox, it was admired by Smithyman for its iconic character, but others might consider it merely an elegant but superficial exercise in the seventeenth century manner.

Joseph ranges in fact through a wide variety of verse forms, styles, and voices, showing a talent for imitation sometimes deliberately turned to parody and pastiche. His themes and interests also range widely. The experience of war continued to mark his work long after, and this was probably the source of the strong sense of public events, of the wide world in which poets as well as ordinary men and women lived, apparent in many poems. His deft satire of the complacencies of the 1950s had considerable appeal.

Twopence Coloured (1951) was Charles Spear's only book, a collection of curious poems, much loved by anthologists. Brief, conventional in form, they originated mainly as dreams and are remarkable for the clarity and polish with which strange visions of beauty or terror are expressed. Like Joseph's, this is a mind nourished by books, not by society or landscape, and the poet's personal experience is nowhere to be found. Glimpses of far-off European history, single moments from a novel, fragments of Greek myth, jostle with pictures of twentieth century city life. Each word is chosen with the utmost care by one who knows its weight and history but has a weakness, all the same, for bells, chimes, stars, swords, and butterflies, and for colours like azure, opal, and violet. The exquisite surface of the poems, however, is pierced from time to time by witty and ironic barbs, reminiscent of the early Eliot. And behind the carefully cultivated romance and glamour are the sounds of distant and not so distant wars. This ironic, mannered voice is very much of its age, but not particularly of its place.

A poet like Keith Sinclair shows the limitations of a simple division between post-war romanticism and modernism, for he effortlessly straddles both. To a young man returned from the war, full of intellectual and creative energy, the post-war years were a time of excitement and promise. Later the teaching and writing of history absorbed most of Sinclair's formidable abilities but in the 1940s and 1950s his poems appeared as often as Smithyman's and Baxter's in journals and anthologies. By 1962 three books had been published. He is kin to Curnow and Smithyman in his method of proceeding by the inventive deployment of resemblances, sometimes exploding line after line, sometimes wittily developed throughout the course of a poem. However, his poems always have a visceral energy and the effect is often strongly sensual. Their repeated, indeed obsessive, theme is love. In *Songs for a Summer*, for example, Donne and Dylan Thomas father a multitude of songs, lively, flamboyant, occasionally trapped in verbal excess but exhibiting a natural lyric talent.

Perhaps only Baxter of the post-war generation owed as clear a debt to his elders, and Curnow was quick to note in some of Sinclair's poems the imaginative use of the historical subject. However, Sinclair's continuing nationalism is not anxious or neurotic; he mocked 'the no-monoliths-on-our-hills or the South Island school of poets who perpetually reflect on the fact of our brief residence in these islands', and approached national themes and subjects in a direct, matter-of-fact, and generally optimistic way. Ambitious and eager, he wished 'to help make New Zealand less "sheep and gold", more storied, through art and ideas more real and enhanced'. Thus the famous 'Memorial to a Missionary', 'Ihumatao', and especially 'The Ballad of Meola Creek', accept the place in all its solid detail and, even more boldly, the people who had already lived there for centuries. Similarly, in the love poetry, as a southern reviewer noted, images of hot Auckland summers, beaches, birds, and boats 'in the brown months', show a poet completely at ease with his environment.[110]

The Politics of Poetry, 1951–60

Discussion about the nature of poetry in New Zealand, initiated by Curnow in the Caxton anthology, quickly became vigorous in the years that followed. The 1951 Writers' Conference in Christchurch struck a rare note of harmony and optimism among New Zealand writers. Its star turn was Baxter's speech on 'Recent Trends in New Zealand Poetry', in which he mentioned a group of poets writing in Wellington, where he himself had moved in 1949, who seemed to be making a 'fresh start'.[111] Often known as the 'Wellington group', they included W.H. Oliver, Alistair Campbell, Louis Johnson, and Hubert Witheford, as well as Baxter himself. The terms in which Baxter spoke of them ('free from the schizophrenia of the New Zealander who cannot distinguish himself from his [colonial] grandfather'), and some of their own declarations elsewhere, suggested that these young men saw themselves in opposition to the older generation who controlled most of the publication outlets, and especially to Curnow and the naïve nationalism they attributed to him. This was the beginning of a feud which lasted well into the 1960s, separating Baxter and Curnow, and breaking the precarious harmony of May 1951.

Louis Johnson, who became the central figure of the Wellington group, was yet another prolific young poet. His first two books, *The Sun Among the Ruins* and *Roughshod Among the Lilies* (both 1951), present intense, ungainly poems concerned with love, death, and the role of the artist. He proclaimed a new abstraction in New Zealand poetry,[112] and a general vagueness is certainly one of the flaws of his early verse.

But Johnson was more important as an energetic and unfailingly generous editor and promoter of poets and poetry. No one did more during the 1950s and 1960s to encourage new talent and to create an audience, in a country and at a time when such a task might have seemed foolish. In 1951 he established the *New Zealand Poetry Yearbook* as 'an annual collection of the best New Zealand poetry' and edited it until its demise in 1964 (he simultaneously ran the Capricorn Press, publishing volumes of poetry, and was an editor of a quarterly, *Numbers*). Each issue of the *Yearbook* included work by thirty to forty poets, both new and established, and was introduced by an editorial in which Johnson commented on the current scene and included a list of recently published volumes. Reviews (of which Curnow's were the most acerbic) consistently mentioned a certain laxity of critical standards in the selection. Curnow argued, characteristically, against 'easy publication' on the grounds that it failed to develop rigorous critical understanding in an audience; on the other hand, Johnson, also characteristically, showed a commendable willingness to chance his arm by welcoming newcomers — six or seven in each issue — and by a generous catholicity of taste. The yearly collection became a subject of lively debate.

Although personalities and regional antagonisms between Auckland and Wellington fuelled the debate, it was primarily a generational conflict, the inevitable response of a new generation to what seemed the outdated concerns of its predecessors, as Johnson later recognized. In a 1954 lecture on 'Symbolism in New Zealand Poetry', Baxter claimed that 'the myth of insularity . . . has proved something of a stilt-house against the tide of new development', that Curnow's devotion to it explained his neglect of Johnson, Campbell, and Joseph in the 1951 revised anthology, and that 'the specifically *New Zealand* features of our writing are not . . . what appeals to the overseas reader, but the sense of reality suffered, which is much the same in any time or country'. A nationalist strait-jacket, he implied, was being imposed on an exciting new poetry of more universal concerns. Curnow, for his part, switched the argument away from content towards poetics, persistently attacking the poetry of the Wellington poets, including Baxter, for what he saw as a deplorable return to the neo-Georgian sins of sentimentality, literariness, vagueness, and rhetoric.[113]

Were the younger poets in Wellington really writing a different kind of poetry? Did the national/universal division correspond in any way to the distinction proposed in this History between romantic and modernist poets? Was there a modernist plot to discredit romantic poetry?

As we have seen, Baxter, Campbell, and Witheford began writing in a romantic mode, a style for which Curnow had decreasing sympathy, but which at first drew upon the New Zealand landscape, its loneliness and grandeur, for image and symbol. However, they had never been much interested in New Zealand identity *per se*, and it is possible to see a gradual movement in these poets away from the natural scene to a more direct, more austere treatment of 'the concerns of the human heart'.[114] W.H. Oliver, whose *Fire Without Phoenix* appeared in 1957, drew on landscape observed in both New Zealand and Britain, to address personal and sometimes spiritual matters.

Johnson was primarily a romantic poet, with 'his own dark angel, fluent, expressive, persistent, persuasive'; his work had an almost baroque extravagance which made a virtue of private feeling. However, it owed little to the *Lyrical Ballads*, and a good deal more to the French poets of the nineteenth century. For Johnson, and later for a further group of Wellington poets writing from the mid-1950s (Charles Doyle, Peter Bland, and Gordon Challis), romantic poetry had decisively left the hills and the seashore to inhabit the modern city. The 'reality' of personal experience in a contemporary urban environment was what they hoped to convey in their verse.[115] Love, marriage, and parenthood in a domestic setting were repeated themes; but these poets also turned their pens and their passions towards the bland, self-satisfied society in which they were living, writing poetry of social comment which was well aware of its New Zealand context. Poems in Johnson's third collection, *New Worlds for Old* (1957), have titles like 'A Backstreet of the Welfare State' and 'Suburban Train'.

This shift of focus was not peculiar to the romantic poets, however. The modernists had taken the same road earlier, and the modernist movement in New Zealand was in part a move from public and prophetic pronouncement to deliberate linguistic artefact using material that might well be personal or social. At the same time, some romantic poets continued to draw on the natural world. There was in fact considerable flexibility and variety in the 'reality' to which all poets were attentive, and the 1950s marked an extension of subjects about which poetry was possible.

Wellington writers were themselves increasingly prey to modernist influences. In *A Way of Saying*, Smithyman went so far as to describe Wellington poetry simply as one type of 'academic' writing: the 'School of Johnson'. Certainly many of the younger poets in both groups showed interest in perfecting traditional forms (sestinas flourished throughout the land), pursued the unexpected — even bizarre — image, were resistant to holistic explanations of human behaviour, and increasingly inclined towards indirect and ironic expression of meaning, and the use of invented personae or miniature fictions. An interesting attack by Witheford on Baxter for not writing like Pound shows the way the Wellington wind was blowing.[116]

Curnow's influence was powerful, but other interpretations of the contemporary scene were certainly heard. The Oxford *Anthology of New Zealand Verse*, selected by Robert Chapman and Jonathan Bennett, appeared in 1956. Although it did not have the impact of Curnow's anthology, it conducted a few minor subversions of its own, preserving the Curnow canon but making a somewhat wider entrance-way for younger poets. In his introduction, Chapman placed himself squarely beside Johnson by asserting that, by the mid-1950s, poets were able 'to feel so at ease with their environment that they can simply assume it and find themselves freed to deal directly with the concerns of poetry everywhere'.[117]

But Curnow's new anthology, *The Penguin Book of New Zealand Verse* (1960), claimed flatly that '[n]owhere in the last decade have there been any poetic departures worth mentioning'. In the opening paragraph of his introduction, he eloquently reaffirmed his belief that '[w]hatever is true vision belongs, here, uniquely to the islands of New Zealand', and much of his account of the history and character of New Zealand poetry which followed implied similar views, expressed somewhat more dogmatically than before.[118] He was also careful, sensing opposition, to repeat the claim that there is no contradiction between a poetry responsive to its location, and one of universal application: 'if they are good, they cannot but be news of the human condition'. But he no longer spoke of new personal and universal themes, and there was a disparity between the general tenor of his argument and the way in which his own poetry was developing.

Curnow's introduction has by now become part of the culture which it describes. Such was the success of the Penguin volume that his words defined the tradition, and largely still do for the thousands that read them. But, as Baxter and other reviewers were quick to point out, other readings were possible. Neither in the introduction to the Penguin nor in its selection of poems was Curnow willing to grant to the new generation anything like the potency of their predecessors.

Romanticism in Retreat, 1960-72

During the 1960s, there was a gradual change in the prevailing view of what constituted a poem. Post-war romanticism was modified, adapted, and altered so that, by the early 1970s, the modernist poem was the generally accepted model.[119] In the process, poets and poetry became more diverse, and the affixing of labels or the defining of groups is not always the most useful way of describing them. Romantic poems continued to be written, and the most popular poets, such as Hone Tuwhare and later Sam Hunt, tended to be romantics, since the notion of poetry in the wider public mind had altered little. But the poets who emerged in the late 1950s and early 1960s had been suckled on Eliot, and had grown up into a less optimistic world in which grand prophetic statements seemed inappropriate. At the same time, many of the post-war romantics were adjusting their practice towards a more 'objective' verse, more condensed, more informal, and more self-conscious in its expression.

The sense of place, and the visual, symbolic, and nationalistic uses to which New Zealand landscape had been put, ceased to attract the poetic imagination in the same way. The younger poets had travelled abroad, often for some years; some, like Fleur Adcock, emigrated permanently; others, like Peter Bland, were English immigrants. Isolation was less potent, foreign wars seemed uncomfortably close, and New Zealand was by no means immune from the cultural changes experienced by most Western countries in those years.

For many poets writing in the 1960s, personal experience seemed the most certain point at which to begin; but the challenge was how to use this 'felt' life in a way that gave the poem its own validity. Modernist techniques (such as Smithyman's 'ostensive' and 'social' fictions,[120] and the use of wit, irony, and word play), or more romantic ones (such as the rewriting of myth), were possible solutions. Some saw the 1960s as introducing, in verse by Louis Johnson, Fleur Adcock, and Peter Bland, a new, informal, personal speaking voice into New Zealand poetry.

Social and political themes had not been prominent in the years after the war, but in the 1950s Baxter and Louis Johnson had increasingly revived in poems the anti-Puritanism so persistent in fiction and so familiar in pre-war verse. Satire of suburb and bureaucracy featured in the work of younger Wellington poets like Bland and Doyle, and a political consciousness was active in the poetry of Stead and Tuwhare. Irony was the predominant tool, and only Baxter was driven to pronouncements of national chastisement.

Most poets in the post-war years had been conservative in their approaches to form. In general they used regular forms, but without rigidity and with a conscious attempt to accommodate the natural stress-based rhythms of speech. Many poets showed an Audenesque interest in reviving old verse forms; half-rhyme was common, and that old warhorse, the iambic pentameter, had a good antipodean run. The modernist poets were profoundly interested in the technical structure of a poem, but the full formal implications of Curnow's insistence on the real were only in the late 1950s beginning to be realized, in, for example, 'A Small Room . . .'. This development continued in the 1960s, with looser, freer forms becoming widespread and the whole matter becoming a subject of debate.

This was not simply a question of technique. The authoritative, ordering power of the poet (of which form is but an aspect), the vatic role, held increasingly less appeal. The careers of both Baxter and Curnow to some extent register this change, but it is far more striking in the very different attitudes of the poets emerging at the end of the 1960s.

The mid-1960s was a period of stocktaking. Smithyman's *A Way of Saying* (1965), Baxter's 1967 lecture on 'Aspects of New Zealand Poetry', and to a lesser degree Johnson's editorial in the last *New Zealand Poetry Yearbook* (1964), all cast a retrospective look at poetry since the war; collected volumes of Fairburn and Mason and an influential 1963 essay on Curnow by C. K. Stead[121] recalled an established tradition. Charles Doyle's modest anthology *Recent Poetry in New Zealand* (1965) was not intended to be definitive or authoritative. It claimed to present 'work in progress', was chiefly interesting for the poets' comments introducing each selection, and attempted to balance the Penguin by giving generous representation to poets like Adcock, Johnson, Bland, Gordon Challis, and Owen Leeming.

It also included the young poet C.K. Stead. Stead's astute and provocative comments on New Zealand poetry were already beginning to sharpen the critical discourse, and although Stead was clearly sympathetic to Curnow's position, he was never simply a Curnow spokesman. His poetry, of a piece with his criticism, developed its own characteristics and strengths.

The 'Truth' of poetry, according to Stead's apologia in the Doyle anthology, 'is the world, but a concentration of it so great that it brings the world nearer to us'.[122] This might describe the activity of his second book, *Crossing the Bar* (1972), which collected poems of the 1960s along with a selection from his first book, *Whether the Will is Free, Poems 1954-62* (1964). Much of Stead's early work reflected time spent in Australia and Great Britain, and an admiration for Yeats and somewhat later for Pound and Eliot. There are strong romantic traits in his first book, and his technical skill, verbal control, and musical sense are immediately evident, usually operating within traditional verse forms. The voice is developing, trying out different methods of utterance and composition, occasionally breaking out of a young man's solemnity into wit and satire.

The surgical attacks made on the poems which reappeared in *Crossing the Bar* excise all luxuriance, emotional or verbal, and adapt them for a very different setting. This collection marked the quite distinct development of a poet into his own voice, a modern, indeed modernist, one, with a sharp ironic accent still recognizable in much later work. The lyric qualities of which Stead is capable are little to be seen here, and a deep political anger seems to have provoked the tight, spare, concentrated style. The verse is looser in form and more colloquial in manner, relying on a good ear for speech rhythms and phrases, but Stead is absolutely precise in his choice of words, with puns and allusions doing double time. Some of the poems are deft epigrams for person or occasion, others are swift Poundian images. The longer poems work by quick stabs or fragments, alternating voices, contrasting scenes, juxtaposing images. In 'April Notebook' and 'A Small Registry of Births and Deaths', shots of American imperialism cut to glimpses of a son at play or an Auckland garden. The Curnow generation's sense of isolation and separation, which had latter-day echoes in Stead's first book, is now turned on its head as he sees his own life and family infected by American power in Vietnam. Images are repeatedly drawn from the Roman Empire, a context he would frequently plunder for a tone or angle on contemporary life. Caesar is the political leader, the American president, God, or poet — potentates all. The novelist is the poet's *alter ego* (the same anger was producing *Smith's Dream*) and this collection is full of invented people, small narratives, conversations and exchanges. Stead's personality is strongly present throughout, not in its intimate private self, but as an alert intelligence engaged with the world, interpreting it with wit and feeling.

Doyle was surely right also to draw attention to Fleur Adcock, by an attractive and convincing selection. Some might argue (and she has done so herself)[123] that she is an English poet, having spent part of her childhood and almost all her adult life in Britain, having had all but one of her books published there, and writing verse that fits well in the English tradition. She did, however, begin publishing poetry in New Zealand in the late 1950s and early

1960s, and was closely associated with the Wellington group during her marriage to Alistair Campbell.

Her early work has affinities with Mary Stanley's. Poems arise almost always out of personal associations, and particularly out of the closest human relationships. The poet is rarely alone, but addresses her words to another, a son, a lover, a husband; she writes with poise, ease, and often wit about the most intimate and private moments. Yet the involved and passionate participant is also a detached, analytical observer, with a wry and clear-eyed view of love, its cruelties and passing, as well as its pleasures. Her language is direct, unpretentious, and easily accessible. Her poems, the well-known 'To a Five-Year-Old' for example, or the chilling 'Incident', are beautifully constructed, using a firm but almost imperceptible control. She admits to a conservatism of form,[124] and leans towards rhyme and regular rhythms. But these are always subordinate to the contours of an informal, personal speaking voice, flexible and responsive to nuance.

Another young poet, Vincent O'Sullivan, was not included in Doyle's book, but by a nice irony was the editor of the next major anthology of New Zealand verse in 1970. Like Stead and Adcock, he was well-educated, well-travelled, and well read, and he has always been a highly sophisticated and cerebral writer, drawing on an impressive knowledge of European culture. He has consistently been drawn to myth as a profound explanatory pattern of human existence shared with a wide community past and present. His early work returns again and again to classical mythology, rewriting old stories, adapting them to present situations, siting them in contemporary Mediterranean landscapes. By implication, New Zealand is a land without myth, for it appears rarely in these poems; though he does increasingly attempt to write myths — or anti-myths — for that less heroic civilization too.

Kevin Ireland was a founder of the magazine *Mate*, a more sensitive register of poetry in the 1960s than *Landfall*, and many of his poems first appeared there. Although he subsequently lived in Britain for many years, he remained a very active participant in New Zealand literary life, and all his major collections have been published in New Zealand. He claims his first masters were Mason, Fairburn, and Glover, whose accents certainly show; but he also shared a common modernist predilection for the metaphysical poets.[125] The poems of his first three books, *Face to Face* (1963), *Educating the Body* (1967), and *A Letter from Amsterdam* (1972), are spare, crisp, and witty, with a poise which belies their considerable craft and labour. There is surprisingly little interest in exile or separation, and Ireland writes best and most frequently about love, happy to use traditional themes and highly patterned forms. The lover's voice is skilfully placed at the centre of the poems, stylish, self-mocking, bawdy, but thoroughly of its time. The engagement with the woman involves dialogue, exchange, game, an active structure dependent on the wits. Ireland manages in these minimal verses to balance a cool scepticism with a warm passion, in a style already distinctive.

Peter Bland's talents as a poet are allied to his abilities as a comic actor. An

English immigrant and friend of Louis Johnson, Bland wrote an energetic and mostly humorous verse characteristically seen in his first substantial collection, *My Side of the Story* (1964). He was vociferous in attacking 'tradition-hunting and nationality-chasing' and in claiming a place for the personal. However, his poems are not strikingly personal, and are notable for the relish and comedy with which they comment on New Zealand suburban life. Specific details are freshly observed, but the plaster gnomes are sitting ducks; and sometimes the emotional response seems trite or sentimental. It was when the reading of William Carlos Williams and other Americans in the mid-1960s encouraged a more relaxed and less moralizing tone,[126] and when his flair for dramatic invention propelled him towards fantasy in poems like 'The Building' and 'Landfall, with Cannibals, Goats and Mirrors', that he wrote his best. *Mr Maui*, a collection published after his return to England in 1968, includes some particularly crisp and vivid inventions.

Two other Wellington immigrant poets, Charles Doyle and Gordon Challis,[127] are in retrospect modest if respectable talents. Doyle wrote on exile and, later, on suburban and family life with a dusting of satire; Challis was a more skilled and careful craftsman, his best poems thoughtfully developed metaphors of the human condition.

While the poets that gathered around Johnson in Wellington benefited from shared ideas and enthusiasms, others, working largely in isolation, serve to emphasize the growing diversity of the art. Janet Frame and Hone Tuwhare, for example, drew on very different traditions and habits.

Janet Frame as poet is original, as one would expect. Her poems are as rich and strange as her prose. It is probable that Frame never thought of herself very seriously as a poet, and the poems densely packed into her single collection, *The Pocket Mirror* (1967), have an occasional air and a higgledy-piggledy variety of themes, tones, and forms. Those who call her novels 'poetic' are suggesting presumably that language carries more than its usual share of meaning in 'realistic' contexts; certainly metaphor is pervasive in the poems, which are at once full of concrete detail and of signals of truths beyond. Death remains a persistent concern; so do the falsities and hypocrisies of contemporary life, which might include a Southeast Asian war or a commercial radio advertisement; and so always do the powers, deceits, temptations, and pleasures of words themselves: clichés and facile formulas are unpacked relentlessly, often with wit. Frame prefers an easy colloquial mannner, using rhyme and stress patterns as they come along, and is hostile to the strait-jacket of conventional forms — which she calls 'their merry-go-round of words and postures known'. In some of the poems most of the words are invented; in others, familiar words are cut up and their parts examined — characteristic games, revelling in the raw material and exploring its arbitrary and fragile nature. The guileless certainty with which fantasy, symbol, and disjunction are conveyed, often in the matter-of-fact tones of nursery rhyme or fable, is as convincing and as disturbing as in the novels.

The appearance in the late 1950s of poems by Hone Tuwhare, a boilermaker who had been encouraged to write by R.A.K. Mason, only drew attention to the almost total absence, since early sentimentalities, of poems in English by or about Māori. While some fiction-writers were writing on Māori topics, few poets — Sinclair and Rawlinson are exceptions — even acknowledged their presence; and the richness of the oral tradition in Māori was little known among Pākehā. Curnow, after criticism of the Caxton anthology, included English versions of some Māori 'poems' in the Penguin, and with the establishment of the magazine *Te Ao Hou* in 1952 and especially when Margaret Orbell was editor in the 1960s, a small gateway was opened for the publishing of work, usually in English, by Māori writers. *Mate* was also hospitable to Māori writing, and Barry Mitcalfe persistently drew attention, in his own writing and in his editorial and publishing activities, to the power of the Māori oral tradition.[128]

Tuwhare's first collection, *No Ordinary Sun* (1964), was reprinted eleven times. Its powerful lyric quality, notably in short poems of nostalgia, regret, or grief ('The mana of my house has fled, / the marae is but a paddock of thistle'), was widely praised. The directness and 'uncommon emotional honesty' (Baxter's phrase)[129] of Tuwhare's verse was unusual, and drew its solidity and confidence from the oral strengths of the two communities to which he belonged — the Māori, and the working class. The beautifully expressed sense of a spiritual presence in the natural world was seen as an aspect of Tuwhare's Māori heritage (though of course 'animism' had been praised and practised by Baxter and others in the romantic tradition) but the poetry also records the rapid urbanization of the Māori in the post-war years, and several powerful poems address the threat to traditional Māori values of modern technology.

Here
alien sounds are struck.
Nowhere is there greater fuss
to tear out the river's tongue.

Blue hiss and crackle
of the welding rod,
compressed sigh of air
and the whump and whoof
fuse to the rising clamour
of the rivet gun.

('The Sea, to the Mountains, to the River')

Tuwhare's poetry is often described as 'free verse' but, as MacD. P. Jackson shows, it has strong rhythmic patterns and other kinds of repetition; it owes more to the Bible than to contemporary fashions in poetry.[130] Tuwhare's robust, disrespectful vigour became more political in *Sapwood and Milk* (1973), undermining public clichés, asserting through a tough command of the vernacular the strength and compassion of ordinary people — it is dedicated 'to anyone who may feel left out, and bloody glad of it'. If the modernists and their

411

successors might be suspected of writing for an educated élite, Hone Tuwhare was quite consciously claiming a popular role for poetry.

*   *   *

These new poets moved into a scene already peopled and always changing. One of the most distinctive developments of the 1960s is the way in which the post-war romantic poets modified their verse. Some did so more than others.

Ruth Dallas remained throughout these years, in three separate collections, a fully paid-up romantic. The isolated poet's perceptions of the natural world and a wistful sense of time passing, expressed in exquisite lyric form, were still what she preferred, though she felt the study of Chinese poetry had led to developments in her style. She regarded the loosening-up of her rhythms as experimental, but it is a superficial change; aiming for a greater 'brevity and density', she only intensified the simple, sensuous quality of her language — at its best in her many songs. In *Shadow Show* (1968) there was a greater variety of themes and moods, but her poetry always carries its heart on its sleeve and its meaning on its surface. Dallas continued as a fine lyric poet, producing carefully crafted pieces; she seemed, however, to be increasingly isolated from the whole field of human engagement — people remain memories or images — and in particular from any contemporary discourse about poetry.

While Dallas marked time, Brasch's last three volumes, *Ambulando* (1964), *Not Far Off* (1969), and the posthumous *Home Ground* (1974), show him under the pressures of a new-found experience of love and the imminence of death, working out of romanticism towards a different kind of utterance. The change is, superficially at least, familiar — a more compressed line, more informal in manner, more personal in attention. In *Ambulando* the poems are noticeably less visual and the focus on place, local or national, almost gone; the language is tighter, and there is some interest in the light word-games dear to the modernists. The poet introduces himself with unexpected deliberateness, the onset of middle age allowing a little self-irony in the opening and closing poems, 'Ambulando' and 'Cry Mercy'. Personal identity and its ultimate significance are a constant subject of exploration in these three books. The relations between the one and the all, individual and humanity, poet and audience, separateness and unity, single life and natural process, now and forever — characteristically romantic themes — are treated in a variety of moods and voices. Attracted by 'the Hindu idea of the continuity of all being',[131] the poet repeatedly uses images of the extinction of personality in a wider process: '. . . a self and its leaf-selves / Living dispersed through all / With the salt grains of the sea'. This is clearly an image of death; and also of its twin, love. In two matching poems, 'In Your Presence' and 'Chantecler', the first praises the harmony of physical love, but the second asserts the prideful self, 'playing with one and all my faithless part'. While the tone of 'In Your Presence' recalls the solemn intensity of 'The Estate', 'Chantecler' in its cynical sharpness presents another voice, an ironic opposite, the polarity carrying a dramatic recognition of the impurity of things which in the end the poet must face. The abnegation of the artist before the real also signals an artistic shift — from a poetry of cool, meditative statement to the poem which enacts itself, in which contrarieties and ambiguities might cohabit, in which meaning might be complex and various rather than single and luminous.

In a revealing study of 'Home Ground', the major poem in Brasch's posthumous collection, Ian Wedde shows how this eloquent and moving work brings Brasch's lifelong pursuit of meaning simultaneously to artistic and philosophic resolution.[132] In twenty-six parts, only half of which had appeared before Brasch died, it is a ritual preparation for death. It returns to a particular place, the poet's home ground of Dunedin, the City, where he sits, 'writing in my book and watching in my glass'. The sections are fragments of the mind, the ebb and flow of the reflections of a dying man, but they are also different ways of regarding death, from the cynical to the sacramental; many romantic characteristics are still present in the verse, but this poem asks to be read in a different way from 'The Estate': 'The spur-winged plover steps and probes.' The familiar images of the dispersal of self in the natural world acquire now the vivid actuality of scattered ashes. But the poet's identity remains, as the poem declares in several ways, in his own speech:

> Silence will not let him go
> Entirely; allowed a few notes
> At the edge of dusk
> He will be recalled before long
> And folded into rock
> Reassumed by the living stream.

The poet of New Zealand rootlessness, who had sung a land where 'none knows where he will lie down at night', now uses images reminiscent of Wordsworth's Lucy poems to reach, in his final verse, an acceptance of place which is also a recognition of his own humanity.

The poetry of Denis Glover and Alistair Campbell in these years also showed unexpected evolution. For both men, a major private trauma led to a radical change from a formal romantic verse to a personal poetry, a focus on private relationships, a more colloquial idiom, and a terser, less luxuriant style.

Campbell's breakdown in 1960 revived his creative energy after a dry decade. He wrote an important group of 'Personal Sonnets' and several other related poems, in which he struggled to come to terms with the people and events of a painful childhood: these disciplined and modest poems introduce a new clarity of language, indebted more to speech than to literature. A closely connected development was Campbell's awakening interest in the great Māori chief Te Rauparaha, whose striking fortress, the island of Kapiti, he could see from his house: a dramatic sequence for radio, 'Sanctuary of Spirits' and particularly its final, and somewhat separate, poem, 'Against Te Rauparaha', enact with energy and anger the inner pain the poet was suffering. This vivid

413

and theatrical use of Māori character and history was unusual in its private force (contrasting with the strong sense of community in Tuwhare's poems), but it marks very clearly the way in which Campbell's growing desire to address his Polynesian origins introduced a new directness into his verse, without the loss of the magical and lyrical qualities of his earlier poems. The same period also saw some fine love poems dedicated to his wife.

Ten years later, a poet in his late fifties was disarmed by love. Glover's *To a Particular Woman* (1970), and the longer, more polished *Diary to a Woman* (1971), record in verse the course of a love affair. The direct, personal quality of this poetry and its looser rhythms and conversational language surprised admirers of *Sings Harry*. But the dramatic sense of the rises and falls in the relationship, the robust presence of the woman herself, affectionate but independent in response, and the poet's own attractive self-awareness and humour, make these moving poems.

In the year in which Louis Johnson edited the last *Poetry Yearbook*, 1964, he also published his last collection, *Bread and a Pension*, before leaving New Zealand for twelve years. He still wrote as a romantic. The settings are suburban and domestic, there is some sardonic humour here and there, and the poet makes frequent use of fictional scenes as well as personal incidents. The tendency, though, is always from the felt particular to the moral generalization, spelled out discursively from poet to reader. Unfortunately, Johnson's fluency and verbosity sometimes detract from his sharper insights — most convincing in the poems about children — and blur the intended irony. A poet open to a great variety of impulses and ideas, he often seems, in the context of the poetry that followed, to be insufficiently aware of the way words were being used, insufficiently rigorous, and too easily reliant on substance — for which he had an excellent eye — and superficial flair.

The dominating presence of the late 1960s and early 1970s was the poet of whom a newspaper billboard could say at his death: 'James K. Baxter 1926–1972 Friend'. The course of his final years seems in retrospect to have followed an almost inevitable pattern, a myth enacted before the nation's eyes. Yet for all the publicity Baxter's activities attracted, the myth is best and most lastingly embodied in his poems. Baxter 'wrote' his own life and death.

By the early 1960s admiration for Baxter's verse was waning, and there were signs that his early rhetorical manner had become stale. A gradual and quite conscious change began to appear in his work; this change is immediately seen in *Pig Island Letters* (1966). In these poems, especially in the title sequence (written in 1963), the grand voice is more muted and the verse forms have relaxed: this poetry is surely what he was referring to in 1965 as 'a loose hencoop, erected by rule-of-thumb bush carpentry, fathered by nobody, with half-rhymes and speech rhythms'. In acknowledging these changes later, Baxter claimed 'an advantage in spontaneity . . . and in authenticity', qualities not noticeable in his early verse.[133] His reading of the later Yeats, Lawrence Durrell, and Robert Lowell had helped him in these developments, but they are also connected to an increasing emphasis on social concerns. In 'Lament for

Barney Flanagan', the Wildean 'A Rope for Harry Fat', and the election-year 'Ballad of Calvary Street' he had already shown a taste and a talent for the satirical ballad in the tradition of Fairburn and Glover, and he continued to write poems of this kind, of varying quality, for the rest of his life. This capacity to re-energize popular traditions against the powerful and the bureaucratic, deliberately addressing a non-literary audience, allies him to Tuwhare; but the use of demotic language, the emphasis on impersonal narrative and concrete detail, and the formal mastery required, must all have fed into his other work, as some of the 'Pig Island Letters' show. In those same years, Baxter was writing the verses for children eventually published in *The Tree House* (1974); much loved by children, much neglected by critics, they share, though in less savage form, similar characteristics.

The thirteen 'Pig Island Letters' are poems of the city, bitter indictments of the lack of love in modern urban life. In varying forms and lengths, each letter is distinct, and they are carefully orchestrated as variations on a theme rather than in any logical sequence. The thought is consistent with the early poems, reiterating a personal myth of the loss of innocence and the spiritual journey through chaos, the Abyss, towards love;[134] but here, and increasingly, this is seen as inseparable from the search for a just society. The family appears as repressive and isolating: for example, in the second poem with its catalogue of separate family members, or in the ninth, where 'the poet as family man' is a divided self, an invalid, a victim 'scarred' and 'flayed'. Marriage, always for Baxter an ambiguous state, is here denial; sexual love, similarly complex, is here 'the place where father Adam died'; and the images of women are coarse and harsh, notably in the fourth poem. Political action 'becomes the jail it laboured to destroy'; bureaucracy a 'glass castle'.

In this impressive sequence, every aspect of the poet's experience is relevant and available for poetry. Personal memories, the remarks of friends, his father's searing history as a World War I conscientious objector, images from Dante, a prayer of the soul to Mary at death (Baxter had become a Roman Catholic in 1958), all are part of the poet's vision of a sick world. The directness of the language accommodates and validates this mix, intermingling the spiritual and the banal.

A return to Dunedin in 1966 as the Burns Fellow reactivated childhood memories, which reappear in his poetry alongside Otago landscapes now seen with his own family. But he was already deeply involved in the protest movement against New Zealand's participation in the Vietnam War, an experience which brought him in touch with a student population rebelling against authority. Baxter's 'call' to go north to found a community at a place called Jerusalem on the Wanganui River is not difficult to understand in the context of his own thinking and his growing distaste for conventional city and family life. It was also a step very characteristic of the times. Whatever cultishness there was, however, about Baxter's transformation into a long-haired guru matters little in relation to the poetry, which interprets that experience in a powerful and convincing way.

Baxter's poems of the city were savage satire against the 'depersonalisation, centralisation, desacralisation' of urban life;[135] the Jerusalem poems (in *Jerusalem Sonnets*, 1970, *Jerusalem Daybook*, 1971, *Autumn Testament*, 1972, and several other posthumous collections) are poems of the community, or the 'tribe', whose central value is aroha. They do not 'tell about' a social experiment; they stand for a different way of life, an alternative scale of values which drew strongly on Māori spirituality. Their success depends on how far they actualize those beliefs, that sanctified world, to their readers.

A different kind of poetry was clearly required, though it had already been in preparation. The Jerusalem poems astonish in their extreme simplicity and lucidity. Drawing on the language of the vernacular, they use a natural economy of diction and sparseness of images, and simple syntactic structures linked by parataxis. The verse forms are minimal, predominantly loose sonnets in unrhymed paired lines often running over to a mid-line caesura. In two of the volumes the poems are closely associated with prose pieces, and it seems Baxter wanted to reduce the difference between the forms.

He uses clear, concrete detail, sometimes shocking and ugly (lice, dog turds) sometimes offering beautiful glimpses of trees or flowers, but often simply mundane and domestic. The several poem sequences seem intended to give a sense of the day-to-day activity of the community (the words 'daybook' and 'testament' imply this) at the simplest levels of the preparation of food, the planting of seeds, the building of a hencoop. The members of the 'tribe' come and go, their words and their names entering the text; they are often identified as damaged by that other place, the city, 'the old fat sow who smothers her children'. Christ himself, often called Te Atua, is 'incurably domestic' and sociable; and figures from Māori mythology appear, as Baxter increasingly identified with the Māori sense of communal and spiritual life. The poems are also messages from the new Jerusalem, often addressed to friends outside. This gives them, in contrast to the 'Pig Island Letters', the modesty and intimacy of personal communication, and also provides a continuing comparison between community and city, a comparison evoked also by memories, dreams, anecdotes. Among the most poignant of these communications is 'He Waiata mo Te Kare' addressed to the poet's wife.

The Jerusalem poems are also, like all Baxter's work, a spiritual diary. The poet is preparing to die, to die unto the World and the Flesh; and in some senses the poems are an allegory of the conquering of self. Pain and physical degradation, including acts of fasting and self-flagellation, are personal aspects of the new order. The characteristic element of self-dramatization has not entirely disappeared, and the poet plays many roles — father, leader, old man, ex-poet, scapegoat. But the interpreting, posing poet is now constantly subjected to humiliation, which in literary terms becomes irony. This is done in part through the vivid social setting in which the voices of everyone, from God down to stray dogs, assert themselves against him:

I think the Lord on his axe–chopped cross
Is laughing as usual at my poems,

My solemn metaphors, my ladder–climbing dreams

But it is also done most convincingly and movingly through the language and verse structure, their plainness and anonymity a means of submission and self-denial. In a 1971 interview he contrasted the 'closed in' nature of his early set-piece poems with what he was now writing: 'I prefer one that is like a house with all its doors open. Anything could happen . . . .'[136]

The imminence of death grows more certain throughout these poems and pervades *Autumn Testament*. The powerlessness of the poet is reinforced, and waiting, 'the lifelong grave of waiting', becomes a persistent metaphor. Words and language are on several occasions in the last poems 'not enough'. Prayers are among the last poems he wrote; but though there were mystic elements in his writing, he kept returning to images of human communion.

Yet at times the road comes down to a place
Where water runs and horses gallop

Behind a hedge. There it is possible to sit,
Light a cigarette, and rub

Your bruised heels on the cold grass. Always because
A man's body is a meeting house,

Ribs, arms, for the tribe to gather under,
And the heart must be their spring of water.

('Te Whiore o te Kuri')

Much of Baxter's poetry was unpublished in his lifetime, and some of it is so apparently simple that its power is difficult to describe. His greatness in twentieth century New Zealand poetry is assured; a poet of a distinctive mythopoeic talent and of an intensity of vocation which allowed no choice between perfection of the life and of the work, a poet who spoke to many and who yet remains oddly isolated in the poetic landscape and not easily accommodated by theory. In the wider cultural sense his use, angry and passionate, of poetry as a public force to challenge the spiritual poverty of a nation was unprecedented; his whole-hearted inclusion of Māori cultural and social values in his vision of a just society is a continuing legacy. Reality was indeed for Baxter 'local and special' at the point where he 'pick[ed] up the traces' — his poems could have been written nowhere else — but it was in the power and eloquence with which he pushed beyond that point that he became a major poet.

'Quests & Discoveries': The 'Young' Poets, 1969-72

An Anthology of Twentieth Century New Zealand Poetry, edited by Vincent O'Sullivan, appeared in 1970. It was a thoughtful selection, which favoured recent work and generously restored to favour those slighted or ignored by Curnow in 1960. But its timing was unlucky: it missed out on the last poems of both Brasch and Baxter; and it failed to notice the baby boom. Noisy, numerous, and self-consciously 'new', the poets born just after World War II shared the exhilaration, idealism, and confidence of their educated middle-class contemporaries in those heady years of the late 1960s. Several of them, Sam Hunt, Bill Manhire, and Ian Wedde, began to be seen in *Landfall* from 1967. Alan Loney, somewhat older, joined them in *Mate* soon after. Quite suddenly the *New Zealand Universities Literary Yearbook*, edited by Wedde in 1968 and Manhire and John Dickson in 1969, became unexpectedly lively and interesting; and some of these poets appeared around the same time in *Argot*, a journal associated with Victoria University. But the most celebrated expression of this new poetic vitality was the five issues of the Auckland student magazine, *Freed*, (of which the first in 1969 was called *The Word is Freed* and the last in 1972, with satisfaction as well as wit, *Freed at Last*). Founded by Alan Brunton, it proclaimed a new poetic order: 'a new theory of perception in the lurkhole of our inspiration; new heroes ripped into our world but of the belly of now'. Murray Edmond edited numbers 3 and 4; Russell Haley number 5. All contributed poems, and other prominent contributors were David Mitchell and Bob Orr.[137] Wedde and Manhire also appeared, but discreetly.

Freed was an exuberant act of rebellion: 'Master Alan decided to replace the whisper of dependence with a shout'. The literature of national identity was once more out the window, but with cheek and flair. English models ceased to have potency for this generation; they turned to the United States, particularly to the post-war poets in Donald Allen's anthology, *The New American Poetry* (1960), where the strain of modernism that came through Pound and William Carlos Williams to Charles Olson and Robert Creeley, the colour and vitality of the New York poets, and the explosive energy of the Beat poets, gave them a stimulating sense of possibilities and powers. Several of them stressed the teaching of American poetry at Auckland University, but it was in Dunedin that Alan Loney first found a copy of Olson's *Maximus Poems*, and Bill Manhire was reading Creeley. The 1972 *Universities Literary Yearbook*, in reminding its readers that 'Russell knows Murray and Murray knows Ian, Ian knows Sam and Sam knows Murray, Murray knows . . .', was in fact drawing attention to a vital 'information network'.[138]

There were other American sources too. On the powerful tide of the media came the popular culture of the 'youth revolution' with its songs of protest, lyric appeal to the natural and the simple, mockery of entrenched structures and institutions, and its sense that poetry, politics, and people might be brought together. Also attractive, especially to Brunton and Edmond, was an irreverent zany humour which went back to Dada and the surrealists and, in political terms, to the anarchists.

These poets were young, they were individualistic, and their work was experimental. Few memorable poems were written, and they developed no coherent body of theory; but they have been taken, most notably by C.K. Stead,[139] to represent a significant change in direction for New Zealand poetry, and their ideas and practice have been thought to have considerable historical importance.

They were united in their distaste for the discursive poem. Edmond quotes Susanne Langer, 'For there is an unexplored possibility of genuine semantic [*sic*] beyond the limits of discursive language'; Brunton says 'poetry is the mimesis of men's actions beyond the intellect'. Poetry should eschew the logical ordering of argument or the sequential ordering of narrative in favour of a freer use of language. These poets all saw the poem as image, in the classic modernist sense, accepting a separation of poem and reality but opening the poem to any means which might reduce the space between them. Particularity was stressed. So too was the idea that the image cuts across time, its effect 'to carry the reader out of the sequential, linear world into its own moment: as it were, Snap'. This concept of the poem requires, as does a Curnow poem, the reader's co-operation; as Wedde puts it, 'people reading my poems are questing *with* me not being told *by* me'.[140]

The *Freed* poets also shared the modernist view of the poem as artefact — Brunton used the phrase 'verbal exercise'. The language sources drawn on were deliberately various, from erudite items of European literature to popular culture. They rejected the idea that there was a certain kind of language suitable for poetry, and were keen to welcome into verse any of the words they collided with daily. The poetry of Peter Olds used the language and image of the pub, the road, and the rougher parts of town. There was a vigorous anti-élitism in their position that took them beyond the intellectuality of Curnow and Smithyman, and a desire to break down the wall between high and low culture: 'no sound is dissonant that tells of life'. This alertness to language in all its occasions includes an openness before the raw material, seeing it as a communal possession. Both Manhire and Wedde show an unwillingness to muscle in on their own behalf, to act the heroic poet, but prefer to regard the poet's role, as Manhire says, as '*bricoleur*', collator of collages.[141]

For many readers, what appeared to distinguish these poets were the superficial signs of 'open form', the absence of traditional verse forms. In fact there had been a gradual relaxing of these structures over a number of years in New Zealand poetry, as poets sought to balance some formal control against the contours of ordinary speech. To the 'new' poets, form was not a major issue. For a poet who saw a poem as representing reality in its particularity on the one hand and in its variety, complexity, and plurality on the other, a predetermined form seemed a very blunt instrument. These poets were just as committed to pattern, repetition, rhythm as traditional versifiers were, but their use of them was determined by individual context along the lines of Creeley's famous comment, 'Form is never more than an extension of content'.

The interest in daily linguistic usage and in the natural units of speech was part of a restoration of the oral aspects of poetry and a stress on performance, matters not given much attention by the New Zealand modernists. The poetry of both Brunton and Edmond shows their interest in theatre; Sam Hunt became a popular performer of his own work. The closeness of poetry and music was often mentioned; Mitchell's poems owed much to folk and rock music, and there are strong lyric qualities in Manhire and Wedde too.

Fruitful possibilities were seen in general in relating poetry more closely to the other arts. These poets, particularly Loney, were interested in the visual effect of the poem on the page, and in the use of typography and layout to suggest meaning. The titles of early books by Wedde and Loney were *Homage to Matisse* and *dear Mondrian*; and the continuing association between Manhire and the painter Ralph Hotere is an example of the rich exchange between words and pictures in New Zealand modernism.

Any further generalizations would put at risk the very real individualities of these poets. Arthur Baysting's anthology, *The Young New Zealand Poets* (1973), which collected nineteen of them (Jan Kemp was the single woman),[142] reveals a range of practice — and of quality — and gives a strong sense of excited adventure: none of the poets had appeared in O'Sullivan's anthology, and the contrast with Doyle's 1965 volume is dramatic. But the anthology also carries a whiff of mortality: already the self-consciousness of the experimental was beginning to look mannered. It captures a moment which no one expected to last. Some of these poets would disappear into obscurity, some would go abroad, some would turn to other genres; others, like Wedde and Manhire, would become important poets of the 1970s and 1980s.

The 'young' poets of the late 1960s had proclaimed their own historic importance, and Stead agreed with them in suggesting they first introduced Poundian modernism, or 'open form', into New Zealand poetry; others, and probably the poets themselves, would describe their work as post-modern. But though it suited them to stress discontinuity with the New Zealand past, there were more links with New Zealand modernism than at first appear. Curnow had not published for some time, but it is illuminating to find Smithyman, long ago mining the American lode, in the company of these young men in journals like *Edge* and *Argot*, to read his sympathetic and perceptive Afterword in Baysting's anthology, and to note Murray Edmond's admiration of him.[143] A perspective which sees modernism as already present in New Zealand poetry and already subject to development and change will interpret many of their innovations as extensions of that tradition.

Their major significance lies perhaps in their rejection of the privileged discourse of high culture, their determination to broaden out the language and function of poetry, and their less confident assertion of the poet's role in the poem. They might be called, in the words of Wystan Curnow, 'laid-back modernists'.[144]

Ways of Saying, 1972-90

Poets and poems proliferated in the 1970s and 1980s. There were now several generations writing at the same time: the elders like Curnow and Smithyman, the well-established like Stead and O'Sullivan, the 'young' poets of the late 1960s like Wedde and Manhire, and finally a confident new generation in the 1980s which would include Leigh Davis and Anne French. But poets simultaneously ranged across a kind of poetic spectrum, which included a broad mainstream of Curnow, for example, alongside Stead and French, with Lauris Edmond on the right, or romantic, wing and Leigh Davis on the far left, or avant-garde. These distinctions, more extreme and more complex than the contrast between romantics and modernists earlier, owed much to the debate about 'open form' which was a long-range consequence of the activities of the 'young' poets of the late 1960s. There was also, particularly in the 1980s, a profound change of critical attitude which questioned the 'pure' eye of both poet and reader and saw them as creatures of culture, subject to their social and economic circumstances and especially their sex and their race. As a result, the dominant position accorded to male Pākehā poets in the European tradition was challenged, and the alternative values of poetry by women and by Māori explored, with strong emphasis on the remarkable emergence of women poets from the mid-1970s, and on new work by Māori in both English and Māori.

Controversy about 'open form' broke out as the 1970s moved into the 1980s, and was retrospective in focusing on the changing character of New Zealand poetry in the 1970s and what that might suggest about its future direction. The controversy was begun by C.K. Stead in a 1979 lecture called 'From Wystan to Carlos', in which he attempted to give an overview which might advance the historical perspective from the point at which Curnow had left it in 1960.[145] Like Curnow, he insisted he was simply describing what he saw; but like Curnow he was both a poet and an intelligent and persuasive thinker, and his remarks were quickly taken as propounding a new orthodoxy.

His thesis was simple: New Zealand poetry, by following English models, had missed out on the modernist revolution until the appearance of *Freed*, which first introduced the Pound-Williams-Olson line, or 'open form'. He claimed that during the 1970s this had become established as the 'mainstream', the way things were inevitably proceeding. He defined open form, or modernism, as not simply the relaxation of traditional forms, but an attempt to bring life and literature closer together, a way of writing poetry that more closely approximated the multi-layered, disorganized nature of actual experience. Disparate fragments could be 'aggregated' into longer sequences by the method of 'field composition', that is, the unity given by a single poetic sensibility. He stressed also the creative and rhythmic use of speech patterns, and a quality of incompleteness, suggestiveness, which might involve the reader more intimately in the poetic experience. He believed that Curnow and Baxter had moved closer to this kind of poetry, and pointed to poets like Mitchell and Wedde as characteristic practitioners of 'open form'.

Stead thus shared Curnow's emphasis on the 'real' as separate from the poem, but articulated a shift away from attention to the nature of that reality, towards how the poem might capture it. Debates about national identity were superseded by arguments about poetry that depended on international, especially American, precedent and terminology.

At about that time Alistair Paterson, poet and editor of *Mate*, who had proselytized for contemporary American models for some time and organized a visit by Creeley in 1976, produced an anthology called *15 Contemporary New Zealand Poets* — intended, like the anthologies of Baysting and Doyle, to present new work. This collection had a strong point of view (similar to that expressed by Stead, with whom Paterson had been closely associated) and aimed to show the victory of 'open form'. It included some unlikely bedfellows, ranging from Curnow to several much younger and little-known poets. Paterson followed it by a booklet on the same subject, *The New Poetry: Considerations Towards Open Form* (1981). His own poetry had been experimenting with American forms for some time, and he developed the so-called 'double margin field' form, later taken up by other poets.[146]

Neither lecture nor anthology was very well received by fellow poets, and criticisms suggested that simplistic interpretations of American poetic history and misunderstanding of terms like modernism and open form had led to a distorted picture of the New Zealand scene. Roger Horrocks claimed that by sweeping up a range of poets into a single mainstream derived from Pound, Stead had blurred the true diversity of contemporary poetic practice. He pointed out that there were major changes in American poetry from Pound to Olson and from Olson beyond, changes to which some New Zealand poets were responsive. Alan Loney, a poet particularly attentive to these more recent developments, used a review of Stead's poetry to make the same points, seeing Stead's position as conservative and nowhere near the leading edge of innovation. The dominance of a mainstream was precisely what the 'young' poets had been opposing, and Murray Edmond, in a vigorous review of Paterson's anthology, clearly showed his distaste at what he saw as the re-establishment of a canon.[147] On the other side were poets of a more traditional disposition, like Kevin Ireland, who resisted a picture of contemporary poetry which defined them as anachronistic.

No one could deny that in the 1970s traditional verse forms had virtually disappeared. But this is a trivial statement. Most discussions of open form agreed that its 'openness' was more than this; but exactly what it was they could not agree on. The same can be said of terms like 'modernism' and 'post-modernism'. This debate certainly alerted readers to the broad general movement of New Zealand poetry towards modernism and beyond, and especially to a loosening-up of form and language which made room for diversity, variety, and experiment. But it also gave notice of the appearance of a number of radically different assumptions, often irreconcilable, about the nature and function of poetry.

The Young Poets Grow Older, 1972-90

Even the poets of the *Freed* generation were nothing like as homogeneous as they are sometimes made to seem. A complex and energetic poet like Ian Wedde cannot be captured in categories. While he shared some characteristics with his contemporaries, his third book in particular, *Earthly, Sonnets to Carlos* (1975), revealed a poet who was past mere posturing, and who had assimilated American influences, and many others besides.

An easy 'I' in Wedde's poems attracts immediate attention — the personal is restored with intensity. Much of Wedde's private and emotional life might be traced in the progress of his poems but, like Matisse (the subject of an early poem), he is 'unable to distinguish between the feeling I have for life and my way of expressing it'.[148] The poem locates the feeling, but in the process it acquires an independent existence. Wedde's many lyric passages have the freshness of direct feeling, irrespective of their occasion.

Wedde is deeply aware that language is shared property, believing that the poet has a particular commitment to tend it and pass it on intact, respecting all its users, past and present. In theory this is a radical revision of the modernist notion of tradition as a privileged culture, though his practice was always highly sophisticated. He writes almost always in an 'easy vernacularism', and phrases from daily discourse and from popular culture pervade his work. But they are not taken at face value: they are acted upon as creatively by the poet as are his private emotions. The transformation may be ironic — unsettling clichés in other language settings —, or lyric — reviving the bittersweetness of a line from a song; always alerting readers to codes and signs which they didn't know they knew. The way such material is used often constitutes a direction on how to read the poem — what Wedde calls 'tone'. Ironic play with the common phrases 'we shall not be moved' (in 'Off/Of') and 'for life' (in 'Pathway to the Sea') is part of the satiric effect in two poems assailing ecological destructiveness.

In so far as language is communally owned, Wedde considers himself, as he says, 'accountable'.[149] He has an inherent suspicion of the accepted, the orthodox, the codified, not to mention the powerful. A profoundly iconoclastic habit of mind, which is seen also in his treatment of New Zealand history (in *Tendering*, 1988, and in his novel *Symmes Hole*) and in his approach to New Zealand poetry in two Penguin anthologies, allies him with many of the other 'young' poets. The collections of his mid-career, *Castaly* (1980), and *Georgicon* and *Tales from Gotham City* (both 1984), include a number of overtly political poems, angry, witty, and irreverent:

> This
>   poem
> is for the commonwealth heads of state meeting in London, they
> won't read it or
>   hear it but that's okay it's
> almost
>   why it's getting written . . .

>   ('Don't Listen')

If there is one 'main obsession' throughout Wedde's work, it is the interconnectedness of things, 'worlds within worlds'. Everything that exists is at the intersection of an infinite number of systems or networks; each network is sensitive to the individual link. This perspective can be seen as biological, historical, or political, but it is chiefly for Wedde a powerful imaginative vision of wholeness and of the value of the single and particular being or instant. It supports both metaphor and myth, and it can provoke comic or tragic responses. A vivid manifestation of this vision is a kind of private language which includes key words, talismanic phrases, or memories of particular significance to the poet;[150] these are woven backwards and forwards through all his writing. Not only do they give his entire work — including his fiction — an unusual coherence, but very quickly the reader learns the language too. The pleasure of reading a Wedde poem is immeasurably increased by reading others, as awareness of the connecting tissue grows. The extent of this elaborate network can be shown by the reappearance in *Tendering* of a phrase ('man pen meander') which occurred in a poem in *Freed* nearly twenty years before; words like 'heart', 'net', 'paradise', along with phrases from other poets (Dante's 'dark wood', for example) or from pop songs, begin to carry powerful resonances. Like any language, this one balances familiarity with multifarious possibility, and gives to Wedde's work a sense of the richness of human experience. It also reveals that apprehension of fragmentation and simultaneous desire for order which is a characteristically modernist habit of mind.

The passion for all-inclusiveness explains Wedde's continuing interest in longer poems and sequences (clear too in his selections for the two Penguin anthologies). Here too (but on a lower level) he works 'like a dog backtracking and crisscrossing a terrain in search of an odour's source', the text gradually yielding significance through dynamic patterns of repetition and variation. *Earthly*, a sequence of sixty sonnets on the birth of his son, established Wedde as the most admired poet of the new generation. A passionate response to the event, it simultaneously celebrates the daily awakening to the world, the constantly renewing process of awareness, the cycle of night and day, of winter and spring, and especially the freshness of love. The lines extend backwards to the moment of conception and to the poet's own parents, outwards to war and violence, upwards to the universe. The overarching image is that of the 'earthly paradise', which sets up many echoes, not least with Curnow and Baxter, but by its contradictory character denies a Calvinistic (or Baxterian) interpretation of the Fall in favour of a tender acceptance of human imperfection: 'The world's greedy anarchy I love it!' The structure of the sequence, 'a reticulation of the worn and the marvellous', mocks distinctions between open and closed form. Each sonnet has fourteen lines of ten syllables, but rhyme is not regular; all the conventional ways of grouping lines are used, but the syntax and rhythm play against the structure constantly, with caesuras, enjambement of line and often of sonnet to create an effect of rich and spontaneous luxuriance. Wedde has himself drawn attention to the mathematically precise arrangement of the sonnets within the sequence, every tenth and twentieth sonnet recapitulating those before, so that the whole structure is an amazing web of connection exactly appropriate to the theme.[151]

'Pathway to the Sea' is more detached and ironic in tone, but again chooses and exploits a form precisely organized for the occasion. In nine-line verses, three groups of three lines (echoing William Carlos Williams), the poem proceeds in a superbly controlled headlong rush (echoing A.R. Ammons), almost without a sentence break, as the poet tells a mythic narrative — of digging a drain. The mood is anecdotal and relaxed, and the language supple and witty; digressions swoop out and bend back, phrases echo and re-echo, as Wedde once more develops ideas of relation. Like most myths, 'Pathway' has social and biological implications, and these are constantly brought before the reader as themes of service, responsibility, and the proper use of effort, themes which are relevant also to the writing of poetry itself.

In *Gotham City* even poetry had become a subject of some anxiety, and some wondered if he had written himself to a standstill; but *Tendering*, related to *Symmes Hole* but with its own elegant shape, showed a new strength. The differences and distances between *here* and *there*, *I* and *you*, expressed in the imagery of harbours, oceans, and voyages of discovery familiar from earlier New Zealand poetry, are shaken up, restored, and made new in three tightly knit groups of poems. Wedde's complex layers of language and subtle interplay of registers remain an intense response to what we assume exists outside language; but the poem in his hands is a skilful and brilliant illusion, made at 'the edge where see turns to seem'.

For Bill Manhire the poem is an 'elaboration' (*The Elaboration* was the title of his first book), or a 'fiction', which he too sees as beginning in the known of experience but arriving at the unknown of art.[152] Where Wedde is energetic and excitable, Manhire is restrained and polite. A Manhire poem is brief, apparently simple in syntax and vocabulary, usually without regular patterns of metre or rhyme, and very often strangely enigmatic and elliptical.

His output is small, perhaps little more than a hundred poems in twenty years. He was encouraged by Brasch and he has himself been a mentor for a new generation of poets in the 1980s. With Wedde he has been a conduit for overseas models into New Zealand poetic practice, and readily admits the formative influence of the post-war American poets on his own work. The particular impact of Creeley is very evident in Manhire's simple short lines and the musical phrasing they suggest. American culture also encouraged him to open his poetry to the full diversity of his experience in all its muddle and banality.[153] Like Wedde, but more secretly, he raids the quotidian for cliché and exhausted idiom, and his ear for mimicry is acute.

What makes Manhire's poems at once both fascinating and difficult is that it is not always clear how the language of the poem relates, or if it relates, to the world outside it. There are sometimes signs, for example, that it is operating as allegory or emblem, and renaissance and medieval poetry show their traces; but sometimes, at the other extreme, Manhire seems to be playing language games — a recent poem is a five-page 'concrete poem', and 'The Pickpocket' and 'The Cinema' are almost entirely made up of 'found' phrases.[154] In other poems an external situation is easily identified — his first collection consists of love poems, and *Good Looks* (1982) includes poems about the death of his father and about his own family. But most often his strategy in a poem is suddenly and unexpectedly to shift the way language is being used from one function to another, teasing and testing the reader's alertness: possibilities of 'meaning' are constantly being held out only to vanish before our eyes. In 'Declining the Naked Horse', a simple linguistic paradigm takes on in the last line the character of spoken words in an actual situation; in 'The Buried Soap' the conclusion turns the whole poem into pastiche:

'So first
it was the trees

went purple then
went green.' Dis-

gusting, how
obscene. I think

that's just a wicked
thing to want

to say, Charlene.

In the moving poem 'Children', a rather solemn vision of his children's lives and deaths is given a gentle comic twist by the bluff final cliché: 'and he's just a kid / but watch him grow'.

Some poems have the qualities of song — sensuous, rhythmic, delicate — and dream; imagery of great clarity suggests surreal states or events — snow, stars, water, and stones feature repeatedly. Manhire's presence in the poem is less distinct than Wedde's, though he focuses frequently on his own personal relationships, domestic circle, and childhood. He also works in complex and subtle ways with pronouns, the 'I' and 'you' often elusive and creating a kind of mysterious intimacy.

The poet's modesty and the austerity of his means combine with a dazzling invention and linguistic playfulness. He shares, surprisingly perhaps, some qualities with Charles Spear — the delight in building a magical structure, the attention to detail, the hidden laughter. Manhire gives a very pleasurable sense of what language can be made to do if released from the dull duty of surface meaning.

Of the other 'young New Zealand poets' Murray Edmond is probably the most determined survivor; and his four collections have been written alongside a very active involvement in theatre. For all that Edmond's editorial in *Freed* repudiated a poetry which 'name[d] them hills', his own poetry is very much tied to concrete particulars of this place. It circles repeatedly round home, family, and city, but increasingly it also encounters New Zealand landscape and history; not of course as mere description, but as part of a growing and maturing study of the relationships of 'facts' and language, the way in which we use words and stories to live by. Always impatient with orthodoxies, Edmond has moderated an earlier rhetoric to a more detached voice, interested like Manhire in poems that can be made by 'framing' language heard or remembered.

David Mitchell was older than the *Freed* group, but his long poem, 'the singing bread', was one of its highlights. Written in loose open lines, it shows a marked lyric gift which pervades his 1972 book *Pipe Dreams in Ponsonby*, extravagantly admired at the time, but unfortunately without successors. An opening note says, 'all th poems in this book have been read aloud in public', and the musical resonances of these poems of love and war explain why he preferred that method of publication.

Alan Brunton's energetic, pacy cadences too show a strong desire to move off the page and into the throat. His work is dense with allusions from unlikely sources, and it can be bombastic and self-indulgent; its comic anarchism resists the expected or predictable at every turn. Brunton's sheer delight in language and its subversive possibilities is distinctive. However he became increasingly involved in theatre, and after three slim collections he went overseas for ten years, only returning and publishing in New Zealand again in 1988-9.[155]

A contemporary of Mitchell's, Alan Loney also had a long period of silence in the 1980s. The most faithful disciple of American poetic theory, he later became an editor of the 'post-modern' journal *Parallax*, as well as publishing at his Hawk Press a number of collections by himself and others which show his careful attention to typographic appearance. Loney's work was not universally well received and he, along with Brunton and Graham Lindsay, another poet sometimes working with considerable skill,[156] demonstrates one extreme of a divide which developed during the 1970s and 1980s between a marginal, avant-garde poetry and a more accessible and traditional romantic/modernist practice.

Sam Hunt stands on the other side of the divide. Ironically, by turning poetry into popular entertainment, a travelling roadshow of man, dog, and bottle, Hunt was the 'young' poet who most successfully reached a wider audience. His activities, as he often points out,[157] show up the intellectuality of most of his contemporaries and their inclination to see popular culture as input rather than output. Hunt works in the New Zealand romantic tradition, having landed on Alistair Campbell's doorstep as a schoolboy, and being an admirer of Glover and Fairburn, and a friend of Baxter. Much of his appeal was simply in this old-fashioned style — most of his poems are expressions of feeling in a single surface line which leads to a poignant close. His own experience is his single subject, moments in the life of a sentimental bloke. Themes of love and its loss are insistent, often expressed in the context of the poet's surroundings of seashore or one-horse town. Some poems about his father, mother, and son have the strength of original creations, but many of the love songs suffer from a gap the poet seems not to perceive between the feelings expressed and the situations implied; eloquence comes too easy for a man who really wants to travel on.

Outside Baysting's anthology were a few new and quieter voices, less interested in a dramatic break with the past, and less indebted to American experimentalism. Hilaire Kirkland, for example, wrote a handful of curious poems which appeared in student journals along with work by the 'young' poets. They come from a very different stable; out of Swinburne by the Metaphysicals, they are poems of sardonic anger and bitterness in love, clothed in a startling baroque sensuality that cleverly undermines the conventions of love poetry:

> allot to me a thankful and submissive role —
> that I perhaps can blight
> sweet-mouthed and deceptively, your mind
> and lovingly corrode your flesh.

> ('Song for my Love')

Kirkland's early death in 1975 (a single volume, *Blood Clear and Apple Red*, appeared posthumously in 1981) was a significant loss.

Iain Lonie was a poet unjustly neglected by critics and anthologists. A classicist by training, he wrote (in four collections between 1967 and 1986) a discursive, meditative, and measured verse. His last two books in particular, *Courting Death* (1984) and *The Entrance to Purgatory* (1986), are forced out of abstraction by the intensity of a personal experience (the death of his wife), and contain a number of moving, skilfully made poems: 'no end to the sentence / but mastering language / and shift of mood'.[158]

The same melancholy subject occurs in poems by Michael Jackson, another somewhat isolated poet, who was, however, included in O'Sullivan's anthology, and who received several awards.[159] In his work, a thoughtful, intelligent mind roams about the world (Africa, Greece, the Côte d'Azur), reflecting on places and mores: the poem becomes a necessary framework of understanding, particularly of mythic pattern or cultural contrast in a post-colonial world.

Old Masters, 1972–90

Allen Curnow was a 'sixty-year-old smiling public man' by the time he published *Trees, Effigies, Moving Objects* in 1972 and like Yeats he now produced a series of masterly works. *An Abominable Temper* quickly followed, but when in the preface to his 1974 *Collected Poems* he wrote, 'I hope I have not finished yet', few could have guessed how firmly he would put paid to any notion that it was a valedictory volume. *An Incorrigible Music* (1979) and *You Will Know When You Get There* (1982) were major collections, with further new poems appearing in *The Loop in Lone Kauri Road* (1986) and *Continuum* (1988). Less than a hundred poems in all, they must be considered among the finest written in the language anywhere in the 1970s and 1980s.

Curnow was no longer, however, the dominating critical presence of earlier years; the discourse about New Zealand poetry had fallen into other hands, and much of the creative and critical ferment of the time implicitly criticized the assumptions behind his verse. For other readers his work remained challenging, and he was consistently reluctant to rely on superficial charm or popular appeal. He accurately describes his audience as 'anyone, anywhere, who reads poetry in English and knows the tradition'.[160] A poet of high culture he remained.

A number of writers have suggested that Curnow's new work represented a significant change towards the now fashionable 'open form'. But the striking character of *Trees, Effigies* is its continuity with a poetry which showed, on a formal level, a creative flexibility in harmony with some measure of control: the rich variety of poetic shape in Curnow's later poems is evidence of a poet confident and skilled enough to invent appropriate forms, and one who had long ago assimilated Pound's and Williams's ideas and practice.[161] Similarly, in its verbal and philosophic texture, the Curnow poem had always been sceptical, exploratory, and dense with alternative meanings. A resistance to 'closed' lines of meaning is a lifelong stance; irony its natural expression.

The Curnow voice, too, is unmistakable in the new work: never intimate, always individual; as Leigh Davis points out, it is almost prosaic, making casual observations which begin to buckle with unexpected implications.[162] Above all, Curnow's preoccupations remain constant. He pursues a continuing philosophic enquiry into the relationship between word and world, and the earlier poems about language find many successors, such as 'A Balanced Bait in Handy Pellet Form' and 'The Parakeets at Karekare'. Mythic visions of human experience are still pervaded with Christian imagery, and theological terminology a habitual means of expressing them; death as judgement or sacrifice is still a predominant concern. Curnow remained an acute observer of the tangible and especially the phenomenal world, evoking with vivid clarity the light, colour, and movement of the West Auckland coast, or the ordinary detail of a city street, or the generative energy of living things. His attention to fact and detail is, as ever, precise and erudite, a number of poems depending on a skilfully established 'facticity'.

Changes there are too, as this poet reacts to a changing world and to his own experiences of travel, politics, ageing, domestic life. If the Fall was the insistent myth behind his earlier work, interpreted sometimes in the context of the colonial condition, now it is succeeded in a post-nuclear world by visions of the Apocalypse. Scenes of violence, murder, destruction abound: planes crash, trees tumble, clouds threaten, and winds blow. This sense of impending doom is accompanied by a heightened awareness of the past, which recalls the public poems of the 1940s. A historical past (in a Renaissance murder, for example), a personal past (in poems of childhood), a family past (in the re-creation of an ancestor) all offer patterns of contrast or similarity, ways of exploring the nature and meaning of time, the dilemmas presented by guilt, loss, identity, and memory. In a note to *Continuum*, Curnow refers to 'the way past and present things shift about in some of the poems',[163] and his sense of the presentness of the past is often manifest, particularly for example in *An Incorrigible Music*, where two murders five hundred years apart remind us that

> All the seas are one sea
> the blood one blood
> and the hands one hand.

These opening lines of 'Moro Assassinato' echo the preceding poem, 'Can'st Thou Draw out Leviathan with an Hook?', in which a kahawai is caught off the rocks of Auckland's west coast; the geographic poles of here and there, New Zealand and the world beyond, which had preoccupied the young poet, also recur here, though their terms have changed. Italy/New Zealand in *An Incorrigible Music*, the United States/New Zealand in *Trees, Effigies*, carry different tensions from the earlier colonial anguish but show Curnow continuing to pick away at questions of national identity; this bifurcated way New Zealanders have of looking at the world has been for Curnow a constantly fruitful metaphor of the human condition.

The eighteen poems of *Trees, Effigies, Moving Objects* are densely packed, economical, allusive, and enigmatic. The sequence welds together the personal, the philosophic, and the public in poems of varied forms and styles, and with settings as different as a New Zealand rain forest and a Washington cocktail party. But they appear as fragments assembled under pressure, intersecting and moving apart. A repeated question, 'Where is the world?', might suggest the multiple anxieties of the volume. A natural world, powerful and mysterious in the 'trees' of the title, appears in some poems almost beyond the reach of words; in others the 'effigies' (fictions, or 'semblances') we erect to express thought or belief or order, in such massive forms as the Lincoln Memorial or the statue of the Virgin at Paraparaumu, or the fragility of metaphor, or the arrogance of American Idealism, are Curnow's subject; the 'moving objects' are the transient aspects of the world no human device can halt, and several poems concern age. Many motifs are displaced from one poem to another, as a complex sense of growing tension moves towards a final apocalyptic vision, 'when the ground blinked, / disclosing what never should be seen'.

'An Abominable Temper' seems a poem of surprising simplicity after *Trees, Effigies* but it can be seen as an experiment by the poet in assuming a mask, entering in a dramatic fashion the character of his forebear. It is also a continuation of themes of colonial settlement, and of relations, personal and theological, between father and son.

The dramatic and powerful 1979 sequence, *An Incorrigible Music*, is unified by homicidal violence. The idea of ritual slaughter in particular, to appease the god in a sacrificial act or to cleanse the body politic in assassination, is a natural spur to Curnow's mythopoeic imagination. Two longer poems, 'Can'st

Thou . . . ?' and 'In the Duomo', on the 1478 murder of Giuliano de Medici in the duomo at Florence, along with some related shorter poems, were complete when Curnow went to Italy for several months in early 1978, only to find the crowning act, the kidnapping and death of the Prime Minister Aldo Moro, played out before his eyes. 'Moro Assassinato' became the centre of the new collection. In 'Can'st Thou . . . ?' symbolic overtones predominate, with man and fish, murderer and victim, shifting about in a fluid matrix to become interchangeable; 'In the Duomo', with its strong hints of Dante and Eliot, links political and religious sacrifice in images of the Mass but contrives black comedy and drama as well as reflection from the character and dilemma of Montesecco, the soldier who will not kill in church; again in 'Moro Assassinato' Curnow unwinds a dramatic narrative superbly, by switching from one player to another, by emphasizing time and its passage, by stressing in concrete detail and actual quotation the human character of a historical event. In both poems the leap from particular person to universal myth is made with a daring and economical use of language: 'and Gesù! he saw them / coming, the rods in our hands'.

You Will Know When You Get There takes up the subject of death — most spectacularly in 'Organo ad Libitum', an audacious nine-part poem which begins with the reader's own death and includes bizarre scenes from a sophisticated movie, the Mt Erebus plane crash, and a hotel bedroom, in an elaborate, imaginative and essentially joyful work. 'A Fellow Being', the other long poem in the book, is in part another character study. But here the poet quite deliberately plays with this act of imaginative transference in a way which allows him full ironic mockery of an Auckland dentist ('with an eye to surgery and the costs of extraction' who amassed a fortune by the destruction of kauri forests), but which also acknowledges a shared identity:

> he being
> dead for one thing and in
> the light of such darkness
> a fellow being . . .

Like the murderers and victims of the previous book, both poet and dentist are 'on collusion course', equally guilty and subject to death; but yet, in a classic poetic closure, the natural cycle continues

> in March on my roof the bursting
>
> cone wakes me like hail the soul
> flies this way and that in the thinning
> dawn dark where the paths cross and the
> young trees know only how to grow.

Kendrick Smithyman made no sudden reappearance like Curnow but worked away from year to year, alert and determined, his published work only a fraction of his total output: 'Existence is / like this. You live, contracted, engaged', says the dwarf at the end of the billiard cue. There was, however, a marked change in his poetry from the late 1960s towards the more relaxed and more accessible verse seen at its finest in *Stories About Wooden Keyboards* (1985). The change was gradual; it was stimulated in part, he acknowledges, by the persistent criticism of obscurity in his work, but a more dramatic jolt to poetic habit was the impact of a trip abroad in 1969. The poems of *Earthquake Weather* (1972) and *The Seal in the Dolphin Pool* (1974) show both in their form and their subject Smithyman's excited reaction to new (old) places: 'I was too busy to bother about experimenting with forms, I was going mad with seeing — and touching . . . .'[164] Rhyme and regular stanzas almost disappear, sentences are shorter, syntax on the whole less convoluted. Place is the primary subject of these two books; an English chapel or a Californian bridge provoke characteristically intricate meditations but some of the best poems, 'An Ordinary Day beyond Kaitaia', 'Where Waikawau Stream Comes Out', and 'Tomarata', return to his favourite New Zealand places and simultaneously his favourite, his essential, theme of language. Place for Smithyman frequently intersects with history: a deserted village or a ruined abbey has a positively eighteenth century effect upon him, leading, albeit in a wry, ironic, modern way, to thoughts on the vanity of human wishes.

You could see these poems as a conscientious record of the human encounter with the world of phenomena; the central poetic persona observes and discovers facts, things, history, geography, geology. Personal relationships are almost absent and people are alienated from place: 'We lack precedent. / Latecome we are, our type, intruders.' The poet recognizes mysteries which cannot be grasped by the plodding human intellect: 'The fact is most the mystery is about'. Several poems, 'A Showing Forth by Day of the Nankeen Kestrel', for example, speak of the effortless, unconscious perfection achieved by non-human things. This world beyond speech draws and grips us, and, for this poet of facts, is ultimately what poetry is about: 'Puzzling / hits deeper than any sound plummeted'.

The self-deprecatory poet becomes his own 'puzzling' character, 'doodling mementoes, cryptically muttering', and increasingly turns his enquiries into spoken words, conversation, dialogue. The two subsequent collections, *Dwarf with a Billiard Cue* (1978) and *Stories about Wooden Keyboards*, (1985) are noticeably more social in character. His comic inclinations, always latent, are now let rip and poems of observation and reflection intermingle with poems of anecdote and character; a habitual urge towards rotund generalization is diminished and the same curious facts are transformed into stories, a distinctive kind of poetry not seen in New Zealand before.

Dwarf, though, is a bleak volume, its comedy grotesque or bizarre, its communities (in 'Science Fiction', for example) under threat, the poet, especially in the long final poem, 'Monodies For', grimly confronting pain, sin, failure: 'I give you my word, word of another / bastard, in a bastard world'. Language *is* deceit. But poetry is possible as social exchange with friends and also, attractively, with literary texts: 'About Setting a Jar on a Hill' is a mock-heroic creation in tribute to Stevens' well-known poem. This much more explicit response to other writers continues in *Stories*, with a list of debts to Russian writers in particular. It is a more cheerful book, its tone perhaps struck by the presence of love, as well as language, landscape, and learning, in poems like 'Waitomo' and 'Small Sonata'. The sometimes exotic sources and settings give the book a richness, an exciting sense of connections, but do not take the poet away from his usual preoccupations. 'Reading the Maps An Academic Exercise' was seen by Wedde and Harvey McQueen as the 'touchstone' of their *Penguin Book of Contemporary New Zealand Poetry* (1989) and is perhaps the kind of poem Smithyman was aiming for when he wrote to Charles Brasch in 1950, 'In honesty I hope to write some day poetry with various characters and as worthy of regard as the poetry of our time or of our history which I regard as worthy . . .'.[165] Though it starts as a poem about map-reading, and indeed does describe in precise detail two routes by map in Northland and in Yorkshire, it would not be too grand to say this is a long poem about truth. The poet explores the truths that maps — or poems — propose, making endless play of words like legend, symbol, reference, but also the truths of ambition and hope; disappointment is inevitable, schemes fail to match experience, one map misses the road's end, another leads in a circle: 'If everything is anywhere in flux / perhaps we may not read the same map twice'. The territory changes — 'sands are on the move' — and there is also 'your un- / certainty in seeing'. Smithyman's maps have something in common with Curnow's effigies and with what both see as the limitations of language — 'Metaphor too and parable / long since outmoded' — which are also the limitations of being human. Yet a stubborn optimism, an irrepressible pleasure in the word, keeps returning and makes of his 1987 collection, *Are You Going to the Pictures?* a *tour de force* of charm and comedy and an answer yet again to Smithyman's perennial question, 'How shall I know / where I stand, until I say what I see?' This poet of seeing and saying, of the sentence, indicative or interrogative, yields nothing to time, as interesting in the 1980s as he was thirty years before.

The Middle Generation, 1972-90

C.K. Stead's essay, 'From Wystan to Carlos', was the most provocative critical study of the period; it was also a way of declaring his allegiance to a modernism which derived from Pound. Stead was never a prolific poet, but he produced seven books from 1975 to 1990 in which this poetic can be clearly seen. One of its characteristics is the idea of a tradition inherited, acknowledged, and passed on. A powerful sense of the texts that have gone before pervades his work — which may range from translations of Baudelaire and Japanese *uta* through 'adaptations' of Catullus and Baxterian sonnets to echoes of Eliot and Pound. His many poems of travel not only continue the preoccupying contrast between 'here' and 'there' but also dramatize, make visible, that recognition of earlier writers: his poem 'Paris', for example, is about an idea, a dream, a memory as much as it is about a place. To the charge that his writing is simply derivative one can say that in poetry, as in fiction, Stead is always eager to experiment, to test his capacities further; but he also means to participate in a dialogue with the past, 'a continuum which passes through the poet'.[166] He enjoys this encounter and it obviously stimulates his own creative powers, nourishing a flexible and responsive style.

In 'Quesada', for example, he writes a poem markedly different from its predecessors and owing much, he says, to an odd alliance between Whitman and Cervantes.[167] The Whitman line enables him to convey a passionate heroic stance, a quite unfashionably romantic tragic grandeur which was strong enough to take a punning anti-literary counterpoint without collapsing totally. The emotional aspects of poetry have always been at least as attractive to Stead as the cerebral.

'From Wystan to Carlos' explained how modernism, with its 'openness to experience *as it occurs*', had allowed a revival of the long 'process poem'.[168] Stead's collections through the 1970s and 1980s show him on a number of occasions writing such a poem, with obvious debt to Pound's *Cantos* and following on from *Crossing the Bar*. These poems were personal and particular, but also firmly mimetic: 'What he always wanted why should he argue it was / what they called the real because he saw the rock / in the word . . . .' In some ways the loose fragmentary structure suited Stead's hyperactive mind, tracking simultaneously in many directions but clear and economical in its expression.

Stead projected a five-part long poem of which only three parts, each quite independent, have so far appeared. 'Walking Westward' consists of 'fragments of memory' ranging over several countries and decades and through different moods and rhythms. Particularly noticeable are switches from evocation or image to awareness of the poem's making, from experience to language, the rock in the word. As the title suggests (hinting Donne and Wordsworth), movement over the face of the earth and through time drives the poem. 'Scoria' (in *Geographies*, 1982) concentrates on Auckland, its history, geology, and legend, in league with the poet's childhood memories. The poem attempts a dramatic recovery of the past through swift movements from private detail to public event, the city's volcanic cones potent and dominant symbols. 'Paris', the third poem, is a more formal poem about a more imaginary location. Probably the best of these poems is 'Yes T. S.', outside the plan though similar in kind; it follows the poet's solitary progress in a ring around the world, 'to make real / distances / real'.

The continuity of Stead's books from one to the next is seen also in his interest in the Baxterian, or 'open', sonnet which he used over several years for a wide variety of occasions and moods. He takes over from Baxter little more than the shape, though it may be some tribute that these poems are mostly set at home rather than away. 'The Clodian Songbook', the adaptations from Catullus, flows over two books also, gaining increasing strength and freedom from the perfect match of poets, sensual, tender, savage, and witty. *Between*

(1987) and *Voices* (1990) suggest that Stead has exhausted the long poem; certainly a shorter poem like 'After the Wedding', where lessons learned from Pound, Curnow, Baxter, Yeats, are absorbed into a complex yet lucid vision of childhood, man and nature, Eden and the Fall, shows Stead's 'natural grace' at its best.

Vincent O'Sullivan, who had wandered much in Greece, was not at all sympathetic to the recently proclaimed revolution in poetic practice. The second edition of his anthology (1976) included Wedde, Manhire, Mitchell, and Hunt, but a new prefatory note mentioned a 'decline in the standards and expression of criticism, an over-eagerness to find print, and the sterile energies of faction' in spite of a 'hospitable climate' for poetry. For O'Sullivan poetry was a deliberate activity implying a critical and interpretive approach to experience, working towards a moral vision through metaphor and myth. He continued to write short rounded lyrics, but the two collections of 'Butcher' poems, with their invention of a mythic character, his 'mean knife' poised 'between chops', released his considerable dramatic and satiric talents (apparent in his fiction and drama), his black humour, and his unparalleled ear for the kiwi vernacular in 'the Age of the Meat Man'. Likened to Glover's Harry,[169] Butcher and the poems he inhabits are far more complex. B. is crass, cynical; he dreams absurdly of male heroes, but he has visions which disturb him too. By a subtle and dense use of language and the ironic shifting of position in and out of Butcher's mind, O'Sullivan is able here to solve the perennial difficulty of the New Zealand fiction writer in handling the 'big questions' ('God, sex, and death — savvy?') through a male character of limited apprehension:

> *Here* may be the horn
>   to outhorn Roncevalles
> the boot to fill Eden Park
> a heart so chocker with love for all things born
> it shines self-contained as the host in a church's dark.

These bold switches of register and context are characteristic of O'Sullivan's skill. A thin thread of narrative allows a growing if only partial self-understanding by Butcher and dynamic exchanges with other 'characters', especially the cerebral Baldy and his wife (classically called Sheila).

O'Sullivan was still writing fine personal lyrics of a philosophic kind (in *Brother Jonathan, Brother Kafka*, for example). In *The Pilate Tapes* (1986), however, he sharpened his satiric blade again, bringing Pontius Pilate into the twentieth century as a sentimental liberal and 'the first modern', and replaying the Crucifixion with a savage wit.

Kevin Ireland has written appreciatively of O'Sullivan's work, suggesting that enthusiasm for 'fractured modern verse' had led to underestimation of a good poet. Ireland's poems have nothing like the complexity of O'Sullivan's (which K.O. Arvidson justly calls a 'poetry of ideas')[170] but his deft wit and elegant craft turned out poems with easy appeal. The tidy lyric with end-stopped lines and regular stanzas, cleverly unwinding a metaphysical conceit, remained his stock-in-trade. His characteristic self-irony is pervasive in *Literary Cartoons* (1977), which systematically disarms any criticism likely to be made of his verse:

> so he decided to stray
> behind his time
> to be unfashionable
> risk misreading be un-new . . .

It is an attractive surface brilliance, but by 1980 in *The Dangers of Art* it was wearing a bit thin. *Practice Night in the Drill Hall* (1984) includes attempts at longer lines and more oblique kinds of meaning, with mixed success. The poet's return home, celebrated in cosmic bathos and comic nostalgia in *The Year of the Comet* (1987), rejuvenated his talents; a third Roman strolls abroad in *Tiberius at the Beehive* (1990), a nicely sustained sequence in political satire. In both books themes of exile and separation, so strangely absent earlier, are insistent.

After his return to New Zealand in 1980, Louis Johnson wrote four subsequent volumes. Informal, expansive, they include honest and direct confrontation of his own immediate experiences, especially his discomfort in a changed literary scene and his delight in his two new children. The poet now gained strength from the past ('Memory is rich as gravy') and the fine posthumous collection, *Last Poems* (1990), is strongly elegiac in tone, its final poems showing a new tightness and moving gravity.

Other poets writing outside the prevailing fashion included the Dunedin poet, Brian Turner, whose work had been appearing in journals for some time and whose first collection, *Ladders of Rain* (1978), was soon followed by four others. He was often outspoken in his criticism of modish 'trends' and his poetry, modest and meditative, expressed his belief that 'our relationship with the people and the land of our upbringing is a big and important subject'.[171] At a time when most poets glimpsed the natural world only through city or suburban window, Turner's lyric treatment of mountain, rock, and stream and the human engagement with them, of close personal relations and the passage of time, recalled the earlier Otago romantics, Brasch, Dowling, and Dallas. But his blunt economical language, austere verse structure, and barely suppressed anger at mankind's destructiveness place him in a later age.

Michael Harlow, identified as a 'surrealist' poet, was mentioned by Roger Horrocks among those unjustly pushed aside by Stead's 'mainstream'. An immigrant of cosmopolitan background, he was burdened by neither English nor New Zealand tradition; working, from a background of Jungian psychology, with dream and fantasy, he produced calculated performances in a range of forms from prose poem to lyric.[172]

Fleur Adcock's poetry was widely read in New Zealand throughout the 1970s and 1980s. There i: a remarkable consistency in her work and, in three new collections and a selected poems, the sense of a distinct, confident but never ostentatious poetic world, themes and images echoing to and fro in 'language which is natural . . . and that of [her] own voice'.[173] The acuteness of her observation, both physical and emotional, is always striking. 'Script' cleverly uses the image of radio to describe the poet's dual task: 'there will be / always the taking-in and the sending-out'. The range of observation broadens in *The Scenic Route* (1974) to include a vivid attention to place (Ireland, India) and an increasing focus on the past. Her stance is English but New Zealand as an aspect of personal identity is constantly alluded to and becomes, like the members of her family or the continuing mystery of the erotic, one of the poet's fixed points of reference. *The Inner Harbour* (1979) is the most impressive of the later books, with its range of interests, its technical mastery, and its gracefulness of tone. Poems like 'Future Work' and 'A Way Out' explore a simple conceit with effortless style and lightness of touch. Most skilfully developed in some of these pieces is the sense of the poet watching herself writing a poem, an ironic eye which forbids portentousness or rhetoric. 'A Poem Ended by Death' approaches a difficult subject by gentle mockery of her own poetic styles; 'A Message' is brought to an end by explicit resistance to the declamatory generalizations of romantic closure:

> Gardens are rife with sermon-fodder. I delve
> among blossoming accidents for their designs
> but make no statement. Read between these lines.

In such subtle uses of poetic voice, in the intimacy and flexibility she brought to the language of poetry, Adcock offered to poets like Lauris Edmond and Anne French a distinct and confident way of speaking.

Three Women

The appearance in 1975 of first books by Lauris Edmond, Rachel McAlpine, and Elizabeth Smither, along with a number of others by women, was rapidly considered to mark a historic moment, and the publication in 1977 of *Private Gardens*, an anthology of New Zealand women poets (edited by Riemke Ensing, herself a poet) reinforced it. In the fifteen years that followed, the number and the talent of women publishing poetry have not diminished; it could be argued that Anne French, Cilla McQueen, Jenny Bornholdt, and Michele Leggott *were* the 'young' poets of the 1980s, and to them could be added Elizabeth Nannestad, Janet Charman, Keri Hulme, Bernadette Hall, Dinah Hawken, Heather McPherson, and Kim Eggleston. Up to this time the dominance of men in the poetry of the years since World War II was dramatic; they were the major figures, and the two most distinct 'groups', the Wellington group and the *Freed* poets, included perhaps one woman poet each. These facts were even noted by some of the men themselves.[174]

Those women who did succeed in writing and publishing poetry were isolated and often neglected or belittled, but they maintained an affirmative yet ironic discourse down through the generations. There is also obviously some connection between the strength of the women's movement in New Zealand by 1975 — International Women's Year — and the appearance of new women poets. Lauris Edmond and Rachel McAlpine both readily admit that feminist ideas played some part in their beginning to write and although none of the three was a radical feminist, the movement gave them a sense of community and commitment and a confidence to resist if necessary the current poetic orthodoxy. These women were not young but had already lived half a life in daily contact with the eternal verities. A certain emotional maturity thus perhaps accounts for their distinctiveness of personal style.

In the 1970s and 1980s Lauris Edmond became one of the best-known New Zealand poets. Her audience was a very different one from Hunt's or Tuwhare's but the popularity of all three suggests there might be a different way of looking at the mainstream. Certainly they show, in their very separate ways, that a powerful romantic current still flows, a current which a large number of readers identify as New Zealand poetry. Though she was fifty-one when her first book appeared, Lauris Edmond was of an age with Campbell, Baxter, and Johnson, and her conception of poetry seems to have been formed at an earlier time. (She speaks warmly of Hyde and addresses a poem to Stanley.) She writes accomplished lyrics which have their source in intensely felt personal experience and move gracefully towards a rounded, often generalized, conclusion: 'I seem to want to go right into the middle of an experience and write about that'. There are poems called 'Catching it' and 'Epiphany'. Syntax is simple, language translucent, mediating without complexity between emotion and external reality; the cadences and vocabulary are those of civilized middle-class discourse. Edmond has often been hostile to the New Zealand modernist line which she sees as a 'male poetry which is about the intellectualising of ideas and doesn't work very well in poetry'.[175] She dislikes any poetry which might be considered the clever deployment of language for its own sake.

The sense of a warm, intelligent, compassionate personality and the generous sharing of a full but not unusual life account for a large part of her appeal. She draws repeatedly on the tension between the self's aloneness and its social needs and obligations:

> The pronoun is
> a tiny instrument we use
> to unpick our lives; so 'I'
> and 'you' begin to show
> beneath the old shared knots
> of 'us', so 'ours' is spoilt for 'mine'.

('Signs')

From this tension spring her acute observation of the physical world, her absorbing attention to her family as it grows and changes, her complex reaction to foreign places (especially fine in the Menton poems in *Catching It*), her amused sense of her own public role, her honest and sometimes painful treatment of love in middle age. What might have become an exclusive reliance on a discriminating poetic sensibility is saved by attention to craft[176] and often challenged by recognition of forces the persona cannot fully grasp or control — doubt is the inverse of affirmation in Edmond's work, 'knowing that nothing is mine'.

Death is the chief of these forces and a continuing obsession. It first took particular shape in her second book, *The Pear Tree*, written out of grief at the death of a daughter. These poems and the sequence called *Wellington Letter*, which returns to this death, are among her finest. Emblem of her own — and our — mortality, it comes back repeatedly. It is there again in the last poem of her latest book, *Summer Near the Arctic Circle*; it lines up with other deaths, of friends, of a cat, of a marriage. But it also links with the many poems addressed to the poet's living children, and in later years their children as well. Edmond denies that she writes of or for women, but her poetry affirms, with what one can only call wisdom, the natural processes and patterns with which women have customarily been more at ease and more familiar than men. She is the great New Zealand poet of parents and children, 'this absurd nesting of mothers and daughters', and a vision of a mystic continuity of women down through time lies behind much of her work. Her 'second life' has enabled her to celebrate the bearing and nurturing of her first.

Rachel McAlpine was a lesser poet than Edmond ('I write to have fun'[177]) and indeed after having produced a handful of books in quick succession, ending with a selected poems, she turned her energies more fully to drama and fiction. Her compulsive, charming lyrics looked to be written at speed and without too much labour; they were refreshing in their casual, chatty manner, their lack of piety, and their clever inventiveness. Sam Hunt first set McAlpine writing, and her work has many affinities with the new poetry of the late 1960s.

However, it exhibits also a nervy, slightly hysterical sense of herself as a woman. Edmond's decision to leave a marriage was interiorized before the act of making poems; but with McAlpine the cork is just out of the bottle, and excitement, anger, depression are all there in the verse. Women's liberation, however, was not necessarily the same as sexual liberation, and in much of McAlpine's poetry this caused confusion. The poet's frank and lively expression of her own sexuality too easily became a coy and flirtatious attempt at seeking male approval. *Recording Angel* (1983) is McAlpine's best collection, written on a fellowship in Australia and showing a widening of perspective and a more confident style. Her acknowledgement of fairy tale, nursery rhyme, and the Bible as dominant influences might suggest why she handles dream and fantasy with such success here.[178]

Not particularly motivated by feminism, though sharp with some of its insights, Elizabeth Smither is a distinctive and idiosyncratic poet. She has no obvious kinship with any other New Zealand writer but a very clear idea (from Dickinson, Stevens, Larkin perhaps) of what she wants a poem to be. She professes an admiration for Smithyman and they stand happily together:[179] she reads voraciously and uses this knowledge and passion everywhere in her work; and she is also reticent about the direct expression of personal emotion. But where his poetry is expansive, hers is quick, tight, and concentrated. Her poems are a dozen or so lines, though some later ones are longer, usually in regular stanzas with unrhymed lines. They give a formal impression, and control — including some rhyme — has increased in her later work. They seem curiously timeless, rather like mottoes, epigrams, or inscriptions — all formalized saws or paradoxes for public occasions. Where Edmond and McAlpine reject the intellectual in verse, Smither revels in it. Ideas excite her, and she enjoys a witty and eccentric analogy which strikes a sudden light on a philosophic or religious question; her poems often end with a startling simile, idea flowering into image. (In 'A Cortège of Daughters', a late poem, the unusual sight of a coffin with female pallbearers is in the final lines likened to a 'dark lake' 'sometimes surrounded by irises'.) She leaps with the greatest ease from literature to theology to clothes to camellias, though the reader may not always be nimble enough to pursue the 'rush' of this original and fertile mind. People excite her too, and for a time she played deft variations on legendary characters: Casanova, St Teresa, the Princess (who slept on the Pea), observing with amusement the paradoxes of personality. She often writes of other authors, but treats them as vivid presences, still alive. Here, unquestionably, is Wordsworth:

> And the far solitary man
> Spoon-fed by women
> Surfaces under
> Day wide as windows

Each of these lines, for all its simplicity, is rich with implication and shows the exactness and originality of this poet at her best.

The Age of Anthologies: New Poets of the 1980s

The anthologies of New Zealand poetry from 1945 give significant clues about how contemporaries saw the poetry of their time. In the late 1980s such acts of definition abound — five anthologies appeared between 1985 and 1990, as well as a much-extended edition of O'Sullivan's Oxford anthology. All place strong emphasis on recent poetry, four of them exclusively. Two anthologies define their limits. *Yellow Pencils*, edited by Lydia Wevers, anthologizes women's poetry, and *The New Poets*, edited by Murray Edmond and Mary Paul, remembering Doyle and Baysting, presents a fresh generation. To these could be added the important collection of Māori writing, *Into the World of Light* (1982), edited by Witi Ihimaera and Don Long, which included poetry. Two

Penguin anthologies, *The Penguin Book of New Zealand Verse* (1985), edited by Ian Wedde and Harvey McQueen, and *The Penguin Book of Contemporary New Zealand Poetry* (1989), edited by Wedde, McQueen, and Miriama Evans, give generous overviews. All anthologists were at pains to stress 'difference' and 'variousness', words from the covers of *The New Poets* and *Yellow Pencils* respectively. Only Wedde in his already historic introduction to *The Penguin Book of New Zealand Verse* attempted the old national identity game. But while Curnow had focused on the local referent, it was characteristic of the times that Wedde should see language and its 'growth into its location' as the distinguishing mark of a 'New Zealand' poetry. This process he considers in terms faithful to the early 1970s as a trend away from the language of high culture ('hieratic') towards a broader vernacular, immediate and flexible ('demotic'). While it is hard to avoid noticing what such a theory narrowly conceived might omit from serious consideration, it shared the prevailing resistance to a 'tradition' as a single authoritative line and to conventional ideas of 'excellence' with which this is associated.

Expressed in a highly sophisticated form, this is a view held by the poet and critic who was this decade's generational rebel, Leigh Davis. The four-issue magazine *And* (1983-5), of which Davis was a co-editor, and his long poem or sequence, *Willy's Gazette* (1983), were part of a single revolutionary programme to unsettle the assumptions on which 'New Zealand literature', both idea and practice, had been based. If Loney had been the purest follower of Olsonian post-modernism, Davis wrote from a post-structuralist position heavily indebted to Barthes and other French critics. He rejected completely the familiar idea that 'literature originated with an author and his encounter with things', seeing it instead as a historical and cultural product with no claim to universal truth or mimetic value. Thus he found most contemporary poetry anachronistic, likening Curnow (in a now notorious comparison) to a 1957 Chrysler.[180] Davis and the group at Auckland University associated with him (Roger Horrocks and Alex Calder in particular) were trying to get readers to look freshly at what actually went on when reading a poem, to recognize the baggage a reader brought to it, to be more conscious about the whole process. Poetry is a language construct, that is to say employing a set of 'arbitrary signifiers', or conventional signs functioning according to rules internalized by all members of the language community. *Willy's Gazette* is a rich, clever, and sophisticated exploration (in mock sonnet form) of the arbitrary and purely conventional nature of cultural signs — it is a poem pre-eminently 'about' language, to be enjoyed purely on its surface because that is all, in Davis's view, that poems are. The poem is cluttered with verbal material from literature, business, high technology, pop culture, fashion, used with confidence and panache: the effect Davis desires is an improvised, busy immediacy lasting only a moment — the photocopied A4 format proclaims the poem as transient, disposable, like any cultural product. And indeed Leigh Davis himself, after administering severe shocks to the literary establishment, ceased to be active as poet or critic.

And was a convincing piece of marketing, but its long-term effect was probably most dramatic in critical theory and practice, where articles conducting a wholesale re-examination of important New Zealand literary texts have continued to be influential. Leigh Davis's poetry, along with poetry on similar lines by Roger Horrocks and Wystan Curnow, was a pure version of many ideas that were in the air, and poets, as we have seen, were becoming increasingly aware of the opacity of language.

The stress on plurality in all the anthologies was not simply a tribute to the multiplicity of talents. It was also a key element in contemporary cultural attitudes, carrying intense pressure because of its post-colonial and racial implications. Acceptance of difference was one of the ways in which New Zealanders struggled during the 1980s to grasp and to celebrate the presence of a hitherto neglected indigenous culture in their midst. Most of the 1980s anthologies — the two Penguins, *The New Poets*, and *Yellow Pencils* — saw revisionism as part of their brief: attempting to rescue poets whose work had been neglected by a tradition perceived as male, Pākehā, and élitist. Such moves were in keeping with widespread middle-class opinion, as their publishers were quick to recognize; and though it is true that a new cultural orthodoxy may have been in the making, it is also the case that the egalitarian temper of the 'young' poets-turned-anthologists was in ways like this, making poetry accessible and possible to people who might have once found it intimidating.

The anthologists were particularly hospitable to work by women, but the strength and variety of poetry by women in the 1980s hardly needed the leg-up of affirmative action. Even Vincent O'Sullivan, who was less sympathetic to the cultural tide, gave strong representation to women among his new contributors. During the 1980s women predominated as winners of the New Zealand Book Awards for Poetry, and two of them won major overseas awards.

But the women were not a homogeneous group either. In the past it was too easy to restrict poetry by women to a special category, seen as charming but harmless. The force of feminism, which is present simply as a matter of consciousness in the verse of all these women, pushes emphatically and impressively towards individuality. Repeatedly this involves, as Lydia Wevers points out, an explicit awareness of the place of language in establishing gender roles. Anne French, a highly accomplished poet working out of a thorough knowledge of the English tradition, published three collections in the late 1980s; much of her poetry is an elegant and ironic exploration of the interrelationships between truth and falsehood, men and women: the titles of two of her books are *All Cretans are Liars* and *The Male as Evader*. Michele Leggott, on the other hand, who has written a major critical study of the American poet, Louis Zukovsky, coaxes words to come forward, to stand freshly, to shimmer and dance in the sensual and miraculous world of mother and child.[181] The author of five collections, Cilla McQueen interprets experience in terms of shopping lists, timetables, items to be managed and controlled. In New York, where she wrote most of her single collection, *It Has No Sound and is Blue* (1987), Dinah

Hawken struggles to hold contemporary chaos at bay. 'You have to laugh and you have to cry steeply / — without friction, fluently — in this climate to stay alive.'

The modernist interest in art and the nature of the poem, and a feminist interest in the woman as artist, are also recurring concerns. McQueen, well known as a performance artist, frequently steps out of the realist illusion (in her landscape poems, for example) to reveal the fact of artifice. In Bernadette Hall's poem, 'Mills and Boon', in *Of Elephants Etc.* (1990), the poet moves to a recognition that the fantasy of romance is a fiction which she controls and thus can abolish: 'I have almost forgotten his name'. In her attractive and unusual collection, *Moving House* (1989), Jenny Bornholdt explores the difficulties of transfixing the slipping, sliding human condition in art.[182]

The power of words in naming, bearing witness to what has been taken for granted, ignored, or undervalued, is important to many of these poets. Their poems are dense with detail, often ugly, tasteless, physical detail of life lived close to the margins; and they are full of talk, energetic and active. Janet Charman and Heather McPherson are explicitly feminist poets attempting to develop a self-sufficient female context and mythology, a place in language beyond a male discourse perceived as rational, ordered, and hierarchic.[183]

For poets like Keri Hulme and Roma Potiki, the role of language in establishing and maintaining identity is seen in relation to race as well as gender. As Hulme says, 'I think the word sets the whole thing up'. Both Penguin anthologies, as part of their salvage policy, include a substantial number of poems in Māori, chosen with the aid of specialist editors Margaret Orbell and Miriama Evans; this determined effort to recognize the rich Māori oral tradition as part of 'New Zealand literature' met with some hostility.[184] What is noticeable, however, is the small number of poems in English by Māori poets in both collections (and in the other anthologies), by contrast with the exciting explosion of prose fiction in English by Māori writers during the 1980s. Editor Miriama Evans suggests, in her introduction to *The Penguin Book of Contemporary New Zealand Poetry*, that the tradition is being renewed in its own language.

Hone Tuwhare remains a major figure, though he has been less prolific in recent years. Mark Williams takes his 'We, Who Live in Darkness' as a brilliant political poem, relying on the tension between two different views of the Māori creation myth.[185] But Tuwhare's effortless control of a tough, rhythmic, demotic language is always impressive too:

> Tomorrow, sure as eggs
> the rain will drop by like
> a fresh friend . . .
>
> ('A Festival Letter . . .')

Another older poet important in this context is Alistair Campbell, whose dramatic rediscovery in the late 1970s of his mother's family in the Cook Islands generated two small but moving sequences, *The Dark Lord of Savaiki* (1980) and *Soul Traps* (1985). These short lyrics, relying not on traditional forms but on an economy and clarity of language and on the poet's still flawless evocative powers, draw on Tongarevan legend and stories of his own family. *Soul Traps* is strongly elegaic in tone, and recalls the passage of poet and poetry from the artificiality of the 'Elegy' which so excited the public in 1950. Hulme's *The Silences Between* (1982) was her first book and showed immediately a strongly individual voice, a range of language from sweeping rhetorical grandeur to blunt, earthy vernacular, and above all an inclusion of Māori myth, phrase, and world view that was unforced and powerful. Apirana Taylor's *Eyes of the Ruru* (1979) expressed the anger and alienation of the dispossessed twentieth century Māori. Rowley Habib was a significant Māori poet in the 1970s, writing on similar themes with something of Tuwhare's sense of language and rhythm. Roma Potiki, Arapera Blank, Bub Bridger, and Trixie Menzies are poets writing in English in a direct informal style with a strong awareness of being both Māori and female.[186]

Keri Hulme points out that the possession of two languages is 'like having another pair of eyes and ears . . . you see things differently and you literally see relationships in different ways. . . . It also makes people like me more prone to experiment with language.'[187] During the 1980s, English speakers in New Zealand became increasingly familiar with Māori words, phrases, and concepts, and by 1990 some knowledge of Māori language can be assumed in her readers by a younger Pākehā poet like Anne French in several places in her collection, *Cabin Fever*, where she also quite comfortably uses expressions in French and German.

The movement out of a monolingual consciousness has also reinforced in contemporary poets the obsessive and self-conscious interest in language, the stuff of which poems are made. It is at a pitch in the work of David Eggleton, for example; a gripping performance poet, he was billed to British audiences as the 'Mad Kiwi Ranter', but his fast-talking, streetwise, rhyming patter does not entirely conceal a deliberate and sophisticated craft resistant as much to literary cliché as to media slogan. Gregory O'Brien is another young poet whose magical arrangement of words and pictures creates a strange delight; John Newton uses the language and imagery of a later age to revisit the rural contexts of mid-century poets.[188]

*   *   *

From the minute particulars of Bethell's observation of the Akaroa Harbour in the 1930s, in 'The Long Harbour', and Curnow's intense, memory-laden image of Lyttelton Harbour a decade later, in 'At Dead Low Water', New Zealand poets played many variations on the relationship between language and its occasions. In a 1989 poem, Dinah Hawken was writing of a different harbour in a different way, a poetic voice recognizably of the 1980s:

The harbour is hallucinating. It is rising
above itself, halfway up the great
blue hills. Every leaf of the kohuhu
is shining. Cicadas, this must be the day
of all days, the one around which
all the others are bound to gather.

The blue agapanthus, the yellow fennel, the white
butterfly, the blue harbour, the golden grass,
the white verandah post, the blue hills, the yellow
leaves, the white clouds, the blue
book, the yellow envelope, the white paper.
Here is the green verb, releasing everything.

But there are unmistakable continuities also. For Hawken, as for Bethell and
Curnow, poetry is a continuing and mysterious act of faith in the transforming
power of 'the green verb, releasing everything'.

Children's Literature

BETTY GILDERDALE

Nineteenth Century Settler and Adventure Fiction

Two themes dominated the twenty-nine children's books about New Zealand written in the nineteenth century: the reactions of the early settlers to the vicissitudes of an alien and remote environment very different from Europe, and relationships with the Māori (or 'New Zealanders' as they were then called). Of the two main genres, the more popular was undoubtedly the pioneering family tale of emigration and settlement, the earliest example of which was Mrs J.E. Aylmer's *Distant Homes; or, the Graham Family in New Zealand* (1862). But there was also a considerable amount of conventional adventure fiction, modelled on the then fashionable formulae of later nineteenth century Anglo-European imperialist stories, much of it prompted by the events of the Land Wars of the 1860s and written outside the country. The boundaries between the settler tale and the adventure story were never absolute: the former could include elements of adventure, and the latter often introduced descriptions of spectacular landscapes and of unusual flora and fauna. Nevertheless there are significant distinctions between the family focus of the settler tales, which were usually written by women, and the more plot-centred sensationalism of the adventure stories, written mainly by men.

The first two books about New Zealand which might claim to be children's stories were in fact closer to tracts and guidebooks than to fiction: *Stories About Many Things, Founded on Facts* (1833) and *Emily Bathurst* (1847), both published anonymously in London. The former has the structure of a series of questions from a small boy to his mother. He is given information about dogs, ants and trees, and also about 'New Zealanders'. His mother tells him how one of Captain Cook's men was massacred by the natives, but is at pains to point out that the sailors may have provoked the anger that caused the tragedy. A reconciliatory attitude also characterizes *Emily Bathurst*, which includes a spirited portrayal of a drawing room debate in England in which an archdeacon of the Church Missionary Society, opposed to the alienation of Māori land, roundly condemns the Treaty of Waitangi as 'little more than a mere legal fiction'.[1]

The archdeacon's uncompromising viewpoint certainly does not recur in W.H.G. Kingston's *Holmwood; or, The New Zealand Settler* (1868) and *Waihoura; or, The New Zealand Girl* (1872), the latter reprinted on at least half a dozen occasions over the next thirty years, with its subtitle changed in the last edition (*circa* 1905) to *The Maori Girl*. In both books there is an underlying equation of Christianity with Britishness, and an assumption that 'Maories' were savages before being converted but exemplary Christians afterwards. The evils of drink are also emphasized, especially in *Waihoura*, whose young English heroine believes she has a sacred duty to instruct a convalescent Māori girl in Christianity and temperance. A strongly religious theme, though without Kingston's racism, is also evident in Emilia Marryat's *Amongst the Maoris, a Book of Adventure* (1875), whose title was changed in the second edition of 1891 to *Jack Stanley; or, The Young Adventurers*. The literal quest of the young hero is to discover the man who had ruined his father, but this geographical search becomes a journey of the soul during the course of which he comes to terms with his bitterness. His travelling companion, Colonel Bradshaw, is a veritable encyclopaedia of knowledge about the country and its inhabitants, and much is made of the opportunity to provide a detailed picture of the landscape, flora, and fauna, as well as of Māori customs and beliefs. Marryat's was the last novel whose main theme was evangelism, and one of the few to attempt to understand the Māori people. For the rest of the century books with a Māori component were more concerned to exploit the opportunities for action-packed adventure and sensation provided by the Land Wars.

Within the mainstream of settler fictions which began with Aylmer's *Distant Homes* there are predictable differences between stories based in the North Island, where there is much greater emphasis on the impact of meeting the Māori, and those written about the South Island, where the focus is more on the physical environment and the pioneering drive to carve out a living from it. Aylmer had never visited New Zealand, a fact abundantly evident from her inaccurate geographical and botanical references; but the Graham family were relatives of the author, and like so many subsequent books based on letters and diaries of settlers, it provides (despite its descriptive blunders) an authentic picture of pioneering life in Canterbury in the period. Nevertheless it must be borne in mind that these were the records of literate settlers; few genuine 'early settler' books describe life from any other point of view. Like so many others the Grahams came to New Zealand because they were suffering financial hardship in England, and in spite of their genteel background they demonstrate a commendable ability to adapt to menial work never previously contemplated.

By far the most vivid early-settler stories, however, are three collections written by Lady Barker in the early 1870s: *Stories About* (1870), *A Christmas Cake in Four Quarters* (1871), and *Boys* (1874). Lady Barker had come to New Zealand in 1865, newly married to her second husband Frederick Napier Broome, and they farmed a sheep station in Canterbury until 1868 when they returned to England after losing nearly all their sheep in a fierce snowstorm. Although Barker is better known for her adult books, her three collections for children share the same incisive prose style and freshness of perspective. All the New Zealand stories in these volumes describe young emigrant men, from the cadet-farmer to the more lowly shepherd, and they highlight the foolishness of coming to 'the Colonies' with no capital, as if 'large fortunes could be made in a few years just by changing the air'.[2] The stories also convey the humour and pathos of farming and domestic life in the backblocks (including a powerful story of the accidental death of a surveyor by starvation), and include a lively narrative of an unconventional New Zealand Christmas Day full of comic incidents and sharp observations of settler idiosyncrasies. Barker does not minimize the difficulties of pioneering life, but she does convey the sense of exhilaration and freedom experienced by people who had had the courage to come to a new land offering seemingly limitless possibilities.

Barker wrote at a time when stories about the colonies were becoming increasingly popular with young men in British Public Schools, who were being encouraged to seek adventure (and a career) overseas. A typical picture of such an experience is given in Ernest Simeon Elwell's *The Boy Colonists; or, Eight Years of Colonial Life in Otago* (1878): 'a simple, brief, and plain narrative of what occurred to a settler in the Province of Otago . . . during the years 1859-67'.[3] Like most settler books it graphically describes the hardships of the outward voyage and first impressions of the Māori. It is more vociferous than most on the subject of flies, fleas, drunkenness, and the inadequacies of wayside inns and colonial doctors. It also shares the happy ending common to so many settler stories, a return to England and civilization after the difficulties of colonial life.

While most genuine early-settler books were exploring the relative calm of the South Island, overseas writers such as Jules Verne, George Henty and Reginald Horsley were exploiting the wars in the North Island as a subject for fast-paced sensational adventure stories. Verne in particular, in books such as *Among the Cannibals* (translated from the French *Les Enfants du Capitaine Grant: Voyage autour du Monde*, 1867), painted a lurid and exaggerated picture of Māori 'savagery'. Henty, writing in the 'blood and thunder' tradition which concentrated almost exclusively upon action, at least occasionally had some regard for historical fidelity. In his *Maori and Settler, A Story of the New Zealand War* (1891), the hero is a genteel English settler who has bought a farm in Hawke's Bay and finds himself vulnerable to attacks from the Māori leader Te Kooti Arikirangi. The novel incorporates fantastic elements typical of the genre, however, when he is helped by an almost superhuman friend of herculean proportions, encyclopaedic knowledge and Einstein-like powers of deduction who single-handedly saves the family from annihilation; and it ends typically with the convenient resolution of financial difficulties and a return to England. Horsley's *In the Grip of the Hawk: A Story of the Maori Wars* (1907), also about Te Kooti, has a liveliness in the telling, but in its cavalier attitude to facts, its sensationalizing of the atrocities of the Hauhau, and (as in Henty's fiction) its constant disparagement of the Māori, it reveals a total lack of understanding of the reasons behind the conflict. Such books were representative of the adventure genre of the time.

One of the few settler stories with a domestic setting in the North Island was H.A. Forde's *Across Two Seas, A New Zealand Tale* (1894). Here for the first time in New Zealand children's fiction, is the portrayal of a refreshingly strong and adventurous mother who emigrates on her own with her seven children rather than have them adopted out after her husband's death. Mrs Vaughan is an educated woman who rears her sons and daughters without any discrimination of role, teaching both to knit socks on the voyage out and, when they settle near Auckland, insisting that they all learn history and literature even though such subjects might not be immediately useful in their present way of life. She is the policy-maker and supporter of her family, whose characters and relationships are warmly drawn. Unlike most fictional settler women, Mrs Vaughan refuses to become overwhelmed by domesticity, instead delegating chores and maintaining her own intellectual and artistic interests in books, writing, and music. Her organizational talents and firm philosophic grasp of education result in a dynamic family who never become enslaved by the utilitarian routine of farming.

After 1900 there was only one settler story written in the evangelical tradition of the previous century: Louisa H. Bedford's *Under One Standard; or, The Touch that Makes Us Kin* (1916). The unifying Christian standard is indeed the hope of the Godwin family in their relationships with the Māori. However the overall image of pioneering and of the Māori, despite the idealism of the novel's title, is ambivalent. Mrs Godwin, made of less stern stuff than Forde's Mrs Vaughan, returns to England with her family, worn down by the wartime upheavals of pioneering life in Taranaki in the 1860s. Her brother remains, becoming a Selwyn-inspired clergyman, and the novel concludes with his disparaging comments about Te Whiti and his 'garbled Old Testament religion'. Bedford's treatment of the wars in Taranaki, and of their impingement on the lives of settlers like the Godwins, maintains a degree of sympathy for the Māori cause. There is a moving description of Māori passive resistance at Waitara and of Selwyn's urgent pleas for an understanding of the Māori viewpoint, and the intransigence of settler attitudes is vigorously spelt out: 'The Bishop's just a crank where Māoris are concerned. It's a big mistake for a man to try to mix up politics and religion.'[4]

One of the central threads in Bedford's novel was the divided loyalty of a Māori boy befriended by the Godwin family and converted to Christianity. It was in fact the second novel within three years to explore the theme of Māori-Pākehā friendship, which subsequently became a major preoccupation in New Zealand literature for children. The first, William Satchell's *The Greenstone Door* (1914), was a landmark in articulating for the first time an indigenous view of the wars and of the tragic destruction they created in personal relationships. By ensuring that his European hero, Cedric Tregarthen, had been reared in a Māori pā, Satchell was able to highlight the ambivalence felt by Cedric when hostilities erupt between his foster family and his own race. This is especially poignant when at the novel's climax Cedric observes the Battle of Orakau where his stepmother, stepsister and many friends are besieged, and in the immediate aftermath witnesses the summary execution of his beloved foster-father as a traitor. *The Greenstone Door* is thus much more than an adventure story. It accentuates the plight of people born in New Zealand for whom the Wars had deep personal consequences. It is the first book which, for its examination of complex issues and emotions and the depth of its characterization, warrants acceptance as both a children's book and as a work for adult readers.

Local Fantasy and the Family Story, 1900-1930

The settler and adventure stories which dominated nineteenth century writing for children were never thought of as contributing to an indigenous literature. Often written (and always published) overseas they were intended as 'reports' of immigrant experiences for the British market, or simply used New Zealand as an exciting or exotic setting to satisfy the demand for novelty on which adventure yarns depended. By the end of the nineteenth century, however, a new generation of children born in New Zealand had emerged, and writers began to notice the lack of local material for younger readers. In Great Britain fiction written exclusively for children was still in its infancy; the usual diet for younger readers consisted of fairy stories and legends. It was to this fantasy genre — and especially to Māori myths and legends — that New Zealand authors initially turned in an attempt to fashion an indigenous body of stories for children. The first book for children to be published in New Zealand was entitled *Fairy Tales and Folklore of New Zealand and the South Seas* (1892), its author (Edward Tregear) a politician, poet, Fellow of the Royal Geographical Society, linguist, and a keen amateur ethnologist. His interest in folklore was in keeping with its scholarly revival in Europe, and he dedicated his book to Andrew Lang, a scholar whose works such as *Myth, Ritual and Religion* (1887) were having a profound effect upon children's literature overseas.

Tregear avoided the main Māori myths and concentrated instead upon fairy tales and folklore: how the Māori were taught to make fishing nets by the fairies, or the story of Pare and Hutu and Rua's stolen wife. His aim seems to have been to record plainly rather than to embellish his narratives, unlike Kate McCosh Clark, who published *Maori Tales and Legends* four years later in 1896. A number of her stories overlap with Tregear's, but although their dramatic momentum is heightened, the style is flowery and sentimental and the language sometimes lapses into archaisms. Scholarly notes are provided at the back to interest adults. Five years earlier Clark had written and illustrated *A Southern Cross Fairy Tale* (1891), whose aim was to reconcile children to a midsummer Christmas in the southern hemisphere. Lacking red holly berries they gather red roses, and in a dream they encounter a youthful (presumably antipodean) Santa Claus who takes them on a conducted tour of the beauties of New Zealand. This contrived tale highlighted the problem of fantasy writing for young New Zealanders at this period. Most authors were first generation immigrants, whose inner landscapes were peopled by northern images of witches, wizards, wolves, and hobgoblins, creatures bred from mists and winter snows. Attempts to amalgamate these with the very different features of the local environment invariably seemed artificial.

Of the main three authors of children's fantasy between 1900 and 1914 —

Amy Dora Bright, Marie Alexander and Edith Howes — Bright appeared the most aware of this problem. In her preface to *Three Xmas Gifts and other Tales* (1901), the first of three fantasy books, she admits that bringing northern folklore into the southern hemisphere may well produce 'some old faces tattooed', but hopes there may be no need for apology:

> Folklore and fable . . . are not indigenous only to the Old World, but are born of the spirit that broods over the bush and the music that sings on the beaches. Our future literature will be, in form and tunefulness, peculiarly our own.[5]

The eleven stories in *Three Xmas Gifts* are all set in New Zealand, but fail to integrate the mixture of European and Māori folklore Bright draws on in order to explain features of birds and plants. Alexander's books were all published in New Zealand — *Children's Tales Written in New Zealand for Little New Zealanders* (1900), *Rudolph, A tale of Fairyland* (1906), and *Bushi's Adventures, A Wonderful Dream* (1910) — and exemplified, despite occasional realistic touches, the Victorian propensity to use fantasy for didactic purposes: the fate of dreadful children was a key component of her work. It is hardly surprising that some years later Hilaire Belloc in England saw fit to satirize this type of story in his *Cautionary Tales*: like Matilda's Lies, Alexander's narratives make one 'gasp and stretch one's eyes' at their obvious overstatements and retributive idea of punishment.

Alexander's books were also extremely poorly produced, but overseas it was becoming increasingly evident that young children deserved good pictures in an attractive format; Beatrix Potter's first book had appeared in 1900. Mrs Ambrose E. Moore's *Fairyland in New Zealand, A Story of Caves* (1909) was the most elegantly produced book to date issued by a New Zealand publisher, Brett of Auckland, in which the delicate pictures by Emily C. Harris harmonized finely with the good overall design and typography. Unfortunately the text was scarcely worthy of such elevated treatment. Like her contemporaries, Moore explained her aims in a preface:

> Why should not the children of New Zealand have fairy stories all their own, like the little German children . . . is the question I asked myself, so I sat down to write some.[6]

Anyone who could so misunderstand the nature of traditional tales as to think they could be so effortlessly fabricated is likely to produce exactly the sort of far-fetched story that *Fairyland in New Zealand* proved to be.

The year before, in 1908, Johannes Carl Andersen's *Maori Fairy Tales* was published by Whitcombe and Tombs of Christchurch, the first children's book issued by a company which over many decades was to make a significant contribution to indigenous publishing for New Zealand children. Andersen's volume, which drew on his ethnographic research into Māori legends, was significantly more authentic than the fairy tales contrived by Moore, and he was also a personal friend of Edith Howes, author of a score of full-length books (and numerous shorter stories in the Whitcombe's Story Book series), who was to dominate New Zealand children's literature for the next thirty years. Howes was a teacher (at Wellington Girls' College, then at Gore) with particular interests in science and nature study, and ahead of her time in many of her ideas, but she nevertheless used the currently fashionable gossamer-winged fairies as a vehicle of her didactic intentions.

These were most evident in *The Cradle Ship* (1916, reprinted in many editions including French, Italian and Danish translations), whose aim, daringly advanced for the time, was to teach children the facts of life. Twins, who wish to know where a new baby comes from, are taken by their parents on a voyage in the 'Cradle Ship', during which they observe every variety of animal with its young, beginning with insects and fish who abandon their eggs, progressing to the more nurturing birds, marsupials and animals, until they finally understand that human babies 'grow beneath their Mother's heart'. Howes believed firmly in the power of knowledge and deplored the prevailing secrecy in sexual matters. Fourteen years later, in an adventure story for older readers, *The Golden Forest* (1930), she left readers in little doubt that a young man had died of venereal disease. *The Singing Fish* (1921) explored gender stereotyping: a brother who scorns his sister because she is 'only a girl' is changed into a 'cock-a-bully' fish by the Mischief Fairy (clearly a representative of the movement for women's rights at the time) who ensures that he has enough unpleasant underwater experiences never to repeat his error: 'Boys who say, "you're only a girl" become men who say "you're only a woman"'.[7]

When liberated from the sentimental 'flower fairy' syndrome, Howes wrote directly and well, and her popularity was not undeserved. She was eager that children should know their flora and fauna, and in the first really indigenous adventure story, *Silver Island* (1928), a group of shipwrecked children survive because they are familiar with bushcraft and the sea. Knowledge of native birds was crucial, too, for the children of *Young Pioneers* (1934), in which Howes combines instruction about nature study and history in a well-managed 'early settler' story. In her last book of all, *Riverside Family* (1944), she again abandoned the fantasy of earlier years and wrote an unembellished account of the daily life of a family. Despite her ability to construct good plots, all Howes's fantasy books have suffered from changes in literary fashion, and their overt didactic emphases were also endemic to the period in which she wrote. She was, however, innovative in establishing the survival-story format in local adventure fiction, and in her willingness to tackle unconventional subjects she remains one of the most significant writers of children's literature in New Zealand.

Most of Howes's longer books were published in England, often by Cassell, who provided her with illustrators of the calibre of Florence Mary Anderson and Frank Watkins. In general, her books published in New Zealand received less lavish treatment. This was not, however, the only reason for sending manuscripts to London. The home market was at that time so small that royalties dependent on the number of sales would have been minimal. It was financially important to capture the larger British market, but at a time when England was still considered 'Home' by many, it was also psychologically and professionally important to prove that a colonial writer could produce material worthy of London publication. The major disadvantage of this arrangement (apart from the pressure to conform to the fictional subjects and styles required by the overseas market) was that authors could be in danger of not being known in their own country. Howes *was* widely known in New Zealand: partly, perhaps, because her shorter fictions were frequently published by Whitcombe and Tombs, and partly because the didactic nature of her work meant that her work was well-known in educational circles. The pressure that linked children's writing to the market provided by educational institutions was beginning to play an increasingly important role, for better and worse, in the growth of local children's literature.

Isabel Maud Peacocke lived in Auckland, and like Howes published overseas, almost exclusively with Ward, Lock of London. Her output was prolific, but she was to boast that whole editions of her books were sold out before any reached New Zealand — this perhaps explains why she was less widely known in her own country than Howes, whose *Cradle Ship* had been a best seller. *My Friend Phil* (1914, illustrated by Margaret Tarrant) was Peacocke's first novel, and the first New Zealand novel which could be called a 'family story', in the tradition of overseas writers like Louisa May Alcott in the United States, L.M. Montgomery in Canada, and Ethel Turner in Australia. Unlike the earlier settler stories in which families contend with the difficult external circumstances of a pioneering environment, the family story is more concerned with human relationships in everyday domestic surroundings, and thus more than any other genre tends to reflect changing social conditions and attitudes. Peacocke's novels in retrospect are more valuable as a reflection of their period than for their literary quality. Her twenty-two children's books span the years 1914 to 1939, and in addition to these she wrote seventeen adult novels (under the name of Cluett), four smaller fantasy stories, and many abridged classics for the popular Whitcombe's Story Book series. She also wrote plays and poems for radio, regularly contributed items of general interest to the *New Zealand Herald*, and was a founding member (later president) of the New Zealand Penwomen's Club.

Although she was the first teacher at the Anglican Dilworth School, established for boys from disadvantaged backgrounds, Peacocke did not use her experiences there as material for the genre of school stories popular at the time. Her interest lay less in interaction between children than in relationships between parent and child. Her association with Dilworth is evident in the way parents are depicted throughout her fiction: at best they are snobbish, at worst irresponsible. The wise and good-humoured adults in her books are kindly uncles and aunts who take over where parents fail. Central to a number of stories is the problem of guardianship; others have parents who blatantly place their own interests before those of the child. *Little Bit O' Sunshine* (1924) and *His Kid Brother* (1926) include irresponsible fathers who are on the wrong side of the law; and mothers such as the singer in *The Adopted Family* (1923) and the writer in *Brenda and the Babes* (1927) are seen as selfishly abandoning their children in pursuit of their own careers. Peacocke's children, by contrast, are invariably high-spirited but well-intentioned: their misdemeanours (unlike those of their elders) arise from unselfish motives coupled with inexperience of adult reactions. The twin heroes of *The Misdoings of Micky and Mac* (1919), for instance, in a munificent gesture fill their uncle's room and pockets with beans in varying stages of preservation, after taking literally his statement that he could not afford to marry because he 'hadn't the beans'.

Living as she did in affluent Remuera, Peacocke often emphasized the effects of snobbery. In both *Quicksilver* (1922) and *Marjolaine* (1935) obstacles to friendship between children of differing social backgrounds come not from the children themselves, but from the well-to-do parents of one of them, and Peacocke often presents such attitudes as reinforced by authoritarian educational regimes. However, although her experiences as a teacher ensured that her observations of children are accurate, her novels are usually written from an adult point of view. Her books are likely to have appealed to older sisters, amused to see the gaucheries of the younger ones recorded in print. Only in *The Cruise of the* Crazy Jane (1932) and *Cathleen with a 'C'* (1934) is a child's-eye view achieved through the use of a first-person narrator.

Peacocke's main weakness is an unevenness of style. At its best her prose is incisive and satirical; at its worst it is self-consciously slangy and coyly sentimental. Her strengths (most evident, perhaps, in the decade following *The Misdoings of Micky and Mac*) lie in her strong sense of place, well-developed plots, memorable episodes, and sheer ability to keep readers turning the pages. The stories are often enlivened by the humour of the author's commentary on her characters and by the comic inventiveness of the incidents that take place. Her work taken as a whole provides a vivid picture of social life at the time. Soldiers leave for and sometimes return from the First World War, many children are fatherless, and unemployment and consumption claim their victims. She is also one of the few New Zealand authors to set all her novels, apart from *My Friend Phil*, firmly in Auckland. Domestic dramas are enacted on trams travelling along Karangahape Road, in large houses in Remuera or in smaller ones in Mount Eden. Brief forays take place into the Waitakere Ranges or to off-shore islands, and in *When I Was Seven* (1927) she writes warmly about her own childhood home in Cheltenham and Devonport on Auckland's North Shore. No novelist up to this time had provided children with so unforced and immediate a recognition of the urban and suburban domestic settings in which most lived, with their surrounding environments of bush and beach.

Throughout the 1920s Peacocke's family stories for older readers and Howes's fantasy stories for younger children continued to appear regularly. But in Christchurch one of their contemporaries was also energetically engaged in promoting children's literature, profoundly influencing its development though she produced relatively few books herself. Esther Glen came from a newspaper family and worked as a freelance journalist, and when she realized how few good indigenous articles and books were available for children she started a children's supplement in the Christchurch *Sun*, encouraging children themselves to write. Abounding in ideas and enthusiasm she invited professional writers (including Howes) to talk to children, turned her office into a venue where they brought not only their writing but their paintings, their hobbies and even their pets, and organized picnics, play productions and concerts. When the *Sun* disappeared in a merger in 1935, Glen transferred to the Christchurch *Press*, but continued to work for children. It was this vigorous encouragement of the imaginative life of children, and her influence on the quality and professionalism of children's journalism, as much as her own four books, which led the New Zealand Library Association to give her name to an award it instituted in 1945, for 'the most distinguished contribution to New Zealand literature for children'.

Her lasting reputation as an author rests predominantly on two novels, *Six Little New Zealanders* (1917) and its sequel *Uncles Three at Kamahi* (1926). The title of the first clearly alluded to Ethel Turner's *Seven Little Australians*, drawing on the same nationalistic impulse and aiming, similarly, to move away from the Victorian didactic tradition. The opening sentences of the story gesture ironically to that tradition: 'Take an atlas. Don't be afraid, this isn't a geography lesson. Really and truly, it's the only improving piece in the whole book.' The narrator, Ngaire Malcolm, is as good as her word. She is twelve years old, the fourth child in a family of six whose ages range from nineteen to nine. When their mother has to go 'Home' to England for medical treatment the children stay on their uncles' farm at Kamahi in Canterbury, and since the family has been city-reared in Auckland, and the uncles are rural bachelors, both parties suffer severe culture shock, with amusing results. The two novels are much more than slapstick comedy, however. There is a very convincing portrayal of the children's relationships with each other and with their long-suffering uncles, and the character of Ngaire's older sister Jan, in many ways reminiscent of Jo in Louisa May Alcott's *Little Women*, is poignantly drawn. Glen's crisp style and acute powers of observation are in the same tradition as Lady Barker's, and there is a similar exuberant feeling for South Island back-country landscape — for clear mountain air and for the freedom and independence of sheep station life.

Christchurch in the 1920s presented a lively literary scene. Glen attracted into her circle of speakers not only Howes, H.C.D. Somerset and Jessie Mackay, but also Mona Tracy, another journalist working on the *Press*. Tracy had begun her working career at the age of thirteen, when she persuaded the editor of the New Zealand *Weekly News* to employ her. Later she underwent the rigorous training given to its journalists by the *New Zealand Herald* in Auckland. She was one of the first women reporters in New Zealand, and when she transferred to the South Island to work for the *Press* during the First World War, she became the first woman journalist to sit at the press bench during Court hearings. She subsequently became editor of the Women's Page, but retired after marriage and the birth of her children. Tracy's research into New

Zealand history gave her the material for many radio talks as well as for adult non-fiction and poetry. She had been born and brought up near Paeroa in a Māori-speaking district, attended school with Māori girls and certainly spoke some Māori herself. These interests led her to write ten stories for older readers (published under the title *Piriki's Princess and Other Stories of New Zealand*, 1925) in which for the first time Māori women protagonists appeared and problems of identity for characters of mixed Pākehā-Māori ancestry were sympathetically explored. Two stories deal with love affairs between Pākehā women and Māori men, their unhappy endings reflecting the fact that such relationships were socially unacceptable, although marriages between Pākehā men and Māori women did not suffer the same stigma.

Tracy's first novel, *Rifle and Tomahawk* (1927) explores the theme of friendship between Māori and Pākehā boys which had occurred the previous decade in Satchell's *The Greenstone Door* and Bedford's *Under One Standard*. Set in Hawke's Bay at the time of the Hauhau rebellion, it recounts how the Māori hero Hori Te Whiti, whose tribe had joined the forces of Te Kooti, takes the risk of warning his best friend Ron Cameron of the danger of an uprising. The exciting story describes how the Cameron children are separated, how Ron's sister Isbel is taken to Te Kooti's pa, and how Hori and Ron effect her escape. Tracy had carefully researched the period and was much more sympathetic to the Māori cause than most writers of the time. The Pākehā boy, Ron, speaks fluent Māori, and at the end of the book proposes a toast to the time when the Māori will be permitted to come back to their own lands and to realize the dream for which they have suffered. Tracy's writing was not predominantly didactic, however. Her interest was mainly in writing readable historical fictions, and until recently she was the only significant children's novelist whose books were all published in New Zealand. Her subsequent novels are set even earlier than *Rifle and Tomahawk* — in Australia, among sealers in Doubtful Sound, and among warring factions in the Waitemata — and their brisk tempo highlights the 'Lawless Days' (as she describes them in one of her titles) of early Australasian exploration.

In *Piriki's Princess* Tracy explored conflicts of personal and cultural identity in Māori-Pākehā relations. In 1934 Theodore A. Harper and Winifred Harper raised a question of identity in more explicitly nationalistic (and more narrowly Pākehā) terms: whether the New Zealand-born European was still 'British', or a new breed — a 'New Zealander'. Most of the Harpers' novels were stirring adventure stories set in America and Siberia, but *Windy Island* (1934) and its sequel, *Seventeen Chimneys* (1938), were set in Canterbury at the end of the century. They concentrate upon a young man, Bob, growing up in a prosperous home modelled on the family mansion ('Bridewell') in Devon. Life in the Canterbury 'Bridewell' exactly matches that of the Devonshire one, and parental expectations are that Bob will go 'home' to Oxford. However Bob resists, explaining to his father, 'Every boy in New Zealand wants to go Home sometime, though it's not like you and Mother think it is — you see we are *Colonials*.' He later amplifies his preference for New Zealand: 'I want to get the hang of the thing, to see where we come in . . . where New Zealand comes in.'[8] However, the resolution is ambivalent. In *Seventeen Chimneys*, Bob's parents return to England after losing all their money and Bob stays behind, training as a mining engineer at the Government School of Mines in Thames, where he works at the Martha mine; but at the end he leaves for the United States. There is a probing of motives and a depth of characterization in these novels, heightened by what may well be an autobiographical emphasis, and their conscious questioning of New Zealand identity parallels the concern of much of the adult literature of the time.

The Emergence of the School Story, 1930-50

In the 1930s, alongside the continuing productivity of Howe, Peacocke and Tracy, a new genre came into prominence: the school story. The influence of Angela Brazil in England cast a wide net, and local examples of the genre, like hers, were often set in boarding schools. However New Zealand's first school story, Phillis Garrard's *Hilda at School: A New Zealand Story* (1929), unlike its English counterparts, is set in a day school in Taihape. In this story and its three sequels Hilda skirmishes her way through the primary and secondary departments with a teacher, Ian Macdonald, who by a convenient quirk of fate is constantly promoted to more senior classes with her. *Hilda at School* is as much about Hilda at home, where she lives with a widowed father and a faithful retainer, the latter the only stereotyped character in the series. Characteristically, books about day schools lack the cloistered atmosphere of those set in boarding schools; out-of-school activities are equally as important as in-school activities. Priscilla, in *The Doings of Hilda* (1932), has lived in a number of countries (like Garrard herself, who had lived in England, Canada and Bermuda before settling in Taihape), and the freshness of vision she brings to the New Zealand school system suggests that her perspective is close to the author's own. She finds the use of the strap, for instance, 'delightfully primitive and old-fashioned, quaint even', and in a preface the author claims consciously to show 'a mixed school with an atmosphere very different from that of an English school, but which aims at making its pupils hardy and self-reliant as well as educated'.[9]

The books are certainly not museum pieces about the education system of the time; they were reissued in an omnibus edition in 1958 and again in the 1980s. They are infused with the vitality of Hilda, a high-spirited, engaging character whose strong will is tempered by disarming honesty. Through her eyes, extremes of landscape and climate are acutely registered: sweltering summer heat, and sharp winter frosts which freeze the ink in the inkwells. Garrard also writes sympathetically about her protagonist's simple (often irksome) everyday routines: her daily pursuit of her horse Roger the Red around the paddock before she can catch him to ride to school, her dislike of the necessity of wearing stockings, her cheerful participation with classmates in banter and pranks which are still instantly familiar to younger readers.

The sturdy self-reliance inculcated at Hilda's country school is very different from the picture of Otago Boys' High School in C.R. Allen's *A Poor Scholar; a Tale of Progress* (1936), a book of sociological rather than literary interest which chronicles the struggle of a poor boy to achieve university education even in egalitarian New Zealand at the beginning of the century. Peacocke's anti-snobbery theme is echoed in Allen's treatment of an encounter between the gauche boys from the High and the fine young gentlemen of Christ's College, Christchurch. There is a recapitulation, too, of the Harpers' exploration of national identity when the 'poor scholar' tells the English girl who later becomes his wife, 'I don't suppose you can understand what it is to have all your thoughts turned to a place [England] you've never seen.'[10]

The last of Garrard's 'Hilda' stories was published in 1944, and three years later the author who became her most widely-read successor in the genre of the school story, Clare Mallory (Winifred McQuilkan), published *Merry Begins*, the first of a number of boarding school stories. McQuilkan, later Hall, lectured until 1979 in the English Department of Victoria University College, but the 'Merry' books were based on her experiences as a teacher and later as headmistress at a private girls' school in the South Island, which must have been very like the fictional Mary Tremayne Ladies' College of Dunedin, the setting for the 'Merry' books. The novels are notable for the quality of their style, at a time when few well-written children's books were appearing, and because they use the conventional school adventure story format to explore the nature of authority and its place in the school system. Several have a central character who questions the discipline imposed by staff and prefects and has to come to terms with the reasons for her rebellion. Mallory take the liberal stance of defending authority and discipline as long as it is self-inculcated rather than imposed by external rules. The underlying theme of the books is summarized by the headmistress when she has cause to reprimand one of the characters in *Merry Again* (1947): 'Rebels sometimes do great good in the world. But people who rebel against the rules for their own selfish ends do good to no one, they are even most unkind to themselves. You are at Tremayne's to learn, not only French and Science. What you need to learn most is how to discipline yourself.'[11] Ultimately the girls at Tremayne have to learn that the authority of prefects and, indeed, of teachers, has been earned through academic or sporting excellence rather than arbitrarily imposed from above. Two Mallory books, published in 1950, are set in day schools: *Leith and Friends* and *The Pen and Pencil Girls*. The first has an unusual heroine who loves Jane Austen's novels, and the second describes the activities of a group of girls in a South Island classroom who form a 'Story Club' and discover that the best writing derives from personal experience rather from imitating literary fashions. Such a message was to be vigorously promoted by educationalists Sylvia Ashton-Warner and Elwyn Richardson some years later.

The school stories of Clare Mallory were undoubtedly the best books to

461

appear in the 1940s and early 1950s, otherwise a period of general dearth in children's literature. The upheavals of the Depression years, followed by the Second World War, tended to isolate New Zealand from overseas publishing, and there were few local editors with experience in children's books. In those that did appear the quality of paper used, because of wartime shortages, was often poor, and the standard of illustrations and production remained very uneven. Although wartime conditions had a similar effect on the quality of book production in England, a long-lasting perception arose among many New Zealand readers at this time that local children's books were necessarily inferior. One effect of this was a vigorous drive in the 1940s, across a range of institutions and organizations, to improve the climate in which children's literature might be written, promoted and read.

In the 1940s the character of the *School Journals* began to change. They had been established in 1907 to meet the urgent need for a reliable supply of books in schools, at a time when text books were not only very expensive to import but a year might elapse between their ordering and delivery. Initially the Department of Education decided to publish its own school texts, and the *Journals* were issued as history and geography readers (in three parts for junior, middle and senior pupils), copies being given to individual children to keep. Gradually they assumed the character of more general readers until in the 1940s the non-fiction subject matter was siphoned off into quarterly *Bulletins*, while the *Journals*, now kept in class sets by schools rather than issued individually, provided the main reading material. With their new emphasis on literary and imaginative quality, and strengthened by the fact that they had no need to conform to the real or imagined demands of the commercial market, they exercized a major influence on subsequent children's literature. Some of the best known names in New Zealand literature, such as Alistair Campbell, James K. Baxter, Maurice Duggan, and Louis Johnson were to work at various times on the editorial committee, and a number of New Zealand's most notable writers, including Margaret Mahy, had their stories first published in the *Journals*.

The 1940s also saw a considerable expansion in library services for children. A Boys' Recreational and Reading Room had been established at the Leys Institute in Auckland as early as 1909, and by 1910 Junior Reading Rooms had been set up in the Newtown branch of the Wellington Public Library as well as in Dunedin. Dunedin also provided the venue for the first library conference in the same year, which advocated the setting up of juvenile libraries and reading rooms in all municipal centres. Despite these initiatives the lack of specialized training for children's librarians, which had been emphasized in the Munn–Barr Report on New Zealand libraries in 1934, remained a major problem. As a result two librarians, Dorothy Neal (later White, then Ballantyne) and Kathleen Harvey, were sent to the Carnegie Library School in Pittsburgh to train as children's librarians, and on their return they exercised a strong influence on the quality and professionalism of library services for children. In 1946 the New Zealand Library School was at last established, and for the first time New Zealand public librarians for children began to be trained in their own country.

The School Library Service began in 1942, and although its precise terms of operation were to change over the years, its purpose of making available the best in fiction and non-fiction to children and teachers remained constant. Despite the vulnerability of such state-funded services to shifting economic and political circumstances, which often meant that library services to children suffered a tortoise-and-hare existence of sudden growth and long retrenchments, libraries were to become increasingly active in promoting indigenous literature. It was at a New Zealand Library Association Conference in 1945 that the Esther Glen Award was instituted. It carried no monetary recompense, and aimed at improving the quality of children's writing and book production by careful discrimination in the awards it made. During its first twenty-five years there were only six.

The first recipient of the Esther Glen Award was Stella Morice's *The Book of Wiremu* (1944). Although its artificial rendering of Wiremu's broken English speech was later to date badly, it was the first book for several decades — apart from Tracy's works — to attempt an inner portrayal of Māori characters. The theme of Morice's brief narrative is self-respect, the restoration of mana, within the extended family of the whānau. Living a simple life with his uncle and grandmother, Wiremu is able to demonstrate pig-hunting and eeling to a visiting Pākehā boy, and consequently gain in self-worth. Reprinted in 1958, and again in 1966, the story was an early example of what was to become a renaissance of interest in Māori culture, especially from the 1960s onwards.

Two other books from the later 1940s also reflected this quickening of interest. The second recipient of the Esther Glen Award was A.W. Reed for his *Myths and Legends of Maoriland* (1946). A.W. Reed, whose firm became increasingly active in the field of children's publishing in the 1940s, had previously written some amusing (if lightweight) fantasies, but his interest in the folklore and myths of the Māori was to result in eight books over the next twenty-eight years. James Rich in *Teko-Teko in Waitomo* (1949) introduced another perspective which was a development of Morice's in *The Book of Wiremu*: the search for a Māori identity independent of European culture. Kaira, a young Māori girl, had broken away from the traditions of her elders, and 'knew hardly anything about Maoriland or Maoris or colonial history'. Instead, 'she went to school and to the movies . . . so she knew a lot more than old Maoris who had never been brought up properly and believed in tabu [*sic*] and what they should and shouldn't do'.[12] The story takes Kaira to the Waitomo Caves, where three teko-teko (carved figures at the gateway to a pā) assist her to regain the heritage she had lost. Rich's short novel is poorly written, but like Morice's it heralded a change in the fictional portrayal of Māori children in later books.

New Impulses, 1950–70

In the two decades of the 1950s and 1960s almost as many children's books were published as in the previous half century, and there was an increasing diversity of subject matter and approach. However, the pattern of growth was uneven, particularly in the 1950s. Some of the most popular books of that decade, like Avis Acres's illustrated *Hutu and Kawa* series for younger readers, were sentimental throwbacks to the 'flower fairy' era. Other books, by a new generation of authors, focused on controversial contemporary social issues. Fantasy writing, with a very small number of notable exceptions, remained weak, but from the later 1950s there was a revival of the adventure story genre, and especially, a new interest in revisiting New Zealand history (the settler period and the Land Wars) as part of a more general impulse to explore issues of New Zealand's social, cultural and national identity. In the 1960s, also, new Māori themes emerged strongly in individual books and authors.

In a great deal of the fiction for older readers a new seriousness of purpose was apparent. This was partly a reflection, perhaps, of the high-minded aims behind the educational and other government-sponsored initiatives that had begun in the 1940s, and partly a response to a new concern about New Zealand children and the need for local literature to engage relevantly with their 'real' experience of life in New Zealand in the 1950s and 1960s. However, such high seriousness often had its own drawbacks. If, by comparison, much of the earlier children's literature now seemed sentimental and escapist, the tendency in some of the new writing to project adult preoccupations and anxieties into the fictional world of the book, and the wish to use literature to mould children in socially acceptable ways, could often result in a new kind of didacticism. The continuing weakness of fantasy as a genre, which at its best connects deeply *at the child's level* with often unarticulated wishes, hopes, fears and needs, was perhaps symptomatic.

There were fitful signs of improvement in the quality of picture books for younger readers, and in the 1960s photographic books began to appear in some quantity as well, made possible by improvements in the technology of local book production. By the early 1960s, also, the influence of the School Publications branch of the Department of Education was beginning to be felt. However, a feature of the period as a whole was the number of authors who produced only one or two books: a clear indication that a stable professional base for New Zealand children's authors had yet to be established. Although there was considerable expansion in the local publication of children's books, with new firms like Blackwood and Janet Paul competing with the two established publishers in the field (Reeds and Whitcombes), the vast majority of full-length books were still published overseas, primarily in England, though occasionally in joint publication arrangements with local firms.

In 1950 New Zealand's first picture book of high quality appeared: Joan Smith's *The Adventures of Nimble, Rumble and Tumble*. There had been no New Zealand picture books for children before the 1940s (and only five published in that decade), although there were many illustrated books in which the function of the pictures was mainly to lighten the text. In Smith's book, story and pictures were genuinely integrated, interacting with each other. The pleasing lithographs made restrained use of colour, yet despite the fact that the book's achievement was promoted by the prize of the Esther Glen Award, there were few successors in the 1950s. The immensely popular *Hutu and Kawa* series by Avis Acres, in which two pohutukawa fairies engage in mischievous pranks in the bush or on the beach, used a picture book format with illustrations by the author, but the sentimental 'flower fairy' format harked back to fantasy stories at the beginning of the century. It was not until the 1960s that technical advances in printing could achieve the lavishly coloured productions which eventually turned the picture book into a New Zealand growth industry.

Improved technology also resulted in a number of photographic books in the 1960s intended for a wider age range, mostly prompted by an earnest and urgent desire to teach children about New Zealand. Their aim was not only to show 'life in New Zealand' on farm, on sea shore, and in the high country, but also to offer positive images of the Māori. Titles provide a good indication of their contents: Jane Hill's *Hey Boy!* (1961), Gay Kohlap's *David, Boy of the High Country* (1964), Pat Lawson's *Kuma is a Maori Girl* (1961), Valerie and Colin Salt's *My Cobber* (1967, the 'cobbers' being a Māori and a Pākehā boy), and Ans Westra's controversial *Washday at the Pa* (1964), which was first published as a School Bulletin. Based on a two-day stay on the East Coast of the North Island, the fine photographs show the rather squalid living conditions of a Māori family who were shortly to move into a State house. The Bulletin, however, aroused considerable public controversy and it was withdrawn on the grounds that it would give a wrong impression of the Māori people, although the author insisted that her aim was to show 'what an intelligent coloured race can do with civilization when they are given a chance by being treated as human beings'.[13]

Only two fantasy stories in the period are worthy of mention. In 1950 Daphne Goomes's *The Laughing Hours* appeared, the first New Zealand fantasy story to use a 'time-slip', a valuable device enabling children who quickly identify with present-day events and settings to realize that the past is also an inescapable fact. In *The Laughing Hours* the location of a family holiday on a familiar beach plausibly slips back to a time when the children's grandmother received the gift of a pearl from a Māori girl. It is an evocative story, with a well-realized landscape, and because the footing in a particular time and place is firm the time-slip is credible. The book is a landmark in New Zealand fantasy writing, although its author wrote no others.

Apart from Goomes's novel, nothing in the fantasy stories of the period anticipated Maurice Duggan's *Falter Tom and the Water Boy* (1958), a classic fantasy tale without a trace of moralism or self-conscious nationalism. Although the novel can be visualized in New Zealand terms, its setting in time and place is unspecific, as the tale unfolds of Old Falter Tom who accepts the Water Boy's invitation to explore under the sea and finally decides to stay there. The story is told with the relaxed ease of an accomplished storyteller.

Within the framework of fantasy, characters and dialogue are totally plausible, and many of the universal ingredients of fairy tales are present: the adult hero, the magic talisman, the need to choose which is offset by the fatefulness of commands which may not be gainsaid. Cause and effect create their own internal logic and give firm shape to the narrative. *Falter Tom and the Water Boy* also won the Esther Glen Award and has remained a New Zealand classic, enjoying considerable success overseas after its re-publication in the 1970s and 1980s.

A greater contrast could hardly be imagined than between Duggan's mythic resonances and the deliberate social realism of Brian Sutton-Smith's *Our Street*, a controversial book which appeared in 1950, drawing attention to the social alienation of a younger generation of boys in working-class urban environments. Sutton-Smith was an educationalist who subsequently moved to the United States, where he developed a special expertise in children's play, and *Our Street* — together with its sequels (*Smitty Does a Bunk*, 1961, and *The Cobbers*, 1976) — were intended to highlight the lack of good recreational facilities for working-class boys in cities. The noveis' social realism (initially influenced, the author has said, by his experience of reading Morice's *The Book of Wiremu* to children at Brooklyn School in Wellington) came as a shock to the reading public, accustomed as it was to a tradition of family stories, like Peacocke's and Glen's, which were basically conceived as entertainment. Hero Smitty and his friends in *Our Street* seem to have little love or respect for parents or teachers, and there is almost no communication between adult and child. The boys are dishonest and deceitful, and Sutton-Smith's style is uneven, although it is presumably an attempt to stay within the language of the milieu he describes. A plethora of prefaces by a school principal, by Dorothy White, and by the author himself all suggested that because such behaviour does occur the book should be used by teachers for discussion with their classes. It was the first time that a book had been so openly promoted for the value of its social objectives, independently of questions about its literary merit.

Sutton-Smith's book was in fact a lone foray into urban realism in the 1950s. A much cosier view of life in New Zealand, especially of country life, informed children's literature during that decade of increasingly comfortable affluence for most New Zealanders. Because it was increasingly felt that children should become familiar with their own country there was a rash of books — mostly undistinguished — whose 'New Zealand' titles clearly indicated their purpose: *George and Albert Snowywhiskers Visit New Zealand, On a Farm in New Zealand, A New Zealand Alphabet, New Zealand Birthday, Verena Visits New Zealand, The New Zealand Twins, New Zealand Nature Books*, and so on. Joyce West was the most distinguished of the authors of rural fiction at this time. Her idyllic picture of the country first appeared in *Drover's Road* (1953), part of a trilogy set in sheep-farming country on the East Coast of the North Island. But whether there, or in the dairy-farming country further north in books such as *The Year of the Shining Cuckoo* (1961), West was a shrewd observer of rural life, and achieved the same slightly nostalgic purpose for predominantly urban and suburban children as her friend Mary Scott achieved in her light rural romances for adult readers. West's is a world of freshly-baked scones, of shelves groaning beneath home-made jams and bottled fruit, and of rivalries at agricultural shows. The seasonal country calendar is punctuated by lambing and shearing, its daily rhythms by milking or the ebb and flow of tides on causeways. Excitement is provided by equestrian events, or by storms, floods, or landslips. This settled way of life is reflected in the largely tranquil human relationships and a humorous acceptance of idiosyncrasies. West was a natural successor to Glen in delineating children growing to maturity with the warm acceptance of their families and communities.

The growing national awareness of New Zealand writers in the 1950s led, towards the end of the decade and in the 1960s, to a revival of the adventure story genre, with what seems a remorseless insistence on the inaccessibility of the country's terrain, the vagaries of its climate, and the ever-present risk of earthquakes. The novels describe a land abounding in mountains, forests and rushing rivers, in which rainfall is heavy, and sudden and devastating downpours result in slips, floods, and drownings. In short, the New Zealand adventure story has a love affair with a land that is both beautiful and cruel, and with a climate that can never be trusted. The same ambivalence haunted books written by the early settlers, and it is perhaps no coincidence that where the one genre ends the other begins. The first adventure story of this type had been Howes's *Silver Island* (1928), published just twelve years after the last of the settler books, Bedford's *Under One Standard.* If the new adventure stories had historical antecedents in the settler genre, they owed nothing to the 'blood and thunder' tradition of nineteenth century authors like Henty. Their overseas models were Defoe's story of survival, *Robinson Crusoe*, the detective yarns of Arthur Conan Doyle, and Robert Louis Stevenson's *Treasure Island.*

The simple formula that resulted, requiring only that the story be moved briskly along, and relying heavily upon stereotyped two-dimensional characterization as well as on the coincidence of exciting events, admirably suited cadet writers, many of whom wrote only one adventure story before moving in more challenging directions. A model plot for the new genre of New Zealand adventure stories might be constructed as follows: 'Twins on a New Zealand sheep station learn that their aunt in England has been killed in a car crash and that their orphaned cousin is to come to live with them. After his arrival they decide to introduce him to the bush and they embark, suitably equipped, on a tramping holiday. Unfortunately they lose their way and narrowly escape drowning when they unwisely camp by a river and are trapped during a sudden flood after heavy rain in the mountains. They finally find shelter in a cave, where they discover Māori artefacts, but they become aware that other people are also searching for the artefacts to smuggle them abroad. The sinister intruders are South Americans. The children escape and manage to attract the attention of a helicopter which has been sent to search for them. Once restored to their family they set out to track down the smugglers, helped by an old hermit who lives in a rabbiter's whare. The smugglers are brought to justice and the children are guests of honour when the artefacts are presented to the local museum.'

Such stories abound, and fit admirably with the overwhelming didacticism of telling a new generation of city and suburban-born children about the bush and how to survive in it, as well as inculcating respect for Māori culture. They also frequently include a New Zealand stereotype common in adult writing — the hermit. He appears in earlier books as a 'sundowner', in later ones as a miner who has stayed on (like Glover's Arawata Bill) in deserted goldfields, or as an old rabbiter living in a tumbledown whare. Significantly it is an old man, rather than a young one, who is unconventional in his thinking and lifestyle, demonstrating a freedom from the constraints imposed by city and suburban living.

The most accomplished of the adventure story writers was the Christchurch author Phyl Wardell, whose first book, *Gold at Kapai*, was published in 1960. Subsequently, over three decades, her lucid, unpretentious writing not only celebrated the New Zealand landscape but effectively appealed for its preservation. Most of her stories are set in remote areas of the South Island where a forgotten Māori tribe, a surviving moa, or greenstone artefacts might be concealed, and where paua shell smugglers are foiled in *Hazard Island* (1976). In *The Nelson Treasure* (1983), Wardell moves the setting to the North Island, where property developers are prevented from encroaching upon dense bush. The author's young protagonists are bright and alert, trained in bushcraft and quick to detect any threat to their native environment. The covert message of these well-managed stories is that young people who respond to the quiet mystery of remote places are better equipped to face the vicissitudes of daily living.

School Publications also began to have a marked effect upon children's literature (including the adventure genre) in the early 1960s. Stories which first appeared in the *Journals* or *Bulletins* were now occasionally published, although not always with great success, since what made interesting episodic reading did not necessarily transmute itself into a satisfactory novel. Nevertheless books such as Ruth France's *The Shining Year*, O.E. Middleton's *From the River to the Tide*, and Barry Mitcalfe's *The Long Holiday* (all published in 1964) indicated an increasing sophistication in the fictional treatment of the local scene and of the theme of New Zealand identity. In 1965 and 1966 School Publications also issued for the first time a number of stories with a historical focus, a genre which (with two exceptions in the 1950s) had been in abeyance for many decades.

The exceptions were Ronald Syme and Eileen L. Soper. Syme, English-born but educated at Wanganui Collegiate School, spent a large part of his working life in the Pacific Islands, and became well known for stirring adventure stories set in the Pacific. In *Gipsy Michael* (1954) and *The Spaniards Came at Dawn* (1959), however, he turned to New Zealand for his settings and themes. *Gipsy Michael* is a highly readable and well-researched yarn which takes its hero Michael Benson at breathless pace from England in 1862 to every trouble spot in both the North and South Islands during the Land Wars and the gold rushes.

The Spaniards Came at Dawn is based on two known facts (the puzzling find in Queen Charlotte Sound of a large European cross, possibly belonging to the seventeenth century, and the discovery of a Spanish morion in Wellington Harbour), out of which Syme constructs a plausible children's adventure fiction: Spanish pirates are blown off course to New Zealand and become involved in various conflicts with local tribes. Syme was a most accomplished teller of tales, with a skill in arousing children's interest in the past. Eileen Soper achieved the same interest in history in *Young Jane: A Tale of New Zealand in the Sixties* (1955), although the pace of her novel is very different from those of Syme. It is the first book to portray a child's-eye view of early-settler life in the 1860s, rendering sensitively the period atmosphere and day-to-day life of a South Island sheep station, where Jane is brought up after the death (by drowning) of her parents.

The historical fictions sponsored in the next decade by School Publications were also set in the 1860s, but focused primarily on the Land Wars in the north. Roderick Finlayson's *The Springing Fern* (1965) began life as a series in the Primary School *Bulletins*, and tells the story of a Māori family living on the Manukau Harbour from the 1830s to the 1920s. It traces the disillusionments endured by successive generations, but also shows the gradual recovery of self-respect in later decades through the revival of a sense of Māoritanga. Other stories which contributed to this revisionist account of the past and which initially appeared episodically in the *School Journals* were F.L. Comb's *Ben* (1966), which included an unusually amusing account of the outwitting of a novice British officer by the Hauhau as they escape from a surrounded pā; David Jensen's *They Came to Cook Strait* (1966), telling of skirmishes with Te Rauparaha; and A.H. Messenger's *Children of the Forest* (also 1966), an autobiographical account of a Taranaki childhood during which Messenger's father had been captain in charge of a redoubt.

The main thrust of historical fiction, however, was a revival of interest in the early settlers. Helen Sandall and Elizabeth Henniker Heaton's *The Emigrants* (1963) is reminiscent of Forde's *Across Two Seas* as an account of a professional family arriving in a new land. It also includes an acerbic study of a dominating father, who as a doctor provides the authors with a convenient opportunity to describe in detail the hazards and miseries of the outward voyage. Cecil and Cecilia Manson's *The Lonely One* (also 1963) depicted a settler family of which the eldest son is prematurely driven out to work, and through his friendship with Ranginui (a Māori who is likewise living alone) comes to find meaning in life by working with horses. The Mansons' *The Adventures of Johnny van Bart* (1965) depicted a colourful Hungarian character, and this introduction of settlers other than British occurred in a number of books of the time. In Margery Godfrey's *South for Gold* (1964) the two main protagonists are Slav and German. In Doris White's *The Family that Came Back* (1965) the device of a time-slip enables the heroine to meet the ghosts of her great-grandparents and discover that her ancestors were variously Welsh, Scots, Irish, French, and

Dalmatian. Colin Bell's *Po-Ling, the Cook from Ti-Tree Point* (1965), a picture book, was the first to portray a Chinese settler.

An author who began writing for children in the 1960s was Elsie Locke, whose novel *The Runaway Settlers* (1965) revealed the scrupulousness of her research as well as her strong sympathy for the underdog, and became one of the most widely read of all the settler stories. Like the widow Mrs Vaughan in *Across Two Seas*, the central character in *The Runaway Settlers*, Mrs Small, is a single parent, but in her case independence is an act of will: she has left a drunken husband in Australia, changing her name to Phipps in order to make a new start. The book gives an unusually authentic picture of poorer European settlers and of life on the Banks Peninsula and on the goldfields. Mrs Phipps herself is indomitable, obviously cast in the mould of those settler women who cause their weaker sisters to pale: able to walk vast distances, cultivate large gardens, and build or renovate houses, they at the same time manage to keep their large families firmly in order. Furthermore, Mrs Phipps suffers no nonsense from men in authority: when she finds that the employer of her two older sons has failed to honour his contract she speaks to him very plainly indeed, as few women of the period would have dared.

In two later books, *The End of the Harbour* (1968) and *Journey Under Warning* (1983), Locke casts new light on old disputes, again through the originality of her research. In the first a family strategically placed on the Manukau Harbour witnesses the beginnings of the Land Wars, and in the second a young man is unwittingly caught up in the Wairau Affray, a dispute between Nelson settlers and Te Rauparaha over the prospecting of the Wairau Plain. Her most recent book, *A Canoe in the Mist* (1984), is an absorbing account of the eruption of Mount Tarawera seen through the eyes of two eleven-year-old girls. Locke's books are closer, perhaps, to historical documentary than to fiction. They present Māori perspectives and are based on careful reconstructions of actual events, angled from the viewpoint of a young protagonist.

Attempts by Pākehā writers to offer a more truthful perspective on the Māori experience of colonization, and to avoid the sentimental or disparaging stereotypes which had occurred in so much earlier writing, were not confined simply to historical fictions set in the distant past. In 1963 a novel was published which sensitively portrayed a twentieth century crisis in Māori identity. *The Parting of the Mist* by Lyndon Rose is set in the 1930s. The young hero's paternal grandfather is chief of a central North Island tribe, but his maternal grandfather, with whom he lives, is an Anglican parish priest. He feels torn between the values of traditional Māori culture and Anglicized Maoridom. This conflict initially lands him in Borstal; and it is not until after his overseas army service during the Second World War that he begins to resolve the problem. No children's novel up to that time had so acutely portrayed the perplexity of a people at the crossroads of their culture. The novel also conveys a powerful contemporary sense of the crisis resulting from the drift of young Māori from the country to the cities after the war. Had it been published in New Zealand instead of Australia, and reached a wider local readership, its challenging perspective on New Zealand race relations might have received much more notice than it did.

Lesley Cameron Powell's dignified story for younger children, *Turi, the Story of a Little Boy* appeared that same year and was complemented by the moving photographs of Pius Blank. It was the first of a number of books to feature the Māori extended family, conveying poignantly yet without sentimentality the warmth of Turi's relationship with his grandmother and his sadness at her death. This honest yet compassionate treatment of old age and death set a pattern for what was to become an unusual and distinguishing feature of New Zealand children's literature in the English-speaking world.

Boys and their grandmothers also occur in two books by R.L. Bacon, *The Boy and the Taniwha* (1966) and *Rua and the Sea People* (1968). In both, grandmothers initiate their grandsons into the legends and customs of the Māori people. Not only are these books well written; they are beautifully illustrated by Para Matchitt, who uses traditional Māori patterns to reinforce the feeling of the text rather than simply to represent events. A headmaster in South Auckland, Bacon was in the forefront of the revival of māoritanga, insisting that New Zealand children be made aware of Māori legends, in books whose production and illustrations were of the highest quality. Three of his later books, *The House of the People* (1977), *The Fish of Our Fathers* (1984) and *The Home of the Winds* (1986) described the building of the first meeting house, the construction of a war canoe, and the erection of the first fortified pa. All three books were illustrated by the artist R.G.H. Jahnke, and *The House of the People* was the first recipient of a newly instituted award for illustration, the Russell Clark Award. Their stylization in typically Māori colours of brown, ochre and black richly complemented the poetic style of the narration. Amongst his many books for children Bacon's only novel to date is *Again the Bugles Blow* (1973), in which by means of a time-slip a Māori boy sees his ancestors at the Battle of Orakau. It bears the hallmark of all of Bacon's writing, the ability to construct a good story in language that demonstrates a thorough grasp of natural speech rhythms.

Growth and Diversity, after 1970

If the 1950s and 1960s were decades of uneven but steady growth, the years after 1970 saw a spectacular transformation in both the quantity and quality of New Zealand children's literature. A small number of writers from the previous decade — Wardell, Locke and Bacon — continued to develop their careers as children's authors, but the 1970s and 1980s were largely marked by an upsurge of new writers across the whole spectrum of genres in children's literature. In 1969 alone four significant authors published their first books: Ruth Dallas, Anne de Roo, Joy Cowley, and Margaret Mahy, who was subsequently to achieve international acclaim. In the 1970s these were joined by a steady stream of new authors — among them Joan de Hamel, Margaret Beames, Eve Sutton and Philip Holden — and in the 1980s by a host of writers, amongst whom those who quickly established substantial reputations were Lynley Dodd (in the genre of picture books), Joanna Orwin, Caroline Macdonald, William Taylor, Maurice Gee, Barry Faville, and Tessa Duder.

This renaissance reflected an acceptance by New Zealand readers of the value of locally-written children's literature. It was reinforced by an increasing emphasis on creative New Zealand content in the school curriculum and in training colleges. Several of the new authors were themselves teachers, or closely connected with the education system. There were also changes in the publishing industry, with new promotional and professional initiatives for children's books. For the first time — especially in the 1980s — a majority of children's books were published in New Zealand (mirroring developments in the field of adult fiction), as the main commercial firms developed children's lists alongside new, purely local publishers like Mallinson Rendel. In 1969, under the initiative of Tom Fitzgibbon at Auckland's North Shore Teachers' College, the Children's Literature Association of New Zealand was established, and its many promotional activities strongly influenced the climate in which local children's books were read and discussed. In the 1970s the larger metropolitan newspapers (and the *New Zealand Listener*) began reviewing children's books on a reasonably regular basis, occasionally with special columns. Between 1979 and 1985 a children's literary magazine, *Jabberwocky*, edited by Jo Noble, an Auckland bookseller, provided a lively forum for creative writing by children. In the late 1970s, and especially in the 1980s, the New Zealand Literary Fund began to develop specific policies designed to promote the growth of children's literature: an author-support programme of annual grants (the Choysa Bursaries), a publication subsidy scheme, and promotional activities pursued through a Writers-in-Schools programme and through the establishment (in 1982) of annual national awards for the Children's Book of the Year and the best picture book, sponsored by the Government Printing Office.

Such developments made possible at least the beginnings of a stable professional base for children's authors, and they were accompanied by a growing interest in writing *about* children's literature. Before the 1970s, with the exception of the work of the librarian Dorothy Neal White, almost nothing had appeared. White's *About Books for Children* (1949) had introduced the most appropriate literature available for children at the time, and it was followed in 1954 by *Books Before Five*, a highly influential book in educational circles which combined her library expertise with observations of the reading tastes and habits of her daughter from the age of two to five. From 1972 the Children's Literature Association Yearbook, produced annually, provided a regular forum for critical commentary on overseas and indigenous children's literature, as well as for annotated bibliographies. In the 1970s Dorothy Butler, who ran a specialist children's bookshop on Auckland's North Shore, published the first of several books that revealed her passionate commitment to the value of books in children's personal development. *Cushla and her Books* (1979), based on research she had done at the University of Auckland, chronicled the stories enjoyed by her handicapped granddaughter during her first five years, and the remarkable impact they had had on her personal development and her acquisition of literacy. It was followed by two equally dynamic books in the 1980s: *Babies Need Books* (1980), covering the ages one to five, and *Five to Eight* (1986).

The 1980s saw the first scholarly and critical books to appear on New Zealand children's literature. J.B. Ringer's *Young Emigrants* (1980) included an essay alongside its chronicle of books and short stories with a New Zealand background between 1813 and 1919. Diane Hebley's *Off the Shelf* (1980) provided an annotated listing of selected titles published after 1958. The first complete history, of more than eight hundred titles, appeared in 1982: Betty Gilderdale's *A Sea Change, 145 Years of New Zealand Junior Fiction*. One result of this was the inception of a reprint programme (the Kotare Series of Hodder and Stoughton) aimed at making early New Zealand children's classics available: nine titles were reissued during the 1980s. In 1984 Ian F. McLaren's *Whitcombe's Story Books, A Transtasman Survey* discussed this well-known series in addition to providing a bibliography, and in 1985 Hugh Price published a bibliography of *School Books Published in New Zealand up to 1960*, a listing of special value since such books were omitted from the five-volume *New Zealand National Bibliography*. In 1986 the Auckland College of Education published the first edition of *Tea-tree and Iron Sands*, a guide to current New Zealand children's writers, edited by Tom Fitzgibbon and Margaret Spiers; the guide contained annotated listings, biographical notes, and informative comments by authors. A second edition appeared in 1989, and in 1988 the first edition of *Matapihi* appeared (a pioneering companion volume on current New Zealand children's book illustrators, compiled by the same editors on the same principles as *Tea tree and Iron Sands*). In 1987 the first biography of a children's author written for children, *Introducing Margaret Mahy*, was written by Betty Gilderdale.

A considerable amount of the new fiction of the 1970s and 1980s represented a continuation of the themes and genres introduced in the previous decade. The realistic impulse to 'tell children about New Zealand' remained strong, and was one of Ruth Dallas's motivations in her sequence of four books — *The Children in the Bush* (1969), *The Wild Boy in the Bush* (1971), *The Big Flood in the Bush* (1972), and *Holiday Time in the Bush* (1983) — set in the 1890s and sparked off (like much of her poetry) by her familiarity with the southern region of the South Island. Dallas had grown up, she said, in 'an English storybook world unrelated to life as I knew it'.[14] Building on the re-awakened interest in early-settler stories, she chose for her key character (as Locke did) a mother bringing up her children on her own, a widow who works as a district nurse in order to support her family. The children profit from their mother's frequent absences to get into various very credible scrapes whose pace and scope are exactly right for young readers.

Dallas's fiction signalled a move away from conventional nuclear family settings to a more intense personal focus on individual children or on unusual relationships. Unconventional older people feature in two later books, *The House on the Cliffs* (1975) and *Shining Rivers* (1979). In the latter, set in the early-settler period, the guidance and generosity of an old goldminer tempers the disenchantment felt by a young immigrant boy at the diggings. The contemporary setting of *The House on the Cliffs*, from which a solitary old lady is threatened with removal to an old people's home, is reminiscent of Dallas's poetry, and images of sea and coast provide insight into the delicate balance between loneliness and independence. The many stories and poems contributed by Dallas to the *School Journals* on animal themes also came to fruition in *A Dog Called Wig* (1970), an unusual animal story in which a boy grows in self-knowledge when he discovers that his dog prefers the boy's father. Dallas's novels were published in Methuen's 'Easy to Read' format, but vocabulary restrictions are seldom evident: her economical style and evocative poet's eye ensure a rapport with her young readers.

The same interest in individual (often isolated and confused) characters in authentic New Zealand settings, who are engaged in the exploratory process of 'learning about themselves and their relationships with other people', informs the fiction of Anne de Roo, who describes her aim as:

Exploring New Zealand, its people and scenery and history and what it means to be a New Zealander, Maori or Pakeha, with the hope that the reader will find something of herself or himself, that the real world and the book world will not be as completely divorced as they were when I was a child, when books were all set in Europe or America and life had to be lived in a country that had no words to describe it.[15]

Few New Zealand authors of children's fiction have explored as many genres or developed such a range of themes as Anne de Roo has. *The Gold Dog* (1969), *Moa Valley* (1969) and *Scrub Fire* (1977) are adventure stories; *Boy and the Sea Beast* (1971), *Cinnamon and Nutmeg* (1972), and *Mick's Country Cousins* (1974) all show how responsibility for an animal can act as a catalyst in human relationships; *Traveller* (1979) and *Because of Rosie* (1980) are early-settler stories; *Jacky Nobody* (1983) and its sequel *The Bat's Nest* (1986) are historical novels about Hone Heke; and *Friend Troll, Friend Taniwha* (1986) is a fantasy story for younger children.

Amid such a diverse output there are, nevertheless, certain constants. Animals — a dolphin, a calf, a goat and numerous dogs — play important roles in many books, and often provide the only consolation in the frustrated life of a lonely or unusual individual. Indeed, de Roo's main characters frequently perceive themselves to be outsiders: the academic non-sporting boy, the independent elderly man, the only boy in a family of girls, a young and homesick immigrant. In several books the feeling of isolation and confusion is heightened by being torn between two cultures. In *Mick's Country Cousins* Mick resents the fact that he looks Māori yet feels himself to be European. Jacky Nobody, reared in a mission school after his Pākehā father deserts him, is shocked to discover that he is related to Hone Heke. Even in the amusing fantasy *Friend Troll, Friend Taniwha* the Norwegian Troll, accidentally imported to New Zealand, feels alienated until befriended by a Taniwha. The underlying seriousness of de Roo's books is often lightened by humour, however, and by the warmth of her sympathetic projection into the thoughts and feelings of her troubled characters.

Three other authors emerged during the 1970s whose work extended the scope of the adventure genre, and often combined it with an interest in New Zealand's past alongside the more typical registering of New Zealand's physical environment and landscape. These were Margaret Beames, Eve Sutton, and Joan de Hamel. Beames's contemporary adventure story *Greenstone Summer* (1977) established her as a skilful teller of colourful, event-laden tales, but she turned to historical fiction in the 1980s with *Hidden Valley* (1983), in which a Taranaki settler family import a valuable bull which escapes. A later novel, *The Parkhurst Boys* (1986), draws on a factual event of 1842: the transportation to New Zealand of some English boys from the Parkhurst Prison. The narrative traces the many experiences of two of these boys during the journey out, and after their arrival in early colonial Auckland. In these well-researched and lively books enjoyment of the story is paramount, although the reader unconsciously absorbs knowledge of the period.

Eve Sutton's first book was the text of an outstanding picture book (*My Cat Likes to Hide in Boxes*, 1973) which won the Esther Glen Award in 1975. The book was illustrated by Lynley Dodd, who subsequently became one of New Zealand's most successful picture-book artists. The text ingeniously exploited a lively contrast between exotic foreign cats and the humble indigenous one. Sutton later turned to New Zealand's history and pre-history, beginning with three specialized historical adventure stories for either beginner readers or older children who required a simple text. *Green Gold* (1976), *Tuppenny Brown* (1977) and *Johnny Sweep* (1977) all focused shrewdly and credibly on immigrant teenage boy heroes who for one reason or another find themselves alone in Auckland with only their wits to survive on. Such is Sutton's narrative strength that neither the restricted vocabulary required by these books, nor their author's meticulous research, is ever obtrusive. The books are set in gum fields and kauri forests, on a whaling ship and among criminals, and trace the character development of boys who arrive in raw new environments and grow through hardship to purposeful self-acceptance.

After these shorter stories Sutton moved on to longer books, which enabled her to develop her interest in historical research, and provided more scope for her skills of plotting and characterization. The search for a sense of purpose is also the major theme of *Moa Hunter* (1978), in which the young hero, a chief's son, is permanently maimed in a rash attempt to catch a moa, and has to adjust to a future in which his disability will prevent him from ever succeeding to his father's position. He eventually finds self-fulfilment as a tohunga who carves greenstone and introduces kūmara to his tribe. *Surgeon's Boy* (1983) is narrated by a young man accompanying his doctor-father on convict ships and whaling stations, and *Kidnapped by Blackbirders* (1984) has as its background the repugnant practice of taking Pacific Islanders as slave labour on Australian sugarcane plantations. Sutton's most recent novel, *Valley of Heavenly Gold* (1987), turns to the South Island goldfields for its setting, and builds into the excitement of its events the theme of racial prejudice against Chinese immigrants.

Joan de Hamel's first book, *X Marks the Spot* (1973), combined the conventional 'survival' and 'detection' themes of adventure stories, as three children are forced to survive in the Westland bush and inadvertently uncover a plot to smuggle the rare kākāpō parrot out of the country. Whether portraying the exhilaration of the high peaks or the coastal strip of Otago, de Hamel has a keen eye for landscape, and she acutely explores contemporary New Zealand issues such as the problems of a multi-racial society, and the conservation of the environment and of animals and birds — the latter a preoccupation, if not obsession, in an increasing number of adventure stories in the 1980s, such as Wardell's *The Nelson Treasure* (1983) and Beverley Dunlop's *The Dolphin Boy* (1982). De Hamel's *Take the Long Path* (1978) is a complex, haunting book in which the protagonist's difficult relationship with his father is resolved partly through recognition of his family problems mirrored in a penguin family, and partly through his imaginative identification with the spirituality of an old Māori man who urges him to rediscover a lost whalebone club. The old man had 'taken the long path' from the dead in order to pass on a family anxiety, and by the novel's end the protagonist has also taken the long path towards an understanding of himself and of the complexities of human behaviour. De Hamel also draws on local Māori legend in *The Third Eye* (1987), set in Tasman Bay, a novel which broaches questions of Māori land rights and the destructive inroads of tourism, as well as containing the same vividly realized sense of place and landscape as her other novels.

The novels of de Roo, Sutton and de Hamel all contributed to a revitalization of the genre of adventure fiction, making it the vehicle of much richer studies of character and introducing contemporary social themes. Animals, and relationships with animals, are often important in such studies, as catalysts for character development or as part of the theme of respect for the natural environment, but Philip Holden is one of the very few New Zealand authors to produce books in which the animal itself functions as the hero. Human responsibility for animals had been stressed in earlier books such as Peacocke's *Tatters* (1928) and Neil McNaughton's *Tat, the Story of a New Zealand Sheep Dog* (1970), while numerous 'true' stories devoted themselves to famous animals such as the dolphins Opo and Pelorus Jack. Holden was a seasoned hunter whose love of the chase was finally overcome by his admiration of the prey. His books stand alone in featuring an animal in its natural setting with no hint of sentimentality or of anthropomorphism. *Fawn* (1976), *Stag* (1980), *White Patch* (1981) — all on the subject of the red deer — and *Razorback* (1984) all create an evocative picture of the silences of the bush and of the poignant battle for survival waged by its animal inhabitants.

However, the genre whose emergence in the 1970s signalled the biggest shift in New Zealand children's literature, notwithstanding Howes's early efforts at the beginning of the century, was fantasy. In 1969 two writers who excelled at this genre published their first books: Joy Cowley and Margaret Mahy. It should perhaps be pointed out that while bad fantasy (of which there have been many examples in New Zealand) is disastrously easy to write, good fantasy is a most exacting medium. Credulity is quickly strained unless the initial flight of fancy is most firmly disciplined into a satisfactory shape, the characterization believable, and the language stimulating. It is the genre which sees the best and worst writing for children.

Not since Duggan's *Falter Tom and the Water Boy* in 1958 had a New Zealand fantasy story reached the international standard of Joy Cowley's *The Duck in the Gun* (1969), first published in the United States. Cowley initially wrote for adults, and this new departure was a picture book suitable for six- to eight-year-olds, an age group to which most of her subsequent work has been directed. Written with sparkling humour, her stories always have a contemporary moral purpose, seriously exploring alternatives to conflict, and challenging gender and racial stereotypes. By laying her eggs in a gun the duck averts a war. A pirate is subdued by a strong woman because he fears the dark (in *The Fierce Little Woman and the Wicked Pirate*, 1984); another pirate is persuaded by his wife to write down swear words rather than say them (*Captain Felonius*, 1986); and a giant is prevailed upon to stop bullying a city when butterflies tickle him (*Brith the Terrible*, 1986). Only *Salmagundi* (1985) presents a less than optimistic picture: just as an arms race appears to have been halted, two armament manufacturers resume their plotting, since 'True wickedness does not lie quiet for long'. Cowley has written only one novel for older children, *The Silent One* (1981), which won the newly-established Children's Book of the Year Award in 1982. This is a moving modern reconstruction of a myth: that a sea creature like the kelpie sometimes comes to live among human beings, bringing confusion and catastrophe. The Silent One is a mysterious deaf mute who befriends a white turtle. Increasingly he becomes the scapegoat for every natural disaster which occurs on his Pacific Island, until he finally withdraws into the sea and changes into a great white turtle himself. The emotional depth and mythic resonances of the story, and the stylistic elegance of its telling, ensure that it will remain a children's classic.

Margaret Mahy, New Zealand's most highly acclaimed and prolific children's author, was trained as a librarian. As well as winning the Esther Glen Award four times she has twice been the recipient of the Carnegie Medal in Great Britain (for *The Haunting*, 1982, and *The Changeover: a Supernatural Romance*, 1984), and has won prizes in Holland and Italy as well as the English *Observer*'s Award for Young Adult Fiction (for *Memory*, 1987). By 1990 she had written twenty-two picture book texts, eleven collections of stories, five junior novels, six novels for older readers, and more than thirty-six texts for emergent reader series. Ironically, when she began writing in the early 1960s local demand was for stories with an overtly New Zealand atmosphere and setting, and her archetypal fantasy tales of lions, witches and wizards were consistently rejected by local publishers. Her work was, however, accepted for the *School Journals*, and it was when these were exhibited in the United States that it attracted the notice of the overseas publishers who were to continue to publish it: Franklin Watts in the United States, and Dent in England. It was only after she had attracted international attention that she was recognized in New Zealand, and the continuing overseas publication of her work remains a significant exception to the general trend towards local publication.

At the core of Mahy's art is her vitality of language, combined with a strong sense of humour ('I think humour has a more spiritual function than many people are prepared to admit', she has commented), and a seemingly inexhaustible fund of ideas. Like the works of Eleanor Farjeon and Walter de la Mare, her books demonstrate that children may apprehend even when they cannot comprehend, revealing an intuitive grasp of children's imaginative processes, and avoiding either condescension or moralizing. She shares with children a gift for both precision and hyperbole: precision of observation and exaggeration of numbers, as when a boy is followed home by first one, then four, then nine, then twenty-seven, and finally forty-three hippopotomuses, in *The Boy Who Was Followed Home* (1977). Another story is entitled *17 Kings and 42 Elephants* (1987). Alongside literature she has strong interests in philosophy and astronomy. She is fascinated by the implications of quantum physics, and the outward exuberance of her work is underpinned by considerable philosophic depth. She herself sees her fantasy stories as 'shadows cast in the conscious world by unconscious actions and journeys . . . crests of icebergs made possible by the hidden experiences that produce them', and as consistent with a 'true rationality which I see as having more emotional and intuitive components than is commonly acknowledged'.[16]

Whether written for younger children or teenage readers, her books explore the inevitable tension between the constraints of everyday living and the demands of imaginative freedom. Her pirates, robbers or crocodiles are adventurous, socially unacceptable free spirits, who refuse to be bound by convention or by gender expectations, and who burst into the lives of ordinary 'respectable' people, charge them with energy, whirl them around, and leave them with altered perspectives. In the picture book *The Man Whose Mother Was a Pirate* (1972) a neat little man and his unorthodox mother run away to sea. In a teenage novel *The Catalogue of the Universe* (1985) the young aspiring astronomer Tycho, desperately juggling between reason and emotion, realizes that in astronomical terms the universe itself is unpredictable, that 'only common sense is tidy, Truth wobbles and hides'.[17] If Mahy has a dominant theme it is the exploration of the unpredictable, and the need to be open to its demands. The penalty of having a closed mind is manifest in *The Haunting* (1982); when the grandmother discovers her magic powers, she suppresses them by constant ordering and tidying until her creative imagination withers and dies.

Although she continued to write for younger children, during the 1980s Mahy also turned to science fiction and novels for teenage readers. Many of the same preoccupations are evident in these as in her earlier books, but the longer form afforded the opportunity for a more expansive exploration of human relationships, and for her enthusiasm of style to be tempered to a controlled precision of expression. Until recently Mahy consistently portrayed family warmth in her fiction, particularly between mothers and daughters, but in *The Tricksters* (1986) relationships are more complex and disturbing. This book's seventeen-year-old central character, herself writing a novel, unintentionally activates the ghost of a drowned youth, son of the original owner of the beach house where she is staying with her family. The ghost takes the multiple form of three 'Tricksters' (Ovid, Felix, and Hadfield) who represent the Heart, Head, and Instincts, and their presence not only serves to reveal previously undisclosed secrets relating to the youth's death, but poses a considerable threat to the outward harmony of the family.

The Tricksters, a complex book, set in a recognizable Banks Peninsula, is an example of Mahy's increasing use of local settings in her writing. *Memory* (1987), also a novel for 'young adults', is set in Christchurch, and presents the city as a place where unemployment, drunkenness, and violence make the streets unsafe for women. When Jonny, an intoxicated teenager, meets Sophie, an old woman suffering from Alzheimer's disease who is wandering the streets one night, his anxiety for her safety leads him to see her to her home, and an unusual friendship develops between them. It is one of Mahy's few books with no resonance of fantasy. Its central preoccupation is with the nature of memory. Sophie's fragmented reminiscences form a counterpoint to Jonny's troubled recollections of his sister's death, and of his fears that he may have caused it. The portrayal of the poignancy and humour of Sophie's dementia is movingly authentic. For all her eccentricities Sophie never loses dignity, and her childlike ability to impose what the author calls her 'inner society' upon the outside world contrasts with Jonny's struggle to balance the 'inward' and 'outward' facets of his experience. Ultimately, he is freed from the tyranny of memory through realizing that memories 'are always in the process of being revised, updated or having different endings written upon them'.[18]

The influence of Mahy's example, and especially of educational initiatives like those of Dorothy Butler and Marie Clay (whose research on young children's reading at the University of Auckland had achieved international recognition), contributed a great deal to the huge increase in picture book publications in the 1980s — perhaps the single most important new factor in the continuing renaissance of children's literature during that decade. In the 146 years between 1833 and 1979 ninety-one picture books were published in New Zealand. In the six years alone between 1980 and 1986 a further 141 appeared. Many of these were designed to teach reading through the use of texts with a high interest-level rather than through the older 'graded reader' systems. Educational publishers such as Ashton Scholastic, Shortlands Publications (with their Jellybeans series), and Heinemann (with their Sunshine Books series) provided high-quality production, and established writers such as Bacon, Cowley and Mahy contributed many of the titles alongside award-winning illustrators like Robyn Belton. But whereas books especially designed for children's reading had previously been available only for the 'captive' educational market in schools, they were now sold much more widely in bookshops, and many of the major publishers increased their picture book quota, often selling to overseas markets in advance of New Zealand publication. Television may also have contributed to the trend, strongly evident overseas as well, towards increased visual content in stories generally, and towards more picture books for older children.

The picture book of the 1980s reflected the same general thematic preoccupations and shifts as fiction for older readers, but within the more restricted vocabulary scope of the genre. In particular, Māori legends and traditional art forms had a strong influence on picture-book art in the 1980s. The pioneering efforts of Bacon (with the illustrators Matchitt and Jahnke) were expanded and developed in the 1980s. Māori artists such as Katarina Mataira and Robyn Kahukiwa used the decorative patterns of Māori carvings and weaving to excellent effect. *The Kuia and the Spider* (1981) by Patricia Grace, a story about a spinning competition between an old Māori lady and a spider, was illustrated by Kahukiwa, and written in the hope that 'Māori children will see themselves, and that their family values will be reinforced for them'. In *Watercress Tuna and the Children of Champion Street* (1984), also illustrated by Kahukiwa, Grace hoped that 'children from different ethnic backgrounds will recognize themselves, and [that] the multicultural nature of our society will be promoted'.[19] Both books were separately issued in Māori-language editions (the latter also in a Samoan-language edition), and dual-language or separate editions have become increasingly common since the first such book, Jill Bagnall's *Crayfishing with Grandmother* (1973), appeared in the previous decade. Miriam Smith's *Kimi and the Watermelon* (1983), *Roimata and the Forest of Tane* (1986) and *Annie and Moon* (1988) were three fine examples, and dual Māori and English texts also appear in the large, strikingly-coloured versions of Māori myths and legends by Peter Gossage. Their mood is serious and often severe. By contrast, the cartoon-like *Pukunui* series by James Waerea uses English in the text and Māori in the speech-bubbles to give a light-hearted account of the adventures of a pre-European Māori boy.

Amongst picture books on more general themes two of the best-known authors both in New Zealand and overseas are Lynley Dodd and the New Zealand-born expatriate writer, Ronda Armitage. Both made use of lively language to create memorable characters. In an early book, *The Nickle Nackle Tree* (1976) — a splendidly alliterative counting book — Dodd revealed her inventive sense of the aural and alliterative possibilities of words. In a later series of six books (so far) beginning with *Hairy Maclary of Donaldson's Dairy* (1983), which she wrote and illustrated herself, Dodd invented a number of canine and feline protagonists with such inspired names as Schnitzel von Krumm (for a dachshund) and Slinky Malinky (for a black cat). The popularity of these books lies not only in their cheerfully rhyming cumulative texts, complemented by jaunty, amusing pictures, but also in the fact that although the animals have distinctive personalities, Dodd is rarely tempted to anthropomorphize the events they become involved in, which are confined to the typical activities of their species. Her dogs go to the vet, steal bones, and chase cats up trees. In *The Apple Tree* (1985) a possum steals apples, in *The Smallest Turtle* (1985) a newly-hatched turtle has to make its way to the sea, and in *Wake Up, Bear* (1986) a bee succeeds in wakening a bear after hibernation where other animals have failed.

Ronda and David Armitage's picture books *The Lighthouse Keeper's Lunch* (1977), *The Lighthouse Keeper's Catastrophe* (1986), and *The Lighthouse Keeper's Rescue* (1989) are widely read both in New Zealand and in Great Britain. All three pose a dilemma which must be solved. In the first, seagulls steal the lighthouse keeper's lunch, but his wife devises a plan to thwart them. In the second, there is a *cata*strophe when Hamish the cat is accidentally locked in the lighthouse with the keys left inside, and in the final story the lighthouse keeper loses his job. Ronda Armitage, the writer, works closely with her artist husband David who supplies the colourful pictures, and she carefully balances what needs to be said in the text with what can be left to the illustrations. The Armitages' other picture books include *Don't Forget Matilda* (1979), *The Bossing of Josie* (1981), *One Moonlit Night* (1983), and *Grandma Goes Shopping* (1984). Their subject matter is always close to children's experience (a birthday present, forgetting essential equipment, camping out at night, or going shopping), and food is always an important ingredient in the stories. Ronda Armitage's language is distinguished by its precision, including the use of long words if appropriate: the lighthouse keeper is 'conscientious', his wife 'concocts delicious lunches', and her plan is 'ingenious'. The author comments:

> Unlike books for older children, picture books are for reading aloud, so the story must flow smoothly and each sentence needs to be rhythmic. This form of writing is perhaps more akin to poetry than to prose in the sense that each word has to play its part — after all, there aren't many of them.[20]

Ronda Armitage's expatriation, in 1974, was to England. Pamela Allen, another expatriate, moved to Sydney where she writes and illustrates her books herself, allowing the lively pictures with their vitality of line and clarity of colour to carry the weight of the narrative, and keeping the texts minimal. Her first two books, *Mr Archimedes' Bath* (1980) and *Who Sank the Boat?* (1982) amusingly demonstrated scientific problems of water displacement and balance, while two later stories, *Bertie the Bear* (1983) and *The Lion in the Night* (1985) turned to human problems, demonstrating the positive effects of changes of attitude through sudden humorous reversals in the narrative. Thus a bear who is chased turns round and entertains its pursuers, and a lion who has kidnapped a baby princess returns her one night to her castle and invites everyone to breakfast. Fraternal jealousies feature in two more recent books, *Herbert and Harry* (1986) and *I Wish I had a Pirate Suit* (1989). In the former a character wastes his life in concealing treasure from his brother, and in the latter a boy turns the tables on his previously dominant older brother.

Gwenda Turner and Gavin Bishop are two local author/artists whose work focuses specifically on New Zealand settings. Gwenda Turner uses a naturalistic style to illustrate books for the very young, such as *New Zealand ABC* (1985) and *Snow Play* (1986). 'After writing my story', she has commented, 'I then go looking for animals, people and so forth, because my style of illustrating is true-to-life and I research everything I draw.'[21] Gavin Bishop trained as a painter, and his controlled use of colour and strong sense of design produce a distinctive artistic effect. In his first book, *Mrs McGinty and the Bizarre Plant* (1981), he began to incorporate into his work features of the South Island landscape and architecture. Christchurch factories such as Edmonds and Aulsebrooks, the Roman Catholic Cathedral, and a variety of domestic architectural styles occur both in *Mrs McGinty* and in *Mr Fox* (1982). In *Bidibidi* (1982), the story of a sheep's journey in search of a rainbow, the land-forms and birds of the Southern Alps are sharply delineated, as well as old buildings such as the deserted 'Leg o' Mutton Arms — established 1870'. But although the land-forms are starkly realistic, they sometimes take on a threatening, surrealistic quality, in keeping with the themes of the stories. In his original stories, *Mrs McGinty*, *Bidibidi*, and *The Horror of Hickory Bay* (1984), and in his retellings of traditional tales, *Mr Fox*, *Chicken Licken* (1984), and *Mother Hubbard* (1986), Bishop's characters are all at some stage subjected to menace. Mrs McGinty is initially harassed by a plant which gets out of control, Bidibidi only just escapes being eaten, and the monster of Hickory Bay invests the whole coastal landscape with an atmosphere of malevolence. Chicken Licken's companions and Mr Fox are, true to tradition, graphically devoured. Usually, however, the threat is overcome: Mrs McGinty finds friends, Bidibidi meets the rainbow maker, and the Horror of Hickory Bay is overcome.

The most successful picture books are those which achieve a synthesis of mood in text and pictures. This is possible when the author is also the artist and thus fully in control of the total effect, but becomes more difficult when collaboration between a separate author and illustrator is required. Philip Temple and Chris Gaskin in *The Story of the Kakapo* (1988), *Moa, the Story of a Fabulous Bird* (1985), and *The legend of the Kea* (1986) provide one example of a highly successful collaboration. Their books combine a story format with a considerable amount of information about the birds, and the pictures by Chris Gaskin match these qualities of the narrative with a fine blend of accurate detail and expressive feeling. The authors Jenny Hessell and Dorothy Butler have been teamed with a variety of illustrators. Hessell's sensitive treatments of difficult subjects — sexual molestation in *What's Wrong with Bottoms?* (1987), coping with death in *Nobody's Perfect* (1989), and reproduction in *Rebecca's Babies* (1988) — have been particularly well interpreted by Mandy Nelson's illustrations. Several of Dorothy Butler's entertaining texts for young children have been illustrated by Lyn Kriegler: a counting book *A Bundle of Birds* (1987), *Bears, Bears, Bears* (1989), and *Lulu* (1990), the story of an independent cat. The

Kriegler/Butler team also produced a charming picture book for rather older readers, *Come Back Ginger* (1987), based on a true incident during the Northern Wars of 1845, when a settler family about to be evacuated to avoid a Māori attack suddenly discover that their cat has found a rare bird.

Come Back Ginger reflected a growing trend towards the production of picture books for older children. In two popular cartoon books, *Terry and the Gunrunners* (1982) and *Terry and the Yodelling Bull* (1986), Bob Kerr and Stephen Ballantyne attempted to create a popular New Zealand hero, as an alternative to film- and television-inspired American superheroes of the 'cops and robbers' genre. The books are accomplished in their sophisticated humour and quick action plots set in familiar New Zealand landscapes, and maintain a fine balance between text, pictures, and overall design.

However, it is the work of the Canterbury short story writer Anthony Holcroft which most strikingly indicates the creative possibilities of extending the picture book genre to include older age groups. Holcroft first attracted attention with an early story, 'The Girl in the Cabbage Tree', in an anthology edited by Dorothy Butler, *The Magpies Said* (1980), and his stories have increasingly been interpreted in picture book format. *The Old Man and the Cat* (1984) and *The Oldest Garden in China* (1985) were illustrated by Fifi Colston, and in 1989 *Rosie Moonshine* was expressively visualized by Lyn Kriegler. The latter story, which first appeared in a collection by Holcroft, *Tales of the Mist* (1987), is remarkable for the lucidity of its prose and the quality of its storytelling. Holcroft explores archetypal themes, but locates his exclusively adult characters in deeply felt and penetratingly observed South Island landscapes. In almost all the tales a supernatural visitant challenges the protagonists to reassess their values. Greed and possessiveness result in the destruction not only of human relationships, but frequently of the land itself, whose barren soil symbolizes the impoverishment of the human spirit. Holcroft's achievement lies in his ability to tether the archetypal firmly to the landscape of New Zealand, and marks a significant development of indigenous fantasy writing for children.

In the 1980s, fiction for older children saw a continuing expansion of earlier preoccupations as well as some discernible new directions. One of these was in the more varied picture given of family relationships; another, the development of science fiction which has often focused on contemporary social and political issues.

Joanna Orwin, by profession a botanist, described her fictional aims in what were by now very familiar terms: 'to write about New Zealand experiences in a way that rings true, and to express for our children a sense of belonging to a particular place and time'.[22] An author for older children, Orwin's first two novels (illustrated by Robyn Kahukiwa) were about the pre-European Māori. *Ihaka and the Summer Wandering* (1982) describes the summer migrations of the moa-hunters, and its sequel, *Ihaka and the Prophecy* (1984), shows how Ihaka is apprenticed to a tohunga and learns how to select and fell a mighty totara tree prior to constructing a canoe. Orwin's next novel, *The Guardian of the Land*

(1985), uses a time-slip construction to take a Māori boy, Rua, and his Pākehā friend David to pre-settler days, where they sail with the whalers and witness a seal hunt and a raid upon a pā. As a result of their adventures in the past they discover a whalebone pendant which is important to Rua's tribe, and David learns to change what at the beginning of the novel are distinctly racist attitudes towards Maoridom. *Watcher in the Forest* (1987) also evokes the Māori past, as it traces the journey of a group of young trampers through a vividly realized landscape of bush, lake, and mountains.

Alongside the growing focus on Māori subjects in the 1980s, there has been a continuing fascination with the Pākehā past during the settler period and later. An interest in family history set Phyllis Johnston researching to produce a series of books (beginning with *No-one Went to Town*, 1980) which are reminiscent of Locke in their careful detailing of the daily life of pioneers from the 1890s to the 1920s, in the rugged settings of inland Taranaki and the King Country. A number of other books dealing with the more recent past draw on autobiographical experience. In the 1970s Mary Cox in *Wild Manes in the Afternoon* (1976) and Barbara Murison in *Buster Bee Stories* (1977) had initiated this trend: the former a warmly sympathetic tale of girlhood in the central North Island before World War II, the latter an amusing and memorable account of childhood in Auckland and Wellington in the 1930s. Gloria Gibson's *Mouse in the Attic* (1980) and *Mouse in School* (1983) were set in the 1920s, and the same period was chronicled in Peggy Dunstan's *A Fistful of Summer* (1981).

A strong autobiographical element also appears in Beverley Dunlop's *The Poetry Girl* (1983), a novel which looks back on a troubled girlhood in the 1940s, first in Nelson, then in the Waikato. As in a number of teenage stories of the 1980s, the family situation is an unhappy one. The heroine, Natasha, suffers from asthma, and this hinders her progress at school, occasioning the sarcasm of a series of male teachers. Her quarrelling parents and an attempted suicide by her father cause her to retreat into poetry, which satisfies where human relationships have failed. Dunlop had been a prolific contributor to the *School Journals* over a number of years, and it was not until the early 1980s (assisted by the Choysa Bursary) that she began to extend the range of her writing. *The Dolphin Boy* (1982) was partly conceived out of concern for the preservation of dolphins, but the Dolphin Boy, who understands the language of dolphins and can explain their power to communicate and heal, also acts as a catalyst to resolve conflict in the relationship between a child and his foster family. In *Earthquake Town* (1984) Dunlop drew upon the memories of people who had actually experienced the Napier earthquake in 1931, and as in *The Dolphin Boy*, the central event acts as a catalyst in human relationships and in the process of self-discovery. The teenage narrator, Megan, covers every hour of that extraordinary day, during the course of which her own domestic problems are brought sharply into perspective against the real tragedy she witnesses. Dunlop's most recent novel, *Spirits of the Lake* (1988), turns to the same theme as Orwin's in *Watcher in the Forest*, drawing on Māori legendary history of Lake

Waikaremoana to suggest a supernatural dimension in otherwise inexplicable events in the present.

Two other recent books, Jack Lasenby's *The Mangrove Summer* (1988) and Maurice Gee's *The Champion* (1989), draw upon their authors' memories of the Second World War. In the first, Lasenby describes how a family on holiday in their Coromandel bach learns that the Japanese have bombed Pearl Harbour and that their father has been taken prisoner. The oldest girl becomes preoccupied with a fear of Japanese invasion and insists that the other children join her in taking a boat and hiding in the mangrove swamps. For a while they manage to survive, but the expedition ends in disaster with the accidental drowning of the youngest of the children. Gee's *The Champion*, which became a television serial, is set in West Auckland. Always at his best with adult characters, the author takes time to introduce some memorable and eccentric local inhabitants, but the arrival of three American soldiers, two white Southerners and a Black, Jackson Coop, acts as a dramatic catalyst to bring to the surface the suppressed racism of the community, with tragic results. The twelve-year-old protagonist's empathy with the victim, Coop, echoes that of the young Bruce Mason for Firpo in his play *The End of the Golden Weather* (1962), and the novel primarily enacts his movement out of innocence to a realization of the underlying adult tensions of the community. Gee had explored the theme of discrimination in an earlier book, *The Fire Raisers* (1986). The story, which was originally written for television and only later adapted as a novel, is set in a small South Island town during the First World War. The victim of discrimination in this instance is a German woman, persecuted by the activities of an arsonist which ignite first the passions and then the xenophobia inherent in the community. With their small-town settings and acute dissection of social dynamics, these children's novels have a similar bearing to Gee's adult novels such as *In My Father's Den* and *Prowlers*.

In realistic children's fiction with a contemporary setting, two marked developments in the 1980s are the willingness of a number of authors to explore aspects of personal relationships that were previously considered unsuitable, and to create strong female protagonists whose behaviour demonstrates the possibility (and desirability) of breaking away from stereotyped expectations. In Jack Lasenby's novel for teenagers, *The Lake* (1987), the central character leaves home because she is being molested by her step-father. During a period in which she is learning self-sufficiency in the bush she is befriended by a hermit, formerly guilty of incest, who rescues her from rape by shooting her would-be attacker. A father who may molest his daughter appears in William Taylor's *Possum Perkins* (1987), in which a lonely and withdrawn girl whose interests are narrowly focused on her school studies is helped by a cheerful, outgoing boy and his large Catholic family when they cooperate in trying to rear a young possum.

Taylor's experiences as a teacher in the central North Island have enabled him to write shrewdly on a range of social issues, and several of his characters fall foul of the law. *Shooting Through* (1986) is the story of two escapees from

Borstal, one Māori the other Pākehā. In *My Summer of the Lions* (1986) a young boy, emotionally unstable after his mother's death from cancer, takes to stealing hubcaps when he learns that his father is to remarry. *The Kidnap of Jessie Parker* (1989) chronicles in spare, terse narrative how a thirteen-year-old is kidnapped and held hostage by bank robbers. More sentimental writers might have concluded the novel with Jessie's escape, but Taylor takes time to explore the aftermath of the episode. Jessie is puzzled by the ambivalence of her feelings towards one of her captors, and a novel which begins as a fast-paced adventure narrative becomes a study of the psychology of the relationship between oppressor and oppressed. In contrast to the seriousness of approach in such socially conscious novels, Taylor reveals considerable comic talent and an acute ear for children's vernacular in three stories about students of the fictional Greenhill Intermediate School, *The Worst Soccer Team Ever*, *Break a Leg*, and *Making Big Bucks* (all 1987), which were later televised. These light-hearted books all have underlying, though never intrusive, explorations of the value of cooperation rather than competition, of the difficulties of peer-group pressure, and of emerging feminism. One of the most entertaining characters is Lavender Gibson, who makes a memorable stand on women's issues, such as the right of girls to play soccer and to protest against a Wet T-Shirt competition. This, she asserts, 'goes dead against the person-hood of being a woman. It turns us feminists into objects and it's disgusting'.[23]

Lavender is one of an increasing band of strong and unorthodox female characters to appear in fiction of the 1980s, true successors of Mahy's Pirate Mother. Mahy herself continued to invent such women. The Mother in *Jam* (1985) is 'the cleverest of the whole family': 'She could whip up a pot of atomic porridge. She could tuck a computer into bed and sing it to sleep with a lullaby.'[24] Her scientific expertise is such that 'important scientists' send for her to help cure sun spots, and in the end she returns to the professional workforce leaving her husband at home to care for the family. In two similarly exuberant and amusing books, *The Wrestling Princess* (1986) and *Oskar and the Ice-Pick* (1988), Judy Corbalis, a New Zealand-born author living in England, introduces not only a princess who wrestles and drives a fork-lift truck, but a queen who is a champion racing-car driver, a mother who is a mountaineer, and a grandmother who abandons ballet dancing in favour of underwater swimming.

The most powerful creation of a strong central female character occurs in Tessa Duder's *Alex* (1987) and *Alex in Winter* (1989), set in the later 1950s and 1960s. In *Alex* the title-character is a high-flying young fifteen-year-old who aims not only to become a national swimming champion but also to play First XI hockey, take examinations in ballet and piano, and pass School Certificate. Her plans are complicated by the stress of a relationship with an older boy who is subsequently killed in an accident, and by the treadmill of training and racing, especially against her main rival who is totally single-minded and has fewer outside commitments. The novel ends as Alex wins the 100 Metres Women's Freestyle race, a victory which should ensure her a place in the national

Olympic team for the Rome Olympics, but its sequel, *Alex in Winter*, traces the protagonist's continuing reaction to her boyfriend's death and her increasing impatience with the bureaucracy and insensitivity of swimming officialdom. Her unhappiness heightens her perceptions of the society around her, and she becomes sharply critical of the chauvinism of the rugby scene, the '6 o'clock swill' caused by the closing of New Zealand bars at 6 p.m., and the sending of an all-white team of All Blacks to South Africa. In this middle book of a planned trilogy the bitterly self-preoccupied Alex has moved far from the ebullient girl at the beginning of the first novel, and the prose style is as spare and compelling as her plight.

Although these are works of fiction, they undoubtedly have a strong autobiographical basis in Duder's experiences as a champion Commonwealth swimmer, and in the convincing detail of the novels' description of the routines of competitive swimming: rising at dawn for daily practices, emerging from the water with green-tinged hair and with eyes smarting from chlorine. Two earlier novels, *Night Race to Kawau* (1982) and *Jellybean* (1985), also reflect Duder's own enthusiasm for sailing and music. The former recounts how a mother and her children struggle to manage their yacht (and succeed) after the father is accidentally injured. In the latter, Geraldine (or 'Jellybean') is the daughter of a solo mother who is a professional musician. She accepts without question the succession of babysitters and attendance at rehearsals and concerts, but finds life suddenly complicated by the arrival of a former friend of her mother who suggests that she should consider the unusual career of becoming a conductor. Duder has always frankly insisted that 'I write primarily for myself, to release inner tensions, to explore the intricacies of family life; not "for children" or for any supposed market'.[25] No novelist since Peacocke has so firmly set her books in middle class and professional Auckland society, and her strong sense of place ensures that the Hauraki Gulf, and the urban world of Auckland's North Shore and Queen Street, spring vividly to life.

Alongside the increased range of personal relationships within the contemporary realistic novel, the 1980s also saw significant growth in the genre of fantasy writing for older children. Maurice Gee classified his five earlier books for children (other than his two realistic novels of the later 1980s, *The Fire-Raiser* and *The Champion*) as 'adventure stories falling somewhere between science fiction and fantasy'.[26] The first two, *Under the Mountain* (1979) and *The World Around the Corner* (1980), have firm settings in this world; the first in Auckland, the second near Nelson. The underlying theme of both is that children can assist Good to triumph over Evil in other worlds, and thus, potentially, in this world. To effect this, talismen (stones of power in one, and magic glasses in the other) have to be discovered and suitably disposed of. A similar motif underlies the Tolkienesque trilogy *The Halfmen of 'O'* (1982), *The Priests of Ferris* (1984) and *Motherstone* (1985). The world of 'O' is under threat, having lost the balance between Good and Evil, and only the reunification of the two separated halves of 'O' can save it from annihilation, since by the third book both sides have such powerful weapons that they could destroy their world. The act of joining the two halves is performed by Susan, heroine of the three books, although in so doing she knows that 'O' will revert to the Stone Age. All of Gee's fantasy worlds carry strong contemporary concerns and are rooted in the New Zealand landscape. His books emphasize the need for conservation of the environment, and for the reconciliation of conflict. In the world of the Grimbles (in *The World Around the Corner*) trees have been felled and hills levelled, and the inhabitants live in smoke-filled cities while their factories manufacture weapons of war. The implied political statement is particularly evident in *The Priests of Ferris*, which examines the nature of power and the manipulation of ideas.

The planet under threat from weapons of mass destruction or from pollution provided the focus of a number of science fiction novels in the 1970s and 1980s. The first of the genre was Diana Moorhead's *Gullman's Glory* (1976), which visualized a post-holocaust age after genetic engineering, and in Marc Alexander's *The Mist Lizard* (1977) contemporary children are warned by visitants from another planet that they live in an 'Age of Waste'. Margaret Mahy's *Aliens in the Family* (1986) introduces a student from another planet who returns to study Earth because it was the home of his forebears.

A sophisticated first novel by Barry Faville, *The Keeper* (1986), depicts New Zealand several generations after nuclear war, as a primitive society reduced to subsistence living, with a paranoid fear of non-conformity. His second book, *The Return* (1987), is set in a small community on the East Coast in an indefinite past where, some sixty years previously, visitors from outer space had, against orders, conducted a genetic experiment. Now two of their descendants return, disguised as a mother and son, to discover the results. They are also anxious to ascertain the reasons for a surge in scientific knowledge on Earth, and are particularly concerned about recently invented weapons of mass destruction, which give rise to speculation 'about the state of mind of a race that could so eagerly invent and manufacture them'.[27] Faville's crisp, economical prose presents so credible a picture of Wilkes Beach and its ordinary inhabitants that the reader willingly suspends disbelief in the fantastic events that occur there. In *Stanley's Aquarium* (1989) genetic engineering is again the subject: the title-character, a megalomaniac, is selectively breeding piranha which he intends to release into Lake Taupo. His plan is foiled by the observant teenage girl who mows his lawn, and who becomes fascinated by his mysterious domestic life and the strangeness of his garden, which is planted like a South American jungle.

Elements of science fiction and fantasy also recur in a number of the novels of Caroline Macdonald, a major children's author to emerge in the 1980s. Ecological, philosophic, and scientific dilemmas underpin three of them, *Elephant Rock* (1983), *Visitors* (1984), and *The Lake at the End of the World* (1988), but her overwhelming preoccupation is with young people isolated from any peer group, 'characters who are for some reason removed from the usual process of conditioning'.[28] The child alone is inevitably more dependent on adults, and her multi-layered novels are sensitive explorations of parent/child relationships which often suffer from a breakdown in communication.

Elephant Rock, her first book, daringly and uncompromisingly examines the situation of a twelve-year-old girl whose mother is dying of cancer, avoiding the pitfall of sentimentality through the use of a time-slip device which enables the girl to relive her mother's youth and consequently understand and more readily accept the impending bereavement. In *Visitors* a lonely boy, who is paid little attention by his affluent parents, uses his video-recorder to receive messages from beings from outer space who have been trapped in this world for hundreds of years. The book develops a counterpoint of differing cross-threads of communication. The boy, able to receive but not to understand the messages of the aliens, is assisted by a physically handicapped girl who is able to communicate only through the use of a word-processor, and who has more insight into the meaning of the messages. The problems of the Visitors reflect and intensify the lack of communication within the family, and the solving of one predicament assists in the resolution of the other.

The Yellow Boarding House (1984) and *Joseph's Boat* (1988) both highlight a communication failure between parent and child. In the former, a New Zealand mother and her daughter are stranded without money in Melbourne. The mother has to go out to work, and in her absence the daughter inadvertently becomes involved with a drug-smuggling gang. The relationship between mother and daughter is astutely portrayed: the mother, under stress, still protectively treating her daughter like a child, and the daughter, emerging into adulthood, resentful at not being given responsibility or taken into her mother's confidence. In *Joseph's Boat*, a long picture-book story finely illustrated by Chris Gaskin, a father is immersed in the daily toil of farming on an offshore island, and fails to realize that his son is lonely until the son takes a boat and is nearly lost at sea.

The Lake at the End of the World takes place in the year 2025 in a world which has virtually died from pollution, except for a lake and its environs in New Zealand. Unbeknown to each other, two groups live near its shores: one, a highly structured community which inhabits underground caves; the other, a small family of father, mother, and daughter who eke out a subsistence living above ground. When teenage Hector from the underground community meets the daughter, Diana, it becomes clear that their differing upbringings have generated widely divergent attitudes and beliefs, but both have to cooperate when the leadership of the formerly utopian underground community declines into tyranny. The novel is not only a perceptive study of the two teenage protagonists but explores important questions about the nature of power and social institutions, and about the direction of agricultural management and the effects of industrial pollution. A potent contrast is drawn between the authoritarian but protected regime of the underground community, and the very different life of the family, vulnerable to the contingencies of weather, accidents, and illness. It is, however, the family which retains its myth-making capacity; in the technological community the voices of poets have been silenced.

During the 1970s and 1980s a diverse tradition of imaginative writing for children took root, and for the first time in the English-language literary history of the country it has achieved a richness and vitality which parallels that of adult literature. It is no longer possible to dismiss children's literature as a lesser or weaker form, and besides, in much recent ostensibly adult fiction — as with Satchell's *The Greenstone Door* earlier in the century — the boundaries between adult and children's writing have become increasingly blurred. Fiction as diverse as C.K. Stead's *Smith's Dream*, the short stories of Witi Ihimaera and Patricia Grace, and Gee's *In My Father's Den*, are widely read by adolescents as well as by adults, just as fictions such as Margaret Mahy's *The Haunting* and *Memory* are as challenging to adult readers as they are to older children.

The generic history of children's literature reveals the same complex pattern of evolution and transformation as adult fiction. The older, seemingly clear-cut boundaries between genres like the adventure story, the family story, and fantasy have begun to break down. The adventure story has developed a much stronger focus on individual character and group relationships, alongside its traditional dependence on plot. The family story has developed a vastly broader canvas, with considerable emphasis on conflict and its resolution, including densely-grained studies of individual (often isolated and lonely) children, relationships in single-parent families, specialized relationships between members of families, and (in stories by Māori authors especially) the extended family relationship of the whānau. The fantasy story has developed a vigorous sense of specific, recognizable New Zealand place and landscape as the setting for fantastic events, often creating an effect akin to 'magic realism' in adult fiction.

Recent junior fiction reflects a growing awareness of the power of technology and of New Zealand's vulnerability in a world threatened by global catastrophe and ecological disaster. It also reveals changes in family structures and in gender roles. Through its exploration of the past it examines New Zealand's dual heritage and the increasing cultural diversity of contemporary life, while attempting to avoid the stereotypes which dominated the country's earlier literature for children.

Popular Fiction

TERRY STURM

The Publishing Context

In 1908 the influential New York publishing firm of Doubleday Page offered some friendly advice to G.B. Lancaster (the pen-name of Edith Lyttleton, 1873–1945), whose fourth book they had recently published. The advice took the form of a complaint, that the 'tremendous power' of her work was not being 'used to best advantage because it had never been turned into producing a novel along more usual and conventional lines':

> If you would write a novel or two, more of the sort that people are accustomed to buy in this country, it ought to be possible to secure a public here which would thereafter take anything good that you cared to put before them. But in the books so far, the people, the surroundings, the conditions and even the language, are all so foreign to any experiences or ideas which the average American has, that it is extremely difficult for him to establish that basis of human sympathy which a man has got to have for the characters in a novel in order to thoroughly enjoy it.[1]

There was enormous pressure on colonial writers like Lyttleton to conform to the requirements of the market overseas. New Zealand was too small to sustain a publishing industry of its own, or a local readership large enough to provide authors with a regular income. Nevertheless the country has produced a remarkable number of authors who have been able to make a professional career as novelists in the main popular genres of romance, mystery, adventure, and crime fiction. With very few exceptions, however, the broad popular market needed to sustain such professionalism has had to be primarily an overseas one. Authors have been forced to address the publishing priorities of the major British and American firms catering for that market, no matter how interested they might be, as Lyttleton always was, in depicting 'the people, the surroundings, the conditions and even the language' of their own country.

However, a great deal of care needs to be taken not to apply this fact of dependence on overseas markets reductively, as if all popular writers are locked into fixed formulas, and hence largely homogeneous. High-cultural dismissals of popular culture have been very powerful in New Zealand (one of the most visible signs, in fact, of the persistence of a colonial consciousness), and as elsewhere they tend to promote various stereotypes, implying that popular authors (in a kind of unholy alliance with publishers motivated by profit) are engaged in a conspiracy to exploit readers by pandering to their escapist fantasies, their baser natures, or simply their nostalgia for an idealized colonial past, solely for commercial gain. At least until recently, few of the authors discussed in this section have been treated seriously in commentaries on New

Zealand writing, despite the fact that they are the most widely read of all New Zealand writers, both inside the country and overseas. Popular authors are no more (nor less) creatures of the marketplace than are serious authors, although they are often intimidated into self-disparagement by the puritanical fervour of negative stereotyping of their genres. Ngaio Marsh (1899-1982), arguably one of New Zealand's most original novelists, and one who renovated the genre of crime fiction in England in significant ways, often downplayed her achievement as a writer, at least in New Zealand; so did Mary Scott (1888-1979), a highly skilled and successful author of light family romances set in backblocks New Zealand.

There is considerable variety of purpose and achievement amongst New Zealand's popular novelists, for a number of reasons. For one thing, there has always been a diversity of attitude towards New Zealand writing among the competitive overseas publishers to whom authors over the years became attached. Some publishers were more receptive to New Zealand work than others. Nelle Scanlan (1882-1968), for example, who began her career with lightweight English society novels in the early 1930s, was persuaded to turn to the New Zealand setting and themes of her highly successful Pencarrow novels by an Englishman, Robert Hale, then employed by Scanlan's publisher, Jarrold. When Hale set up his own firm later in the decade he became a major publisher of New Zealand authors, both serious and popular, for the next forty years.

There were also significant differences between the British and American popular markets, and these provided an alternative set of options for aspiring New Zealand authors. From the nineteenth century at least until the 1930s the market for British publishers *included* the colonial market, and American editions were not generally made available to the New Zealand market. By the turn of the century most major British publishers had developed special colonial lists, and encouraged at least some fiction with local colonial settings and themes, especially in the genres of adventure and romance. Ideally, such fiction needed to appeal not only to the broad colonial market (Australasia, Canada, and the Indian subcontinent) but also to the 'home' market in England, where there was a substantial body of readers interested in exotic peoples, locales and actions, and in the progress of Empire in the lands to which millions of their fellow-subjects and relatives had emigrated. The reading interests of these markets overlapped, but increasingly, by the turn of the century, they did not wholly coincide. The result was that a great deal of the tension in the adventure and romance plots of the New Zealand writers of the time was provided by conflict between British stereotypes and emergent colonial stereotypes (male and female), which required considerable ingenuity (and a huge amount of sheer plot contrivance) to resolve.

Such resolution, as Lydia Wevers shows in her section on the short story elsewhere in this volume, commonly took the form of a reformation of the British characters (educated in the school of hard knocks provided by the harsh conditions of a raw colonial environment), and a testing and affirmation of the moral fibre of the colonial-born characters, whose quintessential Britishness was revealed — at the end, through the discovery of lost inheritances or concealed blood ties — and celebrated by marriage. This pattern could in fact include a considerable amount of satire of the effeteness of British civilization, but such satire was always incidental to the central message: that the colonies provided a breeding ground for Britishness, perhaps even carried its destiny, more effectively than Great Britain itself. The pattern has remained very powerful in New Zealand popular fiction published in Great Britain, not only in later forms of historical romance which returned to the country's nineteenth century colonial past, but in continually recycled contemporary versions of it. At least until the 1960s, one of the commonest plots in New Zealand light romance was the emigration of a young English heroine to rural New Zealand where, after appropriate romantic vicissitudes, she marries the eligible owner or inheritor of a prosperous sheep station, thus discovering her roots in a 'British' gentility and ease of living that would not have been possible if she had not had the courage to leave 'home' and seek her destiny in New Zealand.

Entry into the large American market, on the other hand, was both simpler in theory and more difficult in practice, since what was required (as Doubleday Page's letter to Lyttleton spelt out) was an accommodation purely and simply to that market's own *internal* needs: addressing the 'experiences or ideas' of the 'average American', whatever that might mean to an ambitious New Zealand author on the other side of the world. Lyttleton's immediate response was to write a romantic adventure novel set in the Australian outback, giving it the transparently American title, *Jim of the Ranges* (1910). Dealing with issues of frontier law and lawlessness (though she also managed to sneak in some material on her favourite theme of colonial identity), the novel was very obviously aimed at the internal American market for action novels of the Wild West, and even included a minor character with the quite improbable name, in Australia, of the 'Cisco Kid. It had little immediate success in the United States (although a decade later it was made into a Hollywood silent feature film); and in the meantime Lyttleton, having gone to London, addressed herself successfully to the British market (especially for North American tourists) with *The Honourable Peggy* (1911). This novel was a curious combination of a tourist guidebook to the cathedrals, castles, and literary shrines of Great Britain and what might be called a 'vehicular romance'. In the somewhat cramped conditions of a Riley touring car, an effete Englishman of impeccable aristocratic stock and a clean-cut Canadian frontiersman of shady origins compete for the hand of the Honourable Peggy under the watchful eye of her guardian, who in a denouement of quite outrageous improbability turns out to be the Canadian's natural father and the prime mover of the plot.

Lyttleton was a very talented writer who struggled throughout her career to accommodate her serious literary interest in colonial life and history with the economic necessity to earn her living by writing for overseas markets. Louisa Alice Baker (1858-1926), the author of sixteen romantic novels (who wrote under the pen-name of 'Alien'), had a similar struggle, never quite establishing herself in the American market (though nearly half of her novels achieved publication in New York), and complaining bitterly, of the British market, that 'a story with an English setting is of three times the value in London, commercially, of one with a colonial background':

> When I was living in a small East Coast fishing town I saw how French sardines were made. The sprats were caught, dressed, and tinned in the local factory, and labelled there — the labels were sent from France. So it seems with colonial artists, they are bred under the Southern Cross, held cheaply there — and labelled in London.[2]

There were also other complications in the history of the local New Zealand market for popular fiction. As Lawrence Jones shows elsewhere in this history, almost all nineteenth century New Zealand novels were written in one or other of the then-popular genres of melodrama and the sensation novel, but they were the casual by-products (rarely more than one or two novels per author) of lives primarily devoted to some other career. This is the main reason why most of them are so unreadable today, such amateurishly written examples of their genres. An early emigrant author like B.L. Farjeon, who produced three novels in the 1860s and decided that he wished to embark on a professional career as a novelist, promptly returned to England.

However in the 1880s and 1890s, at a time when the population of native-born New Zealanders began to outnumber immigrants, the first of two highly significant local institutional developments occurred: the emergence of a relatively stable base of regular weekly journalism, alongside the older established newspapers. It would be hard to underestimate the importance of these local journalistic outlets (including Australian publications like *The Bulletin*) as initial testing-grounds for aspiring popular authors. Both Baker and Lyttleton served their apprenticeships in such journals, and the pattern they established was to be regularly repeated. For many years Mary Scott wrote humorous newspaper sketches about a young backblocks wife, Barbara, before becoming a novelist in the early 1950s. The first book by Grace Phipps (1901-1983), *Marriage With Eve* (1955), initially appeared as a series of sketches in the *New Zealand Mirror*, and she also edited the 'Over the Teacups' column of the *New Zealand Women's Weekly* for many years. Essie Summers (1911-), New Zealand's most prolific Mills and Boon author, contributed poems, sketches, and articles to local (and overseas) newspapers and weeklies for at least two decades before her first novel was published in 1957.

The second local development, though it was much slower in making its effects felt, was the emergence of a fledgeling publishing industry for popular fiction. Until the Second World War there were no publishers who regularly published novels, though firms which had established themselves earlier in the century (like Reed, and Whitcombe and Tombs) had occasionally included a popular novel in their lists, such as Frank Anthony's backblocks romance, *Follow the Call* (1936). After the war, however, there was a significant expansion of local publishing, and both firms began to publish fiction on a more regular (though still small-scale) basis. They also began to enter into joint publication arrangements with overseas firms. The effect of these shifts was to reinforce the apprenticeship role of popular journalism. From the 1940s and 1950s onwards a typical pattern for a significant number of New Zealand's emergent popular novelists — Mary Scott, Dulce Carman, Mavis Winder, and Grace Phipps, among others — was an initial apprenticeship in the weekly journals, followed by book publication with Reed or Whitcombe and Tombs, and then by a graduation to the regular lists of one of the major overseas publishers.

One way of looking at these shifting patterns in the overseas and local markets for popular fiction is to see them as offering not simply a set of constraints on authors, but a variety of options — about the kinds of fiction they might want to write and the kinds of reader they might wish to address. By the middle decades of the twentieth century these commitments had come to vary considerably amongst individual novelists. The crime novelist Ngaio Marsh, and the romantic mystery novelist Dorothy Eden (1912-1982), reflected the persistence of the older pattern, and published wholly overseas, where they lived for much of their lives. Others, like Essie Summers, graduated directly from journalistic outlets to the lists of overseas firms. Mary Scott, on the other hand, always published her novels locally as well as overseas, and thus retained her commitment to the New Zealand scene. A rare instance of a bestselling New Zealand author who has remained largely unpublished outside this country is Barry Crump, whose first book, *A Good Keen Man*, appeared from Reed in 1960 and by 1968 had achieved sales of 50,000 copies.[3] 'Bestselling' in such a description, however, is a relative term. By 1980 the number of copies of Essie Summers' forty-six novels sold on the international market was seventeen million.[4]

Even within the more specialized market operations of the 1970s and 1980s, changes continued to occur. In the 1980s, for example, Mills and Boon established a Sydney-based Australasian publishing operation, and this development led to a very distinct shift in the settings and plots and characters of a newer generation of authors, including Rosalie Heneghan, Daphne Clair, Robyn Donald, and Susan Napier: much less emphasis on Anglo-New Zealand actions set in rural New Zealand, much more on locally-based, up-market, urban professional circles. In the 1980s New Zealand produced one novelist, Yvonne Kalman, whose New Zealand historical sagas (in the mould of Colleen McCullough) managed to break into the new American blockbuster market.

In what follows, which is an internal history of popular fiction in New Zealand, the dynamics of the publishing industry and of readership, as sketched above, provide an essential context. Because popular fiction so closely addresses what its authors perceive to be the fundamental values and behaviour (and often the wishes or needs) of their large readerships, it also provides rich insights (directly or indirectly) into New Zealand society and history, into its sustaining myths about the past, about race relations, about gender relations, and about the institutions and norms that support those relations. Such myths are often directly visible on the surface of popular texts, in ways that tend not to occur in the 'serious' texts of high culture, which often address the general culture metafictionally by attacking or undermining the conventions and stereotypes of the popular genres that celebrate it. Writers as diverse as Jean Devanny, Frank Sargeson, Maurice Gee, and Marilyn Duckworth, to mention only a few, manipulate and play with the conventions of romance, the vernacular yarn, the thriller, and the Gothic tale, in order to criticize or question the social norms and values on which they are based. The boundary line between popular and 'serious' authors can never be absolute, of course, and the same kind of interplay is active in the work of poets like Allen Curnow, James K. Baxter, and Ian Wedde, as well as in the work of a playwright like Mervyn Thompson. This section, which will consider only fiction, takes as its provisional starting point those writers who, in terms of the number of books they published and the number of copies they sold, have successfully reached the broad popular markets they wrote for.

Three Late Victorians

Baker and Lyttleton, and their near contemporary, Isabel Maud Peacocke (1881-1973), were all born in the second half of the nineteenth century, and although almost all of their fiction was written in the twentieth century, it was strongly influenced by the Victorian middlebrow popular tastes of their youth. Of the three, Baker's novels are closest to full-blown Victorian domestic melodrama. Her long, convoluted romances, dealing with the theme of marriage, usually contain at least two or three deathbed scenes of excruciating pathos, and she is particularly fond of the effect of a sentimental domestic tableau: errant characters seem regularly, after many years of absence, to discover loved ones — parents, spouses, children — at the precise moment when they are singing some long-forgotten song or playing some long-forgotten melody. Set mainly in Australasia, they also contain a curious mixture of *fin de siècle* religiosity and eroticism, exaggerated scenic descriptions of the more spectacular features of New Zealand's landscape (the rugged mountain scenery of the South Island, the sounds, Rotorua at the time of Mt Tarawera's eruption), and rhetoric derived from the contemporary movement for women's rights. Elizabeth M. Smith, the author of the first historical survey of New Zealand fiction (1938), commented that Baker's books showed 'a succession of women, always in the right and always self-sacrificing'.[5]

Baker's central fictional subject is the renovation of the institution of marriage, and she uses the conventional form of the romance to engage in a passionate moral crusade against, in her own words, 'any sort of marriage that does not give a trinity of union, body, soul and mind'.[6] For Baker, the emancipation of women was an essential first step in the evolution of a higher Christian consciousness that would eventually transform society by transforming the quality of relations within the institution of marriage and the family on which it was based. Emancipation meant primarily the release *into* marriage of women's currently stunted emotional and intellectual capacities. By ceasing to regard women simply as their physical property, men too would be transformed, making possible a higher form of equal union between the sexes.

Conflict in the novels is provided by seemingly endless variations on what the publisher of her first novel, *A Daughter of the King* (1894), called 'a picture of the wedded state without love'.[7] In this novel, set at Governor's Bay near Christchurch, a young woman marries a minister who is apparently at the point of death after an accident, believing that she is only temporarily separating herself from his cousin, the man she really loves. Unfortunately her selfless act backfires. The minister inconveniently recovers and demands that she fulfil her 'marital duty' to him. After enduring several years of loveless marriage, the woman causes a parish scandal by leaving him, taking their young daughter by claiming (falsely) that her husband is not the father. The rest of the novel is concerned to bring the woman to an understanding of the causes of her appalling situation, and to an appropriate course of action. The setting shifts to inner-city Melbourne, where she is deeply affected by a production of Ibsen's *A Doll's House* ('terrible because it is true') and sees the appalling slum conditions in which women and children live. Assisted by a male friend who is platonically devoted to her (a mute artist, whose life's achievement is a majestic painting, 'Daybreak', showing a woman lifting herself from earth, expressing the emotions of 'questioning, hunger and hope'), she embarks on a process of intellectual and artistic self-improvement, only to find her life seemingly shattered again, when she is about to achieve public triumph as a violinist, by the death of this friend, in a scene of truly Victorian pathos. His death, however, and her realization of his lifelong, mutely self-sacrificing devotion to her, is the final stage in her moral re-education. She hears that her husband is dying (again), and in the final pages goes back to him, to participate this time in a real deathbed scene, with the full panoply of confessions and repentances, reconciliations, even a form of re-marriage and re-dedication, the whole foreshadowing Baker's social ideal of a truly Christian marital union.

Baker's novels all follow the basic pattern laid down in her first. Her heroines find themselves trapped in destructive marital relationships, rebel against (as one of them puts it) 'a sense of intolerable wrong, wrong to her womanhood, to her equality of nature and intellect',[8] and courageously undertake an independent process of self-discovery. The final stage is invariably a re-directing of those rebellious energies, now informed with moral and intellectual awareness, *back* into the institution of marriage:

[I]f men wait, and fit themselves in the time of waiting, they will find the womanhood which went off on that pilgrimage of research will, after testing every mile of the long journey, travel in a circle back to them again, for man and woman are indissolubly one. They cannot have separate suns and systems, and live in separate worlds, for the mysterious creation of one soul and one flesh can never be explained away.[9]

Baker's fiction was warmly received by the religious press in England, and much of her popularity probably derived from its regular recommendation of her work. However, there were some dissenting voices, at least in New Zealand. Clara Cheeseman, in the first full-length published article on New Zealand fiction (1903) described Baker as 'somewhat too fond of what may be called regrettable incidents', and an *Evening Post* reviewer of *The Perfect Union* (1908) described it as belonging to a class of 'decadent books . . . in which evil suggestions are conveyed wrapped up in high-flown language'.[10] The possibility that readers might overlook the strong moral patterning of the novels and dwell instead on the sordid details of 'the wedded state without love' (or, on occasion, as in *The Perfect Union*, on the temptations of the unwedded state *with* love) was always present in Baker's novels, since the mode of narration of *all* events is so constantly heightened, so close to the methods of the sensation novel. Furthermore, Baker was unusual in insisting that 'the trinity of union, body, mind and soul' genuinely *include* the body.

It is this aspect of Baker's writing which links her most closely with her New Zealand contemporary, Edith Searle Grossmann, and it also looks forward to the anti-puritan themes of novelists like Jane Mander. In fact, the destructive effects of the repression of sexuality are found as early as Baker's second novel, *The Majesty of Man*. It portrays a guilt-tormented man who is torn between the claims of a long-suffering wife whom he has left, believing mistakenly that in marrying her he had betrayed her love for another man, and the higher claims (of renunciation of the flesh) of Sister Lilian, whose humanitarian feminist order he joins in the slums and opium dens of Melbourne, as an act of expiation. There is no doubt at the end where Baker stands, despite her lavish distribution of sympathy all round, though it requires a deal of quite improbable plotting to restore the spouses to a renovated marriage, and to declare Lilian's belief that the body should be renounced in favour of the higher dictates of the intellect and soul, to be spurious. At the end Lilian dies pathetically and at length in the domestic bosom of the restored spouses, clutching their child (whom they have named 'Lilian' after her) and whispering, 'My baby'. The narrative adds, 'The woman of ideas became almost imperceptibly a woman of love.'[11] Lilian thus finds her true vocation, at the moment of death, in surrogate motherhood. Readers might be excused for seeing it instead, like the many other deaths and maimings Baker inflicts on her wayward characters, as a punishment.

In one or two of Baker's later novels, her potentially subversive insistence that marriage include sexual satisfaction for both partners becomes even stronger. *His Neighbour's Landmark* (1907) has as one of its central themes a young wife's dissatisfaction with a partner whose attitudes are merely protective, affectionate, and courteous to her. The familiar pattern of enforced separation occurs, in this case aided by the seemingly supernatural agency of the Mt Tarawera eruption (a tragedy whose fictional victims in popular novels, like those of the Napier earthquake, exceed the actual toll by many thousands), in which the husband believes his wife has been killed. However, the resolution which eventually confirms their new relationship depends on one of the hoariest of colonial clichés. The heroine discovers that her true identity is as heiress of an English estate, a mere stone's throw from the estate which the hero has already inherited after being falsely accused and sent to New Zealand as a remittance man. New Zealand, in this novel, is thus the domain of plot complication, and England the domain of plot resolution, where they live happily ever after. There could be no clearer illustration of the author's colonial consciousness at work.

Edith Lyttleton's fiction drew on very different late Victorian conventions. Reacting against a rigid upbringing that confined her reading to genteel ladies' magazines and *Sundays at Home*, she later devoured the work of Kipling and Stevenson, and when she began writing novels and stories in the early 1900s, she turned to the conventions of the picturesque action novel of strongly plotted adventure and romance, as written by men. Thomas Hocken dismissed her early books with the phrase 'A coarsely told story — locality New Zealand', and later New Zealand critics, on the rare occasions when the existence of her work was acknowledged, echoed Hocken's judgement. However, the *Bulletin*'s editor, A.G. Stephens, who for a number of years was uncertain whether the 'G.B. Lancaster' whose stories he regularly published was a man or a woman ('the betting in trouser-buttons is about even'), saw her as a skilled exponent of 'a rapidly evolving type of Australasian novel' whose origins lay in American fiction: 'a type of the novel of action, dealing with the primitive passions of men and women, face to face with the wilder aspects of Nature'.[12]

Although she came from a patrician Canterbury background (born in Tasmania, and brought up on the family station, 'Rokeby', near Ashburton), the emphasis in much of Lyttleton's fiction (thirteen novels and hundreds of short stories) often falls on tragedy and the frustration of colonial aspirations — increasingly so, in her later novels, for her central female protagonists. Her expatriation in London, from 1909 to 1925, was also unusually complex, less a displaced colonial's yearning for 'Home' than a condition of 'inner exile', and much of her life was a restless search for spiritual roots in the countries of her colonial forebears (New Zealand, Australia, and Canada), and in exotic, geographically remote parts of the world.

The Tracks We Tread (1907), set on a back-country South Otago station, is representative of Lyttleton's early male-focused, Kiplingesque writing. The novel's unity is less a unity of plot or character than of place, and the remorseless shaping power of the environment (subject to storm, gale, flood, landslide, as well as providing moments of quite spectacular beauty) is a central theme, requiring for those who work in it unusual qualities of endurance and physical courage. The novel traces a round of seasonal events on the station, and it narrates these events largely from the point of view of the working men themselves, conveying their tribal loyalties and individual rivalries, their hard drinking, their sentimentalizing of women, and above all their absolute pride in their skills as bushmen. There is an almost anthropological sense of the social codes which hold this world together, in which traditional hierarchies of birth or wealth are abolished, and new gradations, based on physical prowess and manual skill, take their place, rigidly excluding the coward and the physical weakling. An unusual feature of this and other early novels is the seemingly unconscious explicitness with which Lyttleton conveys the homosexual undertones of mateship: so intense, in the relationship between the station's head man and a workman victimized for cowardice whom he is forced to sack, that the head man eventually resigns in order to pursue the younger man he feels he has betrayed ('He's weak as a girl, an' I loves him as I'll never love a girl.') He eventually locates his mate in Queensland, near to death, and a deathbed reconciliation occurs that is as tear-jerking as any in Baker's novels. It is as if Lyttleton's innocent eye, drawing on the gender-based conventions of heterosexual romantic love, observed what was repressed in male constructions of mateship. Although the scene is overwritten, like much else in Lancaster's early writing, the clash of conventions is unmistakable. Jimmie dies with his arm hooked around his friend's neck, 'and nothing would loose it until the end came'.[13]

Between *The Tracks We Tread* and *Promenade* (1938), a late novel in which Lyttleton returned to a New Zealand historical setting, eight further novels were published, almost all with impressive publishing histories, and all revealing an increasing professional skill in handling popular conventions. *The Law Bringers* (1913), a romantic epic of the colonization of Canada's rugged North-West, represented a key technical advance, as well as revealing Lyttleton's increasing doubt about the law of evolutionary progress, which she had earlier invoked to justify the ethic of colonialism:

> We white men make and enforce the criminal laws of a country. But it is not sufficiently taken into consideration that in very many cases we also make the conditions, which, later on, call for the enforcements of those laws. So that punishment, when it falls, often falls on the wrong person . . .. We make laws. And at the same time we are making criminals.[14]

The Law Bringers was a remarkably successful novel in Great Britain and Canada, leading to the reprinting of almost all her earlier fiction, as well as lucrative contracts with several British general magazines for all the short stories she cared to write, and it was later made into an extremely popular Hollywood silent film under the title, *The Eternal Struggle*. It also foreshadowed Lyttleton's ambitious move (amounting almost to a new start, late in her writing career) to the genre of the family saga, in the three 'Dominion-historical' novels she wrote between 1933 and 1943. Lyttleton described them as belonging to the Galsworthian genre of 'the family novel — the book which starts its story many years ago, and works down gradually to the present day, bringing in perhaps three generations of one family in the process'.[15]

The first of these novels, the Tasmanian saga *Pageant*, was ill-served by its British and Australian distributors, but highly successful in the United States, where it sold 40,000 copies within a few months and was described by Carl Van Doren as 'a frontier novel with a difference'. Its theme of antagonism between settled colonists and convicts was, in his view, 'not racial, as in the familiar type of frontier novel, but social':

> The privileged are ranged against the underprivileged, with the result that the people in the story live always on the precipice of collapse or near the crater of insurrection.[16]

Promenade followed in 1938, and *Grand Parade*, a saga of British colonization in Nova Scotia (where Lyttleton also had family ancestors), in 1943. All three novels are the works of her maturity, in which she found the genre most suited to her interests: her fascination with history, especially the colonial experience in Australia, New Zealand, and Canada; her personal search to understand her own roots; and her abiding interest in what she called the 'real picturesque', the unsung heroism, beauty, and pathos of ordinary lives struggling for self-realization against 'the inevitable law of change', in which 'nothing stands without . . . love . . . and courage'.[17] The recurrent leitmotif expressed in the titles of all three novels — the notion of life as a pageant, promenade, or parade — hints at the ironic scepticism that underpins these later parallel explorations of colonial societies. A central theme of *Promenade* is 'the clash between those who wanted to work for the country and those who worked for their own ends', with its 'endless chance for humour and tragedy'.[18] Set initially in Kororareka, next in commercially expanding Auckland, then in Canterbury during the 'Golden Age' of the big sheep stations, with brief codas evoking the Boer War and the First World War, the novel also traces conflict between Māori and Pākehā, between parents and children, and between a tradition-bound immigrant generation and an emergent colonial-born generation seeking to make something different of the new country. In particular it attempts to explore the pioneering experiences of women in colonial New Zealand.

In all the later novels, which are loosely based on the main events of colonial history, Lyttleton is freed from the constraints of intricate plotting, and employs vivid characterization, a supple, ironic style, and a variety of comic or tragic incidents whose purpose is always the revelation of character. *Promenade* is rich in such characterizations: Sir Peregrine Lovel, the patriarchal 'self-made autocrat', a 'self-contained soul rotating continually on its own axis', with 'an ego spreading across the world'; his sister-in-law, Lady Caroline Lovel, 'ornately vulgar in the best Victorian manner', who 'considered herself drama and so often turned out to be comedy'; the shady, opportunist trader and speculator, Nick Flower; Sir Peregrine's recalcitrant children, members of the 'lost' first generation who resist the traditions of their father but never succeed in making or discovering their own; above all, the persistent generations of strong women, Sir Peregrine's sister-in-law Darien, his daughter Tiffany, and in the later stages of the novel a young woman of the third generation, Prue Greer (almost certainly an autobiographical portrait). Independent-spirited, intelligent and humane, refusing 'the Holy Immolation of Matrimony', and caustic, often, in their comments on the stupidities they observe around them, they represent a kind of civilizing possibility, beyond what is seen elsewhere — in these later novels which revisit Lyttleton's earliest themes — as the ironic comedy and farce of mainstream colonial history.

Isabel Maud Peacocke's writing career spanned forty years, from her first novel for young readers, *My Friend Phil* (1914) to her last, for adults, *Change Partners* (1955), and her books appeared at the rate of one (and sometimes two) a year for most of that period. Although she is better known as a children's author who popularized the family story in New Zealand, she also wrote sixteen adult novels (all of them published in London by Ward, Lock), five during the decade 1918-29, and the remainder between 1943 and 1955, after she had stopped writing for children. In fact, however, the boundaries between Peacocke's children's fiction and adult fiction were never as clear-cut as this distinction implies. Betty Gilderdale has commented that the first four children's books were 'more romances than juvenile novels',[19] and her adult novels often include children as significant characters (in *Concerning the Marlows* (1950), for example, the child of a broken marriage is instrumental in bringing his parents together again). Peacocke's adult novels are also written out of the same strong regional feeling for Auckland and its surrounding environs as her children's books, often using the landscape in a crudely symbolic way or for 'poetically' heightened scenic set-pieces.

Where the adult novels do differ, however, is in the didacticism that underlies their deceptively light, often whimsical surface. They are primarily fictionalized tracts for the times, carrying an unmistakable message that marriage as an institution is under threat, and that young women, in particular, will be vulnerable if it collapses. Often the novels work with the conventions of the moral fable, especially in the way they draw on fairy-tale elements, or quote, at key moments, from popular sentimental poems or songs. The earlier novels focus on courtship, defending the value of marriage and of premarital chastity for both men and women, but especially for her heroines, who are constantly tempted into premarital sexual relationships. The later novels turn to marital breakdown, promoting the resolution of marital problems within marriage rather than through separation.

The 'Cinderella' of her first adult novel, *Cinderella's Suitors* (1918), which was serialized in both Great Britain and the United States, is an orphaned Auckland typist suddenly thrust into wealth by an aunt's legacy of £5000 a year, with the proviso that she does not marry. The novel thus becomes a simple test of the niece's — and her suitors' — willingness to marry for love, rather than for money and possessions. Initially intoxicated by the prospects opened up to her, the typist travels overseas, but she rejects her would-be suitors one by one: a genteel Englishman, and the villainous Lord Wendover who attempts to seduce her by force (Peacocke's heroines may be 'very ordinary human prototypes', as their author claims, but they move in a world of utterly conventional Victorian melodrama), and, back home, an egotistical MP who makes fiery socialistic speeches and has made his wealth in pork sausages. Eventually she forfeits the legacy and marries her long-time lover and protector, a struggling journalist, only to find, a year later, that the legacy is confirmed, since they have survived the test of hardship and achieved what the aunt initially desired, the 'old-fashioned virtue' of 'domestic felicity'.[20]

The Guardian (1920) is a much more intricately plotted novel, but its central action, as in most of her novels, is a testing and purification of the motives of the heroine, in this case a twenty-year-old 'girl-woman', a child of nature brought up on Auckland's remote west coast. In the city she falls prey to the attentions of a plausible scoundrel, Dion Westaway, a married man who has abandoned his wife, and who flippantly mocks 'time-honoured institutions', arguing that those who truly love should follow 'the law of nature', not 'the laws of society'. It is only by the most strenuous efforts of her loving guardian, and by the aid of a bushfire (Westaway's near-destruction in quicksands on an earlier visit to the west coast, in nefarious pursuit of the heroine, had not deterred him) that the villain is finally smoked out and the heroine brought to her senses, choosing marriage to her protector, who articulates the novel's philosophy:

> Convention is not such a bad old road to follow. It's been laid down by the pioneers who have gone before us . . ... Some of the signs seem ridiculous and some unnecessary, but on the whole it's a good road to follow. One can't be a law unto oneself.[21]

London Called Them (1946), one of Peacocke's late adult novels, includes the same kind of trial-by-suffering for her heroine, in this instance a young Auckland writer who seeks to make a literary career for herself in London, and ends up in a squalid marriage to a would-be modern poet who turns out to be a cocaine addict. He forces her to burn the manuscript of her novel about their lives, which might have established her as a writer in London. Fortunately he is killed in the war, and the heroine returns to New Zealand where she marries another of Peacocke's 'guardian' figures, a young New Zealand pavement artist who had fallen in love with her in London during the depths of her despair, but refused to ask her to lower her 'white standard' or 'adventure bravely into muddy waters' by abandoning her marriage. The novel provides a great deal of edged comment on the pretentiousness of the London literary scene, and the difficulties of breaking into it ('The whole thing's been a farce — me coming here to set the Thames on fire when I couldn't even make the Waitemata smoke'[22]), but its main theme is a defence of the institution of marriage. The romantic formula, as Peacocke used it in all her adult fiction, was primarily a means of ensuring that her heroines were rewarded for their acts of self-denial — preserving their virginity, or staying in difficult marriages.

1930–1950: Five Professionals

Baker, Lyttleton, and Peacocke remained much less widely read in New Zealand than overseas, primarily because of poor distribution arrangements by their British publishers. It was not until the 1930s that authors began to appear who attracted a significantly wide local readership. The two figures who were instrumental in this shift in reading habits were Rosemary Rees (1876–1963) and Nelle Scanlan. Rees began writing novels relatively late in life, after an earlier career on the stage. She wrote her first (*April's Sowing*, 1924) in five weeks, after the collapse of a comedy company she had set up to tour New Zealand (among its members was a youthful Ngaio Marsh), which left her 'practically penniless, and very deeply in debt'.[23] She produced a novel a year for the next two decades (publishing them in the United States as well as in numerous editions in Great Britain), then less regularly in the 1950s until her last, *The Proud Diana*, in 1962, a year before her death at the age of eighty-eight.

Rees was a key transitional figure in the emergence of the light romance in New Zealand, away from the high melodrama of the late-Victorian domestic romance that Baker and Peacocke had specialized in, to the simplified plots, single-character emphases, and simple romantic affirmations suggested by titles such as *Lake of Enchantment* (1925), *Wild, Wild Heart* (1928), *Hetty Looks for Local Colour* (1935), *Home's Where the Heart Is* (1935), *You'll Never Fail Me* (1939), and *I Can Take Care of Myself* (1940). In her novels, Rees occasionally hints at social themes (problems of courtship and marriage, Māori-Pākehā relations, economic insecurity in the farming industry), though E.M. Smith saw her as largely 'contenting herself with lavish applications of local colour in place of ideas', and her prime concern was entertainment of an undemanding kind. Robin Hyde reported, at the New Zealand Authors' Week Conference in 1936, that Rees 'made no bones about writing to sell: "The highbrows take themselves much too seriously. Come along and have a cup of tea."' In her travelogue, *New Zealand Holiday* (1933), Rees also made no bones about her politics, describing mid-Depression New Zealand as 'a happy, comfortable country . . . notwithstanding the outcry from the Labour party about the bitterly hard lot of the unemployed'.[24]

Lake of Enchantment provides an early instance of Rees's attitude to premarital and extramarital sexual relations, which remained a recurrent issue in her romances, as in Peacocke's. The heroine is an actress-novelist (very like Rees herself) who returns to New Zealand after fourteen years overseas, seeking a quiet environment in which to reassess her life after a nervous breakdown. In the tranquil bush setting of an inland Otago run she meets an engineer, also living alone near the site of a hydroelectric project, and they fall in love. While they are stranded together one night on an island in the 'Lake of Enchantment' (the locale of numerous intensely romantic Māori legends of love), she reveals to him that she had allowed herself to be cited as the co-respondent in a divorce case involving a married man she believed she loved, and that her earlier life had also included a succession of unsatisfying love affairs ('I thought I was modern — thought I believed a woman had the right to live her own life — all that sort of thing.') After these revelations, which appear to express the heroine's anxiety that she might be perceived as 'damaged goods', the engineer expresses an ethic of tolerance and an awareness of double standards which she finds unusual among men:

I think men's ideas of women — their moral standard for women — takes its rise in pure, primitive jealousy . . . .. That's why a man prates about purity for women, and has one standard for a woman, and another for himself.[25]

Shortly afterwards, it is revealed that he is himself married to a woman who is a violent drug addict, who leaves him for long periods, but whom he feels he cannot abandon because of her illness. There is thus a double complication: the heroine has a 'past', and the hero is already married, and both are thus tempted to have an extramarital affair.

However, the complications of this situation are in the end crudely evaded. It turns out that, although the heroine has a 'past', she has always stopped short of losing her virginity (even during the divorce episode); and the engineer's marital problem is solved by the simple expedient of his wife's death. Rees's plots almost invariably have this kind of cheating in them, ostensibly espousing attitudes of tolerance against judgemental views of 'irregular' sexual behaviour, but in the end rigidly reinforcing the older conventions of romantic love, with their prohibitions on premarital and extramarital sex, and on divorce. Whether such contradictions represented Rees's own uncertainties, or whether they were a shrewd estimate of the wishes of her readers to eat their cake and have it, it is impossible to say.

The same element of cheating occurs in Rees's treatment of Māori themes. Ostensibly, her novels espouse what from the 1930s to the 1950s was a 'progressive.' Pākehā assimilationist version of race relations, which did include, on occasion, criticism of racial prejudice and of the failures of Pākehā policies on race relations. Rees was brought up in Gisborne, and Sir Apirana Ngata assisted her in her travels through the East Coast while she was gathering material for *New Zealand Holiday*. However a novel like *Penelope Waits* (1947) resolves one of its central themes — the love that develops between an unsettled English emigrant, David Holt, and an ostensibly half-caste heroine, Heine Bates (the Penelope of the title) — by the crude plot expedient of a revelation that Heine is not, after all, half-caste. Moreover, her real identity (Lois Lindley) makes her the niece of a Pākehā lawyer who had been instrumental in blocking his own son's marriage to her *because* she was half-caste, and she now has a large claim on her real parents' legacy, which had earlier gone to the same lawyer as next-of-kin. Again, however, this comment on racism has a double edge to it. It evades the question of whether David Holt would have married Heine if she *were* half-caste, and allows a romance resolution in the purest terms: Holt marries Lois Lindley, heiress, not Heine Bates, half-caste, and Mrs Bates conveniently returns to her tribe, apparently delighted to renounce any claims on the young woman to whose upbringing she has devoted a large part of her life.

Like Rees, Nelle Scanlan also began writing relatively late in life: 'I was never young and full of promise. I was once young, but my first novel wasn't published until I was nearly fifty. Because I was a late starter my books are limited in number — about fifteen.'[26] Before her first novel in 1931 she had made a name as a journalist, initially (until the end of the First World War) in the provincial press, then as a free-lance overseas correspondent in the United States and (from 1923) in Great Britain, where she became a practised public speaker and a sprightly reporter of social news, especially of public events involving royalty. The story of these years is the subject of the last book she wrote, the autobiographical *Road to Pencarrow* (1963), disappointingly thin on her life as a novelist, and much of it based on an earlier account of her travels which she had written in the form of a novel, *Ambition's Harvest* (1935). Between 1933 and 1948, when she finally retired to New Zealand, Scanlan travelled regularly between England and New Zealand, living for five or six years at a time in each country. Her novels reflect this dual residency: six are set overseas, mainly in London, the other nine in New Zealand.

Scanlan's first novel, *Primrose Hill* (1931), was set in a London boarding house, and revealed a slight talent for social comedy, including lightly drawn sketches of eccentrics, colonials abroad, and stereotypes drawn from the English professional class, loosely held together by the romantic interests of the characters. In her later London novels, Scanlan attempted much more ambitious romantic comedies of manners of the professional and leisured upper middle classes. But plot was never her forte, and the writing itself (in a novel like *Kit Carmichael*, 1947) is rarely sophisticated or witty enough to convey anything other than the banality and social parasitism of the stereotypes whose romantic and domestic dilemmas provide her subject. By far the best of these London novels is *The Marriage of Nicholas Cotter* (1936), which explores with some tact the unusual relationship between a middle-aged bachelor lawyer and an eighteen-year-old woman, and the devastating effect this relationship has on his older, unmarried sister, with whom he has shared a life of settled, comfortable routine for many years.

Scanlan's most original achievement undoubtedly lay in her nine New Zealand novels, all of them variants on the formula which made the first novel of the Pencarrow tetralogy, *Pencarrow* (1932), so resounding a popular success. Writing about Scanlan in 1962, by which time 'some 30,700 copies of *Pencarrow* alone [had] been sold in this country and more than 80,000 of the series', Alan Mulgan argued that Scanlan had done more than anyone to prepare a local market for New Zealand fiction:

> Every later New Zealand novelist is in her debt. She did this because, coming at the right time, she gave New Zealand a saga of ordinary New Zealand people: farmers and lawyers, mothers and fathers, sons and daughters, men and women who go about the familiar business of making a living, falling in love, bringing up their children well or badly, spurred by ambition and hampered by weaknesses — a family world within a world, a family of loyalties and misfits, of affection and jealousies, of wisdom and stupidity, of success and failure, 'most remarkable like' you and me. And this chronicle is readable; otherwise it would not have caught the public fancy.[27]

Pencarrow and its successors, *Tides of Youth* (1933), *Winds of Heaven* (1934), and *Kelly Pencarrow* (1939) constitute a pioneering dynastic saga, dealing with the domestic, romantic, and occupational histories of an individual family as it consolidates (and occasionally dissipates) its power during three generations, from the early days of Wellington to the beginning of the Second World War. The first volume, focusing on the founding pioneers, Matthew and Bessie Pencarrow, and on the ascendancy of their sons and daughters — especially Miles (later Sir Miles) Pencarrow, who becomes a prosperous and powerful Wellington lawyer — has the broadest chronological sweep. In the second and third volumes, in which the narrative advances to the First World War and then to the mid-Depression years, the grandchildren occupy centre stage, with two strongly drawn rebellious central characters, Kelly and Genevieve, children of Miles and Norah. In the fourth volume, which introduces a new generation during the period of the ascendancy of the Labour Government in the second half of the 1930s, a considerable weakening of the initial drive of the series occurs, as if the author's own interest were flagging. Despite the title, such coherence as the novel achieves resides in the now ageing figure of Genevieve, who has become a forthright, and on occasion acerbic, commentator on the foibles of other family members.

There is a powerful implication throughout the series that the ramifying history of the Pencarrow family parallels the history of European colonization of New Zealand. Māori are almost completely excluded from this history, which represents civilization in New Zealand as an alliance of the Pencarrow's agricultural interests with the city-based professional and commercial interests represented by the legal firm of Miles Pencarrow. There is also a potential contradiction throughout (as in all family sagas) between the short-term temporal pattern of episodes, in which individual rivalries and confrontations are often so intense that the dynasty seems on the point of collapse, and the overarching pattern of cyclical repetitions — so often carried by women as the stable, matriarchal, domestic centre of the action — that frames the text. However, the overwhelming feeling is of celebration. The first three novels are remarkably skilled in their manipulation of local conflict, exploiting it to the full but knowing when and how to absorb it into the novel's powerful general illusion of a universal drama of civilization and progress.[28] It is the lack of any conscious engagement with ideas in the novels, their seemingly endless proliferation of domestic episodes told with humour and pathos (scenes of childhood, romantic entanglements, marriage and family crises, death), which in the end makes them such powerful ideological statements of their time, and which explains their immense appeal to middle-class readers at the height of the Depression. E.M. Smith commented astutely on the historical ambience of the series:

> [It] is not so much based on actual history as placed in an historical atmosphere which has not enough substance to get the authoress into difficulties with any authorities upon the subject, but which is typical enough of New Zealand to make most readers feel that it is true.[29]

Scanlan's novels have nothing of Jean Devanny's or Jane Mander's analytical interest in their material, nor of Robin Hyde's and Edith Lyttleton's historical curiosity and questioning. Politics, economics, race relations — even the workings of the two central institutions on which the prosperity of the family is based: farming and the law — barely touch the novels in their own terms, but simply provide occasions for the unfolding of a drama whose true centre lies in the power relations of the domestic life of the family. It is only in the fourth novel, where Scanlan allows Genevieve to articulate a largely negative view of New Zealand's new Labour Party politics of the Welfare State (that it will undermine the independence of working people and of the young, and 'kill enterprise, ambition, initiative')[30] that the otherwise 'invisible' political assumptions of the saga as a whole are made clear.

After a decade in which she had produced lengthy novels at the rate of one a year, Scanlan's last five were produced at a much more leisurely pace. The three New Zealand novels among them rehearsed what was by now familiar territory. *March Moon* (1944) is the most 'pastoral' of all her novels. Set in the locale of the author's childhood (near Picton), it traces the development of a youthful romance against a background of intense hostility between an eccentric middle-aged couple (brother and sister), on an inherited farm which has gradually fallen into decay because of their longstanding feud. Like much of Scanlan's fiction, which portrays a relatively narrow middle-class world as representative of New Zealand, the novel never quite avoids the impression of overwriting trivial events, sentimentalizing the commonplace.

The Rusty Road (1948) is the best of the later novels, capturing something of the ambience of the Pencarrow books, as a small-scale family chronicle set on a modest farm near Wellington, with its mixture of domestic and romantic events involving births, marriages, and deaths. At its centre is the wise matriarchal figure of Katty Harty, who through long experience becomes 'the focal centre of [the] home; its unifying influence, and its strength under stress'. She practises an ethic of compromise, not holding 'too tight a rein' on her husband and children, and learning to 'assert her influence, but in subtle ways', 'not defiantly, just a little manoeuvring'. *The Rusty Road* primarily attempts to convey the stresses to which any 'normal' marriage is subject (including an episode in which Katty experiences the temptation of sexual indiscretion with a travelling salesman), while defending and celebrating the institution itself. The novel preaches, none too subtly, a kind of pragmatic ethic of tolerance *within* traditional moral conventions: 'Without system, life would be chaotic, yet a rigid adherence to plans was impossible.'[31]

Ngaio Marsh published her first novel, *A Man Lay Dead*, in 1934. It was followed by thirty-one more novels, written over five decades. By 1949, when the millionth copy of her books was sold, she had already become one of the four *grandes dames* of international detective fiction, alongside Agatha Christie, Dorothy Sayers, and Margery Allingham.

Only four of Marsh's novels are set in New Zealand. *Vintage Murder* (1937) occurs in 'Middleton', a small New Zealand town, and *Colour Scheme* (1943) in a thermal spa on the Northland coast. *Died in the Wool* (1944) turns to a high-country South Island sheep station, and *Photo-Finish* (1980) has a spectacular lake setting in Westland. Most of her other novels are set in England, in genteel rural or urban locales, and several have theatrical settings, reflecting the author's other abiding passion, the theatre. However, there is often a kind of displacement of New Zealand material into novels otherwise remote from the New Zealand scene. The backgrounds of *Enter a Murderer* and *The Nursing-Home Murder* (1935) were provided by her local experiences (the former set in a theatre, the latter in a convalescent hospital). *A Surfeit of Lampreys* (1941) was based on an eccentric aristocratic family the author had first met in New Zealand, and it also includes a central New Zealand character, a kind of innocent abroad, who directs the reader's sympathies throughout. New Zealanders also turn up in a considerable number of the later novels. Martyn Tarne in *Opening Night* (1951) — dedicated to 'the Management and Company of the New Zealand Student Players of 1949' — is a young actress recently arrived from New Zealand, who plays a significant role as a catalyst of events in the novel. Jenny Williams (a New Zealand postgraduate scholar and teacher) plays a similar role in *Dead Water* (1963). Peregrine Jay, a passionate young Shakespearean director from New Zealand, appears in *Death at the Dolphin* (1967) (alongside a part-Māori drama student) and again in Marsh's last novel, *Light Thickens* (1982).

Despite the often-expressed view, especially among New Zealand critics, that Marsh's was an essentially outdated colonial Anglophile sensibility,[32] there was in fact considerable complexity in the relationship between 'New Zealand' and 'English' elements in her life and art, and her affinities were much closer to the new high-cultural nationalist-realist impulses of the 1930s and 1940s than to the earlier literature of colonial exile. Her sensibility was divided. There was a division between her work as a popular detective novelist (living overseas for half of each year), in which she addressed a large international readership, and her work as a theatrical director in New Zealand, where she struggled to establish a tradition of locally-based professionalism in an environment which was the polar opposite of her fictional milieu. There was also a division of purpose within her imagination. Her first effort at a novel was a piece of New Zealand realism that aimed to break from 'the well-worn rails of the colonial novel' and confront what she called 'the problem of background': the need to construct characters who 'grew out of' their surroundings, and to present landscape as expressing 'the spiritual and mental experiences of human beings'.[33] She never published this novel, and afterwards resisted the temptation to turn to 'straight' fiction, but these ideas about New Zealand literature remained constant in her thinking. They recur in her New Zealand novels (in comments voiced by her detective-hero, Roderick Alleyn), in a published 'Dialogue with Allen Curnow' of 1945,[34] and, later, in her autobiography, *Black Beech and Honeydew*.

Most revealing of all, in this context, was the *nature* of her contribution to the detective novel as a genre. Essentially, she took the classic plot-centred conventions of the genre, as it had been popularized by Doyle, Christie, and Sayers, and nudged it in the direction of realism, in the direction of precisely those elements of expressive characterization, human interest, and naturalness of background that she saw as necessary for a 'straight' novel. Much of this realism lay in the invention of a detective (Alleyn) of 'comparative normalcy', without 'mannerisms tied like labels round his neck', as had occurred with the 'celebrated eccentrics' of Doyle and others.[35] In his thoroughgoing professionalism, his empirical approach to crime solving, his compassion and understated humour, and in the occasional glimpses the author allows us of his domestic life with Agatha Troy (who has her own career as a painter), Alleyn anticipated the more realistic detective-stereotype of post-war British television drama. Marsh also developed a supple language which could be witty and intelligent, register subtle or sudden emotional shifts, and convey dialogue effortlessly and economically. Increasingly, too, her novels expressed an ironic social focus which allowed, as Julian Symons put it, 'a little light from the outside world'[36] into the relatively closed, genteel worlds of the form she inherited.

Crime fiction, for Marsh, was thus never simply a form of escape. She was always interested in theoretical readings of the genre (psychological and anthropological, as well as political), but deeply sceptical of them, and in this she was true to the modernist intellectual formation which linked her to the new impulses in New Zealand literature in the 1930s and 1940s. In comments about her own detective fiction, she saw herself as practising an 'impure' form of the genre derived from Wilkie Collins and Dickens, in which a concern for three-dimensional characterization tends to override the demands of the clue-puzzle. Although she always presents the 'pure', Poe-derived, classical form as a higher (because more aesthetically unified) form, and the 'impure' form as a weaker hybrid, constantly torn between the demands of character and of plot, it is also clear that Marsh regards the hybrid form as more realistic and more serious. Characterization in the 'pure' form is two-dimensional, and in the presentation of death the 'pure' form observes a kind of 'necrophiliac etiquette': 'The horror but not the unspeakable degradation of death is admitted.' True to the 'impure' mode, Marsh also commented that she invariably started her novels not with a plot, but with people, in settings 'as far as possible within the confines of my own experience':

> Very often I begin to write about these people in their immediate situation with no more than the scantiest framework for a plot and its denouement. This is a cockeyed method of setting about a strictly conventional form and it lands one with a great deal of re-writing. But it's the only way I can work and I fancy it illustrates one of the occupational hazards of the second stream of crime-writing.[37]

Marsh's other reservation about the 'impure' form is not so much technical as moral, an anxiety about the 'endless duplicity' the author practises around the guilty person, in a mode which otherwise relies on a truthful presentation of characters-in-the-round:

> While the author can be honest, penetrating and exhaustive about all the characters except one, he is obliged to be devious and misleading in his handling of that one — the guilty person. It is this flaw, I think, that sets three-dimensional detective writing, however brilliant, in a minor category.[38]

This tension is focused especially in Alleyn's contradictory relationship to Marsh's narratives. In novel after novel he argues that the consideration of motive (one of the primary means by which characters-in-the-round are developed) is irrelevant in solving crimes, preferring to work by an empirical testing of hypotheses based on the patient accumulation of facts. Alleyn's is a bleakly pessimistic view of human nature: almost anyone is capable of murder, there is always a plethora of motives, and in any case the motives which drive people to murder are extraordinarily varied and often contradictory. Consideration of motives, in Alleyn's view, thus invariably obscures, complicates, and inhibits the process of identifying the actual murderer from amongst the many others who, the more that is known of their background circumstances and psychology, *might* have committed the crime. Alleyn is thus both Marsh's protagonist *and* her antagonist, his victories an exposure of the author's own 'endless duplicity' — even collusion — in the structure of lies, evasions, and silences that protect the murderer from discovery.

The leisurely pace of Marsh's openings (usually the murder does not occur until at least a third of the way into the narrative, and often much later than that) is also an expression of her interest in scene-setting and character development. Where her novels work most successfully, the denouement, after Alleyn's arrival on the scene with his empirical investigative procedures, goes hand in hand with a continuing retrospective revelation of her characters' lives. *Died in the Wool* is a fine example of this technique. In this novel, an unsolved murder mystery on a high country sheep station in Canterbury is re-opened, as a result of the inability of the main characters (all except the murderer, who lies) to live with the aftermath of suspicion and scandal. For close to half the novel, Alleyn functions as a psychoanalyst, waiting for a key fact to emerge as the main characters reconstruct their different understandings of the personality of the dead woman, whose enigmatic portrait dominates the setting where the self-revelations occur, and where a typical plethora of motives — money, sex, espionage — emerge. It is only at this point that new events are set in motion and a trap set in place to identify the person whose self-revelation is a lie, an elaborate subterfuge. And these events go along with a continuing unfolding of the past, and of the personality of the dead woman.

Died in the Wool is dedicated to 'The lexicographers', an indication of the correctness Marsh aimed at in her use of the technical language of the shearing shed, and of her lifelong interest in language. Her handling of New Zealand English in her earlier novels is uneven, often serving as a crude comic foil for the educated standard English of Alleyn, and in fact one of the reasons she once gave for not setting more of her books in New Zealand was the poverty of New Zealand speech:

> I write very largely in dialogue, and I'm afraid I do think, by and large, that the New Zealand dialogue is monotonous and I do think that the average New Zealander has a very short vocabulary . . . . They haven't got many individual idiosyncrasies in expressing themselves.[39]

The Anglocentric side of Marsh's sensibility is nowhere more strongly revealed than in this attitude to New Zealand speech, whose alleged deficiencies she never tired of berating, on radio and elsewhere. Her own linguistic imagination, in her novels, lends itself to sophisticated play with manners and ideas. She delights in flamboyant (often theatrical) characters who display their idiosyncrasies in their speech, and thus function as foils for the dispassionate, coolly pragmatic Alleyn. Marsh's own voice, one suspects, lies somewhere between these extremes. On occasion, key clues in her novels are linguistic (the most ingenious, turning on an archaic usage of the word 'lover' as a verb, occurs in *Off With His Head*, 1957), and her novels are rich in literary allusions, occasionally basing themselves wholly on a literary idea: the biography of Shakespeare in *Death at the Dolphin*, and the interpretation of *Macbeth* in *Light Thickens*. Discussions of Freud, Jung, and mythology occur in the novels, and scholarly sources are often acknowledged in prefatory notes. Most interesting of all, in the linguistic play in the novels, are the patterns of cross-reference from one novel to another, and the recurrence of minor characters. Almost all of her novels have a literary self-consciousness of their genre explicitly built into them, either through characters who are themselves readers of thrillers, or through Alleyn's consciousness of himself as a 'real life' detective whose methods expose the myths and stereotypes of other merely fictional detectives.

The author who most rivalled Ngaio Marsh in the level of sheer professional skill she achieved in her chosen genre — the novel of romantic mystery and suspense — was Marsh's close contemporary, Dorothy Eden. Eden also came from Canterbury, where she was born in 1912 and grew up on a farm, before leaving home at the age of sixteen to work as a secretary in legal offices (in Ashburton, then Christchurch) from the time of the Depression to the end of the Second World War. By then she had published several novels (the first in 1940), and decided to devote herself full-time to a professional career as a writer. She moved to London in the 1950s, where she remained for the rest of her life, publishing her fortieth novel in the year of her death (1982) as well as writing short stories prolifically for the international magazine market.

By 1960 Eden had published nineteen novels, eight of them with New Zealand settings or associations. Her best-selling novel of that year, *Sleep in the Woods*, was an early settler romance set in Taranaki during the Land Wars. After this, however, when she had become permanently settled in London, almost all of her novels had Anglo-European settings, and included an increasing number of Gothically-tinged historical romances alongside the contemporary romantic mysteries. Several of the historical novels are set in Victorian England (*The Bird in the Chimney, Bella,* and *Speak To Me of Love*); others are set, variously, in Ireland at the time of the celebrated love affair of Parnell and Kitty O'Shea (*Never Call It Loving*), at Mafeking (*Siege in the Sun*), and in Peking during the Boxer Rebellion (*The Time of the Dragon*); and one is a Gothic novel of pioneering life in New South Wales (*The Vines of Yarrabee*). Apart from England, the settings of her contemporary novels include Italy, Ireland, and especially Scandinavia, the locale of Hans Christian Andersen's fairy tales (a long-time favourite author of Eden's, alongside the Brothers Grimm). It was not until her last novel, *An Important Family,* another Gothic historical romance, that she returned to a New Zealand setting, in fact to the home territory (the remote farming hinterland of Canterbury) of her very first novel, *Singing Shadows.*

Eden's special skill as a novelist is her manipulation of plot, especially her timing of the introduction of new events and of the release of bits of information about her characters, to create suspense and uncertainty. The typical general pattern of her Gothic romances is an initially casual destabiliza- tion of an apparently normal surface of events (a slightly unusual coincidence, a slightly ambiguous or evasive word or phrase or gesture amongst her characters), followed by an intensifying momentum in which the narrative is detached entirely from 'normality' and the heroine engulfed in a nightmare world of terror, menace, and macabre events, and often threatened with physical violence. Because the narratives remain close to the consciousness of their central characters, the reader is drawn particularly intimately into the destabilizing momentum, sharing the heroine's anxieties about whether she is initially overreacting to events, or even suffering from paranoid delusions, and then suspending disbelief as nightmare displaces the familiar world.

Eden draws on the whole panoply of Gothic tricks and devices to initiate and sustain her performances. In *Bride By Candlelight* (1954), set in an isolated, decaying homestead in Canterbury, threatening notes are slipped into the heroine's room, a woman is 'accidentally' burnt in a fire and then 'imprisoned' in a mental hospital, bizarre events take place at night when the power is cut off by snowstorms, and the characters include a handsome villain with a scarred face, and an apparently senile and demented elderly woman who lives in an upstairs room. The plot itself hinges on the impersonation of a dead man by his married brother, who attempts to contract a bogus marriage with the heroine in order to inherit money from her uncle. Although the novel is itself maimed, at the end, by its need to provide a longish explanation of events (in the later novels the denouements themselves carried such clarifications, without the need for clumsy explanatory interventions), it also includes a powerful characterization device which Eden increasingly exploited to intensify the sense of isolation and vulnerability experienced by her heroines: a male character who appears to be a loyal friend and confidant (and actually does turn out to be so), but who during the course of the nightmare also becomes an object of the heroine's anxieties and uncertainties. The device is used particularly effectively in *Waiting for Willa* (1970).

The conventional Gothic setting of the haunted house — the large, rambling edifice brooding over its shadowy secrets — repeatedly features at the centre of the novels. In *The Shadow Wife* (1968), set in Denmark, a mysteriously locked turret room eventually yields the secret which explains the motives of the villain in contracting a sham marriage with the heroine and then disowning her. In this novel, Eden points to the larger symbolic dimensions generally carried by such edifices in all of her novels, when she refers to the villain's 'smiling serenity covering the dark dungeons hidden within him'.[40] In *An Important Family* (1982), a woman addicted to laudanum is murdered by her husband, who wishes to marry the heroine. The murder occurs in a remote homestead which had once been the scene of the death of a woman in childbirth, whose large black cat survives to terrorize the room's new incumbent.

The other recurrent element in Eden's mode of Gothic romance (again, a 'classic' feature of the genre) is the repeated suggestion of fairy-tale events and atmosphere. Preternaturally heightened feelings are often invested in landscapes: the sinister lakes and forests of Scandinavia in *The Shadow Wife* and especially in *Waiting for Willa*, the snow-bound sub-alpine New Zealand settings of *Bride By Candlelight* and *An Important Family*, the Taranaki bush setting of *Sleep in the Woods*. The narratives often contain, at base, the simplest storylines from fairy tales, in which the heroine searches for, and eventually marries, Prince Charming. In both *Sleep in the Woods* and *An Important Family*, the heroines are Cinderellas from English and Irish servant-class backgrounds, who emigrate to colonial New Zealand seeking to better themselves through marriage; and both novels carry an implicit theme of New Zealand as a society without rigid class distinctions. Other fairy-tale elements occur simply in casual references and images. In *The Shadow Wife*, the heroine's situation evokes the image of the Lady of the Lake, and in *Waiting for Willa* there are repeated references to the Ice Maiden (of death).

Eden's novels impinge on the broader world of politics and society only in the most conventional ways, and only in terms of popular imperial stereotypes of 'famous' events, such as the Boxer Rebellion and the siege of Mafeking. In *The Shadow Wife*, the unmasking of the villain's past involves a history of Nazi collaboration during the war and of Viking racial arrogance, and in *Waiting for Willa*, the revelations relate to the operations of an international Stockholm-based Soviet spy network. In each case, as in *Bride By Candlelight* earlier, villainy is not simply the isolated act of an individual, but part of a network involving accomplices and fellow-conspirators and others (especially wives) terrorized into silence: such revelations of multiple villainy provide an essential element in Eden's plausible motivation of feelings of vulnerability, isolation, and paranoia in her heroines. In both *Sleep in the Woods* and *An Important Family*, the perspectives on New Zealand's nineteenth century history are equally conventional and Eurocentric, including (in the former) acknowledged elements of invention and embroidery in the account of Hauhau history, and (in the latter) an underlying criticism of the aristocratic villain's idealistic commitment to Wakefield's vision of colonization, for failing to take 'human nature' into account: 'the usual components of love and hate, greed, envy, bad tempers, craftiness, guile . . . . [The] perfect colony can't banish the things we all carry on our backs.'[41]

However, like all Gothic novels, Eden's novels imply a great deal about the politics of gender relations, and are unusually explicit in their presentation of sexuality, with a total absence of the moralizing endemic to the more conventional kinds of courtship and family romance. Although the goal of Eden's heroines is marriage, they are quite matter-of-fact in their acceptance of premarital sexual relations. *Bride By Candlelight*, for example, ends with the promise of marriage, but with the lovers actually about to sleep together: 'Darling, now I have only a cotton nightdress.' 'Even that,' he said briefly, 'is more than enough.'[42] In *An Important Family*, the heroine's relationship with the villain develops in intimacy throughout the novel (though it stops short of sexual relations), without moralizing on either Eden's or her heroine's part, despite the fact that he is married. In *Sleep in the Woods*, there are some remarkably explicit scenes in which one of the female characters fantasizes about the sexual attractiveness of young Māori men. However the overwhelming atmosphere of the novels is one in which the 'natural' sexual impulses women feel have to function and survive in a world where males are generally predatory and threatening, and often actually violent. In *Bride By Candlelight* the villain is a philanderer. In *Sleep in the Woods* the central conflict is between the heroine's desire to use marriage to advance her social status and her husband's brutal assertion of his sexual 'rights'. In *An Important Family* there is a strong suggestion of incest in the relationship of the villain to his sexually uninhibited, immature daughter, as well as to an adolescent girl he 'adopts' as his daughter after the other marries and returns to England.

In all of Eden's novels, the essential problem for the heroine is how to 'read' the language and gestures of the males she is surrounded by, how to recognize the tiniest clue or hint that might separate the man who is genuinely and selflessly interested in loving her, from the many others who profess to be so but are secretly concerned to manipulate, threaten, and abuse her. The most perfunctory, and least plausible, elements in Eden's novels are their happy endings.

Mary Scott (1888-1979), from the time she turned to writing novels in the early 1950s, away from the local sketches she had been publishing in newspapers for twenty years, also achieved a wide international readership, especially in Germany, Holland, and Scandinavia. But she always saw herself, unlike any of the writers previously discussed, as writing primarily for New Zealand readers, and was in fact New Zealand's first successful popular author to set and publish all her work there: five collections of 'Barbara' stories, presenting the comedy and pathos of life as a backblocks farmer's wife, three collections of playlets for use by Women's Institutes, and thirty-three novels, including five competent thrillers set in New Zealand and written in collaboration with the children's author, Joyce West. In a finely written autobiography, *Days That Have Been* (1966), Scott told the story of the grinding struggle of life on remote backblocks farms inland from Kawhia in the earlier decades of the century, and of her beginnings as a writer, prompted by the need to supplement the family income during the Depression years. The book also conveys, throughout, her vision of the essentially New Zealand social values she saw as originating in the country's rural communities, 'the unfailing kindness and help shown by everybody in times of crisis', which she celebrates even in the lightest of her 'light romances':

> In sickness, death, accident, or any disaster whatsoever, your neighbours stood by you and you by them. That was the unwritten law of the backblocks, and necessary for self-preservation.[43]

Although she was self-effacing about the 'fatal facility' of her writing, and frustrated at times by being 'thoroughly typed' as a 'light-hearted writer',[44] Scott did write one 'serious' novel in the late 1930s. Drawing on autobiography, but with primarily fictional events and dates, it was a realistic account of a woman's struggle to survive in the backblocks and become a writer, and was eventually revised and published in 1957 as *The Unwritten Book*. The title is intriguing: it refers, literally, to the book (with the grim title, *Toll*) which the protagonist never completes; but it also suggests that there might be another kind of 'narrative' of the backblocks, altogether grimmer, which Scott herself might have written if she had not chosen, instead, to focus on the domestic comedy of backblocks life. In *The Unwritten Book* the emphasis falls, unrelentingly, on dark events which hardly ever occur in her light novels: the death of the protagonist's husband in a bush accident, leaving her deeply traumatized and struggling bitterly to survive on her own for many years; the breakdown of their neighbours' marriage (the result of the wife's increasing frustration, as her husband withdraws dourly into an endless routine of farm work); illness, poverty, and the destructive toll of poor soil, animal disease, and natural disasters like fire, in an environment remote from the normal amenities of civilization.

On the rare occasions when such events occur in Scott's other fiction, they are always on the periphery of the narratives, or are presented in ways which emphasize the character-shaping qualities of the backblocks. The sharing of hardship brings spouses closer together. Remoteness brings out qualities of neighbourliness and community spirit. Improvised entertainment and social life, since it has to be actively made by the community, not passively consumed from outside, is more authentic and socially cohesive. And the absence of civilized amenities (with the exception of the telephone, a crucial 'social asset'[45] always present in the novels) encourages not only a spirit of resourcefulness largely absent or in decline in the cities and suburbs, but a sturdy quality of independence and a belief in values other than the materialistic.

Scott's early 'Barbara' stories make light comic play out of such perspectives, and are full of inventively contrived, largely domestic incidents in the life of a young, irrepressible backblocks wife in an environment in which she is continually thrust on to her own resources and wits. The sketches were published by the same firm, Reed, which popularized the comic 'Me and Gus' stereotypes invented by Frank Anthony in the 1920s, and they complement Anthony's male comic vision of rural life. Oddly, however, the comic foil for Barbara's ingenious schemings is provided not by another female character, but by her long-suffering husband, who narrates the stories with a mixture of mock exasperation and resignation. Probably quite intuitively, Scott thus hit on a format which in different ways appealed to both female *and* male readers, and to both rural and urban readers. It was not until Scott's first novel (*Breakfast at Six*, 1953) that she developed a female duo, the high-spirited Larry Lee and her more prosaic foil, the narrator, Susan Russell; and this pair regularly reappeared in novels throughout the rest of Scott's career, including her last (written twenty-five years after her first), *Board But No Breakfast* (1978).

The pattern of all the later novels is remarkably stable, and it represents a re-working, and a localizing, of older colonial conventions to a key phase in the *internal* social history of New Zealand. In the older colonial pattern, England represented 'civilization', against which and in terms of which the development of a pioneering society, and a pioneering 'character', was defined. In Scott's novels, 'civilization' is represented, wholly internally, by New Zealand's own now-established cities and suburbs. The older colonial polarity between Great Britain and New Zealand is thus replaced by a local polarity between town and country.

Very few of her characters are not New Zealanders, though there are occasional reminders of the older pattern. Colonel Gerard, a pompous, status-obsessed English pukka sahib in *Breakfast at Six*, learns true 'civilization' in the backblocks, and becomes an accepted member of the close-knit community at Te Rimu in the subsequent novels set there. His English cousin, Ursula Maitland, undergoes the same process in *Turkey at Twelve* (1968), but is only partially reformed, and returns to England. In most of the novels, however, the motif of emigration from England to New Zealand is replaced by the motif of an internal emigration, from city sophistication to backblocks freedom. Legacies occur frequently in Scott's novels, often enabling characters to give up nine-to-five city careers, even if only for a few months, in order to pursue long-held dreams of discovering their true selves in the country; but the legacies are almost always provided by the city-based wealth of deceased aunts and uncles in New Zealand, not England. By far the commonest adaptation of stereotype, however, is that of the colonial 'new chum'. The almost invariable pattern of Scott's novels entails the introduction of 'sophisticated' outsiders from the city (usually young women) who are ignorant of country ways and often innocently patronizing, and full of missionary zeal to bring the benefits of civilization to the natives. The outsiders then undergo a process of self-discovery through their involvement in the affairs of the local community, most commonly through the complications of a romantic entanglement whose satisfactory resolution is the final sign that they have fully absorbed the new values of the backblocks.

In *Breakfast at Six*, the 'new chum' thus abruptly transplanted from the city is the narrator herself, a youthful Susan Russell, recently married to a stolid local farmer, and she gradually learns the values of the backblocks through her close friendship with her ebullient neighbour, Larry Lee. Romantic interest is provided, alongside the domestic action of settling into marriage, by the wives' engineering of the marriage of Anne Gerard to yet another taciturn backblocks farmer and returned serviceman, in defiance of the wishes of Anne's father, the English colonel. These characters, together with Miss Adams, who runs the local store and telephone service, provide the 'core' backblocks community around which later novels are built, and against which outsiders are tested, to be welcomed into the community or excluded from it. In *Dinner Doesn't Matter* (1957) there is a particularly carefully contrived reformation of two outsiders who are polar opposites: Susan's younger sister, an immature, flighty, 'modern girl' from the city, who needs to learn a sense of responsibility, and Rachel Wayne, also from the city, who is overly serious, overly efficient, mousy, and needs to learn to enjoy life. Backblocks life transforms both these outsiders by offering, in the end, a kind of happy medium, confirmed as always by the suitable marriages each makes. Throughout the novels set at Te Rimu, which also include *Tea and Biscuits* (1961) and *Strangers for Tea* (1975), the main values of backblocks life are located in the domestic environment of parents and children, whose security is rooted in the seasonal round of farm work and the reliability of neighbours in emergencies, and whose pleasures are confirmed in the social life of dances, Christmas parties (*Turkey at Twelve*), marriages, picnics, Women's Institute theatricals (*Breakfast at Six*), and such larger district events as race meetings and dog trials.

Politics and economics impinge only lightly on this world, whose values are primarily those of a *petit bourgeois* ethos of hard work and individual initiative (the later novels introduce increasingly negative comments about the Welfare State). Nevertheless, Scott is careful to introduce into all her novels elements designed to qualify what might otherwise be seen as a simple idealization of rural New Zealand. One of these elements is the social range of backblocks life, though it rarely includes Māori communities except on the periphery. In almost all the novels there are explicit rural disparities of wealth and class, with their attendant snobberies and exclusions. An *internal* breaking down of such barriers often occurs (again, primarily through romance actions), *alongside* the reformation of outsiders. Another complicating element is provided by gender differences. Backblocks life is not only rigidly divided along gender lines (husbands the providers of economic security for the family, wives the makers of family and social life); it also contains its share of unreconstructed characters: philandering bachelor-farmers, and immature, status-driven young rural women who become rivals to the heroine in her pursuit of the few decently eligible bachelors around.

Although Scott saw herself as becoming 'thoroughly typed', her novels are remarkably inventive in the range of events they draw on to set the pattern in motion. They also trace a kind of internal social history of the backblocks themselves, the breaking down of remoteness, during the quarter century over which Scott wrote them: the improvement of roads, the modernization of amenities and services (in *Turkey at Twelve* Miss Adams's country store has become a small supermarket), the influx of tourists. So much so that in one of the last novels she wrote, *Away From It All* (1977), Scott explores the questions: do the backblocks still exist? did they *ever* exist? The answer is unequivocally provided by the outsider figure, Adrian Medway, a light novelist who has come to the country to write 'the Great New Zealand Novel':

> You might live all your life in the big city and not meet with such spontaneous friendliness. They tell me the backblocks don't exist any more, but I know of a community a little out of the way of traffic and excitement where live a few people who have cut themselves off from the rat race, and are the happier for it.[46]

Scott's novels are rich in their allusions, throughout, to the literary culture and reading habits of New Zealanders, and a central aspect of her town-country polarity is an opposition between high culture (which belongs in cities) and popular culture (whose province is the country). Susan Russell, also an aspiring writer, mocks currently fashionable authors read by the intellectuals in cities (including Eliot and Yeats), and the obsession of sophisticated urban writers to produce the Great New Zealand (realistic) Novel, since by definition such writers are locked out of the 'real' New Zealand of the backblocks. New Zealand's literary culture also provides a subsidiary theme in the trilogy of 'Freddie' novels Scott wrote in 1956, 1960, and 1965 (*Families are Fun, No Sad Songs*, and *Freddie*). In the voice of the independent-spirited Anna Lorimer (a light novelist in these novels, who lives in the backblocks) Scott perhaps presents her strongest defence of the 'truth' she saw her own family romances as exploring:

> Marriage troubles aren't hereditary. Some of them are very happy and most of them are all right, in spite of our modern novelists.[47]

And beneath the ironies in the following passage, which alludes unmistakably to the killing of a cat in Frank Sargeson's 'Sale Day', Scott implies very clearly that Anna Lorimer's rural romances, for all their 'lightness', embody a realism that is superior to the fake realism of the high-cultural intellectuals writing in the city:

> 'I'm quite content to amuse my readers harmlessly and write about people and things I know. Not what the intelligentsia approves.'
> 'But you read a lot of modern stuff,' Stephen persisted.
> 'And admire a great deal of it, but it's not for me. My experience has been regrettably limited. I've never known anyone who would put a live cat into a hot stove, and my

521

friends don't seem to murder their mistresses or seduce each other's wives. Now, don't let's talk about dull things. What about those horses, Stephen?'[48]

The 1950s: Four Romance Writers

In their own specialized popular forms, Marsh, Eden, and Scott dominated the 1950s and 1960s, and all continued writing strongly throughout the 1970s. In the 'mainstream' form of light romance and the family novel, the 1950s were transitional years, before the virtual takeover of the market for light romance by the firm of Mills and Boon from the 1960s onwards, as the influence of other publishers in the field declined. By the mid-1950s Peacocke and Scanlan had ceased writing, and Rees's popularity had waned, but there were a considerable number of other romance authors who were now widely read, and whose publishing history often reflected the wider shift taking place in the international market. Dulce Carman (1883-1970) continued the New Zealand connection established by Rees with the firm of Wright and Brown. Dorothy Quentin wrote nearly sixty novels between 1939 and 1969, all of them published by Ward, Lock (Peacocke's publisher), before shifting briefly at the end of her career to Mills and Boon. Mavis Winder published twenty-five novels between 1949 and 1973: some under the name of Mavis Areta (for Wright and Brown), others under the name of Mavis Winder (for Herbert Jenkins, then Robert Hale), often in co-publication with Reed or Whitcombe and Tombs. Less prolifically, Grace Phipps (1901-1983) began her career in the early 1950s with comedies of family life (suburban equivalents of Scott's rural domestic comedies), then shifted in the mid-1960s to more conventional courtship romances, especially of the doctor-nurse variety, with the firm of Robert Hale.

Like Scott, Dulce Carman turned to writing novels relatively late, after many decades during which, despite the demands of raising a family (in Dannevirke, then Hastings), she published hundreds of stories and numerous children's serials in local newspapers and magazines. She was born in England, and emigrated with her parents to New Zealand in 1892. An early novel was published in 1924, but the next did not appear until 1948, and it was followed by a further twenty-five over the next two decades — all, like Scott's, with settings in rural areas of the North Island. Although Carman preferred to describe her novels as 'family stories — suitable for all ages' rather than light romances,[49] any further resemblance to Scott is purely coincidental.

Carman's special field was what her publishers called the 'romance of Maoriland', although the author, somewhat astonishingly, seems to have seen herself as a realist, claiming never to have 'any definite plot in mind before starting to write', and advising writers 'to allow their stories to portray the life about them and their characters to live and move amid scenes of which the authors themselves have first hand knowledge'.[50] In fact, the actions and resolutions of her novels are often so bizarre, and so much complicated material (of the kind that would normally fill a Victorian three-decker) is crammed into the space of little more than 200 pages, that there is almost no room for character development, and it is often difficult to discern any central theme. The plot of *Neath the Maori Moon* (1948) hinges on an initial deathbed revelation (which turns out to be false) that the heroine, raised in England to inherit the manorial acres, has Māori blood in her — a revelation that so shatters her that she promptly flees in despair to stay with friends in Hawke's Bay, under an assumed name. Here, the manager of the very next farm, also living under an assumed name, turns out to be the 'real' (not racially tainted) heir to the selfsame manorial acres. The heroine, as the plot thickens, is pursued to New Zealand by her villainous stepsister who, jealous that a relationship might develop between the two which will thwart her own design to marry the real heir, repeatedly besmirches the heroine's reputation, then attempts to have her killed by a runaway pedigree bull, and finally tries to run her over with her car. In the novel's final revelations, equally bizarre, it turns out that the heroine is not half-caste at all ('Then I — am white — *all* white!', she whispers), and is thus free to marry the heir. In fairy-tale fashion, she returns to the English estate in the novel's final scene, and the purity of the aristocratic blood line is at last seen to have been preserved.

Improbable as it might seem, Carman developed a substantial reputation as an author who wrote sympathetically about race relations in New Zealand, and claimed to have consulted Māori elders to check that her Māori lore was accurate. Her sympathy is present only occasionally at rhetorical moments on the surface of the novels. Their fundamental perspective is deeply patronizing, based on an Anglocentric idea of assimilation in which Māori are seen as in need of special assistance to learn the values of Pākehā civilization. In *The Maori Gateway* (1963), a sequel to *The Wailing Pool* (1961), the Pākehā foster-son of a Waikato chief plans to set up 'a small community of the best brains in the tribes, [to] teach them the white man's *outlook* on life, and how to appreciate the fact that life is not a series of hand-outs, but that where benefits are received, payment must be made, and responsibilities accepted'. The aim of this community will be to teach farming skills, employing Māori only, except for 'one or two super-grade [white] men to direct operations, with integration in mind'. The chief not only approves this plan enthusiastically, but is described as having reared the foster-son for this very purpose ('to be a leader of the young Maoris of the Waikatos . . . a sort of scoutmaster to bring out the best in them'), and he donates a specially carved gateway as a symbol of 'a life of complete integration in all ways with the white man who lives beside him'.[51]

The other side of this Anglocentric moral vision of a 'fine Maori race' which might become integrated into society by leaving savagery behind and learning the arts of white civilization, is the actual animus often directed at contemporary Māori people, apart from those, like the Waikato chief, who support and articulate the integrationist position. In *The Tapu Tree* (1954) Māori are described as 'mostly of two calibres, the very good, and the lazy loafer', and in *The Maori Gateway*, despite a scene in which two young women are protected from a gang of local bodgies by three young Māori men, there are numerous heavily loaded comments on the behaviour of contemporary Māori:

> The trouble in the world today, so far as the Maori is concerned, is that he has too much money, too much time to waste, access to drink, which is fatal to them, and — insecurity.[52]

Just as Māori characters and events are invariably presented in sub-plots, subsidiary to the main actions of the novels, which centre on the property concerns and marital destinies of Pākehā characters, Māori legendary material is almost always appropriated out of its Māori cultural context in order to romanticize, and reinforce, the central Pākehā actions and destinies. The clearest example occurs in *The Tapu Tree*, a novel about a longstanding feud between two Pākehā families, with a typically convoluted pattern of unknown identities and a cross-weaving of romantic conflicts, whose moral purpose appears to be that 'the solution of all the world's problems could be summed up in one word — friendliness — being good neighbours'. The feud is finally resolved when long-buried gold is discovered beneath the mysterious tree, a tōtara, and shortly after the feuding families have been united and marriages confirmed, the tree suddenly falls. 'Its mission is ended', comments one of the characters.[53] This kind of cultural appropriation of local myth and legend has a long history in New Zealand writing, in popular fiction and in some 'serious' fiction, in children's literature, and in poetry, drama, and non-fiction. In the work of Carman, its underlying political and cultural meanings are especially clear.

Carman's view of race relations reflected the confident monocultural optimism of New Zealand in the 1950s. Dorothy Quentin's romances reflected this optimism in a different way, celebrating the country's post-war affluence and materialism and offering an image of New Zealand as a kind of paradisal private enterprise society. Quite a few of her many novels are set in rural New Zealand, especially in the Thames area, and others are set in England and Italy, occasionally focusing (as Rees had done) on the world of theatrical entertainment. She was also New Zealand's first author to specialize in the hospital romance. A novel like *Rainbow Valley* (1960) is typical. In it a young English woman goes to work at 'Rainbow Valley', a private children's hospital a hundred miles south-west of Auckland, where she eventually marries the local doctor-in-charge, after an appropriate series of misunderstandings involving a career-driven woman medical scientist and the seductive Latin American attractions of the jet-setting son and daughter of a visiting international philanthropist.

If the plot is flimsy, the celebration of New Zealand is not. From the moment the heroine glimpses the wonder of the newly-opened Auckland Harbour bridge as her flying-boat lands, the perfection of the country she has come to seems to know no limits. Auckland is like 'one of those old mediaeval tapestries, full of clear soft colours'. Queen Street has huge shop windows 'bright with beach wear and model frocks and men's sports' wear that shouted of America. Many of the gleaming big cars were American, too.' The doctor who meets her looks 'like Gregory Peck, her favourite screen actor', has a crimson Bentley 'with long rakish lines and plenty of chromium plating about it', and within minutes has informed her that in New Zealand 'we don't have the word "stranger" in our vocabulary':

> [Y]ou'll settle down in a country that doesn't admit any class-distinctions or colour-bar . . . and I mean that. Maoris here are just the same as ourselves — citizens of a new country, with the same opportunities.

As she travels to 'Rainbow Valley' she learns that in 'this great little country' New Zealanders 'spend every available moment in the garden and on the beaches':

> We have a forty-hour week. Shops and offices are closed all day Saturdays annd Sundays, so everyone can get out for the weekend.

Rural New Zealand is also paradisal, with 'small, clean towns set in the midst of miles of rolling pastoral country', all with 'wooden-verandah'd shops, petering out among the bright-painted cheerful bungalows set in their pretty gardens'; and the 'primeval forest' offers 'a world of indescribable beauty'. When the heroine arrives at the farmhouse next to the hospital it is as if Scott's backblocks do not exist. It has a 'stainless-steel kitchen with its hatch through to the simple dining room', and 'everything was electric — the washing machine, the washing-up machine, the cake-mixer . . . a mail-order home'. Even the routines of farm life are idyllic, as the heroine wakes to a morning that seems 'like the beginning of the world' and notices the 'orderly spectacle' of milking, in which 'even the animals seemed to be part of the disciplined team'.[54]

There is only one threat to this gadget-ridden, Americanized private enterprise paradise, and that is the socialist threat of the Welfare State. 'Dad's dream', the doctor-in-charge tells the heroine, was to maintain the hospital as a private concern:

> [H]e believed in people . . . .. He thought it was good for wealthy people to give, voluntarily, rather than have the money taxed out of them by the State. He thought it was nicer for the children to know they were being helped by loving benefactors, rather than by a Social Welfare Act.[55]

In the end, the threat to the hospital is avoided by the generosity of the international philanthropist, and paradise is confirmed, for the heroine, by marriage. What is significant, in such light romances, is the close relationship between the pattern of courtship and marriage, and the intensely conservative political status quo it reinforces. Quentin, following Rees, confirmed this pattern in all her New Zealand novels, and it was to be repeated, in seemingly endless variations, by many of the romance writers who followed.

In Mavis Winder's novels, where romantic resolutions are sometimes reinforced by a none-too-subtle Christian message about the values of home and family and the evil of divorce, there are occasional surface resistances to the pattern of a kind never found in Quentin. This is because Winder typically begins her narratives with a distinctly contemporary social problem, and because so much narrative intensity is invested in the moments of conflict these problems cause. In *Shadowed Journey* (1955), a happily married woman suddenly suffers a nervous collapse when her husband becomes infatuated (so she mistakenly believes) with another woman at work. Sent away to recuperate, she suffers amnesia as a result of the Tangiwai train disaster and is mistakenly identified in hospital as another woman. At the end she only just avoids marrying another man, before her husband discovers her and the marriage is restored. *Render Unto Caesar* (1957) also deals with marital breakdown, this time as a result of a financier-husband's obsessive pursuit of money and status, his neglect nearly precipitating a divorce when his wife becomes attracted to another man.

The Stubble Field (1956) and *The Glitter and the Gold* (1967) both have at their centre domineering older women, whose possessiveness threatens the well-being of the heroines. In the first, a foster-mother's persistent harshness towards the heroine from early childhood reduces her to a state of pathological timidity, until she is prompted to assert her independence and regain her self-respect by the foster-mother's son. In the second, which has slightly more subtlety, a lonely grandmother becomes pathologically obsessed with rearing her son's only child after the death of his wife, and uses the child unscrupulously in a campaign to thwart her son's remarriage. *The Gulf Between* (1958) deals with the relationship between a young woman who has inherited a large department store in Christchurch, and an embittered man gaoled for embezzlement, whom she meets as a prison visitor. There is a sharp emphasis on the ostracism he suffers after his release, and on his difficulties in regaining employment, although the novel ends conventionally with the revelation of his innocence.

In *Folly is Joy* (1973), one of Winder's late novels, the theme is the generation gap, and the action involves the gradual reformation of an orphaned heroine who initially revolts against her aunt's upbringing of her — rejecting convention, baiting authority, and joining anti-Vietnam War demonstrations. Although innocent, she then finds herself arrested at Christchurch Airport for carrying drugs, which she believes were planted on her by a young medical student she met on the aeroplane. Bitter about her conviction, she eventually comes across the young man again (he is now a doctor with a promising research career), and blackmails him into promising to marry her, as a means of revenge and of regaining status in society. The rest of the novel, which brings her into intense conflict with the young man's snobbish and wealthy Takapuna parents, traces the gradual transformation of the relationship, despite the initial bitterness and hatred on both sides, into a conventional romantic pattern.

Although Winder's novels invariably end with the neatness of moral fables, there is considerable pressure from the material she works with — marital and family problems, generation breakdowns, and acquisitive behaviour — to resist such easy containment. The anti-Vietnam War rebel, who thumbs her nose at conventional morality and fights ostracism after her drugs conviction, is considerably livelier, as a character, than the sugary romantic heroine she becomes at the end. The result is that, overall, the kind of contemporary 'New Zealand' conveyed in Winder's novels is extremely different from Quentin's unproblematic celebrations of affluence.

Grace Phipps, in her best-known early fiction of the 1950s, focused less on courtship than on marriage, and on the humour and sentiment (from a housewife's point of view) of managing husbands and raising children and adolescents in the burgeoning quarter-acre suburban house-and-gardens of the period. Her early books were primarily episodic in the manner of Scott's *Breakfast at Six*, reflecting the origins of much of their material in serial journalism, and they seem refreshingly unselfconscious in comparison with either Quentin or Winder. Eve McCullock, the central character in *Marriage With Eve* (Reed, 1955) and its sequels, and Molly Craig in *The Women of the Family* (Reed, 1956), are both sagely benevolent suburban matriarchs very much in the mould of Scanlan's and Scott's rural wives-and-mothers, who are deeply committed to the values of home and family. The comedy and irony of events, in Phipps's work, invariably reinforce those values. In one of the episodes of *Marriage With Eve*, entitled 'Marriage is a Career', Eve is initially envious of an old school friend who appears to have made a glamorous and successful career as a journalist, but after finding that the woman is deeply unhappy she reflects:

> I suppose making a success of marriage and bringing up a family to be a credit to the community is just about as important a job for a woman as becoming famous.[30]

In another episode, Eve's husband receives a promotion in his insurance job, after what seems a disastrous series of culinary mishaps when the manager comes to dinner, because the manager 'thinks a family has a steadying influence on a man', and in 'The Girl Friend' Eve learns that the best way to ensure that her sons do not get involved with girls of whom she disapproves is not to preach. Towards the end of the novel the family moves from St Albans to a small orchard on the outskirts of Christchurch, seeking a less materialistic lifestyle, and Phipps allows Eve to voice her 'deeper emotions', which lay at the heart of the book's appeal to women readers in the 1950s:

> She could prattle, nineteen to the dozen, about the small things of life, but concerning her deeper emotions, she was inarticulate.
> She wanted to tell Sam that she was proud of his integrity, of the way he'd handed out those bonuses in the face of his own misfortune, of the sort of courage he'd had to throw up a good-paying position in the city and take on an orchard because he thought that was a better way to live. She was proud of their four boys, of the old-fashioned love and unity that bound them all together. She was proud that, at the core of their being, there was faith in God.

Sam blew out another cloud of smoke and looked at his wife. He understood, without any telling, what she was thinking.[57]

The Women of the Family traces very similar themes, and gives food- and tea-making rituals even greater prominence. No less than sixteen domestic events and crises (ranging from revelations of pregnancy and death to the announcement of business failure and of crises in a younger daughter's romantic life) are talked through, celebrated, or resolved over cups of tea, and Phipps's target readership is regaled with regular accounts of the preparation of roasts, stews, scones, apple turnovers, fish pie, marmalade, and gooseberry jam. In her later novels, Phipps specialized in the more conventional genre of the doctor-nurse romance, suppressing much of the humour which often lightened the sentimentality of the earlier books. In her last, *Nurse Penney's Patients* (1981), the main theme is abortion. The novel is little more than a moral tract, using the romance pattern (and Nurse Penney's manipulation of her pregnant flatmate's relationships) to ensure that happy marriage is a reward for refusing the options either of abortion or of adopting the baby out.

The 1960s and after

In genres other than light romance, the period after 1960 was marked by an upsurge in the number of new writers, though none matched either the authority or anything like the quantity of books of earlier authors. The strongest growth, in the wake of Ngaio Marsh's achievement, was in the thriller. In the last eight years of her life Elizabeth Messenger (?1909-1965) wrote nine thrillers (as well as an historical novel, *Golden Dawns the Sun*, 1962, set in Otago and based on family papers), and she was the first author to attempt to acclimatize the crime genre wholly to New Zealand settings, alongside the collaborative efforts of Mary Scott and Joyce West in the early 1960s. Beginning with the Nelson-Marlborough locales she knew intimately (Queen Charlotte Sound for *Murder Stalks the Bay*, 1958, and Takaka for *Dive Deep for Death*, 1959), Messenger then shifted to tourist locations, a shrewd move which enabled her to introduce overseas characters for the benefit of an international readership: a fishing lodge at Taupo in *Material Witness* (1959), the Bay of Islands in *A Heap of Trouble* (1963), and Fiordland in *Uncertain Quest* (1965).

The 1960s also saw a significant increase in the number of male authors in the field of popular fiction, though with the exception of Barry Crump, none matched the achievements of the major women writers in the field. Simon Jay (a pseudonym for Colin Alexander) produced a successful thriller in 1964, *Death of a Skin Diver* (in which the detective is a pathologist), and followed it with an espionage thriller set in Auckland, *Sleepers Can Kill* (1968), both novels appearing from Marsh's publisher, Collins. Terence Journet wrote a number of thrillers in the 1960s and 1970s, and in the early 1970s Colin Peel produced the first of a number of novels based on contemporary international events, including espionage (*Adapted to Stress*, 1973), nuclear power struggles (*One Sword Less*, 1973), and the international oil crisis (*Flameout*, 1976). George Joseph, whose sporadic career as a novelist and short story writer (alongside a career in law) had begun much earlier, in the 1930s, produced a number of sex-and-violence thrillers for the American Bloodhound series in the later 1950s (most of them set in the United States), and turned to the New Zealand scene in 1957 with *Lie Fallow My Acre*. He continued to produce locally-based novels sporadically thereafter, including *Trial and Error* (1978), a courtroom thriller written with considerable urbanity and professional skill.

In the 1980s, the most distinguished successor to these various crime writers, along with Colin Peel, was Laurie Mantell, who published her first thriller, *Murder in Fancy Dress* (set in Lower Hutt) in 1978. Throughout the 1980s she continued to produce highly readable thrillers — their titles always reminiscent of Marsh's — distinguished by the ingenuity of their plotting and solutions, by their convincing outward reference to the contemporary social context in which crimes of violence occur, and by the developing characterization of her detective, Steven Arrow and his colleagues.

Although the thriller on occasion includes elements of mystery and suspense, there have been few successors to Dorothy Eden in New Zealand. One exception was Miriam MacGregor, who in the late 1960s and early 1970s wrote half a dozen novels, with New Zealand settings, in the Eden mould (a heroine as protagonist, subject to personal threats of violence, in mysterious Gothically-tinged settings), before she turned to light romances for Mills and Boon. However, there was quite a strong revival of the 'straight' adventure yarn, which had been largely in abeyance since the late nineteenth century except for the *Bulletin*-influenced work of writers like Frank Morton and Will Lawson in the earlier decades of the twentieth century, and the early fiction of Edith Lyttleton. Frank Bruno (St Bruno, 1910-1967), who described himself as pursuing a 'tough, unhallowed career' as, variously, 'a law clerk, cartoonist, hobo, professional fighter, feature writer, machine-gunner, lightning carica-turist, crime writer, columnist, and boxing and sports writer',[58] produced five lurid action novels in the early 1960s, set mainly in the nineteenth century. They include *The Hellbuster*, his best known, located in the Bay of Islands in 1843, *Black Noon at Ngutu*, a sensationalized treatment of the Land Wars in Taranaki in the 1860s, and *Fury at Finnegan's Folly*, an equally sensational portrayal of life on the West Coast goldfields in the 1860s.

James Tullett, writing at the same time, began with an historical novel, *Tar White* (1962), set on the Te Awaiti whaling station in the Marlborough Sounds (also the setting for James Heberley's narrative in Ian Wedde's *Symmes Hole*), and then turned to contemporary adventure stories relating to recently developed New Zealand industries, including aerial top-dressing in *Red Abbott* (1964), the forestry industry in *White Pine* (1965), and search-and-rescue operations in deer-stalking territory in *Hunting Black* (1966). More sophisticated (and more carefully researched) historical adventure narratives were written by James Sanders, from the early 1970s onwards. Sanders published an autobiography, *The Time of My Life*, in 1967, describing his early years in various farming jobs, his war experiences, and his post-war involvement in journalism and the advertising industry. His novels revisit the major subjects of New Zealand historical fiction, including early ships carrying convicts to Australasia (*The Green Paradise*, 1971, and *The Shores of Wrath*, 1972), the Coromandel gold rush (*High Hills of Gold*, 1973), whaling (*Kindred of the Winds*, 1973), and the Land Wars of the Waikato (*Fire in the Forest*, 1976).

New Zealand's best-selling male author by far, however, was Barry Crump, who wrote not in any of the standard adventure and action genres, but in an episodic, yarn-spinning mode primarily local in origin, although general models existed outside the country in American writers, and in the Australian sketches of Henry Lawson and his successors. Within New Zealand, this mode had been established quite early in journalism; and Lydia Wevers, elsewhere in this History, traces its continuities into the serious short fictions of Frank Sargeson. As a continuing popular form in the twentieth century, it had predecessors, for Crump, in the 'Me and Gus' sketches of Frank Anthony. It also survives (for a primarily female readership) in the 'Barbara' sketches of Mary Scott and the episodic 'Eve McCullock' novels of Grace Phipps. All of these authors were published by Reed (in what were clearly seen as distinct, complementary men's and women's markets for such fiction), and Reed also published Crump's books until the early 1970s, when he took over their marketing himself.

Crump's first book, *A Good Keen Man*, appeared in 1960 (its title quickly becoming part of the New Zealand vernacular), and it was followed immediately by *Hang On A Minute Mate* (1961). By 1962 each had sold nearly 50,000 copies, and within half a dozen years the former had been reprinted fourteen times and the latter nine. By 1972 twelve books had appeared. Thereafter there was something of a gap until new books began to appear in the 1980s, although the recycling of the earlier ones continued unabated. In 1990 Crump's total sales had been estimated at a million copies.[59]

The basic formula of a Crump story is relatively simple, though not the professional skill with which he continued to work towards producing variations of it.[60] In *A Good Keen Man* an apparently naïve male narrator, who finds life in the cities and suburbs stultifying and bureaucratic, describes a series of episodes in his life in the back-country Ureweras as a government-employed deer-culler. He is Man Alone, who values his independence above everything else. Initially a new chum to back-country life, he learns (always by experience, not by book-learning) to be inventive and resourceful, and becomes intimately knowledgeable about the bush, the terrain, the vagaries of climate and weather, the habits of the animals he hunts and of the dog who is his closest friend, and the quirks and foibles of the variety of characters (similarly on the run from city life) who are assigned each season to assist him. The popularity of the stories resided not only in the power of the myth of maleness they constructed (or reinforced) in the fantasies of city-based male readers, but also in the seemingly artless way the stories were told. The narrators speak a version of New Zealand male vernacular speech which is colloquial (but not excessively so — there is not a great deal of swearing in Crump's dialogue, and no obscenity), and which moves at a fairly rapid pace from one eight-to-ten-page, event-laden episode to another. Characterization, while not wholly rudimentary (especially as far as the narrators are concerned), remains fixed on externals.

Crump developed a considerable number of variations, always *within* this pattern, over successive books. In his second, *Hang On A Minute Mate*, he introduced the stylistic device of the yarn within a yarn. It gave him the freedom to range over a much greater variety of comic material, and enabled him to focus at least a little attention on the motivation of the narrator, Sam Cash, who passes on the dubious benefits of his experience to an increasingly dependent younger mate, Jack Lilburn. The books also vary the contexts in which independence, the avoidance of social ties of any kind, is asserted, occasionally with a slightly edged awareness of its consequences. In *Hang On A Minute Mate*, Sam Cash eventually opts out of a continuing relationship with Jack Lilburn ('We're getting to depend on each other a bit too much anyway. A man's only half a man when he can't live on his own.'[61]), and at the end, in gaol for failing to pay maintenance to his wife, he refuses even to see Jack when he comes to visit him.

In *Hang On A Minute Mate*, marriage is also a threat to the independence his male characters desire, a theme conveyed often with a great deal of stereotypical misogynist humour. *A Good Keen Girl* (1970), about a marriage that ends in disaster, conveys Crump's typical perspective. Although there are notional gestures towards the ignorance and shortcomings of the narrator, the overwhelming impression is that women are a completely different, unpredictable species. Crump loads the narrative against women by giving the wife a bizarre obsession with astrology: the husband's well-meaning obtuseness is thus opposed, without hope of success, to his wife's manic irrationality.

Puha Road (1981) includes a variation on the same theme. It begins with a shift of locality from the country to the city, and the narrative includes a variety of comic incidents in the lives of two itinerant male characters working at casual jobs around Auckland, before they decide to shift to Northland. Here Muxy, the narrator's mate, happily marries, only to be killed in a plane crash shortly afterwards. The overt message is that the eccentric Muxy's luck has run out: his adventures invariably have chance outcomes, since he is largely incapable of managing his own life. The covert message, however, seems specifically directed to marriage, and the consequences of relationships of any kind with women: the vitality the narrative has invested, throughout, in the eccentric Muxy, simply cannot survive marriage, even in as remote an environment as Puha Road.

*　　*　　*

By far the most vigorous growth from the late 1950s onwards occurred in the genre of light romance published by Mills and Boon, and to a lesser extent by the firm of Robert Hale. There were three especially prolific new New Zealand authors in the late 1950s and early 1960s: Ivy Preston, who wrote more than thirty novels through to the 1980s, Nora Sanderson, who specialized in doctor-nurse romances, and Essie Summers, the most famous of all New Zealand's authors of light romance. These were joined in the later 1960s and early 1970s by Mary Moore, Gloria Bevan, Rilla Berg, and Karin Mutch, and in the later 1970s and early 1980s by a new generation, including Rosalie Heneghan, Daphne Clair, Robyn Donald, and Susan Napier.

Essie Summers' first novel, whose title (*New Zealand Inheritance*) indicated a theme that was to run through all of them, was published in 1957, and more than fifty had been written by the mid-1980s when she retired from authorship. By 1981 her books had sold a remarkable seventeen million copies worldwide, and were available in at least a dozen languages.[62] In 1974 she published an autobiography, *The Essie Summers Story*, gossipy, entertaining, and rich in anecdotes about her life as the wife of a Presbyterian minister, and about her apprenticeship years as a contributor of articles, poems, and stories to local newspapers (the *Timaru Herald*, the *Christchurch Star*, the *Hawke's Bay Herald-Tribune*) and then to overseas weeklies. Summers also comments with engaging frankness about her practice as a writer, and offers a rare insight into the motivations and attitudes of an author of light romance.

The book quickly dispels any notion that formula writing is undemanding, as one might expect from Mills and Boon's own claim that only three manuscripts are accepted out of every thousand submitted.[63] Summers was a copious note-taker, constantly on the look-out for any unusual event which might spark a novel. Her most common settings are sheep stations, but she also includes drapery and fashion design backgrounds (as well as teaching and nursing), drawing on her own early experience in a large Christchurch department store. She also carefully researched the local history, geography, and geology of the places she wrote about, and was a rigorous reviser of her work. *No Orchids By Request* (1965) was originally based on a poem she had contributed to *Good Housekeeping*. Rejected by Mills and Boon in 1954, it was subsequently re-worked to include a shift of setting as well as substantial structural changes. Summers' account of the revision reveals how thoroughly professional she became, over the years:

> Many years later I tackled this story from a different angle, used another setting [Banks Peninsula] which brought hero and heroine into more constant meeting, brought the hero in from the first chapter, and made him keep his thoughts to himself. He proved — finally — one of my most popular heroes.[64]

Despite Summers' prolific output, there are a number of constants in her fiction. The main one is the theme of inheritance itself, which in her novels has less to do, overtly, with the achievement of wealth and status than with the discovery, or recovery, of family connections — becoming part of an extended, multi-generational family, rooted in a particular place (especially the farming communities of inland Otago), whose continuities are traced back to British sources in quite specific (Scottish or English or Welsh) ancestral networks. A strong rural–urban tension thus exists in the novels, though Summers' remote enclaves of civilized living in the South Island are very different from Mary Scott's harsher, relatively unhistoried North Island backblocks communities. Summers' New Zealand or English heroines, at the beginnings of her novels, are invariably displaced, drifting characters — intelligent and sensitive, usually at least in their mid-twenties, half-committed to careers as teachers or nurses or in offices or fashion stores, often without parents or from broken homes, and often disillusioned by some earlier romantic relationship.

The typical romance pattern in Summers begins for the heroine with a sudden destabilizing event, often engineered by well-meaning relatives (aunts, uncles, grandparents), which abruptly moves her from her urban environment to the country, and brings her immediately into contact with the hero, thence into an intense, complicated drama of mutual suspicion, whose resolution (marriage) carries with it the integration or reintegration of the heroine into a larger family network. Although on occasion Summers relies heavily on coincidence in the unfolding of this drama, she is generally very skilled at motivating the heroine's and the hero's suspicion of each other, while at the same time preserving the reader's faith in their essential decency and integrity. Often, an extremely delicate balance is required in the writing, especially where the heroine's mistrust of the hero centres on a suspected sexual misdemeanour in the past. In *The Gold of Noon* (1974), for example, the heroine had broken off an engagement five years before because she believed she had discovered the hero in an affair with a married woman. As the drama of their new encounter unfolds, Summers has to tread a very fine line in describing the conflict within the heroine, between her repressed and dormant positive feelings for the hero, and her repugnance for the person she believes him to be. Often these feelings are complicated by the introduction of a rival: invariably conventionally sophisticated and beautiful (and usually from the city) if a woman, and invariably staid, unexciting, and 'brotherly' if a man. Since the narratives are told so closely from the heroine's point of view, readers cannot be allowed even to begin to think that the heroine's sexual feelings might be involved in a relationship with any man other than the hero; *his* apparent involvement with another woman, on the other hand, invariably reinforces her suspicions about his sexual betrayal of her.

If the heroine's anxiety usually expresses her uncertainty about the hero's sexual loyalty and integrity, the hero's suspicion almost invariably expresses his anxiety about the heroine's mercenary motives for marriage. One of Summers' earliest novels, *Bachelors Galore* (1958), for example, was based on a comment in the Report of Special Committee on Moral Delinquency in Children and Adolescents (the Mazengarb Report, 1955) that New Zealand had many surplus bachelors: 'the heroine would not, of course, come out to New Zealand in search of one, but the hero could think this was her design.'[65] The format of Summers' hero–heroine relationships is thus premised on a gender role division of which the novels wholeheartedly approve, and marriage, in the end, is a kind of trade-off of sex and property. The ritual courtships which her characters perform assume *her* exclusive possession of sexuality, which in marriage she agrees to share with him, and *his* exclusive possession of property, which in marriage he agrees to share with her.

Of greater interest, however, are the recurrent enabling devices which eventually allow suspicions about sexuality and property to be resolved, since they form a quite distinctive pattern in Summers' fiction, and often seem more important than the primary romantic action. Occasionally Summers draws on the traditional devices of melodrama for these (dramatic rescues by the hero or heroine in conditions of storm and flood occur, for example, in *Bride in Flight*, *The Gold of Noon*, and *A Lamp for Jonathan*), but such climactic moments usually reinforce a pattern that has been developing quite independently. Its essential elements involve children, the wider extended family, the landscape, history, and poetry.

Summers' novels are unusual in the closeness of the relationship they depict between children and both the heroine *and* the hero. For the hero, the heroine's capacity to look after children provides an essential test of her suitability as a marriage partner, but the same also applies in reverse. A fundamental message to young women in Summers' novels is: choose a man who *enjoys* the company of children. Again and again, the heroine's doubts about the integrity of the hero come into conflict with her actual observation of his naturalness in the presence of children and his liking for them. At the beginning of *A Lamp for Jonathan* the heroine's shock encounter with the hero after a gap of five years occurs as she is driving and he is out walking with his young nephew and niece. One of them has a ball which rolls across the road, forcing her to stop. He then asks the heroine to fix the broken elastic on his niece's knickers. This very ordinary incident is highly typical of Summers, and it carries a clear message for her readers, right at the start of the novel, if not at this stage for the confused heroine: a man who behaves so naturally with children simply cannot be the mercenary villain she believes him to be; the novel provides the explanation on its penultimate page.

Members of the extended families of the hero and heroine also play important roles as catalysts in Summers' plots, and in her manipulation of readers' sympathies. The fact that the hero is liked, for example, by a family member whom the heroine trusts (especially by grandparents) provides a further complication in the drama of her conflicting feelings towards him, and confirmation of the reader's belief in his integrity. The sense the novels often give of an encompassing family ambience, in which the resolution of romantic conflict is willed by relatives, adds to the impression that marriages in Summers are not so much between individuals as between family and ancestral networks, which are often cross-linked at other levels through intermarriage and property relations.

Finally, these immediate familial bondings are heavily reinforced by an almost poetic sentiment of place, landscape, and history, far more than is usually the case in the genre of light romance. The novels invest a great deal of sentiment in landscape description, and at key moments hero and heroine experience healing intimacies in the shared contemplation of a landscape they both regard as Edenic. The capacity to respond to landscape thus becomes a test of the presence of that inner integrity each is seeking in the other, and often Summers reinforces these moments with direct quotations from her own or others' poems. *Beyond the Foothills* (1976) is a particularly rich instance of such associational writing, since the whole novel, in terms of its key names and place-names, is conceived as a tribute to one of Summers's favourite authors, the Canadian L.M. Montgomery.

The final stage in the rescue of the heroines from rootlessness and drift is the recovery of historical continuity. This aspect of the pattern is deeply metaphorical of New Zealand's colonial experience, expressing a strong conservative aspiration towards British ties of history and sentiment. In *Anna of Strathallan*, the plotting of Anna's recovery of her historical roots is unusually clear. 'Every child,' her grandmother says, 'should have a heritage of songs and tales handed down from one generation to the next, especially of their immediate forebears.' The reader is also told that the Strathallan homestead to which Anna comes is built 'foursquare like those Georgian homes . . . in Britain, with small-paned windows, painted white, which show up against the natural stone', and as the heroine becomes familiar with farm life, she comments:

> How marvellous to be accepted like this, striding over the paddocks with knowledgeable farmers, one of their fraternity; she knew she belonged here, with generations of sheepmen behind her from the hills and glens of Scotland.⁶⁶

The specific ties that bind Summers' heroines, via New Zealand family networks, to Great Britain and Europe, vary from novel to novel, but always in relation to a landscape in which '[t]ourists . . . would wonder aloud if they were in the Southern hemisphere or the middle of Europe'.⁶⁷ Scotland and England feature strongly throughout. In *Autumn in April* (1981) the connection is both Scottish and French; in *A Mountain for Luenda* it is Welsh; in *The Gold of Noon* it includes the alpine landscape of Austria; and in *South Island Stowaway*, unusually, the connection is American, to a Puritan heritage deriving from Maine, with the heroine enacting the legendary story of one of the earliest women to emigrate to the remote Marlborough sound in which the tightly-knit family has survived for generations. Summers' use of history is thus never simply for background or local colour: it is part of the deeply ideological character of her fiction as a whole, its unrelenting, seductive, conservative nostalgia.

In the hands of Summers' contemporaries and near-contemporaries the light romance was much more simplified, with a tendency to concentrate the narrative focus more narrowly on the hero and heroine. The simplification of style (perhaps aimed at a younger or less literate readership) is particularly noticeable in novels like Mary Moore's *Rata Flowers are Red* (1960) and Ivy Preston's *Island of Enchantment* (1963), the latter built on the slightest of storylines about a young woman who eventually frees herself from a possessive fiancé and marries a dark, handsome vet she had met during a camping holiday in Stewart Island: 'Instinctively she glanced down at his hands, the hands of a healer. She could imagine them moving surely and confidently to ease the suffering of some helpless animal.' Preston's *Magic in Maoriland* (1962) includes a racial theme, presented equally simplistically. The author resolves the 'problem' of the heroine's romantic attachment to a young Māori by the brutal expedient of inventing as a rival a young Māori woman who is so jealous of the heroine that she attempts first to drown her, and then to injure her by causing her horse to bolt, explaining to her later that 'We have not always been a civilized race. Violence has been part of our heritage.'[68] Not surprisingly, the heroine backs out of the relationship, and is rewarded at the end by the chance discovery, in Wellington, of a Pākehā New Zealander she had briefly met, years before, in England.

Most of Preston's novels are set in the South Island or on cruise ships, and she shared her friend Summers' distaste for explicit descriptions of physical intimacy, complaining of new developments in the 1980s: 'I'd always thought of books of romance as rather old-fashioned and innocent — and certainly stopping at the bedroom door.'[69] However, her novels are remarkable for the frenzied intensities of feeling aroused in the heroine by the slightest and most innocent of physical gestures from the hero (even by his mere physical proximity), all of them rigorously repressed in the deceptively calm front she presents to him. In Preston's fiction, as in most of the Mills and Boon romances of the 1960s and 1970s, this internal drama of the heroine's sensations is almost always contrived and melodramatic, full of secretive observations of the hero while his attention is elsewhere, and it certainly lacks any explicitly sexual focus. But it is very different from Summers, who places much less weight on the immediate physical relationship of heroine and hero, much more on the wider family networks and social environment within which the heroine's speculations about the suitability of the hero occur.

In the fiction of Gloria Bevan, the narrowing of focus evident in Preston and others on to what might be called the exclusive drama of the couple — the heroine and hero locked in isolated combat — becomes even more pronounced, and anticipates some of the new terms in which such relationships were presented in Mills and Boon fiction of the late 1970s and 1980s. Bevan began publishing in the mid-1960s, and much of her writing over the next decade remained within the standard formulas: most of her novels begin by transferring their heroines from England to New Zealand, often as a result of inheritance, and most are set on North Island sheep stations, although several have Pacific Island settings. Increasingly, however, in Bevan and others, such formulas are emptied of content. They function simply as devices to isolate the heroine from any sustaining social or family context and to confront her with a hero who is an absolute stranger and equally without a sustaining context or background. The result is that the encounter becomes much more explicitly sexual in character.

What these shifts reflected (at least as far as later New Zealand Mills and Boon writers were concerned) were a number of major changes in the general culture: the decline of the family, the new sexual 'freedom' of the 1970s and 1980s, the transfer of wealth from its traditional base in the rural sector to the new breed of up-market, atomized, ruthlessly competitive, financial empires in the cities. Much of the new fiction (by Rosalie Heneghan, Daphne Clair, Robyn Donald, and Susan Napier) is set in the tall office blocks, penthouse apartments, and wealthy beach and tourist playgrounds of this world, especially in or near Auckland, and it is very different from the South Island rural bias of the more traditional Mills and Boon writers. Despite the glossy appearances of that world, the heroines, often struggling to succeed in professional careers, are fundamentally alone in it. The essential narrative, in the form of romance that results, is thus presented as a narrative of self-discovery, especially sexual self-discovery.

The personality of the hero in such romances is a pure expression of the ruthless acquisitiveness of these new market forces. His arrogance, self-assertion, 'hardness', and sexual aggressiveness have to be matched, and eventually controlled (after a considerable number of tension-building delays), by the heroine's discovery and acceptance of her own sexuality, and of her capacity for self-assertion. The ostensible result, in the romance resolution that brings marriage or the promise of it, is a relationship of equality: the hero's lawless, often violent sexual instincts are 'humanized' and accommodated to the heroine's needs; the heroine's over-socialized 'passivity' is replaced by a willingness to act on her new awareness of self. It is as if a conditioned absoluteness of sexual difference is broken down, and 'resolved' happily ever after, through the joint discovery of a middle ground, in which each takes on some of the attributes of the other.

One of Bevan's late novels, *Master of Mahia* (1981), illustrates the new pattern, as well as the unusually difficult questions of interpretation and judgement it raises. In this novel an English heroine, destitute in Samoa after being abandoned by the wealthy woman she accompanied there as a nurse-companion, is in effect blackmailed and kidnapped by the hero, who 'rescues' her, 'imprisons' her on his sheep station at Mahia, and subjects her to a regime of apparently humiliating sexual overtures. Yet she finds that when she is 'free' to leave, she does not wish to, because she is held to him by the sheer force of a sexual attraction which throughout the novel's various intimate episodes engulfs her in waves of feeling she seems powerless to control:

Their glances clashed and held and once again she found herself powerless to combat the electric excitement flashing between them. Fighting the waves of dizzying emotion that were all but submerging her, she swallowed, turning away. 'So long as I know!' she flung at him, and made her escape.
It was only later, lying in bed in the quietness of her upstairs room, that she asked

herself what she had been escaping *from*. The scorching memory of his threat, 'If you don't behave yourself there'll be more of that!' still burned in her mind. Or could it be that she was fleeing from herself? She didn't dare pursue the matter to its logical conclusion for fear of what the answer might be.[70]

Such a passage, with its typically heightened melodrama of physical sensations, is meant to carry a key moment of self-awareness for the heroine, but it does so in a context that suggests sado-masochistic fantasy, and even (at least to some commentators) pornography, celebrating as the discovery of authentic sexual desire what is in fact a degrading sexual self-abasement to male domination.[71] In *Master of Mahia* the hero is meant to be seen as changing during the course of the novel: his apparently dormant capacity for love emerges, and 'explanations' are offered for his earlier callousness. But the process of change is quite implausible.

In one sense, such novels can be seen as making explicit the repressed or displaced sexual politics hidden beneath the reticence of earlier Mills and Boon novels, but they do so only to confirm such politics as part of a universal drama of fixed sexual 'instincts' or 'impulses'. Robyn Donald and Susan Napier evoke this primary drama repeatedly, and often absurdly, in their evocation of the fantasy lives of their heroines. In Napier's *Love in the Valley* (1985) the heroine fantasizes:

Weren't feet and hands supposed to indicate the size of a man's vital parts? Julia blushed at the involuntary tingling sensation that invaded her as she remembered the large, capable hands on the Maserati's wheel.[72]

In Donald's novels the commonest adjective describing male sexuality is 'feral', and although genital organs are not named as such, there are quite specific formulations to indicate male erections, and heroines are regularly excited by the sensation of the involuntary 'peaking' of their nipples as they think about the hero.

The degree of sexual explicitness varies among the novelists of the 1980s. Rosalie Heneghan, for example, is considerably more reticent than Donald and Napier, even though a novel like *Spell of the Mountains* (1989) is a perfect example of the new pattern. A wealthy hotelier-hero, callous and aggressive in his business and personal relationships to begin with, is finally accepted by the heroine (who initially hates his male arrogance) only when she has actively reconstructed him and made it possible for him to *say* the word 'love' to her.[73] As in *Master of Mahia*, this reconstruction of the hero is utterly implausible, and is in fact one of the weakest elements in the new pattern. Since so much of the dramatic tension of the narrative resides in the heroine's frightened and thrilled reaction to the hero's phallic 'hardness' and domineering personality, his transformation generally has to be very sudden (it also has to be a *partial* transformation only, since the hero needs to retain his 'hardness' if the heroine's newly discovered sexual desire is to be satisfied), and it is often reinforced by transparently artificial plot expedients, the 1980s equivalents of the melodramatic devices of nineteenth century romance. The robot-like ruthlessness of the hero in *Spell of the Mountains* is suddenly revealed as having its secret source in his repressed anxiety that he was responsible as a young adolescent for the deaths of his father and brother in a road accident.

Odd as it might seem, the new pattern can also include quite a strong awareness of feminist discourse about sexual politics in the 1970s and 1980s.[74] Daphne Clair, in particular, often alludes to such discourse. The heroines seem to lead independent lives, and they are much more strongly committed to careers than in earlier romance, though not, in the end, at the expense of marriage and children. Episodes in which the hero asserts his sexual will against the heroine are often described in the vocabulary of rape, and on occasion evoke, or imply, a general social context of violence against women. Moreover, the heroes who engage in sexual behaviour akin to rape are invariably wealthy, powerful, respectable pillars of the new up-market society. In *Spell of the Mountains* the heroine initially dislikes the hero because he stereotypes women and speaks slightingly of them in an interview he gives to a glossy magazine. Donald often produces a Gothic effect in the way she portrays highly educated career women, in executive positions, surrounded by threatening, predatory males ready to pounce on them if they make a mistake, and in both *A Bitter Homecoming* (1989) and *No Guarantees* (1990) the heroines are trained in self-defence, the latter containing a scene in which the heroine disables a would-be rapist who enters her bedroom. In Clair's *Take Hold of Tomorrow* (1986), a title which suggests a general message for her younger women readers, the heroine is the managing director of a computer firm, and has to resist the stereotyping of executive women by some of those whom she employs (including an office harasser), and assert her right to develop a relationship with a younger man.

Such details suggest that the Mills and Boon romance in the 1980s at least acknowledges changes in the position of women in the last two decades, as well as registering the impact of feminist critiques of existing gender relations. But the key question, as feminist debate about the romance has emphasized, is how such 'incidental' details relate to the recuperative pattern of the structure as a whole. If the novels are read wholly in terms of their overall moral patterning, they do indeed seem to be deeply reactionary, offering simple, fantasy solutions to matters of profound social conflict in contemporary society: violent men are miraculously transformed and their violence explained away; sexuality is defined, exclusively, as heterosexuality; and the only form of relationship envisaged throughout is marriage or the promise of marriage. However, the evidence of studies of the readership of such romances (like that of Janice Radway in the United States)[75] suggests that the novels are never read in so linear and passive a fashion; that there is always a potential space between the pattern of resolution and the material that provides the novel's central conflicts — always a potential, that is, for that material to be read differently from the way its authors (and the market researchers) intended. This is particularly so in

1980s romance, where so much of the material emphasizes male sexual aggression (without clearly visible initial signals of integrity, like the opening image of the hero in the company of children in Summers' *A Lamp for Jonathan*), and where so much of the writing deals in the highly volatile area (for characters and readers) of sexual fantasy.

This space, in which readers actively construct or reconstruct the meaning of what they read, exists in all writing, and it can be especially significant in highly formularized genres like the romance, where even the slightest shift in conventions may carry a very powerful signal. For many readers, the event most remembered in Donald's *No Guarantees* might be the 'minor' plot detail of the disabling of the rapist. One is reminded of Clara Cheeseman's anxiety that some readers might ignore the moral of Louisa Baker's novels and be attracted by the 'regrettable' actions of heroines who walk away from unsatisfactory marriages. The existence of this space is also, of course, one of the reasons why all genres have changing histories, and why the typical concerns of the romance have altered over the century, in New Zealand as elsewhere, in response to the changing pattern of gender relations in the general culture.

The same kind of space exists in the novels of Yvonne Kalman, who achieved a very substantial international readership, especially in the American blockbuster market, by reviving the genre of the historical romance in the form of the colonial dynastic saga. Kalman was a schoolteacher until she turned to fiction in the later 1970s, initially publishing a children's story about a pet possum, *Sparkles* (1979), followed by two novels described by the author as 'pretty torrid'[76], released only as mass-market paperbacks on the American market (*Summer Rain* and *Midas*, 1980). She then accomplished her major breakthrough into the blockbuster market with a trilogy, *Greenstone Land* (1981), *Juliette's Daughter* (1982), and *Riversong* (1985), and has since published a further half dozen novels, including a second successful venture into the pioneering historical saga with *Mists of Heaven* (1987) and its sequel *After the Rainbow* (1989).

Kalman was the first novelist after Edith Lyttleton in the 1930s to revive the historical romance in a major way, although there had been sporadic ventures into the territory during the intervening period, by authors writing primarily in other genres, and in occasional notable individual examples like Georgina McDonald's *Grand Hills for Sheep* (1949), a workman-like account of Scottish Presbyterian pioneering consciousness in Otago, and *Stimson's Bush* (1954), dealing with pioneering in late nineteenth century Southland. The difference, in Kalman's work of the 1980s, lies in the massive scale of her writing (the *Greenstone Land* trilogy alone adds up to more than 1300 pages), and in the way her novels reflect a much more contemporary historical and social consciousness, although they are primarily written as spectacular, fast-moving entertainments.

Like Lyttleton's *Pageant* and *Promenade* and McDonald's *Grand Hills for Sheep*, Kalman's novels are well-researched, especially in the social customs, lifestyle, and conventions of dress, hairstyle, and cuisine, in colonial society, and in the broad outlines of colonial power politics, against which the romantic and domestic narratives unfold. The *Greenstone Land* trilogy begins in Kororareka in the late 1830s, but its central focus quickly turns to nineteenth century Auckland and the rise to prominence of the fictional Peridot-Yardley-Bennington dynasty, whose business interests span shipping, trading emporia, and property, and whose complicated, internecine family feuds, private scandals, and romantic entanglements are presided over by the ruthless matriarchal figure of Maire Peridot-Yardley. In *Mists of Heaven* and its sequel, the setting is Canterbury, with the same mix of complicated domestic entanglements set against a background of pioneering, and of provincial politics and power struggles amongst the colonial élite of Christchurch. Overall, Kalman's novels evoke New Zealand's colonial past in accordance w'th traditional conventions as they had taken root in the country. There is an emphasis on raw adventure, violent events and passions, vivid local colour. But there is a strong contemporary sense of the struggle her confused, independent-minded heroines engage in to assert themselves against the self-seeking, predatory, and often brutal egos (male and female) they are surrounded by. The novels are also somewhat more sensitive to racial issues than predecessors in the genre, and in *Juliette's Daughter* racial conflict is one of the major themes.

The revival of the genre of the historical romance in the 1980s, in Kalman's highly professional hands, is thus not simply an accident, nor is it simply a reflex of the international market. Like other kinds of romance in New Zealand, historical romance has its own internal history, and just as Lyttleton turned to the form in the 1930s at a time of heightened general interest in (and questioning of) the country's colonial past, Kalman's interest reflects the general quickening of historical consciousness in New Zealand in the 1980s, which occurred in 'serious' fiction as well. Her work also illustrates the central proposition of this account of New Zealand's popular fiction: that it has never been simply a literature of escape, but has developed in close and varying relation to general social and cultural changes on the one hand, and to the practice of 'serious' writers on the other. The main concerns of its central figures (all women) reveal just how broad its imaginative scope has been: Lyttleton's and Kalman's interest in colonial society, Scanlan's representation of middle-class values and attitudes, Marsh's high cultural innovations in crime fiction, Eden's Gothic focus on gender relations, Scott's insights into the tensions between rural and urban life in New Zealand, and Summers' deeply conservative, nostalgic celebrations of the family and of the ties between New Zealand and Europe.

Publishing, Patronage, Literary Magazines

DENNIS McELDOWNEY

1

This chapter is an enquiry into how the works considered in the other chapters came to be published, in books and periodicals and (briefly mentioned) the electronic media. It shows how patrons, mainly the State, came to assist both writers and publishers. In default of any other, it includes an outline history of book publishing and literary magazines in New Zealand. The story of publishing runs parallel to but is not the same as the story of printing. Printing, as the mechanical multiplication of copies, is but one step in the process of publishing, which selects and edits the text before it is printed and sells or otherwise distributes it after.

The beginning of printing in New Zealand is simple to relate. Disregarding William Yate's few ineptly printed hymns and catechism of 1830, the honour goes to William Colenso. His story, as he told it in Napier more than fifty years later, in a lecture subsequently printed by his friend Robert Coupland Harding,[1] has often been retold, and deserves to be. It is all a pioneer story should be. The Church Missionary Society, having had Colenso trained for the job, ordered equipment without consulting him, so that when the Stanhope press arrived at Paihia, crucial items (even paper) were found to be missing. He contrived substitutes with the help of a joiner living in the bay, and attempted to recruit Maori assistants, who proved quick to learn but unwilling to stand for hours in one spot. He discovered trained pressmen among the crews of American whalers, industrious, silent men, one of whom chewed tobacco. With their help, in 1835, he printed (on writing paper) the Epistles to the Ephesians and Philippians in Māori, using pink blotting paper for the cover. The New Testament in Māori was completed on the second-to-last day of 1837.

This first printing was part of an act of publishing, which began with the missionary William Williams translating the text and continued with the distribution (sometimes the sale) of printed copies among Māori tribes. But was it the first publishing in New Zealand? In a wider sense, words had been published in Aotearoa long before that. People of the late twentieth century are in a better position than Westerners have been for centuries to appreciate how arbitrary it is to equate publishing with the printing press or even with literacy. Data processing and transmission through collective memory, if it can be put that way, had gone on for centuries before Colenso brought his press ashore on a platform lashed across two canoes. Although Māori eagerly acquired the new literacy for practical purposes, especially for letter-writing and even for polemical journalism, oral transmission was still preferred. To quote Sir Apirana Ngata, 'education through the ear, conveyed by artists in intonation and gesticulation' was preferred by 'the genius of the race' to 'mute transference through the eyes'.[2] This undoubtedly explains why few Māori took to writing books before the late twentieth century, and then mainly in English.

Even books had been published though not printed in New Zealand before Colenso's arrival. Thomas Kendall's *A Karao no New Zealand; or, The New Zealander's First Book*, printed in Sydney in 1815, Samuel Lee's *A Grammar and Vocabulary of the Language of New Zealand*, printed in London in 1820, the Book of Common Prayer in Maori, printed in Sydney in 1833,[3] and several others were intended for distribution in New Zealand by the Church Missionary Society, through its depots in New Zealand. They must be accounted New Zealand publications.

But many early publishers of writings related to New Zealand had no more idea of being New Zealand publishers than their authors had of contributing to New Zealand literature. Hawkesworth, Parkinson, the Forsters and other narrators of Cook's voyages, were published in eighteenth century fashion by consortiums of London booksellers. The early nineteenth century explorers and adventurers were published by the new breed of independent publishers, none of whose names recurs often enough to suggest a special commitment to the subject. Only the missionary societies were consciously 'New Zealand publishers'. The C.M.S. example in sending Colenso into the field was quickly followed by the Wesleyans, in 1837, and some years later by the Society of Mary. They were soon directing tracts against one another.[4]

Once colonization was in the air secular publishing began to look purposeful. So much New Zealand Company propaganda was published by Smith, Elder and Co., already a respectable firm although young George Murray Smith had not yet signed up Thackeray, Charlotte Brontë and Ruskin, that a special relationship is an inescapable inference. Jerningham Wakefield, however, went to an even more notable publisher, John Murray, with *Adventure in New Zealand*. Such individual choices remained the norm throughout the century, when publication was thought of. Many of the authors now most valued were not writing for publication at all. Most London publishers had guides to emigrants on their lists, either to individual colonies like New Zealand or to the whole range of destinations. Some, like Edward Stanford, specialized in the topic.

Printing presses were stowed in the first emigrant ships as a matter of course and newspapers, official proclamations, and commercial announcements were being peeled off them within days of landing. Books were much longer coming, especially any that might be termed literature. Which is not to repeat the fallacy that the settlers were too busy breaking in the soil to put pen to paper. Many settlers wrote enthusiastically, especially political broadsides against one another, and religious ones as well. Sometimes the two subjects coincided. When war came in the forties and again in the sixties, the C.M.S. was roused both in London and locally to defend the missionaries against accusations of land-grabbing and sedition, and to counter-attack against settler politicians. All this activity does not indicate a flourishing publishing industry. Printers or (less often) booksellers might put their imprints on the title pages, but most pamphlets were certainly paid for by the authors. This was also true of the first collection of verse, *New Zealand Minstrelsy* (1852) by William Golder, who 'followed the old balladmonger's tradition of personally canvassing for subscribers and hawking his books for sale'.[5] It was probably true of the first locally published 'novel', H.B. Stoney's *Taranaki: a Tale of the War*, of which one of the earliest monthlies, *Chapman's New Zealand Magazine*, asked 'Is this the very worst, or only the second worst book we ever met with!'

This was in 1862. It had taken twenty years, and probably the 'native crisis', for the first signs of a sense of identity to appear, or at least of a body of local knowledge. The first locally published book still known to literate New Zealanders, Maning's *Old New Zealand*, appeared in Auckland the following year, from the proprietors of the *Southern Cross* newspaper. (It was published simultaneously in London by Smith, Elder.) The first systematic publishing list emerged at the same time, from George Chapman, the Auckland bookseller whose name appeared on the magazine. His list was strictly practical: 'handy books' to gardening and beekeeping, gazetteers and tourist guides, a Māori grammar, a ready reckoner for goldminers. They were small and plain, but intelligent, well arranged, and well printed. The magazine was more ambitious — the most ambitious, apart from a couple of rapidly aborted efforts in Wellington in the fifties, that the colony had seen. It included fiction, most of it imported but some local, verse by local poetasters, serious articles on earthquakes and the establishment of a local university (urging the London rather than the Oxford model), tales of Māori life and retellings of Māori legend. Like the success of *Old New Zealand* this shows a fascination with the people the colonists had just been at war with, and were about to be again, an intricate mixture of attraction and hostility. The crop of imitation *Punch*es at this time specialized in crudely racist jokes and cartoons. Certainly the Māori could not be ignored. Chapman's Māori grammar (by H.T. Kemp) was advertised as essential for all businessmen.

Chapman's magazine, which by excluding political controversy gave itself a bland air, lasted less than six months. It was replaced in 1863 by the *Southern Monthly Magazine* ('southern' in relation to the northern hemisphere, rather than to the geography of New Zealand), which took over some of the same features (including gardening notes). Its founders were a group of young professional men of recognizable talent. Hocken mentions Joseph Giles, a physician, and Hugh Lusk, a lawyer. Lusk contributed an article on Hauhauism to the *Fortnightly Review* in 1865;[6] but the *Southern Monthly*, like *Chapman's*, was modelled on the *Cornhill* and similar magazines rather than on the quarterlies and reviews. Its appearance was smoothly professional, its printing equal to its models. It did not exclude political controversy.

The *Southern Monthly Magazine*, again, enshrines colonial ambiguities. It gave early expression to New Zealand nationalism, or rather to prophecy that nationalism would eventually arise. But this was in the context of the Waikato war, which was defended with some literary sophistication (or sophistry).

> The questions with which we in New Zealand have found ourselves compelled to grapple are of a more subtle and complicated character [than politics in England]. We have to reconcile conflicting elements. We have to encroach upon the possessions of others without committing injustice, to seize by force that which we most require for our own uses without exhibiting a spirit of rapacity, to rescind treaty engagements without breaking faith, to civilize with the edge of the sword, to secure the interests of humanity and progress by a process of war, conquest, and confiscation, to induce a race of men who always suspected our friendship while our swords were sheathed, to believe in it now when we press upon them with increasing forces, drive them from their habitations, and occupy their land.[7]

This elegant paradox led to no equally elegant resolution, but to common settler beliefs: that the makers of the Treaty of Waitangi were in error in believing that aboriginal inhabitants had any right to 'unused' land, and that in any case the Māori would inevitably die out, an outcome not to be regretted, although not to be inhumanely hastened.

At about the time Samuel Butler was writing to his father that in Canterbury 'it does not do to speak about John Sebastian Bach's "Fugues" or pre-Raphaelite pictures', the *Southern Monthly Magazine* was publishing a long note on Matthew Arnold's *Essay in Criticism* on its first appearance. The local content of the *Southern Monthly* was still largely utilitarian: practical advice predominated. Again there was imported fiction, catering, said the editors, for 'that large class of readers . . . who look to the periodical Magazine as a means of relaxation and amusement', and again limping local verse, along with (pirated?) pieces by Premier Domett's friend, Robert Browning, and his wife.

The *Southern Monthly Magazine* survived until 1866. Its nearest successor, aside from the long series of journals issued in Dunedin by the monomaniac J.G.S. Grant,[8] was the Dunedin quarterly *New Zealand Magazine* of 1876-7. Dr Giles as a contributor provided an element of continuity, but the model this time was the intellectual quarterlies. There was no fiction and definitely no gardening notes. 'We believe', said the introductory remarks hopefully, 'that among the 400,000 of our population there is a larger proportion of those who are able to appreciate and willing to support such an undertaking as this than in any other country.'

The group behind this venture were the first professors at the University of Otago and Canterbury University College, several clergymen, and a businessman, Robert Gillies.[9] Contributors included some of the more philosophically inclined politicians. High seriousness prevailed. The nearest approach to light relief was a satire on biblical criticism, showing by its methods that Oliver Cromwell was unlikely to have existed. Poetry was mainly translations of Catullus and Horace. New Zealand politics and social questions were considered at a remove from the hurly-burly, from first principles derived on the one hand from Mr Mill and on the other from Mr

Spencer. The implications of what F.W. Hutton called the Doctrine of Evolution were canvassed in many articles. It may reflect this ferment that within a decade most of the clergymen who contributed were in secular employment.

2

George Chapman's publishing in the 1860s and 1870s was practical and modest. When in the 1880s Henry Brett, owner of the *Auckland Star*, and his editor T.W. Leys began publishing books, they were few in number but on a grand scale. *Brett's Colonists' Guide and Cyclopaedia of Useful Knowledge* (1883) was the apotheosis of the emigrants' guide which had been standard publishing fare for forty years. A royal octavo of 830 pages (over 1200 in later editions), fully illustrated with wood engravings, it told isolated settlers how to build a house or a haystack, cure their cows or their children, cook the dinner, make butter, prune fruit trees and perform a hundred other tasks. Soon afterwards, in acknowledgement that even colonists did not live by practical advice alone, they provided an icon for the colonial table to go alongside those elaborate Victorian editions of the Bible, *The Pilgrim's Progress*, and *Foxe's Book of Martyrs*. T.W. Gudgeon's *The Defenders of New Zealand, Being a Short Biography of Colonists Who Distinguished Themselves in Upholding Her Majesty's Supremacy in These Islands* (1887) was illustrated with eighty-two full-page portraits and several coloured lithographs, was bound in half morocco on heavy boards, and included an engraved presentation plate. Thomas Bracken's 359-page *Musings in Maoriland* of 1890, printed in Leipzig and published with the Dunedin imprint of Arthur T. Keirle (though probably essentially self-published), was another sacred object. Dedicated (it does not say with permission) to Alfred Lord Tennyson, with introductions by Sir George Grey and Sir Robert Stout, it was a local companion for similar editions of Tennyson himself, Longfellow and Robert Burns.

The last of the grand European scientific expeditions was that of the Austrian vessel *Novara* in 1859 whose results were still being published in Vienna in the 1880s. The New Zealand Institute, to become in the twentieth century the Royal Society of New Zealand, was established in 1867 and its *Transactions and Proceedings* became the accepted vehicle for scientific work. The shift from religion to science as the dominant intellectual interest was symbolized by William Colenso, a frequent contributor to the *Transactions* on philological and botanical subjects. He provides another tenuous bridge to the twentieth century through Robert Coupland Harding whom he first saw as one of two small boys eyeing books at a Napier auction. Thinking such an interest ought to be encouraged he bought them one apiece. Harding, son of a local newspaper proprietor, remained a friend of Colenso's, who bequeathed to him much of his material including the composing stick he had taken to Paihia. He became a knowledgeable typographer, publisher of a journal *Typo* (1887-97) and of sundry books and pamphlets. He 'led the way back to simplicity, proportion, and basic, if older, typography' and corresponded 'with leaders of the craft in England'.[10] Harding belongs in a tradition of marrying print and writing, even though he never managed to ally his craft with writers of comparable interest.

Colenso had been the first *de facto* government printer in the Bay of Islands in 1840. The Printing Office was established in 1842 in Auckland, abolished four years later on the grounds that it would be cheaper to farm out official work to commercial printers, and re-established in 1864. Its miscellaneous publications in the next few decades included a handy book for coroners, a far from handy book (1244 pages) for justices of the peace, drill manuals for volunteers, Thomas Kirk's *Forest Flora of New Zealand*, the *Official Year Book*, and the ubiquitous emigrants' handbooks. It is not possible, though, to look at these titles and discern the planning of a list. Many were printed at the behest of other departments. Private printers were quick to protest at anything from the Government Printer that appeared to be unofficial. A committee investigating one complaint in 1885 gave an assurance that any such work was undertaken for the dissemination of useful knowledge which would not otherwise have been published, and that 'no pecuniary profit from the printing resulted either to the Government Office or to the authors'. Seven years later another committee recommended that no printing should be executed at the Government Printing Office 'which is not official in its character'.[11]

The government itself was responsible for one of the Office's largest undertakings, John White's vast, ill-organized *Ancient History of the Maori*, which was also one of the earliest instances of state patronage of writers, in the narrow sense of employing them to do a specific job. White, like several other sons of missionaries, had been used in negotiating the purchase of Māori land. From 1879, in another manifestation of the Pākehā's ambiguous relationship towards things Māori, he was employed by the government to record the traditions of the despoiled and 'dying' race. His remuneration varied, according to which ministry was in power, from £450 per annum to £200. White at one stage estimated that twenty-one volumes would be required, but only six had been completed when he died in 1891.[12]

The general publishing scene remained, *Typo* complained, 'chaotic'.

> There is no means by which the numerous books that issue from the press can be recorded and classified. When it is made compulsory to send copies to some State library, there will be an official register; at present it is impossible to know what works appear in the colony . . . . The most useful books published in New Zealand have at the best but a provincial reputation, and works that if placed properly before the trade, would sell rapidly by hundreds, go off slowly by dozens.[13]

Several private firms, in widely scattered localities, were following the examples of Chapman and Brett with small-scale but apparently planned publishing. A.D. Willis, a Wanganui printer and one-term Member of the House of Representatives, published local guides and histories, scenic pictorials, fictional sketches, a comic annual, a freethought review, Edward Tregear's *The Maori Race*, and a number of school textbooks.[14]

Providing textbooks designed for New Zealand schools was the most significant development in local publishing in the late nineteenth century. It is obscured in Bagnall's *National Bibliography* which excludes most schoolbooks. Its significance is that out of it eventually grew the experience and the financial base for general publishing. As early as the 1870s, the Rev. Thomas Adolphus Bowden, a former inspector of secondary schools and principal of Wellington College, was publishing textbooks in nearly a dozen subjects, written or edited by himself, through his New Zealand Educational Book Depository in Wellington. Many of them were co-published with George Philip and Sons in London. Other firms with textbook lists were Wise and Caffin of Dunedin, James Horsburgh, also of Dunedin, and Upton and Co. in Auckland. Geography was the subject most obviously demanding local texts, and English benefited from local examples, but formal subjects (as they were then) like arithmetic, chemistry, grammar, even handwriting copybooks were successfully published in competition with imported material.[15]

The imprint of Whitcombe and Tombs began to appear on schoolbooks in the early 1880s. The partnership was formed in 1882: its antecedents were unpromising. George Whitcombe, son of a British army officer, was in his late twenties. He had come to New Zealand from England in his teens and served briefly in the Armed Constabulary before trying a variety of jobs, including several unsuccessful bookselling partnerships in Christchurch, one of them with the Rev. Mr Bowden. George Tombs, eighteen years older, was a jobbing printer in Cathedral Square handicapped by antiquated equipment. The partners became booksellers and printers in Cashel Street, and in 1883 were among the first to register a limited liability company, under the Companies Act of the previous year, to help them raise the capital lacking in Whitcombe's previous ventures.[16]

Whitcombe was literate, ambitious, enterprising, and this time successful. He became a respected member of the Canterbury Club, but among unionists gained the reputation of being intransigent and ruthless, and was embroiled in a dispute with the printers' union in the key year of 1890.[17] Tombs retired as early as 1889 and died in 1904.[18] Two of his sons joined the business; one died young, and the other, Harry, eventually set up on his own. The firm became a Whitcombe domain. All eight of George Whitcombe's sons were employed in it.

By the late 1880s graded series had been systematically developed in most school subjects. Some had been taken over from other bookseller-publishers. Later came the famous Whitcombe's Story Books, paper-covered reprints and abridgements of imperial adventures like *Coral Island* and *Martin Rattler*, of Scott, Dickens, and Hawthorne, of classics for younger children, and of a number of original works with New Zealand and Australian settings, sold for a few pence.[19] By the early twentieth century Whitcombe's were finding a market for their books across the Tasman.

3

> Colony though it may be, New Zealand is a nation — not yet beyond its embryonic form, but still a nation; and . . . *Zealandia* has been established as a distinctively national literary magazine. Its contributors will be all New Zealanders, and no subject will be dwelt upon in its pages that is not of interest, directly or indirectly, primarily to New Zealanders. It is nothing to us that it may prove of interest, secondarily, to all the world beside.

This was the manifesto, in July 1889, of *Zealandia, a Monthly Magazine of New Zealand Literature by New Zealand Authors*. Published in Dunedin by William Freeman (pseudonym for William Freeman Kitchen) *Zealandia* promised to be popular while maintaining a high standard. Continuity with the *New Zealand Magazine* was provided by Sir Robert Stout, who wrote in a high philosophic vein. The editor's notes, called 'Arrow Heads', often had a radical tinge. *Zealandia* was also an early vehicle for coming writers of the 1890s. W.P. Reeves contributed a short story, there were poems by Mary Colborne-Veel and Edith 'Howat' [Howitt] Searle, later Grossman, who were both about twenty-six (the same age as the editor), and a sketch by A.H.A., who may have been the seventeen-year-old Arthur H. Adams. There were fashion notes, children's pages (very moralistic), chess and draughts notes, nature notes, acrostics and rebuses and other forerunners of the crossword puzzle, and a page of feeble jokes. The fiction, said *Typo* with justification, was 'almost without exception rubbish, — a medley of old material with a few local names thrown in. Of local color there is not a trace, and the imaginary natives introduced are unlike any people who ever dwelt on the face of the earth.'[20] Only in the occasional rural yarn (especially by Thomas Cottle) is there a glimpse of reality.

Having proclaimed its nationalism, *Zealandia* seemed at a loss where to find it, other than in some of the editor's topical comments, in descriptions of tourist resorts, and in retelling Māori legends. After a year, having finished its melodramatic serial (which was unusual for these short-lived journals), *Zealandia* put up its shutters. Later in 1890 Kitchen took a role in the maritime strike as editor of a union daily, the *Globe*. He left for Australia in 1891 and in 1893 let it be known that he had died, leaving a grieving widow and children. He reappeared under another name as Svengali to an eighteen-year-old fortune-teller, Madame Aramanda.[21]

Serious-minded readers (including Harding writing in *Typo*) preferred the contemporary *Monthly Review*, published in Wellington and much more a successor to the *New Zealand Magazine*. Its topics included Darwinism, biblical criticism, and the Baconian theory of the authorship of Shakespeare's plays, but it had more New Zealand content, including Thomas McDonnell's memoirs of the wars, and a series by Gudgeon on the 'manners, customs, and modes of thought of a past generation of Maoris, a race of people very unlike [and superior to, it is made clear] their modern representatives'. There was no examination of the ethos of colonial society in the *Monthly Review*, and very little in *Zealandia*. Yet both published enthusiastic articles about Ibsen, the author of the one in the *Monthly Review* being a fellow Scandinavian, Oscar [O.T.J.] Alpers. It was as if something was being said at one remove.

Even after another decade some readers must have felt a sense of recognition when the first issue of the *New Zealand Illustrated Magazine* appeared in 1899 exuding the same confidence in being wanted: 'there is an often-expressed desire amongst patriotic literary men and general readers to have a Magazine with a distinctive New Zealand colouring'. Not that it looked like any of its predecessors. In the meantime half-tone photo-engraving had arrived and the pages of the *Illustrated* were clearly modelled on the new London monthlies, pitched rather higher than the *Strand* òr *Pearson's*; perhaps the *Windsor*? It was published in Auckland by the New Zealand Literary and Historical Association; the founding editor was Frederick Ehrenfried Baume, lawyer, city councillor, university college councillor, Zionist, founder of the New Zealand Natives' Association,[22] married to a graduate from California. His future was to be as K.C. and M.P., not (like *Zealandia*'s Kitchen) as con man; but again there was continuity, provided by his right-hand man, Thomas Cottle, and by many other contributors. The *Illustrated* achieved a coverage of the writers then active far more complete than any of its precursors. The one notable absentee seems to have been William Satchell. Not only writers were represented: Frances Hodgkins for one illustrated several stories. The *Illustrated* also achieved more consistency of tone: middle-brow, without academic pretensions, but also without marking off fiction as an indulgence for idle moments. Jane Mander (writing as Mary J. Mander) tentatively explored marriage and what her contemporaries called 'the sex problem'; G.B. Lancaster's characters were tough bushmen.[23] The English popular novelists Marie Corelli and Ouida may have stood behind other writers; there was often a tone of elevated pathos and romance. O. Henry was another clear influence. But most of the writers of fiction believed in what they were doing.

The factual articles, however, were nearly all descriptive; there was virtually no social or political analysis or criticism. As in *Zealandia*, 'New Zealand' stood for 'scenic wonderland'; and for a more distinctive national identity they still looked to the Māori. With writers like Elsdon Best, James Cowan, Johannes Andersen, Apirana Ngata, there was more depth and accuracy than hitherto, but as J.O.C. Phillips has said, 'This was not a multi-cultural movement; but one that answered strictly Pakeha needs — an effort to provide instant history and mythology in a new and unlettered land.'[24]

Even this degree of nationalism faded, and the *Illustrated* lost its way among articles about Windsor Castle and the Battle of Trafalgar before its career was ended in 1905. The cue was taken up by its immediate successor, the *Red Funnel*, published in Dunedin by the Union Steam Ship Company but, it was made clear, as a literary magazine, not a tourist guide-book. It disclaimed any intention to be 'local': 'It is the ambition of its publishers to extend its circulation throughout the Empire.' A strong Australian content, including articles on federal politics by W.A. Holman and serials by Ethel Turner, became dominant over time, supplemented by material from elsewhere in the Pacific and from Europe. The dream of an Empire-wide circulation proved a chimera and the *Red Funnel* folded in 1909.

With literary magazines appearing at such widely spaced intervals, like meteorological stations in a sea with few islands, they provide only a spasmodic view of writers' preoccupations. What outlets did writers have in between? Some of the dailies, and especially their weekly editions, had room for creative writing. William Satchell appeared in the *New Zealand Graphic* (Brett's weekly) during the 1890s, over his anagrammatic pseudonym Saml. Cliall White. But this was unusual for the *Graphic*. As in other newspapers, most fiction (especially serials) was syndicated from overseas. Alan Mulgan explained years later that in buying a story by a writer with a 'name' for a trifling sum, 'the editor knows that [it] will be of suitable size, and cut nearly [neatly?] into proper lengths with the right notes of suspense at the ends of chapters, whereas a locally written story may have to be worked over'.[25] Local poetry was sometimes published, and publication usually considered sufficient reward. In 1908 Blanche Baughan was inciting Johannes Andersen to join in a 'strike': 'Miss Mackay has already: we have resolved to allow nothing of ours to be printed without pay.'[26] The overwhelmingly English or American 'creative' content in local journals underlines the fracture in the mind between literary culture and the known environment, and explains the inadequacy of the stumbling attempts to overcome it. Yet most of these journals — the *Otago Witness*, the *Weekly Press*, the *Auckland Weekly News* and the rest — had periods when they were hospitable to local writers. They have hardly been explored as yet. W. H. New suggests that here, in the sketches of local life rather than in the more formal fiction and poetry, is the reservoir from which later writing drew.[27]

Satchell resorted to another expedient — his own journal, *The Maorilander*, a penny weekly written entirely by himself, launched with great fanfare in 1901, and lasting seven weeks.[28] There were several short-lived local imitations of the Sydney *Bulletin*. Above all there was the *Bulletin* itself. According to one calculation, about ten percent of the items printed in the *Bulletin* between 1890 and 1900 came from New Zealand; according to another, sampling over a longer period, there were slightly more contributions from New Zealand than from Queensland, considerably more than from South Australia. Nor did New Zealanders have to write like Australians to be acceptable to the *Bulletin*. As Phillips shows, there was little larrikinism or bush balladry in New Zealand writing in the *Bulletin*. 'The image of New Zealand in the *Bulletin* was of a rather genteel and British place, unfortunately rather prudish and respectable'.[29] For those who did not conform even to those indulgent expectations, there were other Australian outlets. *The Lone Hand* was one, for Katherine Mansfield and more substantially for G.B. Lancaster. Mansfield, in her Wellington year, 1907-8, had *fin-de-siècle* 'vignettes' published in E.J. Brady's *Native Companion*. At home, a vignette appeared in *The Triad*, a story in the *Feilding Star* (apparently; all trace of it has gone) and another in *The Dominion* (if a 1987 attribution is accepted). The following year there was one in the *Evening Post* (which Antony Alpers thinks may have been lifted from some English publication).[30] It was not a bad record for a young, tentative writer, but emphasizes that there was nothing in New Zealand to which she could *naturally* turn.

The Triad was an exception to the norm of short-lived journals. Published in Dunedin from 1893, it was very much the personal expression of its editor and proprietor, C. N. Baeyertz, and his confederate Frank Morton. They wrote most of what was not clipped from overseas publications. Baeyertz was more interested in music than literature. He was the scourge of amateur performers and visiting professionals alike. Baeyertz and Morton shared an unamiable but possibly necessary quality as literary as well as music critics: they were unmoved by, except possibly to enjoy, the writhing of their victims. A damning review, unsigned but almost certainly by Morton, of a book of verse by one J. Maclennan impelled a pained correspondent to reveal that the author was a sick man who hoped with his book to provide an income for his wife and children in the event of his death. *The Triad* was unabashed. It ridiculed the naïvety of the expectation. The review had pilloried not only Maclennan but Jessie Mackay, who had written an introduction.

> Miss Mackay has written some good and charming verse, some harmless tripe, and some irreparable rubbish. Wherefore, she has now become a critic, and is (I pray you, men, tread softly!) literary adviser to the firm of Whitcombe and Tombs. I, who love and honour the sweet creature Woman, and am her meekest slave and tiniest poetaster in these seas, I imagine Miss Mackay . . . pouring the vials of her maidenly contempt on the work of all wicked and virile creatures like myself . . . .

Another shocked response again brought no repentance: 'To say that Miss Mackay is no critic is simply to declare her very woman — shall she complain for that[?]'[31]

This talent for invective has given *The Triad* a reputation for fearless tilting at colonial conventionalities. Its lush and sentimental taste in illustrations gives it away. 'Morton' as K.K. Ruthven wrote, 'admired writers who bravely ruffled the flag on top of the Establishment building but made no attempt to rock the foundations'; and Ruthven has entertainingly described Morton's brush with Ezra Pound in defence of sanity against Imagism and Vorticism.[32] Notwithstanding the Mansfield fragment, *The Triad* did not discover or nurture any strikingly interesting writers. Frank Morton had a lively mind and ready dexterity in verse, but was not serious in exercising them; and if Pound discovered 'the faint beginnings of salvation' in another frequent contributor, Alice Kenny, the least that can be said is that he was mistaken. When *The Triad* moved to Sydney during the First World War the local scene became a little duller but nothing fundamental had happened.

It is not only the exclusion of most schoolbooks from the *New Zealand National Bibliography* which has obscured the extent of Whitcombe's publishing. Whitcombe's seem to have regarded their publishing mainly as providing work for the printery and stock for the bookshops. In their own descriptions of themselves, publishing took a minor part — as it did in terms of people employed specifically for that purpose. But by any standard they were major publishers. One estimate is that twelve million copies of the Story Books were printed between 1908 and 1962.[33] Title after title was reprinted every three or four years in runs of 5000, 10,000, and even 20,000.

General publishing was on a smaller scale, and much of it was heavily practical. *Colonial Everyday Cookery* ranked with the rather later *Edmonds' Cookery Book* as a best seller. Manuals for gardeners and farmers followed suit. But especially after the appointment of James Hight as editor in 1901 (Hight was also lecturer in political economy and constitutional history at Canterbury College), there was a growing list of standard works in history, biography, ethnology, and natural history, and reprints of such colonial classics as Maning's *Old New Zealand* and Jerningham Wakefield's *Adventure in New Zealand*. There were many slim volumes of verse (and some less slim), but fiction was rare. Blanche Baughan's *Brown Bread from a Colonial Oven* was an exception.

One thing authors of general works gained from Whitcombe's educational publishing was their professionalism. By the turn of the century Whitcombe's authors were signing standard printed agreements, a refinement which some New Zealand publishers hadn't attained sixty years later. Payment was usually by a royalty of ten percent, often rising progressively with later editions. Sometimes, especially with the cheaper books, the royalty was expressed in monetary terms. A royalty of twopence on a ninepenny book was a generous twenty-two percent. The author of a number of successful textbooks, and there were several such authors, could be making £300-400 a year, probably more than they earned from teaching. Even Blanche Baughan probably earned as much, in the purchasing power of that time, from her *Brown Bread* and her *Poems from the Port Hills*, as the author of equivalent books would earn today.

Whitcombe's did exact their *quid pro quo*. A clause which remained unchanged in their agreements from at least 1903 until the 1980s provided that 'the publisher reserves the right to make such alterations to the manuscript as he may deem advisable in the interests of all parties'. In all Baughan's agreements, even for her tourist guides, this clause was vigorously scored out, but it was not until the early 1980s that it became usual for a typed addition to make any alteration subject to the agreement of the author.

In the days before inflation, with no pressing need to realize on capital before its value eroded and apparently no pressure on warehouse space, even a single edition could produce pocket money for its author for a very long time. Whitcombe's catalogues of the 1920s included the original editions of titles published twenty and even thirty years before. Nearly all volumes of poetry, however, were paid for by the authors and sold by Whitcombe's on commission (Baughan again being an exception, along with Arthur Adams). *A Treasury of New Zealand Verse* (1926) earned the two editors, Alexander and Currie, a five percent royalty apiece, but there appears to have been no provision for paying the poets.

By 1907 Hight was so busy at the university college, of which he was eventually rector, that a protégé was installed at Whitcombe's. Arnold Shrimpton, a history graduate and part-time lecturer, remained editor for forty years, until his death in 1947.[34] Major publishing decisions, however, continued to be made by top management. This was especially true during the long reign of George Whitcombe's eldest son and successor, Bertie (his baptismal name, not a diminutive), who was managing director from his father's death in 1917. Commercial considerations, which had always been paramount, became if anything more so. Decorum was equally important. An admiring bookshop employee, who stressed Bertie's 'kindliness only equalled by his sense of humour', also told of his rebuking a fellow member of his club for wearing brown shoes with a navy-blue suit.[35] Whitcombe's publishing, speaking metaphorically, was never about to commit such a solecism. Arnold Shrimpton was no more likely than his employer to do so.

Other booksellers continued to publish from time to time. Some of them even developed lists of textbooks, often finding it expedient to sell out to Whitcombe's thereafter. The Government Printer continued to publish quite widely, despite earlier strictures. Among the most active institutions were the Polynesian Society and the Board of Maori Ethnological Research. Their books, and the *Journal* of the Society, were often printed by Thomas Avery and Son of New Plymouth, because of their ability to set Māori and other Polynesian languages, and on their own account Avery developed a small list, concentrating on regional Taranaki history. But none of this threatened Whitcombe's near monopoly of New Zealand publishing, which with their conservatism had come to induce complacency and dullness.

When Whitcombe's undertook responsibility for the sale of a book of verse, even if the cost had been paid by the author, it appeared with the full Whitcombe and Tombs imprint. A title page reading 'Printed for the author by Whitcombe & Tombs Ltd' indicated that they took no responsibility for its sales. They acknowledged even less responsibility for a tiny booklet entitled *The Beggar* by a nineteen-year-old not long out of Auckland Grammar School, R.A.K. Mason. It has no imprint at all, except discreetly on the last page. The outcome of this self-publishing venture entered literary folklore early. The story of how Mason dumped 200 copies of *The Beggar* off Queen's Wharf (not the entire remainder as some later versions have it) had by 1935 been told at least three times, by A.R.D. Fairburn, Robin Hyde, and Pat Lawlor. As befits its mythological status there is more than one version. One of them has Mason stuffing bundles under the washhouse copper.[36]

Fairburn described 'the general get-up' of *The Beggar* as displaying 'that colossal lack of imagination which seems to be the outstanding characteristic of

New Zealand publishers'. The answer to that, both for Mason and for New Zealand writers in general, was already simmering at Mason's old school where a sixth-former, Bob Lowry, was introduced by two of his teachers to a printing press, on which he produced class magazines, menus for class dinners, and programmes for class theatricals. His enthusiasm spilled over into long letters to a former classmate, now living in Christchurch, Denis Glover. When Lowry, early in 1930, won a Lissie Rathbone Scholarship to university his former headmaster wrote: 'I trust that you will concentrate on your work and not allow undue time to be taken up by hobbies and amateur journalistic distractions.'[37] Mr Mahon's trust was misplaced.

5

If we accept Allen Curnow's 'hard judgement' that 'almost nothing that matters was added to New Zealand's verse between 1906 and 1930',[38] a corollary, and possibly a cause, is the scarcity of outlets. There were student magazines, the magazine supplements of some daily and weekly newspapers, a few popular monthlies (the *New Zealand Railways Magazine* was one), and annuals intended mainly as gifts for overseas relatives or (like the *New Zealand Artists' Annual*) primarily as an outlet for cartoonists. There were three or four attempts to establish reviews modelled on the *Spectator* or *New Statesman*, each of which lasted a few months at most. There were virtually no literary magazines, however 'little' or humble. Even university magazines were largely unaware of modern literary movements.

J.C. Beaglehole, who wrote poetry throughout the 1920s, published only in the Victoria University College magazine *Spike* (which for a time he edited), in two issues of the short-lived *New Nation*, and in three anthologies, *The Old Clay Patch*, the Alexander and Currie *Treasury of New Zealand Verse*, and Quentin Pope's *Kowhai Gold*.[39] A.R.D. Fairburn between 1927 and 1930 published frequently in the *Auckland Star*, the *Auckland Sun*, the Auckland University College magazine *Kiwi*, in *Kowhai Gold*, and in two overseas periodicals, the *New Triad* of Sydney and *Poetry* of Chicago.[40] Beaglehole's verse in this decade was accomplished in its formal attributes and mellifluous, sometimes dealt in a playful kind of way with metaphysical or scientific notions, and had a sentimental tinge. And this was Fairburn the 'lily-white lad . . . full of pretty love-tales heigho the holly'.[41] They were in tune with their market, or wrote for it; who can say? Short stories, even less ambiguously, were written by those who knew what editors required. M.H. Holcroft's autobiography tells the story of a young man who survived, just, by writing fiction, but not in New Zealand and seldom with New Zealand fiction.[42]

The first sign of lasting improvement came through Harry Tombs, that son of George Whitcombe's printing partner who had set up on his own account in Wellington. He had aesthetic interests, had studied the violin in Germany in his youth and was a Sunday watercolourist.[43] In 1928 he founded the quarterly

Art in New Zealand. Although it emphasized the visual arts, some literary content was intended from the first and a literary editor appointed. Charles A. Marris was at that time fifty-four. As associate editor of the Christchurch *Sun* earlier in the 1920s he had decided to 'throw open its column [*sic*] to this country's literary talents . . . .. The startling news spread to the uttermost parts of the islands and from those districts and nearer home, Mss. streamed in, a steady spate, until seemingly there was no end to them.'⁴⁴ In 1925 he moved to Wellington to revitalize the ailing Liberal daily, the *New Zealand Times*, which nevertheless died in 1927: Marris continued to edit its sporting offshoot, the *New Zealand Referee*.⁴⁵

In 1931, Tombs made a sortie into the market for the illustrated 'Christmas number' with an annual called *Rata*, again with Marris as editor and again with some literary content. It lasted three years. The two had a longer partnership in the annual *New Zealand Best Poems*, part anthology, part vehicle for new work, which began in 1932 and lasted until 1943. After Beaglehole returned to New Zealand in 1930 from study abroad he became a regular contributor to all three Marris publications, but Fairburn made only one appearance, in the 1935 *Best Poems*. By then, the scene was transformed.

'It began in the Literary Club at Auckland University, with the fortuitous coincidence of a number of the literary-minded — still occasionally to be found in such societies — and a young freshman with a private press and unlimited enthusiasm.' A club periodical was planned; after vacation air had gone to the editor's head the plan was extended, 'to launch out beyond the confines of this college, and try to establish something of dominion significance'. This explanation was given in the first, March 1932, issue of *The Phoenix* (nowadays usually known simply as *Phoenix*, the style adopted for the fourth and last issue). The 'young freshman' printer was of course Bob Lowry; the editor was James Bertram, aged twenty-one and in Lowry's words 'a most refined young fellow, of the very perfectest thing in taste in every dashed thing under the sun'. Lowry also described to Glover his way of impressing the refined young fellow: 'I've got a picturesquely Italian black sateen working shirt that I scrambled into for his benefit and timbered round doing technical things to the presses, things I'd only learnt a day or two before, as if all this sort of thing was catsmeat to me ever since childhood.'⁴⁶ Besides establishing a periodical, they were acting out another enduring and influential literary legend.

There are two distinct *Phoenix*es, each with two numbers. 'The background of the *Phoenix* is literary, its policy aesthetic', the introduction declared; the model was Middleton Murry's *Adelphi*, and D.H. Lawrence was invoked in the title and the device. Physically the first issue was an octavo printed one page at a time in a variety of undistinguished types though with an obvious typographical flair. By the second issue Lowry had got hold of a good Monotype face (Imprint) and was rapidly learning how to use it, though the effect was still tentative.

The most influential of the friends with whom Bertram shared the planning of *Phoenix* were Charles Brasch, Ian Milner, and Jack Bennett who all, like

Bertram himself, went on to distinguished careers. They were in agreement on the need to be serious. Brasch said many years later that 'the change I see in the verse of the thirties is from treating poetry as a toy and decoration to using it as a means of apprehending reality, or recording experience of it.'[47] In *Phoenix* itself he wrote of 'that Drinkwaterish simpering which is the curse of most colonial poetry when it has passed the first, wild-west stage'.

R.A.K. Mason contributed poetry written while at the height of his powers, Brasch and Curnow struggled to find a new and appropriate language. 'We shall expect great things of Mr Curnow, when he has really found himself', said Bertram, reviewing a number of university magazines. Writers of stories were even further from finding themselves; they were still waiting for Sargeson to lead them away from a rather precious muse. But poetry and fiction were less prominent than criticism. Politics was not absent but wore an aesthetic and philosophical face.

Bertram disappeared after the second issue, to take up a Rhodes scholarship at Oxford, and Mason — 'a fierce man exploring politics and a man of granite when he had made up his mind'[48] — was appointed to succeed him. The 1933 issues of *Phoenix* were visibly manifestoes. Lowry the typographer had struck form to produce substantial quartos with large margins, large (12-point) type, heavy headings and page folios in the still comparatively new Gill sanserif, bold linocuts on buff paper, some in two colours, most with political or industrial themes.

Mason was in his late twenties and his most prominent contributors were likewise not students. 'Some, indeed, may feel', explained the introduction, a trifle disingenuously, 'that this issue discriminates unfairly against our University contributors. If that is so, then it is due to accident. The material was prepared under great difficulties and in haste at a time when most University men were hard to find, or, if found, too tired to respond.'

The aestheticism of the previous year was repudiated. Mason wrote more vigorously than his predecessors, and there was no doubt about his message. 'This is no time to be studying the tonal value of the minor works of T.E. Brown[e]. It is the greatest hour in history . . . . This is no time for optimism, no time for pessimism: the hour for realism is here.' Soviet art was applauded — 'The cinema as an art-form is possible only in Russia', said Clifton Firth — bourgeois art condemned. It was sex rather than politics that caused trouble, however. A murkily argued article by Eric Cook claimed that 'this Faustian syphilization' must be saved by sexual and communist revolutions. Martin Sullivan, president of the Students' Association and a future dean of St Paul's in London, read this article in page proof and insisted on its removal (an episode he looked back on in his autobiography with astonishment). Some copies had already been bound with the article, and these were duly sold; the rest appeared with two blank pages and a note explaining that the article which formerly occupied pages 35 and 36 had been removed by order of the Students' Association Executive. Mason, who had not thought much of the article, welcomed this opportunity to show up authority.[49]

Generalizations don't describe the whole. Although Mason included some self-consciously Marxist verse, J.C. Beaglehole's long, brooding 'Decline of the West' is quite different in its assumptions, and other poets were not political at all. The fourth issue, like both the previous year, has a poem by C.R. Allen, a blind Dunedin man in his forties whose attitudes and poetic practice were both conservative.

A fifth issue of *Phoenix* was prepared, but Bob Lowry, in debt, in trouble with the Students' Association for unauthorized expenditure, and excluded from university courses, fled to Christchurch. 'Overwork has taken my nerves so badly that I can't think straight to clear up the mess, and I'm cutting my losses.'[50] This established a pattern which Lowry followed through life.

One can agree with Brasch that 'only Mason's poems seem memorable now',[51] and still admire the energy and panache. It was however the memory of *Phoenix* which was so potent, especially the memory of the first *Phoenix*, of 1932. It was in the minds of its first begetters that *Phoenix* continued to ferment. 'That great advance must not be abandoned, and from the time *Phoenix* died, James, Ian, Jack Bennett, other friends and I began talking about another journal to succeed it.'[52]

Phoenix Mark II had the most immediate successor. In Christchurch 'the nicest, quietest, kindliest man in the country', Kennaway Henderson, 'was preparing to demolish the System'[53] by publishing a weekly journal called *Tomorrow*, of which the first issue appeared on 11 July 1934. Henderson was a journalist, watercolour painter, and cartoonist in his fifties who had been twice imprisoned during World War I for resisting conscription. Without means so far as his friends could tell apart from the occasional commission to paint pictures, he worked full-time on *Tomorrow* without pay.[54]

His efforts were seconded by the English department of Canterbury University College, that is to say by the professor, Frederick Sinclaire, and the lecturer, Winston Rhodes, both of them recent arrivals from Melbourne (though Sinclaire was an Aucklander originally). It was Sinclaire who wrote, in a specimen issue used in canvassing,

> We inhabit a land of dreadful silence. New Zealand is the country in which no one says anything, in which no one is expected to say anything. . . . We have no dogmas to thrust down the throats of our readers. We have nothing to sell them. We appeal to them to help us in breaking the uncanny and ill-boding silence.

Henderson's model, for the title as well as the content, was A.R. Orage's *The New Age*, as he had read it before World War I. He was prepared, Glover said, 'to accept any contribution for *Tomorrow* that showed clear thinking and a certain amount of ability to write'.[55] The tone was radical but, at least in early years, by no means single in voice. The tone was also, often enough, witty and satirical, and an increasingly lively correspondence column was headed 'The Tumult and the Shouting'. Every week there was one of Henderson's own cartoons, which were sometimes described as 'ferocious', but were ferocious only in their gallery of abstract types: newspaper editors, militarists, Rotarians, bishops. Caricatures of actual people were surprisingly benign, even of Forbes and Coates, the villains of those Depression years, even of Adolf Hitler.

While the emphasis was on political comment and current affairs generally, *Tomorrow* from the first was hospitable to poets and writers of fiction. A reader thumbing through the volumes will suddenly find familiar words springing out:

> I do not dream of Sussex downs
> or paint old England's quaint old towns:
> I think of what will yet be seen
> in Johnsonville and Geraldine[56]

(but spot the differences from the definitive version), or the story which begins, 'My uncle wears a hard knocker. His wife put him up to it.'[57]

Denis Glover was a prolific contributor from the first, of both prose and verse. He wrote satirical verses, squibs, and epigrams over his own name, initials, and a variety of pseudonyms. Fairburn and Curnow did the same. They all contributed serious poetry, as did Mason, Beaglehole, Brasch, Hyde, and others less well remembered. Sargeson's first appearance in *Tomorrow* was also with satirical verse, but it was in its pages that he developed as a story writer, very much on his own at first. Until a first story by Roderick Finlayson, 'Wi gets the Gospel', appeared on 23 June 1937, stories by other writers tended to be satirical, or political, or even old-fashioned plotted tales, of which some of the most polished were by M.H. Holcroft.

New Zealand books as they appeared were perceptively reviewed, but there were not many of them. Nor was local writing the main interest of the two English department contributors. Sinclaire's columns were *causeries* of a traditional kind; he had a particular affinity with early nineteenth century essayists, especially Hazlitt. Rhodes's sympathies were much wider. One of his enthusiasms was G.K. Chesterton, but he could also write familiarly of Ezra Pound. His recurrent interest, however, was in Soviet literature. He warned that Western readers 'must resolutely forget all the axioms and slogans of bourgeoisdom, and imagine themselves in a country where, incredible as it may seem, human nature is being changed'. He introduced readers to the concept of socialist realism, 'a realism which is not at all like that of the passive photographer, but rather is filled with the fervour and purposiveness of the author who knows the life that he describes because he lives it and takes part in it'.[58] Marxist rhetoric had its uses locally. It allowed artists to express their alienation. Thus M.T. Woollaston: 'The antidote to an easy, wistful idealism about life and art is a thorough realisation of the implacable enmity which exists between an artist who retains the intensity of his calling, and the bourgeoisie: an enmity which is not at any point to be bridged.'[59] It was closely related, too, to the continuing discussion about the proper language for a New Zealand writer. Fairburn (not a Marxist, though as given to anti-bourgeois rhetoric as the best of them) had expressed the opinion in *Art in New Zealand* that

Huckleberry Finn was more relevant to New Zealanders than any other fictional character: in *Tomorrow* he welcomed Sargeson's first small collection of stories, *Conversation with My Uncle*, because it underlined that fact. Sargeson's own tribute to Sherwood Anderson[60] was part of the same discussion.

There were, naturally, some writers who would not have been comfortable with *Tomorrow*, nor *Tomorrow* with them. Ursula Bethell never appeared there. During the 1930s she published in J.H.E. Schroder's literary page in *The Press*, and also in a rural weekly newspaper, the *North Canterbury Gazette*, published (in Rangiora) by Oliver Duff, after he resigned as editor of *The Press* because of a disagreement with its owners about the Christchurch tramway strike in 1932.

This preference of Bethell's was anomalous in one way, for a change was happening in the 1930s of which Bethell was very much a part. Until that time most of the influential figures on the literary scene (Whitcombe's editors excepted) were journalists. So were many of the practising writers. From Pat Lawlor's many reminiscences one would infer that poetry, fiction, criticism, and history were what journalists did in their spare time and in their more reflective moments. Lawlor himself was a representative if lightweight figure, editor of the New Zealand edition of the Australian humorous magazine, *Aussie*, and of its offshoot the *New Zealand Artists' Annual* (until the Depression killed them); editor of a series of 'Hori'-type *Maori Tales* which, it was claimed, had outsold any other New Zealand books; later, New Zealand representative of the *Bulletin* and founder in 1934 of the New Zealand centre of the international writers' organization, P.E.N. He described himself as a 'bookman' and his interests as 'bookish'. For many years in a succession of periodicals he published a column of literary gossip under the pseudonym of 'Shibli Bagarag'.

Although the links between journalism and literature were never entirely broken, increasingly from the 1930s literary activities were in the hands of academics, or of people with academic connections and inclinations. A sentiment shared by these people was scorn for newspapers and the people who worked for them. The slobbering, trap-weaving spiders of Kennaway Henderson's cartoons, and the 'slow dripping of water on mud;/thought's daily bagwash, ironing out opinion' of Fairburn's *Dominion* were typical. Marris steadfastly refused to acknowledge this shifting power base: 'in contrast to the influence of the University colleges in letters say, thirty years ago, those "centres of learning" today are playing an insignificant role'.[61]

Art in New Zealand and *New Zealand Best Poems* still gathered in many writers of verse. So did the *New Zealand Mercury*, a monthly 'little magazine', of poetry only, published between 1933 and 1936 by two Wellington women, Helen Longford and Violet Foote. Its Georgian allegiance was averred in its title (from Sir John Squire's *London Mercury*), it held monthly competitions, and its poets were largely those of the Marris publications. Glover saw these and the *Tomorrow* poets as 'on one side . . . the music makers and the dreamers of dreams, and on the other a group making a different and even discordant din in what is thought a new and fearful manner', and accused *Best Poems* and the *New Zealand Mercury* of 'transplanting Georgians and their hothouse tradition'.[62] The irony is that Glover himself has often been described as a Georgian; and neither he nor Marris admitted how much overlap there was. Glover conferred a kind of immortality on Marris, though even more in latter days on himself as a male chauvinist, with his *Arraignment of Paris*.

> — But who are these, beribboned and befrilled?
> Oh can it be the ladies' sewing guild?
> But no, they follow Paris — it is clear
> these are his sheep, and he their pastor dear.
> Our lady poets these: hermaphroditic
> he is at once their guide, their friend, their critic.
> And with them go a few who by their faces
> should be in shoulder-straps instead of braces.[63]

Allen Curnow's more moderate verdict (much later in date) was that 'Marris printed much bad work. But he made and kept an audience of sorts for a few of the better writers: Robin Hyde, Eileen Duggan, and J.R. Hervey, among others'. Among the 'others' were several more whom Curnow included in his own anthologies: J.C. Beaglehole, Douglas Stewart, Arnold Wall, Gloria Rawlinson. One clearly anomalous name was that of Anton Vogt, an iconoclast and modernist, yet a frequent contributor to the later issues of *Best Poems*.[64]

6

By the mid-thirties poets had alternatives to Whitcombe and Tombs. R.A.K. Mason's *No New Thing*, self-published with the imprint Spearhead Publishers, was printed by the Unicorn Press which Lowry (back from Christchurch) had set up in Mason's house. Moving the press into the city, he was joined by Ronald Holloway in the first of his many partnerships. Together they printed and published D'Arcy Cresswell's *Lyttelton Harbour*, Sargeson's *Conversation With My Uncle*, and Arthur Sewell's essay on Katherine Mansfield.[65]

Even more substantial things were happening in Christchurch, initially through Lowry's inspiration. Having enthused Glover with his own love of printing, Lowry took on the role of mentor. Selling him early in 1933 a press and a font of type, Lowry recommended Glover to keep his 'eyes skinned' for samples of good and bad typography, to study the better trade journals and anything by Eric Gill, Stanley Morison, or D.B. Updike, and to send him once a month a sample of everything he had done 'for a free crit'.[66]

The authorities Lowry recommended to Glover help to explain why in the early printing of both — in the disposition and balance of type and space, in the choice of paper, above all in the emphasis on the design of the typeface itself — there was as much a break from the ambitious 'fine printing' of the established houses as from run-of-the-mill jobbing. They understood the value of reticence, and Glover especially held that printing was to serve the word printed and not to draw attention to itself. There were marks of the amateur, the learner, in the work of each; yet they had made a qualitative leap, and the fact that they had been able to do so without overseas experience shows that at least some libraries and bookshops were enlightened enough to stock books by typographers and examples of their work.

Glover's early adventures were an echo of Lowry's. Like Lowry he set up his press in a basement at the university college, calling it the press of the Caxton Club, and printed a magazine, *Oriflamme*. Like Lowry he tangled with a student president later to be a pillar of the establishment (Joseph Ward, grandson of a recent Prime Minister and heir to his baronetcy), and both the subject (sex) and the author (Eric Cook) of the offending article were the same as they had been in *Phoenix*. In Glover's case the college authorities themselves came down on him.[67]

In 1935 the Caxton Club equipment was moved to rented premises, a power-driven press was added to it, Glover found a partner, John Drew, and the Caxton Press was in business. From the beginning it was a serious commercial firm, which gave it the financial base for its publishing. It quickly became well known for elegant design and competent machining of mundane objects like letterheads and account forms, and was especially favoured for church newsletters and orders of service.

The first Caxton Press publication was *Another Argo*, a booklet containing one poem each from Fairburn, Curnow, and Glover, and a frontispiece by Leo Bensemann (who later joined the staff). 'There were meant to be 150, but only 70 complete copies survived the paper storm around the machine', says a disarmingly frank early catalogue. 'Through the ink the type may be seen to be Garamond 14-point. Note 0 for O on title-page and cover.'[68]

The contributors to *Another Argo* were to be the mainstay of the Caxton list in its early years, together with Mason and Ursula Bethell. Within two and a half years the Press had published collections or long poems by all of these, together with several lampoons by Glover, Allen Curnow's essay *Poetry and Language*, D'Arcy Cresswell's repudiation of the Copernican universe, *Eena Deena Dynamo*, two anthologies of poetry from *Tomorrow*, two books of brilliant caricatures by J. T. Allen, and one of Leo Bensemann's distinctively fantastic drawings. Fairburn's *Dominion* came out in March 1938 and Curnow's *Not in Narrow Seas* a year later. In what one writer has called 'that unhappily brief period of euphoria between the Depression and war'[69] the Caxton Press was defining not only its own role, but how New Zealand writing (poetry at least) in the 1930s would be seen for a long time to come.

It was still on a very small scale, however. Much of the poetry was hand-set, editions were small (although they were not 'limited editions' in the sense familiar to private presses in Europe), and authors expected no financial return. Sustained prose was rare because of the cost, the capacity of the press, and 'the absence of a single good local linotype face'.[70] Caxton published no novels in the

1930s or for years afterwards. In 1940, however, they celebrated the availability from a trade house of linotype Baskerville with the publication of two seminal works, Frank Sargeson's second collection of stories, *A Man and His Wife*, and M.H. Holcroft's long essay on 'cultural influences in New Zealand', *The Deepening Stream*. These were probably the first Caxton books to make a real impact on a wider public.

If Whitcombe and Tombs were conscious of increasing competition during the 1930s (which is doubtful, since their educational base was untouched) the source was not the Caxton Press or the Unicorn Press, but a Dunedin importer and occasional manufacturer of Sunday school supplies, Alfred Hamish Reed.[71] The published history of the house of Reed is misleadingly subtitled 'Fifty years of New Zealand publishing, 1907-1957', but as the book itself makes clear their publishing properly dates from 1932, when Reed was invited to join with the large printing firm of Coulls Somerville Wilkie in publishing *The Letters and Journals of Samuel Marsden*, edited by J.R. Elder, Professor of History at Otago. The project appealed to the evangelical in Reed; he put up half the capital, and set out to sell the book in the only way he then knew, by direct mailing.

Marsden's Lieutenants followed two years later, and by that time Reed had a taste for publishing. He brought out several more books, mostly biographies and reminiscences of clergymen and missionaries. Then the veteran James Cowan, who was possibly writing too much to be accommodated by established publishers, submitted his *Tales of the Maori Bush*. Reed accepted it, at the urging of his young nephew, Alexander Wyclif Reed, who had recently opened a branch in Wellington, and thus embarked on secular publishing. In 1935, six books were published with the imprint of A.H. & A.W. Reed, in 1936 ten, in 1937 nine. History, biography and pioneering reminiscences predominated.

The list was not pre-planned, but selected from work submitted. Manuscripts seem hardly to have been edited; many were rambling and disorganized. Yet they obviously appealed to a public becoming aware of its past. And from the beginning the firm did attract known writers: Cowan himself, H. Guthrie-Smith, Arnold Wall, and W. Downie Stewart among them.

Among the few novels were two by C.R. Allen, little remembered now but admired then. A more lasting reputation attached to a novel which was little noticed at the time, Frank Anthony's *Follow the Call*. Anthony had died in 1927 (the memoir included in the book mistakenly said 1925), before any of his work had appeared in volume form, and his mother and sister negotiated publication of *Follow the Call* with A.H. Reed. He liked the book, but: 'In view of undertakings we are already committed to . . . we should not be able to risk having our money laid out for a considerable time'. Anthony's mother therefore paid the cost, about £100 (Reed accepted a down payment of £25, a nest-egg Mrs Anthony had put aside for a rainy day) and received half the retail price of copies sold. Publication in late 1936 had taken just six months from Mrs Anthony's initial enquiry. Early sales were dismal. Reed pressed the family to sell the book among their neighbours in Taranaki, but they thought it would seem 'too much like "skite" '. War brought a happy ending. Imported books were scarce, and almost anything local sold, including *Follow the Call*, which was out of print by 1944.[72]

With a few exceptions (Mona Tracy's fiction for children was all published by Whitcombe's), novelists were still obliged to look overseas; and overseas publication was still the ambition of writers of all genres. Jonathan Cape's acceptance in 1936 of James Cowan's stories of trading among the Pacific Islands, *Suwarrow Gold*, must have been a highlight in his long career, even though sales (unlike the reviews) were disappointing. He kept all the correspondence with Cape, but not with local publishers.[73]

New Zealand authors were published during the first half of the twentieth century by a wide spectrum of London publishers, from the lowbrow (Jarrolds and Robert Hale, both of whom published Nelle Scanlan) to the high (Faber with D'Arcy Cresswell's *The Poet's Progress*), from sober, established houses like Chapman and Hall (William Satchell, Rosemary Rees), Cassell (Edith Howes) and Macmillan (Satchell again) to specialists in juvenile books like Ward, Lock (Isabel Maud Peacocke). But some London publishers seemed readier than others to publish New Zealand authors. It is tempting to look for associations in explanation. Dent published a number of New Zealand titles whose sales potential could hardly alone have commended them: *Kowhai Gold*, O.N. Gillespie's anthology *New Zealand Short Stories*, Alan Mulgan's *Spur of Morning*, volumes of essays by Mulgan, Schroder, and F. L. Combs. J.M. Dent's son had emigrated to New Zealand for his health and served as vicar of several Anglican parishes. He impressed his father on a visit home with his belief that New Zealand 'was solving most of the problems, both political and social, that this old country was still struggling with'. Although J.M. Dent died before the flurry of New Zealand publishing occurred, the vicar's brother took over from him. Allen and Unwin, with a yet more solid New Zealand list (successive editions of Reeves's *The Long White Cloud*, Beaglehole's *New Zealand: A Short History*, A.J. Harrop's historical works, Eileen Duggan's poems, John Pascoe's *Unclimbed New Zealand*), also had family connections. Sir Stanley Unwin combined business with visits to three brothers who lived in New Zealand. Walter Nash for a time was his active sales agent, and represented Dent as well.[74]

For many years there was a notorious 'New Zealand mafia' in the Oxford University Press — Kenneth Sisam, John Mulgan, Dan Davin, Robert Burchfield, and others less renowned. Oxford (*in* Oxford) after World War II counted almost as a New Zealand publisher. As late as the 1960s, the local manager complained that there was no point in his developing a local list since anything really good would be snaffled by Clarendon. For a New Zealand scholar the imprint of the Clarendon Press, Oxford's academic arm, was the ultimate accolade.

American publication was rare and, when it was achieved, nearly always negotiated by the London publisher. Edith Lyttleton, who was a consummate businesswoman, dealt directly with a succession of American publishers; but she was an exception.[75]

But there was a price to be paid for overseas publication. In the days before airmail there was the frustration of slow communication, and many New Zealand authors were unable to read their proofs — a fact made obvious by literals which no New Zealander would pass. More serious, especially for novelists, was the self-consciousness induced, the delayed acceptance of the New Zealand scene as natural. Nelle Scanlan's novels are full of explanations of New Zealand geography and customs; those few of Ngaio Marsh's early books set in her native land draw embarrassed attention to New Zealand idioms. Publishers probably didn't require such guidebook gestures: Mansfield managed without. But writers thought they did.

There was also a more tangible price on publication in London. Copies sold in New Zealand, although it was a local author's main market, were deemed 'export sales', and royalties were paid on the wholesale not the retail price. It was, moreover, a lower wholesale price than applied to the 'home' market. This was a hangover from the 'colonial edition', when an overrun from the main edition was offered to colonial booksellers at reduced rates, so that in spite of additional freight a novel published at 7s.6d. in the United Kingdom was sold in New Zealand at 6s. Even after the term 'colonial edition' was dropped the system continued, although the advantage it gave to the New Zealand bookbuyer was obscured after 1933 by an unfavourable rate of exchange.[76]

A detailed documentation of the system is enshrined on the first page of Frank Sargeson's autobiographical trilogy, faithfully reproduced in successive editions. Chronicling the disquiet which led to his abortive trip to the King Country and his past, Sargeson mentions 'a statement from my publisher, from which I inferred that the New Zealand public had by now probably paid somewhere about £500 for my recent book [*I Saw in My Dream*]. My share of the amount would be somewhere about £25. It was the sort of thing I just couldn't take. Not at the moment, anyhow.' A footnote exonerates John Lehmann: 'It is quite usual for an author to be paid ten per cent of what his publisher receives on copies of his book sold overseas: on copies sold in Great Britain he is paid ten per cent of the published price: best-seller rates are somewhat higher, of course.'[77] £25 is an effective royalty of five percent on sales worth £500. Since local publishers were seldom willing to publish novels, and even less willing to pay competitive royalties for them, there was no apparent way out.

7

Members of the Labour ministry which took office at the end of 1935 shared a number of attitudes which predisposed them to favour cultural activities by government. Most had little formal schooling but several had gained a wide education through books and W.E.A. courses. They respected scholars and writers, and believed their fruits should be widely shared. And they were New Zealand nationalists, who intended to practise economic insulation and independence in foreign policy.

The forthcoming centennial of European settlement in New Zealand provided an occasion to express these beliefs. The recently appointed Secretary of Internal Affairs, Joseph Heenan, was given the task of organizing the celebrations. A series of historical publications was his idea.[78] By the end of 1936 Heenan had chosen the first full-time employee: a young Cambridge graduate, Eric Hall McCormick, who had been in charge (part-time) of the Hocken Library in Dunedin. Together they planned a series of monographs, scholarly but accessible to the general reader, and another of pictorial surveys published fortnightly, *Making New Zealand*, with a more directly popular appeal. The most ambitious project, which was never completed, was a historical atlas.

The programme was supervised by an impressive National Historical Committee, of which McCormick was secretary, but the committee seldom met. A small but eager staff was employed. Oliver Duff was editor; John Pascoe, a Christchurch law-clerk, passionate mountaineer, and photographer, was illustrations editor; David Hall, who with a small private income had been trying to survive as a writer, was publicity officer. All except Duff were young; they were available because, in McCormick's words, they were all 'more-or-less misfits or failures'; none (again excepting Duff) had any training for or experience of editing or publishing. But they quickly acquired formidable expertise and worked together harmoniously to achieve nearly all this ambitious programme nearly on time. Joseph Heenan, whom McCormick has likened to 'a ballet impresario, a Diaghilev', was justly proud of them.[79]

They set up office among the mouldering national archives in the attic of the General Assembly Library, later moving to an old wooden building in Sydney Street which they called Centennial House. At the end of 1938 Duff left to found the *Listener*; McCormick succeeded him, and J.C. Beaglehole was brought in as typographical adviser. Beaglehole, independently of Glover and Lowry, had also been inspired by the typographical movement, although not himself a practising printer. He had designed for the Carnegie-financed Council for Educational Research, whose books often reached a wider than strictly educational audience, and had persuaded out of Whitcombe and Tombs (by then equipped with some of the best Monotype faces) work of a distinction which still eluded them in their own publishing. His typography for the centennial publications was equally authoritative.[80] A large subsidy enabled the casebound monographs to be sold for the low price, even then, of five shillings (in editions of 2000 copies); *Making New Zealand* was 1s.6d. an issue. Authors were paid £100 for the 30,000 word monographs, £15 for 5,000 words in *Making New Zealand* — reasonably generous rates for the time.

Like a movie still, this short-term, intense enterprise freezes a developing generation into the attitudes of the moment. It shows them on the road between the beliefs of their parents and those which a later generation (and they themselves, often enough) would regard as the norm. It shows that some were making this journey more wholeheartedly than others, or moving faster along some roads than along others.

The team were nearly all versed in the rigour of modern scholarship, and endeavoured to choose authors with similar backgrounds. Several of the surveys (for example Leicester Webb on government and F.L.W. Wood on New Zealand in the world) broke new ground. The editors were embarrassed by the manuscripts initially turned in by two older authors, Cowan on *Settlers and Pioneers* and S.H. Jenkinson on *New Zealanders and Science*, both of which had been commissioned on the insistence of Heenan. But some of their other decisions reflected their period.

They were all interested in the arts, and McCormick's own survey, *Letters and Art in New Zealand*, was to be a landmark of criticism, but the popular market for *Making New Zealand* was assumed to have no such interest. Three issues on sport were included and none on the arts, except architecture, which seems to have gained its place because buildings were a working part of the material environment, like trains and ships. Paintings provided many of the illustrations, but music, the theatre, and 'reading' were confined to sections of the issue on 'recreation'.

In October 1937 McCormick addressed a memorandum to Heenan stressing the need for a theme to unite the centennial surveys.

> Now the 'idea' which seems to me of fundamental importance in any consideration of New Zealand history is this; that 100 years ago a sample of nineteenth century society and civilization was transferred to New Zealand and has since been reshaped and adapted, with varying degrees of success, to conform to the conditions of a new environment — i.e. natural surroundings and climate, a new order of society, special economic conditions, a native people and all the other elements which constitute environment in its widest sense. It is this process of adaptation with its record of trials and errors and its continuous subjection to fresh influences from outside which it seems to me might be the underlying theme of the surveys.

In this way, McCormick said, 'we should avoid the type of history that is a bare chronicle of events without interpretation'.[81]

Although the memorandum was circulated to all·the commissioned authors, McCormick later doubted whether more than two or three heeded it. Yet he probably articulated commoner thoughts than he then realized. There was no celebration of imperial glory; the creation of a unique society by the interaction of imported elements with a given environment was the theme. Yet the imported element was 'a sample of nineteenth century society and civilization'; the native people who were displaced were the fourth-mentioned of the environmental factors.

There was no Māori on the National Historical Committee. When a meeting of the standing committee in June 1937 considered a preliminary list of surveys, 'Dr. Scholefield pointed out the omission of any survey of Native Affairs in the list of suggestions before the Committee. Mr. Heenan, in reply, emphasised the delicate nature of this matter, and advised that it be left, meanwhile, in abeyance.'[82] There were suggestions that the field might be left to the volume which I.L.G. Sutherland was known to be editing.[83] Finally, Sir Apirana Ngata was commissioned to write a survey, but never did.

Nor were there any women on the committee. One L. Griffith of Dunedin wrote to the Minister: 'It seems to us [although she did not claim to be writing on behalf of a group] that it is in the interests of the Dominion Centennial Committee, women should be appointed co-equally with the rest of the committee.'[84] No reply is on record. Women on the staff were at junior and secretarial levels. There was discussion about whether a survey should be devoted to women. Duff wrote in a memorandum to Heenan:

> The only question here is whether it is logical, and necessary, to separate men and women historically. While I cannot believe that it is, I can see a prudential case, perhaps we should call it a domestic-political case, for giving women a volume to themselves if they want one. I do not think they *will* want one unless someone suggests to them that they should have it.[85]

In the event, there was a survey on women.

It is well known (because the author made it known) that another of the volumes originally announced failed to appear, because it was turned down by the Prime Minister, Peter Fraser. W.B. Sutch's survey, which was meant to be about social welfare but was mainly about the lack of it, was troubling Centennial House well before the Prime Minister came into the picture. Nearly all the members of the editorial committee had doubts about it, not always for the same reason. To McCormick, it was too long, badly arranged, and clumsily written. Beaglehole also disliked its style. Duff doubted its scholarship, A.D. McIntosh thought Sutch had selected evidence to support a Marxist interpretation, Hall was concerned about the government's reaction. Before Heenan, let alone the Prime Minister, had seen it, Sutch was asked to rewrite. McCormick approved the second version, and passed it for publication as his last act before joining the army at the end of 1940; but Heenan still disapproved:

> it is not so much the omissions as the general tone of the work that seems, to my mind, to strike a discordant note in a series of Centennial publications, the purpose of which is really to show the bright side of our national progress.[86]

In any case, Fraser had specifically asked to see the manuscript, and forbade publication. Both versions were brought out by private publishers.[87]

Less well known is the fact that a chapter was excised from Cowan's *Settlers and Pioneers*, apparently because it dealt with the confiscations of Waikato land and the attitude of settlers to the Māori. Cowan grumbled to I.L.G. Sutherland, who replied: 'How can good relations between two peoples be maintained on the basis of falsehoods, or suppression of the truth?'[88]

Literary competitions were also held, judged largely by professors of English, for a novel, short story, play, long essay, long poem, and short poem. Prizes went to J.R. Hervey, Frank Sargeson, Roderick Finlayson, and M.H.

Holcroft, as well as to people now unknown; a reasonably perspicacious result. Reporting on the novels, Professor Herbert Ramsay of Otago thought that of 106 entries probably a dozen merited publication. The fact that only one is known to have been published was later used as an argument for a literary fund; but that one, Beryl McCarthy's *Castles in the Soil* (third equal), scarcely supports the case.

War overtook Centennial House and the historical atlas was first postponed and eventually abandoned. The true successor of the Centennial Publications was the immense war history project following 1945, which led to the establishment of the Historical Publications branch of Internal Affairs. When the centennial of the settlement of Otago was celebrated in 1948, A.H. McLintock, later parliamentary historian, organized regional histories on a remarkable scale, and the *Otago Daily Times* chimed in with a novel competition. It was a late echo of Centennial House.

8

An early casualty of World War II was the *New Zealand Railways Magazine*; a more serious one was *Tomorrow*.

From March 1936 Kennaway Henderson gave up the struggle to produce a weekly paper. *Tomorrow* henceforth appeared fortnightly. There were more subtle changes. The late 1930s were a difficult time for leftists. The rise of Hitler, the Spanish Civil War, and the Japanese incursions in China shook the pervasive pacifism of earlier in the decade and Stalin's purges cast doubt on the workers' paradise. Two of *Tomorrow*'s current affairs commentators clashed over the Moscow trials and one ceased to publish there. As Glover later put it, 'It was most important that you should be either on the side of the shooters or the shot. A majority of the editorial committee was all for the shooters'.[89]

Tomorrow began to express an editorial viewpoint. Contrary opinions were still printed, but might be argued against in the same issue. The result was that *Tomorrow* became less attractive to some of its previous writers. Glover remained faithful (though stroppy), so did Rhodes and Sargeson. But Sinclaire and Holcroft last appeared in 1937, Curnow and Beaglehole in 1938; and Fairburn contributed rarely in its last two years. The rift widened in 1939 when *Tomorrow* defended the Nazi-Soviet pact and opposed the war. So when the police, under war regulations, warned the printer in 1940 of the risk he was taking, resulting in its effective suppression, *Tomorrow* already appealed to a narrower audience. It left a sizeable gap, however, only partly filled by the *New Zealand Listener*, which began publication under Oliver Duff's editorship in July 1939. Book reviews were prominent from the first, and Gordon Mirams's pioneering film reviews even more so, but most of its space was committed to radio publicity, especially as newsprint became short; what could be spared was used for topical articles. Both during and after the war, the *Listener* was an important forum on current issues. It was a main outlet for

Fairburn the essayist and polemicist. There he recalled his prickly meeting with Frances Hodgkins, or called for the establishment of a National Trust. But the Duff *Listener* was not central to the creative writing of the period. Sargeson did appear as early as 1940 and spasmodically thereafter and was later joined by A.P. Gaskell and the very early Janet Frame, and a good many others less memorable. But poetry, apart from humorous and satirical verse, was quite rare, and that little so various (Fairburn and Vogt, Arnold Wall and Alan Mulgan) as to make it difficult to judge of Duff's judgement. The *Listener* had to await Holcroft's editorship, beginning in 1949, to move nearer the hub of things.

In 1941 and 1942 Caxton published six issues of the slim but typographically attractive *Book*, described as a miscellany, which was mainly a showcase for Caxton authors and a sampler of Caxton books. In the same years an élite of New Zealand writers achieved a very large audience indeed through John Lehmann's *Penguin New Writing*. In the thirties Frank Sargeson had become proficient in recycling his locally published stories in avant-garde (but paying) periodicals overseas, notably the American *New Directions* and Lehmann's *Folios of New Writing* and *New Writing and Daylight*. The style and milieu of Sargeson's stories struck a chord with Lehmann, who was both socialist and aesthete, and his interest extended to other Caxton writers. In a passage frequently quoted from his autobiography, Lehmann asked

> Why was it then that out of all the hundreds of towns and universities in the English-speaking lands scattered over the seven seas, only one should at the time act as a focus of creative activity in literature of more than local significance . . .?

Penguin New Writing appeared during the war on flimsy grey paper. Wartime emotion in Britain, both patriotic and vaguely socialist, turned it for a time into a best seller, and Sargeson, Curnow, Finlayson, Glover, and half a dozen other New Zealanders were carried with it. Caxton writers may have defined New Zealand writing by defining themselves; although Lehmann's words were written much later, his approval at the time must have felt like objective confirmation.[90]

An imitation appeared in Wellington, edited by Ian A. Gordon, a young Scot who had arrived to fill the chair of English at Victoria College in 1937. Although its fiction at least was nearly all in the mode of colloquial realism, and it obviously welcomed first-hand proletarian or wartime experience, *New Zealand New Writing* made no overtly political statement. Alongside its Australian counterpart (edited by Katharine Susannah Prichard among others) it was positively bourgeois. But its four 64–80 page issues, published from 1942 to 1945, are the most comprehensive collection of the writing of the time. It included some (but only a few) of the writers of the thirties, those interesting transients Anna Kavan and Greville Texidor, and several who were transitory as writers. It also began to define a post-war generation, nearly all of whom were serving in the forces, among them Kendrick Smithyman, Keith Sinclair, Hubert Witheford, David Ballantyne, Helen Shaw, and Bill Pearson.

9

New Zealand New Writing was published by the Progressive Publishing Society, a wartime phenomenon in itself. During the thirties, left-wing co-operative bookshops were established in the three largest centres (later joined by a fourth in Dunedin), which acted as agents for Victor Gollancz's Left Book Club and Moscow's foreign language publishing house, besides stocking Penguin Specials, Phaidon Press art books and new fiction and poetry. They were close to *Tomorrow*'s public. Several of the shops began publishing in a small way early in the war, mainly pamphlets on 'post-war reconstruction'. In 1942 the bookshops combined to launch the Progressive Publishing Society in Wellington, chaired initially by Sutch. This was to be a demonstration of the co-operative principles which, according to many of the books they published, were to rule after the war. With Russia in the war, there was no conflict between moderate Labourites and the followers of Moscow, and support for the war effort was one of the strongest themes of their political tracts. But the Society also took over authors and projects from Caxton, who with most of their staff away were finding it difficult to keep up with job printing, let alone publishing. They reissued Sargeson's *A Man and His Wife*, published new collections by Curnow and Vogt, new essays by Sinclaire and Holcroft, and *We New Zealanders*, Fairburn's assault on national complacency. They published so much so quickly that they overran the country's capacity for good printing. The typography was often frightful. (Much of the country's printing capacity, and scarce paper, was being used during the war to make up for the lack of imports by printing overseas best sellers — not only Ngaio Marsh, who was an obvious choice, but such writers as Frances Parkinson Keyes and Marcia Davenport. Penguin books were also printed in New Zealand).[91]

The Progressive Publishing Society was an exciting venture at the time, but financial control was loose, some directors had philosophical problems about budgeting for a profit, and a number of odd publishing decisions were made. What market was envisaged for *Three Essays on Czech Poets*, by Frederick Ost? The end of the society came almost with the end of the war.[92]

10

The debates on 'post-war reconstruction' provided the context for a specific debate on state patronage of writers. It had never been entirely absent, since the days of John White and his *Ancient History of the Maori*. For twenty years from 1910 Elsdon Best was employed as ethnologist at the Dominion Museum, beginning at a salary of £180, which increased eventually to £500. His brief was to research and write a series of bulletins on pre-European Māori life and culture; one of the first tasks he set himself was to show up deficiencies in White's work — as later critics were to do with his. During and after World War I James Cowan, who had been a publicist in the Tourist Department, was employed by the Internal Affairs Department to write *The New Zealand Wars*, published by the Government Printer in two volumes, 1922-3.[93]

The Labour government in its first few years showed its friendly intentions towards the arts by granting civil list pensions to Cowan, Jessie Mackay, William Satchell, and Eileen Duggan.[94] Three of these were compassionate grants to old and ailing writers; Duggan was in a different category, but was generally understood to be a lady of retiring and delicate character. Assistance for creative writing to the young and fit was another matter. D'Arcy Cresswell called on John A. Lee at the Ministry of Housing:

> [I] told him of my situation in Auckland and suggested that some position should be found for me, without prejudice to my broadcasting and my literary work. Lee thought so too, and talked to Heenan at the Department of Internal Affairs by telephone; when I heard them agreeing, it seemed, that the best aid for a sad case like mine was an annuity, and regretting that there was no provision for such a thing in the country. 'What can you do?' asked Jack. 'I can be a Judge,' I said; at which he laughed, as if I could not.[95]

Cresswell had a way of organizing patronage which the unsympathetic called bludging on friends, but which his destiny as a poet, he believed, fully justified.[96] Lee on this occasion arranged for a job in a state forest near Auckland, but another friend, Alan Mulgan, served him better by commissioning readings from literature for the radio. From this time the broadcasting service, for which Mulgan had become supervisor of talks, was increasingly a financial resource for writers.

Sargeson had been able to take advantage of other resources: the dole during the Depression, and later an invalid benefit for a tuberculous condition. When his recovery threatened his livelihood, Heenan, on the intervention of McCormick, arranged for a pension from art union profits.[97] Heenan, with the encouragement of Peter Fraser, was making a practice of these *ad hoc* grants from lottery funds, to other arts as well as literature; since he was secretive about them it is difficult to say how many — it may not have been as many as rumoured. But Fairburn's ire would shortly be aroused, and other artists were also suspicious.[98]

M.H. Holcroft, whose prestige as a literary thinker was at its height, advocated in *The Waiting Hills* (1943) a state editorial board to select works for marketing through commercial publishers at a nominal price with a government subsidy.[99] He also pointed to the need for republishing 'classics' (Lady Barker, F.E. Maning, Jerningham Wakefield and the like) which readers could not become acquainted with outside reference libraries and the second-hand market.

E.H. McCormick, with whom the Sutch fiasco still rankled, was sceptical.

He imagined a 'state editorial board', composed of such people as M.H. Holcroft, Frank Sargeson, Eileen Duggan, and Allen Curnow, resolving 'with one dissentient' to sponsor a faulty but powerful first novel, *Cliffs of Fall*, by an unknown author, Dan Davin. When it is published there is an outcry against 'this outrageous slur on the character of New Zealand womanhood' and 'this flagrant abuse of the taxpayers' money'. But if a state editorial board *were* established, said McCormick (speaking to a Library Association conference in 1946) 'it would be largely composed of people with standing in the community' who would encourage 'the safe and the second-rate'.[100]

Holcroft, returning to his advocacy in 1947, asked: 'Are there likely to be many cases of the kind mentioned by Mr McCormick? And would the possibility of occasional rejections — even if they are rejections to be lamented — destroy the value of the Literary Fund as an incentive to good writing?' He also saw the value of providing leisure for established writers.

> A man who has shown himself capable of overcoming the difficulties of an unfavourable environment, and who has developed a talent which promises still better work in the future, deserves all the assistance the State can give him . . . it becomes increasingly hard as he grows older to find the energy for creative tasks that must be done while he is earning his living in some other way.

He was opposed, however, to providing younger writers with abundant leisure, not because it would make them creatures of the State but because 'The struggle against difficulties is an indispensable part of the creative process, especially in the formative years . . . . A man's talent is hardened by adversity.' A 'man' had to be in a state of internal conflict before he could do good work, and if he were given security for several years and told to go ahead and write books 'No doubt the books would be written; but I think they would lack purpose and vitality'.[101]

The best-remembered opponent of state patronage is A.R.D. Fairburn. There is good copy in his quarrel with Frank Sargeson and in his couplet about mushrooms growing in the open and toadstools under trees. The most formed expression of Fairburn's views is found in a late essay, 'The Culture Industry' (1956). He had always conceded that works of public record (historical and biographical) could properly be assisted by state funds: 'Yet even here we should be extremely circumspect. It would be easy to arrive by slow stages at the point where history is re-written to order by State-employed professionals, as happened in Nazi Germany, and as has become the standard procedure in the U.S.S.R.' He was adamant about poetry and fiction. They should 'remain completely exempt from State patronage. . . . Put a novelist on the pay-roll of the State and sooner or later you turn him into a tomcat (*arrangé*) that comes to the kitchen door for its milk and in return begs prettily or catches mice.' The maximum demand of the serious artist 'as has often been said, is to be *let alone*. The careerists and parasites who clamour for "recognition" (meaning, not the sort of *understanding* the genuine artist values more than any other thing, but does not expect to be able to command at will — but *money*) should be ignored.'[102]

Holcroft and Fairburn, despite their differences in emphasis, shared a view of the artist and of how art comes about which was at once puritan and romantic, and which may also be seen as an idealization of how they had themselves conducted their lives.

It is striking that one argument was not used. Those who opposed state patronage argued from the side of literature: they feared that the state would corrupt writers. No one argued that it was inappropriate for the state to support literature, or that it was an improper use of taxpayers' money. Or rather, nobody who was taken seriously argued so. If such opinions were expressed it was likely to be by *New Zealand Truth*, and therefore easily dismissed as philistine. The unexpressed premise was that there was a hierarchy of values, in which some activities were of more worth than others. The capacity of people to judge differed according to their attainments and education, and even people of discernment might honestly differ about the place on the ladder of particular writers, but that there was a ladder was not to be doubted, nor that Shakespeare stood higher on it than Edgar Wallace. No one was going to call such a view élitist. A government's proper concern was to make the best in art and literature, like education, available to the widest possible public.

While all these opinions were in the air, the establishment of the Literary Fund was the consequence, finally, of lobbying by P.E.N., which at the time had a small membership heavily weighted with Wellington gentleman amateurs. A deputation led by the president, C.A.L. Treadwell (a lawyer who had written textbooks and a popular book on notable New Zealand trials), met the Minister of Internal Affairs, W.E. Parry, in November 1944. Briefing the minister beforehand Heenan showed that he was reluctant to give up the direct patronage he had been exercising (in the name of the Minister, of course). He suggested 'that you indicate to the P.E.N. the Government would be prepared from time to time to give due consideration to representations made by it as a responsible body of men and women qualified to offer responsible advice.'[103] Instead, Parry advised a delegation to the Prime Minister — who was in San Francisco helping to found the United Nations. A second delegation to Parry a year later was given the same advice. This time the Prime Minister was off to London for the inaugural meeting of the U.N. General Assembly.

The P.E.N. proposal was based broadly on the Australian Commonwealth Literary Fund. They asked for an annual grant of £1200 to be administered by a committee of seven, of whom three should be members of P.E.N. An ambitious programme for spending the £1200 included subsidies for historical works, and for 'belles lettres, poetry or prose', grants to authors, prizes for young writers, reprinting New Zealand classics, and a subsidy to P.E.N. for professional assistance and advice to authors.[104]

By the time a persevering P.E.N. renewed its pressure in mid-1946, Heenan had changed his mind. With growing protest from other artists about the secret use of 'slush funds', and the Labour government running short of electoral support, he may have concluded that the days of informal grants were numbered. He became a strong supporter of the proposal. He suggested an annual grant of £2000, rather than the £1200 asked for by P.E.N., and fought down a Treasury attempt to reduce it to £500. In October 1946 he met the new president, Sir James Elliott (a surgeon who had published an autobiography and the biography of a schoolmaster), along with Ian Gordon and Pat Lawlor, and told them the government would set up a literary fund 'after the election'.[105]

P.E.N. welcomed the decision in its October *Gazette*; but the only public notice of it was in *John A. Lee's Weekly*; this was followed by a stream of letters from Lee to several ministers advising how the fund should be administered (avoid academics, he warned), and laying advance claim to subsidies for reprinting his own books. There was no public announcement until August 1947, by which time the members of the advisory committee had been chosen, and they had met and decided on their priorities. Open government was not a fad of the 1940s.

P.E.N.'s three representatives on the advisory committee were Sir James Elliott (elected first chairman), Ian Gordon and G.H. Scholefield. In addition Pat Lawlor was honorary secretary. Government appointees were Oliver N. Gillespie, of the Prime Minister's information staff, Pei Te Hurinui Jones, Māori scholar and adviser to the King movement, Mrs Mary Mackenzie, a neighbour and friend of Walter Nash, Ngaio Marsh, J.H.E. Schroder, and Ormond Wilson M.P. They were precisely such 'people with standing' as McCormick had predicted, people who could be trusted not to let £2000 go to their heads. As a further safeguard, final decisions were to rest with the trustees of the Fund, who were the Prime Minister and the Ministers of Finance and Internal Affairs.

The priorities decided by the Committee at its first meeting in July 1947 were (1) grants towards publishing costs of historical works, contemporary creative literature, reprints of New Zealand classics, and Māori literature; (2) grants to New Zealand authors for approved projects; (3) grants towards critical books and studies; and (4) 'such other means as the Committee with fuller knowledge gained from its experience might deem desirable'.

Nine years later contemporary creative literature was placed ahead of historical writing; otherwise the Committee's announced terms of reference remained much the same for many years.[106] One other modification stemmed from the Committee's early experience. At first it was not clear, to the Committee or anyone else, whom the grants to assist publication were to go to. A flood of applications from authors of reminiscences, of works on astrology, of poetry which had lain in a bottom drawer for forty years, quickly persuaded the Committee that applications should preferably come from publishers committed to undertaking the work if given a grant.

Quite bold decisions were taken by these 'people with standing'. Some of the early grants were impressively large, in relation both to the money available and to costs at the time. £300 given to the Caxton Press to assist the publication of M. H. Holcroft's trilogy of essays, *Discovered Isles*, might be worth $12,000 to a publisher faced with 1990 printing costs. The sum of £375 given to Antony Alpers to assist him in gathering material for his biography of Katherine Mansfield was supplemented by grants of £200 and £150 in subsequent years. Even more boldly, £625 was given to Allen Curnow to enable him to travel overseas, on the application not of Curnow himself but of Glover and Holcroft, 'with supporting letters from well-known writers'. Peter Fraser as a trustee objected on the grounds that 'there was no security of any definite literary return'; Schroder went to see him and argued forcefully that Curnow had much to gain from the experience; and that it was obvious from past performance that he would go on writing. Fraser was convinced.[107]

The grant to Curnow did not pose the kind of question McCormick had foreseen: whether the Committee would support a book like Davin's *Cliffs of Fall* and whether, if they did so, public opinion would be outraged. The nearest test came in 1948. David Ballantyne, whose first novel, *The Cunninghams*, was about to be published by the Vanguard Press in New York, applied for assistance to write another. The advisory committee recommended a grant of £100. Pat Lawlor took home from the meeting the manuscript of *The Cunninghams* with which Ballantyne had supported his application, read it, decided it was pornographic, and withheld the recommendation from the trustees until he had had an avuncular talk to Ballantyne, whom he advised to think of his mother. Ballantyne eventually got his grant and there was no outcry, but the episode helps to explain the tone of an article about the Fund which Ballantyne published in New York the following year. The hope had been, he said, that 'under Premier Peter Fraser's canny eye . . . the Dominion might even produce another Katherine Mansfield — and wouldn't that be something!' He saw no sign of it. Conceding that 'this correspondent' had received a grant 'after some fantastic interviews' he said that 'no other grants to fiction writers have been announced at this writing', and that 'official encouragement of literary art has largely taken the form of subsidies for the printing of pioneers' letters and of new editions of out-of-print books nobody much cares to see in circulation again', while Antony Alpers had received ' "a substantial grant" . . . to do a biography of — guess who — Katherine Mansfield.'[108]

By 1951 the Minister of Internal Affairs alone was responsible for approving grants and Ian Gordon was chairman; in 1955 Pat Lawlor was replaced as secretary by a senior member of the Internal Affairs staff, Andrew Sharp; a long-term regime was established.[109]

11

Denis Glover returned in 1944 from service in the navy, stimulated by meeting John Lehmann and other literary figures and also some of the best printers and typographers in Britain. He immediately took Caxton into the forefront again, with typographical design showing a new flair and professionalism. The first year after his return saw the publication of the eighteen-year-old James K.

Baxter's first collection, Curnow's *Book of New Zealand Verse*, Glover's own *The Wind and the Sand*, Sargeson's *When the Wind Blows* and his anthology *Speaking for Ourselves*, and Burdon's *New Zealand Notables Series II*. By the mid-fifties Caxton had introduced Kendrick Smithyman, Keith Sinclair, Ruth Dallas, Paul Henderson, Janet Frame, Greville Texidor, John Reece Cole among others, as well as publishing established writers and such projects as Ursula Bethell's *Collected Poems* and Robin Hyde's *Houses by the Sea*. But after a time Glover's drive faltered. He was restless — some of his friends thought he had been more affected by his war experiences than he admitted. He was drinking heavily. He got into financial difficulties, both personally and commercially. One of his partners took over financial control of the Press while continuing to employ Glover, but eventually (in 1953) sacked him.[110]

If Caxton now led in literary publishing, Reeds dominated the popular field. The Dunedin office had been closed in 1940, when A.H. Reed ostensibly retired from day-to-day participation. He continued to oversee minute aspects in long weekly letters to his nephew and as late as the 1970s vetoed a book on the New Zealand wine industry, because, whatever the house editor might say in arguing for wine as a social grace, 'It's alcohol, isn't it?'[111] His main contribution to his firm, however, was as an author. He and the even more prolific A.W. learned during the war to supply gaps in the market. Much of their early writing was Sunday school material (in which their efforts were supplemented by that relict of *The Triad*, Alice Kenny), but they ranged from party games to a manual on map-reading. In time A.W. specialized in Māori language and folklore, A.H. in historical works which appealed to bookbuyers more than to scholars.

The post-war list was largely the creation of two young men, Ray Richards and Tom Kennedy, both returned servicemen and both former Sunday school pupils of A.H.'s and office boys with him in Dunedin. Few Reed books of the 1940s and 1950s appear in literary histories confined to poetry and the serious novel. Yet they plugged into the national psyche with books that nowhere else would have been probable best sellers. An early portent was Peter Newton's *Wayleggo*, the unsophisticated memoirs of a high-country musterer. In 1951 they published the first of a series of *Me and Gus* books, Frank Anthony's stories in the radio-script versions of Francis Jackson. This strain culminated in Barry Crump's *A Good Keen Man* in 1960 (almost a caricature of the genre), and Mona Anderson's much more homely *A River Rules My Life* in 1963. New Zealanders found in such books confirmation of their belief in themselves as outdoor individualists; and together with rugby and other sporting books, they composed the Reed image, which other publishers began to emulate. It was a distorted image in reality: the Reed list ranged from gardening books and cookbooks, through scenic colour books, to standard works on natural history and Māori studies. Fiction was by no means absent, but it was mostly domestic humour (Mary Scott, Jillian Squire), Mills-and-Boon-type romance (Mavis Winder), and adventure.

Caxton continued to publish after Glover's departure, but in an environment of increasing competition, even in the 'quality' field, in which some of their authors preferred to go elsewhere. Glover for a time joined a navy friend and Christchurch advertising agent, Albion Wright, who had established the Pegasus Press to do much the same kind of publishing and printing as Caxton. *Arawhata Bill* was published there, and Janet Frame, whose *The Lagoon* Caxton had taken a long time to produce, went to Pegasus with *Owls Do Cry*.

A Hamilton bookseller (and contributor to *Phoenix*), Blackwood Paul, worked in Wellington during the war for the Army Education and Welfare Service (A.E.W.S.), and sat on the board of the Progressive Publishing Society. There he met Janet Wilkinson, who had assisted J.C. Beaglehole in designing books for the Department of Internal Affairs. Her chief interest in joining the P.P.S. board was to improve their typography. She and Paul married, and over the next two decades, first in Hamilton and then in Auckland, published an increasing number of books with the nicely old-fashioned Paul's Book Arcade imprint. They took over from P.P.S. the production of Gordon Mirams's *Speaking Candidly*, which exploited his popularity as the *Listener* film critic, and stocks of other P.P.S. titles, and compiled a book, *Our Own Country*, from wartime A.E.W.S. bulletins. Their first best seller (in their terms at that time — 3000 copies) was Helen Wilson's autobiography, *My First Eighty Years*, which Janet had persuaded her to write. Another early book was a reprint of John Mulgan's *Man Alone*, which had not sold widely in the original Selwyn and Blount edition, and now became a standard text in schools. The Paul list showed thus early its characteristic combination of literary and typographical quality with a shrewd assessment of market possibilities. Recruiting Phoebe Meikle brought dedicated care to textual editing and the experience to develop an educational list. Their greatest financial coup was to persuade Mary Scott, whose novels had been published by Hurst and Blackett, that a full royalty on New Zealand sales outweighed the kudos of an overseas imprint. With a novel every eighteen months selling 7000 copies, Mary Scott enabled the Pauls to be more adventurous in their literary publishing.[112]

By the early sixties Pauls' had displaced Caxton as the leading publisher of poetry (more often than not printed by Caxton, however), and were publishing more fiction than Caxton had ever done, jointly with overseas publishers where possible. Their writers included Maurice Duggan, M.K. Joseph, Ruth France, Bill Pearson, A.E. Batistich, and also Frank Sargeson with the *Collected Stories*, but not *Memoirs of a Peon*, with which Blackwood Paul was 'out of sympathy'. Children's fiction was another Paul specialty. But it was all being done from the month-by-month cash return. There was virtually no capital.

The dominant position of Whitcombe and Tombs, especially in educational publishing, was undermined after the war not only by competing firms but by the burgeoning School Publications branch of the Education Department. The *School Journal* had provided supplementary reading (and inculcated social values) since early in the century. Now, using techniques pioneered by the A.E.W.S., the branch launched a series of bulletins to supplement or replace textbooks. Drawing on many of the country's best writers and illustrators (and employing some of each full-time) its imaginative work made the Whitcombe's texts look drab and old-fashioned.[113] The Story Books succumbed to the competition of cheap and attractive imports, Puffins and the like.

When Arnold Shrimpton died in 1947 he was succeeded as Whitcombe's editor by Carl Straubel, another historian — though he had hitherto earned his living in journalism and public relations. He had far more typographical sensitivity than his predecessor and soon transformed the appearance of Whitcombe's books. He and his successor David Lawson (still under the watchful eye of Bertie Whitcombe, who was in control until his death at eighty-seven, in 1963), achieved some distinguished and successful publishing, but it never again seemed possible to characterize a 'typical' Whitcombe's book, except that it was like a typical Reed book, but better-looking. There was an exception in one area. For a time Whitcombe's became the most frequent publisher of fiction, usually in joint imprint with Robert Hale of London. Their choice was eclectic, embracing detective stories and romances as well as serious novels, with, at first, one restriction. For a long time their chief manuscript reader was a retired Scottish Congregational minister who had an aversion to 'the sex problem'. By 1959, however, they were prepared to publish Maurice Shadbolt's *The New Zealanders* with Gollancz.

In these cases an author's contract was with the English publisher, who continued to pay reduced royalties on 'export' (including New Zealand) sales. It was only when ambitious younger authors, especially those with literary agents, became willing to engage in tough negotiation, that some overseas publishers conceded New Zealand could be a 'home' market.[114] This period also saw the novelty of some writers (David Ballantyne, Janet Frame, Sylvia Ashton-Warner) being published first in New York. Because of the customary apportionment of world markets between British and American publishers, such books could not normally be sold in New Zealand until they were published here or in Britain, which might mean delays of several years, while some never appeared in New Zealand bookshops at all. The most sustained programme of New Zealand literary criticism was in the Twayne World Authors series, whose publishers seemed to be indifferent to the New Zealand market, so that local buyers had to exercise ingenuity and patience to get them.

University publishing was another post-war development. After thirty years of discussion by the University of New Zealand Senate the New Zealand University Press published its first books in 1947. It was a part-time operation, run by a board of management whose most active members were Beaglehole and Gordon. Its *magnum opus* was a manual for buttermakers, but it published Fairburn's *Three Poems* and Baxter's Macmillan Brown lectures, *The Fire and the Anvil*, and such standard works as Keith Sinclair's *The Origins of the Maori Wars*, Ernest Beaglehole's *Mental Health in New Zealand*, and Ian Gordon's *English Prose Technique*. Its leisurely, amateur ways irritated some of its authors, but a valuable list was distinguished by Beaglehole's typography, and after fourteen years its initial capital was still intact. When the University of New

Zealand was abolished in 1961 the Press went with it, and the new autonomous universities were left to pick up the pieces. Otago was the first to do so.[115]

In Auckland Bob Lowry continued to produce the occasional book under a succession of imprints as he was discarded from one partnership after another. His typographical wit was displayed most exuberantly in Fairburn's *How to Ride a Bicycle in Seventeen Lovely Colours*; among the best of his more formal works was D'Arcy Cresswell's *The Forest*. Denis Glover moved to Wellington where he worked for a time for Harry Tombs, who was publishing modestly with his renamed Wingfield Press. Glover himself continued to publish small books under several imprints, notably the Catspaw Press. There were other amateur presses, among them Mervyn Taylor's Mermaid, Louis Johnson's Capricorn, and Noel Hoggard's Handcraft. The publishing scene was lively and among the larger battalions apparently profitable; and it was almost entirely a local phenomenon.

12

No publisher in the twenty years after World War II had the influence on letters in New Zealand which was exercised from its beginning by *Landfall*, the quarterly first published in March 1947. Throughout the thirties, when he was working on archaeological sites in North Africa and at a school for disturbed children in England, Charles Brasch had nurtured his dream of a periodical which would be a *Phoenix* grown up. Conversations with Glover, on leave from the navy, matured the dream into a plan: 'We talked over the prospect again and again, at all times of day and night, even while Denis lay soaking and talking in the bath, a large pink almost hairless octopus'.[116] Brasch returned to New Zealand after the war and widened his talks among the intellectuals of his generation, at first with the intention of establishing a sort of collective responsibility for the proposed journal. But it soon became clear that he must take it on himself, if only because he alone, with an inherited income, had the time to do so. The Caxton Press took financial responsibility for publishing *Landfall*; contributors were paid ('the only way of ensuring a high standard, since it carries the right to reject what is not good enough'[117]), but the editor was not; yet he was able to make it a full-time job.

The first issue could scarcely have been more austere, in cover, in typography, and (to a large degree) in content, yet undoubtedly this was welcomed by most of those to whom it was directed. One who did not agree was the reviewer in the *Southland Daily News*, whose comments were reproduced with more favourable ones on the cover of the second issue: 'In no way will it compare with the many good magazines annually tossed off by the University Colleges and . . . there have been school magazines turned out which, for vitality, originality, and humour would wipe the floor with this first number'. This hit on the point precisely. Enough college magazines had been 'tossed off'; it seemed time for something solid, sober, and authoritative.

Brasch did not intend his quarterly to be confined to the arts. 'To rediscover a just relationship between the arts and men's other activities, and a single scale of values to which all can be referred — that must be the constant aim of those who care about them', the 'Notes' in the first issue said. '. . . It is hoped that each number of *Landfall* will include some contribution which has no apparent connection with the arts.' The 'single scale of values', although here used in a specific context, was a controlling idea in Brasch's editorship, and so was a 'sense of truth as something to be pursued throughout life, imaginative truth above all', a degree of dedication which he suspected even Glover did not share.[118]

Brasch feared beforehand that not enough material would come in to sustain the standard he aimed for. But *Landfall*'s arrival coincided with a burst of writing in New Zealand, and in part inspired it, especially writing of a length and complexity for which there had previously been no home. Its attraction to writers and the generosity of Brasch's response are attested by the names in the index to the first five volumes. Looked at more closely, *Landfall* does reveal Brasch's preferences. Among the young writers of fiction he encouraged were Maurice Gee, Maurice Duggan, Janet Frame, and the last two names show that he was not afraid to move away from realism and into stylistic innovation; but a certain decorum was still required, and he was suspicious of anything savouring of retreat into fantasy or emotionalism. Thus he only ever published one story by Helen Shaw and turned down some of her best.

Nor was Brasch a passive editor. John Geraets, author of a thesis on Brasch's *Landfall*, who read much of the correspondence between Brasch and his contributors, came to the conclusion that while Brasch considered a work of art an inviolable whole, he often had, in his mind, that 'whole' as a platonic ideal to which the actual script had more or less relation. This 'led him to see it as his responsibility to ensure that each work offered for publication should be brought as close to its (to his mind) ideal potential as possible'; and he did not hesitate even to draft out an alternative ending to a story.[119] It is not surprising that some authors saw it as Brasch imposing himself on their work. It was seldom quite that, but he was naturally more in sympathy with some writers than others. From her first diffident submission he encouraged and guided Ruth Dallas towards her own maturity; his relations with Kendrick Smithyman were much more prickly. While recognizing Smithyman's ability, Brasch expected (in Geraets's words) 'a progressive logical statement', whereas Smithyman's poetry offered 'a lattice-work of intersecting possibilities'. Smithyman, by no means dependent on *Landfall*, learned to submit to Brasch the work he was most likely to accept.[120]

The availability of *Landfall* also led to the writing of some notable literary, or literary-cum-social, criticism. Among early examples, Bill Pearson's 'Fretful Sleepers' (September 1952) and Robert Chapman's 'Fiction and the Social Pattern' (March 1953), helped to set the terms of debate for decades to come. In reviewing, *Landfall* may not have scored more than the average number of hits and misses. Brasch did not allow one critic to review any author more than once, short of a full critical survey — partly in reaction to the practice of the *Listener*, in which David Hall for many years reviewed virtually all New Zealand fiction. The result is apparent, in the review columns, in the lack of a deliberately cumulative view of any of the writers dealt with.

For articles on topics outside literature Brasch always preferred good writing to technical expertise; so that they tended to be the views of articulate amateurs. It might be seen as one of the last appearances anywhere of the renaissance man — or as what a later generation referred to disparagingly as 'top of the head stuff'. With the growth of scholarly publication on the one hand and of investigative journalism on the other it was becoming difficult to sustain even by the end of Brasch's editorship.

Besides setting its own agenda, *Landfall* throughout the Brasch years set that of the competing 'little magazines'. (In Geraets's terms *Landfall* was not a 'little magazine' but an 'established periodical'.) Editorial policies were defined by their relation to *Landfall*. Not that this could be said about the longest-running of them, Noel Hoggard's *Arena*. Hoggard, a man without literary talent and with little literary judgement, but with a passion for being in the literary swim, published a succession of little magazines from the early thirties until shortly before his death in 1975. *Letters* from 1943, renamed *Arena* in 1946, was laboriously hand-set and printed in a backyard shed. Some of the contributors to its two or three issues a year would not have been published anywhere else; there were older writers who found that fashion had passed them by, established writers going through a crisis of confidence or wanting to experiment. *Arena*'s most valuable function was to give the experience of publication to several generations of young writers, many of whom became well known — a long list stretching from Keith Sinclair and David Ballantyne to Fiona Kidman and Ian Wedde would be a fitting epitaph. And there was another element: of the eighty-one issues, Louis Johnson contributed to sixty and Kendrick Smithyman to thirty-nine. Neither of them needed to. Genuine affection and admiration possibly tinged with pity must have moved them.

Of the post-*Landfall* magazines, the first was *Hilltop* in 1949, which became *Arachne* (there were three issues under each name). Although it was produced by the Victoria University College Literary Society, it was 'not a student magazine', its first issue declared. Its prime movers were John M. Thomson, Lorna Clendon, and Pat Wilson. Alistair Campbell remembers that '*Hilltop* was to be an alternative to *Landfall*, which we considered stuffy and academic'[121] but there is not much sign of this in the first issue, and it was a little early for *Landfall*'s characteristics to have been defined sufficiently to be reacted against. On the other hand, waiting for *Hilltop* were the poets who became known as the Wellington group, and it was already clear that *Landfall* didn't have the space for everything being produced. Brasch normally restricted authors to one story or one group of poems a year.

By the time *Hilltop* became *Arachne* the editorial group consisted of Louis Johnson, Erik Schwimmer (a young Dutch immigrant with an un-New Zealand interest in literary theory), Hubert Witheford, and W.H. Oliver, and there was more indication that it was an alternative to *Landfall*. It gave prominence, for one thing, to Helen Shaw. But *Arachne* did not last beyond 1951. When in 1954 much the same group of writers brought out *Numbers* it was more assertive, not to say aggressive. An editorial invoked the spirit of Dada 'the iconoclastic': 'We are interested in printing work which, by its experimental nature or forthrightness, may frighten more timid editors.' Holcroft, presumably one of the 'more timid editors', headed a *Listener* editorial 'Lisping in Numbers' and dismissed the manifesto as 'juvenile nonsense'. There was a long-running war between Holcroft and Louis Johnson of which this was neither the first nor the last shot. Holcroft continued to print Johnson's poetry, nonetheless.[122]

In the fourth issue Baxter rejected entirely the concept of 'standards' upheld by Brasch, Holcroft, and (especially) Curnow, who two years before had said that 'easy publication . . . plays the devil with public taste'.[123] In retrospect, while the fireworks remain entertaining, *Numbers*, like most little magazines, was primarily a welcome vehicle for writers publishing wherever they could, and a special one for a few, of whom the most notable, now, is J.C. Sturm.

Holcroft was always sensitive to what he felt as a slight on the *Listener* as a literary magazine, but he had a point in maintaining that there were more openings for writers than there had ever been. The *Listener* was now regularly publishing both poetry and stories, and Holcroft had been battling with broadcasters to ensure that it remained in that role. There were constraints, though, especially for stories. They could rarely be longer than 2000 words, and for family reading there was a limit to possible topics. Nevertheless, as anthologies prove, good stories were printed.

C.A. Marris retired from *Art in New Zealand* in 1942; there was no designated literary editor but a noticeable infiltration of Caxton poets in its remaining four years. For the seven issues of the *Arts Year Book* (there were many variations in the title) which succeeded the quarterly, Fairburn edited a selective showcase of the year's poetry. Louis Johnson in effect, if not by design, took over the role from 1951 with his *New Zealand Poetry Yearbook*, edited on the inclusive principles which provoked Curnow's strictures on easy publication.

Fairburn was also one of those behind *Here and Now*, a current affairs monthly which made a false start in 1949 and revived more modestly a year later. The title both remembered *Tomorrow* and defined the difference. Stylishly edited and printed by Bob Lowry — the most stable activity in his career — and coinciding with Sid Holland and the waterfront dispute, the Cold War and McCarthyism, it was bound to be anti all that; but it did not deal in Utopias. Even so, much of the verse and fiction was overtly political. Much was not, and it had the distinction of publishing Sylvia Ashton-Warner (under the pseudonym of 'Sylvia') before *Spinster* had made her famous. *Here and Now*'s interest in literature faded after three or four years, and it faded itself in 1957. Its line of succession forked, as it were, into *Comment*, which at its beginning was both liberal and Catholic, and the more orthodoxly leftist *New Zealand Monthly Review*. Both published poetry but were scarcely literary reviews.

Lowry printed, though he did not publish, two literary magazines from 1957-8 until, oppressed by unfinished work, he killed himself in 1963. *Image* was edited by Robert Thompson, an industrial chemist and poet, and had a private patron to pay its bills; its image was largely the Auckland of Smithyman, Sinclair, Chapman. The first issue of *Mate* was edited by John Yelash and Kevin Jowsey (who became Ireland); they were unavailable for a second issue and it was taken over by a twenty-two-year-old *Star* reporter, Robin Dudding, who thus began a long career of literary editing. His co-editors and successors included Anthony Stones, Tom McWilliams and Bert Hingley. The egalitarian, mateship connotations of the title seemed to be confirmed by the discovery of Barry Crump, but the founders and later editors were alive to other overtones: spouse or sexual partner and the cognate verb, more sinister meanings in chess and Māori. *Mate* drew more comprehensively from New Zealand writers, including those to be best known in the future, than any contemporary except *Landfall*. Nor was it afraid of demanding writing: it published Kendrick Smithyman's critical series on New Zealand poetry which became *A Way of Saying*.

Brasch had his disagreements with authors (Maurice Shadbolt finally refused to submit anything to him) and his blind spots (which included the growing influence of American poetry, so that he printed as the work of a New Zealander an adaptation of a poem by W.S. Merwin[124]); but it is still the files of *Landfall* to which one goes for the heart of the writing of the time and to which the little magazines remain peripheral. When Brasch resolved to retire in 1966, after twenty years, and began with Caxton a long and sometimes anguished search for a successor, it was Dudding of *Mate* he finally wanted, although Dudding had not applied. Or rather, of several possibles canvassed, Dudding was the only one willing to contemplate the kind of job it would have to be.[125]

Permanence was part of the original concept of *Landfall*. Brasch thought it a weakness in the English monthly *Horizon* to be so identified with Cyril Connolly that it had to die when he quit after ten years. Yet in hindsight it might have been wiser to accept the same fate for *Landfall*, if only for practical reasons. No successor would be able to make *Landfall* a full-time occupation. Brasch lived *Landfall*; it was hardly possible to have a conversation with him without becoming aware that the ideas expressed were being tested in his mind for possible *Landfall* use. He was able to travel the country, visiting writers and seeing paintings, take sabbaticals overseas, and employ an assistant, at no expense to the publishers. But the final decision on the future of *Landfall* was in any case Caxton's. An established periodical with a growing subscription list was not something to throw away lightly.

At first it was university teachers who were considered for the editorship; but Brasch was wary of *Landfall* becoming an English department organ. Then Caxton's publishing editorship became available and Dudding was appointed to that, with *Landfall* included. Brasch genuinely retired and did not try to influence his successor; nevertheless, the Dudding *Landfall* succeeded to his authority, though new writers were introduced (as Brasch would have done) and non-literary contributions gradually faded out. But Dudding needed *Landfall* to be primary and the daily pressures of his job often made it secondary. In 1972 Dudding was dismissed by the Caxton directors after an issue failed to appear on time; the occasion was so trivial that it must have been the breaking-point of accumulating strain. Brasch was distressed and helped Dudding found *Islands*, on which the apostolic succession visibly settled.

Landfall continued under the editorship at first of one of the Caxton directors, Leo Bensemann, better known as a painter and typographer than as a literary man. Many writers obviously relished the fact that there were now two large quarterlies to take their work, but editorially *Landfall* had a tentative air. When Peter Smart, head of the English department at Christ's College, took over he said that he was prepared 'to publish some stories and poems which I feel are only partly successful, because I want this magazine to voice a whole range of writers, old and new',[126] and some issues did look as if he was letting the whole class have a go. Under later editors, *Landfall* found a place for itself further to the left (in a literary sense) than *Islands*. Both *Landfall* and *Islands* attended to other arts besides writing, and *Landfall* was distinguished by fine colour reproductions on its covers, but neither any longer noticed current affairs in general. In the eighties, largely for financial reasons, the appearances of *Islands* became erratic and then apparently ceased. Its space was occupied from 1988 by a substantial semi-annual, *Sport*, published by a new, vigorous 'Wellington group' under the editorship of Fergus Barrowman.

Many writers were published first in student magazines, which from time to time, depending on their editors, transcended their origins. From the Auckland University Literary Society, which in 1932 produced *Phoenix*, came *Freed* ('the word is freed') thirty-seven years later. C.K. Stead has wondered whether 'a proper perspective might not teach students of our literature' to see this as an event 'of comparable symbolic significance'.[127] It was a thought which had already occurred to the editors. A cartoon on the back cover of the last issue showed an academic doing a Ph.D. on *Freed*.

An excited manifesto written by Alan Brunton for the first issue proclaimed that

> The rule of Elders must
> > describe
> its own povery [*sic*] and will itself
> gracefully into non-being

Familiar sentiments, which in the fifth issue Bert Hingley described as 'poetic egofever and arselicking in a dadaist explosion a few decades too late'. The real achievement, Hingley continued, was 'four good poets, Brunton, Haley, Edmond and Mitchell, who have used FREED as a platform at a time when many others would not publish their work'. For once this was not an adequate summary. Brunton's invocations to 'words as things and not as signs', 'the poet as his own hero, his own jaunt through the patois of the tribe', to the names of Carlos Williams, Olson, Creeley, Black Mountain, did achieve the resonances which by the late eighties had impelled the Auckland University library to keep its file 'in the glass case'.

Yet, as Stead was aware, as a myth *Freed* was even more mythical (in the popular meaning of the word) than usual. *Frontiers* of Christchurch had been printing poems-as-objects for a year or two and even had an editor resident in New York (Michael Harlow) to keep it in touch with the hub. And it was the rare editor who would not publish the *Freed* poets. The years around 1970 saw an explosion of little magazines and the *Freed* poets were appearing simultaneously in *Argot* (in which David Mitchell had been exhibiting 'open form' since the early sixties), *Edge*, and the *Universities Yearbook*. *Landfall* and *Islands*, still under the rule of Elders, took only a little longer to catch up. *Mate* (which became *Climate*) was soon an apostle of open form, under the editorship of an older poet, Alistair Paterson.

Little magazines usually had brief lives. In the late seventies and the eighties this became deliberate, an expression of flux. Planned impermanence was a mark of such journals as *Splash*, *And*, *Parallax* and *Rambling Jack*; another (except in the last named) was a high ratio of theory to practice.

Creative writing that was in the widest sense political was still found in the feminist journals, particularly *Broadsheet*. Art that spoke only of itself was no part of their agenda. There was no specifically Māori literary magazine, as an outlet for the other distinctive voice of those years. Even the journal which described itself as multi-cultural and multi-lingual, *Cave* (which became *Pacific Moana Quarterly*, which became *Crosscurrent*) found more contributors among Pacific Islanders than among Māori. From the early fifties Māori writers were encouraged by *Te Ao Hou*, published by the Maori Affairs Department, and its successors published by the Department and the Maori Council. Pākehā editors of *Te Ao Hou* — Erik Schwimmer, Bruce Mason, Margaret Orbell — were distinguished interpreters of Māori to European and had, at that time anyway, mana in the Māori world; yet a paternalistic not to say maternal air rises from the files of *Te Ao Hou*. Writers it introduced, Patricia Grace, Rowley Habib, Witi Ihimaera among them, have since been widely published; but the literary magazine has not become a Māori form.

Deliberately ephemeral little magazines echoed the real world where advertising (which had taken over the word 'creative') and television attracted vigorous writers with promises of a livelihood but no immortality. But print survived. The post-Holcroft *Listener* expanded in size, colour, and circulation but retained through a succession of editors (though with some more strongly than others) a commitment to writing and criticism. There may have been fewer stories but they were often longer. Some of the glossy magazines, like *Metro* and the house journals of airlines and credit-card companies, provided another outlet (and pay) for some writers of fiction. There were signs, hardly conclusive yet, that they might be having some influence on the settings (in the executive class), and on the style (hard glitter).

13

Publishing in New Zealand had never become a fully independent activity, except for some companies for parts of their careers. Booksellers, printers, and institutions were its traditional sponsors. After 1960 a fourth became dominant — the British publisher with local management, accountants, warehouse, and sales staff already in place, to which an editor or two was a minor addition.

Collins Brothers Limited, a subsidiary of Collins Publishers of Glasgow and London, had been established in Auckland since 1888 as an importer and manufacturer of stationery and agent for the parent firm's books. Diaries were published, a few school books, particularly atlases, the very occasional general book. In the late 1950s it was concluded that sales staff would be more welcome to booksellers if they were selling New Zealand books as well as British.[128] Collins embarked on a programme with advice from John Reid, Associate-Professor of English at the University of Auckland, literary critic, broadcaster, film reviewer, a founder of the Mercury Theatre, Catholic apologist, and raconteur. Into a list dominated by natural history, family-life sketches, memoirs of lawyers and surgeons, Reid managed at first to insinuate Smithyman's *A Way of Saying*, a collection of Charles Doyle's poetry, and Doyle's anthology, *Recent Poetry in New Zealand*; but it was soon clear that 'literature' was unprofitable. Collins's publishing continued to be practical and reliable, a reflection of Glasgow's business face.

Collins was followed by Heinemann Educational, whose interest was in the expanding educational market of the prosperous early sixties. Its managing director, David Heap, like most executives of the new transnationals, insisted that he ran an indigenous New Zealand company, but they all had the benefit of a stronger capital base and access to expertise and overseas connections. Heap became known as one of the most astute operators in the business, publishing books exactly tailored to carefully researched requirements, printed plainly and economically, and reasonably priced. He was not averse to general literature, if it fitted his plans. Witi Ihimaera was one of his finds.

Hodder and Stoughton was the next comer. In 1967 an editorship was created for Neil Robinson, literary editor of the *Weekly News*. His list appealed to the *Weekly*'s audience, reflecting a wholesome outdoor life and an interest in local history. He did however begin publishing fiction, and shrewdly picked up Maurice Shadbolt's *Strangers and Journeys*, published in 1972. After he retired, Bert Hingley developed this side of the list, maintaining against received wisdom that fiction could be published profitably without subsidy. Other firms followed his example until by the late eighties it had become normal for New Zealand publishers to publish novels, and for New Zealand novels to be published in New Zealand. This, and the growth in publishing for children, were the most significant shifts in local publishing during this decade.

The Oxford University Press also became a New Zealand publisher, headquarters having become less inclined to take on regional work. They began tentatively in the 1960s, more confidently in the following decade when Bridget Williams and Wendy Harrex returned to New Zealand from editorial experience in Oxford. Large works requiring long lead-times, such as the *Oxford History of New Zealand*, became their particular mark, along with more rapidly produced and profitable anthologies, and one of the best lists for children.

Local people who just liked the idea of being publishers continued to appear. John McIndoe was the third-generation head of a printing firm in Dunedin which bore his grandfather's name (which was also his). He took on one book at his own risk, and was beguiled by the experience. With his first editor, Peter Stewart, he emphasized regional work; with his second, Brian Turner, while retaining the regional base, he added both poetry and fiction. It was hardly profitable if by profit is meant maximum return on capital invested, but he enjoyed it — and ensured a niche for himself in New Zealand's intellectual history. John Dunmore was Professor of French at Massey, and entered publishing with a quarterly 'newspaper' in French for secondary schools. With the cash-flow from this enterprise and the help of his daughter he expanded into books, especially historical and sociological works useful to university classes. For a time the Dunmore Press published fiction jointly with overseas publishers, filling in usefully after Whitcombe's enthusiasm for fiction waned and before Hodder and Stoughton's began.

Alister Taylor began his spectacular career by publishing in his own name a New Zealand version of the sixties-generation subversive text, *The Little Red School-Book*, while he still worked for Reed Educational. He followed it up with *Bull-Shit and Jellybeans* by the student activist Tim Shadbolt, promoted younger poets in collections printed on coloured Abbey-Mill paper, and graduated to expensive, limited-edition art works. The Wellington firm of Price Milburn, general and academic publishers from 1957, capitalized from the 1960s on Beverley Price's genius for devising supplementary infant readers which used minimal vocabularies to tell actual stories. Enormous sales followed, overseas as well as locally (including a series in Welsh).

Publishing by the newly independent universities developed during the sixties. Otago was the first to use the imprint 'University Press', followed by Auckland and Victoria. All three were directed by committees of academics; all three published widely, but each took a characteristic direction. Otago's honorary editor for many years was the librarian, their books being produced and distributed by McIndoe. They remained the more austere, working through overseas associates rather than local booksellers in publishing medical textbooks and studies of Greek literature, though also producing literary essays and the collected poems of Brasch and Dallas. Auckland was the first to appoint a full-time editor; from 1966 their books were distributed by Oxford with a joint imprint, which gave them academic standing but hindered their independent reputation, since it tended to be assumed that Oxford was editorially responsible for their books. Their strengths were in historical works which often broke new ground, a series of New Zealand fiction reprints, and a considerable poetry list. Victoria, which Price Milburn assisted with capital as well as production and distribution, developed complementary lists in play scripts (the first sustained publishing of New Zealand drama) and short story collections. Canterbury's publications committee sponsored a volume or two a year, becoming a University Press in 1988. The other universities published occasionally for their own requirements.

The universities contributed to their presses staffing, accommodation, accounting services, and small cash grants. Sales had to cover most printing and distribution costs and authors' royalties. The subsidized overheads permitted smaller editions than commercial publishers could afford, but they still had to be larger than the small academic community could sustain by itself. Truly esoteric work was therefore seldom published, and each press walked a razor's edge between commitment to scholarship and the need to sell. In theory, it was absurd to have several university presses in one small country; in practice, close daily association within the universities was probably the only way their anomalous presence would be tolerated.

The growth of New Zealand publishing was aided by the long-term decline in the value of the New Zealand dollar. By using low-cost Asian printers, New Zealand publishers were able to keep the prices of their books just below, at times considerably below, British and American imports, at least in hardback. A recognizable publishing profession emerged, though entry into it was still haphazard and training mainly on the job. More attention to sales and marketing became imperative, and there was more competition for manuscripts. Some authors had the new experience of being courted. This also meant, though, that publishers looked for works to fill perceived gaps, and an author became the channel for realizing the publisher's ideas. For ease in selling there was a desire to place books in recognizable categories, and a reluctance to entertain what didn't fit. All this may have been new in New Zealand; it would have been familiar to Grub-street writers in eighteenth century London. On the positive side, the thumbs-down of one publisher did not seem as final. Once published, however, New Zealand books faced the competition of many more New Zealand books; growth in publishing did not mean a matching growth in sales of individual books.

Titles turned over more rapidly. With the need for fast return on capital, books could no longer be kept in print indefinitely. One reason short stories were preferred to novels by local publishers in the forties and fifties was that they seemed more definitive. A collection of stories, summing up an author's work over several years, promised a corresponding sales life. A single novel seemed much more ephemeral. When the planned life of all books was reduced, novels no longer suffered from the comparison.

The need for growth capital was a major reason for what began to happen among locally based companies. Blackwood Paul died in 1965, shortly after the publishing had been separated from the bookshops to become Blackwood and Janet Paul Ltd. (It was an innovation for a woman's name to appear on an imprint, even in tandem with a man's.) Their publishing was expanded to generate income to meet overheads no longer shared with the bookshops, but still virtually without capital. By 1967, when an economic downturn coincided with heavy expenses, the lack proved fatal. Mark Longman of the long-established English firm came to the rescue: Longman Paul Ltd was announced as a merger, but the reality was a takeover. Janet Paul and her staff were soon out of the business, which kept on the profitable titles, expanded the education list, and eventually made a name for encouraging Māori and Polynesian writers, including Patricia Grace and Albert Wendt.[129]

A.H. Reed was knighted at ninety-nine and died nearly a year later, in 1975. A.W. Reed retired formally but retained control through his shareholding. It may be that some quality of assurance went out of the business, even while it seemed to be booming, perhaps even attested by a few gestures towards literature (Frame, Curnow, Sargeson). A.W. Reed claimed, whimsically no doubt, to have the mind of a ten-year-old.[130] Younger editors continued to be aware of the public they had to reach, but not because they shared its tastes — which may themselves have been changing. They also faced more competition: rugby and other sporting books, for example, became the sole concern of a couple of new publishers. In later years, in a complicated series of events, control alternated between outside chairmen and John Reed of the third generation; there were reports of retrenchments and recriminations. The *Singapore Times* bought a controlling interest for the purpose, it turned out, of detaching the Australian subsidiary. The New Zealand business was eventually sold to Associated Book Publishers, of Britain, who were already publishing locally under the Methuen imprint.[131]

Following Bertie Whitcombe's death in 1963, the immediate effect was expansion rather than retrenchment. Whitcombe and Tombs merged with their largest printing rival Coulls Somerville Wilkie to create the Printing and Packaging Corporation, which used the portmanteau name of Whitcoulls for its retail shops and eventually for its publishing.

Publishing began to look like any other business. Managing directors arrived at publishers' meetings in sleek cars shadowed by fresh-faced accountants. Successful executives were poached by rival firms. Editors became unionized and negotiated an award. The one overseas phenomenon not yet seen was the payment of giant advances to best-selling authors. When the new pattern seemed to be settling down in the 1980s, however, it suddenly became clear that takers-over were themselves vulnerable, especially to events overseas. For this and other reasons, publishing in the late eighties, like business and finance in general, was as unstable and difficult to keep track of as the patterns in a kaleidoscope. There was the repeated spectacle of executives being ordered from their offices at an hour's notice by new owners who had learnt their corporate manners from television soaps. By 1990 most major publishers, and many smaller ones, had been caught up in mergers and takeovers, retrenchments and reconstructions — often in a succession of them — and there is no reason to suppose the landscape has stabilized simply to meet a deadline for describing it. It is even less possible to predict the ultimate effect on the kind and quality of publishing.

When the lifespan of a publishing house has come to resemble that of an insect, venerability is rapidly acquired. As a consistent New Zealand publisher Penguin goes back no further than the eighties but has become notably innovative and entrepreneurial, at the same time strengthening its traditional links by acquiring the Whitcoulls (by then Pacific) backlist when Brierley, having acquired the Printing and Packaging Corporation, divested it of its publishing arm. Penguin was also responsible for introducing an American name to New Zealand publishing by using that of its New York partner, Viking, as its hardback imprint. The acquisition by Random House in 1989 of several publishing and distributing companies, and its use of the imprint Random Century, may have turned an innovation into a trend.

Continuity was represented more strongly by the Oxford University Press. Its career in New Zealand was chequered by retrenchments and reorganizations, but a strong list and excellent production were maintained through the editorial strengths of Bridget Williams, Wendy Harrex, and Anne French. Anthologies, children's books, poetry (including selected editions) and reprints of New Zealand 'classics' were joined increasingly by academic works proper, across the arts but especially in history and law.

Among smaller firms: John McIndoe and his brothers, wishing to retire, sold to Alliance Textiles; the Caxton Press partners, for the same reason, sold to another Christchurch printer, Bascands. Publishing would seem to have continued by grace and favour rather than from economic imperative.

Ray Richards left Reeds to become a publishing consultant and New Zealand's first literary agent. Several former corporate executives followed his example by setting up as consultants, 'book packagers', and specialist publishers. One example was Wendy Harrex, from O.U.P., who tapped a feminist market through the New Women's Press. Women had become more prominent generally in publishing. When the editorship of the Auckland University Press was advertised in 1966 none of the twenty-five or so applicants was a woman; twenty years later about half the applicants and all those on the short list were women. Bridget Williams left Oxford to found (with partners) the Port Nicholson Press which became the New Zealand arm of Allen and Unwin, up-market general publishers, and then, in 1990, Bridget Williams Books. Ann Mallinson of Mallinson Rendel showed that a small New Zealand–owned firm with a general list remained a possibility. Wendy Pye followed with flair and enthusiasm the earlier example of Price Milburn in achieving enormous overseas sales for children's readers.

And as always there was a coming and going of small presses giving exposure to new writers or pursuing personal objectives: among them Kevin Cunningham's Amphedesma Press, Alan Loney's Hawk Press, Barry Mitcalfe's

Coromandel Press, Warwick Jordan's Hard Echo Press, Robert de Roo's Moana. Longest lasting of them was Ronald Holloway's Griffin Press, which in 1988 brought out Roderick Finlayson's *In Georgina's Shady Garden*, fifty years after it took over the same author's *Brown Man's Burden* in mid-publication from Lowry's expiring Unicorn.

14

During the fifties and sixties the Literary Fund settled into a routine largely governed by finance. From establishment in 1947 the basic annual vote remained at £2000 for fifteen years. Although inflation was much less severe than it later became, the value of the grant steadily eroded. Even so, most significant writers appear on the lists of grants; some of them, like Bruce Mason and Janet Frame, at critical moments in their careers. The emphasis was still on grants to publishers and periodicals, however. In three years, 1954–7, 14 percent of the money granted went directly to writers, 49 percent to publishers, and 30 percent to periodicals (including the *Poetry Yearbook* whose grant in those years was the same as for *Landfall*). Of the grants to publishers, the percentages were 8 for poetry, 28 for fiction, 9 for criticism, 51 for other non-fiction, and 4 for one non-fiction reprint. Writers pressed for a larger share, and in 1956 £500 was added to the Fund's grant for an annual scholarship in letters. The first scholar was E.H. McCormick ('a wise and sober choice', noted *Landfall*); subsequent holders were nearly all novelists. The following year a further £100 was added for an award for achievement, given first to Janet Frame. In 1962 the scholarship and award became a charge on lottery funds and the departmental vote for them was added to the basic grant, the first such increase.[132]

The Fund's public relations were only occasionally ruffled. The issue of *Numbers* for February 1959 was 'A Special Issue of Wellington Writing to mark the City's First Festival'; not surprisingly it directed a few shafts at the city's philistines. Both Wellington dailies tried to work up a row. 'SALACIOUS TALES BY N.Z. AUTHORS' was an *Evening Post* headline on 10 February: 'Helped by State Literary Fund'. There was an acrimonious correspondence for a couple of weeks, but no later echoes.

Charles Brasch had never been suspicious of state patronage *per se*. In his quarterly 'Notes' he followed the work of the Fund in a mainly friendly fashion, and he applied for and accepted a grant even though it was restricted to paying the authors of 'literary' contributions. But by 1962 he began to run out of patience.

The list of new books sponsored by the Committee of the Literary Fund which went out of office last August at the end of its three-year term is no doubt unexceptionable, but it is deadly safe . . . .. There is nothing . . . which a good publisher would consider dangerously speculative. It may be that nothing of the sort turned up in those three years; we cannot tell, not knowing what work came before the Committee besides that which it subsidized. But now and then the bush telegraph reports that some work seemingly speculative (in this sense) has been refused a grant, and since such reports are unlikely to be always wrong, they cause disquiet . . . . In the case of fiction particularly, might it not put more faith in the judgment of the responsible adventurous publisher with a reputation at stake? It puts such trust — it is bound to — in the judgment of editors, who ask for a grant for their journals as a whole and not for particular items in them . . . .

Brasch further suggested that there should be a limit to the number of unbroken terms served by any member of the Committee, preserving continuity by staggering retirements, and that Professor Gordon, as chairman, should be 'granted a long rest'.[133]

Gordon was still chairman two years later when for the first and only time the Committee attempted to interfere with the content of a subsidized periodical. On a 'divided vote', that year's grant to the *Poetry Yearbook* was made conditional on the removal of six poems by James K. Baxter (who was himself a member of the Committee). Louis Johnson declined to remove the poems. The argument which arose was nothing to that which erupted when Holcroft defended the Committee, of which he too was a member, in a *Listener* editorial which described Johnson as a poet 'whose persona needs enlargement beyond the making of verse', credited him with 'a devious mind', and maintained that 'the Committee made an editorial judgment which Mr Johnson should have made himself much earlier'. Margaret Dalziel resigned from the Committee in protest, Brasch was appalled, and Holcroft twenty years later admitted that his judgement had been astray.[134]

The following year Brasch was again critical, this time about the appointment to the Committee of the literary adviser to a publisher (meaning John Reid, although he was not named). 'Is it proper for a member of the Literary Fund Committee to be associated with a publisher, even if only in an advisory capacity?'[135] That argument was turned on its head some years later, after Reid had died, when publishers asked how the Committee could make sensible decisions without any knowledge of publishing economics. The point was taken, and a publisher sat on the Committee thereafter.

One conclusion Brasch did not draw is that the Committee might have been more adventurous with more money. At first the reverse happened. In 1967, at a time of financial stringency, Robert Muldoon's first budget reduced the vote for the Fund. Partially restored in 1968 it was slashed again in 1969, although lottery funds helped to make up the deficiency. After the election of Norman Kirk's Labour government, however, when C.K. Stead was appointed chairman, the grant was sharply increased over successive years. The Committee at last felt able to make more direct grants to authors.[136] This worked in tandem with expanding publishing opportunities to stimulate the writing (especially) of novels and books for children.

The Kirk government also moved to compensate authors for the use of their books by libraries. In its purest form, the public lending right, for which Ian Cross especially had been campaigning, is a royalty on each borrowing of a library book. The Authors' Fund as it was implemented was a hybrid. It was paid on a notional figure of library holdings of books by living New Zealand authors, calculated from a five-yearly census of a selected sample of libraries. In theory it was a payment of right for the use of property, not patronage; but since it was paid by the government and not the libraries, and to authors only and not to their estates or publishers, there was still an element of state assistance to authors. The first payout in 1973 was a generous $1.30 per copy (provided fifty or more of each title were held). At the time this made a significant contribution to the income of professional authors. Thereafter the fund suffered the fate of other generous provisions which governments dislike but hesitate to repudiate, in remaining static while inflation raged. The total payout did increase as more books and authors became eligible, but not until 1988 did the rate per copy exceed the original one and the value remained much less.

Authors vied instead for the increasing but still inconsiderable number of fellowships. The Literary Fund's Scholarship in Letters was soon followed by the Robert Burns Fellowship established at the University of Otago by 'a group of citizens' who wished to remain anonymous. They are still officially anonymous, but it has always been assumed that Charles Brasch was the prime mover. The fellow was paid for a year at a rate not lower than that for a university lecturer. A room was provided in the English Department, and the fellow might be asked but not required to deliver a lecture or two. The only requirement was to live in Dunedin. An occasional fellow found this irksome, but Dunedin people certainly appreciated the contribution that successive fellows made to the intellectual life of the city.

The Burns Fellowship remained more generous than any other, and for many years was alone in requiring no state contribution. When provision was made for writers-in-residence at three other universities in 1979-81 they were all lower paid, of shorter duration, and subsidized — but no anonymous citizens came forward to endow them. The Literary Fund did persuade commerce to partly finance several bursaries and awards, though it was the Publishers' Association which initiated the best-known annual competition, the Wattie Book of the Year, sponsored from 1968 by Wattie Industries (later Goodman Fielder Wattie). Publishers and booksellers heavily promoted the short list and eventual winner, and judging conditions were adjusted from time to time to ensure that the books chosen were promotable. The New Zealand Book Awards, another Kirk government innovation, which from 1976 were given in the categories of fiction, non-fiction, poetry, and (from 1980) book production, were designed to confer prestige without commercial taint. There were complaints for years that the purity extended to lack of any effective publicity at all.

At this distance, some of the fears expressed when the Literary Fund was established may seem naïve. No doubt much of the 'safe and second-rate' was supported, but there are few known instances of the first-rate being turned down. Writers have neither become lackeys of politicians nor timid in the face of public opinion. The social climate is the most difficult aspect of the future to prophesy, and a general lessening of reverence for authority and liberation of opinion have armed and protected writers against the foreseen dangers. Overt attempts at political interference have been rare, although in 1982 the National Party caucus attempted to veto P.E.N. nominations of C.K. Stead and Louis Johnson to the Advisory Committee, either from dislike of their politics or (as one M.P. claimed) because they were not women. There have been few outbreaks of public outrage. Nor have those writers supported for a time on public (and private) funds declined into lethargy. Fiction, in particular, has grown in both vitality and purpose, as well as in quantity, as time has been made available to write it.

How much this proves is doubtful. It has not yet been possible for any writer to be given a long period free from financial anxiety (several years that is). The most they can hope for is a succession of fellowships, which often require changes of residence. The necessity to wait on the decisions of committees provides quite enough of the inner conflict which was Holcroft's prerequisite for creative success. Writers who have 'turned professional' have had to subsist on a mix or succession of grants and fellowships, of income from royalties, of part-time or short-term jobs, script-writing, commissioned 'non-books' and journalism, and sometimes of unemployment relief or the support of a spouse. 'Continuity is what I dream of,' Ian Wedde was reported as saying.[137]

Some older writers have been deterred by the pride they learnt in their youth, or from conviction that it is all irrelevant to their purpose, from attempting to board the fellowship roundabout. Most younger writers seem inured to subjecting themselves to judgement in competition with their fellows, but some temperaments are better fitted than others to work the system effectively and survive it emotionally, an ability not necessarily correlated with talent, although not incompatible with talent, either.

Much harder to detect than political or moral influence, would be any tendency to adapt in writing to the perceived literary or philosophical preferences of selection committees. If it were done it would probably be half-conscious and hard to distinguish from whatever other influences incline writers of a generation to conform to one another.

In 1988 responsibility for supporting literature was transferred to the Queen Elizabeth II Arts Council, and the former advisory committee became a committee of the Council. Terry Sturm's chairmanship bridged the transition. His advocacy, a succession of sympathetic Labour government ministers, and the popularity of new lotteries, all played their part in an increase in funding which would have seemed unimaginable a few years earlier. In 1990 the money available to the literature programme of the Arts Council reached a million dollars. This was still a long way short of the ten percent of all arts funding for which P.E.N. had been pressing, but enabled a beginning to be made on another of their aims, two-year writing fellowships.

It has been contrary to expectations in 1947 that in the last years of the Literary Fund regime direct grants to writers were much more significant than assistance to publishers (71 percent of expenditure in 1985-6 direct to writers, 12 percent to publishers, and 7 percent to magazines).[138] One early hope was that books published with Literary Fund support at a 'nominal price' would find a mass market. It was a shock to some early commentators to find books subsidized by the Literary Fund appearing in bookshops at prices no lower than most other books. The Committee recognized that some good books will not sell in large numbers however low the price, and concurred with publishers that its most useful function was to enable publication of small editions at a 'normal' price.

The influence of the Fund can most clearly be traced in broad categories. It was strongest in poetry. For a generation, most volumes of poetry were published with Literary Fund assistance. Virtually no collections of literary criticism appeared without its support, unless specifically designed for an educational market. Steadily over the years it aided the republication of 'New Zealand classics', especially fiction. Most collections of short stories were supported and many novels, but probably even more novels were published independently, either in New Zealand or overseas, and it is difficult to decide which were 'better', though the subsidized novels may occasionally have been more experimental. Its strongest support for the advancing edge of literature was through its continuing grants to magazines. The Fund was least supportive to general non-fiction. When squeezed financially it preferred to support 'creative' writing, until the late 1980s, when special funding was secured for non-fiction.

Not all New Zealand publishers got, or wanted, the assistance of the Fund. The larger, more commercial, and increasingly international publishers tended not to be interested. They preferred to make their decisions on their assessment of market possibilities, and some of them became quite adventurous, especially with fiction. Publishers were also moving, with the support of authors, to extend the market by seeking payment for the photocopying of copyright material. (Some authors, too, were beginning to exploit the market by auctioning their books to publishers.)

Most Literary Fund grants were given to the university presses, small independent publishers, and private presses. This became so marked that a case was revived for sustaining grants to be given to publishers with a proven record of taking on good but unprofitable work, and leaving the particular judgements to the publishers themselves. A parallel system of judgement, it was argued, wasted both money and time. Such a system, however, might prompt questions about the real difference between publishers: is it in the quality of the work published, or in consciousness of the market and ability to exploit it? Do regular grants for, especially, poetry merely accustom buyers to unrealistic prices? Might they, after a period of adjustment, become reconciled to an economic price, as with other commodities formerly subsidized, like milk and bread? This would be a seductive argument to those convinced of the virtues of the market. The problem is that when production is already low, any reduction at all will inordinately increase the unit cost. In the 'real world' a commodity which reaches this point is simply discontinued, or is produced as a frankly expensive article for a luxury or highly specialized trade. We are driven back to the axioms with which the Literary Fund started, that some activities have intrinsic value, and that their products ought to be disseminated as widely as possible. The question now facing the whole arts community is whether the case for intrinsic value still holds, in the face of theories and practice which emphasize the mutable and the ephemeral.

Bibliography

JOHN THOMSON

Introductory Note

This discursive bibliography is divided into four general sections — bibliographies and other works of reference, literary history and criticism, anthologies, and periodicals — followed by individual author entries. While providing the detailed information needed to answer specific inquiries, its aim is to be sufficiently approachable to offer, if read at length, a sense of the nature and range of material available.

Under authors' names an indication of the publishing history is usually provided as well. (Note that the term 'reprinted' is used not in its strict bibliographical sense, but rather to indicate a new edition, usually by a different publisher.) With a few exceptions, only an author's separately published volumes are included. Information about the work of a number of writers who may be known for one book only (for instance Charles Spear, John Reece Cole, and Michael Henderson) is provided earlier in the relevant chapters, and is not repeated here. For a detailed account of the bibliographical record relating to Māori language and literature, readers are referred to Jane McRae's section of this History, 'Māori Literature: A Survey'.

Critical discussions in articles or books devoted to an author are identified under that author's name, but reference is not made there to discussion to be found in books or essays of wider range, for instance *The Penguin History of New Zealand Literature*, or Allen Curnow's introductions to his poetry anthologies. For an indication of the full breadth of criticism available on any author, readers should also use the 'Literary History and Criticism' section of this bibliography. Where critical work is not extensive, fuller reference is provided to university theses, reviews, and magazine articles.

Abbreviations

AL   *Answering to the Language*, by C.K. Stead, Auckland, Auckland University Press, 1989

APL   Auckland Public Library

ATL   Alexander Turnbull Library, National Library, Wellington

B   *Beginnings: New Zealand Writers Tell How They Began Writing*, ed. with an introduction by Robin Dudding, Wellington, Oxford University Press, 1980

BHB   *Bird, Hawk, Bogie: Essays on Janet Frame*, ed. Jeanne Delbaere-Garant, Aarhus, Dangaroo Press, 1978

BWM   *Barbed Wire & Mirrors*, by Lawrence Jones, Dunedin, University of Otago Press, 1987

CENZN   *Critical Essays on the New Zealand Novel*, ed. Cherry Hankin, Auckland, Heinemann Educational Books, 1976

CRNLE   Centre for Research in the New Literatures in English

ed.   edited *or* edited by

ENZL   *Essays on New Zealand Literature*, ed. Wystan Curnow, Auckland, Heinemann Educational Books, 1973

FP   *Flight of the Phoenix: Critical Notes on New Zealand Writers*, by James Bertram, Wellington, Victoria University Press, 1985

FS   *Fretful Sleepers and Other Essays*, by W.H. Pearson, Auckland, Heinemann Educational Books, 1974

HL   Hocken Library, University of Otago, Dunedin

IGC   *In the Glass Case*, by C.K. Stead, Auckland, Auckland University Press, 1981

JCL   *Journal of Commonwealth Literature*

JNZL   *Journal of New Zealand Literature*

LBH   *Look Back Harder*, ed. Peter Simpson, Auckland, Auckland University Press, 1987

NLA   National Library of Australia, Canberra

NZCER   New Zealand Council for Educational Research

NZWW   New Zealand Writers and Their Work

OOC   *Our Own Country*, ed. Sue Kedgley, Auckland, Penguin, 1989

TLS   *Times Literary Supplement*

TWAS   Twayne's World Authors Series

WLWE   *World Literature Written in English*

Bibliographies and other works of reference

General

The essential bibliography for New Zealand literature in the broadest sense is the *New Zealand National Bibliography to the Year 1960*, ed. A.G. Bagnall, 5 vols, Wellington, Government Printer, 1969-85. Volume 1, in two parts, covers the period to 1889, the remaining volumes, with supplement and index, the period 1890-1960. The best of its predecessors was T.M. Hocken's *A Bibliography of the Literature Relating to New Zealand*, Wellington, Government Printer, 1909, reprinted Wellington, Newrick Associates, 1973, which is of interest for its introduction, and for its brief annotations which show Hocken to have been unimpressed by his country's imaginative literature in its early days. The years since 1960 have seen an enormous increase in the number of books of imaginative literature published, and Bagnall's bibliography must be supplemented by the *Current National Bibliography of New Zealand Books and Pamphlets Published in 1961*, annual to 1965, Wellington, National Library of New Zealand, which was issued bound with the *Index to New Zealand*

Periodicals. The *New Zealand National Bibliography* was first published separately for the year 1966, and was annual to 1982, with a subject index and details of new periodicals and of those which had ceased publication. Since then it has appeared annually on microfiche. The National Library's database, New Zealand Bibliographic Network, provides full information, including New Zealand library holdings, from 1982. A retrospective conversion programme is in progress and has covered most of the preceding fourteen years. Most important libraries are linked to the network and are charged for its use. A *Bibliography of New Zealand Bibliographies*, Wellington, New Zealand Library Association, 1967, based on a Library School exercise by S.J. Cauchi, covered manuscripts, newspapers, theses, libraries, Māori literature, theatre, biography, and imaginative literature in English. 'A Bibliography of Library School Bibliographies, 1946-72', ed. Anne Rimmer and William Siddells, Wellington, Library School, 1972, provided both descriptive and evaluative annotations. These bibliographies were not as a rule formally published, but can be borrowed from the National Library within New Zealand through the interloan service. The series 'Bibliographical Work in Progress', *New Zealand Libraries*, annual from 1962, recorded work published as well as work in progress. It has been replaced by *Bibliographical Work in New Zealand: Work in Progress and Work Published*, ed. A.P.U. Millett and F.T.H. Cole, annual since 1980, Hamilton, University of Waikato Library, which includes indexes to New Zealand newspapers, working files in libraries (with a subject index), and a general author and subject index.

The *Union List of Theses of the University of New Zealand 1910-1954*, ed. D.L. Jenkins, Wellington, New Zealand Library Association, 1956, has been supplemented by different editors and under slightly different titles in 1963, 1969, 1972, 1976, 1980, 1984, and 1989, covering the years up to 1985. *New Zealand Books in Print*, Wellington, New Zealand Book Publishers' Association, began triennially in 1957; from 1979 it has been annual (Melbourne, D.W. Thorpe Pty Ltd) and includes book publishers, and other related associations, literary societies, prizes and awards, and a list of New Zealand publishers. G.A. Wood's *Studying New Zealand History*, Dunedin, University of Otago Press, 1988, is of considerable use to students of New Zealand literature. J.E. Traue, *New Zealand Studies: A Guide to Bibliographic Resources*, Victoria University Press for the Stout Research Centre, 1985, covers a wider range of material.

General Literature
The first attempt at a literary bibliography was the not very useful *Annals of New Zealand Literature; Being a Preliminary List of New Zealand Authors and Their Works*, ed. J.C. Andersen, Wellington, New Zealand Authors' Week Committee, 1936. Of wider range and more recent date, but of limited use owing to the exclusion of articles, is *Books and Pamphlets Relating to Culture and the Arts in New Zealand*, ed. Bernard W. Smyth and Hilary Howorth, Christchurch, Department of Extension Studies, University of Canterbury, 1978. *Australian Literature: A Bibliography to 1938* by E. Morris Miller, extended

to 1950 by Frederick T. Macartney, Sydney, Angus & Robertson, 1956, includes some New Zealand writers on the strength of their being born or having lived in Australia, and provides in addition biographical details and brief essays on their work. *New Zealand Literature to 1977*, ed. John Thomson, Detroit, Gale Research Co., 1980, built on and superseded by the present bibliography, has the advantage of title as well as author indexes. W.H. Pearson's 'Bibliography: The Maori and Literature', in *The Maori People in the Nineteen-Sixties*, ed. Eric Schwimmer, Auckland, Blackwood & Janet Paul, 1968, which covers the years 1938-65, is an updating and expansion of Pearson's earlier list in *Journal of the Polynesian Society*, vol. 67, 1958, where some pre-1938 material was also included. Ruth Ensor's bibliography (see below) is much fuller on earlier fiction, but Pearson includes verse, drama, uncollected short stories, popular fiction, and critical material. New Zealand literature appears in the *Annual Bibliography of English Language and Literature* and, very thinly, in the *MLA International Bibliography of Books and Articles on the Modern Languages and Literatures*, but both series are outclassed by the invaluable 'Annual Bibliography of Commonwealth Literature: New Zealand', which has appeared in the *Journal of Commonwealth Literature* beginning with the year 1964. A descriptive essay on the year's literary events accompanies each bibliography.

Poetry
Amongst bibliographies of poetry, P. Serle's *A Bibliography of Australasian Poetry and Verse*, Melbourne University Press, 1925, and Peter Alcock's 'A Select Bibliography of New Zealand Verse and Some Related Writing, 1920-1952', Wellington, Library School, 1952, are of largely historical interest, and E.I. Cuthbert, *Index of Australian and New Zealand Poetry*, New York, Scarecrow Press, 1963, includes only the poems in a few important anthologies. 'New Zealand Poetry: A Select Bibliography, 1920-72', ed. John Weir and Barbara Lyon, Christchurch, The Library, University of Canterbury, 1977, issued in only eleven copies, valuably lists first lines of all poems published by more than twenty poets with details of first appearance and later publication. Critical material is also included. The major living New Zealand poets are to be found in *Contemporary Poets*, ed. James Vinson and D.L. Kirkpatrick, 4th edition, London, St James Press, and New York, St Martin's Press, 1985, which, besides lists of published volumes, also includes comment by each poet and a brief critical essay. Earlier editions include a few poets who have since died. Of more specialized interest are J.E. Weir, 'Five New Zealand Poets: A Bibliographical and Critical Account of Manuscript Material', thesis, University of Canterbury, 1974, which discusses some manuscripts, including letters, by R.A.K. Mason, Ursula Bethell, Eileen Duggan, James K. Baxter, and Alistair Campbell; Margery Walton, 'A Bibliography of Poetry Published and Printed at The Caxton Club Press and The Caxton Press, Christchurch, 1934-63', Wellington, Library School, 1963; and J.R. Winter, 'New Zealand Women Poets: Works Published Since 1970: An Annotated Bibliography', Wellington, Library School, 1977.

Fiction

James Burns, *New Zealand Novels and Novelists 1861-1979*, Auckland, Heinemann, 1981, is a useful quick chronological guide with an author and title index. 'A Bibliography of New Zealand Prose Fiction, 1778-1948', included by Joan Gries in her thesis, 'An Outline of Prose Fiction in New Zealand', University of Auckland, 1951, remains the most thorough bibliography for that earlier period. It includes titles of short stories published in collected volume form. Three Library School bibliographical exercises are of interest especially for their annotations. They are E.M.M. Millen, 'New Zealand Fiction 1947-1957: An Annotated List of Novels and Collected Short Stories', Wellington, 1957; Janet Horncy and Catherine Hutchinson, 'New Zealand Fiction, October 1957-1968: An Annotated List of Novels and Collected Short Stories', Wellington, 1968; and R.M. McKenzie, 'The Short Story and New Zealand Society: A Bibliography', Wellington, 1967, which comments on material published from 1934 on. More specialized is Ruth Ensor, 'The Treatment of the Maori in Fiction: A Bibliography of Novels and Collected Short Stories, 1861-1967, Annotated and Arranged in Chronological Order', Wellington, 1968. *Contemporary Novelists*, ed. James Vinson and D.L. Kirkpatrick, 4th edition, London, St James Press, and New York, St Martin's Press, 1986, provides up-to-date bibliographies of and critical essays on the major New Zealand novelists.

Drama

There are three Library School bibliographical exercises relevant to drama. They are Rosemary Mathias, 'New Zealand Amateur Theatre: A Select Bibliography', Wellington, 1963, Sally Edridge, 'Bibliography of New Zealand Drama, 1953-1963', Wellington, 1964, and Gwen Hopkins, 'A Chronological Survey of Professional Theatre In New Zealand: A Select Bibliography', Wellington, 1968. Howard McNaughton's *New Zealand Drama: A Bibliographical Guide*, Christchurch, The Library, University of Canterbury, 1974, was the first comprehensive list, by playwright's name, of plays for stage, radio, and television, the great majority of them unpublished. The most recent such list is *The Playmarket Directory of NZ Plays and Playwrights*, Wellington, Playmarket, 1985, which includes full-length and one-act plays, plays for children, and musicals and operas. *Contemporary Dramatists*, ed. D.L. Kirkpatrick, 4th edition, Chicago, St James Press, 1988, parallels the volumes for poets and novelists described above.

Māori Literature

Bibliographical aids to writing in Māori (and English translation) include *A Bibliography of Printed Maori to 1900* by H.W. Williams, Wellington, Government Printer, 1924, and 'A Supplement to the Williams Bibliography of Printed Maori', by A.D. Somerville, 1947, a Library School bibliography which covers material published between 1900 and 1947 and adds many pre-1900 items. Two other such bibliographies are Linda Hurst, 'A Select, Annotated Bibliography of Publications on the Myths, Legends and Folk Tales of the Maori', Wellington,

Library School, 1973, and Graeme Siddle, 'Aspects of Maoritanga: A Select Bibliography for Public Libraries', Wellington, Library School, 1975, which has well-annotated sections on language, poetry, action songs, and proverbs. Here may also be mentioned two bibliographies covering the South Pacific: Esther Williams, *South Pacific Literature Written in English*, Suva, University of the South Pacific Library, 1979, and Vibeke Stenderup, *Pacific Islands Creative Writing: A Select Annotated Guide*, Hojbjerb, Vibeke Stenderup, 1985. The New Zealand Film Archive issues catalogues of its Māori and Pacific films.

Related Subjects
Useful for areas related to the study of literature are Kathleen Coleridge, 'A Bibliography of New Zealand English', Wellington, Library School, 1966, Kathryn Rennie, 'New Zealand Journalism: A Selective Bibliography', Wellington, Library School, 1968, and Penelope Griffith, 'Printing and Publishing in New Zealand: A Preliminary Bibliography', Wellington, Library School, 1974.

Biography
Biographical dictionaries are unhelpful as sources of information on New Zealand writers. *A Dictionary of New Zealand Biography*, ed. G.H. Scholefield, Wellington, Department of Internal Affairs, 1940, excluded living people and thus most notable writers. Although the first volume of *The Dictionary of New Zealand Biography*, ed. W.H. Oliver, Wellington, Allen & Unwin and Department of Internal Affairs, covering the years 1769-1869, was published in 1990, volumes covering the writers of the 1930s and later are unlikely to appear for some time. *Who's Who in New Zealand*, published irregularly since 1908, 11th edition, ed. J.E. Traue, Wellington, Reed, 1978, (with a 12th edition announced for 1991) and *Notable New Zealanders*, Auckland, Paul Hamlyn, 1979, provide the usual basic information. Authors who are published in the United States usually appear in the annual *Contemporary Authors: A Bio-Bibliographical Guide to Current Authors and Their Works*, Detroit, Gale Research Co., 1962-78, continued from 1981 as *Contemporary Authors: New Revision Series*. Biographical information is also included in *Contemporary Poets*, *Novelists*, and *Dramatists* (see above).

Serials
Amongst indexes to serial publications the most useful is the annual *Index to New Zealand Periodicals*, Wellington, National Library of New Zealand, which covers the period 1941-86, and which increasingly covered material of New Zealand interest appearing in overseas periodicals. It has been replaced, from 1987, by *Index New Zealand*, available on paper and microfiche, which is a far less usable printout of a database. The database, INNZ, is searchable on Kiwinet, and in that form is much more sensitive to specific inquiries. A charge is made for its use. *The Finding List*, on microfiche, Wellington, National Library of New Zealand, 1987, attempts to keep abreast of current holdings of

serials in New Zealand libraries, and is regularly updated. For newspapers there is D.R. Harvey, *Union List of Newspapers Preserved in Libraries, Newspaper Offices, Local Authority Offices and Museums in New Zealand*, Wellington, National Library, 1987, which covers all New Zealand papers to 1986 and includes microform holdings as well. Library catalogues on microfiche provide in effect published catalogues, though their expense restricts widespread availability.

Manuscripts
Still at an early stage is the *National Register of Archives and Manuscripts in New Zealand*, Wellington, National Library of New Zealand, 1979-. Only a small portion of the country's manuscripts are yet covered, two volumes having been published by 1987, each separately indexed. New material is being entered on a database. *The Union Catalogue of New Zealand and Pacific Manuscripts in New Zealand Libraries*, Wellington, ATL, 1968-9, remains of some use in the meantime. Manuscripts acquired by the ATL have been described in *Turnbull Library Record* since 1967, and important archive collections and accessions in other libraries in *Archifacts* since 1974. Readings of verse and prose are included in *Sounds Historical: A Catalogue of the Sound History Recordings in the Sound Archives of Radio New Zealand*, 2 vols, Wellington, Radio New Zealand, 1983. An archive of recordings specifically devoted to literature is being developed at the Stout Research Centre, Victoria University of Wellington. An interim catalogue is being prepared.

New Zealand English
Early material on New Zealand English of mainly historical interest includes E.E. Morris, *Austral-English: A Dictionary of Australasian Words, Phrases and Usages*, London, Macmillan, 1898, and S.J. Baker, *New Zealand Slang: A Dictionary of Colloquialisms*, Christchurch, Whitcombe & Tombs, 1941. Arnold Wall's *New Zealand English: A Guide to the Correct Pronunciation of English*, 4th edition, Christchurch, Whitcombe & Tombs, 1961, belongs to prescriptive days. George Turner, *The English Language in Australia and New Zealand*, London, Longmans, 1966, concentrates on Australia and on vocabulary. The best book to date on an under-researched subject is *New Zealand English*, Auckland, Heinemann, 1985, by E. Gordon and T. Deverson, which discusses pronunciation and vocabulary for school students, but is of wider value. The same authors' *Finding a New Zealand Voice*, Auckland, New House Publishers, 1989, also for schools, covers the same topics but with more historical content and an emphasis on attitudes to New Zealand English. The *New Zealand English Newsletter*, 1987-, reflects current scholarly research; no. 2, 1988, contains a valuable bibliography on New Zealand English by Tony Deverson. Essays on New Zealand English include those by Jack Bennett (1943), reprinted in *English Transported: Essays on Australasian English*, ed. W.S. Ramson, Canberra, Australian National University Press, 1970, which also contains an essay by George Turner; H.W. Orsman in *British and American English Since*

1900, by Eric Partridge and John Clark, London, Andrew Dakers, 1951; and Arnold Wall (on 'New Zealand Speech') in *An Encyclopaedia of New Zealand* (see below). The most readily accessible short list of specifically New Zealand words was compiled by R.W. Burchfield for *The Pocket Oxford Dictionary*, 5th edition, Oxford, Clarendon Press, 1969. Best regarded as a lively stopgap is *Up the Boohai Shooting Pukakas: A Dictionary of New Zealand Slang*, by David McGill, Lower Hutt, Mills Publishing, 1988. Words and usages peculiar to New Zealand are included in the *Heinemann New Zealand Dictionary*, ed. H.W. Orsman, 2nd edition, Auckland, Heinemann Reid, 1989; *The New Zealand Pocket Oxford Dictionary*, ed. R.W. Burchfield, Auckland, Oxford University Press, 1986, is less full. Until the publication in 1992 of *A Dictionary of New Zealand English*, ed. H.W. Orsman, *A Supplement to the Oxford English Dictionary*, ed. R.W. Burchfield, 4 vols, Oxford, Clarendon Press, 1972–86, provides the richest illustrative and historical examples of New Zealand words and usages.

Māori
Māori has been less well served lexicographically, despite the existence since 1844 of *A Dictionary of the Maori Language*, 7th rev. edition, by H.W. Williams, Wellington, Government Printer, 1971. Recent concise English dictionaries have included Māori words commonly used in New Zealand English, for example, the *Heinemann New Zealand Dictionary*, ed. H.W. Orsman, 2nd edition, Auckland, Heinemann Reed, 1989, and the *Collins New Zealand Compact Dictionary of the English Language*, ed. Ian Gordon, Auckland, Collins, 1985. A descriptive Māori Grammar, considerably more complete than *Let's Learn Maori* by Bruce Biggs, Wellington, Reed, 1969, is being prepared by W.A. Bauer for Routledge, and is likely to appear in 1992.

General Reference
Reference works which are useful sources of general information related to literature are *An Encyclopaedia of New Zealand*, ed. A.H. McLintock, 3 vols, Wellington, Government Printer, 1966, *New Zealand Atlas*, ed. Ian Wards, Wellington, Government Printer, 1976, which also includes a wide variety of descriptive essays, and *Gazetteer of New Zealand Placenames*, Wellington, Department of Lands and Survey, 1968, which gives grid references to the older non-metric maps. *Wises New Zealand Guide: A Gazetteer of New Zealand*, Auckland, Wises Publications, 1979, is less complete but more accessible. The origins and meanings of place-names are described by A.W. Reed in *Place Names of New Zealand*, Wellington, Reed, 1975, and in his *Supplement to Place Names of New Zealand*, Wellington, Reed Trust, 1979.

The *New Zealand Official Yearbook*, Wellington, Department of Statistics, annual since 1893, has for the last forty years included a select bibliography of old and new books on all subjects, including a selection of titles of imaginative literature. The standard New Zealand history is *The Oxford History of New Zealand*, ed. W.H. Oliver, Oxford, Clarendon Press, and Wellington, Oxford

University Press, 1981. Art is covered by Gil Docking, *Two Hundred Years of New Zealand Painting*, Wellington, Reed, 1971; Elva Bett, *New Zealand Art: A Modern Perspective*, Auckland, Reed Methuen, 1986, surveys the period from about 1970. J.M. Thomson has written a *Biographical Dictionary of New Zealand Composers*, Wellington, Victoria University Press, 1990. Nicholas Reid, *A Decade of New Zealand Films*, Dunedin, McIndoe, 1986, examines ten films from the preceding decade, and has an historical introduction. The *Heinemann Dictionary of New Zealand Quotations*, ed. Harry Orsman and Jan Moore, Auckland, Heinemann, 1988, is an entertaining oddity.

Literary history and criticism

General Studies
There are very few books about New Zealand literature, and of these most are collections of essays or are separately published lectures. The earliest historical survey was E.H. McCormick's *Letters and Art in New Zealand*, Wellington, Department of Internal Affairs, 1940, which in its recast form, *New Zealand Literature: A Survey*, London, Oxford University Press, 1959, remained until 1990 the only full-length study. A succinct and appreciative survey, it gave, even in its later form, too little space to work written after 1930, but did consider earlier books of history, travel, and anthropology. (It was preceded by McCormick's fuller 1929 thesis for the University of New Zealand, 'Literature in New Zealand'.) John Reid, *Creative Writing in New Zealand: A Brief Critical History*, Auckland, 1946, is slight in comparison, as is Alan Mulgan, *Literature and Authorship in New Zealand*, London, Allen & Unwin, 1943. But in 1990 appeared *The Penguin History of New Zealand Literature*, Auckland, Penguin, by Patrick Evans, an individual and sometimes provocative study which valuably places the strictly literary part of the history in a much wider context of cultural history, publishing history, and international literary history, all done with admirable verve and brevity. M.H. Holcroft developed an important series of essays in the 1940s, published in three parts, *The Deepening Stream: Cultural Influences in New Zealand*, Christchurch, Caxton, 1940, *The Waiting Hills*, Wellington, Progressive Publishing Society, 1943, and *Encircling Seas*, Christchurch, Caxton, 1946; and as a trilogy, *Discovered Isles*, Christchurch, Caxton, 1950. These essays range well beyond purely literary matters, but at the heart of his argument is his vision of the geographical and cultural isolation of the artist. Widely admired in the 1940s, these essays were almost equally widely criticized in the 1950s, as by D.M. Anderson, *Landfall*, no. 21, 1952. But although it belongs to its time, the trilogy remains the most considerable and coherent work of literary and cultural criticism of its kind yet written. Also of literary interest by Holcroft are the lecture *Creative Problems in New Zealand*, Christchurch, Caxton, 1948, and the three lectures making up *Islands of Innocence: The Childhood Theme in New Zealand Fiction*, Wellington, Reed, 1964. Other shorter studies include Ormond Burton, *Spring Fires: A Study in*

New Zealand Writing, Auckland, Book Centre, 1956, which calls for a passionate enthusiasm of a quasi-religious nature in New Zealand writing, and James Bertram, *Towards a New Zealand Literature*, Dunedin, Hocken Library, University of Otago, 1971, which is a historical survey of New Zealanders' attitudes towards the notion of a national literature.

Alan Mulgan's collection of thirteen essays, *Great Days in New Zealand Writing*, Wellington, Reed, 1962, is the earliest and slightest of a growing number of collected essays and reviews. It was followed by A.R.D. Fairburn, *The Woman Problem and Other Prose*, Auckland, Paul, 1967, essays on society and culture, including literature. W.H. Pearson, *Fretful Sleepers and Other Essays*, Auckland, Heinemann Educational Books, 1974, is mainly a collection of book reviews but includes some important essays. The same is true of *James K. Baxter As Critic*, ed. Frank McKay, Auckland, Heinemann Educational Books, 1978, Charles Brasch, *The Universal Dance*, ed. John Watson, Dunedin, University of Otago Press, 1981, Frank Sargeson, *Conversation in a Train and Other Critical Writing*, ed. K. Cunningham, Auckland, Auckland University Press, 1983, James Bertram, *Flight of the Phoenix*, Wellington, Victoria University Press, 1985, Bruce Mason, *Every Kind of Weather*, ed. David Dowling, Auckland, Reed Methuen, 1986, which includes reviews, articles, and letters on theatre and other cultural events, and Allen Curnow, *Look Back Harder*, ed. Peter Simpson, Auckland, Auckland University Press, 1987. The most valuable collection of essays and reviews by a single author is C.K. Stead, *In the Glass Case*, Auckland, Auckland University Press, 1981. A second collection, *Answering to the Language*, Auckland, Auckland University Press, appeared in 1989. Many of the essays collected in these volumes are detailed under appropriate headings in this bibliography. Also separately listed are the nine pieces in *Essays on New Zealand Literature*, ed. Wystan Curnow, Auckland, Heinemann Educational Books, 1973.

Amongst general articles surveying New Zealand literature are a composite essay by D.O.W. Hall, W.J. Gardner, Nola Millar, W.H. Oliver, and Joan Stevens called 'Literature' in *An Encyclopaedia of New Zealand*, ed. A.H. McLintock, Wellington, Government Printer, 1966, and several by J.C. Reid, in *The Commonwealth Pen: An Introduction to the Literature of the British Commonwealth*, ed. A.L. McLeod, Ithaca, Cornell University Press, 1961, in *The Pattern of New Zealand Culture*, ed. A.L. McLeod, Ithaca, Cornell University Press, 1968, and in *Australia and New Zealand* (with G.A. Wilkes), University Park, Pennsylvania State University Press, 1970. There are essays by William Walsh in his *Commonwealth Literature*, London, Oxford University Press, 1973, R.J. Smithies in *New Zealand Official Yearbook*, 1964, and MacD. P. Jackson in *Thirteen Facets: Essays to Celebrate the Silver Jubilee of Queen Elizabeth the Second, 1952-1977*, ed. Ian Wards, Wellington, Government Printer, 1978, the last a pithy commentary on literary achievements of the previous twenty-five years. W.H. Oliver in *The Oxford History of New Zealand*, ed. W.H. Oliver, Oxford, Clarendon Press, and Wellington, Oxford University Press, 1981, considered the arts generally since 1940, Keith Sinclair, *New Zealand Journal of*

History, vol. 12, 1978, in a review article offered a personal rundown of literary history, and James Bertram in *Towards Maturity*, Wellington, Victoria University Press for The Friends of the Turnbull Library, 1982, emphasized the devoted but numerically few supporters from whom writers in New Zealand had benefited.

Literature before 1930 has commanded little attention since that time. More or less contemporary studies include articles by Hilda Keane, *New Zealand Illustrated Magazine*, vol. 1, 1900, who foresaw with unhappy prescience literary possibilities in scenery and Māori romance, Jessie Mackay, *Art in New Zealand*, vol. 1, 1929, who was defensive about the poverty of past writing, Robin Hyde, *T'ien Hsia Monthly*, vol. 7, August, 1939, reprinted in *Women's Studies Journal*, vol. 5, 1989, who gave more space to nineteenth than to twentieth century writing, Oliver Gillespie, *Tomorrow*, 30 October 1935, who decried New Zealanders' lack of pride in their literature, and, in a brief note which also covered Australia, Jane Mander, *Literary Digest International Book Review*, vol. 1, May 1923. Pat Lawlor's *Confessions of a Journalist*, Auckland, Whitcombe & Tombs, 1935, sometimes provides useful information on writers active in the first three decades of the century. There is a thesis by W.K.J. Gonley, 'New Zealand Life in Contemporary Literature', University of New Zealand, 1932. More recent articles and theses include those by Peter Alcock, *JCL*, vol. 6, 1971, who traces the roots of the new work of the 1930s in the Victorian and Edwardian eras, J.C. Reid, *New Zealand's Heritage*, ed. Ray Knox, Wellington, Paul Hamlyn, 1971-3, pp. 1593-6, who writes on the 1890s, P.J. Hanlon, 'The Development of Literature in New Zealand: A Study of Cultural Conditions in New Settlements', University of Edinburgh, 1955, Bruce Nesbitt, 'Literary Nationalism in Australia and New Zealand 1880-1900', Australian National University, 1968, and Dulcie Gillespie-Needham, 'The Colonial and His Books: A Study of Reading in Nineteenth Century New Zealand', Victoria University of Wellington, 1971.

Comments from those involved in the new work of the 1930s include those by Denis Glover, *Tomorrow*, 30 October 1935, and H. Winston Rhodes, *Tomorrow*, 1 August 1934, 13 May 1936, and 19 July 1939, and *New Zealand Libraries*, vol. 10, 1947. Amongst later essays looking at such matters as the effects of writing in a new country are C.K. Stead's excellent piece in *Distance Looks Our Way: The Effects of Remoteness on New Zealand*, ed. Keith Sinclair, Auckland, Paul's Book Arcade for the University of Auckland, 1961, reprinted in *IGC*; W.H. Pearson, 'The Recognition of Reality' in *Commonwealth Literature: Unity and Diversity in a Common Culture*, ed. John Press, London, Heinemann Educational Books, 1965, reprinted in *FS*; Jack Bennett, *Listener* (London), 21 January 1960; and Peter Simpson, *Untold*, no. 6, 1986, who compares the formalist concept of 'making strange' with the use of the words 'strange' and 'stranger' in the writing of Robin Hyde, D'Arcy Cresswell, and Allen Curnow. Peter Alcock, *WLWE*, vol. 16, 1977, takes a more psychological view of alienation in Katherine Mansfield, John Mulgan, Frank Sargeson, and Janet Frame. Allen Curnow built on the introductions to his anthologies in a lecture printed in *The Future of New Zealand*, ed. M.F. Lloyd Prichard, Christchurch, Whitcombe & Tombs for the University of Auckland, 1964, reprinted in *ENZL* and in *LBH*. R. Seymour, *New Zealand New Writing*, no. 4, 1945, expressed doubts about the adequacy of the Holcroft-Curnow-McCormick formulation of New Zealanders as 'island dwellers'. Alex Calder, *And*, no. 1, 1983, provocatively discovers sexual metaphors in Curnow's and Brasch's critical writing and uses these to argue their blinkered view of reality. The limitations and distortions produced by the concept of 'nationalism' are discussed by Stevan Eldred-Grigg, *Landfall*, no. 163, 1987.

Most of these critical writers had in mind a distanced relationship with England. Writers who have commented on the relationship with the USA are A.R.D. Fairburn, *Art in New Zealand*, vol. 6, 1934, in an historically significant essay which accurately forecast the value of American literature as a source of models for New Zealand, R.T. Robertson, *Hilltop*, no. 1, 1949, who compares early American writing with the contemporary position in New Zealand, and who returns to the theme in *The Literary Half-Yearly*, vol. 18, 1977, and Lawrence Jones, *Review*, 1966, who also compares fiction and poetry from the two countries. Joseph Jones, *Listener*, 19 March 1954, offered an American's view of our 'frontier' literature. The relationship (or lack of relationship) with Australia is the subject of Nettie Palmer, *Meanjin*, vol. 3, 1944, H. Winston Rhodes, *Meanjin*, vol. 27, 1968, and Terry Sturm, *Ariel*, vol. 16, 1985, revised in *Tasman Relations: New Zealand and Australia, 1788-1988*, ed. Keith Sinclair, Auckland, Auckland University Press, 1987.

There has been an increasing number of articles on Māori writing in English and the relationship between Māori and English traditions in literature. Earlier essays are by W.H. Pearson in *The Maori People in the Nineteen-Sixties*, ed. Eric Schwimmer, Auckland, Longman Paul, 1968, reprinted in *ENZL*, which is as much a history of racial attitudes as of the literature in which the Māori appear, K.O. Arvidson, *WLWE*, vol. 14, 1975, which concentrates on the work of Hone Tuwhare, Witi Ihimaera, and Albert Wendt, and H. Winston Rhodes, *Meanjin*, vol. 32, 1973, which distinguishes between the Māori and Pākehā 'search for identity'. N. Simms, *World Literature Today*, vol. 52, 1978, provides an introduction to Māori literature in English, K.O. Arvidson in *Only Connect: Literary Perspectives East and West*, ed. Guy Amirthanayagam and S.C. Harrex, Adelaide, CRNLE, and Honolulu, East-West Center, 1981, discusses cultural interaction in New Zealand literature, and R. Corballis in *A Sense of Place: Essays in Post-Colonial Literature*, ed. Britta Olinder, Göteborg, University of Gothenburg, 1984, writes on contemporary Māori writing in English. Margaret Orbell, *WLWE*, vol. 17, 1978, introduces Māori women's writing, and Miriama Evans, *Landfall*, no. 153, 1985 and *Meanjin*, vol. 44, 1985, the publishing of Māori literature. The first of a series called 'Studies in New Zealand Art and Society', Peter Beatson's *The Healing Tongue: Themes in Contemporary Maori Literature*, Palmerston North, Department of Sociology, Massey University, 1989, consists of brief reflective essays followed by discussions of relevant stories and poems, mostly published in the preceding ten years.

Taking a wider view are Subramani, *Mana Review*, vol. 1, 1976, who looks at literary responses to the mythical ideal of the South Seas island, and Bill Pearson, *Rifled Sanctuaries: Some Views of the Pacific Islands in Western Literature to 1900*, Auckland, Auckland University Press, 1984. Subramani went on to write *South Pacific Literature: From Myth to Fabulation*, Suva, University of the South Pacific, 1985, where he discusses the origin and growth of a literature in English which began only in the 1960s. Norman Simms, *Silence and Invisibility: A Study of the Literature of the Pacific, Australia and New Zealand*, Washington, D.C., Three Continents, 1986, is concerned more with the problems encountered in writing and discussing this literature than with conventional description of it; there is a full bibliography of books upon such problems, as well as of books by Pacific writers and about Pacific writing.

Amongst critics on criticism, Peter Simpson, *Ariel*, vol. 16, 1985, writes on the collected essays and reviews of Sargeson, Brasch, Baxter, Pearson, and Stead. Essays on literary theory in general are not included in this bibliography, but the uses of post-modernist theory in New Zealand are examined by Roger Horrocks, *And*, no. 2, 1984, who laments New Zealanders' anti-theoretical bent, and Simon During, *And*, no. 1, 1983, reprinted in *Southern Review*, vol. 18, 1985, who 'overreads', as he calls it, a Sargeson short story as a lead into a discussion of modernism and post-modernism, and who in *Landfall*, no. 155, 1985, looks at what post-modernism means for New Zealand literature. Leonard Wilcox, in the same issue of *Landfall*, is similarly engaged, and examines the avowedly post-modernist periodicals *Parallax*, *And*, and *Splash*. Jonathan Lamb, *Landfall*, no. 159, 1986, even suggests that modernist and post-modernist theory has been used to endorse the need writers sense for realism.

Writers on other topics include W.J. Cameron in his *New Zealand*, Englewood Cliffs, Prentice-Hall, 1965, who approaches national character through fiction and non-fiction, Dennis McEldowney, *Landfall*, no. 77, 1966, on religion in New Zealand writing, Peter Alcock in *Marriage and the Family in New Zealand*, ed. Stewart Houston, Wellington, Hicks Smith, 1970, on the family in New Zealand literature, James Bertram in *Violence*, ed. J.M. Barrington, Wellington, Department of Justice for the Royal Society of New Zealand, 1971, on violence in New Zealand literature, Wystan Curnow, *ENZL*, on 'the fate of intellectual and imaginative excellence in a welfare state', and Michael Volkerling in a thesis on the social concerns of New Zealand writers, University of Auckland, 1975.

Writing by women has attracted considerable attention in recent years, as will be clear in later sections. General studies are so far few, but include Joan Stevens, *New Zealand Women in Literature*, Wellington, New Zealand Federation of University Women, 1972, who writes on women in fiction and on the woman writer in New Zealand, and Peter Alcock, *WLWE*, vol. 17, 1978, who takes a quick survey of women writers from Lady Barker on.

Moments of Invention, Auckland, Heinemann Reed, 1988, contains photographic studies of twenty-one authors by Robert Cross, with brief literary biographies based on interviews by Greg O'Brien.

Poetry
The first and still the only full-length study of poetry is Kendrick Smithyman's *A Way of Saying*, Auckland, Collins, 1965, which distinguishes between poets of the 1930s and 1950s using the terms 'romantic' and 'academic', 'provincial' and 'regional'. It is a provocative, idiosyncratic book, its packed contents not helped by the lack of chapter headings and index. Several lectures by James K. Baxter were also published separately: *Recent Trends in New Zealand Poetry*, Christchurch, Caxton, 1951; *The Fire and the Anvil: Notes on Modern Poetry*, Wellington, New Zealand University Press, 1955, three lectures on problems of criticism, inspiration, and symbolism; and *Aspects of Poetry in New Zealand*, Christchurch, Caxton, 1967, a fine lecture which also distinguishes between the poets from the 1930s and 1950s. All are reprinted in *James K. Baxter As Critic*, ed. Frank McKay, Auckland, Heinemann Educational Books, 1978.

A.L. (Tony) Kingsbury's thesis, 'Poetry in New Zealand 1850–1930', University of Auckland, 1968, Helen Barnhill's thesis, 'The Pakeha Harp: Maori Mythology in the Works of [Alfred Domett, Arthur Adams, Jessie Mackay and Blanche Baughan]', University of Otago, 1972, and C.B.K. Smithyman's article on social attitudes and the epic prior to 1900, *University of Auckland Historical Society Annual*, 1967, look at the earliest verse. W.S. Broughton, 1966, reprinted in *ENZL*, wrote on the problems of D'Arcy Cresswell, A.R.D. Fairburn, and Geoffrey de Montalk as poets in the 1920s.

The most important writing on the poets of the 1930s generation is found in Allen Curnow's introductions to his anthologies. An earlier essay of his on the poetry appeared in *Meanjin Papers*, vol. 2, 1943, and a more recent one in which he returns to the value of local circumstance in poetry is in *National Identity: Papers Delivered at the Commonwealth Literature Conference, University of Queensland, 1968*, ed. K.L. Goodwin, London, Heinemann Educational Books, 1970; both are reprinted in *LBH*. Arthur Ashworth, *Southerly*, vol. 10, 1949, surveying New Zealand poetry, shows how completely Curnow's new pantheon was accepted. Terry Sturm, *JCL*, no. 2, 1966, reprinted in *ENZL*, wrote on poetry and the Depression. Owen Gager, *Argot*, no. 20, 1969, representing a younger generation, argued that the old cultural isolation was the self-pitying result of lack of interest in overseas writers. Patrick Hutchings, *Literary Half-Yearly*, vol. 18, 1977, shows that poets' responses to landscape, a theme usually associated with Allen Curnow and Charles Brasch, continue to be of significance.

Charles Doyle, *Conspectus*, 1964, also had Curnow feelingly in mind when writing about the 1950s poets. His *Small Prophets and Quick Returns*, Auckland, New Zealand Publishing Society, 1966, is less confident, perceiving a lack of direction in contemporary poetry. M. Bramwell discusses volumes of poems from the mid-1960s by Peter Bland, Louis Johnson, and James K. Baxter in *Poetry of the Pacific Region*, ed. Paul Sharrad, Adelaide, CRNLE, 1984. A.J. Gurr, *JCL*, no. 1, 1965, reprinted in *Readings in Commonwealth Literature*, ed. William Walsh, Oxford, Clarendon Press, 1973, usefully discusses the implications for later writers of Curnow's poetry, though the division between the Curnow and Johnson factions is overstated. Peter Alcock, *WLWE*, vol. 17, 1978, briefly notes the complete break between Doyle's anthology *Recent Poetry in New Zealand* (1965) and Arthur Baysting's *The Young New Zealand Poets* (1973).

Alistair Paterson, *Landfall*, no. 117, 1976, also wrote on this transition and its influences, and in *Pilgrims*, vol. 3, 1978, followed the careers of Baysting's poets. Chris Parr, *Pilgrims*, vol. 2, 1977, wrote on the Pound, Black Mountain, and Beat influences, and outlined what he saw as weaknesses in current New Zealand verse. In *Islands*, no. 38, 1987, reprinted in *The American Connection*, ed. Malcolm McKinnon, Allen & Unwin/Port Nicholson Press in association with the Stout Research Centre, 1988, Bill Manhire recalls his own experience of reading American poets in the 1960s and 1970s. Alistair Paterson's *The New Poetry: Considerations towards Open Form*, Dunedin, Pilgrims South Press, 1981, begins with American and even British theorizing, and distinguishes between the work of C.K. Stead, Ian Wedde, Alan Loney, and Allen Curnow and what he considers to be their American models. Generally recognized as the major statement on New Zealand poetry since Curnow's introductions, C.K. Stead's lecture 'From Wystan to Carlos: Modern and Modernism in Recent New Zealand Poetry', *Islands*, no. 27, 1979, reprinted in *IGC*, argues that New Zealand poetry for a long time derived from the better Georgians and from Auden, and that Eliot's and Pound's influence began only through American poetry in the 1960s; it does not distinguish between modernism and post-modernism. Roger Horrocks, *Parallax*, no. 3, 1983, welcomed Stead's survey, but suggested the most interesting places in new poetry, for example the surrealist tradition, were off his map. Allen Curnow in *New Zealand through the Arts: Past and Present*, Wellington, Friends of the Turnbull Library, 1982, reprinted in *LBH*, attacks the American poet Olson's poetic theory, and although he scarcely mentions New Zealand poetry, he implies that theory's deleterious effect upon it.

Keri Hulme in *Only Connect: Literary Perspectives East and West*, ed. Guy Amirthanayagam and S.C. Harrex, Adelaide, CRNLE, and Honolulu, East-West Center, 1981, introduces Māori poetry, in Māori and English, as moulded by the forces of Māori and Pākehā social and poetic traditions.

In other articles, G. Whalley, *Queen's Quarterly*, vol. 74, 1967, wrote on 'celebration and elegy' in New Zealand poetry, Alan Roddick, *New Zealand Alpine Journal*, vol. 25, 1972, and R.A. Copland in *New Zealand's Nature Heritage*, ed. Ray Knox, Hong Kong, Hamlyns, 1974-6, pp. 2357-63 and 2419-25, discussed mountains and nature respectively in New Zealand poetry, and Ian Wedde examined landscape conventions in poetry in *Te Whenua, te Iwi*, ed. Jock Phillips, Wellington, Allen & Unwin/Port Nicholson Press in association with the Stout Research Centre, 1987. Murray Edmond, *Cave*, no. 4, 1973, suggests the poet ought not to be defined always by publication in book form, Stephen Chan, *Islands*, no. 14, 1975, comments on poetry and politics in New Zealand, and R. Seymour, *Outrigger*, no. 6, 1975, extensively analyses work by and about women poets in earlier issues, to which Lauris Edmond adds a dissenting note. John Davidson, *JCL*, vol. 15, 1980, illustrates the widespread presence of the goddess Venus in New Zealand poetry, Kendrick Smithyman, *JCL*, vol. 17, 1982, in a characteristically dense lecture, finds his contemporary poets have a no-longer-anxious sense of both an historical past and a poetic tradition, and Fleur Adcock, *Listener*, 8 May 1982, offers a personal view of the contemporary scene. W.S. Broughton, *SPAN*, no. 20, 1985, writes on the use of the vernacular idiom (especially by R.A.K. Mason, Allen Curnow, and Vincent O'Sullivan), and Anne Else, *Landfall*, no. 156, 1985, reviews the reviewing of poetry by women in that periodical's first fifteen years.

Surveys of the poetry since 1982, more or less annual, have appeared in *JNZL* in essays by K.O. Arvidson, Ronda Cooper, John Needham, and Peter Alcock. In addition, Kirsty Cochrane, *JNZL*, no. 2, 1984, wrote on the work of Vincent O'Sullivan, Fleur Adcock, Bill Manhire, and Ian Wedde.

Fiction
The only recent general history of fiction is *New Zealand Fiction* by Joseph Jones and Johanna Jones, TWAS, Boston, 1984, a brief study combining chronological and thematic approaches. Two earlier studies are the fuller but superficial *A History of New Zealand Fiction from 1862 to the Present Time with Some Account of Its Relation to the National Life and Character* by E.M. Smith, Wellington, Reed, 1939, and the thesis by Joan Gries, 'An Outline of Prose Fiction in New Zealand', University of New Zealand, 1951. Joan Stevens's *The New Zealand Novel 1860-1965*, 2nd revised edition, Wellington, Reed, 1966, though its comments are brief and note-like, remains a useful guide to early and minor novels. H. Winston Rhodes's short but thoughtful *New Zealand Novels: A Thematic Approach*, Wellington, Price Milburn, 1969, is still useful despite its date. Too brief to be of equal use is his survey of twenty-five writers, *New Zealand Fiction Since 1945*, Dunedin, McIndoe, 1968. Lawrence Jones's *Barbed Wire & Mirrors*, Dunedin, University of Otago Press, 1987, though made up of articles and reviews, amounts to a consistent and developing study of the fiction. In *Leaving the Highway*, Auckland, Auckland University Press, 1990, Mark Williams, referring especially to Frame, Stead, Hulme, Ihimaera, Wedde, and Gee, argues effectively for a complex, deep-rooted tradition in New Zealand fiction which is impoverished and falsified by the repudiation of its earlier fictional manifestations. The history of the short story in New Zealand is covered in a long chapter in W.H. New, *Dreams of Speech and Silence: The Art of the Short Story in Canada and New Zealand*, Toronto, University of Toronto Press, 1987. Essays on individual authors in *Critical Essays on the New Zealand Novel*, Auckland, Heinemann Educational Books, 1976, and *Critical Essays on the New Zealand Short Story*, Auckland, Heinemann, 1982, both ed. Cherry Hankin, are listed separately under authors' names. Dan Davin, *Journal of the Royal Society of Arts*, vol. 110, 1962, attempted to define what seemed specifically New Zealand in the New Zealand novel. A little narrower in scope but with a similar intention, Lawrence Jones's contribution to *Identity and Culture in New Zealand*, ed. David Novitz and Bill Willmott, Wellington, GP

Books, 1989, surveys the expression in fiction of the dream of an ideal society. And in *Where Did She Come From? New Zealand Women Novelists 1862-1987*, Wellington, Allen & Unwin/Port Nicholson Press, 1989, Heather Roberts tries to show, somewhat overlooking their frequent popular success, the critical suppression of women novelists.

There is an early essay on the common lack of truth to reality in what was then recent fiction by Clara Cheeseman, *New Zealand Illustrated Magazine*, vol. 7, January, 1903. Some attention to fiction before 1930 is given by Dennis McEldowney in articles on the Māori–European wars in fiction and on the colonial novel in *New Zealand's Heritage*, ed. Ray Knox, Wellington, Paul Hamlyn, 1971-3, pp. 1149-53 and 1205-10. Joanna Morris wrote a thesis on the development of the fictional heroine, 1890-1939, University of Otago, 1985.

The foundation essay for the study of the 'realist' tradition was Robert Chapman's 'Fiction and the Social Pattern', *Landfall*, no. 25, 1953, reprinted in *ENZL*. Lawrence Jones, *CENZSS*, examines Sargeson's influence on A.P. Gaskell and O.E. Middleton; in *Islands*, no. 20, 1977, he notes the persistence of realism in Dan Davin, Noel Hilliard, and others; and in *Landfall*, no. 160, 1986, continues his examination of realism in past and recent fiction. All three essays are reprinted in *BWM*. R.A. Copland, *CENZSS*, reflects on the similarities amongst the near-autobiographical stories of Dan Davin, James Courage, and John Reece Cole. Ian Reid, *Fiction and the Great Depression: Australia and New Zealand 1930-1950*, Melbourne, Edward Arnold, 1979, takes a stimulatingly fresh approach though he gives more attention to the greater volume of Australian fiction. In a long review, Terry Sturm, *Australian Literary Studies*, vol. 9, 1980, argues that Reid's oversimplified understanding of the relationship between literature and society leads to mistaken conclusions about New Zealand fiction. In an essay with a title deliberately echoing Robert Chapman's, Nick Perry, *Islands*, no. 38, 1987, offers a sociologist's view of the relation between fiction and social life. The 'Man Alone' character in the fiction is discussed by Lawrence Jones, *Journal of Popular Culture*, vol. 19, 1985, in an essay further developed in *BWM*. Appropriately included at this point is an essay by William New in his *Among Worlds: An Introduction to Modern Commonwealth and South African Fiction*, Erin, Ontario, Press Porcepic, 1975, in which he contrasts what he sees as reciprocal elements in New Zealand literature, the ideal new land, and the uncultured conventional society. More specifically, an essay by Peter Alcock, *Quadrant*, vol. 11, 1967, considers fiction's report on sexual inadequacy and alienation, an article by Heather Roberts, *Landfall*, no. 115, 1975, discusses women characters in the novel between 1920 and 1940, and another by Cherry Hankin, *WLWE*, vol. 14, 1975, finds that the preceding hundred years reveal a deepening pessimism in women novelists about the place of women in society. Aorewa McLeod in *Public and Private Worlds*, ed. Shelagh Cox, Allen & Unwin/Port Nicholson Press, 1987, examines recent women's novels for signs of a fiction based on women's sexuality and their skill in relationships. There are theses by J.C. Baxter on the New Zealand national character as exemplified by Frank Sargeson, John Mulgan, and Dan

Davin, University of New Zealand, 1952, by E.J. O'Brien on short stories written after 1930, University of Canterbury, 1949, and by Heather Roberts on the subjective novel, University of Canterbury, 1980.

In a variety of articles taking in more recent fiction, Patrick Evans, in a three-part essay, *Landfall*, nos 117, 119, and 121, 1976-7, discusses the 'provincial dilemma' as dealt with by Ian Cross, Janet Frame, C.K. Stead, and Michael Henderson, and in *Islands*, no. 28, 1980, he argues that New Zealand writers are still blinkered by English traditions and fail to respond to the proletarian element in society. The nature of historical fiction as evidenced in five novels is analysed by David Dowling, *Australian and New Zealand Studies in Canada*, no. 2, 1989. Cherry Hankin, *Landfall*, no. 128, 1978, discusses the 'double scale of values' in criticism, arguing that imaginative vision and imaginative language will render the problem obsolete. Specifically on the short story, H. Winston Rhodes, *Landfall*, no. 81, 1967, on the publication of C.K. Stead's anthology *New Zealand Short Stories: Second Series*, (1966), offered valuable thoughts on the nature and shortcomings of such collections. David Ballantyne, *Kenyon Review*, vol. 32, 1970, commented on the writing and publishing of short stories in New Zealand, and M.C. Bradbrook, in her *Literature in Action: Studies in Continental and Commonwealth Society*, London, Chatto & Windus, 1972, reprinted in *Readings in Commonwealth Literature*, ed. William Walsh, Oxford, Clarendon Press, 1973, suggests reasons for the particular appropriateness of the short story form in New Zealand. Elizabeth Smither, *Islands*, no. 37, 1986, reflects on the continuing shortcomings of the short story as evidenced by Lydia Wevers' anthology *New Zealand Short Stories: Fourth Series* (1984), and Margot Schwass, *JNZL*, no. 3, 1985, discusses stories about and by migrants, especially Amelia Batistich, Yvonne du Fresne, and Renato Amato.

Most writing on fiction by Māori writers concentrates on particular authors. A little wider in range is S.F.D. Hughes, *Modern Fiction Studies*, vol. 27, 1981, who describes the emergence of a Polynesian voice in Heretaunga Pat Baker, Albert Wendt, Witi Ihimaera, and Patricia Grace. Of interest for its attempt to classify by theme is Phoebe Meikle's study of Māori short story writers in *ACLALS Bulletin*, 5th series, no. 1, 1978. The Māori as presented in fiction by non-Māori writers was notably covered by W.H. Pearson in *Journal of the Polynesian Society*, vol. 67, 1958, reprinted in *FS*, and was also the subject of a thesis by Nancy Wall, University of Otago, 1963. J.S. Ryan, *New Literature Review*, vol. 9, 1980, observing that Māori writers concentrate on contemporary Māori life, discusses the recent attempts by some non-Māori writers to capture in fiction the Māori past.

Lawrence Jones, *Islands*, no. 31-32, 1981, reprinted in *BWM*, writes on the non-realist tradition as exemplified by Helen Shaw and Russell Haley. The combination of future settings and a degree of freedom from restraints of conventional novelistic language in four women's novels is noted but not closely analysed by Elizabeth Thomas, *SPAN*, no. 24, 1987. Good critical comment on recent publications and developments is contained in the surveys of fiction, starting from 1982, in *JNZL*; the first four are by Peter Simpson, Elizabeth Caffin, Lawrence Jones, and Mark Williams. *JNZL*, no. 6, 1987, splits the survey into essays on novels by women, novels by men, and the short story, by Gail Pittaway, J.C. Ross and W.S. Broughton respectively. The recent wave of film adaptations of short stories and novels provides material for analysis in Bill Lennox's *Film and Fiction*, Auckland, Longman Paul, 1985, a text for schools. There is also a thesis on the topic by Brian McDonnell, University of Auckland, 1986.

Drama
Little has been written on plays rather than productions of plays, but there are nevertheless two separate books. Howard McNaughton, *New Zealand Drama*, TWAS, Boston, 1981, concentrates on literary analysis of playwrights' themes and technical skills, and John Thomson, *New Zealand Drama 1930-1980: An Illustrated History*, Auckland, Oxford University Press, 1984, looks especially at the relationship of drama and society. An early discussion of the place of drama in New Zealand literature by the 1930s play anthologist Victor Lloyd appeared in *Annals of New Zealand Literature*, ed. J.C. Andersen, Wellington, New Zealand Authors' Week Committee, 1936. An exchange of letters between Bruce Mason and John Pocock, *Theatre in Danger: A Correspondence*, Hamilton, Paul's Book Arcade, 1957, discussed the problems of writing plays, including poetic drama, in New Zealand. Erle Nelson, *Landfall*, no. 66, 1963, emphasized the social conscience of a healthy drama, stressing especially Māori-Pākehā relations. Roger Robinson, *Landfall*, no. 116, 1975, wrote on the publication of New Zealand drama. In *Canadian Theatre Review*, vol. 14, 1977, David Carnegie succinctly covered theatre history, professional theatre, playwrights, publication, and other topics, and in *SPAN*, no. 12, 1981, Howard McNaughton, in a forerunner of the *JNZL* surveys, reviewed new plays of 1979 and 1980. The entire issue of *Australasian Drama Studies*, vol. 3, no. 1, 1984, was devoted to New Zealand theatre. Of particular interest here are Sebastian Black's examination of New Zealand history as revealed in selected plays since 1922, and Howard McNaughton's survey of writing about New Zealand drama (or more accurately, its theatrical presentation). Renée, *Landfall*, no. 153, 1985, briefly considered politics and theatre, and at greater length Helen White, *Australasian Drama Studies*, vol. 3, no. 2, 1985, reviewed roles for women in plays since 1950. Christopher Balme, *Australasian Drama Studies*, no. 15-16, 1989-90, reviews the development of Māori theatre from the 1960s. The year's plays have been surveyed more or less annually since 1982 in *JNZL* in articles providing the most helpful recent criticism; the first four surveys are by Sebastian Black, Howard McNaughton, David Carnegie, and Robert-H. Leek. *Australian and New Zealand Theatre Record*, 1987-, reprints all reviews of productions of New Zealand plays.

Various kinds of information are available on the history of theatre and broadcasting in New Zealand. Peter Downes has written *Shadows on the Stage: Theatre in New Zealand; The First 70 Years*, Dunedin, McIndoe, 1975, and in *Top of the Bill: Entertainers through the Years*, Wellington, Reed, 1979, he follows the careers of some stage performers at home and abroad. Downes was joined by Peter Harcourt in the writing of *Voices in the Air: Radio Broadcasting in New Zealand: A Documentary*, Wellington, Methuen & Radio New Zealand, 1976. There was an earlier history by Ian Mackay, *Broadcasting in New Zealand*, Wellington, Reed, 1953. The theatrical history of New Zealand drama from 1920 to 1970 is recounted by Peter Harcourt in *A Dramatic Appearance*, Wellington, Methuen, 1978.

Biography

Literary autobiography and biography have been notable in recent years. Antony Alpers, in *Biography in New Zealand*, ed. Jock Phillips, Wellington, Allen & Unwin/Port Nicholson Press, 1985, reflected on his own work as a literary biographer. Dennis McEldowney, *JNZL*, no. 2, 1984, reviewed both autobiographies and biographies of Frank Sargeson, Janet Frame, Sylvia Ashton-Warner, Charles Brasch, James K. Baxter, John Middleton Murry, and Katherine Mansfield. Lawrence Jones, *Ariel*, vol. 16, no. 4, 1985, restricted himself to the first four of those writers, but included several others in an extended version of his essay in *BWM*.

Children's Literature

The only full-length study is Betty Gilderdale's *A Sea Change: 145 Years of New Zealand Junior Fiction*, Auckland, Longman Paul, 1982, which covers the years, in thematic chapters, from 1833 to 1978. It has a full bibliography. There are descriptive and critical annotations in the bibliographies by Hazel D. Pitcher, 'Bibliography of New Zealand Children's Books 1920-1960', Wellington, 1960, and J.B. Ringer, 'A Bibliography of New Zealand Juvenile Fiction 1833-1919, with Annotations and Introductory Essays', Wellington, 1977, both compiled for the Library School. J.B. Ringer refashioned his bibliography into an essay on books before 1920, with a full list of titles, in *Young Emigrants: New Zealand Juvenile Fiction 1833-1919*, Hamilton, privately published, 1980. Diane Hebley, in *Off the Shelf: Twenty-One Years of New Zealand Books for Children*, Auckland, Methuen, 1980, gives publishing details and brief accounts of the stories of over 200 books from *A Lion in the Meadow* to books for adolescents. A catalogue called *New Zealand Books for Children Exhibited at the International Youth Library*, Munich, 1981, [Auckland, Exhibition Committee?, 1981], contains a brief history of children's literature and an annotated list, both written by Jill McLaren. *Tea-Tree and Iron Sands*, ed. Tom Fitzgibbon and Barbara Spiers, 2nd edition, Auckland, Auckland College of Education, 1989, a guide to 'present-day' writers, provides brief biographies, synopses of stories, and comments by the authors. A companion volume by the same editors is *Matapihi: A Guide to Contemporary New Zealand Children's Book Illustrators*, 1988. The best source of articles on writing for children is the *Yearbook* of the (New Zealand) Children's Literature Association, 1972-, which has printed many talks on a wide variety of children's books. There is a thesis by C.D. Neutze, University of Auckland,

1981, on the work of L.M. Montgomery, Isabel Maud Peacocke and Ethel Turner. Diane Hebley, *Landfall*, no. 171, 1989, surveys children's literature of the 1980s.

Anthologies

The first anthologies published in New Zealand were of work in Māori, for example the mōteatea and legends collected by Sir George Grey and printed in 1853 and 1854. The first English anthologies brought together Canterbury writing, and the first and major national collection of verse in English was compiled in Christchurch too. The anonymous editor of *Literary Foundlings: Verse and Prose Collected in Canterbury, New Zealand*, Christchurch, The 'Times' Office, 1864, had the good luck to be able to include an essay by Samuel Butler, though contributors are not identified. *The Book of Canterbury Rhymes*, Christchurch, Ward & Reeves, 1866, revised and enlarged, ed. W.P. Reeves, as *Canterbury Rhymes*, Christchurch, 'Lyttelton Times' Company, 1883, contained mostly humorous verse on topical matters collected from local newspapers. Also chosen for local and topical interest were the poems of fifty years of European settlement in *The Jubilee Book of Canterbury Rhymes*, Christchurch, Whitcombe & Tombs, 1900. New Zealand verse was sometimes considered to have an Australasian identity in anthologies which did not distinguish the country of origin of their contents. The first such book was *Australian Ballads and Rhymes*, ed. D.B.W. Sladen, London, Walter Scott, 1888. Later examples are *An Australian Anthology*, ed. Percival Serle, London, Collins, 1927, with a third enlarged edition, Sydney, Collins, 1946, where the New Zealand contributors, though still few, are identified in the index, and *The Oxford Book of Australasian Verse*, ed. Walter Murdoch, London, Oxford University Press, 1918, which in its fourth edition, Melbourne, Oxford University Press, 1950, gave a separate section to New Zealand verse that was edited by Alan Mulgan.

New Zealand Verse, ed. with an introduction by W. F Alexander and A.E. Currie, London, Walter Scott, 1906, was the first and remains the only fully representative and well-considered anthology of nineteenth century New Zealand verse. Poems and extracts by over fifty authors are arranged by subject — emigration, the landscape, the cities, Māori life and legend, lyric poems of love and death. In their sober introduction, the editors note the supremacy of Alfred Domett's poetical powers, the abundance of landscape poetry, the rarity of verse about back-country farming, and the absence of poems about freezing works or 'the results of Universal Franchise and Industrial Arbitration'. A second edition, Christchurch, Whitcombe & Tombs, 1926, is only slightly enlarged and omits the introduction. The first collection of verse by writers connected with a university was *The Old Clay Patch: A Collection of Verses Written in and around Victoria University College*, ed. F. A. De la Mare and Siegfried Eichelbaum, Christchurch, Whitcombe & Tombs, 1910, revised and enlarged in 1920 and again, Wellington, New Zealand University Press, 1949.

A similar compilation, *College Rhymes: An Anthology of Verse Written by Members of Canterbury College 1873-1923*, Christchurch, Whitcombe & Tombs, 1923, is introduced by its editor, O.T.J. Alpers, with an outline of dramatic and literary activities at the College. The most handsome anthology, *Countess of Liverpool's Gift Book of Art and Literature*, ed. A.W. Shrimpton, Christchurch, Whitcombe & Tombs, 1915, included essays, stories, and poems, and was sold for the benefit of disabled soldiers. The same purpose was served in the following World War by *Lady Newall's New Zealand Gift Book*, Wellington, P.E.N. (New Zealand Centre), 1943. Quentin Pope and C.A. Marris completed the representation of verse from the earlier decades of the century. The former's *Kowhai Gold: An Anthology of Contemporary New Zealand Verse*, London, Dent, and New York, Dutton, 1930, exemplifies the work of the previous fifteen years, a time when few poets escaped an unreal, because unexperienced, conception of the 'Home Country', and seemed as a result to run to a sentimental view of their own land and people. C.A. Marris edited an annual series called *New Zealand Best Poems*, Wellington, Harry H. Tombs, from 1932 to 1943, and these, with the anthology *Lyric Poems 1928-1942* of 1944 which rounded the series off, made up the last substantial fling of verse in the tradition of the previous decades. Trixie Menzies, *Landfall*, no. 165, 1988, does her best to rescue the work of Pope and Morris from later customary vilification.

The first anthology of short stories did not appear till 1930. O.N. Gillespie, the editor of *New Zealand Short Stories*, London, Dent, was conscious of having an English audience, chose work descriptive of New Zealand, and felt it necessary to explain the lack of 'any national outlook or distinctive atmosphere'. The nature of outlets for stories is indicated by the provenance of those in this collection: half came from the Sydney weekly *Bulletin* and the Christchurch daily *Sun*. Two other anthologies also represented the short story before Sargeson and Finlayson. *Tales by New Zealanders*, ed. C.R. Allen, London, British Authors' Press, 1938, and the slighter *Pataka (Treasure House): Selected Short Stories by New Zealand Authors*, ed. John Kington, Auckland, K System Publishing Dept, 1936, offer examples of the kind of story written for newspapers and weeklies in the 1920s and 1930s. The enormous increase in dramatic writing in the 1930s was reflected in a series of collections of one-act plays edited by Victor S. Lloyd, published for the use of amateur dramatic societies. The volumes were *Seven One-Act Plays*, Wellington, Radio Publishing Company of N.Z., 1933, *Seven One-Act Plays 1934*, Wellington, Radio Publishing Company of N.Z., 1934, *Six One-Act Plays 1935*, Wellington, National Magazines Ltd, 1935, *Further One-Act Plays 1935*, Wellington, National Magazines Ltd, 1935, and *Clay, and Other New Zealand One-Act Plays*, Wellington, National Magazines Ltd, 1936.

Anthologies of the new and mostly younger poets of the 1930s began with *New Poems*, ed. Ian Milner and Denis Glover, Christchurch, Caxton Club Press, 1934 — poems, the editors believed, which broke with 'that unfortunate tradition in which any sentimental rhapsodising . . . seems to pass for poetry'.

Amongst the ten contributors were Charles Brasch, Allen Curnow, A.R.D. Fairburn, Denis Glover, and R.A.K. Mason. Further collections by this group were *Verse Alive* and *Verse Alive, Number Two*, ed. H. Winston Rhodes and Denis Glover, Christchurch, Caxton, 1936 and 1937, (both of which printed poems drawn from *Tomorrow*), *A Caxton Miscellany of Poems, Verse, Etc.*, Christchurch, Caxton, 1937, and most importantly, *A Book of New Zealand Verse 1923-1945*, ed. Allen Curnow, Christchurch, Caxton, 1945, enlarged edition (1923-1951), 1951. This last established a new canon which has been modifed but not replaced, and was the most influential anthology in the history of New Zealand poetry, both for its verse and for its introduction. It broke with earlier anthologies by printing fuller selections by fewer poets, and deliberately looked for a pattern in the new verse which had been written since the Depression. Few of the poems were more than fifteen years old. This verse was written by New Zealanders, not British immigrants, and for New Zealand not English readers. Curnow found that many of the poems were based on a sense of the insecurity and rootlessness of New Zealanders in these islands.

Precisely what pattern Curnow perceived, and whether it was really there, were questions more fully debated on the publication of Curnow's *Penguin Book of New Zealand Verse*, Harmondsworth, Penguin, 1960. Later developments were not so readily accommodated within Curnow's earlier view of the true strengths of New Zealand verse, and the Penguin anthology is less satisfyingly unified; but with its greatly developed and recast version of the 1945 introduction, this anthology reached more readers than any other before or since, and consolidated the new order. Both of Curnow's introductions are reprinted in *LBH*. Significant reviews of the Penguin include those by A W. Stockwell, *Landfall*, no. 58, 1961, E.A. Horsman, *Comment*, no. 7, 1961, and Ian Reid, *Comment*, no. 30, 1967. John Geraets, *And*, no. 1, 1983, argues that only in the 1980s is it possible to stand outside the definition Curnow gave to the New Zealand poem, and in the same issue, Roger Horrocks re-reads the anthology as an artifice or construct rather than a report on reality. All the same, James K. Baxter in his review of the Penguin, *Education*, vol. 10, no. 1, 1961, had pointed to biases caused by what he called Curnow's piety, and compared the anthology unfavourably to Chapman and Bennett's collection. That *Anthology of New Zealand Verse*, ed. Robert Chapman and Jonathan Bennett, London, Oxford University Press, 1956, was unlike Curnow's Caxton anthology in being the first comprehensive selection of New Zealand poetry since Alexander and Currie's of 1926. In fact, however, four fifths of the poetry in it was written after 1926, and although this book did not have the influence of Curnow's, it did, on the whole, confirm the status Curnow had given to his choice amongst the more recent poets. The introduction is by Robert Chapman. Lawrence Baigent, *Landfall*, no. 39, 1956, wrote a review.

The equivalent anthologies of the short story began with that of Frank Sargeson, *Speaking for Ourselves*, Christchurch, Caxton, 1945, which similarly collected writers writing for their fellow countrymen and not exploiting the country's exoticism for the benefit of English readers, but it had nothing like the effect of Curnow's verse anthology. The job of establishing a new order in the short story was effected by Dan Davin in *New Zealand Short Stories*, London, Oxford University Press, 1953; though they extended back to Lady Barker's, two thirds of the stories were first published after 1937. It was also the first New Zealand anthology to include Katherine Mansfield.

Collections of verse and occasionally prose by school children began in the 1930s with *Yours and Mine: Stories by Young New Zealanders*, ed. Warwick Lawrence, New Plymouth, Thomas Avery, 1936, *An Anthology of High School Verse: A Decade of Verse by Boys of the Christchurch Boys' High School, 1926-1935*, ed. A. Murray Oliver, Christchurch, The Editor, 1936, and *Correspondence School Book of Verse — 1937*, Wellington, Department of Education, Correspondence School, 1937, which also covered the previous ten years. There were few more such collections till the early 1970s, since when they have been frequent, notably in a series edited by Helen Hogan. Work collected specifically for school students began with early post-primary School Bulletins published by the Department of Education which were notable for including non-fiction. The Department's *Writing in New Zealand* series began in 1947 with no. 1, 'Early Journals and Records', no. 2, 'Two Pioneers', no. 3, 'The Short Story', and no. 4, 'Poetry in New Zealand'. Each issue included brief introductory material. Later bulletins in the following ten years covered the early novel 1860-90, early historians, the later novel, contemporary verse, and more varied extracts and examples from novels and short stories. Further bulletins in 1960 and 1973 were restricted to verse.

A.E. Currie's *A Centennial Treasury of Otago Verse*, Christchurch, Caxton, 1949, is an example of the regional anthology in which inclusion can depend on local flavour as much as literary merit. *New Zealand Farm and Station Verse 1850-1950*, ed. Airini E. Woodhouse, Christchurch, Whitcombe & Tombs, 1950, regional in another sense, includes the verse, which Alexander and Currie found so rare, describing rural and especially sheep-farming life from firsthand knowledge. Similarly unpretentious in its contents but of wider suffrage was *Shanties by the Way: A Selection of New Zealand Popular Songs and Ballads*, ed. Rona Bailey and Herbert Roth, Christchurch, Whitcombe & Tombs, 1967. A later anthology of station life, mostly non-fiction prose, was *Alone in a Mountain World: A High Country Anthology*, ed. David McLeod, Wellington, Reed, 1972. *The Kiwi Laughs: An Anthology of New Zealand Prose Humour*, ed. J.C. Reid, Wellington, Reed, 1961, collected short stories and other pieces of comic intent; it had a successor in *The Acid Test: An Anthology of New Zealand Humorous Writing*, ed. Gordon McLauchlan, Auckland, Methuen, 1981.

The next generation of writers is represented in *New Authors Short Story One*, London, New Authors, 1961, and *New Zealand Short Stories: Second Series*, ed. C.K. Stead, London, Oxford University Press, 1966. Stead's introduction to the latter argues for a choice based not on representativeness, description of the country, or intellectual attitude, but on the power of each story to give the artistic pleasure appropriate to the form which is used. The revolt in verse against a supposedly required New Zealand quality led Louis Johnson to edit the eleven volumes of *New Zealand Poetry Yearbook*, Christchurch, Pegasus, 1951-64, as a home for works by those who felt *Landfall* to be dominated by the alleged Curnow requirements. In fact, Johnson, though giving space to possible new directions, proved eclectically inclusive. Owen Leeming, *Landfall*, no. 66, 1963, reviewed the *Yearbook*, focusing on vol. 10. The work of this generation of poets who made their name in the 1950s was anthologized in *Recent Poetry in New Zealand*, ed. Charles Doyle, Auckland, Collins, 1965. Of the generously represented thirteen poets, only Baxter is also to be found amongst the sixteen in Curnow's 1945 anthology. The poets were invited to introduce their own work. Two anthologies of one-act plays tested the market for drama and found it warranted no further collections for another decade. They were *Five New Zealand Plays*, ed. John N. Thomson, Auckland, Collins, 1962, unpublished plays of which the earliest dates from the late 1930s, and *Three Plays by New Zealanders*, Wellington, Price Milburn, 1964, a selection of plays recently entered for the British Drama League's play-writing competitions.

In a wide-ranging collection published at this time, J.C. Reid edited for the general reader *A Book of New Zealand*, Auckland, Collins, 1964, and included much non-fiction prose, along with fiction and verse, arranged under subject headings. This book was revised and enlarged by Peter Cape, Auckland, Collins, 1979.

The first anthology of writing drawn from a single periodical was *Landfall Country: Work from Landfall 1947-61*, ed. Charles Brasch, Christchurch, Caxton, 1962. It is appropriate to mention here a much later anthology of slightly earlier work, Anthony Stones's *Celebration: An Anthology of New Zealand Writing from the 'Penguin New Writing' Series*, Harmondsworth and Auckland, Penguin, 1984, which includes, among other poems, stories, and non-fiction pieces, Sargeson's 'That Summer' and 'When the Wind Blows'. *Review: 1888-1971: A Retrospective Anthology of the Literary Review*, ed. Kevin Jones and Brent Southgate, Dunedin, Bibliography Room, University of Otago, 1972, is selected from the university magazine. Bill Manhire selected two volumes of stories from the *Listener* from 1939 to the mid-1970s, *N.Z. Listener Short Stories* and *N.Z. Listener Short Stories: Volume 2*, Wellington, Methuen, 1977 and 1978.

From the mid-1960s, commercial publishers took over the role School Publications had assumed in 1947 of providing anthologies of New Zealand writing for schools. Peter Smart's *Discovering New Zealand Writing: An Anthology for Third, Fourth, and Fifth Forms*, and *Exploring New Zealand Writing: An Anthology for Senior Students*, both Wellington, Reed, 1964, were substantial selections which continued the practice of introducing students to non-fiction as well as fiction and poetry. A further substantial selection for schools was Helen Hogan's *Nowhere Far from the Sea: An Anthology of New Zealand Poems for Secondary School Students*, Christchurch, Whitcombe & Tombs, 1971. There have been a number of anthologies of stories and poems since which are specifically designed for secondary school use, for example, *A Cage of Words*, ed. Harvey McQueen, Auckland, Longman Paul, 1980. There have also been one or two collections of poems for younger children, for example, *These Islands: A Collection of New Zealand Verse for Young People*, ed. Gwenyth Jones, Auckland, Longman Paul, 1973, and, edited by Dorothy Butler, *The Magpies Said: Stories and Poems from New Zealand*, Harmondsworth, Kestrel, 1980.

The major anthologies of the 1970s began with *An Anthology of Twentieth Century New Zealand Poetry*, ed. Vincent O'Sullivan, London, Oxford University Press, 1970. This did not seriously challenge the choice of poets Curnow had made for the Penguin, but included work of the following ten years, and in its enlarged forms (Wellington, 1976 and Auckland, 1987) has held its place as the standard anthology of verse. More helpful in defining what was new since Curnow was *The Young New Zealand Poets*, ed. Arthur Baysting, Auckland, Heinemann Educational Books, 1973, in which all but one of the nineteen poets were born between 1940 and 1950. Another anthology which attempted to locate a new centre in the country's poetry was *Ten Modern New Zealand Poets*, ed. Harvey McQueen and Lois Cox, Auckland, Longman Paul, 1974, which while including two poets over 50, avoided the 1930s generation and printed no verse written before 1945. The selections are generous, and there are good biographical and critical introductions. *Poetry New Zealand*, a successor to *New Zealand Poetry Yearbook*, and more or less triennial from 1971 to 1984, ed. Frank McKay, Christchurch, Pegasus (volumes 1-3), and Dunedin, McIndoe (volumes 4-6), samples current verse. Elizabeth Caffin edited volume 6. A new series, to appear twice yearly and therefore more properly a periodical, but also called *Poetry New Zealand*, 1990-, consciously continues the initiative of Louis Johnson. Unclear in the significance of its initial date is *The Oxford Book of New Zealand Writing Since 1945*, ed. MacDonald P. Jackson and Vincent O'Sullivan, Auckland, 1983, a very large anthology, really too large to be thought of as a supplement to the Curnow and Sargeson anthologies of 1945. *New Zealand Short Stories, Third Series*, ed. Vincent O'Sullivan, Wellington, Oxford University Press, 1975, represented the decade of work after Stead's collection. O'Sullivan found no increase of sophistication in the form, but a greater insistence on shallow experience, more violence, and a welcome appearance of more work by and about Māori. The only anthology of plays, *Contemporary New Zealand Plays*, ed. Howard McNaughton, Wellington, Oxford University Press, 1974, just pre-dated the sudden success of writing for the theatre in the later 1970s. *The Seventies Connection*, ed. David Hill and Elizabeth Smither, Dunedin, McIndoe, 1980, a decadal anthology of short passages of verse, fiction, and non-fiction, though aimed at schools, has a more general interest too. Special anthology issues of periodicals are not recorded here, but worth noting is vol. 3, nos 1-2, 1974, of the San Francisco *Second Coming*, which was in effect the first anthology of New Zealand verse published specifically for American readers, even if the circulation was small and the selection favoured the Caveman Press stable of poets such as Trevor Reeves and Peter Olds.

Amongst anthologies devoted to special themes are *New Zealand Love Poems*, ed. James Bertram, Dunedin, McIndoe, 1977, *The Iron Hand: New*

Zealand Soldiers' Poems from World War II, ed. Les Cleveland, Wellington, Wai-te-ata Press, 1979, and *Mystical Choice*, ed. Helen Shaw, Auckland, Mandala Editions, 1981, a short collection of meditative, metaphysical, and mystical verse. *Classical New Zealand Poetry*, ed. Richard Matthews, Dunedin, Department of Classics, University of Otago, 1985, prints poems, especially by Mason, Baxter, Adcock, and Stead, with the original Greek or Latin from which they spring, and *Countless Signs: The New Zealand Landscape in Literature: An Anthology*, ed. Trudie McNaughton, Wellington, Reed Methuen, 1986, at a time of conservation consciousness replaces the earlier high-country farm anthologies. *I Have Seen the Sun*, ed. Bernard Gadd, Auckland, Longman Paul, 1986, collects stories of a fantasy or science fiction bent. The increasing number of publications which collect work submitted for prizes, year's work from schools and universities, and work produced by writing groups and original composition classes is a feature of recent times, but such anthologies are too numerous and slight to be detailed here.

Writing in English by Māori is represented by *Contemporary Maori Writing*, ed. Margaret Orbell, Wellington, Reed, 1970, which claims to print the work of the first generation of Māori writers using traditional English forms, mainly the short story. The substantial and in places much more adventurous *Into the World of Light*, ed. Witi Ihimaera and D.S. Long, Auckland, Heinemann, 1982, is more varied and less 'English'. R. Corballis compared the two anthologies in *A Sense of Place, Essays in Post-Colonial Literatures*, ed. Britta Olinder, Göteborg, English Department, University of Gothenburg, 1984. A sampling of stories and verse from the South Pacific is provided by Albert Wendt in *Lali: A Pacific Anthology*, Auckland, Longman Paul, 1980.

The most striking feature of the last fifteen years has been the appearance of volumes devoted to women's writing. It is not entirely unprecedented: *Poems*, ed. Alan Dunlop, New Zealand Women Writers' and Artists' Society, *c.* 1953, is an earlier example. But in 1977 came two substantial collections, *Shirley Temple Is a Wife and Mother: 34 Stories by 22 New Zealanders*, ed. Christine Cole Catley, Whatamongo Bay, Cape Catley, and *Private Gardens: An Anthology of New Zealand Women Poets*, ed. Riemke Ensing, Dunedin, Caveman Press, which contains mostly recent work but also verse by older poets such as Mary Stanley, Gloria Rawlinson, and Ruth Gilbert, which is otherwise not easily found. A more deliberately historical survey is made by *Women Writers of New Zealand 1932-82*, ed. Margaret Hayward and Joy Cowley, Wellington, Colonial Associates for the N.Z. Women Writers' Society, 1982, which includes brief biographies and some examples of work, and *Hyacinths and Biscuits*, ed. Peggy Dunstan et al., Auckland, Ken Pounder, 1985, which was the Diamond Jubilee Book of the Penwomen's Club (NZ), 1925-1985. *In Deadly Earnest: A Collection of Fiction by New Zealand Women, 1870s-1980s*, ed. Trudie McNaughton, Auckland, Century Hutchinson, 1989, is another example, gathering short stories and extracts from novels. *Women's Work: Contemporary Short Stories by New Zealand Women*, ed. Marion McLeod and Lydia Wevers, Auckland, Oxford University Press, 1985, also published as *One Whale Singing;*

And Other Stories from New Zealand, London, Women's Press, 1986, covers the previous eighteen years. Recent stories by women writers have been published in a series called *New Women's Fiction,* Auckland, New Women's Press, edited by Cathie Dunsford, 1986, Aorewa McLeod, 1988, and Mary Paul and Marion Rae, 1989. *The Power and the Glory and Other Lesbian Stories* was edited by Miriam Shapira, Auckland, Papers Inc., 1987. Verse is represented by *Yellow Pencils: Contemporary Poetry by New Zealand Women,* ed. Lydia Wevers, Auckland, Auckland University Press, 1988.

There have been a number of recent general anthologies. *The Oxford Book of Contemporary New Zealand Poetry,* ed. Fleur Adcock, Auckland, Oxford University Press, 1982, chose poetry from about 1970 onwards. It attracted little enthusiasm, the editor, some thought, having been too long an outsider. Far more challenging than anything since Curnow has been *The Penguin Book of New Zealand Verse,* ed. Ian Wedde and Harvey McQueen, Auckland, Penguin, 1985, which includes Māori verse chosen by Margaret Orbell (with her own translations), chronologically placed amongst other entries in English, and which gives prominence to the longer poem. Ian Wedde wrote the introduction, and also discussed his work for the book in *SPAN,* no. 19, 1984, and *Meanjin,* vol. 44, 1985. There are reviews by C.K. Stead, reprinted in *AL,* and Keri Hulme, *Landfall,* no. 155, 1985. With Miriama Evans and Harvey McQueen, Ian Wedde then edited *The Penguin Book of Contemporary New Zealand Poetry,* Auckland, Penguin, 1987, which covers recent verse from about 1980. *The New Poets: Initiatives in New Zealand Poetry,* ed. Mary Paul and Murray Edmond, Wellington, Allen & Unwin, 1987, is restricted to poets who began publishing in the 1980s, and thus highlights new directions. A wider period, successfully enforcing greater discretion than is apparent in the larger Penguin, marks *The Caxton Press Anthology: New Zealand Poetry 1972-1986,* ed. Mark Williams, Christchurch, Caxton Press, 1987. Williams's introduction is thoughtful and balanced. An anthology intended to exemplify the success of 'open form' verse is Alistair Paterson's *15 Contemporary New Zealand Poets,* Dunedin, Pilgrims South Press, 1980. A history of the New Zealand poetry anthology from 1945 to 1985 was written by Mike Doyle for *Ariel,* vol. 16, 1985.

Twelve 'new' stories are collected by John Barnett in *All the Dangerous Animals Are in Zoos,* Auckland, Longman Paul, 1981, and in *'Listener' Short Stories 3,* ed. with an introduction by Michael Gifkins, Auckland, BCNZ Enterprises, 1984, stories of the previous half-dozen years are represented. *New Zealand Short Stories, Fourth Series,* ed. Lydia Wevers, Auckland, Oxford University Press, 1984, covers the previous ten years, and in her introduction the editor notes the almost complete urbanization, the lack of worry about 'New Zealandness', and a greater variety of style in the stories. *The Penguin Book of Contemporary New Zealand Short Stories,* ed. Susan Davis and Russell Haley, Auckland, Penguin, 1989, in 45 stories offers yet another sampling of the previous ten years' work. The only anthology since Davin's to represent all New Zealand stories is *Some Other Country: New Zealand's Best Short Stories,* ed. Marion McLeod and Bill Manhire, Wellington, Unwin Paperbacks with

Port Nicholson Press, Sydney and London, Unwin Paperbacks, 1984; it includes stories by writers from Mansfield to Marshall. A prose anthology which challenges older traditions is *The New Fiction,* ed. with a long introduction by Michael Morrissey, Auckland, Lindon Publishing, 1985, an avowedly post-modernist collection of predominantly younger writers. Whether the writing is either post-modernist or in other ways significantly new has been argued, most aggressively by C.K. Stead, *Islands,* no. 37, 1986, reprinted in *AL,* who suggests the volume is marginal and already dated. There have been no notable recent collections of drama, but a special kind of theatre is represented in *Three Radio Plays,* Wellington, Victoria University Press, 1989.

Periodicals

The commercial difficulties of publishing books in a small community have meant that periodicals have provided space for far more than experimental or youthful work, and have thus played an important part in the country's literary history. All the major as well as most of the recent literary magazines are mentioned here. Other early ones, either short-lived or of only marginal relevance to literature, are listed and annotated in Iris M. Park, *New Zealand Periodicals of Literary Interest,* Wellington, National Library Service, 1962. Note, too, that some publications of the poetry yearbook type are described under 'Anthologies'. The Sydney *Bulletin* in its early years was an important outlet for New Zealand writing, as were local newspapers, but the earliest significant New Zealand magazine was *The Triad,* 1893-1927, 'a monthly magazine of music science and art' edited till 1925 by C.N. Baeyertz. Baeyertz was a cosmopolitan and *The Triad* was never limited to the arts in New Zealand. He was best qualified in music, and literature received less emphasis until the appointment of Frank Morton as assistant editor. It was an extraordinarily lively and well-informed magazine of the arts which succeeded in combining a wide range of intellectual and artistic interests with considerable popular appeal, and was unmatched until the 1940s. Pat Lawlor, twice in *New Zealand Magazine,* vol. 22, 1943, Alan Mulgan in his *Great Days in New Zealand Writing,* Wellington, Reed, 1962, and M.H. Holcroft, *New Zealand's Heritage,* ed. Ray Knox, Wellington, Paul Hamlyn, 1971-3, pp. 1924-28, have written about the editor. A curious relationship between Ezra Pound and *The Triad* is recounted by K.K. Ruthven, *Landfall,* no. 89, 1969. Another early monthly, *The New Zealand Illustrated Magazine,* 1899-1905, included one or more short stories in nearly every issue. A typescript index, compiled by G.C. Heron, 1943, is held at ATL.

The four colleges of the University of New Zealand began reviews soon after their foundation, but these were not at first hospitable to original writing. Otago University's *Review,* 1888-1979, became predominantly and then entirely a literary annual from the 1950s. A selection was published in 1972 — see 'Anthologies'. Literary work began to appear more regularly in the *Canterbury*

University College Review, 1897–1948, from the 1930s. *Kiwi: The Magazine of the Auckland University College*, 1905–66, was from its beginnings a little more open to literary contributions, and became almost exclusively a magazine of comment and the arts in the later 1930s, followed similarly in the 1940s by *Spike: Victoria College Review*, 1902–61. All were irregular in their last years. In a special position is the *School Journal*, 1907–, published in graded parts. In its early years the stress fell on informative articles rather than on imaginative literature, but from the 1940s, fiction by New Zealand authors was more regularly included to encourage children to recognize their independent nationhood. Many of the country's most notable writers, including poets, have written expressly for the *School Journal*. Separate indexes have been published from time to time. The most significant discussion of the *Journal* is by D.R. Jenkins, *Social Attitudes in the New Zealand School Journal*, Wellington, NZCER, 1939, and by E.P. Malone, *New Zealand Journal of History*, vol. 7, 1973, who points to the 'imperial ideology' of its first 25 years. Other comment is made by P.M. Hattaway, *National Education*, vol. 36, 1954, Alistair Campbell, *Education*, vol. 6, 1957, P.R. Earle, *Education*, vol. 20, 1971, K.G. Smythe, *Education*, vol. 23, 1974, and Julie Dalzell, *Designscape*, no. 87, 1976–7.

Two new magazines began in the 1920s. *New Zealand Magazine*, 1921–52, carried frequent notes and articles on literary matters as well as short stories. More significant was *Art in New Zealand*, 1928–46, whose literary editor till 1942 was C.A. Marris. Though mainly devoted to the pictorial arts, each number usually carried a short story and poems, with an occasional essay on a literary topic. A typescript index of volumes 1–14, compiled by Elizabeth Arya, 1943, is held at ATL. It was succeeded by *Year Book of the Arts in New Zealand*, 1945–51, which always included a selection of the year's verse, usually accompanied by a review essay. A literary and artistic magazine of much lighter character was *New Zealand Artists' Annual*, 1926–32. Although only four issues appeared of *Phoenix*, 1932–3, edited successively by James Bertram and R.A.K. Mason, it was a notable independent student magazine devoted to literature and opinion, modelled in both content and its distinguished typographical design on English periodicals, especially the *Adelphi*. Material for a fifth unpublished issue is in the Mason papers, HL. Also appropriate to its decade, and more widely read, was *Tomorrow*, 1934–40, a fortnightly edited by Kennaway Henderson. It covered both national and international affairs of a political, social, and cultural nature. It was not primarily a literary periodical, but it did print many of the early short stories of Frank Sargeson as well as stories and poetry by other authors, and ran reviews of — and occasional essays on — New Zealand literature. Denis Glover, *Rostrum*, 1940, reviewed its achievement in the year of its forced closure, and H. Winston Rhodes recalled its beginnings in *New Zealand Monthly Review*, nos 213 and 214, 1979. J.J. Herd compiled *Index to Tomorrow 1934–40*, Dunedin, University of Otago Press, 1962.

A variety of magazines, reflecting both a new group of writers and a more specialized readership, began in the 1940s. The general contents of the *New Zealand Listener*, weekly since 1939, reflected its function as, until 1988, the official organ of the National Broadcasting Service. However, the first two editors, Oliver Duff and M.H. Holcroft, were both keen to develop a strength in original literary work. Duff was hampered by paper shortages and other difficulties in the war years, but under Holcroft the regular short story became a feature and some important poetry was published. Book reviews and articles on literary topics gradually became more substantial too. Although that emphasis was not always maintained by later editors, it has been largely recovered in recent years under the literary editorship of Andrew Mason, when interviews with and profiles of authors have been a feature. The magazine's sale in 1990 to the newspaper company Wilson & Horton leaves its future character in doubt. The *Listener* reviewed its own progress, anonymously, 24 June 1949, and in articles by Dennis McEldowney, 17 October 1958, and by Peter Bland and others, 26 June 1964. M.H. Holcroft's autobiographical account of his editorship is *Reluctant Editor: The 'Listener' Years, 1949-67*, Wellington, Reed, 1969. Three selections of its short stories have been published — see 'Anthologies'.

Closely modelled on the *Penguin New Writing* of the war years, and presumably designed to catch the same kind of wartime readership, the four numbers of *New Zealand New Writing*, 1942-5, ed. Ian Gordon, printed work by some of the best writers of fiction of the time, though very little poetry. The nine numbers of the miscellany *Book*, 1941-7, ed. Denis Glover, were distinguished by their generally high literary standard and the typographical experimentation of their editor-printer. Olive Johnson compiled *An Index to Book: A Miscellany from the Caxton Press, Christchurch*, Auckland, Department of English, University of Auckland, 1960. *Arena*, 1943-75, ed. Noel Hoggard, ran to 81 irregular issues. It was hand-printed by its editor, and understandably favoured poetry and the shorter short story. Though it seldom carried the best work written during its thirty years of life, few New Zealand authors of the time were not represented in its pages. P. Andrews compiled the cyclostyled 'An Index to Arena, Numbers 1-70', 1970.

By far the most important literary magazine yet established has been *Landfall*, 1947-, founded by Charles Brasch and edited by him for the next twenty years. Amongst later editors have been Robin Dudding and David Dowling. Those who created *Landfall* are agreed that they were determined to introduce a magazine of the kind *Phoenix* had aspired to be. In editing *Landfall*, Charles Brasch also had in mind J. Middleton Murry's *Adelphi* as well as magazines like *Criterion, Dublin Review*, and *Horizon*. Besides original work in verse and prose, *Landfall* printed extensive reviews of New Zealand literary publications. In more recent years, critical essays on New Zealand writing have been frequent. For over twenty-five years, and until the appearance of *Islands*, it was the outstanding literary periodical. A separate index is issued with each five volumes. Charles Brasch, interviewed by Ian Milner, *Landfall*, no. 100, 1971, talked of the founding, editing, and publishing of the periodical during its first twenty years. The earlier editorial files are held at HL. There is a thesis by David Anido, 'The Genesis and Development of Landfall, and its Influence in

Relation to the Culture of New Zealand and the Commonwealth', University of Canterbury, 1972. John Geraets, *And*, no. 3, 1984, provides useful statistics and a cryptic, over-clever but suggestive article on its character under Brasch. He also uses correspondence with Smithyman, *Landfall*, no. 160, 1986, for a case study of Brasch's procedure as an editor. A selection was published in 1962 — see 'Anthologies'.

Two later magazines of current comment, though not primarily literary periodicals, deserve mention. *Here & Now*, 1949-57, frequently included a short story or poem, and reviewed literary publications. *Comment*, 1959-70 and 1977-82, a quarterly of public affairs generally, and political matters in particular, usually carried a few poems, and from time to time printed important critical essays and full reviews of notable literary publications. An index to vols 1-6 appeared in 1966. *Te Ao Hou*, 1952-75, was a quarterly of Māori cultural affairs which soon began to include short stories and poems by Māori writers. Margaret Orbell, *Listener*, 7 May 1965, looked back over the literary contributions. An index appeared in no. 22. *Koru*, 1976 and 1978, an annual for Māori writers and artists, ran to only two numbers after a most auspicious start.

Most post-war magazines of literary interest have been devoted exclusively to the arts, if not specifically to literature, and have consciously distinguished themselves from *Landfall* and later *Islands*. The ten issues of *Numbers*, 1954-9, a magazine associated with Louis Johnson, James K. Baxter, and Charles Doyle, were, it declared, sympathetic to younger writers, while *Fernfire*, 1957-66, aimed to publish fiction, in particular, for the ordinary working man. *Mate*, 1957-77, of which Robin Dudding and Alistair Paterson were the longest-serving editors, was not afraid at first to follow behind *Landfall*, and established a position in the 1960s ahead of its other contemporaries as a magazine of original writing with occasional critical essays. A separate index to numbers 1-12 was published. Its editorial files are held at ATL. It was renamed *Climate: A Journal of Australasian Writing* in 1978, and was absorbed by *Pilgrims*, 1976-80, ed. Stephen Higginson, which in its final numbers worthily continued the original aspirations of *Mate*. *Hilltop*, 1949, which ran to three issues, reintroduced the short-lived student magazine, but though published by the Victoria University College Literary Society, it solicited and received work by a variety of New Zealand writers. It was replaced by the similar periodical *Arachne*, 1950-51. The two are well discussed by James Bertram (1954), reprinted in *FP*. Later versions have been increasingly the work of graduates rather than undergraduates, though the *New Zealand Universities' Literary Yearbook*, 1960-72, was predominantly filled with student writing, and *Argot*, 1962-72, was closely connected with Victoria University. *Freed*, also known from its first issue as *The Word Is Freed*, 1969-72, produced mainly by Alan Brunton, Murray Edmond, and Russell Haley, was very independent in its contents, graphics, and layout. Murray Edmond, *SPAN*, no. 16-17, 1983, described its founding and history. *Edge*, 1971-73, with a seventh number in 1976, ed. Don Long, included an increasing amount of overseas work. *New Argot*, 1973-5, and *Spleen*, 1975-6, were both lively (the latter at times irreverent) reviews of the arts. *Spleen* concentrated on the visual and popular performing arts. The succeeding generation of such periodicals was heavily influenced by new literary theory. *Parallax*, 1982-83, ed. Alan Loney, was subtitled 'A Journal of Postmodern Literature and Art', which also describes *And*, 1983-5, ed. Alex Calder, and *Splash*, 1984-6, ed. Wystan Curnow. All three, of a few issues only, published original post-modernist work as well as critical and theoretical writing on literature, art, and culture. The post-modernist stance of *Parallax* was reviewed by Terry Locke, *Landfall*, no. 147, 1983, and Leonard Wilcox, *Landfall*, no. 155, 1985, examined the post-modernist claims of *Parallax*, *And*, and *Splash*. *Antic*, 1986-, is devoted to post-structuralist and feminist literary theory, but contains an occasional article specifically on New Zealand writing. Similarly rare articles appear in *Sites*, 1984, described in its subtitle as a journal for radical perspectives on culture.

Other literary magazines of the 1970s and 1980s, though some have had strong university links, have sought a more general literary readership. Of these, the most important has been *Islands*, 1972-, founded and edited by Robin Dudding, who continued and developed the traditions of *Landfall*. It has been notable for fiction by both established and new writers, and for its reviews and essays. The poetry has been more variable. There is a separate index to the first five volumes. Editorial files are held at ATL. The internationalism of *Edge* was made a platform of the more substantial *Cave*, 1972-5, ed. Trevor Reeves and Norman Simms, who most notably avoided the policy of *Landfall*, continued in *Islands*, of serving New Zealand writers only, and solicited overseas, and especially American, contributions, but failed to establish the clear identity of its rivals (or of later magazines like *Parallax* or *And*). Undaunted, Simms continued in 1976 with *New Quarterly Cave*, 'An International Review of Arts and Ideas'. The internationalism of this, and of its successor *Pacific Quarterly*, 1978-85, is impressive, but the New Zealand contributions are disappointing. *Morepork*, 1979-81, began its three issues strongly with contributions from well known and lesser known writers, but failed to sustain that momentum. The first issue of *Rambling Jack*, 1986-7, planned as only four issues for poems and (very) short fiction, was also its strongest. An impressive general magazine of literature and the arts of the 1980s was *Untold*, 1984-, edited from Canterbury University and featuring South Island writers. Its first issue was reviewed with a contemporary issue of *Islands* by Alex Calder, *Landfall*, no. 153, 1985. But the twice-yearly *Sport*, 1988-, ed. Fergus Barrowman, at once established itself as currently the leading magazine for poetry and fiction. Reviews are excluded, and critical commentary is rare. *Spiral*, 1976-85, a magazine for writing and art by women, contained in its six numbers few contributors who had yet established a name. Occasional essays with a feminist perspective on literature are to be found in *Women's Studies Journal*, 1984-, and literary articles, reviews and especially interviews appear in the feminist *Broadsheet*, 1972-. The only periodical of note devoted to theatre was *Act*, 1967-75, first edited by Bruce Mason and usually quarterly. It was a general theatre magazine, but particular attention was given increasingly to articles on and reviews of New Zealand plays. Many later issues carried complete playscripts by New Zealand playwrights. It was succeeded by the more frequent but thinner *Act: Theatre in New Zealand*, 1976–86. *Australian and New Zealand Theatre Record*, 1987–, photocopies all reviews of current productions and thus covers all new plays. General articles on the New Zealand literary magazine include one by Alexander Fry, *Listener*, 26 September 1958; those by D.S. Long, *Arts and Community*, vol. 8, no. 5, 1972, *WLWE*, vol. 14, 1975, *New Zealand Libraries*, vols 37 and 39, 1974 and 1976, and *Second Coming*, vol. 3, no. 1-2, 1974; one by Trevor Reeves, *Commonwealth Newsletter*, no. 6, 1974; and most usefully, on the magazines of the 1970s and 1980s, Mark Williams, *JNZL*, no. 5, 1987. There is a thesis on the subject of literary magazines by J.M. Wild, University of New Zealand, 1951.

Individual Writers

Arthur H. Adams 1872–1936. Poet, novelist, and editor. Adams went to Sydney as a young man, where he worked on the *Bulletin* at a time when much New Zealand writing was published there. His early books include *Maoriland, and Other Verses*, Sydney, Bulletin Newspaper Co., 1899, *The Nazarene: A Study of a Man*, London, Philip Welby, 1902, *Tussock Land: A Romance of New Zealand and the Commonwealth*, London, Fisher Unwin, 1904, and *London Streets*, London, T.N. Foulis, 1906. His poetry was brought together as *The Collected Verses of Arthur H. Adams*, Melbourne, Whitcombe & Tombs, 1913. He provided the words for various musical pieces by Alfred Hill, including the cantata *Hinemoa* (1896) and the opera *Tapu* (1903). He also published *Three Plays for the Australian Stage*, Sydney, W. Brooks, 1914. *A Man's Life*, London, Eveleigh, Nash & Grayson, 1929, is an autobiographical sketch in fictional form.

Fleur Adcock 1934–. Poet. Her volumes of poetry are *The Eye of the Hurricane: Poems*, Wellington, Reed, 1964, *Tigers*, London, Oxford University Press, 1967, *High Tide in the Garden*, London, Oxford University Press, 1971, *The Scenic Route*, London, Oxford University Press, 1974, *Below Loughrigg*, Newcastle upon Tyne, Bloodaxe Books, 1979, *The Inner Harbour*, Oxford, Oxford University Press, 1979, *Selected Poems*, Oxford, Oxford University Press, 1983, *The Incident Book*, Oxford, Oxford University Press, 1986, *Hotspur: A Ballad*, Newcastle upon Tyne, Bloodaxe Books, 1986, and *Meeting the Comet*, Newcastle upon Tyne, Bloodaxe Books, 1988. *The Virgin and the Nightingale*, Newcastle upon Tyne, Bloodaxe Books, 1983, contains translations of medieval Latin poems. She has edited *The Oxford Book of Contemporary New Zealand Verse*, Auckland, Oxford University Press, 1982, and *The Faber Book of 20th Century Women's Poetry*, London, Faber, 1987. An autobiographical essay, 'Beginnings', is in *Islands*, no. 26, 1979, and another in *Beyond Expectations*, ed. Margaret Clark, Wellington, Allen and Unwin/Port Nicholson Press, 1986. She was interviewed by Lauris Edmond, *Landfall*, no. 143, 1982, by Harry Ricketts in his *Talking about Ourselves*, Wellington, Mallinson Rendel, 1986, and for an article by D. McGill, *Listener*, 13 March 1976. Useful reviews are by James Bertram (*The Eye of the Hurricane*), *Landfall*, no. 72, 1964, reprinted in *FP*, C.K. Stead (*High Tide in the Garden*), *Landfall*, no. 100, 1971, reprinted in *IGC*, Trevor James (*The Inner Harbour*), *Landfall*, no. 134, 1980, and Pamela Tomlinson (*The Inner Harbour*), *Islands*, no. 29, 1980. A study of her poetry is included in a thesis by Siew Keng Chua, University of Auckland, 1981.

Rewi Alley 1897-1987. Poet. His collections of verse are numerous and many were published in China. Those published in New Zealand include *Gung Ho: Poems*, ed. H. Winston Rhodes, Christchurch, Caxton, 1948, *Leaves from a Sandan Notebook*, ed. H. Winston Rhodes, Christchurch, Caxton, 1950, *This is China Today: Poems*, ed. H. Winston Rhodes, Christchurch, Rewi Alley Aid Group, 1951, *Fragments of Living Peking, and Other Poems*, ed. H. Winston Rhodes, Christchurch, New Zealand Peace Council, 1955, *Human China: A Diary with Poems*, with an introduction by H. Winston Rhodes, New Zealand Peace Council, 1957, *Journey to Outer Mongolia: A Diary with Poems*, Christchurch, privately published, 1957, *Beyond the Withered Oak Ten Thousand Saplings Grow*, ed. H. Winston Rhodes, Christchurch, Caxton, 1962, *The Mistake: Poems*, Christchurch, Caxton, 1965, *What is Sin?: Poems*, Christchurch, Caxton, 1967, *Twenty-Five Poems of Protest*, Christchurch, Caxton, 1968, *Upsurge: Asia and the Pacific: Poems*, Christchurch, privately published, 1969, *73 Man to Be: Poems*, Christchurch, privately published, 1970, *Winds of Change: Poems*, Christchurch, Caxton, 1972, *Poems for Aotearoa*, Auckland, New Zealand-China Society & Progressive Book Society, 1972, *Over China's Hills of Blue: Unpublished Poems and New Poems*, Christchurch, privately published, 1974, *Today and Tomorrow: Poems*, Christchurch, privately published, 1975, *Snow over the Pines: Poems*, Auckland, New Zealand-China Friendship Society and Progressive Book Society, 1977. An autobiography *At 90: Memoirs of My China Years*, Beijing, New World Press, 1986, was reprinted as *Rewi Alley: An Autobiography*, Wellington, New Zealand Government Printing Office Publications Division, 1987. A manuscript collection is held at ATL. A bibliography by A.P.U. Millett, 'Rewi Alley: A Preliminary Checklist of Published Books and Pamphlets' is included in *Rewi Alley Seventy Five*, Hamilton, Secretariat of the National Committee for the Commemoration of Rewi Alley's Seventy Fifth Birthday, 1972, and there is also a Library School bibliography by E. Sun, 'The Publications of Rewi Alley, 1960-1972', Wellington, 1973. *A Learner in China* by W.T.G. Airey, Christchurch, Caxton & Monthly Review Society, 1970, is a biography, as is *Rewi Alley of China*, Auckland, Hodder & Stoughton, 1980, by Geoff Chapple. He was interviewed by David Gunby, *Landfall*, no. 101, 1972.

Antony Alpers 1919-. He is the major biographer of Katherine Mansfield. The early *Katherine Mansfield: A Biography*, New York, Knopf, 1953, London,

Cape, 1954, has been superseded by his fuller *The Life of Katherine Mansfield*, New York, Viking, London, Cape, and Toronto, Clarke Irwin, 1980. In *The Stories of Katherine Mansfield*, Auckland, Oxford University Press, 1984, he has edited the fullest edition of her short stories. He has also written on dolphins, and has retold *Maori Myths & Tribal Legends*, Auckland, Paul, and London, Murray, 1964, and *Legends of the South Sea*, Christchurch, Whitcombe & Tombs, and London, Murray, 1970.

Renato Amato 1928–64. Short story writer. His only collection is *The Full Circle of the Travelling Cuckoo*, ed. Ian Cross and Maurice Shadbolt, with a memoir of the author by Maurice Shadbolt, Christchurch, Whitcombe & Tombs, 1967. A manuscript collection is held at ATL. There are articles, both mainly biographical, by L. Cleveland and Maurice Shadbolt in *Landfall*, no. 71, 1964. Dennis McEldowney, *Landfall*, no. 86, 1968, wrote a full review of the stories.

Johannes Andersen 1873–1962. Historian and ethnologist. His output was large and varied. Historical works include *Jubilee History of South Canterbury*, Auckland, Whitcombe & Tombs, 1916, and *Old Christchurch in Picture and Story*, Christchurch, Simpson & Williams, 1949. An interest in place-names produced *Place Names of Banks Peninsula: A Topographical History*, Wellington, Government Printer, 1927, and *Maori Place-Names, Also Personal Names and Names of Colours, Weapons and Natural Objects*, Wellington, Polynesian Society, 1942. Further ethnographical work included *Maori String Figures*, Wellington, Board of Maori Ethnological Research for the Author, 1927. A special interest in legends produced *Maori Life in Ao-Tea*, Christchurch, Whitcombe & Tombs, 1907, and *Myths & Legends of the Polynesians*, London, Harrap, 1928. *Maori Fairy Tales*, Christchurch, Whitcombe & Tombs, 1908, and *Maori Tales*, Auckland, Whitcombe & Tombs, 1924, are simpler retellings suitable for children. His interest in natural history is represented by *Bird-Song and New Zealand Song Birds*, Auckland, Whitcombe & Tombs, 1926. He also published Danish songs, and several collections of verse.

Frank Anthony 1891–1927. Short story writer and novelist. His published volumes are *Follow the Call*, Dunedin, Reed, 1936, reprinted with an unfinished novel entitled 'Dave Baird', ed. with an introduction by Terry Sturm, Auckland, Auckland University Press, 1975, and *Me and Gus*, Hawera, privately published, 1938, revised for radio with additional material by Francis Jackson and published as *Me and Gus*, Wellington, Reed, 1951, *More Me and Gus*, Wellington, Reed, 1952, and *Me and Gus Again*, Wellington, Reed, 1955, these last three collected as *The Complete Me and Gus*, Wellington, Reed, 1963. The unpublished novel 'Gus Tomlins' included incidents from the published stories; it was presented with the stories, ed. Terry Sturm from the original versions as *Gus Tomlins, together with the Original Stories of 'Me and Gus'*, Auckland, Auckland University Press, 1977. There is a manuscript collection at

ATL. Frank Sargeson's appreciative review of his work, *Islands*, no. 20, 1977, is reprinted in his *Conversation in a Train*, Auckland, Auckland University Press, 1983.

Ronda and David Armitage. Children's writers. Their work includes *The Lighthouse Keeper's Lunch*, London, Deutsch, 1977, reprinted Harmondsworth, Puffin, 1980, *The Trouble with Mr Harris*, London, Deutsch, and Auckland, Hutchinson, 1978, *'Don't Forget, Matilda!'*, London, Deutsch, 1979, *The Bossing of Josie*, London, Deutsch, 1980, *Ice Creams for Rosie*, London, Deutsch, 1981, *One Moonlit Night*, London, Deutsch, 1983, and *Grandma Goes Shopping*, London, Deutsch, 1984.

Sylvia Ashton-Warner 1908–84. Novelist and teacher. Her novels comprise *Spinster*, London, Secker & Warburg, 1958, New York, Simon & Schuster, 1959, reprinted Harmondsworth, Penguin, 1961, London and Auckland, Heinemann, 1972, and with an introduction by Fleur Adcock, London, Virago, 1980, *Incense to Idols*, London, Secker & Warburg, and New York, Simon & Schuster, 1960, *Bell Call*, New York, Simon & Schuster, 1964, reprinted Christchurch, Whitcombe & Tombs, London, Hale, 1971, *Greenstone*, New York, Simon & Schuster, 1966, Christchurch, Whitcombe & Tombs, and London, Secker & Warburg, 1967, and *Three*, London, Hale, and Christchurch, Whitcombe & Tombs, 1971, New York, Knopf, 1973. There is one volume of short stories, *Stories from the River*, Auckland, Hodder & Stoughton, 1986. Her teaching experiences are described in *Teacher*, London, Secker & Warburg, and New York, Simon & Schuster, 1963, reprinted with an introduction by Dora Russell, London, Virago, 1980, *Myself*, New York, Simon & Schuster, 1967, Christchurch, Whitcombe & Tombs, and London, Secker & Warburg, 1968, and *Spearpoint: "Teacher" in America*, New York, Knopf, 1972, and as *"Teacher" in America*, London, Cassell, 1974. *I Passed This Way*, New York, Knopf, 1979, London, Virago, and Wellington, Reed, 1980, is an autobiography; it was reprinted Auckland, Reed-Methuen, 1985. Lynley Hood has written *Sylvia! The Biography of Sylvia Ashton-Warner*, Auckland, Viking, 1988. Lynley Hood, *Listener*, 2 June 1984, and Jack Shallcrass, *Landfall*, no. 151, 1984, gave memorial tributes. Dennis McEldowney, *Landfall*, no. 91, 1969, compares the handling of similar material in the 'fictional' and 'autobiographical' forms. The relationship between autobiography and fiction also interests Carole Durix, *Ariel*, vol. 18, 1987, who had already published three other articles, on the Māori in her fiction in *Literary Half-Yearly*, vol. 20, 1979, on natural patterns and rhythms in *Greenstone* in *Commonwealth*, no. 3, 1977/78, and on her skilful depiction of women in *WLWE*, vol. 19, 1980.

Ron Bacon 1924–. Children's writer. His only novel for children is *Again, the Bugles Blow*, Auckland, Collins, 1973. He has rewritten *Maori Legends* in three small volumes, Auckland, Shortland Educational, 1984. He has also published many shorter picture books, for example, *Rua and the Sea People*, Auckland,

Collins, 1968, *Hemi Dances*, Auckland, Waiatarua Publishing, 1985, and *A Legend of Kiwi*, Auckland, Waiatarua, 1987.

Louisa Baker 1858-1926. Romance novelist. Her fiction, always published under the pseudonym Alien, includes *A Daughter of the King*, London, Hutchinson, and Chicago, Neely, 1894, *The Majesty of Man*, London, Hutchinson, 1895, *In Golden Shackles*, London, Hutchinson, and New York, Dodd, Mead, 1896, *Wheat in the Ear*, London, Hutchinson, and New York, Putnam's, 1898, *Looking Glass Hours*, with Rita (pseudonym), London, Hutchinson, 1899, *The Untold Half*, London, Hutchinson, and New York, Putnam's, 1899, *The Devil's Half-Acre*, London, Fisher Unwin, 1900, *Another Woman's Territory*, Westminster, Constable, and New York, Crowell, 1901, *A Maid of Mettle*, Philadelphia, Jacobs, [1902], London, Digby Long, 1913, *Not in Fellowship*, London, Digby Long, 1902, *Over the Barriers*, London, Isbister, 1903, *A Slum Heroine*, London, Digby Long, 1904, *An Unanswered Question and Other Stories*, London, Digby Long, 1906, *His Neighbour's Landmark*, London, Digby Long, 1907, *The Perfect Union*, London, Digby Long, 1908, *An Unread Letter*, London, Digby Long, 1909, and *A Double Blindness*, London, Digby Long, 1910. Phillipa Moylan offers a feminist critique in a thesis, University of Auckland, 1989.

David Ballantyne 1924-86. Novelist. His volumes comprise *The Cunninghams*, New York, Vanguard, 1948, reprinted Christchurch, Whitcombe & Tombs, and London, Hale, 1963, Christchurch, Whitcoulls, 1976, and Auckland, Oxford University Press, 1986, *And the Glory* (stories), Christchurch, Whitcombe & Tombs, and London, Hale, 1963, *The Last Pioneer*, Christchurch, Whitcombe & Tombs, and London, Hale, 1963, *A Friend of the Family*, Christchurch, Whitcombe & Tombs, and London, Hale, 1966, *Sydney Bridge Upside Down*, Christchurch, Whitcombe & Tombs, and London, Hale, 1968, reprinted Auckland, Longman Paul, 1981, *The Talkback Man*, London, Hale, 1978, Palmerston North, Dunmore Press, 1979, and *The Penfriend*, Palmerston North, Dunmore Press, and London, Hale, 1980. His early interest in American fiction is apparent in a contribution to *Art in New Zealand*, vol. 15, no. 1, 1942, and American interest in him in another to *New Zealand Magazine*, vol. 28, no. 1, 1949; and in an autobiographical article, with selected correspondence, *Islands*, no. 31-32, 1981, he details his relationship with J.T. Farrell. Patrick Evans, in the same issue, considers why his work is underrated and argues a more important place for him in the development of New Zealand fiction, and in a review article on *The Talkback Man*, *Landfall*, no. 132, 1979, reprinted in *IGC*, C.K. Stead also calls for a reconsideration.

Lady Barker 1831-1911. She is best known for her accounts of Canterbury sheep-station life, *Station Life in New Zealand*, London, Macmillan, 1870, most recently reprinted, ed. Fiona Kidman, London, Virago, 1984, and *Station Amusements in New Zealand*, London, William Hunt, 1873, most recently reprinted Auckland, Wilson & Horton, 1970. Stories written for or suitable for children are told in *Stories About:—*, London, Macmillan, 1871, in *A Christmas Cake in Four Quarters*, London, Macmillan, 1871, and in *Boys*, London, Routledge, 1874. Nelson Wattie writes on her in *English Literature of the Dominions*, ed. K. Gross and W. Klooss, Würzburg, Königshausen & Neumann, 1981, and Dorothy Jones, *SPAN*, no. 21, 1985, compares her with other 'gentlewomen' writers in Canada and Australia.

Blanche (B.E.) Baughan 1870-1958. Poet. Her collections of poems include *Verses*, Westminster, Archibald Constable, 1898, *Reuben and Other Poems*, Westminster, Archibald Constable, 1903, *Shingle-Short and Other Verses*, Christchurch, Whitcombe & Tombs, 1908, and *Poems from the Port Hills*, Auckland, Whitcombe & Tombs, 1923. *Brown Bread from a Colonial Oven*, London, Whitcombe & Tombs, 1912, is a collection of sketches. She also published several booklets of scenic description. Alan Mulgan wrote a short tribute in *Landfall*, no. 48, 1958. Peter Alcock, *Landfall*, no. 102, 1972, gives an appreciation of both prose and verse, and in *JCL*, vol. 24, 1984, examines prosody, imagery, and tone in two long poems.

James K. Baxter 1926-72. Poet and playwright. His collections of poems include *Beyond the Palisade*, Christchurch, Caxton, 1944, *Blow, Wind of Fruitfulness*, Christchurch, Caxton, 1948, *Poems Unpleasant* (with Louis Johnson and Anton Vogt), Christchurch, Pegasus, 1952, *The Fallen House*, Christchurch, Caxton, 1953, *The Iron Breadboard: Studies in New Zealand Writing*, Wellington, Mermaid Press, 1957, *The Night Shift: Poems on Aspects of Love* (with Charles Doyle, Louis Johnson, and Kendrick Smithyman), Wellington, Capricorn Press, 1957, *In Fires of No Return: Poems*, London, Oxford University Press, 1958, *Howrah Bridge and Other Poems*, London, Oxford University Press, 1961, *Pig Island Letters*, London, Oxford University Press, 1966, *The Lion Skin*, Dunedin, Bibliography Room, University of Otago, 1967, *The Rock Woman: Selected Poems*, London, Oxford University Press, 1969, *Jerusalem Sonnets: Poems for Colin Durning*, Dunedin, Bibliography Room, University of Otago, 1970, reprinted Wellington, Price Milburn, 1975, *Jerusalem Daybook*, Wellington, Price Milburn, 1971, *Autumn Testament*, Wellington, Price Milburn, 1972, *Runes*, London, Oxford University Press, 1973, *The Labyrinth: Some Uncollected Poems, 1944-72*, Wellington, Oxford University Press, 1974, *The Tree House, and Other Poems for Children*, Wellington, Price Milburn, 1974, *The Bone Chanter: Unpublished Poems 1945-1972*, ed. J.E. Weir, Wellington, Oxford University Press, 1976, *The Holy Life and Death of Concrete Grady: Various Uncollected and Unpublished Poems*, ed. J.E. Weir, Wellington, Oxford University Press, 1976, *Collected Poems*, ed. J.E. Weir, Wellington, Oxford University Press, 1979, and *Selected Poems*, ed. J.E. Weir, Auckland, Oxford University Press, 1982. Baxter also published poems in broadsheet, folder, and pamphlet form.

His volumes of plays include *Two Plays: The Wide Open Cage and Jack*

Winter's Dream, Hastings, Capricorn Press, 1959 (*Jack Winter's Dream* was reprinted Wellington, Victoria University Press, 1979), *The Devil and Mr Mulcahy [and] The Band Rotunda*, Auckland, Heinemann Educational Books, 1971, *The Sore-Footed Man [and] The Temptations of Oedipus*, Auckland, Heinemann Educational Books, 1971, and *Collected Plays*, ed. Howard McNaughton, Auckland, Oxford University Press, 1982. There is an early, unfinished, semi-autobiographical novel *Horse*, Auckland, Oxford University Press, 1985. Amongst much critical and religious writing may be mentioned *Recent Trends in New Zealand Poetry*, Christchurch, Caxton, 1951, *The Fire and the Anvil: Notes on Modern Poetry*, Wellington, New Zealand University Press, 1955, *Aspects of Poetry in New Zealand*, Christchurch, Caxton, 1967, *The Man on the Horse*, Dunedin, University of Otago Press, 1967, and *The Flowering Cross*, Dunedin, New Zealand Tablet, 1970. Frank McKay edited a selection, *James K. Baxter As Critic*, Auckland, Heinemann Educational Books, 1978. 'Beginnings', *Landfall*, no. 75, 1965, reprinted in *B*, is the chief of several wholly or partly autobiographical essays. A large manuscript collection is held at HL.

Bibliographical aids include P.H. Hughes, 'An Annotated Bibliography of Selected Works by, and about, James K. Baxter Published between 1944-1975', Library School, Wellington, 1975, and J.E. Weir and Barbara A. Lyon, *A Preliminary Bibliography of Works by and Works about James K. Baxter*, Christchurch, University of Canterbury, 1979. *James K. Baxter: A Portrait*, by W.H. Oliver, Wellington, Port Nicholson Press, 1983, is an illustrated biography. Frank McKay's *The Life of James K. Baxter*, Auckland, Oxford University Press, 1990, is fuller, admirably dispassionate, and balanced. Pat Lawlor, in *The Two Baxters*, by Pat Lawlor and Vincent O'Sullivan, Wellington, Millwood Press, 1979, prints diary extracts recording his friendship with Baxter. The only substantial interview was with J.E. Weir, *Landfall*, no. 111, 1974, but he talked about his plays with Arthur Baysting, *Listener*, 7 February 1969, and about Jerusalem with Ian Hay-Campbell, *Listener*, 18 October 1971. The best short study is by Vincent O'Sullivan, *James K. Baxter*, Wellington, Oxford University Press, 1976, but Charles Doyle's *James K. Baxter*, TWAS, Boston, 1976, is fuller. Briefer and simpler studies are by J.E. Weir, *The Poetry of James K. Baxter*, Wellington, Oxford University Press, 1970, and Christopher Parr, *Introducing James K. Baxter*, Auckland, Longman Paul, 1983. Frank McKay analysed poetry from *The Rock Woman* and *Autumn Testament* for school students in *Views of English*, no. 2, 1980. The publication of the *Collected Poems* elicited three significant review articles, by Bill Manhire, *Islands*, no. 31-32, 1981, by Vincent O'Sullivan, *Listener*, 25 October 1980, and by Howard McNaughton, *Landfall*, no. 137, 1981, while Trevor James summarized Baxter's life and work in *London Magazine*, vol. 21, no. 12, 1982. Otherwise, apart from a number of retrospective tributes published on Baxter's death, of which James Bertram's, *Listener*, 20 November 1972, is an example, there are few general studies in articles, though in *WLWE*, vol. 22, 1983, Trevor James traces the image of a journey through a labyrinth throughout the verse, and in *Awakened Conscience: Studies in Commonwealth Literature*, ed. C.D.

Narasimhaiah, New Delhi, Sterling Publishers, 1978, Peter Alcock offers a quick survey of the poetry. Vincent O'Sullivan writes well on myth in the earlier poetry in *Islands*, no. 3, 1973, and on religious experience and myth in Baxter in *Poetry of the Pacific Region*, ed. Paul Sharrad, Adelaide, CRNLE, 1984, in an essay reworked from *The Two Baxters*. Christopher Parr, in *English in New Zealand*, September 1979, summarizes his doctoral thesis on certain themes in Baxter's search for a humanistic Christianity.

Early responses to the young Baxter are represented by W. Hart-Smith, *Meanjin*, no. 51, 1952, and by Robert Chapman's review of *The Fallen House*, *Landfall*, no. 27, 1953. Alistair Campbell recalls his early reading of Baxter in *Landfall*, no. 107, 1973. Keith Russell, *SPAN*, no. 21, 1985, reads 'Pig Island Letters' as a sermon preaching the resurrection of energy and the reforming power of art. John Weir, 'Five New Zealand Poets: A Bibliographical and Critical Account of Manuscript Material', thesis, University of Canterbury, 1974, discusses the work of the last six years and is based largely on private correspondence. Articles on the later Baxter often touch on his social and religious activities as well as the poetry. C.K. Stead writes well on the Jerusalem verse in *Islands*, no. 3, 1973, reprinted in *IGC*, and other short studies are by D.C. Walker, *Landfall*, no. 97, 1971, Tony Simpson, *Cave*, no. 2, 1972 (on Baxter as social prophet), W.S. Broughton, *WLWE*, vol. 14, 1975 (on Baxter's poetic development seen from the viewpoint of his Jerusalem period), and Frank McKay, *Landfall*, no. 137, 1981. McKay's essay is the best of several more closely focused on the presence of the religious in Baxter's poetry; others, taking various approaches, are by Owen Leeming, *Landfall*, no. 97, 1971, and Trevor James, *Landfall*, no. 140, 1981, and no. 152, 1984. John Davidson has written several times on Baxter's use of classical myth and motif, in both poetry and drama, in *Islands*, no. 14, 1975, and no. 15, 1976, in *AUMLA*, no. 47, 1977, and in *Landfall*, no. 134, 1980. R. Jackaman adds comments on the Odyssean journey motif, *Landfall*, no. 147, 1983. Baxter's problems with poetic drama are well analysed by H.W. Smith in *James K. Baxter Festival 1973: Four Plays*, Wellington, Manaaki Society, 1973; he writes less critically about *The Band Rotunda* and other early plays in *Landfall*, no. 85, 1968. Howard McNaughton surveys the plays with well-informed insight, *Islands*, no. 4, 1973, and in his introduction to the *Collected Plays*, in a more general account of his dramaturgy, finds space for the playwright's own comments.

J.C. Beaglehole 1901-71. Historian. Amongst his major historical works are *Captain Hobson and the New Zealand Company*, Northampton, Mass., Smith College, 1928, *The Discovery of New Zealand*, Wellington, Department of Internal Affairs, 1939, 2nd edition, 1961, *The Exploration of the Pacific*, London, A. & C. Black, 1934, 3rd edition, largely rewritten, 1966, *New Zealand: A Short History*, London, Allen & Unwin, 1936, *The University of New Zealand*, Wellington, NZCER, 1937, *Victoria University College: An Essay towards a History*, Wellington, New Zealand University Press, 1949, and *The Life of Captain James Cook*, London, Hakluyt Society and A. & C. Black, and

Stanford, California, Stanford University Press, 1974. He edited *The Journals of Captain James Cook on His Voyages of Discovery*, Cambridge, Cambridge University Press for the Hakluyt Society, 4 vols, 1955-74, and *The "Endeavour" Journal of Joseph Banks 1768-1771*, 2 vols, Sydney, Trustees of Public Library of New South Wales in association with Angus & Robertson, 1962. *The New Zealand Scholar*, Christchurch, Canterbury University College, 1954, is the most notable of a number of published lectures. *Words for Music*, Christchurch, Caxton, 1938, is a volume of poems. *John Cawte Beaglehole: A Bibliography*, Wellington, ATL and Victoria University of Wellington, 1972, was compiled by Margery Walton, Julia Bergen, and Janet Paul. An obituary by F. L.W. Wood appeared in *New Zealand Journal of History*, vol. 5, 1971, and a longer biographical sketch by E.H. McCormick in *Landfall*, no. 100, 1971. A. Laing, *Nation*, 14 May 1973, drew the attention of Americans to his fine prose and fine scholarship on Cook.

Margaret Beames 1935-. Children's writer. Her work includes *The Greenstone Summer*, Wellington, Reed, and London, Stanmore Press, 1977, *Hidden Valley*, Wellington, Mallinson Rendel, 1983, *The Plant That Grew and Grew*, Auckland, Ashton Scholastic, 1984, *The Parkhurst Boys*, Wellington, Mallinson Rendel, 1986, and *Clown Magic*, Wellington, Mallinson Rendel, 1989.

Elsdon Best 1856-1931. Ethnologist. Amongst his many publications on the Māori, the more substantial are *The Stone Implements of the Maori*, Wellington, Government Printer, 1912, *Maori Storehouses and Kindred Structures*, Wellington, Government Printer, 1916, *The Land of Tara and They Who Settled It*, New Plymouth, Avery, 1919, *The Astronomical Knowledge of the Maori, Genuine and Empirical*, Wellington, Government Printer, 1922, *Polynesian Voyagers*, Wellington, Government Printer, 1923, *The Maori*, 2 vols, Wellington, Board of Maori Ethnological Research for the Author, 1924, *The Maori As He Was*, Wellington, Dominion Museum, 1924, most recently reprinted 1974, *Maori Religion and Mythology*, Wellington, Government Printer, 1924, *Games and Pastimes of the Maori*, Wellington, Board of Maori Ethnological Research for Dominion Museum, 1925, *Maori Agriculture*, Wellington, Board of Maori Ethnological Research for Dominion Museum, 1925, *The Maori Canoe*, Wellington, Board of Maori Ethnological Research for Dominion Museum, 1925, *Tuhoe: The Children of the Mist*, 2 vols, Wellington, Board of Maori Ethnological Research for the Author, 1925, reprinted Wellington, Reed for the Polynesian Society, 1972 and 1973, *The Pa Maori*, Wellington, Board of Maori Ethnological Research for Dominion Museum, 1927, *Fishing Methods and Devices of the Maori*, Wellington, Government Printer, 1929, *The Whare-Kohanga . . . and Its Lore*, Wellington, Government Printer, 1929, and *Forest Lore of the Maori*, Wellington, Polynesian Society with Dominion Museum, 1942. Most of these books were reprinted by the Government Printer, Wellington, between 1972 and 1977. E.W.G. Craig wrote a biography, *Man of the Mist*, Wellington, Reed, 1964, and in *Historical Review*, vol. 14, 1966 reflected on his study of the man. In the same periodical, vol. 7, 1959, J.H. Starnes had already offered a simple biographical and ethnographical sketch.

Ursula Bethell 1874-1945. Poet. Her collections comprise *From a Garden in the Antipodes*, London, Sidgwick & Jackson, 1929, *Time and Place*, Christchurch, Caxton, 1936, *Day and Night: Poems 1924-35*, Christchurch, Caxton, 1939, and *Collected Poems*, Christchurch, Caxton, 1950. There is a slightly fuller *Collected Poems*, ed. Vincent O'Sullivan, Auckland, Oxford University Press, 1985. Manuscript material is held at University of Canterbury. Biographical reminiscences were collected in *Landfall*, no. 8, 1948, and M.H. Holcroft's study, *Mary Ursula Bethell*, NZWW, Wellington, Oxford University Press, 1975, is as much biographical as critical. Balanced discussion is given by Lawrence Baigent, *Landfall*, no. 17, 1951; and S.A. Grave, *Meanjin*, vol. 13, 1954, relates her response to the New Zealand landscape to her Christian belief and English cultural traditions. Helen Shaw wrote briefly in *Arachne*, no. 3, 1951, and J.M. Morton's thesis on the poetry, 1949, is at Victoria University of Wellington. A later thesis by M.W. Hillock, University of Canterbury, 1982, studies her imagery. John Weir, 'Five New Zealand Poets: A Bibliographical and Critical Account of Manuscript Material', thesis, University of Canterbury, 1974, includes discussion of her ideas about and her method of composing poetry. Vincent O'Sullivan's introduction to *Collected Poems*, 1985, is a succinct review of literary influences and of her poetic development.

Graham Billing 1936-. Novelist. His novels include *Forbush and the Penguins*, Wellington, Reed, and London, Hodder & Stoughton, 1965, New York, Holt, Rinehart & Winston, 1966, reprinted Auckland, Oxford University Press, 1986, *The Alpha Trip*, Christchurch, Whitcombe & Tombs, and London, W.H. Allen, 1969, *Statues*, London, Hodder & Stoughton, 1971, *The Slipway*, New York, Viking, 1973, London, Quartet, 1974, and *The Primal Therapy of Tom Purslane*, Dunedin, Caveman Press, and Melbourne, Quartet Books, 1980. *Changing Countries*, Dunedin, Caveman Press, 1980, is a collection of poems. He has also written non-fiction, including the texts for the photographic volumes, *South: Man and Nature in Antarctica: A New Zealand View*, Wellington, Reed, 1964, London, Hodder & Stoughton, and Seattle, University of Washington Press, 1965, revised edition, Wellington, Reed, 1969, and *New Zealand, the Sunlit Land*, Wellington, Reed, 1966. His manuscript papers are held at ATL. Jill McCracken, *Listener*, 12 June 1972, wrote an article based on an interview, and he was also interviewed by Richard Corballis, *Landfall*, no. 135, 1980. His narrative art is praised by Howard McNaughton, *Landfall*, no. 139, 1981.

Peter Bland 1934-. Poet. His collections of verse include *Habitual Fevers*, in *Three Poets*, by Peter Bland, John Boyd, and Victor O'Leary, Wellington, Capricorn Press, 1958, *Domestic Interiors: Poems*, Wellington, Wai-te-ata Press, 1964, *My Side of the Story: Poems 1960-1964*, Auckland, Mate Books, 1964, *The Man with the Carpet-Bag: Poems*, Christchurch, Caxton, 1972, *Mr Maui: Poems*,

London, London Magazine Editions, 1976, *Primitives: Poems*, Wellington, Wai-te-ata Press, 1979, *Stone Tents*, London, London Magazine Editions, 1981, *The Crusoe Factor*, London, London Magazine Editions, 1985, and *Selected Poems*, Dunedin, McIndoe, 1987. 'Beginnings', *Islands*, no. 30, 1980, is an autobiographical essay. C. Bourke's article, *Listener*, 24 August 1985, is partly biographical, partly about Bland the actor. Two plays, *Father's Day* and *George the Mad Ad-Man*, were published in *Landfall*, no. 83, 1967, and *Act*, no. 3, 1967.

Thomas Bracken 1843-98. Poet. His volumes of verse include *The Haunted Vale: A Legend of the Murray, and Other Poems and Lyrics*, Sandhurst, J.K. Robshaw, 1867, *Behind the Tomb and Other Poems*, Melbourne, Clarson, Massina & Co., 1871, *Flowers of the Free Lands*, Dunedin, Mills Dick & Co., and Melbourne, George Robertson, 1877, *Lays of the Land of the Maori and Moa*, London, Sampson Low, 1884, *Lays and Lyrics: God's Own Country and Other Poems*, Wellington, Brown Thomson & Co., 1893, *Musings in Maoriland*, Dunedin, Arthur T. Keirle, 1890, and *Not Understood, and Other Poems*, Wellington, Richard Brown, 1905. *Not Understood* went through many editions, most recently Christchurch, Whitcombe & Tombs, 1956. *Pulpit Pictures*, Dunedin, Coulls & Culling, 1876, *Paddy Murphy's Budget: A Collection of Humorous "Pomes, Tiligrams, an' Ipistols"*, Dunedin, Mackay Bracken & Co., 1880, *Paddy Murphy's Annual: A Record of Political and Social Events in New Zealand*, Dunedin, Fergusson & Mitchell, 1886, and *The Triumph of Women's Rights*, Auckland, W. McCullough, 1892, contain comic verse and sketches.

Charles Brasch 1909-73. Poet and editor. His major collections of poetry, all published by Caxton in Christchurch, are *The Land and the People and Other Poems*, 1939, *Disputed Ground: Poems 1939-45*, 1948, *The Estate and Other Poems*, 1957, *Ambulando*, 1964, *Not Far Off*, 1969, and, ed. by Alan Roddick, *Home Ground*, 1974. Alan Roddick also edited the *Collected Poems*, Auckland, Oxford University Press, 1984. Brasch translated poems by Amrita Pritam in *Black Rose*, New Delhi, Nagmani, 1967, by Hilde Zisserman in *Gedichte aus Neuseeland*, Dunedin, McIndoe, 1970, and by Esenin (with Peter Soskice) in *Poems by Esenin*, Wellington, Wai-te-ata Press, 1970. For John Crockett's company he wrote *The Quest: Words for a Mime Play*, London, Compass Players, 1946. His major work as editor was the founding and editing for twenty years of the periodical *Landfall*. From this, he selected *Landfall Country: Work from Landfall, 1947-1961*, Christchurch, Caxton, 1962. He also wrote an introduction to his selection of James Courage's stories called *Such Separate Creatures*, Christchurch, Caxton, 1973. A lecture, *Present Company: Reflections on the Arts*, was published in Auckland, Paul, 1966, and was included in a selection of critical prose writings edited by John Watson as *The Universal Dance*, Dunedin, University of Otago Press, 1981. *Indirections: A Memoir*, ed. James Bertram, Wellington, Oxford University Press, 1980, gives a full autobiographical account of Brasch's life in Dunedin and overseas to 1947; the record of his later years remains unpublished. A large manuscript collection is held at HL.

'Charles Brasch: An Annotated Bibliography of Selected Works by and about Charles Brasch' by B.M. Attwood was compiled for the Library School, Wellington, in 1979. Miscellaneous biographical information was provided in a collection of tributes collected in *Islands*, no. 5, 1973. James Bertram, a lifelong friend, wrote a short biography with discriminating critical comment in *Charles Brasch*, NZWW, Wellington, Oxford University Press, 1976. Brasch spoke of his poetry as well as of *Landfall* in an interview with Ian Milner, *Landfall*, no. 100, 1971. There are two important articles on the poetry by Vincent O'Sullivan and Ian Wedde. O'Sullivan, *Landfall*, no. 92, 1969, sees an unprotected, courageous quality in Brasch's fourth and fifth volumes of verse and re-reads the earlier volumes with fresh insight, while Wedde, *Islands*, no. 13, 1975, finds in *Home Ground* a balance finally achieved in the relationship of art and life. Joost Daalder writes on 'disputed ground', *Landfall*, no. 103, 1972, and returns to a colder analysis of the poetry in *Pacific Quarterly*, vol. 3, 1978. J. Geraets discusses the memoir and the critical writings in *Islands*, no. 33, 1984, and E.H. McCormick comments on Brasch as editor in *Southerly*, vol. 33, 1973.

Errol Brathwaite 1924-. Novelist. His novels include *Fear in the Night*, Christchurch, Caxton, 1959, *An Affair of Men*, London, Collins in conjunction with the Otago Daily Times, and New York, St. Martin's Press, 1962, *Long Way Home*, Christchurch, Caxton, 1964, and the trilogy *The Flying Fish*, *The Needle's Eye*, and *The Evil Day*, London, Collins, 1964, 1965, and 1967, all three reprinted Auckland, Collins (Fontana), 1977. He has also written fiction for children, and tourist guides. A talk printed in *Proceedings of the New Zealand Library Association (Otago Branch) Weekend School, Oamaru, 1973*, 1974, is part autobiographical essay, part an account of his historical and geographical research for his books. Dennis McEldowney, *Landfall*, no. 72, 1964, provides one of the fuller reviews of the fiction.

Alistair Campbell 1925-. Poet. His collections include *Mine Eyes Dazzle: Poems 1947-49*, Christchurch, Pegasus, 1950, and as *Mine Eyes Dazzle*, with an introduction by James K. Baxter, Christchurch, Pegasus, 1951, revised edition, 1956, *Sanctuary of Spirits: Poems*, Wellington, Wai-te-ata Press, 1963, *Wild Honey*, London, Oxford University Press, 1964, *Blue Rain: Poems*, Wellington, Wai-te-ata Press, 1967, *Kapiti: Selected Poems, 1947-71*, Christchurch, Pegasus, 1972, *Dreams, Yellow Lions*, Martinborough, A. Taylor, 1975, *The Dark Lord of Savaiki*, Pukerua Bay, Te Kotare Press, 1980, *Collected Poems, 1947-1981*, Martinborough, A. Taylor, 1981, *Soul Traps: A Lyric Sequence*, Pukerua Bay, Te Kotare Press, 1985. *The Frigate Bird*, Auckland, Heinemann Reed, 1989, is the first of a planned trilogy of novels. His only published stage play is *When the Bough Breaks*, *Act*, no. 11, 1970, revised version in *Contemporary New Zealand Plays*, ed. Howard McNaughton, Wellington, Oxford University Press, 1974. He has also written fiction and non-fiction for children. *Island to Island*,

Christchurch, Whitcoulls, 1984, is an autobiography, chiefly of his first twenty-five years. Campbell was interviewed by Diane Farmer, *Listener*, 15 April 1965, by Sam Hunt, *Affairs*, February 1969, and on his plays by Howard McNaughton, *Landfall*, no. 109, 1974. Peter Smart's *Introducing Alistair Campbell*, Auckland, Longman Paul, 1982, is especially valuable for its biographical information. The many drafts of some of the poems are discussed by John Weir, 'Five New Zealand Poets: A Bibliographical and Critical Account of Manuscript Material', thesis, University of Canterbury, 1974. James Bertram traces the growth of Campbell's poetry in a review of *Wild Honey*, *Comment*, no. 22, 1965, reprinted in *FP.* Frank McKay, *Landfall*, no. 127, 1978, illuminates the historical and cultural setting of *Sanctuary of Spirits*, and Howard McNaughton, *WLWE*, vol. 19, 1980, considers the importance of that sequence's original conception as a drama for voices. McNaughton also has a note on the place of the radio play 'The Suicide' in Campbell's development in *Landfall*, no. 112, 1974, and John Thomson a note on a D.H. Lawrence source for the poem 'The Return', *JNZL*, no. 1, 1983. David Gunby, *Landfall*, no. 89, 1969, surveys reviews of Campbell's most successful volume, *Mine Eyes Dazzle*.

Dulce Carman 1883-1970. Romance novelist. Her novels, all (with two exceptions noted) published in London by Wright & Brown, include *The Broad Stairway*, London, Ouseley, 1924, *Neath the Maori Moon*, 1948, *The Riddle of the Ranges*, 1950, *Golden Windows*, 1951, *Where Kowhais Bloom*, 1952, *The Wind from the Hill*, 1953, *The Tapu Tree*, 1954, *Colours in the Sun*, 1955, *Dream of the Dark*, 1955, *The Witching Hour*, 1955, *A Million Dreams Away*, London, Hutchinson, 1956, *The Devil's Rosebowl*, 1958, *The Loveliest Night of the Year*, 1958, *The Moon Witch*, 1959, *Golden Flower*, 1960, *The Shining Hill*, 1960, *The Magic of the Hills*, 1961, *The Wailing Pool*, 1961, *The False Dawn*, 1962, *The Miracle of Tane*, 1962, *The Maori Gateway*, 1963, *The Pool of Wisdom*, 1964, *Tomorrow's Sun*, 1964, *The Youngest One*, 1965, *The Guiding Star*, 1966, *The Necklace of El-Hoya*, 1967, and *The Star Child*, 1967.

James Courage 1905-63. Novelist. His volumes of fiction comprise *One House*, London, Gollancz, 1933, *The Fifth Child*, London, Constable, 1948, *Desire without Consent*, London, Constable, 1950, *Fires in the Distance*, London, Constable, 1952, *The Young Have Secrets*, London, Cape, 1954, reprinted with an introduction by Elizabeth Caffin, Wellington, Allen & Unwin/Port Nicholson Press, 1985, *The Call Home*, London, Cape, 1956, *A Way of Love*, London, Cape, and New York, Putnam, 1959, *The Visit to Penmorten*, London, Cape, 1961, and *Such Separate Creatures: Stories*, ed. with an introduction by Charles Brasch, Christchurch, Caxton, 1973. HL holds a manuscript collection which is itemized in *JNZL*, no. 5, 1987, by Cathe Giffuni, who also provides a full bibliography of works by and about Courage. Phillip Wilson, *Listener*, 21 November 1952, wrote an article based on an interview. R.A. Copland, *Landfall*, no. 71, 1964, discusses the five New Zealand novels, and David

Dowling, *Commonwealth Novel in English*, vol. 1, 1982, reassesses *Fires in the Distance*.

James Cowan 1870-1943. Historian and journalist. His more substantial works include *New Zealand, or, Ao-tea-roa*, Wellington, New Zealand Government Department of Tourist and Health Resorts, 1907, *The Maoris of New Zealand*, Christchurch, Whitcombe & Tombs, 1910, *The Adventures of Kimble Bent*, Christchurch, Whitcombe & Tombs, 1911, *Samoa and Its Story*, Chistchurch, Whitcombe & Tombs, 1914, *The Old Frontier: Te Awamutu, the Story of the Waipa Valley*, Te Awamutu, Waipa Post Printing and Publishing Co., 1922, *The New Zealand Wars*, 2 vols, Wellington, Government Printer, 1922-3, reprinted 1955-6, *Fairy Folk Tales of the Maori*, Auckland, Whitcombe & Tombs, 1925, *The Maoris in the Great War*, Auckland, Whitcombe & Tombs for the Maori Regimental Committee, 1926, *Travel in New Zealand, the Island Dominion*, 2 vols, Auckland, Whitcombe & Tombs, 1926, *Legends of the Maori*, vol. 1 with Hon. Sir Maui Pomare, Wellington, Fine Arts (NZ), 1930, vol. 2 ed. James Cowan, Wellington, H.H. Tombs, 1934, *The Maori Yesterday and Today*, Auckland, Whitcombe & Tombs, 1930, *Tales of the Maori Coast*, Wellington, Fine Arts (NZ), 1930, *Tales of the Maori Bush*, Dunedin, Reed, 1934, *Hero Stories of New Zealand*, Wellington, H.H. Tombs, 1935, *A Trader in Cannibal Land: The Life and Adventures of Captain Tapsell*, Dunedin, Reed, 1935, *Suwarrow Gold, and Other Stories of the Great South Sea*, London, Cape, 1936, *Settlers and Pioneers*, Wellington, Department of Internal Afairs, 1940, *Sir Donald Maclean: The Story of a New Zealand Statesman*, Dunedin, Reed, 1940, and *Tales of the Maori Border*, Wellington, Reed, 1944.

Joy Cowley 1936-. Novelist and children's writer. Her adult fiction includes *Nest in a Falling Tree*, Garden City, N.Y., Doubleday, and London, Secker & Warburg, 1967, reprinted Auckland, New Women's Press, 1984, *Man of Straw*, Garden City, N.Y., Doubleday, 1970, London, Secker & Warburg, 1971, reprinted Melbourne, Sun Books, 1973, *Of Men and Angels*, Garden City, N.Y., Doubleday, 1972, London, Hodder & Stoughton, 1973, *The Mandrake Root*, Garden City, N.Y., Doubleday, 1975, London, Hodder & Stoughton, 1976, *The Growing Season*, Garden City, N.Y., Doubleday, 1978, London, Hodder & Stoughton, 1979, reprinted Auckland, Oxford University Press, 1985, and *Heart Attack and Other Stories*, Auckland, Hodder & Stoughton, 1985. Her work for children includes *The Duck in the Gun*, Garden City, N.Y., Doubleday, 1969, *The Silent One*, Christchurch, Whitcoulls, and New York, Knopf, 1981, London, Methuen, 1982, and *The Terrible Taniwha of Timberditch*, Auckland, Oxford University Press, and Wellington, Kidsarus 2, 1982. From 1984, she has published well over a hundred brief story books, many consisting mostly of illustrations, for young children and children learning to read. There is an interview with Marilyn Duckworth in *Affairs*, March 1971, and Pauline Swain, *Listener*, 22 May 1972, wrote an article based on an interview. David Norton,

Climate, no. 29, 1979, analyses her short story 'The Silk', and Christopher Bates provides a useful introduction to imagery and themes in *Landfall*, no. 139, 1981.

D'Arcy Cresswell 1896-1960. Poet. His collections of verse include *Poems (1921-1927)*, London, Wells Gardner, Darton & Co., 1928, *Poems 1924-1931*, London, John Lane The Bodley Head, 1932, *Lyttelton Harbour: A Poem*, Auckland, Unicorn Press, 1936, *The Voyage of the Hurunui: A Ballad*, Christchurch, Caxton, 1956, and *Sonnets, Published and from Manuscripts*, ed. Helen Shaw, Christchurch, Nag's Head Press, 1976. In the later 1950s he published poems in several small pamphlets and on single sheets. *The Forest*, Auckland, Pelorus Press, 1952, is a verse comedy in three acts. *Eena Deena Dynamo*, Christchurch, Caxton, 1936, and *Modern Poetry and the Ideal*, Auckland, Griffin Press, 1934, are two short essays. *Margaret McMillan*, London, Hutchinson, 1948, is a biography. His two early autobiographical volumes are *The Poet's Progress*, London, Faber, 1930, and *Present without Leave*, London, Cassell, 1939. *The Letters of D'Arcy Cresswell*, Christchurch, University of Canterbury, 1971, was edited by Helen Shaw, who also edited *Dear Lady Ginger: An Exchange of Letters between Lady Ottoline Morrell and D'Arcy Cresswell*, Auckland, Auckland University Press, 1983, London, Century, 1984. There are manuscript collections at ATL and APL. He was remembered by seven New Zealand friends in *Landfall*, no. 56, 1960. In *D'Arcy Cresswell*, TWAS, New York, 1972, Roderick Finlayson gives sympathetic attention to the whole range of his interests. He was interviewed by Phillip Wilson, *Listener*, 10 February 1950. W.S. Broughton (1966), reprinted in *ENZL*, discussed his poetry of the 1920s, and H. Winston Rhodes, *New Zealand Libraries*, vol. 10, 1974, wrote with balanced understanding on the autobiographies.

Ian Cross 1925-. Novelist. His novels comprise *The God Boy*, New York, Harcourt, Brace, 1957, London, Deutsch, 1958, reprinted Harmondsworth, Penguin, 1962, with an introduction by Joan Stevens, Christchurch, Whitcombe and Tombs, 1972, and Auckland, Penguin, 1989, *The Backward Sex*, London, Deutsch, 1960, reprinted Auckland, Oxford University Press, 1987, and *After Anzac Day*, London, Deutsch, 1961, reprinted Christchurch, Whitcoulls, 1979. He has also written *The Unlikely Bureaucrat: My Years in Broadcasting*, Wellington, Allen & Unwin/Port Nicholson Press, 1988. An interview with Marilyn Duckworth, *Affairs*, May 1970, focuses on the fiction, but the best biographical article, Vincent O'Sullivan's in *Listener*, 29 March 1986, covers a fuller range of activity. Well-considered responses to the first two novels are found in reviews by E.H. McCormick and R.A. Copland, *Landfall*, no. 47, 1958, and no. 56, 1960. In a long article spread over *Landfall*, nos 117, 119, and 121, 1976-7, Patrick Evans sets Cross in a society of complacent conformity and outbreaks of violence and warfare, and examines his confrontation of and solution to what Evans calls the writer's 'provincial dilemma'.

Barry Crump 1935-. Novelist. His work, until 1971 published in Wellington by Reed, includes *A Good Keen Man*, 1960 and *Hang On a Minute Mate*, 1961, together reprinted as *Two in One*, 1962, *One of Us*, 1962, *There and Back*, 1963, *Gulf*, 1964, *Scrapwagon*, 1965, *The Odd Spot of Bother*, 1967, *Warm Beer and Other Stories*, 1969, *A Good Keen Girl*, 1970, *"No Reference Intended"*, 1971, *Bastards I Have Met*, Auckland, Crump Publications, 1971, *Fred*, Auckland, Crump Productions, 1972, *The Best of Crump*, Auckland, Crump Productions, 1974, consisting of extracts from eleven of the earlier books, *Shorty*, Henderson, CW Associates, 1980, *Puha Road*, Auckland, C & C Associates, 1981, *The Adventures of Sam Cash* (stories from *Hang On a Minute Mate* and *There and Back*), Auckland, Beckett Publishing, 1985, *Wild Pork and Watercress*, Auckland, Beckett, 1986, *A Barry Crump Collection*, Auckland, Beckett, 1987, *Barry Crump's Bedtime Yarns: A Collection of Short Stories and Poems*, ed. Mandy Herron, Auckland, Barry Crump Associates, 1988, and *Bullock Creek*, Opotiki, Barry Crump Associates, 1989. Two brief biographical sources are an anonymous article, *Listener*, 21 April 1961, and an interview with Tony Reid, *Listener*, 20 November 1982.

Allen Curnow 1911-. Poet and editor. His volumes of poetry include *Valley of Decision: Poems*, Auckland, Auckland University College Students' Association Press, 1933, *Enemies: Poems 1934-36*, Christchurch, Caxton, 1937, *Not in Narrow Seas: Poems with Prose*, Christchurch, Caxton, 1939, *Island and Time*, Christchurch, Caxton, 1941, *Recent Poems* (with A.R.D. Fairburn, Denis Glover, and R.A.K. Mason), Christchurch, Caxton, 1941, *Sailing or Drowning: Poems*, Wellington, Progressive Publishing Society, 1944, *Poems: Jack without Magic*, Christchurch, Caxton, 1946, *At Dead Low Water and Sonnets*, Christchurch, Caxton, 1949, *Poems 1949-57*, Wellington, Mermaid Press, 1957, *A Small Room with Large Windows: Selected Poems*, London, Oxford University Press, 1962, *Trees, Effigies, Moving Objects: A Sequence of Poems*, Wellington, Catspaw Press, 1972, *An Abominable Temper and Other Poems*, Wellington, Catspaw Press, 1973, *Collected Poems 1933-1973*, Wellington, Reed, 1974, *An Incorrigible Music: A Sequence of Poems*, Auckland, Auckland University Press, 1979, *Selected Poems*, Auckland, Penguin, 1982, *You Will Know When You Get There: Poems 1979-81*, Auckland, Auckland University Press, 1982, *The Loop in Lone Kauri Road: Poems 1983-1985*, Auckland, Auckland University Press, 1986, *Continuum: New and Later Poems, 1972-1988*, Auckland, Auckland University Press, 1988, and *Selected Poems, 1940-1989*, London, Viking, 1990. An accomplished verse satirist, he has published under the pseudonym of Whim-Wham *A Present for Hitler and Other Verses*, Christchurch, Caxton, 1940, *Whim-Wham: Verses 1941-1942*, Christchurch, Caxton, 1942, *Whim-Wham, 1943*, Wellington, Progressive Publishing Society, 1943, *The Best of Whim-Wham*, Hamilton, Paul's Book Arcade, 1959, and *Whim-Wham Land*, Auckland, Paul, 1967. There are four plays in verse: *The Axe: A Verse Tragedy*, Christchurch, Caxton, 1949, and *Four Plays* (which adds *The Overseas Expert*, *The Duke's Miracle*, and *Resident of Nowhere*), Wellington, Reed, 1972. He edited two influential anthologies, *A Book of New Zealand Verse 1923-45*, Christchurch, Caxton, 1945, enlarged edition, 1951, and *The Penguin Book of New Zealand Verse*, Harmondsworth, Penguin, 1960. Several significant essays on New Zealand poetry are listed under 'Literary History and Criticism'. Many of his articles and reviews, as well as his influential introductions to the anthologies he edited, are reprinted in *Look Back Harder*, ed. Peter Simpson, Auckland, Auckland University Press, 1987. A collection of manuscript papers is held at ATL.

There is a Library School 'Bibliography of Works by and on Allen Curnow', Wellington, 1976, by Theresa Graham, and Peter Simpson's checklist of his critical prose appeared in *JNZL*, no. 5, 1987. The excellent long interview with MacD. P. Jackson, *Islands*, no. 4, 1973, reprinted in *LBH*, may be supplemented by those with Arthur Baysting (on the plays), *Listener*, 7 March 1969, with Harry Ricketts in his *Talking about Ourselves*, Wellington, Mallinson Rendel, 1986, and with Peter Simpson, *Landfall*, no. 175, 1990. Alan Roddick's *Allen Curnow*, NZWW, Wellington, Oxford University Press, 1980, is the only separate study. An early and still one of the finest articles was by C.K. Stead, *Landfall*, no. 65, 1963, reprinted in *ENZL* and *IGC*, who supports a closely argued philosophical essay with detailed analyses of poems; and in another substantial review article on the publication of the *Collected Poems*, Terry Sturm, *Islands*, no. 11, 1975, studies the relationship of poet to poems over forty years of writing. In other general studies, A.J. Gurr, *JCL*, no. 1, 1965, takes 'Landfall in Unknown Seas' to be the archetypal example of Curnow's search for a local identity, Rob Jackaman, *Pilgrims*, no. 9, 1980, argues that Curnow's earlier 'geographical anxieties' are resolved in *An Incorrigible Music*, Leigh Davis, *And*, no. 3, 1984, in an essay throttled by literary theory, finds postmodernist fault with Curnow's conception of reality, and James Wieland, *Landfall*, no. 136, 1980, examines Curnow's mythopoeic dealings with islands and time. Trevor James in *Poetry of the Pacific Region*, ed. Paul Sharrad, Adelaide, CRNLE, 1984, argues that Curnow's well-known anxiety about place and time was at heart theological and existential rather than nationalistic. In *JCL*, vol. 22, 1987, James returns to the theme of 'philosophical scepticism' in the poetry of the previous eight years. Chris Wallace-Crabbe, *Ariel*, vol. 16, 1985, points to his changing use of language, and Alan Riach, *Landfall*, no. 169, 1989, reflects on Curnow in relation to Charles Olson. Writing on individual collections, Terry Sturm, *WLWE*, vol. 14, 1975, offers a detailed and persuasive reading of *Trees, Effigies, Moving Objects*, and Edward Burman, *Landfall*, no. 153, 1985, demonstrates how 'Moro Assassinato' draws together ideas and images from the earlier poetry. K.O. Arvidson, *JNZL*, no. 1, 1983, perceptively analyses *You Will Know When You Get There*. There are extensive reviews of *Continuum* by MacD. P. Jackson in *Landfall*, no. 171, 1989, and by C.K. Stead in *AL*.

Ruth Dallas 1919-. Poet and children's writer. Her collections of poetry include *Country Road and Other Poems, 1947-52*, Christchurch, Caxton, 1953,

The Turning Wheel: Poems, Christchurch, Caxton, 1961, *Day Book: Poems of a Year*, Christchurch, Caxton, 1966, *Shadow Show: Poems*, Christchurch, Caxton, 1968, *Song for a Guitar and Other Songs*, Dunedin, Otago University Press, 1976, *Walking on the Snow: Poems*, Christchurch, Caxton, 1976, *Steps of the Sun: Poems*, Christchurch, Caxton, 1979, and *Collected Poems*, Dunedin, University of Otago Press, 1987. Her work for children includes *The Children in the Bush*, London, Methuen, 1969, *Ragamuffin Scarecrow*, Dunedin, Bibliography Room, University of Otago, 1969, *A Dog Called Wig*, London, Methuen, 1970, *The Wild Boy in the Bush*, London, Methuen, 1971, *The Big Flood in the Bush*, London, Methuen, 1972, *The House on the Cliffs*, London, Methuen, and Wellington, Hicks Smith, 1975, *Shining Rivers*, London, Methuen, 1979, and *Holiday Time in the Bush*, London and Auckland, Methuen, 1983. 'Beginnings', *Landfall*, no. 76, 1965, reprinted in *B*, is an autobiographical essay. Manuscript papers are held at HL. There is an interview in *Review* (Dunedin), 1975, with J. Gibb, who, in *Pilgrims*, vol. 3, 1978, counters early critical attention to technique with an examination of content. Useful reviews include those by James Bertram (*The Turning Wheel*), *Landfall*, no. 62, 1962, reprinted in *FP*, and Charles Doyle (*Day Book*), *Landfall*, no. 82, 1967.

Dan Davin 1913-90. Novelist. His fiction includes *Cliffs of Fall*, London, Nicholson & Watson, 1945, *For the Rest of Our Lives*, London, Nicholson & Watson, 1947, reprinted Auckland, Paul, and London, Michael Joseph, 1965, *The Gorse Blooms Pale* (short stories), London, Nicholson & Watson, 1947, *Roads from Home*, London, Michael Joseph, 1949, reprinted with an introduction by Lawrence Jones, Auckland, Auckland University Press, 1976, *The Sullen Bell*, London, Michael Joseph, 1956, *No Remittance*, London, Michel Joseph, 1959, *Not Here, Not Now*, London, Hale, and Christchurch, Whitcombe & Tombs, 1970, *Brides of Price*, London, Hale, and Christchurch, Whitombe & Tombs, 1972, *Breathing Spaces* (short stories), London, Hale, and Christchurch, Whitcoulls, 1975, *Selected Stories*, with an introduction by the author, Wellington, Victoria University Press, and London, Hale, 1981, and *The Salamander and the Fire: Collected War Stories*, Auckland, Oxford University Press, 1986. He has also edited volumes of English and New Zealand short stories. *Crete*, Wellington, War History Branch, Department of Internal Affairs, 1953, is a contribution to the New Zealand Official War History, and in *Closing Times*, London, Oxford University Press, 1975, reprinted Auckland, Oxford University Press, 1985, he recalls several literary friends. ATL holds a manuscript collection. James Bertram's *Dan Davin*, NZWW, Auckland, Oxford University Press, 1983, which contains a select bibliography, is biographical as well as critical; it is the only full study, and amplifies an earlier article, *Meanjin*, vol. 32, 1973, reprinted in *FP*. Davin was interviewed on his regular visits to New Zealand, anonymously in the *Listener*, 17 September 1948, by M.H. Holcroft, *Listener*, 3 April 1959, by Ray Knox, *Listener*, 12 September 1969, and by Michael King, *Listener*, 21 October 1978. In a substantial review of *Not Here, Not Now*, *Landfall*, no. 95, 1970, Michael Beveridge also surveys the earlier novels. Winston Rhodes, *CENZN*, discusses the personal voice and the social historian in *Roads from Home*. Lawrence Jones, *Islands*, no. 20, 1977, reprinted in *BWM*, uses Davin to illustrate the persistence of the realistic short story, and the stories are also briefly considered by R.A. Copland, *CENZSS*.

Joan de Hamel 1924-. Children's writer. Her books include *X Marks the Spot*, Guildford, Lutterworth Press, 1973, reprinted Harmondsworth, Puffin, 1976, *Take the Long Path*, Guildford, Lutterworth Press, 1978, reprinted Harmondsworth, Puffin, 1980, *Hemi's Pet*, Auckland, Reed Methuen, 1985, and *The Third Eye*, Auckland, Viking Kestrel, 1987.

Anne de Roo 1931-. Children's writer. Her books include *The Gold Dog*, London, Hart-Davis, 1966, reprinted Wellington, Price Milburn, 1982, *Moa Valley*, London, Hart-Davis, 1969, *Boy and the Sea Beast*, London, Hart-Davis, 1971, *Cinnamon and Nutmeg*, London, Macmillan, 1972, Nashville, Nelson, 1974, reprinted London, Pan, 1974, *Mick's Country Cousins*, London, Macmillan, 1974, reprinted London, Pan, 1977, *Scrub Fire*, London, Heinemann, 1977, reprinted London, Scholastic Publications, 1980, *Traveller*, London, Heinemann, 1979, *Because of Rosie*, London, Heinemann, 1980, *Jacky Nobody*, Auckland, Methuen, 1983, *The Bat's Nest*, Auckland, Hodder & Stoughton, 1986, and *Friend Troll Friend Taniwha*, Auckland, Hodder & Stoughton, 1986.

Jean Devanny 1894-1962. Novelist. Her early work includes the following fiction with a New Zealand setting: *The Butcher Shop*, London, Duckworth, 1926, reprinted with an introduction by Heather Roberts, Auckland, Auckland University Press, 1981, *Lenore Divine*, London, Duckworth, 1926, *Old Savage and Other Stories*, London, Duckworth, 1927, *Dawn Beloved*, London, Duckworth, 1928, *Riven*, London, Duckworth, 1929, *Bushman Burke*, London, Duckworth, 1930, *Devil Made Saint*, London, Duckworth, 1930, and *Poor Swine*, London, Duckworth, 1932. In the twenty years following 1927 she also wrote a further nine Australian novels. 'Jean Devanny: A Biographical and Bibliographical Note' by Ronald E. Store and Richard Anderson appeared in *Australian Academic and Research Libraries*, vol. 1, 1970. Her manuscripts are described in *Women in Australia: An Annotated Guide to Records*, ed. Kay Daniels, Mary Murnane, and Anne Picot, vol. 2, Canberra, Government Printer, 1977. *Point of Departure: The Autobiography of Jean Devanny*, St Lucia, University of Queensland Press, 1986, was edited by Carole Ferrier, who also, in *Hecate*, vol. 6, no. 1, 1980, wrote on her New Zealand novels. Drusilla Modjeska includes a substantial study in her *Exiles at Home*, Sydney, Angus & Robertson, 1981.

Alfred Domett 1811-87. Poet and politician. His volumes of verse include *Poems*, London, Henry Leggatt, 1833, *Venice*, London, Saunders & Otley, 1839, *Ranolf and Amohia: A South-Sea Day-Dream*, London, Smith Elder, 1872, revised edition, London, Kegan Paul, 1883, and *Flotsam and Jetsam: Rhymes Old* *and New*, London, Smith Elder, 1877. *The Diary of Alfred Domett, 1872-1885* was edited with a biographical introduction by E.A. Horsman, London, Oxford University Press, 1953. Dennis McEldowney, *Landfall*, no. 88, 1968, wrote on *Ranolf and Amohia*, and E. Glasgow, *Contemporary Review*, vol. 215, 1969, gave a simple survey of his work in New Zealand.

Marilyn Duckworth 1935-. Novelist. Her novels include *A Gap in the Spectrum*, London, New Authors, 1959, reprinted Auckland, Oxford University Press, 1985, *The Matchbox House*, London, Hutchinson, 1960, New York, W. Morrow, 1961, reprinted Auckland, Oxford University Press, 1987, *A Barbarous Tongue*, London, Hutchinson, 1963, *Over the Fence is Out*, London, Hutchinson, 1969, and, all from Hodder & Stoughton, Auckland, *Disorderly Conduct*, 1984, *Married Alive*, 1985, (reprinted Auckland, Spectre, 1990), *Rest for the Wicked*, 1986, *Pulling Faces*, 1987, and *A Message from Harpo*, 1989, (reprinted Auckland, Spectre, 1990). *Explosions on the Sun*, Auckland, Hodder & Stoughton, 1989, is a collection of stories. *Other Lovers' Children: Poems 1958-74*, Christchurch, Pegasus, 1975, is her only volume of verse. A personal essay on the nature of New Zealanders appeared in the *Listener*, 4 October 1971. There is an interview with Sue Kedgley in *OOC*, and a profile by Marion McLeod, based on an interview, *Listener*, 22 November 1986. Her most frank discussion of her work is in *The Weekend Australian*, 18-19 November 1989. A full review of *Over the Fence is Out* by Patrick Evans appeared in *Landfall*, no. 95, 1970.

Tessa Duder 1940-. Children's writer. Her books for children include *Night Race to Kawau*, Auckland, Oxford University Press, 1982, *Jellybean*, Auckland, Oxford University Press, 1985, *Alex*, Auckland, Oxford University Press, 1987, *Dragons*, Auckland, Shortland, 1987, *Simply Messing About in Boats*, Auckland, Shortland, 1988, and *Alex in Winter*, Auckland, Oxford University Press, 1989. She recounts her childhood in *Through the Looking Glass*, ed. Michael Gifkins, Auckland, Century Hutchinson, 1988.

Yvonne du Fresne 1929-. Short story writer and novelist. Her volumes include *Farvel and Other Stories*, Wellington, Victoria University Press with Price Milburn, 1980, *The Book of Ester*, Auckland, Longman Paul, 1982, *The Growing of Astrid Westergaard and Other Stories*, Auckland, Longman Paul, 1985, *Frédérique*, Auckland, Penguin, 1987, and *The Bear from the North: Tales of a New Zealand Childhood*, London, Women's Press, 1989. Stephanie Edmond, *Listener*, 23 March 1985, in an article based on an interview, is useful. The best review is by Margot Schwass (*The Growing of Astrid Westergaard*), *Listener*, 23 March 1985. Anna Rutherford, in *English Literature of the Dominions*, ed. K. Gross and W. Klooss, Würzburg, Königshausen & Neumann, 1981, discusses *Farvel* in terms of imaginative autobiographical truth, and there is an article on her work generally by Susan Ash, *SPAN*, no. 28, 1989.

Eileen Duggan 1894–1972. Poet. Her collections comprise *Poems*, Dunedin, New Zealand Tablet, 1922, *Poems*, with an introduction by Walter de la Mare, London, Allen & Unwin, 1937, *New Zealand Poems*, London, Allen & Unwin, 1940, and *More Poems*, London, Allen & Unwin, and New York, Macmillan, 1951; *New Zealand Bird Songs*, Wellington, Harry H. Tombs, 1929, contains poems for children. She also published occasionally on aspects of local Irish Catholicism. MS material is held in the archives of the Archdiocese of Wellington and in the NLA (photocopies at ATL). Grace Burgess wrote a simple biography called *A Gentle Poet: A Portrait of Eileen Duggan OBE*, Carterton, G. Burgess, 1981. *Eileen Duggan*, NZWW, Wellington, Oxford University Press, 1977, by Frank McKay, is the only substantial critical study; it also provides a bibliography. Reviews of *More Poems* by Joan Stevens, *Landfall*, no. 21, 1952, and by James K. Baxter, *Listener*, 13 July 1951, are interesting contemporary responses to her last volume, and tributes by Kevin Maher, *Listener*, 15 January 1973, and Dennis McEldowney, *Islands*, no. 6, 1973, contain sensitive critical and personal observations. John Weir, 'Five New Zealand Poets: A Bibliographical and Critical Account of Manuscript Material', thesis, University of Canterbury, 1974, makes good use of comments on poetry found in her letters. Her Georgianism is considered in a thesis by Anne French, Victoria University of Wellington, 1979.

Maurice Duggan 1922–74. Short story writer. His volumes of stories comprise *Immanuel's Land: Stories*, Auckland, Pilgrim Press, 1956, *Summer in the Gravel Pit: Stories*, Hamilton, Paul, and London, Gollancz, 1965, reprinted Auckland, Longman Paul, 1971, *O'Leary's Orchard and Other Stories*, Christchurch, Caxton, 1970, and *Collected Stories*, ed. with an introduction by C.K. Stead, Auckland, Auckland University Press, 1981. His stories for children include *Falter Tom and the Water Boy*, London, Faber, New York, Criterion, and Hamilton, Paul's Book Arcade, 1958, reprinted Auckland, Longman Paul, and Harmondsworth, Kestrel, 1974, Auckland, Penguin, 1984, and *The Fabulous McFanes and Other Children's Stories*, Whatamongo Bay, Cape Catley, 1974. 'Beginnings', *Landfall*, no. 80, 1966, reprinted in *B*, is an autobiographical essay. ATL holds a manuscript collection. Keith Sinclair's memorial tribute appeared in *Listener*, 25 January 1975. The essence of Duggan's method has resisted assay, though two early reviews were unintimidated: R.A. Copland (*Immanuel's Land*), *Landfall*, no. 41, 1957, and Lawrence Jones (*Summer in the Gravel Pit*), *Landfall*, no. 75, 1965. Dan Davin, *CENZSS*, is able to make interesting use of personal correspondence in discussing *Summer in the Gravel Pit*. Terry Sturm, *Landfall*, no. 97, 1971, covers a variety of ideas but is hampered by a story-by-story approach. Factual background to some of the stories is given by Stead in his introduction of 1981, reprinted in *IGC*. Patrick Evans, *Landfall*, no. 142, 1982, persuasively sees Duggan's experiments in terms of a 'provincial dilemma', and with some difficulty Ian Wedde, *Islands*, no. 34, 1984, winds into a sensitive discussion of a wholeness in Duggan's output, found in the themes, the hints of biography, and the struggle with language.

Beverley Dunlop 1935-. Children's writer. Her work, all from Auckland, Hodder & Stoughton, includes *The Dolphin Boy*, 1982, *The Poetry Girl*, 1983, *Earthquake Town*, 1984, *Queen Cat and Other Stories*, 1988, and *Spirits of the Lake*, 1988.

Peggy Dunstan 1924-. Children's writer. Her collections of poems for children include *Sunflowers and Sandcastles*, Wellington, Millwood Press, 1977, *In and Out the Windows*, Auckland, Hodder & Stoughton, 1980, and *Behind the Stars*, Auckland, Hodder & Stoughton, 1986. She has also published collections of verse for adults. *A Fistful of Summer*, Christchurch, Whitcoulls, 1981, and *The Other Side of Summer*, Auckland, Hodder & Stoughton, 1983, are books of childhood reminiscence.

Dorothy Eden 1912-82. Romance novelist. Her novels, published in London by Macdonald until 1959 and Hodder & Stoughton thereafter, except where noted, include *Singing Shadows*, London, Stanley Pool, 1940, *The Laughing Ghost*, 1943, *We Are for the Dark*, 1944, *Summer Sunday*, 1946, *Walk into My Parlour*, 1947, *The Schoolmaster's Daughters*, 1948, *Crow Hollow*, 1950, *The Voice of the Dolls*, 1950, *Cat's Prey*, 1952, *Lamb to the Slaughter*, 1953, *Bride by Candlelight*, 1954, reprinted Auckland, Hodder & Stoughton, 1975, *Darling Clementine*, 1955, *Night of the Letter*, 1955, *Death Is a Red Rose*, 1956, *The Pretty Ones*, 1957, *Listen to Danger*, 1958, *The Deadly Travellers*, 1959, *The Sleeping Bride*, 1959, *Samantha*, 1960, *Sleep in the Woods*, 1960, New York, McCann, 1961, *Afternoon for Lizards*, London, 1962, *Whistle for the Crows*, 1962, *The Bird in the Chimney*, 1963, *Bella*, 1964, *The Marriage Chest*, 1965, *Never Call It Loving*, 1966, *Siege in the Sun*, 1967, *Winterwood*, 1967, *The Shadow Wife*, 1968, *The Vines of Yarrabee*, 1969, *Melbury Square*, 1970, *Waiting for Willa*, 1970, *Afternoon Walk*, 1971, *Speak to Me of Love*, 1972, *The Millionaire's Daughter*, 1974, *The Time of the Dragon*, 1974, *The House on Hay Hill and Other Stories*, London, Coronet, and New York, Fawcett, 1976, *The Salamanca Drum*, 1977, *The Storrington Papers*, 1979, *The American Heiress*, 1980, and *An Important Family*, London and Auckland, Hodder & Stoughton, and New York, Morrow, 1982.

Lauris Edmond 1924-. Poet. Her collections include *In Middle Air*, Christchurch, Pegasus, 1975, *The Pear Tree: Poems*, Christchurch, Pegasus, 1977, *Wellington Letter: A Sequence of Poems*, Wellington, Mallinson Rendel, 1980, *Salt from the North: Poems*, Wellington, Oxford University Press, 1980, *Catching It: Poems*, Auckland, Oxford University Press, 1983, *Selected Poems*, Auckland, Oxford University Press, 1984, *Seasons and Creatures*, Auckland, Oxford University Press, 1986, and *Summer near the Arctic Circle*, Auckland, Oxford University Press, 1988. She has also written a novel, *High Country Weather*, Wellington, Allen & Unwin/Port Nicholson Press, 1984. *Hot October: An Autobiographical Story*, Wellington, Allen & Unwin/Port Nicholson Press, 1989, is supplemented by an autobiographical essay in *Beyond Expectations*, ed. Margaret Clark, Wellington, Allen & Unwin/Port Nicholson Press, 1986.

Interviews include those with David Dowling, *Landfall*, no. 144, 1982, with Anne Else on her novel, *Broadsheet*, no. 126, 1985, with Janet Wilson, *Listener*, 19 April, 1986, on her experience as a writer from schooldays on, with Harry Ricketts in his *Talking About Ourselves*, Wellington, Mallinson Rendel, 1986, in *Broadsheet*, no. 170, 1989, about her autobiography, and with Sue Kedgley in *OOC*. Useful reviews of *Selected Poems* include those by K. Cochrane, *Landfall*, no. 154, 1985, and Fiona Farrell Poole, *Listener*, 5 October 1985.

Murray Edmond 1949-. Poet. His collections of verse include *Entering the Eye*, Dunedin, Caveman Press, 1973, *Patchwork: Poems*, Day's Bay, Hawk Press, 1978, *End Wall: Poems*, Auckland, Oxford University Press, 1981, and *Letters and Paragraphs*, Christchurch, Caxton, 1987. With Mary Paul, he edited *The New Poets*, Wellington, Allen & Unwin, 1987. He was interviewed by Harry Ricketts in his *Talking about Ourselves*, Wellington, Mallinson Rendel, 1986.

A.R.D. Fairburn 1904-57. Poet. His collections include *He Shall Not Rise: Poems*, London, Columbia Press, 1930, *Dominion*, Christchurch, Caxton, 1938, *Recent Poems* (with Allen Curnow, Denis Glover and R.A.K. Mason), Christchurch, Caxton, 1941, *Poems, 1929-41*, Christchurch, Caxton, 1943, *The Rakehelly Man & Other Verses*, Christchurch, Caxton, 1946, *Strange Rendezvous: Poems 1929-1941 with Additions*, Christchurch, Caxton, 1952, *Three Poems: Dominion, The Voyage & To a Friend in the Wilderness*, Wellington, New Zealand University Press, 1952, *The Disadvantages of Being Dead*, Wellington, Mermaid Press, 1958, *Poetry Harbinger* (with Denis Glover), Auckland, Pilgrim Press, 1958, and *Collected Poems*, Christchurch, Pegasus, 1966. He was a prolific author of letters, articles, and booklets. One of his more substantial prose publications was *We New Zealanders: An Informal Essay*, Wellington, Progressive Publishing Society, 1944. Other material was brought together in *The Woman Problem & Other Prose*, selected by Denis Glover and Geoffrey Fairburn, Auckland, Paul, 1967. The *Letters of A.R.D. Fairburn*, Auckland, Oxford University Press, 1981, were selected and edited by Lauris Edmond. Manuscript material is held at the University of Auckland and ATL.

Olive Johnson's *A.R.D. Fairburn 1904-1957: A Bibliography of His Published Work*, Auckland, University of Auckland, 1958, is remarkably thorough. Recent interest has been chiefly biographical. In addition to the *Letters*, there are Denys Trussell's *Fairburn*, Auckland, Auckland University Press, 1984, a well researched biography, and the more free-wheeling *Walking on My Feet: A.R.D. Fairburn 1904-1957: A Kind of Biography*, Auckland, Collins, 1983, by J. and H. McNeish. Apart from two theses, by J.C. Ross on the poem 'Dominion', 1962, and W.S. Broughton on Fairburn, Mason, and Cresswell, 1968, both University of Auckland, and two articles, by MacD. P. Jackson, *Kiwi*, August 1961, and Louis Johnson and Eric Schwimmer, *Numbers*, no. 7, 1957, the only substantial criticism was prompted by the *Collected Poems* of 1966. C.K. Stead, *Landfall*, no. 80, 1966, reprinted in *IGC*, analysed his dislike of the poetry, to which Ian Hamilton replied, *Comment*, no. 32, 1967, placing the poet in his social and geographical environment. W.S. Broughton, *Dispute*, vol. 2, no. 4, 1967, and Vincent O'Sullivan, *Comment*, no. 28, 1966, both discussed the incompatibility between Fairburn's lyrical gift and his social and political beliefs, Broughton pointing to his success in the personal lyric.

Roderick Finlayson 1904–. Short story writer. His volumes of stories include *Brown Man's Burden*, Auckland, Unicorn Press, 1938, reprinted with additional stories as *Brown Man's Burden and Later Stories*, ed. with an introduction by Bill Pearson, Auckland, Auckland University Press, 1973, *Sweet Beulah Land*, Auckland, Griffin Press, 1942, *Other Lovers*, Dunedin, McIndoe, 1976, and *In Georgina's Shady Garden and Other Stories*, Auckland, Griffin Press, 1988. *Tidal Creek*, Sydney, Angus & Robertson, 1948, reprinted with an introduction by Dennis McEldowney, Auckland, Auckland University Press, 1979, and *The Schooner Came to Atia*, Auckland, Griffin Press, 1952, are two novels. *The Springing Fern*, Christchurch, Whitcombe & Tombs, 1965, is historical fiction originally published in Primary School Bulletins. His non-fiction includes the essay *Our Life in This Land*, Auckland, Griffin Press, 1940, *The Maoris of New Zealand* (with Joan Smith), London, Oxford University Press, 1958, and *D'Arcy Cresswell*, TWAS, New York, 1972. HL holds a manuscript collection. He was interviewed by O.E. Middleton, *Listener*, 9 July 1973, and Vincent O'Sullivan, *Listener*, 22 September 1979, wrote a comprehensive article based on an interview. John Muirhead, *WLWE*, vol. 14, 1975, develops a discussion of narrative technique into an excellent introduction to the stories.

Janet Frame 1924–. Novelist and short story writer. Her fiction includes *The Lagoon: Stories*, Christchurch, Caxton, 1951, reprinted as *The Lagoon and Other Stories*, Auckland, Random Century, 1990, *Owls Do Cry*, Christchurch, Pegasus, 1957, New York, Braziller, 1960, London, W.H. Allen, 1961, reprinted Melbourne, Sun Books, 1967, London, Women's Press, and Auckland, Hutchinson, 1985, *Faces in the Water*, Christchurch, Pegasus, and New York, Braziller, 1961, London, W.H. Allen, 1962, reprinted New York, Avon Books, 1971, London, Women's Press, 1980, *The Edge of the Alphabet*, Christchurch, Pegasus, New York, Braziller, and London, W.H. Allen, 1962, *The Reservoir: Stories and Sketches*, New York, Braziller, 1963, *Snowman, Snowman: Fables and Fantasies*, New York, Braziller, 1963, *Scented Gardens for the Blind*, Christchurch, Pegasus, and London, W.H. Allen, 1963, New York, Braziller, 1964, reprinted London, Women's Press, 1982, *The Adaptable Man*, Christchurch, Pegasus, New York, Braziller, and London, W.H. Allen, 1965, *The Reservoir and Other Stories* (containing most of the stories and fables first collected in 1963), Christchurch, Pegasus, and London, W.H. Allen, 1966, *A State of Siege*, New York, Braziller, 1966, Christchurch, Pegasus, and London, W.H. Allen, 1967, reprinted Sydney, Angus & Robertson, 1982, and North Ryde, NSW, Sirius, 1989, *The Rainbirds*, London, W.H. Allen, 1968, Christchurch, Pegasus, 1969, and as *Yellow Flowers in the Antipodean Room*, New

York, Braziller, 1969, *Intensive Care*, New York, Braziller, and Toronto, Doubleday Canada, 1970, Wellington, Reed, and London, W.H. Allen, 1971, *Daughter Buffalo*, New York, Braziller, and Toronto, Doubleday Canada, 1972, Wellington, Reed, and London, W.H. Allen, 1973, reprinted Auckland, Century Hutchinson, 1986, *Living in the Maniototo*, New York, Braziller, 1979, Auckland, Hutchinson, and London, Women's Press, 1981, *You Are Now Entering the Human Heart* (selected short stories), Wellington, Victoria University Press, 1983, London, Women's Press, 1984, and *The Carpathians*, Auckland, Century Hutchinson, New York, Braziller, and London, Bloomsbury, 1988, reprinted London, Pandora, 1989. *The Pocket Mirror*, New York, Braziller, and London, W.H. Allen, 1967, Christchurch, Pegasus, 1968, is a collection of poems.

The early autobiographical essay 'Beginnings', *Landfall*, no. 73, 1965, reprinted in *B*, has been superseded by three volumes of autobiography, *To the Is-Land*, New York, Braziller, 1982, Auckland, Hutchinson, and London, Women's Press, 1983, *An Angel at My Table*, New York, Braziller, Auckland, Hutchinson, and London, Women's Press, 1984, and *The Envoy from Mirror City*, New York, Braziller, Auckland, Hutchinson, and London, Women's Press, 1985. The three were reprinted separately, London, Paladin, 1987, and in one volume as *An Autobiography*, Auckland, Century Hutchinson, 1989. Bibliographies include those of B.N. Moir (written for the Library School, Wellington), 'Janet Frame: An Annotated Bibliography of Autobiography and Biography, Commentary by Janet Frame and Criticisms and Reviews of Her Works', 1975, Carole Ferrier and Michael Coleman, 'Janet Frame: A Preliminary Bibliography', *Hecate*, vol. 3, 1977, W.H. New, 'An Annotated Checklist of Critical Writings on Janet Frame' in the 1978 collection of essays described below, and J.B. Beston, 'A Bibliography of Janet Frame', *WLWE*, vol. 17, 1978. In a rare interview with Marion McLeod, *Listener*, 24 September, 1988, she discussed the writing of *The Carpathians*.

In the two full-length studies, Margaret Dalziel, *Janet Frame*, NZWW, Wellington, Oxford University Press, 1980, offers straightforward analysis of action and character, language and vision; Patrick Evans, *Janet Frame*, TWAS, Boston, 1977, traces the local and biographical experience in the novelist's universal themes, and follows her development novel by novel. Evans has also written an introductory study for schools, *An Inward Sun*, Wellington, Price Milburn, 1971. Jeanne Delbaere edited *Bird, Hawk, Bogie: Essays on Janet Frame*, Aarhus, Dangaroo Press, 1978. Several of these essays are described below; there are others on *Faces in the Water* (Donald W. Hannah), *The Edge of the Alphabet* (Patrick Evans), *Scented Gardens for the Blind* (Wilson Harris), *The Adaptable Man* (Bruce King), *The Rainbirds* (Annemarie Blackmann), and *Daughter Buffalo* (Jeanne Delbaere). Amongst general essays on the novels, Patrick Evans, *Meanjin*, vol. 44, 1985, manages the brief survey unusually well, defining the parable-like nature of the fiction, and in *Modern Fiction Studies*, vol. 27, 1981, argues that there is an obsessive and limiting autobiographical element in her handling of death which is liberated through her linguistic gifts. Peter

Alcock, *Commonwealth*, vol. 1, 1974–75, hints at the psychological edge where he locates both novels and novelist, and Victor Dupont, in *Commonwealth*, ed. A. Rutherford, Aarhus, Akademisk Boghandel, 1971, provides an elementary survey of what he sees as skilfully crafted accounts of diseased or stunted lives. Jeanne Delbaere-Garant, in *Commonwealth Literature and the Modern World*, ed. Hena Maes-Jelenik, Brussels, Didier, 1975, divides the characters, using Heideggerian terminology, according to their attitude to death. Anna Rutherford, *WLWE*, vol. 14, 1975, reprinted in *BHB*, analyses both 'this' and 'that' world, indicating the imprisoned condition of both. Gina Mercer, *Meanjin*, vol. 44, 1985, draws attention to Frame's poetic use of language whether in prose or verse, Elody Rathgen, in *Women's Studies: Conference Papers '83*, ed. Hilary Haines, Auckland, 1984, briefly reviews the response of married and single female characters to the assumption that women marry, and K.F Stein, *Pacific Quarterly*, vol. 9, 1985, points to the dark comedy in Frame's attitude to word-play, the craft of writing, and the writer. In *JCL*, vol. 22, 1987, Carol McLennan runs over Frame's account of the gap between the language of Western values and people's actual experiences, and Gina Mercer in a thesis, University of Sydney, 1989, reads the novels as subversive attacks on patriarchal power structures.

In the first collection of stories, H. Winston Rhodes, *CENZSS*, retrospectively finds a way of seeing which foreshadows later work. Writing about the early novels, Jeanne Delbaere-Garant, *Ariel*, vol. 6, 1975, emphasizes the confrontation with death and the importance of Rilke's Orpheus sonnets, and R.T. Robertson, *Studies in the Novel*, vol. 4, 1972, reprinted in *BHB*, highlights the plight of the artist in a provincial society hostile to the imagination. Carole Ferrier, in *South Pacific Images*, ed. Chris Tiffin, Brisbane, South Pacific Association for Commonwealth Literature and Language Studies, 1978, finds the last novels limited by their characters' collapse of communication and withdrawal into death. Winston Rhodes, *Landfall*, no. 102, 1972, finely argues that parable rather than character and plot is the essence of the fiction, and concentrates on *Scented Gardens for the Blind*. Susan Ash, *JNZL*, no. 6, 1988, highlights but also takes issue with the presentation of the female artist as hero in *A State of Siege* and *Living in the Maniototo*.

A number of other articles are wholly restricted to single works. Philip Griffiths, *Words*, no. 4, 1974, shows the early story 'Swans' to be an accomplished forerunner in theme and imagery of the later fiction, and 'Winter Garden' is well analysed by David Norton, *Climate*, no. 29, 1979. *Owls Do Cry* has attracted most attention. Lawrence Jones, *Landfall*, no. 95, 1970, reprinted in *BWM*, analyses the power of time, death, and a materialistic society over the imagination but enters a caveat on the ethics of Frame's espousal of Daphne's position; Cherry Hankin, *Landfall*, no. 110, 1974, reprinted in *CENZN*, shows how the use of language defines and judges the characters, Peter Alcock, *Landfall*, no. 115, 1975, distinguishes the four Withers children according to their possession of 'this' or 'that' world, unconvincingly arguing that Daphne has neither, and W.D. Ashcroft, *JCL*, vol. 12, 1977, reprinted in *BHB*, links

Daphne's journey into madness with mystical and psychological thought about transcendent inner knowledge. More recently, Ruth Brown, *Landfall*, no. 175, 1990, has questioned Frame's assumption that all except true artists enjoy material prosperity.

Stanley Hyman's review of *Scented Gardens for the Blind*, in his *Standards: A Chronicle of Books for Our Time*, New York, Horizon Press, 1966, is a fascinating first response of an established American reviewer to Frame. The novel is analysed in detail by Jeanne Delbaere-Garant in *The Commonwealth Writer Overseas*, ed. Alastair Niven, Brussels, Didier, 1976, reprinted in *BHB*. Monique Malterre, writing in French, *Etudes Anglaises*, vol. 25, 1972, gives a close reading of *State of Siege*, and writing in English in *Commonwealth*, vol. 2, 1976, reprinted in *BHB*, restricts herself to a 'tentative interpretation'. In *Antic*, no. 3, 1987, Alex Calder points to the use of language to reinforce the threat to the protagonist's body and mind. Dawn Danby, *And*, no. 2, 1984, attacking reductionist male criticism, calls for a less analytical reading, and Roger Horrocks, *And*, no. 3, 1984, suggests how changing cultural politics can call for new readings. *Intensive Care* is compared by David Dowling, *WLWE*, vol. 25, 1985, with the Canadian Hugh MacLennan's *Voices in Time* as an apocalyptic novel. To Victor Dupont, in *Commonwealth Literature and the Modern World*, ed. Hena Maes-Jelenik, Brussels, Didier, 1975, reprinted in *BHB*, it marks a development from the psychological to the didactic, social novel. The widespread inability of reviewers to read *Daughter Buffalo* as a perceptive political text is noted by Shona Smith, *Untold*, no. 8, 1987. Patrick Evans, *SPAN*, no. 18, 1984, argues with some success that *Living in the Maniototo* is Frame's supreme exploration of the relationship between art and life, novelist and reader. C.K. Stead in a review (1979), reprinted in *IGC*, had already hailed that novel's 'post-modernist' complexities. But Robert Ross, *WLWE*, vol. 27, 1987, despite acknowledging the replacement of plot and character by language as the organizing principle, still discusses the book in terms of story and person. Shona Smith, *Untold*, no. 5, 1986, offers a deeper and more lively questioning of the post-modernist (and post-colonial) labels. Lydia Wevers, *Listener*, 21 July 1984, reviewing the second of the autobiographical volumes, usefully considers Frame's qualities as an autobiographer, and T.D. Armstrong, *London Review of Books*, 5 December 1985, reviewing all three autobiographies, comments on the process of her becoming a writer committed to language. Patrick Evans, *Untold*, no. 6, 1986, looks at the relationships of biography, autobiography, and fiction. A study of her poetry is included in a thesis by Siew Keng Chua, University of Auckland, 1981.

Anne French 1956-. Poet. Her collections, all published Auckland, Auckland University Press, include *All Cretans Are Liars*, 1987, *The Male As Evader*, 1988, and *Cabin Fever*, 1990. She was interviewed by Lydia Wevers, *Landfall*, no. 171, 1989.

Phillis Garrard. Children's writer. Her stories include *Hilda at School: A New*

Zealand Story, London, Blackie, 1929, *The Doings of Hilda*, London, Blackie, 1932, *Hilda's Adventures*, London, Blackie, 1938, and *Hilda Fifteen*, London, Blackie, 1944. The first three stories were collected as *New Zealand Schoolgirl*, London, Blackie, 1958.

A.P. Gaskell, pseudonym of A.G. Pickard 1913-. Short story writer. His only collection was *The Big Game and Other Stories*, Christchurch, Caxton, 1947, reprinted with six additional stories as *All Part of the Game*, edited with an introduction by R.A. Copland, Auckland, Auckland University Press, 1978. The earlier volume was reviewed by Frank Sargeson, *Landfall*, no. 1, 1947, and the later volume by W.H. New, *Islands*, no. 25, 1978.

Maurice Gee 1931-. Novelist and children's writer. His fiction includes *The Big Season*, London, Hutchinson, 1962, reprinted with an introduction by Bill Manhire, Wellington, Allen & Unwin/Port Nicholson Press, 1985, *A Special Flower*, London, Hutchinson, 1965, *In My Father's Den*, London, Faber, 1972, reprinted Wellington, Oxford University Press, 1977, Auckland, Oxford University Press, 1984, *A Glorious Morning, Comrade: Stories*, Auckland, Auckland University Press, 1975, reprinted with one new story as *Collected Stories*, Auckland, Penguin, 1986, *Games of Choice*, London, Faber, 1976, reprinted Wellington, Oxford University Press, 1977, *Plumb*, London, Faber, 1978, Wellington, Oxford University Press, 1979, reprinted London, Angus & Robertson, 1981, *Meg*, London, Faber, Auckland, Penguin, and New York, St Martin's Press, 1981, reprinted Harmondsworth, Penguin, 1983, and *Sole Survivor*, London, Faber, Auckland, Penguin, and New York, St Martin's Press, 1983, reprinted Harmondsworth, Penguin, 1984, (the last three novels form a trilogy), *Prowlers*, Auckland, Viking, and London, Faber, 1987, and *The Burning Boy*, Auckland, Viking, 1990. He has also written several stories for children, including *Under the Mountain*, Wellington, Oxford University Press, 1979, *The World Around the Corner*, Wellington, Oxford University Press, 1980, *The Halfmen of O*, Auckland, Oxford University Press, 1982, *The Priests of Ferris*, Auckland, Oxford University Press, 1984, *Motherstone*, Auckland, Oxford University Press, 1985, *The Fire-Raiser*, Auckland, Puffin in association with Oxford University Press, 1986, and *The Champion*, Auckland, Puffin, 1989. Cathe Giffuni compiled a bibliography for *Australian and New Zealand Studies in Canada*, No. 3, 1990. 'Beginnings', *Islands*, no. 17, 1976, reprinted in *B*, is an autobiographical essay about childhood and youth; a talk printed in the *Listener*, 17 January 1987, adds fascinating comment on his novels. Of several interviews, that with David Young, *Listener*, 10 February 1979, is especially useful, though one in *Spleen*, no. 6, 1976, (with Ian Wedde) also has interest. The most recent interview was with Colleen Reilly, in *Australian and New Zealand Studies in Canada*, no. 3, 1990, where there are also two articles on the nature of character in the Plumb trilogy and in *Prowlers* by Leslie Monkman and Susan Braley. The interview was reprinted in *Sport*, no. 5, 1990.

The only full study is by Bill Manhire, *Maurice Gee*, NZWW, Auckland,

Oxford University Press, 1986, which also contains a bibliography. David Hall, *Introducing Maurice Gee*, Auckland, Longman Paul, 1981, is designed for schools. The most substantial article, by Brian Boyd, *Islands*, nos 30 and 31-32, 1980-81, analyses Gee's approval of individual growth and his awareness of the damage caused by judging others, in the context of families growing apart, and analyses *Plumb* in fullest detail. In a simpler article, Donald Hannah, *Kunapipi*, vol. 3, no. 2, 1981, follows Gee's interest in the strains and cruelties within family relationships. Writing on the Plumb trilogy, Lawrence Jones, *Landfall*, no. 151, 1984, with a longer version in *BWM*, points out what the trilogy gains over the three novels read separately, and Trevor James, *WLWE*, vol. 23, 1984, intently pursues the theological implications as Gee's characters work through the anxieties of puritan restriction to an open acceptance of the world. Still more challenging, James, *London Magazine*, vol. 24, no. 11, 1985, discusses the fiction in terms of evil and the metaphysical void. On *Plumb* itself, Dennis McEldowney, in *The Word Within The Word*, ed. W.T.G. James, Hamilton, University of Waikato, 1983, gently comments on the Presbyterian and Unitarian background. The short stories are discussed by Lauris Edmond, *CENZSS*, mainly in terms of characterization and of prevailing cruelty offset by flashes of individual spirit, and David Norton, *Climate*, no. 29, 1979, closely analyses 'A Glorious Morning, Comrade'. In an article based on an interview, Louise Guerin, *Listener*, 13 October 1984, comments on the books for children. Some good critical comment is contained in reviews, including those by Dennis McEldowney (*A Special Flower*), *Landfall*, no. 78, 1966, Jim Williamson (*In My Father's Den*), *Islands*, no. 1, 1972, Russell Haley (*Games of Choice*), *Spleen*, no. 6, 1976, John Thomson (*Games of Choice*), *Islands*, no. 19, 1977, and (*The Burning Boy*), *Listener*, 12 November 1990, Roger Robinson (*Plumb*), *Comment*, no. 6, 1979, and Brian Boyd (*Sole Survivor*), *Listener*, 16 July 1983, and (*Prowlers*), *Listener*, 21 November 1987.

Michael Gifkins 1945-. Short story writer. His stories are collected in *After the Revolution and Other Stories*, Auckland, Longman Paul, 1982, *Summer is the Côte d'Azur*, Auckland, Penguin, 1987, and *The Amphibians*, Auckland, Penguin, 1989. He also edited *Listener Short Stories*, 3, Auckland, BCNZ Enterprises, 1984. Owen Marshall's review of the volume of stories appeared in *Landfall*, no. 146, 1983, and Brian Boyd's in *Islands*, no. 35, 1985.

Esther Glen 1881-1940. Children's writer. Her stories include *Six Little New Zealanders*, London, Cassell, 1917, *Twinkles on the Mountain*, Christchurch, L.M. Isitt, 1920, *Uncles Three at Kamahi*, Auckland, Whitcombe & Tombs, 1926, and *Robin of Maoriland*, Auckland, Whitcombe & Tombs, 1929.

Denis Glover 1912-80. Poet and printer. His collections of poetry include *Several Poems*, Christchurch, Caxton, 1936, *Thirteen Poems*, Christchurch, Caxton, 1939, *Recent Poems* (with Allen Curnow, A.R.D. Fairburn, and R.A.K. Mason), Christchurch, Caxton, 1941, *The Wind and The Sand: Poems 1934-44*,

Christchurch, Caxton, 1945, *Sings Harry and Other Poems*, Christchurch, Caxton, 1951, *Arawata Bill: A Sequence of Poems*, Christchurch, Pegasus, 1953, *Since Then*, Wellington, Mermaid Press, 1957, *Poetry Harbinger* (with A.R.D. Fairburn), Auckland, Pilgrims Press, 1958, *Enter without Knocking: Selected Poems*, Christchurch, Pegasus, 1964, enlarged edition 1971, *Sharp Edge Up: Verses and Satires*, Auckland, Paul, 1968, *To A Particular Woman*, Christchurch, Nag's Head Press, 1970, *Diary to a Woman*, Wellington, Cats-paw Press, 1971, *Wellington Harbour*, Wellington, Cats-paw Press, 1974, *Clutha: River Poems*, Dunedin, McIndoe, 1977, *Come High Water*, Palmerston North, Dunmore Press, 1977, *Or Hawk or Basilisk*, Wellington, Catspaw Press, 1978, *For Whom the Cock Crows*, Dunedin, McIndoe, 1978, *To Friends in Russia*, Christchurch, Nag's Head Press, 1979, *Towards Banks Peninsula*, Christchurch, Pegasus, 1979, and *Selected Poems*, Auckland, Penguin, 1981. *Denis Glover's Bedside Book*, Wellington, Reed, 1963, and *Dancing to My Tune*, Wellington, Catspaw Press, 1974, are two miscellanies of verse and prose, and *Men of God*, Palmerston North, Dunmore Press, 1978, is a short satirical novel. *Hot Water Sailor*, Wellington, Reed, 1962, is an autobiographical sketch of Glover's life to his mid-fifties; it was republished, Auckland, Collins, 1981, with the continuation *Landlubber Ho!* In *D-Day*, Christchurch, Caxton, 1944, he briefly described his experience in the Normandy invasion. An extensive MS collection is held at ATL.

The fullest bibliography is in John Thomson's *Denis Glover*, Wellington, Oxford University Press, 1977, which also offers a general study of the poetry and describes his work for New Zealand writing as printer and publisher at the Caxton Press. *Introducing Denis Glover*, Auckland, Longman Paul, 1983, by Gordon Ogilvie, another general study, contains some more personal biographical information. An interview with Marilyn Duckworth appeared in *Affairs*, June 1970. There are few substantial articles. Amongst the most useful are those by Alistair Campbell, *Comment*, no. 21, 1964, analysing an unsympathetic choice of poems, by Alan Roddick, *Landfall*, no. 73, 1965, offering perceptive notes based on sensitive reading, and by John Thomson, *Landfall*, no. 82, 1967, discussing the interrelated themes of time and youth. Lauris Edmond, *Affairs*, March 1973, gives unusual attention to the comic and satiric verse, and Joost Daalder, *Pacific Quarterly*, vol. 5, 1980, despatches the poetry with cold analysis. A more recent study by an old friend is Allen Curnow's introduction to the *Selected Poems*, 1981, first published in *Islands*, no. 31-32, 1981.

Patricia Grace 1937-. Short story writer and novelist. Her volumes include *Waiariki* (stories), Auckland, Longman Paul, 1975, reprinted Auckland, Penguin, 1986, *Mutuwhenua: The Moon Sleeps*, Auckland, Longman Paul, 1978, reprinted Auckland, Penguin, 1986, *The Dream Sleepers and Other Stories*, Auckland, Longman Paul, 1980, reprinted Auckland, Penguin, 1986, *Potiki*, Auckland, Penguin, 1986, and *Electric City and Other Stories*, Auckland, Penguin, 1987. Stories for children include *The Kuia and the Spider*, Auckland,

Longman Paul, and Wellington, Kidsarus 2, 1981, and *Watercress Tuna and the Children of Champion Street*, Auckland, Longman Paul, 1984. She describes how she tries to define what is genuine in Māori life in *Tihe Mauri Ora*, ed. Michael King, Wellington, Methuen, 1978. There is an interview with Sue Kedgley in *OOC*. Articles based on interviews come from David McGill, *Listener*, 11 October 1975, and Louise Guerin, *Listener*, 15 March 1986. Norman Simms, *Pacific Quarterly*, vol. 3, 1978, is impressed by her skill in using English fictional technique to tell of things Māori. R. Nunns, *Islands*, no. 26, 1979, believes she shows 'at an emotional level . . . what it means to be a Maori', and Keri Kaa, *Spiral*, no. 5, 1982, provides a fragmented but sympathetic Māori response to the stories. J.B. Beston, *Ariel*, vol. 15, 1984, comparing her with Witi Ihimaera, finds strength in her human warmth and weakness in her themes. Bill Pearson, *CENZSS*, writes briefly on the sources and effect of her prose style. Lauri Anderson briefly examines Maoriness and the clash of cultures in *Mutuwhenua* in *WLWE*, vol. 26, 1986.

Edith Searle Grossmann 1863-1931. Novelist. Her novels comprise *Angela: A Messenger* (by Edith Searle), Christchurch, Simpson & Williams, 1890, *In Revolt*, London, Eden, Remington, 1893, *A Knight of the Holy Ghost*, London, Watts & Co., 1907, and *The Heart of the Bush*, London, Sands & Co., 1910. She also wrote the brief biography, *Life of Helen Macmillan Brown*, Christchurch, Whitcombe & Tombs, 1905. Nelson Wattie, *WLWE*, vol. 24, 1984, shows how *The Heart of the Bush* accurately reflects the dual attractions of English and New Zealand cultural life for such a woman as the novel's heroine. A feminist critique of her novels is offered by Phillipa Moylan in a thesis, University of Auckland, 1989.

W.H. Guthrie-Smith 1861-1940. Farmer and naturalist. His books comprise *Birds of the Water, Wood and Waste*, Wellington, Whitcombe and Tombs, 1910, reprinted 1927, *Mutton Birds and Other Birds*, Christchurch, Whitcombe & Tombs, 1914, *Tutira: The Story of a New Zealand Sheep Station*, Edinburgh, Blackwood, 1921, 3rd edition with additional chapters, 1953, reprinted Wellington, Reed, 1969, *Bird Life on Island and Shore*, Edinburgh, Blackwood, 1925, and *Sorrows and Joys of a New Zealand Naturalist*, Dunedin, Reed, 1936. *Crispus*, Edinburgh, Blackwood, 1891, is an historical drama. A.E. Woodhouse wrote a biography, *Guthrie-Smith of Tutira*, Christchurch, Whitcombe & Tombs 1959. H.W. Rhodes discussed the strengths of *Tutira* in *New Zealand Libraries*, vol. 10, 1947.

Russell Haley 1934-. Poet, short story writer and novelist. His collections of verse include *The Walled Garden*, Auckland, Mandrake Root, 1972, and *On the Fault Line and Other Poems*, Paraparaumu, Hawk Press, 1977; and of short stories, *The Sauna Bath Mysteries & Other Stories*, Auckland, Mandrake Root, 1978, *Real Illusions*, Wellington, Victoria University Press, 1984, New York, New Directions, 1985, and *The Transfer Station*, Palmerston North, Nagare

Press, 1989. *The Settlement*, Auckland, Hodder & Stoughton, 1986, and *Beside Myself*, Auckland, Penguin, 1990, are novels. He co-edited *The Penguin Book of Contemporary New Zealand Short Stories*, Auckland, Penguin, 1989, and has written *Hanly: A New Zealand Artist*, Auckland, Hodder & Stoughton, 1989. He was interviewed in *Argot*, no. 20, 1969. Lawrence Jones, *Islands*, no. 31-32, 1981, discusses his stories. *The Settlement* is reviewed by Damien Wilkins, *Listener*, 20 December 1986, where there is also an article on the author by Ian Wedde.

Roger Hall 1939-. Playwright. His published plays include *Glide Time*, Wellington, Price Milburn for Victoria University Press, 1977, *Middle-Age Spread*, Wellington, Price Milburn for Victoria University Press, 1978, *State of the Play*, Wellington, Price Milburn for Victoria University Press, 1979, *Prisoners of Mother England*, Wellington, Playmarket, 1980, *Fifty-Fifty*, Petone, Price Milburn with Victoria University Press, 1982, *Hot Water*, Petone, Price Milburn with Victoria University Press, 1983, and *The Share Club*, Wellington, Victoria University Press, 1988. He wrote the book for the musical *Footrot Flats*, Wellington, Playmarket & INL Print, 1984, and has also written plays for radio and television, and for children. A manuscript collection is held at HL. There is an interview with Gordon Campbell, *Listener*, 23 August 1980. David Groves, *Act*, vol. 3, no. 8, 1978, finds the early plays conformist and intellectually timid, Ian Fraser pays particular attention to *State of the Play* in an afterword to the published text, and Michael Neill, *Act*, vol. 7, no. 5, 1982, appraises the success of the farce *Hot Water*.

Noel Hilliard 1929-. Novelist and short story writer. His volumes include the tetralogy *Maori Girl*, London, Heinemann, 1960, *Power of Joy*, London, Michael Joseph, 1965, *Maori Woman*, Christchurch, Whitcombe & Tombs, and London, Hale, 1974, and *The Glory and the Dream*, Auckland, Heinemann, 1978, *A Piece of Land* (stories), Christchurch, Whitcombe & Tombs, and London, Hale, 1963, *A Night at Green River*, Christchurch, Whitcombe & Tombs, and London, Hale, 1969, *Send Somebody Nice: Stories and Sketches*, Christchurch, Whitcoulls, and London, Hale, 1976, and *Selected Stories*, Dunedin, McIndoe, 1977. There is a Library School bibliography by Jeffrey Downs, 'Noel Hilliard: A Preliminary Bibliography', Wellington, 1976. P. Isaac, *New Zealand Book World*, no. 25, 1976, wrote a slight but informative biographical article. He was interviewed by Peter Beatson, *Sites*, no. 16, 1988. Critical comment comes mainly from reviewers, for example, Bill Pearson, *New Zealand Monthly Review*, no. 16, 1961, who acknowledges the realism of *Maori Girl* but argues that the book is a parable to indict Pākehā society, H. Winston Rhodes, who is sympathetic to *Maori Woman* in *Landfall*, no. 113, 1975, and Patricia Glensor, who gives reasons for her unfavourable response to the tetralogy, *Landfall*, no. 129, 1979. Most helpful is Lawrence Jones on the stories, *Islands*, no. 20, 1977. A descriptive account of social attitudes in his fiction is given in a thesis by Trevor Mullinder, University of Canterbury, 1974.

Merton (Horace Emerton) Hodge 1903-58. Playwright. His published plays comprise *The Wind and the Rain*, London, Gollancz, 1934, *Grief Goes Over*, London, Gollancz, 1935, *The Island*, London, Heinemann, 1937, and *Story of an African Farm*, London, Heinemann, 1938. In addition to these, he wrote other unpublished adaptations of novels as well as other original plays. He rewrote *The Wind and the Rain* as a novel, London, Cassell, 1936. MSS are held at ATL. John Reece Cole summarizes his theatrical career in *New Zealand's Heritage*, ed. Ray Knox, Wellington, Paul Hamlyn, 1971-73, pp. 2387-92.

M.H. Holcroft 1902-. Journalist, critic, and novelist. His novels include *Beyond the Breakers*, London, John Long, 1928, *The Flameless Fire*, London, John Long, 1929, *Brazilian Daughter*, London, John Long, 1931, and, published only in Italy, *Un delitto in ogni porto (A Death in Every Port)* Milan, Mondadori, 1985. Extended essays on literature and society include *Discovered Isles: A Trilogy*, Christchurch, Caxton, 1950, comprising *The Deepening Stream*, Christchurch, Caxton, 1940, *The Waiting Hills*, Wellington, Progressive Publishing Society, 1943, and *Encircling Seas*, Christchurch, Caxton, 1946, *Timeless World: A Collection of Essays*, Wellington, Progressive Publishing Society, 1945, *Creative Problems in New Zealand*, Christchurch, Caxton, 1948, *Islands of Innocence: The Childhood Theme in New Zealand Fiction*, Wellington, Reed, 1964, and *Mary Ursula Bethell*, Wellington, Oxford University Press, 1975. *The Eye of the Lizard: A Selection of Editorials from the New Zealand Listener*, 1949-59, Wellington, Reed, 1960, was followed by a further selection, *Graceless Islanders*, Christchurch, Caxton, 1970, both being republished as *A Voice in the Village: The Listener Editorials of M.H. Holcroft*, Hamilton, Silver Fern Echoes, 1989. Other works include *Lebanon: Impressions of a UNESCO Conference*, Christchurch, Caxton, 1949, *New Zealand*, Wellington, Reed, 1963, *The Shaping of New Zealand*, Auckland, Hamlyn, 1974, *Old Invercargill*, Dunedin, McIndoe, 1976, *The Line of the Road: A History of Manawatu County, 1876-1976*, Dunedin, McIndoe for Manawatu County Council, 1977, and *Carapace: The Motor Car in New Zealand: A Roadside View*, Dunedin, McIndoe, 1979. The early autobiographical essay *Dance of the Seasons*, Christchurch, Whitcombe & Tombs, 1952, was followed by *Reluctant Editor: The "Listener" Years, 1949-67*, Wellington, Reed, 1969, the more comprehensive *The Way of a Writer*, 1984, and *A Sea of Words*, 1986, both Whatamongo Bay, Cape Catley, and *The Grieving Time*, Dunedin, McIndoe, 1989. D.M. Anderson, *Landfall*, no. 21, 1952, subjected *Discovered Isles* to close philosophical scrutiny. There is an appreciation of his work as editor of the *Listener* by J.H.E. Schroder, *Listener*, 12 January 1968, and H. Paske, *Listener*, 23 June 1984, reported on the writing of his autobiography.

Edith Howes 1874?-1954. Children's writer. Her work includes *The Sun's Babies*, London, Cassell, 1910, *Fairy Rings*, London, Cassell, 1911, *Rainbow Children*, London, Cassell, 1912, *Where Bell-Birds Chime*, Christchurch, Whitcombe & Tombs, 1912, *Maoriland Fairy Tales*, London, Ward Lock, 1913,

The Cradle Ship, London, Cassell, 1916, *Wonderwings and Other Fairy Stories*, Auckland, Whitcombe & Tombs, 1918, *Little Make-Believe*, Auckland, Whitcombe & Tombs, 1919, *The Singing Fish*, London, Cassell, 1921, *The Dream-Girl's Garden*, London, Ward Lock, 1923, *The Enchanted Road*, New York, William Morrow, 1927, *Silver Island: A New Zealand Story*, Auckland, Whitcombe & Tombs, 1928, *The Long Bright Land: Fairy Tales from Southern Seas*, Boston, Little Brown, 1929, *Sandals of Pearl*, London, Dent, 1929, *The Golden Forest*, London, Dent, 1930, *The Great Experiment*, London, Dent, 1932, *Mrs Kind Bush*, London, Cassell, 1933, and *Riverside Family*, Auckland, Collins, 1944. She also wrote ten stories for Whitcombe's Story Books and Whitcombe's Nature Story Books, published between 1923 and 1934.

Keri Hulme 1947-. Novelist and short story writer. Her volumes include *The Bone People*, Wellington, Spiral, 1983, reprinted Auckland, Spiral/Hodder & Stoughton, and Baton Rouge, Louisiana State University Press, 1985, New York, Penguin, and London, Pan (Picador), 1986, *Lost Possessions*, Wellington, Victoria University Press, 1985, and *Te Kaihau: The Windeater* (stories), Wellington, Victoria University Press, 1986, and as *The Windeater: Te Kaihau*, London, Hodder & Stoughton, 1986, New York, Braziller, 1987, reprinted Sevenoaks, Sceptre, 1988. *The Silences Between: (Moeraki Conversations)*, Auckland, Auckland University Press, 1982, is a volume of poems. She has also written the text for the illustrated *Homeplaces: Three Coasts of the South Island of New Zealand*, Auckland, Hodder & Stoughton, 1989. Manuscript material relating to *The Bone People* is held at the University of Canterbury. She tells of her roots in Okarito and Moeraki in *Te Whenua, te Iwi*, ed. Jock Phillips, Allen & Unwin/Port Nicholson Press in association with the Stout Research Centre, 1987. There is a wide-ranging interview with Sue Kedgley in *OOC*, and replies to heterogeneous questions in *Broadsheet*, no. 173, 1989. An early interview with Don Long, *Tu Tangata*, no. 7, 1982, was largely about the writing of *The Bone People*. The success of that novel drew many interviews and reviews but few of substance. Amongst exceptions are interviews with Sandi Hall, *Broadsheet*, no. 121, 1984, on her life and opinions as they related to the novel, and with Shona Smith, *Untold*, no. 4, 1985, on matters arising from the novel, and review articles by Merata Mita, *The Republican*, November 1984, and by C.K. Stead, *Ariel*, vol. 16, 1985, revised version *London Review of Books*, 5 December 1985, reprinted in *AL*. Stead's unfavourable response led Margery Fee, *Australian and New Zealand Studies in Canada*, no. 1, 1989, to discuss how other people can write about the work of indigenous minorities. Shona Smith, *Untold*, no. 2, 1984, is especially useful on the religious and mystical sources of the novel, and Judith Dale, *Landfall*, no. 156, 1985, stresses the novel's true centre in the mind, both sensuous and verbal, of the heroine. In *Antic*, no. 3, 1987, Anne Maxwell argues that the commendable post-colonial nationalist aims are in part subverted by novelistic techniques bred of an older cultural dispensation. But Chris Prentice, *SPAN*, no. 23, 1986, thinks the effects of a colonial past on the novel's present are skilfully accommodated in a deliberate ambiguity in matters of race, gender, sexual preference, and certain novelistic techniques. Susan Ash, *WLWE*, vol. 29, 1989, is persuaded of the blacker vision of isolated people in *Te Kaihau* which the commensalist vision of *The Bone People* fails to replace. Harry Ricketts interviewed her on her work as a poet, *Talking About Ourselves*, Wellington, Mallinson, Rendel, 1986.

Sam Hunt 1946-. Poet. His collections of verse include *From Bottle Creek: Selected Poems 1967-69*, Wellington, Poetry Magazine, 1969, *Bracken Country*, Wellington, Glenbervie Press, 1971, *From Bottle Creek*, Wellington, A. Taylor, 1972, *South into Winter*, Wellington, A. Taylor, 1973, *Time to Ride*, Martinborough, A. Taylor, 1975, *Drunkard's Garden*, Wellington, Hampson Hunt, 1977, *Collected Poems 1963-1980*, Harmondsworth, Penguin, 1980, *Running Scared*, Christchurch, Whitcoulls, 1982, *Approaches to Paremata*, Auckland, Penguin, 1985, and *Selected Poems*, Auckland, Penguin, 1987. Colin Hogg's *Angel Gear: On the Road with Sam Hunt*, Auckland, Heinemann Reed, 1989, is biographical. He was interviewed by Jill McCracken, *Landfall*, no. 107, 1973. In *Rapport*, vol. 4, no. 1, n.d., he discusses writing and then publicly 'performing' his poems. Peter Smart's *Introducing Sam Hunt*, Auckland, Longman Paul, 1981, is designed for school students.

Robin Hyde 1906-39. Novelist and poet. Her novels comprise *Check to Your King*, London, Hurst & Blackett, 1936, reprinted with an introduction by Joan Stevens, Wellington, Reed, 1960, also reprinted Auckland, Golden Press, 1975, and Auckland, Viking, 1987, *Passport to Hell*, London, Hurst & Blackett, 1936, reprinted with an introduction by D.I.B. Smith, Auckland, Auckland University Press, 1986, *Wednesday's Children*, London, Hurst & Blackett, 1937, reprinted with an introduction by Susan Ash, Auckland, New Women's Press, 1989, *The Godwits Fly*, London, Hurst & Blackett, 1938, reprinted with an introduction by Gloria Rawlinson, Auckland, Auckland University Press, 1970, and *Nor the Years Condemn*, London, Hurst & Blackett, 1938, reprinted with an introduction by Phillida Bunkle, Linda Hardy, and Jacqueline Matthews, Auckland, New Women's Press, 1986. Her collections of poetry are *The Desolate Star and Other Poems*, Christchurch, Whitcombe & Tombs, 1929, *The Conquerors and Other Poems*, London, Macmillan, 1935, *Persephone in Winter: Poems*, London, Hurst & Blackett, 1937, *Houses by the Sea, and Later Poems*, with a biographical introduction by Gloria Rawlinson, Christchurch, Caxton, 1952, and *Selected Poems*, ed. with an introduction by Lydia Wevers, Auckland, Oxford University Press, 1984. *Dragon Rampant*, London, Hurst & Blackett, 1939, reprinted with an introduction by Derek Challis and a critical note by Linda Hardy, Auckland, New Women's Press, 1984, describes her experiences in China in 1938, and *A Home in This World*, Auckland, Longman Paul, 1984, is an autobiographical fragment about her life as a journalist. She published a collection of her journalism as *Journalese*, Auckland, National Printing Co., 1934. An article on New Zealand literature was reprinted with an introduction by Jackie Matthews, *Women's Studies Journal*, vol. 5, 1989. Auckland University holds a manuscript collection.

Patrick Sandbrook describes some manuscripts, and drafts of her work, in *JNZL*, no. 4, 1986. Two Library School bibliographies cover her literary work and journalism: Jennifer Walls, 'A Bibliography of Robin Hyde (Iris Wilkinson) 1906-39', Wellington, 1960, and Margaret Scott, 'A Supplementary Bibliography of Robin Hyde', Wellington, 1966. Little critical attention was paid to her until recently, though H. Winston Rhodes, *New Zealand Libraries*, vol. 10, 1947, was briefly appreciative of her novels, and James Bertram, *Landfall*, no. 27, 1953, reprinted in *FP*, offered a reassessment concentrating on her later poems. There is a thesis on the later works by Janscie Sharplin, University of Canterbury, 1971, and on the 'writer at work' by Patrick Sandbrook, Massey University, 1985. The only general account of her fiction as a whole is the simple survey by Frank Birbalsingh, *Landfall*, no. 124, 1977, but the introductions noted above may be read on specific novels; the one to *Nor the Years Condemn* is particularly full. For Felicity Riddy in *The Commonwealth Writer Overseas*, ed. Alastair Niven, Brussels, Didier, 1976, *The Godwits Fly* shows her growing dissatisfaction with the loner, and the need for deeper human relationships, Gloria Rawlinson discusses the composition and content of *The Godwits Fly*, *CENZN*, and Patrick Sandbrook, *Landfall*, no. 143, 1982, argues that in this novel Hyde traces her heroine's progress from nationalistic 'colonial England-hunger' to a sense of being a full member of the human race. Shelagh Cox, in *Women's Studies: Conference Papers '82*, ed. Hilary Haines, Auckland, 1983, argues from *Wednesday's Children* that her heroines can build joyous and free worlds only in their imaginations. Colin J. Partridge, *JCL*, no. 5, 1968, examines Hyde's poetic development, concentrating on the later poems.

Witi Ihimaera 1944-. Short story writer and novelist. His volumes include *Pounamu, Pounamu* (stories), Auckland, Heinemann, 1972, *Tangi*, Auckland, Heinemann, 1973, *Whanau*, Auckland, Heinemann, 1974, *The New Net Goes Fishing* (stories), Auckland, Heinemann, 1977, *The Matriarch*, Auckland, Heinemann, 1986, *The Whale Rider*, Auckland, Heinemann, 1987, and *Dear Miss Mansfield: A Tribute to Kathleen Mansfield Beauchamp* (stories), Auckland, Viking, 1989. He also co-edited *Into the World of Light: An Anthology of Maori Writing*, Auckland, Heinemann, 1982. He has been ready to speak of his purpose in writing, notably in *WLWE*, vol. 14, 1975, and in *Tihe Mauri Ora*, ed. Michael King, Wellington, Methuen, 1978, and of his place amongst Māori writers in *New Zealand through the Arts: Past and Present*, Wellington, Friends of the Turnbull Library, 1982. An autobiographical essay on his childhood appeared in *Through the Looking Glass*, ed. Michael Gifkins, Auckland, Century Hutchinson, 1988. Richard Corballis compiled a bibliography, *SPAN*, no. 18, 1984. Amongst interviews, that with J.B. Beston, *WLWE*, vol. 16, 1977, is especially valuable; one with Blanaid Fitzgerald, *Listener*, 9 October 1972, is of interest for its early date. There is also a reply to a written questionnaire in

Speaking of Writing, ed. R.D. Walshe, Sydney, Reed Education for the English Teachers' Association of New South Wales, 1975.

Though written chiefly for school students, *Introducing Witi Ihimaera*, by Richard Corballis and Simon Garrett, Auckland, Longman Paul, 1984, is the fullest, and only separate, study, though Bill Pearson, *CENZSS*, is authoritative on the stories. Sandra Tawake, *Mana*, vol. 8, no. 1, 1983, has written on the village setting of the rural fiction, as has H. Winston Rhodes in his review of *Whanau*, *Landfall*, no. 114, 1975. B.J. Murton, *New Zealand Geographer*, vol. 35, 1979, uses this part of the fiction to add to discussion of the place of land in Māori society. Several writers have noted the change of setting from rural village to city. Graeme Wynn, *International Fiction Review*, vol. 2, 1975, briefly comments on the cultural change involved, Alistair Fox, *Pilgrims*, no. 8, 1980, finds the use of the Wizard of Oz myth in the two collections of stories to have unencouraging social implications, and H. Isernhagen, *WLWE*, vol. 24, 1984, observes a corresponding change from traditional myth to modernist techniques. In related studies, M.S. Martin, *International Fiction Review*, vol. 10, 1983, outlines Ihimaera's attempt to communicate between two cultures, and J. Ben Guigui, *Caliban*, no. 14, 1977, looks at the combination of myth and realism. Some critics are conscious of introducing him to an international audience, but can still be helpful, as is, for example, J.B. Beston on *The New Net Goes Fishing*, *Commonwealth*, no. 3, 1977-78. Norman Simms, *Pacific Quarterly*, vol. 3, 1978, finds his work insufficiently Māori, and apt to be sentimental in a European fashion. Peggy Nightingale, on the other hand, comparing him with Albert Wendt in *Myth and Metaphor*, ed. Robert Sellick, CRNLE, Adelaide, 1982, finds a strength in his characters' Maoriness that promises a more fruitful relationship with European culture. Richard Corballis, *Landfall*, no. 129, 1979, partly in reply to Simms, discerns considerable organizational skill. J.-P. Durix, *JNZL*, no. 1, 1983, focuses on time in the organization and meaning of *Tangi*, and Chris Tiffin writes more generally about the novel in *Awakened Conscience: Studies in Commonwealth Literature*, ed. C.D. Narasimhaiah, New Delhi, Sterling Publishers, 1978. Two long reviews of *The Matriarch*, one interpreting it approvingly as a modern epic, the other alleging novelistic (and political) crudities, are by Alex Calder, *Landfall*, no. 161, 1987, and C.K. Stead, *London Review of Books*, December 1986, reprinted in *AL*. In an article based on an interview, D. Young, *Listener*, 7 June 1986, is factually informative about *The Matriarch*, and Trevor James, *SPAN*, no. 24, 1987, argues that Pākehā cultural preconceptions have obscured Māori spiritual dimensions in the book.

Kevin Ireland 1933-. Poet. His collections of verse include *Face to Face: Twenty-Four Poems*, Christchurch, Pegasus, 1963, *Educating the Body: Poems*, Christchurch, Caxton, 1967, *A Letter from Amsterdam*, London, Amphedesma Press, 1972, *Orchids, Hummingbirds and Other Poems*, Auckland, Auckland University Press, 1974, *A Grammar of Dreams*, Wellington, Wai-te-ata Press, 1975, *Literary Cartoons*, Auckland, Islands/Hurricane House, 1977, *The Dangers* *of Art: Poems 1975-80*, Auckland, Cicada Press, 1980, *Practice Night in the Drill Hall: Poems*, Auckland, Oxford University Press, 1984, *The Year of the Comet: Twenty-Six 1986 Sonnets*, Auckland, Islands, 1986, *Selected Poems*, Auckland, Oxford University Press, 1987, and *Tiberius at the Beehive*, Auckland, Auckland University Press, 1990. He has also published translations from Bulgarian. 'Beginnings', *Islands*, no. 28, 1980, is an autobiographical essay. Another essay on his boyhood and youth appeared in *One of the Boys?*, ed. Michael King, Auckland, Heinemann, 1988. He was interviewed by Adrian Blackburn, *Listener*, 11 August 1979, and by Tony Reid, *Listener*, 26 March 1988.

Michael Jackson 1940-. Poet. His collections of verse include *Latitudes of Exile: Poems 1965-1975*, Dunedin, McIndoe, 1976, *Wall*, Dunedin, McIndoe, 1980, *Going On*, Dunedin, McIndoe, 1985, and *Duty Free: Selected Poems, 1965-1988*, Dunedin, McIndoe, 1989. *Rainshadow*, Dunedin, McIndoe, 1988, is a novel, as is *Barawa and the Ways Birds Fly in the Sky: An Ethnographic Novel*, Washington, Smithsonian Institution Press, 1986. He has also published professionally as an anthropologist.

Louis Johnson 1924-88. Poet. His collections of verse include *Stanza and Scene: Poems*, Wellington, Handcraft Press, 1945, *The Sun among the Ruins*, Christchurch, Pegasus, 1951, *Roughshod among the Lilies*, Christchurch, Pegasus, 1951, *The Dark Glass*, Wellington, Handcraft Press, 1955, *News of Molly Bloom: The Passionate Man and the Casual Man: Two Poems*, Christchurch, Pegasus, 1955, *New Worlds for Old: Poems*, Wellington, Capricorn Press, 1957, *The Night Shift: Poems on Aspects of Love* (with James K. Baxter, Charles Doyle, and Kendrick Smithyman), Wellington, Capricorn Press, 1957, *Bread and a Pension: Selected Poems*, Christchurch, Pegasus, 1964, *Land like a Lizard: New Guinea Poems*, Milton, Queensland, Jacaranda Press, 1970, *Onion*, Dunedin, Caveman Press, 1972, *Selected Poems*, Bathurst, NSW, Mitchell College of Advanced Education, 1972, *Fires and Patterns*, Milton, Queensland, Jacaranda Press, 1975, *Coming & Going: Poems*, Wellington, Mallinson Rendel, 1982, *Winter Apples*, Wellington, Mallinson Rendel, 1984, *True Confessions of the Last Cannibal: New Poems*, Plimmerton, Antipodes Press, 1986, and *Last Poems*, Plimmerton, Antipodes Press, 1990. A manuscript collection is held at ATL. He was interviewed by C. Mooney, *Climate*, no. 30, 1979, and by Harry Ricketts in his *Talking about Ourselves*, Wellington, Mallinson Rendel, 1986. He wrote about his own *Fires and Patterns* in *Pilgrims*, no. 7, 1979, and that collection was reviewed in the same issue by Graeme Turner. *Bread and a Pension* was reviewed by MacD. P. Jackson, *Landfall*, no. 73, 1965.

Michael (M.K.) Joseph 1914-1981. Novelist and poet. His novels comprise *I'll Soldier No More*, London, Gollancz, and Hamilton, Paul's Book Arcade, 1958, *A Pound of Saffron*, London, Gollancz, and Hamilton, Paul's Book Arcade, 1962, *The Hole in the Zero*, London, Gollancz, and Auckland, Paul, 1967, *A Soldier's Tale*, Auckland, Collins, 1976, reprinted London, Collins (Fontana), 1977, *The*

Time of Achamoth, Auckland, Collins, 1977, and *Kaspar's Journey*, Auckland, Brick Row/Hallard Press, 1988. His collections of verse include *Imaginary Islands: Poems*, Auckland, privately published, 1950, *The Living Countries: Poems*, Hamilton, Paul's Book Arcade, 1959, and *Inscription on a Paper Dart: Selected Poems 1945-72*, Auckland, Auckland University Press, 1974. He also wrote *Byron the Poet*, London, Gollancz, and Hamilton, Paul's Book Arcade, 1964. 'Beginnings', *Islands*, no. 27, 1979, is an autobiographical essay, and in *English in New Zealand*, September 1975, he linked science fiction and attitudes towards the future. A brief but useful tribute by Dennis McEldowney appeared in the *Listener*, 14 November 1981. K.K. Ruthven, *Islands*, no. 27, 1979, fully analysed narrative technique in *A Soldier's Tale*, a novel also examined by K. Kuiper and V. Small, *Poetics Today*, vol. 7, 1986; and Norman Simms, *Pacific Quarterly*, vol. 4, 1979, looked briefly at the first two science fiction novels.

Yvonne Kalman 1942-. Romance novelist. Her fiction includes *Summer Rain*, New York, Jove, 1980, the trilogy *Greenstone Land*, London, Macdonald, 1981, *Greenstone Land: Juliette's Daughter*, London, Macdonald, 1982, and *Greenstone Land: Riversong*, London, Macdonald, 1985, *Passion's Gold*, New York, Jove, 1984, *Mists of Heaven*, London, Bantam, 1987, and its sequel *After the Rainbow*, London, Bantam, 1989. *Sparkles*, Auckland, Collins, 1979, is a story for children.

Fiona Kidman 1940-. Novelist and poet. Her fiction includes *A Breed of Women*, Sydney, Harper & Row, 1979, reprinted Auckland, Penguin, 1988, *Mandarin Summer*, Auckland, Heinemann, 1981, reprinted Auckland, Picador, 1988, *Mrs Dixon and Friend: Short Stories*, Auckland, Heinemann, 1982, *Paddy's Puzzle*, Auckland, and Tadworth, Surrey, Heinemann, 1983, also published as *In the Clear Light*, New York, Norton, 1985, *The Book of Secrets*, Auckland, Heinemann, 1987, reprinted Auckland, Picador, 1988, *Unsuitable Friends: Short Stories*, Auckland, Century Hutchinson, 1988, and *True Stars*, Auckland, Random Century, 1990. Her volumes of verse include *Honey and Bitters: Poems*, Christchurch, Pegasus, 1975, *On the Tightrope: Poems*, Christchurch, Pegasus, 1978, and *Going to the Chathams: Poems 1977-1984*, Auckland, Heinemann, 1985. *Search for Sister Blue*, Wellington, Reed, 1975, is a play for radio. She was interviewed by Riemke Ensing, *Landfall*, no. 136, 1980, and by Sue Kedgley in *OOC*. Lance Kendrick compiled 'Traveller in the Countries of the Heart: A Preliminary Bibliography on Fiona Kidman' for the Library School, Wellington, 1976. There is a profile based on an interview by Marion McLeod, *Listener*, 3 October 1987.

Michael King 1945-. Historian. Major works include *Te Puea: A Biography*, Auckland, Hodder & Stoughton, 1977, reprinted 1982, *New Zealand: Its Land and Its People*, Wellington, Reed, 1979, *The Collector: A Biography of Andreas Reischek*, Auckland, Hodder & Stoughton, 1981, *New Zealanders at War*, Auckland and Exeter, N.H., Heinemann, 1981, *Maori: A Photographic and Social History*, Auckland, Heinemann, 1983, *Whina: A Biography of Whina Cooper*,

Auckland, Hodder & Stoughton, 1983, *Death of the Rainbow Warrior*, Auckland, Penguin, 1986, *After the War: New Zealand Since 1945*, Auckland, Hodder & Stoughton in association with Wilson & Horton, 1988, and *Moriori: A People Rediscovered*, Auckland, Viking, 1989. *Being Pakeha: An Encounter with New Zealand and the Maori Renaissance*, Auckland, Hodder & Stoughton, 1985, is autobiographical. R. Mannion, *Auckland Metro*, no. 40, 1984, discussed his experience of writing about Māori people and events.

G.B. Lancaster, pseudonym of Edith Lyttleton 1873-1945. Novelist and short story writer. Her novels include *Sons o' Men*, London, Andrew Melrose, 1904, New York, Doubleday, 1905, *A Spur to Smite*, London, Andrew Melrose, 1905, and as *The Spur*, New York, Doubleday, 1906, *The Tracks We Tread*, London, Hodder & Stoughton, and New York, Doubleday Page, 1907, *The Altar Stairs*, London, Hodder & Stoughton, and New York, Doubleday, 1908, *Jim of the Ranges*, London, Constable, 1910, *The Honourable Peggy*, London, Constable, 1911, *The Law-Bringers*, London, Hodder & Stoughton, and New York, George Doran, 1913, *Fool Divine*, London, Hodder & Stoughton, and New York, George Doran, 1917, *The Savignys*, London, Hodder & Stoughton, and New York, George Doran, 1918, *Pageant*, London, Allen & Unwin, New York, Century, and Sydney, Endeavour Press, 1933, *The World Is Yours*, London, Allen & Unwin, New York, Appleton-Century, and Sydney, Endeavour Press, 1934, *Promenade*, Sydney, Angus & Robertson, New York, Reynal & Hitchcock, and London, John Lane, 1938, and *Grand Parade*, New York, Reynal & Hitchcock, 1943, London, John Lane, 1944. An article on her beginnings, signed H.M., appeared in the *New Zealand Magazine*, vol. 24, no. 2, 1945, and F.A. De la Mare wrote a tribute, *G.B. Lancaster*, Hamilton, privately published, 1945.

John A. Lee 1891-1982. Novelist and politician. His fiction includes *Children of the Poor*, London, T. Werner Laurie, and New York, Vanguard Press, 1934, reprinted London, Bernard Henry, and Auckland, N.V. Douglas, 1949, London, May Fair Books, 1963, Christchurch, Whitcombe & Tombs, 1973, *The Hunted*, London, T. Werner Laurie, 1936, reprinted London, May Fair Books, 1963, Wellington, Price Milburn, 1975, *Civilian into Soldier*, London, T. Werner Laurie, 1937, reprinted London, May Fair Books, 1963, Auckland, Oxford University Press, 1985, *The Yanks Are Coming*, London, T. Werner Laurie, and Wellington, Gordon & Gotch, 1943, *Shining with the Shiner*, Hamilton, F.W. Mead trading as Bond Printing Co., 1944, reprinted London, Bernard Henry, and Auckland, N.V. Douglas, 1950, London, May Fair Books, 1963, *Shiner Slattery*, Auckland, Collins, 1964, reprinted Auckland, Collins (Fontana), 1975, *Mussolini's Millions*, London, Howard Baker, 1970, *Soldier*, Wellington, Reed, 1976, and *The Politician*, Auckland, Century Hutchinson, 1987. Under the loose heading of memoirs can be included *Simple on a Soap-Box*, Auckland, Collins, 1963, *Rhetoric at the Red Dawn*, Auckland, Collins, 1965, *The Lee Way to Public Speaking*, Auckland, Collins, 1965, *Delinquent Days*, Auckland, Collins, 1967, reprinted Christchurch, Whitcoulls, 1978, *Political Notebooks*, Wellington, A. Taylor, 1973, *Early Days in New Zealand*, Martinborough, A. Taylor, 1977, and *The John A. Lee Diaries, 1936-40*, with foreword, commentary, and afterword by John A. Lee, Christchurch, Whitcoulls, 1981. He also published *Socialism in New Zealand*, with an introduction by Rt Hon C.R. Atlee, London, T. Werner Laurie, 1938, *For Mine Is the Kingdom*, Martinborough, A. Taylor, 1975, a fictionalized biography of Sir Ernest Davis, and *Roughnecks, Rolling Stones & Rouseabouts, with an Anthology of Early Swagger Literature*, Christchurch, Whitcoulls, 1977, reprinted Auckland, Penguin, 1989. APL holds a collection of manuscripts. *John A. Lee*, Dunedin, University of Otago Press, 1977, is a biography by Erik Olssen. H. Winston Rhodes, *New Zealand Libraries*, vol. 10, 1947, wrote on the earlier novels, and M.H. Pouilhes and Victor Dupont, *Commonwealth*, no. 1, 1974-75, on the subject of juvenile delinquency in the fiction. Dennis McEldowney, *CENZN*, discusses *Children of the Poor*, and Victor Dupont, *Commonwealth*, no. 2, 1976, *For Mine Is the Kingdom*. Because Lee's fiction is so closely based on personal experience, J.T. Henderson, *Political Science*, vol. 26, 1974, on the personal origins of his political behaviour, is of interest.

Elsie Locke 1912-. Children's writer and historian. Her books for children include *The Runaway Settlers*, London, Cape, and Auckland, Paul, 1965, New York, Dutton, 1966, reprinted Harmondsworth, Penguin, 1971, *The End of the Harbour*, London, Cape, and Auckland, Paul, 1968, *Look under the Leaves*, Christchurch, Pumpkin Press, 1975, *Ugly Little Paua . . .* (stories), Christchurch, Whitcoulls, 1976, *The Boy with the Snowgrass Hair*, (with Ken Dawson), Christchurch, Whitcoulls, 1976, *Explorer Zach*, Christchurch, Pumpkin Press, 1978, *Journey under Warning*, Auckland, Oxford University Press, 1983, and *A Canoe in a Mist*, London, Cape, 1984. Some of her historical books were also written for older children. *Student at the Gates*, Christchurch, Whitcoulls, 1981, is autobiographical.

Robert Lord 1945-. Playwright. His published plays include *It Isn't Cricket*, *Act*, no. 15, 1971, *Meeting Place*, *Act*, no. 18, 1972, *Balance of Payments*, in *Can't You Hear Me Talking to You?*, ed. Alrene Sykes, St Lucia, University of Queensland Press, 1978, *Glitter and Spit*, *Act*, no. 27, 1975, and *Bert and Maisy*, Dunedin, University of Otago Press, 1988. A significant unpublished play is *Well Hung*, first performed in 1974. There is an interview with Sunny Amey, *Act*, no. 24, 1974.

Rachel McAlpine 1940-. Poet and novelist. Her collections of verse include *Lament for Ariadne*, Dunedin, Caveman Press, 1975, *Stay at the Dinner Party*, Dunedin, Caveman Press, 1977, *Fancy Dress*, Auckland, Cicada, 1979, *House Poems*, Wellington, Nutshell Books, 1980, *Recording Angel*, Wellington, Mallinson Rendel, 1983, *Thirteen Waves*, Feilding, Homeprint, 1986, and *Selected Poems*, Wellington, Mallinson Rendel, 1988. *The Limits of Green*, Auckland,

Viking, 1985, *Running Away from Home*, Auckland, Penguin, 1987, and *Farewell Speech*, Auckland, Penguin, 1990, are novels. *The Stationary Sixth Form Poetry Trip*, Wellington, Playmarket, 1980, *Driftwood*, Wellington, Victoria University Press, 1985, *Peace Offering*, Auckland, Heinemann, 1988, and *Power Play*, Wellington, Playmarket, 1990, are plays for secondary school students. *Song in the Satchel: Poetry in the High School*, Wellington, NZCER, 1980, discusses the teaching of poetry in secondary schools. She was interviewed by Michael Harlow, *Landfall*, no. 145, 1983, by Harry Ricketts in his *Talking about Ourselves*, Wellington, Mallinson Rendel, 1986, and by Sue Kedgley in *OOC*.

Sue McCauley 1941-. Novelist. Her novels include *Other Halves*, Auckland, Hodder & Stoughton, 1982, *Then Again*, Auckland, Hodder & Stoughton, 1988, and *Bad Music*, Auckland, Hodder & Stoughton, 1990.

E.H. McCormick 1906-. Critic and biographer. His works include *Letters and Art in New Zealand*, Wellington, Department of Internal Affairs, 1940, part of which was rewritten and expanded as *New Zealand Literature: A Survey*, London, Oxford University Press, 1959, *The Expatriate: A Study of Frances Hodgkins*, Wellington, New Zealand University Press, 1954, *The Fascinating Folly: Dr Hocken and His Fellow Collectors*, Dunedin, University of Otago Press, 1961, *Alexander Turnbull: His Life, His Circle, His Collections*, Wellington, ATL, 1974, *Omai: Pacific Envoy*, Auckland, Auckland University Press, 1977, *Portrait of Frances Hodgkins*, Auckland, Auckland University Press, 1981, and *The Friend of Keats: A Life of Charles Armitage Brown*, Wellington, Victoria University Press, 1989. There are two autobiographical essays, *The Inland Eye. A Sketch in Visual Autobiography*, Auckland, Auckland Gallery Associates, 1959, and 'Beginnings', *Islands*, no. 22, 1957. Vincent O'Sullivan, after an interview, portrayed him as a cultural historian in *Listener*, 18 July 1981.

Caroline Macdonald. Her stories for children include *Elephant Rock*, Auckland, Hodder & Stoughton, 1983, *Visitors*, Auckland, Hodder & Stoughton, 1984, *Yellow Boarding House*, Auckland, Oxford University Press, 1985, *Earthgames*, Melbourne, Rigley, and Auckland, Shortland, 1988, *Joseph's Boat*, Auckland, Hodder & Stoughton, 1988, and *The Lake at the End of the World*, Auckland, Hodder & Stoughton, 1988.

Greg McGee 1950-. Playwright. His published plays include *Foreskin's Lament*, Price Milburn with Victoria University Press, 1981, *Tooth and Claw*, Wellington, Victoria University Press, 1984, and *Out in the Cold*, Wellington, Victoria University Press, 1984. There is useful discussion of *Foreskin's Lament* by Ian Fraser, *Act*, vol. 6, no. 8, 1981, and of *Out in the Cold* by Michael Neill, *Act*, vol. 8, no. 4, 1983. Sebastian Black, *Australasian Drama Studies*, no. 17, 1990, examines the playwright's dramaturgy rather than his social comment, and David Carnegie in the same issue traces the evolution of the script of *Foreskin's Lament*.

Jessie Mackay 1864–1938. Poet. Her collections of verse include *The Spirit of the Rangatira and Other Ballads*, Melbourne, George Robertson, 1889, *The Sitter on the Rail and Other Poems*, Christchurch, Simpson & Williams, 1891, *From the Maori Sea*, Christchurch, Whitcombe & Tombs, 1908, *Land of the Morning*, Christchurch, Whitcombe & Tombs, 1909, *The Bride of the Rivers & Other Verses*, Christchurch, Simpson & Williams, 1926, and *Vigil*, Auckland, Whitcombe & Tombs, 1935. A manuscript collection is held at the Mitchell Library, Sydney (photocopies at ATL). There is a biography, *A Voice on the Wind*, Wellington, Reed, 1955, by N.F.H. McLeod.

James McNeish 1931–. Novelist and journalist. His novels include *Mackenzie*, London, Hodder & Stoughton, 1970, reprinted Harmondsworth, Penguin, 1974, *The Glass Zoo*, London, Hodder & Stoughton, and New York, St Martin's Press, 1976, *Joy*, Auckland, Hodder & Stoughton, 1982, and *Lovelock*, London, Hodder & Stoughton, 1986. *The Mackenzie Affair*, Auckland, Hodder & Stoughton, 1972, is a fictionalized biography, and *The Rocking Cave*, Wellington, Playmarket, 1981, a play. He has also published a variety of non-fiction volumes. A personal comment on life in New Zealand appeared in the *Listener*, 13 September 1971, and N. Forrest, *Listener*, 21 August 1964, recounts the experiences of his early adult years. He was interviewed by Russell Haley, *New Outlook*, Autumn, 1983. *Mackenzie* was reviewed at length by Lawrence Jones, *Landfall*, no. 97, 1971, reprinted in *BWM*.

Cilla McQueen 1949–. Poet. Her collections of verse include *Homing In*, Dunedin, McIndoe, 1982, *Anti Gravity*, Dunedin, McIndoe, 1984, *Wild Sweets*, Dunedin, McIndoe, 1986, *Benzina*, ed. Iain Lonie, Dunedin, McIndoe, 1988, and *Berlin Diary*, Dunedin, McIndoe, 1990. She was interviewed by Marion McLeod, *Listener*, 7 March 1987. Harry Ricketts, *Landfall*, no. 152, 1984, writes of the work in the first two volumes, and Roger Horrocks, *And*, no. 4, 1985, about *Anti Gravity*, about which there is also an article by Ian Wedde, *Untold*, no. 3, 1985.

Margaret Mahy 1936–. Children's writer. Longer stories include *Clancy's Cabin*, London, Dent, 1974, *The Bus under the Leaves*, London, Dent, 1974, reprinted Harmondsworth, Puffin, 1976, *The Pirate Uncle*, London, Dent, 1977, *Raging Robots and Unruly Uncles*, London, Dent, 1981, reprinted Harmondsworth, Puffin, 1985, *The Haunting*, London, Dent, 1982, *The Pirate's Mixed-Up Voyage*, London, Dent, 1983, *The Birthday Burglar, and A Very Wicked Headmistress*, London, Dent, 1984, *The Changeover: A Supernatural Romance*, London, Dent, 1984, reprinted London, Macmillan, 1987, *The Catalogue of the Universe*, London, Dent, 1985, *Aliens in the Family*, Auckland, Ashton Scholastic, 1985, London, Methuen, 1986, *The Tricksters*, London, Dent, 1986, reprinted Auckland, Penguin, 1988, and *Memory*, London, Dent, 1987, reprinted London, Penguin, 1989, Basingstoke, Macmillan, 1990. She has also written a large number of short illustrated story books for young children. One of the earliest and most successful of these was *A Lion in the Meadow*, London, Dent, and New York, Watts, 1969. Collections of her stories include *The First Margaret Mahy Story Book*, London, Dent, 1972, *The Second Margaret Mahy Story Book*, London, Dent, 1973, *The Third Margaret Mahy Story Book*, London, Dent, 1975, *The Chewing-Gum Rescue and Other Stories*, London, Dent, 1982, *Leaf Magic and Five Other Favourites*, London, Dent, and Auckland, Waiatarua Publishing, 1984, and *The Downhill Crocodile Whizz, and Other Stories*, London, Dent, 1986. She was interviewed by Jill McCracken, *Listener*, 3 May 1975, by Murray Edmond, *Landfall*, no. 162, 1987, and by Sue Kedgley, *OOC*. Also in *Landfall*, no. 162, 1987, Claudia Marquis offers a reading of *The Haunting*. Betty Gilderdale's *Introducing Margaret Mahy*, Auckland, Viking Kestrel, 1987, is designed for younger readers.

Clare Mallory, pseudonym of Winifred Hall (McQuilkan). Children's writer. Her work, nearly all published in Melbourne by Geoffrey Cumberlege, Oxford University Press, includes *Merry Begins*, 1947, *Merry Again*, 1947, *Merry Marches On*, 1947, *Tony Against the Prefects*, 1949, *The New House at Winwood*, 1949, *Juliet Overseas*, 1949, *Leith and Friends*, 1950, *The Pen and Pencil Girls*, 1950, *The Two Linties*, 1950, and *The League of the Smallest*, 1951.

Jane Mander 1877-1949. Novelist. Her novels comprise *The Story of a New Zealand River*, London, John Lane, The Bodley Head, and New York, John Lane, 1920, reprinted Christchurch, Whitcombe & Tombs, 1938, Christchurch, Whitcombe & Tombs, and London, Robert Hale, 1960, Christchurch, Whitcombe & Tombs, 1973, *The Passionate Puritan*, London, John Lane, The Bodley Head, and New York, John Lane, 1921, *The Strange Attraction*, New York, Dodd Mead & Co., and London, John Lane, The Bodley Head, 1923, *Allen Adair*, London, Hutchinson, 1925, reprinted with an introduction by Dorothea Turner, Auckland, Auckland University Press, 1971, *The Besieging City*, London, Hutchinson, 1926, and *Pins and Pinnacles*, London, Hutchinson, 1928. A brief note about a young woman's spiritual and political development, *New Republic*, 25 March 1916, is suggestive of autobiography. A manuscript and clipping collection is held at APL. Dorothea Turner, *Jane Mander*, TWAS, New York, 1972, relates biography, especially social and political interests, to the fiction, and includes a bibliography, and in an article on *The Story of a New Zealand River*, *CENZN*, knowledgeably explores that novel's composition, conventions and themes. Lydia Wevers, in *Women in New Zealand Society*, ed. Phillida Bunkle and Beryl Hughes, Auckland, Allen & Unwin, 1980, traces the evolution of the heroines from helpless pioneer to self-liberating, self-sufficient woman.

Bill Manhire 1946-. Poet. His collections of verse include *Malady*, Dunedin, Amphedesma Press, 1970, *The Elaboration*, Wellington, Square & Circle, 1972, *How to Take Off Your Clothes at the Picnic*, Wellington, Wai-te-ata Press, 1977, *Dawn/Water*, Eastbourne, Hawk Press, 1979, *Zoetropes*, London, Murihiku

Press, 1981, *Good Looks*, Auckland, Auckland University Press, 1982, and *Zoetropes: Poems 1972-82*, Sydney, Allen & Unwin, and Wellington, Port Nicholson Press, 1984, Manchester, Carcanet Press, 1985. There is a brief collection of stories, *Locating the Beloved and Other Stories*, Wellington, Single Title Press, 1983; and *The Brain of Katherine Mansfield*, Auckland, Auckland University Press, 1988, and *The New Land: A Picture Book*, Auckland, Heinemann, Reed, 1990, are two further forays into fiction. He has also written *Maurice Gee*, Auckland, Oxford University Press, 1986, and edited several collections of short stories. He was interviewed by Michael Gifkins, *Listener*, 11 June 1990. There are discussions of his poetry by Peter Crisp, *Islands*, no. 24, 1978, and H. Lauder, *Landfall*, no. 147, 1983. Roger Horrocks includes analysis of *Zoetropes: Poems 1972-82* in an article in *And*, no. 4, 1985.

Frederick Maning 1811-83. Best known for his exuberant autobiography, *Old New Zealand*, Auckland, Creighton & Scales, and London, Smith Elder, 1863. *History of the War in the North of New Zealand*, Auckland, George Chapman, 1862, was reprinted with *Old New Zealand*, London, Bentley, 1876. The two have appeared together since, most recently Auckland, Viking, 1987. Joan FitzGerald, *JCL*, vol. 23, 1988, interestingly links his narrative method to *Tristram Shandy*, though she overlooks the prevailing norm of Victorian jocosity. There is a thesis on Maning by David Colquhoun, University of Auckland, 1984.

Katherine Mansfield 1888-1923. Short story writer. For the five main volumes of stories, which have been frequently reprinted, and since 1945 available in collected form, only the first editions are noted here. Together with *Prelude*, they are *In a German Pension*, London, Stephen Swift, 1911, *Prelude*, Richmond, London, Hogarth Press, 1918, *Bliss and Other Stories*, London, Constable, 1920, New York, Knopf, 1921, *The Garden Party and Other Stories*, London, Constable, and New York, Knopf, 1922, *The Dove's Nest and Other Stories*, London, Constable, and New York, Knopf, 1923, and *Something Childish and Other Stories*, London, Constable, and Toronto, Macmillan, 1924, and as *The Little Girl and Other Stories*, New York, Knopf, 1924. *The Scrapbook of Katherine Mansfield*, ed. J. Middleton Murry, London, Constable, 1939, New York, Knopf, 1940, reprinted New York, H. Fertig, 1974, is a miscellany of unpublished fragments, not all fiction. There was one volume of verse, *Poems*, London, Constable, 1923, New York, Knopf, 1924, 2nd edition London, Constable, 1930, New York, Knopf, 1931; a newly selected *Poems of Katherine Mansfield* was edited by Vincent O'Sullivan, Auckland, Oxford University Press, 1988. There is a collection of book reviews, *Novels and Novelists*, ed. J. Middleton Murry, London, Constable, and New York, Knopf, 1930, reprinted Boston, Beacon Press, 1959. A collection of *Dramatic Sketches*, Palmerston North, Nagare Press, was edited with an introduction by David Dowling and Wilhelmina and David Drummond. There have been many selections of the stories, notably *Selected Stories*, ed. with an introduction by Dan Davin,

London, Oxford University Press, 1953. *Collected Stories of Katherine Mansfield*, London, Constable, 1945, remains, in various reprints, most recently London, Penguin, and Auckland, Viking, 1988, the most accessible collection. *The Stories of Katherine Mansfield*, ed. Antony Alpers, Auckland, Oxford University Press, 1984, is textually sounder, and adds some, but not all, uncollected stories. *Undiscovered Country: The New Zealand Stories of Katherine Mansfield*, ed. Ian Gordon, London, Longman, 1974, attempts to arrange the New Zealand material to suggest the growth of a late-Victorian family. *The Aloe, with Prelude*, ed. with an introduction by Vincent O'Sullivan, Wellington, Port Nicholson Press, 1982, prints parallel versions of this story. Margaret Scott has printed a variety of manuscript fragments in *Turnbull Library Record*, vols 3-7 and 12, 1970-79.

The collected letters are being published by Oxford University Press in several volumes. Available up to 1990 are vol. 1, 1903-1917, ed. Vincent O'Sullivan and Margaret Scott, and vol. 2, 1918-1919, ed. Vincent O'Sullivan with Margaret Scott, Oxford, Clarendon, 1984 and 1987. Otherwise the incomplete editions of J. Middleton Murry must be used: *The Letters of Katherine Mansfield*, 2 vols, London, Constable, and Toronto, Macmillan, 1928, New York, Knopf, 1929, and *Katherine Mansfield's Letters to John Middleton Murry, 1913-1922*, London, Constable, New York, Knopf, and Toronto, Longmans, 1951. Murry also edited a collection of material from various sources which he called *Journal of Katherine Mansfield*, London, Constable, and New York, Knopf, 1927, and greatly enlarged, London, Constable, 1954. *Letters between Katherine Mansfield and John Middleton Murry*, London, Virago, 1988, was edited by Cherry Hankin with an admirably non-judgemental introduction. Useful selections of all this are *The Letters and Journals of Katherine Mansfield: A Selection*, ed. C.K. Stead, London, Allen Lane, 1977, and *Selected Letters*, ed. Vincent O'Sullivan, Oxford, Clarendon, 1989. The only freshly edited portion of the notebooks so far published is *The Urewera Notebook*, ed. with an introduction by Ian Gordon, Oxford (i.e., Wellington), Oxford University Press, 1978. *The Critical Writings of Katherine Mansfield*, Basingstoke, Macmillan, and New York, St Martin's Press, 1987, were selected by Clare Hanson. The greatest collection of manuscript material, especially letters and notebooks, is at ATL, but Newberry Library, Chicago, also has much material, particularly manuscripts of her major stories. Manuscripts held by the British Library are listed and described in *British Library Journal*, vol. 14, 1988.

The entry in *The New Cambridge Bibliography of English Literature*, vol. 4, Cambridge, Cambridge University Press, 1972, is the most readily available bibliography. Ruth Mantz, *The Critical Bibliography of Katherine Mansfield*, London, Constable, 1931, provides full bibliographical descriptions of the first editions of the stories in book form, as well as much other information about original periodical publication. The formidably exhaustive *Bibliography of Katherine Mansfield*, Oxford, Clarendon Press, 1990, by B.J. Kirkpatrick, describes in detail all primary material, including lost or rejected articles, musical settings, and most radio and television adaptations. The fullest bibliography of criticism is Jeffrey Meyers, 'Katherine Mansfield: A Bibliography of International Criticism, 1921-1977' in *Bulletin of Bibliography and Magazine Notes*, vol. 34, 1977, well supplemented by Nelson Wattie, 'A Bibliography of Katherine Mansfield References 1970-84', *JNZL*, no. 3, 1985. These bibliographies should be consulted for biographical and critical comment in languages other than English.

There are many biographies and biographical essays. None has the value of Antony Alper's second biography, *The Life of Katherine Mansfield*, London, Cape, New York, Viking, and Toronto, Clarke Irwin, 1980, though Jeffrey Meyers, *Katherine Mansfield: A Biography*, London, Hamilton, 1977, tells a more colourful, 'modern' version. Their attitudes to the problems of writing Mansfield biography are tellingly distinguished in two articles, Antony Alpers in *TLS*, 28 March 1980, and Jeffrey Meyers in *Biography*, vol. 1, 1978. Claire Tomalin's *Katherine Mansfield: A Secret Life*, London, Viking, 1987, is good on her medical history. Gill Boddy's *Katherine Mansfield: The Woman and the Writer*, Ringwood, Victoria, Penguin, 1988, offers a freshly written biographical introduction to the writer, focusing particularly on the letters and journals. To the other innumerable articles and essays describing parts or the whole of her life, the bibliographies listed above must serve as a guide. Recent biographical study is admirably surveyed by Dennis McEldowney, *Ariel*, vol. 16, no. 4, 1985. *Passionate Pilgrimage: A Love Affair in Letters*, ed. Helen McNeish, Auckland, Hodder & Stoughton, and London, Michael Joseph, 1976, and Vincent O'Sullivan, *Katherine Mansfield's New Zealand*, Auckland, Golden Press, 1974, London, Muller, 1975, reprinted Auckland, Viking, 1988, are useful for their photographic record.

Sylvia Berkman's sensitive and balanced *Katherine Mansfield: A Critical Study*, New Haven, Yale University Press, and Christchurch, Whitcombe & Tombs, 1951, London, Oxford University Press, 1952, was the first and remains the best full-length study. In *The Fiction of Katherine Mansfield*, Carbondale, Southern Illinois University Press, and London, Fetter & Simons, 1971, Marvin Magalaner attempts, with considerable success, to define the essence of her fiction. Arthur Sewell, *Katherine Mansfield: A Critical Essay*, Auckland, Unicorn Press, 1936, briefly but admirably attends to the stylistic use and effect of detail. Saralyn Daly, *Katherine Mansfield*, TWAS, New York, 1965, is often suggestive on separate stories but does not draw her perceptions together. Sometimes unconvincing as literary criticism, Cherry Hankin's *Katherine Mansfield and her Confessional Stories*, London, Macmillan, 1983, does show how the stories may cast light on the life, a function also performed by Jeffrey Meyers in *Married to Genius*, London, London Magazine Editions, 1977. Other full-length critical studies include Nariman Hormasji, *Katherine Mansfield: An Appraisal*, Auckland, Collins, 1967, which attempts a psychological interpretation of her authorial personality, and Clare Hanson and Andrew Gurr, *Katherine Mansfield*, London, Macmillan, 1981, surveying critical approaches, with analyses of stories, for senior students. Kate Fullbrook's

Katherine Mansfield, Brighton, Harvester Press, 1986, is a tendentious feminist reading of selected stories and examines her understanding of the social forces holding women in their place in society. Anne Friis, *Katherine Mansfield: Life and Stories* (1946), reprinted Norwood, Norwood Editions, 1977, includes thesis-like analysis of style and technique. Ian Gordon's *Katherine Mansfield*, London, Longman's Green for The British Council and the National Book League, 1954, revised edition London, Longman for The British Council, 1963, is a short general study. There are several other short studies more specifically directed at students, including Antony Alpers, *Katherine Mansfield*, Wellington, School Publications Branch, Department of Education, 1947, Dan Davin, *Katherine Mansfield in Her Letters*, Wellington, School Publications Branch, Department of Education, 1959, Heather Curnow, *Katherine Mansfield*, Wellington, Reed, 1968, and Elizabeth Caffin, *Introducing Katherine Mansfield*, Auckland, Longman Paul, 1982.

Early responses mostly took the form of reviews. Some of the more interesting are by Conrad Aiken (1921, 1922, and 1927), reprinted in *A Reviewer's ABC: Collected Criticism*, New York, Meridian Books, 1958, London, Allen, 1961, Joseph Collins, *New York Times Book Review*, 18 February 1923, and J.C. Squire in *Books Reviewed*, London, Heinemann, 1922. The collections of the early 1920s also prompted a number of essays, including those by Martin Armstrong, *Fortnightly Review*, 1 March 1923, which is perceptive on her stylistic technique, and can be set alongside another early analysis by Edward Wagenknecht, *English Journal*, vol. 17, 1928, S.P.B. Mais, in *Some Modern Authors*, London, Grant Richards, and New York, Dodd Mead, 1923, which welcomes her structural innovations, Alfred C. Ward, in *Aspects of the Modern Short Story: English and American*, London, University of London Press, 1924, Kathleen Freeman, *Canadian Forum*, vol. 7, 1927, which points to the place of detail in characterization and to the non-dramatic plot, Edward Shanks, *London Mercury*, vol. 17, 1928, which emphasizes the 'impressionism' and the pictorial nature of the stories, and George Harper, *Quarterly Review*, vol. 253, 1929. There is also T.O. Beachcroft's essay in *Modern Fiction Studies*, vol. 24, 1978, which recalls her original impact as the first English modernist. In a special position are essays by her husband, J. Middleton Murry, to be found in his *Katherine Mansfield and Other Literary Portraits*, London, P. Nevill, 1949, and, more particularly, *Katherine Mansfield and Other Literary Studies*, London, Constable, 1959, though their late date should be noted.

Publication of the stories in single volumes drew notices, for example, of the 1937 American edition by Ben Belitt (1937), reprinted in *A Preface to Literature*, ed. Edward Wagenknecht, New York, Holt, 1954, and by Katherine Anne Porter (1937), reprinted in *The Days Before*, New York, Harcourt Brace, 1952; of the 1946 English edition by V.S. Pritchett, *New Statesman*, 2 February 1946, who also contributed an essay on the stories to the *Listener* (London), 4 July 1946, and anonymously in *TLS*, 2 March 1946; and of the 1981 edition, amongst many others, by Gillian Tindall, *Encounter*, vol. 65, no. 4, 1985. Virginia Woolf famously reviewed the *Journal* (1927), reprinted in *Collected Essays*, vol. 1,

London, Hogarth Press, 1966, and Orlo Williams the *Journal* and *The Letters* in a review commended by Murry, *Criterion*, vol. 8, 1929. The 1951 edition of the letters prompted James Bertram to a more general essay, *Landfall*, no. 23, 1952, reprinted in *FP*, and the 1954 edition of the 'journal' and Antony Alpers' first biography of 1953 led Vance Palmer to describe the 'new' Katherine Mansfield, *Meanjin*, vol. 14, 1955. There was an anonymous review of the *Scrapbook*, *TLS*, 28 October 1939. Murry's editing of the two editions of the journal was examined by Ian Gordon, *Landfall*, no. 49, 1959, and in more detail by Philip Waldron, *Twentieth Century Literature*, vol. 20, 1974; Ruth Mantz also commented on its inadequacy, *Adam*, no. 370-375, 1972-3. Murry's creation of a 'Mansfield cult' is the contention of Jeffrey Meyers, *Journal of Modern Literature*, vol. 1, 1979. A number of writers have surveyed Mansfield criticism, including Jack Garlington, *Twentieth Century Literature*, vol. 2, 1956, and Nelson Wattie in *The Story Must Be Told*, ed. Peter Stummer, Würzburg, Königshausen & Neumann, 1986. Heather Murray usefully tries to account for the unfavourable views of many British critics, though her own interpretations are not always convincing, in *JNZL*, no. 6, 1988. The French reception was recounted by Pierre Citron, *Revue de Littérature Comparée*, vol. 20, 1940, and Christiane Mortelier, *AUMLA*, no. 34, 1970, and the Italian by J.B. Ringer, *Landfall*, no. 142, 1982. The views of a group of New Zealand writers were canvassed in *Listener*, 11 October 1968.

Essays and criticism of the 1930s and 1940s are represented by Louis Cazamian, on Katherine Mansfield as a letter writer, *University of Toronto Quarterly*, vol. 3, 1934, Virginia Moore, on the metaphysical and spiritual concerns of her last years, in *Distinguished Women Writers* (1934), reprinted Port Washington, N.Y., Kennikat Press, 1968, David Daiches, on her search for 'truth' through the use of detail, in *New Literary Values*, Edinburgh, Oliver & Boyd, 1936, (where he also discusses her part in the development of the short story), and in *The Novel in the Modern World*, Chicago, University of Chicago Press, 1939, (where he also discusses the link between her stories and lyric poetry), Dorothy Hoare in *Some Studies in the Modern Novel*, London, Chatto & Windus, 1938, Litchfield, Conn., Prospect Press, 1940, and H.E. Bates, who also mentions the element of poetry, in *The Modern Short Story: A Critical Survey* (1941), reprinted London, Michael Joseph, 1972. New Zealand comment was provided by Ian Milner, *Phoenix*, no. 1, 1932, Ian Gordon, *New Zealand New Writing*, no. 3, 1944, Pat Lawlor, briefly, on the spiritual side of Katherine Mansfield, *Catholic Review*, vol. 1, 1945, and Frank Sargeson, who places her in a 'feminine tradition', *Listener*, 6 August 1948, reprinted in a fuller version in his *Conversation in a Train*, Auckland, Auckland University Press, 1983. French criticism may be briefly represented by André Maurois (1935), reprinted in *Points of View from Kipling to Graham Greene*, New York, Ungar, 1968, London, Muller, 1969, who includes notes on her 'feminine impressionism'. One of the earliest and long-continuing scholarly debates was over the degree of her indebtedness to Chekhov, both generally and in particular stories. Writers who isolated this theme are D. Brewster and A. Burrell in *Dead Reckonings in Fiction*

(1924), reprinted Freeport, N.Y., Books for Libraries Press, 1969, Elisabeth Schneider, *Modern Language Notes*, vol. 50, 1935, E.M. Almedingen, *TLS*, 19 October 1951, Ronald Sutherland, *Critique*, vol. 5, 1962-63, and Don Kleine, *Philological Quarterly*, vol. 42, 1963. On safer ground, Irene Zohrab, *JNZL*, no. 6, 1988, investigates her part in a review of *The Cherry Orchard*, and a six page biography of Chekhov, and reprints both. Edward Wagenknecht's detection of her knowledge of Dickens and of similarities in their style (1929), reprinted in *Dickens and the Scandalmongers*, Norman, University of Oklahoma Press, 1965, proved uncontroversial. Comparison with, rather than indebtedness to, Virginia Woolf has also been popular, and studies devoted to this include Elizabeth Hamill, in *These Modern Writers*, Melbourne, Georgian House, 1946, A.L. McLaughlin, *Modern Fiction Studies*, vol. 24, 1978, and Angela Smith, *JCL*, vol. 18, 1983. C.K. Stead details the biographical connections, and, less cogently, literary parallels with T.S. Eliot in *AL*.

Later, more general studies include those by Helen Shaw, *Meanjin*, vol. 10, 1951, Elizabeth Bowen (1956), reprinted in *Afterthought; Pieces about Writing*, London, Longmans, 1962, and in a particularly good account of style and form, based on biographical information, C.K. Stead, *New Review*, no. 42, 1977, reprinted in *IGC*. For Cherry Hankin, *Modern Fiction Studies*, vol. 24, 1978, the use of fantasy to bring some of the best stories to a close is psychologically apt, and in *CENZSS* the same author examines the inner life of her characters, especially in some New Zealand stories. Two writers find that her personality flaws her work: for Brigid Brophy (1962), reprinted in *Don't Never Forget*, London, Cape, 1966, it is anger and hatred; for Frank O'Connor, in *The Lonely Voice*, London, Macmillan, 1965, it is lack of heart. Literary affiliations are well dicussed by Frieder Busch, *Arcadia*, vol. 5, 1970, who places her beside French and German 'impressionists', and in another valuable article, Vincent O'Sullivan, *Landfall*, no. 114, 1975, discusses the influence of Wilde and Pater (as well as her Joycean epiphanies and her attitude to sex). Clare Hanson, *JCL*, vol. 16, 1981, traces her reading of symbolist theorists, especially Symons, and demonstrates Mansfield's practice of the theory in 'Prelude'. Symbolism and imagery also occupy Celeste Wright in a number of brief articles, including one on darkness, *Modern Philology*, vol. 51, 1954, Mary Burgan, on childbirth trauma, *Modern Fiction Studies*, vol. 24, 1978, and T.S. Zinman, on images of the flawed condition of human existence, *Modern Fiction Studies*, vol. 24, 1978. Constance Brown, *Centennial Review*, vol. 23, 1979, argues that her stories were deeply affected by World War I. Eileen Baldeshwiler, *Studies in Short Fiction*, vol. 7, 1970, isolates comments which can be grouped to suggest a theory of fiction, and Paul Dinkins, *Descant*, vol. 3, 1958, and James Burns, *Education*, vol. 14, 1965, consider her novel reviews.

Katherine Mansfield was early praised for her portrayal of children, for example, by George Hubbell, *Sewanee Review*, vol. 35, 1927. The frequently noted theme of loneliness was fully explored by Keith Sinclair, *Landfall*, no. 14, 1950. Pat Lawlor, in *The Loneliness of Katherine Mansfield*, Wellington, Beltane Book Bureau, 1950, while commending Sinclair, regrets his omission of the spiritual dimension. In fact, the connection between her working at her craft and a spiritual or religious element was noted on the publication of letters and journal by Orlo Williams and George Harper (see above), and had already been reported by A.R. Orage (1924), reprinted in *Selected Essays and Critical Writings*, London, Stanley Nott, 1935. Later writers who return to this are T.O. Beachcroft, in *The Modest Art: A Survey of the Short-Story in English*, London, Oxford University Press, 1968, and C. Jordis, *La Nouvelle Revue Française*, no. 375, 1984. Some more recent criticism, accepting her place in early twentieth century English writing, has looked for characteristics which can be traced to her New Zealand upbringing, for example, William Walsh, in *A Manifold Voice: Studies in Commonwealth Literature*, London, Chatto & Windus, 1970, Russell King, *JCL*, vol. 8, 1973, and Peter Alcock, *JCL*, vol. 11, 1977. Her expatriate status interests A.J. Gurr in *Writers in Exile*, Brighton, Harvester Press, 1981. Bruce Harding isolates the three 'crime-oriented' colonial stories for analysis in *JNZL*, no. 6, 1988, and the colonial stories are also suggestively re-read by Lydia Wevers, *Women's Studies Journal*, vol. 4, 1988. The best brief summary of the importance of New Zealand to Katherine Mansfield and to her work is by Gill Boddy, *New Zealand Libraries*, vol. 45, December 1988. Linda Hardy, *Landfall*, no. 175, 1990, demonstrates Mansfield's inadequacy, as reflected in some recent New Zealand writing, as a guarantor of cultural identity, and in the same issue Bridget Orr analyses the persistent question of colonial and even racial identity in Katherine Mansfield herself. But Vincent O'Sullivan, in his lecture *Finding the Pattern, Solving the Problem*, Wellington, Victoria University Press, 1989, though he begins in the Pacific, soon concentrates eurocentrically on a writer overwhelmed by the First World War.

Although her gender has certainly not been overlooked, it has only recently been given widespread attention. Mary Benet tries to define the female artist in Katherine Mansfield in *Writers in Love*, New York, Macmillan, 1977, Marie Lederman, *Women's Studies*, vol. 5, 1977, uses her experience of sexual relationships as a lead into that theme's development in her fiction, and Sophie Tomlinson, *Landfall*, no. 156, 1985, accuses Antony Alpers of a male-centered biographical interest in his approach to the stories of his 1984 collection. An issue of vol. 4 of *Women's Studies Journal*, 1988, was largely devoted to feminist views of her life and work, and included a study of Linda Burnell by Heather Murray, with other articles by Anne Else, Ruth Parkin Gounelas, Sara Knox, Alison Laurie, and Isabelle Meyer. Critical and biographical commentary arising out of the centennial year of her birth continues to appear, for example, seven new essays in *Short Fiction in the New Literatures in English*, ed. J. Bardolph, Nice, University of Nice, 1989.

There are many studies of individual stories. With the help of Carco, Russell King subtly analyses 'Je ne parle pas français', *Revue de Littérature Comparée*, vol. 47, 1973. Helen Nebeker, *Modern Fiction Studies*, vol. 18, 1972–3, highlighted the study of sexual implications in 'Bliss', to be followed by Marvin Magalaner, *Modern Fiction Studies*, vol. 24, 1978, and W.E. Anderson, *Twentieth Century Literature*, vol. 28, 1982, and Pamela Dunbar, *Women's Studies Journal*, vol. 4,

1988; Phillip Wilson, *Landfall*, no. 133, 1980, claims Chaucer's 'Merchant's Tale' as a source, and M. Zorn, *Studies in Short Fiction*, vol. 17, 1980, argues for Bertha's potential for love and beauty. Don Kleine writes of 'A Man without a Temperament', *Critique*, vol. 3, 1960. J.F. Kobler points to the implications of the sexless first-person narration of 'The Young Girl', *Studies in Short Fiction*, vol. 17, 1980. There is an early analysis of 'Daughters of the Late Colonel' by Arthur Nelson (1941), in *The Creative Reader*, ed. R.W. Stallman and R.E. Watters, New York, Ronald Press, 1954, and the temporal and spatial relationships in the story are discussed by Don Kleine, *Modern Fiction Studies*, vol. 24, 1978. Maude Morris's provision of factual background and photographs for 'At the Bay', *Turnbull Library Record*, vol. 1, 1968, is one of the best such attempts. 'The Garden Party' has attracted attention to both its social and personal elements, as in Warren Walker, *Modern Fiction Studies*, vol. 3, 1957–8, in Donald Taylor and Daniel Weiss, *Modern Fiction Studies*, vol. 4, 1958–9, in Don Kleine, *Criticism*, vol. 5, 1963, in Anders Iversen, *Orbis Litterarum*, vol. 23, 1968, and in A.J. Sorkin, *Modern Fiction Studies*, vol. 24, 1978. David Dowling argues for the importance of Beryl in 'The Doll's House', *Landfall*, no. 134, 1980. Alex Calder reads 'A Married Man's Story' in terms of narrative/discourse theory in *Landfall*, no. 175, 1990. And 'The Fly' has attracted as much attention as any story, including articles by F.W. Bateson and B. Shahevitch, *Essays in Criticism*, vol. 12, 1962, John Hagopian, *Modern Fiction Studies*, vol. 9, 1963–4, Ted Boyle, *Modern Fiction Studies*, vol. 11, 1965, and Paulette Michel-Michot, *Studies in Short Fiction*, vol. 11, 1974. David Dowling reviewed the quality of her criticism in *JNZL*, no. 6, 1988. A.R.D. Fairburn wrote warmly of her poetry, *New Zealand Artists' Annual*, vol. 1, no. 3, 1928, and Judith Dale, *Landfall*, no. 175, 1990, of some recent dramatized 'lives' of Katherine Mansfield.

Ngaio Marsh 1899-1982. Crime novelist. Only the first editions are noted of her novels, which comprise *A Man Lay Dead*, London, Bles, 1934, *Enter a Murderer*, London, Bles, 1935, *The Nursing-Home Murder* (with Henry Jellett), London, Bles, 1935, *Death in Ecstasy*, London, Bles, 1936, *Vintage Murder*, London, Bles, 1937, *Artists in Crime*, London, Bles, 1938, *Death in a White Tie*, London, Bles, 1938, *Overture to Death*, London, Collins for the Crime Club, 1939, *Death at the Bar*, London, Collins for the Crime Club, 1940, *Death of a Peer*, Boston, Little, Brown, 1940, and as *Surfeit of Lampreys*, London, Collins for the Crime Club, 1941, *Death and the Dancing Footman*, Boston, Little, Brown, 1941, *Colour Scheme*, London, Collins for the Crime Club, 1943, *Died in the Wool*, London, Collins for the Crime Club, 1944, *Final Curtain*, London, Collins for the Crime Club, 1947, *Swing, Brother, Swing*, London, Collins for the Crime Club, and as *A Wreath for Rivera*, Boston, Little, Brown, 1949, *Opening Night*, London, Collins for the Crime Club, and as *Night at the Vulcan*, Boston, Little, Brown, 1951, *Spinsters in Jeopardy*, Boston, Little, Brown, 1953, *Scales of Justice*, London, Collins for the Crime Club, 1955, *Death of a Fool*, Boston, Little, Brown, and as *Off with His Head*, London, Collins for the

Crime Club, 1957, *Singing in the Shrouds*, Boston, Little, Brown, 1958, *False Scent*, Boston, Little, Brown, 1959, *Hand in Glove*, London, Collins for the Crime Club, 1962, *Dead Water*, Boston, Little, Brown, 1963, *Killer Dolphin*, Boston, Little, Brown, 1966, and as *Death at the Dolphin*, London, Collins for the Crime Club, 1967, *Clutch of Constables*, London, Collins for the Crime Club, 1968, *When in Rome*, London, Collins for the Crime Club, 1970, *Tied Up in Tinsel*, London, Collins for the Crime Club, 1972, *Black As He's Painted*, Boston, Little, Brown, 1973, *Last Ditch*, London, Collins for the Crime Club, 1977, *Grave Mistake*, London, Collins, 1978, *Photo-Finish*, London, Collins for the Crime Club, 1980, and *Light Thickens*, Collins for the Crime Club, 1982. She called her autobiography *Black Beech and Honeydew*, Boston, Little, Brown, 1965, London, Collins, 1966, revised and enlarged edition, Auckland, Collins, 1981. She was also recognized as a play producer and wrote *A Play Toward: A Note on Play Production*, Christchurch, Caxton, 1946. *The Christmas Tree*, London, SPCK for the Religious Drama Society of Great Britain, 1962, is a short play. She began her career as an artist and *Perspectives*, Auckland, Auckland Gallery Associates, 1960, is a lecture on the attitudes of New Zealanders to the visual arts. She wrote about her reading from childhood on, *Listener*, 17 December 1965, and briefly surveyed the history of crime fiction, *Pacific Quarterly*, vol. 3, 1978. There is a manuscript collection at ATL. A detailed bibliography of Marsh's English language publications, compiled by Rowan Gibbs and Richard Williams, appeared in the Dragonby Bibliographies series, Dragonby Press, Scunthorpe, 1990. Joan Stevens, *Listener*, 8 May 1972, discussed the full range of her crime fiction. Bruce Harding wrote of her work in *Comment*, no. 15, 1982, and at greater length on the four novels set in New Zealand in *Landfall*, no. 144, 1982. Julian Symons places her achievement in context in *Bloody Murder: From the Detective Story to the Crime Novel*, London, Faber, 1972, and she is one of four authors dealt with by Jessica Mann, *Deadlier than the Male*, New York, Macmillan, 1981.

Owen Marshall 1941-. Short story writer. His collections of stories include *Supper Waltz Wilson and Other New Zealand Stories*, Christchurch, Pegasus, 1979, *The Master of Big Jingles & Other Stories*, Dunedin, McIndoe, 1982, *The Day Hemingway Died and Other Stories*, Dunedin, McIndoe, 1984, *The Lynx Hunter and Other Stories*, Dunedin, McIndoe, 1987, and *The Divided World: Selected Stories*, Dunedin, McIndoe, 1989. He was interviewed by Lawrence Jones, *Landfall*, no. 150, 1984, and this led to an essay in *BWM*; he was also interviewed by Noel O'Hare, *Listener*, 1 August 1987. An autobiographical account of the books in his life, and an essay by Vincent O'Sullivan defensively but also perceptively protecting him from modern literary theory, appeared in *Sport*, no. 3, 1989.

Bruce Mason 1921-82. Playwright. His published plays include *The Pohutukawa Tree*, Wellington, Price Milburn, 1960, revised edition, 1963, *The End of the Golden Weather*, Wellington, Price Milburn, 1962, revised edition,

1970, *Awatea*, Wellington, Price Milburn, 1969, *Zero Inn*, Christchurch, Canterbury Area of the N.Z. Theatre Federation, 1970, *Hongi*, in *Contemporary New Zealand Plays*, ed. Howard McNaughton, Wellington, Oxford University Press, 1974, *Blood of the Lamb*, Wellington, Price Milburn with Victoria University Press, 1981, *Bruce Mason Solo (The End of the Golden Weather, To Russia with Love, Not Christmas but Guy Fawkes*, and *Courting Blackbird*), Wellington, Price Milburn with Victoria University Press, 1981, and *The Healing Arch (Hongi, The Pohutukawa Tree, The Hand on the Rail, Swan Song*, and *Awatea*), Wellington, Victoria University Press, 1987. He also published several short stories. *Theatre in Danger* (with John Pocock), Hamilton, Paul's Book Arcade, 1957, is the most considerable of his critical writings and reviews, of which a generous selection was edited by David Dowling as *Every Kind of Weather*, Auckland, Reed Methuen, 1986. Sebastian Black, *Landfall*, no. 165, 1988, drew attention to this volume's editorial shortcomings, and to the need for qualification of the self-portrait Mason is allowed to present there. 'Beginnings', *Landfall*, no. 78, 1966, reprinted in *B*, is an autobiographical essay. Manuscripts are held at Victoria University of Wellington. Richard Campion, *Listener*, 29 January 1983, provided one of a number of memorial tributes. There is an extensive interview with Howard McNaughton, *Landfall*, no. 106, 1973; other interviews are with Marilyn Duckworth, *Affairs*, May 1971, and with Helen Paske, *Listener*, 15 August 1981. The fullest study is by Howard McNaughton, *Bruce Mason*, NZWW, Wellington, Oxford University Press, 1976, and includes a bibliography. David Dowling, *Introducing Bruce Mason*, Auckland, Longman Paul, 1982, is deliberately simpler, but covers all but the very last plays. Alexander McLeod, *Listener*, 24 June 1960, provides an early comment on Mason's talent as solo performer. His own *New Zealand Drama: A Parade of Forms and a History*, Wellington, Price Milburn, 1973, a text for schools, describes the background and writing of *The Pohutukawa Tree*, and Don McAra, *Landfall*, no. 147, 1983, gives a director's account of producing that play. Bruce Harding, *Landfall*, no. 150, 1984, argues that the seeds of Mason's attacks on irrelevant puritan guilt are in the short story 'Genesis'. Helen White, *Act*, vol. 6, no. 8, 1981, reviews the text and cassette tapes of *Bruce Mason Solo*.

R.A.K. Mason 1905-71. Poet. His collections include *The Beggar*, Auckland, privately published, 1924, *No New Thing: Poems, 1924-29*, Auckland, Spearhead Publishers, 1934, *End of Day*, Christchurch, Caxton, 1936, *Recent Poems* (with Allen Curnow, A.R.D. Fairburn, and Denis Glover), Christchurch, Caxton, 1941, *This Dark Will Lighten: Selected Poems, 1923-41*, Christchurch, Caxton, 1941, and *Collected Poems*, with an introduction by Allen Curnow, Christchurch, Pegasus 1962, reprinted Wellington, Victoria University Press, 1990. The major manuscript collection is at HL. A copy of J.E. Traue's typescript checklist of works by and about Mason, 1963, is held at ATL. There is some biographical information in Doyle and Weir below, and in tributes collected in *Landfall*, no. 99, 1971. Mason discussed his poetry with Sam Hunt, *Affairs*, no. 5, 1969. In the two critical studies, both titled *R.A.K. Mason*,

Charles Doyle, TWAS, New York, 1970, explores themes and literary parallels, and J.E. Weir, NZWW, Wellington, Oxford University Press, 1977, analyses poems individually. The most sensitive and illuminating study is by C.K. Stead, *Comment*, no. 16, 1963, reprinted in *IGC*, and the most substantial attack is by Roger Savage, *Landfall*, no. 67, 1963, in a review. Early comments of historical interest are by A.R.D. Fairburn, *New Zealand Artists' Annual*, vol. 1, no. 4, 1929, and Allen Curnow, *Book*, no. 2, 1941, reprinted in *LBH*. John Weir describes the poet's manuscripts in 'Five New Zealand Poets: A Bibliographical and Critical Account of Manuscript Material', thesis, University of Canterbury, 1974. His Georgianism is considered in a thesis by Anne French, 1979, Victoria University of Wellington, and recent articles include those by Ruth Harley, *Islands*, no. 29, 1980, distinguishing between his poetry and his politics, and several by Joost Daalder including those in *Landfall*, no. 138, 1981, and *WLWE*, vol. 21, 1982. Rachel Barrowman explored his links with the Auckland People's Theatre between 1936 and 1940 in *Sites*, no. 16, 1988.

Katerina Mataira 1932-. Children's writer. Her work includes *Maui and the Big Fish*, Christchurch, Whitcombe & Tombs, and Sydney, Angus & Robertson, 1972, *Maori Legends for Young New Zealanders*, Auckland, Hamlyn, 1975, *The Warrior Mountains*, Raglan, Te Ataarangi Publications, 1982, and *The River Which Ran Away*, Raglan, Ahura Press, 1983.

Ian Middleton 1928-. Novelist. His novels include *Pet Shop*, Martinborough, A. Taylor, 1979, *Faces of Hachiko*, Auckland, Inca Print, 1984, *Sunflower: A Novel of Present-Day Japan*, Auckland, Benton Ross, 1986, *Mr Ponsonby*, Auckland, Lyndon, 1989, and *Reiko*, Tauranga, Moana Press, 1990. Kevin Ireland, *Listener*, 25 March 1989, provides a note on Middleton and *Mr Ponsonby*.

O.E. Middleton 1925-. Short story writer. His collections of stories include *Short Stories*, Wellington, Handcraft Press, 1953, *The Stone and Other Stories*, Auckland, Pilgrim Press, 1959, *A Walk on the Beach*, London, Michael Joseph, 1964, *The Loners*, Wellington, Square & Circle, 1972, *Selected Stories*, Dunedin, McIndoe, 1975, and *Confessions of an Ocelot, and, Not for a Seagull*, Dunedin, McIndoe, 1979. He also published *Six Poems*, Wellington, Handcraft Press, 1951. 'Begininngs', *Landfall*, no. 81, 1967, reprinted in *B*, is an autobiographical essay. A manuscript collection is held at APL, and a smaller one at HL. Middleton comments on his experience of critics' incompetency in *Pilgrims*, no. 8, 1980. Jim Williamson discussed his stories in *Islands*, no. 4, 1973, and Lawrence Jones the short novels in *Pilgrims*, no. 8, 1980, reprinted in *BWM*.

Barry Mitcalfe 1930-86. His writing for children includes *The Long Holiday*, Christchurch, Whitcombe & Tombs, 1964, reprinted Wellington, Price Milburn, 1982, and *Three Stories*, Wellington, School Publications Branch,

Department of Education, 1964. He also wrote fiction and verse for adults, as well as books on Māori life and Māori poetry.

Ronald Hugh Morrieson 1922-72. Novelist. His volumes of fiction comprise *The Scarecrow*, Sydney, Angus & Robertson, 1963, reprinted Auckland, Heinemann Educational Books, 1976, Auckland, Penguin, 1981, *Came a Hot Friday*, Sydney, Angus & Robertson, 1964, reprinted Auckland, Penguin, 1981, *Predicament*, Palmerston North, Dunmore Press, 1974, reprinted London, Hale, and Palmerston North, Dunmore Press, 1981, Auckland, Penguin, 1986, and *Pallet on the Floor*, Palmerston North, Dunmore Press, 1976, reprinted with two short stories and an introduction by Peter Simpson, Auckland, Penguin, 1983. Peter Simpson's study, *Ronald Hugh Morrieson*, Auckland, Oxford University Press, 1982, includes a bibliography. Maurice Shadbolt, *Listener*, 12 February 1973, recalled a visit paid to him. Frank Sargeson and C.K. Stead both wrote commendatory notes on his fictional skills in *Landfall*, no. 98, 1971. Lawrence Jones, *Landfall*, no. 144, 1982, reprinted in *BWM*, comments on Simpson's study and Morrieson's novels. Both are treated less sympathetically by Vincent O'Sullivan, *Listener*, 12 June 1982. In *And*, no. 4, 1985, Alex Calder tries to see what sort of fictional world is postulated by the narrative method of *The Scarecrow*.

Michael Morrissey 1942-. Poet and short story writer. His collections of verse include *Make Love in All the Rooms*, Dunedin, Caveman Press, 1978, *Closer to the Bone: Poems*, Christchurch, Sword Press, 1981, *Dreams*, Christchurch, Sword Press, 1981, *She's Not the Child of Sylvia Plath: Poems*, Christchurch, Sword Press, 1981, *Taking in the View*, Auckland, Auckland University Press, 1986, and (all Auckland, Van Guard Press), *New Zealand, What Went Wrong*, 1988, *Dr Strangeglove's Prescription*, 1988, *The American Hero Loosens His Tie*, 1989, and *A Case of Briefs*, 1989. *The Fat Lady and the Astronomer*, Christchurch, Sword Press, 1981, is a collection of stories. He also edited, with an introduction, the anthology *The New Fiction*, Auckland, Lindon Publishing, 1985. He was interviewed by Suzann Olsson, *Landfall*, no. 146, 1983. His collection of stories is discussed by Lawrence Jones in *BWM*.

Alan (A.E.) Mulgan 1881-1962. Journalist and man of letters. His books include *Maori and Pakeha: A History of New Zealand* (with A.W. Shrimpton), Auckland, Whitcombe & Tombs, 1922, *Three Plays of New Zealand*, Auckland, Whitcombe & Tombs, 1922, *The English of the Line and Other Verses*, Auckland, Whitcombe & Tombs, 1925, *Home: A New Zealander's Adventure* (travel), London, Longmans Green, 1927, *Golden Wedding*, London, Dent, 1932, reprinted with other poems and an introduction by Eileen Duggan, Christchurch, Caxton, 1964, *Spur of Morning* (novel), London, Dent, 1934, reprinted Christchurch, Whitcombe & Tombs, 1960, *A Pilgrim's Way in New Zealand* (travel), London, Oxford University Press, 1935, *Aldebaran and Other Verses*, Christchurch, privately published, 1937, *The City of the Strait: Wellington* *and Its Province: A Centennial History*, Wellington, Reed for the Wellington Provincial Centennial Council, 1939, *First with the Sun* (essays and sketches), London, Dent, 1939, *Literature and Authorship in New Zealand*, London, Allen & Unwin, 1943, *From Track to Highway: A Short History of New Zealand*, Christchurch, Whitcombe & Tombs, 1944, *Pastoral New Zealand: Its Riches and Its People*, Christchurch, Whitcombe & Tombs, 1946, *The Making of a New Zealander* (autobiography), Wellington, Reed, 1958, and *Great Days in New Zealand Writing*, Wellington, Reed, 1962. Manuscript collections are held at ATL and APL. Dennis McEldowney, *Landfall*, no. 71, 1964, surveyed his career as a writer.

John Mulgan 1911-45. Novelist. His only novel is *Man Alone*, London, Selwyn & Blount, 1939, reprinted Hamilton, Paul's Book Arcade, 1949, Auckland, Longman Paul, 1970. *Report on Experience*, with an introduction by J.A.W. Bennett, London, Oxford University Press, 1947, is a long auto-biographical essay; the second edition, Auckland, Paul, 1967, adds an important letter. It was reprinted, Auckland, Oxford University Press, 1984. There are bibliographies in Paul Day's two monographs, that of 1968 being more detailed. Despite Mulgan's importance in the history of New Zealand fiction, critics have been disarmed by the single simple novel and most comment has been biographical, though James Bertram's review of *Man Alone*, *Tomorrow*, 1 May 1940, reprinted in *FP*, is of historical interest as an immediate New Zealand response. Another early comment was Dan Davin's review of *Report on Experience*, *Landfall*, no. 5, 1948, reprinted in *Landfall Country*, ed. Charles Brasch, Christchurch, Caxton, 1962. Paul Day, *John Mulgan*, NZWW, Wellington, Oxford University Press, 1977, is more biographical than his earlier *John Mulgan*, TWAS, New York, 1968, which had elicited biographical comment from James Bertram, *Comment*, no. 39, 1969, reprinted in *FP*. The critical sections of Day's first book developed an article, *Comment*, no. 24, 1965, reprinted in *CENZN*, in which he argued the novel to be about the effects of New Zealand society and the nature of the land on the individual. Colin Partridge, *Commonwealth*, vol. 2, 1976, writes of Mulgan's (and his hero Johnson's) search for forms of courage which will reconcile individualism and communal life. In *Landfall*, no. 128, 1978, Day suggests, tenuously, that the germ of *Man Alone* lay in Mulgan's dissatisfaction with his father's novel *Spur of Morning*. Victor Dupont, *Literary Half-Yearly*, vol. 20, 1979, sees Johnson in terms of other literary wanderers. An interpretation by C.K. Stead, *Islands*, no. 25, 1979, reprinted in *IGC*, emphasizing a Marxist international viewpoint, carries to an extreme a reading noted in passing by Davin in 1948. Correspondence in the following issue predictably attacked Stead's biographical remarks; only W. Easterbrook-Smith offered perceptive comment on the novel. Roland Anderson, *Ariel*, vol. 16, no. 4, 1985, reviews what critics and writers have made of Mulgan's 'man alone'.

Joseph Musaphia 1935-. Playwright. His published plays include *Free*,

Landfall, no. 68, 1963, *Victims, Act*, no. 20, 1973, *Obstacles, Act*, no. 25, 1974, *The Guerrilla*, Sydney, Currency Press, 1976, *Mothers and Fathers*, Sydney, Currency Press, and Wellington, Price Milburn, 1977, and *Shotgun Wedding*, Wellington, Playmarket, 1981. He has written other plays for the stage as well as numerous radio plays. There is a biographical article, based on an interview, by Helen Paske, *Listener*, 10 February 1979.

Joanna Orwin 1944–. Children's and scientific writer. Her books for children, all published in Auckland by Oxford University Press, are *Ihaka and the Summer Wandering*, 1982, *Ihaka and the Prophecy*, 1984, *The Guardian of the Land*, 1985, and *Watchers in the Forest*, 1987. She has also published on ecological subjects.

Vincent O'Sullivan 1937–. Poet, short story writer, dramatist, and critic. His collections of verse include *Our Burning Time*, Wellington, Prometheus Books, 1965, *Revenants*, Wellington, Prometheus Books, 1969, *Bearings*, Wellington, Oxford University Press, 1973, *From the Indian Funeral*, Dunedin, McIndoe, 1976, *Butcher & Co*, Wellington, Oxford University Press, 1977, *Brother Jonathan, Brother Kafka*, Wellington, Oxford University Press, 1980, *The Butcher Papers*, Auckland, Oxford University Press, 1982, *The Rose Ballroom and Other Poems*, Dunedin, McIndoe, 1982, and *The Pilate Tapes*, Auckland, Oxford University Press, 1986. His collections of stories include *The Boy, the Bridge, the River*, Dunedin, McIndoe, and Wellington, Reed, 1978, *Dandy Edison for Lunch and Other Stories*, Dunedin, McIndoe, 1981, *Survivals and Other Stories*, Wellington, Allen & Unwin/Port Nicholson Press, 1985, and *The Snow in Spain*, Wellington, Allen & Unwin, 1990. *Miracle: A Romance*, Dunedin, McIndoe, 1976, is a satirical novel. His plays include *Shuriken*, Wellington, Victoria University Press, 1985, *Jones & Jones*, Wellington, Victoria University Press, 1989, and *Billy*, Wellington, Victoria University Press, 1990. Gay Cusack compiled 'A Bibliography of the Writings of Vincent O'Sullivan', supplement to *Landfall*, no. 140, 1981. He wrote the critical study *James K. Baxter*, NZWW, Wellington, Oxford University Press, 1976, and is editing (with Margaret Scott) *The Collected Letters of Katherine Mansfield*. He also edited *An Anthology of Twentieth Century New Zealand Poetry*, London, Oxford University Press, 1970, enlarged editions, Wellington, 1976, and Auckland, 1987, as well as other volumes of verse and prose. James Bertram's article in the *Listener*, 4 July 1981, is mainly biographical. He was interviewed about *Shuriken* by Phillip Mann, *Illusions*, no. 3, 1986. There are articles on the poetry and the fiction by David Dowling and Gay Cusack respectively in *Landfall*, no. 140, 1981, and K.O. Arvidson analyses *The Butcher Papers* and *The Rose Ballroom* in *JNZL*, no. 1, 1983. *Shuriken* is discussed by Sebastian Black, *Landfall*, no. 157, 1986, and by Michael Neill in a review of the published script, *Australasian Drama Studies*, no. 8, 1986.

Isabel Maud Peacocke 1881–1973. Children's writer. Her stories for children, published in London by Ward, Lock except where noted, include *My Friend*

Phil, 1915, *Dicky, Knight-Errant*, 1916, *Patricia-Pat*, 1917, *Robin of the Round House*, 1918, *The Misdoings of Micky and Mac*, 1919, *Piccaninnies*, Auckland, Whitcombe & Tombs, 1920, *The Sand Playmates*, Auckland, Whitcombe & Tombs, 1921, *Ginger*, 1921, *The Sand Babies*, Auckland, Whitcombe & Tombs, 1921, *Teenywiggles*, Auckland, Whitcombe & Tombs, 1921, *Quicksilver*, 1922, *The Adopted Family*, 1923, *Little Bit 'o Sunshine*, 1924, *His Kid Brother*, 1926, *Brenda and the Babes*, 1927, *When I Was Seven*, 1927, *The Runaway Princess*, 1929, *Haunted Island*, 1930, *The Dwarf of Dark Mountain*, 1931, *The Cruise of the 'Crazy Jane'*, 1932, *The Guardians of Tony*, 1933, *Cathleen with a 'C'*, 1934, *Marjolaine*, 1935, *The Good Intentions of Angela*, 1937, and *Lizbett Anne*, 1939. She also wrote novels for adult readers. She is one of three children's writers discussed in a thesis by C.D. Neutze, University of Auckland, 1981.

Bill Pearson 1922-. Novelist and critic. His only novel is *Coal Flat*, Auckland, Paul's Book Arcade, and London, Angus & Robertson, 1963, reprinted Auckland, Longman Paul, 1970, London and Auckland, Heinemann, 1976, Auckland, Oxford University Press, 1985. Many of his essays and reviews are collected in *Fretful Sleepers and Other Essays*, Auckland, Heinemann Educational Books, 1974. He has also written a few short stories and published books on Henry Lawson in New Zealand and on the Pacific Islands in Western literature. There is an autobiographical essay in *Sport*, no. 5, 1990. Allen Curnow, *Comment*, no. 17, 1963, wrote enthusiastically about the novel's 'major scale'. The review is reprinted in *CENZN*, where it is followed by a much fuller analysis of the novel's virtues. Both essays are reprinted in *LBH*. Frank Sargeson, *Landfall*, no. 84, 1967, in an imaginary conversation, is teasingly suggestive about the novel's strengths and possible weaknesses.

Dorothy Quentin, pseudonym of Madeleine Batten 1911-. Romance novelist. All the titles which follow (except the last) were published in London by Ward, Lock, who sometimes gave Melbourne as an additional place of publication. Her work includes *Brave Enterprise*, 1939, *If I Should Love You*, 1939, *Rhapsody in Spring*, 1940, *Voyage to Paradise*, 1940, *Errand of Mercy*, 1941, *So Shadows Pass*, 1942, *Tomorrow's Bread*, 1942, *Love in Four Flats*, 1943, *Sob-Sister*, 1943, *There's No Escape*, 1943, *Love Go with You*, 1944, *Sell Me Your Life*, 1944, *Sparkling Waters*, 1945, *Briarways*, 1946, *Morning Star*, 1946, *Bright Horizon*, 1947, *Love Sails at Dawn*, 1947, *Maiden Voyage*, 1948, *Tomorrow Is Another Day*, 1948, *The Golden Hibiscus*, 1949, *The Singing Hills*, 1949, *Little Mansions*, 1950, *The Mountains Are Still Green*, 1950, *Reach Me a Star*, 1950, *Flamingo Island*, 1951, *The Winds of Love*, 1951, *Dear Anna*, 1952, *The Honest Heart*, 1952, *The Blue Gum Tree*, 1953, *Harbour My Heart*, 1954, *The Inn by the Lake*, 1954, *The Generous Heart*, 1955, *Inheritance of Love*, 1955, *Prelude to Love*, 1956, *Reflections of a Star*, 1956, *Dream of Love*, 1957, *Forsaken Paradise*, 1957, *The House by the Sea*, 1958, *Love Me by Moonlight*, 1958, *The Unchanging Love*, 1959, *Whispering Island*, 1959, *Lugano Love Story*, 1960, *Rainbow Valley*, 1960, *The Eagle and the Dove*, 1961, *The Prisoner in the Square*, 1961, *Dangerous Affair*, 1962, *Imprudent*

Lover, 1962, *The Dark Castle*, 1963, *The Doctor's Destiny*, 1963, *The Cottage in the Woods*, 1964, *Perilous Voyage*, 1964, *The Healing Tide*, 1965, *The One I Want*, 1965, *Duel across the Water*, 1966, *House of Illusion*, 1966, *Lantana*, 1967, *What News of Kitty?*, 1967, *The Little Hospital*, 1968, and *Goldenhaze*, London, Mills & Boon, 1969.

Alexander Wyclif (A.W.) Reed 1908-79. Publisher, author and writer for children. His books for children include *Poppa Passes: The Adventures of the Vedgie People*, Wellington, Reed, 1943, *The Adventures of Matchbox Max*, Wellington, Reed, 1944, *At the Bottom of the Garden*, Wellington, Reed, 1944, *The Shepherd Boy*, Wellington, Reed, 1945, *Myths and Legends of Maoriland*, Wellington, Reed, 1946, *Wonder Tales of Maoriland*, Wellington, Reed, 1948, *Maori Tales of Long Ago*, Wellington, Reed, 1957, *Maori Fables and Legendary Tales*, Wellington, Reed, 1964, *Maori Fairy Tales*, Wellington, Reed, 1970, and *The Biggest Fish in the World*, Wellington, Reed, 1974.

Rosemary Rees 1876-1963. Romance novelist. Her work, omitting later reprints, includes *April's Sowing*, London, Herbert Jenkins, 1924, *Heather of the South*, London, Herbert Jenkins, 1924, *Lake of Enchantment*, London, Herbert Jenkins, 1925, *"Life's What You Make It!"*, London, Herbert Jenkins, 1927, *Wild, Wild Heart*, London, Chapman & Hall, 1928, *Dear Acquaintance*, London, Chapman & Hall, 1929, New York, Farrar & Rinehart, 1930, *Sane Jane*, London, Chapman & Hall, 1931, and as *Second Romance*, New York, Arcadia House, Toronto, George McLeod, 1940, *Concealed Turning*, London, Wright & Brown, 1932, *Local Colour*, London, Chapman & Hall, 1933, *New Zealand Holiday* (travel book), London, Chapman & Hall,1933, *Hetty Looks for Local Colour*, London, Wright & Brown, New York, Arcadia House, 1935, *Home's Where the Heart Is*, London, Chapman & Hall, New York, Arcadia House, Toronto, Ryerson Press, 1935, *Miss Tiverton's Shipwreck*, London, Chapman & Hall, 1936, *Escape from Love*, New York, Hilman-Curl, 1937, *Turn the Hour*, London, Chapman & Hall, 1937, *Sing a Song of Sydney*, London, Chapman & Hall, 1938, *You'll Never Fail Me*, London, Chapman & Hall, New York, Arcadia House, Toronto, George McLeod, 1939, *I Can Take Care of Myself*, London, Chapman & Hall, 1940, and as *Little Miss Independent*, New York, Arcadia House, Toronto, George McLeod, 1940, *Sackcloth for Susan*, London, Chapman & Hall, New York, Arcadia House, Toronto, George McLeod, 1941, *The Mended Citadel*, London, Chapman & Hall, 1943, and as *Again We Dream*, New York Arcadia House, 1943, *Penelope Waits*, London, Chapman & Hall, Melbourne, Oxford University Press, Toronto, Smithers & Bonellie, 1947, *Displaced Person*, London, Chapman & Hall, 1948, *She Who Loves*, London, Chapman & Hall, Toronto, British Book Service, 1952, *The Five Miss Willoughbys*, London, Chapman & Hall, 1955, *Better to Trust*, London, Chapman & Hall, 1956, *Love in a Lonely Land*, London, Harrap, 1958, and *The Proud Diana*, London, Wright & Brown, 1962.

William Pember Reeves 1857-1932. Historian and poet. His historical works include *The Long White Cloud: Ao Tea Roa*, London, Horace Marshall, 1898, third edition revised and extended by the author with a 'sketch of recent events' by Cecil J. Wray, London, Allen & Unwin, 1924, and *State Experiments in Australia and New Zealand*, London, Grant Richards, 1902. His collections of verse include *New Zealand and Other Poems*, London, Grant Richards, 1898, and *The Passing of the Forest and Other Verse*, London, privately published, 1925. He also published books of scenic description as well as political speeches and articles. There is a biography, *William Pember Reeves*, Oxford, Clarendon Press, 1965, by Keith Sinclair.

Renée 1929-. Playwright. Her published plays include *Secrets* and *Setting the Table*, Wellington, Playmarket, 1984, *Wednesday to Come*, Wellington, Victoria University Press, 1985, and *Pass It On*, Wellington, Victoria University Press, 1986. *Willy Nilly*, Auckland, Penguin, 1990, is a novel. There are interviews with Claire-Louise McCurdy, *Women's Studies Journal*, vol. 1, 1985, with Pamela Payne-Heckenberg and Tony Mitchell, *Australasian Drama Studies*, no. 10, 1987, with Peter Beatson, *Sites*, no. 16, 1988, and with Lee Harris, *Broadsheet*, no. 181, 1990. Rebecca Simpson, *Listener*, 15 September 1984, writes up conversations held during a playwright's workshop. There are reviews of *Wednesday to Come* by Rebecca Simpson, *Listener*, 22 September 1984, and John Thomson, *Act*, vol. 9, no. 5, 1984. Background material to that and the following play is contained in a schools supplement, *Act*, vol. 11, no. 3, 1986.

Frank Sargeson 1903-82. Short story writer and novelist. His fiction includes *Conversation with My Uncle and Other Sketches*, Auckland, Unicorn Press, 1936, *A Man and His Wife* (short stories), Christchurch, Caxton, 1940, revised edition, Wellington, Progressive Publishing Society, 1944, *When the Wind Blows*, Christchurch, Caxton, 1945, *That Summer and Other Stories*, London, John Lehmann, 1946, *I Saw in My Dream* (including, as part one, *When the Wind Blows*), London, John Lehmann, 1949, reprinted with an introduction by Winston Rhodes, Auckland, Auckland University Press, 1974, *I for One . . .*, Christchurch, Caxton, 1954, *Collected Stories, 1935-1963*, with an introduction by Bill Pearson, Auckland, Paul, 1964, reprinted London, MacGibbon & Kee, 1965, and as *The Stories of Frank Sargeson*, with additional stories and updated bibliography but without the introduction, Auckland, Longman Paul, 1973, reprinted Auckland, Penguin, 1982, *Memoirs of a Peon*, London, MacGibbon & Kee, 1965, reprinted Auckland, Heinemann, 1974, *The Hangover*, London, MacGibbon & Kee, 1967, *Joy of the Worm*, London, MacGibbon & Kee, 1969, these last two reprinted together, Auckland, Penguin, 1984, *Man of England Now* with *I for One . . .* and *A Game of Hide and Seek*, Christchurch, Caxton, and London, Martin Brian & O'Keeffe, 1972, *Sunset Village*, Wellington, Reed, and London, Martin Brian & O'Keeffe, 1976, and 'En Route' in *Tandem* (with Edith Campion), Wellington, Reed, 1979. Two plays, 'A Time for Sowing' and 'The Cradle and the Egg', appeared under the title *Wrestling with the Angel*,

Christchurch, Caxton, 1964. *Conversation in a Train and Other Critical Writing*, Auckland, Auckland University Press, 1983, was edited with an introduction by Kevin Cunningham. The autobiographical essay 'Beginnings', *Landfall*, no. 74, 1965, reprinted in *B*, was superseded by the three memoirs *Once Is Enough*, Wellington, Reed, and London, Martin Brian & O'Keeffe, 1973, *More Than Enough*, Wellington, Reed, and London, Martin Brian & O'Keeffe, 1975, and *Never Enough*, Wellington, Reed, and London, Martin Brian & O'Keeffe, 1977, collectively republished as *Sargeson*, Auckland, Penguin, 1981. Peter Alcock quotes from Sargeson-John Lehmann correspondence in *The Library Chronicle* (University of Texas), no. 10, 1978. There is a substantial manuscript collection at ATL.

Sargeson is covered bibliographically by J.W. Hayward, 'Frank Sargeson: An Annotated Bibliography: Works and Critical Comment', 1975, and Kevin Cunningham, 'Frank Sargeson's Critical and Autobiographical Writings: An Annotated Bibliography', 1977, both compiled at the Library School, Wellington. Dennis McEldowney, *Frank Sargeson in His Time*, Dunedin, McIndoe, 1976, is a good, brief, fully illustrated literary biography. *Islands*, no. 21, 1977, was devoted to Sargeson, and contains many personal reminiscences as well as brief critical comments. Amongst several interviews, one with Michael Beveridge, *Landfall*, nos 93 and 94, 1970, is by far the fullest and most rewarding; another with J.-P. Durix, *Commonwealth*, no. 3, 1977/78, reveals an unbuttoned Sargeson talking to a non-New Zealander. There are two separate studies. Winston Rhodes, *Frank Sargeson*, TWAS, New York, 1969, elucidates the solutions found to the problems faced by a novelist in a new country and a new society without indigenous literary traditions, and R.A. Copland, *Frank Sargeson*, NZWW, Wellington, Oxford University Press, 1976, provides perceptive but more conventional analysis of the fiction.

Articles of a comprehensive nature are few and thin. One of the better ones is by Trevor James, *London Magazine*, vol. 22, no. 7, 1982, who emphasizes Sargeson's search for the identity of New Zealand and New Zealanders. J.S. Martin, *Journal of General Education*, vol. 33, 1981, considers the persistent reflection of a claustrophobic society throughout Sargeson's choice of styles and themes. More successful articles focus on the short stories or individual novels. Of largely historical interest is a collection edited by Helen Shaw, *The Puritan and the Waif*, cyclostyled, Auckland, H.L. Hofmann, 1954, with essays by D'Arcy Cresswell, James K. Baxter, Walter Allen, E.P. Dawson, Erik Schwimmer, Helen Shaw, and, of greater value, Dan Davin and Winston Rhodes. Rhodes's essay, reprinted in *Landfall Country*, ed. Charles Brasch, Christchurch, Caxton, 1962, brilliantly investigates the 'moral climate' of the stories. Bill Pearson's introduction to the *Collected Stories* was reprinted in *FS*. E.A. Horsman, *Landfall*, no. 74, 1965, argues that the process of discovery, not the end result, constitutes the stories' value. The strengths and limitations of their narrative technique are well analysed by R.A. Copland, *Landfall*, no. 87, 1968, reprinted in *CENZL*, and are reconsidered by Bruce King in his *The New English Literatures*, London, Macmillan, 1980, in a context described by his title.

King also examines *I Saw in My Dream* as an experimental novel. Helen Shaw, *CENZSS*, returns to the moral climate of the stories, and David Norton, *CENZSS*, believes they have been overpraised and points out shortcomings. In *JNZL*, no. 4, 1986, Joost Daalder labours what he naïvely takes to be Sargeson's approval of violent behaviour. Kai Jensen, *Landfall*, no. 173, 1990, sieves the homosexual masculinity from the stories' manly realism. Simon During takes modern critical theory to 'The Hole that Jack Dug' in *And*, no. 1, 1983, reprinted in *Southern Review*, vol. 18, 1985. Lauris Edmond, *Islands*, no. 6, 1973, looks disapprovingly at the new authorial tone of the last stories, and W.H. New, *Landfall*, no. 143, 1982, contributes a note on narrative as a reflection of society. New shows a similar interest in *I Saw in My Dream*, *WLWE*, vol. 14, 1975, where the hero, like his society, is found to be both shut in and shut out. On *Memoirs of a Peon*, J.B. Ower, *Landfall*, no. 104, 1972, responds to the intellectual complexities but fails to convey the fun, a lack put right by R.A. Copland, *CENZN*, who locates the comedy in the narrative technique. Organizational powers are the subject of a review article on *Joy of the Worm* by Terry Sturm, *Landfall*, no. 93, 1970. The first of the memoirs is held to be the finest account of what it means to be an artist in New Zealand by Kevin Cunningham, *Islands*, no. 6, 1973, and is seen to record lost opportunities by Lawrence Jones, *JNZL*, no. 1, 1983, reprinted in *BWM*.

William Satchell 1860-1942. Novelist. His novels comprise *The Land of the Lost*, London, Methuen, 1902, reprinted Auckland, Whitcombe & Tombs, and London, Methuen, 1938, and edited with an introduction by Kendrick Smithyman, Auckland, Auckland University Press, 1971, *The Toll of the Bush*, London, Macmillan, 1905, reprinted with an introduction by Kendrick Smithyman, Auckland, Auckland University Press, 1985, *The Elixir of Life*, London, Chapman & Hall, 1907, and *The Greenstone Door*, London and Toronto, Sidgwick & Jackson, and New York, Macmillan, 1914, reprinted Auckland, Whitcombe & Tombs, 1935, London, Sidgwick & Jackson, 1936, London, John Spencer, 1961, Auckland, Golden Press in association with Whitcombe & Tombs, 1973, and Auckland, Viking, 1987. His poems and miscellaneous tales have not been considered important. ATL holds a manuscript collection. Phillip Wilson's study *The Maorilander*, Christchurch, Whitcombe & Tombs, 1961, revised and enlarged, with a bibliography, as *William Satchell*, TWAS, New York, 1968, though not uncritical, overvalues the novels. Kendrick Smithyman's introductions to the the reprints discuss the literary origins of Satchell's characters and plot (*Land of the Lost*) and the Hokianga setting (*Toll of the Bush*). An interesting comparison of *The Greenstone Door* and *Great Expectations* as *Bildungsromane* is made by M. Butcher, *Kunapipi*, vol. 5, 1983.

Nelle Scanlan 1882-1968. Romance novelist. Her work includes *Boudoir Mirrors of Washington*, Chicago, John Winston, 1923, *Primrose Hill*, London, Jarrolds, 1931, *The Top Step*, London, Jarrolds, 1931, the Pencarrow tetralogy comprising *Pencarrow*, London, Jarrolds, 1932, *Tides of Youth*, London, Jarrolds, 1933, *Winds of Heaven*, London, Jarrolds, 1934 and *Kelly Pencarrow*, London, Robert Hale, 1939, all four reprinted Christchurch, Whitcombe & Tombs, 1958, *Ambition's Harvest*, London Jarrolds, 1935, *The Marriage of Nicholas Cotter*, London, Robert Hale, 1936, *Leisure for Living*, London, Robert Hale, 1937, *A Guest of Life*, London, Robert Hale, 1938, *March Moon*, London, Robert Hale, 1944, Christchurch, Whitcombe & Tombs, and Toronto, Ryerson Press, 1945, *Kit Carmichael*, London, Robert Hale, and Christchurch, Whitcombe & Tombs, 1947, *The Rusty Road*, London, Robert Hale, 1948, Christchurch, Whitcombe & Tombs, 1949, *Confidence Corner*, London, Robert Hale, 1950, and *The Young Summer*, London, Robert Hale, 1952. *Road to Pencarrow*, London, Robert Hale, and Christchurch, Whitcombe & Tombs, 1963, is an autobiography. There is an obituary notice by S. Perry, *Listener*, 25 October 1968. Alan Mulgan has a chapter on the Pencarrow novels in his *Great Days in New Zealand Writing*, Wellington, Reed, 1962.

Mary Scott 1888–1979. Novelist. Her work includes *Where the Apple Reddens*, London, Hurst & Blackett, 1934, *And Shadows Flee*, London, Hurst & Blackett, 1935, *Barbara and the New Zealand Back-Blocks* (stories), New Plymouth, Thomas Avery, 1936, *Barbara Prospers* (stories), Wellington, Reed, 1937, *Five Little Plays*, Napier, Telegraph Print, c. 1944, *Life with Barbara* (stories), Wellington, Reed, 1944, *More Little Plays*, Hamilton, privately published, c. 1949, *Five Barbara Plays*, Hamilton, privately published, c. 1950, *Barbara on the Farm*, Wellington, Reed, 1953, *Breakfast at Six*, London and New York, Hurst & Blackett, 1953, *Barbara Sees the Queen and Other Stories*, Wellington, Reed, and London, Phoenix House, 1954, *Yours to Oblige*, London and Melbourne, Hurst & Blackett, 1954, *Pippa in Paradise*, London and Melbourne, Hurst & Blackett, 1955, *Families Are Fun*, Hamilton, Paul's Book Arcade, 1956, and a sequel, *Dinner Doesn't Matter*, Hamilton, Paul's Book Arcade, and Sydney and London, Angus & Robertson, 1957, *The Unwritten Book*, Wellington, Reed, and London, Herbert Jenkins, 1957, *One of the Family*, Hamilton, Paul's Book Arcade, Sydney, Angus & Robertson, and Toronto, Ryerson Press, 1958, *The White Elephant*, Hamilton, Paul's Book Arcade, Sydney, Angus & Robertson, and Toronto, Ryerson Press, 1959, *Fatal Lady* (with Joyce West), Hamilton, Paul's Book Arcade, 1960, *No Sad Songs*, Hamilton, Paul's Book Arcade, 1960, *Tea and Biscuits*, Hamilton, Paul's Book Arcade, 1961, *It's Perfectly Easy*, Hamilton, Paul's Book Arcade, 1962, *Such Nice People* (with Joyce West), Hamilton, Paul's Book Arcade, and Sydney, Angus & Robertson, 1962, *The Long Honeymoon*, Hamilton, Paul's Book Arcade, 1963, *The Mangrove Murder* (with Joyce West), Auckland, Paul's Book Arcade, and London, Angus & Robertson, 1963, *A Change from Mutton*, Hamilton, Paul, and London, Angus & Robertson, 1964, *No Red Herrings* (with Joyce West), Hamilton, Paul's Book Arcade, and London, Angus & Robertson 1964, *Freddie*, a sequel to *Families Are Fun* and *No Sad Songs*, Hamilton, Paul, 1965, *Who Put It There?* (with Joyce West), Hamilton, Paul, and London, Angus & Robertson, 1965, *What Does It*

Matter?, London, Hurst & Blackett, 1966, *Yes, Darling*, London, Hurst & Blackett, 1967, *Turkey at Twelve*, London, Hurst & Blackett, 1968, *Strictly Speaking*, Auckland, Hurst & Blackett, 1969, *Haven't We Met Before?*, London, Hurst & Blackett, 1970, *If I Don't, Who Will?*, Auckland, Hutchinson, 1971, *Shepherd's Pie*, London, Hurst & Blackett, 1972, *First Things First*, Auckland, Hurst & Blackett, 1973, *A Mary Scott Omnibus*, containing *Breakfast at Six*, *Yours to Oblige* and *Pippa in Paradise*, Auckland, Hutchinson, 1973, *It Was Meant*, London, Hurst & Blackett, 1974, *Strangers for Tea*, Auckland and London, Hurst & Blackett, 1975, *Away from It All*, Auckland and London, Hurst & Blackett, 1977, and *Board But No Breakfast*, Auckland, Hutchinson, and London, Hurst & Blackett, 1978. *Days That Have Been*, Auckland, Paul, 1966, is an autobiography. An early article about her appeared in *New Zealand Magazine*, vol. 21, no. 3, 1942.

Maurice Shadbolt 1932-. Novelist and short story writer. His fiction includes *The New Zealanders: A Sequence of Stories*, Christchurch, Whitcombe & Tombs, and London, Gollancz, 1959, New York, Atheneum, 1961, reprinted with an introduction by Cherry Hankin, Christchurch, Whitcombe & Tombs, 1974, this edition reprinted Auckland, Hodder & Stoughton, 1986, *Summer Fires and Winter Country* (short stories), Christchurch, Whitcombe & Tombs, and London, Eyre & Spottiswoode, 1963, New York, Atheneum, 1966, *Among the Cinders*, Christchurch, Whitcombe & Tombs, London, Eyre & Spottiswoode, and New York, Atheneum, 1965, reprinted with an introduction by Stephen Becker, Christchurch, Whitcoulls, 1975, revised edition Auckland, Hodder & Stoughton, 1984, *The Presence of Music: Three Novellas*, London, Cassell, 1967, *This Summer's Dolphin*, London, Cassell, and New York, Atheneum, 1969, *An Ear of the Dragon*, London, Cassell, 1971, *Strangers and Journeys*, London, Hodder & Stoughton, and New York, St Martin's Press, 1972, reprinted London, Coronet Books, 1975, *A Touch of Clay*, London, Hodder & Stoughton, 1974, reprinted Auckland, Oxford University Press, 1987, *Danger Zone*, London, Hodder & Stoughton, 1975, reprinted Auckland, Hodder & Stoughton, 1985, *Figures in Light: Selected Stories*, Auckland, Hodder & Stoughton, 1978, *The Lovelock Version*, London, Hodder & Stoughton, 1980, New York, St Martin's Press, 1981, *Season of the Jew*, London, Hodder & Stoughton, 1986, New York, Norton, 1987, reprinted [England], Sceptre, 1988, and Boston, Godine, 1990, and *Monday's Warriors*, Auckland, Hodder & Stoughton, and London, Bloomsbury, 1990. He has published one play, *Once on Chunuk Bair*, Auckland, Hodder & Stoughton, 1982, and a number of geographical and biographical books. A talk on his literary autobiography appeared in *Landfall*, no. 108, 1973. 'Beginnings', *Islands*, no. 31-32, 1981, is a more personal autobiographical essay.

There is a full bibliography by Murray Gadd, *JNZL*, no. 2, 1984. Jacqueline Amoamo, *Listener*, 7 August 1972, bases a brief account of his life on an interview; other interviews include one with Alister Taylor, *Affairs*, February, 1971, and (also for an article) with Tony Reid, *Listener*, 29 January 1977. There is no significant general review of his work. Bill Pearson, *Comment*, no. 3, 1960, reprinted in *FS*, attacked limitations in the matter and style of *The New Zealanders*, and was echoed more abrasively by Ian Hamilton, *Mate*, no. 4, 1960. A concern with the New Zealandness of the characters of those stories interests Lauris Edmond, *CENZSS*. Peter Simpson's straightforward assessment of *Among the Cinders*, *Landfall*, no. 122, 1977, compares it with *Huckleberry Finn*. K.O. Arvidson in a letter to the editor, *Landfall*, no. 100, 1971, most interestingly declined to review *An Ear of the Dragon*. Lawrence Jones, *CENZN*, reprinted in *BWM*, sympathetically re-examines the common view of *Strangers and Journeys* (e.g. Michael Volkerling's review, *Islands*, no. 5, 1973) that its opening strength is dissipated in the later parts. Carole Durix, *Commonwealth Novel in English*, vol. 2, 1983, finds in *A Touch of Clay* the theme of death defining life; more unusually, Patrick Holland, *WLWE*, vol. 21, 1982, compares it with a Canadian novel to illustrate the use of myths to define a people through their geographical environment. Phillip Mann interviewed Shadbolt on the first production of *Once on Chunuk Bair*, *Illusions*, no. 11, 1989.

Helen Shaw 1913–85. Short story writer and poet. Her collections of stories comprise *The Orange Tree*, Auckland, Pelorus Press, 1957, and *The Gipsies and Other Stories*, Wellington, Victoria University Press, 1978. Her collections of verse include *Out of the Dark: Poems*, London, Mitre Press, 1968, *The Girl of the Gods: A Collection of Helen Shaw's Poems*, ed. Amal Ghose, Madras, Diparun Bros, 1973, *The Word and Flower*, Stevenage, Ore Publications, 1975, *In Dream's Glass*, Kingston-upon-Thames, Court Poetry Press, 1979, *Ambitions of Clouds*, Christchurch, Nag's Head Press, 1981, *This Is My Sorrow: As from Heloise to Abelard: A Sequence of Poems*, Auckland, Griffin Press, 1981, *Circles and Stones*, Stevenage, Ore Publications, 1982, *The Sun's Archives*: Poems, Madras, Tagore Institute of Creative Writing International, 1984, *Leda's Daughter: Poems*, Auckland, Griffin Press, 1985, *On a Dark Mirror: Four Romance Poems*, Auckland, Griffin Press, 1985, and *Time Told from a Tower: Poems*, Christchurch, Nag's Head Press, 1985. She also edited a collection of critical essays on Frank Sargeson, letters and poems by D'Arcy Cresswell, and a collection of religious poems. 'Beginnings', *Islands*, no. 23, 1978, is an autobiographical essay. Robin Dudding, *Listener*, 13 July 1985, provides a useful memorial tribute. She discusses the writing of her own stories in *Pilgrims*, no. 8, 1980. Lawrence Jones, *Islands*, no. 31-32, 1981, also writes about her stories. Riemke Ensing, *Islands*, no. 36, 1985, reviews her life as a writer.

Keith Sinclair 1922-. Historian and poet. His historical works include *The Origins of the Maori Wars*, Wellington, New Zealand University Press, 1957, reprinted Auckland, Auckland University Press, 1961, *A History of New Zealand*, Harmondsworth, Penguin, 1959, revised and enlarged edition, London, Allen Lane, 1980, reprinted Auckland, Penguin, 1988, *William Pember Reeves*, Oxford, Clarendon Press, 1965, *Walter Nash*, Auckland, Auckland University Press, 1976, and *A Destiny Apart: New Zealand's Search for National Identity*,

Wellington, Allen & Unwin, 1986. He has edited *The Oxford Illustrated History of New Zealand*, Auckland, Oxford University Press, 1990. His collections of verse include *Songs for a Summer & Other Poems*, Christchurch, Pegasus, 1952, *Strangers or Beasts: Poems*, Christchurch, Caxton, 1954, *A Time to Embrace*, Auckland, Paul's Book Arcade, 1963, and *The Firewheel Tree*, Auckland, Auckland University Press, 1973. In articles based on interviews, Tony Reid, *Listener*, 6 November 1976, discusses the writing of the Nash biography, and Michael King, *Listener*, 31 August 1985, considers generally his work as a New Zealand historian. W.H. Oliver, *New Zealand Journal of History*, vol. 21, 1987, provides a biographical note on his development as a historian, and in the same volume there is a bibliography of his published work.

Elizabeth Smither 1941-. Poet. Her collections of verse include *Here Come the Clouds: Poems*, Martinborough, A. Taylor, 1975, *You're Very Seductive William Carlos Williams*, Dunedin, McIndoe, 1978, *Little Poems*, New Plymouth, T.J. Mutch, 1979, *The Sarah Train*, Eastbourne, Hawk Press, 1980, *Casanova's Ankle*, Auckland, Oxford University Press, 1981, *The Legend of Marcello Mastroianni's Wife*, Auckland, Auckland University Press, 1981, *Shakespeare Virgins*, Auckland, Auckland University Press, 1983, *Professor Musgrove's Canary*, Auckland, Auckland University Press, 1986, *Animaux*, Wellington, Modern House, 1988, and *A Pattern of Marching*, Auckland, Auckland University Press, 1989. *First Blood*, Auckland, Hodder & Stoughton, 1983, and *Brother-love Sister-love*, Auckland, Hodder & Stoughton, 1986, are two novels. She comments on her own *You're Very Seductive William Carlos Williams* in *Pilgrims*, no. 7, 1979. HL holds a manuscript collection. She was interviewed by Maurice Shadbolt, *Pilgrims*, vol. 3, 1978, by David Dowling, *Landfall*, no. 151, 1984, and by Harry Ricketts in his *Talking about Ourselves*, Wellington, Mallinson Rendel, 1986.

Kendrick Smithyman 1922-. Poet. His collections of verse include *Seven Sonnets*, Auckland, Pelorus Press, 1946, *The Blind Mountain & Other Poems*, Christchurch, Caxton, 1950, *The Gay Trapeze*, Wellington, Handcraft Press, 1955, *The Night Shift: Poems on Aspects of Love* (with James K. Baxter, Charles Doyle and Louis Johnson), Wellington, Capricorn Press, 1957, *Inheritance: Poems*, Hamilton, Paul's Book Arcade, 1962, *Flying to Palmerston: Poems*, Wellington, Oxford University Press for the University of Auckland, 1968, *Earthquake Weather*, Auckland, Auckland University Press, 1972, *The Seal in the Dolphin Pool*, Auckland, Auckland University Press, 1974, *Dwarf with a Billiard Cue*, Auckland, Auckland University Press, 1978, *Stories about Wooden Keyboards*, Auckland, Oxford University Press, 1985, *Are You Going to the Pictures?*, Auckland, Auckland University Press, 1987, and *Selected Poems*, edited with an introduction by Peter Simpson, Auckland, Auckland University Press, 1989. *A Way of Saying*, Auckland, Collins, 1965, is a study of New Zealand poetry. He has also edited novels by William Satchell, as well as the short stories of Greville Texidor. An interview with MacD. P. Jackson appeared in

Landfall, no. 168, 1988. Iain Sharp, *Landfall*, no. 156, 1985, wrote a review of *Stories about Wooden Keyboards*, which was also reviewed especially well by Peter Simpson in the *Listener*, 28 June, 1986. There are two articles on his poetry, by Reg Berry and Murray Edmond, in *Landfall*, no. 168, 1988.

C.K. Stead 1932-. Poet, novelist and critic. His collections of poetry include *Whether the Will Is Free: Poems 1954-62*, Auckland, Paul's Book Arcade, 1962, *Crossing the Bar*, Auckland, Auckland University Press, 1972, *Quesada: Poems*, 1972-74, Auckland, The Shed, 1975, *Walking Westward*, Auckland, The Shed, 1979, *Geographies*, Auckland, Auckland University Press, 1982, *Poems of a Decade*, Dunedin, Pilgrims South Press, 1983, *Paris: A Poem*, Auckland, Auckland University Press, 1984, *Between*, Auckland, Auckland University Press, 1988, and *Voices*, Wellington, GP Books, 1990. His novels comprise *Smith's Dream*, Auckland, Longman Paul, 1971, revised edition 1973, *All Visitors Ashore*, London, Harvill, and Auckland, Collins, 1984, reprinted London, Picador, 1986, *The Death of the Body*, London, Collins, 1986, and *Sister Hollywood*, London, Collins, 1989. *Five for the Symbol*, Auckland, Longman Paul, 1981, is a group of short stories. Critical essays on New Zealand literature are collected in *In the Glass Case*, Auckland, Auckland University Press, 1981; *Answering to the Language*, Auckland, Auckland University Press, 1989, includes essays on English and Australian writers as well. Notable amongst other critical writing is *The New Poetic*, London, Hutchinson University Library, 1964, revised as *The New Poetic: Yeats to Eliot*, Philadelphia, University of Pennsylvania Press, 1987, on Yeats, Pound, and Eliot. He gives an account of his life as a poet, *Islands*, no. 9, 1974, reprinted in *IGC*, and discusses his poetry in an interview with Michael Harlow, *Landfall*, no. 148, 1983. There is another interview with Harry Ricketts in his *Talking about Ourselves*, Wellington, Mallinson Rendel, 1986. Early comment on the poetry is found in reviews, for example E.A. Horsman (*Whether the Will is Free*), *Landfall*, no. 71, 1964, and James Bertram (*Crossing the Bar*), *Islands*, no. 2, 1972. Stead himself writes about *Quesada*, *Pilgrims*, no. 7, 1979, reprinted in *IGC*. Alan Loney, *Islands*, no. 30, 1980, analyses verbal features in *Walking Westward*, and Michael Sharkey, *Pacific Quarterly*, vol. 5, 1980, notes an analytical predilection and weakness of language. Mike Doyle, *Landfall*, no. 144, 1982, is more positively appreciative of Stead's technique in *Geographies*, a volume which is well analysed by K.O. Arvidson, *JNZL*, no. 1, 1983. Dell Boldt provides detailed factual analysis of 'Walking Westward' and 'Scoria' in a thesis, Massey University, 1984. Writing on the fiction, R.T. Robertson, *Ariel*, vol. 6, 1975, finds *Smith's Dream* to be based on limited and reactionary premises, Ian Cross, *Listener*, 10 November 1984, praises the cleverness of *All Visitors Ashore* but regrets the lack of heart, and David Young, *Listener*, 13 October 1984, investigates its literary and personal background. J.-P. Durix, *JCL*, vol. 21, 1986, also provides factual background to the novel, and in his *The Writer Written*, Westport, Connecticut, Greenwood Press, 1987, he discusses the novel as metafiction. Patrick

Hutchings, *JNZL*, no. 1, 1983, believes Stead's narrow concept of the imagination lies behind judgements made in *In the Glass Case*.

Douglas Stewart 1913-85. Poet and playwright. Stewart left New Zealand as a young man and established a considerable reputation as an Australian writer and literary editor of the Sydney *Bulletin*, 1940-60. Books with a New Zealand connection include the early verse collections *Green Lions*, privately published, 1936, *The White Cry*, London, Dent, 1939, *Elegy for an Airman*, Sydney, Frank C. Johnson, 1940, and *Sonnets to the Unknown Soldier*, Sydney, Angus & Robertson, 1941; and *A Girl with Red Hair and Other Stories*, Sydney, Angus & Robertson, 1944. *Collected Poems 1936-1967* was published in 1967, Sydney, Angus & Robertson. *The Golden Lover*, in *The Fire on the Snow [and] The Golden Lover: Two Plays for Radio*, Sydney, Angus & Robertson, 1944, is set in a Māori community. His early life is recounted in *Springtime in Taranaki: An Autobiography of Youth*, Sydney, Hale & Iremonger, and Auckland, Hodder & Stoughton, 1983. There are two separate studies: Nancy Keesing, *Douglas Stewart*, Australian Writers and Their Work, 1965, 2nd edition, Melbourne, Lansdowne Press, 1969, and Clement Semmler, *Douglas Stewart*, TWAS, New York, 1974. A fuller bibliography of works and criticism can be found in *The Oxford History of Australian Literature*, ed. Leonie Kramer, Melbourne, Oxford University Press, 1981.

Essie Summers 1912-. Romance novelist. All her work was published in London by Mills & Boon, and includes *New Zealand Inheritance*, 1957, reprinted 1976 as a Mills & Boon Classic, *Bachelors Galore*, 1958, *The Time and the Place*, 1958, *The Lark in the Meadow*, 1959, *The Master of Tawhai*, 1959, *Moon over the Alps*, 1960, *Come Blossom-Time, My Love*, 1961, *No Roses in June*, 1961, *The House of the Shining Tide*, 1962, *South to Forget*, 1963, *Where No Roads Go*, 1963, *Bride in Flight*, 1964, *The Smoke and the Fire*, 1964, *No Legacy for Lindsay*, 1965, *No Orchids by Request*, 1965, *Sweet Are the Ways*, 1965, *Heir to Windrush Hill*, 1966, *Postscript to Yesterday*, 1966, *A Place Called Paradise*, 1967, *His Serene Miss Smith*, 1967, *Meet on My Ground*, 1968, *Rosalind Comes Home*, 1968, *The Kindled Fire*, 1969, *Revolt — and Virginia*, 1969, *The Bay of the Nightingales*, 1970, *Summer in December*, 1970, *The House on Gregor's Brae*, 1971, *Return to Dragonshill*, 1971, *South Island Stowaway*, 1971, *The Forbidden Valley*, 1973, *A Touch of Magic*, 1973, *The Gold of Noon*, 1974, *Through All the Years*, 1974, *Anna of Strathallan*, 1975, *Beyond the Foothills*, 1976, *Not by Appointment*, 1976, *Adair of Starlight Hills*, 1977, *Goblin Hill*, 1977, *The Lake of the Kingfisher*, 1978, *Spring in September*, 1978, *My Lady of the Fuchsias*, 1979, *One More River to Cross*, 1979, *The Tender Leaves*, 1980, *Autumn in April*, 1981, *Daughter of the Misty Gorges*, 1981, *A Lamp for Jonathan*, 1982, *A Mountain for Luenda*, 1983, *Season of Forgetfulness*, 1983, *MacBride of Tordarroch*, 1984, *Winter in July*, 1984, and *To Bring You Joy*, 1985. *The Essie Summers Story*, 1974, is an autobiography. She contributed a piece on how to write (and how she wrote) a novel to *New Zealand Dairy Exporter*, vol. 35, no. 7, 1960, and H. Paske describes her life and work (based on an interview) in *Listener*, 18 April 1981.

Margaret Sutherland 1941-. Novelist. Her novels include *The Fledgling*, London, Heinemann, 1974, reprinted Auckland, Oxford University Press, 1986, *The Love Contract*, Auckland, Heinemann, 1976, and *The Fringe of Heaven*, Owings Mills, Middlesex, Stemmer House Publishers, and Wellington, Mallinson Rendel, 1984. She has also published *Getting Through and Other Stories*, Auckland, Heinemann, 1977.

Eve Sutton 1906-. Children's writer. Her books include *My Cat Likes to Hide in Boxes*, London, Hamish Hamilton, 1973, New York, Parents' Magazine Press, 1974, reprinted Harmondsworth, Puffin, 1978, *Green Gold*, London, Hamish Hamilton, 1976, *Johnny Sweep*, London, Hamish Hamilton, 1977, *Tuppeny Brown*, London, Hamish Hamilton, 1977, *Moa Hunter*, London, Hamish Hamilton, 1978, *Skip for the Huntaway*, Wellington, Price Milburn, 1983, *Surgeon's Boy*, Wellington, Mallinson Rendel, and Auckland, Ashton Scholastic, 1983, *Kidnapped by Blackbirders*, Wellington, Mallinson Rendel, and Barnstaple, Spindlewood, 1984, and *Valley of Heavenly Gold*, Wellington, Mallinson Rendel, 1987.

William Taylor 1940-. Children's writer. His work for children includes *Pack Up, Pick Up and Off*, Wellington, Price Milburn, 1981, *My Summer of the Lions*, Auckland, Reed Methuen, 1986, *Shooting Through*, Auckland, Reed Methuen, 1986, *Break a Leg!*, Auckland, Reed Methuen, 1987, *Making Big Bucks*, Auckland, Reed Methuen, 1987, *Possum Perkins*, Auckland, Ashton Scholastic, 1987, reprinted as *Paradise Lane*, London, Hutchinson, 1987, *The Worst Soccer Team Ever*, Auckland, Reed Methuen, 1987, *I Hate My Brother Maxwell Potter*, Auckland, Heinemann Reed, 1989, *The Kidnap of Jessie Parker*, Auckland, Heinemann Reed, 1989, and *The Porter Brothers*, Auckland, Collins, 1990. Diane Hebley, *Listener*, 8 August 1987, reported on his writing of children's fiction. He has also written novels for adults.

Mervyn Thompson 1936-. Playwright. His published plays include *First Return*, Christchurch, Christchurch Theatre Trust, 1974, *O! Temperance!*, Christchurch, Christchurch Theatre Trust, 1974, *A Night at the Races*, (with Yvonne Blennerhassett Edwards), Wellington, Playmarket, 1981, *Songs to the Judges*, Wellington, Playmarket, 1983, *Songs to Uncle Scrim*, Wellington, Playmarket, 1983, *Selected Plays*, with an introduction by Sebastian Black, Dunedin, Pilgrims South Press, 1984, and *Coaltown Blues*, Wellington, Victoria University Press, 1986, and *Children of the Poor* (an adaptation of John A. Lee's novel), Christchurch, Hazard Press, 1990. *All My Lives*, Christchurch, Whitcoulls, 1980, is an autobiography. There are interviews about his work at the Court Theatre, *Act*, no. 22, 1974, about *First Return*, *Act*, no. 28, 1975, with David Dowling about *All My Lives*, *Landfall*, no. 136, 1980, and with Patrick

McClennan, *Listener*, 8 January 1990, about his work generally. Sebastian Black, *Listener*, 18 August 1984, is useful on the semi-autobiographical play *Coaltown Blues*. Thompson discusses his musical theatre in *Music in New Zealand*, no. 9, 1990. Richard Corballis's review of *Selected Plays*, *Landfall*, no. 157, 1986, drew a long response from the playwright in issue no. 160.

Mona Tracy 1897-1959. Children's writer. Her books include *Piriki's Princess and Other Stories of New Zealand*, Auckland, Whitcombe & Tombs, 1925, *Rifle and Tomahawk: A Stirring Tale of the Te Kooti Rebellion*, Auckland, Whitcombe & Tombs, 1927, *Lawless Days: A Tale of Adventure in Old New Zealand and the South Seas*, Auckland, Whitcombe & Tombs, 1928, reprinted London, Harrap, 1934, and *Martin Thorne — Adventurer*, Auckland, Whitcombe & Tombs, 1930.

Brian Turner 1944-. Poet. His collections of verse include *Ladders of Rain*, Dunedin, McIndoe, 1978, *Ancestors*, Dunedin, McIndoe, 1981, *Listening to the River*, Dunedin, McIndoe, 1983, *Bones*, Dunedin, McIndoe, 1985, and *All That Blue Can Be*, Dunedin, McIndoe, 1989. He has also written on South Island landscape. He comments on his own *Ladders of Rain* in *Pilgrims*, no. 7, 1979. He was interviewed by Harry Ricketts in his *Talking about Ourselves*, Wellington, Mallinson Rendel, 1986.

Hone Tuwhare 1922-. Poet. His collections of verse include *No Ordinary Sun: Poems*, Auckland, Paul, 1964, third edition revised and enlarged, Dunedin, McIndoe, 1977, *Come Rain Hail: Poems*, Dunedin, Bibliography Room, University of Otago, 1970, reprinted Dunedin, Caveman Press, 1973, and Dunedin, Square One Books, 1989, *Sap-Wood & Milk: Poems*, Dunedin, Caveman Press, 1972, *Something Nothing: Poems*, Dunedin, Caveman Press, 1974, *Making a Fist of It: Poems and Short Stories*, Dunedin, Jackstraw Press, 1978, *Selected Poems*, Dunedin, McIndoe, 1980, *Year of the Dog: Poems New and Selected*, Dunedin, McIndoe, 1982, and *Mihi: Collected Poems*, Auckland, Penguin, 1987. He was interviewed by Jan Coad, *Affairs*, August 1970, and Taura Eruera, *New Argot*, vol. 3, 1975, and also *Koru*, no. 1, 1976. A more recent and extensive interview was with Bill Manhire, *Landfall*, no. 167, 1988. MacD. P. Jackson reviewed *No Ordinary Sun*, *Landfall*, no. 74, 1965. Articles include those by Molly Elliott, *Arts & Community*, vol. 5, June 1969, R. Tamplin, *New Quarterly Cave*, vol. 1, 1976, and Bernard Gadd, *Landfall*, no. 149, 1984, who argues that Tuwhare is truly Māori and working-class in his poetry. Tia Barrett, *Commonwealth*, vol. 7, 1985, attempts to capture that 'Maori dimension' in his poetry.

Phyl Wardell 1909-. Children's writer. Her books include *Gold at Kapai*, Wellington, Reed, 1960, *The Secret of the Lost Tribe of Te Anau*, Wellington, Reed, 1961, *Passage to Dusky*, Wellington, Reed, 1967, *Hazard Island*, Christchurch, Whitcoulls, 1976, and *Beyond the Narrows*, Auckland, Hodder & Stoughton, 1985.

Jean Watson 1935-. Novelist. Her novels include *Stand in the Rain*, Christchurch, Pegasus, 1965, Indianapolis, Babbs-Merrill, 1966, reprinted Wellington, Allen & Unwin/Port Nicholson Press, 1986, *The Balloon Watchers*, Palmerston North, Dunmore Press, 1975, *The World Is an Orange and the Sun*, Palmerston North, Dunmore Press, 1978, *Flowers from Happyever: A Prose Lyric*, Wellington, Voice Press, 1980, and *Address to a King*, Wellington, Allen & Unwin/Port Nicholson Press, 1986. Jill McCracken, *Listener*, 3 July 1972, wrote an article based on an interview, and there is an interview with Pat Rosier in *Broadsheet*, no. 142, 1986. In *Landfall*, no. 163, 1987, Warwick Slinn discusses time in her fiction. Anita Segerberg, *Landfall*, no. 173, 1990, considers *Address to a King* in relation to the novella form.

Ian Wedde 1946-. Poet, novelist and short story writer. His collections of poems include *Homage to Matisse*, London, Amphedesma Press, 1971, *Made Over*, Auckland, Stephen Chan, 1974, *Earthly: Sonnets for Carlos*, Akaroa, Amphedesma Press, 1975, *Pathway to the Sea*, Taylors Mistake, Hawk Press, 1975, *Spells for Coming Out*, Auckland, Auckland University Press, 1977, *Castaly: Poems 1973-1977*, Auckland, Auckland University Press, 1980, *Georgicon*, Wellington, Victoria University Press, 1984, *Tales of Gotham City*, Auckland, Auckland University Press, 1984, *Driving into the Storm: Selected Poems*, Auckland, Oxford University Press, 1987, and *Tendering*, Auckland, Auckland University Press, 1988. His fiction includes *Dick Seddon's Great Dive*, Auckland, Islands, 1976, *The Shirt Factory and Other Stories*, Wellington, Victoria University Press, 1981, *Symmes Hole*, Auckland, Penguin, 1986, and *Survival Arts*, Auckland, Penguin, and London, Faber, 1988. He introduced and with Harvey McQueen edited *The Penguin Book of New Zealand Verse*, Auckland, Penguin, 1985, and, with Harvey McQueen and Miriama Evans, edited *The Penguin Book of Contemporary New Zealand Poetry*, Auckland, Penguin, 1989. He has also written on New Zealand art. He was interviewed by G. Campbell on his fiction, *Listener*, 5 December 1981, by David Dowling, *Landfall*, no. 154, 1985, and by Harry Ricketts on his poetry in his *Talking about Ourselves*, Wellington, Mallinson Rendel, 1986. Peter Crisp, *Islands*, no. 17, 1976, and Lawrence Jones, *Pilgrims*, vol. 3, 1978, provide the best review articles on the earlier poetry. Michele Leggott's thesis, University of Canterbury, 1978, covers the same earlier period. John Needham, *Landfall*, no. 137, 1981, adduces *Pathway to the Sea* to refute C.K. Stead's rejection of 'intelligible sequence' in modern verse, and Mark Williams, *Landfall*, no. 153, 1985, also places the poetry in relation to the literary ideas of both Stead and the younger generation of theorists. Leigh Davis, *And*, no. 4, 1985, offers a difficult Lacanian reading of *Georgicon*, which is also the subject of part of Roger Horrocks's article in the same issue. There is less comment on the fiction, but James Bertram, *Islands*, no. 17, 1976, reprinted in *FP*, on *Dick Seddon's Great Dive*, and Patrick Evans, *Listener*, 22 November 1986, and Alan Riach, *Landfall*, no. 160, 1986, both on *Symmes Hole*, offer thoughtful reviews. Cynthia Brophy, *Landfall*, no. 165,

1988, examines *Symmes Hole* using the term 'postmodern' with its social as much as its literary implication.

Albert Wendt 1939-. Novelist, short story writer and poet. His novels include *Sons for the Return Home*, Auckland, Longman Paul, 1973, *Pouliuli*, Auckland, Longman Paul, 1977, and *Leaves of the Banyan Tree*, Auckland, Longman Paul, 1979, London, Allen Lane, 1980. His collections of stories include *Flying-Fox in a Freedom Tree*, Auckland, Longman Paul, 1974, reprinted Auckland, Penguin, 1988, and *The Birth and Death of the Miracle Man*, Harmondsworth, Viking, 1986. His collections of poems include *Inside Us the Dead: Poems 1961 to 1974*, Auckland, Longman Paul, 1976, and *Shaman of Visions: Poems*, Auckland, Auckland University Press, 1984. There are several interviews: with Marjorie Crocombe, *Mana Annual*, 1973, with J. and R. Beston, *WLWE*, vol. 16, 1977, and with Jim Davidson, *Meanjin*, vol. 37, 1978; Helen Paske's article, *Listener*, 25 March 1978, is based on an interview. Roger Robinson, *Landfall*, no. 135, 1980, offers a general assessment. Alienation and the breakdown of traditional Samoan society (with associated symbolism of darkness) are the theme of Helen Tiffin, *Meanjin*, vol. 37, 1978, and of Margaret Nightingale, *New Literature Review*, no. 9, 1980, and (as Peggy Nightingale) in *Myth and Metaphor*, ed. Robert Sellick, Adelaide, CRNLE, 1982. W.D. Ashcroft, *New Literature Review*, no. 9, 1980, more optimistically notes the success of Wendt's heroes in escaping disorientation and gaining a sense of personal balance and achievement. N. Simms, *Commonwealth Novel in English*, vol. 1, 1982, notes a striking development in fictional skills from the first to the third novel. P. Crisp, *Islands*, no. 26, 1979, discusses *Pouliuli*, and K.O. Arvidson, *Listener*, 10 May 1980, wrote a long review of *Leaves of the Banyan Tree*. R. Beston, *WLWE*, vol. 16, 1977, wrote on the poetry.

Joyce West 1908-85. Children's writer. Her books include *Drover's Road*, London, Dent, 1953, *The Year of the Shining Cuckoo*, Hamilton, Paul's Book Arcade, 1961, London, Dent, 1963, New York, Roy, 1964, reprinted Auckland, Hodder & Stoughton, 1985, *Cape Lost*, Auckland, Paul's Book Arcade, and London, Dent, 1963, *The Golden Country*, Auckland, Paul, and London, Dent, 1965, *The Sea Islanders*, London, Dent, and New York, Roy, 1970, and *The River Road*, London, Dent, 1980. She has also written novels for adults.

David McKee Wright 1869-1928. Poet. His collections of verse include *Aorangi and Other Verses*, Dunedin, Mills, Dick & Co., 1896, *Station Ballads and Other Verses*, Dunedin, J.G. Sawell (Wise's), 1897, *New Zealand Chimes*, Wellington, W.J. Lankshear, 1900, *Wisps of Tussock: New Zealand Rhymes*, Oamaru, Andrew Fraser, 1900, and *An Irish Heart*, Sydney, Angus & Robertston, 1918. *The Station Ballads and Other Verses*, ed. with a biographical introduction by Robert Solway, Auckland, John A. Lee, 1945, is a selection of ballads most of which come from the 1897 collection. Wright was literary editor of the Sydney *Bulletin* for all but a few years of the period 1909-26.

Michael Sharkey reveals his numerous pseudonyms in *Notes and Furphies*, no. 12, 1984, appraises him more generally in *Southerly*, no. 4, 1986, and discusses Wright's satire on the 1890s *Bulletin* writers and bohemians, which Sharkey discovered, in *Australian Literary Studies*, no. 4, 1986.

Notes

Māori Literature: A Survey

1. For an outline of the derivation and dialects of the language see Bruce Biggs, 'The Maori Language Past and Present' in Erik Schwimmer (ed.), *The Maori People in the Nineteen-Sixties* (Longman Paul, Auckland, 1968), pp. 65-84.
2. Details of the survey are provided in Richard A. Benton, *The Flight of the Amokura* (NZCER, Wellington, 1981), pp. 15-24. For discussions of the survival/decline of the language, see Bruce Biggs, *The Complete English-Maori Dictionary* (Oxford University Press/Auckland University Press, Auckland, 1981), p. ix; Andrew Pawley, 'Can the Maori Language Survive?' *Hurupaa* 10 (1989), pp. 12-23; and Walter Hirsh (ed.), *Living Languages* (Heinemann, Auckland, 1987), pp. 63-105.
3. See 'The Maori Language Past and Present' pp. 79-81 regarding this debate. The marking of vowel length remains inconsistent, although use of the macron is more common than the double or unmarked vowel.
4. For a review of these policies, see Biggs, 'The Maori Language Past and Present' pp. 73-7.
5. Ibid. p. 73.
6. *Oral Culture, Literacy and Print in Early New Zealand* (Victoria University Press, Wellington, 1985), pp. 15, 18-19.
7. See: Lyndsay Head and Buddy Mikaere, 'Was Nineteenth-Century Maori Society Literate?' *Archifacts* 2 (1988), pp. 17-20; Judith Binney's review of McKenzie in *Political Science* 38, 1 (1986), pp. 185-6; Claudia Orange's review of McKenzie in *N.Z. Listener* (1 August, 1987), pp. 60-2.
8. Michael Jackson, 'Literacy, Communications and Social Change' in I.H. Kawharu (ed.), *Conflict and Compromise* (A.H. & A.W. Reed, Wellington, 1975), pp. 35-44.
9. These include Tamati Reedy, 'Complex Sentence Formation in Maori' (Ph.D. thesis, University of Hawaii, 1974); W.A. Bauer, 'Aspects of the Grammar of Maori' (Ph.D. thesis, University of Edinburgh, 1981); and M.S. Mutu-Grigg, 'The Manner Particles rawa, tonu, noa, kee, and kau in Maori' (M.A. thesis, University of Auckland, 1982).
10. These bibliographies will be extended by a National Library project to re-catalogue, index, and microfiche all printed Māori to 1960. See Sharon Dell, 'The Maori Book or the Book in Maori' *N.Z. Libraries* 45, 5 (1987), pp. 98-101.
11. See J.G. Laughton and Percy R. Thomas, *New Zealand and the World's First Book* (British and Foreign Bible Society, Wellington, 1964), pp. 14-34.
12. Newspapers are listed (incompletely) in the Williams *Bibliography* and supplements. A full listing of all newspapers in Māori is due in the forthcoming bilingual publication from the National Library of Gail Dallimore's 'A Bibliography of Maori Newspapers'.
13. Acts of Parliament are listed under 'Ture' in the index to the Williams *Bibliography*, and number over 100.
14. See: the Foreword, 'Learning and Tapu' in Michael King (ed.), *Te Ao Hurihuri* (Methuen, Auckland, 1975), pp. 7-13; and Michael King, 'Some Maori Attitudes to Documents' in Michael King (ed.), *Tihe Mauri Ora* (Methuen, Auckland, 1978), pp. 9-18.
15. The collection, known as the Grey Maori Manuscripts (GNZMMSS), is housed in the Auckland Public Library. It went first to the South African Public Library at Capetown in 1861, but was returned after negotiations to the Auckland Public Library in 1922-1923.
16. Two examples of his writing can be seen in Jenifer Curnow's 'Te Rangikaheke, Wiremu Maihi; A Book Describing the Murder of Te Hunga, the History of the Wars Formerly Carried on Between the Tribes of Rotorua and Waikato' *Journal of the Polynesian Society* 99, 1 (1990), pp. 7-54; 99, 2 (1990), pp. 128-77. (This journal is subsequently referred to as *JPS*.)
17. Edward Shortland's papers are held in the Hocken Library, Dunedin; the papers of John White, S. Percy Smith, and Elsdon Best (some of which also form part of the Polynesian Society Papers) are in the Alexander Turnbull Library, Wellington, and those of George Graham are located in the Auckland Museum Library and the Auckland Public Library.
18. 'Nga Whawhai o Ngapuhi', Auckland Museum Library MS 165.
19. Himiona Kamira Papers, Auckland Museum Library MS 693.
20. Himiona Kamira, 'The Story of Kupe' *JPS* 66, 3 (1957), pp. 217-48.
21. Auckland Public Library, GNZMMSS 1. A translation of the notebook and history of the faith are given in Paul Clark, *'Hauhau'. The Pai Marire Search for Maori Identity* (Auckland University Press, Auckland, 1975).
22. See Judith Binney, 'Myth and Explanation in the Ringatū Tradition' *JPS* 93, 4 (1984), pp. 345-98; also, William Greenwood, *The Upraised Hand* (Polynesian Society, Wellington, 1942), p. 68.
23. *The Upraised Hand*, pp. 89-90.
24. 'Myth and Explanation in the Ringatū Tradition' p. 380.
25. Mantell Family Papers, MS Papers 83; McLean Papers, MS Papers 32, Alexander Turnbull Library. Letters to McLean published in H. Kamariera, *McLean Papers: Selected Readings in Maori* (Massey University, Palmerston North, 1975).
26. Minute books of the Court are held in the regional offices of the Maori Land Court.
27. The Papatupu Block Committee minute books are held in the Whangarei office of the Maori Land Court.
28. 'A Vienna Journal' *Te Ao Hou* 24 (1958), pp. 38-43; 25 (1958), pp. 20-7.
29. For details about this press and others owned and operated by Māori, see W.J. Cameron, 'A Printing Press for the Maori People' *JPS* 67, 3 (1958), pp. 203-10; and Johannes Andersen, 'Maori Printers and Translators' in R.A. McKay (ed.), *A History of Printing in New Zealand* (R.A. McKay, Wellington, 1940), pp. 33-47.
30. The proceedings are: *Nga Korero o te Hui o te Whakakotahitanga i tu ki Te Tiriti o Waitangi* (Wiremu Makara,

Auckland, 1892); *Paremata Maori o Niu Tireni — Nohonga Tuatahi — i tu ki Te Waipatu* (Webbe & Co., Otaki, 1892); *Paremata Maori — Waipatu* (Wiremu Makara, Auckland, 1893); and *Tuunga Tuawha o te Paremata o te Kotahitanga o te Iwi Maori o Nui Tireni* (Wiremu Makara, Auckland, 1895). They are held in the Alexander Turnbull Library, Wellington.

31. Comments on its influence can be found in Allen Curnow (ed.), *The Penguin Book of New Zealand Verse* (Harmondsworth, Penguin, 1960), p. 71; and in Antony Alpers, *Maori Myths and Tribal Legends* (Longman Paul, Auckland, 1964) pp. 5-6.

32. See: David Simmons, 'The Sources of Sir George Grey's *Nga Mahi a Nga Tupuna' JPS* 75, 1 (1966), pp. 177-88; and Bruce Biggs, 'The Translating and Publishing of Maori Material in the Auckland Public Library' *JPS* 61, 2 (1952), pp. 180-2.

33. There is a transcription and translation by David Simmons, 'The Taonui Manuscript' *Records of the Auckland Institute and Museum* 12 (1975), pp. 57-82.

34. See M.P.J. Reilly, 'John White: An Examination of His Use of Maori Oral Tradition and the Role of Authenticity' (M.A. thesis, Victoria University, 1985), p. 151.

35. These articles appeared in the *Appendix to the Journals of the House of Representatives*, 1880, G-8, pp. 1-31.

36. John White Papers, MS Papers 75B, Alexander Turnbull Library.

37. See 'John White: An Examination of His Use of Maori Oral Tradition . . .' pp. 1-8 and 447-58.

38. See Bruce Biggs and David Simmons, 'The Sources of *The Lore of the Whare-Wananga' JPS* 79, 1 (1970), pp. 22-42.

39. See: T.H. Smith, 'On Maori Proverbs' *Transactions and Proceedings of the New Zealand Institute* 22 (1890), pp. 111-18; S. Percy Smith, 'The History of Otakanini Pa, Kaipara' *TPNZI* 28 (1896), pp. 41-7; and W.L. Buller, 'The Story of Papaitonga, or a Page of Maori History' *TPNZI* 26 (1894), pp. 572-84.

40. See: Timi Waata Rimini, 'The Fall of Manga-a-kahia Pa' *JPS* 1 (1892), pp. 147-53; Takaanui Tarakawa, 'Ko te Hoenga Mai o Te Arawa, Raua ko Tainui i Hawaiki' *JPS* 2 (1893), pp. 220-51; and Paora Tuhaere, 'An Historical Narrative Concerning the Conquest of Kaipara and Tamaki by Ngati Whatua' *JPS* 32 (1923), pp. 229-37.

41. For example, Bruce Biggs, 'The Translating and Publishing of Maori Material . . .' pp. 183-91; and Margaret Orbell, 'Two Versions of the Maori Story Te Tahi-o-te-Rangi' *JPS* 82, 2 (1973), pp. 127-40.

42. Sir Apirana Ngata, *Te Tiriti o Waitangi: He Whakamarama* (Maori Purposes Fund Board, Wellington, 1922); 'The Maori and Printed Matter' in *A History of Printing in New Zealand* (R.A. McKay, Wellington, 1940), pp. 48-9. For a list of Ngata's writing in Māori and English see R.N. Erwin, *Apirana Ngata: A Preliminary Bibliography of his Printed Work* (National Library Service, Wellington, 1964).

43. Two examples of these monographs are: Melodie Watson and Margaret Orbell, *Two Maori Stories from Marlborough* (Christchurch, 1983); and Agathe Thornton, *Te Uamairangi's Lament for His House* (Christchurch, 1986).

44. These were all published by Victoria University, Wellington: Ruka Broughton, *Ko Ngaa Tuhituhi a Te Kaahui Kararehe o Taranaki ki a Te Mete 1893-1906* (Department of Maori Studies, 1984); Hirini Mead, *Nga Taonga Tuku Iho a Ngati Awa: Ko Nga Tuhituhinga a Hamiora Pio, Te Teko (1885 -1887)* (Department of Maori Studies, 1981); and Te Kapunga Dewes, *Nga Waiata Haka a Henare Waitoa* (Department of Anthropology, 1981).

45. See: Robert Te Kotahi Mahuta, 'Whaikorero: A Study of Formal Maori Speech' (M.A. thesis, University of Auckland, 1974); S.M. Mead, 'Imagery, Symbolism and Social Values in Maori Chant' *JPS* 78, 3 (1969), pp. 378-404; Sam Karetu, 'Language and Protocol on the Marae' in King (ed.), *Te Ao Hurihuri*, pp. 31-44; and Te Kapunga Dewes, 'The Case for the Oral Arts' in King (ed.), *Te Ao Hurihuri*, pp. 46-63.

46. See: S.M. Mead, 'Imagery, Symbolism and Social Values in Maori Chants' *JPS* 78, 3 (1969), pp. 381-2; and Miriama Evans, Harvey McQueen, and Ian Wedde (eds), *The Penguin Book of Contemporary New Zealand Poetry* (Penguin Books, Auckland, 1989), p. 19.

47. See: Te Raumoa Balneavis, 'Nga Whakatauki' *Te Wananga* II, 1 (1930), pp. 18-20; Arapeta Awatere and Koro Dewes, *Te Kawa o te Marae* (Department of Anthropology, Victoria University, Wellington, n.d.); *Nga Waiata Haka a Henare Waitoa*; and Timoti Karetu, *Nga Waiata me Nga Haka a Te Kapa Haka o Te Whare Wananga o Waikato* (Waikato University, Hamilton, 1987).

48. See: Raymond Firth, 'Proverbs in Native Life with Special Reference to those of the Maori' *Folklore* 32, 2 (1926), pp. 134-54 and 245-70; and Jane McRae, 'Whakataukii. Maori Sayings' (Ph.D. thesis, University of Auckland, 1988).

49. See: *Nga Waiata Haka a Henare Waitoa* and *Nga Waiata me Nga Haka a Te Kapa Haka o Te Whare Wananga o Waikato*.

50. There is a general note about women composers in Sir Apirana Ngata and Pei Te Hurinui Jones's *Nga Moteatea* Part II (Polynesian Society, 1961), p. xi. See also songs by Topeora in *Nga Moteatea* Part I (A.H. & A.W. Reed, Wellington, 1959), Nos. 48, 49, and 70; and an account of Puhiwahine's life in Pei Te Hurinui Jones, *Puhiwahine: Maori Poetess* (Pegasus Press, Christchurch, 1961).

51. *The Penguin Book of New Zealand Verse* (Harmondsworth, Auckland, 1960), pp. 68-87.

52. See Ian Wedde and Harvey McQueen, *The Penguin Book of New Zealand Verse* (Penguin Books, Auckland, 1985), pp. 53-61.

53. *The Penguin Book of Contemporary New Zealand Poetry* (Penguin Books, Auckland, 1989), pp. 19-23.

54. For example, Maori Publications, Kopeopeo, Whakatane; and Mahia Publishers, Mahia. See also Miriama Evans, 'Politics and Maori Literature' *Landfall* 39 (1985), pp. 40-5.

Non-fiction

1. William Pember Reeves, *The Long White Cloud: Ao Tea Roa,* 2nd edn. (Horace Marshall and Son, London, 1899; first published in 1898), p. 415.

2. Karl Marx, *Capital*, 3 vols. (Progress Publishers, Moscow, 1954), vol. 1, p. 712.

3. A suitably compact statement of the place of writing in a migrant society — in this case Australia — is: Paul Gillen, 'Mightier than the Sword?' in Verity Burgmann and Jenny Lee (eds), *Constructing a Culture* (McPhee Gribble/Penguin,

Fitzroy and Ringwood, 1988), pp. 190-208. See also: P.J. Gibbons, 'A Note on Writing, Identity, and Colonisation in Aotearoa' *Sites* 13 (1986), pp. 32-8.

4. Andrew Sharp, *The Voyages of Abel Janszoon Tasman* (Clarendon Press, Oxford, 1968), p. 36. This book is hereafter referred to as *Voyages*.

5. On the archive and its constitutive effects, see: Daniel Defert, 'The Collection of the World: Accounts of Voyages from the Sixteenth to the Eighteenth Centuries' *Dialectical Anthropology* 7 (1982), pp. 11-20.

6. Sharp, *Voyages*, p. 36.

7. J.C. Beaglehole (ed.), *The Journals of Captain James Cook*, 3 vols. (Cambridge University Press for Hakluyt Society, Cambridge, 1955-1967), vol. 1, p. 278; J.C. Beaglehole (ed.), *The Endeavour Journal of Joseph Banks*, 2 vols. (Trustees of Public Library of New South Wales/Angus and Robertson, Sydney, 1962), vol. 2, pp. 1, 3.

8. Fanny Burney, cited by Beaglehole, *Journals of . . . Cook*, vol. 1, p. ccxliii. On Hawkesworth's work see: W.H. Pearson, 'Hawkesworth's Alterations' *Journal of Pacific History* 7 (1972), pp. 45-72.

9. John Savage, *Some Account of New Zealand* (Murray and Constable, Edinburgh, 1807), pp. v-vi; A.G. Bagnall (ed.), *New Zealand National Bibliography to the Year 1960*, 5 vols. (Government Printer, Wellington, 1969-1985), vol. 1, p. 924.

10. The seminal work is: Bernard Smith, *European Vision and the South Pacific 1768-1850* (Oxford University Press, London, 1960).

11. William Yate, *An Account of New Zealand* (Seeley and Burnside, London, 1835), pp. 80-1.

12. Augustus Earle, in E.H. McCormick (ed.), *A Narrative of a Nine Months' Residence* (Clarendon Press, Oxford, 1966; first published 1832), pp. 88, 114-15, 193.

13. J.S. Polack, *New Zealand: Being a Narrative of Travels and Adventures*, 2 vols. (Bentley, London, 1838), vol. 1, p. 163.

14. Charles Heaphy, *Narrative of a Residence* (Smith, Elder, London, 1842), pp. vii, 66.

15. Alexander Marjoribanks, *Travels in New Zealand* (Smith Elder, London, 1846), p. 167.

16. Hopeful [pseud.], *'Taken In'* (Allen, London, 1887), pp. 140, 176, 182.

17. E.J. Wakefield, *Adventure in New Zealand*, 2 vols. (Murray, London, 1845), vol. 2, pp. 108, 529-30.

18. Ernest Dieffenbach, *Travels in New Zealand*, 2 vols. (Murray, London, 1843), vol. 1, p. 117.

19. Wakefield, *Adventure in New Zealand*, vol. 1, p. 173; Dieffenbach, *Travels in New Zealand*, vol. 2, pp. 171-3.

20. George Grey, *Polynesian Mythology* (Routledge and Sons, London, 1906; first published 1855), pp. vii-xiv; Antony Alpers, *The World of the Polynesians* (Oxford University Press, Auckland, 1987), p. xvi.

21. Richard Taylor, *Te Ika a Maui* (Wertheim and Macintosh, London, 1855), pp. 2-6, 270-8, 465-6.

22. Edward Shortland, *Traditions and Superstitions of the New Zealanders*, 2nd edn. (Longman, Brown, Green etc., London, 1856; first published 1854), pp. 98-9.

23. William Swainson, *New Zealand and its Colonization* (Smith, Elder, London, 1859), p. vii.

24. A.S. Thomson, *The Story of New Zealand*, 2 vols. (Murray, London, 1859), vol. 1, p. iii; vol. 2, p. 341.

25. Ibid. vol. 1, p. 67.

26. Ibid. vol. 1, p. 225; vol. 2, pp. 294-6, 305-7.

27. Octavius Hadfield, *One of England's Little Wars* (Williams & Norgate, London, 1860), pp. 3, 9, 21, 24-5.

28. J.E. Gorst, *The Maori King* (Macmillan, London, 1864), pp. 75, 77, 400, 403.

29. James E. Alexander, *Incidents of the Maori War* (Bentley, London, 1864), pp. vi, 374-5.

30. F.E. Maning, *Old New Zealand* (Creighton, Auckland, 1863), p. 1.

31. Ibid. p. 3.

32. Ibid. pp. 64, 188, 230.

33. Ibid. p. 231. The reading of Maning offered above draws very substantially upon: Joan FitzGerald, 'Images of the Self: Two Early New Zealand Autobiographies' *Journal of Commonwealth Literature* 22, 1 (1988), pp. 16-42.

34. James Belich, *The New Zealand Wars* (Auckland University Press, Auckland, 1986), p. 313.

35. For Virginia see: Peter Hulme, *Colonial Encounters* (Methuen, London, 1986), Chapter 4.

36. William Fox, *The War in New Zealand* (Smith, Elder, London, 1866), p. 261.

37. John Rochfort, *The Adventures of a Surveyor* (Bogue, London, 1853), p. i; Charles L. Money, *Knocking about in New Zealand* (Mullin, Melbourne, 1871), p. 130.

38. Samuel Butler, in A.R. Streatfeild (ed.) *A First Year in Canterbury Settlement* (Cape, London, 1923; first published 1863), pp. 31, 49.

39. Ibid. pp. 33, 54, 66, 76, 119.

40. J.L. Campbell, *Poenamo* (Williams and Norgate, London, 1881), pp. ix, 98, 310, 353, 357.

41. Sarah Amelia Courage, *Lights and Shadows of Colonial Life* (Whitcoulls, Christchurch, 1976; first published c. 1896), pp. 42, 61, 159, 241.

42. James McIndoe, *A Sketch of Otago* (Wheeler, Dunedin, 1878), pp. 2, 3.

43. Thomas Brunner, *Journal of an Expedition* (Printed by Charles Elliott at *Examiner* Office, Nelson, 1848), pp. 12, 13.

44. Quoted in H.F von Haast, *The Life and Times of Sir Julius von Haast* (Haast, Wellington, 1948), p. 423.

45. Arthur P. Harper, *Pioneer Work in the Alps of New Zealand* (Unwin, London, 1896), pp. 140, 199, 315; John Pascoe, *Great Days in New Zealand Exploration* (Reed, Wellington, 1958), p. 180.

46. T.H. Potts, *Out in the Open* (Lyttelton Times, Christchurch, 1882), p. 45.

47. W.L. Buller, *A History of the Birds of New Zealand*, 2nd edn., 2 vols. (Buller, London, 1888), vol. 1, pp. 27, 28-9. See also: Ross Galbreath, *Walter Buller: the Reluctant Conservationist* (Government Printer, Wellington, 1989), pp. 159-66.

48. Some of these matters are discussed in Keith Sinclair, *A Destiny Apart* (Allen and Unwin/Port Nicholson Press, Wellington, 1986), Chapters 3 through 10. An important discussion is: J.O.C. Phillips, 'Musings in Maoriland — or was there a *Bulletin* School in New Zealand?' *Historical Studies* 20 (1983), pp. 520-35.

49. E.M. Bourke, *A Little History of New Zealand*, 2nd edn. (Robertson, Melbourne, 1882: first published in 1881), pp. v, 94.

50. Quoted in Keith Sinclair, *William Pember Reeves: New Zealand Fabian* (Clarendon Press, Oxford, 1965), p. 232.

51. W.P. Reeves, *Long White Cloud*, p. v.
52. Ibid. p. vi.
53. Ibid. pp. 19, 26.
54. Ibid. p. 166.
55. Ibid. pp. 1, 204, 229.
56. Reeves, *Long White Cloud*, 4th edn. (Allen and Unwin, London, 1950), p. 304.
57. W.P. Reeves, *State Experiments in Australia and New Zealand,* 2 vols (Grant Richards, London, 1902), vol. 1, p. v.
58. Elsdon Best, as reported by J.C. Andersen, *The Lure of New Zealand Book Collecting* (Whitcombe and Tombs, Christchurch, 1936), p. 87.
59. Edward Tregear, *The Aryan Maori* (Government Printer, Wellington, 1885), pp. 1, 103, 104.
60. S.P. Smith, *Hawaiki*, 4th edn. (Whitcombe and Tombs, Christchurch, 1921; first published in 1898), p. 13.
61. For a discussion of these matters, see M.P.K. Sorrenson, *Maori Origins and Migrations* (Auckland University Press/ Oxford University Press, Auckland, 1979).
62. Elsdon Best, *Waikare-moana* (Government Printer, Wellington, 1897), pp. iii-iv, 1.
63. James Cowan, 'Domett and his work Ranolf and Amohia' *New Zealand Illustrated Magazine* 5, 3 (December 1901), pp. 214-23, the quotation on p. 216.
64. O.N. Gillespie (ed.), *New Zealand Short Stories* (Dent, London, 1930), pp. v-vii; James Cowan, *Hero Stories of New Zealand* (H.H. Tombs, Wellington, 1935), pp. vii, ix.
65. Ibid. p. x.
66. James Cowan, *The New Zealand Wars*, 2nd edn., 2 vols. (Government Printer, Wellington 1955-1956; first published in 1922-1923), vol. 1, pp. 1, 25-6.
67. J.C. Andersen, *Maori Life in Ao-tea* (Whitcombe and Tombs, Christchurch, 1907), p. v.
68. L. Cockayne, *New Zealand Plants and their Story*, 2nd edn. (Government Printer, Wellington, 1919; first published in 1910), pp. v, 35-6, 103.
69. Ibid. p. 46.
70. Elsdon Best, review in *New Zealand Journal of Science and Technology* 5 (1923), pp. 59-61; W.H. Guthrie-Smith, *Tutira; The Story of a New Zealand Sheep Station* (Blackwood, Edinburgh, 1921), pp. 255, 346-7.
71. Best, review, loc. cit.
72. Guthrie-Smith, *Tutira*, 3rd edn. (Blackwood, Edinburgh, 1953), pp. 327, 329.
73. Henry Brett and Henry Hook, *The Albertlanders: Brave Pioneers of the 'Sixties* (Brett, Auckland, 1927), p. 5.
74. Ibid. p. 135; Robert Gilkison, *Early Days in Central Otago*, 2nd edn. (Whitcombe and Tombs, Christchurch, 1936; first published in 1930), p. 104; Gilkison, Preface to first edition reprinted in *Early Days*, 4th edn. (Whitcombe and Tombs, Christchurch, 1978), p. xii.
75. A.E. Mulgan, *The Making of a New Zealander* (Reed, Wellington, 1958), p. 30; Mulgan, *Home*, Swan Library edn. (Longmans, Green, London, 1934; first published in 1927), p. 145.
76. J.C. Beaglehole, *New Zealand: A Short History* (Allen and Unwin, London, 1936), pp. 158-9. An important essay is: Stevan Eldred-Grigg, 'A Bourgeois Blue? Nationalism and Letters from the 1920s to the 1950s' *Landfall* 41 (September 1987), pp. 293-311. W.L. Renwick, ' "Show Us These Islands and Ourselves . . . Give us a Home in Thought" ' *New Zealand Journal of History* 21 (1987), pp. 197-214, praises the inventors of 'identity' while expressing 'shock' (p. 201) that 'Maori people' were left out of this construction by J.C. Beaglehole and others. See also E.H. McCormick, *Letters and Art in New Zealand* (Department of Internal Affairs, Wellington, 1940), pp. 1-24, 123-5, 148-56.
77. Nancy Taylor (ed.), *Early Travellers in New Zealand* (Clarendon Press, Oxford, 1959), pp. v, vi.
78. J.C. Beaglehole, 'The New Zealand Scholar' in Peter Munz (ed.), *The Feel of Truth* (Reed for Victoria University of Wellington, Wellington, 1969), pp. 235-52, quotation on p. 251. This lecture was first published in 1954. See also Mary Boyd, 'Women in the Historical Profession' *Women's Studies Journal* 4 (September 1988), pp. 76-87.
79. F.L.W. Wood, *New Zealand in the World* (Department of Internal Affairs, Wellington, 1940), p. 133.
80. Harold Miller, *New Zealand* (Hutchinson, London, 1950), p. 7.
81. W.H. Oliver, *The Story of New Zealand* (Faber, London, 1960), pp. 20, 288. See also: K.A. Pickens, 'The Writing of New Zealand History: a Kuhnian Perspective' *Historical Studies* 17 (1977), pp. 384-98.
82. See W.H. Oliver, 'A Destiny at Home' *New Zealand Journal of History* 21 (1987), pp. 9-15.
83. Keith Sinclair, *A History of New Zealand* (Penguin, Harmondsworth, Middlesex, 1959), p. 269.
84. Ibid. pp. 123, 125.
85. Ibid. pp. 276, 296.
86. Keith Sinclair, 'On Writing Shist' *Historical Studies* 13 (1968), pp. 426-32, quotations on p. 429; Sinclair, *History*, pp. 41, 247, 278.
87. Sinclair, 'Writing Shist' p. 427.
88. W.H. Oliver, *Challenge and Response* (East Coast Development Research Association, Gisborne, 1971), pp. 9, 10, 233, 240; Evelyn Stokes, *A History of Tauranga County* (Dunmore, Palmerston North, 1980), p. 10.
89. Oliver Duff, *New Zealand Now* (Department of Internal Affairs, Wellington, 1941), pp. 123-4.
90. John Mulgan, *Report on Experience* (Oxford University Press, Auckland, 1984; first published in 1947), pp. 14-15.
91. D.M. Davin, *Crete* (War History Branch, Department of Internal Affairs, Wellington, 1953), p. 89.
92. John Pascoe, *Unclimbed New Zealand* (Allen and Unwin, London, 1939), pp. 26, 161; Pascoe, *Land Uplifted High* (Whitcombe and Tombs, Christchurch, 1952), p. 19. Barry Brailsford, *Greenstone Trails* (Reed, Wellington, 1984), indicates the extent of Pākehā reliance on Māori knowledge.
93. Pascoe, *Great Days in New Zealand Exploration* (Reed, Wellington, 1959), p. 12; Pascoe, *Uplifted,* p. 207.
94. E.H. McCormick, *Alexander Turnbull: His Life, His Circle, His Collections* (Alexander Turnbull Library, Wellington, 1974), p. xiii.

95. James Clifford, '"Hanging Up Looking Glasses at Odd Corners": Ethnobiographical Prospects' in Daniel Aaron (ed.), *Harvard English Studies in Biography* (Harvard University Press, Cambridge, Massachusetts, 1978), pp. 41-56, quotation on p. 44.

96. Pascoe, *Land Uplifted*, pp. 99-100, 150-1, See also: Pip Lynch, 'Women Mountaineers' *New Zealand Alpine Journal* 38 (1985), pp. 129-30; M.B. Scott, 'Women Climbers of New Zealand' *New Zealand Alpine Journal* 10 (1943), pp. 22-3.

97. N.E. Coad, *New Zealand from Tasman to Massey* (H.H. Tombs, Wellington, 1934), p. 280.

98. Helen M. Simpson, *The Women of New Zealand* (Department of Internal Affairs, Wellington, 1940), pp. viii, 163.

99. A.E. Woodhouse (ed.), *Tales of Pioneer Women*, 2nd edn. (Whitcombe and Tombs, Christchurch, 1940), p. xv.

100. Helen Wilson, *My First Eighty Years*, 4th edn. (Paul, Hamilton, 1955; first published in 1950), pp. 76, 79, 168, 169, 184.

101. Nancy Ellison, *The Whirinaki Valley* (Paul, Hamilton, 1956), p. 205.

102. Jean Boswell, *Dim Horizons* (Whitcombe and Tombs, Christchurch, 1956), pp. 2, 105, 176-7.

103. Amelia Howe, *Stamper Battery* (Paul, Hamilton, 1964), pp. 5, 6, 101, 125.

104. Shelagh Cox and Bev James, 'The Theoretical Background' in Shelagh Cox (ed.), *Public and Private Worlds* (Allen and Unwin/Port Nicholson Press, Wellington, 1987), p. 2.

105. Phillida Bunkle, *Second Opinion* (Oxford University Press, Auckland, 1988), p. ix; Sandra Coney, *The Unfortunate Experiment* (Penguin, Auckland, 1988), p. 9.

106. Michael King, *Being Pakeha* (Hodder and Stoughton, Auckland, 1985), pp. 7, 39-40.

107. Donna Awatere, *Maori Sovereignty* (Broadsheet, Auckland, 1984), pp. 11, 60, 66. See also: Keith Sinclair, *A History of New Zealand*, rev. ed. (Penguin, Harmondsworth, Middlesex, 1988), p. 329.

108. Walter D'Arcy Cresswell, *Present Without Leave* (Cassell, London, 1939), p. 184.

109. Ibid. p. 199.

110. Cresswell, *The Poet's Progress* (Faber, London, 1930), p. 94.

111. Cresswell, *Present Without Leave*, pp. 1-2.

112. See also: Dennis McEldowney, 'Recent Literary Biography' in *Journal of New Zealand Literature* 2 (1984), pp. 47-57; Lawrence Jones, *Barbed Wire and Mirrors* (University of Otago Press, Dunedin, 1987), pp. 222-42.

113. Charles Brasch, *Indirections* (Oxford University Press, Wellington, 1980), pp. 360, 391.

114. Sylvia Ashton-Warner, *I Passed This Way* (Reed, Wellington, 1979), pp. vii-ix, 51.

115. Ibid. pp. 196, 347, 355.

116. M.H. Holcroft, *The Way of a Writer* (Cape Catley, Whatamongo Bay, 1984), pp. 1-2.

117. M.H. Holcroft, *A Sea of Words* (Cape Catley, Whatamongo Bay, 1986), pp. 202-3.

118. M.H. Holcroft, *The Way of a Writer*, pp. 75, 148, 178, 185.

119. M.H. Holcroft, *A Sea of Words*, p. 201.

120. Frank Sargeson, *Once is Enough* (Reed, Wellington, 1973), p. 44.

121. Ibid. pp. 46-8.

122. Ibid. pp. 10-11.

123. Sargeson, *Never Enough!* (Reed, Wellington, 1977), p. 54.

124. Sargeson, *More Than Enough* (Reed, Wellington, 1975), pp. 29-30, 77; Sargeson, *Never Enough!*, p. 73.

125. Sargeson, *More Than Enough*, pp. 92, 111.

126. Ibid. p. 95.

127. Ibid. p. 112.

128. *Never Enough!*, pp. 24-5.

129. *More Than Enough*, p. 149.

130. Ibid. p. 154.

131. Janet Frame, *To the Is-land* (Women's Press in association with Hutchinson, London and Auckland, 1984; first published in 1983), pp. 19, 59, 159.

132. Ibid. pp. 96, 138.

133. Janet Frame, *An Angel at My Table* (Hutchinson, Auckland, 1985; first published in 1984), p. 163.

134. Ibid. pp. 67-8, 75.

135. Janet Frame, *The Envoy from Mirror City* (Hutchinson, Auckland, 1986; first published in 1985), pp. 20, 27, 54.

136. Ibid. pp. 141-2, 176.

137. Ibid. pp. 151-4.

138. Antony Alpers, *Katherine Mansfield* (Cape, London, 1954), pp. 6-7.

139. Ibid. pp. 95, 193.

140. Ibid. pp. 322-3.

141. Lynley Hood, *Sylvia!* (Viking, Auckland, 1988), p. 9.

142. J.C. Beaglehole, *The Life of Captain James Cook* (Black, London, 1974), p. xi; Beaglehole (ed.), *Journals of . . . Cook*, vol. 1, p. cxciii.

143. Beaglehole (ed.), *Journals of . . . Cook*, vol. 2, p. 2.

144. Ibid. vol. 1, pp. ccx-ccxii.

The Novel

1. The basic distinction between Colonial and Provincial (although not in those terms) is, of course, everywhere in Allen Curnow's criticism of New Zealand poetry, most explicitly in his introduction to the *Penguin Book of New Zealand Verse* (1960). Peter Simpson introduced the terminology and defined the periods more systematically in relation to Canterbury poetry in his 'From Colonial to Provincial: The Evolution of Poetry in Canterbury 1850-1950' (*Historical News*,

November 1981, pp. 10-16), and his subdivision of the 'Colonial' into the 'settler' and the 'colonial-born' generations roughly parallels the present distinction between 'Pioneer' and 'Late Colonial'. For the distinction between 'Provincial' and 'Post-provincial', see below, note 58. For an earlier attempt at periodization in New Zealand literature as a whole see Lawrence Jones, 'Versions of the Dream: Literature and the Search for Identity', in *Culture and Identity in New Zealand*, eds David Novitz and Bill Wilmott (GP Books, Wellington, 1989), pp. 187-211.

2. Descriptive advertisement in William Henry Kingston, *Holmwood; or, The New Zealand Settler: A Tale* (Griffin and Farrar, London, n.d., but Burns lists 1869, Turnbull Library copy pencilled 1867), end papers.

3. In addition to his separately published novels, Pyke published in periodicals such stories as 'Under the Wattles: A Pastoral Idyll' (*New Zealand Illustrated Annual*, December 1880, pp. 50-62), which is really a truncated novel. It is possible that other Pyke novels were serialized in periodicals but did not appear (or have not survived) as separate books. *Eustace Egremont*, mentioned by Clara Cheeseman in a critical article of 1903, 'Colonials in Fiction', (*New Zealand Illustrated Magazine*, January 1903, p. 275) was perhaps such a novel.

4. Stoney, (W.C. Wilson, Auckland, 1861), p. 9; Lusk, 'New Zealand Wars, and their Chroniclers', *Chapman's New Zealand Magazine* 1 (1862), pp. 80-84; for this and subsequent notes, when there is more than one reference within a paragraph, the note will include all the references for that paragraph, in order, identified by author or title.

5. (E.A. Howard, Brisbane, 1906), p. 6.

6. Ferguson, Foreword to 4th edn., *Bush Life in Australia and New Zealand* (Sands & Co., Edinburgh, 1908); in the preface to his *Poems of the Heart* (James Horsburgh, Dunedin, 1897), Ferguson refers to *Bush Life* as 'my autobiographical novel'; Bathgate, (Sampson, Low, Marston, Searle, and Rivington, London, 1881), p. v; Cottle, (H. Brett, Auckland, 1891), Preface.

7. See Carol A. Legge, 'A Transcription of Dumont D'Urville's Manuscript *Les Zelandais Histoire Australienne* and the Accompanying Notes, Followed by a Study of Some Literary and Historical Aspects of the Text', Ph.D. Thesis, Victoria University of Wellington, 1989; White, (Sampson, Low, Marston, Low, and Searle, London, 1874), pp. v-vi; Johnstone, (Chapman and Hall, London, 1874), pp. vii-ix.

8. 'H.H.L.', 'A Rolling Stone', *Chapman's New Zealand Magazine* 1 (September-November 1862); Fairburn, (Hall & Co., London, 1867), p. 59; 'Mortimer' (Nimmo, Edinburgh, 1871), 'advertisement'; Rock, (J. Wilkie and Co., Dunedin, 1888), p. 93.

9. For the authorship, see R.C.J. Stone, *The Father and His Gift: John Logan Campbell's Later Years*, (AUP, Auckland, 1987), pp. 145-46.

10. Ellis, (Auckland, 1882), p. vi; for the autobiographical element, see Vera Colebrook, *Ellen: A biography* (The Women's Press, Dublin, 1980), p. 158; Wardon, (Simpson and Williams, Christchurch, 1892), p. 5.

11. Francis Carr, *Archimago; or, the New Zealander on the Ruins of London Bridge* (1864); William De Lisle Hay, *The Doom of a Great City: Being the Narrative of a Survivor, written A.D. 1942* (1880); anonymous, *Europa's Fate; or, The Coming Struggle . . . A History Lesson in New Zealand A.D.2076* (1875); 'Edwina Gibbon' (Charles John Stone), *History of the Decline and Fall of the British Empire* (1884); Henry Crocker Marriott Watson, *The Decline and Fall of the British Empire; or, The Witch's Cavern* (1890). The only New Zealand connection is Watson, a Christchurch vicar and father of the author of *The Web of the Spider*.

12. *The Cradle of 'Erewhon': Samuel Butler in New Zealand* (Melbourne University Press, Melbourne, 1960).

13. *A South Sea Siren*, ed. Joan Stevens (AUP/OUP, Auckland, 1970), pp. 80-81.

14. Butler, *Erewhon or Over the Range* (Associated University Presses, London, 1981), p. 62.

15. *Taranaki*, p. 17; Boldrewood, (Macmillan, London, 1899), p. 91; *Everything is Possible to Will*, p. 229; *A Rolling Stone* (Richard Bentley & Co., London, 1886) I, p. 6; *The Narrative of Edward Crewe* (Sampson, Low, Marston, Low, and Searle, London, 1874), p. 238; *Making His Pile* (Mason, Firth, and McCutcheon, Melbourne, 1891), p. 177.

16. *Martin Tobin* (John Maxwell and Company, London, 1864) II, pp. 123-4; MacPherson, (Tablet, Dunedin, 1889), p. 90; *Macpherson's Gully*, p. 21; Langton, *Mark Anderson: A Tale of Station Life in New Zealand* (J. Wilkie & Co., Dunedin [1889]), p. 16.

17. (Sampson, Low, Marston, Searle, and Rivington, 1878), p. 351.

18. See Dennis McEldowney, Introduction to *Tikera; or, Children of the Queen of Oceania*, trans. Jerzy Podstolski, ed. Dennis McEldowney (Auckland, AUP/OUP, 1972), pp. ix-xiii; *Tikera*, pp. 37-38, 272, 246.

19. *Philosopher Dick* (Unwin, London, 1891) I, pp. 226, 6; I, p. 78; II, p. 442; II, p. 440; II, p. 441; II, pp. 400, 429, 425; II, pp. 497-98; I, p. 53.

20. *A South Sea Siren*, pp. 61, 197.

21. *Making His Pile*, p. 144; *A Rolling Stone*, I, pp. 31-32.

22. *Everything is Possible to Will*, p. iv; *Anno Domini 2000; or, Woman's Destiny* (Hutchinson and Co., London, 1884), pp. 28-29.

23. *Taranaki*, pp. 5, 89, 8-9; *Henry Ancrum*, (Tinsley Brothers London, 1872), I, pp. 147-48; 'Comus', *The Last of the Waikatos* (Daily Southern Cross, Auckland, 1873), p. 27.

24. *Tikera*, pp. 43, 23, 264; Rev. Jos. Spillmann, S.J. *Love Your Enemies*, trans. from the German (B. Herter, Freiburg im Breisgau, 1895), pp. 6, 34.

25. Churchward (Swan Sonnenschein & Co. London, 1892) I, p. 57; *The Rebel Chief* (F.V. White & Co., London, 1896), pp. 225, 232, 97, 91; *'War to the Knife'*, pp. 73, 88.

26. *'War to the Knife'*, p. 146. For further laments of Māori extinction, see *Dickey Barrett* (Taranaki Herald, New Plymouth, 1890), p. 109; *The Rebel Chief*, p. 293; *The Web of the Spider*, 3rd edn. (E.W. Cole, Melbourne, n.d.), pp. 372-73; *Maoria*, p. 189. For narrative predictions of the coming Māori doom, see *Number One* (Simpkin, Marshall & Co., 1862), pp. 277-78; *Amongst the Maoris* (Frederick Warne & Co., London, n.d.), p. 256; *Hine-Ra* (W.H. Williams, Melbourne, 1887), p. 24; *Ena* (Smith, Elder and Co., 1874), p. 1; *Tikera*, pp. xxvi. For hopes of Māori survival, see *'War to the Knife'*, p. 345; *Ngamihi*, pp. 226-34.

27. *Jem Peterkin's Daughter*, I, pp. 34, 37, 16.

28. Cheeseman, 'Colonials in Fiction', p. 282; Shadbolt, remarks during 'An Evening with Maurice Shadbolt', New Zealand Writers' Week, 16 April, 1989, Dunedin.

29. Allen as late as 1950-51 published a slight, serialized novel, *Local Habitation*, in his literary periodical *The Wooden Horse*.

30. According to Satchell's solicitor, Eric S. Cowell, there had been 'at least one serial story' published in 'a Southern daily' before the novels, and there was a (probably later) novel about horse racing in early New Zealand which was never published, as well as some later manuscripts worked on after the re-publication of *The Greenstone Door* in 1935 (William Satchell papers, Alexander Turnbull Library).

31. Dorothea Turner, *Jane Mander* (Twayne Publishers, New York, 1972), pp. 24, 97, 98, 135, 25, 115; quoting a letter to the *Triad* in 1909, an article in the *Maoriland Worker* in 1911, an article in the *Mirror* in 1934, a letter in the Auckland *Star* in 1924, an article in the Christchurch *Press* in 1934.

32. *The Cave of Endor* (John Long, London, 1927), pp. 176-77; *Captain Sheen* (Unwin, London, 1905), p. 306; *Oak Uprooted* (Skeffington & Son, London, 1928), p. 231; *The Counterfeit Seal* (Otago Daily Times and Witness Co., James Horsburgh, H. Wise and Co., Dunedin 1897), p. 140; *In the Shadow of the Bush* (Sands and Co., London, 1899), p. 317; *Tussock Land* (Unwin, London, 1904), pp. 279, 286; *Land of My Children* (Paul, Hamilton, 1955), p. 213.

33. *The Counterfeit Seal*, p. 140. For further justification of the destruction of the bush see *In the Shadow of the Bush*, p. 2; *Tussock Land*, pp. 272-73; *Spur of Morning* (Whitcombe and Tombs, Wellington, 1960), p. 139; Annabella Forbes, *Helena: A Novel* (William Blackwell and Son, Edinburgh, 1905), p. 317. For further Māori laments, see *Ko Meri* or *'A Cycle of Cathay': A Story of New Zealand Life* (Eden Remington and Co., London, 1890), pp. 181, 389; *Zealandia's Guerdon* (John Long, London, 1902), pp. 213-15; *Captain Sheen*, p. 195; *Helena*, p. 181; *Maori Witchery* (Dent, London, 1929), p. 206; *Spur of Morning*, p. 140; *Tussock Land*, pp. 34, 31. For fears of Māori reversion, see *Ko Meri*, pp. 319, 390; *Haromi* (James Clarke & Co., London, 1902), p. 240; *Half-Caste* (The Macquarrie Head Press, Sydney, 1929), p. 32.

34. 'Colonials in Fiction', p. 282; 'Dave Baird' in *Follow the Call* ed. Terry Sturm (AUP/OUP, Auckland, 1975), pp. 136, 129; *Helena*, pp. 82-83; *Blacklaw* (Methuen, London, 1914), pp. 115, 253; *Spur of Morning*, p. 265; *In the Shadow of the Bush*, p. 38; *The Angel Isafrel* (Upton and Co., Auckland, 1896), p. 21.

35. *Solemn Boy* (Chatto and Windus, London, 1927), p. 32; *My Restless Years* (Max Parrish, London, 1962), p. 36; *Solemn Boy*, p. 29.

36. *Solemn Boy*, p. 241.

37. *Tussock Land*, p. 218; *The Law Bringers* (Hodder and Stoughton, London, 1913), p. 37; Lancaster is writing of Canada, but the evolutionary-imperial ethic runs through all of her fiction.

38. *Patmos* (Gordon & Gotch, London, 1905), p. 299; *A Daughter of the King* (Hutchinson, London, 1896), p. 186; *The Road the Men Came Home* (National Labour Press, London, 1920), p. 121; *A Pagan's Love* (T. Fisher Unwin, London, 1905), pp. 217, 307, 312; *Limanora* (Oxford University Press, Oxford, 1931), p. 44.

39. *The Knight of the Holy Ghost*, pp. vii, 246; *Angela*, p. 53; 'The Growth of Colonial Sentiment' in *Empire Review* 9 (1905), p. 72.

40. *Contemporary Review* 89 (1906), 850; *In Revolt*, p. 387. For publishing details of Grossmann's novels, see the Bibliography section. In the notes that follow, such detail has been omitted for all novelists who receive listings in the Bibliography section, when the first edition has been cited.

41. *The Heart of the Bush*, pp. 227, 332.

42. *The Toll of the Bush*, ed. Kendrick Smithyman (AUP/OUP, Auckland, 1985), pp. 96-97; *The Elixir of Life*, pp. 110-11, 64.

43. *The Greenstone Door* (Golden Press, Auckland, 1980), pp. 242, 278-79, 325; *The Toll of the Bush*, p. 96; *The Land of the Lost*, ed. Kendrick Smithyman (AUP/OUP, Auckland, 1971), p. 207; *The Toll of the Bush*, p. 242.

44. *The Passionate Puritan*, p. 63; *The Story of a New Zealand River*, p. 302; Turner, *Jane Mander*, p. 38, quoting from a letter used in O.N. Gillespie, 'Jane Mander: A Radio Portrait' in Alexander Turnbull Library; *The Story of a New Zealand River*, pp. 51, 39-40; *Allen Adair*, ed. Dorothea Turner (AUP/OUP, Auckland, 1971), p. 48; *The Besieging City*, p. 204.

45. *The Passionate Puritan*, pp. 41-2; *The Strange Attraction*, p. 58; *The Passionate Puritan*, p. 13; *The Strange Attraction*, p. 3; *The Story of a New Zealand River*, p. 318.

46. Turner, *Jane Mander*, p. 29, quoting from a biographical note to J.C. Andersen in the Alexander Turnbull Library; *The Story of a New Zealand River*, pp. 27, 29; Sargeson, from his 1938 review of the second edition of *The Story of a New Zealand River*, quoted in Turner, *Jane Mander*, p. 139.

47. Review of *The Story of a New Zealand River* in *Novels and Novelists* (Constable, London, 1930), p. 218.

48. *The Besieging City*, p. 116; letter to the Auckland *Sun*, 1928, quoted in Turner, *Jane Mander*, p. 89.

49. *Lenore Divine*, p. 115; *The Butcher Shop*, ed. Heather Roberts (AUP/OUP, Auckland, 1981), p. 206.

50. *Lenore Divine*, p. 231; *Poor Swine*, p. 270; *Dawn Beloved*, p. 65; *Lenore Divine*, pp. 82, 127-28.

51. Originally the overt didacticism may have been even more blatant, as Devanny told Nelle Scanlan in 1926 that her publisher had required that she cut several chapters in which she 'fully explored' her 'philosophy' and which were 'really the key to the story' (quoted in Bill Pearson, 'The Banning of *The Butcher Shop*', in *The Butcher Shop*, ed. Roberts, p. 228).

52. *Dawn Beloved*, pp. 38, 223.

53. *Bushman Burke*, p. 17.

54. *Poor Swine*, p. 267. By this time Devanny had probably read some Lawrence (whose early works had been published by Duckworth), for she records in *Point of Departure* that she read *Lady Chatterley's Lover* in 1931, and had read (and not liked) *Kangaroo* earlier (*Point of Departure: The Autobiography of Jean Devanny*, ed. Carole Ferrier [University of Queensland Press, St. Lucia, 1986], p. 137).

55. Gorrie, *Phoenix* I, 2 (July 1932), p. 52; Mulgan, 'The New Zealand Novel', in *Annals of New Zealand Literature*, issued by New Zealand Authors' Week Committee, April 1936, p. 11; Gillespie, 'The Golden Year for New Zealand Literature: Varied Achievement in the Art of Letters', *New Zealand Railways Magazine*, XIII (July 1938), pp. 14, 16; *Letters and Art*

in New Zealand, (Department of Internal Affairs, Wellington, 1940), p. 170; *Creative Writing in New Zealand: A Brief Critical History* (Auckland, Whitcombe and Tombs, 1946), pp. 54, 58; Chapman, 'Fiction and the Social Pattern: Some Implications of Recent New Zealand Writing', *Landfall* 25 (March 1953), p. 26.

56. McCormick, *New Zealand Literature: A Survey*, pp. 159-60; Brasch, 'Notes', *Landfall* 48 (December 1958), p. 299; Stevens, *The New Zealand Novel: 1860-1965*, p. 112; Brasch, 'Notes', *Landfall* 70 (June 1964), pp. 112-13.

57. Joseph, review of *Beneath the Thunder*, p. 170; Bettica, *N.Z. Listener*, 3 December 1965, p. 18; Gurr, review of *Power of Joy* and *An Absence of Angels*, *Landfall* 76 (December 1965), pp. 388-90; Taylor, review of *Another Man's Role*, *Landfall* 85 (March 1968), p. 105; Brasch, 'Correspondence', *Landfall* 87 (September 1968), pp. 340-41; Brasch was replying to a letter from Peter Crisp, *Landfall* 86 (June 1968), pp. 229-30.

58. The distinction between 'Provincial' and 'Post-provincial' has been made most explicitly by Peter Simpson in his *Ronald Hugh Morrieson* (OUP, Auckland, 1982), pp. 54-60, and by Patrick Evans, especially in his 'The Provincial Dilemma', *Landfall* 117 (March 1976), pp. 25-36; 119 (September, 1976), pp. 247-58; 121 (March 1977), pp. 9-22. Both Simpson and Evans tend to use the terms as an evaluation; for a fuller discussion, see Lawrence Jones, *Barbed Wire & Mirrors: Essays on New Zealand Prose* (University of Otago Press, Dunedin, 1987), pp. 146-52.

59. *Sweet White Wine* (Robert Hale, London, 1956), p. 6; *The New Zealand Novel*, p. 95; Cross, from a talk given to the University of Otago Literary Society, reported in *Critic*, 21 July 1959, pp. 8-9.

60. *Landfall* 19, (September 1951), pp. 164-72.

61. 'Writers in New Zealand: A Questionnaire', *Landfall* 53, (March 1960), p. 44.

62. Sargeson, 'Two Novels by Ronald Hugh Morrieson: An Appreciation', *Landfall* 98 (June 1971), pp. 133-37; Stead, 'Ronald Hugh Morrieson and the Art of Fiction', *Landfall* 98, (June 1971), pp. 137-45; Shadbolt, 'Introduction' to Morrieson, *Predicament* Dunmore Press, Palmerston North, 1982), p. 12; Peter Simpson, *Ronald Hugh Morrieson*. After 1982, Davin and Maurice Gee were added before the series lapsed.

63. Sargeson, 'Writing a Novel', in *Conversation in a Train and Other Critical Writings*, ed. Kevin Cunningham (AUP/ OUP, Auckland, 1983) p. 62; 'Chris Bell', 'A Transfer', *Landfall* 20 (December 1951), pp. 276-87; 'Fretful Sleepers', *Landfall* 23 (September 1952), pp. 201-30; for the composition of the novel, see Pearson, 'Writers in New Zealand: A Questionnaire', *Landfall* 53 (March 1960), pp. 62-3, and *Contemporary Novelists*, 2nd edn., ed. James Vinson (St. James Press, New York, 1976), p. 1013.

64. 'Writers in New Zealand: A Questionnaire', *Landfall* 53 (March 1960), p. 44.

65. Simpson, *Ronald Hugh Morrieson*, p. 59; Gillespie, 'Preface', *New Zealand Short Stories* (J.M. Dent and Sons, London, 1930), pp. v-vi; Chapman, 'The Writers' Conference', *Landfall* 19 (1951), pp. 224-26.

66. Sargeson, p. 60; Chapman, pp. 53-54; A. Mulgan, 'Correspondence', *Landfall* 28 (December 1953); *Man Alone* (Longman Paul, Auckland, 1969), p. 82.

67. Ian Reid, *Fiction and the Great Depression: Australia and New Zealand 1930-1950* (Edward Arnold, Melbourne, 1979); Sargeson, 'Mr Rhodes's Heroic Novelists', in *Conversation in a Train*, p. 20; Lee, letter to Reid in *Fiction and the Great Depression*, p. 125; Chapman, 'Fiction and the Social Pattern', p. 58.

68. Chapman, ibid., p. 5.

69. Lawrence Jones, 'Stanley Graham and the Several Faces of Man Alone', in *Barbed Wire & Mirrors*, pp. 210-21.

70. Chapman, ibid., pp. 57, 55.

71. *Faces in the Water* (W.H. Allen, London, 1962), p. 11.

72. Sargeson, *Conversation in a Train*, p. 61; Evans, 'The Provincial Dilemma: After *The God Boy*', *Landfall* 117 (March 1976), p. 34.

73. *Sydney Bridge Upside Down*, (Longman Paul, Auckland, 1981), p. 208.

74. Ballantyne, 'Sargeson in 1944', *Islands* 21 (March 1978), p. 293; *The Empty Hills* (Robert Hale, London, 1967), p. 264.

75. Chapman, 'Fiction and the Social Pattern', p. 32; Evans, 'The Provincial Dilemma: 2. "The Bit in between"', *Landfall* 119 (September 1976), pp. 246-58.

76. *The Little Country* (Thomas Nelson and Sons, London, 1937), p. 412.

77. Copland, *Landfall* 66 (June 1963), pp. 195-96; Curnow, '*Coal Flat* Revisited' in *Critical Essays on the New Zealand Novel*, ed. Cherry Hankin (Heinemann Educational, Auckland, 1976), p. 105; Rhodes, *New Zealand Monthly Review* (July 1963), p. 16; Sargeson, 'Conversation in a Train: or, What Happened to Michael's Boots', in *Conversation in a Train*, p. 140; Pearson, Personal Letter, 16 May 1986.

78. Sargeson, 'One Hundred Years of Story-telling', in *Conversation in a Train*, p. 72-76; Pearson, 'Correspondence', *Journal of New Zealand Literature* 4 (1986), p. 86; Sargeson, 'One Hundred Years of Story-telling', p. 75.

79. Sargeson, *Sargeson*, (Penguin, Auckland, 1981), pp. 50, 354; Hyde, *Wednesday's Children*, ed. Susan Ash (New Women's Press, Auckland, 1989), p. 143; Hilliard, *The Glory and the Dream*, (William Heinemann, Auckland, 1978), p. 258; Chapman, 'Fiction and the Social Pattern', p. 58; Pearson, p. 230.

80. Chapman, ibid., p. 41; Davin, *For the Rest of Our Lives* (Nicholson and Watson, London, 1947), p. 337.

81. Reid, *Fiction and the Great Depression*, p. 60.

82. *Point of Origin*, (The Bodley Head, London, 1962), p. 135.

83. *Bell Call* (Simon and Schuster, New York, 1964), p. 15; *Incense to Idols* (Secker and Warburg, London, 1960), pp. 170, 164.

84. *After Alienation: American Novels in Mid-Century* (World Publishing Company, New York, 1965), pp. 13-32.

85. *The Sullen Bell*, p. 100; *Brides of Price*, p. 35.

86. See McDonald, *Grand Hills for Sheep* (1948), *Stinson's Bush* (1954); Preston, *Harvest of Daring* (1957), *Great Refusals* (1958), *Who Rides the Tiger* (1980).

87. Sargeson, *Conversation in a Train*, p. 54; Fairburn, 'Some Aspects of New Zealand Art and Letters', *Art in New Zealand* 6 (1934), pp. 216-17; Mander, 'New Zealand Novelists: An Analysis and Some Advice', *The Press*, 10 November 1934, p. 17.

88. Bertram, 'John Mulgan: Between Two Wars', in *Flight of the Phoenix*, p. 42; (originally in *Tomorrow* 6, 13 [1 May 1940]); Sargeson, 'Conversation with Frank Sargeson: An Interview with Michael Beveridge', in *Conversation in a Train*, p. 157.
89. 'Sargeson in 1944', pp. 292-3; 'The Outlook for the New Zealand Author', *New Zealand Magazine* 28, 1 (Autumn 1949), p. 9; 'An American Influence', *Islands* 31-32 (June 1981), p. 41.
90. All quotations from Cross, Lecture on *The God Boy* at the University of Otago, 1962, typescript, Hocken Library.
91. Copland, 'The Goodly Roof: Some comments on the fiction of Frank Sargeson', *Landfall* 87 (September 1968), p. 323; Chapman, review of *The Cunninghams*, *Landfall* 10 (June 1949), pp. 182-85.
92. *Contemporary Novelists*, p. 977.
93. Gurr, p. 390; Sargeson, 'Katherine Mansfield', in *Conversation in a Train*, pp. 28-33.
94. *The Modes of Modern Writing: Metaphor, Metonymy, and the Typology of Modern Literature* (Edward Arnold, London, 1977), p. 40.
95. Letter to *Southland Times*, 10 October 1936, quoted in D.I.B. Smith, 'Introduction' to *Passport to Hell* (AUP, Auckland, 1986), p. xviii; *Nor the Years Condemn*, with an introduction by Phillida Bunkle, Linda Hardy, and Jacqueline Matthews (New Women's Press, Auckland, 1986), p. 33; letter, in Introduction, *Passport to Hell*, p. xviii.
96. Author's Note, in *Nor the Years Condemn*, p. 7.
97. *Sydney Bridge Upside Down*, p. 5.
98. Afterword, in *Figures in Light: Selected Stories*, pp. 237, 241.
99. 'Conversation with Frank Sargeson', p. 179; *Sargeson* pp. 387, 399.
100. Statement in *World Authors 1950-1970*, ed. John Wakeman (H.W. Wilson, New York, 1975), p. 1287; 'Books and Writers in New Zealand: A Novelist's View', a lecture given in the Winter Series, University of Auckland, 1974 (from the typescript); 'The Making of a Book', *Landfall* 108 (December 1973), pp. 279-80, 278.
101. Copland, review of *The Big Season*, *Landfall* 64 (December 1962), p. 393; 'Maurice Shadbolt Interviewed', *The New Zealander*, 30 July 1968, p. 19.
102. *The Hangover*, p. 21.
103. *Earthenware* (Pisces Print, [Christchurch], 1977), p. 73; *In My Father's Den*, p. 131.
104. 'Conversation with Frank Sargeson', p. 185.
105. *Strangers and Journeys*, p. 109.
106. Evans, 'A Survey: Responses', *Landfall* 122 (June 1977), p. 110; Thomson, 'Like Father, Like Son?', *Islands* 19 (October 1977), p. 93.
107. Nunns, 'Two Novels', *Islands* 17, (March 1977), p. 316; Cochrane, 'Cowley vs Sutherland', *Landfall* 121 (March 1977), p 90.
108. McCauley, *Listener*, 4 August 1979, p. 73; *The World is an Orange and the Sun* (Dunmore Press, Palmerston North, 1978), p. 38.
109. *Then Again* (Hodder and Stoughton, Auckland, 1986), p. 21.
110. *Man of Straw* (Secker & Warburg, London, 1970), p. 10.
111. *A State of Siege*, pp. 50, 20-21, 169.
112. *Forbush and the Penguins* (A.H. and A.W. Reed, Wellington, 1965), p. 189; Billing, Interview with Richard Corballis, *Landfall* 135 (September 1980), p. 255.
113. *Balloons* (Robert Hale, London and Whitcombe & Tombs, Christchurch, 1973), p. 183; Robinson, Review, *Listener*, 8 July 1978, p. 60.
114. *Waiting for Einstein* (Benton Ross, Auckland, 1984), p. 155.
115. 'Why I Write', *World Literature Written in English* XIV (1975), p. 118; 'Maori life and literature: a sensory perception', in *New Zealand Through the Arts: Past and Present*, the Turnbull Winter Lectures 1981 (Friends of the Turnbull Library, Wellington, 1982), pp. 52-53; *The Matriarch* (Heinemann, Auckland, 1986), p. 427.
116. *Potiki* (Penguin, Auckland, 1986), p. 132.
117. *The Eye of the Thorn* (Tauranga Moana Press, Tauranga, 1984), pp. 4, 5; *The Bone People* (Spiral, Wellington, 1983), pp. 462, 2, 406.
118. *O.E.* (Benton Ross, Auckland, 1986), pp. 251-52.
119. *The Matriarch*, p. 195.
120. *Blackball 08* (Collins, Auckland, 1984), p. 241.
121. Wilson, review of *A Multiple Texture*, *Landfall* 111 (September 1974), p. 267; *A Multiple Texture* (Robert Hale, London, 1973), p. 160; David Young, 'Tenants of Fiction', *Listener*, 13 October 1984, p. 32.
122. *The Pepper Leaf* (Chatto and Windus, London, 1971), p. 214.
123. *Intensive Care*, p. 5.
124. *The Godmothers* (The Women's Press, London, 1982), pp. 145, 181.
125. *Time and the Forest* (John McIndoe, Dunedin, 1986), p. 309; *Mackenzie* (Hodder and Stoughton, London, 1970), p. 354; *Through the Eye of the Thorn*, p. 169; *The Matriarch* p. 109; *Potiki*, p. 52.
126. *The Rainbirds*, p. 164.
127. Baxter, 'Beginnings', in *Beginnings: New Zealand Writers Tell How They Began Writing*, ed. Robin Dudding (Oxford University Press, Wellington, 1980), p. 47; *Disorderly Conduct* (Hodder and Stoughton, Auckland, 1984), p. 160; *Sole Survivor*, p. 231.
128. *Strangers and Journeys*, p. 500.
129. 'An Hour with Patricia Grace', New Zealand Writers' Week, Dunedin, 9 April 1989.
130. 'Language is the Hawk', in *In the Glass Case*, p. 131. See Mark Goulden's account in *Mark My Word* and Frame's own 'innocent' account in *The Envoy from Mirror City*, the third volume of her autobiography.
131. See Curnow, *An Incorrigible Music: A Sequence of Poems* (Auckland University Press, Auckland, 1979), pp. 22-23; Ruthven, 'Joseph's Tale', *Islands* 27 (November 1979), pp. 521-30.

132. *The Settlement* (Hodder and Stoughton, 1986, Auckland), pp. 44, 134.

The Short Story

1. Mark Williams, *Leaving the Highway* (Auckland University Press, 1990), p. 192.
2. Clare Hanson, *Short Stories and Short Fictions, 1880-1980* (Macmillan, London, 1985), p. 12
3. George Cotterill, *Literary Foundlings* (The Times Office, Christchurch, 1864), p. 23.
4. Henry Lapham, *We Four and the Stories We Told* (Otago Daily Times Office, Dunedin, 1880), p. 18.
5. Ibid., p. 39.
6. Chas. Owen, 'The Disappearance of Letham Crouch', *New Zealand Illustrated Magazine* 4 (July 1901), pp. 777-81.
7. G.B. Lancaster, 'God Keep Ye, Merrie Gentlemen', *New Zealand Illustrated Magazine* 5 (December 1901), pp. 167-76.
8. William Freeman, Editorial, *Zealandia* No. 1 (July, 1889), p. 2; John C. Thomson, Letter, *Zealandia* No. 6 (December 1890); Clara Cheeseman, 'Colonials in Fiction', *New Zealand Illustrated Magazine* 7 (January 1903), pp. 275-6.
9. Bill Pearson, 'Attitudes to the Maori in some Pakeha Fiction', *Fretful Sleepers and Other Essays* (Heinemann, Auckland, 1974), p. 49.
10. Ibid.
11. A.A. Grace, *Tales of a Dying Race* (Chatto and Windus, London, 1901), p. vii.
12. A.A. Grace, *Maoriland Stories* (Alfred G. Betts, Nelson, 1895), pp. 99, 136; *Tales of a Dying Race*, p. 84.
13. Alice A. Kenny, 'The Justice of the Kaianga', *New Zealand Illustrated Magazine* 12 (August 1905), pp. 361, 364. *Note* 'Kaianga' is a misspelling of the word 'kāinga' (family).
14. William Baucke, *Where the White Man Treads* (Wilson and Horton, Auckland, 1905), p. 4.
15. Clara Cheeseman, 'Married for his Money', *Australian Ladies Annual*, 1878. In Elizabeth Webby and Lydia Wevers (eds), *Happy Endings* (Allen and Unwin/Port Nicholson Press, Wellington, 1987), p. 64.
16. G.B. Lancaster, 'His Daily Work', *The Huia* (December 1903), p. 15.
17. G.B. Lancaster, *Sons O' Men* (Hodder and Stoughton, London, 1914), p. 53.
18. Ibid., pp. 136-7.
19. Ibid., p. 16.
20. W.H. New, *Dreams of Speech and Violence: The Art of the Short Story in Canada and New Zealand* (University of Toronto Press, Toronto, 1987), p. 128.
21. B.E. Baughan, *Brown Bread from a Colonial Oven* (Whitcombe and Tombs, Christchurch, 1912), p. 33.
22. Mona Tracy, 'The Return', *Art in New Zealand* (September 1928), p. 45.
23. W.H. New, *Dreams of Speech and Violence*, p. 113.
24. Clare Hanson and Andrew Gurr, *Katherine Mansfield* (Macmillan, London, 1981), p. 27.
25. Antony Alpers (ed.), *The Stories of Katherine Mansfield* (Oxford University Press, Auckland, 1984), p. xiv. All subsequent references are to this text, cited as *Mansfield*. The notebook Alpers refers to has been published as *The Urewera Notebook*, ed. Ian A. Gordon (Oxford University Press, Auckland, 1978).
26. Ian A. Gordon (ed.), *Undiscovered Country: The New Zealand Stories of Katherine Mansfield* (Longman, London, 1974), p. xviii.
27. *Mansfield*, pp. 111, 112.
28. Hanson and Gurr, p. 16.
29. See Andrew Gurr, *Writers in Exile: The Identity of Home in Modern Literature* (Harvester Press, Brighton, 1981)
30. Accepting all the stories to which Gordon attributes New Zealand locations (in *Undiscovered Country*) makes the total just under half. Even if some of his attributions are queried (for example, 'The Fly', which seems to argue an English setting since 'the girls' have just been over to see the war graves), by far the most common scene is New Zealand.
31. *Mansfield*, pp. 278, 279; John Middleton Murry, Introduction, *The Scrapbook of Katherine Mansfield* (Constable, London, 1939), p. vii; for 'plotty' stories, see letter to Dorothy Brett, 12 November 1921.
32. Hanson and Gurr, p. 113.
33. All quotations from *Mansfield*, p. 453.
34. Ibid., p. 464.
35. Ibid., p. 117.
36. O.N. Gillespie (ed.), *New Zealand Short Stories* (Dent, London, 1930), p. v.
37. Review of John Guthrie, *So They Began*, *Evening Post*, 18 January 1936.
38. Jean Devanny, *Old Savage and Other Stories* (Duckworth, London, 1927), p. 280.
39. E.H. McCormick, *New Zealand Literature, A Survey*, (Oxford University Press, London, 1959), pp. 96-7.
40. Allen Curnow, 'New Zealand Literature: The Case for a Working Definition', *Essays on New Zealand Literature (ed. Wystan Curnow) (Heinemann, Auckland, 1973), p. 141.*
41. C.K. Stead, *Islands* 21 (March 1978), p. 213.
42. W.H. New, *Dreams of Speech and Violence*, p. 143.
43. H. Winston Rhodes, 'In the Beginning', *Islands* 21, p. 217; review of E.H. McCormick, *Letters and Art in New Zealand*, *Dominion* (1 February 1941), p. 15; Roger Horrocks, 'The Invention of New Zealand', *And* 1 (October, 1983)), pp. 10-11.
44. Editorial, *New Zealand Railways Magazine*, (1 May 1933); Oliver Duff, review of *A Man and his Wife*, *New Zealand Listener*, 25 October 1940, p. 19.
45. *Tomorrow* (18 August 1937), p. 656; 'Conversation with Frank Sargeson: an Interview with Michael Beveridge', in (ed.) Kevin Cunningham, *Conversation in a Train and Other Critical Writing* (Auckland University Press and Oxford University Press, Auckland, 1983), p. 169.
46. *Conversation in a Train*, pp. 15, 16.

47. Simon During, 'Towards a Revision of Local Critical Habits', *And* 1, pp. 75-92.
48. 'City and Suburban', *The Stories of Frank Sargeson* (Longman Paul, Auckland, 1973), p. 291.
49. Lawrence Jones, *Barbed Wire & Mirrors, Essays on New Zealand Prose* (University of Otago Press, Dunedin, 1987), p. 53.
50. 'Conversation with Frank Sargeson', p. 50.
51. See W.H. New, pp. 137-53.
52. John Reece Cole, in (ed.) Cherry Hankin, *It Was So Late and Other Stories* (Auckland University Press and Oxford University Press, Auckland, 1978), p. 36.
53. Ibid., p. 61.
54. Greville Texidor, 'Goodbye Forever', in (ed.) Kendrick Smithyman, *In Fifteen Minutes You Can Say a Lot* (Victoria University Press, Wellington, 1987), p. 207.
55. James Courage, *Such Separate Creatures* (Caxton Press, Christchurch, 1973), p. 43.
56. Bill Pearson, Introduction to Roderick Finlayson, *Brown Man's Burden and Later Stories* (Auckland University Press and Oxford University Press, Auckland, 1973), p. xxiii.
57. Ibid., pp. 26, 27, 45.
58. Ibid., pp. 76, 53.
59. Noel Hilliard's three collections, *A Piece of Land* (1963), *Send Somebody Nice* (1976), and *Selected Stories* (1977), are social realist stories, many of which focus on the social consequences of the Māori shift from the country to the city: displacement, deracination, poverty, discrimination.
60. C.K. Stead notes that in Duggan's copy of *Speaking for Ourselves*, Duggan has scored over the pages of his work and written at the end, 'What embarrassing crap!' Introduction to *Collected Stories* (Auckland University Press, Auckland, 1981), p. 21.
61. Ibid.
62. See W.H. New, p. 164.
63. *Collected Stories*, p. 101.
64. Ibid., pp. 196, 198.
65. V. Cunningham, review of *Collected Stories* in *The Times Literary Supplement* (9 April 1982), p. 404; *Collected Stories*, p. 9.
66. *Collected Stories*, pp. 361, 364.
67. Janet Frame, *An Angel at My Table* (Hutchinson, Auckland, 1984), p. 111.
68. *The Lagoon* (Caxton Press, Christchurch, 1961), pp. 7, 10.
69. Ibid., p.11.
70. W.H. New, p. 162.
71. *The Reservoir* (George Braziller, New York, 1963), pp. 64, 40.
72. *The Gypsies and Other Stories* (Victoria University Press and Price Milburn, Wellington, 1978), p. 93.
73. *An Olive Tree in Dalmatia and Other Stories* (Paul's Book Arcade, Auckland and Hamilton, 1963), p. 8.
74. 'A Little Talk About Our (Winter) District', in (ed.) Lydia Wevers, *New Zealand Short Stories* 4 (Oxford University Press, Auckland, 1984), p. 40.
75. *The Growing of Astrid Westergaard and Other Stories* (Longman Paul, Auckland, 1985), p. 20.
76. A pub scene in 'The Makutu on Mrs Jones' is framed in terms of a Western movie.
77. W.H. New, p. 173.
78. *The New Net Goes Fishing* (Heinemann, Auckland, 1977), pp. 57, 173.
79. *Waiariki* (Longman Paul, Auckland, 1975), p. 5.
80. Patricia Grace, 'The Maori in Literature', in (ed.) Michael King, *Tihe Mauri Ora: Aspects of Maoritanga* (Methuen, Auckland, 1978) pp. 81-2; *Waiariki*, p. 47.
81. *Waiariki*, pp. 85, 88.
82. Editorial, *Te Ao Hou* 1 (Winter 1952).
83. *Te Ao Hou* 34 (March 1961), p. 26.
84. *Te Ao Hou* 28 (September 1959); *Te Ao Hou* 27 (June 1959), p. 16.
85. Apirana Taylor, *He Rau Aroha, A Hundred Leaves of Love* (Penguin, Auckland, 1986), *Ki Te Ao* (Penguin, Auckland, 1990); Bruce Stewart, *Tama and Other Stories* (Penguin, Auckland, 1989).
86. For discussions of the oral quality of Māori writing in English, see Norman Simms, *Pacific Moana Quarterly* 3 (July 1978), and Richard Corballis, *Introducing Witi Ihimaera* (Longman Paul, Auckland, 1984).
87. Rora Paki, 'Ka Pu te Ruha Ka Hao te Rangatahi', *Te Ao Hou* 15 (July 1956).
88. Clare Hanson, *Short Stories and Short Fictions*, p. 113; Maurice Shadbolt, 'Author's Afterword', *Figures in Light, Selected Stories* (Hodder and Stoughton, Auckland, 1978), p. 237-8.
89. Cherry Hankin, Introduction to *The New Zealanders* (Whitcombe and Tombs, Christchurch, 1974), p. 1.
90. Maurice Shadbolt, *Figures in Light*, p. 242.
91. A.K. Grant, *New Zealand Listener* (27 October 1973), pp. 26-7.
92. *Dandy Edison for Lunch and Other Stories* (McIndoe, Dunedin, 1981), p. 129.
93. Ibid., p. 152.
94. *The Snow in Spain* (Allen and Unwin, Wellington, 1990), p. 72.
95. *The Master of Big Jingles & Other Stories* (McIndoe, Dunedin, 1982), p. 160; *The Day Hemingway Died and Other Stories* (McIndoe, Dunedin, 1984), p. 67.
96. Michael Gifkins, quoted on the back cover of *The Lynx Hunter and Other Stories* (McIndoe, Dunedin, 1987); 'Bravo, Echo, Victor', *The Day Hemingway Died*, p. 89.
97. *The Lynx Hunter*, pp. 71, 72, 98.
98. C.K. Stead, *Five for the Symbol* (Longman Paul, Auckland, 1981), pp. 139, 166.

99. John Barth, *Atlantic* v. 220, 20 (1967), p. 69; Frederic Jameson, 'Postmodernism, or the Cultural Logic of Late Capitalism', *New Left Review* 57 (1984), p. 146.
100. Introduction, *The New Fiction* (Lindon Publishing, Auckland, 1985), pp. 16, 18, 19.
101. Ibid., p.34.
102. Ibid., p. 75.
103. See Chris Else, *The New Fiction*, pp. 144-53; Introduction, p. 57; Ian Wedde, *The Shirt Factory* (Victoria University Press and Price Milburn, Wellington, 1981), p. 7.
104. *The Amphibians* (Penguin, Auckland, 1989), p. 88.
105. Ibid., p. 167.
106. John Cranna, 'Visitors', *Visitors* (Heinemann Reed, Auckland, 1989), p. 2.
107. Bill Manhire, *The New Land: A Picture Book* (Heinemann Reed, Auckland, 1990), p. 104.
108. Joy Cowley, Prologue, *Heart Attack and Other Stories* (Hodder and Stoughton, Auckland, 1985), p. 8.
109. Ibid., p. 93.
110. Fiona Kidman, *Mrs Dixon and Friend* (Heinemann, Auckland, 1982), p. 4.
111. Margaret Sutherland, *Getting Through and Other Stories* (Heinemann, Auckland, 1977), p. 7.
112. Annabel Fagan, 'Laughing Girl', in (ed.) Miriam Saphira, *The Power and the Glory and Other Lesbian Stories* (Papers Inc., Auckland, 1987), p. 41.
113. Janet Frame, *The Lagoon*, p. 93.
114. Barbara Anderson, 'Una Benchley thinks about David Hockney', *Sport* 3 (1990), p. 7.
115. See Fiona Farrell Poole, *The Rock Garden and Other Stories* (Auckland University Press, Auckland, 1989); Stephanie Johnson, *The Glass Whittler* (New Women's Press, Auckland, 1988); Anne Kennedy, *100 Traditional Smiles* (Victoria University Press, Wellington, 1988); Sue Reidy, *Modettes* (Penguin, Auckland, 1988).
116. *The Glass Whittler*, p. 47.
117. Rosie Scott, *Queen of Love and Other Stories* (Penguin, Auckland, 1989).
118. Wendy Pond's stories have appeared in *Sport* and *Landfall*, and in several women's anthologies.
119. *Modettes*, pp. 23, 26.

Drama

Note: The recent discovery by Peter Harcourt of more than thirty manuscripts (or synopses) of plays, dating from 1886-1926, registered under the Copyright Law of 1877 with the Justice Department, and now deposited in the National Archives in Wellington, occurred too late for incorporation in the first and second sections of this chapter. A description of the material, which was written by 'amateur authors and those aspiring to be professional', is provided by Peter Harcourt in *Australasian Drama Studies* 18, April 1991, and thanks are due to the author, and to the editor of this issue of *ADS*, Sebastian Black, for permission to mention the discovery here.

1. The model of hybridity to account for the culturally syncretic nature of post-colonial texts was developed by Homi Bhabha in *'Of Mimicry and Man: The Ambivalence of Colonial Discourse' October* 28 (Spring 1984), pp. 125-33. The model has attracted considerable following and is presented in accessible form in Bill Ashcroft, Gareth Griffiths, and Helen Tiffin (eds), *The Empire Writes Back* (Routledge, London, 1989), pp. 33-6, 97-104.
2. *Daily Telegraph*, 6 October 1863. The circumstances of the production are briefly outlined in Raewyn Dalziel, *Julius Vogel, Business Politician* (Auckland University Press and Oxford University Press, Auckland, 1986), p. 39.
3. Farjeon may also have been the author of *Home Sweet Home* which premiered in London in 1876, and is listed in Allardyce Nicoll's *History of English Drama, 1660-1900* vol. 5 (Cambridge University Press, Cambridge, 2nd edn. 1959), p. 361. If this is so, it would be the first book publication of a New Zealand play. However, it is not mentioned in any biographical reference to Farjeon, nor is it held in copyright libraries with substantial Farjeon holdings, such as Cambridge University.
4. The presentation of these plays is covered in detail in Karen Annette Sherry, 'Theatre in Colonial Auckland, 1870-71' (Masters thesis, University of Auckland, 1987). The large proportion of local material analysed in the thesis has not been paralleled in other comprehensive scrutinies of nineteenth century New Zealand theatre records, such as Howard McNaughton's 'New Zealand Theatre Annals', held on computer files at the University of Canterbury. The thesis does draw attention to the fact that knowledge of local drama performed on the colonial stage is very limited, and there may well have been other periods in which local play-writing briefly flourished.
5. Joe Graham, *An Old Stock-actor's Memories* (John Murray, London, 1930), p. 42f.
6. *New Zealand Herald*, 15 June 1871, p. 5.
7. *New Zealand Herald*, 6 April 1870, p. 5.
8. *New Zealand Herald*, 9 April 1870, p. 5.
9. *Daily Southern Cross*, 9 April 1870.
10. *Otago Witness*, 25 September 1880, p. 22.
11. *Otago Witness*, 27 September 1880, p. 20.
12. Griffen, *Kainga of the Ladye Birds* (Academy of Music, Wellington, 1879), p. 14. The rediscovery of this script was by Fiona Farrell Poole.
13. *Otago Witness*, 27 November 1880, p. 20.
14. See Veronica Kelly, 'The Banning of Marcus Clarke's *The Happy Land*: Stage, Press and Parliament', *Australasian Drama Studies* 2, 1 (1983), p. 71.
15. *Press*, 23 February 1880, p. 2.

16. Firth's political views are detailed in Mona Gordon, *The Golden Age of Josiah Clifton Firth* (Pegasus Press, Christchurch, 1953), pp. 243-4.

17. *Lyttelton Times*, 6 March 1885, p. 4.

18. Darrell's career is the subject of Eric Irvin's *Gentleman George — King of Melodrama* (University of Queensland Press, St Lucia, 1980).

19. *Press*, 11 January 1890, p. 5.

20. Ibid.

21. Leitch, *The Land of the Moa* (Victoria University Press, Wellington, 1990).

22. *New Zealand Sporting and Dramatic Review*, 16 June 1904, p. 18.

23. *New Zealand Sporting and Dramatic Review*, 21 April 1904, p. 18. For Australian production, the play was retitled 'The Unseen Hand', but the New Zealand setting was retained (*New Zealand Sporting and Dramatic Review*, 16 June 1904, p. 18).

24. Ibid.

25. Victor S. Lloyd, Foreword to *Seven One-Act Plays, 1934* (Radio Publishing Co, Wellington, 1934), p. 7.

26. Victor S. Lloyd, Foreword to *Seven One-Act Plays* (Radio Publishing Co, Wellington, 1933), p. 7.

27. Ibid.

28. Letter to the author by Joan Sheppard, 25 May 1989.

29. Levy, 'God Made Two Trees' in *Seven One-Act Plays, 1934*, p. 24.

30. Ibid., p. 23.

31. 'Play Competition', *Art in New Zealand* 10 (1937), p. 90.

32. Typescript in author's possession, Act 3, Scene 3, p. 3.

33. Ibid., Act 1, Scene 1, p. 1.

34. *Seven One-Act Plays* (1933), p. 38.

35. Ibid., p. 38f.

36. *'Clay' and Other New Zealand One-Act Plays* (National Magazines, Wellington, 1936), p. 11.

37. Ian Hamilton, 'Theatre Prospect', *Tomorrow*, 9 November 1938, pp. 22-4.

38. R.A.K. Mason, 'To Save Democracy', *Tomorrow*, 27 April 1938, p. 408.

39. The attribution is made by Rachel Barrowman in 'Culture and the Left in New Zealand, 1930-50' (Masters thesis, Victoria University, 1987). Barrowman has published part of her research as 'R.A.K. Mason and the Auckland People's Theatre, 1936-1940', *Sites, A Journal for Radical Perspectives on Culture* 16 (1988), pp. 6-18.

40. Frank Sargeson, 'Mr Hamilton's Play', *Tomorrow*, 12 April 1939, p. 377.

41. Curnow, *Four Plays* (Reed, Wellington, 1972), pp. 7-8.

42. Roddick, *Allen Curnow* (Oxford University Press, Wellington, 1980), p. 38.

43. Mason and Pocock, *Theatre in Danger* (Paul's Book Arcade, Hamilton, 1957), pp. 11-13, 23-4.

44. Ibid., pp. 91-4, 100.

45. Mason, *The Healing Arch* (Victoria University Press, Wellington, 1987), p. 95.

46. Ibid., p. 102.

47. Mason, *New Zealand Drama: A Parade of Forms and a History* (New Zealand University Press, Wellington, 1973), pp. 62-3. Mason frequently commented on such paintings at greater length, as in *The Healing Arch* pp. 296-7.

48. Ibid., p. 63.

49. Frank McKay (ed.), *James K. Baxter as Critic* (Heinemann Educational Books, Auckland, 1978), p. 217 [paraphrased from original].

50. Ibid., p. 213.

51. J.E. Weir, 'Interview with James K. Baxter', *Landfall* 111 (September 1974), p. 243.

52. Baxter, 'Some Possibilities for New Zealand Drama' (1967), p. 11 [radio talk].

53. McKay, pp. 214-15.

54. Mason, *Every Kind of Weather* (Reed Methuen, Auckland, 1986), contains extracts of an unpublished history of the Players which details the funding.

55. Bertram, review of *The Tree*, *Landfall* 59 (September 1961), p. 267.

56. Diane Farmer, 'Inside the Outsider', *New Zealand Listener*, 15 April 1965, p. 5.

57. *The Observer*, 12 January 1969.

58. *New Zealand Theatre* 168 (August 1969), p. 12.

59. David Carnegie, *Act* 4, 9 (November 1979), p. 72.

60. Day, *Act* 2, 6 (August 1977), p. 31.

61. Mason, 'Authentic Fury', *New Zealand Listener*, 14 December 1974.

62. Harrison, correspondence, *Act* 3, 10 (December 1978), p. 83.

63. Thompson, *Selected Plays* (Pilgrims South Press, Dunedin, 1984), p. 182.

64. *Act* 14 (July 1971), p. 17.

65. McGee, *Foreskin's Lament* (Victoria University Press, Wellington, 1981), pp. 45, 54.

66. McGee, 'Out in the Cold', *Islands* 7, 5 (November 1979), pp. 459-66.

67. Helen White, 'Paths for a Flightless Bird: Roles for Women on the New Zealand Stage since 1950', *Australasian Drama Studies* 3, 2 (April 1985), p. 111.

68. *New Zealand Listener*, 4 September 1982, p. 110. See also the interview in *Australasian Drama Studies* 10 (1987), pp. 21-28, and 'Suffering's Cyclical Nature' by Rebecca Simpson, *New Zealand Listener*, 22 September 1984, p. 37.

69. *New Zealand Times*, 14 November 1982, p. 12.

70. Neill, *Act* 8, 1 (February 1983), p. 5.

71. White, *Act* 8, 4 (August 1983), p. 41.

72. Sebastian Black, 'Ways of Seeing: Vincent O'Sullivan's *Shuriken*', *Landfall* 157 (March 1986), p. 66.

73. Ibid., p. 66.
74. Hoar, *Squatter* (Victoria University Press, Wellington, 1988), p. 54. The biblical account is in *II Samuel* 12, 1-7.
75. Press release for Maunder's *Te Tutakitanga I Te Puna*, in author's possession.
76. Kaa, *Act* 10, 6 (December 1985), p. 70.
77. Programme to *Te Tutakitanga I Te Puna*, in author's possession.

Poetry

1. James K. Baxter, *The Man on the Horse* (University of Otago Press, Dunedin, 1967), pp. 131-2.
2. *An Anthology of Twentieth Century New Zealand Poetry*, Vincent O'Sullivan (ed.) (Oxford University Press, London, 1970, 3rd edn. Auckland, 1987), p. xviii.
3. *New Zealand Listener*, 11 July 1987, p. 8.
4. Allen Curnow's phrase in *The Penguin Book of New Zealand Verse*, Allen Curnow (ed.) (Penguin, Harmondsworth, 1960), p. 62. Curnow was not, of course, implying any simple equation between the poem's 'reality' and what was 'prior' to it; *The Penguin Book of New Zealand Verse*, Ian Wedde and Harvey McQueen (eds) (Penguin, Auckland, 1985), pp. 458-9.
5. Richard Wilbur, in *Poet's Choice*, Paul Engle and Joseph Langland (eds) (Dial Press, New York, 1962), p. 193; Wei T'ai is quoted by Geoffrey Grigson, *The Private Art: A Poetry Note-Book* (Allison and Busby, London and New York, 1982), p. 135.
6. F.W. Bateson, *English Poetry and the English Language* (Clarendon Press, Oxford, 1934), p. vi; *Penguin Book of New Zealand Verse* (1985), pp. 23, 29. 'Hieratic' (of the priesthood) is used by Wedde to denote 'language that is received, self-referential, encoded *elect*, with a "high" social threshold emphasizing cultural and historical continuity'; and 'demotic' (of the people) denotes 'language with a spoken base, adaptable and exploratory codes, and a "lower" and more inclusive social threshold emphasizing cultural mobility and immediacy'.
7. Samuel Taylor Coleridge, *Biographia Literaria*, George Watson (ed.) (Dent, London, 1906, 1965), p. 198.
8. Lines quoted are from the following poems: Curnow, 'Landfall in Unknown Seas' (*Sailing or Drowning*, 1943) and 'A Reliable Service' (*You Will Know When You Get There*, 1982); Baxter, 'Wild Bees' (*The Fallen House*, 1953) and 'Sonnet 42' (*Autumn Testament*, 1973); Domett, *Ranolf and Amohia* (Smith, Elder, London, 1872), p. 7; Glover, 'Songs' (*Sings Harry*, 1951).
9. Tony Kingsbury, 'Poetry in New Zealand 1850-1930' (Ph.D. dissertation, University of Auckland, 1968), pp. 104-5; Bob Orr, *Passages* (Auckland University Press, Auckland, 1991).
10. Ian Wedde, 'Pathway to the Sea' (*Castaly*, Auckland University Press, Auckland, 1980); Maurice Gee, *Plumb* (Faber, London, 1978), p. 12.
11. Charles Brasch, *Indirections* (Oxford University Press, Wellington, 1980), p. 20.
12. Alistair Campbell, response to 'A Survey', *Landfall* 122 (June 1970), p. 105.
13. J.C. Reid, *Creative Writing in New Zealand* (The Author, Auckland, 1946), p. 11.
14. The passages quoted come from the following volumes: Bowen, *Poems* (Union Office, Christchurch, 1861); Broome, *Poems from New Zealand* (Houlston and Wright, London, 1868); Domett, *Ranolf and Amohia*, p. 21; Barr, *Poems and Songs, Descriptive and Satirical* (John Greig, Edinburgh, 1861); Randle, *Lilts and Lyrics of New Zealand* (James Horsburgh, Dunedin, 1893); Mackay, *The Spirit of the Rangatira* (George Robertson, Melbourne, 1889); Rogers, in *New Zealand Verse*, W.F. Alexander and A.E. Currie (eds) (Walter Scott, London, 1906), which has also provided the text for the Randle extract; Ollivant, *Hine Moa, the Maori Maiden* (A.R. Mowbray, London and Oxford, [1879]).
15. *The Penguin Book of Victorian Verse*, George MacBeth (ed.) (Penguin, Harmondsworth, 1969, 1975), p. 24; ibid., p. 161.
16. Alexander and Currie, *New Zealand Verse*, pp. xiv-xv.
17. Northrop Frye, 'Conclusion', in *Literary History of Canada: Canadian Literature in English*, Carl F Klinck (ed.) (University of Toronto Press, University of Toronto, 1965), pp. 830-2.
18. God is 'Wisdom's Great Dictator' in T.E.L. Roberts, 'Trickling Water', in *Rimu and Rata* (The Author, Christchurch, 1920), p. 20; Mackay, *The Spirit of the Rangatira*, p. 18; Hulme, *Speculations*, Herbert Read (ed.) (Kegan Paul, Trench, Trubner, London, 1936), p. 232; Burn, *The Monthly Review*, II.5 (May, 1890), p. 280.
19. Khaldun's statement is noted by Geoffrey Grigson, *The Private Art*, p. 87; Bateson, *English Poetry and the English Language*, pp. 111, 123-4; Tennyson, quoted by Vincent O'Sullivan (ed.), *An Anthology of Twentieth Century New Zealand Poetry* (1987 edn.), p. xviii; Baughan, letter to Johannes C. Andersen, 6 May 1908, Auckland Institute Manuscript Collection.
20. Sir George Grey, *Polynesian Mythology* (J. Murray, London, 1855), pp. 65-6; Domett, *Ranolf and Amohia*, pp. 122-3.
21. One nineteenth century New Zealand poet certainly imitated 'The Raven': Andrew Kinross's 'The Dying Soldier' ('On the field of battle sighing lay a youthful warrior dying, / Slowly ebbed his blood away, ebbed away for evermore'), in *My Life and Lays* (John Ward, Invercargill, 1899), even has a 'Nevermore' refrain; *Polynesian Mythology*, p. 239; *Ranolf and Amohia*, pp. 162-3.
22. *Ranolf and Amohia*, pp. 132-4, extracted by Alexander and Currie as an anthology piece; Alexander and Currie, *New Zealand Verse*, p. xxviii.
23. *Everyman's Book of Victorian Verse*, J.R. Watson (ed.) (Dent, London, 1982), pp. xiv-xv; the phrases are from the first two stanzas of William Pember Reeves's 'A Colonist in his Garden', reprinted by Alexander and Currie and discussed below; 'David Lowston', included in Ian Wedde's *Penguin Book of New Zealand Verse* (1985), was made available in *Shanties by the Way*, Rona Bailey and Herbert Roth (eds) (Whitcombe and Tombs, Christchurch, 1967), pp. 12-13 — this is a useful source of other New Zealand popular songs and ballads; Catherine H. Richardson, 'The First News frae Auld Scotland'; William Pember Reeves, 'New Zealand'; Charles C. Bowen, 'The Old Year and the New'; all in Alexander and Currie, *New Zealand Verse*, pp. 15-16, 1-2, 5-6.
24. *Ranolf and Amohia*, p. 232; Kingsbury, 'Poetry in New Zealand', p. 29. I am considerably indebted to this brilliant

thesis, which draws attention to the peculiarities of Bracken's poem, discussed below. E. H. McCormick, *New Zealand Literature: A Survey* (Oxford University Press, London, 1959), p. 68, quotes some verses from *Colonial Couplets* (Simpson and Williams, Christchurch, 1889) by G.P. Williams and W.P. Reeves, which joke about the New Zealand use of 'gully' and 'bush', rather than 'valley', 'dell', 'forest', and 'leafy glade'.

25. Thomas Bracken, *Flowers of the Free Lands* (Mills, Dick, and Co., Dunedin, 1877), p. 51.

26. *New Zealand Minstrelsy* (R. Stokes and W. Lyon, Wellington, 1852), p. v.

27. *The New Zealand Survey* (The Author, Wellington, 1867), preface.

28. *Shanties by the Way*, p. 44. This anthology contains a good selection of Thatcher's work, as well as verses (1889-1893) by Arthur Desmond, and Edwin Edwards's lively 'Waitekauri Everytime!'.

29. Bowen, *Poems* (1861), p. 66; Broome, *Poems from New Zealand* (1868), p. 36.

30. *Musings in Maoriland* (Arthur T. Kierle, Dunedin, 1890), pp. 104-5.

31. Kingsbury, 'Poetry in New Zealand', p. 80; Sir George Grey, Correspondence (Auckland Public Library, Grey Collection).

32. Andrew Kippis, *A Narrative of the Voyages Round the World Performed by Captain James Cook* (Bickers, London, 1883), p. 370.

33. In the revised edition of 1883, Domett rearranged the opening, as explained by Dennis McEldowney, 'The Unbridled Bridal Pair: "Ranolf and Amohia"', *Landfall* 88 (December 1968), 374-83. My quotations are from the original text of 1872.

34. *Ranolf and Amohia*, pp. 46-7.

35. *Ranolf and Amohia*, p. 152.

36. *Ranolf and Amohia*, pp. 232, 301, 212-13, 265.

37. Jessie Mackay, 'Concerning New Zealand Letters', *Art in New Zealand* I.3 (March 1929), 161-5; *Literary Essays of Ezra Pound* (Faber, London, 1954, 1960), pp. 4, 9;

38. Nellie F.H. Macleod, *A Voice on the Wind* (Reed, Wellington, 1955), p. 5; *Literary Essays*, p. 294; 'mystic miraculous moonshine' is from Swinburne's self-parody 'Nephilidia'.

39. *Poetical Works of Henry Lawson* (Sydney, 1925), p. vii; Wright's boast about his humble origins is in an autobiographical note in the second edition of *The Station Ballads and Other Verses*, Robert Solway (ed.) (John A. Lee, Auckland, 1945), p. 62.

40. *Station Ballads* (J.G. Sawell, Dunedin, 1897), pp. 106-8.

41. *The Passing of the Forest and Other Verse* (The Author, London, 1925), pp. 13-14.

42. Letter to Miss G. Colborne-Veel, 25 April [1925], quoted by Keith Sinclair, *William Pember Reeves* (Clarendon Press, Oxford, 1965), p. 341.

43. *The Penguin Book of New Zealand Verse*, Allen Curnow (ed.) (1960), p. 311.

44. Ibid., p. 38; P.C.M. Alcock, 'A True Colonial Voice: Blanche Edith Baughan', *Landfall* 102 (June 1972), p. 170.

45. Letter to Johannes C. Andersen, 12 May 1907, bound into Auckland Institute copy of Baughan's *Verses* (1898).

46. Among the many other poets who addressed the theme was Alan Mulgan in 'Dead Timber' in *The English of the Line* (Whitcombe and Tombs, Auckland and Christchurch, [1925]); Mulgan's poem was included in *Kowhai Gold: An Anthology of Contemporary New Zealand Verse*, Quentin Pope (ed.) (Dent, London and Toronto, Dutton, New York, 1930); Matthew Arnold, 'Stanzas from the Grande Chartreuse'.

47. *The Penguin Book of New Zealand Verse* (1960), pp. 38-9.

48. Robert Chapman and Jonathan Bennett (eds), *An Anthology of New Zealand Verse* (Oxford University Press, London, 1956). Hubert Church, *The West Wind* (The Bulletin, Sydney, 1902), *Poems* (Whitcombe and Tombs, Wellington, [1904]), *Egmont* (T.C. Lothian, Melbourne, 1908), *Poems*, (T.C. Lothian, Melbourne, 1912).

49. Introduction to R.A.K. Mason, *Collected Poems* (Pegasus Press, Christchurch, 1962), p. 9.

50. C. K. Stead, *In the Glass Case: Essays on New Zealand Literature* (Auckland University Press, Auckland, 1981), p. 174; Mason's journals are quoted by J.E. Weir, *R.A.K. Mason* (Oxford University Press, Wellington, 1977), pp. 7, 12.

51. Stead, *In the Glass Case*, p. 183; Robert Frost, *Selected Poems*, Ian Hamilton (ed.) (Penguin, Harmondsworth, 1973, 1984), p. 15.

52. *James K. Baxter as Critic*, Frank McKay (Heinemann, Auckland, 1978), p. 72.

53. Personal recollection of memorial talk on Fairburn, given by Mason to the Auckland University College Literary Society, April 1957. A version has been published as R.A.K. Mason, *Rex Fairburn* (Press Room, University of Otago, Dunedin, 1962). Fairburn's own poem on a similar theme, 'Laughter', is no less typical of its author in its poetic strategy; whereas 'Judas Iscariot' is essentially a sustained metaphor, Fairburn worked a series of images into ironic couplets, such as 'If you've swindled a friend, or betrayed your love, / a hearty laugh will fit like a glove'. In a letter to Mason, 24 June 1932, Fairburn pointed out that Hazlitt's essay 'Good Nature' 'hits the same nail as your poem does'; *The Letters of A.R.D. Fairburn*, Lauris Edmond (ed.) (Oxford University Press, Auckland, 1981), p. 78.

54. James Bertram, *The Flight of the Phoenix* (Victoria University Press, Wellington, 1985), p. 86.

55. Fairburn, letter to Muriel Innes, 14 June 1934, *Letters*, p. 87; John Needham, 'Recent Poetry and Coleridgean Principles', *JNZL: Journal of New Zealand Literature* 3 (1985), p. 40.

56. Kingsbury, 'Poetry in New Zealand', p. 271.

57. M. H. Holcroft, *Mary Ursula Bethell* (Oxford University Press, Wellington, 1975), p. 30. This booklet gives helpful biographical information, but Holcroft (like John Weir, whom he cites, p. 8) misreads 'Trance'.

58. *Mary Ursula Bethell*, p. 39; Kingsbury, 'Poetry in New Zealand', p. 280.

59. C.K. Stead demonstrated in *The New Poetic* (Hutchinson, London, 1964) that the best of Marsh's Georgians were revolutionary in their time, opening the way for Pound and Eliot. But it is to the later and lesser Georgians that the *Kowhai Gold* poets are mainly indebted. Trixie Te Arama Menzies reappraises the anthology in '*Kowhai Gold* — Skeleton

or Scapegoat?', *Landfall* 165 (March 1988), pp. 19-26. *Kowhai Gold*, like *New Zealand Verse* before it, lists all the verse volumes of the poets represented.

60. James K. Baxter, *James K. Baxter as Critic*, pp. 59-60, saw merit in Alan Mulgan's *Golden Wedding* (Dent, London, 1932) and in 'Success' in *Aldebaran and other Verses* (The Author, Christchurch, 1937). Allen Curnow's Caxton *Book of New Zealand Verse* of 1945 included interesting work by J.C. Beaglehole, whose *Words for Music* was published by the Caxton Press, Christchurch, 1938.

61. *The Penguin Book of New Zealand Verse*, Ian Wedde and Harvey McQueen (eds), p. 34; Dick Davis, review of the Penguin anthology, *P.N. Review* 13.2 (1986), p. 67 (which prints 'vicars' '); Curnow, Caxton *Book of New Zealand Verse* (1945, 1951), p. 23; Alan Mulgan, *Great Days in New Zealand Writing* (Reed, Wellington, 1962), p. 94; Fairburn, letter to Muriel Innes, 16 July 1934, *Letters*, p. 89; Baxter, *James K. Baxter as Critic*, p. 151. F.M. McKay gives an enthusiastic account of Duggan's verse in *Eileen Duggan* (Oxford University Press, Wellington, 1977).

62. Quoted by Peter Simpson in his introduction to Allen Curnow, *Look Back Harder*, p. xvi, from a review, 'Three New Zealand Poets', in *The Press* (Christchurch), 27 July 1940; the phrase 'local signs' is Curnow's.

63. *James K. Baxter as Critic*, pp. 60, 87-8.

64. E.H. McCormick, *New Zealand Literature: A Survey* (1959), p. 124; Lydia Wevers, introduction to Robin Hyde, *Selected Poems* (Oxford University Press, 1984), p. xvi. 'Young Knowledge' is included in Ian Wedde's Penguin anthology (1985). A short poem not in *Selected Poems* but showing Hyde at her sardonic best is 'The English Rider', in *Persephone in Winter*; it was anthologized by Chapman and Bennett in their *Anthology of New Zealand Verse*.

65. Another poet who wrote in the vein of the *fin de siècle* English aesthetes was Dick Harris, who died in 1926 at the age of thirty-nine. His verse — ridiculed by Fairburn in a letter to Denis Glover, 6 May 1936 (*Letters*, p. 100) — was gathered by Pat Lawlor in *The Poetry of Dick Harris* (New Century Press, Sydney, 1927). Harris specializes in such forms as the triolet, pantoum, villanelle, rondel, rondeau, and ballade.

66. Denys Trussell, *Fairburn* (Auckland University Press and Oxford University Press, 1984), p. 16; this biography contains some of the most perceptive criticism of Fairburn's verse; for life as 'a search for meaning', see 'What Life Means to Me' in A.R.D. Fairburn, *The Woman Problem and Other Prose* (Paul, Auckland, 1967), pp. 79-83.

67. Note appended to *Three Poems*, reprinted in A.R.D. Fairburn, *Collected Poems* (Pegasus Press, Christchurch, 1966), p. 58; Robin Skelton (ed.) *Poetry of the Thirties* (Penguin, Harmondsworth, 1964) is full of poems that recall Fairburn for a reader familiar with his verse. The introduction is relevant to an understanding of Fairburn and his New Zealand contemporaries. Compare, for instance, Louis MacNeice's 'An Eclogue for Christmas', a dialogue between 'A' and 'B', with Fairburn's 'Dialogue' between 'A' and 'B' in *Dominion*.

68. Allen Curnow (ed.), *The Penguin Book of New Zealand Verse* (1960), p. 319; 'What Life Means to Me', in *The Woman Problem*, p. 82.

69. The accusations about cosiness and sentimentality are by C.K. Stead, *In the Glass Case*, p. 165, and Ian Wedde, *The Penguin Book of New Zealand Verse* (1985), p. 41. Stead, though offering a fairly negative view of Fairburn's achievement, is one of the few critics to see the exceptional promise of *He Shall Not Rise*; *Penguin Book* (1960), p. 47.

70. 'What Life Means to Me', in *The Woman Problem*, p. 83. Fairburn's neo romantic transcendentalism and his outbursts against 'the army of the unliving' have their closest twentieth century parallels in the verse of E.E. Cummings, though stylistically the two poets are worlds apart. The stress on 'the immortal moment' links Fairburn with Blake, Shelley, Wordsworth, and Browning, among others.

71. Allen Curnow, *Penguin Book of New Zealand Verse* (1960), p. 47.

72. Fairburn, letters to Charles Brasch, 8 April 1947 and 14 May 1947, *Letters*, pp. 157, 159; *Penguin Book* (1960), p. 316.

73. The quoted phrase ('a load of debt . . .') is from Fairburn's *Dominion*. There is a careful discussion of 'New Zealand Poetry and the Depression' by T.L. Sturm in *Essays on New Zealand Literature*, Wystan Curnow (ed.) (Heinemann, Auckland, 1973), pp. 16-28; Fairburn, letter to R.A.K. Mason, 1 February 1930, *Letters*, p. 31. To Fairburn himself, de Montalk was writing about 'the New Zealand school of poets' and 'the New Zealand group of poets' and their 'proud rank among the masters' as early as 1926; see W.S. Broughton, 'Problems and Responses of Three New Zealand Poets in the 1920s', in *Essays on New Zealand Literature*, p. 4; Fairburn, letter to Denis Glover, 8 June 1935, *Letters*, p. 95. Among the better known poets included in Marris's annual were J.C. Beaglehole, Douglas Stewart (who became an Australian poet), Gloria Rawlinson, and Arnold Wall; there were even a couple of pieces by Charles Brasch, and Fairburn himself was once represented without his permission.

74. Fairburn, letter to Denis Glover, 29 August 1935, *Letters*, p. 96; not Glover's phrase, but Gerard Manley Hopkins's in 'Pied Beauty'.

75. Allen Curnow, *Penguin Book of New Zealand Verse* (1960), p. 50.

76. Charles Brasch, *Collected Poems*, Alan Roddick (ed.) (Oxford University Press, Auckland, 1984), p. 17. As first published, the poem consisted of three stanzas of four, four, and six lines. Brasch suppressed the rather too explicit and abstract second quatrain. His alteration of 'Birds and fishes visit us and come no more' seems to me an error of judgement: not only is the closer rhyme preferable within the shorter poem, but 'come no more' is plainly untrue.

77. Curnow diagnosed 'geographical anxieties' in his prefatory note to his *Collected Poems 1933-1973* (Reed, Wellington, 1974), p. xiii.

78. The poet's own words, quoted on the cover of the Kiwi gramophone record of his reading of the poem to Lilburn's music, played by the Alex Lindsay String Orchestra (Kiwi Record LD-2, Reed, Wellington, [1960]).

79. *Look Back Harder*, pp. 3-5.

80. J.R. Hervey, *Selected Poems* (1940), *New Poems* (1942), *Man on a Raft* (1949), *She Was My Spring* (1955); all Caxton Press, Christchurch.

81. Allen Curnow, introduction to *A Book of New Zealand Verse, 1923-45* (Caxton, Christchurch, 1945), pp. 14-15; reprinted in Allen Curnow, *Look Back Harder: Critical Writings, 1935-1984*, Peter Simpson (ed.) (Auckland University Press, Auckland, 1987), p. 43. All further references to Curnow's critical writings will be to this volume.

82. *Look Back Harder*, p. 49.

83. For examples of his resistance to the word 'myth', see his 1951 review of *New Zealand Poetry Yearbook*, 1, *Look Back Harder*, pp. 107-8, and in a 1953 review of M.H. Holcroft's *Dance of the Seasons*, *Look Back Harder*, p. 124; but in 'Aspects of New Zealand poetry' (1943), writing of Mason and Fairburn, he says, 'I am convinced that the impulse towards a formed myth of place and people is the chief energizing principle among those of their generation', *Look Back Harder*, p. 38. See also *Look Back Harder*, p. 49.

84. For example, in the comment '. . . some poets are making a home for the imagination, so that more personal and universal impulses may be set at liberty', *Look Back Harder*, p. 45; or the interesting remark in a review of Baxter's second book, *Blow, Wind of Fruitfulness*, 'the older poets still living and writing have been seeking a way back to more personal and universal themes, lest their discovery of New Zealand should end in isolation', *Look Back Harder*, p. 100.

85. For example, the essay which appeared in *Meanjin Papers* in 1943 entitled 'Aspects of New Zealand Poetry', *Look Back Harder*, pp. 32-41.

86. A.R.D. Fairburn, 'Poetry in New Zealand', in *First Year Book of the Arts in New Zealand*, H. Wadman (ed.) (Tombs, Wellington, 1945), p. 127; James Bertram, 'Robin Hyde: a reassessment', *Landfall* 27 (September 1953), p. 184; reprinted in *Flight of the Phoenix: Critical Notes on New Zealand Writers* (Victoria University Press, Wellington, 1985), p. 18 (all further references to Bertram's critical writings will be to this volume). J. R. Hervey, *Selected Poems* (Caxton, Christchurch, 1940), *New Poems* (Caxton, Christchurch, 1942), *Man on a Raft* (Caxton, Christchurch, 1949), *She Was My Spring* (Caxton, Christchurch, 1955).

87. W.H. Oliver, *Arachne* 2 (February 1951), p. 2; Kendrick Smithyman, *A Way of Saying: A Study of New Zealand Poetry* (Collins, Auckland, 1965), pp. 80ff.

88. Hubert Witheford, *Shadow of the Flame*, Poems 1942-7 (Pelorus, Auckland, 1950), *The Falcon Mask* (Pegasus, Christchurch, 1951), *The Lightning Makes a Difference* (Brookside, London, 1962), *A Native, Perhaps Beautiful* (Caxton, Christchurch, 1967), *A Possible Order* (Ravine, Harrow, 1980).

89. George Turner, review of *The Falcon Mask*, *Landfall* 22 (June 1952), p. 155.

90. James K. Baxter, *The Fire and the Anvil: Notes on Modern Poetry* (New Zealand University Press, Wellington, 1955), p. 27; reprinted in *James K. Baxter as Critic*, Frank McKay (ed.) (Heinemann, Auckland, 1978), p. 25. All further references to Baxter's critical writings will be to this volume.

91. See Bill Manhire, 'Events & editorials: Baxter's *Collected Poems*', *Islands* 31-32 (June 1981), p. 102; *James K. Baxter as Critic*, p. 11.

92. James K. Baxter, introductory note to *A Selection of Poetry by James K. Baxter* (Poetry Magazine, Wellington, 1964), p. [6].

93. See Baxter's view that 'Animism is an essential factor in the artist's view of the world', *James K. Baxter as Critic*, p. 3.

94. See the note by Baxter on the selection of his poems in Charles Doyle (ed.), *Recent Poetry in New Zealand* (Collins, Auckland, 1965), p. 29.

95. *A Way of Saying*, p. 59.

96. *James K. Baxter as Critic*, p. 89.

97. Ruth Gilbert, *Lazarus and Other Poems* (Reed, Wellington, 1949), *The Sunlit Hour* (Allen and Unwin, London, 1955), *The Luthier* (Reed, Wellington, 1966), *Collected Poems* (Black Robin, Wellington, 1984); Gloria Rawlinson, *Gloria's Book* (Whitcombe and Tombs, Christchurch, 1933), *The Perfume Vendor* (Hutchinson, London, 1936), *The Islands Where I Was Born* (Handcraft, Wellington, 1955), *Of Clouds and Pebbles* (Paul's, Hamilton, 1963).

98. 'Paul Henderson' (Ruth France), *Unwilling Pilgrim* (Caxton, Christchurch, 1955), *The Halting Place* (Caxton, Christchurch, 1961).

99. See Smithyman's comments, *A Way of Saying*, pp. 206-7.

100. See Hubert Witheford, 'The silver tongue', *New Zealand Poetry Yearbook* 3 (Reed, Wellington, 1953), pp. 52-8.

101. *Look Back Harder*, p. 292; Allen Curnow, 'Note', *Trees, Effigies, Moving Objects* (Catspaw, Wellington, 1972), p. [5].

102. *Look Back Harder*. p. 1; see Curnow's comments about the 'enormous pains' of composition in Harry Ricketts, *Talking About Ourselves: Twelve New Zealand Poets* (Mallinson Rendel, Wellington, 1986), p. 103.

103. T.S. Eliot, 'Shakespeare and the Stoicism of Seneca' in *Selected Prose*, J. Hayward (ed.) (Penguin, Harmondsworth, 1953), p. 53.

104. *Look Back Harder*, p. 257; *Look Back Harder*, p. 294.

105. See John Geraets's article on Smithyman's difficulties with Brasch, 'Kendrick Smithyman and Brasch's *Landfall*', *Landfall* 160 (December 1986), pp. 443-57.

106. *A Way of Saying*, p. 131.

107. Reginald Berry, 'Hard yakker: Kendrick Smithyman's colorless green ideas', *Landfall* 168 (December 1988), p. 388-402; Interview with Smithyman by MacD. P. Jackson, *Landfall* 168 (December 1988), p. 414; John Geraets, 'Kendrick Smithyman and Brasch's *Landfall*', p. 453.

108. *Look Back Harder*, p. 199; Interview, *Landfall* 168 (December 1988), p. 406.

109. Introductory note to the selection of his poems in *Recent Poetry in New Zealand*, p. 164.

110. *Look Back Harder*, p. 169; Keith Sinclair, review of Hubert Witheford, *Shadow of the Flame*, *Here & Now* 1 (October 1949), p. 32; Keith Sinclair, 'Memories of T.H. Scott', *Landfall* 54 (June 1960), p. 182; J.E.P. Thomson, review of Keith Sinclair, *A Time to Embrace*, *Landfall* 72 (December 1964), p. 374.

111. *James K. Baxter as Critic*, p. 4.

112. Louis Johnson, editorial, *New Zealand Poetry Yearbook* 2 (Reed, Wellington, 1952), p. 10.

113. See interview with Johnson in *Talking About Ourselves*, p. 147; *James K. Baxter as Critic*, p. 53; see also Erik Schwimmer, 'Commentary' in *Poetry Yearbook* 1 (Reed, Wellington, 1951), pp. 65-70; L. Johnson, editorial, *Poetry Yearbook* 2 (Reed, Wellington, 1952), pp. 7-12; Charles Doyle, 'Anger or apathy?', *Poetry Yearbook* 8 (Pegasus, Christchurch, 1959), pp. 12-16; Allen Curnow, *Look Back Harder*, p. 107.

114. Robert Chapman, review of James K. Baxter, *The Fallen House*, *Landfall* 27 (September 1953), p. 210.

115. *A Way of Saying*, p. 220; in *Poetry Yearbook* 8 (1959), p. 10, Johnson notes that of the 104 contributors to date, only seven lived outside the four main centres.

116. *A Way of Saying*, p. 6; Hubert Witheford, 'The silver tongue', *Poetry Yearbook* 3 (Reed, Wellington, 1953), pp. 52-58.

117. Introduction to *An Anthology of New Zealand Verse*, Robert Chapman & Jonathan Bennett (eds) (Oxford University Press, London, 1956), p. xxxii.

118. *Look Back Harder*, p. 174; *Look Back Harder*, p. 133.

119. Smithyman gives a similar analysis of contemporary developments in *A Way of Saying*, a remarkably astute study given its closeness to the subject.

120. Smithyman writes, '. . . where the more academic writer offers us fictions as ostensible entertainments (his ostensive fictions) the writer with more of the romantic to him offers us statements of social significance, his social fictions . . .', *A Way of Saying*, p. 202ff.

121. C.K. Stead, 'Allen Curnow's Poetry', *Landfall* 65 (March 1963), pp. 26-45; reprinted in *In the Glass Case: Essays on New Zealand Writers* (Auckland University Press, Auckland, 1981), pp. 189-206.

122. *Recent Poetry in New Zealand*, p. 179.

123. Introduction to Fleur Adcock (ed.), *The Oxford Book of Contemporary New Zealand Poetry* (Oxford University Press, Auckland, 1982), p. [x].

124. *Recent Poetry in New Zealand*, p. 18.

125. Kevin Ireland, 'Beginnings', *Islands* 28 (March 1980), p. 31.

126. *Recent Poetry in New Zealand*, p. 46; Peter Bland, 'Beginnings', *Islands* 30 (October 1980), p. 233.

127. Collections by Charles Doyle include, *A Splinter of Glass* (Pegasus, Christchurch, 1956), *Distances* (Paul's, Hamilton, 1963), *Messages for Herod* (Collins, Auckland, 1965), *A Sense of Place: Poems* (Wai-te-ata, Wellington, 1965), *Earth Meditations: 2* (Alldritt, Auckland, 1968), *Earth Meditations: 1-5* (Coach House, Toronto, 1971), *Stonedancer* (Auckland University Press, Auckland, 1976), *A Steady Hand* (Auckland University Press, Auckland, 1983); Gordon Challis's single volume is *Building* (Caxton, Christchurch, 1963).

128. See Robert Chapman's comment, 'No Maori poet has written in English, and the translations have been inadequate to establish communication between the traditions', *An Anthology of New Zealand Verse*, p. xxviii; Barry Mitcalfe, *Poetry of the Maori: Translations* (Paul's, Hamilton, 1961), *Maori Poetry: The Singing Word* (Price Milburn/Victoria University Press, Wellington, 1974).

129. *James K. Baxter as Critic*, p. 209.

130. MacD. P. Jackson, review of *No Ordinary Sun*, *Landfall* 74 (June 1965), pp. 189-93; see also the interview with Tuwhare by Bill Manhire, *Landfall* 167 (September 1988), p. 266.

131. 'Conversation with Charles Brasch', *Landfall* 100 (December 1971), p. 370.

132. Ian Wedde, 'Captivating invitation: getting on to Charles Brasch's "home ground"', *Islands* 13 (Spring 1975), p. 315-27.

133. See, for example, C.K. Stead, 'James K. Baxter: a loss of direction', *In the Glass Case*, pp. 211-15; *Recent Poetry in New Zealand*, p. 30; interview with Baxter by J.E. Weir, *Landfall* 111 (September 1974), p. 244.

134. Here and elsewhere I am indebted to Vincent O'Sullivan's commentaries on Baxter in *James K. Baxter* (Oxford University Press, Wellington, 1976) and in 'After Culloden: remarks on the early and middle poetry of James K. Baxter', *Islands* 3 (Autumn 1973), pp. 19-30.

135. *Autumn Testament* (Price Milburn, Wellington, 1972), p. 6.

136. Interview, *Landfall* 111, p. 245.

137. Bob Orr, *Blue Footpaths* (Amphedesma, London, 1972), *Poems for Moira* (Hawk, Taylors Mistake, 1979), *Cargo* (Voice, Wellington, 1983), *Red Trees* (Auckland University Press/Silverfish, Auckland, 1986).

138. [Bert Hingley], *Freed At Last* (1972), p. 24; Stephen Chan, 'Editor's indulgence', *A Charlatan's Mosaic: New Zealand Universities Literary Yearbook 1972* (New Zealand Universities Arts Council, Auckland, 1972), p. [4]. Ian Wedde uses the phrase 'information network' in *Talking About Ourselves*, p. 49.

139. C.K. Stead, 'From Wystan to Carlos: modern and modernism in recent New Zealand poetry', *In the Glass Case*, p 139-59.

140. Murray Edmond, 'Creating a potent image: notes on the magazine *The Word is Freed*', *Span* 16-17 (April/October 1983), p. 62; Alan Brunton, editorial, *The Word is Freed* 1 (July 1969), p. 1; Bill Manhire in *The Young New Zealand Poets*, Arthur Baysting (ed.) (Heinemann, Auckland, 1973), p. 122; Ian Wedde in *The Young New Zealand Poets*, p. 185.

141. Peter Olds, *Lady Moss Revived: Poems* (Caveman, Dunedin, 1972), *Freeway* (Caveman, Dunedin, 1974), *Doctor's Rock* (Caveman, Dunedin, 1976), *Beethoven's Guitar* (Caveman, Dunedin, 1980), *After Looking for Broadway* (One Eyed Press, Christchurch, 1985); the line, 'no sound is dissonant . . .', which is almost identical to the last line of Coleridge's 'This Lime-tree Bower my Prison', occurs in Alan Brunton, 'Ottery St Mary', *Messengers in Blackface* (Amphedesma, London, 1973); Bill Manhire, 'Breaking the line: a view of American and New Zealand Poetry', *Islands* 38 (December 1987), p. 152.

142. Jan Kemp, *Against the Softness of Woman* (Caveman, Dunedin, 1976), *Diamonds and Gravel* (Hampson Hunt, Wellington, 1979), *Ice-breaker Poems* (Coal-Black, Auckland, 1980).

143. 'Creating a potent image', p. 61.

144. Wystan Curnow, 'Speech balloons & conversation bubbles', *And* 4 (October 1985), p. 126.

145. *In the Glass Case*, pp. 139-59.

146. Alistair Paterson, *Caves in the Hills* (Pegasus, Christchurch, 1965), *Birds Flying* (Pegasus, Christchurch, 1973), *Cities and Strangers* (Caveman, Dunedin, 1976), *The Toledo Room* (Pilgrims South, Dunedin, 1978), *Qu'appelle* (Pilgrims South, Dunedin, 1982), *Odysseus Rex* (Auckland University Press, Auckland, 1986), *Incantations for Warriors* (Earl of Seacliff Art Workshop, Auckland, 1987).

147. Roger Horrocks, 'Off the map', *Parallax* 3 (Winter 1983), pp. 247-55; Alan Loney, 'Some aspects of C. K. Stead's

"Walking westwards [*sic*]" ', *Islands* 30 (October 1980), pp. 240-50; M. Edmond, 'Please classify and file', *Islands* 31-32 (June 1981), pp. 161-6.
148. This appears as the epigraph to 'Homage to Matisse', which was first published separately by Amphedesma Press, London, in 1971 and later appeared in *Made Over* (1974).
149. *Talking About Ourselves*, p. 54.
150. The phrase, 'main obsessions', comes from a prefatory note to Castaly: 'Nevertheless my main obsessions (sometimes called "themes") have remained the same . . . .'; Wedde several times refers to the private language a child has with an imaginary friend as the starting point for his poetry: interview with Wedde by David Dowling, *Landfall* 154 (June 1985), p. 173; *Talking About Ourselves*, p. 53.
151. *The Young New Zealand Poets*, p. 185; Wedde expressed surprise at Stead's use, in 'From Wystan to Carlos', of *Earthly, Sonnets to Carlos* to demonstrate 'open form': 'if ever there was a closed thing . . .', *Landfall* 154 (June 1985), p. 166; ibid.
152. See a concluding note in *The Elaboration* (Square & Circle, Wellington, 1972), p. 29.
153. See Bill Manhire, 'Breaking the line'.
154. Ibid., p. 152.
155. Red Mole, the theatrical collective founded by Brunton in 1974, had as one of its 'five principles', 'to escape programmed behaviour by remaining erratic'; Alan Brunton, *Messengers in Blackface* (Amphedesma, London, 1973), *Black and White Anthology* (Hawk, Taylors Mistake, 1976), *O Ravachol* (Red Mole, Auckland, 1979), *And She Said* (A. Fisher/Red Mole, New York, 1984), *New Order* (A. Fisher/Red Mole, New York, 1986), *Day for a Daughter* (Untold, Wellington, 1989), *Slow Passes* (Auckland University Press, Auckland, 1991).'
156. Alan Loney, *The Bare Remembrance* (Caveman, Dunedin, 1971), *dear Mondrian* (Hawk, Taylors Mistake, 1976) *Shorter Poems 1963-77* (Auckland University Press, Auckland, 1979), *Swell* (Black Light, Wellington, 1987); Graham Lindsay, *Thousand-eyed Eel* (Hawk, Taylors Mistake, 1976), *Public* (Ridge-Pole, Dunedin, 1980), *Big Boy* (Auckland University Press, 1986).
157. For example, in an interview with Jill McCracken, *Landfall* 107 (September 1973), p. 226.
158. Iain Lonie, *Recreations* (Wai-te-ata, Wellington, 1967), *Letters from Ephesus* (Bibliography Room, University of Otago, Dunedin, 1970), *Courting Death* (Wai-te-ata, Wellington, 1984), *The Entrance to Purgatory* (McIndoe, Dunedin, 1986).
159. Michael Jackson, *Latitudes of Exile: Poems 1965-1975* (McIndoe, Dunedin, 1976), *Wall* (McIndoe, Dunedin, 1980), *Going On* (McIndoe, Dunedin, 1985), *Duty Free: Selected Poems 1965-1988* (McIndoe, Dunedin, 1989).
160. Interview with Curnow by Peter Simpson, *Landfall* 175 (September 1990), p. 302.
161. Stead's lecture 'From Wystan to Carlos' suggested that Curnow had moved towards 'open form', and so did the inclusion of poems by Curnow in Paterson's anthology, *15 Contemporary Poets*. Wedde also makes a similar claim, *Talking About Ourselves*, p. 50. For Curnow's reading of Pound and Williams, see his lecture, 'Olson as oracle: "projective verse" thirty years on', *Look Back Harder*, pp. 305-18.
162. Leigh Davis, 'Solo Curnow', *And* 3 (October 1984), p. 51ff.
163. See also Curnow's remark, 'I like to think poetry can — perhaps even that it does — substitute a kind of simultaneous order for the linear, chronological . . . order that we assume for most practical purposes', interview, *Landfall* 175, p. 306.
164. Interview with Smithyman by MacD. P. Jackson, *Landfall* 168 (December 1988), pp. 411, 418.
165. Quoted in Geraets, 'Kendrick Smithyman and Brasch's *Landfall*', p. 448.
166. Interview with Stead by Michael Harlow, *Landfall* 148 (December 1983), p. 450.
167. C. K. Stead, 'On Quesada', *In the Glass Case*, p. 275.
168. 'From Wystan to Carlos', *In the Glass Case*, p. 148; interview, *Landfall* 148, p. 459.
169. Vincent O'Sullivan (ed.), *An Anthology of Twentieth Century New Zealand Poetry* (2nd edn., Oxford University Press, Wellington, 1976), p. xxix; James Bertram, 'Vincent O'Sullivan: enter the Butcher', Flight of the Phoenix, p. 138.
170. Quoted in Carroll du Chateau, 'Deb Poets Society', *Metro* (December 1990), p. 139; Kevin Ireland, review of *Brother Jonathan, Brother Kafka*, *Landfall* 135 (September 1980), p. 300; K. O. Arvidson, 'Curnow, Stead, and O'Sullivan: major sensibilities in New Zealand poetry', *Journal of New Zealand Literature* 1 (1983), p. 47.
171. *Talking About Ourselves*, p. 72.
172. Michael Harlow, *Edges* (Lycabettus, Athens, 1974), *Nothing but Switzerland and Lemonade* (Hawk, Eastbourne, 1980), *Today is the Piano's Birthday* (Auckland University Press, Auckland, 1981), *Vlaminck's Tie* (Auckland University Press, Auckland, 1984).
173. Fleur Adcock, 'Comment', in *Private Gardens: An Anthology of New Zealand Women Poets*, Riemke Ensing (ed.) (Caveman, Dunedin, 1977), p. 15.
174. Riemke Ensing, *Making Inroads* (Coal-Black, Auckland, 1980), *Letters: Selected Poems* (Lowry, Auckland, 1982), *Topographies* (Prometheus, Auckland, 1984), *Spells from Chagall* (Griffin, Auckland, 1987); Elizabeth Nannestad, *Jump*, (Auckland University Press, Auckland 1986); Kim Eggleston, *From the Face to the Bin: Poems 1978-1984* (Strong John, Greymouth, 1984), *25 Poems: The Mist Will Rise and the World Will Drip With Gold* (Strong John, Greymouth, 1985); see Baxter's remarks mentioned in note 96 and also Baysting's introduction to *The Young New Zealand Poets*, p. 4.
175. *Talking About Ourselves*, p. 61; interview in Sue Kedgley, *Our Own Country: Leading New Zealand Women Writers Talk About Their Writing and Their Lives* (Penguin, Auckland, 1989), p. 187.
176. See introduction to Mark Williams (ed.), *The Caxton Press Anthology: New Zealand Poetry 1972-1986* (Caxton, Christchurch, 1987), p. 23.
177. Interview with McAlpine by Michael Harlow, *Landfall* 145 (March 1983), p. 75.
178. Ibid., p. 74.
179. *Talking About Ourselves*, p. 90.
180. Leigh Davis, 'Set up', *And* 1 (October 1983), p. 3; Leigh Davis, 'Solo Curnow', *And* 3 (October 1984), p. 61.

181. Michele Leggott, *Like This?* (Caxton, Christchurch, 1988), *Swimmers, Dancers* (Auckland University Press, Auckland, 1991).
182. Bernadette Hall, *Heartwood* (Caxton, Christchurch, 1989), *Of Elephants Etc.* (Untold, Wellington, 1990); Jenny Bornholdt, *This Big Face* (Victoria University Press, Wellington, 1988), *Moving House* (Victoria University Press, Wellington, 1989).
183. Janet Charman, *2 Deaths in 1 Night* (New Women's Press, Auckland, 1987); Heather McPherson, *A Figurehead: A Face* (Spiral, Wellington, 1982), *The Third Myth* (Tauranga Moana, 1986).
184. For example, in C. K. Stead, 'Wedde's inclusions', *Landfall* 155 (September 1985), pp. 289-302.
185. *The Caxton Press Anthology*, p. 26.
186. Arapera Blank, *Nga Kokako Huataratara* (Waiata Koa, Auckland, 1986); Bub Bridger, *Up Here on the Hill* (Mallinson Rendel, Wellington, 1989); Trixie Te Arama Menzies, *Uenuku* (Waiata Koa, Auckland, 1986), *Papakainga* (Waiata Koa, Auckland, 1988).
187. *Our Own Country*, pp. 103-4.
188. David Eggleton, *South Pacific Sunrise* (Penguin, Auckland, 1986), *People of the Land* (Penguin, Auckland, 1988); Gregory O'Brien, *Location of the Least Person* (Auckland University Press, Auckland, 1987), *Dunes and Barns* (Modern House, Auckland, 1988), *Man with a Child's Violin* (Caxton, Christchurch, 1990), and *Malachi: an entertainment* (Wellington Plains, 1990); John Newton, *Tales from the Angler's Eldorado* (Untold, Christchurch, 1985).

Children's Literature

1. Anon., *Emily Bathurst at Home & Abroad* (Wertheim, London, 1847), p. 100.
2. Lady Barker, *Boys* (Routledge, London, 1874), p. 10.
3. Ernest Simeon Elwell, *The Boy Colonists* (Simpkin Marshall, Oxford, 1878), t-p.
4. Louisa H. Bedford, *Under One Standard; or, the Touch that Makes Us Kin* (Society for the Promotion of Christian Knowledge, London, 1916), pp. 215, 92.
5. Amy Dora Bright, *Three Xmas Gifts* (Wilding, Shrewsbury and Simpkin, London, 1901), p. iii.
6. Ambrose E. Moore, *Fairyland in New Zealand* (Brett, Auckland, 1909), Preface.
7. Edith Howes, *The Singing Fish* (Cassell, London, 1921), p. 144.
8. Theodore and Winifred Harper, *Windy Island* (Doubleday, New York, 1934), p. 209.
9. Phillis Garrard, *The Doings of Hilda* (Blackie, London, 1932), p. 157.
10. C.R. Allen, *A Poor Scholar* (Reed, Wellington, 1936), p. 227.
11. Clare Mallory, *Merry Again* (Oxford University Press, Melbourne, 1947), p. 110.
12. James Rich, *Teko-Teko in Waitomo* (Richlake Studios, Rotorua, 1949), p. 37.
13. Ans Westra, in *Photography*, September 1964.
14. Ruth Dallas, in *Tea-tree and Iron Sands* (eds Tom Fitzgibbon and Barbara Spiers, 2nd edn., Auckland College of Education, Auckland, 1989), p. 34.
15. Anne de Roo, *Tea-tree and Iron Sands*, p. 38.
16. Margaret Mahy, in *Tea-tree and Iron Sands*, p. 91; 'Talk to the Children's Literature Association', published in the *Children's Literature Association Yearbook*, 1976; *Tea-tree and Iron Sands*, p. 91.
17. Mahy, *The Catalogue of the Universe* (Dent, London, 1985), p. 44.
18. Mahy, *Memory* (Dent, London, 1987), p. 171.
19. Patricia Grace, in *Tea-tree and Iron Sands*, p. 63.
20. Ronda Armitage, *Twentieth Century Children's Writers* (St James's Press, Chicago/London, 1989), p. 31.
21. Gwenda Turner, in *Tea-tree and Iron Sands*, p. 122.
22. Joanna Orwin, ibid., p. 104.
23. William Taylor, *Break a Leg* (Reed Methuen, Auckland, 1987), p. 65.
24. Mahy, *Jam* (Dent, London, 1985), n.p.
25. Tessa Duder, in *Tea-tree and Iron Sands*, p. 44.
26. Maurice Gee, ibid., p. 56.
27. Barry Faville, *The Return* (Oxford University Press, Auckland, 1988), p. 79.
28. Caroline Macdonald, *Twentieth Century Children's Writers*, (St James's Press, Chicago/London, 1989), p. 615.

Popular Fiction

1. Letter from Henry Lanier of Doubleday Page and Company to Edith Lyttleton, 12 August 1908. Held privately in family papers.
2. Quoted by 'The Sage' in 'Literary Chat', *New Zealand Illustrated Magazine* 7 (February 1903), pp. 404-5.
3. See *The House of Reed, 1957-1967*, no author (Reed, Wellington, 1968), p. 15.
4. Essie Summers interviewed by Helen Paske, *New Zealand Listener* (18 April 1981), p. 18.
5. E.M. Smith, *A History of New Zealand Fiction* (Reed, Wellington, 1939), p. 47.
6. Louisa A. Baker, 'The Editor and His Contributors', *New Zealand Illustrated Magazine* 7 (March, 1903), pp. 424-5.
7. 'Alien', *A Daughter of the King* (Hutchinson, London, 1894), endpage.
8. *His Neighbour's Landmark* (Digby, Long and Company, London, 1907), p. 60.
9. *A Daughter of the King*, p. 186.

10. Clara Eyre Cheeseman, 'Colonials in Fiction', *New Zealand Illustrated Magazine* 7 (January, 1903), p. 279; E.M. Smith, *A History of New Zealand Fiction*, p. 71.
11. *The Majesty of Man* (Hutchinson, London, 1896), p. 342.
12. T.M. Hocken, *A Bibliography Relating to the Literature of New Zealand* (Government Printer, Wellington, 1909), pp. 461, 474; A.G. Stephens, *The Bulletin* (6 September 1906), Red Page; A.G. Stephens, *The Bulletin* (19 December 1907), Red Page.
13. G.B. Lancaster, *The Tracks We Tread* (Doubleday Page and Company, New York, 1907), pp. 232, 279.
14. *The Law Bringers* (Hodder and Stoughton, London, [1913]), pp. 298-9.
15. Lyttleton interviewed in the *Auckland Star* (26 November 1937).
16. Carl Van Doren, in the journal of the United States Literary Guild, *Wings* 7, 2 (February 1933), p. 8.
17. G.B. Lancaster, 'Tasmania Speaking', *Wings* 7, 2 (February, 1932), p. 12, and *Pageant* (Penguin, Ringwood, 1985), p. 378.
18. Lyttleton, letter to Rutger Bleecker Jewett, Appleton-Century Company, 12 December 1933. Held privately in family papers.
19. Betty Gilderdale, *A Sea Change* (Longman Paul, Auckland, 1982), p. 73.
20. Isabel M. Peacocke, *Concerning the Marlows* (Ward, Lock, London, 1950), p. 137; *Cinderella's Suitors* (Ward, Lock, London, 1918), p. 316.
21. *The Guardian* (Ward, Lock, London, 1920), pp. 100, 162, 240, 256.
22. *London Called Them* (Ward, Lock, London, 1946), pp. 109, 107.
23. Rosemary Rees, 'How I Wrote My First Novel', typescript [*circa* 1931], held at ATL.
24. E.M. Smith, *A History of New Zealand Fiction*, p. 27; Robin Hyde's comment is cited in Heather Roberts, *Where Did She Come From? New Zealand Women Novelists 1862-1987* (Allen and Unwin/Port Nicholson Press, Wellington, 1989), p. 46; *New Zealand Holiday* (Chapman and Hall, London, 1933), p. 40.
25. *Lake of Enchantment* (Herbert Jenkins, London, 1925), pp. 161, 162.
26. Nelle M. Scanlan, *Road to Pencarrow* (Robert Hale and Whitcombe and Tombs, London and Christchurch, 1963), p. 133.
27. Alan Mulgan, *Great Days in New Zealand Writing* (Reed, Wellington, 1962), pp. 96-7.
28. See Christine Bridgwood, 'Family Romances: the Contemporary Popular Family Saga', in Jean Radford (ed.), *The Progress of Romance: the Politics of Popular Fiction* (Routledge and Kegan Paul, London, 1986), pp. 167-93.
29. E.M. Smith, *A History of New Zealand Fiction*, p. 39.
30. *Kelly Pencarrow* (Robert Hale, London, 1939), p. 204.
31. *The Rusty Road* (Robert Hale and Whitcombe and Tombs, London and Christchurch, 1949), pp. 24, 16, 18, 274.
32. The most recent is Patrick Evans, who describes Marsh as spending 'years writing about an English never-never-land', *The Penguin History of New Zealand Literature* (Penguin Books, Auckland, 1990), p. 74.
33. Ngaio Marsh, 'The Novelist's Problem', Christchurch *Press* (22 December 1934).
34. Allen Curnow and Ngaio Marsh, 'A Dialogue by Way of Introduction', *First Year Book of the Arts in New Zealand* (1945), pp. 1-8.
35. Marsh, 'Birth of a Sleuth', MS in the Ngaio Marsh Papers, ATL.
36. Julian Symons, *Bloody Murder, From the Detective Story to the Crime Novel: A History* (Faber and Faber, London, 1972), p. 123.
37. Marsh, 'Death at a Remove', MS in the Ngaio Marsh Papers, ATL; 'Troy', typescript in the Ngaio Marsh Papers, ATL; untitled typescript of an article for *Mystery and Detective Magazine*, in the Ngaio Marsh Papers, ATL.
38. 'Death at a Remove'.
39. Quoted in Bruce Harding, 'The New Zealand Stories of Ngaio Marsh', *Landfall* 144 (December 1982), p. 452.
40. Dorothy Eden, *The Shadow Wife* (Hodder and Stoughton, London, 1968), p. 135.
41. *An Important Family* (Hodder and Stoughton, London, 1982), p. 12.
42. *Bride by Candlelight* (Macdonald, London, 1954), p. 208.
43. Mary Scott, *Days That Have Been* (Blackwood and Janet Paul, Auckland, 1966), p. 103.
44. Ibid., pp. 198-9.
45. Ibid., p. 68.
46. *Away From It All* (Hurst and Blackett, London, 1977), pp. 178-9.
47. *Families Are Fun* (Paul's Book Arcade, Hamilton and Auckland, 1956), p. 167.
48. Ibid., pp. 75-6.
49. Phyl Wardell, 'Her Target: 20 Novels', *New Zealand Home Journal*, 1959.
50. V. May Cottrell, 'She Starts at the End', *New Zealand Women's Weekly* (11 October 1951), p. 15.
51. Dulce Carman, *The Maori Gateway* (Wright and Brown, London, 1963), pp. 10, 142, 140.
52. *The Tapu Tree* (Wright and Brown, London, [1954]), p. 200; *The Maori Gateway, p. 139*.
53. *The Tapu Tree*, p. 215.
54. Dorothy Quentin, *Rainbow Valley* (Ward, Lock, London, 1960), pp. 8, 20, 18, 19, 31, 33, 37, 47, 55, 54.
55. Ibid., p. 36.
56. Grace Phipps, *Marriage With Eve* (Reed, Wellington, 1955), p. 30.
57. Ibid., pp. 55, 191-2.
58. Frank Bruno, quoted on the dustjacket of *The Hellbuster* (Robert Hale, London, 1959).
59. Information provided in the Sunday Magazine of the *Dominion Sunday Times* (19 August 1990), p. 26. The preface to *A Barry Crump Collection* (Beckett Publishing, Auckland, 1987) claimed that a Russian translation of *Gulf* (1964), Crump's fifth book (about crocodile-hunting in the Gulf of Carpentaria), had sold 100,000 copies.
60. Even in 1970, after Crump had published ten books, Frank Sargeson described him as 'a primitive, or virtually a primitive [writer]'. See Kevin Cunningham (ed.), *Conversation in a Train* (Auckland University Press and Oxford University Press, Auckland, 1983), p. 156.

61. Barry Crump, *Hang On A Minute Mate* (Reed, Wellington, 1961), p. 170.

62. See note 4.

63. Information provided in Bernadette Little, 'A Life of Pure Bliss', *New Zealand Herald* (16 September 1986).

64. Essie Summers, *The Essie Summers Story* (Mills and Boon, London, 1974), p. 89.

65. Ibid., p. 95.

66. *Anna of Strathallan* (Mills and Boon, London, 1975), pp. 33, 71, 94.

67. *The Gold of Noon* (Mills and Boon, London, 1974), p. 66.

68. Ivy Preston, *Island of Enchantment* (Robert Hale and Whitcombe and Tombs, London and Christchurch, 1963), pp. 48-9; *Magic in Maoriland* (Wright and Brown, London, 1962), p. 135.

69. 'Ivy will stay out of the bedroom', *New Zealand Times* (17 October 1982). In her autobiography Summers had commented: 'With regard to depicting life, I deplore coarse writing, because I feel it atrophies the reader's imagination, clips its wings. As far as the bedroom door and no further isn't prudery, it's consideration for the reader. The lack of reticence in some writing fails in its purpose . . . it is trying to describe the indescribable.' (p. 110)

70. Gloria Bevan, *Master of Mahia* (Mills and Boon, London, 1981), p. 124.

71. See Ann Barr Snitow, 'Mass Market Romance: Pornography for Women is Different', in Ann Barr Snitow, Christine Stansell, and Sharon Thompson (eds), *Powers of Desire: the Politics of Sexuality* (Monthly Review Press, New York, 1983), pp. 245-63.

72. Susan Napier, *Love in the Valley* (Mills and Boon, Sydney, 1985), p. 57.

73. Tape-recordings of Rosalie Heneghan discussing her fiction are held in the archives of the Stout Research Centre, Victoria University of Wellington.

74. See Ann Rosalind Jones, 'Mills & Boon Meets Feminism', in Jean Radford (ed.), *The Progress of Romance: the Politics of Popular Fiction*, pp. 195-218.

75. Janice A. Radway, *Reading the Romance: Women, Patriarchy, and Popular Literature*, University of North Carolina Press, Chapel Hill, 1984.

76. Yvonne Kalman interviewed by Toni McRae, 'A best-selling writer's revenge for a bad read', *Auckland Star* (5 October 1988).

Publishing, Patronage, Literary Magazines

1. William Colenso, *Fifty Years Ago in New Zealand* (R. C. Harding, Napier, 1888). Originally delivered as a lecture to the Hawke's Bay Philosophical Institute, 17 Oct. 1887.

2. Sir Apirana Ngata, 'The Maori and Printed Matter', in R. A. McKay (ed.), *A History of Printing in New Zealand, 1830-1940* (Wellington House of Printing House Craftsmen, 1940), pp. 48-49.

3. Details of these three books come from A.G. Bagnall's *New Zealand National Bibliography to the Year 1960*, 5v. [i.e. 6v., v.1 being in two parts] (Government Printer, Wellington, 1969-85), which is the foundation of any study such as this. See also Johannes Andersen, *The Lure of New Zealand Book Collecting* (Whitcombe and Tombs, Christchurch, 1936), pp. 11-15, and 'Early Printing in New Zealand' in McKay, *History of Printing in New Zealand*, pp. 2-15; A.G. Bagnall and G.C. Petersen, *William Colenso, Printer, Missionary, Botanist, Explorer, Politician; His Life and Journeys* (Reed, Wellington, 1948), pp. 42-54; D.F. McKenzie, *Oral Culture, Literacy & Print in Early New Zealand: the Treaty of Waitangi* (Victoria University Press, Wellington, 1985), *passim*; Tolla Williment (comp.), *150 Years of Printing in New Zealand* (Wellington, Government Printer, 1985), pp. 9-17.

4. Fiona Macmillan, *The Spread of Printing, Eastern Hemisphere, New Zealand* (Vangendt & Co., Amsterdam, 1969), pp. 19, 21-23.

5. Roderick Cave, *The Private Press* (2nd ed., Bowker, New York, 1983), p. 58.

6. T.M. Hocken, *A Bibliography of the Literature Relating to New Zealand* (Government Printer, Wellington, 1909), p. 233; H. Lusk, 'Maori Mahommedanism', *Fortnightly Review*, ii (1 Nov. 1865), pp. 731-7.

7. 'Our colonization and its ethics', p. 548.

8. R.M. Burdon, *New Zealand Notables, Series Two* (Caxton, Christchurch, 1945), pp. 166-85.

9. Judith M. Wild, 'The Literary Periodical in New Zealand', (M.A. thesis, University of New Zealand (Victoria) 1951), pp. 11-12.

10. C.R.H. T[aylor], in A.H. McLintock (ed.), *An Encyclopaedia of New Zealand* (Government Printer, Wellington, 1966), ii, p. 871; D.F. McKenzie (ed.), *Selections from Typo, a New Zealand Typographical Journal 1887-1897 edited by R. Coupland Harding* (Wai-te-Ata Press, Wellington, 1982).

11. W.A. Glue, *History of the Government Printing Office* (Government Printer, Wellington, 1966), pp. 84, 89.

12. Bagnall, *New Zealand National Bibliography*, v.1, pt.2, pp. 1116-17 (items 6028-30); Andersen, *The Lure of New Zealand Book Collecting*, pp. 77-90.

13. McKenzie (ed.), *Selections from Typo*, p. 95 (from iv.43, 26 July 1890).

14. L.J.B. Chapple, *A Bibliographical Brochure . . . of New Zealand Literature* (Reed, Wellington, 1938), pp. 28-29; Hugh Price, 'Who are New Zealand's Book Publishers?' (unpublished typescript, 1987), pp. 29-30. Mr Price's generosity in sharing his knowledge of New Zealand publishing is reflected throughout this chapter.

15. Hugh Price, 'School Books Published in New Zealand to 1960', (draft typescript, 1985).

16. Typescript outlines of the Company's history in Whitcoulls' archives; Ian F McLaren, *Whitcombe's Story Books, a Trans-Tasman Survey*, (University of Melbourne Library, Parkville, 1984). When I consulted Whitcoulls' archives in 1987-8 they were still in the possession of Whitcoulls Ltd and were not classified in any way. They are now (1990) in the possession of Penguin Books, who plan to present them to the Alexander Turnbull Library.

17. Anne Crichton, 'The Whitcombe and Tombs Dispute, 1890' (Research Essay, University of Canterbury, 1983).

18. McKenzie (ed.), *Selections from Typo*, p. 69 (from iii.33, Sept. 1889); Christchurch *Press*, 11 July 1904.
19. Price, 'School Books Published in New Zealand to 1960'; McLaren, *Whitcombe's Story Books*.
20. McKenzie (ed.), *Selections from Typo*, p. 89 (from iv.40, 26 April 1890). This obviously refers to *Zealandia* without naming it.
21. H. Roth, 'Radical Writers of the Nineties — William Freeman Kitchen', *Fern Fire* 13 (December 1965), pp. 17-19.
22. On this see Keith Sinclair, *A Destiny Apart* (Allen and Unwin, Wellington, 1986), chap. 3.
23. See *Illustrated* stories by Mary J. Mander and G.B. Lancaster reprinted in Elizabeth Webby and Lydia Wevers (eds), *Happy Endings: Stories by Australian and New Zealand Women 1850s-1930s* (Allen and Unwin, Wellington, 1987), pp. 92-118.
24. J.O.C. Phillips, 'Musings in Maoriland — or Was There a *Bulletin* School in New Zealand?', *Historical Studies*, xx.81 (October 1983), p. 534.
25. Alan Mulgan, *Literature and Authorship in New Zealand* (Allen and Unwin for P.E.N., London, 1943), p. 45.
26. Baughan to Andersen, 9 Aug. 1908, Andersen papers (MS7), Auckland Institute and Museum Library. (I am grateful to Peter Gibbons for this reference.)
27. W.H. New, *Dreams of Speech and Violence, the Art of the Short Story in Canada and New Zealand* (University of Toronto Press, 1987), p. 117.
28. Phillip Wilson, *The Maorilander, a Study of William Satchell* (Whitcombe & Tombs, Christchurch, 1961), pp. 54, 61.
29. Bruce Nesbitt, 'Aspects of Literary Nationalism in Australia and New Zealand with Special Reference to the *Bulletin*, 1880-1890' (Ph.D. thesis, Canberra, 1968), p. 459; Phillips, 'Musings in Maoriland', pp. 521-2, 523-4.
30. Antony Alpers (ed.), *The Stories of Katherine Mansfield*, (O.U.P., Auckland, 1984), p. 545; Brownlee Kirkpatrick, 'In Quest of KM', *NZ Listener*, 11 July 1987, p. 24.
31. *The Triad*, xv.10 (Jan. 1908), p. 11; xv.11 (Feb. 1908), p. 5.
32. K.K. Ruthven, 'Ezra Pound, Alice Kenny & the "Triad"', *Landfall* 89 (March 1969), pp. 73-84.
33. McLaren, *Whitcombe's Story Books*, p. vii.
34. *Who's Who in New Zealand*, 1908 (Hight); Christchurch *Press*, 28 Mar. 1947 (obituary of Shrimpton).
35. Untitled, unsigned, undated typescript in Whitcoulls' archives.
36. Fairburn, 'A New Zealand poet', *N.Z. Artists' Annual*, i.4 (August 1929), p. 69; Hyde, *Journalese* (National Printing Company, Auckland, 1934), p. 48; Lawlor, *Confessions of a Journalist* (Whitcombe & Tombs, Christchurch, 1935), p. 231; Jean Alison, 'R.A.K. Mason, 1905-71', *Landfall* 99 (September 1971), p. 225.
37. H.J.D. Mahon to Lowry, as copied by Lowry to Glover, 8 February 1930, MS Papers 418 (Denis Glover), Folder 3 (see also Folders 1 and 2), Alexander Turnbull Library.
38. Allen Curnow, *Look Back Harder, Critical Writings 1935-1984*, ed. Peter Simpson (Auckland University Press, 1987), p. 213.
39. *John Cawte Beaglehole, a Bibliography*, (Alexander Turnbull Library and Victoria University of Wellington, 1972), pp. 8-14.
40. Olive Johnson, *A.R.D. Fairburn 1904-1957: a Bibliography of His Published Work* (University of Auckland, 1958), pp. 15-25.
41. 'Rhyme of the Dead Self', *Collected Poems* (Pegasus, Christchurch, 1966), p.[220].
42. M.H. Holcroft, *The Way of a Writer* (Cape Catley, Queen Charlotte Sound, 1984).
43. Harry Tombs to Jean Stevenson, 28 Feb. 1933, Whitcoulls' archives; see also MS Papers 1973 (Harry H. Tombs), Alexander Turnbull Library.
44. C.A. Marris. 'Our Younger Generation of Writers', *Annals of New Zealand Literature* . . . (New Zealand Authors' Week Committee, Wellington, 1936), p. 18.
45. *Who's Who in New Zealand* 1941, 1950 (obituary); Pat Lawlor, *Confessions of a Journalist*, pp. 60, 229-30.
46. Lowry to Glover, 25 Feb. 1932, MS Papers 418, Folder 3, Alexander Turnbull Library.
47. Brasch to James K. Baxter, 28 July 1961, cited in John Geraets, '"Landfall" under Brasch' (Ph.D. thesis, Auckland, 1982), p. 154.
48. Elsie Locke, *Student at the Gates* (Whitcoulls, Christchurch, 1981), p. 78.
49. Alison, 'R.A.K. Mason', p. 227.
50. Lowry to Glover, 22 Sept. [1933], MS Papers 418, Folder 5, Alexander Turnbull Library; Jean Alison, 'R.A.K. Mason', p. 227; Keith Sinclair, *A History of the University of Auckland* (Auckland University Press, 1983), p. 168. For the whole tortuous story, see Peter Hughes, '"Sneers, Jeers . . . and Red Rantings": Bob Lowry's Early Printing at Auckland University College', *Turnbull Library Record*, xxii.1 (May 1989), pp. 5-31.
51. Charles Brasch, *Indirections* (Oxford University Press, Wellington, 1980), p. 186.
52. Brasch, *Indirections*, p. 187.
53. Denis Glover, *Hot Water Sailor* (Reed, Wellington, 1962) p. 108.
54. H. Winston Rhodes, 'The Beginning of Tomorrow', *New Zealand Monthly Review*, xx.214 (September 1979), p. 14; see also H. Winston Rhodes, *Kennaway Henderson, Artist, Editor and Radical* (Publications Committee, University of Canterbury, 1988).
55. Glover, *Hot Water Sailor*, p. 108.
56. Denis Glover, 'Home Thoughts', *Tomorrow*, 21 August 1935, p. 16.
57. Frank Sargeson, 'Conversation with My Uncle', *Tomorrow*, 24 July 1935, pp. 6-7.
58. *Tomorrow*, 25 Nov. 1936, p. 47; 13 March 1935, p. 13.
59. *Tomorrow*, 29 April 1936, p. 22.
60. *Tomorrow*, 6 November 1935, p. 14-15, reprinted in *Conversation in a Train* (Auckland University Press, 1983), pp. 15-17.
61. *Annals of New Zealand Literature*, p. 19.

62. 'Pointers to Parnassus', *Tomorrow*, 30 October 1935, p. 17.

63. Denis Glover, *Selected Poems* (Penguin, Auckland, 1981), pp. 7-8.

64. Allen Curnow, introduction to *The Penguin Book of New Zealand Verse* (Harmondsworth, Penguin, 1960), reprinted in *Look Back Harder*, p. 160; see also, Trixie Te Arama Menzies, 'Kowhai Gold — Skeleton or Scapegoat?', *Landfall* 165 (March 1988), pp. 19-26.

65. Ronald Holloway, 'Remembering Bob Lowry', *Landfall* 69 (March 1964), p. 56.

66. Lowry to Glover, 12 March 1933, MS Papers 418, Folder 5, Alexander Turnbull Library.

67. Glover, *Hot Water Sailor*, pp. 87-97.

68. *A Catalogue of Publications from the Caxton Press Christchurch up to February 1941*, p. 9; the best outline of Glover's printing and publishing is in J.E.P. Thomson, *Denis Glover* (New Zealand Writers and Their Work, Oxford, Wellington, 1977).

69. Antony James Booker, 'The Centennial Surveys of New Zealand, 1936-41' (B.A.(Hons) research essay, Massey University, 1983), p. 109.

70. *Catalogue of publications . . . 1941*, p. 25.

71. The rise of the house of Reed has been described in: [A.H. and A.W. Reed], *The House of Reed, Fifty Years of New Zealand Publishing, 1907-1957* (Reed, Wellington, 1957); [A.W. Reed], *The House of Reed 1957-1967* (Reed, Wellington, 1968); A.H. Reed, *An Autobiography* (Reed, Wellington, 1967); A.W. Reed, *Young Kauri 1875-1975: Personal Recollections of Sir Alfred Hamish Reed CBE* (Reed, Wellington, 1975); A.W. Reed, *Books Are My Business: the Life of a Publisher* (My Life and My Work series: Reading, Educational Explorers, 1966). Of these the last-named is the liveliest and most revealing about the firm's publishing.

72. Terry Sturm, introduction to new edition of *Follow the Call* (New Zealand Fiction series, Auckland University Press, 1975); correspondence between A.H. Reed and Annie Anthony and Muriel Kerrisk, 1936-44, Frank Anthony Papers, Acc. 78-38, Alexander Turnbull Library.

73. MS papers 39 (James Cowan), Folder 39, Alexander Turnbull Library.

74. Hugh R. Dent (ed.), *The Memoirs of J.M. Dent* (Dent, London, 1928), p. 133 (the Auckland University Library copy of this book is inscribed by its editor to Walter Nash 'with kindest messages'); *Crockford's Clerical Directory*, 1915, 1927, 1932; Sir Stanley Unwin, *The Truth About a Publisher* (Allen and Unwin, London, 1960), pp. 117, 297.

75. Information kindly provided by Terry Sturm; Edith Lyttleton, typescript of address to Penwomen's Club, 1937.

76. Alan Mulgan, *Literature and Authorship in New Zealand*, pp. 49-50.

77. Frank Sargeson, *Sargeson* (Penguin, Auckland, 1981), p. 11.

78. This account owes much to Antony Booker's research essay, 'The Centennial Surveys of New Zealand', and to discussions of it with Dr E.H. McCormick.

79. McCormick interview, 8 December 1987.

80. See Dennis McEldowney, 'The Typographical Obsession', *Islands*, 28 (March 1980) pp. 59-70.

81. McCormick to Heenan, 11 Oct. 1937, IA 62/8/1 pt 1, National Archives; also transcribed, not with entire accuracy, as an appendix to Booker, 'Centennial Surveys'.

82. Minutes of Standing Committee, 21 June 1937, IA 62/8/1 Pt 2, National Archives.

83. Published in 1940 as *The Maori People Today* (Wellington, N.Z. Institute of International Affairs and N.Z. Council for Educational Research, 1940).

84. L. Griffith to W.E. Parry, 25 June 1937, IA 62/7, National Archives.

85. Duff to Heenan, 3 May 1938, IA 62/8/1 Pt 2, National Archives.

86. Heenan to Nash, 5 March 1941 (but not sent), cited Booker, 'Centennial Surveys', p. 46; the summary of events derives from Booker, pp. 37-47.

87. The first version as *The Quest for Security in New Zealand* (Penguin, Harmondsworth, 1942) and the second as *Poverty and Progress in New Zealand* (Modern Books, Wellington, 1941).

88. Sutherland to Cowan, 2 September 1940, MS papers 39 (James Cowan), Folder 3, Alexander Turnbull Library; see also Booker, pp. 36-37.

89. Denis Glover, 'Back Pages from "Tomorrow"', *Rostrum*, [ii] (August 1940), p. 31.

90. John Lehmann, *The Whispering Gallery: Autobiography I* (Longmans, London, 1955), p. 263. Anthony Stones (ed.), *Celebration* (Harmondsworth, Penguin, 1984) reprints all the New Zealand-related contributions to *Penguin New Writing*.

91. The author has Penguin editions of Christopher Isherwood's *Mr Norris Changes Trains*, W.W. Jacobs's *The Lady of the Barge*, and Dorothy Parker's *Here Lies*, all printed in New Zealand in 1944.

92. Rachel Barrowman, '"Making New Zealand Articulate": the Progressive Publishing Society, 1942-1945', *New Zealand Journal of History*, xxii.2 (October 1988), pp. 152-68.

93. E.W.G. Craig, *Man of the Mist, a Biography of Elsdon Best* (Reed, Wellington, 1964), pp. 137-40, 177, 195, 211, 216; *A.J.H.R.*, H.22, 1918 p. 8, 1919 pp. 11-12, 1920 pp. 4-5, 1921-2 p. 9 (for Cowan).

94. *P.E.N. Gazette*, no. 12 (November 1945), p. 1.

95. D'Arcy Cresswell, *Present Without Leave* (Cassell, London, 1939), pp. 252-3.

96. Cresswell, *Present Without Leave*, *passim*; Ormond Wilson, *An Outsider Looks Back* (Port Nicholson Press, Wellington, 1982), pp. 38-41.

97. Dennis McEldowney, *Frank Sargeson in His Time* (McIndoe, Dunedin, 1976), p. 39.

98. Frederick Page, *A Musician's Journal* (McIndoe, Dunedin, 1986), pp. 97-98.

99. M.H. Holcroft, *The Waiting Hills* (Progressive Publishing Society, Wellington, 1943), pp. 97-98.

100. E.H. McCormick, 'The State as a Publisher of Books and Periodicals', *New Zealand Libraries*, ix.2 (March 1946), pp. 31-32.

101. M.H. Holcroft, *Creative Problems in New Zealand* (Caxton, Christchurch, 1948), pp. 30-31, 33.

102. A.R.D. Fairburn, 'The Culture Industry', *Landfall* 39 (September 1956), pp. 198-211 (reprinted in *The Woman Problem and Other Prose* (Paul, Auckland, 1967), pp. 136-52).
103. Heenan to Parry, 22 November 1944, I.A. 86/1, National Archives.
104. *P.E.N. Gazette* 12 (Nov. 1945), pp. 1-2.
105. I.A. 86/1, National Archives.
106. *The New Zealand Literary Fund 1946-1970* (Government Printer, Wellington, 1970), pp. 1-2.
107. Advisory Committee minutes, 24 February, 25 August 1948.
108. David Ballantyne papers, Acc. 88-12, Boxes 1 (iii), 3 (iii), Alexander Turnbull Library; Advisory Committee Minutes, 30 June, 21 July, 25 August, 4 October 1948; Ballantyne, 'New Zealand Letter', *New York Times Book Review*, 12 June 1949, p. 12.
109. *The New Zealand Literary Fund*, pp. 2-3
110. Thomson, *Denis Glover*, p. 28.
111. A.W. Reed papers, Acc.76-14, Box 1, Alexander Turnbull Library; A.W. Reed, *Young Kauri*, p. 45.
112. Interview with Janet Paul, 10 November 1987; Mary Scott, *Days That Have Been* (Blackwood & Janet Paul, Auckland, 1966), p. 198.
113. Price, 'School Books Published in New Zealand', pp. 120-38; 'Who are New Zealand's Publishers?', p. 25.
114. Information from Barbara Cooper and Maurice Shadbolt.
115. Hugh Parton, *The University of New Zealand* (Auckland University Press, Auckland, 1979), pp. 78-79; Denys Trussell, *Fairburn* (Auckland University Press, Auckland, 1984), p. 250.
116. Brasch, *Indirections* (O.U.P., Wellington, 1980), p. 388.
117. Ibid.
118. *Indirections*, pp. 388-9.
119. Geraets, '*Landfall* under Brasch', p. 191.
120. Ibid., pp. 224-46, 260; John Geraets, 'Kendrick Smithyman and Brasch's *Landfall*', *Landfall* 160 (December 1986), pp. 443-57.
121. Alistair Campbell, *Island to Island* (Whitcoulls, Christchurch, 1984), p. 116.
122. *Listener*, 16 July 1954; M.H. Holcroft, *Reluctant Editor* (Reed, Wellington, 1969), p. 42.
123. Allen Curnow, 'The Poetry Yearbook: a Letter to Louis Johnson', *Here and Now*, iii.7 (May 1953), p. 28 (reprinted in Curnow, *Look Back Harder*, p. 109).
124. Bill Manhire, 'Breaking the Line: a View of American and New Zealand Poetry', *Islands* 38 (December 1987), pp. 146-7.
125. Geraets, '*Landfall* under Brasch', pp. 334-7, 343-5; interview with Robin Dudding, 24 May 1988.
126. *Landfall* 116 (December 1975), p. 268.
127. C.K. Stead, *In the Glass Case: Essays on New Zealand Literature* (Auckland University Press, Auckland, 1981), p. 148.
128. Information from Mr W.E. Forde; *Quenching the Thirst for Knowledge: One Hundred Years of Publishing in New Zealand* (Collins, Auckland, 1988).
129. Janet Paul interview, 10 November 1987; *N. Z. Herald*, 2 October 1968.
130. A.W. Reed, *Books Are My Business*, p. 94.
131. Karen Jackman, 'The House That Reed Built', *Listener*, 14 July 1979, pp. 14-15; Paul Bradwell, 'Boiled-sweet days demise', *Dominion Sunday Times*, 24 April 1988.
132. *The New Zealand Literary Fund 1946-1970*, pp. 3-5, 10-12; W.H. O[liver], 'Notes', *Landfall* 43 (September 1957), p. 188.
133. 'Notes', *Landfall* 61 (March 1962), pp. 3-5.
134. *Listener*, 13 March 1964, p. 8; *Otago Daily Times*, 28 April; 'Notes', *Landfall* 70 (June 1964), pp.114-15; M.H. Holcroft, *A Sea of Words* (Cape Catley, Queen Charlotte Sound, 1986), pp. 77-88. (As an annual the *Yearbook* was not officially considered a periodical: hence the need to submit its contents.)
135. 'Notes', *Landfall* 79 (September 1966), p. 217.
136. *The New Zealand Literary Fund 1946-1970*, p. 4; annual reports of the Department of Internal Affairs, *A.J.H.R.*, G.7, 1973-5.
137. Quoted by Michael Gifkins, 'Bookmarks', *New Zealand Listener*, 20 December 1986.
138. Neil Scotts, Lewis Holden, Jenny Neale, *Art Facts, a Statistical Profile on the Arts in New Zealand* (Department of Internal Affairs, Wellington, 1987), p. 93 (percentages rounded).

Index

Subjects are indexed under headings given in small capitals. Apart from HISTORICAL EVENTS, the headings all correspond to the titles of the first nine chapters. Other entries are mainly for names of persons, publishing houses, small presses, and selected organizations, and for the titles of anonymous works, anthologies, magazines, and newspapers. Titles of works by known authors are not indexed separately, but page-references to them are given in the entries for the authors' names, whether or not the author's name is mentioned in the same place as the title. Note: (1) that Māori personal names beginning with 'Te' are indexed under 'Te', but the titles of Māori publications beginning with 'Te', 'Ko' or 'Nga' are indexed under the following word; and (2) that page numbers from p. 603 on refer to the bibliography and end-notes, which have been indexed more selectively than the rest of the book.

Acheson, Frank O.V., 126
Acres, Avis, 464, 465
Act, 312, 635-6
Act Bulletin, 312
Adams, Arthur H.: novels, 124, 127, 128-9, 130; poetry, 344, 360-2, 374; plays and operas, 281, 282; short story, 222; other refs., 552, 557, 636
Adams, Robert Noble, 126, 128
Adcock, Fleur, 406-10 *passim*, 436-7, 630, 636-7
Addison, Doris, 152, 153, 160
Adsett, Dell, 148, 153, 164
Airey, W.T.G., 70-1
Alexander, Colin, 528
Alexander, James E., 41-2
Alexander, Marc, 488
Alexander, Marie, 454
Alexander, W.F. see: *New Zealand Verse* (ed. Alexander and Currie, 1906); *A Treasury of New Zealand Verse* (ed. Alexander and Currie, 1926)
'Alien' see Baker, Louisa Alice
Allan, Ruth, 70
Allen, C.R.: novels, 124, 127, 130, 140, 461; other refs., 561, 566
see also: *Tales by New Zealanders* (ed. C.R. Allen, 1938)
Allen, J.T., 565
Allen, Pamela, 481-2
Allen and Unwin, 567, 594
Alley, Rewi, 637
Alone in the World (novel, 1886), 113
Alpers, Antony, 38, 99-100, 101, 216, 579, 622, 637-8, 682
Alpers, O.T.J., 66, 364, 553
Amato, Renato, 190, 638
Amey, Sunny, 309
Amphedesma Press, 594
And, 441, 589, 635
Andersen, Johannes, 62, 89, 363, 454, 554, 605, 638
Anderson, Barbara, 263-4, 267, 268
Anderson, Florence Mary, 455
Anderson, Mona, 580
Andrews, Isobel, 289, 299, 324
Andrews, Philip, 158
Another Argo (Caxton Press, 1935), 380, 565
An Anthology of New Zealand Verse (ed. Chapman and Bennett, 1956), 365, 394, 405-6, 625
An Anthology of Twentieth Century New Zealand Poetry (ed. O'Sullivan, 1970, 1976), 394, 418, 420, 428, 435, 442, 628
Anthony, Frank, 75, 129, 223-4, 496, 566-7, 580, 638-9
Anvil, 237
Te Ao Hou, 17, 243, 248-50, 411, 589, 634
Ko Aotearoa, 13
Appendices to the Journals of the House of Representatives, 11

Arachne, 585, 634
Arena, 585, 633
'Areta, Mavis' see Winder, Mavis
Argot, 418, 420, 589, 634
Armfelt, Nicholas, 158
Armitage, Ronda and David, 481, 639
Art in New Zealand, 282, 284, 558-9, 562, 563, 586, 632
Arvidson, K.O., 435, 614, 728 (n. 170)
Ashcroft, W.D., 708
Ashton Scholastic, 479
Ashton-Warner, Sylvia: autobiography, 91-2; biography of, by Lynley Hood, 102; novels, 140, 145, 157-8, 169; other refs., 461, 582, 586, 639
Associated Book Publishers, 593
Atkinson, A.S., 58
Auckland Star, 124, 558
Auckland Sun, 558
Auckland University Press, 591-2, 594
Auckland Weekly News, 554
Aussie, 563
Australian Journal, 205
Avery, Thomas, and Sons, 557
Awatere, Arapeta, 19, 21
Awatere, Donna, 88-9
Aylmer, Mrs J.E., 449

Bacon, Ron L., 471, 479, 480, 639-40
Baeyertz, C.N., 555; see also: *Triad*
Bagnall, A.G., 77, 551, 604
Bagnall, Jill, 480
Baigent, Laurence, 157
Baines, William Mortimer, 110, 117
Baker, Heretaunga Pat, 187, 249
Baker, Louisa Alice, 123, 127, 130, 495-7, 498-501, 505, 506, 540, 640
Ballantyne, David: novels, 144, 150, 151, 154, 162-3, 164, 169, 171, 177, 182; other refs., 574, 579, 582, 585, 640
Ballantyne, Stephen, 483
Ballekom, Manu van, 19
Balneavis, Te Raumoa, 19
Banks, Joseph, 30-1, 69
Barker, Lady, 47-8, 81, 205, 450-1, 575, 640-1
Barlow, Cleve, 5
Barr, John, of Craigilee, 345, 353-4
Barr, John A., 116
Barrer, Nina A.R., 81
Barrowman, Fergus, 588
Barrowman, Rachel, 722 (n. 39), 733 (n. 92)
Bartle, Frank, 114
Bates, Peter, 173, 177, 181-2
Bathgate, Alexander, 111, 112
Batistich, Amelia, 186, 190, 243, 244, 245, 581
Batten, Francis, 317

Baucke, William, 210-11
Baughan, Blanche E.: novels, 80; poetry, 345, 349, 362-4, 374; short stories, 207, 210, 213-14, 215, 217; writings on NZ scenery, 54; other refs., 554, 556, 557, 641
Baume, Eric, 127, 129
Baume, Frederick Ehrenfried, 553
Baxter, Archibald, 76
Baxter, James K.: autobiography, 193; biographies of, 101-2; novel, 158; plays, 296-9, 301, 304, 307; poetry, 341, 342, 343, 390-3, 403-7 *passim*, 414-17, 579-80, 596; other refs., x, 335, 367, 374, 375, 394, 401, 411, 462, 582, 586, 606, 641-3
Baysting, Arthur, 420; *see also: The Young New Zealand Poets* (ed. Baysting, 1973)
Beaglehole, Ernest, 86, 88, 582
Beaglehole, J.C.: and Centennial publications, 569, 571, 572, 581; historical writings, 68-9, 70, 92, 102, 104, 567; poetry, 374, 558, 559, 561; other refs., 572, 582, 643-4
Beaglehole, Pearl, 86, 88
Beames, Margaret, 471, 475, 644
Beardsley, Eric, 189
Beaton, Hilary, 328-9, 330
Bedford, Louisa H., 452
Bedggood, David, 80
Beer, Christina, 338-40
Belich, James, 43, 103
Bell, B.V., 183
'Bell, Chris' *see* Pearson, Bill
Bell, Colin, 470
Bell, George, 126
Bell, Gerda, 103
Bell, John, 123, 127, 128, 129
Belton, Robyn, 480
Bennett, F.O., 153, 160
Bennett, J.A.W., 380, 559
Bennett, Jonathan *see: An Anthology of New Zealand Verse* (ed. Chapman and Bennett, 1956)
Bensemann, Leo, 565, 588
Benton, Richard, 5
Berg, Rilla, 532
Berkman, Sylvia, 682
Berry, Ken, 181
Berry, Reginald, 726 (n. 107)
Bertram, James, 91, 162, 300, 380, 387, 559-60, 612, 613, 615, 647, 653
Best, Elsdon: ethnographic works, 59, 60, 68; and Maori writing, 9, 16; other refs., 63, 64, 553, 574-5, 644-5
Bethell, Ursula, 369-73, 380, 387, 563, 565, 606, 645
Bettica, Thomas, 141
Bevan, Gloria, 532, 536-8
Bible, translated into Maori, 6, 545
Bidwill, J.C., 33, 34
Biggs, Bruce, 5, 10, 16, 18-19
Billing, Graham: novels, 172, 177, 178, 182, 194, 195, 196; plays, 306; other refs., 645
Binney, Don, 177, 189
Binney, Judith, 78, 86-7
Bishop, Gavin, 482
Black, Sebastian, 330
Blackwell, E.M., 62, 74
Blackwood and Janet Paul Ltd, 593
Bland, Peter, 303, 304, 405-7 *passim,* 409-10, 645-6
Blank, Arapera, 21, 249
Blank, Pius, 471
Bledisloe, Viscount, 89
Boddy, Gill, 682
Boldrewood, Rolf, 109, 112, 117, 121, 122
Bolitho, Hector, 68, 124, 127, 129, 130
Book, 573, 633

The Book of Canterbury Rhymes (ed. Reeves and Ward, 1866), 364, 623
Book of Common Prayer in Maori, 546
A Book of New Zealand Verse (ed. Curnow, 1945, 1951), 357, 365, 384, 385-6, 387, 388, 393, 394, 404, 411, 564, 625
Booth, Laurence, 273-4, 280
Booth, Pat, 157, 158-9, 159, 160, 164
Bornholdt, Jenny, 437, 443
Boswell, Jean, 82-3
Boucicault, Dion, 278
Bourke, E.M., 53-4, 80
Bowden, Boyce, 373
Bowden, Thomas Adolphus, 551
Bowen, Charles C., 344, 354, 360
Bowman, Edward, 307-8
'Bowman, Hildebrand', 115
Boyd, Mary, 713 (n. 78)
Bracken, Thomas, 351-2, 354-5, 357-8, 360, 370-1, 549, 646
Bradbrook, M.C., 620
Bradwell, Eric, 285, 286
Brady, E.J., 554
Brasch, Charles: autobiography, 91, 343; ed. of *Courage, Such Separate Creatures,* 234; poetry, 342-3, 380, 381-2, 387, 388-9, 412-13, 562, 591; verse script of mime play, 291; other refs., 140-1, 143, 154, 165, 425, 559-60, 595-6, 597, 646-7; *see also: Landfall*
Brathwaite, Errol, 144, 144-5, 156, 158, 160, 188, 647
Brave Days (ed. Wilson, Barrer, and Spurdle, 1939), 81-2
Brett, Henry, 65-6, 454, 549
Brett's Colonists' Guide and Cyclopedia of Useful Knowledge, 549
Bridger, Bub, 444
Bridget Williams Books, 594
Bright, Amy Dora, 454
Broadhead, H., 57
Broadsheet, 83, 266, 589, 635
Broome, Frederick Napier, 345, 354
Brophy, Charles Hamilton, 111, 121
Brougham, A.E., 20
Broughton, Ruka, 19, 22
Brown, J. Edward, 183, 186
Brown, John Macmillan, 126, 130, 131
Brown, Michael, 193
Browne, C.R., 125, 128
Brunner, Thomas, 49-50, 77
Bruno, Frank, 529
Brunton, Alan, 418-20 *passim,* 427, 588
Buchanan, M.H.A., 110
Buck, Sir Peter, 16, 67-8, 290
Buick, Lindsay, 65, 89, 103
Buller, Walter, 17, 51-2
Bulletin (Sydney), 208, 210, 364, 496, 501, 529, 554, 563, 633
Bulletins (school publications), 462, 468, 469
Bullock, Margaret Carson, 114
Bullock, Marie, 299, 324
Bunkle, Phillida, 84-5, 670
Burchfield, Robert, 567, 610
Burdon, R.M., 77, 78, 148, 580
Burn, David Will M., 348
Burns, Carolyn, 327-8
Burton, Ormond, 611-12
Butler, Dorothy, 472-3, 479, 482-3
Butler, Samuel, 45-6, 47, 54, 115-16

Cadey, Prudence, 129
Calder, Alex, 441
Caldwell, Campbell, 300, 301
Cameron, Bertha, 125, 129
Cameron, Ian, 156
Campbell, Alistair: plays, 304, 305-6, 307, 312; poetry, 387,

390-1, 403, 404, 413-14, 443-4; other refs., 409, 427, 462, 585, 606, 647-8
Campbell, Sir John Logan, 46-7, 78, 102, 103, 114
Campbell, Lady, 109, 113, 117, 122
Campion, Edith, 181
Campion, Richard, 301
Canterbury University Press, 592
Cape, Jonathan, 567
Capricorn Press, 404, 583
Carey, Patric and Rosalie, 301
Carman, Dulce, 497, 522-4, 648
Carnegie, David, 311, 621
Carrick, Robert, 115
Casey, R., 158
Cassell, 455, 567
Cathie, Diarmid, 158
Catley, Christine Cole, 84
Cave, Roderick, 731 (n. 5)
Cave, 589, 635
Caxton Press, 380, 384, 385, 387, 391, 564-7, 573, 578-81 *passim*, 583, 587, 594, 630
Celebrating Women (ed. Catley, 1984), 84
Challis, Derek, 670
Challis, Gordon, 405, 407, 410
Chamier, George, 109-10, 116, 118-20, 123
Chaplin, Judith, 86-7
Chapman, George, 547
Chapman, Robert: criticism, cited or discussed, xii, 140, 146-7, 149, 151, 155-6, 164, 165, 584, 619; other refs., 587; *see also: An Anthology of New Zealand Verse* (ed. Chapman and Bennett, 1956)
Chapman and Hall, 567
Chapman's New Zealand Magazine, 114, 547
Charman, Janet, 437, 443
Cheeseman, Clara: novel, 113, 116, 117, 120; short story, 211; other refs., 122, 129, 208, 500, 540, 619
Children's Book of the Year Award, 477

CHILDREN'S LITERATURE
bibliography, 622-3
periods: 19th cent. settler and adventure fiction, 449-53; local fantasy and the family story (1900-30), 453-60; emergence of the school story (1930-50), 460-3; new impulses (1950-70), 464-71; growth and diversity (after 1970), 471-90

Children's Literature Association of New Zealand, 472
Christchurch Star, 532
Christie, John, 131, 125
Church, Hubert, 125, 342-3, 365, 374
Church Missionary Society, 32-3, 545, 546
Churchward, W.B., 113, 116, 121, 122
Clair, Daphne, 497, 532, 537, 539
Clark, Kate McCosh, 453
Clarke, Neva, 141, 153, 160
Clay, Marie, 479
Clayden, Arthur, 35
Clendon, Lorna, 585
Climate, 258, 589, 634
Coad, N.E., 80-1
Cochrane, Kirsty, 179, 618
Cockayne, Leonard, 63
Cody, J.F, 160
Colborne-Veel, Mary, 365, 552
Cole, John Reece, 230, 232, 233, 234, 580
Colebrook, Vera, 715 (n. 10)
Colenso, William, 50-1, 57, 77, 545, 546, 549-50
Collins, 528, 590
Colonial Everyday Cookery, 556
Colston, Fifi, 483
Combs, F.L., 469, 567

Comment, 154, 586-7, 634
Condliffe, J.B., 68, 70-1
Coney, Sandra, 84-5
Cook, Eric, 560, 565
Cook, Harvey, 126, 127, 128
Cook, James, 30-1, 32, 69
Copland, R.A., 154, 164, 174, 617, 697
Coppard, J.A.S., 285-6
Corbalis, Judy, 486
Corballis, Richard, 614, 642
Coromandel Press, 595
Cotterill, George, 204
Cottle, Thomas, 111, 122, 552, 553
Coulls Somerville Wilkie, 566, 593
Courage, James: novels, 140, 143-4, 159, 160, 161; short stories, 230, 234-5; other refs., 648-9
Courage, Sarah Amelia, 48
Cowan, James: biographical and historical writing, 61-2, 87, 89, 188, 566, 567, 570, 571, 575; other refs., 102, 553, 649
Cowley, Joy: novels, 172, 174-5, 180, 195; short stories, 254, 263, 264; writing for children, 471, 477, 479; other refs., 649-50
Cox, Mary, 484
Cox, Nigel, 183
Cox, Shelagh, 83
Craik, G.L., 32, 54
Cranna, John, 262-3
Crawford, J.C., 51
Cresswell, D'Arcy: autobiography, 89-90, 380, 567; letters, 101; play, 291, 583; poetry, 380, 387, 564; other refs., 565, 575, 650
Crookes, Marguerite, 62-3
Cross, Ian: novels, 140-1, 144, 150, 151-2, 163-4; other refs., 142-3, 146, 596, 650
Crosscurrent, 589
Cruise, R.A., 32
Crump, Barry, 235, 497, 528, 530-1, 580, 587, 651
Cunningham, Kevin, 594
Curnow, Allen: criticism cited, xii, 154, 155, 340, 364, 374, 379, 385-6, 387, 397, 398, 403, 558, 564, 565, 616, 617; plays, 290-1, 296-7, 299, 300, 303, 311; poetry, 174, 198, 341, 380, 381, 382-4, 385, 387, 397-40, 419-21 *passim*, 428-31, 560, 562, 565; and 'Wellington group', 403-8 *passim*; other refs., x, 344, 572, 573, 579, 593, 614, 651-2; *see also: A Book of New Zealand Verse* (ed. Curnow, 1945, 1951); *The Penguin Book of New Zealand Verse* (ed. Curnow, 1960)
Curnow, Jenifer, 9
Curnow, Wystan, ix, 260, 420, 442, 612, 615
Current Thought, 210, 214
Currie, A.E. *see: New Zealand Verse* (ed. Alexander and Currie, 1906); *A Treasury of New Zealand Verse* (ed. Alexander and Currie, 1926)

Dallas, Ruth: poetry, 387-8, 389, 412, 591; writing for children, 471, 473-4; other refs., 580, 584, 652-3
Daly, Saralyn, 682
Dalziel, Margaret, 596, 660
Dalziel, Raewyn, 78
Dampier, Alfred, 281
Darrell, George, 278-9, 280
Darwin, Charles, 31
Davey, F.L., 274
'David Lowston' (ballad), 350
Davidson, Janet, 85
Davidson, William, 207, 212
Davies, Sonja, 84
Davin, Dan: novels, 140, 143-4, 156, 157, 159, 160, 161; short stories, 230, 231, 232, 233, 238; war history, 75-6; other

refs., 567, 576, 579, 618, 653–4; *see also: New Zealand Short Stories* (ed. Davin, 1953)
Davis, C.O.B., 13, 15
Davis, Leigh, 342, 421, 429, 441-2
Davis, Michael, 160
Day, Paul, 313, 692
de Hamel, Joan, 471, 475, 476, 654
de Mauny, Erik, 148
de Montalk, Geoffrey, 380
de Roo, Anne, 471, 474–5, 476, 654
de Roo, Robert, 185, 193, 195, 196, 595
Delahunty, Sarah, 327
Dent, J.M., 478, 567
Devanny, Jean, 124, 125, 131, 137–40, 146, 223, 224, 654
Dewes, Te Kapunga (Koro), 19, 20
Dibble, Warren, 304–5, 306, 307, 324-5
Dickon, Julian, 307
Dickson, John, 418
A Dictionary of New Zealand Biography (Scholefield), 66, 608
The Dictionary of New Zealand Biography (ed. Oliver), 22-3, 608
Dieffenbach, Ernest, 37-8, 103
Dillon, Peter, 31
Dodd, Lynley, 472, 475, 480-1
Domett, Alfred, *Ranolf and Amohia*: 54, 61, 112, 341, 345, 349, 350, 355-7, 654-5
Dominion (Wellington), 216, 225, 554
Donald, Robyn, 497, 532, 537, 538, 539, 595
Dorman, T.F., 186
Doubleday Page, 493, 495
Doughty, Ross, 182
Douglas, Charles, 77
Dowling, Basil, 384, 389-90
Downes, Cathy, 330
Dowrick, Stephanie, 187
Doyle, Charles, 405, 407, 410, 590, 616, 642, 690; *see also: Recent Poetry in New Zealand* (ed. Doyle, 1965)

DRAMA:
bibliography, 607, 621-2
introduction, 271-2
periods: drama of colonization (19th cent.), 272-81; amateur movement (1900-45), 281-90; early post-colonial period (1945 to early 1960s), 290-303; foundation of community theatres (mid-1960s), 303-11; Playmarket and its playwrights (1970s), 312-22; new impulses in the 1980s, 322-32; theatres, companies, and organizations: Amamus Theatre, 317, 318, 332
Association of People's Artists, 291
British Drama League, 282-4, 287, 288, 302, 306, 312, 324; Central Theatre, 309
Christchurch Comedy Club, 282
Circa Theatre, 320
Community Arts Service, 299, 324
Depot Theatre, 332
Downstage Theatre, 303, 305, 306, 307, 309, 310, 312
Garrick Club, 277
Globe Theatre, 298, 301
Grafton Theatre, 282
Mercury Theatre, 309, 324, 315
New Independent Theatre, 313
New Theatre, 302
New Zealand Drama Council, 312
New Zealand Drama School, 302
New Zealand Players, 300, 301
New Zealand Theatre Federation, 312
The People's Theatre, 287, 288
Playmarket, 311, 312-22, 324, 607
radio, 285, 288, 296-308 *passim*, 310, 312, 321

Repertory theatre societies, 282–4, 291
Sunnyside Dramatic Class, 278
television, 294, 295, 296, 302, 307, 308, 315, 321, 323-4
'Theatre Action', 317
Theatre of the Eighth Day, 318, 332
Unity Theatre, 287, 289, 291, 293
Working Title Theatre, 325

Drew, John, 565
Drummond, James, 53, 62
Drummond, Yolanda, 175
Dryland, Gordon, 173, 175-6, 182, 183, 190, 312, 313, 315, 318
du Fresne, Yvonne, 174, 186, 195, 243, 244-5, 263, 655
Duckworth, Marilyn, 144, 157, 158, 171-2, 178-80 *passim*, 191, 194, 655
Dudding, Robert, 587-8
Duder, Tessa, 472, 486-7, 655
Duff, Oliver, 74-5, 226, 563, 569, 571, 572, 633
Duff, Roger, 85
Duggan, Eileen: poetry, 374-5, 381, 387, 394, 395, 564, 567; short stories, 230; other refs., 575, 606, 656
Duggan, Maurice: short stories, 203, 237-9, 242, 581, 584; writing for children, 465-6, 477; other refs., 462, 656
Dunlop, Beverley, 476, 484, 657
Dunmore, John, 70, 591
Dunmore Press, 591
Dunstan, Peggy, 484, 657
During, Simon, 228, 615
D'Urville, Dumont, 111

Earle, Augustus, 33, 54, 102
Early Travellers in New Zealand (ed. Taylor, 1959), 69
Ebbett, Eve, 84
Eden, Dorothy, 497, 514-17, 541, 657
Edge, 420, 589, 634, 635
Edmond, Lauris, 84, 101, 190, 194, 421, 437-9, 657-8
Edmond, Murray, 418-20 *passim*, 426-7, 588, 617, 658
see also: The New Poets (ed. M. Edmond and M. Paul, 1987)
Edmonds' Cookery Book, 556
Eggleston, Kim, 437
Eggleton, David, 342-3, 444
Elder, J.R., 65, 92, 566
Eldred-Grigg, Stevan, 183, 614, 713 (n. 76)
Elliot, Wilhelmina Sherriff, 125
Elliott, Sir James, 125, 578
Ellis, Ellen R., 114, 117, 120
Ellison, Nancy, 82
Else, Chris, 258, 260
Elwell, Ernest Simeon, 451
Emily Bathurst (children's book, 1847), 449
Ensing, Riemke, 437
Erihi, Riki, 249
Escott, Margaret, 158
Esther Glen Award, 463, 466, 475, 477
Evans, Charlotte, 113
Evans, Claude, 291
Evans, Miriama, 22, 443, 614
Evans, Patrick, 150, 152, 178, 183, 197, 620, 660; *see also: The Penguin History of New Zealand Literature*
Evening Post, 222, 500, 554-5, 595
Ewing, Barbara, 186

Faber and Faber, 567
Fagan, Annabel, 721 (n. 112)
Fairburn, A.R.D.: biography of, by Trussell, 101; letters, 101; cited, 374, 380, 381; and Huckleberry Finn, 161, 562-3; and R.A.K. Mason, 368-9, 557-8; poetry, 374, 376-9, 380, 393, 559, 565, 573; other refs., 387, 572, 574, 575, 576-7, 583, 586, 617, 658-9; *see also: Year Book of the Arts in New Zealand*

Fairburn, Edwin, 114, 115
Farjeon, Benjamin L., 109, 112, 273, 496
Faulkner, Alun, 288
Faville, Barry, 472, 488
Featon, John, 115, 120–1
Feilding Star, 554
Ferguson, Carlyle, 130
Ferguson, Dugald, 109, 110, 114, 123
15 Contemporary New Zealand Poets (ed. Paterson, 1980), 422, 630
Finlayson, Roderick: novels, 143, 148, 155, 184; short stories, 230, 235–6, 562; writing for children, 469; other refs., 571, 573, 595, 650, 659
Firth, Josiah Clifton, 277, 560
Firth, Raymond, 67, 68
Fitzgerald, James Edward, 364
FitzGerald, Joan, 680, 712 (n. 33)
Fitzgibbon, Tom, 473
'Fonthill, Arthur', *see* Firth, Josiah Clifton
Foote, Violet, 563
Forbes, Annabella, 128, 129
Forde, H.A., 451–2
Forsters (narrators of Cook's voyages), 546
Forsyth, Archibald, 126, 131
Foster, J.B., 5
Foston, Herman, 125, 131
Fowler, Leo, 160
Fox, William, 44
Frame, Janet: autobiography, 97–9; novels, 108, 140, 145–51 *passim*, 155, 168–9, 171, 174, 178, 180–1, 192, 193, 196–9 *passim*; poetry, 410; short stories, 237, 240–2, 258, 266, 268; other refs., x, 230, 573, 580, 581, 582, 584, 593, 595, 659–62
France, Ruth: novels, 141, 144, 158; poetry, 395; writing for children, 468; other refs., 581
Frances, Charles, 152
Franklin Watts, 478
Fraser, Alexander, 112
Fraser, Malcolm, 260
Fraser, Peter, 571, 575, 578, 579
Freed, 418–19, 421, 423, 424, 426, 427, 588–9, 634
Freeman, Sue, 183, 186
Freeman, William *see* Kitchen, William Freeman
French, Anne, ix, 343–4, 421, 437, 442, 444, 594, 662
Frontiers, 589
Froude, J.A., 36
Fullarton, J.H., 156, 160

Galbreath, Ross, 78
Gallagher, Kathleen, 327
Gant, Phyllis, 179, 190, 195
Gardner, W.J., 73
Garrard, Phillis, 460–1, 662–3
Gaskell, A.P., 230, 231, 233, 573, 663
Gaskin, Chris, 482, 489
Gee, Maurice: novels, 170, 172, 174, 176–7, 178, 181, 182, 194–5, 490; short stories, 253, 254; writing for children, 472, 484, 487–8; other refs., 342, 584, 663–4
Geraets, John, 584, 585, 634, 726 (n. 125)
Gibson, Colin, 191
Gibson, Gloria, 484
Gifkins, Michael, 260, 261–2, 664
Gilbert, G.R., 160, 230
Gilbert, Ruth, 395
Gilderdale, Betty, x, 473, 504, 622, 679
Giles, Joseph, 547, 548
Gilkison, Robert, 66
Gillespie, Oliver N., 61, 140, 146, 222, 373, 567, 578, 613; *see also: New Zealand Short Stories* (ed. Gillespie, 1930)
Gillies, John, 153
Gillies, Robert, 548

Glen, Esther, 457–8, 664; *see also* Esther Glen Award
Glenday, Alice, 173, 175
Globe, 552
Glover, Denis: autobiography, 90; essay on D-Day and prose sketches, 76; poetry, 341–2, 380–1, 387, 393, 413, 414, 562; printing and publishing, 380, 387, 558, 564–7, 579–80, 580–1, 583; other refs., 561, 562, 563–4, 572, 573, 613, 664–5
Glue, W.A., 731 (n. 11)
Godfrey, Margery, 469
Godley, Charlotte, 80, 81
Golder, William, 352–3, 547
Good Housekeeping, 532
Goodbye to Romance (ed. E. Webby and L. Wevers, 1989), 264
Goodwin, Arnold, 286
Goomes, Daphne, 465
Gordon, Ian A., 216, 573, 578, 579, 582, 596
Gordon, Mona, 63, 80, 722 (n. 16)
Gorrie, Rilda, 140
Gorst, John, 13, 41, 88
Gossage, Peter, 480
Goulden, Mark, 718 (n. 130)
Government Printer, 550, 557, 575
Grace, Alfred A., 123–4, 126, 208–10, 213, 235–6
Grace, John Te H., 16–17
Grace, Patricia: novels, 173, 184, 185, 195–6, 199; short stories, 243, 245–51 *passim*, 263, 490; writing for children, 23, 480; other refs., 589, 593, 665–6, 720 (n. 80)
Graham, George, 9
Graham, Jeanine, 78
Graham, Stanley, 148
Grant, A.K., 253–4, 321
Grant, Alison, 374
Grant, J.G.S., 548
Gray, Alison, 179
Greenwood, Hélène, 126
Greenwood, Lisa, 179, 195
Grey, Lady Eliza, 11 12
Grey, Sir George: biography of, by Rutherford, 77–8; and Bracken, 549; and Domett, 349; and Maori song, 20; and Maori writing, 8–9, 11–12, 14–15, 16, 57; *Polynesian Mythology*, 14, 38, 349
Griffen, Mr, of Wanganui, 275–6
Griffin Press, 595
Griffith, L., 571
Grossmann, Edith Searle, 80, 124, 131–2, 149, 500, 552, 666
Grove, Neil, 20
Grover, Ray, 141–2, 148, 164, 187
Growden, Oliver, 114
Gudgeon, T.W., 549, 552
Gurney, Mary, 230
Gurr, Andrew J., 141, 165, 216, 219, 616–17, 682
Gustafson, Barry, 78
Guthrie, John, 153, 160
Guthrie-Smith, W. Herbert, 63–4, 75, 92, 277, 566, 666
Guyan, Alexander, 302

Haast, H.F. von, 77
Haast, Julius von, 50
Habib, Rowley, 249, 444, 589
Hadfield, Octavius, 41
Te Haeata, 6
Hale, Robert, 494, 522, 532, 567, 582
Haley, Russell: novels, 192, 198, 199; short stories, 258–9, 261; other refs., 418, 588, 666–7
Hall, Bernadette, 437, 443
Hall, David, 18, 569, 585
Hall, J., 111
Hall, Roger, 298, 320–2, 326, 331, 667

Hall, Sandi, 192, 193, 197
Hall, Winifred *see* Mallory, Clare
Hamilton, Ian, 287, 288-9, 314
Hammond, R.T., 277
Hankin, Cherry, 682
Hanson, Clare, 203, 216, 219, 251, 682
Happy Endings (ed. Webby and Wevers, 1987), 719 (n. 15)
The Happy Land (play, 1880), 276
Harawira, K.T., 4
Hard Echo Press, 595
Harding, Bruce, 688, 730 (n. 39)
Harding, Robert Coupland, 545, 549-50; *see also: Typo*
Hardy, Linda, 670
Hare, Ngakuru Pene, 9-10
Harkness, C.M., 110
Harlow, Michael, 436, 589
Harlow, Ray, 5, 19
Harper, Arthur, 50
Harper, Theodore and Winifred, 459-60
Harrex, Wendy, 594
Harris, Dick, 725 (n. 65)
Harris, Emily C., 454
Harrison, Craig, 186, 191, 312, 314-15, 318
Harrison, Pakariki, 23
Harrop, A.J., 68, 567
Harvey, Norman, 164, 191
Hawke Press, 427, 594
Hawken, Dinah, 437, 442-3, 444-5
Hawkes Bay Herald-Tribune, 532
Hawkesworth, John, 31, 32, 104, 546
Hayter, Adrian, 191
Head and Shoulders (ed. Myers, 1986), 84
Heap, David, 590
Heaphy, Charles, 35
Heaton, Elizabeth Henniker, 469
Heber, Davy, 125
Hebley, Diane, 473, 622, 623
Hecate, 266
Heenan, Joseph, 569, 570, 571, 575, 577-8
Heinemann, 479
Heinemann Educational, 590
Henderson, Jim, 75, 77
Henderson, Kennaway, 561-2, 563, 572
Henderson, Michael, 176, 195
'Henderson, Paul' *see* France, Ruth
Heneghan, Rosalie, 497, 532, 537, 538-9
Henty, George, 451
Here and Now, 586, 634
Hervey, J.R., 381, 384, 387, 564, 571
Hessell, Jenny, 482
Hight, James, 556
Hill, Alfred, 281
Hill, Jane, 465
Hilliard, Noel, 141, 145, 152-3, 155, 236-7, 667
Hilltop, 585, 634
Hineira, Arapera, 444
Hingley, Bert, 587, 588, 590

HISTORICAL EVENTS:
    Bastion Point confrontation (1978), 184, 315, 316; gold
        rushes, 73, 112-13, 273, 284-5, 468; Land Wars,
        40-5, 62, 72, 103, 110-13 *passim*, 120-2, 133, 126, 210,
        273-5 *passim*, 279, 450-3, 468 *passim*
    Mt Tarawera eruption (1886), 114, 279, 281, 500
    Queen Street riot (1932), 147, 148, 167, 176
    Springbok tour (1981), xii, 177, 178, 295, 317, 321, 325,
        332
    Treaty of Waitangi (1840), xii, 3, 6, 34, 103, 121, 315,
        382, 449, 548
    Waterfront strike (1951), 152, 176, 199, 325

World War I (1914-18), 76, 147, 215, 287, 318, 332, 457,
    485
World War II (1939-45), 75-6, 84, 155-6, 182, 198, 232,
    233, 318, 329-30, 485

Hoar, Stuart, 331
Hoare, James O. Bryen, 126
Hocken, Thomas, 54, 501, 604
Hodder, W.R., 126
Hodder and Stoughton, 590
Hodge, Merton (Horace Emerton), 286, 289, 668
Hodgkins, Frances, 553
Hodgson, William, 365
Hoggard, Noel, 583, 585
Hohepa, Pat, 5, 18-19, 23
Te Hokioi, 13, 88
Holcroft, Anthony, 483
Holcroft, M.H.: autobiography, essays, and local history,
    92-3, 566, 611; editor of *NZ Listener*, 387, 573, 586, 596,
    633; novels, 92; and state patronage, 575-9 *passim*, 596;
    other refs., 571-2, 645, 668
Holdaway, Linda, 4
Holden, Anne, 151, 152
Holden, Philip, 472, 476
Holloway, Ronald, 564, 595
Hongi Hika, 4, 33
'Honnor of Ashburton', 114
Hood, Archibald, 122
Hood, Lynley, 102, 639
Hook, Henry, 66
Hooker, John, 158
Hooper, Peter, 173, 192, 193, 196, 199
'Hopeful', 36
Horrocks, Roger, 225-6, 422, 441, 442, 615, 617
Horsburgh, James, 551
Horsley, Reginald, 451
Hotere, Ralph, 420
Howe, Amelia, 83
Howes, Edith, 284-5, 454-6, 458, 477, 567, 668-9
Huata, Te Okanga, 22
Hughes, Eve, 312
Hughes, Peter, 732 (n. 50)
The Huia, 210, 211
Huia Tangata Kotahi, 14
Hulme, Keri: novel, 170, 173, 185-6, 195, 196; poetry, 437,
    443, 444; short stories, 186, 245; other refs., 23, 617,
    669-70
Hunt, Sam, 406, 418, 419, 427-8, 435, 439, 670
Hunter, Edward, 125, 130
Hutchinson, Ivy, 187
Hutton, F.W., 64
Hyde, Robin: journalism, 80; novels, 140, 143, 147-51
    passim, 155, 166-7, 168; one-act play, 284; poetry, 374,
    375-6, 381, 387, 562, 564; short stories, 230; other refs.,
    506, 670

Ihaka, Kingi, 21
Ihimaera, Witi: novels, 173, 184-5, 188-9, 191, 195-6, 199;
    short stories, 23, 243, 245-51 *passim*, 490; other refs.,
    248-9, 589, 590, 671-2; *see also: Into the World of Light*
    (ed. Long and Ihimaera)
Image, 587
In Deadly Earnest (ed. McNaughton, 1989), 264, 629
'Inglewood, Kathleen', 125, 129
Innes, Wayne, 196
Into the World of Light (ed. Long and Ihimaera, 1982), 248,
    440, 629
Ireland, Kevin, 409, 422, 435-6, 587, 672-3
Irish Writing, 237
Isitt, Kate Evelyn, 125, 129
Islands, 224, 225, 258, 263, 588, 635

Te Iwi o Aotearoa, 17
Izett, James, 277

Jabberwocky, 472
Jackson, Francis, 580
Jackson, Laurence, 187
Jackson, MacD. P., 411, 727 (n. 130)
Jackson, Michael, 4, 428, 673
Jacobs, Henry, 364
Jahnke, R.G.H., 471, 480
Jarrold, 494, 567
Jay, Simon, 528
Jeffery, Margaret, 150, 153, 160, 161, 182
Jenkins, Herbert, 522
Jenkinson, S.H., 570
Jenner, Ted, 260
Jensen, David, 469
John A. Lee's Weekly, 578
Johnson, Louis: poetry, 403-7 *passim*, 414, 436; other refs.,
    462, 583, 585, 586, 596, 598, 673; *see also: New Zealand
    Poetry Yearbook*; *Numbers*; 'Wellington group'
Johnson, Mike, 173, 192, 195, 199
Johnson, Stephanie, 264, 268
Johnston, Gordon, 153
Johnston, Phyllis, 484
Johnston, Stuart, 154
Johnstone, Capt. J.C., 111, 122
Jones, Bob, 191
Jones, Joseph, 115
Jones, Lawrence, 229, 618, 622, 715 (n. 1)
Jones, Lloyd, 176
Jones, Norman P.H., 160
Jones, Pei Te Hurinui, 17, 18, 19, 20, 578
Jones, Stella, 300-1, 324
Jordan, Warwick, 595
Joseph, George, 529
Joseph, M.K.: novels, 140, 144, 156, 157, 171, 190, 191, 198;
    poetry, 397, 402, 581; science fiction, 171, 192-3, 197;
    other refs., 111, 673-4
Journal of the Polynesian Society, 17, 18, 57, 58, 59, 88, 557
Journet, Terence, 528-9
Jowsey, Kevin *see* Ireland, Kevin
Joyce, Alexander, 115
The Jubilee Book of Canterbury Rhymes (ed. O.T.J. Alpers,
    1900), 364, 623

Kaa, Keri, 332
Kacem, Alie, 126
Te Kaea, 250
Te Kahiti o Niu Tireni, 6
Kahukiwa, Robyn, 480, 483
Kalman, Yvonne, 497, 540-1, 674
Kamira, Himiona, 10
Kang, Jye, 186
Te Karanga, 17
Karanga Hokianga, 22
Kararehe, Te Kaahui, 19
Te Karere o Nui Tireni, 6
Karetu, Timoti, 4, 19, 21
Katene-Horvath, Dovey, 21
Kavan, Anna, 573
Kawau, Piri, 9
Kaye, Bannerman, 126, 129
Keane, Hilda, 613
Keane, M.C., 365
Keesing, F.M., 86
Keesing, Nancy, 704
Kehu, 49-50
Keinzley, Florence, 153, 167-8
Keirle, Arthur T., 549
Kelly, John Liddell, 346-7

Kelly, Leslie G., 16-17
Kemp, H.T., 547
Kemp, Jan, 420
Kendall, Thomas, 4, 546
Kennaway, L.J., 47
Kennedy, Anne, 264, 267
Kennedy, Tom, 580
Kenny, Alice, 127, 210, 555, 580
Kerekere, Wiremu, 21
Kerr, Bob, 483
Kerr, Walter, 125
Kerr, Wharetoroa, 19
Kerry-Nicholls, J.H., 34
Keulemans, J.G., 51
Kidman, Fiona: novels, 174, 175, 176, 190, 194; short stories,
    254, 263, 265, 266; other refs., 585, 674
King, Michael, 87-8, 674-5
Kingsbury, Tony, 616, 723 (nn. 9, 24)
Kingston, William Henry G., 449-50, 715 (n. 2)
Kinross, Andrew, 723 (n. 21)
Kippenberger, Howard, 75
Kippis, Andrew, 355
Kirby, Joshua Henry, 113, 120, 122
Kirk, Thomas, 550
Kirkland, Hilaire, 428
Kitchen, William Freeman, 207, 552, 553
Kiwi, 558, 632
Koea, Shonagh, 254, 263, 267
Koebel, W.H., 127
Kohere, Reweti, 20
Kohlap, Gay, 465
Te Korimako, 6
Kotare series (Hodder and Stoughton), 473
Kowhai Gold (ed. Pope, 1930), 373-4, 375, 567, 624
Kriegler, Lyn, 482-3

Laing, R.M., 62, 74
Lancaster, G.B. *see* Lyttleton, Edith
Landfall, 91, 94, 141, 144, 145, 154, 178, 234, 253, 258, 263,
    304, 307, 394, 409, 418, 583-5, 587-8, 595, 627, 633-4
Langford, Gary, 312
Langton, William, 110-11, 118
Lapham, Henry, 205-6, 212
Lasenby, Jack, 485
Lawlor, Pat, 127-8, 557, 563, 578, 579, 613
Lawson, David, 582
Lawson, Pat, 465
Lawson, Will, 529
Lay, Graeme, 183
Lee, John A.: novels, 123, 140, 143, 147, 148, 150; other refs.,
    330, 575, 578, 675-6
Lee, Samuel, 4, 546
Leeming, Owen, 306-7, 407
Left Book Club, 287
Legge, Carol A., 715 (n. 7)
Leggott, Michele, 437, 442, 707
Lehmann, John, 568, 573
Leitch, George, 279-80
Le Rossignol, J.E., 57
Letters, 585
Levy, Ilma Maude, 284
Leys, T.W., 549
Leys Institute, 462
Lilburn, Douglas, 383, 398
Lindauer, Gottfried, 61
Lindsay, Graham, 427
Literary Foundlings (ed. Cotterill, 1864), 204, 623
Literary Fund, 300, 472, 577-9, 595-600
LITERARY MAGAZINES *see* PUBLISHING, PATRONAGE, LITERARY
    MAGAZINES
LITERATURE IN MĀORI *see* MĀORI, LITERATURE IN

The Little Red School-Book, 591
Locke, Elsie, 470, 471, 676
The Lone Hand, 210, 554
Loney, Alan, 418, 419, 422, 427, 594
Long, D.S. *see: Into the World of Light* (ed. Long and Ihimaera, 1982)
Longford, Helen, 563
Longman Paul Ltd, 593
Lonie, Iain, 428
Lord, Robert, 309-11, 312, 318, 676
Lowry, Bob, 380, 558, 559-61 *passim*, 564-5, 583, 586, 587, 595
Lusk, Hugh H., 110, 114, 547
Lyttleton, Edith: novels, 123, 130, 140, 493, 495, 496, 498, 501-4, 505, 540, 541; poetry, 365; short stories, 207, 211-13, 216; other refs., 567-8, 675

McAdam, Constance Clyde, 127, 130
McAlpine, Rachel: novels, 173. 191, 193, 197; plays, 326-7; poetry, 437, 438, 439; other refs., 676-7
McCarten, Anthony, 337-40
McCarthy, Beryl, 140, 160, 572
McCarthy, Lilian, 289
MacCartie, Justin Charles, 111, 116, 117, 120
McCauley, Sue, 174, 179, 181, 184, 181, 677
McClenaghan, Jack, 148, 157, 158
McCormick, E.H.: autobiographical essay, 90; biographies, 78-9; and Centennial publications, 568, 570, 571; criticism, x, xi, 102, 140, 298, 570, 611; and Literary Fund, 575-9 *passim*, 595; other refs., 223, 225, 677
Macdonald, Caroline, 472, 488-90, 677
McDonald, Georgina, 160, 540
McDonnell, Thomas, 552
McEldowney, Dennis, 101-2, 615, 622, 697, 715 (n. 18), 724 (n. 33)
McEldowney, W.J., 591
McEwen, J.M., 16-17
McGee, Greg, 304, 322-4, 326, 329, 330, 677
McGregor, John, 20
MacGregor, Miriam, 529
McIndoe, James, 48-9
McIndoe, John, 591, 594
McIntosh, A.D., 571
McKay, Frank, 102, 642
Mackay, Jessie: non-fiction, 80; poetry, 345, 348, 358, 374; other refs., 357, 458, 554, 555, 575, 613, 678, 724 (n. 37)
McKenzie, D.F, 3, 731 (nn. 3, 10)
Mackenzie, Mary, 578
Mackrell, Brian, 187
McLaren, Ian F, 473, 731 (n. 16)
McKay, R.A., 731 (n. 2)
McLean, Donald, 12
McLean, Mervyn, 18
Maclennan, J., 555
McLeod, Catherine, 178, 190
McLeod, Marion, 629
McLeod, N.F.H., 678
McLintock, A.H., 73, 572
Macmillan, 567
McNab, Robert, 64-5
McNaughton, Howard, x, 621, 689
McNaughton, Neil, 476
McNeill, Brian, 308-9, 312, 318, 330, 331
McNeish, James: novels, 173, 177, 186-7, 188, 189, 193, 196; play, 309; other refs., 678
McPherson, Heather, 437, 443
MacPherson, Rachel, 117-18
McQueen, Cilla, 437, 442, 443, 678
McQueen, Harvey *see The Penguin Book of New Zealand Verse* (ed. Wedde and McQueen, 1985); *The Penguin*

Book of Contemporary New Zealand Poetry (ed. Wedde, McQueen, and Evans, 1989)
Mactier, Susan, 125, 126, 127, 129
McWilliams, Tom, 587
Magalaner, Marvin, 682
Mahuta, Robert Te Kotahi, 19
Mahy, Margaret: biography of, by Gilderdale, 473; writing for children, 471, 477-9, 486, 488, 490; other refs., 462, 678-9
Makgill, Sir George, 127, 129
Making New Zealand, 568, 569
Mallinson, Anne, 594
Mallinson Rendel, 472, 594
Mallory, Clare, 461, 679
Mander, Jane: novels, 124-5, 134-7, 500; other refs., 92, 161, 553, 613, 679
Manhire, Bill: poetry, 418-20 *passim*, 421, 425-6, 435; short stories, 260, 263; other refs., 617, 663, 679-80, 726 (n. 91), 727 (nn. 130, 140, 141)
Maning, F.E., 42-3, 54, 547, 556, 575, 680
Mann, Jessica, 688
Mann, Philip, 193, 197
Mansfield, Katherine: biographies of, by A. Alpers, 99-100, 101, 579; journals and notebooks, 218-9; letters, 101, 219, 681; plays about, 308-9, 330; poetry, 374, 375; short stories, 165, 166, 215-22, 229, 230, 238, 243, 568; other refs., x, 554-5, 564, 680-7
Manson, Cecilia, 469
Mantell, Laurie, 529
Mantell, W.B.D., 12
Te Maori, 250
Maori Ethnological Research, Board of, 557
Maori Language Commission, 2, 18

MĀORI, LITERATURE IN:
    bibliography, 607-8
    historical and contemporary setting, 1-3
    oral tradition: in manuscript, 7-11; in print, 14-17, 17-20 *passim*
    orthography, dictionaries, grammars, linguistic studies, 3-5, 18-19, 23
    writing (19th cent.): church and government publications, 5-7; letters, 11-12; minute-books, 12-13; newspapers, 13-14; writing (20th cent.): collections, 18, 20; commentaries and literary criticism, 19, 20; journals and newspapers, 17-18; monographs and editions, 18-19, 22; original prose and poetry, 19, 20-4; theses, 19, 20

Maori Publication Fund, 23
The Maori Recorder, 13
Maori Tales (series, ed. Lawlor), 563
The Maorilander, 554
Maranga Mai, 317
Marjoribanks, Alexander, 36
Markham, Edward, 102, 450
Marriott, James, 272
Marris, Charles A., 380-1, 559, 563, 564, 586, 632
Marryat, Emilia, 122
Marschel, Barrie, 280
Marsden, Samuel, 32, 65, 92, 566
Marsh, Ngaio: crime novels, 494, 497, 510-14, 528, 541, 568; theatre work, 282, 286, 290, 291, 309, 506, 511; other refs., 574, 578, 687-8
Marshall, Heather, 181, 190
Marshall, Owen, 253, 254, 255-7, 688
Martin, William, 41
Mason, Bruce, 291-6, 300, 303, 311, 312, 589, 595, 688-9
Mason, R.A.K.: plays, 287-8, 289, 312; poetry, 335-40, 362, 365-9, 373, 374, 380, 387, 557-8, 562, 564, 565; other refs., 411, 560-1, 686-7

Mataira, Katerina, 21, 23, 480, 690
Matawhaanui, 18
Matchitt, Para, 471, 480
Mate, 258, 411, 418, 422, 587, 589, 634
Matthews, Jacqueline, 670
Maughan, William, 197
Maunder, Paul, 317-18, 332
Maunsell, William, 4, 6
May, Philip, 73
Mead, S.M. (Hirini), 4, 14, 18-19, 249
Meikle, Phoebe, 581, 620
Melbourne, Hirini, 21, 23
Menzies, Trixie, 444, 624, 724 (n. 59)
Messenger, A.H., 469
Messenger, Elizabeth, 528
Metge, Joan, 86
Methuen, 474, 593
Metro, 589-90
Michael, Shona, 173
Middleton, Ian, 186-7, 190, 690
Middleton, O.E., 148, 152, 230, 233, 468, 690
Millar, Nola, 300, 301, 302
Millen, Julia, 84
Miller, Harold, 70
Miller, John, 70
Milner, Ian, 559
Mills and Boon, 496, 497, 522, 529, 531, 532, 537, 539
Mincher, Philip, 252-3
Mirams, Gordon, 572, 581
Mitcalfe, Barry, 20, 187, 411, 468, 594-5, 690-1
Mitchell, David, 418, 420, 427, 435, 588, 589
Mitchell, June, 187, 195
Moana Press, 595
Money, Charles L., 45
Montgomery, Eleanor, 277
Monthly Review, 348, 552-3
Moore, Mrs Ambrose E., 454
Moore, Mary, 532, 536
Moorfield, John, 5
Moorhead, Diana, 488
'Morgan, Alun', see Faulkner, Alun
Morice, Stella, 463, 466
Morrieson, Ronald Hugh, 144, 145, 150-1, 153-4, 164, 691
Morrissey, Michael, 258, 259-60, 691; *see also: The New Fiction* (ed. Morrissey, 1985)
'Mortimer, Algernon Reginald Hillen', 114
Morton, Frank, 529, 555
Nga Moteatea, 18, 19
Mountain, Julian, 153
Mountjoy, Laura, 192, 193, 197
'Moyhanger', 32
Muir, Robin, 152
Mulcock, Anne, 178-9
Mulgan, Alan: non-fiction, 67, 68, 90-1, 611, 612; novel, 123, 127-30 *passim*, 142, 146, 283; plays, 282; poetry, 374, 573; other refs., 508, 554, 567, 575, 691-2
Mulgan, John: autobiography, 75; criticism, 611, 612; novel, 142, 143, 147, 148, 151, 161-2, 166-7; other refs., 567, 581, 692
Murison, Barbara, 484
Murray, John, 546
Murry, John Middleton, 216
Musaphia, Joseph, 304, 312, 318, 319-20, 692-3
Musgrove, H., 127
Mutch, Karin, 532
Myers, Virginia, 84

Nahe, Hoani, 15
Nannestad, Elizabeth, 437
Napier, Susan, 497, 532, 537, 538
Nash, Walter, 567

Native Companion, 216, 554
Neate, Frank, 178
Needham, John, 369
Neighbourhood Watch, 331
Neill, Michael, 328-9
Nelson, Mandy, 482
New, W.H., 213, 241, 554, 618, 619
The New Chum, 222
The New Fiction (ed. Morrissey, 1985), 258, 260, 261, 631
New Nation, 558
The New Poets (ed. M. Edmond and M. Paul, 1987), 440, 441, 442, 630
New Women's Fiction series, 264, 630
New Women's Press, 594
New Zealand Artists' Annual, 558, 563, 632
New Zealand Authors' Fund, 596-7
New Zealand Authors' Week Conference (1936), 140, 506
New Zealand Best Poems (annual, ed. Marris, 1932-43), 380-1, 559, 563, 564, 624
New Zealand Book Awards, 597
New Zealand Company, 35, 36, 54
New Zealand Council for Educational Research, 569
New Zealand Country Journal, 51
New Zealand Educational Book Depository, 551
New Zealand Gazette, 6
New Zealand Graphic, 554
New Zealand Herald, 230, 456, 458
New Zealand Illustrated Magazine, 61, 206, 208, 209, 210, 222, 364, 553
New Zealand Listener, 92, 93, 141, 183, 253, 263, 387, 472, 569, 572-3, 586, 589, 627, 630, 632-3
New Zealand Literary and Historical Association, 553
New Zealand Literary Fund, 300, 472, 577-9, 595-600
New Zealand Magazine, 548, 552, 632
New Zealand Mercury, 563, 564
New Zealand Mirror, 496
New Zealand Monthly Review, 587
New Zealand National Bibliography, 473, 551, 556, 604
New Zealand New Writing, 573-4, 633
New Zealand Observer, 147
New Zealand Poetry Yearbook, 394, 404, 407, 414, 586, 595, 596, 627
New Zealand Railway Magazine, 226, 558, 572
New Zealand Reader (schoolbook, 1895), 54
New Zealand Referee, 559
New Zealand Short Stories: (ed. Gillespie, 1930), 61, 146, 222, 223, 567, 624; (ed. Davin, 1953), 233, 626; (ed. Stead, 1966), 243, 626; (ed. O'Sullivan, 1975), 628; (ed. Wevers, 1984), 630; (OUP series as a whole, 1953-84), 239-40, 263
New Zealand Theatre, 312
New Zealand Times, 559
New Zealand Universities' Literary Yearbook, 418, 589, 634
New Zealand University Press, 582-3
New Zealand Verse (ed. Alexander and Currie, 1906), 347-50, 357, 360, 363, 364-5, 623
New Zealand Whole Earth Catalogue, 260
New Zealand Women's Weekly, 496
New Zealand Writers and Their Work (OUP series), x, 101, 145, 642, 645, 647, 653, 660, 663, 689, 690, 692, 693, 697
Newton, John, 444
Newton, Peter, 77, 580
Ngata, Sir Apirana, 18-21 *passim*, 86, 88, 507, 545-6, 553, 571
Ngawai, Tuini, 21
Nicholas, J.L., 32, 54
Nicholls, Marjory, 373-4
Nisbet, Hume, 109, 112, 121, 122
Nolan, Iris, 187

NON-FICTION:
   introduction and conclusion, 29-34, 102-4
   'Archive of Exploration' (1642-1840), 29-34; voyages
      and exploration, 29-31; visitors' accounts, 31-4
   'Literature of Invasion' (1840-1890), 34-52
   colonization and migration propaganda, 35-8
   exploration, mountaineering, topography, 49-50
   natural history, 50-2
   pioneer narratives, 45-9
   writings on NZ wars and on the Māori, 38-45
   'Literature of Occupation' (1890-1930), 52-68
   anthropology, 67-8
   bibliography, 54
   biography and autobiography, 66-7
   ethnology, 57-60, 62
   history and local history, 54-7, 64-6, 68
   myth-making, 60-2
   natural history, 62-4
   topography, 54; 'Literature of National Identity'
      (1930-1990), 68-89
   history, 68-73
   local history, 73-4
   writing by and about Māori, 85-9
   writing by and about men, 74-9
   writing by and about women, 79-85
   'Literary Biography and Literary Autobiography'
      (1930-1990), 89-102, 622
   autobiography, 89-99
   biography, 99-102

Nonweiler, Barry, 182
Noonan, Michael Anthony, 302
Norman, Philip, 321
Norman, Waerete, 19

NOVEL:
   bibliography, 607, 618-21
   development of a local tradition, 108-9, 123, 140-2,
      170-1
   novelists and their careers, 109-10, 123-5, 142-6, 171-4
   periods: 'Pioneer' (1861-89), 108-23; 'Late Colonial'
      (1890-1934), 123-40; 'Provincial' (1935-64), 140-69;
      'Post-Provincial' (from 1965), 170-99
   principal modes and types, 110-16, 125-8, 159-69,
      187-99; *Bildungsroman*, 127-8, 135-6, 138-9;
      didacticism, 110, 114-16, 125-6, 131-2, 160; future
      fiction, 115, 191-4; historical novel, 133-4, 160,
      187-91; impressionism, 165-9, 195-6; Māori
      romance, 112, 126; melodrama, 110, 112-14, 126-7,
      133-4, 136-7, 138; metafiction, 197-9, 498; realism
      of various kinds ('naïve', 'critical', 'solid'),
      110-12, 116, 125, 135-6, 159-65, 169, 194-5; satire,
      115-16, 196-7; sensation novel, 113-14
   principal themes, 117-22, 128-31, 146-59, 174-87:
      criticism of society, 118-20, 129-30, 137-40, 147,
      151-2, 153-5; existentialism and
      'accommodation', 156-9; expatriation, 186-7;
      feminism, 120, 131, 137-40, 192, 194; individual at
      odds with society, 155; Man Alone *and* Woman
      Alone, 117, 147-50, 151, 174, 178, 181-3, 186; Māori
      life and Māori-Pākehā relations, 120-2, 128-9, 133,
      138, 152-3, 183-6; marriage and personal relations,
      177-81; myth-making, 133-4, 160, 187-94; progress
      towards Pastoral Paradise and/or Just City, 108,
      117-22, 128-31, 132-3, 134, 137-8; puritanism,
      129-30, 134-7, 138-40, 146, 150-1, 174-6;
      temperance, 130; *see also* POPULAR FICTION

North Canterbury Gazette, 563
Numbers, 243, 404, 586, 595, 634
Nunns, Rachel, 179

O'Brien, Gregory, 444
O'Connor, Frank, 203
O'Farrell, P.J., 77-8
Official Handbook of New Zealand, 36
Official Year Book of New Zealand, 36, 550
Olds, Peter, 419
Oliver, W.H.: biography, 101-2, 608; history, 71, 74, 610;
   poetry, 387, 403, 405; other refs., 585
Ollivant, Joseph Earle, 346
Oppenheim, Roger, 17, 21
Orange, Claudia, 103
Orbell, Margaret, 16, 19, 20, 21, 102, 411, 443, 589, 614
Oriflamme, 380
Orr, Bob, 342, 418
Orwin, Joanna, 472, 483-4, 693
Osmond, Sophie, 126
Ost, Frederick, 574
O'Sullivan, Vincent: novel, 191, 196; plays, 304, 318, 329,
   330, 332; poetry, 342, 409, 421, 435; short stories, 253-5;
   other refs., 335, 642, 693; *see also: An Anthology of
   Twentieth Century New Zealand Poetry* (ed.
   O'Sullivan, 1970, 1976); Mansfield, Katherine: letters
Otago Daily Times, 572
Otago University Press, 583, 591-2
Otago University Review, 631
Otago Witness, 109, 554
Ovenden, Keith, 177, 187
Owen, Charles, 127, 128, 281, 719 (n. 6)
Owen, William, 153
Oxford University Press, x, 101, 145, 567, 591, 592, 594

P.E.N., 563, 577-8, 598
Pacific Moana Quarterly, 589
'A Pakeha Maori', *see* Maning, F.E.
Te Paki o Matariki, 14
Paki, Rora, 249, 720 (n. 87)
Parallax, 258, 427, 589, 635
Paraone, Te Hemara Rerehau, 13
Park, Ruth, 150
Parker, Dean, 312, 313-14, 325
Parkinson, Sydney, 546
Parkman, Francis 62
Parry, W.E., 577
Pascoe, John, 76-7, 80, 567, 569
Paterson, Alistair, 422, 589, 617
PATRONAGE *see* PUBLISHING, PATRONAGE, LITERARY
   MAGAZINES
Paul, Blackwood and Janet, 464, 581, 593
Paul, M. *see: The New Poets* (ed. M. Edmond and M. Paul,
   1987)
Peacocke, Isabel Maude: novels, 123, 498, 504-5, 506, 522;
   writing for children, 455-6, 476, 567; other refs., 693-4
Pearson, Bill: criticism, xii, 208, 209, 584, 606, 612, 614, 615,
   716 (n. 51), 719 (n. 9), 720 (n. 56); novel, 141, 142, 145-6,
   154-5; other refs., 574, 581, 694
Peel, Colin, 528-9
Penberthy, Brent, 173, 184
Penfold, Merimeri, 4, 21
Penguin Books, 574, 594
The Penguin Book of Contemporary New Zealand Poetry (ed.
   Wedde, McQueen, and Evans, 1989), 433, 440-1, 442,
   443
The Penguin Book of New Zealand Verse: (ed. Curnow,
   1960) 21, 225-6, 341, 394, 406, 411, 441, 625; (ed. Wedde
   and McQueen, 1985) 21, 338, 340, 424, 440-3 *passim*,
   630
The Penguin History of New Zealand Literature (Evans),
   xiii-xiv, 603, 611, 730 (n. 32)
Penguin New Writing, 573, 627, 633
Petersen, G.C., 77
Pewhairangi, Ngoi, 21

Phillips, Jock, 103, 553, 554
Phipps, Grace, 496, 497, 522, 527-8
Phoenix, 140, 203, 224, 380, 559-60, 583, 588, 632
Te Pihoihoi Mokemoke, 13, 88
Pio, Hamiora, 19
Te Pipiwharauroa, 6, 18
Plarr, Victor, 374
Pocock, John, 291
Podstolski, Jerzy, 715 (n. 18)

POETRY:
   bibliography, 616-18
   controversies: between Curnow and 'Wellington
      group' (1951-60), 385-6, 403-6; over 'open form'
      (1972-90), 421-2, 617
   introduction: words and the inner and outer worlds,
      335-44
   periods: Victorian period, 344-64; poets of 1920s and
      1930s, 364-84; 1945-60: 385-403; 1960-72: 406-20;
      1972-90: 423-45
   principal groups: *Phoenix* group and others, 364-84;
      post-war Romantics, 386-95, 412-17; modernists,
      396-403, 428-33; the 'middle generation', 406-12,
      433-40; the 'young' poets, 418-20, 423-8; the 'new'
      poets, 440-5

Pohuhu, Nepia, 15, 17
Polack, J.S., 33
Polynesian Society, 17, 18, 57, 58, 88, 557
Pond, Wendy, 268
Ponika, Kohine, 21
Poole, Fiona Farrell, 267, 327
Pope, Quentin, 373-4, 558

POPULAR FICTION:
   periods: 'Late Victorian', 498-505; '1930-1950: Five
      Professionals', 505-22; 'The 1950s: Four Romance
      Writers', 522-8; 'The 1960s and after', 528-41
   principal types: action and adventure, 501-2, 529;
      backblocks comedy and romance, 517-22; crime
      fiction, 510-14, 528-9; Gothic romance, 514-17;
      historical family saga, 502-4, 528, 540-1; light
      romance, 506, 522-8, 531-41; melodramatic
      romance, 498-501, 504-5; yarns, 530-1
   publishing context, 493-8
   see also: NOVEL

Port Nicholson Press, 594
Porter, Frances, 78
Potatau, Hemi, 23
Potiki, Roma, 443, 444
Potts, T.H., 51, 54
Powell, Lesley Cameron, 471
The Power and the Glory (ed. Saphira, 1987), 266, 630
Press (Christchurch), 124, 299, 563
Preston, Florence, 149, 150, 160
Preston, Ivy, 532, 536
Price, Beverley, 591
Price, Hugh, 473
Price Milburn, 591, 592, 594
Private Gardens (ed. Ensing, 1977), 437, 629
Progressive Publishing Society, 574, 581
Public and Private Worlds (ed. Cox, 1987), 83-4

PUBLISHING, PATRONAGE, LITERARY MAGAZINES:
   literary magazines: early, 547-9; late 19th, early 20th
      cent., 552-5; 1920s and early 1930s, 558-64; late
      1930s, early 1940s, 572-4; 1947-90: 583-90
   patronage, 574-9, 595-600
   publishing: early, 545-7; late 19th cent., 549-51; early
      20th cent., 556-8; 1930s, 564-8; Centennial,

568-72; 1940s and 1950s, 574, 579-83; 1960-90:
   590-5; of popular fiction, 493-8

Pugsley, Christopher, 76
Puhiwahine, 21
*Te Pukapuka o Nga Kawenata e Waru . . . a Te Haahi
   Ringatu*, 11
Pulseley, Daniel, 122
Pye, Wendy, 594
Pyke, Vincent, 54, 109, 112, 113, 114

Quentin, Dorothy, 522, 524-5, 694-5
'Quivis' (*Evening Post* reviewer), 222

Rambling Jack, 589, 635
Ramsden, Eric, 65
Randle, Marie R., 345
Rata, 559
Ratana, Tahupotiki Wiremu, 11, 335
Rawlinson, Gloria, 149, 167, 395, 564, 670
Recent Poems (Caxton Press, 1941), 380
Recent Poetry in New Zealand (ed. Doyle, 1965), 407, 420,
   590, 627
Red Funnel, 553-4
Redman, Frederick Taylor, 126
Reed, A.H. and A.W., 18, 463, 464, 496, 497, 522, 530,
   566-7, 580
Reed, Alfred Hamish, 566, 580, 593
Reed, Alexander Wyclif, 20, 126, 463, 566, 580, 593, 610,
   695
Reed, G.M., 126, 129
Reed, John, 593
Reedy, Kuini, 22
Rees, Arthur, 129
Rees, Rosemary, 123, 506-7, 522, 525, 567, 695
Rees, W.L., 118
Reeves, William Pember: biography of, by Sinclair, 78;
   historical writing, 54-7, 68, 70, 71; poetry, 349-50,
   359-60, 364, 371; other refs., 27, 54, 552, 567, 696
Reid, Ian, 156, 717 (n. 67)
Reid, John C., 140, 590, 596, 611, 612, 627
Reidy, Sue, 264, 267, 268
Reilly, Colleen, 174, 181
Reilly, M.P.J., 16
Religious Tract Society, 109, 112
Renée, 324-7, 621, 696
Renwick, W.L., 713 (n. 76)
Rhodes, Winston: and *Tomorrow*, 225, 561, 562, 572; other
   refs., 154, 613, 614, 618, 620, 697, 732 (n. 54)
Rhythm, 216
Rich, James, 463
Richards, Max B., 302-3, 307, 311
Richards, Ray, 580, 594
Richardson, Elwyn, 461
Rimini, Timi Waata, 17
Ringer, J.B., 473, 622
Ritchie, James, 86
Ritchie, K.W., 187
Roberts, Heather, xiv, 619, 730 (n. 24)
Robinson, Belinda, 183
Robinson, Neil, 590
Robinson, Roger, 708
Rochfort, John, 45
Rock, Gilbert, 114
Roddick, Alan, 291
Rogers, D.H., 345-6
Rose, Lyndon, 470-1
Rosier-Jones, Joan, 184
Ross, D.M., 374
Ross, James Clark, 31
Ross, Kathleen, 289-90, 291-2, 324

Ross, William, 113
Roth, H.O., 723 (n. 23), 732 (n. 21)
Rout, Ettie, 80
Rowan, Diana, 325
Ruhen, Olaf, 156
Rusden, G.W., 44, 80
Russell, G. Warren, 126
Russell Clark Award, 471
Rutherford, James, 77-8
Ruthven, K.K., 198, 555
Ryan, P.M., 5

Salmond, Anne, 16, 86
Salt, Valerie and Colin, 465
Sandall, Helen, 469
Sanders, James, 529-30
Sanderson, Nora, 532
Sandford, Kenneth, 76
Sandys, Elspeth, 190
Saphira, Miriam, 266
Sargeson, Frank: autobiography, 94-7; essay on, by D.
    McEldowney, 101-2, 697; novels and novellas, 140-4
    passim, 148-50 *passim*, 162, 164, 167, 171, 174, 182-3, 189,
    194, 199; plays, 299, 300, 303, 311; radio talks on
    writing a novel, 145, 146, 149-50, 155, 161, 165; short
    stories, 222, 224-9, 230, 231, 563, 564, 566, 574, 581; and
    state patronage, 571, 575, 576; tribute to Sherwood
    Anderson, 162, 226, 563; and younger writers, 163, 175,
    199, 229-30, 233, 235, 237 *et passim*; other refs., x, 145,
    151, 155, 288, 341, 359, 568, 572, 580, 593, 696-8; *see
    also*: *Speaking for Ourselves* (ed. Sargeson, 1945)
Satchell, William: biography and study of, by Wilson, 101;
    journalism, 554; novels, 124, 132-4, 140, 160, 188, 452-3,
    490; other refs., 553, 567, 575, 698
Savage, John, 31-2, 54
Savage, Michael Joseph, 335
Scanlan, Nelle: autobiography, 90, 508; novels, 123, 140,
    494, 506, 507-10, 522, 541, 568; other refs., 698-9
Scholefield, G.H., 66, 578, 608
School Journal, 462, 468, 469, 474, 478, 484, 581-2, 632
School Publications Branch, 464, 468, 469
Schroder, J.H.E., 563, 567, 578, 579
Schwimmer, Erik G., 248, 585, 589, 726 (n. 113)
Scott, Dick, 74, 79-80
Scott, Margaret, 101
Scott, Mary, 494, 496, 497, 517-22, 528, 541, 580, 699-700
Scott, Robert H., 110, 122
Scott, Rosie, 268, 327
Scott, T.H., 389
Seager, E.W., 278
Semmler, Clement, 704
Sewell, Arthur, 564, 679
Shadbolt, Maurice: non-fiction, 76, 197; novels, 172, 174,
    176, 177-8, 181, 183, 188-91 *passim*, 194, 197, 582, 590;
    short stories, 252, 253; other refs., 122, 145, 170, 195,
    590, 700-1
Shadbolt, Tim, 591
Sharkey, Michael, 709
Sharp, Andrew, 85-6, 579
Sharples, Pita, 21
Shaw, Helen, 101, 230, 242-3, 574, 584, 586, 701
Shelley, James, 282, 284, 298
Sherry, Karen Annette, 721 (n. 4)
Shirley Temple Is a Wife and Mother (ed. Catley, 1977), 264,
    629

SHORT STORY:
    bibliography, 607, 618-22
    introduction, 203-4
    periods: colonial short fiction to Mansfield, 204-22;
        nationalism and social realism (1920s-1950s),
222-43; writing as Other; Other writing (1960s
    and after), 243-68;
principal types: adventure story, 204-5, 222, 230;
    colonial yarn, 204-5, 212-13, 222, 230; Dalmatian
    and Danish immigrant stories, 243-5; family
    story, 242-3; 'free' story, 251-8; ghost story,
    205-7; Māori story, 208-11, 234-7, 245-51;
    post-modern story, 258-63; romance, 211-12, 222,
    223, 230; sketch, 214-15, 222, 223; *see also*
    Sargeson, Frank; social realist story, 230-5; *sui
    generis*: *see* Duggan, Maurice; Frame, Janet;
    Mansfield, Katherine; women's fiction (1980s),
    263-8

Shortland, Edward, 9, 16, 39, 45
Shortlands Publications, 479
Shrimpton, Arnold W., 24, 67, 68, 557
Simmons, David, 16, 86
Simms, Norman, 708
Simpson, Helen M., 81
Simpson, Peter, 613, 615, 691, 714 (n. 1)
Simpson, Tony, 79-80
Sinclair, Keith: biographical and historical writing, 71-3,
    78, 582, 696; poetry, 397, 402-3; other refs., 574, 580,
    585, 587, 612-13, 701-2
Sinclair, Margaret A., 351
Sinclair, Mary, 350
Sinclaire, Frederick, 561, 562, 572
Sisam, Kenneth, 567
Sissons, Jeffrey, 19
Skinner, H.D., 85
Slatter, Gordon, 144, 156-7, 164
Sligo, John, 181
Smart, Peter, 588
Smith, D.I.B., 670
Smith, Elizabeth M., 498, 506, 509, 618
Smith, Joan, 464-5
Smith, Miriam, 480
Smith, S. Percy: ethnographic and historical writing, 16,
    58-9, 60-1, 85; and Maori writing, 9, 16, 17, 19
Smith, Elder and Co., 109, 546
Smither, Elizabeth: novels, 173, 183, 186, 187; poetry, 437,
    439-40; other refs., 620, 702
Smithyman, Kendrick: criticism, cited or discussed, 387,
    393, 396, 400-1, 405, 407, 590, 616; poetry, 400-2,
    419-20, 421, 431-3; other refs., 574, 580, 584, 585, 587,
    590, 698, 702-3
Somerset, H.C.D., 75, 458
Somerville, Dora, 307
Soper, Eileen L., 468, 469
Soper, F.G., 289
Sorrenson, M.P.K., 102
Southan, W.M., 113, 120
Southern Cross, 547
Southern Monthly Magazine, 547-8
Southland Daily News, 583
Southland Times, 93
Speaking for Ourselves (ed. Sargeson, 1945), 237, 625-6
Spear, Charles, 157, 397, 402
Spiers, Margaret, 473
Spike, 558, 632
Spillmann, Joseph, 111, 121
Spiral, 266, 635
Splash, 589, 635
Sport, 258, 588, 635
Spurdle, Flora, 81
Squire, Jillian, 580
Stanford, Edward, 546
Stanley, Mary, 394-5
Stead, C.K.: criticism, cited or discussed, 197, 224-5, 365,
    407-8, 421-2, 612, 729 (n. 184); novels, 173, 177, 178, 190,

191, 199, 490; poetry, 342, 343–4, 407–8, 419, 421, 433–5; short stories, 257–8; other refs., 145, 237, 596, 598, 703–4
Stelin, Ebba, 126
Stevens, Joan, x, 80, 102, 141, 142, 615, 618
Stewart, Bruce, 250–1
Stewart, Douglas, 77, 564, 704
Stewart, Mary Anne *see* Barker, Lady
Stewart, Peter, 591
Stewart, W. Downie, 57, 566
Stokes, Evelyn, 74
Stone, R.C.J., 78, 103
Stones, Anthony, 587, 733 (n. 90)
Stoney, Henry Butler, 108, 109, 110, 117, 120, 199, 547
Stories About Many Things, Founded on Facts (children's book, 1833), 449
Story, Elsie, 126
Stout, Sir Robert, 549, 552
Stowell, H.M., 4
Straubel, Carl, 582
Sturm, J.C., 243, 245–6, 249, 586
Sturm, Terry, 598, 638
Sullivan, Martin, 560
Summers, Essie, 496, 497, 532–5, 536, 541, 704–5
Summers, John, 175
Sun (Christchurch), 559
Sutch, W.B., 79, 571, 574
Sutherland, I.L.G., 86, 571
Sutherland, James, 190
Sutherland, Margaret, 174, 179, 180–1, 194, 263, 264, 265–6, 705
Sutton, Eve, 471, 475–6, 705
Sutton-Smith, Brian, 466
Swainson, William, 39–40
Syme, Ronald, 468–9
Symons, Julian, 688

Talbot, Thorpe, 112–13
Tales by New Zealanders (ed. Allen, 1938), 230, 624
Tales of Pioneer Women (ed. Woodhouse, 1940), 81–2
Taonui, Aperahama, 15
Tapsell, Hans, 61
Tarakawa, Takaanui, 17
Targuse, Violet, 283–4, 285
Tarrant, Margaret, 456
Tasman, Abel, 29–30, 54
Tautoko, 17
Tawaewae, Hami, 17
Taylor, Alister, 591
Taylor, Anthony, 309
Taylor, Apirana, 23, 250, 251, 444
Taylor, Brian, 181
Taylor, Denis, 141–2, 147
Taylor, Ellen, 127
Taylor, Mary, 80
Taylor, Mervyn, 583
Taylor, Nancy, 69
Taylor, Richard, 16, 38–9
Taylor, William, 173, 176, 177, 182, 184, 472, 485–6, 705
Te Kooti Arikirangi, 11
Te Puea Herangi, 21
Te Rangi Hiroa *see* Buck, Sir Peter
Te Rangikaheke, Wiremu Maihi, 9, 18
Te Rauparaha, Tamihana, 9
Te Ua Haumene, 10–11
Te Wheoro, Wi, 15
Te Whiwhi, Matene, 8–9
Te Wiata, Inia, 292
Temple, Philip, 77, 173, 187, 190, 482
Temuera, Paora, 88
Texidor, Greville, 230, 233–4, 573, 580

Thatcher, Charles Robert, 354
Thompson, Mervyn, 315–17, 318, 322, 330, 331, 705–6
Thompson, Nola, 160
Thompson, Robert, 587
Thomson, A.S., 40
Thomson, G.M., 62–3
Thomson, John C., 207
Thomson, John E.P., x, 178, 606, 621
Thomson, John M., 585, 611
Thornton, Agathe, 19
Thornton, Guy, 125
Timaru Herald, 532
Tiramorehu, Matiaha, 19
Tirohia, 250
Te Tiupiri, 14
Te Toa Takitini, 14, 18
The Tomahawk (play, 1870), 274
Tombs, George, 551, 558
Tombs, Harry, 558, 559, 583
Tomorrow, 225, 226, 286, 287, 288, 299, 561–3, 565, 572, 574, 632
Topeora, 21
Torrens, J.M., 126
Tracy, Mona, 215, 373, 458–9, 567, 706
Transactions and Proceedings of the New Zealand Institute, 17, 51, 549
Traue, J.E., ix, 605, 608
Treadwell, C.A.L., 577
A Treasury of New Zealand Verse (ed. Alexander and Currie, 1926), 365, 557, 558, 623
Tregear, Edward, 5, 57–8, 126, 365, 453, 551
Tremewan, Philip, 332
Triad, 127, 208, 216, 554, 555, 580, 631
Trollope, Anthony, 36
Trussell, Denys, 101
Truth, 317, 577
Tu Tangata, 17, 250
Tuhaere, Paora, 17
Tullett, James, 529
Tumohe, Wiremu Toetoe, 13
Te Tumu Korero, 22
Turnbull, Alexander Horsburgh, 54
Turner, Brian, 436, 591, 706
Turner, Dorothea, 679
Turner, Gwenda, 482
Turner, Samuel, 50
Tuwhare, Hone, 406, 407, 411–12, 443, 706
Twayne's World Authors Series, x, 101, 582, 642, 650, 660, 679, 682, 692, 697, 698, 704
Tyerman, Daniel, 31
Tynan, Kenneth, 308
Typo, 549, 550, 552

Unicorn Press, 564, 595
Untold, 258, 635
Unwin, Sir Stanley, 567
Upton and Co., 551

Vaile, E.E., 66
Veitch, Ishbel, 373
Verne, Jules, 109, 121, 451
Victoria University Press, 592
Victory, Louis H., 357–8
Vogel, Harry B., 124, 127
Vogel, Julius, 115, 118, 120, 273, 277
Vogt, Anton, 564, 573

Wade, William, 34
Wadman, Howard, 291
Waerea, James, 480
Waikato (chief), 4

Waititi, Hoani, 4
Waitoa, Henare, 19, 20
Te Waka Karaitiana, 6
Te Waka Maori o Niu Tireni, 6, 13
Te Waka o Aotearoa, 13
Te Waka o Te Iwi, 13
Wakefield, Edward Jerningham, 36–7, 38, 102, 546, 556, 575
Walker, William Sylvester, 126–7, 128
Wall, Arnold, 365, 564, 566, 573, 609, 610
Wallis, Redmond, 157
Te Wananga, 13, 17, 19
Ward, Joseph, 364, 565
Ward, R., 112
Ward, Lock, 456, 522, 567
Wardell, Phyl, 468, 471, 476, 706
Wardon, Reve, 114–15, 118
Watkins, Frank, 455
Watson, Henry Brereton Marriott, 112, 118, 122
Watson, Jean, 158, 172, 179, 195, 707
Wattie Book of the Year, 597
Webb, Alice, 213, 214–15
Webb, Leicester, 570
Webby, Elizabeth, 264, 719 (n. 15)
Wedde, Ian: criticism, cited or discussed, 340–3, 374, 413, 441, 617; novels, 173, 183, 189, 191, 195, 198, 199; poetry, 344, 418–20 *passim*, 421, 423–5, 435; short stories, 237, 258, 260, 261; other refs., 585, 598, 707–8; *see also*: *The Penguin Book of New Zealand Verse* (ed. Wedde and McQueen, 1985); *The Penguin Book of Contemporary New Zealand Poetry* (ed. Wedde, McQueen, and Evans, 1989)
Weekly News, 458, 590
Weekly Press, 554
Weir, J.E., 641, 642, 690
'Wellington group' (of poets), 403–6, 409
Wendt, Albert, xi–xii, 186, 593, 708
Wentworth, C. Merton, 153
West, Joyce, 160, 230, 466–7, 528, 708
Westbury, Frank Atha, 114
Western, A., 274–5, 278
Weston, Jessie, 123, 127, 128, 129
Westra, Ans, 465
Wevers, Lydia, 264, 440, 441, 442, 629, 630, 670, 719 (n. 15)
Te Wharekura, 17
Whatahoro, H.R., 16
Te Whetu Marama o Te Kotahitanga, 11
Te Whetu o Te Tau, 13
Whitcombe, Bertie, 557, 582, 593
Whitcombe, George, 551, 557
Whitcombe and Tombs, 454, 456, 464, 496, 497, 522, 551, 556–7, 569, 582, 593
Whitcombe's Story Books, 455, 456, 473, 551, 556, 666
Whitcoulls, 593
White, Doris, 469–70
White, Dorothy Neal, 462, 466, 472

White, Helen, 326, 329, 722 (n. 67)
White, John: ethnographic writing, 15, 57, 550, 574–5; and Maori writing, 9, 15, 16; novels, 111, 112
Whitworth, Jess, 168
Whitworth, Robert, 112, 122
Wi Hongi, Wiremu, 19
Wikiriwhi, Jean, 23
Wilcox, Dora, 350
Williams, Bridget, 591, 594
Williams, Herbert W., 5, 6, 14, 607, 610
Williams, George Phipps, 360
Williams, Mark, xii, 203, 443, 618
Williams, W.L., 4, 6
Williams, William, 4, 5, 545
Williamson, J.C., 275
Willis, A.D., 550–1
Wilson, Anne Glenny, 123, 127
Wilson, George, 112, 122
Wilson, Guthrie, 142, 144, 156, 157, 160, 161
Wilson, Helen, 81–2, 128, 581
Wilson, J.G., 66
Wilson, Len, 190
Wilson, Pat, 585
Wilson, Phillip, 101, 141, 145, 152, 156, 158, 159, 698
Wilson, Ormond, 578
Winder, Mavis, 497, 522, 526–7, 580
Winn, Lucy, 230
Winstanley, Kate, 327
Wise and Caffin, 551
Wiśniowski, Sigurd, 109, 116, 118, 121, 122, 123
Witheford, Hubert, 390, 396, 403–5 *passim*, 574, 585
Women's Studies Journal, 83, 635
Women's Work (ed. McLeod and Wevers, 1985), 264, 629
Wood, F.L.W., 70, 570
Wood, Mrs Nugent, 205
Woodhouse, A.E., 81–2
Woollaston, M. Toss, 77, 562
Wordsworth, Jane, 173, 184
Workers' Educational Association, 287
Wright, Albion, 581
Wright, David McKee, 358–9, 708–9
Wright, Stanley, 128
Wright and Brown, 522
Writers' Conference (Christchurch, 1951), 403

Yate, William, 32–33, 545
Year Book of the Arts in New Zealand, 385, 387, 394, 586, 632
Yelash, John, 587
Yellow Pencils (ed. Wevers, 1988), 440, 441, 442, 630
Young, David, 718 (n. 121)
The Young New Zealand Poets (ed. Baysting, 1973), 341, 420, 428, 628

Zealandia, 114, 207, 210, 552–3